COMMERCIAL REPORTS

AREA STUDIES SERIES

EDITORIAL DIRECTOR   Professor J J O'Meara
RESEARCH UNIT DIRECTOR   T F Turley
ASSISTANT DIRECTOR   S Cashman

CHIEF EDITORIAL ADVISERS

P Ford
Professor Emeritus, Southampton University
Mrs G Ford

SPECIAL EDITORIAL CONSULTANT FOR
THE UNITED STATES PAPERS

H C Allen
*Commonwealth Fund Professor of American
History, University College, London*
*Director of the London University Institute of
United States Studies*

RESEARCH EDITORS
Johann A Norstedt
Marilyn Evers Norstedt

This Series is published with the active co-operation of
SOUTHAMPTON UNIVERSITY

WITHDRAWN

IRISH UNIVERSITY PRESS AREA STUDIES SERIES

BRITISH PARLIAMENTARY PAPERS

UNITED STATES OF AMERICA

31

Embassy and consular
commercial reports
1885–86

IRISH UNIVERSITY PRESS
Shannon   Ireland

PUBLISHER'S NOTE

The documents in this series are selected from the nineteenth-century British House of Commons *sessional and command papers*. All of the original papers relating to the United States of America are included with the exception of two kinds of very brief and unimportant papers. Omitted are (1) random statistical trade returns which are included in the larger and complete yearly trade figures and (2) returns relating to postal services, which are irregularly presented, of tangential USA relevance, and easily available in other sources.

The original documents have been reproduced by photo-lithography and are unabridged even to the extent of retaining the first printers' imprints. Imperfections in the original printing are sometimes unavoidably reproduced.

Many papers in this reprint are enlargements from the original octavo format.

© 1971 Irish University Press Shannon Ireland
Microfilm, microfiche and other forms of micro-publishing
© *Irish University Microforms Shannon Ireland*

ISBN 0 7165 1531 8

Printed and published by
Irish University Press Shannon Ireland
DUBLIN   CORK   BELFAST   LONDON   NEW YORK
T M MacGlinchey *Publisher*   Robert Hogg *Printer*

Contents

IUP Page Number

For ease of reference IUP editors have assigned a continuous pagination which appears on the top outer margin of each page.

Commercial Reports

Commercial report no. 4 on correspondence respecting the negotiation of a treaty regulating trade between the British West Indies and the United States
1884–85 [C.4340] LXXI 9

Commercial report no. 24 on the finances of the United States, 1882–84
1884–85 [in C.4528] pt. IV, LXXVI 37

Commercial report no. 41 on Chicago, 1883; Philadelphia, 1884; St. Paul, 1883
1884–85 [in C.4240] pt. X, LXXVII 100

Commercial report no. 5 on Charleston, 1884; Galveston, 1884
1884–85 [in C.4356] pt. II, LXXVII 276

Commercial report no. 6 on Baltimore, 1884
1884–85 [inC.4364] pt. III, LXXVII 295

Commercial report no. 10 on Mobile and Alabama, 1884; New Orleans, 1884
1884–85 [in C.4391] pt. IV, LXXVII 309

Commercial report no. 17 on Boston, 1884
1884–85 [in C.4444] pt. V, LXXVIII 356

Commercial report no. 20 on Los Angeles and Wilmington, 1884; New York, 1884; Puget Sound district, 1884; SanDiego, 1884; California, 1884
1884–85 [in C.4524] pt. VII, LXXVIII 364

Commercial report no. 21 on Astoria, 1884; Newport, 1884; Oregon and Washington Terrotory, 1884
1884–85 [in C.4525] pt. VIII, LXXIX 480

Commercial report no. 22 on Minnesota, 1884
1884–85 [in C.4526] pt. IX, LXXIX 535

Commercial report no. 3 on production of borax in the United States; notes from the reports of the governors of the territories of Idaho, Montana, Dakota, New Mexico, Arizona, Alaska
1884–85 [in C.4336] LXXXI 559

Commercial report no. 11 on the cotton centennial exhibition at New Orleans
1884–85 [in C.4415] pt. II, LXXXI 563

Commercial report no. 25 on the fish commission; consumption of spirits, wine, beer and wine production in the United States
1884–85 [in C.4529] pt. III, LXXXI 577

Commercial report no. 9 on the United States
1884–85 [in C.4386] LXXXI 583

Commercial report no. 5 on Baltimore, 1885; New Orleans, 1885
1886 [in C.4654] LXV 593

Commercial report no. 6 on Boston, 1885; Mobile, 1885
1886 [in C.4657] LXV 609

Commercial report no. 10 on North and South Carolina, 1885; New York, 1885; California, 1885; Portland, 1885
1886 [in C.4737] LXVI 627

Continued

Contents

Continued

IUP Page Number

Commercial report no. 12 on Galveston, 1885; Puget Sound district and Washington Territory, 1885–86
1886 [in C.4761] LXVI 681

Commercial report no. 8 on coinage and depreciation of the silver dollar; imports and exports in the United States
1886 [in C.4733] LXVII 697

Commercial report no. 18 on labour unions in the United States
1886 [in C.4781] LXVII 713

Commercial report no. 20 on the United States
1886 [in C.4783] LXVII 769

Commercial report no. 21 on the United States
1886 [in C.4784] LXVII 780

As most commercial reports are extracted from larger papers, the reader should note that a particular report may lack a proper title page.

COMMERCIAL. No. 4 (1885).

CORRESPONDENCE

RESPECTING THE

NEGOTIATION

OF A

TREATY REGULATING TRADE

BETWEEN THE

BRITISH WEST INDIA COLONIES

AND THE

UNITED STATES.

Presented to both Houses of Parliament by Command of Her Majesty.
March 1885.

LONDON:
PRINTED BY HARRISON AND SONS.

To be purchased, either directly or through any Bookseller, from any of the following Agents, viz. :
Messrs. HANSARD, 13, Great Queen Street, W.C., and 32, Abingdon Street, Westminster;
Messrs. EYRE and SPOTTISWOODE, East Harding Street, Fleet Street, and Sale Office, House of Lords;
Messrs. ADAM and CHARLES BLACK, of Edinburgh;
Messrs. ALEXANDER THOM and Co. (Limited), or Messrs. HODGES, FIGGIS, and Co., of Dublin.

[C.—4340.] *Price* 3½*d*.

TABLE OF CONTENTS.

No.	Name.	Date.	Subject.	Page
1	Treaty between Great Britain and United States	July 3, 1815	Articles respecting trade between the United States and the British Colonies	1
2	,, ,,	Oct. 20, 1818	Extending the Treaty of 1815 for ten years	2
3	,, ,,	Aug. 6, 1827	Extending the Treaty of 1815 indefinitely, reserving power to either side to denounce it	2
4	To Mr. West	May 28, 1884	To ask that the British West Indies may be admitted to most-favoured-nation treatment	3
5	Mr. West	June 10,	Note in accordance with No. 4	3
6	To Mr. West	26,	Approves note in No. 5	4
7	Mr. West	July 18,	Note from United States. British West Indies are already in enjoyment of most-favoured-nation treatment, and cannot receive special favours without negotiating a Reciprocity Treaty	4
8	To Colonial Office	Sept. 3,	What instructions should be sent to Mr. West?	5
9	Colonial Office	Oct. 7,	The proposed negotiation should be begun at once. Mr. Lubbock would go to Washington to be consulted on technical points	6
10	To Mr. West	25,	Bases for a Convention with the United States for a mutual reduction of the duties on the principal articles of trade between the British West Indies and the United States	6
11	Colonial Office	Nov. 3,	Jamaica will join the other West India Islands in the Convention with the United States	7
12	To Mr. West	4,	Informs of above	8
13	Mr. West	13,	Note to United States' Government in accordance with No. 10	8
14	,, ,,	20,	Result of the negotiation. The United States desire a wider basis for the Convention, and that its advantages shall not be conceded gratis to third parties under most-favoured-nation clauses	9
15	,, ,,	Dec. 5,	Sends draft Treaty embodying wishes of United States	10
16	,, ,,	5,	Report on draft Treaty in No. 14. Mr. Lubbock's opinion of its value	18
17	,, ,,	6,	High opinion of assistance rendered by Mr. Lubbock	19
18	To Mr. West	Feb. 12, 1885	Reasons why Her Majesty's Government cannot accept draft Treaty in No. 14. Proposals in No. 10 could be modified so as to secure the same ends without infringing the most-favoured-nation clause as usually interpreted	20
19	To Colonial Office	12,	Further economic reasons for rejecting the draft Treaty	23

Correspondence respecting the Negotiation of a Treaty regulating Trade between the British West India Colonies and the United States.

No. 1.

Extract from the Treaty between Great Britain and the United States of July 3, 1815.

ARTICLE I.

THERE shall be between the territories of the United States, and all the territories of His Britannic Majesty in Europe, a reciprocal liberty of commerce. The inhabitants of the two countries respectively shall have liberty freely and securely to come with their ships and cargoes to all such places, ports, and rivers in the territories aforesaid to which other foreigners are permitted to come; to enter into the same, and to remain and reside in any parts of the said territories respectively; also to hire and occupy houses and warehouses for the purposes of their commerce; and generally the merchants and traders of each nation respectively shall enjoy the most complete protection and security for their commerce, but subject always to the laws and statutes of the two countries respectively.

ARTICLE II.

No higher or other duties shall be imposed on the importation into the United States of any articles, the growth, produce, or manufacture of His Britannic Majesty's territories in Europe, and no higher or other duties shall be imposed on the importation into the territories of His Britannic Majesty in Europe of any articles, the growth, produce, or manufacture of the United States, than are or shall be payable on the like articles being the growth, produce, or manufacture of any other foreign country; nor shall any higher or other duties or charges be imposed in either of the two countries on the exportation of any articles to the United States or to His Britannic Majesty's territories in Europe respectively than such as are payable on the exportation of the like articles to any other foreign country; nor shall any prohibition be imposed on the exportation or importation of any articles the growth, produce, or manufacture of the United States, or of His Britannic Majesty's territories in Europe, to or from the said territories of His Britannic Majesty in Europe, or to or from the said United States, which shall not equally extend to all other nations.

No higher or other duties or charges shall be imposed in any of the ports of the United States on British vessels than those payable in the same ports by vessels of the United States; nor in the ports of any of His Britannic Majesty's territories in Europe on the vessels of the United States than shall be payable in the same ports on British vessels.

The same duties shall be paid on the importation into the United States of any articles the growth, produce, or manufacture of His Britannic Majesty's territories in Europe, whether such importation shall be in vessels of the United States or in British vessels, and the same duties shall be paid on the importation into the ports of any of His Britannic Majesty's territories in Europe of any articles the growth, produce, or manufacture of the United States, whether such importation shall be in British vessels or in vessels of the United States.

[177]

The same duties shall be paid and the same bounties allowed on the exportation of any articles the growth, produce, or manufacture of His Britannic Majesty's territories in Europe to the United States, whether such exportation shall be in vessels of the United States or in British vessels; and the same duties shall be paid and the same bounties allowed on the exportation of any articles the growth, produce, or manufacture of the United States to His Britannic Majesty's territories in Europe, whether such exportation shall be in British vessels or in vessels of the United States.

It is further agreed that in all cases where drawbacks are or may be allowed upon the re-exportation of any goods, the growth, produce, or manufacture of either country respectively, the amount of the said drawbacks shall be the same, whether the said goods shall have been originally imported in a British or American vessel; but when such re-exportation shall take place from the United States in a British vessel, or from the territories of His Britannic Majesty in Europe in an American vessel to any other foreign nation, the two Contracting Parties reserve to themselves respectively the right of regulating or diminishing, in such case, the amount of the said drawback.

The intercourse between the United States and His Britannic Majesty's possessions in the West Indies and on the Continent of North America shall not be affected by any of the provisions of this Article, but each party shall remain in the complete possession of its rights with respect to such an intercourse.

No. 2.

Extract from the Treaty between Great Britain and the United States of October 20, 1818.

ARTICLE IV.

ALL the provisions of the Convention "to regulate the commerce between the territories of His Britannic Majesty and of the United States," concluded at London on the 3rd July, in the year of our Lord 1815, with the exception of the clause which limited its duration to four years, and excepting also so far as the same was affected by the Declaration of His Majesty respecting the Island of St. Helena, are hereby extended and continued in force for the term of ten years from the date of the signature of the present Convention, in the same manner as if all the provisions of the said Convention were herein specially recited.

No. 3.

Extract from the Treaty between Great Britain and the United States of August 6, 1827.

ARTICLE I.

ALL the provisions of the Convention concluded between His Majesty the King of the United Kingdom of Great Britain and Ireland and the United States of America, on the 3rd July, 1815, and further continued for the term of ten years by the IVth Article of the Convention of the 20th October, 1818, with the exception therein contained as to St. Helena, are hereby further indefinitely, and without the said exception, extended and continued in force, from the date of the expiration of the said ten years, in the same manner as if all the provisions of the said Convention of the 3rd July, 1815, were herein specifically recited.

ARTICLE II.

It shall be competent, however, to either of the Contracting Parties, in case either should think fit, at any time after the expiration of the said ten years—that is, after the 20th October, 1828—on giving due notice of twelve months to the other Contracting Party, to annul and abrogate this Convention; and it shall, in such case, be accordingly entirely annulled and abrogated, after the expiration of the said term of notice.

No. 4.

Earl Granville to Mr. West.

Sir,   *Foreign Office, May* 28, 1884.

THE Secretary of State for the Colonies has been in communication with me with regard to the present position of trade between the British Colonies in the West Indies and the United States.

In consequence of recent Treaties, or of Treaties which it is supposed are about to be negotiated, trade carried on between the United States and the Sandwich Islands, Mexico, Central America, the Spanish West India Islands, and San Domingo, has been, or is likely to be, placed on a more favourable footing than trade between the British West Indies and the United States. You are well aware of the importance of this branch of the commerce of these Colonies. In consequence, however, of the Treaties referred to, it will probably, within a short period, be injured, a result which cannot fail to be disadvantageous to the interests in the United States connected with the several British Colonies, as well as to these possessions themselves.

The United States enjoy as matter of fact, without express stipulation in any diplomatic Agreement, complete most-favoured-nation treatment in these Colonies. Her Majesty's Government therefore consider themselves justified, in this altered state of things, to ask that complete most-favoured-nation treatment shall likewise be extended in the United States to articles the growth, produce, or manufacture of the British West India Colonies.

I have accordingly to request that you will make a representation to the United States' Government to this effect, and that you will ask that the stipulations contained in Article II of the Treaty of the 3rd July, 1815, shall be extended, so as to be made applicable to trade between the United States and the British West India Colonies. You may state that you are authorized to sign a Convention or Declaration, whichever form of document the United States' Government may prefer, to carry into effect an Agreement, to which I trust that they will assent, for this purpose.

I am, &c.
(Signed)   GRANVILLE.

No. 5.

Mr. West to Earl Granville.—(*Received June* 24.)

My Lord,   *Washington, June* 10, 1884.

I HAVE the honour to acknowledge the receipt of your Lordship's despatch of the 28th ultimo, and to inclose herewith copy of a note which I have addressed to the Secretary of State, representing the present position of trade between the British Colonies in the West Indies; asking that the stipulations contained in Article II of the Treaty of the 3rd July, 1815, shall be extended so as to be made applicable to trade between the United States and the British West India Colonies, and stating that I am authorized to sign a Convention or Declaration to carry into effect an agreement to this purpose.

I have, &c.
(Signed)   L. S. SACKVILLE WEST.

Inclosure in No. 5.

Mr. West to Mr. Frelinghuysen.

Sir,   *Washington, June* 10, 1884.

I HAVE the honour to inform you that Her Majesty's Government have had under consideration the present position of trade between the British Colonies in the West Indies and the United States. It appears to them that in consequence of recent Treaties or of Treaties which may be negotiated, trade carried on between the United States and the Sandwich Islands, Mexico, Central America, the Spanish West India Islands, and San Domingo, has been, or is likely to be, placed on a more favourable footing than trade between the British West Indies and the United States, and that such a result cannot fail to be disadvantageous to the interests of the United States connected with the several British Colonies. Her Majesty's Government point out that the United States enjoy as a matter of fact, without express stipulation in any diplomatic agreement, complete most-favoured-nation treatment in these Colonies, and they therefore feel themselves justified in this altered state of things to ask that complete most-favoured-nation treatment shall likewise be extended in the United States to articles the growth, produce, or manufacture of the British West India Colonies.

Earl Granville has accordingly instructed me to make a representation to the United States' Government to this effect, and to ask that the stipulations contained in Article II of the Treaty of the 3rd July, 1815, shall be extended so as to be made applicable to trade between the United States and the British West India Colonies.

I am to add that I am authorized by Her Majesty's Government to sign a Convention or Declaration, whichever form of document may be preferred by the United States' Government, to carry into effect an agreement to which they trust that the United States' Government will assent for this purpose.

I have, &c.
(Signed) L. S. SACKVILLE WEST.

No. 6.

Earl Granville to Mr. West.

Sir, *Foreign Office, June* 26, 1884.

I APPROVE the note addressed by you to the United States' Secretary of State, a copy of which is inclosed in your despatch of the 10th instant, asking on behalf of Her Majesty's Government that the stipulations contained in Article II of the Treaty of the 3rd July, 1815, shall be extended so as to be made applicable to trade between the United States and the British West India Colonies, and also stating that you are authorized to sign a Convention or Declaration to carry into effect an agreement for this purpose.

I am, &c.
(Signed) GRANVILLE.

No. 7.

Mr. West to Earl Granville.—(*Received August* 1.)

(Extract.) *Washington, July* 18, 1884.

WITH reference to your Lordship's despatch of the 28th May last, I have the honour to inclose herewith copy of a note which I have received from the Secretary of State in answer to the communication which, by your Lordship's instructions, I addressed to him, proposing a Convention or Declaration whereby the most-favoured-nation treatment stipulated in Article II of the Treaty of 1815 should be made applicable to trade between the United States and the British West Indies.

It will be seen that it is asserted in this note that agreements giving specific and exceptional advantages do not fall within the most-favoured-nation clause of existing Treaties.

Inclosure in No. 7.

Mr. Frelinghuysen to Mr. West.

Sir, *Department of State, Washington, July* 16, 1884.

I HAVE the honour to acknowledge the receipt of your note of the 10th ultimo.

You therein indicate the view of Her Majesty's Government that in consequence of recent Treaties or of Treaties which may be negotiated, trade carried on between the United States and the Sandwich Islands, Mexico, Central America, the Spanish West Indies, and San Domingo has been, or is likely to be, placed on a more favoured footing than trade between the United States and the British West Indies.

Your Government thereupon points out that the United States as a matter of fact enjoy complete most-favoured-nation treatment in those Colonies, and accordingly asks " that complete most-favoured-nation treatment shall likewise be extended in the United

States to articles the growth, produce, or manufacture of the British West India Colonies."

To this end Lord Granville instructs you to propose a Convention or Declaration whereby the most-favoured-nation treatment stipulated in Article II of the Treaty of the 3rd July, 1815, shall be made applicable to the trade between the United States and those Colonies.

His Lordship's proposition cannot fail to attract consideration on the part of this Government, especially now when it is the desire of the United States to cultivate, by means of carefully-studied conditions of reciprocity, trade between this country and its neighbours of the American continent by which their products may be bartered for our manufactures on bases of mutual favour.

The terms upon which an arrangement is proposed by Lord Granville do not, however, appear to meet the conditions of the question. His Lordship observes that the United States receive in the British West Indies the same commercial treatment as the most favoured nations. This is true, and it is true also of the treatment which the products and manufactures of the United States receive in Mexico, Central America, the Spanish West Indies, and San Domingo, the countries mentioned in your note, and is true also of the French, Danish, Dutch, and other possessions in the West Indies and South America.

This Government would, however, be glad to secure more intimate commercial relations with the countries of the American continent which can best be obtained through agreements giving specific and exceptional advantages, and therefore not falling within the most-favoured-nation clause of existing Treaties.

The details by which such results are to be reached are necessarily to be varied to fit the different conditions of each province, but the general scope would tend to assimilate trade between them and the United States to the conditions which apply to productions and shipping in the domestic coasting trade, or the trade of a country with its own dependencies.

Lord Granville's proposition does not appear to contemplate the concession to the United States of any special privileges for goods or ships like those which, in the view of this Government, are necessary to any such agreement. For instance, the British West Indies impose customs and export duties, similar to those which in negotiating with the countries named by you, the United States would require to be removed or essentially modified by them as a condition of placing their staples on our free list.

It is clear the the IInd Article of the Treaty of 1815 has not authorized, and could not authorize Great Britain to ask for the products or shipping of the United Kingdom, favours identical with or equivalent to those which Spanish-American and West India Colonial products and shipping may receive in the ports of the United States by reason of special Reciprocity Treaties. The formal extension of this Article to the British West India Colonies, therefore, would not give them other rights than those now enjoyed by the United Kingdom. Those Colonies possess, as a matter of fact, and without express stipulation, the complete most-favoured-nation treatment now accorded to the mother country. British vessels and their cargoes from any part of the world are admitted into ports of the United States on the same terms as to duties, imposts, and charges, as those of the United States.

It may, in view of the limited formulation of Lord Granville's proposition, be premature to assume that his Lordship contemplates the negotiation of a Reciprocity Treaty which shall secure for the trade of the West India Colonies with the United States special favours, although the negotiation of the Canadian Reciprocity Treaty of 1854 would show that this class of international engagements, applying only to particular Colonies, is not in violation of the policy of Her Majesty's Government.

I therefore at present only ask you to acquaint Lord Granville with the interest awakened by his proposal, and to say that any further suggestion of Her Majesty's Government on the subject will be most carefully considered.

I have, &c.
(Signed)   FREDK. T. FRELINGHUYSEN.

No. 8.

Mr. Lister to Sir R. Herbert.

(Extract.)   *Foreign Office, September* 3, 1884.

I AM directed by Earl Granville to observe that the proposed negotiations with the United States' Government relative to trade between the United States and the British

Colonies in the West Indies have to be considered with reference to public interests and opinion in this country as well as in the West Indies. It would therefore seem to be advisable that, before further instructions are sent to Mr. West, the Colonial Office should consider and specify distinctly the bases on which it is wished that the further communication relative to the negotiation of the proposed Reciprocity Treaty should be made to the United States' Government. A question may arise at the outset whether any goods, the produce or manufacture of the United States, are to be admitted into the British West Indies on terms more favourable than similar goods the produce or manufacture of the United Kingdom. It will be necessary to supply Mr. West with instructions on this point.

No. 9.

Mr. Meade to Mr. Lister.—(Received October 7.)

Sir, *Downing Street, October* 7, 1884.

I AM directed by the Earl of Derby to acknowledge the receipt of your letter of the 3rd ultimo, respecting the proposal to enter into negotiations with the Government of the United States, with a view to such reciprocal Tariff arrangements as may procure the admission of raw sugar, the produce of the West India Colonies, duty free into the United States.

2. Lord Derby has had this subject under his serious consideration, and continues to receive the strongest assurances that this matter is becoming of vital importance to the West India Colonies, and he has been led to the belief that unless some measure is speedily taken which may restore confidence in those Colonies, the consequences may be deplorable in the extreme.

3. It appears that the planters are already curtailing their operations, and the merchants stopping their advances; and it is anticipated that the immediate result will be that large numbers of labourers will be thrown out of work. If no employment should be procurable, the support of the Indian immigrants may partly or wholly devolve upon Her Majesty's Government. It is further represented that the period within which any effectual action can be taken to prevent this suspension of the sugar industry is now narrowed down to a very few months.

4. The West India Governments are prepared to defray any expense which may attend the attempt to obtain the free entry of their sugar into the United States, and, under all the circumstances, Lord Derby is of opinion that the proposed negotiations should be pressed on with energy. It is believed that Mr. West would find it of great advantage in the conduct of negotiations on this subject, to have the presence of some gentleman thoroughly conversant with the sugar interests of the West India Colonies, whom he could consult on all technical points that may arise. Mr. Nevile Lubbock, the Chairman of the West India Committee, is ready to proceed to Washington to give information to Her Majesty's Minister as to the wishes and requirements of the Colonies.

5. Lord Derby is of opinion that this is the most satisfactory and generally acceptable arrangement which can be made for insuring the proper representation of West India interests at the proposed negotiations; and he will arrange that Mr. Lubbock shall discuss with this Department, in the first instance, the bases of negotiation which Her Majesty's Government is prepared to adopt.

I have, &c.
(Signed) R. H. MEADE.

No. 10.

Earl Granville to Mr. West.

(Extract.) *Foreign Office, October* 25, 1884.

I HAVE now to inform you that Her Majesty's Government, on behalf of the British Colonies of Trinidad, Barbados, and the four Windward Islands, the Leeward Islands, and British Guiana, are prepared to enter into negotiations with the Government of the United States for the admission of sugar the produce or manufacture of the aforesaid British Colonies free of duty, or with a material reduction of the present duty, into the ports of the United States.

2. The minimum reduction of duty on sugar which would be accepted by the aforesaid Colonies as an equivalent for the concessions hereinafter by them offered would be one-half of the duties levied under the Tariff of the 3rd March, 1883.

3. The Colonies aforesaid are prepared to abolish the import duties in their respective ports levied upon the under-mentioned articles, the greater portion of which is imported from the United States:—

    Bread and biscuits.
    Butter.
    Cheese.
    Corn and meal of all kinds.
    Flour.
    Lard.
    Lumber.
    Kerosene oil.
    Oil meal and cake.

The Islands of Barbados, Grenada, St. Lucia, St. Vincent, and Tobago, and the Colony of the Leeward Islands, are further prepared to abolish the duties on meats of all kinds, shooks and staves, and the Colony of British Guiana is prepared to abolish, in addition to the duties on the articles above mentioned, the duty on hams and other dried meats.

Her Majesty's Government conceive that the arrangements may take something the form of the Treaty between the United States and Mexico dated the 20th January, 1883, but they would wish to avoid all implication of differential treatment such as is contained in the stipulations of Article V of that Convention.

Her Majesty's Government would reserve to the Colonial Governments full liberty to impose export duties on the articles mentioned in any arrangement which may be concluded.

No. 11.

Mr. Wingfield to Lord E. Fitzmaurice.—(*Received November* 3.)

(Extract.)   *Downing Street, November* 3, 1884.

I AM now to inform you that the Government of Jamaica have consented that that Colony shall be included in the negotiations, and to inclose, for transmission to Mr. West, a short additional instruction to cover the case of Jamaica. And I am also to request that Lord Granville will cause Mr. West to be informed that the various Colonial Governments have been directed to communicate with him by telegraph if it is their desire to abolish or reduce their duties on articles not included in the instructions.

Inclosure in No. 11.

Additional Instructions to Her Majesty's Minister at Washington as to Jamaica.

THE Government of Jamaica desire that that Colony may be included in the negotiations with the United States for reciprocal commercial arrangements between the United States and the West India Colonies, and are prepared, in return for the admission of sugars produced in Jamaica free of duty into the ports of the United States, to abolish the import duties now levied in the ports of Jamaica upon the following articles, viz.:—

    Bread and biscuits.
    Butter.
    Cheese.
    Corn and meal of all kinds.
    Flour.
    Lard.
    Kerosene oil.

[177]

No. 12.

Earl Granville to Mr. West.

(Extract.) *Foreign Office, November 4, 1884.*

JAMAICA wishes to join in the stipulations in regard to British Colonies in the West Indies set forth in my despatch of the 25th ultimo. I accordingly inclose, for your information and guidance, copies of a letter and its inclosure from the Colonial Office on the subject.*

No. 13.

Mr. West to Earl Granville.—(Received November 25.)

My Lord, *Washington, November 13, 1884.*

I HAVE the honour to acknowledge the receipt of your Lordship's despatch of the 25th ultimo, informing me that Her Majesty's Government, on behalf of the British Colonies therein mentioned, are prepared to enter into negotiations with the Government of the United States for the admission of sugar, the produce or manufacture of the aforesaid British Colonies, free of duty, or with a material reduction of the present duty, into the ports of the United States, and that those Colonies are prepared to abolish the import duties in their respective ports levied upon certain specified articles. I accordingly informed the Secretary of State to this effect in a note, copy of which I have herewith inclosed.

It appeared to me from the correspondence which had passed on this subject, that the object which Her Majesty's Government had in view was to open negotiations at once, and that this could be attained, considering the strong proclivities of the Secretary of State for Reciprocity Treaties, by a simple statement of what Her Majesty's Government on behalf of the Colonies was prepared to do in this respect. At an interview which I had this day with Mr. Frelinghuysen, he told me that he had considered my communication and found it acceptable for opening negotiations. I then told him that Mr. Lubbock had come to Washington for the purpose of giving any technical information in regard to points which might come under discussion, and he expressed his satisfaction at Mr. Lubbock's presence in Washington as well as his desire to see him and hear what he had to say.

In conclusion, he said that he hoped sincerely that we might come to some satisfactory arrangement.

I have, &c.
(Signed) L. S. SACKVILLE WEST.

Inclosure in No. 13.

Mr. West to Mr. Frelinghuysen.

Sir, *Washington, November 7, 1884.*

WITH reference to your note of the 16th July last, in answer to mine of the 10th June, I have the honour to inform you that Her Majesty's Government, on behalf of the British Colonies of Jamaica, Trinidad, Barbados, and the four Windward Islands, the Leeward Islands, and British Guiana, are now prepared to enter into negotiations with the Government of the United States for the admission of sugar, the produce or manufacture of the aforesaid British Colonies, free of duty, or with a material reduction of the present duty, into the ports of the United States.

In return, the British Colonies aforesaid are prepared to abolish the import duties in their respective ports levied upon the undermentioned articles, the greater portion of which is imported from the United States:—

1. Bread and biscuits.
2. Butter.
3. Cheese.
4. Corn and meal of all kinds.
5. Flour.
6. Lard.
7. Lumber.
8. Kerosene oil.
9. Oil meal and cake.

* No. 11.

The Islands of Barbados, Grenada, St. Lucia, St. Vincent, and Tobago, and the Colony of the Leeward Islands are further prepared to abolish the duties on meats of all kinds, shooks and staves, and the Colony of British Guiana is prepared to abolish, in addition to the duties on the articles above-mentioned, the duty on hams and other dried meats.

In communicating to you this proposal of Her Majesty's Government for the improvement of the trade of the West India Colonies with the United States, I feel sure that the interest which it cannot fail to awaken will insure for it the most careful consideration on the part of the Government of the United States, and I avail, &c.

(Signed)　　L. S. SACKVILLE WEST.

No. 14.

Mr. West to Earl Granville.—(*Received December* 3.)

(Extract.) *Washington, November* 20, 1884.

I HAVE the honour to report to your Lordship that numerous informal discussions have taken place daily between Mr. Adee, Mr. Lubbock, and myself, on the subject of the proposed Treaty with the West India Colonies.

I told Mr. Adee that, as regarded the carrying trade and the question of tonnage dues which it involved, I should be unable to negotiate without reference to Her Majesty's Government, and he said that he was of opinion that if Her Majesty's Government were not prepared to accept this basis it would be better that the negotiation should be broken off before it had assumed any official form. There was, however, no reason why we should not endeavour to elaborate the reciprocal advantages which both parties were willing to accord. Mr. Adee said that he thought that the Treaty with Salvador which the United States' Government were actually negotiating was more applicable in the case of the West India Colonies than the Mexican Reciprocity Treaty as regarded the articles to be placed on the free list, and he produced the draft of this Treaty, together with the Schedule of articles. As I at once saw another difficulty which was likely to arise in the proposal for the adoption of this free list, I told Mr. Lubbock, to whom I referred it, that however satisfactory it might be to obtain the abolition of the duty on sugar under it, I could not consent to any modification of existing arrangements with regard to the said commodities without further instructions from Her Majesty's Government. I made this statement in consequence of incidental mention having been made of coal, textile fabrics, machinery, wood, and lumber to be placed on the free list of articles imported into the Colonies from the United States, and of Mr. Lubbock saying he thought there would be no difficulty on this head.

Mr. Lubbock has impressed upon me, in view of the conclusion of the Treaty with Spain, the necessity of obtaining by the proposed Treaty similar advantages for the West India Colonies, and more especially as the British Colonies are excluded from all most-favoured-nation treatment. He said that in fact it was a matter upon which the future well-being of the Colonies depended. I told him that I thought that by consenting to the proposed form of negotiation and to the consideration of the proposals we were now discussing, Her Majesty's Government had given sufficient proof of the interest which they took in the welfare of the West India Colonies, but at the same time it must be borne in mind that there were questions of Imperial policy involved in the proposed negotiations which could not be lost sight of, and that I could not depart from the general nature of the instructions which I had received. I may now state to your Lordship the result arrived at from the informal conversations which have been held:—

1. The United States' Government are willing to negotiate a Reciprocity Treaty with Great Britain on behalf of the West India Colonies.

2. They concede the abolition of the duty on sugar not above No. 16, Dutch standard, and are willing to abolish the duties on a number of other articles the produce of the Colonies.

3. They desire that the benefits of the Treaty, so far as the carrying trade is concerned, shall be confined to the two countries.

4. They ask for no advantages whatever over Great Britain or her Colonies.

5. In order to establish a thorough reciprocity in the trade, they wish to widen the scope of the proposal of Her Majesty's Government for the abolition of the sugar duties, in return for the abolition on the part of the Colonies of the duties on the

[177]

articles specified therein, so as to embrace the provisions, more or less, for the free lists in the Treaties with Mexico, Salvador, San Domingo, and Spain, which countries place on their free list, among many others, coal, wood, lumber, machinery of all kinds, and certain textile fabrics coming from the United States.

6. They wish to guard against extending any of the advantages of the Treaty to other countries, by interpreting the most-favoured-nation treatment to mean that favours should be extended only with the condition of reciprocity attached.

7. They manifest a desire, by means of such a Treaty as above indicated, to attach the West India Colonies, by the creation of commercial interests, to the United States, and to assimilate trade between them to the conditions which apply to productions and shipping in the domestic coasting trade or the trade of a country with its own dependencies.

The above I believe to be the objects which the United States' Government have in view, and which they are desirous of effecting by means of the proposed Reciprocity Treaty.

No. 15.

Mr. West to Earl Granville.—(*Received December* 17.)

My Lord,   *Washington, December* 5, 1884.

I HAVE the honour to inclose to your Lordship herewith copy of a note which has been addressed to me by the Secretary of State, covering a Project of Convention which is submitted to Her Majesty's Government as a counter-project to the one proposed in my note of the 7th ultimo, copy of which was inclosed in my despatch of the 13th ultimo.

In order to save the post, I am obliged to defer my Report on the negotiations which have led to this result.*

         I have, &c.
    (Signed)   L. S. SACKVILLE WEST.

Inclosure 1 in No. 15.

Mr. Frelinghuysen to Mr. West.

Sir,   *Washington, December* 4, 1884.

REFERRING to your note of the 7th ultimo, in which you acquainted me with the proposal of Her Britannic Majesty's Government, on behalf of certain of the British Colonies in the West Indies and in Guiana, to enter into negotiations for the conclusion of a reciprocal Agreement for admitting certain productions of either into the ports of the other free of duties or under a reduction of duties; and referring also to my note of the 15th November in acknowledgment thereof, in which I stated the pleasure I would have in considering and discussing that proposal, with a view to reaching some mutually beneficial agreement thereon, and especially to my intimation that the benefits of such a Treaty should extend to the carrying trade as well, by reserving their privileged enjoyment to the vessels of the two countries, I have now the honour to hand you a draft proposition for a Convention of Reciprocity to accomplish those ends. This draft may be regarded as a counter-project to the proposal formulated in your note of the 7th November.

In personal conferences with you, while considering the special needs of the British Colonies in the premises, and bearing in mind their interests no less than our own, I have taken occasion to intimate that the concurrent favouring of the goods and also the shipping of the two countries engaged in carrying those goods between the United States and those islands, under express conditions which would not throw the reserved privileges open to other countries under the operation of favoured-nation clauses of other Treaties, was to my mind an indispensable condition to the conclusion of such Convention. The present counter-draft makes those points clear.

         I have, &c.
    (Signed)   F. T. FRELINGHUYSEN.

---

* See No. 16.

Inclosure 2 in No. 15.

(Draft, November 28, 1884.)

(Confidential.)

Project of a Convention for Commercial Reciprocity between the United States of America and certain Possessions of Her Majesty the Queen of Great Britain.

THE Government of the United States of America and Her Majesty the Queen of Great Britain, equally animated by the desire to strengthen and perpetuate the friendly relations happily existing between them, and being also desirous to regulate the commerce and navigation between their respective territories and people, and more especially between the United States and certain of Her Majesty's possessions in the West Indies and upon the South American continent, to wit: Jamaica, Barbados, Trinidad, Antigua, St. Christopher, Nevis, Montserrat, Dominica, Virgin Islands, St. Vincent, St. Lucia, Grenada, Tobago, and in addition thereto British Guiana; in such manner as to render the same reciprocally beneficial and satisfactory; especially recognizing that by reason of the close proximity of the said possessions of Her Majesty the Queen of Great Britain to the shores of the United States, intimate and beneficial relations of trade have sprung up between them; and, moreover, equally sharing the belief that the establishment of such commercial intercourse as shall further and devolop trade and good-will will be mutually advantageous to their respective citizens and subjects, have resolved to enter into a Commercial Convention. For this purpose the President of the United States has appointed as his Plenipotentiary,

And Her Majesty the Queen of Great Britain,

who, after exhibition of their respective full powers, found in good and due form, have agreed upon the following Articles;—

ARTICLE I.

For and in consideration of the rights and privileges to be granted by the British Colonies aforesaid, in the present Convention, and as an equivalent therefor, the United States of America hereby agree to admit into the ports of the United States open to commerce as declared ports of entry, all the articles named in the following Schedule (A) free of import duties, and all the articles named in the following Schedule (B) at a reduction of 25 per centum from the rates of customs duties now fixed or which may hereafter be fixed during the continuance in force of this Convention by the Customs Tariff of the United States with respect to the several articles so enumerated in said Schedule (B): *Provided,* That the articles named in Schedules (A) and (B) be the growth or manufacture or production of the aforesaid British Colonies: *And provided further,* That said articles be carried in vessels under the registry and flag of one or the other of the Contracting Parties.

Schedule (A).

Articles of aforesaid British Colonial Production to be admitted free of Duties into the United States.

1. Asphaltum, crude or refined.
2. Balsams and gums, crude, for the manufacture of medicinal extracts and preparations.
3. Beeswax.
4. Bones, hoofs, and horns, unmanufactured.
5. Bones, shells, guano, and other animal remains or deposits, employed as fertilizers.
6. Cinchona, quassia, and other barks or woods yielding medicinal alkaloids.
7. Cocoa, crude and manufactured.
8. Coffee.
9. Cork bark and scrap cork, unmanufactured.
10. Cotton, hemp, sisal, heniquen, palm, and other vegetable textile fibres, unmanufactured.
11. Dye-woods and dye-stuffs of all kinds, animal or vegetable.
12. Esparto, bamboo, and other grasses, and pulp of, for the manufacture of paper.
13. Fruits, vegetables, and nuts, edible, of all kinds, fresh.

14. Ginger, dried or preserved.
15. Gold and silver coin, or unrefined bars thereof.
16. Hides and skins, undressed, whether dried, salted, or pickled.
17. Honey, in comb or strained.
18. India-rubber and gutta-percha, crude, and the milk of the same.
19. Indigo.
20. Ivory, animal or vegetable.
21. Leather, old scrap.
22. Lime juice and orange juice.
23. Meat, fresh, whether beef or mutton.
24. Minerals and ores, of precious or common metals.
25. Molasses and melada.
26. Palm or cocoa-nut oil.
27. Pimento, pepper, cinnamon, cloves, nutmegs and allspice, crude.
28. Phosphates, crude, for fertilizers.
29. Sponges.
30. Sarsaparilla.
31. Starch, arrowroot, and other amylaceous products.
32. Sugar, not above No. 16, Dutch standard, in colour.
33. Turtle, live, or prepared products thereof.
34. Vanilla and Tonquin beans.
35. Wood and lumber of all kinds, in the rough state, whether as logs, planks, sticks, or strips.

Schedule (B).

Articles of aforesaid British Colonial Production to be admitted into the United States at a Reduction of Duties of 25 per centum.

1. Bitters, aromatic.
2. Cordials in bottles consisting of rum aromatized and sweetened.
3. Fruit preserves, fruit jellies, and comfits.

ARTICLE II.

For and in consideration of the rights and privileges to be granted by the United States of America in the present Convention, and as an equivalent therefor, the Government of Great Britain, in behalf of the British Colonies aforesaid, hereby agree to admit into the ports of said Colonies all the articles named in the following Schedule (C) free of import duties, and all the articles named in the following Schedule (D) at a reduction of 50 per centum from the rates of customs duties now fixed, or which may hereafter be fixed, during the continuance in force of this Convention by the Customs Tariff of the aforesaid British Colonies with respect to the several articles so enumerated in said Schedule (D); *Provided,* That the articles named in said Schedules (C) and (D) be the growth or manufacture or production of the United States of America: *And provided further,* That said articles be carried in vessels under the registry and flag of one or the other of the Contracting Parties.

Schedule (C).

Articles of the Production of the United States to be admitted free of Duties into the aforesaid British Colonies.

1. Acids, commercial, for manufacturing purposes.
2. Animals, alive: mules, cattle, sheep, goats, and hogs; and horses for breeding.
3. Asphalt, bitumen, tar, pitch and resin, crude or refined.
4. Belting for machinery, of leather, canvas, or india-rubber.
5. Books, bound or unbound, pamphlets, newspapers, and printed matter, in all languages.
6. Bricks, fire-bricks, tiles, artificial stone, terra cotta, slate, and asbestos, for building.
7. Bridges of iron or wood, or of both combined.
8. Bristles and hair, raw or waste.
9. Brooms, brushes, and whisks of bristles or broom straw.
10. Carts, cars, and barrows, with or without springs, for agricultural use
11. Clocks, mantel or wall.
12. Cocoa and cacao and products thereof, prepared for food.

13. Copper, brass, bronze, zinc, and lead articles, plain or nickel-plated, for industrial and domestic use, and for building.
14. Cotton, hemp, flax, jute, and other vegetable fibres, not spun or woven.
15. Cotton-seed and its products.
16. Crucibles and melting-pots of all kinds.
17. Eggs.
18. Fertilizers of all kinds, natural or artificial.
19. Fire-arms for hunting and sporting purposes, and the cartridges therefor.
20. Firewood.
21. Fish and edible fish products of all kinds, but only when fresh, canned, or tinned.
22. Fishing apparatus of all kinds.
23. Flour and meal, of whatever kind of grain except wheat.
24. Fruits and vegetables, fresh, canned, tinned, bottled, dried, pickled, or preserved.
25. Furniture, comprising beds, tables, sofas, chairs, arm-chairs, desks, toilet tables, wardrobes, book-cases, sideboards, and other household furnitnre, whether plain or upholstered.
26. Fuse and wick for mines.
27. Gas fixtures and pipes.
28. Gelatine, refined, for food.
29. Glass, in plates or sheets, rough or polished.
30. Glassware of all kinds, plain or decorated.
31. Glue.
32. Gold and silver coin of the United States, and refined bullion in bars or powder.
33. Gum and gutta-percha goods, including fabrics and clothing rendered wholly waterproof by means of india-rubber or gutta-percha.
34. Hay.
35. Hides and skins, undressed or dressed.
36. Houses of wood or iron, complete.
37. Ice.
38. Instruments, scientific and surgical, of all kinds.
39. Iron and steel tools, utensils and implements for agriculture, composed of iron or steel, or both, or of these metals, or either of them, combined with other metals, or with wood, including any separate extra parts and pieces pertaining thereto.
40. Iron and steel locks, sliding bolts, hasps, hinges, handles and the like (including porcelain or other knobs or fittings necessary thereto)—commonly known as "builders' hardware."
41. Iron, cast, pig, and scrap.
42. Lamps and lanterns.
43. Lime, quick or slaked.
44. Lithographic stones.
45. Locomotives, railway rolling-stock, rails, railway ties, and all materials and appliances for railways and tramways.
46. Marble or alabaster, in the rough or squared, worked or carved, for constructions or monuments.
47. Meats of all kinds, but only when fresh, canned, or tinned.
48. Medicinal extracts and preparations of all kinds, of which the formula is known, exclusive of quinine or preparations of quinine, opium in gum, extract or tincture, gange, and bhang.
49. Milk, canned, condensed, or preserved.
50. Minerals and ores.
51. Mineral waters, natural or artificial.
52. Mirrors and mirror plates, plain or silvered.
53. Moulds and patterns for the arts.
54. Naphtha and benzine.
55. Paint and varnish brushes.
56. Paints, dry or ground, and turpentine, wood spirit, dryers, and varnishes.
57. Paper of all kinds for printing.
58. Pens of any metal not silver or gold.
59. Photographic apparatus and chemicals.
60. Pianos and other musical instruments.
61. Porcelain, china, and earthen and stone ware, plain or decorated.

62. Printers' ink, all colours.
63. Printers' types, rules, spaces, and all accessories for printing.
64. Printing presses.
65. Quicksilver.
66. Rags or cloth for the manufacture of paper.
67. Sewing machines, and all parts and accessories thereof.
68. Ship-building materials and accessories of all kinds, when used in the construction, equipment, or repair of vessels or boats of any kind, except rope and cordage of all kinds, including wire rope.
69. Shooks, staves, headings, hoops, and cooperage of all kinds, and wooden boxes for packing.
70. Spices, condiments, and alimentary sauces prepared for use, in packages, tins, or glass.
71. Steam and power engines, and machines, machinery, and apparatus, whether stationary or portable, worked by power or by hand, for agriculture, irrigation, mining, the arts and industries of all kinds, and all necessary parts and appliances for the erection or repair thereof or the communication of motive power thereto.
72. Steam-pipes.
73. Steam-boilers.
74. Stoves, ranges, and furnaces, for heating, culinary, or manufacturing purposes.
75. Straw of all kinds.
76. Sulphur.
77. Tan bark of all kinds, whole or ground.
78. Teasels, vegetable or of wire, mounted ready for all uses.
79. Telegraph-wire and telegraphic, telephonic, and electrical apparatus and appliances of all kinds for communication or illumination.
80. Tin-ware, for arts, industries, and domestic uses.
81. Trees, plants, vines, and seeds and grains of all kinds, for propagation or cultivation.
82. Wall-papers.
83. Watches, when not cased in gold or silver; and watch movements, uncased.
84. Water-pipes, of all classes, materials, and dimensions.
85. Willow-ware and wicker-ware.
86. Wire barbed for fences, with the hooks, staples, nails, and the like appliances for fastening the same.
87. Wood prepared in shape suitable for building, including doors, sashes, frames, blinds painted or unpainted, and similar necessary parts of buildings, but not including shingles, beams, rafters, planks, boards, flooring, joists, or laths.
88. Wooden ware and implements of all kinds for agricultural, mechanical, or household use.
89. Wool, raw, washed, or carded.
90. Zinc, tin, and lead, in sheets, asbestos, tar-paper, and other roofings.

SCHEDULE (D).

Articles of the Production of the United States to be admitted into the aforesaid British Colonies at a Reduction of Duties of 50 per centum.

1. Biscuits and other food preparations of flour or meal.
2. Butter, but no imitation thereof shall be classed as butter.
3. Cattle food, prepared, and feed cakes of all kinds.
4. Cheese.
5. Flour of wheat.
6. Grain of all kinds, not including rice and oats.
7. Lard.
8. Leather, fine or common, and all articles in which leather shall be the principal material.
9. Matches.
10. Petroleum and its products, refined, for illuminating and lubricating purposes.
11. Pitch pine.

It is, however, agreed that the privileges attaching under this Convention to the articles of merchandize numbered 29, 30, 49, 52, 60, 61, in Schedule (C) shall not accrue when the said articles are imported into the Colony of Jamaica; and, moreover, that the articles described under No. 69 of the aforesaid Schedule (C) are excepted from free admission into the Colony of Trinidad.

15

ARTICLE III.

The Governments of the two Contracting Parties shall respectively have the power to issue such laws, rules, regulations, instructions, and orders as they may deem proper to protect their revenues and prevent fraud, in order to prove that the merchandizes included in the above Schedules annexed to the 1st and IInd Articles of this Convention are produced or manufactured in the United States of America or in the aforesaid British Colonies respectively, and are therefore entitled to the special benefits which are granted upon their importation into the declared ports of entry of the respective countries.

The Government of each of the Contracting Parties shall have, moreover, the power to amend, modify, or amplify the laws and regulations issued in the exercise of the power conferred by this Article whenever it deems proper, to protect its revenues and prevent fraud.

The Contracting Parties, however, mutually agree that the proofs of origin contemplated in this Article shall be of fact only, and that the carriers of the goods which may be found to contravene the precautionary measures established in virtue hereof shall not be amenable to fine or imprisonment, nor the vessels carrying said goods to penalty, unless upon proof of an attempt on their part to defraud the revenues.

ARTICLE IV.

No export duty or charges shall be imposed in the United States or in the British Colonies aforesaid upon any of the articles proposed to be admitted into the ports of the said Colonies or into the ports of the United States under the Ist and IInd Articles of this Convention, except as hereinafter provided, nor shall any of said articles, coming from the United States or from said Colonies and imported into the territory of the other, be subject to internal excise or consumption dues greater than those which are or may be imposed upon similar articles of national production. The export duties in the said Colonies for immigration and other purposes are not to exceed the following rates: Sugar, one pound sterling (1*l.*) per ton; molasses, five shillings (5*s.*) per ton; cocoa, one pound ten shillings (1*l.* 10*s.*) per ton; coffee, one pound ten shillings (1*l.* 10*s.*) per ton; asphalt, two shillings six pence (2*s.* 6*d.*) per ton; logwood, two shillings (2*s*). per ton.

ARTICLE V.

Vessels of the United States coming directly from any port or ports of the United States with cargo wholly the growth, produce, or manufacture of the United States, or in ballast, for the purpose of lading with cargo for the United States, shall pay upon entering any port or ports of entry of any one or more of the aforesaid Colonies the same tonnage, clearance, and other duties as are levied by the Colonial Government upon national vessels of like tonnage engaged in the domestic coasting or intercolonial trade, and coming directly from any port or ports of the same Colony or of any one or more of the Colonies hereinbefore enumerated; and as to municipal or local dues, such as pilotage, port, wharf, and hospital charges and the like, they shall pay the same charges as are levied upon national vessels of like tonnage and description coming from like ports and carrying like cargo or in ballast: And conversely, vessels of Great Britain trading with the aforesaid Colonies coming from any port or ports of any one or more of said Colonies, with cargo wholly the growth, produce, or manufacture of said Colonies or in ballast, for the purpose of lading with cargo for said Colonies, shall pay upon entering any port or ports of entry of the United States the same tonnage, clearance, and other dues imposed by the Federal Government as are levied upon national vessels of like tonnage and description engaged in the domestic coasting trade and coming directly from any other port of the United States with cargo or in ballast; and as to municipal or local dues, such as pilotage, port, wharf, and hospital charges and the like, they shall pay the same charges as are levied upon national vessels of like tonnage and description coming from like ports and carrying like cargo or in ballast. And the vessels of either Contracting Party, so laden and coming directly from any port or ports of the United States, or from any port or ports of any one or more of the aforesaid Colonies, shall be free to proceed from any one port of entry for foreign commerce to any other like port or ports of entry in the country or in any one or more of the aforesaid Colonies to which they are bound, unlading cargo duly consigned to such several ports subsequently visited in the course of the same voyage on the same terms as the vessels of that country of like tonnage and description engaged in the coasting or intercolonial trade thereof: *Provided,* That nothing in this Article shall give to vessels of the United States or of

[177]

Great Britain the right to take on board in a port of the aforesaid Colonies or of the United States cargo destined for another port thereof when such right is exclusively reserved for the domestic coasting or intercolonial trade under the laws of the respective countries.

ARTICLE VI.

If any vessel of the United States, proceeding from a port or ports of the United States to a port or ports of any one or more of the aforesaid Colonies, shall carry any cargo not the growth, produce, or manufacture of the United States, whether the same be shipped in the United States or at any intermediate foreign port, the favoured treatment stipulated in the preceding Article V shall not be obligatory in respect of said vessel, but said vessel shall be treated, as to tonnage and other shipping dues, and as to the customs duties on said cargo of foreign origin, on the same footing as a vessel of like tonnage of Great Britain coming from the United States laden in like manner; and, conversely, if any vessel of Great Britain, proceeding from a port or ports of any one or more of said Colonies to the United States, shall carry any cargo not the growth, produce, or manufacture of said Colonies, whether the same be shipped in said Colonies or at any intermediate port, the favoured treatment stipulated in the preceding Article V shall not be obligatory in respect of said vessel, but said vessel shall be treated, as to tonnage and other shipping dues, and as to the customs duties on said cargo of foreign origin, on the same footing as a vessel of the United States of like tonnage coming from the aforesaid Colonies laden in like manner; but this Article shall not affect any cargo or part of cargo of such vessels being the growth, produce, or manufacture of the United States or of the aforesaid Colonies; and as to such cargo as they may carry coming under the provisions of Article I or Article II, as the case may be, the privileges stipulated in those Articles shall apply.

ARTICLE VII.

Vessels of the United States, with or without cargo, coming from any foreign countries and entering the ports of the aforesaid Colonies, and British vessels engaged in trade with said Colonies, with or without cargo, coming from foreign countries and entering the ports of the United States, whatever may be the place of origin of their cargo or the destination thereof, shall enjoy under all circumstances, on their entry into port, during their stay, and on departing, the same treatment as national vessels and their cargoes coming from the same places and with like cargo.

ARTICLE VIII.

Vessels of the United States or British vessels trading with the aforesaid Colonies, having entered a port of the United States or of the aforesaid Colonies voluntarily or in distress, with or without cargo, and sailing from said port without transacting any commercial operation, shall be exempt from all tonnage, clearance, navigation, or port dues or charges levied by the general Government; and as to local charges, they shall pay no more than national vessels under like circumstances. In case of entrance in distress, the discharge, reloading, or transhipment caused thereby, the necessary expense for provisioning the crew, and the sale of the damaged merchandize shall not be considered as a commercial transaction when the proper Customs official shall have previously authorized it.

ARTICLE IX.

No fees named in the Tariff of Consular Fees of the United States or of Great Britain shall be charged or collected by Consular officers of either the United States or of Great Britain for official services to the vessels of the United States and of Great Britain engaged in the trade between the United States and the aforesaid Colonies, or respecting such cargo or parts of cargo conveyed by said vessels as may be entitled under this Convention to the privileges of the Schedules of Articles I and II hereof.

ARTICLE X.

Vessels of the United States and of Great Britain, whenever referred to in this Convention, shall be understood to be vessels duly registered and *bonâ fide* owned exclusively by citizens of the United States or British subjects; and no evasion whatever of these requirements for the benefit of other vessels or ship-owners shall be recognized.

17

ARTICLE XI.

The Government of the United States on the one hand, and Her Majesty the Queen on behalf of her aforesaid possessions on the other, bind themselves to extend each to the other reciprocally all favours and privileges in regard to Customs Tariff, commerce, property, and persons which either of them may have conceded or may concede to a third Power, freely if freely granted to such third Power, or for an equivalent consideration if granted to such third Power in virtue of a compensating arrangement.

ARTICLE XII.

The stipulations contained in this Convention shall not prevent either of the Contracting Parties from making such changes in its Customs Tariffs and navigation dues as its respective interests may require, either by legislation or in virtue of Treaties with other Governments. But in case such changes are made, the party affected by the same may denounce this Convention, even before the term specified in Article XVI, and the present Convention shall be terminated at the end of six months from the day on which such notification may be made.

ARTICLE XIII.

The Contracting Parties, however, mutually agree that the conditional privileges which this Convention expressly reserves and confines to the goods and vessels of the respective countries under the national flags are not, under the operation of favoured-nation clauses in existing Treaties which either of them may have concluded with other countries, to be deemed as extending to the goods or vessels of such other countries without equivalent consideration on the part of such other countries; and if any foreign country should claim, under existing favoured-nation engagements, to share in the benefits of the commercial intercourse which this Convention creates as between the United States and the several British Colonies aforesaid, and should either party deem such claim to be allowable, it is hereby engaged that the party affected thereby shall have the right to denounce the present Convention under Article XII hereof; or else that any such Treaty with any foreign country, so far as it may be contrary to the terms of this Convention, may be denounced and terminated so soon as the terms of such Treaty may permit, in which case the alternative right of denunciation of the present Convention shall not be exercised.

ARTICLE XIV.

Nothing in this Convention shall be construed as affecting or impairing any rights of commercial intercourse between the United Kingdom of Great Britain and Ireland and the Colonies aforesaid, or between any other possession of Great Britain and said Colonies, or between the said Colonies themselves, which may now or hereafter exist; but it is agreed that in respect of the articles mentioned in the Schedules of Article II hereof the United States shall be placed on the same footing as Great Britain and her possessions.

ARTICLE XV.

The present Convention shall take effect as soon as it has been ratified by both Contracting Parties according to their respective constitutional procedure, and in respect of each British Colony aforesaid as soon as the necessary laws have been passed by the United States and that Colony respectively, and a notification given by the British Minister at Washington to the United States' Government that such Colony has passed the necessary laws in due form, the said laws to be passed in six months from the date of the exchange of the ratifications to which Article XVII refers.

ARTICLE XVI.

Upon the present Convention taking effect, it shall remain in force for six years from the date in which it may come into operation according to the foregoing Article, and shall remain in force until either of the Contracting Parties shall give notice to the other of its wish to terminate the same, and further until the expiration of twelve months from the date of said notification. Each of the Contracting Parties is at liberty to give such notice to the other at the end of said term of six years, or at any time thereafter or before, as provided in Articles XII and XIII of this Convention.

ARTICLE XVII.

The Ratifications of the present Convention shall be exchanged at as soon as possible.

In faith whereof the respective Plenipotentiaries have signed the present Convention, and have affixed thereto their respective seals.

Done in duplicate, at the city of   , this   day of   , in the year of our Lord 1880.

No. 16.

Mr. West to Earl Granville.—(*Received December* 19.)

(Extract.) *Washington, December* 5, 1884.

I HAVE the honour to inform your Lordship that the informal negotiations which have been in progress with the Department of State, consequent upon the instructions conveyed to me in your Lordship's despatch of the 25th October last, have now taken a definite form in a proposed draft of Treaty, which has been submitted to me by the Secretary of State as a counter-proposal to that made in my note of the 7th ultimo, copy of which was inclosed in my despatch of the 13th ultimo. Copy of this draft of Treaty, as well as copy of the note covering it, were transmitted to your Lordship in my preceding despatch. At a formal interview which I had yesterday with the Secretary of State, he expressed his great satisfaction at the result of the informal negotiations which had been initiated, and which had thus enabled him now to meet the important proposal which had been made by Her Majesty's Government, for a Commercial Treaty with the United States on behalf of the West Indian Colonies, in what he considered to be a satisfactory sense, and he drew my attention in this connection to the paragraph in the President's message, in which he states that by reciprocally reducing tariff burdens many of the embarrassing elements in the great national conflict between free trade and protection might be turned to good account.

I have now the honour to report to your Lordship the course of the preliminary negotiations which have led to the counter-proposal of the United States' Government.

Your Lordship's instructions excluded the question of differential duties, and this appeared to me to be the main object which Her Majesty's Government had in view. As I at once perceived that there was no intention on the part of the Government of the United States to ask for differential treatment, I saw no objection to the discussion of enlarged schedules of articles in the interests of the West India Colonies. With regard to the liberty reserved to the Colonial Governments to impose export duties on Treaty commodities, I conceived that Her Majesty's Government was desirous to secure to them the means of raising revenue, and that this question could be dealt with according to their interests. As I was unable to deal with the main difficulty, namely, the *sine quâ non* on the part of the United States' Government, that the advantages to be accorded by the Treaty should be limited to articles the produce or manufacture of Great Britain, her Colonies, and the United States, carried by ships of British, Colonial, or United States' nationality, I urged the necessity of embodying our proceedings at once into a draft Treaty as a former counter-proposal on the part of the United States' Government, and the text of which, through the prompt action of the Secretary of State and his Department, I was enabled to transmit to your Lordship this day in printed form.

I may here state to your Lordship that I conceive that the object of the Article to this effect might be obtained by an exchange of notes, which course would obviate the necessity of its insertion in the body of the Convention, and with respect to Article IX (Consular fees), that not much importance was attached to it.

The negotiation having now assumed a formal character, I requested Mr. Nevile Lubbock to report to me upon the bearing of the proposed Convention with regard to the interests of the West India Colonies, and I have the honour to inclose to your Lordship herewith copy of a letter which I have received from him.

He states that the loss of revenue to the United States in respect to this Convention cannot be estimated at less than 2,500,000*l.*, while the loss of revenue to the Colonies will only be 180,000*l.*, and that the proposal of the United States' Government is one which would prove highly beneficial to the West India Colonies.

In view of the possible coming into operation of the Reciprocity Treaties between the United States, Mexico, Spain, Salvador, and San Domingo, and of the critical position in which the sugar industry of the West India Colonies would be placed if similar advantages could not be secured for them, I trust that your Lordship will approve of the steps which I have taken.

Inclosure in No. 16.

Mr. Lubbock to Mr. West.

Sir, Washington, *December* 5, 1884.

IN accordance with your wish I beg to inform you that I have carefully examined the schedules of articles which, under the counter-proposition for a Convention which has been submitted by the United States' Government, it is proposed should be favoured, on the one hand by the United States, and on the other by the British West India Colonies, and I beg to report as follows:—

1. With regard to the articles produced in the West Indies and which are to be favoured on their entrance into the United States. The proposition of Her Majesty's Government was that the United States should reduce the duty charged upon sugar by one-half, and no reduction of duty on other articles was suggested. Under the proposed Convention, sugar under No. 16 will be admitted entirely free of duty; no less than thirty-four other articles, comprising practically, with the exception of rum, all the leading articles of production of the West Indian Colonies, are also to be admitted free. In addition to which, bitters, cordials, and preserved fruits are to be admitted at a reduction of duty of 25 per cent.

The loss of revenue to the United States in respect of this Convention cannot be estimated at less than 2,500,000*l.*

2. With regard to the articles which it is proposed should be favoured in the West Indies when coming from the United States, you will remark that it comprises a large number of items which have not been alluded to in my instructions from the Colonial Office. On the other hand, some of the articles, the duty on which Her Majesty's Government proposed to abolish entirely will, it is proposed, still be subject to duties, but the existing duties upon them are to be reduced by one-half. The total amount of revenue which I estimate will be lost by the West Indian Colonies under the Convention is about 180,000*l.*, whilst the revenue which would have been lost under the proposition submitted by Her Majesty's Government would have been about 250,000*l.*

From the foregoing remarks I think it is sufficiently evident that the proposal of the United States' Government is one which would prove highly beneficial to our West Indian Colonies if it should become law.

I have, &c.
(Signed) NEVILE LUBBOCK.

No. 17.

Mr. West to Earl Granville.—(*Received December* 19.)

My Lord, Washington, *December* 6, 1884.

I HAVE the honour to inform your Lordship that Mr. Nevile Lubbock, who was appointed to confer with me in the late negotiations for a Commercial Convention between Great Britain on behalf of the West Indian Colonies and the United States, left Washington this day on his return to England. I take this opportunity of expressing to your Lordship my high appreciation of the zeal, assiduity, and intelligence displayed by Mr. Lubbock in dealing with the details involved in the schedules of the proposed Treaty, and also of the sincere desire manifested by Mr. Adee and the State Department generally to bring about a cordial understanding on all matters connected with it.

I have, &c.
(Signed) L. S. SACKVILLE WEST.

No. 18.

Earl Granville to Mr. West.

Sir,   Foreign Office, February 12, 1885.

HER Majesty's Government have given their most careful consideration to the draft Treaty inclosed in your despatch of the 5th ultimo, which has been proposed by the Government of the United States in the place of the bases submitted to them by you.

The principal object which Her Majesty's Government had in view was to secure a reduction of the heavy customs duties which prevent the sugars produced in the British West India Colonies from finding a remunerative market in the United States. The Treaties negotiated by the latter country with Hawaii and with Mexico, and others now awaiting ratification, indicated that the United States did not propose any longer to limit their supply of sugar to the amount produced on their own territory exclusively; and it even seemed that the many profitable industries which are called into existence by a plentiful supply of cheap sugar were not improbably about to induce the United States to abrogate altogether the protective duties on that article.

Under existing Treaties, Her Majesty's Government are not entitled to claim for the West India Colonies most-favoured-nation treatment in the United States. As, however, the system of reserving the whole or portions of the colonial trade to the mother country, under which this exception of the West Indies from most-favoured-nation treatment took place, had long since been abandoned by Her Majesty's Government, and the United States are now gratuitously admitted to that trade, not only on the footing of the most favoured foreign nation, but on the footing of the other Colonies and of the mother country herself, a request was in the first instance made that the produce of the British West Indies might be similarly admitted to most-favoured-nation treatment in the United States. This request was met on the part of the latter by the statement that the privilege asked had already been granted without any Treaty stipulation, but that the terms of the Treaty of 1815 did not, and could not, authorize Great Britain to claim for the trade and produce of even the United Kingdom itself the special favours granted, or about to be granted, by the United States to particular countries in return for reciprocal favours which the latter had granted, or might grant, to the United States. As, however, Mr. Frelinghuysen's note also expressed a desire to hear the details of any proposals which might be made on the part of Great Britain, and as Her Majesty's Government were anxious to see the West India sugars admitted to the United States' markets on equal terms with the sugars of the most favoured nation, they refrained, for the moment, from taking exception to the interpretation of the most-favoured-nation clause involved in the above statement, and they endeavoured to find a basis of negotiation which should include reductions of duty on both sides, and should secure special advantages to the United States of the nature of those secured by other means in such Treaties as those with Mexico and Hawaii, but without involving differential treatment. This they accordingly endeavoured to effect by selecting for modification of duty those articles in the West India Tariffs which are imported exclusively, or almost exclusively, from the United States. In your note of the 7th November you accordingly submitted to the Secretary of State the proposals of Her Majesty's Government, under which, while the United States were asked to reduce the duty on sugar by 50 per cent. at least, Her Majesty's Government undertook to admit duty free to the West Indies certain articles of natural, agricultural, and dairy produce. The articles selected are some of those in which the producers of the United States need hardly fear competition in Western Europe, much less, therefore, in regions so near the place of production as the West Indies. It may be said, indeed, that these articles are exclusively imported from the United States, and that the United States would therefore reap the advantage of the abolition of duty.

On the 7th ultimo Mr. Frelinghuysen transmitted to you a counter-proposal on the part of his Government.

This counter-draft has received, as I stated at the beginning of this despatch, the most careful consideration on the part of Her Majesty's Government, not only on account of the precision with which its stringent provisions have been elaborated, but also on account of the economic principles which it involves, and the revolution which the principles it contains would, if universally accepted, effect in the value of the Conventional stipulations as to commerce now existing between the various nations of the earth.

Articles I and II are so framed that the reductions made in them are not to be general, but are to be confined to the goods of the country with which the Convention is made, and the important reservation is introduced that the advantage of these reductions of duty are not to apply unless the goods are carried in British or United States' ships.

Article XI is a species of most-favoured-nation clause, but it contains words providing that the clause is not absolute, but is only to apply where an equivalent consideration is given. It is obvious that such a clause is totally different from the stipulation usually called the most-favoured-nation Article. Thus, if there were a Treaty between Great Britain and the United States containing such a clause, and Great Britain were to reduce the duty (say) on Turkish tobacco in consideration of a Treaty with Turkey reducing, say, the Turkish light dues, the United States would not have a right to claim a reduction on United States' tobacco unless they gave up something equivalent to the Turkish light dues. And if the United States were to reduce their duties on French silks and cottons in consideration of a reduction of the French duties on United States' corn, Great Britain would not have a right to the reduction on her silks and cottons unless she gave the United States something equivalent to the French reduction on corn. It is obvious that, with such an addition, the most-favoured-nation clause loses its value and becomes a fruitful cause of dispute.

Article XII reserves to each Party the Power to make changes in Tariffs and Navigation Dues. But it adds a proviso, which is new to international law, to the effect that any changes made by one Party in its Tariff shall authorize the other to denounce the Treaty. In other words, every change in the Tariff of any one of the British West India Islands would have to be submitted for the approbation of the United States, and *vice versâ*, if the security of the Treaty was to be kept intact.

Article XIII expressly provides that the privileges conceded by the Treaty are not to be granted by either Party to other nations by reason of the most-favoured-nation clause existing in any Treaty with such nations, unless any such nation give what, in the opinion of the other Party, is an equivalent. But Her Majesty's Government are decidedly of opinion that the exception to most-favoured-nation treatment thus contemplated would be an infraction of the most-favoured-nation clause as hitherto interpreted in the law of nations. To take an example, such a clause governs the trade between the British West Indies and Belgium. Her Majesty's Government cannot conceive how the claim of Belgium to have her imports, if she had any, into those islands, placed on the same footing as the similar imports from the United States when any favour is granted to these latter, can be rejected by alleging a subsequent agreement come to between Great Britain and the United States, to which Belgium had not been a party.

The interpretation of the most-favoured-nation clause involved in the United States' proposals is, that concessions granted conditionally and for a consideration cannot be claimed under it. From this interpretation Her Majesty's Government entirely and emphatically dissent. The most-favoured-nation clause has now become the most valuable part of the system of Commercial Treaties, and exists between nearly all the nations of the earth. It leads more than any other stipulation to simplicity of Tariffs and to ever-increased freedom of trade; while the system now proposed would lead countries to seek exclusive markets and would thus fetter instead of liberating trade. Its effect has been, with few exceptions, that any given article is taxed in each country at practically one rate only. Thus in France, although there exists a General Tariff and although France has by separate Treaties with various countries engaged to reduce the duties of the General Tariff on various articles, the list of which varies in each Treaty, yet, owing to the operation of the most-favoured-nation clause existing in each of those Treaties, the goods of all nations having such an Article in their Treaties are taxed in accordance with the "Conventional" Tariff, which accordingly becomes the combination of all the lowest duties on each article appearing in the separate Treaties. But should the system contemplated by the United States be widely adopted, there will be a return to the old and exceedingly inconvenient system under which the same article in the same country would pay different duties varying according to its country of origin, the nationality of the importing ship, and, perhaps at some future time, varying also with the nationality of the importer himself.

It is, moreover, obvious that the interpretation now put forward would nullify the most-favoured-nation clause; for any country, say France, though bound by the most-favoured-nation clause in her Treaty with Belgium, might make Treaties with any other country involving reductions of duty on both sides, and, by the mere insertion of a statement that these reductions were granted reciprocally and for a consideration, might yet refuse to grant them to Belgium unless the latter granted what France might consider an equivalent.

Such a system would press most hardly on those countries which had already reformed their Tariffs, and had no equivalent concessions to offer, and, therefore, Great Britain, which has reformed her Tariff, is most deeply interested in resisting it.

Her Majesty's Government are aware that the draft Treaty foresees the possibility of one or the other of the Contracting Parties being unable or unwilling to withhold the advantages of it from Governments that might claim them under the most-favoured-nation clause; but they cannot admit the soundness of a commercial policy based upon Treaties which may at any moment have to be broken either owing to the provisions of other Treaties previously made by one of the Contracting Parties, or owing to the subsequent conclusion of Treaties extending the area of the policy in question; and which, if so broken, are naturally liable to be denounced at the will of the other Contracting Party.

A less general but equally serious objection to the United States' proposals is, in the opinion of Her Majesty's Government, the restriction it would place on the liberty of each Party to deal freely with its own Tariffs without the constant fear that the changes contemplated may lead to the denunciation of the Treaty. In the present instance, this consideration would press much more heavily on the West Indies than on the United States. For it is evident that should the former, owing to the Treaty having provided them with a market for sugar, continue to make that article their principal produce, would suffer much more by the denunciation of the Treaty than would the United States, who, with their larger base of commercial operations, could replace the lost supplies of sugar with far greater ease than the West Indies could find another market for their produce. Their sugars might indeed have then been specially adapted to the requirements of the United States, and be unfit for any other market.

The counter-proposals of the United States require further, as I have already pointed out with reference to Articles 1 and 2 of the counter-draft, that the advantages reciprocally granted shall be confined to goods carried in vessels belonging to one or the other of the Contracting Parties. Thus, United States' ships, when engaged in the West India trade, would be on a better footing than other foreign ships engaged in the same trade. This stipulation would, in the opinion of Her Majesty's Government, be inconsistent both with the most-favoured-nation clauses in Treaties made by this country, and also with the concession of national treatment for shipping contained in many of those Treaties. It is also at variance with the policy pursued by Her Majesty's Government since the repeal of the old navigation laws. Since that time no distinction whatever has been made or allowed in respect of difference of flag. Perhaps in no respect have the steps taken by this country in the direction of free trade been so largely followed by foreign countries as in this matter.

This policy has been eminently successful, and has helped not a little to put at the disposal of the manufacturers and producers of all countries the vast fleets of carrying ships which now keep up communication between all parts of the world, and enable them to find markets which would have remained inaccessible had the old navigation restrictions been maintained.

For these reasons Her Majesty's Government are unable to accept the counter-proposals communicated to you by Mr. Frelinghuysen. They do not, however, abandon the hope of coming to an agreement in this matter; on the contrary, they are glad that the Secretary of State, by preparing a definite draft, enabled them to see precisely and clearly the objects the United States sought to obtain in the negotiation.

After examining and analysing the United States' proposals, Her Majesty's Government are confirmed in the opinion that the United States' Government make it a *sine quâ non* of a reduction of the duties on West India produce that reductions shall be made in the duties on United States' produce imported into the West Indies, and that these latter reductions shall profit the United States only.

The produce of the United States is so varied, and the West India Colonies are geographically so near to the United States, that it will not be difficult to ascertain what are the articles which are supplied exclusively, or nearly so, by the United States.

Her Majesty's Government consider that the list of articles in my despatch No. 65, Commercial, of the 25th October last, fulfils this condition; but they are prepared to consider any additions to it which the United States may wish to propose.

With regard to the desire of the United States to limit the carrying trade between that country and the United Kingdom to the ships of the Contracting Parties, Her Majesty's Government think that the United States will find, on examination, that foreign flags participate in that trade to so slight an extent that their competition may safely be left out of consideration.

The United States wish that the West India trade may be assimilated to the conditions which apply to the productions and shipping in the domestic coasting trade, or to the trade of a country with its own dependencies. The United States are no doubt aware that in the British dominions both these trades are free to the flags of all nations. The proposals of Her Majesty's Government will, they conceive, realize the wish of the

Government of the United States, not by setting up artificial restrictions tending to create unnatural channels for trade, but by removing on both sides the obstacles now placed in the way of trade, and thus establishing between those Colonies and the United States the far more solid and lasting ties of free exchange of the merchandize which each produces most easily.

I have to request you to make known the substance of this despatch to the Secretary of State, and, if you think fit, to communicate to him a copy of it.

I am, &c.
(Signed) GRANVILLE.

No. 19.

Lord E. Fitzmaurice to Sir R. Herbert.

Sir, *Foreign Office, February* 12, 1885.

I AM directed by Earl Granville to transmit to you, to be laid before the Earl of Derby, the accompanying copy of a despatch to Her Majesty's Minister at Washington,* stating that Her Majesty's Government are unable to accept the counter-proposals put forward by the United States' Governement for a Convention respecting trade between the United States and Her Majesty's West Indian Colonies, and requesting that the original proposals made by Her Majesty's Government may be reconsidered by the Government of the United States.

The reasons which have led Her Majesty's Government to reject the proposals in question are fully set forth in the despatch to Mr. West in so far as they relate to the United States and to the foreign relations of Great Britain, but there are other considerations which have contributed to this decision, and which Lord Granville is of opinion should be placed on record.

In the first place, it must be remembered that the seeming promise to the West Indian Colonies is much less than it appears at first sight to be.

In regard to the equivalent reductions of duty to be granted to West Indian produce, it is to be observed that the articles to be free of customs duties in the United States are chiefly colonial raw produce, which, with the important exception of sugar, are already on the free list of the United States' Tariff. It is true that this freedom from duties would acquire additional security from a Treaty stipulation, but, on the other hand, it must be remembered that the policy of the United States is to foster manufactures artificially, and that raw produce is little likely to be taxed in a country pursuing such a policy, more especially where, as is the case in the United States, there is no probability of raw material having to be taxed for the purpose of raising revenue.

With regard to the free admission of sugar, the expectation no doubt is that the whole of the sugar duty remitted by the United States will be a pure gain to the sugar producers of the West Indies, and this it will be while there is any surplus of sugar imported at a duty of 10*l.* per ton. But it is very improbable that there will be any such surplus for any length of time.

Similar Treaties, if the United States carry out the policy of the present proposals, will no doubt be concluded with the other sugar producing countries of the American continent, whose aggregate production will certainly be able to keep pace with the demand of the United States, even though free sugar should cause a very large increase of the consumption of that article; or the United States may come to look on sugar as a raw produce, and adopt a free-trade policy in regard to it. In either case the demand for West Indian sugar will depend on the competition of home-grown sugar in the United States, and of the various foreign sugars which may be admitted into that country. The proposed Treaty cannot, therefore, be reckoned on as guaranteeing an exclusive market to the West Indies. The United States have already negotiated, or are already endeavouring to negotiate, Treaties involving a reduction of the duty on sugar from Hawaii, Mexico, Cuba, Porto Rico, St. Domingo, and certain of the Central American Republics.

If, on the other hand, the proposed remission of duty is looked upon as a step taken by the United States in the direction of free trade, it is, to say the least, probable that the same step will at no distant date be taken by that country without involving any such sacrifices of principle as the present proposal involves.

In regard to the power reserved of terminating the Treaty at six months' notice in certain eventualities, it may be true that the United States might not exercise their

* No. 18.

right on account of every trivial Tariff change effected in the West Indies or on account of the equivalents given by other Powers in consideration of receiving the Tariff treatment proposed to be accorded to the United States; but it must be remembered that the United States' market is of far greater importance to the West Indies in the present state of the trade of those islands than is the West Indian market to the United States. Should the United States wish at any time to terminate the Treaty, its provisions are of a kind which could hardly fail to furnish them at any moment with legitimate grounds for so doing, and it is thus evident that the proposed arrangement is deficient in the element of stability which Her Majesty's Government consider to be essential to the value of any Commercial Treaty.

I am, &c.
(Signed) EDMOND FITZMAURICE.

COMMERCIAL. No. 4 (1885).

CORRESPONDENCE respecting the Negotiation of a Treaty regulating Trade between the British West India Colonies and the United States.

Presented to both Houses of Parliament by Command of Her Majesty. March 1885.

LONDON:
PRINTED BY HARRISON AND SONS.

(325)

United States.

Report by Mr. Helyar on the Finances of the United States of America for the fiscal years ending June 30, 1883, and June 30, 1884.

THE revenue of the United States during the twelve months ending the 30th June, 1883, amounted to 82,876,580*l.*, and the expenditure to 55,293,362*l.*, leaving a surplus of 27,583,218*l.*

Revenue, 1882–83.

The different items of the revenue stood as follows:—

Branches.	Amount.	Increase or Decrease.	
		On 1882.	Per cent.
	Dol. c.	Dol. c.	
Customs	214,706,496 93	− 5,704,233 32	− 2·6
Internal revenue	144,720,368 98	− 1,777,226 47	− 0·8
Sales of public lands	7,955,864 42	+ 3,202,724 05	+ 68·1
Tax on circulation and deposits of national banks	9,111,008 85	+ 154,214 40	+ 1·7
Profits on coinage, bullion deposits, and assays	4,460,205 17	+ 343,511 44	+ 8·4
Customs fees, fines, penalties, &c.	1,436,236 34	+ 92,888 34	+ 7·1
Fees, Consular letters patent, and lands	3,322,361 64	+ 683,370 67	+ 26·3
Repayment of interest by Pacific Railway Companies	1,556,866 90	+ 716,312 53	+ 85·3
Sinking Fund for Pacific Railway Companies	1,322,103 11	+ 525,831 69	+ 66·5
Deposits by individuals for surveying public lands	1,221,611 76	− 830,694 60	− 41·6
Sales of Government property	285,055 02	− 29,904 83	− 9·6
Sale of Post Office property in New York City	648,694 82	+ 648,694 82	None last year
Indian trust funds	121,000 00	− 5,584,243 22	− 97·9
Donations towards liquidating the Public Debt	964,426 87	+ 964,426 87	None last year
Japanese Indemnity Fund	1,839,533 99	+ 1,839,533 99	Ditto
Immigrant Fund	231,476 50	+ 231,476 50	Ditto
Revenues of the District of Columbia	1,970,938 47	+ 255,762 06	+ 15·0
Miscellaneous sources	2,413,332 18	− 970,113 25	− 28·7
Total ordinary receipts	398,287,581 95	− 5,237,668 33	− 1·3

Expenditure, 1882-83.

The ordinary expenditure from all sources for the year was as follows:—

Branches.	Amount.	Increase or Decrease. On 1882.	Per cent.
	Dol. c.	Dol. c.	
Civil expenses	22,343,285 76	+ 4,300,899 34	+ 23·9
Foreign intercourse	2,419,275 24	+ 1,111,692 05	+ 85·5
Indians	7,362,590 34	− 2,374,157 06	− 24·4
Pensions	66,012,573 64	+ 4,667,379 69	+ 7·6
Military establishment	48,911,382 93	+ 5,349,888 74	+ 12·3
Naval establishment	15,283,437 17	+ 251,390 91	+ 1·7
Miscellaneous, including public buildings, lighthouses, and revenue collection	40,098,432 73	+ 5,559,195 23	+ 16·1
Expenditure of District of Columbia	3,817,028 48	+ 486,484 61	+ 14·7
Interest on Public Debt	59,160,131 25	+ 11,917,075 54	+ 16·8
Total ordinary expenditure	265,408,137 54	+ 7,426,697 97	+ 2·8

Surplus applied to redemption of debt.

leaving a surplus of revenue over expenditure of 132,879,444 dol. 41 c.; add, drawn from Treasury cash balances, 1,299,312 dol. 55 c.; total surplus, 134,178,756 dol. 96 c., which was applied as follows:—

	Dol. c.
To the redemption of—	
Bonds for the sinking fund	44,850,700 00
Fractional currency for the sinking fund	46,556 96
Funded Loan of 1881, continued at 3½ per cent.	65,380,250 00
Loan of July and August 1861, continued as above	20,594,600 00
Funded Loan of 1907	1,418,850 00
Funded Loan of 1881	719,150 00
Loan of February 1861	18,000 00
Loan of July and August 1861	266,600 00
Loan of March 1863	116,850 00
Loan of July 1882	47,650 00
Five-twenties of 1862	10,300 00
Five-twenties of 1864	7,050 00
Five-twenties of 1865	9,600 00
Ten-forties of 1864	133,550 00
Consols of 1865	40,800 00
Consols of 1867	235,700 00
Consols of 1868	154,650 00
Oregon War Debt	5,450 00
Refunding certificates	109,150 00
Old demand, compound interest, and other notes	13,300 00
Total	134,178,156 96

Revenue for 1883-84.

The revenue for the year ending the 30th June, 1884, amounted to 72,608,306*l.*; the expenditure was 60,607,599*l.*, leaving a surplus of 12,000,707*l.*

The ordinary revenue from all sources was as follows:—

Branches.	Amount.	Increase or Decrease. On 1883.	Per cent.
	Dol. c.	Dol. c.	
Customs	195,067,489 76	−19,639,007 17	− 9·1
Internal revenue	121,586,072 51	−23,134,296 47	−15·9
Sales of public lands	9,810,705 01	+ 1,854,840 59	+23·5
Tax on national banks	3,108,730 13	− 6,002,278 72	−65·9
Profits on coinage, bullion deposits, and assays	4,250,609 30	− 209,595 87	−47·6
Customs fees, fines, penalties, &c.	1,074,665 46	− 361,570 88	−25·8
Fees, Consular, letters patent, and lands	3,248,937 57	− 73,424 07	− 2·2
Repayment of interest by Pacific Railway Companies	1,371,363 21	− 185,503 69	−12·4
Sinking fund for Pacific Railway Companies	2,045,775 05	+ 723,671 94	+55·6
Deposits by individuals for surveying public lands	664,111 78	− 557,499 98	−46·4
Sales of Government property	546,634 74	+ 261,579 72	+91·6
Indian trust funds	76,115 63	− 44,884 37	−37·1
Donations towards liquidating the Public Debt	63,314 97	− 901,111 90	−93·3
Immigrant Fund	224,286 50	− 7,190 00	− 3·1
Soldiers' Home Permanent Fund	367,092 04	+ 367,092 04	None in 1883
Sale of condemned naval vessels	200,000 00	+ 200,000 00	None in 1883
Revenues of the District of Columbia	1,970,726 13	− 212 24	− 0·001
Miscellaneous sources	2,843,240 13	+ 429,907 95	+18·0
Total ordinary receipts	348,519,869 92	−49,767,712 03	−12·5

N.B.—The items "Sale of Post Office property in New York City" and "Japanese Indemnity Fund," do not appear this year.

[621]

Expenditure for 1883-84.

The ordinary expenditure from all sources for the same period was as follows:—

Branches.	Amount.	Increase or Decrease. On 1883.	Per cent.
	Dol. c.	Dol. c.	
Civil expenses	22,312,907 71	− 20,378 05	− 0·1
Foreign intercourse	1,260,766 37	− 1,158,508 87	−48·3
Indians	6,475,999 29	− 886,591 05	−12·1
Pensions	55,429,228 06	−10,583,345 58	−16·0
Military establishment, including river and harbour improvements and arsenals	39,429,603 36	− 9,481,779 57	−19·4
Naval establishment, including vessels, machinery, and improvements at navy yards	17,292,601 44	+ 2,009,164 27	+13·2
Miscellaneous expenditure, including public buildings, lighthouses, and revenue collection	43,939,710 00	+ 3,841,277 27	+ 9·6
Expenditures on account of the District of Columbia	3,407,049 62	− 409,978 86	−10·8
Interest on the Public Debt	54,578,378 48	− 4,581,752 77	− 7·7
Total	244,126,244 33	−21,281,893 21	− 8·0
Sinking fund	46,790,229 50*	..	..
Total ordinary expenditure	290,916,473 83	..	..
Leaving a surplus of	57,603,396 09	..	..

which was applied to the redemption of—

	Dol. c.
Oregon War Debt	650 00
Loan of 1858	5,000 00
Loan of February 1861	55,000 00
Loan of July and August 1861	202,650 00
Loan of March 1863	28,700 00
Five-twenties of 1862	4,150 00
Five-twenties of 1864	1,000 00
Five-twenties of 1865	1,200 00
Ten-forties of 1864	72,300 00
Consols of 1865	65,400 00
Consols of 1867	178,850 00
Consols of 1868	21,700 00
Funded Loan of 1881	171,450 00
Loan of July 12, 1882	52,260,650 00
Certificates of deposit	990,000 00
Refunding certificates	65,900 00
Old demand, compound interest, and other notes	12,255 00
Increase of cash in the Treasury	3,466,541 09
Total	57,603,396 09
Making with the sinking fund of	46,790,229 50
A total diminution of	104,393,625 59

* Fully expended in the redemption of Sinking Fund Bonds.

UNITED STATES.

From a preliminary Return lately published it appears that the revenue for the year ending the 30th June, 1885, was, in brief, as follows:— *Fiscal year 1884-85. Preliminary Return.*

REVENUE.

	Dol.	c.	£
Customs	181,471,939	34	
Internal revenue	112,498,725	54	
Lands	5,705,986	44	
Miscellaneous	24,014,055	06	
Total	323,690,706	38	= 66,740,351

EXPENDITURE.

	Dol.	c.	£
Civil and miscellaneous	87,494,258	38*	
War Department	42,670,578	47	
Navy Department	16,021,079	67	
Indians	6,552,494	63	
Pensions	56,102,267	49	
Interest on debt, including 3,876,090 dol. 72 c. Pacific Railroad interest	51,386,256	47	
Total	260,226,935	11	= 53,613,801

This leaves a surplus of 63,463,771 dol. 27 c., or 13,085,313*l*., for the redemption of debt, partly by the sinking fund and partly by direct refunding operations, 45,588,150 dollars being redeemed by the former, and 17,875,621 dollars by the latter process.

For the year ending the 30th June, 1886, the revenue has been roughly estimated at 330,000,000 dollars, or, 68,750,000*l*.; and the expenditure, including sinking fund, at 323,911,394 dollars, or, 67,481,540*l*.; leaving a surplus of 6,088,606 dollars, or, 1,268,460*l*. *Estimates for fiscal year 1885-86.*

The most important branch of the United States revenue is the customs. The serious reductions under this head, viz., of 5,704,233 dol. 82 c., or 2·6 per cent., in 1882-83 as compared with 1881-82, and of 19,639,007 dol. 17 c., or 9·1 per cent., in 1883-84 as compared with 1882-83, followed by a still further reduction of 13,595,550 dol. 42 c., or 7·0 per cent., in 1884-85 as compared with 1883-84, is no doubt mainly to be attributed to the general depression of business throughout the United States. *Customs.*

---

* This large increase of 17,000,000 dollars over the previous year is chiefly distributed as follows:—

	Dollars.
Debenture and charges, Customs cases	5,000,000
Deficiency in postal revenue	4,500,000
Alabama claims	3,500,000
Sinking fund for Pacific Railroads	3,500,000
Total	16,500,000

[621]

The following Tables will give some idea of the condition and progress of this important source of revenue:—

(1.)—AMOUNT of Duty collected on the eight principal dutiable articles during three years.

Articles.	1881–82.	1882–83.	1883–84.
	Dollars.	Dollars.	Dollars.
1. Sugar, molasses, and confectionery	49,207,279	46,172,378	48,923,465
2. Wool, and manufactures of ditto	29,253,016	32,320,893	32,001,226
3. Silk, manufactures of	22,633,137	19,654,946	18,962,210
4. Iron and steel, and manufactures of	24,175,547	16,590,504	14,799,117
5. Cotton, manufactures of	12,227,103	12,234,371	11,479,942
6. Flax, hemp, and jute, manufactures of	Not stated	10,149,103	9,418,484
7. Tobacco, and manufactures of	Not stated	7,661,638	6,945,652
8. Spirits and wines	6,771,483	8,741,958	5,730,646

(2.)—IMPORTS, dutiable and free, entered for consumption during the three years.

	1881–82.	1882–83.	1883–84.
	Dollars.	Dollars.	Dollars.
Dutiable	505,491,967	493,916,384	456,295,124
Free	210,721,981	206,913,289	211,280,265
	716,213,948	700,829,673	667,575,389
Average *ad valorem* rate of duty on dutiable merchandize		42·646	41·702
Ditto on dutiable and free merchandize		30·055	28·503

(3.)—EXPENSES of Collection in the three years.

	1881–82.	1882–83.	1883–84.
	Dol. c.	Dol. c.	Dol. c.
Expense	6,549,595 07	6,591,224 51	6,709,485 76
Increase or decrease on previous year	+130,250 00	+41,629 00	+118,261 00

In 1882–83 the amount of duties collected at New York was 147,082,333 dol. 23 c., and at all other ports, 67,624,163 dol. 70 c.; together, 214,706,496 dol. 93 c.

These figures are not given for the year 1883–84.

It will be noticed that, in spite of the large decrease in the imports in two years, viz., 49,000,000 dollars on dutiable merchandize alone, and a corresponding decrease of over 25,000,000 dollars in the Customs revenue, the cost of collection increased in the same period by 160,000 dollars, or, to put the matter differently, in 1881-82 the cost of collection only amounted to 2·9 per cent. of the revenue collected, while in 1883-84 it had risen to 3·4 per cent. of the revenue.

The stationary condition of the imports of free merchandize, combined with the large decrease in the imports of dutiable articles, leads directly to the conclusion that, concurrently with the undoubted depression of general business throughout the United States during the last few years, another cause has been at work, viz., the deleterious influence of the high protective Tariff on the import trade.

The following Table shows the decrease and increase in the importation of the most important dutiable articles in which the most material changes have taken place in the last three years:—

Articles.	1881–82.	1882–83.	1883–84.
	Dollars.	Dollars.	Dollars.
1. Sugar and molasses	100,105,729*	99,196,408*	103,884,274
2. Wool and manufactures of	37,361,520†	44,274,952†	53,542,292
3. Silk, and manufactures of	51,875,959	50,807,610	49,949,128
4. Coffee	46,041,609	42,050,513	49,686,705
5. Iron and steel, and manufactures of	51,377,633	40,796,007	41,464,965
6. Cotton, and manufactures of	34,351,292	36,853,689	30,454,476

Through a change in the form of the Tables the three years' import of sugar and molasses, and of wool and its manufactures, cannot be compared; but a diminution in sugar and molasses of nearly 1,000,000 dollars in 1882-83 over 1881-82 is shown, and also a diminution of over 1,000,000 dollars in the same period under wool and its manufactures.

In silk there is a diminution in the two years of nearly 2,000,000 dollars; in coffee an increase (the only one) of over 3,600,000 dollars; in iron and steel a decrease of nearly 10,000,000 dollars; and in cotton and its manufactures a decrease of nearly 4,000,000 dollars.

The following Table shows briefly similar statistics with regard to the exports in general:—

* Not including white sugar.   † Not including raw wool.

	1882–83.	1883–84.
	Dollars.	Dollars.
Products of agriculture	619,269,449	536,315,318
Products of manufacture	111,890,001	111,330,242
Products of mining, including petroleum	51,444,857	56,822,529
Products of the forest	9,976,143	9,465,330
Products of the fisheries	6,276,375	5,614,111
Other products	5,366,807	5,417,322
Total domestic merchandize	804,233,632	724,964,852

In 1881–82 the total export of domestic merchandize was 733,239,739 dollars.

	Dollars.
The total imports and exports during 1881–82, including exports of foreign merchandize and specie imported and exported, was	1,567,071,700
And the similar total in 1882–83 was	1,607,330,040
While the total in 1883–84 was	1,512,770,947
Thus giving an increase in 1882–83 over the previous year of	40,258,340
But in 1883–84 a decrease on the previous year of	94,559,093

Custom-house fees. The reform of the system of custom-house fees and the consolidation of Customs districts (alluded to in Mr. Drummond's Financial Report of January 1882*) have continued to be earnestly recommended by the Secretary of the Treasury, but apparently without immediate results.

Consolidation of Customs districts. The consolidation of Customs districts would, it is estimated, save the revenue some 500,000 dollars annually. The frauds on the revenue from the practice of undervaluing invoices of merchandize consigned to the agents of European manufacturers continue to be a subject of complaint; but it is admitted that these frauds are inseparable from the present condition of the *ad valorem* Tariff.

Tariff Act of March 3, 1883. The Secretary of the Treasury states, in his latest Report, that the Tariff Act has simplified official work, especially with regard to cotton and silk fabrics, and that the mode of collecting sugar duty according to saccharine strength seems to have given general satisfaction, and has removed the opportunity for evading the revenue by artificial colouring.

Hawaiian Sugar Commission. Extensive frauds on the revenue in connection with the exemption from duty of sugars imported from Hawaii having been alleged, a Special Commission has inquired into and reported on this question. It appears

* See "Commercial No. 16 (1882)."

from their Report that the Treaty with Hawaii has been fairly carried out, and that the character of the sugar imported continues essentially the same as before the conclusion of the Treaty. The Report having stated that the Hawaiian sugar interest was largely non-American, the Hawaiian Government have stated, in reply, that, out of 15,886,800 dollars of assessed plantation property, over 10,000,000 dollars was in American hands.

The Tariff Commission, in its Report to Congress, anticipated a considerable reduction in revenue under the new Tariff; but this was not realized, for, instead of an anticipated reduction of 45,000,000 dollars, there has been only a loss to the revenue of 20,000,000 dollars, and with a probable revival of business in the future, even this will tend to disappear.

The late Secretary of the Treasury proceeds to recommend reductions in the duties on raw materials, and on sugar, molasses, &c.; but since then a Democratic Administration has taken office, and at present their intentions respecting Tariff reform are unknown, while the prospects of such legislation in Congress are extremely dubious.

The late Secretary also strongly recommends the appointment of a Commission of impartial men to inquire into the whole question of free trade and protection, and supports this suggestion with the argument that the United States, when unfettered by a high protective Tariff, will become the most dangerous competitor of Great Britain in the markets of the world.

Internal revenue.

The diminution in this branch of revenue amounted to 1,777,226 dollars, or 2·8 per cent., in 1882-83 as compared with 1881-82, and to 23,134,296 dollars, or 15·1 per cent., in 1883-84 as compared with 1882-83, while in 1884-85 it was 9,087,347 dollars, or 7·4 per cent., as compared with 1883-84.

The decrease in 1883-84 is almost entirely due to reduction of taxation, but the continuous decline affords some additional evidence of the general depression of business.

The following comparative Tables show the amounts received under each separate heading during the years 1881-82, 1882-83, and 1883-84 from spirits, cigars, cigarettes, snuff, tobacco, and beer on which taxes were paid during the period under review:—

334 UNITED STATES.

(1.)—Comparative Statement of Receipts for the last two fiscal years.

The receipts from the several objects of taxation under the Internal Revenue Laws during the last two fiscal years are shown in the following Table:—

Objects of Taxation.	Amount of Tax paid during fiscal years— 1882.	1883.	Increase.	Decrease.
	Dol. c.	Dol. c.	Dol. c.	Dol. c.
Spirits.				
Spirits distilled from fruit	1,095,164 60	1,127,950 25	32,785 65	...
Spirits distilled from grain and other materials	63,683,592 37	67,957,906 48	4,274,314 11	...
Rectifiers (special tax)	184,483 67	189,800 12	5,316 45	...
Retail liquor dealers (special tax)	4,455,355 55	4,624,587 77	169,232 22	...
Wholesale liquor dealers (special tax)	439,018 86	455,915 51	16,896 65	...
Manufacturers of stills (special tax)	1,410 03	1,160 43	...	249 60
Stills or worms manufactured (special tax)	4,783 00	4,020 00	...	763 00
Stamps for distilled spirits intended for export	9,600 10	7,434 00	...	2,166 10
Interest on tax upon spirits	...	0 64	0 64	...
Total	69,873,408 18	74,368,775 20	4,495,367 02	...
Tobacco.				
Cigars and cheroots	18,245,852 37	16,895,215 15	...	1,350,637 22
Cigarettes	972,570 10	929,974 73	...	42,595 37
Snuff	778,650 87	736,022 82	...	42,628 05
Tobacco, chewing and smoking	25,033,741 97	22,136,402 53	...	2,897,339 44
Stamps for tobacco, snuff, and cigars intended for export	6,554 40	876 00	...	5,678 40
Dealers in leaf tobacco (special tax)	84,585 63	54,535 12	...	30,050 51
Dealers in manufactured tobacco (special tax)	2,094,536 21	1,233,812 93	...	860,723 28
Manufacturers of tobacco (special tax)	8,762 48	5,697 88	...	3,064 60
Manufacturers of cigars (special tax)	143,859 66	96,899 00	...	46,960 66
Peddlers of tobacco (special tax)	22,875 22	14,813 63	...	8,061 59
Total	47,391,988 91	42,104,249 79	...	5,287,739 12
Fermented Liquors.				
Ale, beer, lager-beer and porter	15,680,678 54	16,426,050 11	745,371 57	...
Brewers (special tax)	195,824 31	184,885 49	...	10,938 82
Dealers in malt liquors (special tax)	277,417 57	289,680 21	12,262 64	...
Total	16,153,920 42	16,900,615 81	746,695 39	...
Banks and Bankers not National.				
Bank deposits	4,096,102 45	3,026,208 32	...	1,069,894 13
Bank capital	1,153,070 25	722,003 93	...	431,066 32
Bank circulation	4,283 77	782 35	...	3,503 42
Total	5,253,458 47	3,748,994 60	...	1,504,463 87
Miscellaneous.				
Bank cheques	2,318,455 14	1,946,272 10	...	372,183 04
Friction matches	3,272,258 00	2,920,545 20	...	351,712 80
Patent medicines, perfumery, cosmetics, &c.	1,978,395 56	2,186,236 16	207,840 60	...
Penalties	199,830 04	305,803 57	105,973 53	...
Back taxes under repealed laws	81,559 00	71,852 43	...	9,706 57
Total	7,850,497 74	7,430,709 46	...	419,788 28
Aggregate receipts	146,523,273 72	144,553,344 86	...	1,969,928 86

(2.)—COMPARATIVE Statement showing the Receipts from the several objects of internal taxation in the United States during the fiscal years ended the 30th June, 1883 and 1884.

Objects of Taxation.	Amount of Tax paid during fiscal years— 1883.	Amount of Tax paid during fiscal years— 1884.	Increase.	Decrease.
	Dol. c.	Dol. c.	Dol. c.	Dol. c.
Spirits.				
Spirits distilled from fruit	1,127,950 25	1,023,350 85	...	104,599 40
Spirits distilled from grain and other materials	67,957,906 48	70,631,860 48	2,673,954 00	...
Rectifiers (special tax)	189,800 12	183,872 92	...	5,927 20
Retail liquor-dealers (special tax)	4,624,587 77	4,597,139 33	...	27,448 44
Wholesale liquor-dealers (special tax)	455,915 51	448,840 51	...	7,075 00
Manufacturers of stills (special tax)	1,160 43	1,241 67	81 24	...
Stills or worms manufactured (special tax)	4,020 00	2,920 00	...	1,100 00
Stamps for distilled spirits intended for export	7,434 00	16,159 50	8,725 50	...
Interest on tax upon spirits	0 64	...	...	0 64
Total	74,368,775 20	76,905,385 26	2,536,610 06	...
Tobacco.				
Cigars and cheroots	16,895,215 15	10,368,805 27	...	6,526,409 88
Cigarettes	929,974 73	454,409 01	...	475,565 72
Snuff	736,022 82	448,211 58	...	287,811 24
Tobacco, chewing and smoking	22,136,402 53	13,488,047 41	...	8,648,355 12
Stamps for tobacco, snuff, and cigars intended for export*	876 00	...	...	876 00
Dealers in leaf tobacco (special tax)	54,535 12	48,595 82	...	5,939 30
Dealers in manufactured tobacco (special tax)	1,233,812 93	1,136,786 20	...	97,026 73
Manufacturers of tobacco (special tax)	5,697 88	5,117 49	...	580 39
Manufacturers of cigars (special tax)	96,899 00	97,962 19	1,063 19	...
Peddlers of tobacco (special tax)	14,813 63	14,465 01	...	348 62
Total	42,104,249 79	26,062,399 98	...	16,041,849 81
Fermented Liquors.				
Ale, beer, lager-beer, and porter	16,426,050 11	17,573,722 88	1,147,672 77	...
Brewers (special tax)	184,885 49	187,988 82	3,103 33	...
Dealers in malt liquors (special tax)	289,680 21	323,242 41	33,562 20	...
Total	16,900,615 81	18,084,954 11	1,184,338 30	...
Miscellaneous.				
Collections not otherwise provided for	10,873,900 49	248,156 36	...	10,625,744 13
Penalties	305,803 57	289,144 12	...	16,659 45
Total	11,179,704 06	537,300 48	...	10,642,403 58
Aggregate receipts	144,553,344 86	121,590,039 83	...	22,963,305 03

The cost of collection in the three years amounted to:—

		Dol. c.	
In 1881–82	..	5,113,734 88	or 3·5 per cent.
1882–83	..	5,105,957 09	3·5 ,,
1883–84	..	5,100,451 84	4·2 ,,

* Tax repealed 8th August, 1882.

The diminished receipts in the last year not carrying with them a corresponding diminution of staff, naturally caused an increase in the percentage of the cost of collection.

The Act of the 3rd March, 1883, affected internal revenue considerably. It abolished all adhesive stamps taxation, viz., that on proprietary medicines, bank cheques, friction matches, &c., on and from the 1st July, 1883. The tax on bank deposits and capital ceased on the 1st January, 1883, and the taxation on all kinds of tobacco was diminished one-half on the 1st May, 1883. The consolidation of collection districts, commenced in 1882-83 and concluded in 1883-84, has reduced the number of these districts from 126 to 85, thereby effecting an estimated annual saving of 125,000 dollars. The new Act having superseded and altered many classes of stamps, the stocks remaining on hand were utilized by having them specially marked, at a cost of 20,000 dollars.

The general state of the internal revenue appears to be satisfactory, and the Commissioner of Internal Revenue states his belief that no extensive revenue frauds are being perpetrated.

Tobacco. — The total amounts collected by ordinary and special taxes and stamps on all classes of tobacco are—

	Dol.	c.
For 1881-82	47,391,988	91
1882-83	42,104,249	74
1883-84	26,062,399	98

The reduction in taxation under the Act of the 3rd March, 1883, accounts for this large falling-off, which began to show itself in 1883. And the effect would have been greater but for the increase in the production of all forms of tobacco, as shown from the following comparison of 1881-82 with 1883-84:—

	Tobacco and Snuff.	Cigars and Cigarettes.
	Lbs.	Number.
1881-82	184,833,667	4,451,643,225
1883-84	172,153,816	3,662,973,076
Increase	12,679,851	788,670,149

The following Tables show the receipts from and the

production of manufactured tobacco, snuff, cigars, and cigarettes for the two years under review :—

(1.)—RECEIPTS.

	1882–83.	1883–84.
Receipts from Tobacco and Snuff.	Dollars.	Dollars.
Manufactured tobacco, at 16 cents per lb.	17,860,456	None
,, at 8 cents per lb.	4,275,947	13,486,900
Snuff, at 16 c. per lb.	626,546	1,147
,, at 8 c. per lb.	109,477	448,211
Total ..	22,872,425	13,936,258
Decrease on previous year	2,939,967	8,936,167
Receipts from Cigars and Cigarettes.		
Cigars taxed at 3 dollars per 1,000	2,472,119	10,364,909
,, 6 dollars ,,	14,423,096	3,896
Cigarettes taxed at 50 cents per 1,000	76,214	453,972
,, 1 dol. 75 c. per 1,000	853,079	..
,, 3 dollars ,,	33	436
,, 6 dollars ,,	648	..
Total ..	17,825,190	10,823,214
Decrease on previous year .	1,393,232	7,001,975

(2.)—Production.

	1882-83.	1883-84.
Tobacco and Snuff.	Lbs.	Lbs.
Tobacco, taxed at 16 cents per lb.	111,627,846	7,174
,, at 8 cents ,,	53,449,340	168,586,245
Snuff, taxed at 16 cents per lb.	3,915,913	..
,, at 8 cents ,,	1,368,459	5,602,645
Total quantity removed for consumption	170,361,558	174,196,064
Tobacco and snuff removed for exportation	10,951,756	10,637,603
Total apparent production	181,313,314	184,833,667
Total increase of production over previous year	9,159,498	3,520,354
Cigars and Cigarettes.	No.	No.
Cigars and cheroots taxed at 6 dollars per 1,000	2,403,849,392	649,407
Ditto, at 3 dollars per 1,000	884,039,600	3,454,969,610
Cigarettes taxed at 1 dol. 75 c. per 1,000	487,473,743	246
,, 50 cents ,,	152,428,760	907,945,140
,, 6 dollars ,,	107,950	..
,, 3 dollars ,,	11,200	145,337
Cigars removed in bond for export	2,773,375	1,690,000
Cigarettes ,, ,,	76,888,060	86,243,485
Total product	3,947,572,080	4,451,643,225
Total increase of production over previous year	284,599,004	504,071,145

The cigars imported during the year 1882-83 were as follows:—

	Lbs.
Aggregate in quantity	829,777
Of this quantity there were exported	55,584
Leaving to be withdrawn for consumption	774,193
Allowing 13½ lbs. to the 1,000 as the weight of imported cigars, the number would be	57,347,629
Number of cigars withdrawn in 1882	54,190,889
Increase in number of cigars for the fiscal year 1882-83	3,156,740

Owing to the changes introduced by the Act of the 3rd March, 1883, these statistics are not given for the year 1883-84.

The number of manufacturers and dealers in tobacco were—

1881-82	415,355
1882-83	473,392
1883-84	496,853

UNITED STATES.

The drawback allowed on exported tobacco, &c., was—

	1881-82.	1882-83.	1883-84.
	Dollars.	Dollars.	Dollars.
Tobacco	5,069	5,604	6,053
Cigars and cigarettes	1,406	5,195	5,674

The Act of the 3rd March, 1883, reduced the rates of tax on all manufactured tobacco, snuff, and cigars to one-half, and on cigarettes weighing not more than 3 lbs. per thousand to two-sevenths of the previous rate. All special taxes on tobacco manufacturers and dealers were reduced fully 50 per cent. These reductions took effect on the 1st May, 1883, and their effects are clearly shown in the above Tables.

The production of spirits during the two years was as follows:— *Spirits.*

	1882-83.	1883-84.
	Gallons.	Gallons.
Produced and deposited in warehouse—		
Bourbon whiskey	8,662,245	8,896,832
Rye whiskey	4,784,654	5,089,958
Alcohol	10,718,706	12,385,229
Rum	1,801,960	1,711,158
Gin	545,768	641,724
High wines	8,701,951	6,745,688
Pure neutral or Cologne spirits	28,295,253	28,538,680
Miscellaneous	10,502,771	11,426,470
Total	74,013,308	75,435,739

The following Table gives some additional particulars respecting the production of spirits:—

	1881-82.	1882-83.	1883-84.	Average for last five years.
Quantity of grain used in the production of spirits	27,459,095	18,644,787	18,927,982	24,065,879
Quantity of molasses used in the production of rum	2,121,804	2,373,106	2,259,536	2,514,988
Average yield of spirits from each bushel of grain	3·792	3·874	3·895	3·694 (In 1880-81)

The increase in the yield of spirits is believed to be due mainly to improved methods of preparing the grain for distillation.

(Table 3.) — MOVEMENT of Spirits through the Warehouses during the two years.

	1882–83.	1883–84.
	Gallons.	Gallons.
Remaining in warehouse—		
July 1, 1882	89,962,645	..
July 1, 1883	..	80,499,993
Produced in the year ended—		
June 30, 1883	74,013,308	..
June 30, 1884	..	75,435,739
Together	163,975,953	155,935,732
Withdrawn on payment of tax	75,441,087	78,342,474
Lost by leakage or evaporation	2,291,013	3,858,494
Withdrawn for export	5,326,427	9,586,738
Withdrawn for scientific purposes, and for the use of the United States' Government	28,725	20,837
Withdrawn for transfer to manufacturing warehouses	203,938	214,050
Lost by casualty, theft, &c.	184,770	410,588
Remaining in warehouse—		
June 30, 1883	80,499,993	..
June 30, 1884	..	63,502,551
Total	163,975,953	155,935,732

The following statement shows the quantity of spirits, as per original gauge, withdrawn from warehouse for all purposes during the last five years, and the amount and percentage of leakage allowed thereon by law:—

	1879–80.	1880–81.	1881–82.	1882–83.	1883–84.
	Gallons.	Gallons.	Gallons.	Gallons.	Gallons.
Total quantity withdrawn	78,199,283	84,335,900	80,281,611	83,291,013	92,022,593
Leakage allowed	75,834	811,466	1,231,336	2,291,013	3,858,494
Percentage of withdrawals	·096	·962	1·533	2·750	4·193

This great increase in leakage is attributed to the large increase in the withdrawals of Bourbon and rye whisky, on which there is always a larger leakage, owing to the longer period in which they are habitually retained in bond.

The drawback allowed on distilled spirits exported from the United States was, in 1881-82, 1,966 dollars, in 1882-83, 4,608 dollars, and in 1883-84, 8,352 dollars.

The amount of distilled spirits which went into consumption during the fiscal year ended the 30th June, 1885, is 69,156,902 gallons, and the amount of malt liquors on which tax was paid during the same period is 19,185,953 barrels. The amount of wine consumed in the country during the year 1884 is estimated at 20,508,345 gallons.

The Commissioner of Internal Revenue recommends the withdrawal of the privilege granted to manufacturers of vinegar of separating the alcoholic vapours from fermented mash or wort, and using it in the production of vinegar, on the ground that the privilege leads to the illicit distillation of spirits. Legislation would, however, be necessary to effect this object.

Direct tax of 1861. The collection of the direct tax of 1861, consisting of a single levy of 20,000,000 dollars raised by quotas from the different States and Territories, remains in a complicated and unsatisfactory state, there being 3,000,000 dollars unpaid in 1883, 2,750,000 dollars of which were due from the eleven Southern States. The Commissioner recommends that measures be taken to collect this unpaid balance. No doubt the cause of the deficiency lay in the general depression and poverty of the South in the years succeeding the war, in consequence of which much leniency has been shown to individuals from whom the tax was due.

Expenditure. The expenditure of the United States, which had recently been diminishing, has now again begun to increase, owing to a great extent to large amounts spent in 1884-85 under the heading of "Civil, Miscellaneous, and Public Buildings," which may be only temporary, but also to the growth of the enormous Pension List. *Pensions.* It is true that the expenditure under this head was less in 1883-84 than in the two previous years, but in 1884-85 it has again begun to increase, and will probably continue to do so. The following is a short summary of this branch of expenditure.

The number and classification of the persons receiving pensions from the United States' Government in the two last years are as follows:—

Classification.	On June 30, 1883.	On June 30, 1884.
Army invalids	198,643	218,956
Army widows, minor children, and dependent relatives	74,373	75,836
Navy invalids	2,468	2,616
Navy widows	1,907	1,938
Survivors of the war of 1812	4,831	3,898
Widows of ditto	21,336	19,512
Total	303,658	322,756
New pensioners added, and dropped pensioners restored to the roll during the year	38,958	35,413
Dropped from the roll for various causes	20,997	16,315
Net increase	17,961	19,098

	1882-83.	1883-84.
	Dollars.	Dollars.
Aggregate annual value of all pensions during the year	32,245,192	34,456,600
Amount paid to newly-allotted pensions as first payments	29,906,754	23,413,815
Total	62,151,946	57,870,415
Actual net expenditure on pensions	60,064,009	56,908,597

The Act of the 3rd March, 1883, enacted that all persons then or thereafter receiving a pension who, in the military or naval service of the United States and in the line of duty, had lost a hand or foot, or were otherwise incapacitated for manual labour to an equivalent extent, should receive a pension of 24 dollars a-month, and those who had lost an arm above the elbow or a leg above the knee, or were similarly disabled, should receive 30 dollars a-month. The effect of this was to increase pensions of 18 dollars a-month to 24 dollars and pensions of 24 dollars to 30 dollars.

The effect on the Pension List was of course immediate and remarkable, as is apparent in the Tables given above. Another cause has also operated to swell the numbers of pensioners. From 1879 to 1882 a large mass of arrears of claims had accumulated, and the clerical force of the Pension Office was largely increased to meet it by an Act passed in 1882.

Consequently great numbers of new claims have been granted in the last few years solely owing to the wiping out of arrears as above described.

These two causes have produced the present swollen condition of the Pension List. With regard to the future, it is estimated that there were living, in 1883, 962,201 individual soldiers and sailors, and there were then living the pensionable relatives of 72,340 deceased pensioners, none of whom had then applied for pensions.

It was anticipated that the whole of the latter, and a good percentage of the former, class would make application sooner or later, but that probably the majority of the former class would, from various causes, not apply.

Since 1883 something has been done towards reducing this great roll of possible claimants, but in the immediate future still further increase of the Pension List seems inevitable.

Besides the Pension List, there has no doubt been in recent years an increased disposition to liberality in expenditure in various minor directions as already mentioned, as appears from the Returns of Expenditure in 1884-85. [See Table appended to this Report.]

But the new Administration has already shown a strong determination to check extravagance in every branch of expenditure.

In the future, increased expenditure on the navy, the system of coast defence, and fortifications seem probable. This question, however, although it has frequently been brought before Congress, remains untouched, and it is still quite uncertain whether the naval defences of the United States will or will not receive the attention they so much need.

The question of reduction of taxation has, as is well known, been much agitated recently in the United States. The surplus of revenue over expenditure has of late years been very large, amounting, as before shown, to the following amounts, including the sinking fund and also such sums as were taken from cash balances for the reduction of debt:— *Reduction of taxation, and available surplus.*

	1881–82.	1883–84.	1884–85.
	Dollars.	Dollars.	Dollars.
Sinking fund	60,137,855	44,897,256	45,588,150
Remaining surplus	106,143,650	89,281,500	17,875,621
Total	166,281,505	134,178,756	63,463,771

The whole of these sums were applied to the reduction of the Public Debt. There was thus a steady decline in the available surplus, and the rapidly decreasing revenue and stationary or slightly increasing expenditure appear to be approaching an equilibrium, so that at the present rate it is doubtful whether in a year or two any margin available for the reduction of taxation or of debt will remain. It is also true, of course, that, as will be shown under the head of Public Debt, there will soon be no class of Public Debt left available for reduction until 1891 (and then only a limited amount); but that in no wise affects the question of reduction of taxation.

Giving its due weight to the reduction already made in taxation by the Act of the 3rd March, 1883, the main cause of the decline in the revenue seems to be the general depression of business.

Nevertheless, certain facts appear to justify the general expectation which undoubtedly exists in the United States of a revival of business, and consequently of revenue.

For instance, although in the seven months ending with July 1885 the aggregate bank clearings of the United States were 23 per cent. below those for the corresponding period of 1884, the clearings for the month of July 1885 alone exceeded those for July 1884 by no less than 271,033,000 dollars, or 8·5 per cent., and were 162,000,000 dollars above the maximum month for the year.

In the event of such a revival, there is no doubt that proposals for further reduction of taxation will be brought before Congress, and the late Secretary of the Treasury, in his Report for 1884, submitted the following recommendations on this head:—

1. That the existing import duties on raw materials to be used in manufactures should be removed in the interest of the United States' foreign trade.

2. That the duties on articles used or consumed by those who are the least able to bear the burden of taxation should be reduced.

3. That most of the internal revenue taxes should be removed, as indirectly pressing on the agricultural interest, always excepting, however, the tax on whisky.

Such sweeping changes as these are, of course, not within the immediate range of probability, but it is generally believed that the new Administration will bring some proposals for the lowering of the Customs Tariff at any rate before Congress at its next Session.

The two policies of reducing the Tariff and of largely strengthening the navy are, in the present state of the revenue, clearly incompatible, and it is only through a revival of business that they could be carried out on the ordinary Budget.

The following Tables will show the great reduction in the Public Debt of the United States during the three years ending the 30th June, 1885:— *Public Debt.*

STATEMENT of the Public Debt of the United States for the Month of June 1883.

INTEREST-BEARING DEBT.

Title of Loan.	Authorizing Act.	Rate.	When Redeemable.	Interest Payable.	Amount Outstanding. Registered	Amount Outstanding. Coupon.	Amount Outstanding. Total.	Interest Due and Unpaid.	Accrued Interest.
		Per cent.			Dollars.	Dollars.	Dollars.	Dol. c.	Dol. c.
Funded Loan of 1881	July 14, 1870, and January 20, 1871	5*	May 1, 1881	F., M., A., and N.	32,082,600	...	32,082,600	23,645 20	187,118 50
Loan of July 12, 1882	July 12, 1882	3	Option, U.S.	A., N., F., and M.	304,204,350	...	304,204,350	33,052 74	1,521,021 75
Funded Loan of 1891	July 14, 1870, and January 20, 1871	4½	Sept. 1, 1891	M., J., S., and D.	191,829,250	58,170,750	250,000,000	478,587 61	937,500 00
Funded Loan of 1907	July 14, 1870, and January 20, 1871	4	July 1, 1907	J., A., J., and O.	576,869,950	160,716,350	737,586,300	900,615 83	7,375,863 00
Refunding Certificates	February 26, 1879	4	...	...	...	...	355,900	56,941 00	3,559 00
Navy Pension Fund	July 23, 1868	...	...	...	...	...	14,000,000	210,000 00	210,000 00
Aggregate of Interest-bearing Debt					1,104,986,150	218,887,100	1,338,229,150	1,702,815 38	10,235,092 25

* Continued at 3½ per cent.

UNITED STATES.

DEBT ON WHICH INTEREST HAS CEASED SINCE MATURITY.

Title of Loan.	Authorizing Act.	Rate.		Amount Outstanding.	Interest Due and Unpaid.
		Per cent.		Dol. c.	Dol. c.
Old Debt	Various, prior to 1837	4 to 6	Matured at various dates prior to January 1, 1837	57,665 00	64,174 81
Mexican Indemnity Stock	August 10, 1846	5	at various dates in 1851 and 1852	1,104 91	85 74
Loan of 1847	January 28, 1847	6	December 31, 1867	1,250 00	22 00
Bounty-Land Scrip	February 11, 1847	6	July 1, 1849	3,175 00	210 06
Texan Indemnity Stock	September 9, 1850	5	December 31, 1864	20,000 00	2,945 00
Loan of 1858	June 14, 1858	5	after January 1, 1874	7,000 00	875 00
Loan of 1860	June 22, 1860	5	January 1, 1871	10,000 00	600 00
Five-twenties of 1862 (called)	February 25, 1862	6	December 1, 1871, and at subsequent dates	359,600 00	5,067 92
Five-twenties of June 1864 (called)	June 30, 1864	6	November 13, 1875, and at subsequent dates	50,400 00	832 40
Ten-forties of 1864 (called)	March 3, 1864	5	February 15, 1876, and at subsequent dates	61,150 00	14,809 20
Consols of 1865 (called)	March 3, 1865	6	July 9, 1879, and at subsequent dates	251,150 00	33,268 66
Consols of 1867 (called)	March 3, 1865	6	August 21, 1877, and at subsequent dates	342,000 00	9,699 67
Consols of 1868 (called)	March 3, 1865	6	April 1, 1879, and at subsequent dates	727,050 00	105,485 52
Loan of February 1861	February 8, 1861	6	July 4, 1879	118,850 00	13,605 33
Funded Loan, 1881 (called)	July 14, 1870; January 20, 1871	5	December 31, 1880	64,000 00	4,500 00
Funded Loan, 1881 (called)	July 14, 1870; January 20, 1871	5	May 21, 1881, and at subsequent dates	411,250 00	368 32
Oregon War Debt	March 2, 1861	5*	December 23, 1882, and at subsequent dates	3,001,300 00	15,424 05
Loan of July and August 1861	July 17 and August 5, 1861	6	July 1, 1881	7,500 00	1,525 50
Loan of July and August 1861 (called)	July 17 and August 5, 1861	6*	June 30, 1881	412,700 00	2,334 00
Loan of 1863 (1881's)	March 3, 1863	6	December 24, 1881, and at subsequent dates	821,100 00	9,775 03
Loan of 1863 (1881's), called	March 3, 1863	6*	June 30, 1881	98,050 00	964 40
Treasury Notes prior to 1846	Various, prior to 1846	$\frac{1}{10}$ to 6	August 1, 1882, and at subsequent dates	460,300 00	4,822 75
Treasury Notes of 1846	July 22, 1846	$\frac{1}{10}$ to 6	at various dates from 1838 to 1844	82,525 35	2,668 06
Treasury Notes of 1847	January 28, 1847	6	at various dates in 1847 and 1848	5,900 00	200 60
Treasury Notes of 1857	December 23, 1857	3 to 6	at various dates in 1848 and 1849	950 00	57 00
Treasury Notes of 1861	March 2, 1861	6	at various dates in 1858 and 1859	1,700 00	99 00
Seven-thirties of 1861	July 17, 1861	$7\frac{3}{10}$	March 1, 1863	3,000 00	364 50
One-year Notes of 1863	March 3, 1863	5	August 19 and October 1, 1864	16,250 00	1,091 45
Two-year Notes of 1863	March 3, 1863	5	at various dates in 1865	40,665 00	2,045 35
Compound-interest Notes	March 3, 1863; June 30, 1864	6	at various dates in 1866	31,100 00	1,472 47
Seven-thirties of 1864-65	June 30, 1864; March 3, 1865	$7\frac{3}{10}$	June 10, 1867, and May 15, 1868	213,620 00	43,709 91
Certificates of Indebtedness	March 1, 17, 1862; March 3, 1863	6	August 15, 1867, and June 15 and July 15, 1868	137,150 00	19,829 06
Temporary Loan	June 30, 1861	4 to 6	at various dates in 1866	4,000 00	253 48
Three per Cent. Certificates (called)	March 2, 1867; July 25, 1868	3	October 15, 1866	2,960 00	244 19
			February 28, 1873	5,000 00	394 31
Aggregate of Debt on which Interest has ceased since maturity				7,831,415 26	366,524 74

* Continued at 3½ per cent.

348 UNITED STATES.

DEBT BEARING NO INTEREST.

Title of Loan.	Authorizing Act.	Amount Outstanding.	Interest Due and Unpaid.
		Dol. c.	Dol. c.
Old Demand Notes	July 17, 1861; February 12, 1862	58,985 00	...
Legal-tender Notes	February 25, 1862; July 11, 1862; March 3, 1863	346,681,016 00	...
Certificates of Deposit	June 8, 1872	13,375,000 00	...
Gold Certificates	March 3, 1863; July 12, 1882	82,378,640 00	...
Silver Certificates	February 28, 1878	88,616,831 00	...
Unclaimed Pacific Railroad Interest		...	4,619 96
Fractional Currency	July 17, 1862; March 3, 1863; June 30, 1864 ... $15,376,624 81		
Less amount estimated as lost or destroyed, Act of June 21, 1879 ... 8,375,934 00		7,000,690 81	...
Aggregate of Debt bearing no Interest		538,111,162 81	4,619 96

RECAPITULATION.

		Principal.	Interest.	Totals.
	Dol. c.	Dol. c.	Dol. c.	Dol. c.
Interest-bearing Debt—				
Bonds at 5 per cent., continued at 3½ per cent.	32,082,600 00			
Bonds at 4½ per cent.	250,000,000 00			
Bonds at 4 per cent.	737,586,300 00			
Bonds at 3 per cent.	304,204,350 00			
Refunding Certificates	355,900 00			
Navy-Pension Fund	14,000,000 00			
		1,338,229,150 00	11,937,937 63	
Debt on which Interest has ceased since Maturity	...	7,831,415 26	366,824 74	
Debt bearing no Interest—				
Old Demand and Legal-tender Notes	346,740,001 00			
Certificates of Deposit	13,375,000 00			
Gold and Silver Certificates	170,995,471 00			
Fractional Currency	7,000,690 81			
		538,111,162 81		
Unclaimed Pacific Railroad Interest	...	...	4,619 96	
Total Debt	...	1,884,171,728 07	12,309,382 33	1,896,481,110 40
Total cash in the Treasury	...	...	...	345,389,902 92
Debt, less cash in the Treasury, July 1, 1883	...	...	...	1,551,091,207 48
Debt, less cash in the Treasury, June 1, 1883	...	...	...	1,569,189,408 91
Decrease of Debt during the month.	...	...	...	18,098,201 43
Decrease of Debt since June 30, 1882	...	...	...	137,823,253 24

Current Liabilities.		Available Assets.	
	Dol. c.		Dol. c.
Interest due and unpaid	1,702,845 38	Cash in the Treasury	345,389,902 92
Debt on which interest has ceased.	7,831,415 26		
Interest thereon	366,824 74		
Gold and Silver Certificates	170,995,471 00		
United States' Notes held for Redemption of Certificates of Deposit	13,375,000 00		
Cash balance available July 1, 1883	151,118,346 54		
	345,389,902 92		345,389,902 92

UNITED STATES.

BONDS ISSUED TO THE PACIFIC RAILWAY COMPANIES, INTEREST PAYABLE BY THE UNITED STATES.

Name of Railway.	Authorizing Acts.	Rate.	When Payable.	Interest Payable.	Principal Outstanding.	Interest Accrued and not yet Paid.	Interest Paid by the United States.	Interest repaid by Companies. By Transportation Service.	Interest repaid by Companies. By Cash Payments: 5 per Cent. Net Earnings.	Balance of Interest Paid by the United States.
Central Pacific	July 1, 1862, and July 2, 1864	Per cent. 6	30 years from date	January and July	Dol. c. 25,885,120 00	Dol. c. 776,553 60	Dol. c. 22,676,001 67	Dol. c. 4,592,158 25	Dol. c. 648,271 96	Dol. c. 17,435,571 46
Kansas Pacific	,,	6	,,	,,	6,303,000 00	189,090 00	5,940,243 09	2,969,049 59	...	2,971,193 50
Union Pacific	,,	6	,,	,,	27,236,512 00	817,095 36	24,140,755 05	8,933,292 87	...	15,207,462 18
Central Branch, Union Pacific	,,	6	,,	,,	1,600,000 00	48,000 00	1,501,808 26	152,157 10	6,926 91	1,342,724 25
Western Pacific	,,	6	,,	,,	1,970,560 00	59,116 80	1,609,132 14	9,367 00	...	1,599,765 14
Sioux City and Pacific	,,	6	,,	,,	1,628,320 00	48,849 60	1,415,447 89	121,355 39	...	1,294,092 50
Totals	...	...	...	...	64,623,512 00	1,938,705 36	57,283,388 10	16,777,380 20	655,198 87	39,850,809 03

Statement of the Public Debt of the United States for the Month of June 1884.

INTEREST-BEARING DEBT.

Title of Loan.	Authorizing Act.	Rate.	When Redeemable.	Interest Payable.	Amount Outstanding. Registered.	Amount Outstanding. Coupon.	Amount Outstanding. Total.	Interest Due and Unpaid.	Accrued Interest.
		Per cent.			Dollars.	Dollars.	Dollars.	Dol. c.	Dol. c.
Loan of July 12, 1882 ...	July 12, 1882 ...	3	Option, U.S.	A., N., F., and M.	224,612,150	...	224,612,150	28,644 43	1,123,060 75
Funded Loan of 1891 ...	July 14, 1870, and January 20, 1871	4½	Sept. 1, 1891	M., J., S., and D.	195,940,900	54,059,100	250,000,000	532,317 88	937,500 00
Funded Loan of 1907 ...	July 14, 1870, and January 20, 1871	4	July 1, 1907	J., A., J., and O.	590,437,600	147,224,100	737,661,700	886,756 33	7,376,617 00
Refunding Certificates .	February 26, 1879 ...	4	...	...	...	...	290,000	58,000 00	2,900 00
Navy Pension Fund ...	July 23, 1868 ...	3	...	...	...	...	14,000,000	...	210,000 00
Aggregate of Interest-bearing Debt ...		...	...	...	1,010,990,650	201,283,200	1,226,563,850	1,505,718 64	9,650,077 75

UNITED STATES.

DEBT ON WHICH INTEREST HAS CEASED SINCE MATURITY.

Title of Loan.	Authorizing Act.	Rate.		Amount Outstanding.	Interest Due and Unpaid.
		Per cent.		Dol. c.	Dol. c.
Old Debt	Various, prior to 1837	4 to 6	Matured at various dates prior to January 1, 1837	57,665 00	64,174 81
Mexican Indemnity Stock	August 10, 1846	5	at various dates in 1851 and 1852	1,104 91	85 74
Loan of 1847	January 28, 1847	6	December 31, 1867	1,250 60	22 00
Bounty-Land Scrip	February 11, 1847	6	July 1, 1849	3,175 00	210 06
Texan Indemnity Stock	September 9, 1850	5	December 31, 1864	20,000 00	2,945 00
Loan of 1858	June 14, 1858	5	after January 1, 1874	2,000 00	125 00
Loan of 1860	June 22, 1860	5	January 1, 1871	10,000 00	600 00
Five-twenties of 1862 (called)	February 25, 1862	6	December 1, 1871, and at subsequent dates	355,250 00	4,271 67
Five-twenties of June 1864 (called)	June 30, 1864	6	November 13, 1875, and at subsequent dates	49,400 00	825 43
Five-twenties of 1865 (called)	March 3, 1865	6	February 15, 1876, and at subsequent dates	59,950 00	6,915 26
Ten-forties of 1864 (called)	March 3, 1864	5	July 9, 1879, and at subsequent dates	178,850 00	15,460 19
Consols of 1865 (called)	March 3, 1865	6	August 21, 1877, and at subsequent dates	276,600 00	1,098 81
Consols of 1867 (called)	March 3, 1865	6	April 1, 1879, and at subsequent dates	548,200 00	56,990 89
Consols of 1868 (called)	March 3, 1865	6	July 4, 1879	97,150 00	16,026 13
Loan of February 1861	February 8, 1861	6	December 31, 1880	9,000 00	2,640 00
Funded Loan, 1881 (called)	July 14, 1870; January 20, 1871	5	May 21, 1881, and at subsequent dates	234,600 00	4,924 22
Funded Loan, 1881 (called)	July 14, 1870; January 20, 1871	5*	December 23, 1882, and at subsequent dates	533,200 00	14,242 71
Oregon War Debt	March 2, 1861	6	July 1, 1881	6,850 00	1,822 50
Loan of July and August 1861	July 17 and August 5, 1861	6	June 30, 1881	210,050 00	4,717 50
Loan of July and August 1861 (called)	July 17 and August 5, 1861	6*	December 24, 1881, and at subsequent dates	254,850 00	1,402 30
Loan of 1863 (1881's)	March 3, 1863	6	June 30, 1881	69,350 00	305 40
Loan of 1863 (1881's), called	March 3, 1863	6*	August 1, 1882, and at subsequent dates	37,750 00	1,428 34
Loan of July 12, 1882 (called)	July 12, 1882	3	December 1, 1883, and at subsequent dates	16,106,850 00	75,462 09
Treasury Notes prior to 1846	Various, prior to 1846	1/10 to 6	at various dates from 1838 to 1844	82,525 35	2,668 06
Treasury Notes of 1846	July 22, 1846	1/10 to 6	at various dates in 1847 and 1848	5,900 00	200 60
Treasury Notes of 1847	January 28, 1847	6	at various dates in 1848 and 1849	950 00	57 00
Treasury Notes of 1857	December 23, 1857	3 to 6	at various dates in 1858 and 1859	1,700 00	99 00
Treasury Notes of 1861	March 2, 1861	6	March 1, 1863	3,000 00	364 50
Seven-thirties of 1861	July 17, 1861	7 3/10	August 19 and October 1, 1864	15,850 00	1,019 39
One-year Notes of 1863	March 3, 1863	5	at various dates in 1865	59,465 00	1,085 85
Two-year Notes of 1863	March 3, 1863	5	at various dates in 1866	30,300 00	1,394 55
Compound-interest Notes	March 3, 1863; June 30, 1864	6	June 10, 1867, and May 15, 1868	207,660 00	42,553 67
Seven-thirties of 1864-65	June 30, 1864; March 3, 1865	7 3/10	August 15, 1867, and June 15 and July 15, 1868	133,800 00	19,283 91
Certificates of Indebtedness	March 1, 17, 1862; March 3, 1863	6	at various dates in 1866	4,000 00	253 48
Temporary Loan	June 30, 1864	4 to 6	October 15, 1866	2,960 00	244 19
Three per Cent. Certificates (called)	March 2, 1867; July 25, 1868	3	February 28, 1873	5,000 00	394 31
Aggregate of Debt on which Interest has ceased since maturity				19,656,205 26	347,214 06

* Continued at 3½ per cent.

UNITED STATES.

DEBT BEARING NO INTEREST.

Title of Loan.	Authorizing Act.	Amount Outstanding.	Interest Due and Unpaid.
		Dol. c.	Dol. c.
Old Demand Notes	July 17, 1861; February 12, 1862	58,440 00	...
Legal-tender Notes	February 25, 1862; July 11, 1862; March 3, 1863	346,681,016 00	...
Certificates of Deposit	June 8, 1872	12,385,000 00	...
Gold Certificates	March 3, 1863; July 12, 1882	98,392,660 00	...
Silver Certificates	February 28, 1878	119,811,691 00	...
Unclaimed Pacific Railroad Interest		...	4,229 96
Fractional Currency	July 17, 1862; March 3, 1863; June 30, 1864 ... $15,355,995 31		
Less amount estimated as lost or destroyed, Act of June 21, 1879 ... 8,375,934 00		6,980,061 31	...
Aggregate of Debt bearing no Interest		584,308,868 31	4,229 96

RECAPITULATION.

		Principal.	Interest.	Totals.
	Dol. c.	Dol. c.	Dol. c.	Dol. c.
Interest-bearing Debt—				
Bonds at 4½ per cent.	250,000,000 00			
Bonds at 4 per cent.	737,661,700 00			
Bonds at 3 per cent.	224,612,150 00			
Refunding Certificates	290,000 00			
Navy pension Fund	14,000,000 00			
		1,226,563,850 00	11,155,796 39	
Debt on which Interest has ceased since Maturity	...	19,656,205 26	347,214 06	
Debt bearing no Interest—				
Old Demand and Legal-tender Notes	346,739,456 00			
Certificates of Deposit	12,385,000 00			
Gold and Silver Certificates	218,204,351 00			
Fractional Currency	6,980,061 31			
		584,308,868 31		
Unclaimed Pacific Railroad Interest	...	...	4,229 96	
Total Debt	...	1,830,528,923 57	11,507,240 41	1,842,036,163 98
Total cash in the Treasury	...	...	...	391,985,928 18
Debt, less cash in the Treasury, July 1, 1884	...	...	...	1,450,050,235 80
Debt, less cash in the Treasury, June 1, 1884	...	...	...	1,459,267,492 60
Decrease of Debt during the month	...	...	...	9,217,256 80
Decrease of Debt since June 30, 1883	...	...	...	101,040,971 68

Current Liabilities.		Available Assets.	
	Dol. c.		Dol. c.
Interest due and unpaid	1,505,718 64	Cash in the Treasury	391,985,928 18
Debt on which interest has ceased	19,656,205 26		
Interest thereon	347,214 06		
Gold and Silver Certificates	218,204,351 00		
United States' Notes held for Redemption of Certificates of Deposit	12,385,000 00		
Cash balance available July 1, 1884	139,687,439 22		
	391,985,928 18		391,985,928 18

UNITED STATES.

BONDS ISSUED TO THE PACIFIC RAILWAY COMPANIES, INTEREST PAYABLE BY THE UNITED STATES.

Name of Railway.	Authorizing Acts.	Rate.	When Payable.	Interest Payable.	Principal Outstanding.	Interest Accrued and not yet Paid.	Interest Paid by the United States.	Interest Repaid by Companies. By Transportation Service.	By Cash Payments: 5 per Cent. Net Earnings.	Balance of Interest Paid by the United States.
		Per cent.			Dol. c.	Dol. c.	Dol. c.	Dol. c.	Dol. c.	Dol. c.
Central Pacific	July 1, 1862, and July 2, 1864	6	30 years from date	January and July	25,885,120 00	776,553 60	24,229,108 87	4,784,617 43	648,271 96	18,796,219 48
Kansas Pacific	,,	6	,,	,,	6,303,000 00	189,090 00	6,318,423 09	3,055,291 60	...	3,263,131 49
Union Pacific	,,	6	,,	,,	27,236,512 00	817,095 36	25,774,945 77	10,006,107 79	...	15,768,837 98
Central Branch, Union Pacific	,,	6	,,	,,	1,600,000 00	48,000 00	1,597,808 26	162,401 27	6,926 91	1,428,480 08
Western Pacific	,,	6	,,	,,	1,970,560 00	59,116 80	1,727,365 74	9,367 00	...	1,717,996 74
Sioux City and Pacific	,,	6	,,	,,	1,628,320 00	48,849 60	1,513,147 09	131,138 32	...	1,382,008 77
Totals	...	...	...	...	64,623,512 00	1,938,705 36	61,160,798 82	18,148,923 41	655,198 87	42,356,676 54

UNITED STATES.

"OLD FORM" of Statement of the Public Debt of the United States for the Month of June 1885.

INTEREST-BEARING DEBT.

Title of Loan.	Authorizing Act.	Rate.	When Redeemable.	Interest Payable.	Amount Outstanding. Registered.	Amount Outstanding. Coupon.	Amount Outstanding. Total.	Interest Due and Unpaid.	Accrued Interest.
					Dollars.	Dollars.	Dollars.	Dol. c.	Dol. c.
Loan of July 12, 1882	July 12, 1882	3	Option, U. S.	A., N., F., and M.	194,190,500	...	194,190,500	15,696 19	970,952 50
Funded Loan of 1891	July 14, 1870, and January 20, 1871	4½	Sept. 1, 1891	M., J., S., and D.	199,007,500	50,992,500	250,000,000	532,988 75	937,500 00
Funded Loan of 1907	July 14, 1870, and January 20, 1871	4	July 1, 1907	J., A., J., and O.	601,587,350	136,132,500	737,719,850	867,167 83	7,377,198 50
Refunding Certificates	February 26, 1879	4	...	...	...	...	240,600	57,744 00	2,406 00
Navy Pension Fund	July 23, 1868	3	...	...	...	...	14,000,000	...	210,000 00
Aggregate of Interest-bearing Debt					994,785,350	187,125,000	1,196,150,950	1,473,596 77	9,498,057 00

UNITED STATES.

DEBT ON WHICH INTEREST HAS CEASED SINCE MATURITY.

Title of Loan.	Authorizing Act.	Rate.		Amount Outstanding.	Interest Due and Unpaid.
		Per cent.		Dol. c.	Dol. c.
Old Debt	Various, prior to 1837	4 to 6	Matured at various dates prior to January 1, 1837	57,665 00	64,174 81
Mexican Indemnity Stock	August 10, 1846	5	at various dates in 1851 and 1852	1,104 91	85 74
Loan of 1847	January 28, 1847	6	December 31, 1867	1,250 00	22 00
Bounty-Land Script	February 11, 1847	6	July 1, 1849	3,175 00	210 06
Texan Indemnity Stock	September 9, 1850	5	December 31, 1864	20,000 00	2,945 00
Loan of 1858	June 14, 1858	5	after January 1, 1874	2,000 00	135 00
Loan of 1860	June 22, 1860	5	January 1, 1871	10,000 00	600 00
Five-twenties of 1862 (called)	February 25, 1862	6	December 1, 1871, and at subsequent dates	335,850 00	2,519 12
Five-twenties of June 1864 (called)	June 30, 1864	6	November 13, 1875, and at subsequent dates	48,550 00	639 25
Five-twenties of 1865 (called)	March 3, 1865	6	February 15, 1876, and at subsequent dates	37,150 00	2,691 73
Ten-forties of 1864 (called)	March 3, 1864	5	July 9, 1879, and at subsequent dates	99,350 00	7,617 18
Consols of 1865 (called)	March 3, 1865	6	August 21, 1877, and at subsequent dates	228,250 00	707 77
Consols of 1867 (called)	March 3, 1865	6	April 1, 1879, and at subsequent dates	474,100 00	42,089 86
Consols of 1868 (called)	March 3, 1865	6	July 4, 1879	86,800 00	13,407 53
Loan of February 1861	February 8, 1861	6	December 31, 1880	8,000 00	2,640 00
Funded Loan, 1881 (called)	July 14, 1870; January 20, 1871	5	May 21, 1881, and at subsequent dates	198,500 00	275 78
Funded Loan, 1881 (called)	July 14, 1870; January 20, 1871	5*	December 23, 1882, and at subsequent dates	302,700 00	7,204 78
Oregon War Debt	March 2, 1861	6	July 1, 1881	4,050 00	838 50
Loan of July and August 1861	July 17 and August 5, 1861	6	June 30, 1881	156,250 00	1,041 50
Loan of July and August 1861 (called)	July 17 and August 5, 1861	6*	December 24, 1881, and at subsequent dates	202,600 00	151 10
Loan of 1863 (1881's)	March 3, 1863	6	June 30, 1881	32,750 00	542 90
Loan of 1863 (1881's) called	March 3, 1863	6*	August 1, 1882, and at subsequent dates	19,750 00	176 67
Loan of July 12, 1882 (called)	July 12, 1882	3	December 1, 1883, and at subsequent dates	1,246,300 00	7,238 24
Treasury Notes prior to 1846	Various, prior to 1846	$\frac{1}{10}$ to 6	at various dates from 1838 to 1844	82,525 35	2,068 06
Treasury Notes of 1846	July 22, 1846	$\frac{5}{10}$ to 6	at various dates in 1847 and 1848	5,900 00	200 60
Treasury Notes of 1847	January 28, 1847	6	at various dates in 1848 and 1849	950 00	57 00
Treasury Notes of 1857	December 23, 1857	3 to 6	at various dates in 1858 and 1859	1,700 00	99 00
Treasury Notes of 1861	March 2, 1861	6	March 1, 1863	3,000 00	364 50
Seven-thirties of 1861	July 17, 1861	$7\frac{3}{10}$	August 19 and October 1, 1864	15,850 00	1,015 74
One-year Notes of 1863	March 3, 1863	5	at various dates in 1865	38,085 00	1,916 35
Two-year Notes of 1863	March 3, 1863	5	at various dates in 1866	29,950 00	1,359 55
Compound-interest Notes	March 3, 1863; June 30, 1864	6	June 10, 1867, and May 15, 1868	202,730 00	41,597 22
Seven-thirties of 1864-65	June 30, 1864; March 3, 1865	$7\frac{3}{10}$	August 15, 1867, and June 15 and July 15, 1868	132,200 00	19,038 00
Certificates of Indebtedness	March 1, 17, 1862; March 3, 1863	6	at various dates in 1866	4,000 00	253 48
Temporary Loan	June 30, 1864	4 to 6	October 15, 1866	2,960 00	244 19
3 per Cent. Certificates (called)	March 2, 1867; July 25, 1868	3	February 28, 1873	5,000 00	394 31
Aggregate of Debt on which Interest has ceased since Maturity				4,100,995 26	227,199 52

* Continued at 3¾ per cent.

356. UNITED STATES.

DEBT BEARING NO INTEREST.

Title of Loan.	Authorizing Act.	Amount Outstanding.	Interest Due and Unpaid.
		Dol. c.	Dol. c.
Old Demand Notes	July 17, 1861; February 12, 1862	57,950 00	...
Legal-tender Notes	February 25, 1862; July 11, 1862; March 3, 1863	346,681,016 00	...
Certificates of Deposit	June 8, 1872	29,785,000 00	...
Gold Certificates	March 3, 1863, and July 12, 1882	140,323,140 00	...
Silver Certificates	February 28, 1878	139,901,646 00	...
Unclaimed Pacific Railroad Interest		...	4,229 96
Fractional Currency	July 17, 1862; March 3, 1863; June 30, 1864 ... 15,340,109 88		
Less amount estimated as lost or destroyed, Act of June 21, 1879 ... 8,375,934 00		6,964,175 88	...
Aggregate of Debt bearing no Interest		663,712,927 88	4,229 96

RECAPITULATION.

		Principal.	Interest.	Totals.
	Dol. c.	Dol. c.	Dol. c.	Dol. c.
Interest-bearing Debt—				
Bonds at 4½ per cent.	250,000,000 00	...	...	
Bonds at 4 per cent.	737,719,850 00	...	...	
Bonds at 3 per cent.	194,190,500 00	...	...	
Refunding Certificates	240,600 00	...	...	
Navy Pension Fund	14,000,000 00	1,196,150,950 00	10,971,653 77	
Debt on which Interest has ceased since Maturity	...	4,100,995 26	227,199 52	
Debt bearing no Interest—				
Old Demand and Legal-tender Notes	346,738,966 00	...	...	
Certificates of Deposit	29,785,000 00	...	...	
Gold and Silver Certificates	280,224,786 00	...	...	
Fractional Currency	6,964,175 88	663,712,927 88	...	
Unclaimed Pacific Railroad Interest	...	...	4,229 96	
Total Debt	...	1,863,964,873 14	11,203,083 25	1,875,167,956 39
Total cash in the Treasury	...	...	...	488,612,429 23
Debt, less cash in the Treasury, July 1, 1885	...	...	...	1,386,555,527 16
Debt, less cash in the Treasury, June 1, 1885	...	...	...	1,395,549,520 91
Decrease of Debt during the month	...	...	...	8,993,993 75
Decrease of Debt since June 30, 1884	...	...	...	63,494,708 64

Current Liabilities.		Available Assets.	
	Dol. c.		Dol. c.
Interest due and unpaid	1,473,596 77	Cash in the Treasury	488,612,429 23
Debt on which interest has ceased	4,100,995 26		
Interest thereon	227,199 52		
Gold and Silver Certificates	280,224,786 00		
United States' Notes held for Redemption of Certificates of Deposit	29,785,000 00		
Cash balance available July 1, 1885	172,800,851 68		
	488,612,429 23		488,612,429 23

UNITED STATES.

BONDS ISSUED TO THE PACIFIC RAILWAY COMPANIES, INTEREST PAYABLE BY THE UNITED STATES.

Name of Railway.	Authorizing Acts.	Rate.	When Payable.	Interest Payable.	Principal Outstanding.	Interest Accrued and not yet paid.	Interest Paid by the United States.	Interest Repaid by Companies. By Transportation Service.	Interest Repaid by Companies. By Cash Payments: 5 per Cent. Net Earnings.	Balance of Interest Paid by the United States.
		Per cent.			Dol. c.	Dol. c.	Dol. c.	Dol. c.	Dol. c.	Dol. c.
Central Pacific	July 1, 1862, and July 2, 1864	6	30 years from date	January and July	25,885,120 00	776,553 60	25,782,216 07	5,134,185 31	648,271 96	19,999,758 80
Kansas Pacific	,, ,,	6	,,	,,	6,303,000 00	189,090 00	6,696,603 09	3,284,294 23	...	3,412,308 86
Union Pacific	,, ,,	6	,,	,,	27,236,512 00	817,095 36	27,409,136 49	10,647,579 36	283,162 99	16,478,394 14
Central Branch, Union Pacific	,, ,,	6	,,	,,	1,600,000 00	48,000 00	1,603,808 26	219,746 48	6,926 91	1,467,134 87
Western Pacific	,, ,,	6	,,	,,	1,970,560 00	59,116 80	1,845,599 34	9,367 00	...	1,836,232 34
Sioux City and Pacific	,, ,,	6	,,	,,	1,628,320 00	48,849 60	1,610,846 29	178,659 68	...	1,432,186 61
Totals	...	...	...	...	64,623,512 00	1,938,705 36	65,038,209 54	19,473,832 06	938,361 86	44,626,015 62

REVISED STATEMENT of the Public Debt of the United States for the Month of June 1885.

INTEREST-BEARING DEBT.

Title of Loan.	Authorizing Act.	Rate.	When Redeemable.	Interest Payable.	Amount Outstanding.			Interest Due and Unpaid.	Accrued Interest.
					Registered.	Coupon.	Total.		
		Per cent.			Dollars.	Dollars.	Dollars.	Dol. c.	Dol. c.
Loan of July 12, 1882	July 12, 1882	3	Option, U. S.	A., N., F., and M.	194,190,500	...	194,190,500	15,696 19	970,952 50
Funded Loan of 1891	July 14, 1870, and January 20, 1871	4½	Sept. 1, 1891	M., J., S., and D.	199,007,500	50,992,500	250,000,000	532,988 75	937,500 00
Funded Loan of 1907	July 14, 1870, and January 20, 1871	4	July 1, 1907	J., A., J., and O.	601,587,350	136,132,500	737,719,850	867,167 83	7,377,198 50
Refunding Certificates	February 26, 1879	4	...	J., A., J., and O.	...	...	240,600	57,744 00	2,406 00
Navy Pension Fund	July 23, 1868	3	...	Jan. and July	...	...	14,000,000	...	210,000 00

Amount.	Date of Maturity.	Average Date of Maturity.						
Dollars.								
2,362,000	January 16, 1895	⎫						
640,000	November 1, 1895	⎬ March 19, 1895						
1,600,000	January 1, 1896	⎭						
1,440,000	,, ,,	⎫ January 18, 1896						
640,000	February 1, 1896	⎭						
4,320,000	January 1, 1897	January 1, 1897						
9,712,000	,, 1898	,, 1898						
29,904,952	,, 1899	,, 1899						
14,004,560	...	...						

Bonds issued to Pacific Railroads .... | | | | | 64,623,512 | ... | 64,623,512 | 15,269 96 | 1,938,705 36

Aggregate of Interest-bearing Debt .... 1,059,408,862 | 187,125,000 | 1,260,774,462 | 1,488,866 73 | 11,436,762 36

UNITED STATES.

DEBT ON WHICH INTEREST HAS CEASED SINCE MATURITY.

Title of Loan.	Authorizing Act.	Rate.		Amount Outstanding.	Interest Due and Unpaid.
		Per cent.		Dol. c.	Dol. c.
Old Debt	Various, prior to 1837	4 to 6	Matured at various dates prior to January 1, 1837	57,665 00	64,174 81
Mexican Indemnity Stock	August 10, 1846	5	,, at various dates in 1851 and 1852	1,104 91	85 74
Loan of 1847	January 28, 1847	6	,, December 31, 1867	1,250 00	22 00
Bounty-Land Scrip	February 11, 1847	6	,, July 1, 1849	3,175 06	210 06
Texan Indemnity Stock	September 9, 1850	5	,, December 31, 1864	20,000 00	2,945 00
Loan of 1858	June 14, 1858	5	,, after January 1, 1874	2,000 00	125 00
Loan of 1860	June 22, 1860	5	,, January 1, 1871	10,000 00	600 00
Five-twenties of 1862 (called)	February 25, 1862	6	,, December 1, 1871, and at subsequent dates	335,850 00	2,519 12
Five-twenties of June 1864 (called)	June 30, 1864	6	,, November 13, 1875, and at subsequent dates	48,550 00	659 25
Five-twenties of 1865 (called)	March 3, 1865	6	,, February 15, 1876, and at subsequent dates	37,150 00	2,691 73
Ten-forties of 1864 (called)	March 3, 1864	5	,, July 9, 1879, and at subsequent dates	99,350 00	7,674 18
Consols of 1865 (called)	March 3, 1865	6	,, August 21, 1877, and at subsequent dates	228,250 00	707 77
Consols of 1867 (called)	March 3, 1865	6	,, April 1, 1879, and at subsequent dates	474,100 00	42,089 86
Consols of 1868 (called)	March 3, 1865	6	,, July 4, 1879	86,800 00	13,407 53
Loan of February 1861	February 8, 1861	6	,, December 31, 1880	8,000 00	2,640 00
Funded Loan, 1881 (called)	July 14, 1870; January 20, 1871	5	,, May 21, 1881, and at subsequent dates	198,500 00	275 78
Funded Loan, 1881 (called)	July 14, 1870; January 20, 1871	5*	,, December 23, 1882, and at subsequent dates	302,700 00	7,204 78
Oregon War Debt	March 2, 1861	6	,, July 1, 1881	4,050 00	808 50
Loan of July and August 1861	July 17 and August 5, 1861	6	,, June 30, 1881	156,250 00	1,041 50
Loan of July and August 1861 (called)	July 17 and August 5, 1861	6*	,, December 24, 1881, and at subsequent dates	202,600 00	151 10
Loan of 1863 (1881's)	March 3, 1863	6	,, June 30, 1881	32,750 00	542 90
Loan of 1863 (1881's) called	March 3, 1863	6*	,, August 1, 1883, and at subsequent dates	19,750 00	176 67
Loan of July 12, 1882 (called)	July 12, 1882	3	,, December 1, 1883, and at subsequent dates	1,246,300 00	7,238 24
Treasury Notes prior to 1846	Various, prior to 1846	5/10 to 6	,, at various dates from 1838 to 1844	82,625 35	2,668 06
Treasury Notes of 1846	July 22, 1846	1/10 to 6	,, at various dates in 1847 and 1848	5,900 00	200 60
Treasury Notes of 1847	January 28, 1847	6	,, at various dates in 1848 and 1849	950 00	57 00
Treasury Notes of 1857	December 23, 1857	3 to 6	,, at various dates in 1858 and 1859	1,700 00	99 00
Treasury Notes of 1861	March 2, 1861	6	,, March 1, 1863	3,000 00	364 50
Seven-thirties of 1861	July 17, 1861	7 3/10	,, August 19 and October 1, 1864	15,850 00	1,015 74
One-year Notes of 1863	March 3, 1863	5	,, at various dates in 1865	38,085 00	1,916 35
Two-year Notes of 1863	March 3, 1863	5	,, at various dates in 1866	29,950 00	1,359 55
Compound-interest Notes	March 3, 1863; June 30, 1864	6	,, June 10, 1867, and May 15, 1868	202,730 00	41,597 22
Seven-thirties of 1864-65	June 30, 1864; March 3, 1865	7 3/10	,, August 15, 1867, June 15 and July 15, 1868	132,200 00	19,038 60
Certificates of Indebtedness	March 1, 17, 1862; March 3, 1863	6	,, at various dates in 1866	4,000 00	253 48
Temporary Loan	June 30, 1864	4 to 6	,, October 15, 1866	2,960 00	244 19
3 per Cent. Certificates (called)	March 2, 1867; July 25, 1868	3	,, February 28, 1873	5,000 00	394 31
Aggregate of Debt on which Interest has ceased since Maturity				4,100,995 26	227,199 52

* Continued at 3½ per cent.

UNITED STATES.

DEBT BEARING NO INTEREST.

Title of Loan.	Authorizing Act.		Amount Outstanding.
		Dol. c.	Dol. c.
Old Demand Notes	July 17, 1861; February 12, 1862	...	57,950 00
Legal-tender Notes	February 25, 1862; July 11, 1862; March 3, 1863	...	346,681,016 00
Certificates of Deposit	June 8, 1872	29,785,000 00	
Less amount held in Treasurer's cash	...	200,000 00	
			29,585,000 00
Gold Certificates	March 3, 1863; July 12, 1882	140,323,140 00	
Less amount held in Treasurer's cash	...	13,593,410 00	
			126,729,730 00
Silver Certificates	February 28, 1878	139,901,646 00	
Less amount held in Treasurer's cash	...	38,370,700 00	
			101,530,946 00
Fractional Currency	July 17, 1862; March 3, 1863; June 30, 1864	15,340,109 88	
Less amount estimated as lost or destroyed, Act of June 21, 1879	...	8,375,934 00	
			6,964,175 88
Aggregate of Debt bearing no Interest	...	...	611,548,817 88

RECAPITULATION.

		Principal.	Interest.	Totals.
	Dol. c.	Dol. c.	Dol. c.	Dol. c.
Interest-bearing Debt—				
Bonds at 4½ per cent.	250,000,000 00			
Bonds at 4 per cent.	737,719,850 00			
Bonds at 3 per cent.	194,190,500 00			
Refunding Certificates, at 4 per cent.	240,600 00			
Navy Pension Fund, at 3 per cent.	14,000,000 00			
Pacific Railway Bonds, at 3 per cent.	64,623,512 00			
		1,260,774,462 00	12,925,629 09	1,273,700,091 09
Debt on which Interest has ceased since Maturity	...	4,100,995 26	227,199 52	4,328,194 78
Debt bearing no Interest—				
Old Demand and Legal-tender Notes	346,738,966 00			
Certificates of Deposit	29,585,000 00			
Gold Certificates	126,729,730 00			
Silver Certificates	101,530,946 00			
Fractional Currency, less 8,375,934 dollars, estimated as lost or destroyed	6,964,175 88			
		611,548,817 88	...	611,548,817 88
Total Debt	...	1,876,424,275 14	13,152,828 61	1,889,577,103 75
Less cash items available for reduction of the Debt	...	...	263,666,023 42	
Less reserve held for redemption of United States' Notes	...	...	100,000,000 00	
				363,666,023 42
Total Debt, less available cash items	...	...	...	1,525,911,080 33
Net cash in the Treasury	...	...	...	40,676,930 68
Debt, less cash in the Treasury, July 1, 1885	...	...	...	1,485,234,149 65
Debt, less cash in the Treasury, June 1, 1885	...	...	...	1,494,391,011 28
Decrease of Debt during the month, as shown by this statement	...	...	...	9,156,861 63

UNITED STATES.

Cash in the Treasury.

	Dol.	c.	Dol.	c.
Available for reduction of the Public Debt—				
Gold held for Gold Certificates actually outstanding	...		126,729,730	00
Silver held for Silver Certificates actually outstanding	...		101,530,946	00
United States' Notes held for Certificates of Deposit actually outstanding	...		29,585,000	00
Cash held for matured debt and interest unpaid	...		5,817,061	51
Fractional currency	...		3,285	91
Total available for reduction of the Debt	...		263,666,023	42
Reserve Fund—				
Held for redemption of United States' Notes, Acts of January 14, 1875, and July 12, 1882	...		100,000,000	00
Unavailable for reduction of the Debt—				
Fractional silver coin	31,236,899	49		
Minor coin	868,465	64	32,105,365	13
Certificates held as cash—				
Legal-tender	200,000	00		
Gold	13,593,410	00		
Silver	38,370,700	00	52,164,110	00
Net cash balance on hand	...		40,676,930	68
Total cash in the Treasury, as shown by Treasurer's General Account	...		488,612,429	23

362 UNITED STATES.

RECONCILIATION.

	July 1.		June 1.		Resultant Differences.	
	Dol. c.	Dol. c.	Dol. c.	Dol. c.	Increase. Dol. c.	Decrease. Dol. c.
Total Debt, old form ...	...	1,875,167,956 39	...	1,875,119,930 18	...	Inc. 48,026 21
Increased by:—						
Pacific Railroad Bonds	64,623,512 00		64,623,512 00			
Accrued interest thereon	1,938,705 36		1,615,587 80			
Interest due and unpaid thereon	11,040 00		11,910 00			
		66,573,257 36		66,251,009 80		
		1,941,741,213 75		1,941,370,939 98		
Decreased by:—						
Gold Certificates in cash	13,593,410 00		14,371,350 00			
Silver Certificates in cash	38,370,700 00		35,575,590 00			
Certificates of Deposit in cash	200,000 00		315,000 00			
		52,164,110 00		50,261,940 00		
Total Debt, new form ...	...	1,889,577,103 75	...	1,891,108,999 98	Dec. 1,531,896 23	
Cash in the Treasury, old form	...	488,612,429 23	...	479,570,409 27	...	Inc. 9,042,019 96
Reduced by certificates as above	52,164,110 00		50,261,940 00			
Assets not available	32,105,365 13		32,590,480 57			
		84,269,475 13		82,852,420 57		
Cash in the Treasury, new form	...	404,342,954 10	...	396,717,988 70	7,624,965 40	
Made up of—Cash available for reduction of Debt	363,666,023 42		366,624,966 74			
Balance	40,676,930 68		30,093,021 96			
Debt, less cash in the Treasury, old form	...	1,386,555,527 16	...	1,395,549,520 91	...	8,993,993 75
Debt, less cash in the Treasury, new form	...	1,485,234,149 65	...	1,494,391,011 28	9,156,861 63	

It will be observed that a different form of stating the Public Debt has been introduced by the new Secretary of the Treasury, thereby in appearance increasing the net total of the debt, less cash in the Treasury, on the 1st July, 1885, by 99,321,376 dollars. Of course there is no real increase, the difference, which is merely a matter of account, being explained as follows:—

The Pacific Railroad bonds, and interest thereon, amounting in all to 66,573,257 dollars, formerly not included in the Public Debt, are now included therein; the gold and silver certificates and certificates of deposits, in all 52,164,110 dollars, formerly stated as part of the Public Debt, and also re-stated as part of the cash in the Treasury, are now omitted from both.

The gross total of the Public Debt is consequently increased in appearance, through these two changes, by the difference between the two amounts, viz., 14,409,146 dollars.

The cash in the Treasury, diminished by the omission of the certificates, is again further diminished by 32,105,365 dollars of fractional silver and minor coin, described as "assets not available for reduction of Public Debt," and the final net result of this change in the form of account, as before stated, is an apparent increase in the net debt of not far from 100,000,000 dollars.

This revised form of statement, which is no doubt more accurate, has been adopted as the definitive form of account for the future.

The main features of the redemption of debt during this period may be thus summarized: the refunding operations have been steadily continued, and the remainder of the 3½ per cent. bonds, amounting on the 1st November, 1882, to 162,499,600 dollars, have been paid off, while a reduction in the new 3 per cent. bonds, issued under the Act of the 12th July, 1882, and repayable at the option of the United States, has been effected to the extent of 110,000,000 dollars. These bonds, which were gradually issued under the above-mentioned Act on and after the 1st August, 1882, reached a maximum amount of 305,000,000 dollars on the 31st October, 1883, and have since then been steadily diminishing, until on the 1st July, 1885, they had sunk to 194,190,500 dollars. This is the only class of debt

Redemption of debt.

now available for redemption by the United States' Treasury, and at the present rate this amount will have been paid off in less than three years, or by the end of 1887. There will then be no outlet for the surplus revenue (if any) of the United States until the 1st September, 1891, when the 250,000,000 dollars of the 4½ per cent. funded loan of 1891 will become available for redemption.

The Secretary of the Treasury, in his Report for 1883, gave certain calculations as to the relation between the accumulations of surplus revenue and the repayment of the debt, arriving at the conclusion that if the Treasury were free to redeem debt at its option, the whole could be paid within fifteen years, or before the end of the century. But the fluctuations in the surpluses of different years vitiate this calculation, and the available balance of the year ending the 30th June, 1885, was far below the average.

The reduction of debt in the sixteen years ending the 1st November, 1884, amounted to no less than 1,076,452,604 dollars, carrying with it a reduction in the annual interest charge of 79,084,511 dollars, and the average rate paid fell from 5·8 per cent. to 3·92 per cent. during the period.

The following minor operations of debt redemption have also been effected: 1,834,000 dollars United States' bonds of different issues, known as the "Japanese Indemnity Fund," were cancelled in 1883, and in the same year 954,600 dollars in bonds, left as a legacy to the United States' Government by the late Joseph L. Lewis, were likewise cancelled.

There are two ways in which the United States' Debt is reduced:—

1. By the action of the sinking fund, under which 1 per cent. of the entire debt (on which reduction can be effected) is redeemable yearly, and the application to the same purpose of the interest on available sinking fund bonds.

2. By the application of surplus funds to the direct redemption of those classes of debt which are by law from time to time redeemable. The two operations taken together make up the reduction of debt for the year.

In July 1885, 7,000,000 dollars, and in August

1885, 2,879,052 dollars, of Public Debt were redeemed, bringing the statistics up to date. But some doubt has been thrown on these figures, owing to recent transactions in fractional currency between the United States' Treasury and New York banks to the extent of some 6,000,000 dollars. It is asserted in some quarters that this fractional currency in its unsatisfactory state should not be used at all, but the United States' Treasury is of a different opinion.

The Returns respecting the National Banks of the United States, made up as usual to October in each year, give the following results for 1883 and 1884.

On the 1st November, 1883, there were 2,522 National Banks in operation, being an increase over all former years; 261 new banks were organized during the twelve months, the greatest number in any year since 1865. The capital of these new banks was 28,654,350 dollars, and their circulation 7,909,150 dollars, about one-fourth of the capital, such proportion being permitted by the Act of the 12th July, 1882. On the 2nd October, 1883, the total capital of the National Banks was 509,699,787 dollars, an increase during the year of 26,595,574 dollars; their surplus was 102,000,482 dollars, circulation 314,931,575 dollars, and individual deposits 1,049,437,700 dollars, both amounts showing a decrease; loans 1,303,450,790 dollars, and specie 107,817,983 dollars, both showing an increase.

The corporate existence of 307 banks expired during during the year, but 273 renewed it under the recent Act.

Turning to 1884, the corresponding figures are:—

November 1, 1884: Number of National Banks 2,672. Number of banks organized 191, with a capital of 16,042,230 dollars, and a circulation of 3,854,530 dollars.

October 1, 1884: Aggregate capital of the National Banks 524,266,345 dollars, surplus 147,045,833 dollars, circulation 289,775,123 dollars, individual deposits 975,259,295 dollars, loans and discounts 1,240,070,797 dollars, and specie 128,609,474 dollars.

Eleven National Banks, with a capital of 1,285,000 dollars, failed during the twelve months.

The corporate existence of 89 expired, and 83 renewed it under the Act.

In 1885 it is estimated that the corporate existence

366 UNITED STATES.

of 721 banks, with a capital of 189,071,475 dollars, will expire.

The following Tables give the resources and liabilities of the National Banks on the 2nd October, 1883, and the 1st October, 1884, and also a summary for the eleven years ending 1883:—

(1.)—SHOWING the Resources and Liabilities of the National Banks at the close of business on the 2nd day of October, 1883; the Returns from New York City, Boston, Philadelphia, and Baltimore, from the other reserve cities, and from the remaining banks of the country, being tabulated separately.

	New York City.	Boston, Philadelphia, and Baltimore.	Other reserve Cities.*	Country Banks.	Aggregate.
	48 banks.	103 banks.	97 banks.	2,253 banks.	2,501 banks.
RESOURCES.	Dollars.	Dollars.	Dollars.	Dollars.	Dollars.
Loans and discounts	245,108,332	200,815,928	151,364,826	706,161,705	1,303,450,791
Overdrafts	361,471	57,643	372,486	5,002,391	5,793,991
Bonds for circulation	18,277,500	49,002,050	27,232,250	256,901,050	351,412,850
Bonds for deposit	820,000	661,000	4,153,000	11,447,000	17,081,000
United States' bonds on hand	2,296,050	334,150	2,508,000	8,454,850	13,593,050
Other stocks and bonds	13,017,588	7,430,507	5,487,844	45,178,092	71,114,031
Due from reserve agents	...	22,902,211	17,896,779	84,119,738	124,918,728
Due from other National Banks	17,336,757	14,457,637	8,147,081	25,772,754	65,714,229
Due from other banks and bankers	2,800,515	1,729,484	3,436,345	10,299,931	18,266,275
Real estate, furniture, and fixtures	10,727,222	6,581,347	4,070,900	26,958,196	48,337,665
Current expenses	1,077,693	732,879	829,821	4,167,935	6,808,327
Premiums	632,153	690,818	1,031,892	5,709,210	8,064,073
Cheques and other cash items	2,696,132	1,170,960	797,656	8,917,945	13,582,693
Exchanges for Clearing-house	69,207,772	18,272,166	7,304,803	1,568,472	96,353,213
Bills of other National Banks	1,812,886	2,842,064	3,094,672	14,924,183	22,673,805
Fractional currency	45,399	38,416	53,508	306,628	443,951
Specie	50,274,174	13,079,936	13,210,679	31,253,195	107,817,984
Legal-tender notes	17,117,605	8,222,711	15,097,081	30,245,600	70,682,997
United States' certificates of deposit	2,560,000	4,405,000	2,410,000	585,000	9,960,000
Five per cent. redemption fund	857,994	2,200,489	1,213,349	11,319,192	15,591,024
Due from United States' Treasurer	190,320	132,222	152,178	520,968	995,688
Totals	457,217,563	355,759,618	269,865,150	1,289,814,034	2,372,656,365
LIABILITIES.					
Capital stock	50,350,000	80,298,330	51,366,500	327,684,957	509,699,787
Surplus fund	23,875,025	23,313,375	12,731,471	82,080,611	142,000,482
Undivided profits	11,282,715	6,966,434	5,481,854	37,820,956	61,551,959
National Bank notes outstanding	15,384,205	43,521,339	23,955,758	227,656,555	310,517,857
State Bank notes outstanding	39,078	21,396	...	123,883	184,357
Dividends unpaid	223,163	915,649	204,001	1,886,413	3,229,226
Individual deposits	221,672,303	152,012,932	120,938,735	554,813,731	1,049,437,701
United States' deposits	420,095	439,451	2,694,564	6,629,087	10,183,197
Deposits of United States' disbursing officers	225,400	...	1,036,712	2,718,148	3,980,260
Due to National Banks	96,578,148	37,287,071	28,133,291	24,830,167	186,828,677
Due to other banks and bankers	37,167,431	10,727,517	20,853,616	14,853,508	33,602,072
Notes and bills rediscounted	...	...	1,290,648	6,096,889	7,387,537
Bills payable	...	256,124	1,178,000	2,619,129	4,053,253
Totals	457,217,563	355,759,618	269,865,150	1,289,814,034	2,372,656,365

* The reserve cities, in addition to New York, Boston, Philadelphia, and Baltimore, are Albany, Pittsburgh, Washington, New Orleans, Louisville, Cincinnati, Cleveland, Chicago, Detroit, Milwaukee, Saint Louis, and San Francisco.

UNITED STATES.

(2.)—ABSTRACT of the Resources and Liabilities of the National Banks at the close of business on the 30th day of September, 1884, the condition of the New York City, Boston, Philadelphia, Baltimore, and other reserve city banks being tabulated separately from the other banks of the country.

	New York City.	Boston, Philadelphia, and Baltimore.	Other reserve Cities.*	Country Banks.	Aggregate.
	44 banks.	104 banks.	99 banks.	2,417 banks.	2,664 banks.
RESOURCES.	Dollars.	Dollars.	Dollars.	Dollars.	Dollars.
Loans and discounts	205,353,277	199,238,078	142,624,980	692,854,461	1,240,070,796
Overdrafts	120,238	135,977	336,806	4,630,275	5,223,296
Bonds for circulation	15,602,500	43,009,950	26,263,600	242,558,950	327,435,000
Bonds for deposits	820,000	675,000	4,413,000	10,932,000	16,840,000
United States' bonds on hand	4,064,950	180,400	2,279,900	7,054,350	13,579,600
Other stocks and bonds	13,020,739	7,156,090	5,324,615	45,862,033	71,363,477
Due from reserve agents	...	17,184,005	15,156,895	79,652,120	111,993,020
Due from other National Banks	17,352,436	14,227,847	8,681,931	26,073,331	66,335,545
Due from other banks and bankers	2,118,897	1,496,653	3,723,646	8,494,787	15,833,983
Real estate, furniture, and fixtures	9,745,176	6,475,467	4,835,973	28,844,271	49,900,887
Current expenses	731,631	763,139	862,642	4,556,097	6,913,509
Premiums	1,031,284	1,052,509	1,227,986	8,320,853	11,632,632
Cheques and other cash items	2,391,517	1,216,748	708,819	8,786,015	13,103,099
Clearing-house loan certificates	1,690,000	...	...	...	1,690,000
Exchanges for Clearing-house	44,005,521	14,605,905	6,441,564	1,204,128	66,257,118
Bills of other National Banks	2,208,406	2,903,904	3,232,968	14,913,576	23,258,854
Fractional currency	31,832	46,750	56,866	333,576	469,024
Specie	63,113,318	15,351,275	14,906,706	35,238,176	128,609,475
Legal-tender notes	22,885,808	8,668,237	15,097,774	30,396,440	77,048,259
United States' certificates of deposit	4,145,000	7,495,000	2,060,000	500,000	14,200,000
Five per cent. redemption fund	684,105	1,936,086	1,166,497	10,518,328	14,305,016
Due from United States' Treasurer	2,584,758	179,600	164,255	502,677	3,431,290
Totals	413,701,393	343,998,620	259,567,423	1,262,226,444	2,279,493,880
LIABILITIES.					
Capital stock	46,250,000	80,721,260	53,015,600	344,279,485	524,266,345
Surplus fund	22,632,580	23,741,408	13,709,459	86,962,386	147,045,833
Undivided profits	11,091,112	6,911,290	6,160,929	39,069,611	63,232,942
National Bank notes outstanding	13,203,362	37,936,931	23,236,334	215,398,496	289,775,123
State Bank notes outstanding	37,843	20,854	...	120,956	179,653
Dividends unpaid	243,254	1,362,469	223,824	1,856,613	3,686,160
Individual deposits	207,195,659	144,386,221	112,920,281	510,757,135	975,259,296
United States' deposits	428,871	474,508	3,054,781	6,378,038	10,336,198
Deposits of United States' disbursing officers	219,984	...	803,381	2,653,443	3,676,808
Due to National Banks	82,476,635	37,272,743	25,845,386	28,381,130	173,975,894
Due to other banks and bankers	29,922,093	10,915,936	18,118,770	13,465,116	72,421,915
Notes and bills rediscounted	...	...	1,173,598	9,869,965	11,043,563
Bills payable	...	255,000	1,305,080	3,034,070	4,594,150
Totals	413,701,393	343,998,620	259,567,423	1,262,226,444	2,279,493,880

* The reserve cities, in addition to New York, Boston, Philadelphia, and Baltimore, are Albany, Pittsburgh, Washington, New Orleans, Louisville, Cincinnati, Cleveland, Chicago, Detroit, Milwaukee, Saint Louis, and San Francisco.

UNITED STATES.

(3.)—COMPARATIVE Statement showing the Resources and Liabilities of the National Banks for eleven years, at nearly corresponding dates, from 1874 to 1884 inclusive.

In millions of dollars.

	October 2, 1874.	October 1, 1875.	October 2, 1876.	October 1, 1877.	October 1, 1878.	October 2, 1879.	October 1, 1880.	October 1, 1881.	October 3, 1882.	October 2, 1883.	Sept. 30, 1884.
	2,004 banks.	2,087 banks.	2,089 banks.	2,080 banks.	2,053 banks.	2,048 banks.	2,090 banks.	2,132 banks.	2,269 banks.	2,501 banks.	2,664 banks.
RESOURCES.											
Loans	954·4	984·7	931·3	891·9	834·0	878·5	1,041·0	1,173·8	1,243·2	1,309·2	1,245·3
Bonds for circulation	383·3	370·3	337·2	336·8	347·6	357·3	357·8	363·3	357·6	351·4	327·4
Other United States' bonds	28·0	28·1	47·8	45·0	94·7	71·2	43·6	56·5	37·4	30·7	30·4
Stocks, bonds, &c.	27·8	33·5	34·4	34·5	36·9	39·7	48·9	61·9	66·2	71·1	71·4
Due from banks	134·8	144·7	146·9	129·9	138·9	167·3	213·5	230·8	198·9	208·9	194·2
Real estate	38·1	42·4	43·1	45·2	46·7	47·8	48·0	47·3	46·5	48·3	49·9
Specie	21·2	8·1	21·4	22·7	30·7	42·2	109·3	114·3	102·9	107·8	128·6
Legal-tender notes	80·0	76·5	84·2	66·9	64·4	69·2	56·6	53·2	63·2	70·7	77·0
National Bank notes	18·5	18·5	15·9	15·6	16·9	16·7	18·2	17·7	20·7	22·7	23·3
Clearing-house exchanges	109·7	87·9	100·0	74·5	82·4	113·0	121·1	189·2	208·4	96·4	66·3
United States' certificates of deposit	42·8	48·8	29·2	33·4	32·7	26·8	7·7	6·7	8·7	10·0	14·2
Due from United States' Treasury	20·3	19·6	16·7	16·0	16·5	17·0	17·1	17·5	17·2	16·6	17·7
Other resources	18·3	19·1	19·1	28·7	24·9	22·1	23·0	26·2	28·9	28·9	33·8
Totals	1,877·2	1,882·2	1,827·2	1,741·1	1,767·3	1,868·8	2,105·8	2,358·4	2,399·8	2,372·7	2,279·5
LIABILITIES.											
Capital stock	493·8	504·8	499·8	479·5	466·2	454·1	457·6	463·8	483·1	509·7	524·3
Surplus fund	129·0	134·4	132·2	122·8	116·9	114·8	120·5	128·1	132·0	142·0	147·0
Undivided profits	51·5	53·0	46·4	44·5	44·9	41·3	46·1	56·4	61·2	61·6	63·2
Circulation	334·2	319·1	292·2	291·9	301·9	313·8	317·3	320·2	315·0	310·5	289·8
Due to depositors	683·8	679·4	666·2	630·4	668·4	736·9	887·9	1,083·1	1,134·9	1,063·6	993·0
Due to banks	175·8	179·7	179·8	161·6	165·1	201·2	267·9	294·9	259·9	270·4	246·4
Other liabilities	9·1	11·8	10·6	10·4	7·9	6·7	8·5	11·9	13·7	14·9	15·8
Totals	1,877·2	1,882·2	1,827·2	1,741·1	1,767·3	1,868·8	2,105·8	2,358·4	2,399·8	2,372·7	2,279·5

The security for circulating notes held by the National Banks on the 2nd October, 1883, amounted to 352,877,300 dollars of United States' bonds, being a reduction of 9,613,350 dollars during the year; 201,327,750 dollars of United States' 3 per cents. were held as a basis of circulation. The late Secretary of the Treasury, in his Report for 1883, pointed out that all these 3 per cents. were likely to be called for payment within a few years, while there is little or no profit on circulation based on the 4 per cent. and 4½ per cent. bonds at the present premium. Consequently a continued payment of the 3 per cents. tends to produce, and actually has produced, a large reduction in the bank circulation, for on the 1st October, 1884, the total of United States' bonds to secure the circulation had sunk to 327,435,000 dollars and the United States' bonds to secure deposits, &c., amounted to 30,419,600 dollars.

The following Table shows the kind and amount of bonds held on the 1st November, 1883, and the 1st November, 1884:—

Bonds.	Nov. 1, 1883.	Nov. 1, 1884.
	Dollars.	Dollars.
Four and a-half's	41,319,700	49,537,450
Fours	106,164,850	116,705,450
Three and a-half's	632,000	None
Threes	201,327,750	155,604,400
Pacific sixes	3,463,000	3,469,000
Total	352,937,300	325,316,300

The Secretary of the Treasury, in treating the question how, in face of these facts, the National Banks' notes are to be kept in circulation, mentions the suggestion of a refunding operation, consisting in the issue of a new bond at a low rate of interest for a long period, to replace the 4 per cents. and 4½ per cents. as security for circulation, which would present certain advantages to the investor, amongst others, that of not commanding a high price in the first instance. But in view of the undesirability on general principles of creating a new class of debt, the abolition of the present tax on circulation is preferred as a counter-stimulus.

The tax produces about 3,000,000 dollars a-year, but the loss of this amount would, it is calculated, be more

370 UNITED STATES.

than compensated by the stimulus given to the circulation of the National Bank notes. And it is further suggested that the tax falls somewhat unjustly on the banks in question.

The acceptance of the 3·65 per cent. bonds of the District of Columbia guaranteed by the United States, and an increase of the issue of notes to the face value of the bonds deposited, are also suggested as remedial measures, while the great service done to the Government by the National banking system in the collection of revenues, and the advantages of a bank note circulation of uniform value and safe beyond question, are pointed out. Lastly, the Secretary of the Treasury insists on the impossibility of postponing such or similar remedial measures any longer. It is evident that this important question must be brought before Congress shortly.

Bank notes outstanding.

The following Statement by the Comptroller of the Currency, issued on the 1st August, 1885, shows the amounts of National Bank notes and legal-tender notes outstanding at the dates of the passage of the Acts of the 20th June, 1874, 14th January, 1875, and the 31st May, 1878, and at date, together with the increases and decreases:—

	Dollars.
National Bank notes—	
Amount outstanding June 20, 1874	349,894,182
Amount outstanding January 14, 1875	351,861,450
Amount outstanding May 31, 1878	322,555,965
Amount outstanding at date (circulation of National gold Banks not included, 419,194 dollars)	316,911,148
Decrease during the last month	1,720,180
Decrease since August 1, 1884	20,391,324
Legal-tender notes—	
Amount outstanding June 20, 1874	382,000,000
Amount outstanding January 14, 1875	382,000,000
Amount retired under Act of January 14, 1875, to May 31, 1878	35,318,984
Amount outstanding on and since May 31, 1878	346,681,016
Amount on deposit with Treasurer, United States, to redeem notes of insolvent and liquidating banks, and banks retiring circulation under Act of June 20, 1874	39,084,373
Decrease in deposit during the last month	18,780
Decrease in deposit since August 1, 1884	474,934

State and private banks.

The following Table gives the aggregate amounts of the capital and deposits of the various State and private banks as compared with the National Banks for the seven years ending with the 30th November, 1882, when these banks ceased to be required to make Returns for taxation purposes:—

UNITED STATES.

Years.	National Banks. No.	National Banks. Capital. (Millions of dollars)	National Banks. Deposits. (Millions of dollars)	State Banks, Private Bankers, &c. No.	State Banks, Private Bankers, &c. Capital. (Millions of dollars)	State Banks, Private Bankers, &c. Deposits. (Millions of dollars)	Savings Banks with Capital. No.	Savings Banks with Capital. Capital. (Millions of dollars)	Savings Banks with Capital. Deposits. (Millions of dollars)	Savings Banks without Capital. No.	Savings Banks without Capital. Deposits. (Millions of dollars)	Total. No.	Total. Capital. (Millions of dollars)	Total. Deposits. (Millions of dollars)
1876	2,091	500·4	713·5	3,803	214·0	480·0	26	5·0	37·2	691	844·6	6,611	719·4	2,075·3
1877	2,078	481·0	768·2	3,709	218·6	470·5	26	4·9	38·2	676	843·2	6,579	704·5	2,120·1
1878	2,056	470·4	677·2	3,799	202·2	413·3	23	3·2	26·2	668	803·3	6,450	675·8	1,920·0
1879	2,048	455·3	713·4	3,639	197·0	397·0	29	4·2	36·1	644	747·1	6,360	656·5	1,893·5
1880	2,076	455·9	900·8	3,798	190·1	501·5	29	4·0	34·6	629	783·0	6,532	650·0	2,219·9
1881	2,115	460·2	1,039·9	4,016	206·5	627·5	36	4·2	37·6	629	862·3	6,796	670·9	2,667·3
1882	2,239	477·2	1,131·7	4,403	231·0	747·6	38	3·9	41·3	622	929·8	7,302	712·1	2,850·4
1882*	2,308	484·9	1,119·8	4,473	228·4	779·0	42	4·0	43·5	625	960·2	7,448	717·3	2,902·5

* In the last Table of the series the Returns are given for the six months ending May 31, 1882, and also for the six months ending November 30 of the same year.

372 UNITED STATES.

Treasury Reserve Fund.

On the 1st November, 1882, the Treasury Reserve Fund (less coin and currency certificates) amounted to 240,954,707 dollars, or 39 per cent. of the liabilities. On the 1st November, 1883, it had risen to 258,688,528 dollars, or 46·4 per cent., and on the 1st November, 1884, it had again fallen back to 247,256,089 dollars, or 42·7 per cent. The average for the six years ending with 1884 was 236,896,201 dollars, or 39·5 per cent. The lowest percentage during the period was 32·2 per cent. in January 1883, and the highest was 46·4 per cent. in November of the same year.

The gross assets of the Treasury on the 1st November, 1883, 1st November, 1884, and the 1st August, 1885, are shown in the following Table :—

Coin held by the Treasury.

	Nov. 1, 1883.	Nov. 1, 1884.	Aug. 1, 1885.
	Dollars.	Dollars.	Dollars.
Gold coin	147,037,093	166,679,599	} 249,471,030
Gold bullion	62,392,847	55,856,761	
Standard silver dollars	116,036,450	142,926,725	170,243,256 including silver bullion
Fractional silver coin	26,712,424	29,346,757	31,275,261
Silver bullion	4,936,365	4,646,497	See above
Deposits with National Bank depositaries	7,987,693	10,063,053	10,738,516
United States' notes	37,113,037	33,942,172	48,366,408
National Bank notes	6,428,180	10,171,655	2,741,670 National Bank notes 5,405,991 Ditto, in process of redemption
Total assets	408,644,089	453,633,219	518,242,132
Total net demand liabilities	247,821,544	305,562,929	
Excess of assets	160,822,545	148,070,290	

It will be noticed that the assets continue to increase rapidly, principally in the amounts of gold coin and standard silver dollars held, while the increase in the liabilities is accounted for by an increase in the gold and silver certificates.

Clearing-house transactions.

The following Table gives a summary of the Clearing-house transactions during the period under review :—

	Year ending June 30, 1883.	Year ending June 30, 1884.
	Dollars.	Dollars.
Cheques sent to the Clearing-house	129,980,110	116,666,000
Cheques received from the Clearing-house	327,302,309	295,541,948
Balances due to the Assistant Treasurer	1,662,264	1,331,880
Balances due to the Clearing-house	198,984,463	180,207,828

The kinds of money used in the settlement of these balances were as follows:—

	Year ending June 30, 1883.	Year ending June 30, 1884.
	Dollars.	Dollars.
Gold coin	41,225,000	None
Gold certificates	134,637,000	179,328 000
United States' notes	3,692,463	879,828
Transfers in silver certificates	14,741,000	None
Sundry credits	4,689,000	None

The Treasury continues to be the debtor of the Clearing-house to a very large amount, but this indebtedness decreased somewhat in 1883-84. The existing arrangement between the Treasury and the Clearing-house is undoubtedly advantageous to the former in aiding resumption and saving the useless handling of money.

In his latest Report the Treasurer of the United States points out that from the inability of the Treasury to use either silver or silver certificates in its transactions with the New York Clearing-house, where most of its disbursements are made, the available gold ran down from 155,429,600 dollars on the 1st January, 1884, to 116,479,979 dollars on the 12th August, 1884, while the silver dollars and bullion not represented by silver certificates outstanding increased from 27,266,037 dollars to 48,603,958 dollars.

As a temporary expedient, United States' notes were then used in these payments to the extent of one-half, but the amount of these notes has become so reduced that they are no longer available. Consequently the Treasurer states that the question of employing silver dollars or certificates in some fixed ratio in making these payments will shortly have to be decided upon.

On the 30th June, 1884, there were still outstanding

Gold certificates.

of gold certificates of the old issue under the Act of the 3rd March, 1863, 2,614,700 dollars. There had been redeemed in 1882-83, 1,533,580 dollars, and in 1883-84, 888,840 dollars.

Of the issue authorized by the Act of the 12th July, 1882, there were nominally outstanding on the 30th June, 1883, 78,875,100 dollars, and on the 30th June, 1884, 95,777,960 dollars, an increase of 16,902,860 dollars.

The amount held by the Treasury increased in the same period from 22,571,270 dollars to 27,246,020 dollars, thus leaving actually outstanding 68,531,940 dollars, or 12,228,110 dollars more than on the 30th June, 1883. On the 1st November, 1884, the total amount nominally outstanding was 117,758,940 dollars, of which the Treasury held 32,477,750 dollars.

Silver certificates. The amount of silver certificates outstanding on the 1st November, 1882, was 73,607,710 dollars, of which there was held by the Treasury 7,987,260 dollars; on the 1st November, 1883, the total was 99,579,141 dollars, of which 14,244,760 dollars was held by the Treasury; and on the 1st November, 1884, the total was 131,566,531 dollars, of which 30,814,970 dollars was held by the Treasury. These certificates tend to increase largely with the increase in the coinage of "standard silver dollars," which will be considered further on.

Coins and coinage. The Director of the Mint states in his Reports that the coinage executed in the years 1882-83 and 1883-84 as follows:—

Description.	1882-83. Pieces.	1882-83. Value.	1883-84. Pieces.	1883-84. Value.
		Dollars.		Dollars.
Gold	2,407,022	35,936,928	1,827,739	27,932,834
Silver	35,308,076	28,835,470	34,775,793	28,773,388
Minor	60,951,526	1,428,307	55,955,029	1,174,710
Total	98,666,624	66,200,705	92,558,561	57,880,922

It will be observed that the coinage of gold was about 8 millions less in 1883-84 than in the previous year. This was caused in part by the diminished receipt of gold bullion at the San Francisco Mint, where the deposits of gold of domestic production fell off 3,500,000 dollars, and the total deposits of gold about 3,000,000 dollars (at this Mint about six-sevenths of the gold coinage of the country is struck); and in part by a lessened coinage of gold at the Philadelphia Mint, which was principally occupied in coining silver and minor coins.

About three-fourths of the gold coinage was in double eagles, while the silver coinage consisted almost entirely of "standard silver dollars."

The deposits and purchases of gold and silver in the two years were as follows:—

	1882–83.	1883–84.
	Dollars.	Dollars.
Deposits of gold bullion	46,347,106	46,326,678
Gold bars made and re-deposited	2,798,453	4,030,090
Total gold operated on	49,145,559	50,356,768
Silver deposited and purchased	36,869,835	36,520,290
Silver bars made and redeposited	1,742,760	1,078,095
Total silver operated on	38,612,595	37,598,385

In addition to the coinage, the Mint and Assay officers made and issued 18,269,205 dollars in gold bars and 8,050,602 dollars in silver bars in 1882-83, and in 1883-84, 23,875,586 dollars in gold bars and 7,639,724 dollars in silvers bars.

The following Table gives the production of gold and silver in the United States and throughout the world for the last ten years as estimated by the United States' Mint:—

Production of precious metals in United States of America.

Years.	Production of Gold.		Production of Silver.	
	United States.	World.	United States.	World.
	Dollars.	Dollars.	Dollars.	Dollars.
1874	33,500,000	113,500,000	37,300,000	82,000,000
1875	33,500,000	113,500,000	31,700,000	82,000,000
1876	39,930,000	114,000,000	38,780,000	98,000,000
1877	46,900,000	114,000,000	39,800,000	81,000,000
1878	51,200,000	119,000,000	45,281,000	94,900,000
1879	38,900,000	108,700,000	40,800,000	96,170,000
1880	36,000,000	106,400,000	39,200,000	96,700,000
1881	34,700,000	103,000,000	43,000,000	102,150,000
1882	32,500,000	98,700,000	46,800,000	110,000,000
1883	30,000,000	94,000,000	46,200,000	114,200,000
Total	377,130,000	1,084,800,000	408,861,000	957,120,000

[621]

UNITED STATES.

The production for the calendar year 1884 is estimated at approximately the same total figure as in 1883, showing, however, a slight increase in the production of silver and a decrease in that of gold.

Imports and exports of precious metals.

The imports and exports of precious metals during the two years were as follows:—

	1882–83.			1883–84.		
	Gold.	Silver.	Total.	Gold.	Silver.	Total.
IMPORTS.	Dollars.	Dollars.	Dollars.	Dollars.	Dollars.	Dollars.
Bullion	3,334,708	2,475,968	5,810,676	4,997,571	2,910,451	7,908,022
Coin—						
American	8,112,265	670,192	8,782,457	3,824,962	686,182	4,511,144
Foreign	6,287,176	7,609,082	13,896,258	14,008,784	10,998,312	25,007,096
Totals	17,734,149	10,755,242	28,489,391	22,830,317	14,594,945	37,426,262
EXPORTS.						
Bullion—						
American	4,118,455	12,551,378	16,669,833	23,052,183	14,241,050	37,293,233
Foreign	...	319,900	319,900	2,400	494,240	496,640
Coin—						
American	4,802,454	150,894	4,953,348	12,242,051	690,381	12,932,438
Foreign	2,679,979	7,197,273	9,877,252	5,785,383	10,625,755	16,511,108
Total	11,600,888	20,219,445	31,820,333	41,081,987	26,051,426	67,233,413

Consumption of precious metals.

From statistics furnished to the Director of the Mint from private sources, it appears that in 1884, when more complete Returns were obtainable than previously, 14,500,000 dollars of gold and 5,500,000 dollars of silver coin and bullion of all descriptions were employed for manufacturing purposes, out of which 6,000,000 dollars is estimated to have been gold bullion of American origin and 4,500,000 dollars American silver.

Coin circulation in the United States.

The total coin circulation of the United States was estimated on the 1st July, 1883, at 765,000,000 dollars, of which 537,000,000 dollars was gold and 228,000,000 dollars silver coin. This estimate takes into consideration imports and exports of coin, and also the melting down by manufacturers during the year of 2,500,000 dollars of gold coin and 75,000 dollars silver coin.

On the 1st July, 1884, the total coinage had risen to 802,000,000 dollars, of which 552,000,000 dollars was gold and 250,000,000 dollars silver: 4,875,000 dollars gold coin was used in the arts, and 6,000,000 dollars trade dollars were not in circulation, neither of which are consequently included in the above totals.

The following Table shows in detail the changes in the coinage and circulation for the years 1883 and 1884:—

UNITED STATES.

	Gold.	Silver.	Total.
	Dollars.	Dollars.	Dollars.
Circulation, June 30, 1882	500,882,185	199,573,360	700,455,545
Year's coinage, less deposits for re-coinage	35,562,798	28,198,541	63,761,339
Excess of imports over exports	3,309,811	519,298	3,829,109
Total	539,754,794	228,291,199	768,045,993
Less amount used in the arts	2,500,000	75,000	2,575,000
Circulation, July 1, 1883	537,254,794	228,216,199	765,470,993
Year's coinage	27,932,824	28,773,388	56,706,212
Total	565,187,618	256,989,587	822,177,205
Less net exports	8,417,059	4,199	8,421,258
Deposits for recoinage	263,117	152,031	415,148
Used in the arts	4,875,000	216,000	5,091,000
Trade dollars withdrawn from circulation	..	6,000,000	6,000,000
Total loss	13,555,176	6,372,230	19,927,406
Circulation on July 1, 1884	551,632,442	250,617,357	802,249,799
Net gain during the year	14,377,648	22,401,158	36,778,806

The circulation is estimated to have been held on the 1st July, 1884, as follows:—

Held by—	Gold.	Silver.			Total United States' gold and silver Coins.
		Legal tender.	Subsidiary.	Total.	
	Dollars.	Dollars.	Dollars.	Dollars.	Dollars.
Treasury	89,190,346*	39,133,905†	29,600,720	68,734,625	157,924,971
National Banks	97,682,848*	8,978,833	3,000,000‡	11,978,833	109,661,681
Other banks	30,000,000‡	} 127,243,091	42,660,808	169,903,899	534,663,147
Private banks	334,759,248				
Totals	551,632,442	175,355,829	75,261,528	250,617,357	802,249,799

* Less outstanding certificates.
† Includes Treasury and Clearing-house certificates.   ‡ Estimated.

Besides the coinage actually in circulation, the Mints and Assay Offices held on the 1st October, 1883, 61,683,816 dollars gold bullion and 5,107,911 dollars silver bullion ready for coinage, and on the 1st October, 1884, they held 53,000,000 dollars of gold bullion and 5,000,000 dollars of silver bullion.

It may be mentioned in passing that the San Francisco Mint have undertaken and carried out during 1883-84 the coinage of silver coins to the nominal value of 1,000,000 dollars for the Government of Hawaii,

[621]

UNITED STATES.

these coins having the weight and fineness of standard United States' coins.

Values of foreign coins.

The following changes were made in the official values of foreign coins:—

The continuous decline in the value of silver necessitated corresponding reductions in the values of silver coins. By Circular of the 1st January, 1883, the Austrian florin was reduced from 40·6 to 40·1 cents; the Bolivian boliviano, the Ecuador peso, the Peru sol, and the United States of Colombia peso all from 82·3 to 81·2 cents; the India rupee from 39 to 38·6 cents; the Japan yen from 88·7 to 87·6 cents; the Mexico dollar from 89·4 to 88·2 cents; the Russia rouble from 65·8 to 65 cents, and the Tripoli mahbub from 74·3 to 73·3 cents.

No changes were made in the values of gold coins, but the gold peso of the Argentine Republic having been established as the monetary unit of that country by law of the 5th November, 1881, its value was estimated at 96·5 cents.

By Circular of the 1st January, 1884, the values of foreign silver coins were again reduced as follows;— the Austrian florin from 40·1 to 39·8 cents; the Bolivia boliviano, the Ecuador peso, the Peru sol, and the United States of Colombia peso from 81·2 to 80·6 cents; the India rupee from 38·6 to 38·3 cents; the Japan yen from 87·6 to 86·9 cents; the Mexico dollar from 88·2 to 87·5 cents; the Russia rouble from 65 to 64·5 cents, and the Tripoli mahbub from 73·3 to 72·7 cents.

Proportion of notes to coin.

With a view of showing the proportion of notes to coin in the United States, both in the Treasury and in the hands of the general public, in 1883-84, I add the following Table:—

Description.	November 1, 1883.		
	In Treasury.	In private hands.	Total.
	Dollars.	Dollars.	Dollars.
Gold coin and bullion	273,179,117	308,791,137	581,970,254
Silver coin	157,933,165	84,768,767	242,701,932
Legal-tender notes	} 175,570,682	523,124,121	{ 346,681,016
National Bank notes			352,013,787
Total	606,682,964	916,684,025	1,523,366,989

UNITED STATES.

Description.	November 1, 1884.		
	In Treasury.	In private hands.	Total.
	Dollars.	Dollars.	Dollars.
Gold coin and bullion	277,784,954	307,826,918	585,611,872
Silver coin	185,012,536	90,722,903	275,735,439
Legal-tender notes	} 187,504,997	492,735,832	{ 346,681,016
National Bank notes			333,559,813
Total	650,302,487	891,285,653	1,541,588,140

The proportion of currency to coin varied, therefore, in the following ratios :—

At the Treasury the currency was on the former date in the ratio of 40·7 per cent. to the coin and bullion, while on the latter date it had declined to 34 per cent.

The currency in private hands was on the former date in the ratio of 132·1 per cent. to the coin and bullion, while on the latter date the proportion had sunk to 123·1 per cent.

And the proportion of currency to coin and bullion in the whole country, which was on the former date in the ratio of 84 per cent., had sunk on the latter date to 79 per cent.

Before discussing the question of the standard silver dollar, the minor coinage calls for passing notice. It is estimated that there are some 75,000,000 dollars of fractional silver in the country, nearly 30,000,000 dollars of which were held by the Treasury. These latter were practically unavailable as an asset, a large portion being in a badly abraded condition through long use. It was estimated that it would require about 4,000,000 ounces of silver to increase their bullion value so as to bring them up to the same weight proportionately as the silver dollar. The Secretary of the Treasury, writing at different times, recommends measures for the improvement of these minor coins, both in regard to their appearance, convenience, and individual distinctiveness, in all which respects they are defective, those of smaller value resembling too closely the more valuable coins. He further states that at present there is a marked diversity in weight among coins of the same nominal value, but they are also characterized by too great

Subsidiary coins.

variety and "exceeding inelegance of design and lack of artistic merit."

There being no further reason for making fractional silver coins subsidiary to the dollar, and the price of silver being exceptionally low, the Secretary recommends the immediate recoinage of these minor coins, and states that this could be done by the Mints in five years without increase of official staff or interference with the regular coinage of the country. The Director of the Mint in particular recommends the discontinuance of the coinage of the gold dollar as too small for practical use, and also of the 3-cent copper-nickel piece as inconvenient and not in demand.

Standard silver dollar.

This burning question now agitating the United States seems to require separate treatment, and can only be dealt with imperfectly here. The following are the latest statistics published on the subject:—

TABLE showing the Amount of Standard Silver Dollars coined, on hand, distributed, and outstanding at the close of each year since the Coinage was resumed.

Fiscal year ended June 30—	Annual Coinage.	Total Coinage to date.	On hand at close of year.	Net Distribution during year.	Outstanding at close of year.
	Dollars.	Dollars.	Dollars.	Dollars.	Dollars.
1878	8,573,500*	8,573,500	7,718,357	855,143	855,143
1879	27,227,500	35,801,000	28,358,589	6,587,268	7,442,411
1880	27,933,750	63,734,750	45,108,296	11,184,043	18,626,454
1881	27,637,955	91,372,705	63,249,300	9,496,951	28,123,405
1882	27,772,075	119,144,780	87,524,182	3,497,193	31,620,598
1883	28,111,119	147,255,899	112,362,510	3,272,791	34,893,389
1884	28,099,930	175,355,829	135,810,368	4,652,072	39,545,461

* Coinage began in March.

The amount outstanding on the 31st October, 1884, in the Treasuries of the United States had risen to 143,404,093 dollars, of which 32,607,492 dollars was at the United States' Mint at San Francisco, and 26,208,000 dollars at the New York Sub-Treasury.

The amount in actual circulation on that date was 41,326,736 dollars, making a total coinage, up to the 1st November, 1884, of 184,730,829 standard silver dollars.

The increase in circulation for the year was only 1,260,346 dollars.

The following figures published in the New York press from official sources bring these statistics up to the latest date:—

STATEMENT showing the exact Condition of the Silver Coinage and the Amounts of Silver Dollars and Silver Certificates in the Treasury on the 1st September, 1885.

	Dollars.
Silver certificates, representing silver dollars	138,792,186
Less amount in Treasurer's hands	42,712,890
Certificates outstanding	96,079,296
Silver dollars in the Treasury	170,620,411
Less certificates outstanding	96,079,296
Silver dollars owned by Government	74,541,115
Entire coinage in circulation from February 28, 1878, to June 30, 1885	203,884,381
Coined in July and August 1885	4,347,000
Total coinage	208,231,381
Silver dollars and bullion in United States' Treasury	170,620,411
Amount in circulation	37,610,970

Under the provisions of the Bland Act of 1878, which enacted that 24,000,000 silver dollars of 412·5 grains weight should be coined annually, the total amount of these coins has increased to the above-mentioned portentous extent. Between 1873 and 1878 no such coinage had taken place, although silver dollars were always legal tender. But now the stock on hand overflows the vaults of the Treasuries of the United States in every direction, and new vaults have to be built to receive it, one having been just completed at Washington with a capacity of 50,000,000 dollars, and another under construction at New Orleans to hold 28,000,000 dollars. And the present vaults at New Orleans being wholly insufficient to contain the increasing mass, it was found necessary to transfer several millions of these dollars to Washington, two vessels of the United States' navy being employed for the purpose.

The Treasury has, in fact, found it impossible to force these dollars into circulation.

Owing to the continual and increasing depreciation of silver, the market value of these dollars has fallen to

83 cents, and even, recently, to below 80 cents, and it is mainly their use in the payment of customs duties which prevents them from falling even lower. The decrease in the amount in circulation on the 1st September, 1885, is noticeable. The Secretary of the Treasury, writing in 1884, states that, if this coinage is allowed to continue, silver will practically become the standard of value; gold will cease to be a circulating medium, and severe contraction must follow. To avert the detriment to general business, and danger to the national credit now threatening, if Government is compelled to use silver or silver certificates to pay gold obligations, he recommended the repeal of the Bland Act and the suspension of silver coinage. Admitting that the immediate effect might be to depreciate further the market value of silver, he calculated that the necessities of the commercial world, of those Oriental and of some Western nations who use silver as coinage exclusively, and of others who do so partially, must eventually take up the available supplies of silver; and he pointed out, in connection with this point, that the annual production of silver seemed to have reached its maximum, and that of gold was diminishing. As a secondary measure of relief he suggested the withdrawal from circulation by the action of Congress of the 1-dollar and 2-dollar notes, leaving the silver dollars to take their place. The amount of 1-dollar notes in circulation is 26,763,097 dollars, and that of 2-dollar notes 26,778,738 dollars, and such a withdrawal would afford sensible relief to the country, though of course the Treasury would gain nothing. He considered that the inconvenience caused by the change would be only temporary, and even suggested the eventual withdrawal of the 5-dollar notes, to be replaced by gold coins.

No action has, however, been taken by Congress, owing to the strong influence in that body of what is called the "Silver Ring," or group of large owners of silver mines, to whose interest it of course is that the Government should continue a large purchaser of silver.

Meanwhile, a very strong agitation has been growing in the country for the repeal of the Bland Act, which has now (September 1885) assumed formidable proportions. The press is full of the question, meetings of leading bankers and capitalists to discuss the subject are being held throughout the country, and it is publicly stated that the present Secretary of the Treasury has expressed his sympathy with these views, and will support the repeal of the Bland Act.

A compromise has been proposed by Mr. Warner, a Member of Congress, in the shape of a Bill providing for the issue of silver certificates down to 1 dollar, the lowest limit at present being 10 dollars. These are to replace the 1-dollar and 2-dollar notes, which the Treasury has recently ceased to issue, but are not to be legal tender between private parties. Further, that certificates shall be issued on silver bullion according to its market value, payable in silver bullion or greenbacks, at the option of the Government, the Treasury to fix the market rates at which these certificates shall be redeemable.

In support of this project it has been urged that as these silver certificates would be issuable from time to time at the actual market value of silver, there would be no danger of accumulation of the metal in the Treasury. and that such certificates would have many recommendations as a paper currency.

The power of the silver interest in Congress will, it is considered, prevent the passing of a Bill totally repealing the Bland Act. But the Warner compromise is unacceptable to the leading bankers and capitalists of the country, who consider it would perpetuate the evils of the Bland Act under another name. These views were strongly expressed at the recent Bankers' Convention at Chicago.

Although public opinion is divided on the withdrawal of 1-dollar and 2-dollar notes, the general view seems to be in favour of the plan, as affording an outlet for the surplus silver.

The question of the silver certificates, representing, as they do, "standard silver dollars," already alluded to, forms part of the general subject. In a recent article the New York "Tribune" shows how, by a reduction in the issue of these certificates, the present Secretary of the Treasury has succeeded in greatly increasing the proportion of gold received in payment of duties.

It gives the following figures:—In the last week of August 1885, only 9·6 per cent. of the duties in New

York was paid in silver certificates, while 54 per cent. was paid in gold certificates.

During August the proportion paid in silver was only 13·9 per cent., against 34 per cent. in July, 37·8 per cent. in June, 37·8 per cent. in May, and 41·3 per cent. in April. And whereas in the two years from the 2nd March, 1883, to the 1st March, 1885, the additional issue of silver certificates was 43,400,000 dollars, there has been a reduction in their issue since the new Administration came into power of no less than 16,000,000 dollars.

Trade dollar. This dollar, coined under the Act of 1873, and having a higher value than the silver standard dollar, was originally intended for exportation, and principally for the use of Asiatic peoples. Its value is, however, only 86 cents at present prices, and the Secretary of the Treasury has strongly recommended its withdrawal from circulation. He denies that it can be recognized as legal tender. The whole issue of the coin has been only 35,960,446 dollars. It is estimated that from 1,000,000 to 2,000,000 dollars thereof disappeared in manufactures, and five-sevenths of the whole went abroad. Much of this is supposed to have been melted down in China, and some in India. Chinese bankers, by stamping the coin with their own marks, are also supposed to have defaced a considerable portion. From 6,000,000 to 8,000,000 dollars are estimated to remain in the United States. The Secretary of the Treasury recommends their purchase at a slight advance on their market bullion value, and recoinage as standard dollars. To meet the obvious objection that this would again swell the total of standard silver dollars, he replies that such purchases should be counted in as part of the regular bullion purchases for silver coinage. However, if the Bland Act is repealed, this latter suggestion will evidently fall to the ground. The whole question urgently calls for the action of Congress.

In conclusion, it remains to acknowledge the debt due to the official Reports for 1883 and 1884 of the Secretary of the Treasury, the Commissioners of the Inland Revenue, of Customs, and of the Currency, the Director of the Mint, the Treasurer of the United States, and the Commissioner of Pensions, in which these subjects are very fully treated, and from which the facts and figures contained in this Report are mainly compiled. Use has been made in a minor degree of other trustworthy sources of information.

H. A. HELYAR.

Washington, September 1885.

Receipts and Expenditures of the Government from 1855 to 1885.

RECAPITULATION OF NET REVENUE BY FISCAL YEARS.

Year.	Customs.	Internal Revenue.	Direct Tax.	Sales of Public Lands.	Premiums on Loans and Sales of Gold Coin.	Other Miscellaneous Items.	Net Revenue.	Surplus Revenue.
	Dol. c.	Dol. c.	Dol. c.	Dol. c.	Dol. c.	Dol. c.	Dol. c.	Dol. c.
1856	64,022,863 50	...	...	8,917,644 93	...	1,116,190 81	74,056,699 24	4,485,673 45
1857	63,875,905 05	...	...	3,829,486 64	...	1,259,920 88	68,965,312 57	1,169,604 91
1858	41,789,620 96	...	...	3,513,715 87	...	1,352,029 13	46,655,365 96	27,529,904 43*
1859	49,565,824 38	...	...	1,756,687 30	...	1,454,596 24	53,486,465 64	15,584,511 10*
1860	53,187,511 87	...	...	1,778,557 71	709,357 72	1,088,530 25	56,064,607 83	7,065,990 56*
1861	39,582,125 64	...	...	870,658 54	10,008 00	1,023,515 31	41,509,930 39	25,036,714 50*
1862	49,056,397 62	...	1,795,331 73	152,203 77	33,630 90	915,122 31	51,987,455 43	422,774,363 48*
1863	69,059,642 40	37,640,787 95	1,485,103 61	167,617 17	68,400 00	3,741,794 38	112,697,290 95	602,043,434 22*
1864	102,316,152 99	109,741,134 10	475,648 96	588,333 29	602,345 44	30,331,401 25	264,626,771 60	600,695,870 27*
1865	84,928,260 60	209,464,215 25	1,200,573 03	996,553 31	21,174,101 91	25,441,556 00	333,714,605 08	963,840,619 37*
1866	179,046,651 58	309,226,813 42	1,974,754 12	665,031 03	11,683,446 89	29,036,314 23	558,032,620 06	37,223,203 07
1867	176,417,810 88	266,027,537 43	4,200,233 70	1,163,575 76	38,083,055 68	15,037,522 15	490,634,010 27	133,091,335 11
1868	164,464,599 56	191,087,589 41	1,788,145 85	1,348,715 41	27,787,330 35	17,745,403 59	405,638,083 32	28,297,798 46
1869	180,048,426 63	158,356,460 86	765,685 61	4,020,344 34	29,203,629 50	13,997,338 65	370,943,747 21	48,078,469 41
1870	194,538,374 44	184,899,756 49	229,102 88	3,350,481 76	13,755,491 12	12,942,118 30	411,255,477 63	101,601,916 88
1871	206,270,408 05	143,098,153 63	580,355 37	2,388,646 68	15,295,643 76	22,093,541 21	383,323,944 89	91,146,756 64
1872	216,370,286 77	130,642,177 72	...	2,575,714 19	8,892,839 95	15,106,051 23	374,106,867 56	96,588,904 89
1873	188,089,522 70	113,729,314 14	315,254 51	2,882,312 38	9,412,637 65	17,161,270 05	333,738,204 67	43,392,959 34
1874	163,103,833 69	102,409,784 90	...	1,852,428 93	11,560,530 89	17,075,042 73	289,478,755 47	2,344,882 30
1875	157,167,722 35	110,007,493 58	...	1,413,640 17	5,037,665 22	15,431,915 31	288,000,051 10	13,376,658 26
1876	148,071,984 61	116,700,732 03	93,798 80	1,129,466 95	3,979,279 00	17,456,776 19	287,482,039 16	29,022,241 83
1877	130,956,493 07	118,630,407 83	...	976,252 68	4,029,280 58	18,031,655 46	259,000,586 62	30,340,577 69
1878	130,170,680 20	110,581,624 74	...	1,079,743 37	405,776 58	15,614,728 09	257,763,878 70	20,799,551 90
1879	137,250,047 70	113,561,610 58	...	924,781 06	317,102 30	20,585,697 49	273,827,184 46	6,879,300 93
1880	186,522,064 60	124,009,373 92	33 85	1,016,506 69	1,505,047 63	21,978,525 01	333,526,610 98	65,883,653 20
1881	198,159,676 02	135,264,385 51	1,516 89	2,201,863 17	110 00	25,154,850 98	360,782,292 57	100,069,404 98
1882	220,410,730 25	146,497,595 45	160,141 69	4,753,140 37	...	31,703,642 52	403,525,250 28	145,543,810 71
1883	214,706,496 93	144,720,368 98	108,156 60	7,955,864 42	...	30,796,695 02	398,287,581 95	132,879,444 41
1884	195,067,489 76	121,586,072 51	70,720 75	9,810,705 01	...	21,984,881 89	348,519,869 92	104,393,625 59
1885	181,471,939 34	112,498,725 54	...	5,705,986 44	...	24,014,055 06	323,690,706 38	63,463,771 27

* Expenditures in excess of revenue.

UNITED STATES.

RECAPITULATION OF NET ORDINARY EXPENDITURES BY FISCAL YEARS.

Year	Civil and Miscellaneous — Premium on Loans and Purchase of Bonds, &c.	Civil and Miscellaneous — Other Civil and Miscellaneous Items.	War Department.	Navy Department.	Indians.	Pensions.	Interest on Public Debt.	Net Ordinary Expenditures.
	Dol. c.	Dol. c.	Dol. c.	Dol. c.	Dol. c.	Dol. c.	Dol. c.	Dol. c.
1856	...	32,124,214 07	16,948,196 89	14,091,781 03	2,769,429 55	1,298,208 95	1,953,822 37	69,571,025 79
1857	...	28,164,532 97	19,261,774 16	12,747,976 83	4,267,543 07	1,312,043 01	1,678,265 23	67,795,707 66
1858	...	26,429,609 57	25,485,383 60	13,984,551 09	4,926,738 91	1,217,488 47	1,567,055 67	74,185,270 39
1859	385,372 90	23,700,295 14	23,243,822 38	14,642,989 73	3,625,027 24	1,220,378 29	2,638,463 96	69,070,976 74
1860	363,572 39	27,976,434 22	16,409,767 10	11,514,964 96	2,949,191 34	1,102,926 19	3,177,314 62	63,130,598 39
1861	574,443 08	23,267,010 46	22,981,150 44	12,420,887 89	2,841,358 28	1,036,064 06	4,000,173 76	66,546,644 89
1862	...	21,408,491 16	394,368,407 36	42,668,277 09	2,273,223 45	853,095 40	13,190,324 45	474,761,818 91
1863	...	23,256,965 39	599,298,600 83	63,221,963 64	3,154,357 11	1,078,991 59	24,729,846 61	714,740,725 17
1864	...	27,505,599 46	690,791,842 97	85,725,994 67	2,629,858 77	4,983,924 41	53,685,421 69	865,322,641 97
1865	1,717,900 11	43,047,658 01	1,031,323,360 79	122,612,945 29	5,116,837 08	16,338,811 13	77,397,712 00	1,297,555,224 41
1866	58,476 51	41,056,961 54	284,449,701 82	43,324,118 52	3,247,064 56	15,605,352 35	133,067,741 69	520,809,416 99
1867	10,813,349 38	51,110,223 72	95,224,415 63	31,034,011 04	4,642,531 77	20,936,551 71	143,781,591 91	357,542,675 16
1868	7,001,151 04	53,009,867 67	123,246,648 62	25,775,502 72	4,100,682 32	23,782,386 78	140,424,045 71	377,340,284 86
1869	1,674,680 05	56,474,061 53	78,501,990 61	20,000,757 97	7,042,923 06	28,476,621 78	130,694,242 80	322,865,277 80
1870	15,996,555 60	53,237,461 56	57,655,675 40	21,780,229 87	3,407,938 15	28,340,202 17	129,235,498 00	309,653,560 75
1871	9,016,794 74	60,481,916 23	35,799,991 82	19,431,027 21	7,426,997 44	34,443,894 88	125,576,565 93	292,177,188 25
1872	6,958,266 76	60,984,757 42	35,372,157 20	21,249,809 99	7,061,728 82	28,533,402 76	117,357,839 72	277,517,962 67
1873	5,105,919 99	73,328,110 06	46,323,138 31	23,526,256 79	7,951,704 88	29,359,426 86	104,750,688 44	290,345,245 33
1874	1,395,073 55	69,641,593 02	42,313,927 22	30,932,587 42	6,692,462 09	29,038,414 66	107,119,815 21	287,133,873 17
1875	...	71,070,702 98	41,120,645 98	21,497,626 27	8,384,656 82	29,456,216 22	103,093,544 57	274,623,392 84
1876	...	66,958,373 78	38,070,888 64	18,963,309 82	5,966,558 17	28,257,395 69	100,243,271 23	258,459,797 33
1877	...	56,252,066 60	37,082,735 90	14,959,935 36	5,277,007 22	27,963,752 27	79,124,511 58	238,660,008 93
1878	...	53,177,703 57	32,154,147 85	17,365,301 37	4,629,280 28	27,137,019 08	102,500,874 65	236,964,326 80
1879	...	65,741,555 49	40,425,660 73	15,125,126 84	5,206,109 08	35,121,482 39	105,327,949 00	266,947,883 53
1880	2,795,320 42	54,713,529 71	38,116,916 22	13,536,984 74	5,945,457 09	56,777,174 44	95,757,575 11	267,642,957 78
1881	1,061,248 78	64,416,324 71	40,466,460 55	15,686,671 66	6,514,161 09	50,059,279 62	82,508,741 18	260,712,887 59
1882	...	57,219,750 98	43,570,494 19	15,032,046 26	9,736,747 40	61,345,193 95	71,077,206 79	257,981,439 57
1883	...	68,678,022 21	48,911,382 93	15,283,437 17	7,362,590 34	66,012,573 64	59,160,131 25	265,408,137 54
1884	...	70,920,433 70	39,429,603 36	17,292,601 44	6,475,999 29	55,429,228 06	54,578,378 48	244,126,244 33
1885	...	87,494,258 38	42,670,578 47	16,021,079 67	6,552,494 63	56,102,267 49	51,386,256 47	260,226,935 11

NOTE.—The expenditures for interest on the Public Debt include amounts paid for interest on bonds issued to the Pacific Railroads as follows:—

	Dol. c.		Dol. c.		Dol. c.		Dol. c.		Dol. c.		Dol.[1] c.
1866 ...	49,227 04	1869 ...	1,794,857 65	1872 ...	3,877,387 02	1875 ...	3,883,950 72	1878 ...	3,878,441 24	1884 ...	3,873,480 72
1867 ...	54,786 47	1870 ...	4,484,360 25	1873 ...	3,874,710 72	1876 ...	3,881,250 72	1879 ...	3,878,970 72	1885 ...	3,876,090 72
1868 ...	485,028 35	1871 ...	3,874,145 58	1874 ...	3,862,350 72	1877 ...	3,890,258 53	1880 ...	3,874,830 72		
								1881 ...	3,878,250 72		
								1882 ...	3,875,430 72		
								1883 ...	3,877,887 27		

Treasury Department, Warrant Division, September 1, 1885.

UNITED STATES.

CHICAGO.

Report by Vice-Consul Dunn on the Trade and Commerce of Chicago for the Year 1883.

The principal business carried on in this city is dealing in grain flour, and cattle, and the shipment of meats, cured and prepared in various ways to European, West Indian, and South American ports and for domestic use. Chicago is the great market for all the products of the west and north-west.

The following tabular statement of the cereal crops raised in the State of Illinois, and the quantities dealt in in this city during last year may be of interest:—

	Bushels raised in Illinois.	Estimated value of Crop.	Bushels received in Chicago from all points.	Bushels shipped from Chicago on Direct Bills lading to European Ports.	Average price in Chicago for 1883.
		Dol.			Dol.
Wheat	20,347,592	19,337,063	31,225,302	2,124,441	1·04 No. 2 spring
Corn	186,583,558	80,000,000	74,412,319	2,893,870	0·59 ,,
Oats	104,299,230	27,403,706	36,502,283	..	0·33 ,
Rye	4,695,448	2,244,646	5,892,361	65,739	0·58 ,,
Barley	674,338	398,901	9,099,800	..	0·65 ,,

Nine-tenths of the grain received here was reshipped, mainly to Eastern ports, and there distributed. The direct exports of grain to European ports was not large.

In addition to grain, the following are some of the principal exports from this city to European ports on direct bills of lading:—

Articles.		Quantity.
Flour	Barrels	636,583
Corn meal	,,	66,029
Clover and other seeds	Tons	4,676
Pork	Barrels	24,879
Lard	Tierces	319,922
Butter	Tons	1,107
Oatmeal	Barrels	110,672
Oilcake	Tons	15,790
Oil	Barrels	15,913
Bacon and hams	Boxes	321,650 of about 200 lbs. each.
Canned meats	Cases	247,136
Cheese	Tons	5,548
Miscellaneous goods	,,	13,620

CHICAGO. 1893

The oil mentioned above is the product of cotton seed or linseed. This statement shows an increase of about one-fourth over the exports of last year.

The number of cattle and hogs received in Chicago for packing or shipment were as follows :—

	Received.	Shipped.	Packed.
	Head.	Head.	Head.
Cattle	1,878,944	966,758	697,033
Hogs	5,697,163	1,363,759	4,222,780

The number and tonnage of vessels which cleared from this district in 1883 were as follows :—

	Number.	Tonnage.
Vessels in the coasting trade	11,731	3,885,101
Foreign vessels to foreign ports	100	38,295
American vessels to foreign ports	184	57,477
Total	12,015	3,980,873

The 100 vessels classed as foreign vessels were Canadian steamers and sailing craft under the English flag, and all of which cleared for Canadian ports.

The following statement shows the articles imported into this district.

1894   UNITED STATES.

STATEMENT showing the value of Imported Merchandise entered for Consumption, and Duties collected thereon at Chicago during the year 1883.

Commodities.	Value.	Duty.
	Dol.	Dol. c.
Ale, beer, and porter	24,570	7,998 03
Artists' materials	42,140	10,487 15
Barley	62,706	11,606 35
Books and printed matter	58,728	14,633 15
Brushes	25,384	8,969 60
Cheese and cheese colouring	2,759	945 12
Chemicals	55,123	29,927 49
China, glass, and earthenware	381,527	176,979 50
Caustic soda	178,543	83,356 51
Cigars and tobacco manufactures	266,736	262,447 33
Clocks and clock materials	25,070	7,326 80
Cutlery	12,681	5,542 35
Diamonds	137,145	13,714 50
Dressed furs	41,712	8,664 50
Dried fruits and nuts	123,802	37,408 55
Druggists' sundries	61,978	16,632 68
Dry goods	4,796,564	2,361,434 93
Fish	45,651	8,092 34
Gelatine	6,033	1,894 60
Grease	753	144 80
Guns	48,058	16,080 80
Hops	10,902	1,051 44
Ink	1,094	349 70
Iron, pig	24,397	10,357 62
Iron, manufactures of	103,328	41,905 09
Iron, wire rope	28,126	15,791 96
Jewellers' goods	34,038	5,799 90
Leaf tobacco	306,742	171,779 29
Leather, manufactures of	150,242	70,743 35
Lead	119	45 77
Looking glass plates	2,518	676 34
Maple sugar	48,856	9,098 67
Metals, manufactures of	52,698	21,646 45
Millinery goods	9,886	3,749 45
Musical instruments	246,254	66,407 23
Needles	37,613	9,446 36
Paintings	14,498	2,846 48
Paper hangings	13,567	3,772 20
Paper, manufactures of	9,752	2,987 90
Pickles and sauces	6,782	2,364 25
Plate glass, window	13,105	5,323 40
Prepared vegetables	13,281	3,906 90
Rice	18,250	3,650 40
Rubber, manufactures of	7,296	1,695 96
Salt and saltpetre	142,637	59,158 55
Seeds, bulbs, and plants	25,715	4,906 40
Smokers' articles	34,497	24,341 27
Spices	116	84 00
Steel bars	11,915	3,034 92
,, blooms	46,920	26,446 33
Stone and marble	12,267	3,436 70
Tin plates	650,244	180,795 29
Toys and fancy goods	109,809	47,836 54
Varnish	5,471	2,202 00
Wines and liquors	214,443	143,978 95
Wood, manufactures of	28,121	9,742 70
Miscellaneous goods	84,419	29,524 01
Goods exempt from duty	1,536,117	.. ..
Total	10,453,701	4,075,166 85

There are no records of export beyond the figures already given on the previous two pages. It must be borne in mind that the great bulk of the exports from this district are sent to New York, Philadelphia, Boston, and Baltimore, and there exported, and tend to swell the figures of exports at those points.

This city now stands the third in the Union in manufacturing industries. The principal of these are as follows, the values of their products being set against each item:—

	Dollars.
Meat packing and canning	85,324,371
Clothing	18,948,000
Iron and steel manufactures	23,114,713
Furniture and lumber products	16,111,937
Printing and publishing	6,016,295
Agricultural implements	9,778,230
Boots and shoes and leather products	9,184,321
Oils	4,048,893
Liquors, distilled and malt	7,887,278

According to the census of 1880, 90,000 people and upwards were actually employed in these industries, and this number has no doubt since been largely increased.

The direct trade with Canada, principally in manufactured articles, is constantly increasing.

The receipts and shipments of wool and hides for 1883 were as follows:—

	Received.	Shipped.
	Tons.	Tons.
Wool	20,162	22,180
Hides	35,503	49,265

This State produced last year (used almost entirely for home consumption) 10,508,791 tons of bituminous coal, the mining of which gave employment to nearly 25,000 men and boys. The average value of the coal at the mouth of the mine was 1 dol. 46 c. The average rate of wages paid to miners is 90 c. per ton. The wages actually paid last year in Macoupin county, the largest coal-producing county, was 63 c. per ton in summer and 75 c. in winter. Attempts have been and are now being made to produce a marketable coke from Illinois coal. Up to the present the product is too soft for manufacturing purposes, as it crushes too easily under heavy weights.

This State has about 18 large rolling mills and steel works, with a capacity of about 870,000 tons of rails, bars, and other iron products. Three of these mills are located in this city or its immediate neighbourhood.

The total acreage of this State is 34,384,494, of which 26,307,867 may be classed as improved lands and 8,076,627 as unimproved lands.

The following statement shows the area of land in cultivation in 1883:—

	Acres.
Corn	7,132,762
Meadows	2,945,432
Winter wheat	2,876,432
Spring „	44,091
Oats	2,722,432
Rye	270,961
Barley	26,849
Buckwheat	3,491
Flax	29,338
Broom corn	33,922
Sorghum	14,023
Tobacco	3,092
Beans	1,091
Orchards	316,466
Irish potatoes	116,604
Sweet „	2,696
Turnips and roots	4,361
Pastures	4,663,217

During the last few months there have been in this State cases of cattle disease, which it was at first feared was the contagious foot and mouth disease. Careful investigation by the State veterinarian and other competent authorities shows that the disease is a species of foot-rot (technically known as Panaritium), due to atmospheric or telluric influences, aggravated by local causes, such as exposure to wet and filth, to frost, and poor food. The disease is of a sporadic and entirely non-contagious nature, and is found only to affect animals in poor condition, and under two years old. I am advised that no further traces of the disease have shown themselves beyond those that appeared in the first cases. Some cases of apparent pleuro-pneumonia in Pike county on examination proved to arise from digestive causes, owing to frosted and damaged corn having been fed to the cattle.

Nothing is heard in this State of disease among hogs. The State Board of Agriculture report swine in general good condition after the winter, which was both severe and long.

The population of the State of Illinois in 1880 (date of last census) was 3,077,871, and of Chicago 503,185. The population of Chicago December 31, 1883, was estimated at over 600,000. The births in this city in 1883 were about 14,000, and the deaths 11,555.

The State of Illinois has no debt. The county, township, and city debt on July 1, 1882 (the latest available return), was 51,727,283 dol., of which 17,863,500 was due from this city.

The valuation of property in the State (for purposes of taxation) for 1883 was:—

	Dollars.
On real estate	587,390,292
„ personal property	169,209,626
„ railroad	61,304,803
Total	817,904,721

The valuation of property in Chicago (for taxation) was as follows:—

	Dollars.
On real estate	101,796,795
„ personal property	28,490,486
Total	130,287,281

This is probably about one-third of the actual value.

The rate of taxation in Chicago was 3·41 per cent. on the above valuation.

The rate of interest on money is lower now than ever before known. It is difficult to get 7 per cent. on loans, unless made in small sums, and many loans have been effected on desirable property during the last year at 6 per cent., and in one or two exceptional cases at 5 per cent.

The freight rates between Chicago and Liverpool have varied considerably. They were 46 c. per 100 lbs. for grain in February, and 25 c. in May and June; 72½ c. per 100 lbs. on provisions in February; and 39 to 42 c. in May and June. At present the rates are even lower, grain being now carried to the seaboard at 12½ c. per 100 lbs.

Chicago, March 31, 1884.

PHILADELPHIA.

Report by Consul Clipperton on the Trade, Commerce, and Navigation of the Port of Philadelphia, and the Industries and Products of the Consular District of Philadelphia for the Year 1883 *and part of the Year* 1884.

Consular District.—Composed of the States of Pennsylvania, Ohio. Illinois, Indiana, Michigan, Iowa, Wisconsin, and Minnesota.

Population therein	17,894,967
Of which foreign	3,033,385
Area in square miles	422,215
Assessed wealth, real estate, and personal property	£1,869,117,819
Number of traders in business	301,287
Capital invested	£221,976,760
Manufactures:—	
Number of establishments	104,629
Capital	£220,312,218
Products	£4,012,214,000
Imports at Philadelphia	£6,562,010
Exports at Philadelphia	£7,732,493

INTRODUCTION.

General business has been fairly prosperous during the year 1883 within this Consular district; capital has earned a remunerative though reduced interest; manufacturers have suffered from no source except that of over-production; no epidemics have scourged the land; agriculture has experienced no distress; the minerals have made large returns; shipping and internal transportation have enlarged their trade and the facilities for conducting it, and on the whole the year's results may be considered in a favourable light. Yet the year has been marked by a larger number of failures than in any year since 1878. In Philadelphia alone the number of business failures in 1883 was 174, with liabilities amounting to 3,589,349 dol., while in 1878 the number was 257, with liabilities amounting to 10,373,700 dol.; throughout the Union the failures figured 9,184, and the liabilities 173,000,000 dol. Reckless speculation and over-production are assigned as the reasons for the increased number of failures. It is fortunate, perhaps, for the legitimate channels of trade that stock speculators have not the control of the financial condition of the whole country, and that the recent crashes (May, 1884) in railways, bank, and other securities in Wall Street, New York, have not spread over the business industries of the nation. These sudden and almost unprecedented collapses of banking houses and stock manipulators were started by ambitious and young financiers, who, scorning the slow but safer course of their predecessors, rush on to carve their way in the world by buying and selling stock securities which belong to others. In their strenuous efforts to amass wealth they produce nothing tangible in trade, but by the circulation of false reports, gigantic strides in speculation and eventual utter desperation pull down the structures that have cost millions to build up. These men buy and sell stocks, cotton, wheat, coffee, oil on a few dollars' margin, and take their chances against other speculators upon the changing quotations of the markets. They never see a share of stock, nor a bale of cotton, a bushel of grain, or a pound of coffee. The end of it all is, as in every system of habitual gambling, poverty and despair. This numerous class is, as a general rule, possessed of ability to make a respectable livelihood in any honest vocation in life, provided they could submit to the patience, thought, and labour of any productive industry, and rid themselves of the foolish notion that they can make vast fortunes out of nothing. The temptation to be looked upon as a brilliant operator in grain, petroleum, wool, or pork is too great for this class of fortune-hunters in all the large American cities. Relieved of these feelings, such men will have taken the first step towards quitting the road to ruin and turning towards the quieter but safer, and, in the end, more prosperous path of honest labour.

Shipping Interests have maintained their ground fairly at the port of Philadelphia. The exports were 38,662,467 dol., and imports 32,810,045 dol., and the number of entrances from foreign countries were 1,103, with a tonnage of 806,294, while the clearances were 920, with a tonnage of 732,628, which is slightly under the results of the year previous. The aggregate foreign trade of the United States for the year 1883 showed a balance of trade in favour of this country of 102,000,000 dol. of exports over imports. At the Port of New York the imports exceeded the exports by 184,000,000 dols., or, in figures, New York imported 472,809,885 dol. out of a total of 720,762,227 dol. of foreign goods, and exported from that port but 368,832,431 dol. of domestic products. While New York imports more than four-sevenths per cent. of all the foreign merchandize brought into the country, it exported considerably less than half the domestic products shipped to foreign countries, showing that the efforts of other cities on the Atlantic seaboard have succeeded in acquiring the control of a decided majority of the export trade of domestic products to foreign countries. American shipping continues to decline. It appears to be impossible to build steamers and ships in this country in competition with the English shipbuilder, and the costs of equipment and running under the American system are much greater. Hence the gradual subsidence of the American flag on the oceans. It costs the American 15 to 30 per cent. more than any other nationality to keep his vessel afloat, causing him to withdraw his capital and place it in other channels. The "American Line" from this port is the only line crossing the Atlantic flying the "Stars and Stripes," and as a paying line it has signally failed. The four American boats are virtually superseded by five superior British steamers chartered by the line, which render it possible for the Company to continue afloat. It is no longer profitable to place either American steam or sailing vessels in the North American trade, which is now practically conducted by British shipowners. The American shipping is confined to the coasting traffic (where there can be no foreign competition under the law), and some part of the West Indian and South American ports, and in the case of wooden sailing ships built in the State of Maine to the long voyages of three and six months' duration around Cape Horn or the Cape of Good Hope, to the East Indies or Pacific coasts.

The Freight Market has undergone much depression. The increased ship-building of the past two or three years so greatly enlarged the mercantile fleets of the world that freights were subjected to unusual competition. The products of the world to be carried have not kept pace with the ship-building. Not long ago ships were getting 18 dol. and 20 dol. a ton to carry wheat from San Francisco to Liverpool, while at the beginning of the year (1884) there was a fleet at San Francisco awaiting cargoes, and unable to get better rates than 6 dol. or 7 dol. per ton. An American ship recently left New York for Calcutta with oil at 20 c. to 21 c. per five-gallon case; a freight that would scarcely pay the expenses of the outward voyage. The shipping business should yield to those who embark their capital in it five or six per cent. over all expenses, depreciation, and insurance. To do this the earnings must be enough to cover the high premiums on marine risks, generally at or over 10 per cent. per annum, and probably as much more to cover depreciation and repairs. No American ship, it is claimed, can at present do this.

In the year 1862 at the beginning of the exportation of the petroleum trade, freights ranged on sailing vessels from 8s. to 9s. per barrel for the continent of Europe. There is, however, a better outlook for the autumn trade, which will commence as soon as the year's cereals move to the seaboard, and a large addition to the ocean tonnage is looked for at Philadelphia. The American Steam Ship Company, of which Messrs. Peter Wright and Sons are the agents, will shortly double their tonnage, the steamships "Lord Clive," "British King," "British Crown," "British Queen," and the American Steamer "Ohio," returning to the line, swelling their list of steamers to ten. The Allan Line from this port to Glasgow is meeting with success, running a steamer every fortnight with full cargoes, including shipments of live cattle for Liverpool at fair freights. The cargoes westward have been small but fairly remunerative, while those eastward have been full, composed of grain, flour, molasses, tobacco, and general produce. Another line hence to Belfast, the first steamer, the "Lord O'Neill," being now outward bound to this port. A rapidly increasing commerce with Ireland is looked forward to.

Financial.—Early in the year 1884 gold was once more quoted at a premium and the first gold shipment to England of the year was made. The premium was but one-eighth of one per cent. and the shipment only 40,000*l.*, but it is believed to be the forerunner of higher premium and larger shipments if the Federal Government continue the coinage of silver, which has become a drug in the channels of finance. One coinage, known as the "Trade Dollar," no longer passes in the channels of trade or is received at the banks, and is quoted at a discount of from 10 to 15 per cent. Statements of the condition of the banks have a special interest under these circumstances. The condition of all the National Banks, December 31st, 1883, shows the coin reserves to have been 102,002,000 dol. of gold, and 8,470,000 dol. of silver, or 110,472,000 dol. in all. From May 6th, 1881, to May 6th, 1882, when the flow of gold abroad put a definite check to the unusual prosperity of the previous years, the specie holdings of the banks ran down from 128,000,000 dol. on the date first named to 109,000,000 dol. on the date last named. The specie held by the banks was, therefore, decidedly above that at present held; but the loans two years ago were only 1,114,000,000 dol. against 307,500,000 dol. now; and the deposits 1,114,700,000 dol., their highest point up to that time, against 1,120,300,000 dol. at present, the highest ever reached. In two years, therefore, while the deposits of the banks have remained stationary and their specie fallen nearly a tenth, their loans have increased nearly a sixth. The State Banks and Trust Companies returns show that their loans have advanced without any corresponding advance in their specie, although their deposits have increased faster than their loans. The loans of these banks were 352,700,000 dol. in 1881, and 462,000,000 dol. in 1883, while their deposits rose from 293,700,000 dol. in 1881 to 500,300,000 dol. in 1883. It is also noticeable that the savings banks, which from 1873 to 1879 carried a heavy share of currency and specie in their assets, held in 1883 only 129,980,000 dol. cash against 170,072,680 dol. in 1880, while deposits had increased from 819,107,000 dol. to 1,024,856,000 dol. The total resources rose, it is true, from 881,677,000 dol. to 1,118,790,000 dol. and the savings banks were probably never stronger than they are to-day. It is evident that while the banking has expanded during the past two years, in which the shrinkage of values has been great and trade profits small, the reserve of specie and of lawful money has not expanded in like proportion.

The National Debt in March, 1884, was 1,872,138,019 dol., or 374,423,604*l.*, bearing interest from 3 to 4½ per cent. The United States have issued and have now outstanding bonds to the Pacific Railway Companies, the interest upon which at 6 per cent. the Government pays to the amount of 64,623,512 dol. The interest upon these bonds paid by the United States amounts to 61,160,798 dol. 82 c., of which there has been repaid by the companies 17,966,821 dol. 12 c. in transportation service, and in cash payments (5 per cent. net earnings) 655,198 dol. 87 c. The accrued interest not yet paid amounts to 969,352 dol. 68 c. The receipts and expenditures of the United States for the fiscal years ending June 30th, 1883 and 1884 were as follows:—

Receipts.	1883.	1884.
	Dollars.	Dollars.
From Customs	214,706,496	195,627,291
„ internal revenue..	144,720,368	122,004,498
„ miscellaneous	38,560,716	30,534,944
Total ..	398,287,581	348,166,734

Expenditure.	1883.	1884.
	Dollars.	Dollars.
Ordinary..	140,235,432	134,915,689
Pensions..	66,012,573	56,003,995
Interest..	59,160,132	54,578,893
Total ..	265,408,137	245,498,577

Amount of outstanding debt June 30th, 1884, was about 1,226,000,000 dol., upon which the annual interest charge was about 47,000,000 dol.

Manufactures of the city of Philadelphia—the largest manufacturing city in the Union—are given in detail in this report, compiled by Lorin Blodget, Esq., for the authorities of the city, and form one of the most interesting and valuable returns of the report. The figures were compiled in 1882-83, but they can be accepted for the official statements for 1883-84. It is not likely that a similar exhaustive return will be made until the national census of 1890. These returns show that the productive force aggregates 242,106 persons, and the value produced 486,751,670 dol. exclusive of the mint product, of which 3,309,395 dol. in value is purely manufacture, making the total 490,061,065 dol. The total coinage of the mint was 48,309,395 dol., and the total including the mint amounts to 538,410,460 dol. for the calendar year 1882.

Trade and Commerce.—The article under this heading gives a brief outline of the depression experienced in all branches of the country's industries, and a detailed account of the movements of grain at Philadelphia and the Western States of this Consular district. The growth of the trade in the Western Cereals has been enormous, and the receipts for six months at eight of the western cities now average 112,000,000 bushels. The trade is traced in all its details at both inland cities and on the seaboard.

Immigration fell off from 730,349 in 1882 to 570,316 in 1883, a decrease of 160,033. The figures and nationalities are given in detail.

Iron and Steel are treated in an exhaustive manner with official tabulated statements. The history of the trade is traced down to its present condition of prostration, short time, low wages, and ruinous prices.

Railroads are referred to for the whole country, showing extent, cost, indebtedness, and earnings. 65 different railroads, whose figures are used, show their capital stock 648,427,220 dol., or 22,115 dol. per mile, and their funded and floating debts 700,861,599 dol., and the aggregate cost of construction of 1,251,729,029 dol., or 42,693 dol. per mile. Their total gross earnings for 1883 were 214,146,915 dol.

The Coal fields of Pennsylvania, both anthracite and bituminous, are reported upon in detail, as well as the products by States of the whole United States, together with the output cost of production, prices at market points, number of miners employed, and the wages paid.

Labour and Wages.—The depressed condition of the labour market in the United States is worthy of the attention of all persons contemplating emigration to this country at the present time. No families should think of leaving England for America unless they have engaged places before embarking and have sufficient means to tide them over the first few weeks or months after landing. The over-stocked labour-markets and the fall in wages, especially in all branches of manufactures, high rents, dear provisions, and change of climate are sufficient, in most instances, to render miserable all immigrants not robust and of the most sanguine temperaments.

Petroleum and Natural Gas.—These articles are prepared with great care and give accurate statistics of the trade in this wonderful product of nature. "Natural gas" is the last development and extension of the petroleum deposits, and a perusal of the article will show what an important factor it is about to become to the manufacturing interests of Pennsylvania and the lighting of cities and country towns.

Agriculture.—That portion of the report referring to agriculture in detail, the crops for 1882–83, area under cultivation, farm labour, wages, prices of products, &c., together with the favourable reports of the enormous crops now coming forward of the first part of the year 1884.

Tobacco.—The growth, manufacture, and consumption of tobacco are attracting universal attention in this country. The tendency to the use of narcotics is increasing and the habit is not confined to tobacco in the form of cigars and chewing, but cigarette smoking by young people, set forth in this article.

Live Stock and Cattle Diseases are reported upon, with details of live stock at the various shipping points, with remarks as to stock raising and the diseases with which cattle in great herds are afflicted.

Population.—It is accepted, at least as an interesting fact, adverted to in the remarks under this heading, that the female portion of the population of the United States is decreasing in numbers, and that were it not for the influx of male immigration, the subject would become a matter worthy of grave enquiry.

Special attention is called to the report of Vice-Consul Treherne,[*] for the State of Minnesota, and the territory of Dakota. The growth, productions, and trade of these north-western districts of the Union, especially of the railways centres of St. Paul and Minneapolis, are unsurpassed by any section of the United States during the entire history of the Republic. Mr. Treherne's report is the first Consular paper prepared for publication on this north-western section, and, notwithstanding its length, it is so exhaustive and accurate as to claim the attention of the public. Mr. Vice-Consul Dunn's report of the trade and commerce at Chicago is worthy of public attention.

TRADE in British Ships at the Port of Philadelphia.

Year.	Number of Ships.	Tonnage.
Entrances for the year 1858	79	14,044
,, ,, ,, 1870	308	112,557
,, ,, ,, 1879	635	658,029
,, ,, ,, 1880	485	541,018
,, ,, ,, 1881	440	647,153
,, ,, ,, 1882	369	345,096
,, ,, ,, 1883	375	387,554

STATEMENT showing Number, Nationality, and Tonnage of Vessels Arriving at and Departing from the Port of Philadelphia during the Years 1882 and 1883.

ENTRANCES.

Nationality.	1882. Number.	1882. Tonnage.	1882. Crews.	1883. Number.	1883. Tonnage.	1883. Crews.
American	456	283,374	..	412	212,594	..
Austrian	33	18,981	..	27	16,031	..
British	369	345,096	7,738	375	387,554	9,294
Belgian	8	21,039	..	11	24,482	..
German	19	13,663	..	25	20,167	..
Italian	153	82,857	..	139	76,713	..
Norwegian	104	66,367	..	80	48,271	..
Russian	17	11,460	..	10	7,092	..
Swedish	9	5,337	..	9	6,052	..
Switzerland	2	1,536	..	..	..	..
Portuguese	4	967	..	2	888	..
Danish	10	6,359	..	6	4,065	..
Dutch	4	3,269	..	3	4,276	..
Spanish	1	316	..	..	..	..
Haytien	1	315	..	1	145	..
French	..	..	..	2	1,697	..
Finnish	..	..	..	1	368	..

[*] See page 2007.

CLEARANCES.

Nationality.	1882. Number.	1882. Tonnage.	1883. Number.	1883. Tonnage.
American	337	242,883	326	198,188
Austrian	20	16,614	29	17,876
British	311	352,380	304	328,295
Belgian	11	23,581	9	23,876
German	20	15,483	26	20,629
Italian	147	78,122	139	76,477
Norwegian	104	60,292	74	43,592
Russian	16	9,972	14	9,953
Portuguese	4	967	1	239
French	1	1,755	..	..
Spanish	3	1,069	1	87
Swedish	10	5,892	8	5,483
Danish	8	5,717	6	4,064
Dutch	4	3,269	2	2,876
Hawaiian	..	..	1	993

NUMBER and Tonnage of Vessels under the American Flag which Entered and Cleared at the Port of Philadelphia during the following named Years through the Custom-house.

ENTERED.

Years.	From Foreign Countries. Number.	From Foreign Countries. Tonnage.	From other American Ports. Number.	From other American Ports. Tonnage.
1863	388	115,887	4,049	591,770
1871	450	200,928	1,937	521,126
1873	674	397,940	1,366	592,880
1877	469	238,887	1,232	590,714
1879	574	301,041	1,068	555,855
1881	405	259,692	826	531,222
1882	456	283,374	882	543,370
1883	412	212,594	724	418,625

CLEARED.

Years.	For Foreign Countries. Number.	For Foreign Countries. Tonnage.	For other American Ports. Number.	For other American Ports. Tonnage.
1863	305	109,936	1,458	861,613
1871	378	158,979	1,555	636,855
1873	425	202,740	1,561	745,235
1877	447	255,884	1,326	731,609
1879	389	240,797	1,385	747,866
1881	250	203,461	1,254	770,331
1882	337	242,883	1,264	783,541
1883	326	198,188	1,213	576,719

PHILADELPHIA.

Trade in British steamships has been as follows:—

ENTRANCES.

Year.	Number.	Tonnage.	Crews.
1877	32	82,038	621
1878	66	147,461	2,772
1879	162	311,358	5,005
1880	159	468,714	7,794
1881	92	204,032	4,042
1882	109	194,460	5,322
1883	174	261,538	6,848

CLEARANCES.

Year.	Number.	Tonnage.	Crews.
1877	32	82,033	621
1878	63	140,259	2,644
1879	159	306,853	4,885
1880	160	471,570	7,843
1881	88	198,373	3,953
1882	107	190,827	5,219
1883	176	265,111	6,941

Iron shipbuilding in the United States in 1883:—

The following table, compiled from the reports of the United States Treasury, gives the number and tonnage of iron vessels built in the United States in each fiscal year since 1868, when their construction in this country was commenced. The fiscal year ends on the 30th of June.

Fiscal Years.	Sailing. Number.	Sailing. Tonnage.	Steam. Number.	Steam. Tonnage.	Total. Number.	Total. Tonnage.
1868	..	..	..	2,801	..	2,801
1869	..	1,039	..	3,545	..	4,584
1870	..	679	..	7,602	..	8,281
1871	..	2,067	20	13,412	..	15,479
1872	..	..	20	12,766	20	12,766
1873	..	..	26	26,548	26	26,548
1874	..	..	23	33,097	23	33,097
1875	..	..	20	21,632	20	21,632
1876	..	..	25	21,346	25	21,346
1877	..	..	7	5,927	7	5,927
1878	..	..	32	26,960	32	26,960
1879	..	..	24	22,008	24	22,008
1880	1	44	30	25,538	31	25,582
1881	1	36	41	28,320	42	28,356
1882	..	..	43	40,097	43	40,097
1883	1	2,033	34	37,613	35	39,646

From the 30th of June, 1883, to the 31st of December of the same year, there were built seventeen iron vessels, having a tonnage of 17,855 tons. As far as can now be ascertained these vessels were built within the jurisdiction of the following ports.

Ports.	Sailing. Number.	Sailing. Tonnage.	Steam. Number.	Steam. Tonnage.	Total. Number.	Total. Tonnage.
New York	..	..	1	1,064	1	1,064
Philadelphia, Pa..	1	1,997	12	12,258	13	14,255
Wilmington, Del..	..	..	3	2,536	3	2,536
Total	1	1,997	16	15,858	17	17,855

John Roach and Son, of Chester, Pennsylvania, are now engaged in the construction of three cruisers for the United States Navy, which are to be built wholly of steel-hulls, ribs, decks, &c., and the same firm launched from its shipyard at Chester on the 13th of April last the despatch boat "Dolphin," also for the Navy, and also constructed wholly of steel. These are not, however, the first vessels that have been built in the United States with steel instead of iron hulls, but the Government statisticians have counted them all as if built of iron. The hulls of the vessels for the Navy above-mentioned are made of open-hearth steel.

PHILADELPHIA.

Seamen's Wages at Port of Philadelphia 1883 and 1884.

	American Flag, United Kingdom and Continent, North Bayonne.		British and Foreign Flag.									
			United Kingdom and Continent, North Bayonne.		Run.		Continent South Bayonne to Gibraltar.		All Flags, Mediterranean.		West Indies.		South America.		Around Capes Horn or Good Hope.
	Wages.	Advance.	Wages.	Advance.	Wages.	Advance.	Wages.	Advance.	Wages.	Advance.	Wages.	Advance.	Wages.	Advance.	Wages.	Advance.
1883.																
Spring	25	30	30	40	30	40	25	30	20	30	20	25	20	30	18	50
Summer	25	30	30	40	30	40	25	30	20	30	25	30	20	30	18	50
Autumn	25	30	30	40	30	40	25	30	20	30	25	30	20	30	18	50
Winter	25	30	30	40	30	40	25	30	20	30	20	25	20	30	18	50
1884.																
Spring	Same as 1883.															
Summer	Ditto.															
Autumn	Ditto, but no advance.															

Mates .. .. 35 dol. to 45 dol. per month.
Second Mates .. .. .. 25 " 35 " "
Cook and Steward .. .. 30 " 45 " "
Ordinary Seamen .. .. 5 dol. per month less than A.B.

American Shipmasters on Coast and Foreign, 60 dol. to 120 dol.; average 75 dol. or 80 dol.
Coasters on half share of gross freight, pay all wages and provisions, and half all other expenses and Port charges. Owner keeps vessel in repair.

Trade and Commerce.

The year's results in trade did not carry out the expectations entertained at the beginning, and 1883 was a year of steady depression in all branches without any great revulsions. Over-production was the prime cause, nearly all manufactured goods having been largely in excess of demand, engendering a competition which brought down the profits to a minimum, and in many lines of goods to a figure below the costs of manufacture. This condition of things led to mercantile failures, and caused an expansion of credit not healthy to business circles. The community have, however, succeeded in stemming the adverse tide, and, on the whole, the country escaped anything like a commercial crisis.

Grain.—The grain trade of Philadelphia shows an increase during the year. The receipts at this port of all kinds of grain in 1882 were 14,912,854 bushels; while in 1883 they were 17,240,760 bushels; an increase of 2,327,816 bushels. This increase, however, still left the trade much below the year 1881, which showed the receipts of 24,369,967 bushels.

The following tables show the receipts at the port of Philadelphia of the various cereals :—

Year.	Grain.	Corn.	Rye.	Barley.	Oats.
1878	11,394,300	22,832,900	242,200	831,400	3,051,600
1879	20,074,100	18,297,000	687,775	952,000	3,499,800
1880	15,123,330	24,950,750	117,000	1,049,600	3,638,760
1881	8,312,605	11,145,367	107,537	1,211,900	3,432,089
1882	6,732,872	3,801,100	50,512	894,500	3,082,482
1883	5,038,135	7,657,490	10,500	1,053,500	3,417,100

Flour.—The receipts of flour at Philadelphia during the past year show quite a handsome increase over 1882, reaching 1,348,959 barrels. The trade has been moderately active, and the prices have ruled low most of the year, owing, in a great measure, to the low price of wheat. They opened with "Pennsylvania family" selling at 4 dol. 50 c. to 4 dol. 75 c., closing at 4 dol. 75 c. to 5 dol. per barrel. "Patent flours" from the north-west continue to be well received. These flours are made from spring wheat by what is called the "patent process." The flour mills in and about Philadelphia have had a fair business during the past year.

RECEIPTS of Flour at this Port for the past nine years.

Year.	Barrels.
1875	922,190
1876	970,781
1877	740,330
1878	979,380
1879	936,880
1880	933,944
1881	1,009,976
1882	1,268,332
1883	1,348,959

PHILADELPHIA.

Receipts of Live Stock at Philadelphia.—The arrivals and sales of beef cattle at Philadelphia were larger during the past year than they have been for many years past, reaching 214,650 head. This increase was mainly caused by the increased demand for shipment, and the natural increase of the population. Prices have ruled steady. The arrivals and sales of sheep show an increase during the past year, reaching 680,417 head. Good sheep have been in fair demand, and prices have ruled steady most of the year. The arrivals and sales of hogs at the different yards during the past year were larger than they have been for several years past, reaching 383,212 head. The better grades have been in demand, and the prices have ruled steady. The arrivals and sales of cows at the different yards were larger than they have been for several years past, reaching 21,400 head.

The following is a statement of the live stock received and sold at Philadelphia markets during 1883, also a comparison with previous years:—

Year.	Beeves.	Cows.	Hogs.	Sheep.
1850	68,780	15,120	46,900	82,500
1860	90,845	10,637	127,964	324,564
1870	117,903	8,835	189,500	682,900
1872	234,810	11,150	199,610	795,200
1880	201,210	17,396	346,960	623,494
1881	205,912	19,609	367,876	645,792
1882	209,728	20,392	381,402	677,713
1883	214,650	21,400	383,312	680,417

The Grain movement in the early part of 1884 requires a passing notice. Contrary to what seems to be the universal opinion, the aggregate movement has not been light notwithstanding the short crops last year.

It is true that the receipts at the north-western markets have been unusually light since the navigation opened, and in June were the smallest since 1873, with the exception of 1875, 1877, 1878, and 1882, even 1874 and 1876 showing larger June receipts; and we have an increase over railroad mileage 60 per cent., meanwhile, from 74,000 miles at the end of 1875 to 120,000 miles at the end of 1883, so that the same aggregate movement means a great deal less per mile of road engaged in carrying it. But taking the six months ending with June, the north-western grain receipts this year have been exceeded but three times, and then not very much, by 7½ per cent. last year, by 3 per cent. in 1881, and by 12 per cent. in 1880, when they were largest.

The shipments have been larger in proportion than the receipts, and have been exceeded but once in the history of the trade, in 1880, when they were 6⅔ per cent. more than this year. But the shipments were 4 per cent. larger this year than last, though there was much less wheat and corn produced.

While there appears to be no slackness in movement to or from the great north-western markets, there is a marked decrease in the receipts of the Atlantic ports, which, for the six months were not only 24,000,000 bushels (28 per cent.) less than last year, 47,000,000 bushels less than 1881, and 61,000,000 bushels less than 1880, but were 14,000,000 bushels less than in the year 1876 and 8,750,000 bushels less than in 1874. For the past six months, the receipts and shipments at the eight reporting north-western markets (St. Louis, Peoria, Chicago, Milwaukee, Duluth, Detroit, Toledo, and Cleveland) and the receipts of the seven Atlantic ports for 11 years have been, in bushels, flour not included:—

Year.	North-Western Receipts.	North-Western Shipments.	Atlantic Receipts.
	Bushels.	Bushels.	Bushels.
1874	85,287,705	62,451,630	71,870,593
1875	59,718,108	44,671,475	56,376,763
1876	80,718,108	70,535,200	77,491,653
1877	58,119,118	47,764,659	56,053,575
1878	97,407,756	80,270,321	107,929,955
1879	99,466,816	84,970,888	115,927,223
1880	116,279,392	104,218,067	124,068,455
1881	107,737,000	93,576,657	110,208,873
1882	82,366,849	68,586,324	51,129,115
1883	111,730,461	93,489,792	87,131,848
1884	103,918,343	97,748,718	63,135,094

The large shipments from the west have found a market to an unusual extent west of the seaboard. Besides what goes from the reporting markets there are very large shipments made from places that do not report both to the seaboard and to interior points. In 1874 the total Atlantic receipts exceeded the shipments of the north-western reporting markets by 9,000,000 bushels (15 per cent.), in 1878 by 27,000,000 bushels, and in 1881 by 16,500,000 bushels. But since 1881 the tide has turned, exports have fallen off greatly, and the Atlantic receipts have been less than the shipments from the reporting north-western markets—in 1882, 17,500,000 bushels less, last year 6,333,334 bushels less, and this year the immense amount of 34,500,000 bushels (35 per cent.) less. It is remarkable that there should have been such an unusual absorption of grain by the country between the west and the seaboard. Since 1881 the north-western shipments of grain have increased 4,200,000 bushels, while the Atlantic receipts have decreased 47,000,000 bushels. Yet the grain has found a market, apparently, as well this year as ever, and at low prices for wheat only. The shipments were larger than the receipts of the north-western markets this year, which has seldom occurred in June, when the receipts are often the largest of the year. The shipments, however, exceeded the receipts still more in 1880.

The receipts at each of the north-western markets during the half year for the last five years have been, in bushels:—

	1880.	1881.	1882.	1883.	1884.
	Bushels.	Bushels.	Bushels.	Bushels.	Bushels.
Chicago	54,515,803	46,792,530	36,350,594	54,056,039	51,401,482
Milwaukee	7,527,492	8,038,808	7,775,550	9,578,700	8,105,573
Toledo	14,327,457	11,696,850	6,219,896	9,135,278	6,946,353
Detroit	3,875,749	3,661,996	3,154,026	4,947,284	3,749,938
Cleveland	2,238,801	2,288,736	1,490,429	2,051,224	1,622,849
St. Louis	21,797,383	21,336,216	15,780,249	20,493,985	18,976,423
Peoria	10,885,165	13,111,830	11,024,130	10,391,540	12,111,653
Duluth	1,021,542	165,034	571,975	1,076,411	1,004,682
Total	116,279,392	107,137,000	82,366,849	111,730,461	103,918,343

The totals show inconsiderable fluctuations, except in 1882, after the very poor crops of 1881; but there has been some change in the position of the several markets. Since 1880 there has been a decrease of 12,361,000 bushels, in the total receipts, for instance, but it is made up of:—

A loss of	3,114,000 bushels, or	6	per cent. at	Chicago.
,,	7,381,000 ,,	51½	,,	Toledo.
,,	2,821,000 ,,	13	,,	St. Louis.
,,	706,000 ,,	30½	,,	Cleveland.
,,	126,000 ,,	3¼	,,	Detroit.
,,	17,000 ,,	1⅔	,,	Duluth.
Total loss	14,165,000			
A gain of	1,226,000 ,,	11¼	,,	Peoria.
,,	578,000 ,,	7⅔	,,	Milwaukee.

What is most noticeable here is the immense falling off at Toledo and the gain at Peoria. But the changes from 1881 are still more striking. There has been a decrease of only 3,219,000 bushels (3 per cent.) in the total since that year, while at Chicago there has been an increase of 4,600,000 bushels, and a decrease everywhere else except Duluth.

The percentages of the total receipt at each of these places in the several years have been:—

	1880.	1881.	1882.	1883.	1884.
Chicago	46·9	43·7	44·1	48·4	49·5
Milwaukee	6·5	7·5	9·4	8·6	7·8
Toledo	12·3	10·9	9·4	8·2	6·7
Detroit	3·3	3·4	3·8	4·4	3·6
Cleveland	2·0	2·1	1·8	1·8	1·6
St. Louis	18·7	20·0	19·2	18·3	18·2
Peoria	9·4	12·2	13·4	9·3	11·7
Duluth	0·9	0·2	0·7	1·0	0·9
Total	100·0	100·0	100·0	100·0	100·0

Thus the Chicago share has been growing larger every year since 1881; Toledo's is the smallest this year; St. Louis also has its smallest percentage this year, but not much less than in other years, and Peoria has little more than its average percentage.

These cities may be placed in three groups, Chicago, Milwaukee, and Duluth the "north-western" group; Peoria and St. Louis the "interior" group; and Detroit, Toledo, and Cleveland the "Lake Erie" group, and find the percentage of each group to have been:—

	1880.	1881.	1882.	1883.	1884.
North-western	54·3	51·4	54·2	58·0	58·2
Interior	28·1	32·2	32·6	27·6	29·9
Lake Erie	17·6	16·4	13·2	14·4	11·9

The ports west of Lake Michigan gain, as should be expected, as it is a new country tributary to them which has been growing rapidly of late years. A large corn crop might change the percentages, however; it would increase the receipts of St. Louis, Peoria, and Toledo largely, and probably those of Chicago more than all. High rail rates tend to increase the receipts of the lake ports and especially of Chicago and

Milwaukee, and their gains this year have been large notwithstanding very low rail rates.

The receipts at the Atlantic ports have been so small this year that there is not the same interest in their distribution as at times when the exports are large. The domestic trade of the several cities is not much affected by their competition with each other. New Orleans, for instance, in almost any condition of competition, will receive the amount of grain required for itself and the places near by, which it supplies. And this does not vary much from year to year; but the relative rates by river, by lake, and by rail may greatly affect the amount which it receives for export. In 1881, for instance, in the first half of the year it received three times as much as in 1882. Thus the places which export least are likely to have their business affected least by a short crop and light total business. This is so in the case of Boston, which received but 1,600,000 bushels less this year than last, while the decrease at New York was 8,000,000 bushels, at Philadelphia 4,100,000 bushels, at Baltimore 3,500,000 bushels, and at New Orleans 5,000,000 bushels. The total decrease is so great that at almost every important exporting point the falling off is enormous, and must be felt very seriously in trade and for shipping. Compared with 1880, for instance, the decrease was:—

At New York,	25,000,000	bushels, or	47	per cent.
Philadelphia,	16,800,000	,,	75	,,
Baltimore,	9,800,000	,,	47	,,
New Orleans,	5,600,000	,,	19	,,
Boston,	2,000,000	,,	19	,,
Montreal,	1,700,000	,,	40	,,

At Portland the receipts were substantially unchanged, and the aggregate decrease was 60,000,000·9 bushels, which is 49 per cent.

The quantity received at each Atlantic Port during the First Half of the Year for Nine Consecutive Years has been in Bushels.

	1876.	1877.	1878.	1879.	1880.	1881.	1882.	1883.	1884.
	Bushels.	Bushels.	Bushels.	Bushels.	Bushels.	Bushels.	Bushels.	Bushels.	Bushels.
New York	30,500,000	19,900,000	49,100,000	47,500,000	53,800,000	49,200,000	28,700,000	36,700,000	23,700,000
Boston	6,000,000	5,700,000	8,400,000	9,500,000	10,400,000	11,600,000	6,800,000	10,100,000	8,500,000
Portland	1,500,000	700,000	1,400,000	1,000,000	1,600,000	1,100,000	1,000,000	1,700,000	1,600,000
Montreal	4,400,000	2,700,000	3,700,000	3,700,000	4,300,000	4,200,000	2,300,000	4,200,000	2,500,000
Philadelphia	16,000,000	8,300,000	19,800,000	23,000,000	22,400,000	12,000,000	5,300,000	9,700,000	5,600,000
Baltimore	15,500,000	14,200,000	17,900,000	24,400,000	21,000,000	19,700,000	3,700,000	14,700,000	11,200,000
New Orleans	3,600,000	4,500,000	7,600,000	6,800,000	10,600,000	12,000,000	3,300,000	10,000,000	12,000,000
Total	77,500,000	56,000,000	107,900,000	115,900,000	124,100,000	110,200,000	51,100,000	87,100,000	63,100,000

Only in 1877 were the receipts at New York less than this year; Philadelphia's receipts have been much smaller for four years past than previously, while Baltimore shows a tendency to decline in a less degree. New Orleans received less this year than in any other since 1877, except 1882. Boston shows very decided progress of late years, receiving more this year even than in 1878, though the total receipts are 44,800,000 bushels (41 per cent.) less than then. If flour were included, the improvement at Boston would be much more marked. It has but a small export trade in grain, but a very large one in flour.

As before stated, it is not safe to draw conclusions as to the course of the trade at the seaboard by this year's movement, because it has been exceptionally light, and very little exported. Something may be judged from the course of the movement for several successive years; but here, too, it must be borne in mind that the exports for the last three years—even in 1883—were much lighter, and that it is the export trade chiefly which is subject to the competition of the different ports.

Grain Elevators at Philadelphia.—The total exports of all grain from Philadelphia in 1883 were nearly 50 per cent. more than in 1882, all of which passed through some of the following named elevators:—

(Pennsylvania Railroad System.)

GIRARD Point Storage Company.

Elevator.	Location.	Storage Capacity, Bushels.	Receiving Capacity, Cars, Ten Hours.	Delivering Capacity, Bushels, Ten Hours.
A	Girard Point	800,000	150	150,000
B	,, ,,	1,200,000	300	250,000
C	Washington Street	450,000	100	130,000

Pennsylvania Railroad Company's grain: depôt capacity 3,000,000 bushels.

(Philadelphia and Reading Railroad System.)

PHILADELPHIA Grain Elevator Company.

Elevator.	Location.	Storage Capacity, Bushels.	Receiving Capacity, Cars, Ten Hours.	Delivering Capacity, Bushels, Ten Hours.
Port Richmond	Port Richmond	1,000,000	300	3,000,000
20th Street	20th Street	500,000	100	1,000,000

FLOATING Elevators.

Elevator.	Proprietors.	Capacity.
Columbia	Girard Point Storage Company	4,000 bush. per hour.
St. Nicholas	,, ,, ,, ,,	2,500 ,, ,, ,,
Empire	Philadelphia Floating Elevator Association	6,000 ,, ,, ,,

PHILADELPHIA.

Imports in Detail.

The last Tariff Act (March 3, 1883) having introduced an entire change in the preparation of the statistics of imports and exports, this statement was prepared by the United States Customs Officers in compliance with that change, and is rendered for public use in two parts of six months each.

Imports at Philadelphia for the Six Months from January 1 to June 30, 1883.

Free of Duty.

Articles.		Quantity.	Value.
			Dollars.
Argols, crude	Lbs.	606,335	115,421
American products		..	44,153
Barks, medicinal	Lbs.	404,173	135,937
Cork bark		..	36,756
Bolting cloths		..	5,971
Books over 20 years old and for libraries		..	24,135
Chemicals		..	471,678
Chloride of lime	Lbs.	6,683,563	64,931
Cochineal	"	21,940	4,539
Coffee	"	3,527	415
Cutch	"	23,620	1,715
Dyewood, sticks	"	568,183	77,808
Fur skins, raw		..	3,116
Guano	Tons	550	8,184
Gum	Lbs.	407,380	43,296
Gypsum, unground	Tons	4,731	4,581
Hair, raw	Lbs.	270,014	36,822
Hides and skins, raw		..	69,136
Household effects		..	6,772
India-rubber, crude	Lbs.	1,373	582
Indigo, crude	"	79,115	70,982
Madder		47,265	3,640
Volatile oil	Lbs.	3,261	2,024
Paintings		..	2,637
Rags	Lbs.	355,544	14,409
Paper material	"	2,817,632	80,537
Seeds		..	7,676
Soda, nitrate of	Lbs.	11,055,099	209,935
Sulphur, crude	Tons	10,470	235,060
Tea	Lbs.	936	414
Tin, in bars	Cwt.	283	6,815
Wood, rough		..	19,606
Animals		..	39,442
Aluminum		..	57
Antiquities		..	194
Chalk	Tons	13,747	10,141
Charcoal		..	67
Cocoa fibre	Lbs.	12,955	2,065
Cocoanuts		..	32,307
Church vestments		..	917
Down		..	2,234
Dried flowers		..	518
Fashion plates		..	46
Goldbeaters' skin		..	971
" moulds		..	5,803
Green ginger		..	2
Gut skins		..	338
" strings		..	1,746

1916   UNITED STATES.

IMPORTS at Philadelphia for the Six Months from January 1 to June 30, 1883—continued.

FREE OF DUTY.

Articles.		Quantity.	Value.
			Dollars.
Hones	..	..	231
Horns	..	..	3,196
Instruments for colleges	..	..	5,388
Japan wax	Lbs.	3,736	378
Juniper berries	,,	7,056	104
Kainite	Tons	5,012	23,540
Kryolite	,,	548	7,337
Lithograph stones	..	..	1,691
Magnets	..	..	6
Mica plates	..	..	18
Minerals for colleges	..	..	52
Models	..	..	26
Old bones	..	..	117,684
,, coins for colleges	..	..	34
Olives	..	..	995
Orris roots	Lbs.	1,162	117
Palmnuts	..	..	1,681
Platinum	..	..	59,455
,, retort	..	..	4,335
,, pan	..	..	1,811
Quicksilver	Lbs.	141,623	47,747
Quills	..	..	22
Shells	..	..	166
Silk waste	Lbs.	236,732	64,288
Skeletons for colleges	..	..	150
Soap stock	Lbs.	297,060	23,436
Sauerkrout	..	..	1,542
Specimens for colleges	..	..	15
,, of natural history	..	..	3
Stuffed birds	..	..	99
Stones (water of Ayr)	..	..	192
Printed matter	..	..	30
Pumice stone	Lbs.	212,316	1,859
Terra alba	Tons	1,697	7,259
Tonka beans	..	..	15
Turtles	..	..	6
Whetstones	..	..	352
Total free of duty, January to June, inclusive	..	..	2,281,781

SUBJECT TO DUTY.

Articles.		Quantity.	Value.
			Dollars.
Animals	..	..	50
Ale and beer	Gallons	11,459	7,156
Books	..	..	35,734
Brass, and manufactures of	..	..	15,071
Oats	Bushels	585	757
Rice	Lbs.	44,800	1,043
Meal	..	..	1,491
Farinaceous food	..	..	3,733
Bristles	Lbs.	1,629	827
Buttons	..	..	25,881

PHILADELPHIA.

IMPORTS at Philadelphia for the Six Months from January 1 to June 30, 1883—continued.

SUBJECT TO DUTY.

Articles.		Quantity.	Value.
			Dollars.
Chemicals	..	..	275,953
Chicory, ground	Lbs.	54,262	1,411
Coal, bituminous	Tons	207	507
Cocoa, manufactured	Lbs.	4,941	1,962
Copper, old	,,	17,048	2,079
,, manufactures of	..	..	1,535
Cottons—			
Bleached	Sq. yards	419,481	50,021
Coloured	,,	619,207	100,007
Hosiery	..	..	204,888
Jeans, denims, &c.	Sq. yards	18,996	3,753
Cottons, manufactures of	..	..	801,261
Earthenware	..	..	271,287
Fancy goods	..	..	28,358
Sardines	..	..	3,796
Flax, manufactures of, by yards	..	..	397,460
,, ,, other	..	..	310,730
Fruits	..	..	681,814
Furs	..	..	27,919
Glass—			
Window	Lbs.	594,198	21,176
Rough plate	Sq. feet	27,124	2,610
Polished plate	,,	33,929	8,956
Silvered plate	,,	14	10
Manufactures of	..	..	52,282
Hair, manufactures of	..	..	11,603
,, other, &c.	..	..	28,730
Hemp, raw	Tons	52	6,930
,, manufactures of	..	..	7,942
Honey	..	..	2,139
India-rubber, manufactures of	..	..	12,195
Iron—			
Pig	Lbs.	47,090,104	392,119
Castings	,,	291	39
Bar	,,	954,219	19,647
Band-hoop, &c.	..	..	1,385
Sheet	Lbs.	453,267	13,552
Old and scrap	Tons	4,124	82,608
Machinery	..	..	90,907
Fire-arms	..	..	6,382
Steel, in ingots	..	..	111,336
Cutlery	..	..	23,584
Files	..	..	3,056
Iron and steel manufactures	..	..	344,248
Jewellery	..	..	1,045
Jute, raw	Tons	6	2,839
Leather—			
All kinds	..	..	167,475
Manufactures of	..	..	14,608
Gloves	..	..	1,751
Marble and stone manufactures	..	..	42,645
Metals	..	..	22,889
Musical instruments	..	..	12,001
Oils—			
Cod liver	Gallons	17	22
Olive, salad	,,	5,102	9,768
,, not salad	,,	3,402	2,189
Vegetable	,,	55,471	324

IMPORTS at Philadelphia for the Six Months from January 1 to June 30, 1883—continued.

SUBJECT TO DUTY.

Articles.		Quantity.	Value.
			Dollars.
Volatile	Lbs.	4,714	7,712
Opium	,,	33,847	91,537
Paintings	..	..	34,864
Painters' colours	..	..	27,019
Paper manufactures	..	..	11,383
Perfumery	..	..	3,270
Potatoes	Bushels	23,512	13,295
Precious stones	..	..	39,042
Provisions	..	..	12,923
Salt	Lbs.	50,570,296	86,399
Seeds	..	..	14,488
Silk, hosiery	..	..	17,644
,, manufactures of	..	..	304,441
Soda, ash	Lbs.	25,557,212	291,184
,, caustic	,,	3,288,348	74,696
Spices	,,	81,327	14,862
Straw manufactures	..	..	3,114
Sugar, brown	Lbs.	105,257,315	4,497,028
Molasses	Gallons	8,792,075	1,743,667
Candy	..	..	36
Tin plates	Cwts.	289,248	1,184,894
,, manufactures of	..	..	871
Tobacco, leaf	..	..	611
Cigars	..	35	143
Tobacco, manufactures of	..	..	30
Watches	..	..	17,150
Spirits, in casks	Half gallons	50,150	53,602
,, in bottles	Dozen	206	3,695
Wine, in casks	Gallons	89,052	68,035
,, in bottles	Dozen	9,550	88,165
Wood, manufactures of	..	..	27,882
Other lumber	..	..	1,949
Wood, unmanufactured	Lbs.	1,504,519	233,491
Shoddy	,,	62,068	30,582
Shawls	..	..	19,120
Carpets	Sq. yards	12,953	16,612
Dress goods	,,	1,788,361	408,596
Hosiery	..	..	9,517
Woollens	..	..	573,650
Asphaltum	..	..	11,742
Bitumen	Lbs.	112,268	600
Blacking	..	..	374
Bricks, fire	..	..	4,565
Brushes	..	..	14,534
Candles	..	..	136
Cement	Barrels	17,881	2,297
Chalk	..	..	929
Cider	Gallons	71	24
Chocolate	Lbs.	510	147
Clay	..	..	27,568
Clocks	..	..	10,440
Cork, manufactures of	..	..	102
Fuller's earth	..	..	578
Ginger ale	..	..	6,231
Glue	..	..	3,083
Grease for soap stock	Lbs.	62,579	1,915
Hops	..	..	200
Ink	..	..	4,859

PHILADELPHIA.

IMPORTS at Philadelphia for the Six Months from January 1 to June 30, 1883—continued.

SUBJECT TO DUTY.

Articles.		Quantity.	Value.
			Dollars.
Iron ore	Tons	51,742	117,211
Jelly			23
Oilcloths			2,344
„ (Nainsook)			482
Pickles			11,222
Plants			2,013
Quills			603
Rice roots	Lbs.	1,018	201
Rosin			25
Sand			70
Sauces			26
Soap	Lbs.	118,098	12,061
Tiles			8,709
„ encaustic			1,374
Varnish			1,200
Vegetables			1,850
Vinegar			155
Wax, bees	Lbs.	2,179	483
Sponges			1,118
Total subject to duty, January to June, inclusive			15,120,148

IMPORTS at Philadelphia for the Six Months from July 1 to December 31, 1883.

FREE OF DUTY.

Articles.		Quantity.	Value.
			Dollars.
Cattle		531	126,653
Horses		19	2,124
Sheep		1	195
All other animals			386
American products			277,643
Art works			6,812
Asphaltum	Lbs.	1,053,290	5,826
Bolting cloths			26,811
Books			22,590
Argols	Lbs.	56,738	12,864
Bark, Cinchona	„	533,481	175,255
Cochineal	„	2,000	535
Logwood	Tons	2,103	38,177
Other dye woods			8,344
Gum Arabic	Lbs.	182,616	22,963
Other gums	„	31,081	4,163
Cutch	„	111,487	5,664
Chloride of lime	„	6,256,145	81,647
Liquorice root	„	1,518,692	33,485
Mineral waters, not artificial			9,486
Potash, muriate of	Lbs.	2,772,409	42,409
Quinia, sulphate	Ounces	426,991	543,604
Soda, nitrate	Lbs.	3,617,701	61,202
Sulphur, crude	Tons	14,277	305,382

IMPORTS at Philadelphia for the Six Months from July 1 to December 31, 1883—continued.

FREE OF DUTY.

Articles.				Quantity.	Value.
					Dollars.
Other chemicals	..	..	..	..	148,640
Cocoa	..	..	Lbs.	5,857	784
Coffee	..	..	,,	472	70
Cork, unmanufactured	..	..	..	..	30,980
Diamonds, uncut	..	..	..	..	12
Farinaceous substances	..	..	..	..	820
Guano	..	..	Tons	202½	11,739
Phosphates, crude	..	..	,,	6,744	63,468
Other phosphates	..	..	..	..	19,108
Lobsters, canned	..	..	..	..	1,650
Bananas	..	..	..	..	38,846
Cocoanuts	..	..	..	..	34,864
Other fruit	..	..	..	..	1,167
Furs and fur skins, undressed	..	..	..	..	9,152
Hair	..	..	..	..	52,021
Goat skins	..	..	..	..	13,019
Other skins	..	..	..	..	51,301
Household effects	..	..	..	..	13,509
India rubber, crude	..	..	Lbs.	15,100	422
Oils, fixed	..	..	..	..	10,765
,, volatile	..	..	Lbs.	14,074	3,601
Rags, other than woollen	..	..	,,	3,815,373	107,751
Other rags	..	..	..	..	73,266
Plaster of Paris, unground	..	..	Tons	7,796	7,248
Platinum, unmanufactured	..	..	Lbs.	531,720	57,373
Plumbago	..	..	Cwts.	799	807
Seeds, not medicinal	..	..	..	..	11,196
Silk waste	..	..	Lbs.	283,724	69,470
Nutmegs, unground	..	..	,,	1,783	1,253
Pepper, unground	..	..	,,	129,981	17,097
Other spices, unground	..	..	,,	46,203	4,902
Tea	..	..	,,	798	451
Wood, unmanufactured	..	..	..	..	21,369
Antiquities	..	..	..	..	1,657
,, old coins	..	..	..	..	148
Aluminium	..	..	..	..	235
Bismuth	..	..	Lbs.	13,070	20,961
Bells, old	..	..	,,	1,880	193
Bones, old	..	..	,,	..	53,223
,, ground	..	..	..	..	35
Catgut	..	..	..	..	1,662
Chalk	..	..	Tons	6,271	3,299
Cliffstone	..	..	,,	1,426	1,845
Church vestments	..	..	..	..	1,541
Charcoal	..	..	..	..	106
Curry powder	..	..	..	..	28
Cocoa fibre	..	..	..	..	2,310
Dried flowers	..	..	..	..	47
Eiderdown	..	..	Lbs.	2,122	2,227
Goldbeaters' skins	..	..	..	..	4,866
Hones	..	..	..	..	41
Hoofs, old	..	..	..	..	100
Instruments for colleges	..	..	..	..	7,589
,, for United States	..	..	..	..	551
Ivory, not manufactured	..	..	..	..	351
Lithographic stones	..	..	..	..	3,589
Medals	..	..	..	..	36
Magnets	..	..	..	..	12

PHILADELPHIA.

Imports at Philadelphia for the Six Months from July 1 to December 31, 1883—continued.

Free of Duty.

Articles.		Quantity.	Value.
			Dollars.
Minerals for colleges	..	..	105
Models for colleges	..	..	137
Oakum	Lbs.	5,004	263
Parchment	..	..	1,013
Platinum retort	..	..	1,857
Pumice stone	..	..	4,157
Plants	..	..	6,735
Polishing stones	..	..	57
Skeletons	..	..	527
Skulls	..	..	151
Specimens of natural history	..	..	1,202
Spunk	..	..	96
Spurs for earthenware	..	..	733
St. John's bread	..	..	436
Sausage casings	..	..	357
Soap stock	Lbs.	190,573	12,415
Shells	..	..	241
Sauerkraut	Lbs.	157,260	2,497
Teasels	..	..	166
Venice turpentine	Gallons	3	25
Terra, alba	Tons	770	3,791
Types	Lbs.	1,595	149
Whetstones	..	..	105
For Penna Museum	..	..	1,042
Total, free of duty, July to December inclusive	..	..	2,831,270

Subject to Duty.

Articles.		Quantity.	Value.
			Dollars.
Horses	..	3	245
Other cattle	..	..	33
Art works	..	..	13,200
Books	..	..	55,165
Brass, manufactures of	..	..	17,698
Barley	..	..	421
Oatmeal	Lbs.	64,944	2,776
Breadstuffs	..	..	247
Bristles	Lbs.	2,266	1,241
Brushes	..	..	19,323
Buttons	..	..	54,229
Cement	..	..	25,274
Coal tar dyes	..	..	20,241
Glycerine	..	..	1,748
Logwood	..	..	42,863
Opium, crude	Lbs.	80,042	179,687
Soda—			
Bicarbonate of	Lbs.	16,928	288
Ash	..	..	329,867
Caustic	Lbs.	3,182,143	111,300
Other salts	..	..	2,333
Sumac, ground	..	..	95,125
„ other	..	..	143,792

IMPORTS at Philadelphia for the Six Months from July 1 to December 31, 1883—continued.

Subject to Duty.

Articles.		Quantity.	Value.
			Dollars.
Clay, tons		2,829	21,353
Clocks		..	16,998
Watches		..	28,192
Coal, bituminous	Tons	3,030	5,236
Copper, unmanufactured		145	14
,, manufactures of		..	1,258
Cottons—			
Coloured		..	48,971
Bleached		..	17,203
Embroideries		..	244,835
Knit goods		..	73,126
Yarn		..	6,693
Other manufactures of		..	243,413
Chinaware—			
Not decorated		..	54,074
Decorated		..	66,032
All other		..	18,245
Beads and ornaments		..	716
Dolls and toys		..	41,334
Fans		..	13,429
Feathers, natural		..	1,763
,, artificial		..	104
Perfumeries		..	4,885
Pipes		..	3,148
Fancy articles		..	20,449
Sardines and anchovies		..	6,389
Other fish		..	42
Hemp, unmanufactured	Tons	64	10,417
Jute, unmanufactured	Tons	9	747
Bags		..	736
Burlaps		..	244,702
Linens		..	1,376
Thread and twine		..	10,358
Flax yarn		..	8,443
Flax, other manufactures of		..	449,384
Figs		..	7,959
Lemons		..	35,128
Oranges		..	25,570
Prunes	Lbs.	1,010,204	63,076
Raisins		..	73,113
Preserved fruits		..	12,296
Other fruits		..	81,246
Almonds		..	8,464
Other nuts		..	7,162
Furs		..	93,225
Bottles		..	11,768
Glass—			
Window, unpolished	Lbs.	740,584	21,421
Cylinder and crown, polished		..	4,247
Fluted, rolled, or rough	Sq. feet	22,705	2,978
All other		..	35,937
Hair		..	23,939
Hats and bonnets, and materials for		..	31,753
Hops	Lbs.	2,078	783
India rubber, manufactures of		..	18,467

PHILADELPHIA.

Imports at Philadelphia for the Six Months from July 1 to December 31, 1883—continued.

Subject to Duty.

Articles.		Quantity.	Value.
			Dollars.
Iron—			
Ore	Tons	118,678	269,175
Pig			360,521
Old			59,870
Old steel			4,535
Bar iron	Lbs.	1,144,749	22,907
Hoop iron	"	63,759	1,163
Steel sheets	"	224,000	1,810
" ingots			20,131
Taggers' iron			24,575
Tin plates			1,561,379
Wire rods			14,204
" rope			21,706
Anvils			8,633
Chains	Lbs.	131,042	5,082
Cutlery			25,813
Files			592
Firearms			58,783
Machinery			88,788
Needles			1,005
Iron and steel, other manufactures			100,388
Jewellery			2,830
Precious stones			134,272
Lead, manufactures of			5,869
Bending leather			2,760
Calfskin, dressed			23,700
Morocco skins			35,800
Upper leather			98,086
Gloves, kid and leather			11,555
Leather, all other manufactures			21,373
Malt liquors, bottles and jugs			1,173
" " not bottles or jugs			6,571
Marble, manufactures of			37,528
Stone, "			16,605
Metal, "			101,030
Mineral substances			100
Musical instruments			39,550
Oil—			
Fish			788
Olive			16,175
Volatile			1,142
Paints			35,195
Paper, manufactures of			36,061
Meat, extracts of			4,086
" other			399
Butter	Lbs.	2,480	819
Cheese			8,096
Rice	Lbs.	52,700	1,197
Salt			121,878
Seeds, not medical			19,497
Silk—			
Clothing			9,641
Dress and piece goods			3,247
Laces			13,739
Ribbons			32,751
All other manufactures of			371,776
Soap, fancy	Lbs.	121,292	10,177
" other	"	66,908	5,973

IMPORTS at Philadelphia for the Six Months from July 1 to December 31, 1883—continued.

SUBJECT TO DUTY.

Articles.		Quantity.	Value.
			Dollars.
Spices, ground	Lbs.	48,844	13,263
Brandy, proof	Gallons	3,199	14,086
Other spirits		..	25,172
Sponges		..	1,020
Molasses	Gallons	990,479	129,088
Sugar, Dutch Standard, not above No. 13	..	..	3,109,698
Sugar, Dutch Standard, above No. 13	Lbs.	4,311	183
Confectionery		..	2,005
Leaf tobacco	Lbs.	298	177
Cigars		..	475
Other manufactures, tobacco		..	617
Potatoes	Bushels	4,053	1,302
Pickles and sauces		..	4,736
Other vegetables, raw		..	15,122
,, ,, preserved		..	5,140
Wine—			
Champagne	Dozen	1,278	13,713
In casks		..	12,615
In bottles	Dozen	1,515	10,809
Wood—			
Lumber		..	30,809
Cabinet ware and house furniture		..	6,111
Other manufactures		..	34,926
Wool—			
Clothing		..	124,225
Combings	Lbs.	4,260	1,382
Carpets and other similar	,,	2,700,386	340,639
Carpet	Sq. yards	50,558	62,524
Clothing, ready-made		..	25,555
Cloths		..	13,124
Dress goods	Sq. yards	973,787	276,811
Knit ,,		..	82,508
Rags	Lbs.	31,115	12,244
Shawls		..	19,354
Yarns	Lbs.	168,665	97,796
Woollens, all other		..	685,341
Asphaltum, partly manufactured	Lbs.	109,996	394
Brandy colouring	Gallons	9	26
Blacking		..	1,072
Brooms		..	663
Bass-wood fibre	Lbs.	4,712	453
Black lead		..	33
Brown grease	Lbs.	19,859	611
Candles		..	12
Chocolate	Lbs.	2,081	448
Cocoa	,,	840	340
Cork manufactures		..	20
Cotton and rubber rags		..	121
Chalk		..	1,576
Coal dust	Lbs.	2,000	3
Clocks		..	72
Dried moss		..	153
,, natural flowers		..	2,277
Oilcloth		..	2,793
,, floor		..	30
Oiled nainsook		..	1,125
Gun wads		..	3,559

IMPORTS at Philadelphia for the Six Months from July 1 to December 31, 1883—continued.

SUBJECT TO DUTY.

Articles.		Quantity.	Value.
			Dollars.
Ginger ale	..	..	4,805
Grease	Lbs.	70,120	2,083
Honey softener	..	..	221
Ink	..	..	9,340
Lead pencils	..	..	605
Microscopic objects	..	..	170
Mats	..	..	391
Percussion caps	..	..	14,812
Philosophical instruments	..	..	2,973
Plaster-cast models	..	..	162
Peat	..	..	12
Photographs	..	..	19
Polishing powder	..	..	65
Polished heel-ball	..	..	40
Plumbago	..	..	22
Pickles	..	..	7,225
Quills	..	..	118
„ trimmings	..	..	183
Roofing, felt	..	..	2
Rags	..	..	722
Rubber rags	Lbs.	35,532	146
Rosin	..	..	23
Sand	..	..	29
Sponges	..	..	1,492
Straw baskets	..	..	974
Sugar drainings	..	..	52
Sealing-wax	..	..	564
Tin cans	..	..	600
„ manufactures	..	..	172
Teeth, manufactured	..	..	65
Umbrella stretchers	..	..	55
Umbrellas	..	..	279
Varnish	..	..	286
Vinegar	..	..	230
Vegetables	..	..	114
Total subject to duty, July to December, inclusive	..	..	12,577,846

1926   UNITED STATES.

ENTERED for Immediate Transportation without Appraisement, under section No. 2,990, Revised Statutes, from Philadelphia to other Ports, for the Year 1883.

Ports.	Value.
	Dollars.
Wilmington, Delaware	2,090
Baltimore, Maryland	2,859
Georgetown, District of Columbia	101
New York, New York	38,578
Boston, Massachusetts	1,072
Buffalo, New York	337
Detroit, Michigan	1,168
Pittsburgh, Pennsylvania	124,668
Cleveland, Ohio	1,380
Cincinnati, Ohio	209,753
Indianoplis, Indiana	1,551
Louisville, Kentucky	4,136
Milwaukee, Wisconsin	16,979
Chicago, Illinois	1,256,806
St. Louis, Missouri	7,094
Kansas City, Missouri	480
San Francisco, California	402
Total	1,669,454

STATEMENT of Articles Exported from the Port of Philadelphia from January 1 to June 30, 1883.

Articles.		Quantity.	Value.
			Dollars.
Acids	Lbs.	73,407	3,438
Agricultural Implements—			
Fanning mills	Number	17	1,000
Horse-power	”	24	4,250
Ploughs and cultivators	”	21	433
All other, not elsewhere specified			10,744
Animals, living—			
Horned cattle	Number	7	565
Mules	”	24	3,150
Sheep	”	100	700
Bark for tanning			5,665
Beer, ale, and porter, in casks	Gallons	320	122
Books, pamphlets, maps, &c.			15,256
Brass, and manufactures of			852
Bread and breadstuffs—			
Bread and biscuit	Lbs.	71,761	3,346
Indian corn	Bushels	4,571,540	3,111,828
” cornmeal	Lbs.	9,675	34,311
Oats	Bushels	3,173	1,828
Rye	”	8,782	6,992
Wheat	”	1,986,622	2,344,140
” flour	”	156,360	925,725
Other small grain and pulse			13,877
Maizena, farina, &c.			20,464
Bricks, other than fire	Thousands	87	712
Brooms and brushes			711
Candles, tallow and other	Lbs.	6,000	1,108
Carriages, carts, and parts of			4,673
Cars, railroad, passenger, and freight	Number	121	28,465
Clocks			27

STATEMENT of Articles Exported from the Port of Philadelphia from January 1 to June 30, 1883—continued.

Articles.		Quantity.	Value.
			Dollars.
Coffee, cocoa, and spices	..	..	153
Coal, anthracite..	Tons	17,077	77,471
„ bituminous	„	35,331	131,452
Cotton and manufactures of—			
Other unmanufactured	Lbs.	31,067,529	3,748,667
Cordage	„	1,047	106
All other manufactures of	..	..	85,430
Drugs, chemicals, and medicines	..	..	15,848
Dye stuffs	..	..	25,800
Earthen, stone, and china ware	..	..	3,699
Fancy articles	..	..	2,075
Fruits—			
Apples, dried	Lbs.	800	25
„ green or ripe	Bushels	10,456	14,571
Other fruits, green or ripe, or dried.	..	..	13,790
Preserved in cans, or other..	..	..	86
Furs and fur skins	..	..	76,680
Gas fixtures	..	..	91
Glass ware	..	..	1,200
Glue	Lbs.	1,177	159
Hair, manufactured	..	..	1,455
„ manufactures	..	..	4,427
Hats, wool, fur, and silk	..	..	140
Hay	Tons	10	204
Hides and skins	..	..	1,120
Hops	Lbs.	1,458	1,450
India rubber boots and shoes, manufactures, other	..	..	2,309
Iron and steel manufactures—			
Pig	Lbs.	112,000	1,296
Sheet, bands, and hoop	..	48,000	1,500
Castings	..	..	2,310
Car wheels	Number	256	1,147
Stoves..	..	..	40
Steam engines, locomotive	Number	23	279,758
„ „ stationary	„	1	900
Boilers	..	..	6,900
Machinery	..	..	39,700
Nails and spikes	Lbs.	29,800	1,194
All other, of iron	..	..	43,728
Steel edge tools	..	..	203
„ files and saws	..	..	155
„ manufactures	..	..	11,127
Jewellery and other manufactures of gold and silver	..	..	8,924
Leather—			
Morocco and other fine	..	..	57,706
Boots and shoes	Pairs	..	711,768
Saddlery and harness	..	..	165
Lime and cement	..	13	46
Other substances used as manures	..	..	682
Marble, manufactures of	..	..	1,850
Matches..	..	..	1,575
Organs	..	..	900
Pianos	..	..	500
Musical instruments, other	..	..	929
Tar and pitch	Lbs.	35	106
Oil cake..	„	13,280,798	194,860

[612]

1928 — UNITED STATES.

STATEMENT of Articles Exported from the Port of Philadelphia from January 1 to June 30, 1883—continued.

Articles.		Quantity.	Value.
			Dollars.
Oils—			
Petroleum, crude	Gallons	3,419,157	232,899
Refined or manufactured—			
Napthas, benzines, gasolines	"	954,534	56,382
Petroleum, refined	"	26,759,470	2,295,203
Lubricating	"	463,016	80,856
Residuum	Barrels	1,364	4,239
Lard	Gallons	4,420	4,598
Neats foots	"	2,275	4,200
Cotton seed	"	1,211	627
Ore, silver	Cwts.	9,110	36,400
Paints			53
Paintings and engravings			7,140
Paper and stationery			14,148
Plated ware			600
Printing presses and type			6,794
Provisions—			
Bacon	Lbs.	31,309,101	3,467,532
Hams	"	376,840	43,707
Beef, salt	"	2,389,960	179,820
Butter	"	90,144	13,720
Cheese	"	1,388,480	166,788
Fish, pickled	"	349	3,460
" other cured			1,680
Lard	Lbs.	1,922,982	226,710
Meats, preserved			33,610
Oysters			340
Pork	Lbs.	518,120	53,196
Onions	Bushels	5	5
Potatoes	"	509	510
Other vegetables			4,789
Vegetables, preserved			7,914
Rice	Lbs.	315	20
Rags, cotton and linen	"	8,683	350
Scales and balances			485
Seeds, clover	Lbs.	475,281	47,527
" garden			7,414
Sewing machines			5,873
Soap, perfumed			444
" other	Lbs.	145,140	6,492
Spirits from grain	Gallons	41,418	89,776
" turpentine		1,000	475
Starch	Lbs.	12,000	250
Sugar, refined	"	3,844	354
Molasses	Gallons	665,620	157,830
Candy and confectionery			5,029
Tallow	Lbs.	3,210,562	187,779
Tin, and manufactures of			78
Tobacco, leaf	Lbs.	5,274,549	358,128
" cigars	Thousand	3	140
Cigar manufactures, other			64,955
Trunks and valises			45
Umbrellas, parasols, and sun-shades			156
Vessels	Number	1	3,700
Wearing apparel			1,649
Broad planks, &c.		1,442	32,047
Shingles	Millions	73	505
Shooks, other			124,915
Hogsheads and barrels, empty		51,726	108,540
Lumber, other			87,045

STATEMENT of Articles Exported from the Port of Philadelphia from January 1 to June 30, 1883—continued.

Articles.		Quantity.	Value.
			Dollars.
Logs, masts, and spar	..	..	5,980
Furniture	..	..	4,591
Wool manufactures	..	..	892
Wooden ware	..	..	1,377
Wood manufactures, other	..	..	5,692
All other unmanufactured articles	..	..	20,326
„ manufactured articles	..	..	89,587
Total	..	..	19,788,506

The Second Half of the Year.

STATEMENT of Articles Exported from the Port of Philadelphia from July 1 to December 31, 1883.

Articles.		Quantity.	Value.
			Dollars.
Acids	Lbs.	..	1,118
Agricultural implements, all other not elsewhere specified	..	..	888
Animals living—			
Horned cattle	..	365	54,750
Mules	..	30	3,900
Sheep	..	400	2,363
Art works, painting and statuary	..	..	3,113
Bark, for tanning	..	..	41,909
Beer, ale, and porter, in casks	Gallons	840	258
Blacking	..	..	260
Bones and bone dust	Cwt.	..	35
Books, pamphlets, maps, &c.	..	..	19,197
Brass, and manufactures of	..	..	832
Bread and breadstuffs—			
Bread and biscuits	..	86,267	5,516
Indian corn	Bushels	864,102	525,724
„ cornmeal	Barrels	5,529	17,609
Oats	Bushels	5,310	3,074
Oatmeal	Lbs.	4,451,030	115,575
Wheat	Bushels	2,386,155	2,737,914
Wheatflour	Barrels	206,507	1,225,540
Other small grain and pulse	..	..	53,673
Brick, fire	..	..	328
„ other than fire	Thousand	30	250
Brooms and brushes	..	..	572
Carriages and carts and parts of	..	..	4,029
Cars, railroad, passenger and freight	..	116	35,930
Casings for sausages	..	..	590
Clocks	..	..	19
Coffee, cocoa, and spices	..	..	55
Copper—			
Ingots	Barrels	14,346	1,044
Ore, tons	Tons	1,245	74,640
Other manufactures of	..	..	3,899
Coal, anthracite	Tons	39,968	168,138
„ bituminous	„	10,987	39,528
Cotton unmanufactured	Bales	21,279,785	2,600,720
„ all other manufactures of	..	..	45,687

STATEMENT of Articles Exported from the Port of Philadelphia from July 1 to December 31, 1883—continued.

Articles.		Quantity.	Value.
			Dollars.
Roots, herbs, bark	..	..	125
Drugs, chemicals, and medicines	..	..	16,062
Dyestuffs	..	..	5,800
All other chemicals	..	..	20,306
Earthen, stone, and chinaware	..	..	105
Fancy articles	..	..	1,105
Fertilizers	Tons	76	2,093
Apples, dried	Lbs.	500	50
„ green or ripe	Barrels	668	3,047
Other fruits, green, ripe, or dried	..	..	2,646
„ preserved in cans, or otherwise	..	..	476
Glassware	..	..	889
Glue	Lbs.	6,997	990
Hair manufactures	..	..	37,910
Hats, palm leaf, straw, &c.	..	..	63
Hay	Tons	11	225
Hemps, cables, and cordage	Lbs.	15,357	2,918
Hemp manufactures and others	..	..	60
Hides and skins	..	..	11,800
Hops	Lbs.	118,800	26,590
India rubber manufactures, other	..	..	3,854
Iron and steel manufactures—			
Bar	..	8,000	230
Casting	..	..	5,546
Car wheels	..	610	3,253
Stoves	..	..	910
Steam engines, locomotives	..	23	241,730
Boilers	..	..	3,915
Machinery	..	..	40,903
Nails and spikes	Lbs.	99,000	3,685
All other of iron	..	..	3,586
Steel cutlery	..	..	75
„ files and saws	..	..	139
„ fire-arms	..	..	27,805
„ manufactures	..	..	44,474
Jewellery and other manufactures of gold and silver	..	..	3,072
Lamps	..	..	498
Lead and manufactures of	..	..	6,442
Leather, Morocco and other fine	..	..	42,200
„ sole, upper, and all other	..	..	11,839
Boots and shoes	Pairs	342	617
Saddlery and harness	..	..	1,020
„ „ „ manufacturers of	..	..	378
Marble, unmanufactured	..	..	25
„ manufactures of	..	..	4,209
Matches	..	..	177
Organs	Number	3	359
Pianos	„	2	895
Musical instruments, other	..	..	300
Rosin	Barrels	12	34
Tar and pitch	„	153	443
Oilcake	Lbs.	21,540,099	295,258
Turpentine	„	165	333
Oakum	„	2,500	230

PHILADELPHIA.

STATEMENT of Articles Exported from the Port of Philadelphia from July 1 to December 31, 1883—continued.

Articles.		Quantity.	Value.
			Dollars.
Oils—			
Petroleum, crude	Gallons	3,321,410	232,373
Refined or manufactured—			
Naphtha, benzine, gasoline, &c.	,,	566,431	4,080,124
Petroleum, refined	,,	41,856,070	31 274
Lubricating	,,	249,680	49,793
Residuum	Barrels	4,183	9,000
Lard	Gallons	8,848	6,535
Cotton-seed	,,	730	365
Volatile or essential, vegetable	..	..	63
Ore, gold and silver bearing	..	..	237,640
Paraffin and paraffin wax	Lbs.	949,749	27,500
Paints	..	..	107
Paper and stationery	..	..	12,109
Printing presses and type	..	..	2,750
Provisions—			
Beef, canned	..	..	21,255
Bacon	Lbs.	20,497,189	3,311,000
Hams	,,	4,247,589	465,790
Beef, salt	,,	2,164,060	129,186
,, other, cured	,,	1,300	135
Butter	,,	70,539	10,525
Cheese	,,	982,377	114,365
Fish, dried or smoked, cod	,,	3,860	213
,, smoked, other	,,	1,785	143
,, pickled	Barrels	211	2,030
Lard	Lbs.	2,807,195	330,933
Meat, all other products of	..	..	2,875
Oysters	..	..	340
Pork	Lbs.	493,300	35,796
Onions	Bushels	7	5
Potatoes	,,	259	156
Other vegetables, peas, &c.	,,	872	1,145
Vegetables, preserved, canned	..	..	9,624
Grease	..	..	5,522
Rags, cotton and linen	Lbs.	15,150	550
Silk, manufactures of	..	..	1,319
Scales and balances	..	..	1,820
Seed, clover	Lbs.	125,092	11,734
Seeds, timothy	..	11,000	330
,, gardening, and other	..	..	430
Sewing machines	..	..	3,907
Soap, perfumed	..	..	151
,, other	Lbs.	275,379	12,124
Spirits from grain, rye whisky	Gallons	34,089	39,103
Spirit turpentine	,,	44	18
Starch	Lbs.	12,000	480
Stationery, except of paper	..	..	50
Sugar, refined	Lbs.	9,642	816
Molasses	Gallons	429,225	67,474
Candy and confectionery	..	..	5,452
Tallow	Lbs.	2,905,802	188,666
Tin, manufactures of	..	..	25
Tobacco, leaf	Lbs.	5,886,334	426,138
,, manufactures, other	..	..	15,995
Umbrellas, parasols, and sun-shades	..	..	457
Vinegar	Gallons	1,059	284
Wearing apparel	..	..	01
Wine	Dozens	1	7
Broad planks, &c.	Thousand	1,289	26,205

STATEMENT of Articles Exported from the Port of Philadelphia from July 1 to December 31, 1883—continued.

Articles.		Quantity.	Value.
			Dollars.
Shingles..	Thousand ..	101	588
Staves and headings	..	..	152,685
Hogsheads and barrels, empty	Number ..	6,909	6,909
Lumber, other ..	..	..	2,149
Hoop, telegraph and other poles	..	..	40,245
Logs, masts, and spars..	..	..	15,206
Furniture	..	..	4,832
Wooden ware ..	..	..	1,450
Wood manufactures, other	..	..	1,177
Wool, raw and fleecy ..	Lbs. ..	3,600	1,500
„ manufactures ..	..	..	5,491
All other manufactured articles	..	..	26,539
„ unmanufactured ..	..	..	8,604
Total for second half year	..	..	18,873,961
„ first half year	..	..	19,788,506
Total for year	..	..	38,662,467

IMPORTS AND EXPORTS.

The imports and exports at Philadelphia from 1821 to 1883:—

Year.	Imports.	Exports.
	Dols.	Dols.
1821..	8,158,922	7,791,217
1831..	12,124,083	5,513,713
1841..	10,347,698	5,152,501
1851..	14,168,761	5,356,039
1861..	8,004,161	10,277,938
1871..	20,820,374	20,688,551
1873..	29,186,925	29,683,186
1875..	24,011,014	31,836,727
1876..	21,000,000	50,539,450
1877..	20,126,032	37,823,356
1878..	21,048,197	48,362,116
1879..	27,224,549	50,685,837
1880..	38,933,832	56,589,584
1881..	29,774,278	41,162,957
1882..	37,666,489	34,529,459
1883..	32,810,045	38,662,467

IMMIGRATION.

Immigration has continued to flow towards this Continent, almost uninterruptedly since the war of the rebellion. During the past year 570,316 persons of foreign birth emigrated to the United States. In 1862, when the rebellion assumed gigantic proportions, the immigration numbered 89,007. In 1864 when enormous bounties were offered for substitutes to take the places of conscripted citizens, the tide of immigration rose to 193,195, and in 1869, when the issue between the North and the South was effectually settled, the number of immigrants rose to 385,287. In 1877, financial panic year, the number fell off to 130,502 and again in 1881 and 1882, years of great prosperity, the figures were, 720,045 and 730,349, respectively. Of the 570,316 immigrants who arrived in 1883, their nationalities were:—Germany, 184,389; Great Britain and Ireland, 157,361; British North American Provinces, 66,950; Sweden, 32,596; Italy, 29,512; Norway, 21,295; Hungary, 12,308; Switzerland, 11,433; Austria, 11,091; Denmark, 9,747; Russia, 6,907; Bohemia, 6,837; Netherlands, 4,926; France, 4,016; Poland, 2,151; Belgium, 1,673; West Indies, 1,438; Azores, 1,276; Finland, 1,107; Portugal, 650; Australia, 427; Mexico, 411; China, 381; Hawaiian Islands, 284; Greenland and Iceland, 251; Spain, 245; other European countries, 253; other Asiatic countries, 161; Africa, 9; Central America, 26; South America, 67; other islands than those above named, 61; born at sea, 77.

The United States Commissioners of Immigration at the various ports of entry are exacting strict regulations as to the landing of emigrants from Europe. All emigrants who come within the class of inability to maintain themselves through sickness or otherwise, and pauper emigrants, with no points of destination where friends or relatives reside to receive them, are refused a landing and the ships bringing them out are obliged to carry them back.

Manufactures.

The city of Philadelphia has a population verging upon a million of souls, 25 per cent. of whom are directly engaged in productive industries. The actual census of this population shows that 237,000 persons were so employed in 1882. This force is almost without an equal in the history of modern cities, and may be said to be the impulse to Philadelphia's prosperity and wealth. Without these industries the city would be largely depleted of its population. The industrial career of Philadelphia shows that manufactures increase more rapidly than population. The existence of this fact is clearly shown in the history of all American cities during the past 30 years, and Philadelphia, admitted to lead in industrial activity, has fully maintained its ratio of growth during the 10 years from 1870 to 1880. The population of the city increased 25 per cent. from 1870 to 1880, or from 674,022 to 847,170, a gain of 173,148 equal to twenty-five and nine-tenths per cent. and every analogy derived from its past history, as well as from the record of all other cities for the same time, shows that its industries must have increased nearly 50 per cent. during the same period.

Lorin Blodget, Esq., the eminent statistician, has for many months been engaged, assisted by the Mayor and the entire police force of the city, in collating industrial returns for 1882 and 1883, a brief summary of which is herein given by permission.

Mr. Blodget remarks:—" Philadelphia is primarily a city of residence, and its manufacturing is adapted to and in harmony with its character as such, and it is neither built nor occupied as manufacturing cities are elsewhere. No part of the city area is crowded as European manufacturing cities are. There is not one tenement house in it, nor is there any single locality in which employment is enforced or compulsory at any one industry. There are no narrow lanes, with squalid occupants living on the smallest possible wages, and there is no exclusive occupancy or oppressive localization in any part of the city." The following summary, furnished by Mr. Blodget, of the exhaustive details of his labours for the year 1882, presents the manufactures of the city on a reliable basis. It is not likely that any material increase has been made in the year following, and doubtless for some years to come the returns will not be so exhaustive or accurate.

UNITED STATES.

SUMMARY Tabular Statement of the several Industries, the Number of Persons employed, and the Values produced in the City of Philadelphia for the Year 1882.

Industries.	Number of Establishments.	Men.	Women.	Youths.	Total.	Value of Products.
						Dollars.
Acids, sulphuric, muriatic, and nitric	9	313	...	10	323	1,365,000
,, other, with chemicals	...	...	...	...	...	...
Agricultural implements	19	390	...	39	429	710,735
Albums	3	22	4	2	28	35,400
Alcohol and Cologne spirits	8	55	...	...	55	290,500
Ale and porter	8	301	1	...	302	1,328,000
Alum and alum-cake	6	155	...	...	155	775,000
Aluminium manufactures	1	8	...	2	10	18,000
Ammonia, sulphate	2	65	...	...	65	227,500
Ammoniated fertilizers—see Fertilizers	...	...	...	...	...	...
Ammunition and ordnance	2	88	50	25	163	280,900
Animal charcoal	2	48	...	...	48	258,000
Anthracene, from coal tar	2	16	...	...	16	80,000
Aquariums	1	2	...	2	4	6,000
Architects and builders	10	156	...	...	156	471,500
Architectural woodwork	2	35	...	2	37	66,000
Artificial flowers and feathers	13	44	476	40	560	460,000
,, limbs	8	28	3	1	32	48,000
,, teeth	13	137	37	25	199	357,200
,, stones for pavements	3	22	...	...	22	54,000
Art work, bronze statuary	2	10	...	2	12	60,000
,, decorative	6	7	19	2	28	22,400
Artistic pottery and vases	2	8	1	1	10	8,000
Artists in oil, copying only	6	9	2	...	11	38,000
Artists' materials	8	44	8	12	64	96,000
Asbestos packing	1	2	...	1	3	4,500
Asphalte pavements	2	68	...	...	68	204,000
Assayers and refiners	7	73	...	2	75	490,000
Awnings and tents	19	93	20	9	122	183,000
Axle grease	4	15	...	2	17	66,200
Bags, cloth	6	61	165	2	228	684,000
,, paper	14	112	247	93	452	808,500
Bakers, hand	924	2,012	257	326	2,595	6,648,585
,, steam	10	351	139	155	645	1,369,821
Brewers, weiss beer	9	25	...	1	26	105,000
Bricks, pressed, enamelled, and common	62	2,396	...	636	3,032	2,333,000
,, and tiles, fire	13	276	...	26	302	636,300
Bricklayers and builders	49	567	...	35	602	1,304,750
Bristle dressers	2	13	...	...	13	29,500
Bronzes and mixed metals	14	161	4	27	192	2,302,400
Brooms and whisks	47	264	72	89	425	789,701
Brushes, all kinds	29	293	77	610	980	824,093
Brush blocks	2	21	...	15	36	36,000
Butchers' blocks	2	2	...	1	3	4,500
Butter	3	5	...	2	7	12,300
Butter and oleomargine	2	105	21	11	137	585,000
Buttons, cloth-covered	3	7	25	7	39	33,100
,, bone and ivory	2	108	13	45	166	179,000
,, and studs, pearl shell	13	164	62	63	289	250,600
,, fasteners and novelties	2	4	2	...	6	1,500
Buttonhole strips for shoes	10	72	127	16	215	139,750
Calcium lights and oxygen	1	9	...	...	9	16,200
Canes, whips and handles	7	41	...	18	59	75,700
Canned vegetables and fruits	2	14	140	7	161	241,500
Cardboards and cards, fine	1	69	138	61	268	754,000
Cards, fancy	5	20	15	6	41	42,600
,, playing	1	7	23	1	31	36,000
,, notes, and invitations engraved and printed	5	41	84	12	137	175,000
Carpenters and builders	406	3,734	...	97	3,831	7,129,700
Carpets, Brussels tapestry, ingrain, &c.	237	6,402	3,622	1,019	11,043	20,300,445
,, rag, list, and chain	99	169	10	8	187	235,000
,, wood	1	50	...	5	55	82,500
Carriages and waggons	137	1,929	4	128	2,061	2,956,528
,, children's	7	92	3	43	138	193,100
Carriage materials, wood	9	112	2	15	129	242,000
Cars, railroad	14	2,041	0	80	2,121	6,365,000
Car springs - see Steel springs	...	...	...	...	...	...
Baking powder	7	28	23	7	58	119,300
Barrels, sugar and flour, new	5	257	...	21	278	557,732
Baskets and school bags	31	64	9	11	84	108,950
Bath tubs, wood, and zinc	3	20	2	...	22	39,600
Bedding and mattresses	36	151	154	23	328	802,400
Bed springs	6	33	1	4	38	68,400

PHILADELPHIA.

SUMMARY Tabular Statement of the several Industries, the Number of Persons employed, and the Values produced in the City of Philadelphia for the Year 1882—continued.

Industries.	Number of Establishments.	Men.	Women.	Youths.	Total.	Value of Products.
						Dollars.
Bellows	1	1	...	1	2	2,000
Belting, cotton	1	3	8	...	11	44,000
,, leather	7	59	...	8	67	388,600
Belts, dress and uniform	2	5	7	...	12	21,600
Billiard balls	2	5	...	...	5	6,200
,, tables	3	11	...	1	12	21,600
Bird cages—also see Wire	2	7	...	2	9	13,500
Blacking, for stove polish	6	15	21	9	45	68,800
,, ,, leather	4	39	103	12	154	431,200
Black lead, crucibles	5	67	6	1	74	259,000
Blacksmiths and horseshoers	248	804	...	54	858	1,232,200
Blank books	25	290	145	154	589	1,178,000
Bleachers, straw	4	8	8	1	17	25,500
,, yarns and cloth	15	125	...	20	145	300,000
Blocks, pumps, and shop fittings	8	78	...	6	84	145,300
Blueing and wash powders	10	23	11	6	40	54,000
Boats and barges, not steam	12	94	...	6	100	190,400
Bobbins and spools	11	71	10	33	114	163,550
Bookbinders	41	520	946	145	1,611	1,524,000
,, materials	3	20	...	4	24	43,200
Book printers and publishers	18	789	327	195	1,311	2,259,800
,, publishers, not printers	62	487	121	79	687	3,493,010
Boots and shoes	996	6,490	2,863	663	10,016	12,495,800
Boot and shoe uppers	17	62	59	12	133	149,500
,, ,, cut stock	2	9	11	4	24	43,200
,, ,, findings	7	15	1	4	20	24,300
,, ,, tools, not knives	2	2	2	1	5	6,300
Bottling and mineral waters	37	176	1	24	201	436,000
Boxes, cigars and wooden	14	68	46	39	153	242,700
,, paper	36	248	1,545	126	1,919	1,377,400
,, for packing, wooden	46	382	...	33	455	853,300
Boxwood, blocks—see Engravers' block	...	...	...	...	...	...
Brass founders and finishers	47	764	50	152	966	2,366,070
Brewers, ale and porter	8	301	1	...	302	1,328,000
,, beer	75	1,205	9	6	1,220	5,851,000
Chains—see iron chains	...	...	...	...	...	...
Chemicals, not designated	29	1,196	186	91	1,473	6,241,925
Chemical fertilizers	4	270	...	10	280	1,350,000
China decorators	4	14	4	...	18	9,600
Chronometers	1	2	...	...	2	2,000
Cigars	490	2,321	383	350	3,054	3,164,000
Cigar moulds, of wood	2	14	...	9	23	25,000
Clothing, men's and boys'	562	9,193	10,269	934	20,396	31,220,958
,, women's suits and cloaks	276	211	2,881	70	3,132	3,138,333
,, men's shirts and underware	109	358	3,305	141	3,804	4,010,450
,, women's and children's lace-trimmed articles	39	117	1,048	45	1,210	1,511,000
,, suspenders and web goods	12	26	112	11	149	149,000
,, neckwear and scarfs	9	49	231	15	295	324,500
,, of rubber cloth	3	16	62	6	84	110,000
,, of oiled cloth	2	...	15	...	15	30,000
,, cloth, finishing, woollen	3	24	...	...	24	52,800
Coal tar products	2	16	...	...	16	See anthracene.
Coffee roasters and grinders	11	51	...	5	56	360,700
Coffins, caskets, and undertakers' articles	35	165	24	21	210	370,200
Coinage, United States Mint, all	1	181	129	...	310	48,309,395
Colour works	2	9	...	...	9	38,000
Combs	5	54	2	4	60	74,200
Compressed fuel	1	11	...	...	11	16,500
Confectioners	204	823	738	391	1,952	5,345,650
,, moulds and tools	3	18	...	1	19	25,000
Coopers	60	508	...	42	550	848,530
Copper coinage—see Coinage	...	...	...	...	...	385,811
,, manufactures	7	114	...	9	123	354,700
Copying presses	2	40	...	5	45	67,250
Cordage and twine, flax and hemp	9	427	244	320	991	1,973,000
Corks and manufactures of cork	9	50	22	13	85	101,750
Costumers and manufacturers of costumes	5	8	28	2	38	47,500
Cotton yard goods	81	3,332	5,019	1,172	9,523	13,100,333
,, ,, finishers	7	162	26	49	237	472,500
Cotton coverlets	18	242	196	46	484	697,800

1936 UNITED STATES.

Summary Tabular Statement of the several Industries, the Number of Persons employed, and the Values produced in the City of Philadelphia for the Year 1882—continued.

Industries.	Number of Establishments.	Men.	Women.	Youths.	Total.	Value of Products.
						Dollars.
Cotton towels, separate establishments	4	31	47	3	81	113,400
,, laps and wadding	3	5	2	2	9	9,500
,, thread, cord, and twine	3	12	8	2	22	37,800
,, webbing, binding, &c.	4	46	298	70	414	522,000
,, yarns	15	219	304	260	783	1,245,200
,, waste, for packing	5	32	38	...	70	87,500
Cutlery and steel tools	27	297	5	85	387	524,500
Dental instruments, steel	13	437	33	110	580	956,100
Dentists' materials	4	23	8	9	40	185,000
Designers and card stampers	8	35	2	20	57	71,250
Diamond cutting and setting	9	57	1	3	61	220,400
Disinfectants	2	15	...	...	15	19,000
Distillers and rectifiers	8	63	1	3	67	519,000
Dolls and doll bodies	5	4	15	5	24	30,000
Drug mills	4	50	...	2	52	98,600
Dyes and dye extracts	5	43	1	3	47	225,000
Dye and print works, cloths	6	401	69	85	555	3,889,000
,, works, general	80	1,385	44	110	1,539	3,032,200
Dyers and printers of silk yarns	4	61	20	10	91	255,000
,, of straw braids	2	8	...	...	8	72,000
,, and scourers	49	97	31	6	134	160,800
Earthenware and pottery	4	126	11	43	180	257,900
Electric light machinery and apparatus	16	178	29	22	229	343,750
Electroplaters, gold and silver	5	45	1	13	59	88,500
Electrotypers	5	125	8	45	178	251,600
Elevators and hoisting machinery	9	200	1	7	208	385,000
Embroidery and stamping	8	11	92	4	107	149,800
Enamelling	2	4	2	2	8	15,000
Engravers, bank note	2	37	10	10	57	135,000
,, general	38	202	10	81	293	386,175
,, steel and copper-plate	5	38	8	13	59	120,500
,, of music	2	6	...	2	8	14,000
,, on wood	16	52	5	11	68	85,700
,, blocks, boxwood	3	43	...	8	51	76,500
,, plates, steel, &c.	2	12	...	...	12	23,200
Envelopes and tags	8	58	164	14	236	361,000
Extracts, medicinal—see Pharmaceutical products	...	...	...	...	...	...
,, and fruit flavours	6	27	6	2	35	52,500
,, of beef	1	7	1	2	10	18,000
Feathers, dyed and finished	3	2	5	...	7	18,400
Feather dusters	2	4	2	...	6	9,000
Felting and cement covers	1	2	...	...	2	2,000
Fertilizers, chemical	4	270	...	10	280	1,420,000
,, animal matter	6	74	...	2	76	279,500
Files—see steel	8	381	2	231	614	684,000
Firebrick and tile	13	276	...	26	302	636,300
Fish preserving	1	8	...	...	8	22,000
Fishing tackles and nets	6	25	4	5	34	51,000
Flask, demijohns of glass, covered	4	14	28	51	93	237,000
Florists and seedsmen	65	168	28	28	224	352,300
Flouring mills	24	160	1	21	182	2,430,000
Foundry facings	2	32	...	...	32	160,000
Fruit, jellies, and preserves	5	189	81	57	327	510,100
Fruits, dessicated and evaporated	2	12	1	12	25	85,900
Furniture and chairs	271	4,273	189	491	4,953	7,594,979
Furs, hatters, cut	1	20	...	5	25	50,000
Fur, manufacturers, clothing	29	130	278	32	440	929,986
Galvanizing—see iron	9	460	2	33	495	2,165,000
Gasworks	9	2,611	...	6	2,617	3,691,152
Gas fixtures	10	486	49	51	586	915,500
,, meters—not generators	3	233	7	27	267	534,000
,, tanks and apparatus	2	50	...	...	50	90,000
Gilders and bronzers	5	12	1	5	18	27,000
Gas cutters, decorators, and stainers	20	167	38	48	253	379,500
Glassware, flint and green, hollow	12	1,423	353	1,058	2,834	2,734,900
Glass tubes and blowpipes	3	17	3	9	29	28,100
Gloves, not knit	3	12	40	3	55	66,500
Glue and glue products	4	226	35	62	323	869,000
Gold assays—fiscal year	1	10	...	...	10	490,000
,, coinage—calendar year	1	122	120	...	242	35,849,900
,, chains and rings	2	13	...	7	20	30,000
,, leaf and foil	11	159	208	54	421	693,650

PHILADELPHIA.

Summary Tabular Statement of the several Industries, the Number of Persons employed, and the Values produced in the City of Philadelphia, for the Year 1882—continued.

Industries.	Number of Establishments.	Men.	Women.	Youths.	Total.	Value of Products.
						Dollars.
Gold platers, with electro-platers	3	10	...	2	12	...
,, watch cases	12	469	181	212	862	1,386,644
Grinders and polishers, with cutlery and tools	5	15	...	...	15	...
Grindstones	2	10	...	...	10	30,000
Guns, pistols, and sportsmen's articles	16	44	...	10	54	93,600
Hair cloth	3	15	37	4	56	137,500
,, curled	7	219	95	76	390	1,056,300
,, felting (boiler covering) ...	1	3	...	...	3	4,500
,, human	37	39	262	9	310	342,450
,, jewellery	4	5	7	...	12	15,500
,, pins	1	4	5	5	14	18,206
Hanceswood and iron	3	14	...	...	14	28,000
Hardware (not chiefly of iron) ..	22	171	18	42	231	342,450
Harness and saddlery	143	471	11	59	541	838,050
Hat blocks, moulds, wood and iron	4	9	...	5	14	28,000
,, and bonnet frames	2	11	28	4	43	77,400
Hats, and caps, men's and boys' ...	66	1,007	465	321	1,793	2,261,768
,, and bonnets, straw	12	109	434	28	571	713,750
,, ,, trimmed ...	101	11	268	9	306	298,150
Hat bodies	2	45	...	12	57	102,600
,, leathers and tips	4	29	3	11	43	54,500
Hide dressers, salting and cleaning	6	51	...	3	54	486,600
Hoop skirts	3	1	13	...	14	21,000
Horse clothing (with blankets) ...	2	35	300	10	345	385,000
,, sandals	2	4	3	...	7	9,200
Hosiery and knit goods	167	2,222	8,301	1,993	12,516	14,106,640
,, silk, and silk and rubber	6	37	30	8	75	112,500
House furnishing goods	3	22	14	5	41	63,250
Hydrant cases, wooden	2	6	...	...	6	7,500
Ice cream freezers	3	20	...	2	22	39,600
,, wagons and implements ...	4	29	...	...	29	146,200
India-rubber, reclaiming	1	23	...	3	26	39,000
,, clothing	3	16	62	6	84	110,000
Ink, printing	8	82	...	2	84	345,000
,, writing	9	18	11	20	49	82,500
Insect powder	2	2	...	2	4	2,500
Instrument cases	3	10	...	3	13	16,000
Iron manufactures :—						
Blast furnace	1	50	...	...	50	50,000
Rolling mills, bar, sheet, and plate	9	1,405	...	162	1,567	3,449,300
Cut nails and spikes	2	80	...	40	120	210,000
Horse shoes	1	47	...	5	52	104,000
Sheet, galvanized	6	276	...	4	280	1,280,000
Galvanizing works, other ...	9	460	2	33	495	2,165,000
Founderies classified :—						
Car seats	2	20	...	...	20	40,000
,, wheels	1	200	...	...	200	600,000
Hardware specialities	6	340	34	203	577	916,500
Hollow ware and stoves ...	10	1,157	1	147	1,305	1,985,000
Malleable iron castings	4	730	17	150	897	1,479,600
Ship propellers	1	60	...	...	60	120,000
General building foundries ...	48	1,983	...	67	2,050	3,658,811
Wrought iron, classified :—						
Architectural, railways and fire-escapes, plain and galvanized	19	445	...	10	455	875,000
Axles, in part steel	2	54	...	8	62	118,000
Bolts, nuts, and rivets, punched and wrought	9	521	...	84	605	1,369,600
Carriage bolts, wrought ...	6	299	50	168	517	688,000
Chains and cables	4	166	3	49	218	345,200
Hardware, chiefly wrought ...	26	325	12	70	307	435,000
Nails and spikes ,, ...	2	6	...	5	11	15,000
Pipe, wrought and welded ...	6	1,051	...	139	1,190	2,263,000
Railway, switches, and track material	2	380	...	...	380	575,000
Safes and fireproofs	5	126	...	...	126	264,000
Scales and balances	7	143	1	9	153	280,000
Screws for wood and iron ...	4	63	17	33	113	138,000
Ships and ship-building	4	2,440	...	173	2,613	5,620,000
Ship repairs, iron	7	123	...	7	130	253,000
Sheet iron, stamped wares ...	5	120	42	35	197	320,000

1938   UNITED STATES.

SUMMARY Tabular Statement of the several Industries, the Number of Persons employed, and the Value produced in the City of Philadelphia, for the Year 1882—continued.

Industries.	Number of Establishments.	Men.	Women.	Youths.	Total.	Value of Products.
Wrought iron classified—continued						Dollars.
Shovels and hods, stamped	4	183	...	13	196	315,000
Steam heating apparatus	6	131	...	...	131	275,000
Stoves, heaters and ranges	123	875	...	53	928	1,565,000
Wire, drawn	1	25	...	2	27	85,000
,, manufacturers	16	132	6	71	209	300,000
Iron and machinery:—						
Steam engines and boilers	48	920	...	55	975	1,742,500
Locomotives	5	3,793	...	16	3,809	7,506,200
Book makers' machinery	2	49	...	4	53	109,500
Brewers' and maltsters' machinery	2	29	...	2	31	62,000
Brick makers' machinery	5	78	...	4	82	143,500
Cigar ,, ,, iron	2	17	...	4	21	20,000
Coining and mint machinery	2	85	...	14	99	250,000
Confectioners' machinery	2	23	...	1	24	36,000
Die cutters' machinery	1	10	...	5	15	17,500
Elevators and hoisting machinery	9	200	1	7	208	385,000
File making machinery	1	15	...	...	15	17,500
Flouring mill ,,	5	119	...	10	129	225,000
Gas engines	2	158	...	...	158	287,000
,, generating machinery and tanks	8	36	...	...	36	84,000
Hydraulic and pneumatic machinery	3	93	...	...	93	180,000
Iron working machine tools	10	1,203	...	86	1,289	2,255,750
Jewellers and gold working machinery	2	21	...	6	27	45,000
Leather dressing machinery	1	9	...	...	9	15,000
Mining and ore crushing machinery	3	49	...	6	55	114,000
Paper making machinery	3	75	...	13	88	175,100
Printers' presses and machinery	8	109	1	14	124	222,000
Screw making machinery	1	17	...	...	17	31,450
Sewing machines	11	383	7	110	500	867,600
Shafting, exclusively	3	122	...	2	124	248,000
Sugar making machinery	2	24	...	2	26	48,000
Textile manufacturing machinery	40	1,556	19	155	1,730	3,059,250
Wood working machinery	7	383	...	28	411	893,250
Machinery, general, not specified	36	1,021	...	110	1,131	1,973,000
Machinist	28	114	...	14	128	231,250
Ivory and bone turners	6	196	6	77	279	405,300
,, turned, vegetable	1	15	...	...	15	15,000
Japanners	2	19	4	5	28	50,400
Jewellery	79	647	79	123	849	1,458,915
,, and fancy cases	13	78	54	25	157	282,600
Kindling wood	18	90	...	37	127	190,500
Knitting machines	12	113	9	18	140	246,000
Lace goods, curtains, &c.	87	57	617	31	705	844,000
Ladders and house articles	6	14	...	2	16	28,200
Lamps, lanterns, and reflectors	17	133	25	19	177	288,590
Lamp shade, paper, and other	2	8	10	16	34	40,800
Lampblack	4	67	2	7	76	190,800
Lard refiners	6	99	20	26	145	1,805,000
Lasts and last patterns	10	56	...	8	64	80,400
Laundries for manufacturers	3	7	81	...	88	146,000
Lead, pipe, bar, and refining	5	41	...	...	41	945,000
Leather, hides, cleaned, &c.	6	51	...	3	54	486,000
,, curriers	16	131	3	11	145	939,000
,, sole and belting	3	51	...	2	53	209,000
,, morocco	46	1,919	134	499	2,552	1,062,184
,, kid, calf, and glove kid	19	384	20	37	441	1,380,000
,, sheep and fancy	9	109	4	21	134	370,500
,, for whips and ball covers	1	7	...	...	7	10,500
Lightning rods, iron and metal	2	44	...	20	64	351,200
Lights and beacons	2	9	...	...	9	36,000
Lime	3	15	...	...	15	45,000
Lithographers	29	449	96	149	694	954,200
Locks, not of iron	12	134	6	52	192	317,250
Locksmiths, key and bell fitters	28	42	...	8	50	65,000
Looms, iron	8	250	...	...	250	400,000
,, wood and shuttles	6	66	...	4	70	108,000
Maccaroni and farina	2	12	1	2	15	90,000
Machine card clothing	2	25	...	3	28	112,000

PHILADELPHIA.

Summary Tabular Statement of the several Industries, the Number of Persons employed, and the Values produced in the City of Philadelphia, for the Year 1882—continued.

Industries.	Number of Establishments.	Men.	Women.	Youths.	Total.	Value of Products.
						Dollars.
Malt houses	15	193	...	...	193	1,640,750
Mantles, slate	3	49	...	10	59	123,900
Map publishers	6	16	18	23	57	85,500
Marble manufacturers	90	1,198	...	89	1,287	3,311,500
Masonic marks and jewels	2	6	...	2	8	12,000
Masts and spars	4	10	...	2	12	36,000
Matches	7	29	90	25	144	286,200
Mathematical and scientific instruments	10	71	3	23	97	174,700
Mats, cocoa	1	26	5	19	50	85,000
,, wood and rubber	1	6	...	1	7	10,500
Meats cured and packed	67	508	82	67	657	5,563,500
Medicines, proprietary	5	123	105	15	243	1,801,880
Medicine chests	1	7	3	1	11	19,800
Metal foil, lead and tin	1	10	18	5	33	49,500
Metal ware, sheet	6	25	...	10	35	91,000
,, spinners	6	26	...	7	33	57,000
,, solder and soft	4	60	...	12	72	540,000
Microscopes	2	13	...	3	16	28,400
Military and society goods	15	62	85	14	161	227,600
Millstones, burr	2	14	...	...	14	35,000
Mincemeats and fruits	2	38	23	...	61	152,500
Mineral waters	17	138	...	17	155	266,700
,, and soda water apparatus	4	70	...	...	70	175,000
Mirrors and gilt frames	63	598	21	133	752	1,518,590
Models and patterns	23	138	...	16	154	193,000
Music printers and publishers	5	48	20	9	77	154,000
,, typographers	2	10	2	12	24	43,200
Musical instruments, church organs	4	15	...	3	18	35,000
Musical instruments, pianos	5	217	...	15	232	580,000
,, ,, brass and other	31	166	4	36	206	238,660
Needles for sewing and knitting machines	4	10	25	1	36	52,850
Nickel coinage—with coinage	...	...	...	...	...	573,830
,, platers	8	55	...	15	70	138,100
Novelties, house articles	2	3	15	3	21	37,800
Oil cloths	3	426	5	40	471	1,497,850
,, clothing, watermen's	2	12	7	...	19	57,000
Oliene	2	60	15	3	78	390,000
Oil, lard, refined	2	10	...	...	10	75,000
,, animal, lubricating	6	44	...	17	61	403,100
,, ,, refined	5	139	5	6	150	682,000
,, mineral, illuminating	12	2,536	...	611	3,147	9,379,000
,, ,, lubricating	5	24	7	...	31	76,100
,, vegetable, linseed	4	61	...	1	62	309,800
,, ,, rosin	1	9	...	...	9	45,000
Optical goods	18	158	41	30	229	376,900
Paints and varnishes	28	464	11	49	524	3,197,900
Painters, house, sign, and ornamental	283	2,081	...	58	2,139	3,599,930
Paper mills, books, news, and roofing paper	9	467	271	13	751	2,246,000
,, pulp	1	185	...	2	187	748,000
,, hangings, manufacturers'	5	183	3	186	372	681,000
,, hangers, employers only	28	202	20	25	247	446,900
,, boards, covered, for binders, and boxmakers	7	122	3	2	127	445,000
,, boxes, (see boxes)	36	248	1,545	126	1,919	1,877,400
,, cop tubes	2	6	...	2	8	12,000
,, envelopes and stationery	4	28	49	17	94	150,400
Papiermache	1	9	...	6	15	27,000
Parafine, oil and wax	2	17	...	...	17	85,000
Paste for paper boxes, &c.	4	9	...	1	10	16,200
Pens, gold	2	5	...	2	7	8,000
,, steel	2	25	45	10	80	130,000
Perfumery and pomades	20	88	98	40	226	491,300
Pharmaceutical preparations	133	567	168	122	857	2,433,480
Phospor, bronze—see Bronze	...	...	...	...	...	...
Photo-engravers	4	37	...	10	47	87,600
Photographers	50	120	46	22	188	249,710
Photographic publishers	1	8	2	1	11	23,400
Photographers' materials	6	26	14	5	45	76,800
Pickles and sauces	9	43	50	19	112	254,300
Pipes, smoking, wood and other	8	189	28	62	279	365,900

SUMMARY Tabular Statement of the several Industries, the Number of Persons employed, and the Values produced in the City of Philadelphia, for the Year 1882—continued.

Industries.	Number of Establishments.	Men.	Women.	Youths.	Total.	Value of Products.
						Dollars.
Planes, carpenters'	2	6	...	...	6	4,800
Plastering, casks, and stucco works	24	148	21	6	175	329,400
Plate printers	7	51	12	14	77	138,600
Plumbers and gasfitters	236	862	6	180	1,048	1,709,450
,, fittings, and supplies	2	112	...	10	122	309,600
Pocket books and leather bags	12	391	172	174	737	922,000
,, and other flasks	2	4	2	1	7	7,000
Porcelain knobs	2	5	...	...	5	5,600
Pottery and stoneware	7	122	...	12	134	237,314
Printers, job	241	1,859	370	720	2,949	3,783,900
,, and publishers of newspapers and serials	91	1,792	102	177	2,071	6,076,600
Publishers of serials, not printers	23	124	5	5	134	350,000
Printers' frames, rollers, furnishings, &c.	8	43	...	5	48	86,400
Provisions, sausage and prepared meats	13	45	9	11	65	276,800
Pumps, wooden	5	22	1	3	26	45,800
Quilts and coverlets, sewed or handworked	3	19	15	6	40	80,800
Railroad supplies, oils, &c.	2	20	...	8	28	50,400
Rectifiers and refiners of spirits	24	84	2	3	89	824,000
Reeds, heddles, and loom fittings	4	31	3	3	37	59,200
Refrigerators	10	131	6	6	143	214,500
Riggers, for hoisting	3	26	...	...	26	54,600
Roofers, tin, felt, slate, &c.	87	422	4	22	448	707,920
Rubber stamps	5	19	5	8	32	57,600
Sails and ships' rigging	16	145	...	19	164	344,000
Sand and emery paper	2	130	20	39	189	398,000
Sash, doors, and blinds	28	714	...	45	759	1,524,500
Sawmills, mahogany, and cabinet woods	4	82	...	...	82	433,000
Saw and planing mills	23	523	...	11	534	1,675,550
Seed, packing and implements	7	105	83	17	205	358,000
Sewing machines	11	383	7	110	500	867,600
,, machine, repairs	8	18	2	4	24	20,000
Shipbuilders, iron	4	2,440	...	173	2,613	5,620,000
,, wood, (not boats)	3	105	...	...	105	415,000
Ship machinery and repairs, iron	7	123	...	7	130	253,400
Shot, lead	2	10	...	...	10	80,000
Show cards	11	75	11	30	116	162,000
,, cases	8	37	1	5	43	73,100
Signs, metal and glass	7	40	4	5	49	84,600
Signal rockets	1	3	...	...	3	3,400
Silk, tram, organzine, and spun	5	63	234	27	324	710,000
,, machine twist	1	6	50	...	56	140,000
,, spun silks, and noils yarn	4	30	25	30	85	170,000
,, curtains and turcomans	10	171	72	39	282	524,000
,, and mixed upholstery goods	14	587	283	120	990	1,682,000
,, ribbons (in part)	1	44	120	10	174	261,000
,, dress goods (in part)	1	34	146	3	183	329,400
,, and mixed trimmings, fringes, &c.	30	785	2,663	340	3,778	4,166,800
,, gimps	2	34	35	29	93	111,600
,, knit goods	5	38	30	8	76	114,000
,, dyers' yarns, all silk	81	1,900	3,679	614	6,193	8,608,270
Silver ware, solid	10	106	1	24	131	247,700
,, plated ware	33	253	39	54	346	654,600
,, coinage, calendar year 1882 (see coinage)	1	...	...	...	...	11,493,035
Slate mantles	5	82	...	15	97	194,000
Soap, common and candles	31	183	38	32	253	1,182,600
,, perfumed	7	248	64	60	372	1,488,000
Soapstone basins	2	7	...	1	8	14,800
Spices, ground and prepared	10	129	118	9	256	558,200
Sportsmen's goods	5	45	101	12	158	262,400
Starch and starch polish	2	6	12	2	20	28,000
Stationery, not specified	12	17	32	4	53	129,300
Steam packing, waste and felt	8	58	5	9	72	71,700
Steel ingots, rolled, plate, and sheet	6	640	...	...	640	1,659,200
,, springs, car and carriage	11	302	...	14	316	638,000
,, saws	7	499	...	182	681	1,200,120
,, files	18	378	2	215	595	684,000
,, and iron tools	20	453	9	269	731	1,034,800

PHILADELPHIA.

Summary Tabular Statement of the several Industries, the Number of Persons employed, and the Values produced in the City of Philadelphia for the Year 1882—continued.

Industries.	Number of Establishments.	Men.	Women.	Youths.	Total.	Value of Products.
						Dollars.
Steel cutlery and steel tools	27	297	5	85	387	524,500
" wire, tempered for card clothing	1	10	...	...	10	20,000
" forks	2	128	...	17	145	253,750
" cutting, dyes and brands	5	15	...	5	20	29,000
" grate bars	1	10	...	...	10	18,000
Stencils and stamps	10	30	...	7	37	53,650
Stone cutters and stone masonry	35	550	...	19	569	1,332,500
" " tools	3	5	...	1	6	7,200
Stoves and ranges	123	875	...	53	928	1,565,000
Straw goods	12	109	434	28	571	713,750
Sugar refiners	11	1,777	...	12	1,789	27,950,000
Surgical appliances	6	33	10	5	48	76,800
" instruments, steel	17	120	18	23	161	233,450
Suspenders, with clothing	12	26	112	11	149	155,000
Swords, plating and mounting	3	5	...	2	7	12,600
Tags, shipping	6	25	9	16	50	79,500
Tallow and fat melters	3	48	...	1	49	441,000
Tanks and vats, wooden	4	75	...	2	77	169,400
Taxidermists	5	10	...	...	10	9,000
Terra cotta ware and pipe	4	68	...	1	69	207,000
Tin cans	2	47	...	16	63	120,000
" copper, and sheet iron ware	215	951	84	161	1,196	1,821,600
Tobacco manufactures, packing	6	50	40	7	97	485,000
" manufacturers, snuff	4	65	39	37	141	282,000
" " cigars	490	2,321	383	350	3,054	3,164,000
Toys	15	104	77	51	232	237,000
Trunks and valises	26	171	7	35	213	423,000
Trusses	9	81	71	16	168	264,100
Typefounders	4	254	2	159	415	578,645
Types, wood	1	3	...	...	3	3,300
Umbrellas and parasols	36	274	1,201	135	1,610	2,955,450
Umbrella frames, steel and iron	3	81	92	85	258	438,000
" furniture, handles, tips, &c.	3	152	73	115	340	459,000
Undertakers' goods	25	68	9	6	83	132,000
Upholsterers	113	256	131	51	438	754,900
Varnish	8	51	...	1	52	262,000
Velocipedes and bicycles	2	15	...	2	17	25,400
Ventilators, flue and pipe	3	9	...	2	11	13,000
Vinegar	9	30	1	1	32	96,000
Wagon makers	3	232	...	...	232	283,000
Washing and wringing machines	3	8	...	1	9	13,500
Watch cases, silver	1	88	70	60	218	357,800
" makers, dials, and cases	6	16	3	6	25	32,000
" and jewellery, repairs	88	154	4	17	175	226,500
Waterproof, fluid	1	2	5	1	8	12,000
Waxwork, flowers, fruits, &c.	4	2	10	2	14	34,000
Webbing, elastic, mixed	3	40	9	28	77	111,650
Wharf and dock builders	4	196	...	...	196	838,000
Wheelwrights	12	58	...	3	61	104,250
Whips and canes	13	17	4	12	33	45,100
White and red lead	4	265	2	5	272	1,360,000
Whiting and Paris white	6	67	...	1	68	476,000
Window shades and furnishings	35	184	31	46	261	480,650
Wirework, covered and fancy	6	14	1	20	35	54,900
Wood and willow ware	18	138	...	9	147	235,500
" turners and carvers	24	127	...	41	168	230,300
Wool pulling, salting, and cleaning	6	43	...	1	44	124,500
" shoddy	8	56	3	4	63	292,400
Woollen yarns	75	952	444	690	2,086	4,325,400
" flannels	2	125	200	75	400	720,000
" blankets	12	1,044	912	369	2,325	5,245,500
" coatings	3	303	212	113	628	1,411,600
" cashmeres, jeans, and doeskins	11	692	1,013	264	1,969	3,634,400
" shawls	12	138	120	290	287	585,200
" felted goods	2	17	...	2	19	38,000
" Germantown yarns	5	45	59	23	127	304,980
Wool and worsted goods	10	527	484	161	1,172	2,463,410
Worsted yarns	11	435	1,218	610	2,263	4,541,600
" yarns, in other mills	12	...	...	...	...	4,300,000
" zeypher and Shetland yarn	2	30	90	20	140	350,000
" braid and cord	2	22	108	35	165	315,000

SUMMARY Tabular Statement of the several Industries, the Number of Persons employed, and the Values produced in the City of Philadelphia, for the Year 1882—continued.

Industries.	Number of Establishments.	Men.	Women.	Youths.	Total.	Value of Products.
						Dollars.
Worsted coatings and vest goods...	25	2,183	2,196	572	5,104	10,712,100
,, plush	2	60	50	15	125	312,500
,, and silk umbrella cloths...	3	39	105	24	168	332,000
Zinc casting sheets—part of galvanizers...	1	6	...	...	6	25,000
,, retorts—part of crucibles ...	1	3	...	...	3	5,000
United States Mint	1	181	129	...	310	3,309,395
Totals	12,063	147,137	67,050	28,296	242,483	481,226,309

COMPARISON of the Published Returns by the United States Census of 1880 for the Larger Cities of the Union.

	Establishments.	Number.	Men.	Women.	Youths.	Total.	Wages.	Product.	Ratio.
							Dollars.	Dollars.	Dollars.
Baltimore		3,683	34,086	18,137	4,115	56,338	15,117,489	78,417,303	1,392
Boston		3,665	39,810	18,150	1,253	59,213	24,924,009	130,531,993	2,204
Brooklyn		5,201	37,105	7,020	3,462	47,587	22,487,457	177,223,142	3,724
Buffalo		1,183	15,033	1,795	1,193	18,021	7,442,109	42,937,701	2,382
Chicago		3,519	62,431	12,185	4,789	79,414	34,653,462	249,022,948	3,261
Cincinnati		3,276	38,993	10,483	5,041	54,517	19,553,629	105,259,105	1,930
Cleveland		1,055	18,018	2,286	1,420	21,724	8,502,935	48,604,050	2,237
Detroit		919	12,477	2,430	1,203	16,110	6,306,460	30,181,416	1,873
Jersey City		534	7,962	2,426	750	11,138	4,662,655	60,473,905	5,429
Louisville		1,108	13,480	2,829	1,139	17,448	5,835,445	35,423,203	2,030
Milwaukee		844	16,015	3,922	949	20,886	6,446,105	43,473,812	2,081
Newark		1,316	22,151	5,246	2,649	30,046	13,171,339	69,252,705	2,304
New Orleans		915	7,666	1,286	552	9,504	3,717,557	18,808,096	1,978
New York		11,339	146,179	71,745	9,387	227,352	97,030,021	472,926,037	2,080
Philadelphia		11,942	147,137	67,050	28,296	242,483	83,965,518	481,226,309	1,992
Pittsburgh		1,112	32,011	1,681	3,238	36,930	17,168,989	75,915,933	2,055
Providence		1,205	16,050	5,125	1,716	22,891	9,464,110	42,597,512	1,860
St. Louis		2,924	33,980	4,761	3,084	41,825	17,743,532	114,333,375	2,733
San Francisco		2,971	23,662	3,588	1,192	28,442	14,928,534	77,824,299	2,377
Washington		971	5,496	1,389	261	7,146	3,924,612	11,882,316	1,662
Total		59,735	729,742	243,547	57,689	1,049,015	417,506,067	2,266,376,215	2,163

Iron and Steel.

In the Special Report from this Consulate on the production of pig-iron and Bessemer steel in Pennsylvania for the year 1882 (reports from Her Majesty's Consuls for 1882, Part II., page 1528), the history of this industry was carefully traced to its highest activity in the early part of that year, and the causes given for its subsequent decline. Since the publication of that report the decline has been intensified; prices receded slowly and uniformly in the finished products and raw material, but not to an alarming extent. The productions of iron and steel rails in 1883 fell off greatly from that of the previous year. Wages were reduced and shorter periods engaged in labour, but there was no alarming discharge of the working men.

The following tables will show the decline in the prices of iron and steel in the year 1883 and the depressed condition of the trade. In the latter part of the year 1883 the decline was partially arrested, but in the early months of the present year the demand for the product was still more sluggish, and the indications are that the productions in the ensuing months will fall below those of last year.

Wages were not greatly reduced, and the reductions it became necessary to make were acceded to with but slight temporary resistance; nor were a great number of working men discharged because of the depressed trade. The past year was not a year of panic, general disaster, or serious decline in consumption; but it was one of depression.

The total product of pig-iron in the United States for 1883 was 5,146,972 tons of 2,000 lbs. each, against 5,178,122 tons in 1882. The total production of the State of Pennsylvania was 2,638,891 tons in 1883, while in 1882 it was 2,449,256. The number of furnaces in the United States, January 1st, 1884, was 683, of which 271 were in Pennsylvania. Of these 683 furnaces 307 were in blast on that date, of which 142 were in Pennsylvania. On January 1st, 1883, there were 417 furnaces in blast in the country, of which 185 were in Pennsylvania. On July 1st, 1883, there were 334 furnaces in the entire country in blast, of which 151 were in Pennsylvania. Since January 1st, 1884, a good many additional furnaces have gone out of blast, and the market in the first three months of the present year was very dull, and anything in the way of an increased trade appeared more distant than ever. Sales, though not large, have been made at prices below the demand at the close of the year. The standard brands have about held up, but the few changes made tended to still lower figures. This early depression of the present year, it is predicted by practical men in the trade, will continue through the summer months. While, however, at the present writing the demand for steel rails, and for iron and steel for cars and locomotives, for bridges and other structural purposes is less than it was six months or a year ago; that for use in minor and primary stages of manufactures will be increased, such manufactures being extended by the increase of population. Even lower prices for cereals cannot destroy them or arrest their extension. The requirements of the home market will annually furnish a vast amount of business to iron or steel establishments of the country, and the trade cannot entirely collapse. The 120,000 miles of railroad already built must alone require a large number of rails. It is claimed that at least 700,000 tons of rails were used in the United States in 1882 and about 650,000 tons in 1883, for renewals, for new second tracks, and for sidings of old roads. The continual consumption of iron and steel for cars and locomotive will be required to maintain the roads in a fair state of equipment, and the bridges and buildings throughout the country will demand a steady supply from some source. Thus the iron and steel establishments of the country will hold a steady though not extensive trade.

The following is a comparative scale of the ruling rates of wages:—

| | Per Day. ||
	1882.	1883.
	Dol. c.	Dol. c.
Puddlers	3 59	3 00
Puddlers' helpers	2 23	1 65
Heaters	5 01	2 55
Heaters' helpers	1 74	1 30
Rollers	7 24	4 85
Roughers	3 15	2 70
Catchers	3 36	2 25
Hookers	1 50	1 25
Shearmen	1 74	1 30
Straighteners	1 74	1 25
Engineers	2 66	2 40
Millwrights	2 92	2 50
Blacksmiths	2 67	3 15
Machinists	2 50	2 50
Carpenters	2 16	2 00
Nailers	8 00	..
Feeders	2 00	..
Firemen	1 74	1 25
Labourers	1 31	1 25
Boys	0 79	0 79

The wages of working men in iron and steel works for the years 1882 and 1883 were:—

| | Per ton of 2,240 Lbs. ||
	1882.	1883.
	Cents.	Cents.
Heater	63½	63½
Helper	31¾	31¾
Roller	35½	35½
Rougher	21	21
Catcher	16½	16½
Saw boy	8	8
Roller boy	8	8
Straigtener	16½	16½
Hook up	9	12
Buggy man	16½	16½
Stoker	16½	16½
Screw boy	8	8

As bearing upon the prices of pig-iron in the future, attention is called to a recent contract made by a manufacturing firm in the State of Alabama, by which they are to deliver a large quantity of pig iron on the cars for 12 dol. 50 c. This contract is not due to a temporary over-production, but is the result of a mature calculation and is to stand for seven years, with a daily delivery of 70 tons. The estimates of another manufacture of Alabama show the cost of producing this iron to be not quite 10 dol. per ton, showing that the contract is fairly profitable. These manufactures, it is true, are favourably situated as to ore, coal, and lime, and they possess the newest methods of production. In Virginia, pig-iron is produced for 11 dol. 55 c. per ton. The "labour" in these calculations, which the tariff protects at the rate of 6 dol. 72 c. per ton, is paid 1 dol. 50 c. per ton, while another item of costs, "incidentals," is placed at 1 dol. per ton.

Considering the fact that the price of pig-iron on ship board in Scotland is about 10 dol. 50 c. per ton, and for English iron a little more than 9 dol., these are low rates; but when the proposed duty of 6 dol. (instead of 6 dol. 72 c., the present duty) is added, and when cost of transportation, insurance, &c., is included, it is apparent that the manufacturers of pig-iron in the United States have nothing to fear from foreign competition. These figures show what enormous profits have been wrung from the American consumer by operation of a prohibitive duty.

PHILADELPHIA.

The following Table shows the Prices of Iron and Steel for the Years 1882 and 1883, the ton being 2,240 lbs., except for bar iron and nails which are quoted by the pound and keg respectively:—

Months.	Old T-Rails at Philadelphia. 1882.	1883.	New Iron Rails at Mills in Pennsylvania. 1882.	1883.	Steel Rails at Mills in Pennsylvania. 1882.	1883.	Foreign Bessemer Pig Iron at Philadelphia. 1882.	1883.	No. 1 Anthracite Foundry Pig Iron at Philadelphia. 1882.	1883.	Gray Forge Pig Iron at Philadelphia. 1882.	1883.	Common Bar Iron at Pittsburgh, per pound. 1882.	1883.	Nails (gross price) at Pittsburgh, per keg. 1882.	1883.	Gray Forge Pig Iron, all Lake Ore, at Pittsburgh. 1882.	1883.	Gray Forge Pig Iron, Lake Ore mixed, at Pittsburgh. 1882.	1883.
	Dol. c.	Dol. c.	Dol. c.		Dol. c.	Dol. c.	Dol. c.		Dol. c.	Dol. c.	Dol. c.	Dol. c.	Cents.	Cents.	Dol. c.	Dol. c.	Dol. c.		Dol. c.	Dol. c.
January	30 00	22 50	48 50		58 00	40 00	27 50		26 00	25 00	24 00	21 00	2·5	2·2	3 35	3 40	28 00		25 00	21 00
February	30 50	23 00	48 50		55 00	39 50	25 75		26 00	24 50	24 00	20 50	2·5	2·0	3 40	3 40	27 50	No sales.	26 00	20 50
August	26 50	23 50	45 00	No sales.	47 00	38 00	24 50	No sales.	25 50	22 00	21 50	19 00	2·5	2·0	3 60	3 00	...		24 00	18 50
September	27 00	23 50	...		45 00	37 50	24 25		26 00	22 00	22 00	18 75	2·5	2·0	3 40	2 85	...		23 00	18 50
November	27 25	23 00	...		42 00	35 00	23 25		26 00	21 00	21 75	18 50	2·2	1·8	3 40	2 60	24 00		21 75	18 50
December	27 00	22 00	...		39 00	34 00	22 25		25 75	21 00	21 75	18 00	2·2	1·8	3 40	2 50	23 00		21 50	18 00

The Prices for the first four Months of the Year 1884 were—

Months.	Old T-Rails at Philadelphia.	New Iron Rails at Mills in Pennsylvania.	Steel Rails at Mills in Pennsylvania.	Foreign Bessemer Pig Iron at Philadelphia.	No. 1 Anthracite Foundry Pig Iron at Philadelphia.	Gray Forge. Pig Iron at Philadelphia.	Common Bar Iron at Pittsburgh, per pound.	Nails (gross price) at Pittsburgh, per keg.	Gray Forge Pig Iron, all Lake Ore, at Pittsburgh.	Gray Forge Pig Iron, Lake Ore mixed, at Pittsburgh.
	Dol. c.		Dol. c.		Dol. c.	Dol. c.	Cent.	Dol. c.		Dol. c.
January	...	No sales.	34 00	No sales.	20 50	18 25	1·8	2 40	No sales.	18 00
February	...		34 00		20 50	18 00	1·8	2 60		18 00
March	...		34 00		20 50	18 00	1·8	2 50		17 75
April	...		34 00		20 00	18 00	1·8	2 35		17 50

UNITED STATES.

The complete official returns of the United States census of the blast furnaces, rolling mills, steel works, forges, and bloomeries for the year 1880 in the whole United States, are now before the public, and following summary shows the result:—

United States.	Number of Establishments.	Amount of Capital (real and personal) Invested.	Value of all Materials Used.	Value of all Products Made.	Weight of all Products.	Total hands Employed.	Total Amount Paid in Wages.
		Dol.	Dol.	Dol.	Tons.	Number.	Dol.
Total in 1880	1,005	230,971,884	191,271,150	296,557,685	7,265,140	140,978	55,476,785
,, 1870	808	121,772,074	135,526,132	207,208,696	3,655,215	77,558	40,514,981
Percentage of increase in 1880	24·38	89·68	41·13	43·12	98·76	81·78	36·93

The establishments above enumerated were classed as follows:—

	1870.	1880.
Blast furnace establishments	386	490
Rolling mill establishments	310	324
Steel works	30	73
Forges and bloomeries	82	118
Total	808	1,005

The size and capacity of the establishments greatly increased in 1880 over 1870. A complete comparison of the capacity of all the works in the two periods cannot be given, as the capacity of blast furnaces only was given in 1870. The daily capacity of the blast furnaces in 1870 was 8,357 tons of pig iron, and in 1880 it was 19,248 tons, and increase of 130·32 per cent. The number of blast furnaces in 1870 was 574, and in 1880 it was 681, an increase of 18·64 per cent.

The following exhibit shows the number and capacity of the blast furnaces, rolling mills, &c., at the close of the year 1880 in the United States:—

Blast furnace establishments	490
Completed blast furnaces	681
Rolling mill establishments	324
Puddling furnaces, each double furnace counting as two furnaces	4,319
Rotary puddling furnaces (sellers)	1
Dank's puddling furnaces	19
Hammers in iron rolling mills	239
Heating furnaces	2,105
Trains of rolls in iron rolling mills	1,206
Nail machines	3,775
Steel works	73
Bessemer steel converters	24
Open-hearth steel furnaces	37
Pot-holes for crucible	2,691
Trains of roll in steel works	136
Hammers in steel works	219
Forges and bloomeries	118
Forge and bloomery fires	495
Siemen's rotary	1
Hammers in forges and bloomeries	141

PHILADELPHIA.

Daily capacity of blast furnaces			19,248 tons.
,, ,, iron rolling mills			16,430 ,,
,, ,, Bessemer steel converters			4,467 ,,
,, ,, open-hearth steel furnaces			827 ,,
,, ,, open-hearth and Bessemer steel rolling mills			5,223 ,,
,, ,, crucible steel works			445 ,,
,, ,, forges and bloomeries			520 ,,

The capital invested in 1880 in the iron and steel industries of the United States was 230,971,884 dol., while in the year 1870 it was 121,772,074 dol., showing an increase of 109,199,810 dol., or 89·68 per cent.

Of the whole amount invested:—

	Per Cent.
Pennsylvania's share was	46
Ohio	11
New York	9
Missouri	4
New Jersey	4
No other State showing a greater investment than	3

The manufacture of iron and steel has always been a favourite pursuit among the Americans, and primarily in every colony, and subsequently in every State and territory their manufacture has been undertaken wherever the necessary raw materials have been found to exist. The products increased from year to year as population increased, and, with the exception of agriculture, no American industry has been more widely diffused throughout the American Union, or enlisted the energies and progressive spirit of the people.

The total production of the iron and steel works of the United States in 1880 was 7,256,140 tons, while in 1870 it was 3,655,215 tons, showing an increase of 3,609,925 tons, or 98·76 per cent. The phrase "total production" includes the products of all the various processes or operations, although in ascertaining most of these products there is a necessary duplication of the tonnage of raw, or comparatively raw, materials already stated. Thus, rolled iron is mainly produced from pig iron. As the method of stating the production of 1880 is the same that was observed in 1870, a comparison of the results of both periods can be made:—

Iron and Steel Products.	Census Year, 1870.	Census Year, 1880.	Percentage of increase in 1880.	Percentage of decrease in 1880.
	Tons.	Tons.	Tons.	Tons.
Pig iron and castings from furnace	2,052,821	3,781,021	84	..
All products of iron rolling mills	1,441,829	2,353,248	63	..
Bessemer steel finished products	19,403	889,896	4,486	..
Open-hearth steel finished products	..	93,143	..	..
Crucible steel finished products	28,069	70,319	151	..
Blister and other steel	2,285	4,956	117	..
Products of forges and bloomeries	110,808	72,557	..	35
Total	3,655,215	7,265,140	98·76	..

Of the pig iron produced in the year 1880, there were of charcoal and cold blast, 79,613 tons; with charcoal and hot blast, 355,105 tons. The furnace castings amounted to only 4,229 tons; total production 3,781,021 tons, of which 12,875 tons were spiegeleison.

Comparative statement of iron rolling mill products in 1870 and 1880:—

	1870.	1880.
	Tons.	Tons.
Bar iron	488,834	661,211
Rod „	26,087	145,626
Nail plate converted into cut nails	230,225	252,830
Boiler plate iron	} 54,477	{ 89,560
All other plate iron		94,749
Sheet iron	74,753	94,992
Iron rails	531,605	466,917
Skelp iron	2,217	128,321
Muck bar made for sale to other works	33,631	64,469
Structural iron	..	96,810
Rolled iron axles	..	2,630
Hoop iron	..	96,843
Fish-plates and miscellaneous forms of rolled iron	..	48,345
Railroad spikes, horse-shoes, &c., made by rolling mills from rolled iron not included above	..	82,358
Hammered axles	..	21,884
Forgings	..	3,703
Total	1,441,829	2,353,248

Table showing the number of hands employed, hours of labour required, and wages paid in the iron and steel industries of the United States in 1880, compared as far as possible with 1870:—

United States.	Males above 16 Years.	Males below 16 Years.	Females above 15 Years.	Females below 15 Years.	Total Hands Employed.	Average Number of Hours of Labour per Week.	Average Day's Wages for a Skilled Mechanic.	Average Day's Wages of an Ordinary Labourer.	Total Amount Paid in Wages.
							Dol. c.	Dol. c.	Dollars.
Grand total in 1880	133,203	7,709	45	21	140,978	65	2 59	1 24	55,476,785
Grand total in 1870	75,037	2,436	82	...	77,555	...	...	...	40,514,981
Percentage of increase in 1880	77·52	216·46	...	...	81·78	...	...	...	36·93
Percentage of decrease in 1880	...	...	45·12	...	...	...	...	...	...

It should be explained that the figures of "hands employed" and "wages paid" refer to the labour directly employed at the various iron and steel works of the country, and in the mining and other operations conducted in direct connection with these works. They do not include the labour employed in independent and often remote mining operations in the iron and steel industries with ore and coal and other raw materials. Nor do they include any considerable part of the labour employed in the transportation of raw materials from the sources of production to the places of consumption. If the "hands employed" and "wages paid" in these various contributory channels were added to the figures given in the tables, the total number of persons directly supported by the iron and steel industries in 1880, and the total amount of wages paid to them, would be largely increased, and probably doubled.

The decline in prices, as shown by these tables, is very great, equalled only in the decline experienced in years of panic. Steel rails, pig iron, bar iron, and nails fell close to the prices of 1878, which was the worst of the panic years.

The shrinkage in the prices of leading iron and steel products during 1883 was:—No. 1 anthracite foundry pig iron at Philadelphia fell from 25 dol. in January to 21 dol. in December; grey forge pig iron at Philadelphia, from 21 dol. to 18 dol.; grey forge pig iron lake ore mixed at Pittsburgh, from 21 dol. to 18 dol.; steel rails in Pennsylvania, from 40 dol. to 34 dol. 5 c.; bar iron at Pittsburgh, from 2 dol. 2 c. in January to 1 dol. 8 c. in December; nails in the same market, gross price, from 3 dol. 40 c. to 2 dol. 50 c.

The price of Connelsville coke on cars at the ovens fell from 1 dol. 15 c. per net ton in January to 90 c. in midsummer, recovering to 3 dol. in August, and after the close of the year fell again to 90 c. In April, 1884, the price advanced to 1 dol. 10 c.

Best quality of Lake Superior iron ore at Cleveland, Ohio, fell 1 dol. per ton during the year 1883, and since January 1st, 1884, a still further decline has been shown. Season contracts for Lake Superior ore were made in 1883, largely in April and May. In 1884 they have been made chiefly in February. The following table shows the prices for season contracts of both years:—

Kinds of Ore.	Gross Tons.	
	1883.	1884.
	Dol. c.	Dol. c.
Republic..	7 50	6 00
West Republic ..	7 50	6 25
Barnum, Cleveland, and Lake Superior specular	6 50	5 75
Chapin and Menominee	6 00	5 25
Hematites	4 75	4 50

The Production of Pig Iron in 1883.

The production of pig iron in the United States reached its highest point in 1882, when 5,178,122 net tons, or 4,623,323 gross tons, were produced. In 1883 the production was nearly as large, amounting to 5,146,972 net tons, or 4,595,510 gross tons (a net ton is 2,000 lbs., and a gross ton is 2,240 lbs.). The production during the last five years, including the "boom" year, 1879, was:—

Years.	Net Tons.	Gross Tons.
1879	3,070,875	2,741,853
1880	4,295,414	3,835,191
1881	4,641,564	4,144,254
1882	5,178,122	4,623,323
1883	5,146,972	4,595,510

The following table gives in net tons the production of pig iron in the last five years, classified as follows:—

Fuel Used.	1879.	1880.	1881.	1882.	1883.
	Tons.	Tons.	Tons.	Tons.	Tons.
Bituminous	1,438,978	1,950,205	2,268,264	2,438,078	2,689,650
Anthracite	1,273,024	1,807,651	1,734,462	2,042,138	1,885,596
Charcoal	358,873	537,558	638,838	697,906	571,726
Total	3,070,875	4,295,414	4,641,564	5,178,122	5,146,972

The heading "anthracite" includes all the pig iron made with mixed anthracite coal and bituminous coke. For several years this mixture of fuels in the blast furnace has become more and more satisfactory. Of the production of 1,885,596 net tons of anthracite pig iron in 1883, no less than 920,142 net tons, or nearly one-half, were produced with mixed fuel. With the opening up of a new coke field in the Clearfield region of Pennsylvania and the continuance of the present disparity in the prices of coke and anthracite coal, it may reasonably be expected that the use of the latter fuel in the blast furnace will from year to year decline relatively with that of coke and probably absolutely.

Notwithstanding the admixture of coke with anthracite coal, the production of anthracite pig iron in 1883, as compared with 1882, decreased 156,542 net tons, while the bituminous pig iron production, which includes pig iron made with uncoked coal, as well as that made with coke, increased 251,572 net tons. The production of charcoal pig iron steadily increased since 1878, when it amounted to 293,399 net tons, to the year 1882 697,906 net tons, but in 1883 it declined to 571,726 tons, a loss in one year of 126,180 tons (net).

PHILADELPHIA.

The production of pig iron in the different States in 1883 was:—

States.	Net tons.
Pennsylvania	2,638,891
Ohio	679,643
New York	331,964
Illinois	237,657
Michigan	173,185
Alabama	172,465
Virginia	152,907
New Jersey	138,773
Tennessee	133,963
Missouri	103,296
West Virginia	88,398
Kentucky	54,629
Wisconsin	51,893
Maryland	49,153
Georgia	45,364
Colorado	24,680
Connecticut	19,976
Massachusetts	10,760
Indiana	9,950
Minnesota	8,000
Oregon	7,000
California	5,327
Maine	4,400
Texas	2,381
Washington	2,317
Total	5,146,972

The following table shows in detail the production of bituminous coal and coke pig iron in 1883. Fourteen States made this quality of pig iron in that year:—

States.	Net Tons.
Pennsylvania	1,184,108
Ohio	639,115
Illinois	237,657
Virginia	136,023
Alabama	115,080
Tennessee	98,664
West Virginia	88,398
Missouri	69,184
Kentucky	40,648
Georgia	32,319
Colorado	24,680
Wisconsin	12,544
Indiana	9,950
Maryland	1,275
Total	2,689,650

Four States only figured in the production of anthracite pig iron in 1883 as follows:—

States.	Net Tons.
Pennsylvania	1,416,468
New York	203,284
New Jersey	138,773
Maryland	24,071
Total	1,885,596

The production of anthracite, charcoal, and bituminous pig iron in the United States during the past 30 years is shown as follows:—

Years.	Net Tons of 2,000 Pounds.			
	Anthracite.	Charcoal.	Bituminous.	Total.
1854	339,435	342,298	54,485	736,218
1855	381,866	339,922	62,390	784,178
1856	443,113	370,470	69,554	883,137
1857	390,385	330,321	77,451	798,157
1858	361,430	285,313	58,351	705,094
1859	471,745	284,041	84,841	840,627
1860	519,211	278,331	122,228	919,770
1861	409,229	195,278	127,037	731,544
1862	470,315	186,660	130,687	787,662
1863	577,638	212,005	157,961	947,604
1864	684,018	241,853	210,125	1,135,996
1865	479,558	262,342	189,682	931,582
1866	749,367	332,580	268,396	1,350,343
1867	798,638	344,341	318,647	1,461,626
1868	893,000	370,000	340,000	1,603,000
1869	971,150	392,150	553,341	1,916,641
1870	930,000	365,000	570,000	1,865,000
1871	956,608	385,000	570,000	1,911,608
1872	1,369,812	500,587	984,159	2,854,558
1873	1,312,754	577,620	977,904	2,868,278
1874	1,202,144	576,557	910,712	2,689,413
1875	968,046	410,990	947,545	2,266,581
1876	794,578	308,649	990,009	2,093,236
1877	934,797	317,843	1,061,945	2,314,585
1878	1,092,870	293,399	1,191,092	2,577,361
1879	1,273,024	358,873	1,438,978	3,070,875
1880	1,807,651	537,558	1,950,205	4,295,414
1881	1,734,462	638,838	2,268,264	4,641,564
1882	2,042,138	697,906	2,438,078	5,178,122
1883	1,885,596	571,726	2,689,650	5,146,972

The production of spiegeleisen in the United States since 1875 (included in statistics of pig iron production) was—

Years.	Net Tons.
1875	7,832
1876	6,616
1877	8,845
1878	10,674
1879	13,931
1880	19,603
1881	21,086
1882	21,963
1883	24,574

Everything points to a material increase in the production of spiegeleisen in this country. Both native and foreign ores are used. The number of completed furnaces in the United States is shown as follows:—

Years.	Number.
1872	612
1873	657
1874	693
1875	713
1876	712
1877	716
1878	692
1879	697
1880	701
1881	716
1882	687
1883	683

At the close of the year 1882 there were 417 furnaces in blast and 270 out of blast. At the close of the year 1883 there were 307 in blast and 376 out of blast. But few of the largest furnaces were blown out in 1883, the capacity for production, therefore, not being reduced as compared with 1882.

The consumption of pig iron in the United States in 1883 can be approximately shown. The production in gross tons of pig iron was 4,595,510, and the iron imported 322,647 tons, to which are to be added 383,655 tons of domestic pig iron and 14,802 tons of foreign iron held in stock at the beginning of 1883, which give a total supply of 5,316,615 tons for the whole country; deducting from this quantity 476,607 gross tons of domestic pig iron and 5,268 tons of foreign pig iron held in stock at the close of 1883, or a total of 481,875 tons, leaves 4,834,704 tons as the probable consumption of 1883. In 1881 the consumption was similarly estimated at 4,982,565 gross tons, and the consumption of 1882 at 4,963,278 tons.

The production of iron and steel rails in 1883 was as follows:—

Kind of Rails.	1880.	1881.	1882.	1883.
Iron rails	493,762	488,581	227,874	64,954
Bessemer steel rails	954,460	1,330,302	1,438,155	1,286,554
Open-hearth steel rails	13,615	25,217	22,765	9,186
Total	1,461,837	1,844,100	1,688,794	1,360,694

In the following table the total rail production of the country in the last five years is shown:—

	1879.	1880.	1881.	1881.	1883.
Net tons	1,113,273	1,461,837	1,844,100	1,688,794	1,360,694
Gross tons	993,993	1,305,212	1,646,518	1,507,851	1,214,905

The largest production of rails of all kinds in the United States was in the year 1881, aggregating 1,844,100 net tons or 1,646,518 gross tons.* There was a decrease of 155,306 net tons in 1882, or about 8 per cent. The decrease in 1883 was 328,100 net tons, or nearly 20 per cent.

The decline in the production of open-hearth steel rails in the last two years is of slight significance, as that class of steel cannot compete with the Bessemer in the manufacture of rails. The enormous decline in the production of iron rails of recent years indicates the almost total destruction of that branch of the iron industry. The production in 1883 of only 64,954 net tons, or 57,995 gross tons, of iron rails, was a result scarcely to be looked for so soon after the large demand of 1879 and 1880. The reduced price at which Bessemer steel rails can be produced has driven iron rails out of the market.

Included in the production of Bessemer steel rails in 1883 were 32,629 net tons, which were rolled in iron rolling mills, chiefly from imported blooms. The remainder of the year's product (1,253,925 net tons) was rolled directly by the producers of Bessemer ingots.

---

* Gross ton weighs 2,240 lbs., net tons 2,000 lbs.

PHILADELPHIA.

The production of iron and steel rails in the United States since the beginning of the manufacture of Bessemer steel rails in 1867 has been as follows in net tons:—

Years.	Net Tons of 2,000 lbs.				
	Iron Rails, all kinds.	Bessemer Steel Rails.	Open Hearth Steel Rails.	Total Steel Rails.	Total Iron and Steel Rails.
1867	459,558	2,550	..	2,550	462,108
1868	499,489	7,225	..	7,225	506,714
1869	583,936	9,650	..	9,650	593,586
1870	586,000	34,000	..	34,000	620,000
1871	737,483	38,250	..	38,250	775,733
1872	905,930	94,070	..	94,070	1,000,000
1873	761,062	129,015	..	129,015	890,077
1874	584,469	144,944	..	144,944	729,413
1875	501,649	290,863	..	290,863	792,512
1876	467,168	412,461	..	412,461	879,629
1877	332,540	432,169	..	432,169	764,709
1878	322,890	550,398	9,397	559,795	882,685
1879	420,160	683,964	9,149	693,113	1,113,273
1880	493,762	954,460	13,615	968,075	1,461,837
1881	488,581	1,330,302	25,217	1,355,519	1,844,100
1882	227,874	1,438,155	22,765	1,460,920	1,688,794
1883	64,954	1,286,554	9,186	1,295,740	1,360,694

The production of steel rails in 1883 (included in the total production of rails) was 19,440 net tons—a decrease of 2,846 tons upon the production of 1882, which was 22,286 tons. The production in 1883 consisted of 1,970 tons of iron rails, 14,499 tons of Bessemer steel rails, and 2,971 tons of open-hearth steel rails.

Production of Rails of all Kinds.

Years.	Net Tons.
1849	24,318
1850	44,083
1851	50,603
1852	62,478
1853	87,864
1854	108,016
1855	138,674
1856	180,018
1857	161,918
1858	163,712
1859	195,454
1860	205,038
1861	189,818
1862	213,912
1863	275,768
1864	335,369
1865	356,292
1866	430,778
1867	462,108
1868	506,714
1869	593,586
1870	620,000
1871	775,733
1872	1,000,000
1873	890,077
1874	729,413
1875	792,512
1876	879,629
1877	764,709
1878	882,685
1879	1,113,273
1880	1,461,837
1881	1,844,100
1882	1,688,794
1883	1,360,694

Production of Rails of all Kinds by States.

States.	Net Tons.
Pennsylvania	857,818
Illinois	232,005
New York	76,020
Missouri	64,142
Ohio	62,518
Colorado	19,688
Indiana	16,309
Massachusetts	12,465
California	7,460
Wyoming Territory	6,815
Tennessee	2,650
Wisconsin	1,259
West Virginia	775
Alabama	680
New Jersey	60
Total	1,360,694

The distribution of the above-shown production was as follows:—

States.	Net Tons.
Pennsylvania	29,963
Indiana	16,297
Wyoming Territory	6,845
California	2,910
Ohio	2,243
Tennessee	2,050
Wisconsin	1,249
Colorado	1,209
West Virginia	775
Alabama	680
Illinois	650
New Jersey	60
Missouri	23
Total	64,954

The production of Bessemer steel rails from 1874 to 1883 was territorially distributed as follows:—

Years.	Pennsylvania.	Illinois.	Other States.	Total.
	Tons.	Tons.	Tons.	Tons.
1874	66,902	48,280	29,762	144,944
1875	112,843	111,189	66,831	290,863
1876	203,750	133,713	74,998	412,461
1877	250,531	89,519	92,119	432,169
1878	308,093	143,785	98,520	550,398
1879	368,187	197,881	117,896	683,964
1880	495,716	257,583	201,161	954,460
1881	688,276	346,272	295,754	1,330,302
1882	759,624	336,122	342,509	1,438,155
1883	819,544	231,355	235,655	1,286,554

APPROXIMATED Consumption of Rails of all Kinds in the United States from 1867 to 1883 in Net Tons.

Years.	Made in United States.	Imported. Iron.	Imported. Steel.	Approximated Consumption.
	Tons.	Tons.		Tons.
1867	462,108	163,049		625,157
1868	506,714	250,081		756,795
1869	593,586	313,163		906,749
1870	620,000	399,153		1,019,153
1871	775,733	566,202		1,341,935
1872	1,000,000	381,064	149,786	1,530,850
1873	890,077	99,201	159,571	1,148,849
1874	729,413	7,796	100,515	837,724
1875	792,512	1,174	18,274	811,960
1876	879,629	287	..	879,916
1877	764,709	..	35	764,744
1878	882,685	..	10	882,695
1879	1,113,273	19,090	25,057	1,157,420
1880	1,461,837	132,459	158,230	1,752,526
1881	1,844,100	137,013	249,308	2,230,421
1882	1,688,794	41,992	182,135	1,912,921
1883	1,360,694	757	38,220	1,399,671

The annual production of Bessemer steel rails and their average price, and the rates of duty imposed on foreign rails was as follows :—

Years.	Product in Gross Tons.	Price in Currency.	Duty.
		Dol. c.	
1867	2,277	166 00	} 45 per cent. ad valorem.
1868	6,451	158 50	
1869	8,616	132 25	
1870	30,357	106 75	
1871	34,152	102 50	
1872	83,991	112 00	
1873	115,192	120 .50	
1874	129,414	94 25	28 dol. per ton to Aug. 1st, 1872; 25 dol. 20 c. to Mar. 3rd, 1875; 28 dol. from that date to July 1st, 1883. 17 dol. from July 1st, 1883.
1875	259,699	68 75	
1876	368,269	59 25	
1877	385,865	45 50	
1878	491,427	42 25	
1879	610,682	48 25	
1880	852,196	67 50	
1881	1,187.770	61 13	
1882	1,284,067	48 50	
1883	1,148,709	37 75	
1884	..	34 00	

The production of Bessemer steel reached its highest point in 1882, when 1,696,450 net tons of ingots were turned out. In 1883 the production was 1,654,627 net tons, or 41,823 tons less than 1882, being the first decrease in Bessemer steel history. The first blow of basic steel in this country took place at the works of the Pennsylvania Steel Company, May 7th, 1883, with satisfactory results, and it is believed the company will begin the manufacture of this kind of steel as a commercial product at an early date.

The production of Bessemer steel ingots in the United States from 1874 to 1883 was as follows:—

Years.	Pennsylvania.	Illinois.	Other States.	Total.
	Tons.	Tons.	Tons.	Tons.
1874..	85,625	62,492	43,816	191,933
1875..	148,374	136,356	90,787	375,517
1876..	258,452	171,963	95,581	525,996
1877..	328,599	111,299	120,689	560,587
1878..	426,481	179,500	126,245	732,226
1879..	514,165	250,980	163,827	923,972
1880..	643,894	304,614	254,665	1,203,173
1881..	844,501	375,763	318,893	1,539,157
1882..	933,631	397,436	365,383	1,696,450
1883..	1,044,396	273,325	336,906	1,654,627

The decrease of Bessemer steel ingots in 1883 was only 41,823 net tons, as compared with the production of 1882. In 1882 the production of the Bessemer works of the United States (not including the Bessemer steel rails produced in iron rolling mills) was 1,334,349 net tons of Bessemer steel rails, and of 1883 the net tons produced were 1,253,925. Very few of the rails rolled in iron rolling mills in either year were from American blooms. In reducing ingots to finished forms an allowance of about $12\frac{1}{2}$ per cent. must be made for loss in oxidation, and for such crop ends as must be reconverted. Tabulating the figures above given the results were as follows:—

Products.	1882.	1883.	Decrease.	Increase.
	Net Tons.	Net Tons.	Net Tons.	Net Tons.
Bessemer steel ingots	1,696,450	1,654,627	41,823	..
Less about 12 per cent. oxidation and crop ends to be reconverted	212,056	206,828	5,228	..
Bessemer steel in finished forms	1,484,394	1,447,799	36,595	..
Bessemer steel rails produced	1,334,349	1,253,925	80,424	..
Bessemer steel in other finished forms	150,045	193,874	..	43,829

The miscellaneous uses of Bessemer steel embraces steel for bridges and other heavy structures, car and locomotive springs, angles and other shapes for shipbuilding, agricultural implements and machinery, plates and sheets, and wire rods, some of which are, however, imported. The production of barbed wire, which is solely used for fencing purposes, amounted in 1873 to 60 tons only, while in 1883 it amounted to about 100,000 tons.

The production of crucible steel ingots in various sections of the United States was as follows:—

States.	1875.	1876.	1877.	1878.	1879.	1880.	1881.	1882.	1883.
	Tons.	Tons.	Tons.	Tons.	Tons.	Tons.	Tons.	Tons.	Tons.
New England	1,620	1,098	1,974	1,602	1,608	660	2,780	1,000	2,373
New York	2,300	2,300	2,032	2,800	2,300	3,500	4,961	4,693	2,976
New Jersey	7,098	6,806	6,749	7,377	8,651	10,387	14,500	12,400	10,593
Pennsylvania	26,615	28,217	27,983	30,585	43,614	57,077	66,290	65,139	63,687
Western States	1,500	700	1,400	480	605	800	1,231	1,857	800
Southern States	268	261	292	62	2	..	..	..	..
Total	39,401	39,382	40,430	42,906	56,780	72,424	89,762	85,089	80,429

The production of open-hearth steel ingots in the United States from 1875 to 1883, was:—

States.	1875.	1876.	1877.	1878.	1879.	1880.	1881.	1882.	1883.
	Tons.	Tons.	Tons.	Tons.	Tons.	Tons.	Tons.	Tons.	Tons.
New York and New England	3,010	6,085	6,652	8,228	14,660	20,560	24,600	25,536	17,904
New Jersey and Pennsylvania	4,240	7,547	7,771	12,231	19,575	50,736	68,363	73,222	72,333
Western and Southern	1,800	7,858	10,608	15,667	22,055	41,657	53,983	61,784	43,442
Total	9,050	21,490	25,031	36,126	56,290	112,953	146,946	160,542	133,679

The production of blister, puddled, and patented steel in the United States from 1875 to 1883, in net tons, was:—

States.	1875.	1876.	1877.	1878.	1879.	1880.	1881.	1882.	1883.
	Tons.	Tons.	Tons.	Tons.	Tons.	Tons.	Tons.	Tons.	Tons.
New England	1,500	..	..	192	950	72	200	..	713
New York	..	139	..	220	215	617	..	..	1,105
New Jersey	100	652	..	..	..	..	..	..	..
Pennsylvania	7,340	7,601	9,870	8,069	3,004	6,658	2,113	2,114	2,558
Western States	..	1,700	2,034	75	1,000	1,018	734	900	1,222
Southern States	3,667	214	20	..	295	100	..	..	..
Total	12,607	10,306	11,924	8,556	5,464	8,465	3,047	3,014	5,598

1964

The following table gives the production in the United States of all kinds of steel in the twelve years, from 1872 to 1883, in net tons:—

	Net Tons of 2,000 lbs.				
Years.	Bessemer Steel Ingots.	Crucible Steel Ingots.	Open-hearth Steel Ingots.	All other Steel.	Total.
1872	120,108	29,260	3,000	7,740	160,108
1873	170,652	34,786	3,500	13,714	222,652
1874	191,933	36,328	7,000	6,353	241,614
1875	375,517	39,401	9,050	12,607	436,575
1876	525,996	39,382	21,490	10,306	597,174
1877	560,587	40,430	25,031	11,924	637,972
1878	732,226	42,906	36,126	8,556	819,814
1879	928,972	56,780	56,290	5,464	1,047,506
1880	1,203,173	72,424	112,953	8,465	1,397,015
1881	1,539,157	89,762	146,946	3,047	1,778,912
1882	1,696,450	85,089	160,542	3,014	1,945,095
1883	1,654,627	80,455	133,679	5,598	1,874,359

The growth of the pig iron industry is shown by the following return:—

Years.	Gross Tons.
1810	54,000
1820	20,000
1830	165,000
1840	315,000
1850	564,755
1860	821,223
1870	1,665,179
1880	3,835,191
1883	4,595,510

Production of Bars, Shapes, Plates, and other Rolled Iron in 1883.

Rolled iron includes (1) cut nails and spikes; (2) bar, shaped, bolt, rod, skelp, and hoop iron, and rolled axles; (3) plate and sheet iron; (4) all sizes of iron rails.

Omitting iron rails, the production of rolled iron in 1882 was 2,265,957 net tons, against 2,155,346 tons in 1881, being an increase of 110,611 tons. In 1883 the production of rolled iron was (omitting iron rails) 2,283,920 tons, an increase of 17,963 tons over that of the year previous. This increase was more than covered by the extraordinary increase in the production of nail plate for cut nails and spikes. In 1882 the production of nail plate was 307,355 net tons, and in 1883 it was 388,136 net tons, showing an increase of 80,781 tons.

The production of bar, rod, skelp, bolt, hoop, and shaped iron and rolled axles in the United States in 1883 was as follows:—

States.	Net Tons.
Pennsylvania	675,226
Ohio	263,247
New York	104,229
Illinois	94,747
New Jersey	56,839
Massachusetts	47,915
Wisconsin	38,946
Kentucky	36,531
Delaware	22,755
Virginia	22,687
California	20,747
Indiana	18,921
Connecticut	18,491
Maryland	17,459
Rhode Island	14,405
Tennessee	9,786
Missouri	9,642
Maine	8,947
Michigan	8,080
Alabama	6,656
West Virginia	4,964
Wyoming Territory	4,443
Colorado	3,486
New Hampshire	2,132
District of Columbia	141
Total	1,511,422

The production of plate and sheet iron, except nail plate, in the United States in 1883 was—

States.	Net Tons.
Pennsylvania	245,446
Ohio	49,987
Massachusetts	18,626
Kentucky	14,498
Delaware	12,629
Maryland	11,491
West Virginia	7,781
Missouri	6,168
Michigan	3,820
New Jersey	2,305
Maine	1,350
New York	677
California	500
Connecticut	50
New Hampshire	26
District of Columbia	8
Total	384,362

The production of cut nails and spikes from nail plate in the United States in 1883 was (kegs of 100 lbs.):—

States.	Kegs of 100 lbs.
Pennsylvania	2,430,552
West Virginia	1,327,484
Ohio	1,249,700
Massachusetts	677,540
Illinois	526,108
Indiana	413,380
New Jersey	338,107
Tennessee	212,358
Virginia	161,279
Kentucky	144,686
California	111,500
Nebraska	65,000
Colorado	62,969
Alabama	20,000
New York	14,768
Maine	7,306
Total	7,762,737

The most prominent nail manufacturing district in the United States is the Wheeling district, in West Virginia, and that part of Ohio lying near Wheeling. The grand total of iron and steel from 1873 to 1883 in the United States is shown as follows:—

Net Tons of 2,000 lbs.

Products.	1873.	1874.	1875.	1876.	1877.	1878.	1879.	1880.	1881.	1882.	1883.
Pig iron	2,868,278	2,689,413	2,266,581	2,093,236	2,314,585	2,577,361	3,070,875	4,295,414	4,461,564	5,178,122	5,146,972
Spiegeleisen, included above	...	...	7,832	6,616	8,845	10,617	13,931	19,603	21,086	21,963	24,574
Rolled iron, including nails and iron rails	1,837,430	1,694,616	1,599,516	1,509,269	1,476,759	1,555,576	2,047,484	2,332,668	2,643,927	2,493,831	2,348,874
" " and excluding rails	1,076,368	1,110,147	1,097,867	1,042,101	1,144,219	1,232,686	1,627,324	1,838,906	2,155,346	2,265,957	2,283,920
Kegs of cut nails and spikes included in rolled iron	4,024,704	4,912,180	4,726,881	4,157,814	4,628,918	4,396,130	5,011,021	5,370,512	5,794,206	6,147,097	7,762,737
Bessemer steel rails	129,015	144,944	290,863	412,461	432,169	550,398	683,964	954,460	1,330,302	1,435,155	1,286,554
Open hearth-steel rails	...	...	...	...	...	9,397	9,149	13,615	25,217	22,765	9,186
Iron rails	761,062	584,469	501,649	467,168	332,540	322,890	420,160	493,762	458,581	227,874	64,954
Rails of all kinds	890,077	729,413	792,513	879,629	764,709	882,685	1,113,273	1,461,837	1,844,100	1,688,794	1,360,694
Crucible steel ingots	34,786	32,328	39,401	39,382	40,430	42,906	56,780	72,424	89,762	85,089	80,455
Open hearth-steel ingots	3,500	7,000	9,050	21,490	25,031	36,126	56,290	112,953	146,946	160,542	133,679
Bessemer " "	170,652	191,933	375,517	525,996	560,587	732,226	928,972	1,203,173	1,539,157	1,696,450	1,654,627
Miscellaneous steel	13,714	6,353	12,607	10,306	11,924	8,556	5,464	8,465	3,047	3,014	5,598
Steel of all kinds	222,652	241,614	436,575	597,174	637,972	819,814	1,047,506	1,397,015	1,778,912	1,945,095	1,874,359
Blooms from ore and pig iron	62,564	61,670	49,243	44,268	47,300	50,045	62,353	74,589	84,606	91,293	74,758

The Imports of Iron and Steel into the United States during the Years 1880, 1881, 1882, and 1883.

Commodities.	1880. Net Tons.	1880. Value. Dol.	1881. Net Tons.	1881. Value. Dol.	1882. Net Tons.	1882. Value. Dol.	1883. Net Tons.	1883. Value. Dol.
Pig iron	784,968	14,998,212	520,835	8,923,465	604,978	9,896,669	361,266	5,745,999
Castings	114	6,806	632	37,625	2,079	115,691	..	*
Bar iron	126,987	5,721,828	47,820	2,075,161	79,220	3,304,957	47,409	1,914,474
Band hoop and scroll iron	25,322	1,032,026	827	28,296	6,021	204,825	1,003	39,436
Railroad bars of iron	132,459	4,094,550	137,013	3,464,989	41,992	1,077,059	757	21,231
,, ,, of steel	158,230	5,098,351	249,308	7,649,498	182,135	5,403,980	38,220	1,047,609
Sheet, plate, and taggers iron	11,580	951,486	8,411	623,534	13,160	806,648	9,114	684,315
Old and scrap iron	694,273	14,704,879	151,107	2,705,072	164,591	2,736,483	72,000	1,014,863
Anchors, cables, and chains	1,393	140,808	1,520	134,390	1,530	142,108	..	*
Hardware	..	116,253	..	84,013	..	77,966	..	..
Machinery	..	1,601,523	..	1,739,486	..	2,275,753	..	1,635,370
Fire-irons	..	1,083,305	..	1,334,004	..	1,656,349	..	1,258,940
Steel ingots, bar, sheets, and wire	..	5,583,363	..	9,949,918	..	12,990,233	..	*
Cutlery	..	1,894,675	..	1,954,317	..	2,027,496	..	2,061,603
Files	..	159,817	..	168,506	..	169,885	..	*
Saws and tools	..	5,862	..	24,205	..	32,775	..	*
Tin plates, terne plates, &c.	177,015	16,478,110	204,996	14,886,907	239,665	17,975,161	247,781	18,156,773
Other manufactures	..	6,771,508	..	5,771,691	..	6,177,077	..	13,875,693
Total	2,112,341	80,443,362	1,322,439	61,555,077	1,335,371	67,075,125	777,650	47,506,306

* Included in "Other manufactures."

PHILADELPHIA.

The Domestic Exports of Iron and Steel and Manufactures thereof from the United States to all Countries for the Years 1881, 1882, and 1883.

Commodities.		1881. Quantity.	1881. Value. Dollars.	1882. Quantity.	1882. Value. Dollars.	1883. Quantity.	1883. Value. Dollars.
Iron, and manufactures of—							
Pig iron	Net tons	6,897	184,364	4,221	186,221	4,221	111,414
Bar ,,	,,	448	32,325	847	60,628	1,201	72,054
Railroad bars or rails	,,	597	34,262	2,518	126,878	579	31,806
Band, hoop, scroll, plate, and sheet iron	,,	184	14,473	163	14,962	330	29,187
Castings not specified		..	288,005	..	378,884	..	385,262
Cart wheels	Number	13,643	139,222	14,370	149,320	18,217	181,236
Stoves, and parts of		..	142,097	..	213,158	..	232,713
Steam engines, locomotives	Number	104	913,952	174	1,878,528	275	2,650,944
,, stationary	,,	94	88,158	104	183,211	147	170,104
Boilers, separate from engines		..	161,121	..	189,413	..	290,177
Machinery, not specified		..	4,817,698	..	6,129,244	..	5,935,543
Printing presses, and parts of		..	195,261	..	215,619	..	250,407
Nails and spikes	Net tons	4,577	312,059	4,053	320,753	5,724	388,070
All other manufactures of iron		..	5,571,001	..	6,274,604	..	5,289,607

The Domestic Exports of Iron and Steel and Manufactures thereof from the United States to all Countries for the Years 1881, 1882, and 1883—continued.

Commodities.		1881. Quantity.	1881. Value. Dollars.	1882. Quantity.	1882. Value. Dollars.	1883. Quantity.	1883. Value. Dollars.
Steel, and manufactures of—							
Ingots, bars, sheets, and rods	..	235	46,457	501	89,076	257	54,350
Cutlery	..	..	96,552	..	91,994	..	103,732
Saws and tools	..	..	1,157,511	..	1,065,242	..	1,388,562
Fire-arms	..	..	1,018,471	..	927,180	..	1,357,686
Railroad bars or rails	Net tons	87	7,123	1,088	81,350	2,006	102,864
All other manufactures of steel	..	..	562,090	..	453,494	..	..
Total exports of iron and steel	..	..	80,443,362	..	19,029,759	..	19,025,718
Agricultural implements—							
Horse powers	Number	37	9,065	61	20,350	..	38,471
Mowers and reapers	,,	6,210	656,274	11,420	1,127,925	..	1,755,232
Ploughs and cultivators	,,	21,245	180,239	35,564	335,643	..	396,926
All others not specified	..	..	1,576,258	..	1,943,321	..	1,499,280
Scales and balances	..	..	234,777	..	315,898	..	319,041
Sewing machines	..	..	2,179,770	..	2,975,616	..	3,362,971
Fire engines and apparatus	..	..	19,372	..	27,561	..	8,310
Total agricultural implements	..	..	4,855,755	..	6,746,314	..	7,380,231

Up to this date, June, 1884, the market is extremely quiet, No. 1 foundry iron selling for less money this week than ever before in this market. 19 dol. has been taken, and 20 dol. is obtained only in occasional instances. Foundry men have been running with very little iron for several months, but are now disposed to purchase, as there is nothing to be lost by placing orders at 19 dol. to 19 dol. 50 c. No. 2 has been sold at 18 dol. to 19 dol.; grey forge all the way from 16 dol. to 18 dol. Two or three sales of spiegeleisen were made at about 28 dol. for 20 per cent., one being a 500 lot last week. But little Scotch is sold, and Bessemer pig is quoted at 19 dol. 50 c. to 20 dol. Muck bars are nominally 31 dol. Some manufacturers of merchant iron have been booking orders at 2 c. Common iron has been sold at 1 dol. 65 c. Most of the manufacturers report a dull demand, but the prospects for the summer are somewhat fair. Quotations for plate iron range from 2 cents. up. Nothing is done in structural iron out of the usual retail way. Nails are nominally 2 dol. 40 c. to 2 dol. 50 c. per keg of 100 lbs.; the cost forbids little departure from these figures, western production continuing to be above the market requirements. Steel rails are weak and declining, the quotations being nominally from 32 dol. to 32 dol. 50 c., but business can be done at something less. Steel slabs run from 37 dol. 50 c. to 40 dol. Old rails are offered at 19 dol. 50 c. to 20 dol., and much business is likely to be done in old material, as prices have weakened and consumers are in need of stock.

Condition of the Furnaces.—Up to this date, June 1st, there were 106 furnaces in blast, with a weekly capacity of 29,972 tons, and 124 furnaces out of blast, with a weekly capacity of 27,305 tons. On April 1st there were 107 furnaces in blast, with a weekly capacity of 27,612 tons, and 121 furnaces out of blast, with a weekly capacity of 26,605 tons. The following figures show the condition of the bituminous furnaces on the 1st inst., as compared with the 1st of April, excluding Virginia, from which no report was received. On June 1st there were 91 furnaces in blast, with a weekly capacity of 45,312 tons, and 121 furnaces out of blast, with a weekly capacity of 40,821 tons; and on April 1st there were 95 furnaces in blast, with a weekly capacity of 47,125 tons, and 118 furnaces out of blast, with a weekly capacity of 36,740 tons. At Pittsburgh there was possibly a little more doing, but the trade is far from being satisfactory, consumers refusing, as a rule, to anticipate future wants, and demand concessions every time they go on the market to buy. Consumers state that they have no difficulty in obtaining all the neutral mill iron they want from 16 dol. to 16 dol. 50 c. cash, according to quality. Sales are reported of all ore mill at 18 dol. on four months' credit, and it is stated that large blocks of Bessemer iron have been offered at 19 dol. on four months' credit. Foundry iron is being sold from 17 dol. 50 c. to 19 dol., and 19 dol. 50 c. according to quality and brand, with a very light demand.

Steel rails have no demand, and it would appear as if a further reduction would be resorted to. So far there have been no sales at Pittsburgh below 35 dol. cash at mill, but they can be bought elsewhere equal to 33 dol. 50 c. in Pittsburgh. Merchant steel continues quiet and prices remain unchanged: best brands refined cast-steel at $9\frac{1}{2}$ c., ditto crucible machinery at 5 c., and open-hearth and Bessemer ditto at 3 to $3\frac{1}{4}$ c. At New York, Boston, and other cities the same depressed condition of the trade is reported, and little hope is entertained of ordinary activity during the present year and until the Presidential election is settled.

Reports come in from the Western districts that the experiment of restricting the production of pig-iron has not been so satisfactory as was expected it would be. The experiment proved to be successful in one branch of the chemical trade, and it was expected to prove so in the pig-iron trade. In the Cleveland–Ohio district it has not done so. Cheapness of production is the way to create a demand, and the ironmasters may well ask themselves whether it is worth while endeavouring to establish a dead level of production for all makers, whatever their individual capacity, or whether it is not better to leave those makers who cannot make iron as cheap as others to the operation of the natural economic laws. By doing so the end they aim at is more likely to be attained, and a demand will again be created by the cheapness at which the most skilled and enterprising makers can put their iron into the market.

RAILROADS.

The year 1883 has been favourable to railway enterprises. Of 56 lines in this country the earnings have been 290,886,000 dol. against 263,735,000 dol. in 1882, an increase of 27,151,000 dol., or over 10 per cent. Of the 56 roads referred to, all but nine show an increase, the gain in many cases being remarkably large, and the decrease on each of the nine being small. In Pennsylvania 55 new railway companies were chartered during the year. The proposed mileage covers a distance of 1,900 miles, and their total capacity stock is 53,756,900 dol. The majority of these roads are now under way, while others are for future development. In the State of Illinois there were an additional 1,358 miles of road built, which gives to that State alone, adding double tracks and sidings, $10,456\frac{52}{100}$ miles of rail. 65 roads in the United States have reported their statistical condition, which shows their capital stock to be 648,427,220 dol. 45 c., an average of 22,115 dol. 40 c. per mile. The funded debt of the roads reported figures 657,595,734 dol. 14 c., the floating debt 43,265,865 dol. 55 c., and the aggregate of stock, bonds, and floating debt gives the enormous figures of 1,349,288,820 dol.; the aggregate cost of construction being 1,251,729,029 dol. 74 c., or 42,693 dol. 20 c. per mile. Of these 65 corporations now under consideration, the total gross earnings for 1883 were 214,146,915 dol. 55 c., itemised as follows:—Passenger earnings, 59,365,804 dol. 52 c.; freight earnings, 138,077,180 dol. 95 c.; other sources, 16,707,930 dol. 18 c. The figures show an increase for 1883 of 24,793,937 dol. 92 c., that is to say, on passengers 6,582,901 dol. 65 c., on freight 11,309,341 dol. 22 c., other sources 6,901,695 dol. 50 c.

The official returns of the various railway interests of this country in the aggregate for the year 1883 are not as yet given to the public, and the system of railway management is so different from the English that it is thought proper not to cite local instances of prosperity or depression. Competition between gigantic railway management is so mysterious, and statistical representations so conflicting that it is better to leave them to work out their own results, upon which no two men seem to agree.

COAL.

Anthracite.—The coal fields of anthracite are confined to portions of the nine counties of Pennsylvania, in which 310 collieries are now in operation, employing in 1883 the number of 87,303 persons, to whom 33,597,252 dol. was paid in wages. The mines were worked on an average of $221\frac{1}{2}$ days during the year, and the output was 31,240,468 tons of coal. The close of 1883 and the beginning of 1884 leave the anthracite coal trade somewhat depressed, and a system of temporary stoppage of production is resorted to. This depression is in consequence of the condition of the iron trade and the uncertainty as to future tariffs.

Bituminous coal is gaining favour in consequence of its lower cost, especially for manufacturing purposes. Eventually it will, perhaps, be used exclusively for factories, leaving the anthracite for family or domestic use, to which it is so admirably adapted

The total production for 1883, compared with the previous year, was:—

	1883.	1882.
	Tons.	Tons.
Philadelphia and Reading Railroad and Canal	7,506,936	7,064,560
Lehigh Valley Railroad	6,350,559	6,118,351
Pennsylvania and New York Railroad	211,729	188,302
Central Railroad of New Jersey	4,790,797	4,302,104
Delaware, Louisiana, and Western Railroad	5,011,408	4,595,518
Pennsylvania Coal Company	1,481,683	1,438,821
Delaware and Hudson	4,097,219	3,662,037
Shamokin	1,225,086	1,141,506
Lykens Valley	497,755	478,431
St. Louis and Sullivan Railroad	67,296	64,921
Total	31,240,468	29,054,551
Total for 1882	29,054,551	..
Increase	2,185,917	..

The above table shows the production of the year 1883 to have exceeded any previous year. This production has not been reached by forcing the market by auction sales; there has been a steady trade and prices have been fairly remunerative to producers. This was the result of regulating the supply by the demand. The present system of working the mines effects a suspension of mining for three days at stated periods until the demand is sufficiently active to render suspension unnecessary. Without suspension the production would have been much greater during the past year, but the coal would have been sacrificed to unremunerative prices, individual operators broken up, and the trade demoralised generally without any benefit to the small consumer; for it has been clearly demonstrated that when wholesale prices are low the retail dealer reaps the benefit, while the individual consumer pays the same price. The Reading railroad controls all the available avenues to the manufacturing city of Philadelphia for anthracite, and it is hoped that the managers will be willing to allow its consumers to have coal as cheap as it is delivered in Boston—200 miles further off—the cost of freight thence being 1 dol. 25 c. to 1 dol. 50 c. per ton greater.

The following table, carefully compared by Mr. Saward, shows the total production in the United States for the years 1882-83:—

State.	1882.	1883.
	Tons.	Tons.
Alabama	800,000	1,400,000
Arkansas	50,000	75,000
California	260,000	200,000
Colorado	947,749	1,000,000
Dakota	..	50,000
Georgia	175,000	200,000
Idaho	..	10,000
Illinois	9,115,653	10,508,791
Indiana	1,976,470	2,400,000
Indian territory	150,000	175,000
Iowa	3,127,700	3,881,300
Kansas	750,000	850,000
Kentucky	1,300,000	1,650,000
Maryland	1,294,316	2,306,172
Michigan	130,000	135,000
Missouri	2,000,000	2,250,000
Montana	30,000	50,000
New Mexico	146,421	250,000
Ohio	9,450,000	8,229,429
Oregan	30,000	50,000
Pennsylvania, anthracite	29,120,096	31,793,027
,, bituminous	22,000,000	24,000,000
Tennessee	850,000	1,000,000
Texas	..	100,000
Utah	250,000	250,000
Virginia	100,000	225,000
Washington territory	225,000	260,000
West Virginia	2,000,000	2,250,000
Wyoming territory	631,031	700,000
Total	86,849,436	96,159,716

Of the bituminous output in Pennsylvania last year there were 3,219,000 tons of coke, representing 4,830,000 tons of coal, made in 1882. The net increase in production in 1883 was, therefore, 9,310,283 tons, of which 2,672,931 tons were anthracite coal, and the remainder (nearly) 6,737,352 tons bituminous. The total production of bituminous was 64,366,692 tons in 1883, and 57,729,340 tons the year before; of anthracite 31,793,027 tons and 29,120,096 tons respectively.

The coal deposits in the United States, exclusive of the territories, are officially reported as 192,000 square miles in extent; while those in Great Britain are 12,000 square miles, France 2,086 square miles, Germany 1,700 square miles, and Belgium 510 square miles. The total production of the world in 1881, exclusive of China, Sweden, Italy, and Chili, from which no returns have been received, was 360,890,000 gross tons. Great Britain produced, with a coal area of only 12,000 square miles, 154,000,000 tons; and the United States, with an area of 192,000 square miles, produced in 1882 only 92,000,000 tons. In this country the average cost at the mines has been 2 dol. 25 c. for anthracite and 1 dol. 25 c. for bituminous. The heaviest costs are between the mines and the consumer, or the transportation. The coal resources of the United States are believed to be greater than those of all Europe, and they are said to be sufficient to supply the world for ages to come.

Bituminous coal has been largely over-produced during the year 1883, no attempt having been made to regulate the mining. The following table shows the condition of the trade for 1883, so far as the returns have been received:—

PENNSYLVANIA.

	1st District.	2nd District.	3rd District.	4th District.	5th District.	6th District.
Tons of coal produced	7,495,085	4,039,335	1,594,365	2,320,000	289,927	214,549
Number of mines	106	85	90	56	27	48
,, employés, inside	9,274	7,459	4,140	4,128	1,305	3,365
,, ,, outside	1,484	2,188	644	976	587	539
Total number of employés	10,758	9,647	4,784	5,104	1,892	3,904
Number of fatal casualties	17	14	12	8	0	2
,, non-fatal casualties	33	41	26	26	4	1
Total number of casualties	50	55	38	34	4	3
Number of fatal casualties from falls	14	11	11	7	0	2
,, ,, mine cars	3	3	1	1	0	0
Tons of coal produced per life lost	440,887	367,212	129,114	290,000	...	107,214
Number of employés per life lost	633	877	399	638	...	1,453
,, ventilating fans	6	...	9	3	3	3
Tons mined per employé	697	419	324	455	153	74

BITUMINOUS and Semi-Bituminous Coal Production of Pennsylvania in 1883.

In Tons of 2,000 Lbs.

Northern Pennsylvania region—		
Blossburg	1,217,870	
Barclay	371,010	
McIntyre	184,552	
		1,773,432
Central Pennsylvania region—		
Broad Top	196,534	
East Broad Top	97,378	
Snow Shoe	257,230	
Clearfield	2,857,710	
		3,408,852
West Pennsylvania region—		
Alleghany Mountain	458,468	
West Pennsylvania Railroad	399,010	
South-west Pennsylvania Railroad	123,761	
Westmoreland	1,399,702	
Pittsburgh	611,177	
Johnston iron works	775,000	
Add for coke (3,136,400 tons) as coal	5,118,240	
		8,985,348
Total		14,167,632

[612]

UNITED STATES.

The wages paid for digging coal in the various coal districts of the country are reported in the following statement:—

Alabama	45 c. per ton.
Along the Monongahela	2¾ to 3½ c. per bushel.
Angus, Iowa	1 dol. per ton.
Anthracite regions	85 c. per 2 ton car.
Belleville district, Illinois	1½ c. per bushel.
Brazil, Indiana	75 c. per ton.
Bridgeport, Ohio	70 c. ,,
Boulder, Colorado	90 c. ,,
Clarksburg, West Virginia	40 c. ,,
Clearfield region, Pennsylvania	40 c. per net ton.
Connellsville coke region	90 c. per 100 bushels.
Coalton, Kentucky	70 c. per ton, screened coal.
Coal Creek, Indiana	75 c. per ton.
Elk Garden, West Virginia	40 c. ,,
Glen Mary, Tennessee	4½ c. per bushel.
George's Creek, Maryland	50 c. per ton.
Hocking Valley, Ohio	60 c. ,,
Iowa	90 c. to 1 dol. per ton.
Kanawha River, West Virginia	2½ c. per bushel.
Latrobe, Pennsylvania	26 c. per 2,000 pounds.
Leredo Texas (18-inch coal)	1 dol. 50 c. per ton.
Myersdale, Pennsylvania	30 c. per ton.
Missouri	6 c. per bushel.
Mahoning Valley, Ohio	65 c. per ton.
Murphysboro, Illinois	75 c. ,,
Nova Scotia mines	34 c. ,,
Pittsburgh railroad pits	3½ c. per bushel.
Reynoldsville	50 c. per ton for run of mine coal.
St. Clair, Illinois	2½ c. per bushel.

Persons Employed in the Pennsylvania Coal Mines.

Anthracite.

Inside employés—	
Miners	20,345
Miners' labourers	11,095
Company men	6,453
Drivers and runners	5,696
Door boys	2,165
All others	3,426
Outside employés —	
Engineers	1,428
Firemen	1,023
All other mechanics	1,709
Company labourers	8,724
Slate pickers	14,269
All others	4,187
Total	80,520

Bituminous.

Miners	28,372
Inside labourers	1,281
Outside labourers	2,863
Mule drivers	2,412
Blacksmiths and carpenters	616
Overseers and clerks	681
Boys	1,343
Coke oven employés	2,080
All others	385
Total	40,033

PHILADELPHIA.

The number of days worked and the anthracite coal mined in the Wilkes-Barre district, which is the largest of the anthracite coal districts, and the number of tons mined per employé are of interest:—

Names of the Companies.	Days in Operation.	Tons Mined per day.	Persons Employed.	Coal Mined per Year per Employé.
Lehigh Valley Coal Co.	205·22	2,881·1	1,438	411·17
Lehigh and Wilkes-Barre Coal Co.	207·46	8,161·2	4,689	461·08
Delaware and Hudson Canal Co.	237·35	5,907·7	3,065	457·48
Susquehanna Coal Co.	269·98	3,348·6	2,520	358·79
Wyoming Valley Coal Co.	228·90	1,741·5	1,059	375·49
Miscellaneous coal companies	219·52	9,433·9	5,112	405·27
Average	228·07	..	..	394·79
Total	..	30,952·5	17,883	..

Average Prices of Schuylkill Lump Coal at Philadelphia, Tons of 2,240 lbs.

	Dol.	c.
1872	3	74
1873	4	27
1874	4	55
1875	4	39
1876	4	71
1877	2	59
1878	3	25
1879	2	70
1880	4	63
1881	4	50
1882	4	75
1883	4	50

The growth of the coal industry in the United States is shown by the following table:—

ANTHRACITE.

Years.	Total Production.	Increase.	Decrease.
	Tons.	Tons.	Tons.
1878	17,605,262	..	..
1879	26,142,689	8,537,427	..
1880	23,437,242	..	2,705,447
1881	28,500,016	5,062,774	..
1882	29,120,096	620,080	..
1883	31,793,027	2,672,931	..

Increase in five years, 14,187,765 tons.

BITUMINOUS.

Years.	Cumberland District.	Clearfield District.	Blossburg District.	Total.	Increase.	Decrease.
1878	1,679,322	1,295,201	652,577	3,627,120	...	...
1879	1,730,709	1,631,120	874,010	4,235,893	608,719	...
1880	2,136,160	1,739,873	921,555	4,797,588	561,649	...
1881	2,261,918	2,401,987	1,178,581	5,842,486	1,044,898	...
1882	1,790,466	2,838,970	1,165,604	5,795,040	...	46,446
1883	2,544,173	2,857,710	1,217,870	6,619,753	824,713	...

Increased production of coal in the United States from 1870 to 1880 is upwards of 40,000,000 tons, or 10,000,000 tons annually.

	Tons.
In 1870 the total production of coal in the United States was	32,860,690
In 1883 the total production was	96,159,719
Increase in 13 years, 195 per cent., or	63,299,029

A miner in the coal regions of Luzerne county, Penns., writes: "We have men here who worked as miners (and I feel confident they can do as much as any others if the chance is given them), and who earned for the month of June, 1884, only 13 dol. Compare this with the English coal miner and see who is the better paid. The time has come when every intelligent working man around the coal mine will see that the cry of protection is a humbug. How are we being protected? Is it by working half time, signing cut-throat bills, and earning from 13 dol. to 20 dol. per month? If so, we are being protected with a vengeance."

Labour and Wages.

Co-operative associations, so far as they have extended in this country and been properly conducted, have met with success, but as there is no wholesale associations, as in England, it is difficult to obtain accurate statistics respecting their number or the extent of their business. The figures of one of these associations in Philadelphia show the result for the year 1883:—

	Dol.	c.
Capital stock paid in	21,177	21
Sales during the year	241,291	11
Gross profits	20,761	02
Dividends paid to members	16,450	80
Dividends paid to non-members	1,927	93

Compulsory education is advocated by many of the higher grades of working men, who properly argue that it will serve the working people and improve their moral and social position. In the shoe trades strong drink keeps the workmen poor as a rule, and little hope is entertained for the improvement of their condition. Intelligence is low, and strikes, which are frequent, are injurious. Among the women the morals as a rule are good, but intelligence is lacking. Among the trades generally, lack of economy and fondness of drink lead to poverty and immorality. Economy is the sheet anchor of the working man, and a commendable desire to enforce a fair child-labour law is gaining ground. Its opponents are vagabonds who put their children to work in factories to enable themselves to live in idleness. Working men in many trades complain that they are overworked and underpaid, and that "piece work" is ruinous in most instances, as the workmen overwork themselves for a big day's pay: thus the employer is tempted to reduce the price, and the workman is obliged to do the same amount of labour for smaller pay, his wages being measured by what he can be forced to do and not by the value of the work performed.

The brickmakers claim that great injustice is done them by hiring men, say at 15 dol. to 40 dol. per month—few getting the latter figure—and exacting a certain amount of labour per day; and should they break down in the middle of the month and are unable to go on, they lose what they have actually earned, getting no pay for what they have done. If ill they are charged 75 c. for board, and that of the cheapest kind.

Mr. Eayre O. Bartlett, a skilled workman, residing in Pemberton, New Jersey, has recently returned from England, where he was sent to put up some patent furnaces of American ingenuity. He is said to be a rigid protectionist, and he says in public print, " That from what he saw the English working people are better clad than those in America ; that they live quite as well, but more economically ; that they are far more independent, are better organised, have more holidays, and seem to be better contented. Although their wages are not so high as in America, what they earn buys more, which compensates for the difference in rates. Mr. Bartlett states that he did not meet with much of the pauper labour, so freely talked about in this country."

Average Rate of Wages Paid.

Trades.	Per—	Wages.
		Dol. c.
Carpenters	Day	2 50
Ships' carpenters	,,	2 75
Labourers	,,	1 15
Cigar makers	,,	2 00
Jewellers	,,	2 25
Stone cutters	,,	3 50
Stove moulders	,,	1 75
Paper-box makers	,,	1 75
Hat makers	,,	1 75
,, finishers	,,	2 25
Shoemakers	Week	12 00
Blacksmiths	,,	12 50
Miners of iron ore	Day	1 25
Machinists	,,	2 00
Iron moulders	,,	2 25
Puddlers	Week	20 00
Shirt makers (female)	Day	1 00
Carpet factory employés	,,	2 25
Woollen mill operatives	,,	1 40
Cotton mill ,,	Week	6 75
Silk weavers	Day	1 50
Bottle and vial glass blowers	,,	5 00
,, ,, goffer	,,	5 00
,, ,, ,,	,,	3 40
,, ,, moulder	,,	5 00
,, ,, blow and finish	,,	3 02
Window glass blower	Month	100 00
,, flattener	,,	95 00
,, cutter	,,	87 00
Miscellaneous glass workers	Week	12 00
Engine-drivers	,,	15 00
Tinsmiths	Day	2 50
Painters	,,	2 25
Wood turners	Week	9 00
Boiler makers	Day	2 50
File makers	Week	10 00
,, cutters	,,	13 00
Carriage trimmers	,,	10 00
,, painters	,,	10 00
Dyers	,,	8 50
Harness makers	,,	9 00
Tailors	,,	8 00
Designers	,,	18 00
Dressmakers	,,	5 00
Newspaper reporters	Annum	1,500 00
Compositors	Week	16 80
Paper carriers	,,	6 00
Firemen	,,	15 75
Potters	,,	15 00
Cotton and woollen factory hands	,,	8 50
Boot and shoe factory hands	,,	12 00
Bakers	,,	10 00
Brewers	,,	12 50
Tobacco workers	,,	10 00
Saddlers	,,	11 00
Engravers	,,	15 00

Strikes in nearly all branches of trades have been frequent, and continue to occur in nearly all sections of the country. Many thou-

and bricklayers, stonemasons, and plasterers are now out in the city of New York on a demand for nine hours' labour per day instead of ten. The strikers draw weekly payments from the Bricklayers' and Labourers' Unions, and from sums of money donated by other trades and labour organisations. This extensive strike has also been joined by a large body of framers, who declare they will remain out until the nine-hour rule is granted. The coal miners and labourers in the Wilkes-Barre (Pennsylvania) district have also knocked off to the number of over a thousand, because the employers endeavoured to force the men to sign receipts for their pay, less the amount due to the companies' stores by the men, refusing to pay the men unless they so signed. This action the men claim is in violation of the Act of Assembly of 1881, and that it will give their employers almost unlimited power over their wages. The men are determined not to return to work on such conditions, and are supported by the miners of the whole coalfield.

At Bethlehem an extensive iron company announces a reduction in the pay of all hands, including all the officers of the company, of 20 per cent., caused by the recent great fall in the price of steel rails. This action is not likely to lead to any strikes in the iron trades, as the men are aware that the capitalists have enough to do to weather the present ruinous condition of the market.

Some of the worsted mills in New England have given notice of a reduction of 10 per cent. on wages from August 1, 1884.

Iron founders in the upper part of New York State have given notice of a reduction of 10 per cent. Throughout the Eastern States there is a disposition to reduce wages.

PETROLEUM.

The petroleum industry shows evidence of a decline in the supply, and it is probable that prices will be higher in the future. Consumption is at the present time quite equal to the production. Without the discovery of new petroleum deposits, from which the increased consumption can be supplied, the near future will experience a demand for petroleum that will give steadiness to prices and decrease the unhealthy fluctuations in the market at present so unsatisfactory. Over 36,000,000 barrels of oil in stock in the tanks of the pipe-line companies in February 1884 exerted a depressing influence on prices, but as the wants of domestic consumers and the exports are increasing annually, it is claimed that a stability in the market will soon be ensured. The exports in 1883 amounted to 15,600,000 barrels, a gain of nearly 1,100,000 barrels over 1882, 8,000,000 barrels over 1881, and 5,700,000 barrels as compared with 1880.

The average annual exports and domestic consumption were in barrels:—

Years.	Average Annual Exports.	Home Consumption, including Outside Stocks.
1875–76–77	6,649,000	3,926,000
1878–79–80	9,273,000	6,558,000
1880–82–83	15,002,000	6,700,000

Domestic consumption and stocks at refineries and on the seaboard have increased about 160 per cent. in 10 years, and the steady increase of the exportation answers for the superior quality of the American product, enabling it to control the European markets. Notwithstanding the enormous productive powers of the Causcasian fields, the American product is not kept out of Hungary or Austria, and is not likely to be for years to come.

The improved methods of refining, of transportation, and of distribution have sent the American refined petroleum to all quarters of the globe. As a cheap illuminator it occupies the first rank, and its use in manufactures of divers kinds render the product one of almost absolute necessity. Its history dates back to the year 1859, when the aggregate production was only 82,000 barrels, which increased in 1882 to 30,460,000 barrels.

The following table gives the annual production, &c., from the year 1867 to 1868, in barrels:—

Years.	Annual Production.	Exports.	Accumulated Stocks.	Added to Stocks.	Stocks out of Regions and Home Consumption.
	Barrels.	Barrels.	Barrels.	Barrels.	Barrels.
1867	3,583,000	1,596,000	534,000	534,000	1,453,000
1868	3,716,000	2,313,000	265,000	*269,000	1,672,000
1869	4,351,000	2,446,000	340,000	75,000	1,830,000
1870	5,371,000	3,316,000	537,000	197,000	1,828,000
1871	5,531,000	3,800,000	568,000	31,000	1,700,000
1872	6,357,000	3,722,000	1,040,000	472,000	2,163,000
1873	9,932,000	5,800,000	1,625,000	585,000	3,547,000
1874	10,883,000	5,492,000	3,755,000	2,080,900	3,311,000
1875	8,801,000	5,533,000	2,751,000	*954,000	4,222,000
1876	9,015,000	6,080,000	1,926,000	*825,900	3,760,000
1877	13,043,000	8,315,000	2,857,000	931,000	3,797,000
1878	15,367,000	7,914,000	4,307,000	1,450,090	6,003,000
1879	19,827,000	9,944,000	8,094,000	3,787,000	6,096,000
1880	26,048,000	9,961,000	16,606,000	8,512,000	7,575,000
1881	29,638,000	14,804,000	25,333,000	8,727,000	6,107,000
1882	30,460,000	14,574,000	34,335,000	9,002,000	6,884,000
1883	24,000,000	15,628,000	35,715,000	1,380,000	7,291,000

The year 1874 closed the first period of heavy production with a total of 10,883,000 barrels for that year, due to the heavily increased production of a few wells. Prices became depressed, 1 dol. 17 c. per barrel being the average price of crude oil for that year, against 1 dol. 83 c. the year previous. Operations were suspended for three months, and the total production in 1875 was some 2,000,000 barrels less than the year before. In 1875 the price averaged 1 dol. 35 c., in 1876 2 dol. 56¼ c., and in 1877 2 dol. 42 c., which stimulated work in the oil regions; the above table shows the rapid gain in production from that time forward. The average annual price of refined oil at New York has fluctuated quite as much within 20 years as have those of "certificates" or crude oil per barrel at the wells. In 1863 it was 44 c. per gallon, crude then being about 3 dol. 62 c. per barrel. In 1864 it leaped to 74 dol. 6 c. per gollon, during which crude ran from the average of 4 dol 61 c. in the first quarter to 10 dol. 46 c. in the last. From that time the course of prices was downward until 1867, when for the refined the average price was 28½ c. per gallon, and that of crude about 2 dol. 40 c. per barrel range, averaging 1 dol. 82 c.,

* Withdrawn from stocks in tanks in region.

3 dol. 6 c., and 2 dol. 68 c. By 1869 the average annual price of refined had advanced to 32·7 c. per gallon, and that for crude 6 dol. 30 c. per barrel in the first quarter, and 5 dol. 46 c. in the last. The movement of quotations of refined from that time was downward until 1875, when 13 c. per gallon was touched, the close of the first period of heavy production.

In the same period the quotations for crude had dropped from about 5 dol. 70 c. per barrel (1869) to 3 dol. 29 c. in the latter part of 1870, and advanced to about 3 dol. 60 c. in 1872, when a big fall took place, landing prices at 71 c. per barrel as the average during the last three months of 1874. The reaction in 1875 was to 1 dol. 34 c. per barrel as an average for the year. Prior to this year stocks in tank had been accumulating, but for the fiscal year 1875-6 consumption had increased and production fallen off 12 to 13 per cent., requiring the withdrawal of nearly 17,000 barrels from stocks, which had already accumulated to about 1,800,000. In the succeeding fiscal year the consumption demands were larger, and a further draw was made upon the accumulated stocks of nearly 24,000 barrels. Since that time the stocks have steadily increased each year. A decline in production and full consumption, however, advanced prices. In the last quarter of 1876 the average price for refined oil at New York was 19·2 c. per gallon, and for certificates of crude oil 3 dol. 56 c. per barrel. From that time until 1882 prices of both fluctuated, with a net decline. In 1879 refined had dropped 8 c. per gallon, and certificates of crude $67\frac{1}{8}$ c. In 1880 refined averaged $9\frac{1}{8}$ c. per gallon, and certificates which averaged 1 dol. $10\frac{1}{8}$ c. in January were 78 c. in April, and 1 dol. $18\frac{1}{8}$ c. in December. In 1882 production was stimulated and prices much depressed. Refined sank to an average of $7\frac{5}{10}$ c. per gallon, and certificates of crude averaged $83\frac{1}{8}$ c. in January, $54\frac{3}{4}$ c. in June (after touching 49 c.), rallying again to 1 dol. 14 c. in November. In 1883 the average price was 8·14 c. per gallon, and of certificates for the year 1 dol. 52·3 c. per barrel.

The average of monthly quotations for 1883 were :—

1883.	P. L. Certificates Per Barrel.	Crude in Barrels Per Gallon.	Refined Oil, Per Gallon.	Naphtha, Per Gallon.	Case Oil, Per Gallon.
	Dol. c.	Cents.	Cents.	Cents.	Cents.
January	0 $93\frac{3}{4}$	7·18	7·67	6·75	10·93
February	1 01	7·17	7·90	6·75	11·00
March	0 $95\frac{5}{8}$	7·28	8·19	6·75	11·31
April	0 $92\frac{3}{8}$	7·37	8·33	6·24	11·43
May	1 $00\frac{1}{8}$	7·21	7·79	5·34	10·25
June	1 $16\frac{3}{8}$	7·51	7·90	5·61	10·10
July	1 $05\frac{7}{8}$	7·16	7·51	5·18	9·72
August	1 $08\frac{1}{2}$	7·29	7·61	5·11	9·67
September	1 $12\frac{1}{2}$	7·71	8·30	5·30	10·21
October	1 $11\frac{1}{8}$	7·71	8·50	5·80	10·62
November	1 $14\frac{5}{8}$	7·89	8·80	6·00	11·11
December	1 $14\frac{1}{2}$	7·88	9·18	6·23	11·15

Prices of crude oil in barrels per gallon and of naphtha per gallon at New York from 1863 to 1882 inclusive, naturally sympathised to a certain extent with the influence mentioned above.

Natural Gas.

This gas as a fuel has a history, but its importance has received recognition but recently. Where a steady flow has been struck the profits are very large and the outlay very small. One company in Pittsburgh, extended over one ward (a very small area), has an income of 300,000 dol. per annum. Taking coal at 5 c. per bushel, 1,000 cubic feet of gas is worth 8 c., this making the flow of the largest well, Westinghouse, with a flow pressure of 17 lbs., worth 1,200 dol. per day, or upwards of 400,000 dol. per annum. The " gas belt " is stated to extend from the Pennsylvania oil regions in a south-easterly direction to the oil regions of West Virginia. The gas cannot always be struck within this belt. Instances are known of where two wells, sunk 100 feet from each other, one was a success and the other a failure. One drawback growing out of the indiscriminate sinking of wells is that abandoned holes fill with water and tend to seriously interfere with adjoining operations. The eagerness of owners of property near a producing well to secure their share of the gas stored underground simply leads to repeating the outlay to reach it. In some quarters there is a movement to consolidate interests with a view to systematic development.

These liquid or acriform hydro-carbons belong to the same geological series as the bituminous coalfield, extending even to the shales of New York and the salt formations of New York, Michigan, and West Virginia, and probably to all the western bituminous coalfields. The remarkable discoveries of gas in and near Pittsburgh recently made are treated by some writers as novelties, but in fact they are enlarged illustrations of what was well known and frequently utilised in Central and Western New York as early as 1840. Many private houses burned gas as fuel in Ontario and Wayne counties, New York, and the towns of Fredonia and Westfield, Chautauqua county, have for nearly 40 years been lighted by natural gas found in the shales of the carboniferous series cropping out there. Also in Virginia, the salt works of the Upper Great Kanawha Valley have been boiled by the blowing gas of the coal formations there since about 1850; the stratum yielding gas being pierced at a depth in that valley of 1,000 to 2,000 feet. Gas was known and utilised, in fact, long before the oil was believed to have commercial value, although both gas and oil belong to the same geological era, and are almost interchangeable under some conditions. Gas wells were utilised in Eastern Ohio 40 years ago, but they were not so valuable as those in the New York shales and at Erie, Pennsylvania.

25 years after natural gas was found and made valuable the discovery of pretoleum threw everything else into the background, and the hundreds of gas wells developed in boring for oil were almost neglected. The gas was allowed to waste, and when oil was not found the borings were filled up. All the pretoleum formations are full of gas, and the time has come to utilise it simply as fuel. The Pittsburgh basin is a vast reservoir of natural gas, which probably extends to Kanawha on the south, and indefinitely westward beneath the bituminous coal fields and the underlying shales. It is as great a property, possibly, as the oil, and it is co-extensive with the coal. While its transportation to great distances does not now appear practicable, it must be remembered that oil has had a victory over natural impossibilities in the pipe-line transportation that may prepare us for gaspipes hundreds of miles in length. It is noticeable that the sandstones and shales surrounding the coalfields proper are all more or less charged with natural gas. The want of its practical use is, therefore, likely to be even wider than the coal-mining or oil-yielding fields.

Scientific definitions of the quality and compositions of this gas are few. It is a simple hydro-carbon, entirely free from sulphur, and almost absolutely pure. In combustion it yields no smoke or soot, and it does not blacken the stove or the fixture in which it is burned. The heat is intense without the necessity of blowing oxygen or superheated steam into the furnace to make the combustion perfect. With its well-known superiority in this respect it is surprising that it has not been sought for by many smelters of refractory metals, steel makers, and others. On the Great Kanawha the long ranges of salt pans are heated with the precise scale of decreasing temperatures desired to bring the liquid slowly to crystallisation at the remoter pans while very hot when first struck by the gas.

The excitement created at Pittsburgh by the gas wells recently struck there indicates a systematic attempt to utilize it in the iron and steel works in place of coal. In the first trials the gas was brought a long distance from Butler county, and for several years Messrs. Spang, Chalfant, and Co. have used it in their rolling mills at Sharpsburg. The Oliver-Roberts wire rod mill, of South Pittsburgh, began using it on June 14, and the Jefferson Iron Works of Steubenville, Ohio, have struck a very large vein of gas, which they are prepared to use. The Westinghouse well at Pittsburgh, recently struck, is considered ample proof of the abundance of the supply within easy reach of the ordinary borign machinery for all the requirements of the vast iron and steel industries of Pittsburgh and its vicinity. The calculated value of the gas flow of the Westinghouse well as fuel is 1,200 dol. per day, or 400,000 dol. per annum, which is an easier form of raising fuel than by mining so much coal.

Many incidents as to the development of gas in salt boring and coal mining are brought to light in the notices already made public, one important case being as far south as St. Stephens, in Southern Alabama, where the salt wells opened during the late war showed great quantities of gas. The whole of Western Alabama abounds in coal, oil, and gas, and probably the entire basin of the Mississippi, wherever salt water or coal is found, will be available as a source of natural gas.

The use of petroleum for purposes of ordinary heating is rapidly increasing, and all the devices employed for effecting combustion convert the oil into gas as the first step. When this change is effected in pure oils the gas is precisely like the natural gas, and its combustion is without soot or other deposit. When natural gas cannot be found the oil can be used economically as the cheapest of all fuels, in fact, other than gas, since there is no waste, and there need be no heat generated which is not utilised. The natural gas of the blowing wells, however, is incomparably cheaper than oil can be, and if developed as rapidly as now appears likely, it will revolutionise the industries of the Mississippi Valley.

The combustion of natural gas is nearly perfect, what little flame there is attending its burning being of a pure rose colour, and almost entirely free from smoke. The experiments thus far made have not satisfactorily demonstrated the relative merits of gas and coal as fuel, but the results from such trials as have been made are largely in favour of the natural gas.

The town of East Liverpool, Ohio, about 45 miles from Pittsburgh, was the first to utilise natural gas for heating and lighting purposes. Imbued with the idea that their town was on the oil belt, numerous wells were sunk some 25 or 26 years ago, which struck such a heavy vein of gas as to stop further drilling. It was not difficult to discover the highly inflammable nature of the gas, and they set about devising ways and means to put it to use. Pipes were laid through the streets, and connections made with the houses. Experience soon demonstrated that, while it was but poorly adapted for light, its heating properties were undeniably good. It fell naturally into disfavour when the further fact was discovered that it was an unhealthy as well as a poor illuminant, being provocative of headache and languor; but it is still used in the street lamps. It is undeniably cheap, as the company supplying it charged but 20 c. per month per burner for its use, and 2 dol. per month per furnace or stove, with no restriction as to the amount burned. So cheap is it that the street lamps are never extinguished, but allowed to burn day and night. All efforts to regulate the flow were unsuccessful, and it was found impossible to register the amount consumed with ordinary gas meters, and their use was long ago abandoned. The danger of its careless use has been demonstrated in East Liverpool by numerous fires, as well as by an explosion totally destroying a large brick building and causing the loss of several lives.

The duration of life of the gas wells in this place yet remains to be decided, as those first drilled are still producing as largely as at first, or, where there is a diminution, it is caused by the filling up of the well with dirt, and the flow of gas can always be restored to its original volume by cleaning out the casing.

The pressure is immense, and at night, when the gas is lighted, the flow shoots into the air a hundred feet, and its roar can be heard several miles away. Manufacturers are busily engaged in estimating the probable cost of its introduction into their establishments, and many predict that through its general adoption as a fuel the advantages of Pittsburgh as a manufacturing site will be increased a hundredfold, and that within five years it will cease to be known as the Smoky City.

AGRICULTURE.

Pennsylvania.—The returns for the State of Pennsylvania show the agricultural products, consumed and on hand, at the end of 1879, amounted to 129,000,000 dol. Chester county alone produced 6,000,000 dol. The figures have increased since that date, but no accurate data can be found. The dairy industry is one of the leading industries in the State. The whole number of horned cattle in Pennsylvania in 1883 is stated to be as follows:—

	Dollars.
Milk cows, 854,156, at 40 dollars	34,166,240
Other cattle, 861,019, at 20 dollars	17,220,380
Oxen, 15,062, at 40 dollars	602,480
	51,989,100

The dairy products for the year were:—

	Dollars.
Butter, 79,336,012 lbs., at 25 cents.	19,834,003
Milk, 36,540,540 gallons, at 16 cents	5,846,486
Cheese, 1,008,686 lbs., at 12 cents.	121,042
Milk cows, one-fifth of whole number killed for beef (170,831), at 40 dollars	6,833,240
Other cattle, one-third of whole number raised (three years old), 172,205, at 30 dollars	5,166,150
Calves sold as veal (two-thirds of whole number of cows), 569,437, at 5 dollars	2,847,185
Total	40,648,106

While the grand total of the dairy industry amounts to more than the cereal crops, it is not an annual production, only so far as the dairy products go.

The correct average valuation and cost of production of dairy products is shown as follows:—

		Dol.	c.
Annual average price of butter per lb.		0	25
,, ,, ,, cheese ,,		0	12
,, ,, ,, milk per quart		0	04
,, ,, ,, dairy cows		40	00
,, ,, cost of butter per lb.		0	20
,, ,, ,, cheese ,,		0	08
,, ,, ,, milk per quart		0	03
,, ,, ,, dairy cows (3 years old)		30	00

,, ,, percentage of dairy cows raised, 80 per cent.
,, ,, ,, ,, ,, killed, 20 per cent.
,, ,, ,, ,, products sold outside of counties where produced:—
Butter, 22 per cent.
Cheese, 60 per cent.
Milk, 18 per cent.

Whole number of creameries in operation in 1883 194

Market for Dairy Products.—Fifty-two counties supply home markets wholly; fifteen counties sell a portion of their butter and cheese to markets outside the limits of the State.

Breeds of cattle preferred for dairy purposes:—

	Counties.
Jersey or Channel Island	28
Native stock	18
Durham shorthorn	12
Holstein	5
Ayrshire	1
No choice expressed	3
Total	67

Total annual value of dairy products, 40,000,000 dols.

Forests.

	Dollars.
The number of establishments for sawing lumber is	2,827
The value of logs	13,378,589
Annual total sawed	22,457,359

Sheep and Wool.

The number of sheep in the State 1,785,481, at 5 dol. per head	8,927,405
Wool, 8,470,273, at 30 c. per lb.	2,541,081
Total sheep and wool industry	11,468,486

Fruits.

The annual production of the orchards of the State amounts to	4,862,826

Silk Culture.

Establishments in the State for the manufacture of silk	49
Value of raw silk	1,207,795
Gross value of manufactured products	3,491,840

Value of butter, cheese, and milk in Pennsylvania	25,601,531
,, farm implements	35,473,037
,, cereal crops	72,401,736
,, live stock	84,242,877
,, products sold and consumed	129,760,476
Agricultural population	301,112

The following analysis shows the comparative nutritive values, per ton, of farm crops:—Digestible albuminoids, $4\frac{1}{3}$ c. per lb.; digestible fat, $4\frac{1}{3}$ c. per lb.; digestible carbo-hydrates, 9 c. per lb.

	Dol.	c.
Corn meal	22	20
Middlings	21	40
Wheat bran	20	80
Oats	19	40
Timothy hay	13	80
Clover hay	13	80
Hungarian hay	13	20
Meadow hay	12	80
Corn fodder	11	40
Oat straw	8	80
Rye straw	7	00
Milk	6	80
Potatoes	5	80
Beets	7	60
Green cornstalks	4	40
Whey	4	40

Farm Wages in Pennsylvania.—The wages of farm hands for transient service, except harvesting, are 1 dol. 20 c. per day without board, or 85 c. with board. In the year 1866 the wages were as high as 1 dol. 59 c. per day without board, or 1 dol. 10 c. with board. The average monthly wages of farm labourers are, without board, 22 dol. 88 c., or with board 14 dol. 21 c., while in 1866 the rates were 29 dol. 91 c. and 18 dol. 84 c. respectively. In 1879 the rates were the lowest, viz., 19 dol. 92 c. and 11 dol. 46 c. respectively.

The returns of the whole country, for 1883, of the cereal crops, have not been up to the standard expected. The grain has not been as full and solid as in former years. There was an unusual diminution of the crops in the year 1881, except that of oats. In the early part of 1882 the farmers were uneasy as to the results to be obtained, but without desponding they redoubled their efforts, and with the aid of improved implements accomplished more hard work than was ever done in the same period in the United States. The aggregate result for 1882 was a year of general abundance. The corn or maize crop in 1881 fell off 500,000,000 bushels, reducing the supply 300,000,000 bushels below the requirements of consumption and exportation. This demand sent prices up 60 per cent., and caused a determination to secure a large crop the following year.

The crop returns for the various States of the Consular district are given for the year 1882.

PHILADELPHIA.

CORN.

States.	Bushels.
Pennsylvania	41,518,800
Ohio	93,319,200
Michigan	30,081,600
Indiana	107,484,800
Illinois	187,336,900
Wisconsin	30,201,600
Minnesota	21,127,600
Iowa	178,487,600

The wheat consumption for 54,000,000 of people requires 250,000,000 bushels, and for seed 57,000,000 bushels, leaving nearly 200,000,000 bushels for exportation and for filling the severely depleted stocks in the first hands. Such surplus, even if 40,000,000 bushels, in view of the exhaustion of garner and local stocks at the end of the commercial year in August, would be less than that of two years ago, and should not depress prices. The five preceding crops averaged, as estimated, 425,000,000 bushels per annum. The distribution of five years has averaged 429,000,000 bushels, the 20,000,000 difference having been drawn from stocks on hand, reducing the surplus of 1882 to that extent in comparison with 1887. Of this distribution 145,000,000 bushels were exported per annum in wheat and flour, 51,000,000 bushels were used for seed, and 233,000,000 consumed as food. The prices for 1883 ranged from 1 dol. 6 c. to 1 dol. 18 c. per bushel.

The product for 1882 within this Consular district was:—

WHEAT.

States.	Bushels.
Pennsylvania	20,300,700
Ohio	45,453,600
Michigan	33,315,400
Indiana	45,461,800
Illinois	52,302,900
Wisconsin	20,145,400
Minnesota	37,030,500
Iowa	25,487,200

TABLE showing Quantities and Values of Wheat and Wheat Flour Exported during the following Years.

Years.	Wheat.	Wheat Flour.	Total Wheat.	Wheat.	Wheat Flour.	Total Wheat.
	Bushels.	Barrels.	Bushels.	Dollars.	Dollars.	Dollars.
1859	3,002,016	2,431,824	13,945,224	2,849,192	14,433,591	17,282,783
1869	17,557,836	2,431,873	28,501,264	24,383,259	18,813,865	43,197,124
1879	122,353,936	5,629,714	147,687,649	130,701,079	29,567,713	160,268,792
1880	153,252,795	6,011,419	180,304,180	190,546,305	35,333,197	225,879,502
1881	150,565,477	7,945,786	186,321,514	167,698,485	45,047,257	212,745,742
1882	95,271,802	5,915,686	121,892,389	112,929,718	36,375,055	149,304,773

The oats crop in the year 1881 was an exceptionally good one, and this condition was continued through 1882 and 1883. The average yield was 24·7 bushels per acre, which is, however, below the average for 11 years previous, which was 27·6 bushels per acre. In 1874 the lowest average for any single year was 22 bushels. The prices also ranged high, that of 1874, 52 c. per bushel, only exceeding it. When the production of maize fell off in 1881 500,000,000 bushels, the price of oats advanced 10 c. per bushel, and last year averaged at the close 40 c. The value per acre for this series of years is found to be 10 dol., and the statistics of the crops for the following named years show:—

Years.	Total Production.	Total Area of Crop.	Total Value of Crop.	Average Value per Bushel.	Average Yield per Acre.	Average Value of Yield per Acre.
	Bushels.	Acres.	Dollars.	Cents.	Bushels.	Dol. c.
1871	255,743,000	8,365,809	102,570,030	40·1	30·5	12 26
1875	354,317,500	11,915,675	129,499,930	36·5	27·7	10 86
1878	413,578,560	13,176,500	101,945,830	24·6	31·4	7 74
1879	363,761,320	12,683,500	120,533,294	33·1	28·7	9 50
1880	417,885,389	16,187,977	150,243,565	36·0	25·8	9 28
1881	416,481,000	16,331,000	193,198,970	46·4	24·7	11 47

Barley.—This is the only cereal of which a supply for domestic consumption is not produced in this country. While the average production since 1870 has been 36,000,000 bushels, the importation in excess of exports has been about 6,000,000 bushels. Its acreage has increased in nearly the same ratio as the area of wheat, yet the supply is short of the demand, failing to keep pace with the manufacture of beer. The late crops were small, averaging only about 20·5 bushels per acre, the average being for the past decade 24·5 bushels. The influence of price on extension of acreage is well exemplified in the history of this crop. In 1872 there was a large importation, causing some reduction in price. The next year there was no enlargement of the area cultivated, and the price rose from 73·9 c. to 91·5 c. In 1874, the year following, the expansion exceeded 200,000 acres, bringing the price down to 81·3 c., which stopped the increase of area, while better crops and larger imports still further reduced the price. The reduction of 4,000,000 bushels in 1881 sent up the price again from 66·6 c. to 82·3 c. The crop statement is as follows:—

Years.	Total Production.	Total Area of Crop.	Total Value of Crop.	Average Value per Bushel.	Average Yield per Acre.	Average Value of Yield per Acre.
	Bushels.	Acres.	Dollars.	Cents.	Bushels.	Dol. c.
1871	26,718,500	1,177,666	21,541,777	80·6	22·7	18 30
1875	36,908,600	1,789,902	29,952,082	81·3	20·6	16 73
1878	42,245,630	1,790,400	24,483,315	58·0	23·6	13 67
1879	40,283,100	1,680,700	23,714,444	58·9	24·0	14 11
1880	46,165,346	1,843,329	30,090,742	66·6	24·5	16 32
1881	41,161,330	1,967,510	33,862,513	82·3	20·9	17 21

Rye.—This crop shared in the disasters that overtook wheat in the year 1881, and made the lowest yield in 10 years. The average yield per acre of this crop is greater than that of wheat, being nearly 14 bushels for a period of years throughout the country, while that of wheat slightly exceeds 12 bushels only. For the past decade the average has been 11·6 to 15·9 bushels. Pennsylvania, Illinois, New York, Wisconsin, and Iowa are the principal producing States of this cereal, yielding nearly two-thirds of the entire crop. The following table shows the annual production for several years:—

Years.	Total Production.	Total Area of Crop.	Total Value of Crop.	Average Value per Bushel.	Average Yield per Acre.	Average Value of Yield per Acre.
	Bushels.	Acres.	Dollars.	Cents.	Bushels.	Dol. c.
1871	15,365,500	1,069,531	12,145,646	79·0	14·3	11 36
1875	17,722,100	1,359,788	13,631,900	76·9	13·0	10 02
1878	25,842,790	1,622,700	13,592,826	52·6	15·9	8 38
1879	23,639,460	1,625,450	15,507,431	65·6	14·5	9 54
1880	24,540,829	1,767,619	18,564,560	75·6	13·9	10 50
1881	20,704,950	1,789,100	19,327,415	93·3	11·6	10 82

Buckwheat.—This crop has a restricted range. It is annually grown to the extent of about 12,000,000 bushels, of which two-thirds are produced in Pennsylvania and New York. The consumption is in the shape of hot cakes for breakfast in the cities of the seaboard. The acreage has nearly doubled in 10 years. The crop of 1881 was the smallest ever reported, 11·4 bushels per acre. The range has been from this figure up to 20 bushels. The annual production of the eight years named was:—

Years.	Total Production.	Total Area of Crop.	Total Value of Crop.	Average Value per Bushel.	Average Yield per Acre.	Average Value of Yield per Acre.
	Bushels.	Acres.	Dollars.	Cents.	Bushels.	Dol. c.
1871	8,328,700	413,915	6,900,263	82·8	20 1	16 67
1875	10,082,100	575,530	7,166,267	71·0	17·5	12 45
1878	12,246,820	673,100	6,454,120	52·7	18·2	9 59
1879	13,140,000	639,900	7,856,191	59·8	20·5	12 28
1880	14,617,535	822,802	8,682,488	59·4	17·7	10 55
1881	9,486,200	828,815	8,205,705	86·5	11·4	9 86

Potatoes.—The year 1881 was the most disastrous on record for this important vegetable. The range of estimated yields is from 53·5 bushels in 1881 up to 110·5 bushels in 1875. The average for the period is placed at 84·2 bushels, so that in the year 1881 but half a crop was gathered: in some of the States scarcely a third of a crop, while a few had two-thirds of a full yield. The price was higher than ever before, 90 9 c. per bushel at the end of December, and rose still higher as the supply was being exhausted. The lowest price during the period from 1875 to 1881 was 38·9 c. per bushel; in 1875 the average for 11 years being 56·1 c. The loss of 70,000,000 bushels was severely felt, and could not be made good by importation. Though Irish and Scotch potatoes were sold in every market east and west, and the trade acknowledged to have attained extraordinary proportions, but 8,789,860 bushels were brought in, at a cost of 4,660,120 dol., against 2,170,372 bushels in 1880. Six-sevenths of the shortage was not made up, and in 1881 there was a similar scarcity of root crops of all kinds.

ESTIMATED Annual Product, Acreage, and Value of the Potato Crop of the United States for the following named Years.

Years.	Quantity.	Area.	Value.	Value per Bushel.	Yield per Acre.	Value per Acre.
	Bushels.	Acres.	Dollars.	Cents.	Bushels.	Dol. c.
1871	120,461,100	1,220,912	71,836,671	59·6	98·6	58 83
1875	166,877,000	1,510,041	65,019,420	38 9	110·5	48 06
1878	124,126,650	1,776,000	73,059,125	58·9	69·9	41 14
1879	181,626,400	1,836,800	79,153,673	43·6	98·9	43 09
1880	167,659,570	1,842,510	81,662,214	48·3	91·0	44 00
1881	109,145,494	2,041,670	99,291,341	90·9	53·5	48 63

[612]

Hay.—The grass crop, green and dry, is worth more than any other in the country. The hay is worth far less than the pasturage in intrinsic value, and yet grass depastured produces an overwhelming proportion of the growth in flesh of all animals, and bears an important part in the fattening and furnishing of beeves. The following table shows the yield of the hay crop:—

Years.	Quantity.	Area.	Value.	Value per Ton.	Yield per Acre.	Value per Acre.
	Tons.	Acres.	Dollars.	Dol. c.	Tons.	Dol. c.
1871	22,239,400	19,009,052	351,717,035	15 81	1·17	18 50
1875	27,873,600	23,507,964	342,203,445	12 27	1·18	14 56
1878	39,608,296	26,931,300	285,543,752	7 21	1·47	10 60
1879	35,493,000	27,484,991	330,804,494	9 32	1·29	12 04
1880	31,925,233	25,863,955	371,811,084	11 65	1·23	14 38
1881	35,135,064	30,888,700	415,131,366	13 43	1·14	13 43

Crops for 1884.—The prospects for the crops of 1884 are most favourable; an immense harvest is looked for, and the reports that continue to come in show that in some grain districts 36 per cent. larger returns are realised than were last year. Between St. Louis and Sidalia, on the Missouri Pacific Railway, the yield is over 30 per cent. larger than it was last year. Cattle in this vast district will be about the same. Between Kansas city and Omaha grain is reported at a 20 per cent. greater yield; corn or maize is 50 to 75 per cent. greater than the last stock and 15 per cent. greater than last year. Unless some most unforeseen calamity visits this country between now and the autumn, the corn crop will be immense. On the Lexington and Southern Kansas and Arizona branches, grain and corn are reported 21 per cent. better than they were last year; on the Lexington branch the wheat is 10 per cent. better, corn 20 per cent. better, and oats 10 per cent. less than last year. On the Lebanon branch grain and corn 20 per cent. better, and on the Bornville branch 25 per cent. greater. Oats in these districts will fall off 10 per cent. On the Missouri, Kansas, and Texas Railway districts the reports are equally encouraging. At Fort Worth, Alvarada, Waco, Lorena, Troy, Echo, Holland, and Bartlett wheat will increase 30 per cent., corn 10 per cent., cotton 20 per cent., oats 8 per cent., and live stock 25 per cent. In other vast districts of Texas the increase is reported for wheat at 26 per cent., corn 26 per cent., and cotton 19 per cent. In the Kansas districts the increase is reported at 43 per cent. for wheat, 32 per cent. for corn, and 25 per cent. for oats. In the other districts of the west, north-west, and south-west, the acreage in wheat has been increased 15 to 25 per cent., and the estimated increase in yield is put at 25 per cent. as compared with 1883.

TOBACCO.

The domestic tobacco market within the past year or two has been steady in tone and price, evincing no tendency to depression in sympathy with those of other staple articles. This is attributed to the fact that the American manufactured tobacco industry has not succeeded in erecting a production beyond the demand.

The foreign trade in cigars, tobacco, and cigarettes during the past four years shows a heavy gain in the fiscal year of 1883 as compared with 1880.

PHILADELPHIA.

EXPORTS.

		Fiscal Years. 1880.		Fiscal Years. 1883.		Eight Months, Fiscal Years. 1884.		Eight Months, Fiscal Years. 1883.	
		Quantity.	Value.	Quantity.	Value.	Quantity.	Value.	Quantity.	Value.
			Dol.		Dol.		Dol.		Dol.
Leaf	Lbs.	215,910,187	16,379,107	235,628,360	19,038,066	147,221,545	13,095,641	168,007,658	13,902,625
Cigars	Number	2,583,000	67,821	3,885,000	96,901	1,373,000	38,595	2,648,000	62,700
Cigarettes	,,	..	..	..	..	54,159,000	169,478	..	..
Stems and trimmings	Lbs.	..	..	..	..	9,235,705	279,950	..	..
Other manufactures	,,	..	2,095,345	..	2,560,262	..	1,469,664	..	1,769,619

IMPORTS.

		Fiscal Years. 1880.		Fiscal Years. 1883.		Eight Months, Fiscal Years. 1884.		Eight Months, Fiscal Years. 1883.	
		Quantity.	Value.	Quantity.	Value.	Quantity.	Value.	Quantity.	Value.
			Dol.		Dol.		Dol.		Dol.
Leaf	Lbs.	4,759,355	4,911,086	14,893,131	8,548,999	8,902,680	4,005,603	..	2,091,369
Cigars	,,	652,402	2,404,812	829,777	3,137,278	575,971	2,044,984	537,004	..
Other manufactures	,,	..	86,402	..	85,319	..	44,017	..	51,902

Thus the gain in the value of tobacco exported during the fiscal year ended June 30th, 1883, as compared with the record of 1880, was but 8 per cent., while the increased value of importations in 1882-83 as against 1879-80 was 58 per cent., seven-eighths of which was due to increased receipts of leaf tobacco. For the fiscal year ended June 30th, 1881-2, the value of imported leaf tobacco was 6,230,865 dol., of cigars 3,032,038 dol., while other manufactures were 84,859 dol. The gain in value of leaf tobacco was therefore 2,318,134 dol., as compared with 2,051,162 dol., in the two preceding years of Sumatra and Havanah goods. The exports in the fiscal year 1881-82 were valued: of leaf, at 19,067,721 dol., nearly 400,000 dol. less than in the following year; the cigars exported were valued at 113,717 dol., nearly 17,000 dol. more than in the following twelve months; other manufactured tobacco exports were 2,046,092 dol., or over 300,000 dol. less than in the fiscal year ending June 30th, 1883.

The record of eight months of the current fiscal year (ending June 30, 1884) shows a decline in the foreign trade in tobacco. The loss in exports of leaf from July 1st, 1883, to March 31st, 1884, was over 800,000 dol., or 6 per cent; in cigars sent abroad it was over 24,000 dol., or about 38 per cent.; on other manufactured tobacco the decline in the exports was about 70,000 dol. (including exports noted in 1883-84), or about 4 per cent. The percentage of decline in the gross value of the exports of tobacco in eight months, ended March 31st last, as compared with a like portion of the preceding year, was about 223,000 dol., or nearly 1½ per cent. The imports of leaf tobacco in the same period were valued at 573,000 dol. less than in the eight months of 1882-83, a loss of 12 per cent. The loss in imports of cigars was about 46,000 dol., or 2⅓ per cent., and on other manufactured tobacco nearly 8,000 dol., or 15 per cent. The total decline in the eight months was 626,749 dol., or about 9 per cent. It will be observed that the export of cigarettes commenced during the past year. The subject of foreign trade in cigars and cigarettes is one which has attracted considerable attention of late. The trade is not so encouraging as it was supposed it would turn out to be. The receipts of foreign cigars, however, are increasing steadily, and for the eight months ending March 31st, 1884, were 575,971 lbs., as compared with 537,004 lbs. for the previous eight months. Leaf tobacco imports also are nearly 300,000 lbs. and 573,000 dol. ahead, although all other manufactured tobacco returns show a decline, as noted heretofore, of about 8,000 dol. The demand here, therefore, has still to be met largely from abroad. The total importations of foreign cigars in the fiscal year 1882-83 were 57,347,629 cigars, as compared with 54,190,889 in the year previous, an average of one foreign cigar per capita per annum. The exportations were 2,904,425 cigars—say 3,000,000—which was but one-twentieth of the number purchased in foreign lands. Of the total number of cigars manufactured in the United States, New York city makes about one-third, and the manufacture for the whole country was 3,317,860,952, of which only about one-fifteenth of 1 per cent. were exported. Two-thirds of the total, or about 2,289,000,000 were manufactured in the following States:—

States.	Number of Cigars.
New York	1,072,385,970
Pennyslvania	623,846,000
Ohio	277,386,485
Illinois	160,068,150
California	156,829,968

The remaining States made, therefore, something over 700,000,000 cigars. The exports of cigarettes is increasing. The total number sent abroad in eight months of the past fiscal year was 54,159,000, against 76,600,560 in the whole of the preceding fiscal year, being a gain of about 6 per cent. The total number of cigarettes manufactured in the United States in the calendar year 1882 was nearly 600,000,000, or over 10 per capita per annum. Of this New York turned out three-fourths, or 444,092,867 cigarettes. The list of States that manufactured over 100,000 each in that year was:—

State.	Total No. of Cigarettes.
New York	444,092,867
Virginia	88,732,350
Maryland	30,512,095
North Carolina	18,159,260
Louisiana	7,630,918
California	4,050,650
Maine	1,755,955
Ohio	1,259,820
Illinois	981,000
Pennsylvania	682,710
New Hampshire	445,100
Florida	241,410
Texas	238,600

In manufactures of tobacco New York city heads the list:—

Manufactured in New York City.		1882.	1881.
Cigars	Number	802,751,000	759,674,000
Other manufactured tobacco	Lbs.	5,805,726	5,378,569

The enormous growth of the production and consumption of cigarettes in the United States has largely increased within the past dozen years or so. The number of brands or varieties is innumerable, both in the domestic and imported manufactures. The trade in the latter is a growing one, though not developing so rapidly as the domestic product, owing to the heavy protection granted the latter by the tariff, which a good authority pronounces almost prohibitory, being 25 per cent. ad valorem, 2 dol. 50 c. per pound, and the internal revenue tax of 50 c. per 1,000. This amounts to $14\frac{1}{2}$ c. ($7\frac{1}{2}d$) on a package of 20 cigarettes as against a tax on the domestic article of 1 c. per package of 20, being a protection of $13\frac{1}{2}$ c. per domestic package, or about two-thirds of a cent. per cigarette. This accounts for the excessive cost of the foreign article. As to the preference for the foreign or domestic cigarette it is, of course, largely a question of taste; but as to the actual quality of tobacco used, the best is the Havanah made article. Their strength, however, detract somewhat from their popularity. Neither are they rolled as well or so satisfactorily; but the quality of tobacco used is far ahead of most other foreign made cigarettes, and is by those competent to judge alleged to be superior to the more popular American brands. The excessive cost of the Havanahs is explained by the duty. The Government would clearly receive as large, even a larger revenue, if but 50 per cent. ad valorem duty on manufactured tobacco were charged, instead of the existing compound rates. The manufacturers, however, would have to compete, and would make less money.

The tobacco crop in Pennsylvania for 1883 was not so large as in former seasons, and its money value perhaps not so great, yet on the whole it may be considered a fair one, rounding out the farmer's crop year very satisfactorily, and making it one of the most bountiful that he has had for many seasons. The spring was backward and cold, and disagreeable weather continued far into the period when tobacco farmers began operations for the season's crop. The army worm was reported about the middle of July in some sections, but it speedily disappeared. Hailstorms did considerable damage in the latter part of July, and early frosts appearing in September in a measure decreased the yield, but at the close the crop turned out well, though it was not to be termed "first-class." Lancaster, York, and Chester counties are the principal tobacco districts in Pennsylvania, and prices have been well maintained. The cigar industry under the new internal revenue schedule seems to have acquired a fresh impetus, and is prosperous in every direction. In this State many new factories have been started. New packing houses are being erected to accommodate the growing industry. Lancaster city, the great centre of the trade, has been increasing her already large facilities for handling the tobacco crop of Central Pennsylvania. A number of large warehouses have been put up during the year, and the city now has 90 of these establishments, some of them of immense size, and in this particular Lancaster is unmatched by any city in the world.

Tobacco Crop in 1881.

States.	Quantity Produced in 1881.	Average Yield per Acre.	Number of Acres in each Crop.	Value per Lb.	Total Valuation.
	Lbs.			Cents.	Dollars.
Kentucky	163,037,700	700	232,911	·08·8	14,347,316
Virginia	77,649,954	556	139,663	·08·6	2,677,907
Pennsylvania	38,805,661	1,173	33,080	13·0	5,044,735
Ohio	35,419,913	964	36,760	·08·0	2,833,593
Maryland	25,869,218	676	38,265	·08·0	2,069,537
North Carolina	24,827,532	443	56,071	13·5	3,351,716
Tennessee	22,157,300	550	40,286	·07·6	1,683,954
Connecticut	13,763,759	1,572	8,753	16·0	2,202,201
Missouri	12,233,959	877	13,950	·08·3	1,015,418
Wisconsin	8,702,770	866	10,045	12·5	1,087,846
Indiana	7,719,373	717	10,760	·07·5	578,952
New York	6,291,217	1,249	5,037	14·0	880,770
Massachusetts	5,000,964	1,520	3,291	15·0	750,144
Illinois	3,346,195	661	5,062	·08·2	274,387
West Virginia	2,066,531	503	4,112	·08·5	175,655
Alabama	466,133	221	2,110	18·0	83,903
New Hampshire	172,551	1,876	92	12·0	20,706
Vermont	132,736	1,562	85	15·0	19,910
New Jersey	181,689	1,075	169	12·0	21,802
South Carolina	47,528	248	192	14·0	6,653
Georgia	242,758	242	1,004	14·0	33,986
Florida	23,085	216	107	20·0	4,617
Mississippi	436,010	287	1,519	17·0	74,121
Texas	217,950	304	716	18·0	39,231
Michigan	87,706	498	176	12·5	10,963

Opium Smoking.

Opium smoking in the United States is spreading with alarming rapidity under the fostering care of the Chinese, who have a profitable field in this country for laundry work and sinister opium dens. The importation of this drug has increased from 80,075 lbs. in 1881 to 298,152 lbs. in the year ended June 30th, 1883. It is charged by the friends of a Bill offered in Congress to suppress the importation and sale of opium, that the habit of opium smoking once acquired cannot be overcome, and that its victims will not live in any place where the drug cannot be procured. Nearly 50 per cent. of the Chinese population of this country are slaves to the opium pipe, and it is claimed that a stoppage of the drug would cause an exodus of these unpopular people.

Live Stock and Cattle Diseases.

The growth of the cattle trade in the United States during the past 25 years has been wonderful, furnishing a striking American instance of what enormous proportions to which a business can be developed within a comparatively short period. A few head of cattle in Colorado, abandoned by their owner and left to perish in the autumn of 1859, were found fat and in good condition the following spring. Thus it was discovered that cattle could live through the winter in that part of the country without shelter and without other food than the uncut wild grasses found in the valley. To-day there are millions of cattle roving the vast Western plains, branded and "rounded up" in the spring, and fat and ready for the Eastern and European markets. West of the Mississippi river are three great cattle belts—the Northern, the Middle, and the Southern. The first includes Montana and Dakota, tributary to the Northern Pacific Railroad; Colorado, Wyoming, Nebraska, Utah, and the North-Western portion of Kansas belong to the second, which is penetrated by the Union Pacific and the Burlington and Mississippi Railroad; and the third takes in all the territory south of the second, including the Indian territory, New Mexico, Arizona, and Texas, and is tributary to the Great South-Western system of railways. For many years Texas has been noted for its herds of cattle and its nutritious grasses, but for a long time, for want of ready access to market, the cattle had little more than a nominal value. The success which attended the raising of cattle on the Western plains, followed by the opening of the Union Pacific Railroad, led to the driving of vast herds from Texas to Colorado, Wyoming, and adjacent territories, where they were wintered prior to being shipped to the Eastern markets; and this practice is still continued, although since the opening of the South-Western system of railways there is less driving and more shipment direct from the Texas ranges to the Northern markets. The present "native" cattle of the West are a cross of the Texas longhorns and the shorthorns of Kentucky and Northern States. Within a few years past the Western cattlemen have organised associations for the general management of their business. This step became necessary, as stringent laws have been enacted prescribing severe punishments for cattle stealers, and inspectors are employed at all the points where the animals are first unloaded after leaving the plains. Summary punishment by the ranchmen—"Lynch law"—is dealt to cattle stealers on these vast plains.

Chicago is the great central point to which ranch cattle are shipped, although large numbers go to other western termini, as Omaha, Kansas city, and St. Louis. At Chicago the Eastern and Western dealers meet, and in a remarkably short space of time millions of dollars change hands. This business is shown by the following table of the receipts and shipments at Chicago, the valuations including the receipts of all stock:—

Years.	Receipts.	Shipments.	Total Value.
			Dollars.
1866	393,007	263,693	42,765,328
1867	329,183	203,580	42,375,241
1869	403,102	294,717	60,171,217
1874	843,966	622,929	115,049,140
1875	920,843	696,535	117,533,942
1876	1,096,745	797,724	111,185,650
1877	1,033,151	703,402	99,024,100
1878	1,083,068	699,108	106,101,879
1879	1,215,732	726,903	114,795,834
1880	1,382,477	886,614	143,057,626
1881	1,547,498	972,177	183,007,710
1882	1,607,495	931,238	196,670,221
1883	1,909,167	979,429	201,252,772

The receipts in 1883 were beyond those of any previous year. The increase in the shipments of late years has not kept pace with the growth of the receipts. The packing interest and the shipments of fresh beef from Chicago to the Eastern cities in refrigerator cars account for this. The receipts of cattle at the four principal Atlantic ports for the past seven years has been as follows:—

Years.	New York.	Boston.	Philadelphia.	Baltimore.
1877 ..	507,832	155,907	203,470	112,862
1878 ..	543,587	188,385	188,600	117,675
1879 ..	575,159	183,556	206,780	150,829
1880 ..	679,987	230,079	218,606	138,969
1881 ..	592,570	204,928	225,521	122,174
1882 ..	628,843	130,900	163,300	92,614
1883 ..	674,632	161,162	236,050	94,349

It will be seen that while the receipts at Chicago since 1880 have increased over 38 per cent., the receipts at Atlantic ports have actually fallen off, the decrease last year, as compared with 1880, being over 100,000 head. There is a wide difference of opinion as to the ultimate success of the system of carrying fresh beef from 1,000 to 2,000 miles in refrigerator cars. At present, however, a very large percentage of the beef consumed in the manufacturing cities and towns throughout the New England States, New York, and New Jersey is transported in this way. An illustration of the change which has taken place during the past two years is furnished by the city of Paterson, New Jersey, which formerly took 150 to 200 cattle weekly from the New York and Jersey city stockyards; at present the same city does not take more than a cartload weekly. It is estimated that the Western dressed beef which was received at New York and adjacent cities and towns in 1883 was equal to 1,500 head of cattle per week. One firm of Chicago butchers, it is stated, supplies as many as 96 localities in the East with refrigerator beef.

The export trade in both beef and live cattle reached its maximum in 1881, the value of such exports for that year being 26,830,148 dol.; however, it is still more than twice as large as it was six years ago, and more than eight times as large as the average for the eight years from 1866 to 1873 inclusive. The following table shows the exports for the fiscal years ended June 30 for all the United States ports of beef in lbs., and the number of cattle, as well as the value of both combined:—

Years.	Beef.	Cattle.	Value of Beef and Cattle.
	Lbs.	Number.	Dollars.
1866	19,053,800	..	2,766,451
1867	14,182,562	..	1,727,350
1869	27,299,197	..	2,430,357
1874	36,036,537	56,067	4,107,533
1875	48,243,251	57,211	5,301,041
1876	36,596,150	51,593	4,297,007
1877	88,366,143	60,001	9,096,555
1878	93,878,150	80,040	11,879,908
1879	90,076,395	136,720	15,598,658
1880	129,954,666	182,756	23,667,160
1881	146,703,461	185,707	26,830,148
1882	115,486,203	108,110	18,471,664
1883	122,744,996	104,444	20,425,844

There has been a heavy increase in the shipments of both live cattle and beef since the close of the fiscal year ending June 30, 1883, as is indicated by the fact that the shipments for the calendar year ending December 31, 1882, amounted to only 75,377 cattle, while for the past year they were 174,855, and there was a corresponding increase in the exports of beef.

According to the estimates of the United States Department of Agriculture there were 42,547,307 cattle in the country on January 1, 1844, valued at 1,106,715,703 dol., of which 13,501,206 were milch cows, valued at 423,486,649 dol. The number and value are steadily increasing each year, and without doubt will continue to increase for many years to come. Prices are steady, and have been well maintained for more than a year past, although they are not as high as the extreme figures reached in the spring of 1882. Recent reports from the West indicate that the past winter has been favourable to cattle raisers, and that the losses will be light.

The profits of a well-managed range are very large. It is estimated that with 5,000 head of cattle to start a ranch a net profit of 35,000 dol. to 50,000 dol. yearly may be realised after the second year without diminishing the size of the herd.

It is reported by a said-to-be reliable authority in Texas that "cattle raising is here the most profitable business. Calves reach natural growth at three years, and the losses by storms or disease are comparatively unknown. The average expense of raising a beeve is 5 dol., whilst it averages in market 35 dol., thus making 30 dol. clear profit. It is further estimated, from records carefully kept, that each cow will in 10 years through her progeny produce 40 head, which aggregate 1,200 dol. There is no business in the country that yields such enormously large profits, and none that has so uniformly enriched those who have followed it. There was a time when cattle-raising was carried on by methods of a doubtful character, by employing dishonest Mexicans at 50 c. a head for all calves they would brand; but that day is past, and the system now carefully observed is that each cattle raiser brands the calves with the brand of the cows to which they belong, and thus the owners of large herds look only to the markets through their agents for the income arising from the sale of their cattle. This has reduced the business to a system which involves simply the expense of an agent at the various markets, whose duty is to keep a record of the brands of the cattle sold and the price realised."

PHILADELPHIA.

TABLE showing the Total Number and Estimated Value of each kind of Live Stock, with the Average Prices in the early part of 1883 in the States of this Consular District.

States.	Horses. Number.	Horses. Average Price.	Horses. Value.	Mules. Number.	Mules. Average Price.	Mules. Value.	Milch Cows. Number.	Milch Cows. Average Price.	Milch Cows. Value.
		Dol. c.	Dollars.		Dol. c.	Dollars.		Dol. c.	Dollars.
Pennsylvania	536,255	73 24	39,275,316	22,983	85 72	1,970,103	858,427	30 75	26,396,630
Ohio	714,384	57 33	40,955,635	18,702	69 50	1,299,789	751,702	31 15	23,415,517
Michigan	388,354	65 40	25,267,552	5,134	78 33	402,146	388,424	30 20	11,730,405
Indiana	587,258	56 27	33,045,008	51,521	66 20	3,410,690	489,995	26 67	13,068,167
Illinois	1,012,851	58 60	59,353,069	122,045	69 70	8,506,536	874,572	29 40	25,712,417
Wisconsin	363,001	63 50	23,050,563	7,207	77 80	560,705	487,941	26 61	12,984,110
Minnesota	270,146	66 20	17,883,665	9,580	80 15	751,807	294,833	26 40	7,783,591
Iowa	816,092	59 15	48,271,842	45,312	72 34	3,277,870	905,438	27 58	24,971,980
Total for Consular District	4,688,341	62 46	287,102,650	282,284	74 97	20,179,646	5,051,332	28 59	146,062,817
Total for all States and Territories	10,521,554	58 52	615,824,914	1,835,166	71 35	130,945,378	12,611,632	25 89	326,489,510

TABLE showing the Total Number and Estimated Value of each kind of Live Stock, with the Average Prices in the early part of 1883 in the States of this Consular District—continued.

States.	Oxen and other Cattle.			Sheep.			Hogs.		
	Number.	Average Price.	Value.	Number.	Average Price.	Value.	Number.	Average Price.	Value.
		Dol. c.	Dollars.		Dol. c.	Dollars.		Dol. c.	Dollars.
Pennsylvania	884,842	28 70	25,394,965	1,785,481	3 30	5,892,087	1,128,570	11 28	12,730,270
Ohio	1,038,486	27 50	28,558,365	4,951,511	3 10	15,349,684	2,827,200	7 32	20,695,104
Michigan	501,982	27 20	13,653,910	2,320,752	3 12	7,240,746	915,867	7 57	6,933,113
Indiana	851,440	23 30	19,838,552	1,111,516	2 65	2,945,517	2,867,772	6 80	19,500,850
Illinois	1,442,489	26 51	38,240,383	1,026,702	2 85	2,926,101	4,136,213	7 10	29,367,112
Wisconsin	637,752	23 37	14,904,264	1,350,175	2 50	3,375,437	1,117,537	7 50	8,381,527
Minnesota	391,175	21 67	8,476,762	278,302	2 45	681,840	389,043	6 75	2,626,040
Iowa	1,775,427	22 90	40,657,278	482,681	2 82	1,361,160	5,551,571	7 05	39,138,576
Total for Consular District	7,523,593	25 21	189,724,479	13,307,120	2 85	39,772,572	18,933,773	7 68	139,372,592
Total for all States and Territories	23,280,238	19 89	463,069,499	45,016,224	2 37	106,595,954	44,122,200	5 98	263,543,195

Cattle Diseases.—The extension of the more fatal cattle plagues is an unmitigated evil. These diseases must increase as live stock continue to increase, and will become more generally prevalent as the public domain becomes peopled with stock, constituting a great incubus on the progressive development of great natural resources. The cattle scourge has not as yet gained a permanent footing in the Western States, although pleuro-pneumonia pervades, to a limited extent, the small herds of Pennsylvania, New York, New Jersey, and Maryland, with a more or less degree of fatality. The casual existence of this disease has depreciated the exports to the extent of 3,000,000 dol. per annum.

The "foot-and-mouth disease" broke out at Portland, Maine, but it is now claimed that it has been effectually banished. The cases that occurred in the West, especially in Illinois and Iowa, were pronounced cases of "dry gangrene" of the extremities, from feeding on ergotted grasses or smutty corn. The accounts from Missouri and Kansas were, however, very misleading. In Kirksville, Missouri, it was said that the animals had a high temperature, shed their hoofs, and had an eruption of blisters in the mouth. At Neosho Falls, Kansas, the disease prevailed in three adjoining herds, while it respected all surrounding ones, excepting one or two miles distant, into which a cow had been taken from one of the infected herds. The victims were reported to have been fevered, to have blisters and ulcers not only on the feet but also on the mouth and teats, and a calf that had sucked one of the blistered udders had promptly died of violent intestinal inflammation. It was asserted that the source of the infection had been traced to the clothes of two herdsmen who had recently arrived from Scotland, where they had been attending on diseased stock. Add to this that several veterinarians, who had seen the cases, pronounced them to be "foot-and-mouth disease," and the evidence seemed about as conclusive as it well could be. Others, again, as the result of their investigations, pronounced the disease "dry gangrene," or ergotism. It is now generally conceded that the foot-and-mouth disease does not at the present time exist in the United States. There is no law of the general government prohibiting or controlling the importation of sheep, goats, or swine, and no one has any power to quarantine these animals should they arrive at our ports in an infected condition; yet these, together with all cloven-footed animals, are equally susceptible with cattle to the foot-and-mouth disease, and therefore quite likely to introduce it into the remotest part of the country. Some of the States have enacted laws and enforce quarantine on imported cattle. The United States now have a good supply of many of the best breeds of cattle, some of which they probably own more than the countries to which these animals are native and indigenous. The immediate effect of a law prohibiting the importation of live stock for breeding purposes would be to enhance the value of such thoroughbred stock, accruing to the benefit of the breeders and holders of such stock, but at the same time would greatly decrease the purchasing of these for the rapidly extending ranches of the West and South, and thus lead to a very general propagation of a far inferior native stock, and a consequent loss of many millions to the national wealth. The holder of big thoroughbred stock would become rich in a short time at the expense of an incomparably great national loss.

Pleuro-pneumonia in Pennsylvania is being gradually eradicated. For two years Dr. Gadsden reports to the United States Government: 64 herds, numbering 1,252 animals, were placed in quarantine; 324 animals killed, 257 of which were paid for by the commonwealth of Pennsylvania; and the entire cost to the State being only 10,750 dol., of which 4,325 dol. was paid for the animals destroyed. At the present time what little disease exists is confined to one county. The calves of all infected districts have been slaughtered by the State authorities, and are not allowed to be removed into other portions or out of the State, for fear of spreading the infection.

Later.—An order has just been received from the Treasury Department at Washington to place all imported cattle in quarantine for 90 days, and the facilities for importing are restricted by limiting each ship's capacity to the size of the quarantine station.

In the neighbouring State of New Jersey, pleuro-pneumonia has just broken out in a farm not many miles from Philadelphia, and it is feared that the disease will increase. The disease was traced to some young steers purchased for fattening. One animal was ordered to be killed by the State inspector; one lung was found to be entirely collapsed, the other partially so. Five additional animals have been lost. There are a number of valuable Alderneys and Durhams on this farm.

Reports are coming in that a serious disease has broken out among the cattle of the West, said to be Spanish or Texas fever. At the Chicago stockyards a number of cattle have been shot, and all others not apparently affected are closely quarantined. About 500 head have been ordered to be killed. These cattle were from South-Western Kansas. 15 were found dead in the cars, 55 had been thrown out dead on the way, and a great many others were sick and had to be trampled on. The Veterinarian and Health Commissioner pronounce the disease " bloody murrain," and that the disease had evidently existed among the cattle before shipment. It is believed that the trouble will be kept within limits and soon stamped out, whether it be " Texas fever" or " bloody murrain."

POPULATION.

The population of the Consular District	17,894,967
Pennsylvania—	
Manufacturing and mining	528,277
Professional and personal service	446,713
Agriculture	301,112
Trade and transportation	179,965

	1860.	1870.	1880.
Pennsylvania, in toto	2,906,215	3,521,951	4,282,891
Ohio	2,339,511	2,665,260	3,198,062
Indiana	1,350,428	1,680,637	1,978,301
Illinois	1,711,951	2,539,891	3,077,871
Michigan	749,113	1,184,059	1,636,937
Iowa	674,913	1,194,020	1,624,615
Wisconsin	775,881	1,054,670	1,315,497
Minnesota	172,023	439,706	780,793
Total, Consular District	10,680,035	14,280,194	17,894,968
„ United States	31,443,321	38,558,371	50,155,783

MISCELLANEOUS.

Eastern Penitentiary.—*Solitary Confinement.*—Population, January 1st, 1883, 875 white males, 15 white females, 101 negro males, and 4 negro females; total, 995. During the year 1883 there were received 402 white males, 12 white females, 69 negro males, and 7 negro females—total 490—making a total of persons confined and received in 1883,

1,483. Discharged during the year 365 white males, 4 white females, 41 negro males, and 1 negro female—total 409—leaving the population on January 1st, 1884, 1,076. The receptions in 1883 were 490, being 73 more than in 1882. The credit for convict labour was 39,988 dol. 6 c.; the debit cost per diem per capita, 8 c. 1 mill. Of the 490 prisoners received in the year, 101 were total abstainers. The prisoners made by over-work 7,207 dol. 77 c. This is obtained by executing their allotted task, and when that is done, all over-work is credited one-half to the prisoner and the other half to the county.

TAXABLE Property of Philadelphia for 1884.

	Dollars.
Valuation of real estate	516,243,700
Subject to farm rate	38,360,415
Total	554,604,115
Valuation of household furniture	6,475,000
" horses and cattle	2,715,325
" pleasure carriages	694,253
Grand total	564,488,693
Money at interest, assessed as such	82,380,768
Other assessed property	12,690,956
Grand total	659,560,417

Adulteration.—The extent to which adulteration of numerous articles of food in this country has grown is alarming. Butter, cheese, milk, coffee, sugar, spices, mustard, beer, drugs, and many other articles of daily diet are subjected to great injurious manipulation, and the health of the people affected thereby. Butterine and oleomargerine, it is said, are largely manufactured from the fat of the grossest animals, flavoured and coloured so well as to deceive the careless and unwary purchaser. In some States the legislatures are discussing the necessity of limiting, if not prohibiting entirely, the use of deleterious matter in their manufacture. The export trade in butter and cheese for the ten months ending February 29th were nearly 12,000,000 dol., and there is a prevailing opinion that the manufacture of oleomargerine and adulterated cheeses should be prohibited, not only on account of the public health, but also to save the loss of the export trade.

Philadelphia in Brief.

Area	129 square miles.
Paved streets	900 miles.
Unpaved streets	1,100 ,,
Sewers	410 ,,
Gas mains	705 ,,
,, lamps	12,250
Water pipes	730 miles.
City railways	288 ,,
Population	847,000
Building associations, 600; capital	50,000,000 dollars.
Dwelling houses	154,000
Of which are owned by occupants	110,000
Bath rooms	62,000
Water rent	1,186,000 dollars.
Daily consumption	54,000,000 gallons.
Charitable buildings, hospitals, &c.	115
Places of worship	615
Estimated accommodation	450,000
Public schools, 472; value	6,000,000 dollars.
Pupils educated yearly	110,000
Banking capital—national banks	17,000,000 dollars.
Number of factories	11,000
,, steam boilers	3,381
Estimated horse power	113,000
Capital employed	300,000,000 dollars.
Material used	275,000,000 ,,
Hands employed	200,000
Wages paid	110,000,000 dollars.
Value of manufactures	650,000,000 ,,
Exports	38,662,467 ,,
Imports	32,810,045 ,,
Real estate valuation	545,000,000 ,,
Debt of city	45,000,000 ,,
Assets to show for it	58,000,000 ,,
Death-rate	17 2·10 per 1,000

Philadelphia, United States, July 15, 1884.

ST. PAUL.

Report by Vice-Consul Treherne on the Trade and Commerce of St. Paul for the Year 1883.

It may be well to preface my Report with a brief description of the State of Minnesota and of the territory of Dakota, which form the Customs District of St. Paul.

Minnesota occupies the elevated plateau of North America; its streams feed the Mississippi river, the St. Lawrence river, through Lake Superior, and the Red river of the north which, passing the city of Winnipeg in the Canadian province of Manitoba, flows into Hudson's Bay.

It extends from 43° 30' to 49° north latitude, and roughly from 90° to 97° longitude west of Greenwich, and its boundaries are: on the north, the Dominion of Canada; on the south, the State of Iowa; on the east, Lake Superior and the State of Wisconsin; and on the west, the territory of Dakota. Its length from north to south is 375 miles, with a narrow point extending farther northward 23 miles across the western part of the lake of the woods, and its greatest breadth is about 363 miles. Half of the boundaries of the State are formed of navigable waters. On the north are Rainy river, or Rainy Lake river, as it is sometimes called, which is a large navigable stream, very deep, and often widening into lakes or lagoons; and the Pigeon river, which is navigable for small boats from near its source to within 12 miles of its mouth. On the east is the Mississippi river, which separates the south-eastern portion of the State from Wisconsin, and which is navigable for large steamboats to St. Paul and the St. Croix river, which becomes the dividing line between the two States from its junction with the Mississippi river northward to 46° 06' north latitude, and is navigable for steamers for a distance of 25 or 30 miles. On the west, Big Stone Lake, 32 miles long, and Lake Traverse, 28 miles long, are both navigable; and the Red river of the north is navigable northward from 45° 15' north latitude.

The area of Minnesota is 84,286 square miles, or 53,943,379 acres. Of this, 3,608,012 acres are covered by inland lakes and rivers. The State is now divided into 80 counties. Six of these are very large, and will undoubtedly be subdivided as their populations increase. They are in the northern part of the State, and, with one exception, have but few inhabitants. The exception is St. Louis county, in which the town of Duluth is situated. Its population is confined to the vicinity of that town. Several of the others are too large for convenience, and will be divided into two or more in time.

The numerous inland lakes, for which this State is especially famed, occupy nearly all of that part of the area covered by water, no part of Lake Superior being included. In view of this characteristic, Jean N. Nicollet, a French geologist and astronomer, who explored the territory in 1836–7, called the country "Undine." There are about 9,000 lakes, having an average surface of 300 acres each, and several are very large, handsome sheets of water. For instance, Red Lake is estimated to

[612]

cover 340,000 acres; Mille Lacs, 130,000; Leech Lake, 114,000; Winnebagoshish, 56,000; Vermillion, 64,000; and several others upwards of 10,000 acres. As a rule, to which there are few, if any, exceptions, their waters are clear, cold, and pure. They are commonly very deep, with sandy or pebbly bottoms and firm, dry shores, and are nearly all full of fish, amongst which are several varieties highly esteemed for the table.

These lakes are usually grouped on the high plateaus or summits of the divides between the several drainage systems, being largest and most numerous on that between the waters flowing north and south. They are fed mainly by springs, and are the sources of innumerable streams which meander along the higher levels and, ultimately finding paths down the slopes, afford facilities for almost perfect drainage, while furnishing an incalculable aggregate of water power, of which nearly every neighbourhood has sufficient for its local needs. Such streams are the sources of the Mississippi, St. Louis, Red, Rainy Lake, St. Croix, and Minnesota rivers. Many of these lesser rivers and lakes are susceptible of navigation for small steamers, and will in time become important channels for local commerce. Nearly all the larger rivers have also, more or less, waterfalls, that of the Mississippi, at Minneapolis, being the largest, which furnish power for great aggregations of machinery, and about which manufacturing centres are rapidly forming, as the development of the country progresses. It may be appropriately remarked here, however, that St. Anthony Falls, at Minneapolis, represent 125,000 horse power; St. Croix river, in the vicinity of Taylor's Falls, 100,000; St. Louis river, near its mouth, 72,000; Red river, at Fergus Falls, 35,000; Minnesota river, near Granite Falls, 25,000; and a score or more of other falls and rapids, upwards of 20,000 horse power each.

One-third of the surface of the State is covered by forests, and perhaps one-sixth more by groves, fringes of woods, oak openings, and brush lands. In the counties of Cook, Lake, St. Louis, Itasca, Beltrami, Cass, Aitkin, Carlton, Pine, Kanabec, Mille Lacs, Morrison, Crow Wing, Isanti, and Chisago, and in parts of counties lying adjacent to these, there are forests of white pine of probably one-fourth of the entire area. Interspersed among these, along the valleys of streams and on the margins of lakes, and sometimes on the higher plateaus, are belts or patches of deciduous forests hardly less in aggregate extent than the pine-covered areas. The varieties of trees embraces white, black, and burr oak; red, rock, and swamp elm; white, black, and grey ash; hackberry, sugar, and white maple; box elder, linden or basswood; white and red birch; poplar, willow, cottonwood, and a few others.

Swampy localities are frequent on the more northerly highlands, and are often covered with growths of red and white cedar, though more commonly with tamarack: spruce and fir are prevalent in still other places, and in the vicinity of openings or "burnt" districts one finds mountain ash, ironwood, mountain maple, red and choke cherry, balm of Gilead, yew, arbor vitæ, and other similar varieties. In the lowlands there are natural meadows, on the margins of which, where the ground is higher, nearly all the varieties of shrubbery found in similar situations in Northern Indiana and Ohio grow with equal luxuriance, and in the marshes, on both high and low lands, huckleberries, blueberries, cranberries, and wild rice are produced abundantly. In addition to these features there are, all through the wooded parts of the State, small dry prairies, and tracts from which the forest trees have been burned off. Some of these include two or three townships and wherever not overgrown with shrubbery and young trees sustain luxuriant crops of blue joint and other excellent forage grasses. Amongst the shrubs are thousands of gooseberry, currant, raspberry, and blackberry bushes, which bear abundantly.

About the only considerable portion of the State known to be positively uncultivable, is a strip of land comprising apparently about one-third of Cook, one-fourth of Lake, and one-twentieth of St. Louis counties. This extends entirely across the northern portion of the two first-named, counties and a short distance west of Lake Vermillion. In the latter it is known as the "Iron Range," and is said to be the richest and most extensive deposit of that valuable metal found on this continent, if not in the world. The length of the range, as far as discoveries have been made, is upwards of 75 miles, and its width varies from 20 to 40 miles. Ore has been found in nearly every part of this tract, sometimes cropping out among the rocks, and again lying but a few feet below the surface. The ore is a hard, hematite, specular variety, and the results of upwards of 30 specimens taken from different parts of the range show from 65 to 72 per cent. of metallic iron. Experts pronounce the quality of the metal fully equal to the best Swedish iron, and peculiarly well qualified for the manufacture of Bessemer steel and "chill" iron. Mines are now being opened on the range, and two railroads are projected—one being in course of construction from the north shore of Lake Superior. Copper and silver ores are also found in Lake and Cook counties, and mining for both these metals has already been commenced there with, it is alleged, the most flattering promises of success. Plumbago, of good quality, is likewise claimed to have been discovered on Pigeon Point, in quantities sufficient to justify mining, and rumours are circulated from time to time of the finding of other metals and minerals in these localities. The entire north shore of Lake Superior is asserted to be a mineral region of uncommon richness, and its proximity to the lake gives it especial value, because of the facilities for inexpensive transportation thus afforded. Another mineral region is that in the vicinity of the lake of the woods. A beginning has been made on the eastern side of this lake, north of the international boundary, in gold mining, and gold has undoubtedly been obtained there in considerable quantities. Gold has also been found in combination with other metallic and mineral substances near Vermillion Lake, and at several other points along the boundary, and silver ore of high grade is said to be abundant in the vicinity of Hunter's Island. The entire region along the northern boundary may prove to be valuable by reason of its minerals, but that part of it east of Lake Vermillion and north of the latitude of its south shore is pronounced utterly barren, the surface consisting almost wholly of exposed rocks, with scarcely any covering of soil. Its only vegetable products are moss, and an occasional scrub pine of stunted growth.

The soil of Minnesota is very similar in all parts of the State, except where the granitic upheaval is exposed north of Lake Superior. Elsewhere the entire State is covered by alluvial drifts of widely varying depths and somewhat diversified elements. The earlier of these deposits contain a large percentage of alumina. Lying upon this, and more or less intermingled with it, is a deposit of calcareous and silicious elements. Throughout the State these superior deposits are filled with vegetable and animal matter, and, in the wooded regions, covered with a surface layer of vegetable mould. On the prairie, instead of the mould, the animal and vegetable remains are compounded with washings of clay, lime, sand, and ashes of plants, and in some places have the character of alkaloids. Everywhere, however, the combinations of organic remains with the varied bases give the soil an abundant supply of phosphates and other fertilising properties, and the depth of this plant-producing earth is nearly everywhere far beyond the ability of man to render serviceable in cultivation. In appearance the soil is of dark to greyish-brown colour, being darkest in the lower plains and valleys, where it occasionally approaches to blackness, and is quite viscous when wet. It is everywhere exceedingly friable, and so easily worked that a hoe is not needed in the corn or potato field.

The best test of the soil, however, is its record of averages of cultivated vegetable products. The statistical crops reports published by the State, which are known to be from 12 to 20 per cent. less than the actual results, give the following mean averages of the staple crops, viz :— wheat, 14·09 bushels; corn, 30·51 bushels; buckwheat, 11·78 bushels; oats, 32·14 bushels; barley, 24·26 bushels; rye, 15·21 bushels; potatoes, 98·29 bushels; and beans, 11·37 bushels per acre. Instances might be gathered from almost every county in which farming is carried on, where in all of these averages are largely exceeded. Yields of upwards of 20 bushels of wheat, 40 bushels of corn, 45 bushels of oats, 30 bushels of barley, 22 bushels of rye, 15 bushels of buckwheat, 150 bushels of potatoes, and 16 bushels of beans are not at all uncommon, and indeed nearly every careful farmer in the State could show these or greater general averages; but the above are results attained where a considerable proportion of the farmers are unskilful, and many are without the proper tools and implements to till the land thoroughly.

The atmosphere of Minnesota is dry, clear, and pure, and it is seldom that a refreshing breeze is not felt, even on the stillest summer day. The nights of summer, almost without exception, are cool, so as to afford opportunity for refreshing sleep; and although the days are frequently very warm, the heat is rarely oppressive, as is often the case where humid atmospheres prevail. The winters are cold, often severely so; but it is seldom, and only for short intervals, that the term "inclement" can properly be applied to Minnesota weather. The dryness of the air diminishes its capability of conducting heat from the body, and men and animals therefore suffer much less here from cold than where there is even a slightly greater proportion of dampness. Carpenters and other mechanics work at outdoor employments without discomfort, when the thermometer ranges from zero to 10° or 12° below. The intensely cold periods, when the mercury sinks to 20° below zero, or lower, are always of brief duration, the longest never exceeding from three to five days, and more than two or three rarely occur during a single winter. The temperature is variable at all seasons, but especially in winter and spring. In summer and autumn the temperature is more equable. The "blizzards," which are generally exaggerated, are simply high winds accompanied with driving snow, and are no worse or more frequent here than in any prairie country north of the 40th parallel; and meantime this State is almost wholly out of the track of those extensive and terrible cyclones.

The official vital statistics give the average annual death-rate as one person in every 125 of the population.

Minnesota not only possesses the motive power to operate machinery to work up the material, but either does or can produce the material to be operated upon. Her forests supply abundance of pine, cedar, birch, oak, ash, maple, walnut, butternut, basswood, willow, &c., for the manufacture of houses, vessels, cars, wagons, sleighs, agricultural implements and tools, furniture, baskets, tubs, buckets, and almost everything that is made wholly or partially of wood. Her quarries yield granites, syenites, quartzites, limestones, sandstones, slates, &c., and her garnets, jaspers, &c., are not unfrequently used for settings of jewellery. She has the clay for bricks, pottery, delfware, and probably porcelain, and superior white sand for glass. Her fields yield Fife wheat, from which the choicest flour is made, and corn, oats, barley, rye, buckwheat, and potatoes, some of which may be manufactured into breadstuffs, while from others starch, Maltese sugar, &c., can be made.

The amber cane grown here yields a comparatively large percentage of syrup and sugar, and its manufacture by farmers is profitable. Sugar beets grow well in all parts of the State, and contain more than the usual quantity of saccharine. Flax and hemp for the manufacture of linen, cordage, paper, &c., grow flourishingly. Her flocks of sheep, herds of cattle, and droves of hogs can furnish ample supplies of wool and hides for making cloth, flannels, blankets, leather, &c., while the packing and curing of their flesh could be made important and profitable. The mines in the north-eastern counties will afford iron, copper, silver, &c., for manufacturers in those lines. In short, there is ample material to be found in the State for an almost illimitable variety of manufacturing.

The situation of Minnesota at the head of navigation on the Mississippi river, the Great Lakes, and the Red river of the north, places her in possession of enviable natural commercial facilities, the importance of which was recognised by the French explorers who visited this country 200 years ago, and has been the subject of frequent comment by more recent writers. The two former routes enable her with a single transfer of cargo to reach tide-water, and have free access to the markets of the world by the cheapest possible means of transportation, and through the latter steamers may ply between points on her western border and the vast and fertile territory of the north-west, watered by the Assiniboine and Saskatchewan rivers, together with the forest countries bordering on Lakes Winnipeg and Manitoba. Should the scheme of establishing a line of steamers to ply between Fort York, on Hudson's Bay, and Liverpool be successful (which is hardly credible), the Red river puts Minnesota in close proximity to that new oceanic route, and affords her opportunity to share its advantages. It is true that these water routes will not be constantly available; but the benefits accruing from their use during the five or six months of each year can hardly be estimated. They will not only admit of merchandise being carried over them at cheap rates, but will exert a powerful influence in keeping rates of freight by railway at reasonable figures.

The following will show the various roads now operating in the State:—Burlington, Cedar Rapids, and Northern; Chicago and North-Western; Chicago, St. Paul, Minneapolis and Omaha; Minneapolis and St. Louis; Minneapolis, Lyndale, and Minnetonka; Northern Pacific; St. Paul and Duluth; St. Paul, Minneapolis, and Manitoba; Chicago, Milwaukee, and St. Paul. The Burlington, Cedar Rapids, and Northern Railway owns but a few miles (some 30) in this State. It enters from the Iowa border, and runs north to Albert Lea, at which point connection is made with the Minneapolis and St. Louis Railroad and Chicago, Milwaukee, and St. Paul Railway. The Chicago and North-Western Railway, with its branches and leased lines, traverses the State from east to west, and plays a most important part in the railroad system of Minnesota. The Chicago, Milwaukee, and St. Paul operates the largest number of miles of road in the State. Its main line, like that of the Chicago and North-Western, runs east and west, but it has several important branches, which enable it to reach not only St. Paul and Minneapolis on its own rails, but also nearly all the towns of any consequence in Southern Minnesota. The importance of these two latter-mentioned roads to the State is immeasurably great, as by their means direct communication is made with the eastern system of railroads, forming a competition decidedly advantageous to the citizens, as it ensures low rates and speedy passage. Both of these roads are pushing construction very rapidly in all directions. The Minneapolis and St. Louis Railroad is a north and south road, having Minneapolis for its northern terminus, and extending in an almost direct line to Fort Dodge, Iowa, and is being rapidly extended. The Northern Pacific Railroad, starting from its eastern termini, St. Paul and Duluth, traverses the northern part of the State in an almost direct line, to eventually reach its western terminus, Portland, Oregon, on the Pacific coast. An entirely new region of country has been opened up by the advent of this road, and the expectations indulged in when the project of building it was first broached have been more than realised. The value of this road to the State cannot be over-estimated. The St. Paul and Duluth Railroad is essentially a Minnesota road. It traverses the great pine lumber districts of the State, and has for its termini St. Paul and Duluth, as it name implies, at which point connections are made respectively with the eastern and southern systems, and with the Northern Pacific, and also with lake navigation. The Minneapolis, Lyndale, and Minnetonka is but a small local road, affording direct means of reaching the celebrated lake and resorts of Minnetonka from St. Paul and Minneapolis. Not the least important of Minnesota's railroads is the St. Paul, Minneapolis, and Manitoba, which, leaving St. Paul and Minneapolis, takes a western and northern direction, passing through the Red River Valley on its way to Dakota and Manitoba, and making connection at Emerson with the Canadian Pacific. Its branches are directed in all directions, through the western, central, and north-western portions of the State. The St. Paul, Minneapolis, and Omaha Railway, starting from St. Paul, extends through the south-western portion of the State into Iowa, with branches to Dakota, its objective point being some yet undecided upon spot in the Far West. Its main line also runs from St. Paul north-east, and extends through Wisconsin, making connection with the Chicago and North-Western, for Chicago and all eastern points. The total number of miles of railroads now in operation in the State exceeds 4,000.

Probably in no State in the Union has a better or more munificent provision been made for popular education than in Minnesota. Two sections in each township are set apart for this purpose by the Organic Act, and the State Constitution provides that the proceeds of these lands shall remain a perpetual school fund to the State. The proceeds derived from the sale of these lands will eventually amount to at least ±5,000,000 dol., which amount will remain a permanent school fund.

In addition to the direct sale of lands, considerable amounts are realised from the sale of grass and stumpage; the interest on the permanent fund is distributed semi-annually, and this comprises the main support for common schools, except for cities and towns where a special tax is levied to maintain graded schools. Thus an education is guaranteed and placed within the reach of every child in the State. Every means attainable is made use of by the educational authorities to make the common schools of the State equal in their efficiency and standard of scholarship with those of other States. Most of the larger towns have a good system of graded schools, with large and costly buildings. There are three State Normal Schools at Winona, Mankato, and St. Cloud respectively, all well equipped with a faculty of instructors, and with all suitable apparatus for the training of teachers. The State University located at Minneapolis is the crowning grade of the entire educational system. It is fully organised in all its departments. There are also several denominational colleges in the State which are in successful operation.

The government of the State is very similar in its features to that of most of the Northern States of the Union, being divided into three usual branches—legislative, executive, and judicial. The legislative is vested in a legislature of two Houses, a Senate and House of Representatives, which meet biennially. They are elected by senatorial districts, into which the State is apportioned, after every federal or State census, each containing, as near as may be, an equal proportion of population. The sessions of the legislature are limited to 60 days. The members receive 5 dol. for each day from the beginning to the close of each session.

The Executive Department consists of the elected and appointed State officers. The elected officers are: Governor, Lieutenant-Governor, Secretary of State, Treasurer of State, Attorney-General, and Railroad Commissioner, an auditor of State, and a clerk of the Supreme Court. The appointed officers are: Adjutant-General, State Librarian, Governor's private secretary, Superintendent of Public Instruction, Insurance Commissioner, and Public Examiner. The appointment of these officers is confirmed by the Senate.

The Judicial Department of the government is vested in the Supreme Court, District and Common Pleas Courts, Probate Court, and Justices of the Peace. The Supreme Judges, of which there are three, are elected every seven years. There are 12 District Judges and three Common Pleas Judges, each of whom is elected for seven years.

The State of Minnesota derives its name from the principal tributary of the Mississippi river within its boundaries. The name is a compound Sioux or Dakota word. This nation call the Missouri river Minneshoshay—muddy water—and this stream Minnesota. The precise signification of "sota" is difficult to express. Some writers have said it means clear (Schoolcraft) bluish green; others, turbid. Nicollet remarks: "The adjective 'sotah' is of difficult translation. The Canadians translate it by a pretty equivalent word, 'brouillé,' perhaps more properly rendered into English by blear; as, for instance, Minisotah, blear water. I have entered upon this explanation because the word 'sotah' really means neither clear nor turbid, as some authors have asserted, its true meaning being readily found in the Sioux expression, 'ishtasotah,' blear-eyed." From the fact that the word signifies neither white nor blue, but the peculiar appearance of the sky on certain days, the Minnesota Historical Society publications define Minnesota to mean the sky-tinted water, which is certainly poetic, and according to Gideon H. Pond, one of the best Dakota scholars, correct.

The territory of Dakota was once a part of Michigan territory, and afterwards the territory of Wisconsin included all that present State, and all of Iowa and Minnesota and Dakota as far west as the Missouri river. After the organisation of Wisconsin and Iowa as States, Minnesota, while a territory, embraced besides its present area all that portion of Dakota east of the Missouri river; and the boundaries of Nebraska territory from 1857 to 1861 included that portion lying west of the Missouri river. The admission of Minnesota as a State in May, 1858, left all the country west of its diminished boundaries and of North-west Iowa, along the Big Sioux river to the Missouri river on the west, not included in any organisation, and occupied by the Indians. This part was with propriety and by common consent designated by the name of Dakota, from the great associated tribe of Indians known in their own language and among themselves as

Dakotas, and recognised the French word Sioux only when learned by long communication with the whites. The first cession of lands within Dakota was made in 1858 by treaty with a band of the Dakota tribe, called in their language Jancton or Yankton, and with the Poncas, a band of another nation, tribe, and dialect, who claimed a part of it. This purchase opened 25,000 square miles lying in South-Eastern Dakota, and this has gradually been extended by successive treaties with the Sioux or Dakotas, until nearly all that portion east of the Missouri river has been ceded; and in February, 1877, a treaty was ratified and approved by the necessary legislation which ceded and opened the Black Hills in Western Dakota, already celebrated for wealth in the precious metals and in timber. White settlement was begun in 1859, but by reason of the critical and disturbed condition of national affairs, the Act of Congress organising the territory of Dakota was not passed until March 22, 1861. President Lincoln appointed the necessary executive and judicial officers at an early day thereafter, and they came promptly to their posts, so that after June, 1861, Dakota had a government.

The original boundaries as declared by this Act included, besides the present area of the territory, all that region now embraced in Idaho, Montana, and Wyoming, each of which has been created by successive Acts, leaving the western boundary of Dakota the 27th meridian of longitude west from Washington.

In August, 1862, the Indians rose in arms against the whites, and endeavoured to exterminate the pale faces from the prairies of Dakota and Minnesota, and until the spring of 1865, when treaties of peace and friendship were signed, the settlers in Dakota territory had to fight with their red enemies. In 1867–8 immigration was greatly augmented. Towns and villages were located, counties organised, and the land survey extended. From this time on the growth of Dakota has been unprecedented in national history, that of the years 1881, 1882, and 1883 being especially noticeable. In the spring and early summer of 1883 it was estimated that not less than 1,000 settlers per day came into the territory on the various lines of railways. A careful and conservative estimate places the present population at not less than 320,000 people. In its dimensions the territory exceeds many a famous empire of antiquity. It extends through a little more than 6° of latitude, with an average width of about 350 miles, containing in round numbers 150,000 square miles. Its great length from north to south produces a marked difference in climate between the extremes of latitude, and affords a great variety of productions. In the north the surface is level or gently rolling, with a deep black soil containing more or less lime and overlying a subsoil of clay. Some parts, however, are considerably rolling, with a lighter soil, and in the extreme north-west stretches of sandy plains and "bad lands" are found. The extensive wheat fields of North Dakota have rendered the territory famous the country over. A special grade of wheat, known as "No. 1 Hard," is raised, which, while not yielding more per acre than ordinary spring wheat, brings a higher price, from the fact that it is superior in quality, and contains a greater amount of bread-producing material than other wheat. Its cultivation is conducted on a scale of great magnitude, fields of from 1,000 to 5,000 acres being not uncommon. The yield of oats, also largely cultivated, is remarkable, averaging sometimes 70 to 80 bushels per acre, and weighing from 35 to 40 lbs. per bushel. Vegetables and tame grasses, though not as yet extensively cultivated, are said to do well. West of the Missouri river are vast cattle ranges covered with buffalo grass, which possess peculiarly rich qualities, upon which the cattle feed summer and winter. In Central and Southern Dakota the surface is gently undulating, with a deep rich soil, tending to a sandy loam in some localities. General farming and stock raising here take the place of the exclusive grain raising of the north. In the extreme southern part, the soil being strong and warm, large crops of corn are raised, upon which great numbers of cattle and hogs are fattened for market. This has given to the south-eastern counties the name of the "cow counties." Flax is raised in great quantities, and is generally a profitable crop. Wool growing is also extensively engaged in. The farms average much smaller than in the north, containing ordinarily not more than 160 acres. In South-Western Dakota lies a tract of country known as the Black Hills, which was first opened to settlement in 1877. Originally sought for because of its mineral wealth, it has proved to be, contrary to general expectation, a remarkably fine agricultural and grazing country. The hills proper are covered with forests of pine, which afford timber and lumber in abundance. A number of rich and profitable gold mines is now being successfully worked, while the presence of silver, lead, salt, mica, nickel, tin, coal, and other minerals in considerable quantities has been fully established. The valleys and neighbouring plains are covered with fine farms, and farther out are stock ranges estimated to contain not less than 500,000 cattle. It is believed that with established railroad communication the Black Hills district will offer an unequalled field for investment and enterprise. At present the nearest railroad is 200 miles distant, being shut out by the Great Sioux reservation, containing about 35,000 square miles, extending from the Missouri river west to the 103rd meridian, and from the northern boundary of Nebraska to the Cannon Ball river on the north. This reservation is occupied by about 24,000 Sioux Indians with five agencies. An effort is now being made for the opening of a part of this reservation, and an agreement to that effect is now before Congress for ratification. There are several smaller Indian reservations in the territory, among which are the Wahpeton and Sisseton, near the eastern boundary of the territory on Lake Traverse; the Devil's Lake, or Fort Totten reservation in the north; the Mandan in the north-west; and the Crow Creek and Yankton reservations on the Missouri river in the south. The territory is, considering its recent settlement, well supplied with railroad facilities. The Northern Pacific Railroad traverses North Dakota from east to west, crossing the Missouri river at Bismarck. The Chicago and North-Western and the Chicago, Milwaukee, and St. Paul companies have each a main line across the territory as far as the Missouri river, and numerous branches completed and others projected or building. The Missouri river is navigable throughout its entire course within the territory, and numerous steamers are engaged in the transportation of freight on its waters. The Dakota or James river and the Red river of the north are navigable for small steamers for considerable distances, though but little use is made of either stream for purposes of transportation. There are numerous small lakes in the territory, but none of any considerable size, except Lake Traverse and Big Stone Lake on the eastern boundary, and Minne Waken or Devil's Lake in the north. The latter is a salt water lake, very irregular in shape, and about 30 miles long. In most parts of the territory water is easily obtainable in wells of moderate depth. At Yankton and other points in Southern Dakota artesian wells have been sunk to a depth of from 350 to 500 feet, and an unfailing supply of flowing water obtained. The climate is pleasant, healthful, and invigorating. The severity of the cold in winter is everywhere mitigated by the absence of moisture in the atmosphere and the uniformly clear and bright days. The average rainfall has steadily increased for several years as the settlements multiply, and is now ample for the means of vegetation. But little snow falls in winter, except in the northern part and in isolated sections of the central and south-western parts.

There are settlements of Scandinavians, Russians, Bohemians, and Poles scattered over the territory, but the great majority of the people are American born, mostly from the Western States. The large proportion of young men and men not yet past the prime of life is noticeable, and results in a marked and general activity and energy, which account in no small degree for the wonderful development of the country. The railroads keeping pace with or even preceding the settlements have rendered unnecessary the hardships and privations ordinarily incident to the opening of a new country. Schools and churches are numerous and well supported. Two sections of land in each township are reserved to provide a school fund, which will not however become available until after the territory becomes a State. The amount thus reserved will aggregate over 5,000,000 acres. Public institutions are located as follows: The Dakota Hospital for the Insane at Yankton, and another at Jamestown in process of construction, a Deaf-Mute School, and the Dakota Penitentiary at Sioux Falls, with a penitentiary building in course of construction at Bismarck. The financial condition of the territory is good, there being a small debt contracted in the erection of the public buildings named. The greater part of the public domain has been taken up by settlers, except in the extreme north and west of the Missouri river, though in some other localities desirable claims can still be obtained under the homestead and pre-emption laws. There are 10 United States land offices in the territory, located respectively at Yankton, Mitchell, Huron, Watertown, Aberdeen, Fargo, Grand Forks, Devil's Lake City, Bismarck, and Deadwood, with provision for two more on the opening of the Indian reservation west of the Missouri river. A strong effort is being made to divide the territory on the 46th parallel of latitude, and to secure the admission of the southern part into the Union, and there is little doubt that eventually the territory will become two States.

Trade and Commerce.

Exports.—It is impossible to give a correct statement regarding the amount and value of the exports from this district. The value would, however, be included in the returns of the officials at the seaports at which the goods are shipped; I will therefore not attempt it. The main exports at present are flour and cattle. Manitoba and the Canadian North-West are supplied almost wholly from Minnesota and Dakota, and principally from the cities of St. Paul and Minneapolis. No export business is done at the port of St. Paul. Export business is done, however, at Duluth and at Pembina.

What statistics I have been able to collect I have given in the following table:—

	1881.	1882.
	Dollars.	Dol.　c.
Total value of domestic exports	703,122	..
„ declared value of imports	60,820	48,924　00
„ value of commodities from foreign countries entered for transhipment to other foreign countries	2,504,464	4,102,948　00
Portion thereof subject to duty	2,496,491	2,169,150　36

The total tonnage of freight taken from St. Paul by the boats of the St. Louis and St. Paul Packet Company by the Mississippi river was—

		Tons.
For the year 1882	.. ..	8,500
„ 1883	.. ..	6,000

Imports.—The character of the goods imported and the countries from which derived are, in a general way, as follows:—

England: Cotton, woollen, and knit goods, manufactures of iron and rubber, garden seeds, varnishes, and worsted yarns.

Ireland: Linen.

Scotland: Ale and linen goods.

France: Wines, brandies, and cordials, druggists' sundries, church goods, and Parisian fancy articles.

Spain and Portugal: Wines and brandies.

Germany: Knit goods, musical instruments, leather, china ware, wines, felt shoes, toys, paper, and books.

Norway: Fish and cheese.

Sweden: Matches and boxes.

Italy: Painting and statuary.

Austria: Toilet and fancy articles.

Switzerland: Musical instruments.

Bohemia: Glass buttons.

Cuba: Cigars.

China and Japan: Teas.

During the year 1883 the market value of the goods received at the Custom-house in St. Paul was 326,879 dol., and the duties collected upon this valuation was 64,017 dol.—an increase of 22,739 dol. over the duty receipts for 1882. The business for 1883 at the port of Duluth has not yet been tabulated and furnished to me.

I give below a tabulated statement of the yearly business of the Custom-house at St. Paul and Duluth:—

Ports.	1883. Receipts from Duties.	1882. Receipts from Duties.	1882. Receipts from All Sources.	1881. Receipts from Duties.	1881. Receipts from All Sources.
	Dollars.	Dol. c.	Dol. c.	Dol. c.	Dol. c.
St. Paul	64,017	41,278 03	45,247 78	26,983 56	31,809 87
Duluth	..	6,862 56	15,515 87	6,006 81	12,638 80
Pembina	..	..	..	37,377 29	49,120 38

The total tonnage of freight delivered at St. Paul by the boats of the St. Louis and St. Paul Packet Company by the Mississippi river was—

		Tons.
For the year 1882	.. ..	12,750
„ 1883	.. ..	12,000

The following are the statistics of the arrivals and departures of vessels from the port of Duluth now in my possession:—

UNITED STATES.

Arrivals.

AMERICAN VESSELS FROM FOREIGN PORTS.

	1881.	1882.
Steamers, screw	5	..
Total number of vessels	5	14
Tonnage	185	1,528
Number of men	25	86

AMERICAN VESSELS FROM AMERICAN PORTS.

	1881.	1882.
Schooners	243	..
Steamers, screw	324	..
Total number of vessels	567	6,887
Tonnage	359,501	533,001
Number of men	8,511	12,486

FOREIGN VESSELS FROM FOREIGN PORTS.

	1881.	1882.
Schooners	1	..
Steamers, screw	71	..
„ paddle	28	..
Total number of vessels	100	139
Tonnage	60,366	82,320
Number of men	2,760	3,560

Departures.

AMERICAN VESSELS TO AMERICAN PORTS.

	1881.	1882.
Number of vessels	560	692
Tonnage	351,767	525,001
Number of men	9,083	12,707

AMERICAN VESSELS TO FOREIGN PORTS.

	1881.	1882.
Number of vessels	5	11
Tonnage	185	422
Number of men	25	50

FOREIGN VESSELS TO FOREIGN PORTS.

	1881.	1882.
Number of vessels	100	134
Tonnage	60,269	80,164
Number of men	2,777	3,468

The following is a statement furnished me by Bradstreet's Mercantile Agency of the number of mercantile failures during the past three years in Minnesota:—

Years.	Number of Failures.	Assets.	Liabilities.
		Dollars.	Dollars.
1881	95	286,114	548,211
1882	114	251,566	540,671
1883	193	1,037,900	1,599,006

The domestic trade of the district may perhaps be best shown by describing that of the cities of St. Paul and Minneapolis, which form the jobbing centre of the north-west.

During the past 12 months these cities have grown wonderfully in business and population. The jobbing trade is the essential measure of a city's commercial importance, of the relation which it sustains towards the vast territory tributary to it, and of an element which must ever contribute to give certainty and stability to its prospects for the future. The figures show upon what a solid foundation the external and visible growth of these cities is built. By the exclusion in both cities of the grain commission trade, where the element of speculation is present and the number of transfers may swell the aggregate to figures that would not correctly represent wholesale trade so called, the estimate is reduced to the utmost conservatism. Omitting this item altogether and including only the straight jobbing business, as the term is understood in other cities, and the value of goods manufactured and jobbed by the manufacturer, the total jobbing trade of the two cities for the year 1883 is fixed at the magnificent figure of 136,334,771 dol., an increase of 12,236,101 dol. over the figure for 1882, or nearly 10 per cent. The commission business for the same period aggregated 43,815,000 dol. as against 30,485,736 dol. for 1882, making a grand total for straight jobbing, commission, and manufactured goods jobbed, of 180,149,771 dol. against 154,584,406 dol., the total of one year ago.

The figures presented are such as to need little comment. Overleaping as they do, when compared with the figures of a few years ago, all the annals of metropolitan prosperity, they are a witness of the present and an earnest of the future. It is most noticable that the North-west is apparently exempt from those conditions which are even now affecting unfavourably the older communities of the country. The tremendous advance has taken place in the midst of a season that was not a hopeful or confident one in commercial circles. It is the product of an impulse that proceeds from no shortlived trade activity, no local or sectional excitement, but is the result of a material necessity.

2020

I append tabulated statements of the wholesale trade of the two cities:—

STATEMENT of the Wholesale Trade of St. Paul, compiled by the Secretary of the Chamber of Commerce, "Pioneer Press," March 2.

Business.	Number of Establishments.	Number of Employés.	Amount of Sales, 1883.	Increase over 1882.
			Dol.	Dol.
Agricultural implements	9	85	2,163,800	255,800
Beer	14	79	1,157,321	69,167
Blank goods, paper, and church goods	7	87	1,036,000	*200,056
Boots and shoes	5	90	2,910,000	85,000
Cigars and tobacco	18	52	1,267,000	616,700
Clothing	3	73	825,900	25,000
Coffee, tea, spices, &c.	6	60	781,000	89,000
Confectionery, fruit, and bakers' products	7	140	1,502,000	30,750
Crockery and glassware	3	57	479,000	5,000
Drugs, paints, and oils	8	159	2,500,000	740,000
Dry goods and notions	13	374	9,152,000	7,500
Fuel and pig-iron	13	738	4,358,000	1,469,666
Furniture	9	83	533,000	78,000
Grain, flour, feed, and commission	47	95	6,300,000	424,264
Groceries	11	428	13,237,000	*2,960,000
Guns and sporting goods	2	9	110,000	*40,000
Hardware, stoves, and heavy iron	17	269	4,467,750	484,810
Hats, caps, and furs	4	70	1,250,000	75,000
Hides and furs	6	47	716,600	*84,000
Jewellers	4	11	77,500	..
Leather, saddlery, and findings	7	90	981,000	349,374
Lime and cement	3	10	212,000	..
Live stock	9	56	2,572,000	79,856
Lumber	17	1,620	3,660,000	220,378
Machinery and mill supplies	8	129	1,308,000	9,800
Millinery and lace goods	3	42	500,000	..
Musical instruments	6	78	488,300	59,300
Printing material	3	13	181,000	..
Provisions	7	89	1,313,000	112,000
Sash, doors, and blinds	5	116	791,000	99,000
Trunks and valises	2	30	200,000	..
Wines and liquors	14	88	2,060,000	*271,484
Miscellaneous	35	448	2,959,500	..
Total	325	5,815	72,048,771	5,385,365

Miscellaneous includes bar supplies, billiard tables, brewers' supplies, bricks, brooms, brushes, carpets, fish, junk, ice, photographic material, rubber goods, seeds, soap, steam heating, stoneware, surgical instruments, undertakers', upholstery, vinegar, wooden and willow ware, woollen and tailors' trimmings.

* Decrease.

STATEMENT of the Wholesale Trade of Minneapolis compiled by the "Pioneer Press," December 30, 1883.

Business.	Number of Men in House.	Number of Men on Road.	Trade.
			Dol.
Agricultural implements..	185	98	8,762,000
Beer	28	3	405,000
Billiard tables	7	..	90,000
Boots and shoes	22	24	950,000
Broom stock	2	..	50,000
Crockery and glassware	33	7	128,000
Clothing	5	4	200,000
Cigars and tobacco	39	22	1,210,000
Crackers and confectionery	5	4	150,000
Coffee, teas, spices, &c.	10	6	90,000
Curtains, fixtures, mouldings, &c.	8	3	86,000
Drugs, paints, oils, &c.	27	4	385,000
Dry goods	149	35	3,550,000
Fish and oysters	33	4	310,000
Fruits	19	1	485,000
Fuel	16	..	1,750,000
Flour and mill stuff	6	..	1,500,000
Furniture	3	..	50,000
General produce and feed	123	7	2,330,000
Groceries	114	27	7,250,000
Hardware	71	6	887,000
Horses and mules..	..	..	500,000
Jewellery and jewellers' goods	24	8	386,000
Leather, findings, hides, &c.	5	2	155,000
Lime and cement..	31	2	388,000
Lumber jobbers	15	2	170,000
Live stock	..	..	1,390,000
Marble and mantels	3	..	50,000
Machinery, engines, &c.	32	7	830,000
Millinery	13	3	90,000
Oil	27	2	554,000
Plumbers' goods and pumps	25	4	255,000
Printing materials	7	..	70,000
Paper and stationery	28	4	425,000
Rubber goods, belting, &c.	13	6	450,000
Safes, scales, &c.	8	8	95,000
Sportsman's goods	5	..	40,000
Sash, doors, and blinds	16	6	200,000
Seeds	6	..	85,000
Trunks	6	..	15,000
Wines and liquors..	21	6	2,875,000
Total	1,240	315	38,641,000
Total 1883, same classes	1,088	255	35,721,000
Increase	152	60	2,920,000

A comparison—

		Dol.
1883	..	38,641,000
1882	..	35,721,000
1881	..	30,959,562
1880	..	24,299,200
1879	..	14,001,700
1878	..	10,406,250
1877	..	8,147,275
1176	..	5,373,651

Statement of the grain trade of Minneapolis compiled by "Pioneer Press," December 30, 1883.

The grain trade was shown to have been, as compared with previous years, as follows:—

Year.	Number of Men in House.	Number of Men on Road.	Amount of Sales.
			Dol.
1883	113	12	37,415,000
1882	108	12	24,610,000
1881	40	6	16,954,278

STATEMENT of the Jobbing Trade by Manufacturers in Minneapolis, compiled by the "Pioneer Press," December 30, 1883.

Business.	Number of Men in House.	Number of Men on Road.	Trade.
			Dol.
Flour	92	..	17,113,060
Lumber	46	10	4,628,878
Agricultural implements	27	17	1,570,000
Furniture	9	3	845,700
Sash, doors, and blinds	25	8	1,981,000
Boots and shoes	5	4	400,000
Woollen goods	5	1	400,000
Clothing and duck goods	6	2	231,000
Soap and rendering products	9	1	1,350,000
Beer	6	2	575,000
Cigars and tobacco	7	2	225,000
Crackers and confectionery	7	21	799,550
Oil, paints, &c.	5	2	392,000
Pork packing, &c.	6	..	466,000
Bags and jute goods	4	2	360,000
Paper	5	1	250,000
Drain pipe and earthenware	2	..	40,000
Vinegar and pop	2	..	70,500
Organs	2	..	12,000
Trunks, showcases, &c.	2	..	116,000
Iron and tin ware	6	1	160,000
Total for 1883	276	77	31,945,638
„ 1882	200	44	27,610,638
Increase	76	33	4,355,000

SUMMARY, all Classes.

	Dol.
Straight jobbing trade	38,641,000
Jobbed by manufacturers	31,945,000
Grain commission trade	37,515,000
Grand total	108,101,000

It is not to be denied that the general situation, taking the country at large, has not been especially encouraging. Business was generally quiet during the last six months of 1883—more especially during the last two months—and the failure of large houses in different sections has been a feature of trade that has shaken confidence and caused business men to look about them with unwonted carefulness and increased conservatism. To say that St. Paul and Minneapolis have escaped entirely from the depressing influence of this state of affairs would be saying that they are outside of the business world. The low price of wheat has also had a local effect. Farmers have not been disposed to sell their product where they could afford to hold it, and consepuently there has not been that free circulation of money which high prices and eager selling would bring. Again, it is claimed by the merchants that they were never more careful or more conservative in their dealings than they were during 1883; that they scanned mercantile lists closely, and have cut down bills where they thought they were too large; that there has been very little hap-hazard trading in any quarter. Market prices the country over have, moreover, averaged lower, and this fact is to be taken into consideration as an important factor in weighing the figures given above, and yet, in the face of all the adverse tendencies noted above, the volume of trade shows a wonderful increase. Besides the large territory now tributary to St. Paul and Minneapolis, new territory is fast being acquired and supplied by these cities, by means of new railroads and the extension of old ones. Of this new territory, that opened up by the Northern Pacific Railroad is by far the most important. The completion of that road has not only opened up a route for direct trade with China, Japan, and the East, but it has brought to our doors a vast amount of local trade; among others in the Black Hills region, which was supplied largely from Chicago. Last year the grand total shipped viâ Chamberlain by the Chicago, Milwaukee, and St. Paul, and viâ Pierre by the Chicago and North-Western, thence by wagon road, a distance of 215 miles, to Deadwood, aggregated the respectable figure of 20,000 tons. Nothing less than the immediate extension of these two southern railroads into Deadwood, will prevent successful competition viâ the Northern Pacific. Already the initiatory steps have been taken to divert the trade this way, and contracts for 10,000 tons of freight have been signed, which will reach Deadwood viâ the new line from Belfield, in Billings county. Dakota to Deadwood is not over 170 miles, with an excellent road, and is pronounced every way preferable to the present route viâ Pierre.

Should this new route become thoroughly established, St. Paul, as the terminus of the Northern Pacific Railroad, will take the place of Chicago, and be the supply point and jobbing centre for that rich mining region of country, which means an enormous yearly increase to its already astonishing heavy volume of business.

Market Prices.

The quotations given below are for round lots or goods transferred by first hands, and quotations apply to both Minneapolis and St. Paul, unless specially quoted. They represent the market prices on March 25, 1884:—

Builders' Materials.

Glass.—8 × 10, 9 × 10, 10 × 12, 10 × 14, 8 dol.; 12 × 14, 12 × 19, 16 × 20, 6 dol. 50 c., less 60 and 5 per cent. discount.

Lath and Pickets.—Lath per 1,000, 2 dol. 10 c.; pickets per 1,000, 15 dol. Kiln-dried lath, 20 c. extra.

Lime and Cement.—White lime, 1 dol. 15 c. per barrel; Louisville cement, 1 dol. 60 c. per barrel; stucco, 2 dol. per barrel; plastering hair, 30 c. to 35 c. per bushel.

[612]

2024

Lumber, Rough.—Common boards, 14 dol.; first fencing, 16 dol.; second fencing, 11 dol; dimension, 16 feet and under, 12 dol. 50 c.; dimension, 18 feet, 13 dol; dimension, 20 feet, 14 dol.; A stock boards, 40 dol.; B stock boards, 37 dol.; C stock boards, 30 dol.; D stock boards, 17 dol.; common stocks, 14 dol.; second common stocks, 12 dol.

Lumber.—Thick, clears and selects, rough: 1st and 2nd clear wide, $1\frac{1}{4}$, $1\frac{1}{2}$, and 2 inch, 47 dol.; 3rd clears, wide, $1\frac{1}{4}$, $1\frac{1}{2}$, and 2 inch, 42 dol.; A select, wide, 28 dol.; $1\frac{1}{4}$ and 2 inch, 37 dol.; B select, $1\frac{1}{4}$, $1\frac{1}{2}$, and 2 inch, 32 dol.; 2 × 4 clear and select, 24 dol.; 2 × 4 B select, 20 dol.; 2 × 6 and 2 × 8, clear and select, 31 dol.

Lumber, Inch Finishing.—Rough, 1st and 2nd clear, 12, 14, 16, and 18 feet wide, 45 dol.; 3rd clear, 12, 14, 16, and 18 feet wide, 40 dol.; A select, 12, 14, 16, and 18 feet 9 inch and over, 35 dol.; B select, 25 dol.; $\frac{1}{2}$-inch clear panel stuff, 10 inch and upwards, 36 dol.; $\frac{5}{8}$-inch clear panel stuff 10-inch and upwards, 40 dol.; thin, clear, and select, 23 dol.

Lumber Box Boards.—13-inch and over, rough, A box boards, 45 dol.; B box boards, 40 dol.; C box boards, 30 dol.; D box boards, 20 dol.

Dressed Lumber.—Ship-lap and drop-siding, 12-inch ship-lap, plain from C stock, 32 dol.; 8 and 10-inch ship-lap, plain from C stock, 28 dol.; 8, 10, and 12-inch ship-lap, plain from D stock, 19 dol.; 8, 10, and 12-inch common ship-lap, plain, 16 dol.; drop-siding, 8, 10, and 12-inch, same price as ship-lap; drop-siding, 6-inch, same price as flooring.

Lumber Flooring.—Dressed and matched: A flooring, 4 and 6-inch, 38 dol.; B flooring, 4 and 6-inch, 35 dol.; C flooring, 4 and 6-inch, 26 dol.; C flooring, 4 and 6-inch (10 feet), 24 dol.; fencing flooring (selected), 6-inch, 18 dol.

Lumber Siding.—1st and 2nd clear siding tied, 22 dol; A siding, tied, 21 dol.; B siding, tied, 19 dol.; C siding, tied, 14 dol.; fencing siding, selected, tied, 10 dol.; $\frac{3}{4}$-inch or $\frac{7}{8}$-inch drop siding, 6-inch, same price as flooring.

Lumber Ceiling.—Clear ceiling, $\frac{3}{8}$-inch, 4-inch or 6-inch, tied, 23 dol.; A ceiling, $\frac{3}{8}$-inch, 4-inch or 6-inch, tied, 22 dol.; B ceiling, $\frac{3}{8}$-inch, 4-inch or 6-inch, tied, 20 dol.; C ceiling, $\frac{3}{8}$-inch, 4-inch or 6-inch, tied, 15 dol.; clear and A ceiling, $\frac{1}{2}$-inch or $\frac{5}{8}$-inch, tied, 33 dol.; B ceiling, $\frac{1}{2}$-inch or $\frac{5}{8}$-inch, tied, 29 dol.; C ceiling, $\frac{1}{2}$-inch or $\frac{5}{8}$-inch, tied, 25 dol.; $\frac{3}{4}$-inch and $\frac{7}{8}$-inch ceiling, same price as flooring.

Paints.—White lead, standards in lots of 500 lbs., 6 dol. 45 c. per 100 lbs.; less quantity, 6 c. to 7 c. per lb.; standards in lots of 500 lbs., 5 dol. 75 c. American assorted by case, 7 c. assorted; less than a case, $7\frac{1}{2}$ c.

Oil.—Kerosene, 110 degrees test, $12\frac{1}{2}$ c.; Minnesota legal test kerosene, $13\frac{1}{4}$ c.; Minnesota water-white kerosene, $15\frac{3}{4}$ c.; 175 degrees head-light kerosene, $16\frac{1}{4}$ c.; Wisconsin test kerosene, $13\frac{1}{2}$ c.; Wisconsin water-white kerosene, 16 c.; benzine, 20 c. to 26 c.; linseed boiled, 59 c.; raw, 56 c.

Shingles.—No. 20 per 1,000, 3 dol.; No. 10 per 1,000, 2 dol.; extra No. 1 per 1,000, 1 dol. 25 c.; No. 1 per 1,000, 1 dol.; kiln-dried, 10 c. extra.

DRUGS.

Acid, citric, per lb., 53 c.; gallic, per oz., 25 c. to 28 c.; oxalic, per lb., 15 c.; sulphuric, 5 c. to 6 c.; alum, 4 c. to 5 c.; ammonia carb., 20 c. to 22 c.; balsam, copaiba, 55 c.; tolu, 58 c.; blue vitriol, 8 c. to 9 c.; borax, refined, $13\frac{1}{2}$ c.; brimstone, 4 c. to 5 c.; choral hydrate, 1 dol. 50 c. to 2 dol. 25 c.; chloride of lime, 5 c. to 6 c.; chloroform, to 1 dol. 10 c.; cinchonidii sulph., per oz., 70 c.; copperas, per lb., 3 c.

to 4 c.; cream of tartar, pure, 10 c.; cream of tartar, commercial, 20 c. to 22 c.; cubebs, 1 dol.; Epsom salts, 3 c. to 4 c.; glycerine, 24 c. to 26 c.; gum camphor, 25 c.; gum catechu, 9 c. to 10 c.; gum opium, 4 dol. 25 c.; gum opium, powdered, 5 dol. 75 c.; gum shellac, 30 c. to 40 c.; iodine re-sub., 2 dol. 15 c.; morphia, per oz., 3 dol. 75 c.; oil of bergamot, per lb., 2 dol. 15 c. to 2 dol. 25 c.; oil of cassia, 1 dol. 50 c.; castor oil, per gallon, 1 dol. 50 c.; oil of cedar, per lb., 40 c.; oil of lemon, 1 dol. 90 c.; oil of peppermint, 3 dol.; potass of bi-carbonate, 20 c.; potass of bromide, 35 c. to 36 c.; potass of iodide, 1 dol. 50 c.; quicksilver, 50 c.; quinine, per oz., 1 dol. 45 c.; rochelle salts, per lb., 32 c.; sal ammoniac soda, 3 c. to 4 c.; canary seed, 5 c. to $5\frac{1}{2}$ c.; flax seed, 4 c. to $4\frac{1}{2}$ c.; flax seed, ground, $4\frac{1}{2}$ c. to 5 c.; hemp seed, 6 c. to $6\frac{1}{4}$ c.; soda, bi-carbonate, 5 c. to 8 c.; sulphate of flos., 5 c. to 6 c.

Dry Goods.

Prints.—Fancy, Allen's, $5\frac{1}{2}$ c.; American, $5\frac{1}{2}$ c.; Arnold, 6 c.; Cocheco, 6 c.; Dunnell, 6 c.; Eddystone, 6 c.; Gloucester, $5\frac{1}{2}$ c.; Hamilton, 6 c.; Hartel, 6 c.; Knickerbrocker, $5\frac{1}{2}$ c.; Manchester, 6 c.; Merrimac, 6 c.; Pacific, 6 c.; Richmond, 6 c.; Steel River, $5\frac{1}{2}$ c.; Windsor, 6 c.; Lodi, $4\frac{3}{4}$ c.; Belmont, $4\frac{3}{4}$ c.; Fenwick's, $4\frac{1}{2}$ c.; Berwick's, $4\frac{1}{4}$ c.; and Dunkirk, $4\frac{3}{4}$ c.

Shirtings.—Allen, $4\frac{3}{4}$ c.; American, $4\frac{3}{4}$ c.; Merrimac, 5 c.; Regatta, $4\frac{3}{4}$ c.; Southbridge, 4 c.; indigo blue prints, 8 c.; robe and furniture prints, 5 to 8 c.

Ginghams.—Canton dress style, 9 c.; Renfrew dressstyle, $9\frac{3}{4}$ c.; Renfrew jacquards, $10\frac{1}{2}$ c.; Normandie dress styles, $8\frac{1}{2}$ c.; Bates' dress styles, $7\frac{1}{2}$ c.; Clydesdale, 7 c.; Amoskeag checks and staples, 8 c.; Lancaster, 8 c.; Bates' checks and staples, $7\frac{1}{2}$ c.; Berkshire checks and staples, 7 c.; Glenn's Falls, $6\frac{1}{2}$ c.; Lexington, 5 c.

Brown Muslin.—Atlantic A, $7\frac{3}{4}$ c.; Atlantic H, $7\frac{1}{2}$ c.; Atlantic D, $6\frac{1}{2}$ c.; Atlantic P, $5\frac{3}{4}$ c.; Lockwood A, 8 c.; Lockwood B, 7 c.; Graniteville EE, 7 c.; Lawrence LL, $5\frac{3}{4}$ c.; Pepperell E, $7\frac{1}{2}$ c.; Pepperell R, 7 c.; Nashua R, 7 c.

Bleached Shirtings and Sheetings.—New York mills, $10\frac{1}{2}$ c.; Wamasutta, $10\frac{1}{2}$ c.; Fruit 4-4, 9 c.; Fruit, 7-8, $8\frac{3}{4}$ c.; Masonville, 10 c.; Red Bank 4-4, $5\frac{1}{2}$ c.; Hill 4-4, $8\frac{1}{2}$ c.; Hill 7-8, $7\frac{3}{4}$ c.; Lonsdale, $8\frac{3}{4}$ c.; Lonsdale cambric, $11\frac{1}{2}$ c.; Chestnut Hill, 8 c.; Gree, $5\frac{1}{2}$ c.; Androscoggin 9-4, 25 c.; Androscoggin 10-4, $27\frac{1}{2}$ c.; Pepperell, 9-4, $22\frac{1}{2}$ c.; Pepperell 10-4, 25 c.; Hope, 7 c.

Ticking.—Amoskeag ACA, 14 c.; Amoskeag A, 13 c.; Amoskeag B, 12 c.; Amoskeag C, 12 c.; Amoskeag D, $10\frac{1}{2}$ c.; Amoskeag E, 10 c.; Amoskeag F, $9\frac{1}{2}$ c.; Amoskeag G, 9 c.; Amoskeag H, $8\frac{1}{2}$ c.; Old York AAA, $16\frac{1}{2}$ c.; Old York AA, $14\frac{1}{2}$ c.; Old York XX, $11\frac{1}{2}$ c.; Old York X, 10 c.

Cheviots.—Scotch fancies, $12\frac{1}{2}$ c.; Amoskeags, $9\frac{1}{2}$ c. to $10\frac{1}{2}$ c.; Amoskeag stripes, 10 c.; Acton Mills double cable and Acton Mills plaids, 11 c.; Acton Mills double cable XX, $10\frac{1}{2}$ c.; Rugby plaids, $7\frac{1}{2}$ c.; Huntington plaids and stripes, 8 c.

General Produce and Groceries.

Brewers' Supplies.—Barley malt, 75 c. to 80 c. per bushel; pops, 25 c., 28 c., to 30 c. per lb., according to quality.

Butter.—Good and choice creameries, fresh stock, 34 c. to 37 c.; old stock, 23 c. to 26 c.; dairy firsts, 18 c. to 25 c.; seconds, 10 c. to 15 c.; shipping grades of stock, 7 c. to 8 c.

Cheese.—Full cream, 14 c. to 15 c. per lb.; part skim, 8½ c. to 9½ c.; full skim, 6 c. to 7 c.

Cider.—Half-barrels, 4 dol. to 4 dol. 25 c.; barrels, 7 dol. 50 c.; Louisville crab-apple cider, 5 dol. per half barrel; Duffies' New York, 8 dol. per barrel, 25 c. per gallon in casks; champagne cider, half barrels, 5 dol.

Dressed Meats.—Extra Iowa corn-fed steers, 600 to 750 lbs., 10 c.; choice Iowa grade, 600 to 750 lbs., 8¾ c. to 9½ c.; bulls, 8 c. to 8½ c.; cows and heifers, common, 8 c. to 8¼ c.; choice, 8½ c. to 8¾ c.; hogs, 7½ c. to 8 c.; mutton, 8½ c. to 9 c.; veal, weighing 90 to 125 lbs., 9 c. to 11 c.; veal, weighing 150 lbs. and upwards, 8 c. to 10 c.

Fish.—Trout, pike, and whitefish, 10 c.; hallibut, 20 c. to 25 c.; cod, 8 c. to 10 c.; mackerel, 20 c. to 25 c.; herrings, smelts, and pickerel, 7 c.; salmon, 25 c.; brook trout, 30 c.

Flour.—Orange blossom, 6 dol. 35 c.; straits, red cross, 5 dol. 35 c.; capitol, family, 4 dol. 85 c.; bakers' XXXX., 4 dol.; in barrels, 25 c. extra; outside brands, 25 c. to 50 c., lower according to quality; low grades, 2 dol. 50 c. per barrel; Graham, 4 dol. 25 c. to 4 dol. 50 c. per barrel; buckwheat, 6 dol. to 7 dol. per barrel.

Fruits and Nuts.—Apples, good, to choice, 4 dol. 50 c. to 5 dol., according to quality; lemons, 3 dol. to 3 dol. 50 c. per box; bananas, 3 dol. to 5 dol. per bunch, according to size; Malaga grapes, 8 dol. 50 c. per barrel; California pears, 2 dol. 50 c. to 3 dol. per box; Valencias, 6 dol. 50 c. to 8 dol. per case, according to quality; extra large sell at 9 dol. per case; Messinas and Palermos, 3 dol. to 4 dol.; figs, 14 c. to 18 c.; dates, 7 c. per lb.; pea nuts, choice, 11 c. per lb.; hand-picked, 11½ c.; fancy hand-picked, polished, 11 c.; farmers' packing, 7 c. to 8 c.; baked, 1 c. additional; almonds, Tarragona, 20 c. per lb.; California, 20 c.; Languedoc, 22 c.; Ivica, 18 c.; Sicily, shelled, 35 c. per lb.; walnuts, Grenoble, 15 c.; Naples, 17 c.; French, 12 c.; Pecans, 11 c. to 13 c.; filberts, Sicily, 14 c.; Barcelona, 10 c.; Brazil nuts, 12 c.; cocoa nuts, 6 dol. per 100; hickory nuts, shell barks, 1 dol. to 1 dol. 25 c.; large ditto, 75 c.

Furs.—Lynx, 2 dol. 50 c. to 3 dol. 50 c.; mink, 50 c. to 1 dol.; coon, 60 c. to 80 c.; red fox, 1 dol. 25 c. to 1 dol. 50 c.; kitts, 30 c. to 40 c.; silver fox, 20 dol. to 40 dol.; cross, 2 dol. 50 c. to 6 dol.; otter, 4 dol. to 6 dol.; fisher, 6 dol. to 7 dol.; musk-rat, winter, 10 c.; ditto, spring, 12 c.; kitts, 3 c. to 4 c.; badger, 50 c. to 75 c.; wild cat, 50 c. to 60 c.; domestic cat, 10 c. to 4 c.; skunk, 30 c. to 75 c.; martin, 1 dol. 25 c. to 3 dol.; wolverine, 4 dol. to 5 dol.; wolf, 1 dol. 50 c. to 3 dol. 50 c.; prairie wolf, 75 c. to 1 dol.; Lake Superior beaver, 3 dol. per lb.; Hudson Bay beaver, 3 dol. per lb.; Dakota beaver, 2 dol. 25 c. per lb.; bear, 7 dol. to 12 dol.; cubs, 4 dol. to 6 dol.

Hay.—Wild, 7 dol.; Timothy, 9 dol. 50 c.

Hides.—Green hides, 6 c. to 6¼ c. per lb.; green, salted, 7 c. to 7½ c.; dry, salted, 9 c. to 10 c.; long-haired kips, 6½ c. to 7½ c.; veal kips, 8 c.; green calf, 11 c.; dry calf-skin, 12 c. to 13 c.; dry flint hides, 12 c.; damaged, one-third off; lamb-skins, 40 c. to 45 c. each; sheep pelts, 75 c. to 80 c. each.

Honey.—Choice white clover, 18 c. to 20 c. per lb.; common to good, 16 c. to 18 c.

Maple Sugar.—New, 12 c. to 14 c. per lb.

Mill Stuffs.—Ground feed, 18 dol.; coarse corn meal, 17 dol.; sacked bran, 14 dol.; oysters, canned New York counts, 45 c.; selects, 38 c.; standards, 28 c.; mediums, 25 c.; bulk, New York counts, 3 dol. per gallon; selects, 2 dol. 25 c. per gallon; standards, 1 dol. 25 c. per gallon; in shell, 12 dol. per barrel.

Poultry and Game.—Dressed chickens, 15 c. to 17 c. per lb.; dressed turkeys, good to choice, 16 c. to 18 c. per lb., with best stock selling up to 20 c.; ducks and geese, 15 c. to 17 c. per lb.; rabbits, 1 dol. 25 c.

Provisions.—Jobbing prices: mess pork, 18 dol. 75 c. to 19 dol. per barrel; hams, 13½ dol. 14 c.; bacon, clear, 11½ c.; shoulders, 8½ c. to 9 c.; tierce lard, 9¾ c.; keg lard, 10 c.; wooden pails, 20 lb., 10¾ c.; pails, 3 lb., tin, 10¾ c.; 5 lb., 10⅝ c.; 10 lb., 10½ c.; mess beef, 12 dol. to 12 dol. 25 c.; mess beef, extra, 13 dol. to 13 dol. 25 c.; dry beef, quotable at 15 c. to 16 c. per lb.; corned beef, 2 lb. cans, 3 dol. to 3 dol. 25 c. per dozen.

Vegetables.—Potatoes, 30 c. to 35 c.; sweet potatoes, Illinois kiln-dried, 5 dol. per barrel; sweet potatoes, Jersey kiln-dried, 5 dol. to 6 dol. per barrel; celery, 60 c. to 70 c. per dozen; Minnesota lettuce, per doz. bunches, 50 c.; tomatoes, per lb., 15 c. to 20 c.; spinach, per barrel, 3 dol. 50 c. to 4 dol. 50 c.

Wheat.—No. 1, hard, 98 c.; No. 1, regular, 90 c.; No. 2, hard, 93 c.; No. 2, regular, 83 c.

Wool.—Unwashed, 14 c. to 15 c. per lb.; washed, 25 c. to 28 c.

LIVE STOCK.

Cattle.—Good butchers' steers, 5 dol. 50 c. to 6 dol.; good Minnesota steers, 4 dol. 25 c. to 5 dol.; choice butchers' mixed cattle, 3 dol. 50 c. to 4 dol.; cows, 3 dol. 25 c. to 3 dol. 50 c.; calves, 6 dol. to 7 dol.

Hogs.—Packing stock, 5 dol. 75 c. to 6 dol. 50 c.; light, 5 dol. 50 c. to 6 dol.

Sheep.—4 dol. 25 c. to 5 dol.; extra, 5 dol. 25 c.

The different collectors of Customs inform me that the new tariff has made no material difference in the receipts of their respective ports, though the collector at St. Paul thinks increased importations will follow the law, as importers regard it as advantageous.

The following are the commercial laws of Minnesota:—

Acknowledgments.—Deeds must be signed, sealed, and acknowledged by the grantor, and attested by two witnesses. Within the State, acknowledgments may be made before any judge or clerk of a Court of Record, Justice of the Peace, Notary Public, Register of Deeds, Court Commissioner or County Auditor; without the State, but within the United States, by judges or clerks of Courts of Record, Justices of the Peace (whose certificate must be authenticated with certificate of clerk of the Court), and notaries public; also by Commissioners in any of the States or territories of the United States, duly appointed and commissioned by the Governor of this State. In foreign countries before any Notary Public, Minister, Consul, or other diplomatic or commercial agent of the United States there accredited and resident. Arrest for debt not allowed in this State.

Assignments.—Assignments for benefit of creditors must be in writing, signed, acknowledged, and filed in office of clerk of District Court of county where debtor resides, or where business has been principally carried on. Assignee must be resident and freeholder of the State. Assignment void unless all conditions are strictly complied with. Notice of assignment must be published and mailed to each creditor. All claims must be verified by oath of parties making same before payment by assignee, excepting debts due to the United States, the State itself, or for taxes or assessments. Debts are paid in the following order after paying costs and charges of assignment: 1st, all debts due to the United States and the State of Minnesota, and all taxes levied and unpaid, to be paid in full; 2nd, debts owing for wages of servants, labourers, and mechanics, and clerks for labour and service performed by them within three months next preceding the date of assignment, are to be paid in full to the exclusion of all other indebtedness, if there be sufficient wherewith to pay the same in full: if not they shall be paid *pro ratâ*.

Attachments.—Writ will issue when it appears by affidavit that a cause of action exists against defendant, by specifying amount and ground of same that defendant is a foreign corporation or non-resident, or has departed from the State with intent to defraud or delay his creditors, or to avoid service of summons, or keep himself concealed with like intent, or has assigned, secreted, or disposed, or is about to assign, secrete, or dispose of his property with intent to delay or defraud his creditors, or that the debt was fraudulently contracted. In Justices' Court writ cannot issue, except in cases of indebtedness upon a contract express or implied. Attachment allowed in actions for recovery of money at time of issuing the summons, or at any time afterward, against property of the defendant.

Corporations.—Organised under general law. Stockholders in any corporation are liable to the amount of stock held or owned by each of them.

Courts.—Jurisdiction of Justices' Courts co-extensive with limits of county, in action to recover, not to exceed 100 dol.; execution not issued for 10 days after entry of judgment.

Executions.—In District Court may issue at any time after judgment, within 10 years from date of docketing, and to any county where a transcript has been docketed, returnable in 60 days. Executions may be renewed for a period of 60 days for each renewal. In Justice Court no execution can issue until 10 days after entry of judgment, is returnable in 30 days, and may be renewed for same period. In Courts of Record six months' stay is granted on defendant filing bond with two freehold sureties, approved by the Court, conditioned to pay amount of judgment with costs, and interest at the rate of 10 per cent. per annum. Stay in Justices' Courts may be had in same manner, where judgment is under 10 dol., one month; 10 dol. to 25 dol., two months; 25 dol. to 50 dol., three months; 50 dol. to 75 dol., four months; over 75 dol., six months. Real estate sold on execution is subject to redemption for one year from date of sale.

Exemptions.—Books (school or library) and musical instruments for the use of family, wearing apparel of debtor and his family, all stoves and appendages, cooking utensils, household furniture not exceeding 500 dol. in value, 3 cows, 10 swine, 1 yoke of oxen, and a horse, or in lieu, span of horses or mules, 20 sheep and wool from same, necessary food for stock for one year (provided or growing, or both), 1 wagon, cart, or dray, 1 sleigh, 2 ploughs, 1 drag, and other farming utensils not exceeding 300 dol. in value; sewing machine; grain for one year's seed not to exceed 50 bushels wheat, 50 bushels oats, 30 bushels barley, 15 bushels potatoes, and 3 bushels corn; provisions for debtor and family for one year's support (provided or growing, or both), and one year's fuel; tools or instruments of trade and stock-in-trade not exceeding 400 dol. in value; library and implements of any professional man; wages of any labouring man or woman, or their minor children, not exceeding 50 dol., due for services rendered during the 90 days preceding the issuing of process; all the presses, stones, type, cases, and other tools and implements used by any copartnership, or by any publisher or editor of any newspaper, and in the printing or publication of the same not to exceed 2,000 dol. in value, together with stock-in-trade not exceeding 400 dol. in value, homestead not exceeding 80 acres of land, with dwelling-house thereon, not included in the laid-out or platted portion of any incorporated town, city, or village, or instead thereof, at the owner's option land not exceeding one lot, if within the laid-out or platted portion of any incorporated town, city, or village having over 5,000 inhabitants, with the dwelling-house thereon and appurtenances; all moneys arising from insurance of any property exempted from sale or execution when such property has been destroyed by fire.

Garnishment.—In any action in a Court of Record or Justices' Court the property, money, or effects of defendant in the hands of or under the control of any person may be reached by garnishment.

Interest.—For any legal indebtedness, 7 per cent. per annum; contracts in writing may be made for as high as 10 per cent.

Judgments, when filed in the office of the clerk of the Court, become a lien on all real property of debtor in county owned by him at the time of docketing of judgment, or afterwards acquired; lien continues for 10 years. Transcript of docket may be filed in any county where debtor has property.

Limitations.—In actions for recovery of real property, 20 years; foreclosure of mortgage, 10 years; judgments of United States Courts or Courts of any State or territory, 10 years; on contract or obligation, expressed or implied, liability created by statute, other than penalty or forfeiture, for trespass, for taking, detaining, or injuring personal property, for injury to person or rights of another, for relief on ground of fraud, six years; upon action against sheriff, coroner, or constable, upon official liability, upon statute for penalty or forfeiture, three years; action for libel, slander, assault, battery, or false imprisonment, upon a statute for forfeiture or penalty to the State, two years.

Married Women.—All property owned by any married woman, at time or previous to her marriage, shall continue her separate property after marriage; and she may enjoy rents and profits and avails of her industry, free from liabilities on account of husband's debts, and shall be bound by her contracts, and responsible for torts committed by her, same as if unmarried: may make any contract which she might make if unmarried, and shall be bound thereby, except that no conveyance or contract for the sale of real estate, or of any interest therein, other than mortgages on lands to secure purchase money, and leases for terms not exceeding three years, shall be valid, unless husband join; no estate by the courtesy as against purchase money mortgage given by married woman. If husband is insane, she may make such conveyance or contract by joining with guardian of such insane person. No married woman liable for debts of husband, or married man for those of wife, entered into either before or during coverture, except for necessaries furnished wife after marriage; no contract between husband and wife relative to real estate of either, or any interest therein, is valid. Whenever a married woman is deserted by her husband for one year, or would be entitled to divorce for any cause, she may bring action, and obtain decree giving her full authority to a lien to sell, convey, and dispose of her lands without interference of husband. She may sue or be sued as if unmarried, without joining her husband in all cases where husband would not be necessary party, aside from marriage relation. Minority of wife does not affect validity of joint deed.

Mortgages.—Chattel mortgages must be acknowledged and filed in the office of the town or city clerk, both where the mortgagor resides at the time of making the mortgage, and where the property is situated. If these provisions are not complied with, they are void as against creditors, subsequent purchasers in good faith, and mortgagees. A chattel mortgage, coupled with an understanding that mortgagor may retain possession of the property, and sell or dispose of same, without applying proceeds in satisfaction of debt, is fraudulent and void as to the creditors and subsequent purchasers. Real estate mortgages must be recorded in office of registrar of deeds of county where land lies : may be discharged by an entry in the margin of record, signed by mortgagee, his executor, administrator, or assignee; also by satisfaction deed duly executed and acknowledged.

Notes and Bills.—Statute does not define negotiable paper. Liability of indorsers fixed by protest and notice. Notice of protest must be made in writing, and such notice may in all cases be given by depositing the same in the post-office, postage paid, and directed to the party protested against, at his reputed place of residence. Indorsers and makers may all be joined in the case of suit at option of plaintiff. To charge an indorser of demand note, note must be presented on or before 60 days from date. On all bills of exchange payable at sight, or at a future day, certain within this State, and on all negotiable promissory notes, orders, and drafts, payable at sight, or at a future day certain within this State, in which there is not an express stipulation to the contrary, grace shall be allowed in like manner as it is allowed by the custom of merchants on foreign bills of exchange. Grace is not allowed on demand paper. Damages 5 per cent. on domestic, and 10 per cent. on foreign paper protested. Notes obtained by fraudulent representation without negligence on part of maker void; question of negligence, one of fact for jury.

Partnership.—Limited partnership, except for banking or insurance, may be formed by one or more general and one or more special partners, by their making and severally signing certificate containing the name or firm under which said partnership is to be conducted, the nature of the business, names of all the general and special partners interested therein, showing general and special partners, their places of residence, the amount of capital which each has contributed to the common stock, the period at which the partnership is to commence, and which it is to terminate. The certificate to be acknowledged and filed in office of register of deeds of each county where partnership has places of business situated. Copy of certificate must be published. Special partners not liable beyond fund contributed by them to capital.

Revivor.—Part payment, or new promise to pay in writing.

Statute of Frauds.—No action shall be maintained upon any agreement that, by its terms, is not to be performed within one year from the making thereof; upon every special promise to answer for the debt, default, or miscarriage of another; upon every agreement, promise, or undertaking, made upon consideration of marriage, except mutual promise to marry, unless such agreement, or some note or memorandum thereof is in writing, and subscribed by the party charged therewith. Every contract for sale of any goods, chattels, or things in action, for the price of 50 dol., shall be void, unless a note of such contract is made in writing, and subscribed by the parties to be charged, or unless buyer accepts and receives part of such goods, or the evidences, or some of them, of such things in action, or unless buyer at time pays part of purchase money. Grants of trusts are void unless in writing.

Taxes.—Taxes become due and payable December 1st, personal property tax delinquent March 1st; real property delinquent June 1st, penalty of 5 per cent. attached on personal property March 1st, and on real property of 10 per cent. after June 1st. County treasurer to levy distress on goods and chattels, and sell the same at public vendue for personal property tax, and real estate is sold for tax on third Monday in September each year, and is subject to two years' redemption. Tax judgments draw interest at the rate of 1½ per cent. per month from date of sale.

The following are the collection laws of Dakota:—
Acknowledgments of deeds or instruments within the territory may be made before a justice or clerk of the Supreme Court, and within the judicial district county sub-division, or city for which the officer was elected or appointed, before the judge or clerk of any Court of Record, mayor, justice of the peace, register of deeds, or notary public. If without the territory, before any judge or clerk of a Court of Record of the United States, or any State or territory, notary public, or Commissioner of Deeds. In foreign countries before a Minister, Commissioner, diplomatic or Consular agent of the United States, or a judge or notary public of said country. Letters patent from the United States and final receivers' receipts from the United States Land Offices may be recorded without acknowledgment or further proof.

Arrest.—The defendant may be arrested and held to a bill in an action for damages not arising on contract where he is not a resident or is about to remove from the territory, or for an injury to person or character, or for injuring or wrongfully taking, detaining, or converting property, or for money received or property embezzled or fraudulently misapplied by any person in a fiduciary capacity, or to recover property unjustly detained, when it has been concealed, removed, or disposed of, or where guilty of fraud in incurring the obligation, or where he has or is about removing his property to defraud creditors.

Assignments and Insolvency.—Insolvent debtor may in good faith make assignment in trust for benefit of creditors which may provide for any subsisting liability of the assignor, whether absolute or contingent. Such assignment is subject to provisions of the code relative to trusts and fraudulent tranfers. Any debtor may make assignment, with or without consent of creditors, and be thereby discharged from all his debts and liabilities.

Attachment process issues at the time of granting the summons, or at any time afterwards in actions on contracts for the recovery of money only, or for wrongful conversion of personal property against a foreign corporation or non-resident defendant, or when defendant has absconded or concealed himself, or has assigned, disposed of, or secreted his property, or is about to do so with intent to defraud creditors, or that the debt was incurred from property obtained under false pretences. Plaintiff must make affidavit and furnish bond in not less than 250 dol., and equal to the amount specified in District Courts, and at least 50 dol. and not exceeding 300 dols. in Justices' Courts. Real and personal property, debts, moneys, credits, and bank notes may be attached or levied on under execution, but there is no process of garnishment.

Chattel Mortgages.—A chattel mortgage must be in writing, and to be valid as against subsequent purchasers of the property or creditors. It, or an authenticated copy, must be filed in office of register of deeds in county where property is situated, and refiled within 30 days of expiration of three years.

Commercial Travellers.—No license is required.

Corporations.—Private corporations for the purposes of religion, benevolence, education, art, literature, or profit may be organised by three or more persons associating themselves together, and filing a certificate with the secretary of the territory, showing name, object, where place of business to be, term of existence, directors, and capital stock. Each shareholder is liable individually for such proportion of all debts of corporation as stock held by him bears to whole capital stock.

Courts.—Terms and Jurisdiction.—Districts Courts have exclusive Chancery and common law jurisdiction above 100 dol., and where title to real property is concerned. Courts sit twice a year in nearly all the counties. Probate Courts hold six terms a year, and are always open for business. Justices' jurisdiction, 100 dol. District Courts have also concurrent jurisdiction with Justices' Courts for sums less than 100 dol.

Deeds and Mortgages of Real Estate.—They must be recorded in the office of the register of the county to be valid, as against subsequent purchasers and encumbrancers in good faith.

Executions issue as of course at any time within five years after judgment, and must be returned within 60 days. Lands levied on need not be appraised, but notice of sale must be given. Same provisions apply in Justices' Courts as to levy, &c., on personal property. There is no stay law, and execution can only be stayed by order of the Court for irregularity, by injunction, or by appeal with security given.

Real estate sold under execution may be redeemed within one year.

Exemptions.—Homestead, one acre, if within a town plat, and 160 acres if not, with house and appurtenances, unlimited in value. Exemption is absolute except as to taxes, labourers' or mechanics' wages, or for physicians' services, mechanics' lien for work on the homestead, and debts created for the purchase thereof.

Personal property exempt, 1,500 dol., besides wearing apparel, books to 100 dol., provisions for one year, family pictures, &c.

Interest.—Legal rate 7 per cent., but parties may contract in writing for 12 per cent., except in the counties of Lawrence, Pennington, Custer, Mandan, and Forsyth, where the usury law does not apply, and any rate of interest may be charged as may be agreed upon. Usury forfeits all interest.

Interest on open accounts run from date of last item charged, whether debit or credit. Legal rate allowed on judgments.

Judgments of Courts of Record are a lien on all real estate, except the homestead, for ten years from time such judgment is docketed in the clerk's office of the county where the land is situated, and by having execution issued every five years are good for 20 years; in Courts of Record may be obtained within 30 days after service of summons and complaint; in Justices' Courts four days, where no defence is interposed.

Licenses.—Licenses are required to sell, vend, or retail, either at public sale or public auction, any goods, wares, or merchandise. They are granted for one year by the County Commissioner, and the fee is from 10 dol. to 100 dol.

Limitations.—Personal actions, two years; on contract or obligation, six years; on sealed instruments, judgments, or decrees of any Court and in real actions, 20 years.

Married women retain their own real and personal property, and may make contracts, sue, and be sued as if sole. Neither husband nor wife has any interest in the property of the other. Dower and courtesy are abolished.

Mortgages of realty must be in writing with the formalities required in case of a grant of real estate. Wife need not join except in mortgage of homestead. If containing power of sale, may be foreclosed by advertisement without intervention of court. Mortgagee has possession of the premises during the year of redemption after sale.

Notes and Bills of Exchange.—Three days of grace allowed on all bills of exchange or sight drafts, whether foreign or domestic, and on all promissory notes, bills of exchange, and drafts, on the face of which time is specified, and notes on demand for payment of same; acceptances must be in writing by the drawee or an acceptor for honour. To hold indorser the instrument must be presented on the day of maturity and notice of dishonour given. Damages are allowed in favour of holders for value on bills of exchange drawn or negotiated within the territory, and protested for non-acceptance or non-payment. Apparent maturity of a non-interest bearing sight or demand note in ten days after date, in addition to the time required for transmission; on interest bearing notes, one year from date.

Partnerships—General partnerships are controlled by general law; special partnerships may be organised by one or more general and one or more special partners, by their making a certificate showing name and general business of partnership, names and residences of all partners, amount contributed by each special partner and duration of partnership, and filing same, properly verified, in office of register of deeds of each county where business is to be carried on, and publishing same for four weeks in paper in county. The names of the general partners only can appear in firm name, and these only can manage firm.

Replevin.—In action to recover specific personal property, the plaintiff may have same delivered to him pending the action upon giving bond, &c.

Statute of Frauds.—An agreement by its terms not to be performed within one year, to answer for debt, default, or miscarriage of another, upon consideration of marriage, or for sale of chattels of price of 50 dol. and over (unless a partial payment or delivery), must be in writing.

There are 130 banks in the State of Minnesota, with an aggregate capital of **14,411,500 dol.**, and 80 private bankers whose capital is not known; and there are 96 banks in the territory of Dakota, with an aggregate capital of 3,329,000 dol., and 74 private bankers whose capital is not known.

The following is an abstract of the reports to the Comptroller of the Currency since October 3, 1882, arranged by States and reserve cities:—

MINNESOTA.

RESOURCES.

	December 30. 31 Banks.	March 13. 32 Banks.	May 1. 32 Banks.	June 22. 34 Banks.	October 2. 38 Banks.
	Dol. c.	Dol. c.	Dol. c.	Dol. c.	Dol. c.
Loans and discounts	10,525,351 06	10,772,039 96	11,021,011 33	11,618,009 81	12,124,772 45
Bonds for circulation	1,600,000 00	1,572,500 00	1,572,500 00	1,605,000 00	1,664,000 00
United States bonds on hand	5,000 00	5,000 00	11,050 00	17,500 00	20,000 00
Other stocks and bonds	199,373 86	193,889 61	186,876 16	200,253 66	209,162 26
Due from reserve agents	805,023 42	776,359 70	702,768 42	876,462 30	912,393 28
Due from national banks	582,891 41	637,433 99	540,266 18	772,073 41	642,677 21
Due from State banks	125,387 09	169,590 29	184,823 99	253,298 56	200,885 37
Real estate, &c.	376,631 06	402,492 01	424,443 41	439,563 95	467,982 52
Current expenses	68,246 10	81,326 72	125,318 31	148,257 99	69,784 16
Premiums paid	22,400 91	24,588 41	29,219 91	31,711 37	31,245 11
Cash items	205,414 00	178,860 44	196,303 20	173,335 71	286,854 17
Bills of other banks	220,449 60	143,919 00	136,677 00	178,520 00	158,399 00
Fractional currency	3,396 80	3,428 67	3,792 93	3,021 51	4,139 53
Specie	489,231 84	431,260 90	450,753 16	432,235 08	522,708 22
Legal tender notes	669,197 00	489,593 00	453,626 00	501,022 00	538,286 00
Due from United States treasury	78,949 36	81,643 65	88,093 65	90,919 35	81,816 75
Total	15,976,943 81	15,963,926 35	16,127,523 65	17,361,229 70	17,935,096 03

ST. PAUL.

MINNESOTA—continued.

LIABILITIES.

	December 30. 31 Banks.	March 13. 32 Banks.	May 1. 32 Banks.	June 22. 34 Banks.	October 2. 38 Banks.
	Dol. c.	Dol. c.	Dol. c.	Dol. c.	Dol. c.
Capital stock	3,803,700 00	4,070,000 00	4,070,000 00	4,195,000 00	4,451,600 00
Surplus fund	565,287 78	604,110 30	590,110 30	590,110 30	634,484 08
Undivided profits	495,445 05	407,943 58	517,038 03	636,907 34	495,066 42
National Bank circulation	1,415,634 00	1,406,194 00	1,405,434 00	1,436,244 00	1,470,044 00
Dividends unpaid	61,435 00	4,618 62	4,110 62	7,732 62	7,241 62
Individual deposits	8,557,157 60	8,597,794 01	8,648,899 18	9,471,880 89	9,833,906 63
Due to national banks	215,277 66	222,087 78	230,549 27	303,395 54	245,589 85
Due to State banks	448,173 20	162,132 98	114,057 67	263,922 87	441,068 73
Notes re-discounted	411,833 52	444,045 88	544,264 58	453,381 14	305,384 70
Bills payable	3,000 00	45,000 00	33,000 00	5,655 00	50,710 00
Total	15,976,943 81	15,963,926 35	16,127,523 65	17,361,229 70	17,935,096 03

City of St. Paul.

Resources.

	December 30. 3 Banks.		March 13. 3 Banks.		May 1. 3 Banks.		June 22. 5 Banks.		October 2. 5 Banks.	
	Dol.	c.	Dol.	c.	Dol.	c.	Dol.	c.	Dol.	c.
Loans and discounts	7,856,787	41	7,916,653	55	8,065,678	09	11,218,539	12	11,959,731	92
Bonds for circulation	633,500	00	633,500	00	633,500	00	733,500	00	733,500	00
Bonds for deposits	500,000	00	500,000	00	500,000	00	500,000	00	500,000	00
United States bonds on hand			700	00	150	00	2,400	00	200	00
Other stocks and bonds	285,212	67	272,981	02	270,474	84	326,877	90	238,005	44
Due from reserve agents	591,840	32	743,800	70	761,375	38	1,731,019	54	846,534	73
Due from national banks	65,254	52	102,203	80	81,405	38	83,919	35	144,271	91
Due from State banks	230,209	61	85,455	69	107,315	97	187,357	99	146,837	03
Real estate, &c.	60,901	90	57,996	61	58,886	61	153,663	91	188,305	80
Current expenses			19,167	00	27,824	53	45,198	92	25,256	94
Premiums paid							3,684	63	3,252	98
Cash items	12,845	49	12,735	06	43,900	40	48,284	05	26,742	04
Clearing-house exchanges	211,297	29	135,892	62	123,348	63	266,956	13	301,434	97
Bills of other banks	81,175	00	107,320	00	202,551	00	126,405	00	97,212	00
Fractional currency	757	50	1,152	38	904	04	3,142	51	3,739	11
Specie	479,306	49	282,057	20	506,398	52	349,351	29	393,641	26
Legal tender notes	212,897	00	246,541	00	417,812	00	392,842	00	492,796	00
Due from United States treasury	49,675	10	48,165	50	28,753	15	27,945	05	40,549	05
Total	11,271,660	30	11,166,322	13	11,830,278	54	16,201,077	39	16,192,010	58

City of St. Paul—continued.

Liabilities.

	December 30. 3 Banks.	March 13. 3 Banks.	May 1. 3 Banks.	June 22. 5 Banks.	October 2. 5 Banks.
	Dol. c.	Dol. c.	Dol. c.	Dol. c.	Dol. c.
Capital stock	2,200,000 00	2,200,000 00	2,200,000 00	3,906,900 00	4,700,000 00
Surplus fund	655,000 00	655,000 00	655,000 00	655,000 00	805,000 00
Undivided profits	279,829 49	325,083 15	388,703 86	501,558 54	395,777 42
National Bank circulation	554,780 00	570,080 00	567,080 00	558,880 00	656,480 00
Dividends unpaid	50,357 00	105 00	70 00	70 00	588 00
Individual deposits	5,421,423 30	5,288,386 96	5,594,479 02	7,526,444 56	7,202,443 54
United States deposits	172,405 46	130,094 78	156,500 29	125,011 67	78,934 46
Deposits to United States district offices	394,625 61	296,445 91	276,812 72	348,383 48	328,501 64
Due to national banks	664,287 74	824,983 73	775,225 56	1,174,931 69	926,466 93
" State banks	878,951 70	886,162 60	1,216,407 09	1,403,867 45	1,097,818 59
Total	11,271,660 30	11,166,322 13	11,830,278 54	16,201,077 39	16,192,063 00

Dakota.

Resources.

	December 30. 20 Banks.		March 13. 24 Banks.		May 1. 24 Banks.		June 22. 27 Banks.		October 2. 30 Banks.	
	Dol.	c.	Dol.	c.	Dol.	c.	Dol.	c.	Dol.	c.
Loans and discounts	2,668,060	02	2,861,678	37	3,029,947	54	3,284,973	86	3,649,189	85
Bonds for circulation	665,000	00	699,500	00	699,500	00	714,500	00	759,500	00
Bonds for deposits	50,000	00	50,000	00	150,000	00	150,000	00	150,000	00
United States bonds on hand	400	00	20,400	00	1,250	00	12,750	00	50,400	00
Other stocks and bonds	165,908	02	174,114	41	200,062	21	231,502	72	311,878	78
Due from reserve agents	280,016	03	398,401	79	375,445	92	539,741	68	399,554	60
Due from national banks	309,563	40	344,773	64	416,157	85	560,269	11	646,570	41
Due from State banks	246,225	18	260,376	89	341,394	85	292,872	23	284,415	47
Real estate, &c.	238,359	84	279,930	21	282,035	10	302,680	62	333,513	34
Current expenses	25,930	33	64,293	84	80,732	29	101,144	96	76,326	26
Premiums paid	17,830	19	24,069	96	33,471	08	31,799	45	34,973	83
Cash items	60,106	23	39,701	29	50,878	03	88,198	03	75,128	99
Bills of other banks	106,463	00	105,949	00	167,932	00	221,122	00	156,177	00
Fractional currency	1,217	97	2,735	02	1,748	88	2,147	86	2,038	54
Specie	142,506	12	127,587	25	133,560	35	177,358	56	223,975	58
Legal tender notes	281,763	00	300,505	00	399,917	00	357,440	00	363,125	00
Due from United States treasury	35,180	00	32,337	90	32,985	55	34,271	00	35,223	00
Total	5,294,519	33	5,786,354	67	6,397,018	65	7,102,774	08	7,551,990	65

Dakota—continued.

Liabilities.

	December 30. 20 Banks.		March 13. 24 Banks.		May 1. 24 Banks.		June 22. 27 Banks.		October 2. 30 Banks.	
	Dol.	c.	Dol.	c.	Dol.	c.	Dol.	c.	Dol.	c.
Capital stock	1,555,000	00	1,410,000	00	1,425,000	00	1,631,700	00	1,766,700	00
Surplus fund	154,615	02	221,021	68	277,021	08	277,021	08	358,241	72
Undivided profits	304,240	91	283,488	74	288,422	24	364,127	40	329,978	75
National Bank circulation	561,750	00	617,170	00	626,220	00	637,000	00	662,000	00
Dividends unpaid	3,755	00	4,235	00	845	00	845	00	1,345	00
Individual deposits	2,787,349	97	2,966,927	17	3,418,714	43	3,912,630	96	4,082,279	67
United States deposits	33,663	13	43,582	19	167,576	56	95,089	06	134,445	02
Deposits to United States district offices	39,957	65	56,271	62	43,665	23	45,536	84	19,449	20
Due to national banks	31,222	91	15,438	56	12,211	80	33,638	27	43,954	16
Due to State banks	36,665	27	43,586	44	58,274	37	58,687	26	57,682	95
Notes re-discounted	88,899	47	102,941	75	69,443	79	46,438	01	87,914	18
Bills payable	27,400	03	21,692	12	9,624	15	..	..	10,000	00
Total	5,294,519	33	5,786,354	67	6,397,018	65	7,102,774	08	7,551,990	65

AGRICULTURE.

Besides these materials which Nature has bountifully supplied, unaided by human industry, Minnesota is found capable of producing a number of others in sufficient quantities to keep a multitude of factories employed. Already her annual crop of wheat reaches nearly, if not fully, 35,000,000 bushels, very much of which is now ground in her numerous, extensive, and fully-equipped flouring mills, and with each recurring season this product must increase until the entire cultivatable area of the State is brought into subjection to the husbandman. Amber sugar cane, a variety of sorghum or imphee, is also grown here to perfection in constantly increasing quantities, and one large and extensive factory is already in operation at Faribault in extracting its juice and reducing it to syrup and sugar, not a whit inferior to that obtained from the ribbon cane of Louisiana. This industry is bound to increase until it becomes one of the most important of the State. Flax and hemp of best quality grow here luxuriantly, and there is every prospect that the manufacture of linen, cordage, &c., will afford opportunity at an early day for the profitable employment of capital and labour. Butter and cheese are now produced in considerable quantities, and there are already a few small woollen mills and tanneries, but these may and will be almost infinitely increased as the State develops, and her resources are fully drawn upon by the demands of commerce. No doubt this State will hereafter be found capable of yielding yet other products in sufficient quantities to justify the erection of manufactories in her territory by which they can be reduced to marketable forms, thus enabling her people to gain the largest possible profit on their productions. The very circumstance of her having the facilities of manufacturing so convenient will stimulate her enterprising citizens to produce materials for their employment to the full extent ultimately of her resources, and the demands for consumption and export.

Agricultural Products.—Except in her lumbering business and the manufacture of flour, the energies of the people of Minnesota have, up till the present time, been mainly directed to agriculture. Her total cultivated area in 1881, according to the report of the Commissioner of Statistics, was 9,729,536 acres, and the number of farms 81,089. As the average Minnesota farm is about 200 acres in extent, it is clear that only something like one-fourth of each has as yet been improved, and every year will add largely to the cultivated area of these, while at the same time increasing the number by from 5,000 to 6,000. Impressions have obtained currency that only the prairie counties are in reality suited for farming, and that corn and several other products cannot be profitably grown in the northern part of the State : these are mistakes. The small prairies, brush lots, and oak openings scattered throughout the wooded districts are as good farming lands as the prairies, and are scarcely more difficult to prepare for cultivation. So, too, with the woodlands themselves. Even in much of those covered with pines, there is comparatively but little that will not repay cultivation when cleared of its timber, and portions of it are constantly being added to the cultivated area of the State. The trees, however, are far too valuable to be cut and burned on the ground, as was done in the timbered regions of the Central and Eastern States, and even in the older countries here. Wood commands a ready market and good prices, delivered on the line of any railway or navigable stream. Hence the clearing process is slow. Trees are seldom cut until the lumber and fuel can be marketed, and quite as much is realised from the land by the sale of these products as could be gained from cultivated crops.

For this reason the woodlands offer better opportunities to the poorer immigrant, for he can there turn his labour to account immediately for the support of his family, while his house will cost him much less, and fuel can be had for the cutting.

Nor is it true that any important crop grown in the southern part of the State cannot also be grown in the northern part. Corn is now successfully cultivated in Decker, Wadena, and Hubbard counties; also in the valley of the Mississippi, north of Aitken county, the yield being but slightly less than that obtained in localities further south.

Pumpkins, squashes, cucumbers, carrots, parsnips, cabbage, radishes, lettuce, beets, turnips, ruta bagas, &c., flourish there as well as anywhere in the State, and larger and better potatoes than those produced in these northern localities are not grown anywhere. The only place in the State where the cultivation of corn seems not to have succeeded is the Red River Valley, and want of success there is due rather to the character of the soil than the climate. Wheat, oats, rye, and barley grow in all parts of the State wherever there is arable land, and there is but little difference in different localities as to the certainty of these crops or abundance of their yield.

For growing cattle, sheep, horses, and hogs, and for dairying and for butter and cheesemaking, Minnesota excels most other countries on this continent. The dry, pure air, abundance of excellent water, and nutritious grasses all conduce to keep the animals healthy and in good condition. Horses bred here are handsome, strong, and sound, and command ready sale at highest prices in the Eastern markets. Hogs grow rapidly and fatten readily, and their flesh is firm, sweet, and healthy. Sheep are not liable to diseases, the fleece is heavier and finer, and the mutton more palatable than when grown in moister and warmer climates. Cattle raising is likewise more profitable because of the better health of the stock and a much smaller percentage of loss from diseases, and this increased healthfulness tends to make the beef more nutritious, healthy, and palatable, and in greater demand in the markets. The cows also yield more and richer milk from the same causes; and this, with the added advantages of climate and pure spring water, makes Minnesota one of the best countries for butter and cheese-making and dairying. All parts of the State seem about equally adapted to these industries, and in those of the northern counties that are settled, stock of all kinds look quite as well as elsewhere. The prairies, however, afford the largest areas of pasture lands.

The following tabular statements are estimates for 1883, which I have arrived at after a close and searching inquiry:—

ESTIMATE of the Principal Grain Crops for 1883.

Crop.	Minnesota.			Dakota.		
	Acres.	Yield per Acre.	Bushels.	Acres.	Yield per Acre.	Bushels.
		Bushels.			Bushels.	
Wheat	2,600,000	13·0	33,800,000	1,000,000	16·0	16,000,000
Corn	750,000	20·8	15,000,000	250,000	18·2	5,000,000
Oats	950,000	33·1	31,500,000	200,000	42·9	9,000,000

Average Price of Agricultural Products, December 1, 1883.

Crop.	Per—	Minnesota.	Dakato.
		Dol. c.	Dol. c.
Corn	Bushel	0 43	0 45
Wheat	,,	0 80	0 72
Rye	,,	0 50	0 55
Oats	,,	0 28	0 28
Barley	,,	0 47	0 40
Buckwheat	,,	0 73	0 90
Potatoes	,,	0 27	0 30
Tobacco	Lb.	0 10	..
Hay	Ton	4 50	3 75
Sorghum molasses	Gallon	0 57	0 54

Farm Lands.

State.	Acres in Farms.	Value of Farms.	Value per Acre.	Per Cent. of Workers in Agriculture.
		Dollars.	Dol. c.	
Minnesota	13,403,019	193,724,260	14 45	5
Dakota	3,800,656	22,401,084	5 89	49

Incomes from Farming.

State.	Persons in all Occupations.	Persons engaged in Agriculture.	Per Cent. in Agriculture.	Value of Agricultural Produce.	Value per Capita.
				Dollars.	Dollars.
Minnesota	255,125	131,535	52	49,468,951	376
Dakota	57,844	22,508	49	5,648,814	198

In 1858 the territory of Minnesota was admitted into the Union as a State, claiming a white population of 140,000, and two years afterwards, when the United States census was taken, its white inhabitants were found to have increased to 172,023, notwithstanding that the financial depression of 1857 had tended greatly to retard the settlement of all the new States, by occasioning a complete suspension of building railroads and prosecuting other enterprises conducive to the opening up of new countries. The occurrence of the War of Rebellion in 1861 and the Sioux Indian massacre of 1862 interfered still further with the rapid peopling of the new State. But, despite these adverse circumstances, Minnesota's white population in 1865 was found to be 250,099, and its claims to agricultural excellence and healthfulness were by this time so fully established and generally recognised that its future rapid growth was apparently assured. In 1870 its population had increased to 439,407, in 1875 to 597,407, and in 1880 to 780,807. There has been a very considerable increase since the census was taken, and it is fair to presume that the population of the entire State has nearly doubled in the three years that have elapsed since 1880.

The population of Dakota has increased so rapidly during the past few years that an accurate statement cannot be made. It may safely be estimated at 320,000. Some idea of Dakota's increase of population by incoming settlers last year can now be made from land office reports. The grand total of entries by homestead and pre-emption last year was 46,669, which multiplied by the modest figure of three gives a population of 140,007. Each entry represents a head of a family or a single person of age. The average Dakota settler has a good-sized family. The settlement in the Deadwood district is unreported, and the Devil's Lake district has come but recently into the market; yet the settlement in each is numerous, certainly several thousand. To these add settlers on railroad lands and in the villages, and we can credit Dakota with nearly 200,000 of a new population last year. I must again use the statistics of the cities of St. Paul and Minneapolis as a guide to the industries of Minnesota. I have as yet been unable to procure reliable statistics of Dakota.

St. Paul, the capital of Minnesota, and her "sister city," about 11 miles distant, are both situated on the Mississippi river. St. Paul is in latitude 44° 53' north, and longitude 93° 5' west of Greenwich, and is 155 miles from Duluth, 410 miles from Chicago, and 791 by river from St. Louis. The general contour of the city is hilly. The valley of the river is terraced: the lower "bench" or terrace being occupied by the railroad, stockyards, and some few wholesale stores and warehouses on the north bank. The upper bench, encircled by the Bluffs, forms the main business portion of the place to the east and west; the elevation of the Bluffs is maintained upon a prairie plateau, which is covered with residences. To the north the land falls rapidly, and upon the lowlands beyond are located the manufacturing and repair shops of the St. Paul, Minneapolis, and Manitoba Railroad and the Northern Pacific Railroad, and several large foundries, grain elevators, manufacturing establishments, and lumber yards. Still further north and beyond the city limits there is a chain of lakes from which the city waterworks at present derive their supply.

Pierre Parrant and Wm. Beaumette were the first settlers, and in 1841 Fr. Gaultier came here from Dubuque and established a Roman Catholic chapel, which he dedicated to St. Paul, and in a short time this name was adopted by the settlement and has never since been changed. In 1846 a post-office was established; in 1849 the Act creating the territory of Minnesota fixed the seat of government at St. Paul; and in 1851 the town was permanently fixed as the State capital. Since then the place has grown rapidly, and I can think of no better way of evidencing its extraordinary growth than by the population returns since 1838:—

Year	Population
1838	3
1850	840
1855	4,400
1857	9,973
1860	10,600
1865	13,210
1868	20,118
1870	22,300
1871	25,200
1873	27,033
1875	32,178
1880	41,498
1881	50,000
1882	75,885
1883	100,000

By a glance at these figures it will be seen that at no period of its existence, except from 1850 to 1860, has the population of St. Paul increased at a more rapid rate than during the past three years. Business in all branches has increased correspondingly, the wholesale trade having grown from 27,500,000 dol. in 1869 to 36,000,000 dol. in 1879, and to 72,008,771 dol. in 1883. The banking capital is also increasing every year, and now stands at 6,500,000 dol., with the prospect of 500,000 dol. increase during the early part of this year. The real estate business is very large, and by a comparison with Chicago, a city five times as large as St. Paul, its magnitude can be more fully realised. In 1862 the total recorded number of transfers of landed property in St. Paul was 4,447, while in Chicago the real estate transactions for the same period were only 7,528. The real estate transactions in St. Paul for the year 1883 have greatly exceeded in number and value expressed those of any previous year. In numbers they have nearly doubled those of 1881, and in value represented have exceeded those of that year nearly threefold, while the record of 1882 is improved nearly 500 in number of deeds and over 3,000,000 dol. in considerations expressed. In preparing the review here presented only warranty deeds were numbered, and all which expressed a less consideration than 75 dol. were thrown out altogether; although in the review for 1882 every warranty deed was listed, even though the consideration was only 1 dol. I mention this fact to show that the increase in number of deeds as compared with last year is really considerably greater than appears in the comparisons made:—

Years.	Number of Deeds.	Consideration.
		Dollars.
1881	2,831	4,345,991
1882	4,447	9,354,841
1883	4,874	12,981,331

The twelvemonth made up of the last six months of 1882 and the first six months of 1883 showed the period of greatest activity in the St. Paul real estate market, for while the first half of 1883 led the first half of 1882 almost two to one, the last half of 1883 fell slightly below the corresponding time in 1882. To illustrate by figures:—

	Number of Deeds.	Consideration.
		Dollars.
First six months, 1883	2,822	7,992,061
,, ,, 1882	2,318	3,213,387
Excess first half, 1883	504	4,778,674
Last six months, 1882	2,129	5,441,454
,, ,, 1883	2,052	4,989,270
Excess last half, 1882	77	452,184

From information obtained from reliable real estate agents, it is learned that the market of late has been in a very healthy condition; that is, that there is but little speculative demand compared with the purchases for actual improvement. Indeed, it is asserted by the real estate agents, that during the last six months of 1883 there was and is still a much more active market for residence lots than at any time during the extreme activity, as indicated by the volume of transfers.

During the past year a fraction less than 2,000 acres was laid out into building plots, numbering 6,514 lots.

The report of building operations for the last eight months of 1883, as credited to nine principal cities of the United States, exclusive of New York, compiled by Bradstreet's Mercantile Agency, may be of interest:—

Chicago	12,780,000
Cincinnati	11,000,000
St. Paul	9,580,000
Minneapolis	8,310,000
Cleveland	3,750,000
New Orleans	3,000,000
Denver	3,000,000
Des Moines	2,750,000
Detroit	2,580,000

The increase in the value of products manufactured in St. Paul in 1883 over that of the preceding year was 3,811,482 dol., the number of establishments in operation was 758, the number of employés 13,979, and the total value of articles manufactured 25,885,471 dol. Appended below are the tabulated results of the year, as given by the secretary of the Chamber of Commerce, and the totals are handsome enough to prove that St. Paul is not only a great commercial centre, but a hive of manufacturers as well. The increase of the city's manufactures is steady, as is shown by the figure of 1882, when the value of the product was 22,073,989 dol. Contractors and builders head the list in the rates of increase, exceeding the record of 1882 by 787,140 dol. in a total of 4,947,000 dol. In clothing, the total for 1883 2,300,000 dol.; an increase of more than half a million (518,834 dol.) over the preceding year. Furs show an increase of 203,700 dol., manufactured iron for architectural purposes an increase of 155,550 dol., printing and publishing the handsome surplus over 1882 of 293,520 dol., slaughtering and meat packing 235,000 dol., flour and grain milling 113,000 dol., boots and shoes 196,123 dol., crackers and bakery products 199,500 dol., and tins and hardware (including stoves) 232,100 dol.

The only decreases are in agricultural implements, and doors, boxes, and planing mills, trunks and valises.

TABULATED Exhibit of Manufacturing Industries of St. Paul.

Kind of Business.	Number of Establishments.	Number of Employés.	Value of Products, 1883.	Increase over 1882.
			Dollars.	Dollars.
Agricultural implements	2	295	800,000	*64,000
Blacksmiths and wheelwrights	16	75	56,000	9,100
Bookbinding	7	89	90,000	4,146
Boots and shoes	25	407	1,025,000	196,123
Brewers, maltsters, and bottlers	18	193	914,623	106,867
Bricks and tiles	12	250	170,000	11,100
Brooms and brushes	6	42	55,500	250
Cigars	32	492	800,000	28,000
Clothing	78	1,500	2,300,000	518,834
Coffee, spices, and baking powder	6	120	795,000	1,896
Confectionery	9	83	275,000	9,000
Contractors and builders	147	3,921	4,947,000	787,140
Cracker and bakery products	28	300	1,000,000	199,500
Drugs, chemicals, and oils	6	50	405,000	76,100
Flour and grist milling	7	85	1,560,000	113,000
Furniture and upholstery	24	275	560,000	56,100
Furs	7	172	426,000	203,700
Harness and saddlery	18	133	300,000	73,067
Iron, architectural	3	132	265,000	155,550
Jewellery and watchmaking	7	33	52,400	34,000
Machine shops, foundries, and boiler works	16	400	745,000	98,040
Marble and stone cutting	22	422	176,000	51,000
Millinery, lace, and fancy goods	20	94	97,000	9,670
Painting and glazing	12	121	225,000	..
Photography	13	39	63,000	3,360
Pictures and frames	4	17	25,000	..
Printing and publishing	43	1,120	1,698,000	93,520
Railroad repairs and car making	4	1,385	1,417,148	71,939
Sash, doors, boxes, and planing mills	8	400	484,000	*15,500
Slaughtering and meat packing	60	250	1,675,000	235,000
Tin and hardware and plumbing	15	139	450,000	232,180
Trunks and valises	2	92	120,000	*30,000
Wagons and carriages	22	343	612,000	18,000
Miscellaneous	61	510	1,301,800	215,400
Total	758	13,979	25,885,471	3,811,482

Miscellaneous includes awnings and tents, bleachers, boats, brass works, carpet weavers, carriage trimmer, cooperage, cutlery, grinding, dyeing, engraving, fire-proof building material, fireworks, hair goods, hoop and skirt factory, knit goods, lighting companies, mineral waters, musical instruments, opticians, rendering companies, renovators of cloth, sewer and drain pipes, shingle bands, show cases, soap, sporting goods, stamps and seals, steam heating, taxidermists, terra cotta, type foundry, vinegar and catsup, wire works.

The official report of internal revenue collector, Bickel, covering 11 months of the year 1883, with a very close estimate for December, which completes the year's business, is given in the table below. There has been a very marked increase in revenue collections, but it is impossible to give comparisons with 1882, owing to the fact that the two revenue districts of Minnesota were consolidated into one during

* Decrease.

the present year. Collector Bickel could furnish figures for his original district for one-half the year, but the latter half of the year he has had charge of the entire State. Collections up to December 1, 1883 (11 months), amounted to 414,925 dol. Estimating the receipts for December at 29,000 dol., the total receipts for the year will be 443,925 dol. The figures appended give all needed information:—

1883.	Licenses.	Tobacco and Cigars.	Beer Stamps.	Miscellaneous.	Total.
	Dollars.	Dollars.	Dollars.	Dollars.	Dollars.
January	1,252	6,603	9,507	34,455	51,818
February	572	5,888	10,233	236	16,931
March	600	8,532	14,315	80	23,527
April	31,617	7,329	15,612	37	54,597
May	46,235	6,863	18,509	191	71,800
June	5,462	5,251	22,657	127	33,498
July	3,635	4,776	24,358	175	32,945
August	3,284	6,658	24,950	138	35,031
September	3,523	6,466	20,223	457	30,671
October	3,244	8,166	21,903	416	33,731
November	2,733	7,080	20,039	318	39,171
*December	3,000	6,000	19,700	300	29,000
* Total	105,161	79,617	222,010	36,936	443,725

Few cities of the size of St. Paul can make as good a showing as that presented in Comptroller Roche's official statement of the bonded indebtedness of this municipality. The total amount of the city's bonded liabilities is 2,328,040 dol. 71 c., and there is no floating debt, but an item of less than 17,000 dol. payable this year out of the present tax levy. On the credit side of the account, the comptroller finds that the 100,000 inhabitants of St. Paul's own property was assessed two years ago at 43,000,000 dol., the cash value of real estate being 100,000,000 dol. The result of the new assessment will not be known until next August, but Mr. Roche estimates the assessed value of real and personal estate at probably more than 60,000,000 dol. Substantial assets such as these and an unblemished record place the credit of St. Paul high on the list of American cities. It has never defaulted in the payment of any item of principal or interest, and its bonds are eagerly sought for as a safe investment. Of the total bonded debt 72,900 dol. fall due this year, and are to be paid out of the year's taxes; while the interest account, and in effect the principal of the city debt, is substantially lessened by the flourishing condition of her institutions. Thus the new city workhouse promises to be self-supporting. The city waterworks represent half a million of the bonded debt, but the water revenues have paid the interest upon these bonds, as well as upon the mortgage of 160,000 dol., and it is reasonably certain that these revenues will pay the principal of the bonds when due, thus relieving taxpayers from any other share in bearing the burden. The local improvement fund is a revolving fund which must cancel its own bonds at maturity, and the Como Park tract is now worth in cash three times the amount expended in its purchase. The sum which will thus have to be met ultimately by taxation is comparatively small, and the financial condition of the city is a cause for

* Estimated.

just pride. The tax levy for last year, a year of extensive public improvements, is but 24½ mills on the dollar, distributed as follows:—State, 1·8 mills; county, 2·7 mills; educational, 4 mills; school buildings, 2 mills; and city purposes, 14 mills. No recently issued bonds bear more than 5 per cent. interest, and they are eagerly sought at a premium. The official statement indicates the healthiest condition of the city's finances.

MINNEAPOLIS.

Pre-eminently the headquarters of the flour manufacturing interests of the United States in Minnesota is a city of 100,000 inhabitants. It is the county seat of Hennepin county, and is situated on the Mississippi river.

In looking over the figures that lie before me it seems almost impossible to realise that this city was a few short years ago a mere hamlet, and that where now exist flour mills, with an aggregate capacity of 26,660 barrels per day in the year 1882, the Government erected a small grist mill for the convenience of a handful of soldiers. The first lumber mill was not built until 1848, and the village of St. Anthony Falls was surveyed in 1849. In 1854 there was built a flour mill, and the first suspension bridge was thrown across the Mississippi.

The Flouring Interest.—Minneapolis is the largest milling centre in the world, the chief manufacture being its famous flour, which has obtained a reputation for superiority that extends from ocean to ocean, and has penetrated the European markets, giving the city a name and renown of which it has reason to be proud.

The present milling capacity of Minneapolis is shown in the appended table:—

Name of Mill.	Operated by—	Barrels.
West Side—		
Anchor	C. A. Pillsbury and Co.	900
Cataract	D. R. Barber and Son	600
Columbia	Columbia Mill Company	1,000
Crown roller	Christian Bros. and Co.	1,700
Dakota	H. F. Brown and Co.	250
Excelsior	E. V. White and Co.	800
Galaxy	Cahill, Fletcher, and Co.	1,000
Holly	F. S. Hinkle	250
Humboldt	Hinkle, Greenleaf, and Co.	775
Minneapolis	Crocker, Fisher, and Co.	600
National	W. F. Gunn	150
North Western	Sidle, Fletcher, Holmes, and Co.	1,300
Palisade	Washburn Mill Company	1,500
Pettit	J. A. Christian and Co.	1,300
St. Anthony	Hinkle, Greenleaf, and Co.	450
Standard	E. V. White and Co.	1,500
Union	G. W. Goodrich and Co.	310
Washburn, A		3,200
,, B	Washburn, Crosby, and Co.	1,000
,, C		2,000
Zenith	Sidle, Fletcher, Holmes, and Co.	600
East Side—		
Pillsbury, A	C. A. Pillsbury and Co.	5,200
Phoenix	Stamwitz and Schober	275
Total capacity		26,660

On August 24, 1882, the daily capacity was 21,250 barrels. Since that time the North Star and Model Mills, with 600 barrels capacity, have been burned, while the Columbia, Minneapolis, and Excelsior Mills, with a total capacity of 3,400 dol., have been completed and put in operation. The Palisade Mill has been thoroughly remodelled and the capacity increased from 550 to 1,500 barrels per day. Other less notable increases have been in the Washburn A, Galaxy, and National Mills. Another source of increase has been from the mills, while really no machinery was added to them, being able to make more flour on the wheat last fall in a given time than ever before, thus simply giving them a higher record. Of course it is understood by all that in giving the capacity of a mill the maximum figures are universally used.

The milling year closes September 1, and the following figures show the volume of business for the years quoted:—Flour shipments were for 1882–83, 4,089,908; 1881–82, 2,476,807; 1880–81, 2,993,892; 1879–80, 1,787,821 barrels. The local consumption was—1882–83, 140,000 barrels. Flour receipts mainly from small mills in the State were 294,445 barrels. The total product of the past year shows an increase over previous year of 1,099,675 barrels. Exports, since there was any movement in that line, were in 1878 109,183; in 1880, 769,442; and in 1882–83 (12 months), 1,700,750 barrels. Shipments of mill stuffs, 1882–83, were 123,730 tons against 95,836 tons in 1881–82. Wheat receipts in 1882–83, 19,293,375; 1881–82, 16,556,250; 1879–80, 8,775,077 bushels; wheat shipments, 1882–83, 1,423,211; 1881–82, 1,831,750; 1879–80, 74,800 bushels. Add to wheat receipts wheat brought in by wagon 500,000, and the grand total of wheat receipts for the year will reach the enormous figures of 19,793,375 bushels. The foregoing figures when compared show the giant strides made by these mammoth establishments, and there is no doubt the year to come and those to follow will exhibit the same marvellous progress and growth in this department of manufacture.

Next in importance to the flouring interests of Minneapolis ranks the manufacture of lumber, and its rapid growth during the last few years gives the most flattering assurances of permanency and increase. The business has been profitable, and the quotations given of the output for the past three years furnish evidence of increasing prosperity. The extraordinary home demand for lumber verifies the statements as to the growth and building progress of the city. Over 160,000,000 feet were used in 1882. The following table will give the lumber business of Minneapolis for the year 1883:—

Firm.	Lumber.	Shingle.	Lath.
	Feet.	Feet.	Feet.
West Side Mills—			
Minneapolis Mill Company	34,913,257	6,475,000	8,431,000
W. D. Washburn and Co.	7,940,000	3,375,000	1,919,000
J. B. Bassett and Co.	12,652,293	3,193,450	2,050,000
Camp and Walker	22,247,460	3,780,000	3,554,400
James Goodnow	15,363,271	8,746,500	2,887,750
N. G. Leighton	8,657,250	4,517,050	2,986,250
Diamond Mill Company	18,250,220	6,600,000	5,350,000
Total West Side Mills	120,023,651	36,696,200	27,179,300
East Side Mills—			
John Martin and Co.	12,514,560	2,885,000	3,624,750
Eastman, B., and Co.	19,116,237	5,661,000	4,132,450
Merriam, B., and Co.	18,747,178	3,125,000	2,767,710
Cole and Weeks	19,401,346	7,213,250	4,134,000
McMullen and Son	19,000,000	14,700,000	3,000,000
Clough Bros. and Co.	12,730,000	..	3,101,000
Nelson, Tenny, and Co.	12,568,266	..	3,491,700
Trask and Graham	5,091,818	..	1,717,700
Fletcher Bros.	13,000,000	9,000,000	3,500,000
M. A. Lee	4,103,300	1,000,000	..
Smith and Keigan	..	6,780,759	..
Farnham and Lovejoy	19,040,000	3,095,000	3,554,000
Total East Side Mills	152,769,571	53,450,000	32,999,960
Grand total, 1883	272,793,222	90,146,200	60,179,260
,, 1882	314,362,166	188,546,000	61,381,380
Decrease, 1883	41,569,944	47,399,800	1,102,120
Total cut, 1881	233,500,074	86,818,500	49,253,700

	Feet.
Stock on hand December 1, 1882	146,897,590
Manufactured during 1883	272,793,222
Received from other points	47,155,000
Total stock during 1883	466,845,812
Shipments to other points during 1883	126,592,000
Stock on hand December 1, 1883	184,822,098
Total local sales	155,441,714
	Dollars.
Value of production of mills in 1883	4,628,878

	Receipts.	Shipments.
	Feet.	Feet.
1883	47,155,000	126,592,000
1882	48,700,000	134,740,000
1881	40,070,000	156,270,000
1880	20,635,000	162,837,000

The following is a statement of the lumber production of the Minneapolis mills during the last 13 years:—

	Feet.
1870	118,233,100
1871	117,157,000
1872	167,918,820
1873	189,910,000
1874	191,305,680
1875	156,655,000
1876	200,371,250
1877	129,676,000
1878	130,274,100
1879	149,154,500
1880	195,452,200
1881	230,403,000
1882	314,362,166

By many it is believed, and with every show of reason, that even were Minneapolis deprived of her great milling interests she would still become a great manufacturing centre. With the great Falls of St. Anthony at her command, she could build permanent prosperity upon the varied manufactures demanded by the rapid development of the new empire. In agricultural implements Minneapolis is doing an enormous and always increasing business. In miscellaneous manufactures, exclusive of flour and lumber, the city employed 8,945 men in 1882, who produced manufactured articles to the amount of 21,822,862 dol.—an increase in seven years of 18,046,729 dol.

As before stated, there is here a grand field for every variety of industry for the profitable employment of capital and labour. The manufacturing district from the making of lumber and the manufacturing of flour has become very important, and I would call your attention to the fact that this branch of business has fairly outstripped in volume even flour milling, although that industry has been largely responsible for the impetus given to some lines included in the review. This is especially true of the iron-working factories, now fourth in importance and now largely engaged in making mill machinery. The same analogy is found between the lumber business and the sash, door, and blind business, fifth in importance.

The summary of the manufacturing industries, exclusive of flour and lumber, for 1883, was as follows:—

Class of Manufactures.	Number of Hands.	Trade.
		Dollars.
Foundries, machine shops, and machinery other than agricultural	984	2,545,000
Tin, copper, and galvanised iron	143	313,500
Railroad machinery	1,348	4,000,000
Agricultural implements	655	1,645,000
Cooperage	800	1,345,562
Crackers, confections, and spices	249	799,500
Wagons, carriages, and blacksmithing	161	347,500
Sash, doors, and blinds	1,337	1,961,000
Planing mills	161	212,000
Drugs, oils, paints, &c.	64	392,000
Duck goods, tents, &c.	274	445,000
Brick and stone	224	331,000
Gloves, mitts, furs, &c.	54	79,500
Trunks, showcases, &c.	46	116,000
Jewellery	8	21,100
Woollen goods	225	400,000
Rags	65	360,000
Paper	109	250,000
Harness and horse goods	91	126,000
Furniture	506	845,700
Elevator cups, furnaces, belting, &c.	14	91,000
Tanneries, carding, &c.	39	210,000
Fences, wood-working, &c.	185	215,000
Drain pipe and earthenware	26	40,000
Paper boxes	29	12,000
Boots and shoes	175	700,000
Printing, publishing books, &c.	374	761,000
Organs	6	12,000
Patterns	11	22,000
Vinegar, pop, and pickles	50	75,500
Soap and rendering	109	1,350,000
Brooms	30	60,000
Pork and fish packings	69	59,000
Shirts, clothing, &c.	303	351,000
Meerschaum	3	12,000
Cigars	100	225,000
Beer	120	495,000
Total for 1883	8,945	21,822,862
,, 1882	7,388	16,929,734
Increase	1,551	4,893,098

A COMPARATIVE Table.

	Dollars.
1876	3,776,133
1877	4,802,300
1878	5,696,625
1879	8,155,100
1880	10,333,000
1881	12,029,597
1882	16,929,764
1883	21,822,862

Late in the fall of 1882 a sharp advance, particularly in business property, stimulated by some of the magnificent improvements which had been made or begun, led to considerable activity in that line, which bordered on speculation. There was a sharp advance also in all kinds of property predicated on the continued rapid increase of population, and the demand for both residences and stores. The labouring classes had for years been unusually prosperous and steadily employed, and the passion for investing in homes, which is a characteristic of the inhabitants of Minnesota, asserted itself more than ever. The records on file in the office of the register of deeds pretty clearly indicate the periods of unmistakable activity—with the exception, perhaps, of the report for November, which month brought to the surface many deeds for record which had been received before the taxes for the following year became payable. The remarkable growth of the city gave confidence in the stability of its real estate values, which had been previously low. This confidence is still unabated, though not shared in by me.

The following table shows the number of deeds which passed during the year, the amount of the consideration on each, the number of mortgages, and the obligation expressed in each. The table has been compiled directly from the instruments:—

1883.	Number of Mortgages.	Obligations.	Number of Deeds.	Consideration.
		Dollars.		Dollars.
January	370	181,907	571	1,593,934
February	412	587,405	695	1,447,060
March	687	958,872	1,067	2,568,844
April	616	1,222,438	1,062	3,277,591
May	834	1,932,062	1,331	3,243,264
June	640	869,546	1,036	2,792,327
July	469	624,000	782	2,277,513
August	454	736,391	713	1,775,845
September	414	610,396	767	1,601,008
October	512	839,454	932	2,312,942
November	473	1,110,128	922	3,992,697
December	424	526,032	534	1,427,625
Total	6,305	9,397,720	10,220	28,308,550

COMPARISON.

	Number of Deeds.	Consideration.
		Dollars.
Total, 1883	10,220	28,308,550
,, 1882	7,811	19,161,294
,, 1881	5,902	8,425,045
,, 1880	3,161	4,608,017
,, 1879	2,402	3,080,245

It will be observed that the amount in the mortgages is still 33 per cent. of the purchase price—a percentage of debt that is remarkably small, considering the rapid growth of the city, and that a large proportion of its population are young men but beginning the world.

During the past year plats of 147 additions to the city have been filed, containing 13,834 lots, which is largely in excess of the additions of any previous year.

The year 1883 has been one of remarkable activity in real estate in Minneapolis. Sales have been numerous, large, and for greatly advanced prices.

The mineral deposits of Minnesota have as yet been but slightly developed. Iron mining in the northern part of the State has certainly been the principal effort in that direction.

The "Cleveland Iron Trade Review," published on Jan. 14, 1884, gives an account of the extensive development of the Vermillion Lake iron district of Minnesota. The iron ore syndicate, known as the Minnesota Iron Company, is composed of Ohio, Pennsylvania, and Minnesota men. C. Tower, of Philadelphia, is president of the company, and T. L. Blood, of St. Paul, is secretary. The property of the company lies in St. Louis county, Minn. Two mines have already been opened, and the results show that the ore is equal, if not superior, to any mined in the Lake Superior district. The new company owns 22,488 acres in all. The shipping port on Lake Superior for the ore of the district will be Two Harbours, 25 miles north of Duluth. The surveyed line of the Duluth and Iron Range Railroad, the interests of which are substantially identical with that of the Minnesota Company, between the town of Tower, at Vermillion Lake, and Two Harbours, is 72 miles in length. This line will be at once extended to Duluth, and there placed in connection with the railroad system of the United States. The entire length of the road, when completed, will be nearly 100 miles. Work on the road is now in active progress, about 1,000 men being employed. It will be built in the most thorough manner, of standard gauge. The Duluth and Iron Range Railroad Company has also begun building ore piers at Two Harbours. These piers are to be 5 feet higher than those at Escanaba, and 7 feet higher than those at Marquette, thus affording the best possible facilities for loading the largest vessels in the trade. It is now expected that the road will be completed, and shipment will be begun by August, 1884.

The mineral deposits of the territory of Dakota have been, and are being, very extensively developed. The wealth of the Black Hills is simply marvellous, consisting of gold, silver, mica, salt, and coal mines. Rich and profitable gold mines are now being successfully worked in the Black Hills. Coal is also mined along the line of the Northern Pacific Railroad to a considerable extent. I have no statistics of the products of the mining in Dakota at present at my command.

Rates of Wages.

	Dol.	c.		Dol.	c.
Bricklayer	3	50	to	4	00
,, (fronts)	4	00		6	00
Cabinet maker	3	52			
Carpenter	2	50		3	00
,, (finisher)	3	00			
Carver	4	00			
Gasfitter	3	00		3	50
Glazier	2	50			
Labourer	1	50		2	00
Painter	2	50			
Plasterer	3	00		4	00
Plumber	2	75		3	00
Roofer (tin)	3	00		4	00
Slater	3	00			
Stair builder	3	00		5	00
Steam fitter	3	00		3	50
Stonemason	3	00			
Stone cutter	4	00			
Stone setter	4	00			

Of the public works the improvement of the Mississippi and Missouri rivers, the harbours of Duluth and Grand Marais, and the maintenance of the Falls of St. Anthony, form the principal work undertaken by the United States Government. Large sums of money are annually expended on these works. There is no question of more engrossing interest to the people of the North-west than that the improvement of the Upper Mississippi river by the general government, and the account of the work accomplished during the present year by the United States engineer, as well as a casual look over the field in the past, will be most appropriate here. The items are given in detail, covering the improvement of the river between St. Paul and the mouth of the Illinois river. The appropriations for the general improvement of the through navigation of this section are: "Operation of Snag Boats," "St. Paul to Des Moines Rapids," and "Des Moines Rapids to the mouth of the Des Moines River." Under the first head are operated the snag and dredge boats "General Barnard" and "J. G. Parke," whose district extends from St. Paul to the mouth of the Missouri river, a distance of 714 miles. The work of these boats is the removal of snag, trees, and wrecks, assisting steam boats, establishing water gauges and channel marks, making surveys and examinations for new channels, and, when not otherwise engaged, rendering service to the works of permanent improvement. Both boats have been over the entire district during the past season performing the duties mentioned, and in addition the "General Barnard" was used by the United States Senate Special Committee on the Improvement of the Mississippi River, and for an inspection trip from Rock Island to the jetties at the mouth of the river. During the season the boats and crews have removed 199 snags, pulled back on the shore 24 trees which threatened to fall and become snags, and felled and removed 34 overhanging trees, running in connection with this work 2,810 miles. Under the two latter heads of appropriations named are carried on the works of permanent improvement from St. Paul to Grafton, with the exception of the Rock Island and Des Moines Rapids.

Prior to 1878 no permanent work was done on this section of the river except at the Rapids, and a few dams built by the crews of the snag boats. The River and Harbour Bill, approved June 18, 1878, was the first to make appropriation for this work. Since that date there has been appropriated for the river from St. Paul to Des Moines Rapids 950,000 dols., and from Des Moines Rapids to the mouth of the Illinois 515,000 dol. This amount, distributed over five years and over 700 miles of the Father of Waters, has been only sufficient to partially improve some of the worst features of the river. That the work already done has been of great benefit to navigation is now undisputed by those most familiar with the river; but much more remains to be done, and with adequate appropriations this work can be carried on in time to serve the present generation as well as posterity. In evidence of the improved condition of the river, it may be said that the boats of the Diamond Joe line have, with two exceptions, made the irregular trip through from St. Louis to St. Paul, on a stage of water but 2 feet above the lowest on record. A general plan for improvement adopted is, first, to concentrate the whole flow in a single channel by closing with dams constructed of brush mats loaded with stone all sloughs, "chutes," and side channels; then to protect by revetement the heads of islands and cutting banks, which furnish the material for sand bars; and lastly to contract the width of the stream by means of wing or spur dams, to such an extent as will allow the low water discharge to maintain the required depth.

[612]

The Mississippi River Commission, in their first report to the Secretary of War, speak on this subject as follows:—" The system of work in progress on the Mississippi river between St. Paul and the mouth of the Illinois, with the modifications which experience will suggest, is adequate for the improvement of navigation, and should be pushed rapidly to completion. It is further recommended that the entire amount of 1,000,000 dol., estimated by Captain A. Mackenzie for the coming fiscal year for carrying on the adopted improvements between St. Paul and the mouth of the Illinois river, be appropriated in one sum."

Owing to the fact that the last Congress made no appropriations for river improvements, the amount of work done on the river the past season has been comparatively small, being limited to the use of unexpended balances of former appropriations. One tow-boat, with accompanying fleet of launch, quarter boat, pile driver, barges, &c., was employed between St. Paul and Hastings from August 7 until the closing of the river, continuing the work of former years. Nine dams were built, others repaired, and the banks protected at 14 different points. This work required 13,517 cubic yards of brush, 19,062 cubic yards of stone, and cost about 30,000 dols. The above work was done under the personal supervision of the engineer in charge by hired labour, and the purchase of material in open market. Between Minneskia and Brownsville, Minn., a number of dams closing side tunnels and some revetements on caving banks were built under contracts made late the previous season. Near Minneska a small island, which was a serious obstruction to rafts, was dredged out, and the dams built in that vicinity in 1879 were repaired.

The Des Moines Rapids Canal.—During the year much dredging has been done, removing the deposits from the head of the canal and rocks from the channel above. A dry dock for the use of the United States and other vessels is now in process of construction just above the middle lock of the canal. This will be of great advantage to navigation interests, as there is no other similar structure on the river, and at present all boats needing repairs must be hauled out at boat yards. There have also been established at the canal carpenter shops, machine shops, &c., capable of doing most of the repair work incident to the operation of the canal, and a large number of boats now owned by the United States on the river.

A complete list of the improvements is appended, showing at what points the work was done.

Ice Harbour at Dubuque.—Congress, by Act of August 2, 1882, appropriated 20,000 dol. for making a winter harbour at Dubuque, Iowa. Waples Cut was selected as the site of the work, and it has been up to the present time dredged out to a depth of 6 feet below low water, over an area of 400,000 square feet. The work gives great satisfaction, and affords a commodious and safe harbour for a large fleet of steam boats and barges.

Mississippi River, opposite Dubuque.—Some dredging was done on the middle bar between Dubuque and Dunleith, removing a few high points, and an excellent landing was made at the Dunleith warehouses, and a ferry wharf in the same manner.

Rock Island Harbour.—No work was done during the season, the harbour being still in good condition. A survey has been made with a view to laying out dredging work for the future.

Muscatine Harbour.—A dredge was employed during the month of October in removing mud deposits from the front of the Muscatine wharf. The harbour was left in excellent condition.

Fort Madison.—The dam from Smith's Island to the tow-head was begun, and about six courses laid on Niota chute dam; three courses of brush and rocks were laid, bringing it up to about 3 feet above low water.

Des Moines Rapids.—The dam from Montrose Island to Naugoo was brought up to low water mark. This dam is 3,200 feet in length dredge No. 1 was employed in digging broken rock from the cuts on the Rapids; dredge No. 2, 200 feet wide, through the bar at the head of the Rapids.

Warsaw.—The upper dam at Warsaw was strengthened and an additional T head or "grundschwelle" built.

Canton.—A channel was dredged through Howard's Bar, and a gravel dam was built to a height of 2 feet above low water and 1,100 feet long. This dam extends from the island about 500 feet above the Government light, and is intended to maintain the channel at Howard's. Some repairs were made to the Canton and Snooks chute dams.

Quincy.—A large amount of dredging was done in Quincy Bay, and its mouth was cleared of wrecks, logs, &c., and mooring piles were driven. The winter harbour now contains a dredged area of 82 acres. About 7,000 perennial feet of shore below Quincy was protected.

Marion City.—A dam was thrown across the head of Bayou St Charles. This chute, 10 miles in length, drew a large amount of water from the main river. It was gradually becoming wider and deeper, and fears were entertained that the channel might make its way through the bayou, which would have been a serious misfortune, it being so narrow and crooked.

Hannibal.—A dyke of gravel 800 feet in length and with its crest 7 feet above low water was built opposite Hannibal in the spring. During low water this dyke was used as a roadway, and a ferry boat placed its dock on its outer end. Above Hannibal Bridge about 4,000 feet of caving bank was protected.

Gilbert's Island.—Some show shore protection was constructed at the head of Gilbert's Island, and the dam at Denmark Island was raised and strengthened.

Louisiana.—The river below the bridge has been for several years very shoal and the channel crooked, the deepest water being the Buffalo shute, which is very narrow and obstructed by rocks at its lower end. A dam 2,000 feet in length and 7 feet above low water was run out from the Illinois shore. Buffalo chute was closed and some 1,500 feet of the shore of Buffalo Island was protected. The channel is now wide and deep.

St. Paul Levees.—To St. Paul as the head of the navigation of the Mississippi, the question of public levees is one of deep and permanent interest. It has been again brought to the front by the anomalous condition of the appropriation made by the United States Government to aid in the construction of a levee in West St. Paul, which recent developments have made a topic of lively concern. The facts as to the present status of the levee project can be briefly stated. It is proposed to set aside a strip of 200 feet, in minimum width, along the water front of West St. Paul, and for the construction of a levee the city is authorised to issue bonds to the amount of 25,000 dol. Of this 20,000 dol. have been issued, but the proceeds are to be used for the payment of damages to citizens owning the property that will be thus devoted to public uses. Of course the remaining 5,000 of the authorisation will not be sufficient for making even a beginning of work on the levee proper. It was with due knowledge of this that the aid of the Government was sought under the claim that the work under consideration was primarily one of river improvement. With this understanding 15,000 dol. were appropriated in the last River and Harbour Bill for improving the channel and banks of the river on the west side thereof at St. Paul. It has been held by the engineering department, which opinion is supported by the Secretary of War, that the language of the Appropriating Act is not sufficiently explicit to warrant the application of the fund to the contemplated improvement of West St. Paul, and the sum set aside remains unexpended until Congress shall definitely declare its intention.

Railroads form the greatest public works undertaken by private parties. Earlier in my report I have mentioned what roads exist in this district. The capitalisation of these roads may be given approximately as being 15,000 dol. per mile in bonds and 25,000 dol. per mile in stock.

Almost all the railroads operated in Minnesota and Dakota radiate from St. Paul and Minneapolis.

Events move with astonishing rapidity toward the accomplishment of that development of the cities of St. Paul and Minneapolis into the great business centre and distributing point of the whole North-west, which the wisest have always predicted. There is a period in the growth of cities when they must struggle to accomplish even destiny itself, and when every achievement must be won by patient and diligent endeavour. Then there comes a time when, like the bursting of the flower of the fully-matured bud, expansion becomes a law and a process of Nature, and in bewildering succession the events that have been sought and hoped for seem to jostle and crowd each other in their swift and steady advent. That time has now arrived for the two great cities of the North-west. The light has been raised by energy and enterprise above the point of equilibrium, and the next few years are to witness a growth in national importance which has been equalled but once or twice upon this continent and never upon any other. Among the most telling signs of the opening of this new era is the rapid concentration of these focal points of the whole railroad system of the West. That which was prophesied at the opening of through transportation over the Northern Pacific is shaping itself daily into concrete facts of power for the future. Two most important arrangements have recently been entered into with the Northern Pacific, the result of which will be to give to the cities facilities for the accommodation of through traffic and rank as distributing points beyond anything that the past has known. The first of these, the contract entered into between the Northern Pacific and the Minneapolis, St. Marie, and Atlantic companies, by which the latter secures the right to use the terminal facilities of the former, is a great point gained. To the advantage of concentration and of easy interchange of business is to be added the equal or greater advantage of an independent outlet to the east which will be afforded when the new line is completed. The local benefit of this will be immense to both these cities. The interests of the trans-continental line would be subserved by the addition of another to the routes over which its through business may be carried forward, and over which the return supply by which it is to be fed will come, and a powerful impetus will be given to the centripetal force which is ever attracting to and contracting upon this centre the bulk of North-western commerce.

It is generally believed that a similar arrangement has been completed with the Northern Pacific by the Great Chicago, Burlington, and Quincy road. This line, which will have its own track completed to St. Paul before the end of the current year, will use the terminal facilities of the Northern Pacific in this city, and intimate traffic relations between the two will be completed as a matter of course. This agreement entered into by the Burlington system is only another link in the chain of the future greatness of these cities which is now being so rapidly forged. Under any circumstances the approach of so important a line will be fraught with wonderful possibilities of good; but coming as it does, only the first in a race, to reach this point and establish its right to a share of the internal commerce accumulating here, and uniting its interests with those of the Northern Pacific, in a manner which indicates what the policy of the corporations of the West and North-west is to be, it is full of more than ordinary significance. The fact is that it has been admitted by those whose business it is to forecast the future of material development, that the cities of St. Paul and Minneapolis are to constitute the centre to which the commerce of a large population must converge, and through which it is to be distributed. Fixed as was this fact before the completion of the Northern Pacific, it has since assumed a more pressing aspect; and the urgency of the hour is to gain admission to these cities, and participate in the benefits of the vast system of concentration and transfer which shall have here its visible embodiment.

St. Paul New Railroads.—According to common report St. Paul is shortly to have seven new railroads. Six of these will be eastern roads, giving St. Paul important trunk line connections, while the seventh is to be a local road to run between St. Paul and Lake Minnetonka, and to be known as the St. Paul, Minneapolis, and Minnetonka. The others are the Winona, Alma, and Northern, the Minnesota and North-Western, the Lanesboro, Rochester, and St. Paul, the Wisconsin Central, the St. Paul Eastern Grand Trunk, and the Minneapolis, Sault St. Marie, and Ashland. The Winona, Alma, and Northern will probably be the first to enter St. Paul. Its surveyors are now out, and right of way has been secured as far north as La Crosse.

The road is generally acknowledged to be fathered by the Chicago, Burlington, and Quincy. The new line will pass through Hastings, and may enter St. Paul by tunnelling Dayton's Bluff, although that matter is not publicly settled yet. The distance from Chicago to Princeton, thence to Winona, Alma, and on to St. Paul, will be somewhere in the neighbourhood of 390 miles. The Minnesota Northern—or, as it is now commonly called, the new West St. Paul—road has attracted more attention than any of the new lines. According to rumour it is to be an extension of the Illinois Central, which now has a branch line to Mona on the Iowa State line. Mona, by the Iowa and Minnesota division of the Milwaukee and St. Paul, is 115 miles distant from St. Paul; and by the new line the distance will be shortened about 10 miles. The Illinois Central denies that it is building this road, but the general impression is that the new line will, to all intents and purposes, be a north-western extension of that road.

The Wisconsin Central has for some time intended to extend its line from Chippewa Falls to St. Paul, and is now making preparations to begin work upon this extension early in the spring. The work of surveying and locating has already been done, and it is said contractors are now making estimates upon the work. This new line will give the Wisconsin Central a direct line from Milwaukee to St. Paul, and will prove a great advantage to towns along the Central road in Wisconsin. The Wisconsin Central had for years very agreeable traffic arrangements with the Omaha roads for business between St. Paul and Chippewa Falls, but since the Omaha has passed into the hands of the North-Western these traffic arrangements are said not to have been so agreeable. The distance from Chippewa Falls to St. Paul is about 98 miles.

According to the incorporation papers of the Lanesboro, Rochester and St. Paul, filed with the Secretary of State, Jan. 18, the proposed route of the road is from a point on the Iowa line, in Fillmore county, Minn., through Lanesboro and Rochester, and terminating in St. Paul —a distance of about 150 miles.

The St. Paul Eastern Grand Trunk is to connect St. Paul and Minneapolis with Lake Michigan at Oconto, Marinette, and Menominee, on the Green Bay shore, embracing the leading lumbering cities intermediate between these points, and ultimately reaching the Atlantic coast by way of the Sault St. Marie, as well as by way of Milwaukee and the lake system; 15 miles have been completed west from Oconto, and 15 more are ready for the rail. The entire length of the line will be about 300 miles.

The Minneapolis, Sault St. Marie, and Atlantic was incorporated last year, and is to be built from Minneapolis and St. Paul to the Sault St. Marie, there to make connections with the Ontario and Pacific, or some other road that will give an outlet to the Atlantic. The entire distance from Minneapolis to the Sault is 425 miles. The company's surveyors are now in the field locating the line.

The following are the estimated distances of the proposed routes of the new roads:—

	Miles.
Minneapolis, Sault St. Marie, and Atlantic	425
Winona, Alma, and Northern, from Princeton	300
St. Paul Eastern Grand Trunk	300
Lanesboro, Rochester, and St. Paul	150
Minnesota and Northern	105
Wisconsin Central	98
Total	1,378

St. Paul and Minneapolis are now connected by telephone with 16 of the most important cities of Minnesota. During the past season exchanges have been established at St. Cloud, Mankato, and Northfield. Trunk lines have been constructed from St. Paul to Mankato, a distance of 122 miles, giving immediate connection with Farmington, Northfield, Faribault, St. Peter, Kasoto, and Mankato. At each of these places good exchanges are in operation, where a year ago the telephone was not thought of. The business men generally of these cities have taken advantage of the opportunity to place themselves in communication with St. Paul and Minneapolis. A line has also been constructed from Minneapolis to St. Cloud, a distance of 74 miles, connecting with Anoka, Elk River, Clear Lake, and all other points of consequence. Communication has been opened with Winona and Red Wing. This line was completed in July, but could not be placed in operation sooner from the fact that 22 miles of the line was purchased from the Western Union Telegraph Company, and they have but recently vacated it. This gives St. Paul communication with Hastings, Red Wing, Wabasha, Lake City, Reed's Landing, and Winona—a distance of 117 miles.

The biennial report of the State Board of Health has just been issued for the years 1881–82, with revision to Jan. 1, 1883. The statistics of small-pox show that during the time reported upon there were 44 cases, and 499 cases of variola and varioloid. From these diseases 96 deaths resulted, making the average mortality 19·2 per cent.

The annual mean temperature of the State for 1881 was 42·02, and the annual mean humidity 58·61; for 1882, the annual mean temperature was 45·14, annual mean humidity 68·38.

The following meteorological statistics, compiled from observations

ST. PAUL.

taken at St. Paul, and furnished me from the United States Signal Office there, may be of interest.

UNITED States Signal Station, St. Paul, Minn. Lat. 44° 53′ N.; longitude west from Greenwich, 93° 5′.

General mean temperature (average), deduced from the successive annual means 1872 to 1883 inclusive, 45°.

Average temperature, winter season (December, January, and February), 1872–83 to 1883–84, 16·49°.

Average temperature, spring season (March, April, and May), 1872–1883, 40·7°.

Average temperature, summer season (June, July, and August), 1872–1883, 69·8°.

Average temperature, autumn season (September, October, and November), 1872–1883, 44·8°.

Lowest temperature on record for St. Paul, 39·0°; Dec. 25, 1879.

Highest temperature on record for St. Paul, 100·0°; July 1, 1883.

Average annual rainfall (melted snow included), deduced from total annual amounts, from 1872–1883, 29·200.

Greatest amount of rainfall, &c., 39·16 inches in 1881.

Least amount of rainfall, &c., 22·39 inches in 1879.

Mean and extreme depths of snow, no data.

Greatest depth of snow, 2·92 feet; Jan. 31, 1881.

Average hourly velocity of wind, deduced from the total movement from 1872 to 1883, 7·6 miles; prevailing direction, SE and NW.

Highest velocity on record here, 60 miles an hour; from the SE, on April 18, 1880.

The greatest monthly rainfall occurred during June, 1874, when 11·67 inches fell; 2·80 of this quantity fell on the 18th.

The least monthly fall occurred in February, 1877, the total being 0·01 (1 below zero of "Fahrenheit scale").

MONTHLY and Annual Mean Barometer (corrected to "Sea Level"), also Monthly and Annual Mean Temperature and Rainfall.

Month (1883).	Barometer.	Temperature.	*Rainfall.	Remarks.
	Inches.	°	Inches.	
January	30·148	1·1	0·64	Lowest temperature, January, 1883, 31°.
February	30·245	12·1	0·44	
March	30·274	24·4	0·06	Least rainfall during month.
April	29·904	45·1	4·92	
May	29·392	62·2	2·12	
June	29·877	65·1	7·04	Greatest rainfall during mon.
July	29·911	70·2	4·33	Highest temperature 100°, July 1; greatest rainfall during month 2·32, July 6, for one day.
August	29·997	66·5	1·22	
September	30·054	56·5	1·23	
October	30·088	45·2	1·10	
November	30·016	32·8	1·01	
December	30·126	19·8	1·59	
Sums..	360·327	491·0	26·70	
Annual means	30·027	40·9	..	

* Including melted snow.

2062 UNITED STATES.

A correct estimate of the mean and extreme depths of snow is rather difficult to arrive at, as the records only show the amount of snow on the ground at the end of each month.

I annex a copy of a letter I have received from the United States Signal Office regarding the snow-fall of Minnesota:—

United States Signal Office, St. Paul, Minnesota,
March 15, 1884.

H. S. Treherne, Esq.,
British Vice-Consul, St. Paul, Minnesota.

DEAR SIR,—Referring to your letter of the 28th ult., relative to meteorological data, I respectfully enclose as much of the same as could be deduced from the records of this office. In regard to the question "mean and extreme depths of snow," a correct estimate is rather difficult to arrive at, as my records only show the amount of snow on the ground at the end of each month. However, a close approximation to the required quantities may be had as follows: Greatest amount of precipitation on record for winter months in 1880–81, 9·68 inches; assuming that 10 inches of snow would be equal to one of water, the result of the above would be $9·68 \times ·84 = 8·1$ feet of snow; least ·087 inches. Winter of 1876–7, operating as above, $·81 \times ·84 = 6·8$. Average precipitation for winter season is 3·44 inches, and nearly, if not all, is composed of snow. In the above approximation the decrease of snow depth from "thaw" and evaporation is not considered. The amounts express the actual fall during the respective periods.

Very respectfully, P. F. LYONS,
Observer, &c.

Below I give a comparative statement compiled from figures furnished me by the Superintendent Public Instruction:—

	1883.		1882.		1881.
	Dollars.	c.	Dollars.	c.	Dollars.
Total receipts for school purposes	3,018,076	83	2,491,276	85	2,239,345
Total expenditure	2,283,164	43	2,740,904	86	2,287,859
Paid for teaching (wages)	1,070,636	74	1,054,522	50	993,996
Paid for new school	479,450	46	439,005	13	..
Value of houses and sites	4,365,546	00	3,947,857	00	3,703,049

These reports of money received and expended cannot be relied upon as more than approximately correct.

SCHOOL ATTENDANCE.

	1883.	1882.	1881.
Number of scholars enrolled	209,458	196,574	183,386
„ „ teachers	5,402	4,336	5,571

	Dol.	c.
Average wages per month to males	36	52
„ „ females	28	62

This statement gives only the number enrolled in common and graded schools. The attendance at the State University, three normal schools, and private institutions I have no record of.

Insurance.—There were 115 fire and inland insurance companies doing business in the State of Minnesota during 1883. Of this total 20 were British, two Canadian, and three German. The insurance laws of the State allow foreign fire insurance companies to do business within her borders, but they are so worded that permission cannot be granted to foreign life insurance companies. It is intended, I am given to understand, to introduce, at the next session of the Legislature, which meets January, 1885, a Bill amending the present laws, so as to overcome this difficulty. The following table shows the business transacted by fire insurance companies in the State of Minnesota for 1883.

TABLE showing the Fire and Inland Insurance Business transacted in the State of Minnesota for the Year 1883, respecting Risks Written, Premiums Received, Losses Paid, and Losses Incurred: issued by the State Insurance Department, February 11, 1884.

	American Joint Stock Companies.	Foreign.	Mutual Fire.	Township Mutual.	Aggregate.
	Dollars. c.	Dollars. c.	Dollars. c.	Dollars. c.	Dollars. c.
Risks written	156,151,992 00	29,659,029 00	454,375 00	1,219,012 00	187,484,408 00
Premiums received	1,961,843 37	437,915 25	45,421 65	7,148 61	2,452,328 88
Average premium rate	1 25	1 46	...	...	1 31
Losses paid	1,223,334 56	321,234 52	82,178 06	3,516 05	1,630,263 19
" incurred	1,397,702 74	422,477 67	88,043 72	2,236 55	1,910,460 68
Ratio of losses incurred to premiums received	77	96	1 94	31	77

DEPARTMENT OF DAKOTA.

At present the military posts in the North-west, east of the divide of the Rocky Mountains, are included in what is known as the department of Dakota, which embraces within its limits the State of Minnesota and the territories of Dakota and Montana. It was created by order of the President, August 11, 1866, out of the departments of the Missouri and the Platte, and General Alfred H. Terry was assigned to the command. In an order dated from Omaha (Neb.), September 18, 1866, General Terry formally assumed charge of the department, and designated Fort Snelling as his headquarters, but in April following he transferred the headquarters to St. Paul. There were then but 10 posts in the department, viz.: Forts Snelling, Ridgley, Ripley, Abercrombie, Wadsworth (now Sisseton), Randall, Sully, Rice, Thompson, and Buford, which were garrisoned by about 4,000 men, consisting of the 10th, 13th, 22nd, and 31st Regiments of Infantry. There was not a single fort in Montana. The Indian frontier did not seem very remote from St. Paul; indeed the country between the Red and Missouri rivers was a wilderness, while beyond the Missouri was almost a terra incognita, where even military trails were unfrequent, and the Indian roamed at will. Despite the success of the then recent expeditions of General Sibley and Sully, the Indian question was still unsettled. The first step taken by General Terry was to increase the number of posts in the department, and orders were given for the erection of several during the season of 1867. A post was established at Cheyenne river, and Forts Ransom, Totten, Stevenson, Shaw, and Ellis were built. These forts, and others which have since been erected, were located either in the immediate vicinity of the Indian agencies or at strategic

[612]

points, the idea being to keep the Indian within the limits of the reservations, and as far as possible to isolate the various tribes, and prevent them from combining together or communicating with each other. Since 1867 the building of these outposts has kept pace with the progress of the country. Of the 10 original posts, five have been abandoned, but from time to time, as necessity has demanded, others have been added; so that to-day the department contains, including the station at camp, Poplar river, 19 garrisoned posts. In the northeast is situated Fort Pembina. Fort Snelling is the most easterly. In the extreme south lies Fort Randall, while the south-western frontier is guarded by Fort Reade. Near the western line of the department lies Fort Missourla, and in the extreme north-west, and not far from the British boundary, is situated Fort Assinaboine. Since its creation in 1866 no fewer than three regiments of cavalry and 14 regiments of infantry have, at different periods, seen service in the department, and its importance as a military command can readily be estimated from the fact that for a long time fully one-third of the available military force of the United States was on duty within its limits—nor has it been holiday soldiering for these troops—until within the past year almost incessant warfare has been carried on with the Indians, either with single bands or, as in 1876, with the combined force of the Sioux nation. There has been campaigning through the heat and dust of summer, and during the winter cold and through the drifting snows of winter. Besides this the scouting, the escort duty, the guarding of trains, and the usual routine of the garrison have combined to make the lot of the officers and men alike not altogether an enviable one.

As has been remarked, department headquarters were established at St. Paul in April, 1867, after having been located in Fort Snelling four or five months only. Here they remained without change until July, 1878, when there was a sudden hegira to Fort Snelling, in consequence of the enactment of a law by Congress requiring military headquarters to be maintained at points where the Government owns buildings or barracks, unless the Secretary of War shall by an order in writing otherwise direct. The quarters at the fort were, however, so poor and insufficient that permission was granted to return to St. Paul until suitable buildings could be prepared. Two years were spent in the erection of the officers' headquarters and other buildings when the change was effected, and the permanent headquarters of the department were announced at Fort Snelling: since its establishment the department of Dakota has had but two commanders. General A. H. Terry was in charge from April 18, 1866, until May 18, 1869, when he was relieved by Major-General W. S. Hancock, who retained the command for little more than three years. On December 3, 1872, General Terry was a second time appointed commander of the department, and still retains the position.

Minnesota's Militia.—The Minnesota militia, under the title of "The National Guard," is composed of two regiments of infantry of 10 companies each, and one battery of artillery. This is the limit allowed by law, and all the companies are filled. The headquarters of the 1st Regiment are at St. Paul; of the 2nd Regiment at New Ulm. For the support of the militia the State Legislature has appropriated 14,500 dol. per annum. It is stipulated that 300 dol. be allowed to each company every year, this sum to be applied to the purchase of uniforms and the rent of armouries. The latter item alone generally exhausts the appropriation, leaving the uniforms to be paid for out of private funds. Each regiment is compelled to go into camp at least seven days of the year. The State furnishes the transportation, and the soldiers pay for subsistence. The men are allowed 1 dol. 50 c. per day while in camp. If the State furnishes subsistence, 50 c. per day is deducted from the daily money allowance of each man. When the Militia Law was passed, it was supposed the railroad companies would furnish free transportation to the troops going to and from the encampment. This the railroad companies declined to do—except in a very few instances—and at the time of last summer's encampment it was found necessary to cut the compensation of the men down to 1 dol. per day, in order that the fund might hold out. If the railroads are to be paid during the present year, the appropriation will not be sufficient to meet inevitable legitimate expenses. The appropriation for 1883 was entirely exhausted, and an overdraft of some 300 dol. or 400 dol. made, which must be met out of the sum appropriated for 1884. The annual appropriation for 1883, under the circumstances, will not be sufficient to cover what must be paid out, the unexpected item of railroad transportation making serious inroads upon the amount of cash available. When the militia are in active service, each officer and private is allowed 2 dol. per day. The law says that for such service the troops are to be paid from the treasury of the State, upon the requisition of the commander-in-chief.

The Governor, as commander-in-chief, has upon his staff a quartermaster-general and a commissary-general, but they have no organised departments, and are powerless to act in cases of emergency. They have their commissions, but it would do them no good to issue orders, as they could not be carried out. Worse still, there is no provision in the law for equipping these departments. There are no commissary stores, and no authority for ordering or furnishing any. There are no cots, no blankets, no cooking utensils; in short, neither camp nor garrison equipage sufficient for the troops. The State owns just enough tents to shelter one regiment, thus preventing the holding of two encampments at the same time. During the annual encampments the companies generally collect from their homes, and by an expenditure of their private means sufficient utensils to cook their meals; but when the troops are called out they must be boarded at hotels, which is certainly a very expensive and unsatisfactory method. The quartermaster and the commissary departments are myths, so far as the Minnesota National Guard is concerned.

[Copied from the "Daily Yellowstone Journal," published at Miles City, Montana, Saturday, February 23, 1884.]

An Unjust Imputation: An Inquiry as to the Condition of the Sheep in Montana.

Letters of inquiry continue to be received daily in this city by the banks and business men relative to the stock and ranges of Eastern Montana. As was stated in the journal at the time of the reported interview of the Marquis de Mores, in St. Paul, relating to the fatal disease existing in his bands of sheep on the Little Missouri, Eastern Montana would probably suffer from the aspersion, as the article in question directly reflected on this section.

The report went abroad and was copied by all the leading papers of the country, and no one even took the pains to correct the statement as related to Montana. The journal, however, did correct it, and gave its reason for so doing.

Mr. Ladd, of Leighton, Jordan, and Co., on Thursday received a letter from H. S. Treherne, the British Vice-Consul in St. Paul, stating that he had been directed by his Government to make inquiry as to the truth of the new fatal disease existing among sheep on the ranges of Montana, and quotes the reported statement of Marquis de Mores, who is said to have lost 50 per cent. of his sheep, and also states that sheep near Mandan, D.T., have died from similar causes.

After which Mr. Treherne asks Mr. Ladd for any and all information on the subject. Through the kindness of the recipient the journal procured the letter, which corroborates its original prophesy that the article would have a tendency to affect stockmen who were contemplating coming to this section.

It is a harsh, an unjust imputation on this country, and must have been either incorrectly reported, or made up of whole cloth.

The sheep of the Marquis de Mores are not, nor have they at any time been, ranged in Montana, in the first place. The disease, therefore, could not originate therein.

At the time of the reported statement the journal spared no means to ascertain the truth and causes of the ravages made by this disease among the De Mores sheep, and from one and all learned that the prime cause for the decimation arose from the fact that they were driven in when in poor condition, late in the fall, and were unaccustomed to rustle their food; the next cause was that they were poorly looked after and not properly attended to; thirdly, they were unacclimated, and did not seem to thrive on the alkali water; and fourthly, their disease arose from what is known among wool growers as dirt poison, which is accounted for in this way: when pilgrim sheep, not accustomed to rustling, find that they are unable to procure grass near at hand, they are given to the eating of earth, which, when containing alkali, is apt, in most cases, unless the sheep are hardy and fat, to produce the symptoms related by the Marquis. The best evidence of the condition of the sheep in this country is derived from the reports which are from day to day heard from the prominent and experienced wool growers of Montana.

There is not a single case of disease anywhere in this section, and the only disease that ever has been known here was the scab, which, unimportant as it was, has entirely been eradicated.

To give an idea of the prosperity of sheep in this locality, only the other day one of the largest sheep growers was asked what would be his loss this year. In reply he stated that out of a band of 6,400 his loss thus far had been 19; and just so are all the reports, not only as to sheep, but stock generally.

In conclusion, the journal will always take great pleasure in ascertaining the disease, if any exists, and also to repel any unjust imputations cast upon the unexcelled stock ranges of Eastern Montana.

St. Paul, April 7, 1884.

UNITED STATES.

CHARLESTON.

Report by Consul H. P. Walker on the Trade and Commerce of Charleston for the Year 1884.

TRADE AND COMMERCE.

The following tables (Nos. I. to VI., both included) give, *inter alia*, the port receipts of cotton, rice, naval stores, lumber, and crude phosphate rock. By a close examination of them, the products of the Consular district will be understood, and the extent of the trade to which they give rise plainly seen.

Table No. I.—STATEMENT showing the Quantities and Values of Cotton brought to the Shipping Ports of the States of North and South Carolina to August 31, 1884.

States.	Years ending August 31.	Description.	Number of Bales.	Number of lbs. at 450 lbs. to a Bale.	Number of lbs. at 300 lbs. to a Bale.	Average Price per lb. Upland.	Average Price per lb. Sea Island.	Value of £1. Dol. c.	Aggregate Value. Currency. Dollars.	Aggregate Value. Sterling. £	Annual Totals. Currency. Dollars.	Annual Totals. Sterling. £
South Carolina	Annual average of years 1881-2-3	Upland	549,818	247,418,100	...	10 13/16	...	4 76	26,442,909	5,555,233		
,,	,,	Sea Island	11,405	...	3,421,500	...	28 5/16	,,	968,712	203,511		
North Carolina	,,	Upland	153,003	68,851,350	...	...	...	,,	7,444,603	1,563,992	34,856,224	7,322,736
South Carolina	1884	Upland	418,882	188,496,900	...	10¼	...	4 80	19,320,932	4,025,194		
,,	,,	Sea Island	9,419	...	2,825,700	...	40	,,	1,130,280	235,475		
North Carolina	,,	Upland	91,412	41,135,400	...	10¼	...	,,	4,216,378	878,412	24,667,590	5,139,081

CHARLESTON.

Table No. II.—STATEMENT showing the Proportion of the Cotton Crop received at each Receiving Port and Exported therefrom to the United Kingdom, with the like for Three preceding Years.

Port at which Received.	Bales Received.	Percentage of Crop Received.				Bales Exported to United Kingdom.	Percentage of Crop Exported.			
		1884.	1883.	1882.	1881.		1884.	1883.	1882.	1881.
New Orleans	1,515,833	31·69	27·06	24·83	27·52	782,848	31·83	29·60	28·49	32·64
Mobile	253,570	5·30	5·21	5·59	6·69	56,167	2·28	1·16	1·54	2·76
Savannah	656,116	13·72	13·62	15·19	14·96	154,346	6·27	3·75	5·76	7·01
Charleston	428,301	8·95	9·49	10·46	10·67	108,565	4·41	4·48	6·29	6·03
Galveston	595,451	12·45	14·54	9·70	12·09	251,849	10·24	11·02	7·63	11·19
Norfolk	579,015	12·10	17·20	17·19	15·98	253,922	10·32	12·78	13·06	11·05
Wilmington	91,412	1·93	2·46	3·45	2·56	43,413	1·76	1·82	2·24	1·99
New York	117,076	2·44	2·33	3·65	3·02	480,116	19·52	19·36	19·93	14·52
Other ports	545,755	11·42	7·19	9·94	6·50	327,603	13·32	16·03	15·06	12·73
Total	4,782,534					2,458,829				

The shipments from North and South Carolina during the same period (the year ended August 21, 1884) were as follows (in bales):—

Shipped from—	To United Kingdom.	To France.	To Ports in Northern Europe.	To Ports in Southern Europe.	Total Abroad.	To other Ports in the United States of America.	Grand Total.
Charleston, South Carolina	108,565	24,497	79,418	56,090	265,792	145,538	411,330
Beaufort, South Carolina	2,640	...	2,550	...	5,190	...	5,190
Wilmington, North Carolina	43,413	...	...	3,829	47,242	44,816	92,058

In continuation, the following table, showing the receipts, exports, and stocks of cotton for the first four months of the current year, viz., from the 31st August to the 1st January of 1885, in contrast with the same for the corresponding period of the last preceding season, is given.

COMPARATIVE Statement of Receipts, Exports, and Stocks of Cotton at the following Places at Latest Dates.

Ports.	Stocks on hand September 1. 1884.	Stocks on hand September 1. 1883.	Received since September 1. 1885.	Received since September 1. 1884.	Exported from September 1, 1884, to dates. To Great Britain.	To France.	Other Foreign Ports.	Total to Foreign Ports.	Coastwise Ports.	Exported from September 1, 1883, to dates. To Great Britain.	To France.	Other Foreign Ports.	Total to Foreign Ports.	Coastwise Ports.	Stock on hand and on Shipboard. 1885.	1884.
	Bales.	Bales.	Bales.	Bales.	Bales.	Bales.	Bales.	Bales.	Bales.	Bales.	Bales.	Bales.	Bales.	Bales.	Bales.	Bales.
New Orleans ...Jan. 2	16,256	53,629	1,108,959	1,068,302	426,975	162,226	185,233	764,434	232,481	289,009	186,007	152,577	627,593	135,811	419,940	481,765
Mobile " "	1,611	3,203	180,028	194,002	5,604	...	...	5,604	117,277	13,334	...	200	13,534	120,645	54,300	68,197
Texas " "	2,829	17,611	389,245	459,789	113,992	4,937	51,111	170,040	106,981	116,478	24,167	60,736	201,381	160,569	53,086	115,450
Florida " "	...	...	20,319	23,913	...	...	...	...	20,319	1,500	...	...	1,500	22,413	...	...
Savannah—																
Upland " "	1,274	4,235	598,832	547,682	132,085	14,337	150,266	256,688	135,363	103,950	11,730	117,228	232,908	213,614	87,612	105,395
Sea Island " "	82	15	13,598	455	...	...	...	...	...	733	106	...	839	5,312	...	1,057
Charleston—																
Upland " "	453	3,432	431,262	331,814	119,966	19,226	112,565	257,807	112,933	60,348	15,565	83,041	158,954	92,044	53,150	80,125
Sea Island " "	136	9	10,317	4,397	1,992	15	17	2,024	3,103	1,299	32	...	1,331	4,396	5,326	836
North Carolina " "	770	858	79,692	85,048	36,955	...	12,240	49,195	34,731	30,069	...	2,704	32,773	32,679	15,258	20,464
Virginia " "	980	13,934	439,854	577,879	184,960	...	15,039	199,999	130,259	136,169	...	9,613	145,782	368,019	57,733	77,012
New York " "	87,791	114,115	29,460	40,986	289,468	39,220	124,105	461,793	...	181,088	22,272	58,509	261,869	...	105,767	273,984
Other ports " "	19,104	21,065	360,045	90,355	181,582	3,050	42,262	226,844	...	113,657	100	35,011	153,768	...	113,395	43,876
Total ... " "	131,285	232,106	3,661,611	3,424,462	1,491,588	233,011	569,829	2,294,428	893,477	1,052,634	250,979	519,619	1,832,232	1,155,802	1,015,767	1,276,570
Total to date in 1885	232,106	...	3,424,622	...	1,052,634	259,979	519,619	1,832,232	1,155,802	...	...	...	...	...	1,276,570	...
Increase	...	...	236,989	...	438,954	...	50,210	462,196	...	...	...	...	...	...	...	...
Decrease	100,821	...	...	...	...	26,968	...	...	267,355	...	...	...	...	...	260,803	...

Table No. III.—STATEMENT showing the Rice Crop of South Carolina: its Value and its Distribution.

Years ending August 31.	Number of Tierces.	Number of lbs. at 650 lbs. per Tierce.	Price per lb.	Value of £	Value of Product. Currency.	Value of Product. Sterling.	Distribution in Tierces. Consumed.	Distribution in Tierces. Exported.	Distribution in Tierces. Undisposed of.
			c.	Dol. c.	Dollars.	£			
Annual average of years 1881, 1882, and 1883	45,610	29,646,500	5¾	4 79	1,704,674	355,867	15,833	29,467	443
1884	33,738	21,921,700	5⅜	4 80	1,260,957	262,699	10,274	23,054	437

N.B.—Exported abroad, nil.

Table No. IV.—STATEMENT showing the Export of Naval Stores from Charleston, South Carolina, for the Year ended August 31, 1884.

Years ending August 31.	To Great Britain. Barrels.	To Continent of Europe. Barrels.	Coastwise. Barrels.	Total. Barrels.	Of which— Rosin. Barrels.	Of which— Turpentine. Barrels.	Value per Barrel. Rosin. Dol. c.	Value per Barrel. Turpentine. Dol. c.	Total Value. Rosin. Dollars.	Total Value. Turpentine. Dollars.	Value of £ Dol. c.	Grand Total. Currency. Dollars.	Grand Total. Sterling. £
Annual average of years ending 1881, 1882, and 1883	91,134	146,887	83,852	321,873	258,646	63,228	2 22	17 66	574,194	1,116,602	4 79	1,690,796	352,984
Ditto 1884	128,103	186,415	58,442	372,960	304,710	68,250	1 95	13 0	594,184	887,250	4 80	1,481,434	308,632

Table No. V.—STATEMENT showing the Quantity of Lumber exported from Charleston, South Carolina, to August 31, 1884.

Years ended August 31.	Exported to—						Price per Meas. Feet.	Price per £.		Total Value.	
	Great Britain.	Dominion of Canada.	West Indies.	South America.	Continent of Europe.	Coastwise.	Total.			Currency.	Sterling.
								Dol.	c.	Dollars.	Dollars.
Annual average for 1881, 1882, 1883	75,333	...	356,800	...	196,091	32,138,661	32,666,885	Dollars. 15	4 79	490,003	102,295
1884	581,000	90,975	177,872	1,015,213	2,104,617	27,616,776	31,586,453	15	4 80	473,796	93,707

Table No. VI.—STATEMENT showing the Trade in Crude Phosphate Rock, and its Value, to August 31, 1884.

Years ended August 31.	Shipped at	Destined for				Retained for Manufacture.	Total.	Price per Ton.		Value of £		Total Value.		Grand Total.	
		Ports not Designated.	European Continent.	United Kingdom.	Coastwise Ports of United States.							Currency.	Sterling.	Currency.	Sterling.
		Tons.	Tons.	Tons.	Tons.	Tons.	Tons.	Dol.	c.	Dol.	c.	Dollars.	£	Dollars.	£
1884	Charleston	Out Foreign. 13,367	...	...	175,401	53,635	242,403	6	50	4	80	1,575,619	328,254		
"	Bull River and neighbourhood	127,010	...	...	28,744	3,000	158,754	"		"		1,031,901	214,979	2,607,520	543,233
Total		140,377	...	...	204,145	56,635	401,157	...		...		...	...		
Corresponding totals for 1883		19,623	11,360	104,317	174,711	42,620	352,631	6	0	4	79	...	...	2,115,786	441,708
" " 1882		13,183	6,001	105,211	175,073	43,000	342,468	7	0	4	80	...	...	2,407,276	501,515
" " 1881		37,256	4,706	52,580	154,499	38,142	287,183	5	0	4	78	...	...	1,435,915	300,400

CHARLESTON.

Shipping and Navigation.

The following table, No. VII., and the statement thereto appended indicate the extent of British shipping to which the products of this Consular district give employment. This employment consists in the outward transportation of those products only; the importation of British manufactured articles in British or other vessels being inconsiderable. Importations of such are received at northern ports, and are brought southward by American vessels, which have the coasting trade as their exclusive privilege.

Table No. VII.—Showing the Employment of British Shipping within the Consular District of North and South Carolina in the Year 1884.

Direct Trade in British Vessels from and to Great Britain and British Colonies.

Entered.

At—	Total Number of Vessels.			Total Tonnage.			Total Number of Crews.	Total Value of Cargoes.
	With Cargoes.	In Ballast.	Total.	With Cargoes.	In Ballast.	Total.		
Charleston, S.C.	15	34	49	11,871	32,488	44,359	882	£ 12,570
Beaufort, S.C.	1	18	19	1,163	14,495	15,658	313	400
Wilmington, N.C.	8	17	25	3,448	9,809	13,257	293	3,341
Total	24	69	93	16,482	56,792	73,274	1,488	16,311

Cleared.

From—	Total Number of Vessels.			Total Tonnage.			Total Number of Crews.	Total Value of Cargoes.
	With Cargoes.	In Ballast.	Total.	With Cargoes.	In Ballast.	Total.		
Charleston, S.C.	64	...	64	51,576	...	51,576	1,021	£ 1,599,640
Beaufort, S.C.	67	...	67	58,304	...	58,304	1,150	127,200
Wilmington, N.C.	26	1	27	11,765	328	12,093	318	297,646
Total	157	1	158	121,645	328	121,973	2,489	2,024,486

Indirect or Carrying Trade in British Vessels from and to other Countries.

Entered.

At—	Number of Vessels.			Tonnage.			Number of Crews.	Value of Cargoes.
	With Cargoes.	In Ballast.	Total.	With Cargoes.	In Ballast.	Total.		
Charleston, S.C.	8	50	58	3,204	42,952	46,156	927	£ 59,300
Beaufort, S.C.	1	57	58	1,040	51,105	52,145	1,023	270
Wilmington, N.C.	5	18	23	1,436	5,416	6,852	219	7,266
Total	14	125	139	5,680	99,473	105,153	2,169	66,836
,, as above	24	69	93	16,482	56,792	73,274	1,488	16,311
Grand total	38	194	232	22,162	156,265	178,427	3,657	83,147

Cleared.

From—	Number of Vessels.			Tonnage.			Number of Crews.	Value of Cargoes.
	With Cargoes.	In Ballast.	Total.	With Cargoes.	In Ballast.	Total.		
Charleston, S.C.	33	6	39	32,294	2,180	34,474	698	£ 1,122,060
Beaufort, S.C.	10	...	10	9,489	...	9,489	181	17,800
Wilmington, N.C.	10	3	13	3,020	1,649	4,669	115	22,310
Total	53	9	62	44,803	3,829	48,632	994	1,162,170
,, as above	157	1	158	121,645	328	121,973	2,489	2,024,486
Grand total	210	10	220	166,448	4,157	170,605	3,483	3,186,656

CHARLESTON.

APPENDIX.

CLEARANCES.

Periods.	Number of Vessels.	Tonnage.	Value of Cargoes Taken.
			£
Annual average of 12 years to 1883, inclusive	234	133,518	2,328,275
1883..	205	139,787	2,278,527
1884..	220	170,605	3,186,656

Under this heading the following remarks upon the subjects of "Quarantine and Pilotage," and as to the "Engagement of Seamen in American Ports," will not be out of place.

Quarantine.—The quarantine insisted upon at the ports of South Carolina have had the effect of driving away the trade which, years ago, was carried on with the West Indies and South America. The principal importations from these regions—sugar, molasses, and coffee—are no longer brought direct to Charleston, and the line of steamers for the conveyance of merchandise and passengers from Charleston to Havana and back have long ceased to ply.

The stringency of the present quarantine requirements seem unreasonable. West Indian fruits—the direct importation of which the severity of the quarantine regulations forbids—are taken to a port at the north, and brought southward by rail, and are consumed in the city before the lapse of the term of quarantine to which the importing vessel, had she come direct, would have been subjected.

Even vessels that have been to the prescribed regions on a former voyage, that have had no sickness, that have passed quarantine examinations at northern ports, and afterwards visited Charleston, have still been annoyed and delayed by the stringency of the quarantine regulations. It is therefore very desirable that owners and masters of British vessels should not commit themselves to any engagements that may bring their vessels to the ports of South Carolina, during the summer months, after having visited more southern ports.

Pilotage.—Two serious casualties have of late befallen British vessels, outward bound, in their endeavour to cross the bar of Charleston harbour. On each occasion the unfortunate vessels have been in charge of the same pilot. After the occurrence of the second casualty, the Board of Commissioners of Pilotage suspended the offending pilot for three months, and determined that, upon the expiration of that period, he should have what is called a twelve-foot branch only, whereby he would be deprived of the privilege of piloting in or out vessels of greater draught. The vessels which were stranded on the bar, while in charge of the pilot referred to, were respectively of the draught of 15 feet 9 inches and 16 feet 2 inches, and the carelessness which caused the stranding of those vessels, at high water and under favourable circumstances for crossing, amply justified the action of the Board. The mayor of the city, who is the chairman of the Board, has assured Her Majesty's Consul that the "active efforts of the Board will be exerted to punish offenders hereafter," and that "a large majority of the pilots are faithful, intelligent men, and discharge their duties with skill."

Engagement of Seamen in American Ports.—By an Act of Congress, approved on the 26th June, 1884, entitled "An Act to Remove Certain Burdens on the American Merchant Marine, and Encourage the American Foreign Carrying Trade, and for other Purposes," the usual mode heretofore adopted of advancing money to seamen, on account of their wages to be earned by their services at sea, is absolutely prohibited: the payment of such advance money is to be punished by a fine of not less than four times the amount, in addition to which imprisonment, not exceeding six months, may be imposed.

The law is made applicable "as well to foreign vessels as to vessels of the United States," and any violation or connivance to violate the enactment will prevent the vessel affected from obtaining a clearance from any port of the United States.

The following is the enactment referred to:—

"*Advance Wages not to be Paid to Seamen—Assignment of Pay to Wife or Mother.*—Section 10. That it shall be, and is hereby, made unlawful in any case to pay any seaman wages before leaving the port at which such seaman may be engaged in advance of the time when he has actually earned the same, or to pay such advance wages to any other person, or to pay any person, other than an officer authorised by Act of Congress to collect fees for such service, any remuneration for the shipment of seamen. Any person paying such advance wages or such remuneration shall be deemed guilty of a misdemeanour, and, upon conviction, shall be punished by a fine not less than four times the amount of the wages so advanced or remuneration so paid, and may be also imprisoned for a period not exceeding six months, at the discretion of the court. The payment of such advance wages or remuneration shall in no case, except as herein provided, absolve the vessel, or the master or owner thereof, from full payment of wages after the same shall have been actually earned, and shall be no defence to a libel, suit, or action for the recovery of such wages: Provided, that this section shall not apply to whaling vessels: And provided further, that it shall be lawful for any seaman to stipulate in his shipping agreement for an allotment of any portion of the wages which he may earn to his wife, mother, or other relative, but to no other person or corporation. And any person who shall falsely claim such relationship to any seaman in order to obtain wages so allotted shall, for every such offence, be punishable by a fine not exceeding 500 dol., or imprisonment not exceeding six months, at the discretion of the court. This section shall apply as well to foreign vessels as to vessels of the United States; and any foreign vessel, the master, owner, consignee, or agent of which has violated this section, or induced or connived at its violation, shall be refused a clearance from any port of the United States."

The effect of the law, if it were observed, would be to prevent desertion from foreign vessels in American ports, for if seamen received no advance money there would be no establishments at which they could be entertained on shore. But so far as the port of Charleston is concerned it may be safely said that the law is not observed, and that no effort has been yet made to enforce its observance; therefore sailors' boarding houses continue as heretofore, and desertions are just as common as ever.

AGRICULTURE.

Reports from every county in the State of South Carolina have lately been obtained by the enterprise of the "Charleston News and Courier."

The following is a specimen of such reports:—

Abbeville County.—There has been no perceptible change in the condition of the agricultural labourers in Abbeville county as compared with last year, and the supply is sufficient to meet the requirements of the farmers. The supply of labour has not been affected by the emigration of the coloured people to the West. The negroes who have emigrated have generally been the least thrifty and industrious, and their loss will in no way interfere with the operations of the farmers. It is alleged that some of the emigrants have left the county to escape punishment for suspected crimes. They have been told since Cleveland's election that the law against adultery would be strictly enforced, and it is supposed that their guilty consciences have frightened many of them away.

About seven-eighths of the agricultural labourers in this county are coloured and one-eighth white. The labourers are generally making contracts for the new year, and it is quite an easy matter to bring them to terms. There is no difficulty in getting hired hands, most of the one-horse and ox-farmers having been completely broken up. Their failure at farming on their own account has reduced them to such a condition that they are ready to hire themselves out. The rate of wages for farm hands runs from 75 dol. to 100 dol., but most of them prefer to work on the share system, the usual stipulation being one-half of the crop. The coloured labourers are diligent and trustworthy in a few cases. Generally speaking, they feel no responsibility for their debts, and will contract obligations to any amount that their creditors will allow. There has been no improvement in their condition and habits during the past year. In fact, they seem to have grown poorer and more reduced in circumstances. As a rule, the farmers find no trouble in making contracts for hired hands, but good renters are in demand. The landlord in most cases has to furnish the tenant with his supplies, or stand security to the merchant who makes these advances, in order that he may be able to rent his land. The merchants have grown very particular as to whom they will furnish advances. The lien law, they say, is very poor security, and there are few cases where the labourer has any credit of his own.

It is suggested that the negro would be a better and a more willing labourer if there were less discussion of his relations to society. He is generally regarded by our farmers as a better labourer than the white man, but the continual discussion of his position in society and politics has magnified his importance and in the same degree affected his usefulness as a citizen. If the homestead and lien laws could be abolished and creditors empowered to collect their just debts to the full extent of all the property of their debtors, the labourer would soon learn to appreciate his responsibilities, and would doubtless work more diligently and with better results.

And from those reports the following deductions are, it is thought, correctly and justly drawn, viz.:—

At least three-fourths of the agricultural labourers in South Carolina are coloured persons, and their condition is somewhat better than it was a year ago. Provisions are cheap and abundant, so that the wants of the labourers are easily satisfied. The emigration of coloured people from particular parts of the State has not affected the effective supply of labour, as the farmers find that they can hire as many labourers as they need. It is probable, however, that the demand for agricultural labourers is rather diminishing than increasing, inasmuch as the tendency is to increase the use of labour-saving implements and to give more attention than formerly to the crops, which require but little working by hand. In this way a considerable number of labourers

[259]

246   UNITED STATES.

can, perhaps, be spared, but there is abundant room for all industrious coloured people to farm on their own account and become independent.

The coloured labourers have made their bargains, as usual, for the year. The rate of wages paid ranges from 5 dol. to 12 dol. a month, with rations. Where the share system is in vogue, from one-third to one-half of the crop goes to the labourer and the remainder to the landowner. Occasionally, the labourers receive as much as half the crop, any pay half the cost of fertilisers, or furnish one-half the number of work animals required. The estimates of the value of coloured labour differ considerably, but it is agreed that coloured labourers are both diligent and trustworthy, when they are supervised and directed by the whites. When left without supervision, the results are much less satisfactory.

The coloured labourers are reported to be careless and extravagant, spending freely all that they make. Nevertheless, in some counties they are slowly improving their condition. It is a striking fact that "the old-issue" negroes, as they are called—the actual freedmen who were trained as labourers in slavery times—work hard and steadily, and command good wages, while the "new-issue" negroes, who have grown up since emancipation, are disposed to be idle and shirk work. The number of "old-issue" negroes is, of course, diminishing yearly, and the agriculturists of the South cannot prepare too soon for the difficulties they must expect to encounter when they have none but the "new-issue" to depend on.

Population and Industries.

Reference is made to the Analysis of Statistics compiled for the United States Census of 1880, and embodied in the last Annual Commercial Report from this Consulate.

Public Works.

The attempt under the direction and at the expense of the Government of the United States to deepen the approaches to Charleston harbour is of the greatest importance. It has often been referred to in their periodical reports, and as the best possible mode of giving publicity to the present condition of the work and to the results anticipated, a letter from the engineer-in-charge, addressed to the Chairman of the Committee of Harbour Improvements, appointed by the Charleston Chamber of Commerce, is subjoined, together with the remarks of the Press thereon.

The Jetties in Charleston Harbour.

Letter of General Q. A. Gillmore, U.S. engineer, describing the condition and results of the work, and setting forth his reasons for believing that a depth of 30 feet on the bar can be secured:—

"Charleston, S.C., January 22, 1885.
"Hon. S. Y. Tupper,
"Chairman Committee on Harbour Improvements, of Charleston
                     Chamber of Commerce.

"Dear Sir,—Referring to our recent interview, I wish to express my satisfaction with the progress of work on the Charleston jetties under the present contract, and the beneficial results in immediate prospect.

"Captain Bailey informs me that the survey just completed indicates quite plainly that increased scour on the bar between the jetties has been developed.

"Although the concentration of water upon the bar secured by the jetties up to the present time is very small in comparison with what is intended and with what the plan requires, both works being as yet little more than foundation courses, and the south jetty not having yet reached the crest of the bar by about 1,000 feet, I am confident that, even in their present condition, the works are able to maintain a much deeper channel than that which exists between them, and that the time to begin the dredging contemplated in the original estimate has arrived. Proposals for dredging have, therefore, been invited, the object being to aid the scouring power of the accelerated current.

"I wish to reaffirm my confidence in the ability of these works, when completed, to maintain a deep navigable channel across the bar. I believe a depth of 30 feet to be easily attainable.

"Adverse criticisms on the efficacy of submerged jetties have no application to the Charleston works. The latter are strictly tentative in character, and their distance apart was planned with the special object of reserving entire freedom of choice with respect to their ultimate height.

"Their crests can of course be carried up to the height necessary to maintain the desired channel depth between them. Where they cross the bar they are half a mile apart, equal to about one-half of the width of the throat of the harbour between Forts Sumter and Moultrie, where the channel depths are 75 to 80 feet at low water.

"Omitting engineering technicalities, two significant questions may be popularly stated as follows:

"1st. If the flow between Sumter and Moultrie maintains a channel depth of 75 feet where the width is one mile, what portion of that flow will be required between the jetties, where the width is only half a mile, in order to maintain a depth of 28 to 30 feet? The answer suggests itself that not all the water flowing past Fort Sumter will be needed between the jetties. The plan, therefore, allows part of it to pass over their tops, thereby lessening the cost of the works more than one-half.

"2nd. If the flow between Sumter and Moultrie maintains a depth of 75 feet where the width is one mile, what depth would the same volume of flow maintain if it all passed between the jetties where the width is only half a mile? The answer is again evident that, under these conditions, the depth scoured out would be excessive, possibly endangering the stability of the works themselves, and transporting a large body of sand to the seaward slope of the bar beyond the end of the jetties. This would introduce serious complications in the way of new shoals and a new bar. It has been one of the leading objects of the project to avoid such a contingency.

"The principles suggested in the foregoing answers are neither new nor novel. They not only rest on long experience and observation, but are easily demonstrable by approved methods and formulæ. We need not go far for numerous and well-defined illustrations—two or three that are near home will be mentioned.

"At the mouth of St. John's river, where the tide rises and falls about five feet, the low jetties planned on the principles applied to the Charleston works, and not yet half finished, have produced a marked improvement in the gap between them. A channel has there been established by scour alone, of twice the depth existing there six months ago.

"In Savannah harbour, where there is about seven feet rise and fall of tide, the Fig Island jetty, one mile long, with its crest fully four feet below high water, maintains a navigable channel 19 feet deep at high water, through a shoal upon which there was only 11 feet before the improvement was begun. Further down the harbour, at the head of Elba Island and at the Upper Flats, the low jetties, having their crests three feet below high water, are continuously maintaining navigable channels 20 to 23 feet deep through shoals where only 16 feet could be carried at high water before any improvement was made by works or by dredging. These are points where the jetties have been completed a year or more, or long enough to produce a substantial approach to maximum results. At other points where the jetties were finished more recently the scouring is now in progress. In some cases the movement of the sand is so tardy that the deepening process has to be hastened or aided by other means, and this is the object of the dredging which will be commenced in Savannah harbour in a few days.

"It goes almost without saying that the Charleston jetties should not excavate a channel of unnecessary depth between them, with the certain result that the excess of material removed will be deposited outside, where the natural depths are very moderate and the slope of the bottom exceptionally flat, and where we must depend for its removal upon the intermittent and irregular littoral current produced by winds. Where interests of great magnitude are at stake, ordinary prudence suggests that there should be a liberal factor of safety. This is provided in the present project by reserving the power to restrict the volume of flow and the amount of scour between the jetties.

"It has been the subject of profound regret on my part that the importance of this great national work has been recognised in Congress by liberal appropriations. Frequent stoppages and increase in the ultimate cost of the work have been the results of this policy.

"I invite attention to my annual reports for a more lengthy expression of my views on this point.

"Q. A. GILLMORE."

GENERAL REMARKS.

By way of epitomising the foregoing report, it may be said that the Consular district of North and South Carolina during the last year, so shown by the trade with the United Kingdom, which the products of the district have given birth to, has undergone improvement, for although fewer British ships have been employed a greater tonnage has: the diminution of ships is 14, the increase of tonnage is 37,087; and the greater value of products exported by the vessels and tonnage referred to, over former averages, amounts to 858,381*l.* The condition, however, of the bar of Charleston harbour, the irresponsibility of the pilots, the stringency of the quarantine regulations, and the United States law against advances to seamen, threatening severity, but as yet unenforced, present serious obstacles to the advance of commercial interests.

Charleston, South Carolina, January 29, 1885.

GALVESTON.

Report by Consul Lyall on the Trade and Commerce of Galveston for the Year 1884.

The State of Texas, of which Galveston is the principal seaport, possesses an area of 274,356 square miles.

It is bounded on the north by the Indian Territory—as the Government Reservation for various tribes of Indians is called—on the south by the Gulf of Mexico, on the east by Louisiana, and on the south-west and the west by New Mexico and Mexico Proper.

Texas is divided into 226 counties, more than half of which are settled and organised.

At the period of the annexation of Texas by the United States Government, just 40 years ago, the population was little over 200,000: it now (1885) contains nearly two and a quarter million inhabitants.

Texas is fertile and well watered; considerable mineral wealth, as yet unexploited, exists. There are said to be 5,000 square miles of coal produce, strata, and much silver, iron, copper, lead, &c. The soil is chiefly a black or chocolate-coloured "cotton soil," so called in India wherever cotton, as here, happens to be the principal staple.

AGRICULTURE.

Agriculture is generally flourishing, consequent on the fine annual rainfall, which, since the country has been systematically cultivated and planted out, has become still more regular and copious. Any total failure of crops has never yet been experienced. Cotton is and will continue to be the crop *par excellence*, but the growth of any branch of agriculture has been, during the last five years, very marked.

1879.

Cereals.	Acres.	Bushels.	Bushels to Acre—Average.
Maize	2,468,587	29,065,172	11 to 12
Wheat	373,570	2,567,737	6 7
Oats	230,010	4,893,359	20 21
Rye	25,399	3,326	7 8
Barley	5,527	72,786	13 14

1883.

Cereals.	Acres.	Bushels.	Bushels to Acre—Average.
Maize	3,608,362	63,146,300	18
Wheat	506,000	4,301,000	8 to 9
Oats	416,096	9,489,300	22 23
Rye	5,040	57,855	11 12
Barley	7,463	127,030	17

The cotton product has increased during the same period from 805,284 bales to 1,104,825 bales.

The total value of all farm produce has increased since 1880, when it was calculated at 65,204,329 dol. to 89,886,160 dol.

In addition to grain, there is an enormous and increasing (at the ratio of 40 per cent. per annum) production of flax, sugar, molasses, sorghum, hay, honey, bees'-wax, rice, tobacco, potatoes, orchard and garden produce, poultry and eggs. Next to agriculture the most important Texan industry is stock-raising.

Cattle Farming.

In consequence of the rich and abundant pasturage and the mildness of the climate, Texan cattle of improved breed are already counted by millions; yet in some parts of the State the runs or ranches are few in proportion to the area of grazing ground. There is said not to be over one head of cattle per 20 acres of pasturage at present, the total grazing area being reported at 150,000,000 acres.

Sheep have kept pace with horned cattle, the census return of these animals having risen from 100,530 head in 1859 to 4,491,600 in 1883. The average yield of wool for the entire State is over 18,500,000*l*.

To resume, the live stock of all varieties of Texas has nearly trebled itself during the last decade, as the following table will indicate:—

1873.

Live Stock.	Number.	Value.
		Dollars.
Cattle	3,688,436	15,904,312
Horses, mules, and donkeys	706,743	20,782,606
Sheep, goats, and pigs	1,346,865	1,292,824
Total	5,742,044	37,979,742

GALVESTON.

1883.

Live Stock.	Number.	Value.
		Dollars.
Cattle	6,054,488	71,393,319
Horses and mules	1,054,452	27,678,560
Donkeys	4,756	247,320
Sheep	4,491,600	9,228,230
Goats	445,454	517,600
Pigs	1,044,762	1,673,201
Total	13,095,512	110,738,230

Texas possesses over 6,000 miles of railroad, the greater part of which has been constructed within the last 10 years. It is already the sixth State of the Union as to railroad mileage, and the various lines may be said to be doing a good paying business.

COTTON.

The total cotton crop of Texas for 1883–84 may be summarised at 1,104,829 bales.

The following summary shows the amount and value of Texan produce exported during 1883–84:—

	Value.
	Dollars.
Cotton	55,241,250
Wool	3,166,671
Hides	1,346,091
Cattle	12,488,340
Horses	367,410
Timber and shingles	7,426,518
Grain and hay	10,824,719
Cotton seed, cake, and oil	2,415,214
Sugar and molasses	428,516
Miscellaneous products	5,847,116
Total	99,551,845

EDUCATION.

Education is conducted by a School Board, and supported by the interest of nearly 35,000,000 acres of school land; also by a State and county tax. These school lands are expected to realise a fund of 80,000,000 dol. or thereabouts.

There exist at present 3,900 white schools, and 1,148 schools for negroes; 104,591 white children are being educated at the expense of the State, and 37,734 coloured children. There are 31 normal schools for white teachers (total attendance 1,270), and 10 normal schools for black teachers (total attendance 518).

There is already a university for white students at Austin, and another for coloured ones is in contemplation at the same city.

CLIMATE.

The climate in Texas varies considerably. Up the country it is, generally speaking, healthy and temperate, the thermometer ranging from 82° to 92° in July and August, and to 41° and 51° during the cold months. The climate of North-western Texas is specially fine, dry, and bracing.

On the other hand, along the coast and in the low river bottoms the climate is as hot as Northern India, and more unhealthy, in consequence of the sudden changes of temperature which constantly take place.

The port of Galveston is claimed by its inhabitants, and those of the neighbouring towns and settlements on the mainland, to be the natural commercial outlet for the trade and produce not only of Texas, but of many other States lying inland, such as Colorado, Idaho, Wyoming, Montana, Nevada, &c. It is claimed that these inland States, twenty in number, all lie much nearer to the Gulf of Mexico than to the Atlantic seaboard, and that consequently Galveston is destined to "tap" the produce of an enormous radius of country, extending from California and Arizona on the north-west, to Minnesota, Wisconsin, and Illinois on the north-east, in addition to much of the trade of Mexico.

The only drawback to this immense future prosperity lies in the fact of the port of Galveston not at present possessing sufficient water on its bar for the passage of vessels of heavy burden, and the project is to remedy this at any cost. Captain James Eads, the well-known United States engineer, has proposed, for a guaranteed sum of 8,000,000 dol., to produce 30 feet of water on the bar, and this proposition is to come before Congress during its present session. The following data indicate the aggregate resources and population of the interior States above-mentioned, and the distance it is proposed to save by making their sea outlet the Gulf of Mexico instead of the Atlantic, it being confidently believed that had Galveston once an established depth of 30 feet of water on the bar, the whole traffic of the above States would at once choose the gulf route.

TABLE of Distances.

From—	To Galveston.	To New York.
	Miles.	Miles.
California	1,620	2,557
Salt Lake (Utah)	1,349	2,113
Colorado (Denver)	930	1,669
Wyoming	990	1,648
New Mexico	790	1,805
Nebraska	875	1,254
Kansas	680	1,226
Iowa	978	930
Dakota	963	1,282
Arkansas	408	1,153
Total	9,583	15,637

It will be seen that the aggregate distance from the 10 points above selected to the Atlantic at New York is 15,637 miles, and to the Gulf of Mexico at Galveston only 9,583 miles, a difference of 6,054 miles, or near 40 per cent. traffic expenditure.

It therefore appears that the Gulf of Mexico will, should its harbours be adequately opened out, become the regular outlet to the ocean for the people of the whole of the immense territories (now either already colonised and settled, or in rapid course of colonisation and settlement) extending across the basin of the Rocky Mountains and the Pacific slopes.

These twenty States already aggregate a population of over 11,000,000, and an aggregate of wealth—mineral, pastoral, and agricultural—computed at a billion and a half sterling, all which progress has been built up within the last 20 years, and may double before the end of the century.

I may, however, remark with regard to the foregoing, that whatever the prophesied prosperity of Texas in general and Galveston in particular may eventually become, business matters are just now very dull.

The present cotton crop (1883–1884) has turned out less by 400,000 bales than that of the previous year. In the town great numbers of mechanics, artisans, longshoremen, &c., are out of employ, which, in a place where even every unskilled negro thinks he ought to get a dollar and a half a day for his services (and sometimes his food as well), is not surprising.

It is obvious that only a very high rate of commercial prosperity could support such rates of pay; in addition to which the said emancipated negroes, male and female, have, following the example of the whites, voted all domestic service degrading; and consequently, unless carried on according to their notions, which means being put on a par with employers, allowed to go in and out as they choose, to receive friends and visitors at all hours, &c. (in addition to high wages), will have none of it, thus cutting themselves off entirely from a large and lucrative source of subsistence.

Rich people who in Europe would entertain at least half-a-dozen servants, here keep two or three, while those who would keep two or three in Europe, here keep none at all, finding it less trouble, on the whole, to do without them, to say nothing of the saving of expense.

The Chinese, who would have filled up the gap as far as domestic service, garden agriculture, &c., goes, and at a cheap rate, have been expelled the country, mainly of course because they successfully competed with white local labour. Proposals have been already made among his Northern "emancipators" for deporting the negro, and it is quite probable that, if these latter continue to increase and multiply as they are now doing (and eventually compete seriously with the whites in the labour market), it will be discovered that "the nigger," like the Chinaman and the Indian, must go.

Galveston, January 20, 1885.

UNITED STATES.

BALTIMORE.

Report by Consul Donohoe on the Trade and Commerce of Baltimore for the Year 1884.

Shipping and Navigation.

The number of British vessels at this port during 1884 shows a slight improvement on the return for 1883.

ENTERED.

Years.	Vessels.	Tonnage.	Estimated Values of Cargoes.
			£
1880	621	570,824	2,399,309
1881	585	536,948	2,058,366
1882	391	389,324	2,184,179
1883	395	445,732	2,049,859
1884	416	488,203	2,077,134

CLEARED.

Years.	Vessels.	Tonnage.	Estimated Values of Cargoes.
			£
1880	690	623,372	7,720,948
1881	564	516,901	6,970,060
1882	409	396,178	6,058,010
1883	396	445,327	6,578,574
1884	428	485,245	6,168,122

These are nearly all steamships, as very few British sailing vessels now enter at this port.

The Custom-house returns are as follows:—

UNITED STATES.

Arrived from Foreign Ports during 1884.

Months.	Steam-ships.	Ships.	Barks.	Brigs.	Schooners.	Total 1884.
January	40	..	10	..	6	56
February	22	2	8	4	8	44
March	20	..	14	4	7	45
April	41	6	10	6	14	77
May	48	4	14	3	13	82
June	25	1	15	1	20	62
July	41	..	17	3	6	67
August	53	4	10	2	8	77
September	27	3	17	3	4	54
October	28	5	9	2	6	50
November	27	1	17	2	5	52
December	42	1	9	5	1	58
Total 1884	414	27	150	35	98	724
,, 1883	330	33	243	45	135	786

Total amount of tonnage arrived from foreign ports during 1884 .. 639,139
,, ,, ,, ,, 1883 .. 663,311

Decrease, 1884 24,172

Cleared for Foreign Ports during 1884.

Months.	Steam-ships.	Ships.	Barks.	Brigs.	Schooners.	Total. 1884.
January	37	1	12	4	18	72
February	24	..	8	3	20	55
March	26	3	12	4	8	53
April	43	1	21	5	16	86
May	47	4	14	4	19	88
June	27	5	13	2	6	53
July	39	..	14	..	1	54
August	47	1	16	4	2	70
September	42	5	8	3	3	61
October	22	3	16	3	6	50
November	32	3	6	1	9	51
December	41	1	14	3	12	71
Total 1884	427	27	154	36	120	764
,, 1883	380	21	227	50	145	823

Total amount of tonnage cleared for foreign ports during 1884 .. 706,316
,, ,, ,, ,, 1883 .. 787,375

Decrease, 1884 81,059

BALTIMORE.

Freights.—Current rates of freights on grain on or about the first and middle of each month for 1884, per steamer to Liverpool, and to Cork for orders:—

Months, 1884.		To Liverpool, per Steam, per Bushel.		To Cork, for Orders, per Steam, per Quarter.	
		From—	To—	From—	To—
		d.	d.	s. d.	s. d.
January	3	4	..	3 9	..
,,	19	4	..	3 1½	3 3
February	1	3	3½	2 6	2 9
,,	15	2½	3	3 0	..
March	1	2½	..	2 9	..
,,	15	2½	3	3 0	3 3
April	3	3½	..	3 1½	3 3
,,	17	3¾	4	3 3	..
May	3	2½	3	3 3	..
,,	17	2½	..	2 9	3 0
June	6	3	..	2 9	3 0
,,	19	4	..	3 1½	3 6
July	3	4½	..	3 6	3 7½
,,	18	5	..	3 9	4 0
August	1	5½	6	4 0	4 3
,,	15	6	..	4 6	5 0
September	5	3	..	2 6	..
,,	19	3	..	3 6	..
October	3	4	4½	4 3	..
,,	17	4	..	4 4½	4 6
November	1	4½	..	4 6	..
,,	15	5	..	4 9	5 0
December	5	6½	..	4 9	5 0
,,	20	6½	7	5 0	..
Average for the year		4·1-32	..	3 7	..

The Baltimore "Journal of Commerce," on the subject of freights, makes the following remarks:—

"A retrospect of the market during 1884 is not encouraging to the shipping interests, and does not compare favourably as regards the rates of freight with the previous year. The large crops of wheat in other producing countries, the temporary disturbance in sterling exchange consequent on the failures in New York in the latter part of May, the outbreak of cholera in the Mediterranean, and the intense excitement attending the Presidential contest—although the last had probably less influence on the foreign than on the domestic trade—all had an adverse effect.

"Berth rates, until within a short period, have generally been quiet, with a moderate demand; grain accommodation being in relatively less request, until the new crop of wheat began to come forward. Since then the inquiry, though not steady, has been more urgent, particularly so the last few months, from all the export interests, through freight forming a very large proportion. In the table above will be seen the range of quotations on grain to Liverpool the past year, although during the latter part of April of both years 1½d. was accepted, yet a comparison is more favourable to 1883 (7½d. was the quotation for the first two months of that year), except that the rate was 1d. to 1½d. higher in December, 1884, than the same month 1883.

"Grain chartering has not been very satisfactory. The year opened with the market dull and depressed; several steamers previously chartered at 4s. 6d. to 4s. 9d., and just arriving, could only be placed at a loss. Rates continued weak and declining, with an occasional temporary improvement during the first half of the year. In July the certainty of a large crop of wheat at very low prices caused anticipations of a very active trade, and rates advanced, and several fixtures were made in that and the early part of the following month, but the demand slackened and freights declined sharply. Steamers which left Great Britain in ballast in August, when charters were quoted at 4s. 4½d. and 4s. 6d., on their arrival here found the rate 2s. 6d.; it afterwards partially recovered on a limited offering of tonnage, but the market remained quiet until October, when it became more active, and continued strong until the close of the year. The table shows the quotations during the year: compared with 1883 the contrast is marked until the latter part of November, 1884, when they become equal. Sailing vessels, although less in favour than steam, have been taken readily when there was any business, and more could have been done in this line but for a scarcity of tonnage. Rates have not varied much from those for steam.

The exports of petroleum were larger during this than the previous two years. In March and April engagements were made at 2s. to Bremen, and 2s. 1½d. to the Continent; in May tonnage was in demand for the Baltic and 2s. 9d. was paid, afterwards advancing to 3s. 1½d. and 3s. 3d.; rates also became firmer to the Continent, 2s. 7½d., 2s. 9d., and 3s. being successively paid. During July 3s. 6d. and 4s. were paid to the Baltic. In the latter month also heavy engagements were made at 3s. to Bremen, and 3s. to 3s. 4½d. to the Continent. Towards the close of September rates receded and were quoted at 3s. to the Continent, subsequently 2s. 10½d. and 2s. 9d.; in November 2s. 3d.; and in December still lower."

Channel and Approaches to Harbour.—There is now a uniform depth of 27 feet in the Fort McHenry, Brewerton and Craighill branches of the channel, and in the cut-off between the Brewerton and Craighill branches, by which last a saving of nearly a mile in distance has been made, besides an improvement in direction and diminution in cost of maintenance. At the end of the fiscal year, June 30, 1884, the widths in the several divisions of the channel were as follows:—

Fort McHenry to Fort Carroll, 250 feet; Brewerton channel to cut-off, 250 feet; cut-off to Craighill channel, 225 feet, except for a space of one-half mile in length in the central portion where it is but 160 feet wide. Craighill channel is 200 feet wide.

Trade and Commerce.

Statement from the Custom-house Returns of the Value of Imports and Exports of Baltimore during the past Five Years.

Years.	Imports.	Exports.
	Dollars.	Dollars.
1880	18,643,253	73,994,910
1881	16,255,495	55,687,745
1882	14,773,576	43,219,168
1883	12,448,802	50,222,929
1884	11,961,977	42,358,439

BALTIMORE.

The principal articles of import and receipts of produce at this port for the last three years have been as follows:—

Articles.	Quantity.	1884.	1883.	1882.
Coffee	Bags	471,977	279,244	404,270
Cocoa-nuts	Thousands	2,777	3,609	1,751
Cotton	Bales	243,065	323,385	266,639
Flour	Barrels	1,290,598	1,175,521	1,674,813
Corn	Bushels	7,149,974	11,760,338	3,401,208
Wheat	,,	17,781,459	17,146,436	17,898,569
Oats	,,	1,663,277	1,192,462	1,040,843
Rye	,,	685,092	207,386	118,524
Barley	,,	303,788	306,481	310,317
Mackerel	Barrels	20,415	20,012	25,772
Herrings	,,	15,447	15,089	20,055
Guano	Tons	19,464	19,841	19,227
Lemons	Boxes	8,272	5,400	6,715
Oranges	,,	54,317	58,096	28,093
Raisins	,,	1,338	23,800	26,400
Hides	Number of	160,000	165,000	160,000
Pig iron	Tons	7,257	32,110	53,149
Molasses	Hogsheads	7,624	12,588	10,446
Sugar	Bags	753	7,131	9,993
,,	Hogsheads	350	3,458	5,450
Rice	Tierces	14,953	11,115	14,869
,,	Bags	12,556	33,064	6,177
Salt	Sacks	337,136	301,512	277,141
,,	Bushels	64,464	113,000	113,390
Spirits of turpentine	Barrels	22,504	27,321	22,837
Resin	,,	129,771	158,124	141,291
Tar, &c.	,,	13,341	12,452	7,961
Tin-plates	Boxes	475,599	469,190	390,660

Principal articles exported from Baltimore to foreign countries for the past three years:—

Articles.	Quantity.	1884.	1883.	1882.
Bark, quercitron	Bags	53,602	32,036	30,577
Bread	Barrels	9,605	21,956	13,186
Flour	,,	414,941	438,954	465,481
Wheat	Bushels	16,438,965	15,366,296	17,555,084
Corn	,,	5,051,695	10,011,941	1,371,719
Cloverseed	,,	168,857	159,692	82,922
Coal	Tons	59,289	63,526	55,167
Cotton	Bales	209,241	218,666	196,735
Rosin	Barrels	58,749	54,459	40,360
Oil cakes	Packages	10,701	25,960	27,094
Petroleum	Gallons	15,158,733	11,103,599	12,094,479
Bacon	Pounds	3,009,121	2,249,714	211,966
Beef	Tierces and barrels	695	2,009	1,605
Butter	Pounds	12,090	15,235	17,112
Cheese	,,	37,665	64,387	123,325
Lard	,,	4,338,922	9,134,686	4,074,788
Pork	Barrels and boxes	2,291	4,873	2,561
Tobacco	Hogsheads	43,192	43,620	46,239

IMPORTS.

Coffee.—The two last crops of Brazil coffee were in excess of all former years, and the imports into the United States were unusually heavy. The arrivals of Rio and Santos at this port amount to 471,977 bags, against 297,253 bags in 1883. A considerable portion of the late imports were per steamers and destined for the interior. Owing to heavy supplies during the past year prices, which in the beginning ranged from $11\frac{1}{2}$ c. to $13\frac{1}{2}$ c. per pound, gradually declined during the first six months to $8\frac{3}{4}$ c. to $10\frac{1}{2}$ c. per pound, but during the last half of the year the fluctuations have been light, and the closing figures varied but little from those of July.

The stock on hand at the end of December was about 35,000 bags.

Salt.—Supplies of "Liverpool" have been fair during the season, but prices have given way since the beginning of 1884. "Ground Alum," in sacks, which in January was rated at 85 c. to 90 c., in December only fetched from 70 c. to 80 c. per bushel. "Standard," which sold from 1 dol. 40 c. to 1 dol. 50 c., fell in the same time to 1 dol. 20 c. and 1 dol. 30 c. "Turk's Island," which sold for 30 c. to 33 c. per bushel, has gone down to 27 c. and 30 c.

Iron.—There is still a considerable falling off in the importation of iron, as will be seen by the following table:—

Quality.	Quantity.	1884.	1883.	1882.
Pig	Tons	7,257	32,110	53,149
Rails	,,	..	..	5,784
,, steel	Pieces	..	1,000	10,425
,, ,,	Tons	79	..	1,559
,, ,,	Pieces	..	..	5,099
Steel blooms	Number	..	..	2,689
,, ,,	Tons	2,563	7,076	699
,, scrap	,,	..	..	3,170
Iron, scrap	,,	2,380	6,548	2,326
,, ore	,,	185,930	222,596	239,127

American pig iron can now be bought at 19 dol. per ton for the best brands; steel rails at from 27 dol. to 28 dol. per ton. Such prices cannot be competed with by importations from other countries.

Chemicals.—Upon the subject of the importation the "Journal of Commerce" states:—"Trade in English chemicals has been affected during the year by the general depressed condition of the manufacturing interests in the West, where the imports are chiefly distributed."

Sugar and Molasses.—The import trade in these articles at this port has fallen to next to nothing.

EXPORTS.

Cotton.—Receipts for the calendar year embrace eight months of the short crop of 1883 and four months of the crop of 1884. While the aggregate is 80,000 bales short of the previous year, the receipts of the new crop since September are slightly in excess of the same period in 1883. The exports for the year fell off nearly 10,000 bales as compared with 1883, but since the opening of the new crop season, September 1st, are 35,000 bales in excess of the same period in 1883. The increase of ocean steamer lines from this port to Europe, affording more constant and regular facilities for shippers, must continue to attract business in this staple. The consumption for home spinning has been unusually small the past year, most of the mills having suspended work for a portion of the time from a plethora of production and stagnant condition of the markets generally.

RECEIPTS of Cotton for the Past Four Years at the Port of Baltimore.

From	1884.	1883.	1882.	1881.
	Bales.	Bales.	Bales.	Bales.
Charleston	15,824	27,050	33,186	25,680
Savannah	53,170	86,489	92,121	80,082
Virginia and North Carolina	118,330	135,676	111,332	114,293
Per Baltimore and Ohio Railway	46,314	65,500	66,120	31,644
Per Western Maryland Railway	10,000	8,670	..	..
Total	243,438	323,385	302,759	251,699

COTTON Exported for the Year ended December 31 from Baltimore, as compared with Former Years.

	Bales.
To Great Britain	157,237
Bremen	41,586
Holland	2,796
Other countries	7,765
Total, 1884	209,384
„ 1883	215,176
„ 1882	196,735
„ 1881	145,761

COMPARATIVE Prices of Cotton on the 15th of each Month for the past Three Years.

Months.	Ordinary to Middling.		
	1884.	1883.	1882.
	Cents.	Cents.	Cents.
January	$8\frac{3}{4}$ to $10\frac{5}{8}$	$8\frac{1}{2}$ to 10	9 to $11\frac{3}{4}$
February	$8\frac{1}{2}$ $10\frac{1}{2}$	$7\frac{1}{2}$ $10\frac{1}{2}$	9 $11\frac{1}{2}$
March	$8\frac{1}{2}$ $10\frac{3}{4}$	$7\frac{1}{2}$ $10\frac{1}{8}$	$9\frac{1}{4}$ $12\frac{1}{8}$
April	$9\frac{3}{4}$ $11\frac{7}{8}$	7 $9\frac{7}{8}$	$9\frac{1}{2}$ $12\frac{1}{4}$
May	$9\frac{3}{4}$ $11\frac{5}{8}$	8 $10\frac{3}{4}$	$9\frac{1}{2}$ $12\frac{1}{4}$
June	$9\frac{3}{4}$ $11\frac{5}{8}$	$7\frac{1}{2}$ $10\frac{1}{2}$	$9\frac{1}{4}$ $12\frac{1}{2}$
July	$8\frac{3}{4}$ 11	7 10	10 $12\frac{7}{8}$
August	$8\frac{3}{4}$ 11	8 $10\frac{1}{2}$	$10\frac{1}{2}$ 13
September	$8\frac{1}{4}$ $10\frac{5}{8}$	$7\frac{1}{2}$ $10\frac{1}{8}$	$10\frac{1}{2}$ $12\frac{5}{8}$
October	$8\frac{3}{4}$ $9\frac{3}{4}$	$9\frac{3}{4}$ $10\frac{1}{2}$	9 $11\frac{1}{4}$
November	9 $10\frac{1}{8}$	$9\frac{1}{4}$ $10\frac{1}{4}$	9 $10\frac{3}{8}$
December	$9\frac{1}{2}$ $10\frac{3}{4}$	$8\frac{3}{4}$ $10\frac{1}{4}$	9 $10\frac{1}{4}$

UNITED STATES.

Tobacco.

		Hogsheads.
Stock on hand in warehouses, Jan. 1, 1884		15,861
Inspections in 1884—		
Maryland	35,149	
Ohio	5,866	
Virginia and Kentucky	88	
		41,103
Total supply for 1884		56,964
Direct shipments of "Maryland" and "Ohio"—		
To Bremen	8,175	
Rotterdam	6,507	
Amsterdam	514	
France	9,182	
England	547	
		24,925
Shipments viâ New York—		
To Rotterdam	3,428	
Amsterdam	3,088	
France	3,300	
Italy	850	
Northern Europe	477	
		11,143
Shipped coastwise and taken for consumption	2,669	
Baltimore manufacturers	2,885	
,, repackers	959	
Shipments of Virginia and Kentucky	183	
		7,687
		43,755
Stock Jan. 1, 1885		13,209

Grain.—Receipts per Corn and Flour Exchange books for the year 1884 were of wheat, 17,781,459 bushels; corn, 7,149,974 bushels; oats, 1,663,277 bushels; rye, 685,092 bushels; and barley, 303,788 bushels: making in the aggregate 27,583,590 bushels, against 30,613,103 bushels in 1883, and 22,769,461 bushels in 1882.

The receipts of grain per rail, as reported by the different railways, were for the year as follows:—

	Bushels.
Baltimore and Ohio Railway	12,449,115
Northern Central Railway	9,547,729
Western Maryland Railway	1,975,450
Potomac Railway	1,588,357
Total per rail	25,560,651

The following shows the receipts of grain here per the Baltimore and Ohio Railway and the Pennsylvania (or Northern Central) Railway for the last five years:—

Years.	Baltimore and Ohio.	Northern Central.
	Bushels.	Bushels.
1884	12,449,115	9,547,729
1883	11,809,008	14,350,039
1882	9,301,574	10,230,364
1881	14,852,357	19,728,929
1880	25,796,690	21,809,056

The foreign exports of wheat and corn from Baltimore for the same years were as follows:—

Years.	Wheat.	Corn.	Total.
	Bushels.	Bushels.	Bushels.
1884	16,438,965	5,051,695	21,490,660
1883	15,366,296	10,011,941	25,378,237
1882	17,555,084	1,371,719	18,926,803
1881	19,677,131	12,730,939	32,408,070
1880	33,708,985	14,767,408	48,476,393

The following statement, based on the figures of the Corn and Flour Exchange books, shows stock in elevators, December 31, 1883; receipts of wheat and corn during the year 1884; quantity shipped same period; stock on hand, December 31, 1884; and the residue, representing the amount taken for home consumption:—

	Wheat.	Corn.
	Bushels.	Bushels.
Stock in elevators, December 31, 1883	2,010,959	374,931
Receipts during 1884	17,781,459	7,149,974
Total supply ..	19,792,418	7,524,905
Foreign exports	16,524,524	5,051,695
	3,267,994	2,473,210
Deduct stock, December 31, 1884	843,097	247,388
Balance for home consumption and coastwise shipment	2,424,897	2,225,822

The above figures compare very favourably with the movement in grain for two preceding years, especially considering the great competition in the matter of traffic over the rival trunk lines and the efforts made by other seaboard cities to increase their business.

The receipts of wheat show an increase of 635,023 bushels as compared with 1883, and of corn a decrease of 4,610,364 bushels, which latter is to be attributed to the short crop of 1883.

PRICES of Western Mixed Corn on the First of each Month for the Past Year.

Months.	Mixed. From—	Mixed. To—	Steamer. From—	Steamer. To—
	Cents.	Cents.	Cents.	Cents.
January	58	58¼	..	..
February	58¼	58½	53	..
March	59⅝	59¾	..	..
April	55½	56¼	..	..
May	57½	..	..	..
June	61⅝	62	..	..
July	55	55½	..	51
August	..	..	..	..
September	59½	60¾	..	..
October	..	..	..	..
November	..	52	..	..
December	46¾	46	..	..

COMPARATIVE Prices of Southern Wheat on the First of each Month for the Past Year.

Months.	Fultz. From—	Fultz. To—	Longberry. From—	Longberry. To—
	Dollars.	Dollars.	Dollars.	Dollars.
January	1·08	1·11	1·10	1·13
February	1·10	1·13	1·13	1·16
March	1·10	1·14	1·15	1·17
April	1·08	1·10	1·12	1·16
May	1.12	1·15	1·14	1·18
June	1·03	1·10	1·10	1·13
July	1·00	1·07	1·05	1·09
August	90	93	94	95
September	88	91	92	96
October	87	90	93	96
November	85	90	92	95
December	82	84	90	92

EXPORTS of Flour from Baltimore for the Last Two Years.

Destination.	1884.	1883.
	Barrels.	Barrels.
Great Britain	177,232	164,899
Bremen	5,365	11,383
Holland	5,898	8,136
Brazil	222,448	207,107
British North American colonies	1,303	1,345
West Indies	29,319	46,226
Other ports	2,684	143
Total	444,249	439,239

Petroleum.—There is an increase in the export from this port, as will be seen in the table of exports.

Provisions.—There is an increase in the export of bacon, but a considerable falling off as regards lard. This is caused by the restrictions of continental governments on the importation of these products.

Cattle.—The export of cattle from this port was, in 1884, 15,221 head as compared with 14,132 in 1883.

RAILWAYS.

Baltimore and Ohio Railway.

COMPARATIVE Statement of the Leading Commodities received from the West by this Railway, and Delivered to Consignees at Baltimore for the Past Three Years.

Articles.	Packages.	1884.	1883.	1882.
Cotton	Bales	46,314	65,500	66,120
Coal	Tons	2,472,405	1,597,707	1,599,939
Flour	Barrels	715,638	703,338	613,221
Wheat	Bushels	6,918,025	5,762,583	7,417,016
Corn	,,	3,801,297	4,656,975	702,548
Other grains	,,	1,729,793	1,389,450	1,182,010
Lumber	Tons	101,842	93,103	105,953
Provisions	,,	28,728	38,776	20,614

North Central Railway.

RECEIPTS at Baltimore for the above Railway for the Last Three Years Compared.

Articles.	Quantity.	1884.	1883.	1882.
Coal	Tons	767,381	639,949	527,778
General merchandise	,,	283,979	277,954	245,118
Flour	Barrels	696,424	586,930	598,099
Grain	Bushels	9,547,729	14,330,039	10,230,364
Live stock	Tons	57,636	43,573	39,008
Lime and plaster	Bushels	51,379	48,147	44,029
Pig iron and iron ores	Tons	17,305	16,987	27,943
Lumber	Feet	60,869,137	70,271,841	54,130,112
Coal oil	Barrels	158,215	308,811	490,540
Butter	Tons	2,646	3,088	3,646
Provisions	,,	6,035	9,247	11,223

		Tons.
1884		1,618,625
1883		1,713,874
1882		1,414,496
1881		1,595,893

Baltimore and Potomac Railway.

PRINCIPAL Articles at Baltimore over the above Railway for the past Three Years.

Articles.	Quantity.	1884.	1883.	1882.
Coal	Tons	14,826	7,875	1,076
General merchandise	,,	28,381	13,129	22,233
Flour	Barrels	60,440	56,830	44,208
Grain	Bushels	1,588,357	2,360,722	1,166,229
Live stock	Tons	4,301	3,751	5,928
Lime, plaster and stone	,,	1,339	3,231	2,893
Pig iron and ores	,,	3,764	4,368	12,475
Lumber	Feet	13,231,539	20,424,858	11,185,318
Butter	Tons	50	39	20
Provisions	,,	478	185	119

			Tons.
1884	.. ..		126,743
1883	.. ..		135,051
1882	.. ..		98,788
1881	.. ..		49,798

Western Maryland Railway.

CLASSIFICATION of Tonnage Receipts for the Year 1884, compared with Two previous Years.

Articles.	Quantity.	1884.	1883.	1882.
Lumber	Tons	1,316	2,298	19,427
Coal (bituminous)	,,	23,158	12,834	20,701
Miscellaneous	,,	37,061	40,444	79,420
Live stock	,,	12,918	12,804	14,837
Grain and feed	,,	49,386	63,429	36,314
Lime	,,	96	179	4,377
Wood	,,	359	803	1,794
Ores	,,	457	169	5,127
Flour	Barrels	85,293	92,302	90,430

AGRICULTURE.

Maryland Crop Reports.—The annual report of the Department of Agriculture estimates the corn crop of the State of Maryland last year as 15,237,000 bushels from 698,400 acres, representing a value of 7,313,760 dol.; the wheat crop at 8,260,000 bushels from 644,980 acres, representing a value of 6,855,800 dol.; and the oat crop at 1,980000 bushels from 110,000 acres, representing a value of 693,000 dol.

The State agent of Maryland reports: "Winter wheat, owing to the drought and unfavourable circumstances, was sown very late and the area is much less than in 1883. The condition is not flattering on account of the hurried manner of sowing and the ground not being properly prepared."

The State agent of Virginia says: "The area of winter wheat as compared with 1883 is fully one-third less. The condition is bad indeed. A large proportion is not yet up, and much of that seeded during the exceedingly dry weather came up badly and looks puny. The outlook at this time is very discouraging for a crop."

Population and Industries.

Public Schools.—The number of schools in the city under the charge of the Board of School Commissioners is 128, of which 120 were day, and 8 evening schools, containing 40,496 enrolled pupils.

The number of white pupils is 34,599 and of coloured pupils 5,897, The amount expended for white schools is 601,223 dol. 1 c., and for coloured schools 68,776 dol. 99 c. The average salaries of the teachers is 563 dol., and the *per capita* cost of pupils in the several schools as follows:—Baltimore City College, 56 dol.; Female High Schools, 27 dol. 53 c.; Male Grammar Schools 21 dol. 85 c.; Female Grammar Schools 17 dol. 84 c.; English-German Schools 15 dol. 66 c.; Manual Training School, 46 dol. 66 c.; Male Primary, 13 dol. 54 c.; Female Primary, 13 dol. 17 c.; High and Grammar Coloured Schools, 15 dol. 84 c. and Primary Schools, 13 dol. 80 c.

The estimated expenditure for 1885 is 713,500 dol.

Gaol.—The mayor in his message to the city council states that the number of commitments for the year was 9,322 of which 6,559 were for drunkenness and minor offences. This is a large increase over 1883 when the commitments were 7,783, of which 5,323 were for drunkennesss and minor offenses. Most of these cases are where a fine of one dollar is inflicted or thirty days imprisonment. He states that there is no class in a community whose condition more strongly appeals to the humanitarian than these petty offenders, in many cases able-bodied intelligent men, who live in the gaol because they are unable to resist the temptation to drink when out of it. He recommends the council to provide more accommodation as the gaol is overcrowded, and also calls to their attention an Act passed by the State legislature that persons in gaol should be compelled to labour.

Penitentiary.—In this institution are to be found the convicts. At the end of the year there were 522 persons undergoing sentence: of these, 206 were white men, 4 white women, 285 coloured men, and 27 coloured women. Of these 152 are employed at manufacturing wool or merino boots; 153 at furniture and plumbers marble, and 114 at stove and hollow-ware castings. The remainder are employed in various departments of the institution. The warden says: "Our inmates have been obedient and industrious, and have now due to them for overwork 7,079 dol. 34 c., and this after giving their families over 7,000 dol. to assist them. The total receipts were 68,286 dol. 43 c.; expenditure 60,771 dol. 28 c., surplus 7,515 dol. 15 c." From these figures it will be seen that the penitentiary is self-supporting. Further curious statistics given by the warden are as follows:—

"Among the prisoners 124 were labourers prior to conviction; 109 farm-hands; 62 waiters and servants; 26 without occupation; 18 sailors; 15 ostlers; 12 oyster-shuckers; 11 draymen; 10 barkeepers; 9 barbers; 8 cooks, and of shoemakers, carpenters, and plasterers, 7 each. There is also 1 merchant, 1 preacher, 1 bible agent, 1 contractor; 11 are in the prison for murder; murder in the second degree, 29; larceny, 250; burglary, 57; manslaughter, 25; arson, 8; bigamy, 5; rape, 15; perjury, 1, and forgery 12. There are 5 life prisoners; 7 for 21 years, and 2 for 20 years. 95 of the prisoners are strictly temperate; 198 moderate drinkers; 217 are married; 278 unmarried; 23 widowers, and 4 widows; 254 can read and write; 56 can read only; 212 cannot read and write; 385 attended Sunday school; 137 did not attend Sunday school; 443 were convicted for the first time;

51 the second time; 15 the third time; 10 the fourth time, and 3 for the fifth time. The sanitary condition of the institution has been very good, the total number of deaths being two, or ·38 the lowest percentage of mortality on the records of the institution."

Deaths and Births.—The Secretary to the Health Board reports that during 1884 there were 8,035 deaths, divided as follows: White males, 3,480; white females, 3,419; coloured males, 582; coloured females, 554: total whites, 6,899; coloured, 1,136. The annual birth-rate per 1·000 was: whole population, 19·64; white, 19·76; coloured, 18·23; while the death-rate for same period was 20·27 whole population, 18·33 white, and 31·58 coloured. 297 illegitimate births were reported, of which 124 were white, and 173 coloured.

Fire Record.—The fire inspector reports that during the past year there were 389 alarms for fire sounded. The total amount of losses was 617,872 dol. 43 c. The total amount of losses for 1883 was 715,057 dol. 99 c., showing a decrease in favour of the year 1884 of 97,185 dol. 56 c. There were six incendiary fires, and two supposed incendiary, during the year. Four persons were convicted and sentenced to the penitentiary as incendiaries. The inspector recommends the speedy passage by the city council of a suitable building law which will make the erection of " death-traps " impossible, and also suggests the building of a powerful and fully-equipped police and fire boat for the better protection of vessels and buildings along the water-front. During the year there were six persons burned to death and twelve seriously injured at fires. The causes of these fires were as follows; 26 from spontaneous combustion; 26 were chimneys on fire; 98 from carelessness; 31 from matches; 19 from defective flues; 14 from coal-oil lamps: 14 from overheated stoves; 14 from gas-jets; 5 from gasoline; and the others from minor causes.

Coal Trade.—The shipment of coal from the Cumberland district in this State amounted to 2,848,892 tons in 1884 as against 2,482,200 tons in 1883.

Baltimore, February 6, 1885.

UNITED STATES.

MOBILE.

Report by Consul Cridland on the Trade and Commerce of Mobile and Productions of Alabama for the Year 1884.

TAKING into consideration the general depression in the trade and commerce of the United States during the past year, which of course was also felt in this section of the country, this report will show that Mobile has not suffered so heavily as other places, and though the domestic trade has not been as good as last year, yet the exports to foreign ports have been large, and in some branches larger than ever before, especially in the timber and lumber trade, which is steadily increasing, adding much to the prosperity and business of this Gulf port. The latter trade brought a much larger number of vessels to Mobile than in former years, the excess in tonnage over 1883 being about 31,277 tons.

In consequence of the authorities of Alabama not publishing an account of the productions of the State it is very difficult to make any report in reference thereto, and especially the result of the late cotton crop, but the National Cotton Exchange has made public its estimate of the yield of the amount produced in the cotton-producing States for the past season, and the information being exceedingly useful and interesting, is copied here for the benefit of those who may desire to see the result tabulated for each State. It shows that the popular estimate at the end of last August of a crop of 6,000,000 bales exceeded by 200,000 bales the quantity that was produced.

THE COTTON CROP OF ALABAMA AND OTHER SOUTHERN STATES.

The National Cotton Exchange Report, and that of the Agricultural Bureau at Washington, were made public about the middle of last November. The systems vary but little. The National Cotton Exchange basis its estimate of the yield on the fractional parts of a bale per acre, expressed decimally; while the Agricultural Bureau seeks as a basis the number of pounds of lint cotton produced per acre. The former is as follows :—

486 UNITED STATES.

SEASON beginning on the 1st of September, 1883, and ending on the 31st of August, 1884.

States.	Acreage.	Yield per Acre.	Crop.
Virginia	44,629	33	14,728
North Carolina	1,046,024	38	397,491
South Carolina	1,590,374	36	572,535
Georgia	2,965,260	29	859,425
Florida	252,525	29	73,232
Alabama	2,656,970	31	823,661
Tennessee	775,392	35	278,387
Mississippi	2,277,841	35	797,244
Arkansas	1,214,058	42	510,030
Louisiana	893,284	47	419,846
Texas	3,186,594	30	955,978
Missouri, &c.	70,000	33	23,100
Total	16,972,951		5,725,657

Below is a tabulated synopsis of the Agricultural Bureau's Report, the first and third columns giving the acerage and crop in thousands, the second the estimated yield of lint cotton per acre, the fourth the net weight of bales in each State, exclusive of bagging and ties, which are computed at 25 lbs. per bale, but as a fact do not exceed 24 lbs.

States.	Acreage.	Lint per Acre.	Crop.	Weight per Bale.
Virginia	46,000	180	19,000	416
North Carolina	1,061,000	175	408,000	456
South Carolina	1,716,000	152	591,000	453
Florida	268,000	105	62,000	454
Georgia	2,959,000	135	880,000	454
Alabama	2,710,000	130	756,000	471
Mississippi	2,392,000	175	901,000	460
Louisiana	923,000	190	390,000	450
Texas	3,187,000	143	920,000	490
Arkansas	1,259,000	200	534,000	472
Tennessee	815,000	160	276,000	473
Missouri, &c.	60,000	180	23,000	460
Total	17,396,000	153·5 Average Lint.	5,760,000	464·28 Average Weight.

As before stated the average weight of bagging and ties is not more than 24 lbs. per bale, upon which basis there would be a further reduction of 12,000 bales, and a crop of 5,748,000 bales.

Should the American crop reach 5,800,000 bales, and the consumption of the United States, Mexico, and Canada not exceed 1,000,000 bales, the supply of Europe of the current year's growth will be as follows, using Mr. Ellison's estimates of other growths as a basis, all reduced to statistical bales of 400 lbs. :—

MOBILE.

		Bales.
American crop		5,800,000
Consumed in America		2,000,000

		Bales.	Bales.
Available for	Europe	3,500,000	4,275,000
,,	India	1,600,000	1,520,000
,,	Egypt	425,000	697,000
,,	Brazil	375,000	162,000
,,	others	90,000	52,000

European supply, growth of 1884	6,706,000
52 weeks' consumption at 138,000 per week	7,176,000
Excess of consumption	470,000

Should nothing unforeseen occur a substantial advance in prices during this season is indicated, even though the crop of the United States should reach 5,900,000 bales, which is by no means improbable.

As regards the export of cotton to foreign ports, Mobile, like all the old cotton ports, is feeling the effects of the establishment of cotton centres in the interior, from which the cotton is forwarded direct to Europe, or North, in place of seeking its former channel of shipment.

The receipts and shipments of cotton for 1884, as compared with 1882 and 1883, were as follows:—

Cotton received by	1881–2.	1882–3.	1883–4.
	Bales.	Bales.	Bales.
Steamers from the River Alabama	31,989	40,223	30,013
,, ,, ,, Bigbee	45,101	52,390	35,239
,, ,, ,, Warrior	9,545	12,814	5,684
Mobile and Ohio Railroad	119,723	132,043	113,853
,, Montgomery	57,261	74,480	68,745
Wagons	1,421	1,463	1,117
Coastwise from Pensacola	2,096	1,560	..
Total	267,136	314,973	265,040

Of the foregoing were—

Exported to	1881–2.	1882–3.	1883–4.
	Bales.	Bales.	Bales.
Liverpool	36,822	34,840	56,157
Havre	6,313	9,350	..
Other foreign ports	3,231	1,100	1,380
Total to foreign ports	46,366	45,290	57,537
,, United States ports	223,755	266,057	204,795
Local consumption by mills	1,099	630	610
Stock on hand, August 31, 1882	197	..	..
,, ,, ,, 1883	..	3,203	..
,, ,, ,, 1884	..	..	1,611
Unaccounted for	..	..	487
Total	271,417	315,170	265,040

Current rates of cotton and timber, and other freights foreign and coastwise, at the port of Mobile during the years 1882, 1883, and 1884.

A good demand prevailed last year for tonnage, and during the first six months there seemed to be ample tonnage at Mobile and in the lower bay for all purposes, both home and foreign. Cotton room was scarce in the first part of the cotton shipping season, or during the months of November, December, and January, driving the freight to New Orleans for the steamships bound to British ports, but after that vessels coming to Mobile had to take freight at very low rates, and there was much competition between the sailing ships loading at this port and the steamers loading at New Orleans. Early in the year freights for timber and lumber ruled high, but later in the season freights declined. For naval stores there was a very fair supply of tonnage last year, and more shipments were then made to foreign ports than in any previous season.

The range of freights during the past three years has been as follows:—

	1882.		1883.		1884.	
	£ s. d.	£ s. d.	£ s. d.	£ s. d.	£ s. d.	£ s. d.
For cotton—						
To Liverpool	0 0 $0\frac{3}{8}$	to 0 0 $0\frac{13}{32}$	0 0 $0\frac{3}{8}$	to 0 0 $0\frac{15}{32}$	0 0 $0\frac{12}{13}$	to 0 0 $0\frac{5}{16}$
,, Havre...	0 0 $0\frac{1}{2}$	0 0 $0\frac{23}{32}$	...		...	
For timber to foreign ports—						
Sawn	5 15 0	6 2 6	5 15 0	to 6 0 0	4 12 6	to 6 5 0
Hewn	1 17 6	2 1 0	1 18 0	2 2 0	1 10 0	2 2 0
Deals	5 12 6	6 0 0	5 15 0	6 5 0	5 0 0	6 5 0
	Dol. c.	Dol. c.	Dol. c.	Dol. c.	Dol. c.	Dol. c.
Lnmber to the West Indies...	8 00	to 10 00	8 00	to 15 00	7 00	to 11 00
,, Mexico	10 00	12 00	12 00	16 00	12 00	16 00
,, Brazil	20 00	21 00	20 00	21 00	20 00	21 00
,, coastwise	9 00	11 00	8 25	11 00	7 00	10 00
Naval stores—	£ s. d.	£ s. d.	£ s. d.	£ s. d.	£ s. d.	£ s. d.
Rosin, per barrel... ...	0 4 0	to 0 4 3	0 3 9	to 0 4 0	0 3 6	to 0 4 0
Turpentine...	0 6 0	0 6 3	0 6 0	0 6 3	0 5 9	0 6 0

The naval stores were shipped to Great Britain and to continental ports, and also to coast ports of the United States.

MONTHLY Range of Cotton Prices in 1881–82, 1882–83, and 1883–84, Mobile Middling.

Months.	1881–82.		1882–83.		1883–84.	
	Highest.	Lowest.	Highest.	Lowest.	Highest.	Lowest.
September	$11\frac{3}{8}$	$10\frac{3}{4}$	$12\frac{3}{8}$	$10\frac{7}{8}$	10	$9\frac{5}{8}$
October	$11\frac{1}{4}$	$10\frac{3}{4}$	$10\frac{7}{8}$	$10\frac{1}{4}$	$10\frac{1}{2}$	10
November	$11\frac{3}{8}$	11	$10\frac{1}{8}$	$9\frac{5}{8}$	$10\frac{1}{8}$	$9\frac{7}{8}$
December	$11\frac{1}{2}$	$11\frac{1}{8}$	$9\frac{7}{8}$	$9\frac{9}{16}$	10	$9\frac{3}{4}$
January	$11\frac{5}{8}$	$11\frac{1}{8}$	$9\frac{3}{4}$	$9\frac{9}{16}$	$10\frac{5}{16}$	$9\frac{7}{8}$
February	$11\frac{5}{8}$	$11\frac{1}{4}$	$9\frac{3}{4}$	$9\frac{1}{2}$	$10\frac{3}{8}$	$10\frac{5}{16}$
March	12	$11\frac{3}{8}$	$9\frac{5}{8}$	$9\frac{1}{2}$	11	$10\frac{3}{8}$
April	12	$11\frac{3}{4}$	$9\frac{3}{8}$	$9\frac{3}{8}$	$11\frac{3}{4}$	11
May	12	$11\frac{3}{4}$	$10\frac{1}{4}$	10	$11\frac{1}{2}$	$11\frac{3}{8}$
June	$12\frac{1}{4}$	$11\frac{3}{4}$	$10\frac{1}{2}$	$9\frac{3}{4}$	$11\frac{3}{8}$	11
July	$12\frac{5}{8}$	$12\frac{1}{4}$	$9\frac{3}{4}$	$9\frac{1}{2}$	11	$10\frac{3}{4}$
August	$12\frac{5}{8}$	$12\frac{1}{2}$	$9\frac{7}{8}$	$9\frac{1}{2}$	$10\frac{3}{4}$	$10\frac{1}{2}$

Supervision of Cotton at Mobile.

It was stated in the Report of last year that the interests of shippers of cotton to this port were most carefully guarded under the strict supervision then in force. The same has continued during the past cotton season, the Supervision Department at Mobile being complete in all its workings, and giving much satisfaction to all concerned in the trade. The owners of the staple find that their cotton is under espionage from the time of its arrival at this port, while passing through the warehouse and press, and until put on board a ship or a railroad carriage, for export to foreign ports or coastwise.

COMPARATIVE Table of Cotton Exported from Mobile to Foreign and Domestic Ports during the Cotton Seasons of 1881-82, 1882-83, and 1883-84.

Countries Exported to.	1882. Quantity. Bales.	1882. Weight. Lbs.	1882. Value in Currency. Dol. c.	1882. Value in Sterling, at 4·80. £ s. d.	1883. Quantity. Bales.	1883. Weight. Lbs.	1883. Value in Currency. Dol. c.	1883. Value in Sterling, at 4·80. £ s. d.	1884. Quantity. Bales.	1884. Weight. Lbs.	1884. Value in Currency. Dol. c.	1884. Value in Sterling, at 4·81. £ s. d.
Great Britain—												
In British vessels	27,613	13,607,659	1,551,248 48	323,176 15 4	33,840	16,999,033	1,691,682 00	352,433 16 0	46,015	22,817,518	2,374,597 70	493,679 7 1
American vessels	8,344	4,147,478	458,920 00	95,608 6 8	...	...	...	...	1,515	740,384	75,750 00	15,748 8 9
other foreign vessels	865	430,744	47,575 00	9,911 9 2	1,000	810,972	55,000 00	11,458 6 8	8,627	4,249,316	443,656 00	92,236 3 6
Total to Great Britain	36,822	18,185,881	2,057,743 48	428,796 11 2	34,840	17,810,005	1,746,682 00	363,892 2 8	56,157	27,807,218	2,894,003 70	501,663 19 4
France	6,313	3,110,134	354,913 78	73,940 7 5	9,350	4,710,990	465,051 07	96,885 12 9	...	...	...	...
Spain	...	...	...	...	1,100	559,374	55,100 00	11,479 3 4	...	...	...	...
Bremen	3,231	1,600,408	173,500 00	36,146 16 8	...	...	...	...	...	...	...	...
Russia	...	...	...	...	...	...	...	...	1,180	578,360	60,727 00	12,625 3 1
Italy	...	...	...	...	...	...	...	...	200	98,650	10,111 00	2,102 1 7
Total to foreign ports	46,366	22,896,423	2,586,157 26	538,883 15 3	45,290	23,080,369	2,266,833 07	472,256 18 9	57,537	28,484,228	2,964,841 70	516,391 4 0
" United States ports	223,755	110,758,725	12,082,770 00	2,517,243 15 0	266,057	134,402,581	13,475,752 91	2,708,333 6 8	204,795	103,216,680	10,172,167 65	2,114,795 5 5
Total exports	270,121	133,655,148	14,668,927 26	3,056,127 10 3	311,347	157,482,950	15,742,585 98	3,180,590 5 5	262,332	131,690,908	13,137,009 35	2,631,186 9 5

	1882.	1883.	1884.
Average weight per bale	494·68 lbs.	505·81 lbs.	595·09 lbs.
" value "	54 dol. 95 c.	50 dol. 42 c.	49 dol. 67 c.
" " per lb.	11 c.	9 dol. 97 c.	10 dol. 03 c.

Charges on Cotton.

At the commencement of the present season the Cotton Exchange Committee at this port having made some changes in the tariff of charges as compared with last year, and the same having been adopted by those interested, it is deemed necessary to give the tariff as it now stands:—

Factors' Charges.

		Dol.	c.
Wharfage	per bale	0	8
Drayage	,,	0	10
Weighing and checking	,,	0	15
Storage one month	,,	0	35
,, progressive per month	,,	0	5
,, progressive on rejections per month	,,	0	10
Picking, damaged cotton, drayage, and labour	,,	1	25
Wantages	per band	0	7

Buyers' Charges.

		Dol.	c.
Compressing	per bale	0	65
Shipping charges	,,	0	25
Brokerage	,,	0	35
Reweighing	,,	0	8
Wharfage on exports	,,	0	4
Extra ties	per band	0	5
Supervision	per bale	0	1
Stowing	,,	0	50

The charge for compressing is subject to change, and will be governed by the rate ruling at New Orleans.

The Lumber Trade.

This important branch of business, which is one of the leading and growing industries of Mobile and South Alabama, has during the past year held its own, and, notwithstanding the general depression in trade, many shipments have been made to new and important markets, showing as it does that the dealers and exporters who are active and energetic have been alive to any change in the trade, and whenever the demand began to fall off in one direction they did not wait for orders from other places, but sought new and important markets, causing Mobile lumber to become well and favourably known in Europe and many sections of the United States. The trade of the past year, as represented by shipments in vessels, would no doubt have been larger than it was if it had not been for the depressed condition of Northern and Eastern markets, and the stopping, to a great extent, of railroad building in Mexico and Texas. Then, again, the mill men generally prefer to cut sawn timber instead of small stuff when prices are favourable, which was the case the past year, as a very large business was done in sawn timber—in fact larger than any previous year

The shipments in 1884 by rail to the interior and Western markets, also North, were very large, and I am informed by dealers that this branch of the lumber trade was larger than in 1883.

The total shipment of pitch pine last year to foreign and coast ports from Mobile was about 22,200,000 feet against 26,700,000 feet in 1883, showing a decrease of 4,500,000 feet. The exports of lumber to foreign ports in 1884 show an increase of about 372,000 feet as compared with 1883, which was caused by a very large export of the article to Great

Britain, as the total shipment in that direction was larger than one-third of the total exports foreign. The exports to France, Mexico, and Cuba show a heavy decrease, while there was a decided increase in lumber shipments to Germany, Holland, Spain, Trinidad, and Hayti. Large shipments have been made to Belgium, Italy, and Monte Video against none last year.

Although the total shipments foreign exhibit an increase, yet the total value is about 11,650 dol. less than last year, which shows that prices of lumber ruled lower than last season. The following statement does not include shipments by rail and boat to the interior, and some shipments to Southern ports in vessels having coasting license and not reported:—

Shipments to Foreign Ports for the past Three Years.

Ports.	1881-82.	1882-83.	1883-84.
	Feet.	Feet.	Feet.
Mexico	981,975	2,904,213	610,843
Cuba	1,934,826	1,983,390	736,761
Jamaica	1,838,529	1,964,180	1,535,098
Great Britain	1,692,804	2,971,303	6,244,388
Ireland	432,365	125,381	191,348
France	3,762,641	2,608,170	651,839
Germany	44,119	280,318	303,697
Holland	951,250	48,889	578,437
Spain	316,840	97,569	441,687
Africa	1,216,186	566,552	214,512
Hayti	424,437	281,716	494,581
Trinidad	760,151	916,572	1,595,646
Aspinwall	..	1,037,286	..
Various	1,491,041	944,299	1,436,895
Monte Video	..	..	931,829
Belgium	..	..	760,744
Italy	..	..	373,797
Total exports	15,847,164	16,729,838	17,102,102
Value	$252,021 77c.	$239,800 15c.	$238,144 80c.

COASTWISE.

Ports.	1881-82.	1882-83.	1883-84.
	Feet.	Feet.	Feet.
Texas	10,907,643	1,837,514	1,217,166
Boston	2,177,378	3,200,683	1,518,815
Philadelphia	1,913,130	2,051,140	1,329,595
New York	394,671	2,087,814	787,795
Providence	..	495,000	..
Fall River	270,000	35,000	..
Baltimore	..	..	296,618
Various	726,187	316,854	..
Total exports	16,389,009	10,024,005	5,149,989
Total shipments, foreign and coastwise	32,236,173	26,753,843	22,252,091

Exports of Hewn and Sawn Timber.

During the past year this growing branch of business, which is the most important of the pitch pine trade, has greatly increased in importance; and while it cannot be claimed that the business has been particularly remunerative to the shipper, owing to large stocks in Europe, yet the volume of business rapidly increased during the past year, and as Mobile woods have at last been thoroughly introduced into Europe and seem to be in much favour, the port can safely look for an increasing trade with the United Kingdom and the Continent. Mobile is now one of the cheapest and most convenient ports in the United States, and with the advantages offered by the new channel and a safe harbour her timber trade will, it is said, at no distant day be second to none in the South. The timber is not surpassed in quality or manufacture by that shipped from other ports, and hewn timber of special average is difficult to procure at other points, while here there is a never-ending supply, which in itself must recommend this port to buyers and shippers, and finally produce a desirable result.

As previously mentioned the past season was not entirely satisfactory to shippers, as heavy stocks in Europe, held over from last season, and other causes, had their effect here as well as abroad, and the recent failures and suspensions, including the bank of Mobile, also affected the timber trade as well as other branches of business. Notwithstanding the above facts a good demand prevailed in this market for hewn and sawn timber, and producers obtained fair prices during the shipping season. The market opened at 10 c. to $10\frac{1}{2}$ c. per cubic foot for hewn timber, and advanced until it reached $11\frac{1}{2}$ c. to 12 c. in January. From then to May there was very little change, except that in some instances $12\frac{1}{2}$ c. was paid. In June it gradually declined, reaching 8 c. to $8\frac{1}{2}$ c. in August. Sawn timber, which was in good demand, averaged during the season about 10 c. to 11 c. per cubic foot, on a basis of 40 cubic feet average. Owing to the uncertain condition of the timber markets it is almost impossible to predict the result for the season of 1884-85, but the present prospects are encouraging, and may be there will be a change for the better, and what business is done with Europe will be more profitable to the shippers. The exports of 1884 are the largest on record, and show an increase of 120 per cent. over 1883, and over 100 per cent. over the year before, which was previous to 1884 the largest on record. The shipments of hewn timber show an increase of over 1,000,000 cubic feet, while sawn also shows an increase of over 1,000,000 cubic feet; but compared with last year the largest increase is in sawn timber, as the shipments are about 1,600,000 cubic feet, against 484,000 cubic feet in 1883. The shipments in nearly every direction show a marked increase, especially to the United Kingdom of Great Britain and Ireland, as the shipments in that direction are about 1,700,000 cubic feet hewn and 1,100,000 cubic feet sawn, against 805,000 cubic feet hewn and 382,000 cubic feet sawn in 1883. The shipments to Germany and Holland show an increase in both hewn and sawn, but France exhibits a decrease in one and an increase in the other. About 100,000 cubic feet hewn have been shipped to Italy, against none the previous year.

The shipments of timber in 1884, which are valued at 500,000 dol., are a good barometer of the past year's business, and show that probably in the future Mobile will be one of the leading timber ports in the Gulf, especially if the new channel in the bay is deepened to over 20 feet at low tide.

Shipments to Foreign Ports for the past Three Years.

Hewn and Sawn.

Cubic feet in	1881–82.	1882–83.	1883–84.
To Liverpool	466,724	236,094	908,948
England	456,826	653,501	1,190,181
Ireland	128,762	136,499	201,314
Scotland	102,626	139,740	389,824
France	267,342	274,439	247,515
Germany	42,892	44,076	68,670
Holland	143,162	68,172	391,937
Italy	20,979	..	94,421
Africa	..	40,947	..
Various	45,286	59,336	155,256
Total	1,674,599	1,652,804	3,648,066
Value	197,309dol. 27c.	199,331dol. 42c.	504,979dol. 36c.

NUMBER of British and Foreign Ships cleared at Mobile with Timber and Deals for Foreign Ports in the Years

Year	Number.
1880	34
1881	69
1882	77
1883	76
1884	138

Export of Staves in 1884.

Shipments of staves on foreign account were nearly 100 per cent. more than in 1883, but prices were very low and unsatisfactory to producers. This was caused by very large stocks in Europe, which made it almost impossible for shippers to make sales even at very low figures. Over half of the exports were shipped to Great Britain, 11,711 were shipped to Barcelona, and 12,606 to Amsterdam, and the average price of shipments foreign was nearly 116 dol. per 1,200 pieces, which was over 20 dol. per thousand below last year's average value. The highest prices for good staves were 120 dol. for No. 1, and 110 dol. for No. 2. The shipments to foreign ports for the last five years were as follows :—

Year.	Quantity.	Value.
		Dol. c.
1880	121,460	13,351 21
1881	91,462	11,316 27
1882	160,138	23,783 72
1883	35,988	4,910 85
1884	70,803	6,841 00

Manufacture and Export of Shingles.

This important and growing branch of business during the past year greatly improved in volume, which shows that Mobile made shingles are not only of good quality, but low enough in price to compete successfully with those of other markets. A good freshet early in the season, by means of which a large supply of fine cypress was obtained from the swamps, enabled manufacturers to keep well stocked with timber during the entire season. Owing to the large number of shingles made during the past year, there was much competition between manufacturers, which caused prices to decline as the season advanced, and reach such a low figure that the profits were small. These low prices stimulated consumption, and caused not only a large and important business to be done with the interior of this and other Southern States, but many shipments to be made to new and important markets, as the railroads did all they could to foster the trade by giving low rates for shippers to fill all the orders received. Shipments of shingles were made from Mobile to Illinois, Tennessee, Ohio, Indiana, Wisconsin, Kentucky, Mississippi, Georgia and Florida, also coastwise by sail to Boston, Texas, and other points. The demand for machine-made shingles is improving every year, and these, whenever used, give entire satisfaction, which is, no doubt, gratifying to the manufacturers in this district, who have, during the past years, gone to much expense and trouble in adding new and improved machines to their mills.

The shipments foreign, which are principally to the West Indies, show a decrease of 142,958 shingles, while the shipments coastwise show an increase of 24,315 pieces. The falling off in shipments foreign is caused by the decrease in the trade with the West Indies, as in some of the islands the consumption of shingles is growing less, owing to the fact that iron is now used by many for roofing instead of shingles, which is a mistake for a hot climate. The difference in the summer temperature of the top rooms of a building covered with iron or shingles is, that with the former the heat will be at least 10 or 15 degrees more than in the ones that are shingled.

Nearly all the shipments coastwise were to Boston or Texas, as 972,250 shingles were shipped to the former and 807,000 to the latter.

According to the Custom-house clearances of vessels the exports were as follows for the past three years :—

	1882.		1883.		1884.	
	Shingles.	Value.	Shingles.	Value.	Shingles.	Value.
		Dol. c.		Dol. c.		Dol. c.
To foreign ports	2,437,000	13,643 75	1,823,250	8,676 90	1,680,300	6,474 25
Coastwise	806,200	2,337 40	1,764,935	5,295 00	1,789,250	4,473 12
Total	3,243,200	15,981 15	3,588,185	13,971 90	3,469,550	10,947 37

NAVAL STORES.

The influence of the general business depression of the country has been severely felt in this department of trade, and producers have experienced a very unsatisfactory and unprofitable season. In addition to low prices the spring of last year was very cold, and about two to three weeks later than the year before, resulting in serious damage by retarding the flow of gum, and causing the loss of seven or eight chippings. Rain followed in June, the most important month of the season, and kept the atmosphere so cool as to further materially check production. Spirits of turpentine opened early in the season at 38 c. per gallon, but gradually declined to 24 c. per gallon by the last of June, averaging only about 17 dol. 42 c. per barrel for the season. The demand for rosin was good, and the foreign business was the largest ever transacted at this port, the shipments being 31,056 barrels more than the year 1883, and 56,084 barrels over the season of 1882. This gratifying improvement is due in a great measure to the deepening of the harbour, and facilities afforded vessels for loading at the wharves of the port. The better grades of rosin have been principally in demand and have commanded fair prices, while the medium and lower grades were somewhat neglected and relatively cheaper. The foreign shipments have averaged about 1 dol. 55 c. per barrel.

The receipts and values of the past three years have been as follows:—

	1882.		1883.		1884.	
	Barrels.	Value.	Barrels.	Value.	Barrels.	Value.
		Dollars.		Dollars.		Dol. c.
Rosin	172,438	387,986	200,125	400,250	210,512	368,396 00
Turpentine	30,937	665,145	43,870	807,208	41,801	606,114 50
Tar	500	1,625	400	1,600	600	2,400 00
Pitch	1,500	5,250	1,500	3,750	1,200	3,000 00

Exports of Rosin for the past Three Years.

	1882.	1883.	1884.
	Barrels.	Barrels.	Barrels.
To Liverpool	5,725	12,267	5,660
London	..	..	8,370
Bristol	..	..	5,317
Cardiff	..	..	4,093
Russia	..	12,723	3,952
Hamburgh	5,564	13,012	21,751
Antwerp	..	4,025	19,717
Rotterdam	5,902	2,614	5,297
Genoa	..	..	1,213
Barcelona	..	..	500
other ports	2,922	500	327
Total	20,113	45,141	76,197
Value	55,310 dol.	91,310 dol.	118,497 dol.

No record can be obtained of the bulk of shipments of rosin from this port which have been made by coasting vessels or by railroads. At the end of the last season it is estimated that the stock of rosin on hand at the stills amounted to between 15,000 to 20,000 barrels, and 800 to 1,000 barrels of turpentine.

Imports of Salt, Foreign and Domestic.

During the past year a fair business was done in this branch of trade, and prices were lower than last season. Louisiana salt continues to gain favour with buyers, and I am informed that dealers will not pay now more than 5 c. per sack higher for Liverpool, when formerly they would pay 10 c. to 15 c. more for Liverpool than for Louisiana or Vermillion Bay salt.

The agents of the Louisiana salt mines in this port accumulated a very large stock here previous to the end of 1883, which was enough for the past year's trade of Mobile, consequently none was imported direct from the mine in 1884.

The total receipts last year, which were almost entirely from Liverpool, exhibit a decrease, but the imports direct from Liverpool show an increase of over 46 per cent.

The range of prices for coarse salt during the year 1884 were for round lots 70 c. to 90 c., and for small lots 75 c. to 95 c.; Liverpool ruled 5 c. higher. At the present time round lots of salt are selling at 70 c. to 75 c. for Louisiana, and 75 c. to 80 c. for Liverpool. The receipts for the past three years were as follows:—

	1882.	1883.	1884.
	Sacks.	Sacks.	Sacks.
From Liverpool direct	26,698	18,160	26,582
the Louisiana mine	85,677	103,580	..
other ports	7,605	6,741	8,245
Total	119,980	128,481	34,827

Coal and the Coal Mines of Alabama.

The demand for Alabama coal continues good, and the facilities for supplying the same has, during the past year, gradually increased. New mines are being opened, and the quality of the coal of many of them is equal to any, and superior to some, that have been previously worked. The new mines in Walker county, Alabama, are turning out very fine coal for both grate and steam purposes, and I am informed that these mines will before long be able to supply an unlimited demand. The bulk of this coal is shipped to New Orleans and Mobile, and again distributed from both ports. Arrangements have been made by the Mobile and Ohio Railroad, and a wharf constructed for the handling and shipment of coal, which will enable vessels to load from the trucks with ease and despatch.

The receipts of coal at Mobile from the Alabama mines show a falling off last year of nearly 8,000 tons, which was caused by the fact that no shipments of consequence were made from this port, for English coal was obtained at a rate so low that Alabama coal could not be shipped to compete. If a low rate of freight could have been obtained in time, Alabama coal could have been sent to Texas to supply a demand that was necessarily filled in 1884 from other points. The question of sending Alabama coal to the Gulf ports must be governed by the rate of freight that the article can be delivered at Mobile. Notwithstanding the loss of another year's business from the above causes, there is a prospect of some shipments being sent to Texas this season. The retail prices were 5 dol. to 8 dol. for Alabama coal per ton. By the truck, 3 dol. 75 c. to 4 dol. for steam purposes, free on board at the wharf.

The following table shows the receipts of coal at Mobile for the past five years:—

	1880.	1881.	1882.	1883.	1884.
	Tons.	Tons.	Tons.	Tons.	Tons.
Alabama	5,396	8,924	22,345	24,304	17,808
Pennsylvania	1,033	2,701	1,118	1,229	891
Total	6,429	11,625	23,463	25,533	18,699

The last United States Congress appropriated liberal amounts for the improvement of the rivers in the immediate vicinity of the coal mines of Alabama, in order that the coal may be brought down to tide-water; and in all probability other appropriations will be made by Congress until these improvements are completed and the rate of transportation lowered, for it will be almost impossible for Alabama coal to come into competition with English or Pennsylvania coal in foreign markets, however near, until that is done.

In the meantime Alabama coal is attracting much attention both in the South and in the Gulf ports, and every effort is being made to reduce the cost of its transportation from the mines to this port, so that, if possible, it may be carried with profit to the markets of Central and South America. In connection with this subject, General Burke, at present the United States Collector of Customs at this port, has published a statement showing that the object is attainable. An examination of that document, hereto annexed, will show that its contents do not admit of being abridged, and is considered of such interest as to be embodied in this report in full:—

"*The Coal Fields of Alabama.*

"In a few years we will be obliged to deal with the problem of supplying the Gulf of Mexico, the West Indies, the Isthmus of Panama, the countries of South and Central America on the Atlantic and Pacific, and the entire Pacific coast, with cheap coal. This trade, already gigantic in its proportions, is now almost entirely absorbed by Great Britain, mainly for the reason that it is delivered at a less price than coal at present mined in the United States, and the control of this enormous trade has remained for years in British hands, unchallenged. The products of the American mines are almost entirely devoted to home consumption. The great increase of domestic manufactures, of railroads, steam vessels, and in the manufacture of iron, has steadily kept pace with the production of bituminous coal in the United States, and the home demand constantly increasing will, for years to come, be fully equal to the capacity of the mines.

"This is, perhaps, one reason why the export trade in coal is so much restricted.

"There is, however, an additional one, and that is, that the expense of mining coal and delivering it at American tide-water will not justify its extensive exportation in competition with England.

"The long line of water transportation to New Orleans—constantly beset with physical difficulties—and the expensive transportation by rail and otherwise to the Atlantic seaboard are not favourable to a large or profitable exportation.

"To find a portion of our country where these geographical obstacles, distance and locality, cease to be impediments to the development of this trade with the countries named, is what is now much to be desired, in view of the construction of the Panama canal, and the immense influence that great channel of commerce must necessarily exert on our country.

"The object of the present treatise is to present facts showing that the object desired is easily attainable.

"It is only of late years that the existence of coal in Alabama has been brought into general public notice. It is a marvel to practical men how, for years, Pennsylvania sent her coal 2,000 miles to the Gulf, and England carried it over 5,000 miles of ocean to supply our Gulf and Atlantic sea-coast cities and towns, whilst within 250 miles of the tide, right within the heart of our own domains, there existed nearly 6,000 square miles of coal equal in all points of excellence to that of the Northern bituminous fields, and superior in many respects to the British article.

"Even to-day there are some who discredit the statements of those who have published their observations of this magnificent deposit. Slowly but surely the vast mineral treasures of Alabama are becoming utilised; the cheap production of iron rendered possible by the cheap production of coal has led the way to the foundation of an industry whose progress in eight years has been simply marvellous.

"The existence of the coalfields of Alabama was noticed as far back as 1834. A writer in 'Silliman's Journal,' vol. xxxi., in describing them, says: 'This State is very rich in bituminous coal of a most excellent quality. It is in every respect equal if not superior to the very best English coal. It is very heavy, burns with a good flame, and gives out much heat. It also yields the carbureted hydrogen gas in immense quantity. The veins or formation of this coal are quite extensive. It is first seen in the bed of the Black Warrior river, near Tuscaloosa, and next appears on the surface of the ground to the north-east and east of the town.'

"In 1846 Sir Charles Lyell visited Alabama and made an analysis of the coal of the Warrior field, of which he said: 'The most western of the two coalfields has been found by Professor Brumby to be no less than 90 miles long from north-east to south-west, with a breadth of from 10 to 30 miles, extending through the counties of Tuscaloosa, Walker, Jefferson, and Blount on both sides of the Warrior river and its branches. The most eastern coalfield, or that of the Cahawba, is nearly of equal length and width.'

"Notwithstanding the contiguity of this enormous body of coal to the Gulf of Mexico little effort has ever been made to clear away the obstacles that prevented its cheap transportation to the tide. As far back as 1850 coal was mined in the bed of the Warrior and along the banks of the numerous streams tributary to it above Tuscaloosa, and floated to Mobile during the winter freshets of the river, where it was used for fuel and gas purposes with the most satisfactory results. Between the coalfields and continuously navigable water exists obstructions caused by the coal measures themselves, rocky shoals with intervals and long reaches of smooth deep water.

"Before the introduction of railroads the people of that part of the country constructed rude flat boats, quarried the coal out of the dried-up beds of the creeks in summer, after the 'laying by' of their crops, and loading those frail crafts awaited the rise in the Warrior to get over the shoals. With the exception of this very primitive mode of operation there was but little coal mined in the Warrior field, and that was confined to the farmers living on the river, who carried it to Mobile not as a regular business, but as a mere incident to a venture rendered necessary to getting their cotton crops to market. The construction of the South and North Railroad and of the Alabama and Chattanooga Railroad on the eastern and southern boundaries of the Warrior field, the discovery that the coal mined on those lines could be used in the manufacture of pig iron and was pronounced excellent for steam purposes, attracted the attention of capitalists, and in a few years the iron and coal industries on those great lines of railroads increased with astonishing rapidity. Mining towns grew up at once, bringing a large increase of capital and population to the State, and the city of Birmingham sprang into existence and became in a decade an extensive manufacturing centre. In the space of 10 years the whole face of the country was changed by the construction of one line of railroad. In no part of

[359]

the country have the coal and iron industries attained such proportions in so short a space of time.

"*The Warrior Coalfield.*—This magnificent deposit of coal takes its name from the Warrior river, which, finding its source in the mountainous country bordering the coal measures of the State of Alabama on the north, runs directly through them, flowing into the Tombigbee river at Demopolis, Alabama, and thence onward into the Alabama river and the Gulf of Mexico at Mobile. For convenience it has been divided into 'The Plateau or Table-Land region' and 'The Warrior Basin,' the plateaus sinking into the basin proper.

"This basin is composed of the southern portion of Winston, all of Walker, the western part of Jefferson, and the northern part of Tuscaloosa counties. A narrow strip is drained by the Locust Fork or Little Warrior, and the wide expanse of the basin north-west by the Mulberry Fork or Big Warrior. In the plateau region is embraced the coal measures of Jackson, DeKalb, Marshal, Morgan, and Blount, the eastern part of the Fayette, the northern part of Winston, the north-eastern part of Jefferson, and the northern rim of the field in Lawrence, Franklin, and Marion counties.

"The Louisville and Nashville Railroad runs through the eastern edge of the field, the Alabama Great Southern skirting it on the south.

"The Georgia Pacific crosses it, entering it seven miles west of Birmingham, in Jefferson county, and thence through that county westwardly through Walker and Fayette counties to Columbus, Mississippi, where it connects with the Mobile and Ohio.

"This road is built and operated between Atlanta, Georgia, and the Milner coal mines, 10 miles west of Birmingham, and from Columbus, Mississippi, to the western edge of Walker county, leaving an intermediate gap through the very heart of the coal measures of about 36 miles yet to be completed.

"At the present date all coal mined in Alabama is transported by rail, the internal local demand taking the entire product, and the mines being exclusively located in the plateau region spoken of.

"The principal markets for grate coal are New Orleans, Mobile, Galveston, Montgomery, Selma, and the towns and cities in Alabama, Mississippi, and Georgia. A very considerable part is converted into coke and sold to the iron furnaces in Georgia and Alabama, and a large portion is disposed of as steam coal in New Orleans, Pensacola, and Mobile, in those cities entirely superseding foreign coal, and successfully competing with Pennsylvania and Ohio coals. The coal industry in Alabama is in its infancy, but its growth has been almost phenomenal. In 1869 there were produced but 11,000 tons, whilst in 1883 the estimated output of the mines was 1,000,000 tons, and still the product does not keep pace with the demand. The cost of mining a ton of coal in the Warrior field and delivering it on the cars does not exceed 1 dol. The rate of transportation to Mobile is 2 dol., to New Orleans 2 dol. 20 c. It is sold readily in those cities at 4 dol. per ton for steam purposes, leaving the moderate margin of 1 dol. per ton for handling, and profit to the mineowner and the dealer. In this estimate it will be seen that 50 per cent. of the cost of delivery at tide-water is that of transportation, and any means tending to reduce this item is of the greatest importance not alone to this great and increasing industry, but to the commerce of the whole world in the Gulf, West Indies, and South Atlantic.

"The productive area of the coalfields of Alabama is estimated at 5,350 square miles. Of this the Coosa field has 150 square miles, the Cahawba 200 square miles, and the Warrior 5,000 square miles. These divisions take their names from the respective rivers—Warrior, Cahaba, and Coosa—which flow through them. From those streams branch out in all directions innumerable creeks, sub-dividing the coal measures, and affording, especially in the case of the Warrior, many miles of deep water nine months in the year, thus enabling the coal to be mined far up in the interior, and floated to the main stream. Human skill could not have devised a more perfect system of internal canals or auxiliary water courses than nature has provided on the Warrior. Branching off in all directions those creeks cut their way through the measures, and in many cases flow over solid beds of coal. During the summer months this river is not navigable above Tuscaloosa. In fact it is almost at the very verge of the coal measures in Tuscaloosa that the obstructions to navigation commence, caused by the structure of the coal measures themselves. 'At this point the river changes its entire character, forming, during low water, a series of lakes and falls over rocky ledges which completely impede navigation.' In very high stages of the Warrior, and before the construction of railroads, flatboats were successfully carried to Mobile, but the dangerous passage over the shoals, and the losses incurred, caused the ultimate abandonment of that means of transportation, and at the present time the agricultural produce of the Warrior country is carried from 30 to 45 miles to the Louisville and Nashville Railroad at Birmingham, and the business of conveying coal by river entirely suspended.

"The great apparent fact connected with these Alabama coal fields is that, taking into consideration their geographical position, their physical characteristics, the superior quality of their product, and the cheapness with which they may be mined and transported, they constitute the only source of supply in the entire world which can successfully compete with British coal in the Gulf, West Indies, South America, and, on the completion of the Panama canal, on the entire Pacific coast. When the facts on which this assertion is founded are stated, the reality is startling. The coal area of Great Britain is estimated at 11,900 square miles, and that of the United States 192,000 square miles. Thus it is seen that the area of the Warrior coal field alone is nearly equal to half that of Great Britain. In 1880 Great Britain mined 133,808,000 tons of mineral coal, and the United States 59,808,398 tons.

"In 1881 Great Britain exported 18,760,000 tons of coal, to the amount of 40,265,000 dol., and the United States in the fiscal year ending June 30th, 1881, only 653,246 tons, in value 2,831,463 dol.

"The immense bulk of British exported coal is bituminous, and much the larger part of the American exportation is anthracite. During the year 1881 the exportation of bituminous coal by the United States amounted to the contemptible exhibit of 191,038 tons, in value 739,532 dol., and of this the West Indies, Mexico, Central and South America received only 78,672 tons, of the value of 328,726 dol.

"In order to show how completely this trade is controlled by Great Britain the following statement taken from the statistics of the respective countries, and from the reports of our Consuls in those countries, is appended. The exportation to these countries is particularly referred to because they will constitute the nearest and most inevitable market for our Gulf coal in the future.

Bituminous Coal Imported into—	From the United States.	From Great Britain.
	Dollars.	Dollars.
United States of Columbia	23,564	39,000
Mexico	7,326	156,000
British Guiana	..	225,000
Brazil	1,024	948,000
Uruguay	..	350,000
Argentine Republic	..	551,193
Chili	..	437,000
Bolivia	..	30,000
Peru	..	117,000
British West Indies	1,804	207,000
French West Indies	2,400	185,000
Danish West Indies	20,038	127,000
Spanish West Indies	267,541	389,000
Total	323,698	3,761,193

"The amount of American anthracite coal exported to the same countries during the same period amounted to 168,306 dol., but as the exportation of British coal to those countries was mainly bituminous coal, a fairer comparison is made by referring to that kind of coal in treating of American exportation. When we compare the total output of the British mines with those of our own, and then the ratio of our exportation with that of Great Britain, the facts are not flattering to us, but when we are confronted with the statement of the National Bureau of Statistics, that in the year ending June 30, 1881, the importation of British bituminous coal into the United States—having to pay a duty of 75 c. per ton—was 2,008,974 dol., and the exportation of American bituminous coal to all countries was only 739,532 dol., it is a subject of concern to all friends of American trade. The wooden sailing ship is fast disappearing from the seas. In 25 years the great bulk of the ocean-carrying trade will be done by large, commodious freight steamships. The completion of the Panama canal, and the possibility of the construction of the Florida ship canal, will make this matter of coal supply a subject for the consideration of the entire people of the United States. The Gulf of Mexico ought, by right, to be an American lake, but if we have to depend on foreign countries for the supply of cheap steam coal, we never can maintain our position as a great maritime and commercial nation in those waters.

"The proposition is self-evident on the palpable facts now existing that unless a cheaper source of supply is had in this country, so as to render us entirely independent of both Great Britain and Australia on the Atlantic and Pacific, we shall see England maintaining the control of the Isthmus of Panama as absolutely as she now does that of Suez.

"*Comparison of Distances.*—The distance from Mobile to Aspinwall is 1,310 miles, and from Newcastle, England (a principal exporting point for steam coal) 5,340 miles. The American ship loading at Mobile can make at least three voyages and deliver three cargoes whilst the British vessel is delivering but one, and has returned to her home port to reload. The case stands better with the West Indies and Mexico, which countries are at our doors. With Alabama coal delivered at Mobile at 2 dol. per ton, we would see one of the proudest of American commercial triumphs. Within the past year steam coal sold at Newport, England, at 12s. 6d. per ton, or 3 dol. American money. Even with the price of British coal as low as Alabama we still would have the preponderating advantage of distance. But in the matter of cost at tide water it is absolutely certain that with the water-ways to the Gulf of Mexico open to navigation, coal may be delivered at the tide at a lower price than in Great Britain.

"*Mining Comparisons.*—The great advantage possessed by the coals in the Warrior basin is the ease with which they may be mined. Practically, they may be in many places shovelled from the river bank into the coal barges, the inclination of the seams rarely ever exceeding 3°.

"In 1850 Professor Tuomy, the State Geologist, wrote of the coal in the Warrior basin: 'For some years to come a considerable quantity of coal will be procured in the beds of the streams, or where it is but loosely covered by loose, superficial beds, and, in either case, without the investment of much capital. The slight inclination of the beds, and the physical features of the country, will always tend to lessen the expense of mining operations on the Warrior.' (Geological Report, 1850.) During a casual examination of the Warrior basin, made in the summer of 1883, the writer was amazed at the enormous developments of coal. It could be seen in the beds of the rivers and creeks, seam over seam, on the steep banks of the Warrior, in many places eight feet in thickness, and rarely under 28 inches. Truly they are entitled to the appellation of coal fields, for in many places the superficial covering consists of a few feet of clay and shale, and the coal may be literally dug from the earth.

"Regarding the character of the seams on the Mulberry Branch of the Warrior, Professor Tuomy says: 'A very remarkable change takes place in the character of the coal on this branch of the Warrior. It becomes very much cleaner and harder. Although it breaks into small pieces, it rarely produces much slack, and as it comes from the bed it resembles screened coal. This, of all the coal in the State, will best bare transportation, on account of its superior hardness.'

"He then proceeds to give the measurements of 20 outcrops of different seams, measuring in thickness of seams from three to eight feet.

"Of one of those seams he says:

"'On Lost creek some fine exposures occur near the point where the Jasper road crosses it. They are only seen, however, in the bed of the creek. A section of the principal bed is as follows:—

		Inches.
Coal	..	10
Slate	..	14
Coal	..	48

"'There are at least four other beds superimposed on this, which appear higher up the stream. One is remarkable for having a seam of cannel coal on the top of the common coal. The depth of the water prevented me making an examination of this valuable bed, but it is interesting to know that cannel coal exists in the State, and I have no doubt that future explorations will bring thicker seams to our knowledge.

"'These sections will give a fairer view of the Warrior coal field than a whole chapter of description. They are, however, limited to a small portion of the entire area, but it is a part that must always command attention on account of its vicinity to the river.

"Notwithstanding the definite character and value of the information presented here no one feels more sensibly than I do how very inadequately it represents this magnificent formation.'*—(Geological Report, 1850.)

"Thus wrote this accomplished geologist and scientific scholar thirty-three years ago. His luminous mind grasped the idea of controlling with these splendid coal fields the supply of coal to the Gulf countries, and he was the first to give accurate information with a view of advancing this great commercial enterprise.

"The explorations of the field made since his day have more than confirmed his prediction, for there are already mined in the Warrior plateau no less than seven separate seams of coal, varying in thickness from three to six feet, and in the thickness of the coal measures of 2,000 feet, thirty-nine seams of coal have been found.

"In a more recent report on the portion of the Warrior basin referred to, Prof. Stubbs (Professor of Mineralogy and Chemistry in the Agricultural College of Alabama) says:—

"'Heading Lost creek we descended on its right bank till opposite Holly Grove—stopping on West Fork to examine the coal outcrops already mentioned. Near Holly Grove, on Lost creek, are the famous Baker Beds, separated from each other by about 10 feet, the lower being over three feet and the upper nearly two feet. These beds have been worked in the past, and are said to have yielded coal of very fine quality. The relative position of these seams, and their thicknesses, would indicate a continuation of the seams mentioned above. If they are, then we would have them dipping to the east and south, with rate of dip and rate of fall of stream about equal. This would indicate that the centre of our basin was east of Holly Grove. Along the bottom of Lost creek in this vicinity, coal is constantly exposed, varying in thickness from two to three feet. At Guttery's canoe hole, on Dr. Miller's land and other places, the Baker seams occur. There is coal in the well of Dr. Hendon at Holly Grove. Passing on down Lost creek we find coal outcropping at Boschill and Rutledge's. At the intersection of Cane and Lost creeks, numerous outcrops of great thickness and excellent quality occur. Coal has been mined from bed of Cane creek on lands of David Cobb, and is pronounced by Prof. Smith as a 'hard, bright coal, with sufficient bony coal to make it a fine stocking coal, but not enough to injure it as a fuel.' Near Williams' mill on Lost creek, a seam appears in a small ravine, some distance above level of the creek. Lower down the creek, below the mouth of Wolfe, a seam of coal appears in many places, besides forming the bed of the river for several miles. At Mrs. Price's, on Falls branch, it it three feet thick. A shaft was once sunk on left bank of Lost creek near this place, and considerable quantities of coal taken therefrom. This same seam occurs in several places on Fanny's branch and on the east side of the Warrior river in Brake's bend. West of the river, at Vanhoose's mine, it has been profitably mined in ante bellum times.

"'Baker's creek, which empties into the Warrior river several miles above Lost and on same side, is noted for the many outcrops of coal near its headwaters. A seam three to four feet thick of fine working and shipping qualities has been found on lands of Mrs. Bailey, Mr. Key, Mr. Tom Bradley, Mr. Jno. Gaines, Mount Zion church and others. This is the same seam spoken of as the David Cobb's seam on Lost creek, and occurs everywhere in south-west part T. 15, R. 7, upon the tributaries of Lost and Baker creeks. Nor does this seam stop

---

* This magnificent property, from which coal was largely mined in 1855 and up to 1860 is situated on the western bank of the Warrior, and is now owned by the Gulf Coal and Coke Company of Mobile.

here—but going north-east it crops out as Mount Carmel coal bed of over four feet thickness at head of Frog Ague creek and in adjoining section on Big Cane creek of same thickness. It occurs also on the Baugh or Dent bend. Across the river and below Frog Ague, are fine outcrops of coal on Burnt Cane and House creeks.'

"As to quantity, therefore, there is the most abundant testimony to show that there are at least seven workable seams of coal in the Warrior field superimposed one on the other. That towards the basin of the Warrior, that part adjacent to the river, the seams are thicker and almost horizontal. There remains but one subject of investigation, and that is as to the quality of the coal. Here again the testimony is abundant, both practical and scientific.

"The following analyses of Virginia and Alabama coals was made by Sir Charles Lyell:

	Carbon.	Volatile Matter.	Ashes.
Virginia:			
Clover Hill	76·49	13·64	9·87
Black Heath	80·38	10·27	9·35
Deep Run	82·20	10·74	6·36
Powells	86·54	8·76	4·70
Alabama	80·96	12·96	6·08

"The Virginia coals are regarded as the best bituminous coals in the United States.

"From a 'Report of Experiments made on the Evaporative Power and other Qualities of Coals,' made in 1843, by the Navy Department of the United States (Ex. Doc., Vol. 6, 1843), the following results were had in reference to other coals, which are here referred to, to show the superior character of Alabama coal:—

	Carbon.	Volatile Matter.	Ashes.
Liverpool (Eng.)	54·90	39·96	4·62
Newcastle (Eng.)	57·00	35·83	5·40
Scotch	48·81	39·19	9·34
Pittsburg (Pa.)	54·93	36·76	7·07
Carrollton (Ind.)	58·44	33·99	4·97
Cumberland (Md.)	74·53	12·67	10·34

"In this list Cumberland coal stands highest in carbon, but when compared with Sir Charles Lyell's analyses of Alabama coal it is found to be lower in carbon, equal in volatile matter and higher in ash.

"The most accurate and practical test ever made of Alabama coals was made by the Louisville and Nashville Railroad in 1878 with a stationary boiler, to ascertain their evaporative value. Taking Pittsburg as a standard this shows the relative comparative value of the coals used on that railroad.

	Pounds of water evaporated by 1 lb. of fuel.	Per cent. of ash.	Relative evaporative value.
Pittsburgh coal, run of the mine	8·16	13	100
Warrior coal run of the mine	8·15	16	99·9
Pine Hill, block coal (Ky.)	7·63	10 6-100	93·5
Livingston, run of the mine	7·59	19 8-100	93·0
Pittsburgh, not screened	7·44	13	91·0
Guthrie, nut coal (Ky.)	7·00	22	85·7
Pine Hill, run of the mines (Ky.)	6·96	18	85·3
Pender mines, run of the mines, No. 1	6·94	20 5-100	85·0
Pine Hill, run of the mines, No. 2	6·77	16	82·9
New Castle, run of the mines (Ala.)	6·58	22	80·6
Saint Charles, run of the mines (Ky.)	6·51	21 3-100	79·8
Saint Charles, nut coal (Ky.)	6·47	17	79·3
Cahawba, slack (Ala.)	6·09	27	74·6
Fish point, run of the mine (Ky.)	7·18	19 6-100	88·0
Cahawba black-shale bed (Ala.)	7·09	12 5-100	86·0
Sewanee, select (Tenn.)	6·57	8	80·5

"For the coking character of the Black Warrior coals, the subjoined analysis of the best, both from this field and the Cahawba, are given:—

	Water.	Bitumen.	Fixed carbon.	Ash.	Sulphur.
Warrior coal	16	25·09	72·14	2·27	·34
Cahawba	17	25·97	70·10	3·68	·17

"It will be seen from the foregoing statement that the value of Warrior coal, as a generator of steam, is but a trifle lower than Pittsburgh, and almost equal to it. It will also be borne in mind that it came from a new mine on the very edge or rim of the Warrior plateau.

"'*Gas Coal.*—The value of coal for the production of gas, other things being equal, will depend upon the amount of hydrogen they contain.' In the five following specimens Sir Charles Lyell found the hydrogen to stand thus:

Clover Hill (Va.)		5·23
Black Heath "		4·08
Deep Run "		4·77
Powells "		4·23
Alabama		5·13

"There are also highly bituminous coals present among the beds belonging to the Warrior basin, which, being the best for gas purposes, analyses of two of them are here given:

	Bituminous combustible matter.	Fixed carbon.	Ash.	Water.	Sulphur.
No. 1	40·60	54·07	3·09	1·18	1·06
No. 2	34·49	60·09	4·32	·93	·17

"In 1874 a cargo of Alabama coal was shipped to Havana and sold to the Gas Company there. We are permitted to make use of and extract from the letter received after it had been tested.

"'Havana, 13 March, 1874.

"'Peter Knowles, Esq.

"'Dear Sir,—As you are aware, we sold the cargo of Alabama coal, ex. schooner "Evaline," to the gas company, at 9 dols. Spanish gold that they might fairly test the same.

"'They got the following results:
    Montevallo gives 8,740 feet of gas.
    Helena   „   8,743 „   „
    Newcastle „   8,781 „   „ and 1,621 lbs. of coke.
The latter will suit them best as it gives about 200 lbs. per ton more coke than Liverpool.

"'Yours, very truly,
"'Lawton Bros.'"

"The value of coal, as ordinary fuel, is derived from the carbon and hydrogen. Now these analyses in this relation settle the position of Alabama coal.

"(Prof. Tuomy, Geo. Rep. Ala., 1859.)

"'Chemical analyses of coals serve only for comparison, the physical structure being of at least equal importance. The chemist determines the materials which make up the coal, but not the manner in which the constituents are arranged. The heating power is largely dependant upon physical structure, and can only be determined by actual experiment. While the analyses given above place these coals on a par with the best bituminous coals of this country, their physical properties, it is believed, will give to them a very prominent position in the markets of the world.'"—(Prof Stubbs.)

"But the practical value of Alabama steam coal does not rest on the foregoing statements. For the past five years the Government of the United States has been using Warrior coal for steam purposes on its revenue cutters, coast survey vessels, lighthouse tenders and engineer boats in the Gulf. The engineer officers of the Revenue Marine, gentlemen thoroughly skilled in their profession and familiar with the steaming qualities of coals furnished the revenue cutters all over the country, bear the very highest testimony to the quality of the Alabama coal.

"We are permitted to use the following statement, made by Chief Engineer Magee of the United State Revenue Steamer 'McLane,' in corroboration of the foregoing:—

"'United States Revenue Marine, Str. "Louis McLane,"
"'Mobile, Ala., January 29, 1884.

"'Gen. Burke, Collector of Customs,
"'Mobile, Ala.,

"'Sir,—Agreeable to your request, asking for a practical statement of Alabama coals as compared with English coals for steaming purposes, I can say that from an experience of nearly twenty years I have not found an English or other foreign coal that would compare with the coal of the Warrior mine of Alabama. This coal is a good free burner with natural draft; is free from clinker, and has all the qualities of an excellent steaming coal.

"'Very respectfully,
"'Samuel H. Magee,
"'Engineer in Charge.'"

"From all sources come the testimony that, for the production of steam, the soft coal of the Warrior is superior to Welsh steam coal, and for the purposes of the household and the production of gas the compact harder coals of the Warrior basin are unexcelled.

"*Economic Relations.*—From the foregoing statements it is shown that the quantity and quality at Alabama coal are all that can be desired.

"The next subject we shall consider is that of the supply at tide water, in order to build up a great national industry in a section of the country where it is required as an absolute necessity.

"'*National Importance of the work of Improvement.*—The advantage to Alabama of a navigable river which shall traverse the most important coal field in the State, and which shall afford cheap transportation to the Gulf, not only for the coal but also of the other products of the country, cannot be overestimated. A moment's reflection will show that however great may be the benefit to the State of this work of improvement, the advantages to the national government will not be less.

"'An unfailing supply of good and cheap coal at the Gulf is of the first importance to the Navy. The supply of coal has hitherto come by the Ohio river. During the winter months, as is well known, traffic upon that river is often interrupted by ice, and we have lately seen that even during the summer months a coal famine may be experienced in the Lower Mississippi and Gulf regions because of low water in the Ohio.'

"'During the time that the Ohio river is closed by ice, the Warrior would be in its best condition for transporting coal, and there is no likelihood that transportation on this river will ever be interrupted by reason of low water, for during the unprecedented drought of the past summer (1879) there was always a sufficiency of water in the Warrior, had it been provided with locks and dams, to have furnished uninterrupted transportation for the coal barges.'—(Report U. S. Engineer Warrior improvement, 1880.)

"In this connection the national character of this enterprise was recognised as far back as 1828, under the administration of President Jackson, for in that year Congress declared that 'the Tennessee, Coosa, Cahawba and Black Warrior rivers, within the State of Alabama, shall be for ever free from toll for all property belonging to the United States, and for all persons in their service, and for all citizens of the United States, except as to such tolls as may be allowed by by Act of Congress;' and this law may now be found under title 'Rivers and Harbours.'—(Sec. 5244, Revised Statutes United States.)

"In 1836 sales of the public lands were made in Alabama, out of which a fund was created for the improvement of those rivers, and some of the money so raised was expended on the Warrior. The improvements were, however, of such a character as to be of little value. 'The plan appears to be good but the execution was defective,' says Prof. Tuomy. 'The jetties were in many cases not connected with the banks, and not reaching above high water, became dangerous submerged islands to boats coming down at high water. Later improvements were altogether conducted with the view to the removal of obstructions to high water navigation, and consequently it became necessary to undo in many cases what had been done at considerable expense.'

"These facts are mentioned to show that those rivers, and especially the Warrior, were the subjects of national solicitude fifty-five years ago. The longheaded men of those days saw the splendid future before this magnificent coal field and recognised the fact by declaring that the streams that led into it should be for ever free to all citizens of the

United States, great national coal channels, or highways, which at some day would be called to play a most important part in the prosperity and commercial purposes of the country. Nor are we now without the most convincing proofs of their wisdom, for this may be seen from the large saving made by the United States Government at the Gulf ports since the introduction of Alabama coal. As late as 1878 the Government paid for the coal furnished its vessels at the Gulf ports from 8 dol. to 12 dol. per ton. To-day coal is furnished at the rate of 3 dol. 75 c. per ton of 2,000 lbs. at Mobile, and the consequent saving to the Government has been equal to 40,000 dol. in three years. This annual saving is equal to a sum sufficient to pay the annual interest on the money necessary to render the Warrior navigable to coal barges nine months in the year at the rate the Government pays for money.

"Now, the price of coal being 3 dol. 75 c., and the cost of railroad transportation being 2 dol of that amount, it is quite evident that unless a cheaper means of transportation be provided, this great commercial treasure will remain as it is, supplying only the home demand of those localities adjacent to the field. The cost of opening the Warrior to navigation will, in a few years, pay for itself in furnishing to the Government coal at 1 dol. 50 c. per ton less than it now pays, and when these figures are applied to the vast commerce of the Gulf the subject is one of incalculable importance.

"In 1874 Congress voted a small appropriation for the survey and examination of the Warrior, and in 1875 the report of that examination, conducted by an eminent engineer under the direction of Maj. A. N. Damrell (U. S. Engineer Corps), was presented to Congress.

"Again in 1879 another examination and survey was authorised by Congress, and the report of Professor Eugene A. Smith, the accomplished State geologist, was the result. This report, which has done so much towards bringing the immense mineral resources of the Warrior basin to public notice, was made in 1880.

"The report shows that the river can be improved by the use of locks and dams at an estimated cost respectively of 400,553 dol., 760,000 dol. and 1,200,000 dol. depending on the permanency and character of the work to be done. The estimated cost of the improvement, as presented by the report of Colonel Horace Harding in 1875, is 431,000 dol.

"It may be thought by some that the expense of mining on the Warrior river is placed at too low an estimate judging from the expense of mining in other parts of the country and in England and Europe, but when it is considered that the mining in those countries is all done thousands of feet deep in the bowels of the earth and in a manner involving immense cost and mechanical effort it is not to be wondered at. Some of the British shafts are 2,500 feet deep and the Kuttenberger pit in Bohemia had to be abandoned on account of the high temperature at a depth of 3,778 feet.

"For years to come millions of tons of coal may be mined in the Warrior basin by drift mining and by the means of slopes with a very gentle inclination, and delivered to barges at the very mouth of the mine.

"At the present time coal is lower than ever known before, as appears from the following list of prices taken from the 'Coal Trade Journal' of January 2nd, 1884.

"'*Wholesale Prices of Bituminous Coal.*—The following is a recapitulation of the nominal prices current for this variety of coal:—

	Dol. c.	Dol. c.
Cumberland, at Baltimore	3 00 at N. Y.	4 25
Cumberland, at Georgetown	3 00 ,, ,,	4 25
Clearfield, at Baltimore	3 00 ,, ,,	4 25
Clearfield, at Philadelphia	3 50 ,, ,,	4 25
Clearfield, at South Amboy	4 00 ,, ,,	4 25
Westmoreland and Penn Gas, South Amboy	4 50 ,, ,,	4 75
Youghiogheny, Scotts, at Baltimore	3 60 ,, ,,	4 75
Montauk Gas, at Baltimore	3 50 ,, ,,	4 75
Cannelton Gas Cannel, at Newport News	8 50 ,, ,,	9 50
Provincial Gas and Steam coal	— ,, ,,	3 75
Konawha Gas, at Newport News, Va.	3 50 ,, ,,	4 75

"And yet it is confidently expected that, with water transportation on the Warrior and the Cahaba unimpeded to the Gulf, the price of steam coal can, by utilising the abundant sources of American economical methods, be reduced to 2 dol. per ton at Mobile. Arrived at this port there are unrivalled facilities for foreign exportation. Here is one of the finest harbours in the world, perfectly land-locked, with 24 feet of water on the outer bar at low tide. The construction of the ship channel, which admits vessels drawing 17 feet of water to come to the city wharves, and which it is expected will be continued until the depth of 22 feet shall have been obtained, will afford opportunities to coal steamers of the largest size and enable those engaged in the trade to export coal to the Gulf and South America at prices that will virtually exclude foreign coal from those markets.

"The presentation of these views at this time is to draw public attention to the national character of this work. The section of the Revised Statutes of the United States referred to absolutely confines the jurisdiction of the subject to Congress, for no improvement with a view to remunerative profit can be made without its express sanction. It is a very remarkable fact that for fifty-five years little or no effort commensurate with the importance of the subject has been made to inform the country on this singular provision of the law by which Congress has assumed absolute control of those Alabama coal streams. It was only when in the codification of the United States laws it became incorporated as a section of the Revised Statutes that the important fact was noticed. When Congress declared them for ever 'toll free' for all property of the United States, and to all citizens of the United States, it virtually undertook to nationalise them, and as they require improvement in order to render them navigable streams, the conclusion is inevitable that Congress had intended to give effect to this provision of the law and appropriate sufficient to accomplish that which it absolutely prohibits to private enterprise. Any other construction would be senseless, since it would be for ever closing to public use avenues to great wealth which by law were declared to be the property of the whole people of America. It is therefore due to the commercial interests of the country at large, to our just desire to maintain our ascendency in the Gulf of Mexico and on the Isthmus of Panama, to the people of Alabama, that the highways to the magnificent coal fields, the Warrior and Cahawba, should be at once cleared of obstructions to navigation. When this entire subject is gone over and properly considered, it will be found second in importance only to the improvement of the Mississippi river, and in point of economy will reimburse the Government in a few years for the comparatively trifling outlay rendered necessary to complete an undertaking so full of wealth to the country and so valuable an adjunct to our national power and progress.

"In a recent article on 'Iron Shipbuilding in Alabama' the 'New Orleans Times-Democrat' has the following, which on account of its terseness and perspicuity we take the liberty of reproducing here:—

"'*Iron Shipbuilding in Alabama.*—A justly celebrated Southern writer has lately called the attention of Northern capitalists to the promising field for an investment of capital in the coal and iron deposits of Alabama.

"'It is more than probable that the vast extent and the actual value of these important Southern material resources are as yet but feebly comprehended by the general American public. While the Pennsylvania coal and iron deposits are justly celebrated throughout the world for their extent and productiveness, the Alabama mines possess a vast advantage over the former from the fact that the coal and iron deposits are juxtaposited, for the fuel for the working of the iron ore is contiguous to the deposits of the latter. As a consequence, the production of pig iron has already become a prominent Southern industry, while the foundries of the State of Alabama can to-day produce it at the rate of 6 dol. per ton cheaper than it can be made in Pennsylvania.

"'In the latter State this industry, thanks to the protective system that has fostered its infancy and strengthened its growth, is on a most promising footing. The Alabama iron mills, fostered by a few more years of similar protection, will undoubtedly eclipse their Northern rivals, while that Gulf State is destined to take a prominent place among the iron and coal producing regions of the world.

"'While the English iron makers and coal miners are compelled to descend deep into the bowels of the earth to extract the precious deposits, both iron and coal, to an almost inexhaustible extent, are found on the very surface of the ground, in paying quantity and quality, in many localities in Alabama. It has been estimated that Alabama coal can be profitably mined at from 10 c. to 1 dol. per ton. Coal from these deposits is daily hauled by rail to Central Texas, while experts have asserted that it can be placed in New Orleans and retailed at 2 dol. 50c. per ton.

"'As iron and coal exist in juxtaposition in many localities in Alabama, it cannot be a matter of surprise if the iron workers of the State can make pig iron at 6 dol. per ton cheaper than it can be produced in any other part of the Union. If pig iron can be made so cheap there is no reason why a great economy in the production of iron manufactures of all kinds cannot also be obtained, and the rolling mills and foundries of the Gulf State be made to vie with, if not to excel, their rivals of the North, both in cheapness of production and the quality of manufacture. If this premise be true we cannot see why Alabama, with it extended and well-protected sea coast, and its fairly deep water ports, should not, at some time in the near future, build all the iron ships requisite for the freightage of American imports to the markets of the world.

"'We will suppose, for instance, that as the Alabama production of the raw material—pig iron—is 6 dol. per ton cheaper than it is in Pennsylvania, and the preparation of the metal for shipbuilding purposes costs no more in the Alabama mills than in those of Pennsylvania, an iron ship of 3,000 tons can be built at Mobile 10,800 dol. cheaper than on the Delaware; that is, in case the tariff for wages for workmen, &c., rules the same in each locality. The weight of iron used in the construction of a 3,000-ton ship is about 1,800 tons. This, at 6 dol. per ton economy in the production of pig iron, will make 10,800 dol., as above stated.

"'Thus, when the vast coal and iron resources of Alabama become duly appreciated, and ample capital seeks investment in their development, there is no reason why, with cheaper material and equality on other points, the Gulf State should not become the principal iron ship-building locality of the Republic.'"

The Fish and Oyster Trade.

The fish trade of this port was well maintained during the past year, and the superiority of Mobile fish has been recognised even by competing markets. Large shipments were made to New Orleans, Pensacola, Charleston, Atlanta, and other points in the interior, and at times dealers found it difficult to supply the demand. The oyster business, generally so good, was somewhat interfered with last winter by unprecedented cold and bad weather; still the trade was brisk and active, and good profits were realised. The supply continues equal to the demand. The estimated trade of the past three years was as follows:—

	1882.	1883.	1884.
	Dollars.	Dollars.	Dollars.
Value of fish exported	46,500	95,000	100,000
Oysters—plants	30,000	50,000	40,000
" reefers	81,000	100,000	75,000
Total	157,500	245,000	215,000

Production of Vegetables in the Vicinity of Mobile.

This industry has not yet received the attention or assumed the proportions which its value and importance should command, but probably the day is not far distant when the advantages of this district for the raising of early vegetables for the Northern and Western markets will be fully realised, and the pine lands of Mobile County be made profitable. The excellent water and mild climate of this district for eight months of the year, the average healthy condition of the farm hands, and the results of the limited amount of truck farming pursued during the past few years, clearly demonstrate what profits can be derived from the industry. The present small area under cultivation is in the immediate vicinity of the city, and there are 600,000 to 700,000 acres more of just such lands in the county of Mobile awaiting cultivation. An increased acreage was planted in vegetables the past year, and good crops were made, except of cabbages, which were seriously damaged by most unusual and severe weather in January—the mercury having fallen lower than for over forty years in this county—and a general replanting was necessitated, resulting in a very short yield as compared with former seasons. The large production of beans, peas, and tomatoes in a measure counterbalanced the partial loss of the cabbage crop. Prices were somewhat affected by the occurrence of financial disturbances throughout the country during the shipping season, and producers were not as well remunerated as they would have been under more favourable circumstances. The future possibility of this trade cannot be estimated, but it is too valuable to be kept much longer within its present circumscribed limits. The railroads, with characteristic enterprise, have furnished excellent shipping facilities, and there were no complaints of delays or detentions.

The shipments from Mobile for the past three years, with $33\frac{1}{3}$ per cent. added for shipments from other stations in the county by the railroads, were as follows:—

Articles.		1882. Quantity.	1882. Value.	1883. Quantity.	1883. Value.	1884. Quantity.	1884. Value.
			Dol. c.		Dol. c.		Dol. c.
Cabbages	Crates	22,119	99,535 50	27,452	82,356 00	10,212	43,401 00
Potatoes	Barrels	30,769	138,460 50	33,571	75,534 75	34,704	69,048 00
Beans	Boxes	10,910	10,910 00	16,015	20,008 50	35,534	26,650 50
Peas	,,	7,821	7,821 00	6,427	8,033 75	13,062	13,062 00
Turnips	Crates	...	...	...	...	1,178	1,767 00
Cucumbers	Barrels	238	1,071 00	132	396 00	928	2,552 00
Tomatoes	Boxes	32,377	14,569 65	17,693	7,077 20	40,052	16,020 50
Water melons		18,700	2,505 00	8,770	1,315 50	20,651	3,097 65
Various	Packages	116	223 00	132	396 00	978	2,934 00
			275,395 65		195,117 70		178,532 95
Add shipments from country, 33⅓ per cent.	...	...	91,798 55	...	65,039 23	...	59,510 75
Total	...	...	367,194 20	...	260,156 93	...	238,043 70

WOOL.

This branch of trade has been very depressed and unsatisfactory throughout the United States during the past year. The large importation of woollen goods, general business depression, and financial disturbances seriously interfered with the manufacturing interests of the South, and many mills were compelled to suspend operations entirely. Consequently prices were very unsatisfactory to wool growers, and shipments to this market much curtailed. Good stocks are held back and will not be sent to market until better prices are offered. The facilities of this market have steadily improved during the past few years, and the moderate rates of transportation have enabled buyers to pay generally better prices than other southern markets. The season opened in this market at 24½ c. per lb. for unwashed wool and declined, reaching 17 c. to 18 c. in July, which was the lowest price of the season. From then to September there was no change in prices. The prices throughout the past year were as follows:—Washed, 23 c. and 28 c. per lb.; unwashed, 17 c. to 24 c.; barry, 6 c. to 15 c. Receipts and values for the past four years were as follows:—

	Receipts.	Value.
	lbs.	Dol. c.
1881	330,199	95,755 10
1882	343,440	89,294 40
1883	400,000	94,000 00
1884	245,875	50,404 37

COMPARATIVE Statement of Imports of the following Articles into Mobile for the Past Three Years.

Articles.	Measure.	Quantity in 1882.	Quantity in 1883.	Quantity in 1884.
Bacon	Hogsheads	8,877	9,170	7,444
Bagging	Pieces	16,881	27,808	16,645
Bran	Sacks	45,924	48,401	52,491
Butter	Kegs	10,837	9,203	9,688
Candles	Boxes	2,705	1,892	1,621
Cheese	,,	7,434	7,347	3,182
Coffee	Sacks	22,266	24,183	20,437
Coal	Tons	23,463	25,533	18,699
Cotton	Bales	265,040	314,973	265,040
Fertilisers	Sacks	61,778	84,528	95,654
Flour	Barrels	84,975	91,582	97,407
Hay	Bales	24,666	31,853	34,039
Indian corn	Sacks	257,965	217,922	368,406
Iron ties	Bundles	35,865	52,419	37,489
Lard	Tierces	3,463	2,879	2,785
Lime	Barrels	4,340	6,136	4,312
Molasses	,,	6,211	4,062	4,361
Oats	Sacks	67,657	61,662	92,416
Pork	Barrels	2,527	3,588	2,008
Potatoes	,,	17,077	17,970	20,950
Rice	Tierces	3,722	4,361	4,478
Salt	Sacks	119,980	128,481	34,827
Soap	Boxes	22,009	27,008	24,445
Sugar	Hogsheads	4,334	3,184	3,702
Tobacco	Boxes	17,647	19,634	18,971
Whiskey	Barrels	6,732	6,247	5,631
Wool	Pounds	343,440	400,000	245,875

MOBILE.

PRINCIPAL Articles Exported from Mobile to Foreign Ports during the past Three Years, with their Measure, Quantity, and Value.

Articles.	Measure.	1882. Quantity.	1882. Value. Currency.	1882. Value. Sterling, at 4 dol. 80 c. per £.	1883. Quantity.	1883. Value. Currency.	1883. Value. Sterling at 4 dol. 80 c. per £.	1884. Quantity.	1884. Value. Currency.	1884. Value. Sterling, at 4 dol. per £.
Cotton	Bales	46,366	Dol. c. 2,586,157 26	£ s. d. 538,883 15 3	45,290	Dol. c. 2,226,833 07	£ s. d. 472,256 18 9	57,537	Dol. c. 2,964,841 70	£ s. d. 447,992 4 2
Lumber	Super. feet	15,847,128	252,021 77	57,504 10 8	16,729,838	239,800 15	49,958 7 3	17,102,102	228,144 80	47,451 7 1
Rosin	Barrels	20,113	55,310 00	11,522 18 4	45,141	91,310 00	19,022 18 4	76,197	118,497 00	24,635 10 1
Shingles	Pieces	2,437,000	13,643 75	2,842 8 11	1,823,250	8,676 90	1,807 13 4	1,680,300	6,474 25	1,346 0 0
Oak staves	,,	160,138	23,783 72	4,954 18 10	35,988	4,910 85	1,023 1 10	70,803	6,841 10	1,422 4 11
Timber	Cubic feet	1,671,599	197,309 27	41,406 1 0	1,652,804	199,331 42	41,527 7 7	3,810,714	504,979 36	104,985 6 3
Other articles	...	...	21,534 33	4,487 3 0	...	8,406 00	1,751 5 0	...	16,643 54	3,460 3 11
Total	...	...	3,149,760 10	656,301 16 0	...	2,779,268 39	587,347 12 1	...	3,846,421 65	631,272 16 5

[359]

UNITED STATES.

PRODUCTIONS of Alabama Shipped from Mobile, Coastwise or by Railroad, into the Interior of the United States during the past Three Years.

Articles.	Measure.	1882. Quantity.	1882. Currency. Dol. c.	1882. Sterling, at 4 dol. 80 c. per £. £ s. d.	1883. Quantity.	1883. Currency. Dol. c.	1883. Sterling, at 4 dol. 80 c. per £. £ s. d.	1884. Quantity.	1884. Currency. Dol. c.	1884. Sterling, at 4 dol. 81 c. per £. £ s. d.
Cotton	Bales	223,755	12,082,770 00	2,517,243 15 0	266,057	13,475,752 91	2,708,333 6 8	204,795	10,172,167 65	2,114,795 5 5
Pitch pine lumber	Super. feet	16,389,009	259,071 77	53,973 5 8	10,024,005	160,384 00	33,413 6 8	5,419,989	80,436 00	16,722 13 2
Rosin	Barrels	134,325	302,231 25	62,964 19 10	154,984	309,968 00	64,576 13 4	144,315	249,899 00	51,954 1 1
Turpentine	,,	30,937	665,145 00	138,571 17 6	43,870	807,208 00	168,168 6 8	41,801	606,114 50	126,011 6 7
Cypress shingles	Pieces	806,200	3,224 00	671 13 4	1,764,935	6,177 27	1,287 7 9	1,789,250	5,358 00	1,113 18 7
Vegetables	Packages	123,050	367,194 20	76,498 15 10	110,192	260,156 93	54,199 7 2	157,299	238,043 70	49,489 6 8
Wool	Pounds	318,440	82,794 40	17,248 16 8	400,000	94,000 00	19,583 6 8	245,875	50,404 37	10,479 1 6
Fish and oysters	Barrels	...	157,500 00	32,812 10 8	...	245,000 00	51,041 13 4	...	215,000 00	44,698 10 11
Total		...	13,919,930 62	2,899,985 13 10	...	15,358,648 11	3,100,603 8 3	...	11,617,423 22	2,415,264 3 11

BRITISH and Foreign Shipping arriving at the Port of Mobile in 1883; also the Number of Vessels and Tonnage arriving Coastwise.

Nationality.	Number of Vessels.	Tonnage.	Crews.	Value of Cargoes.
				£ s. d.
British	49	32,114	628	20,905 19 2
American	41	7,942	306	
Swedish and Norwegian	45	29,866	598	
Austrian	5	3,445	66	
Russian	4	1,847	39	
Italian	4	1,351	30	
French	3	1,453	34	59,830 0 0
German	3	1,486	29	
Spanish	3	961	28	
Mexican	2	1,416	26	
Netherlands	1	360	12	
Argentine Republic	1	490	10	
Total from foreign ports	161	82,531	1,806	80,735 19 2
,, American coasting	133	40,011	1,336	..
Total	294	122,542	3,142	80,735 19 2

BRITISH and Foreign Shipping departing from the Port of Mobile in 1883; also the Number of Vessels and Tonnage departing Coastwise.

Nationality.	Number of Vessels.	Tonnage.	Crews.	Value of Cargoes.
				£ s. d.
British	48	29,667	584	511,364 19 3
American	51	10,127	391	24,089 19 5
Swedish and Norwegian	40	26,480	522	54,445 8 4
Austrian	6	3,548	70	34,622 1 11
Russian	2	947	20	1,232 14 0
Italian	4	1,821	42	5,980 15 7
French	5	3,034	66	5,716 17 1
German	3	1,486	29	11,562 13 10
Spanish	6	1,563	46	13,554 18 7
Mexican	2	1,416	26	2,233 16 2
Netherlands	1	360	10	533 12 4
Argentine Republic	1	490	12	916 13 4
Portuguese	1	628	14	794 8 0
Total for foreign ports	170	81,567	1,832	667,048 17 10
,, American coasting	78	22,886	705	..
Total	248	104,453	2,537	667,048 17 10

BRITISH and Foreign Shipping arriving at the Port of Mobile in 1884; also the Number of Vessels and Tonnage arriving Coastwise.

Nationality.	Number of Vessels.	Tonnage.	Crews.	Value of Cargoes.
				£ s. d.
British	68	46,387	894	7,050 10 5
American	52	11,504	428	13,757 15 11
Norwegian and Swedish	83	59,970	1,249	390 7 0
Russian	6	2,904	62	..
German	6	1,941	47	36,946 15 6
Italian	5	3,006	56	..
French	2	1,314	25	..
Austrian	1	845	12	6,174 12 9
Spanish	1	400	9	..
Total from foreign ports	224	128,721	2,782	64,320 1 7
„ American coasting	90	25,098	876	..
Total	314	153,819	3,658	64,320 1 7

BRITISH and Foreign Shipping departing from the Port of Mobile in 1884; also the Number of Vessels and Tonnage departing Coastwise.

Nationality.	Number of Vessels.	Tonnage.	Crews.	Value of Cargoes.
				£ s. d.
British	65	46,371	799	480,822 9 5
American	47	9,669	397	33,773 1 11
Norwegian and Swedish	77	53,841	1,143	144,879 0 3
Russian	8	4,258	81	7,643 1 9
German	5	1,941	47	12,039 4 7
Italian	4	2,469	46	1,620 5 10
French	2	1,314	25	1,823 16 6
Austrian	2	1,690	28	34,190 8 9
Spanish	1	400	9	1,039 10 0
Total to foreign ports	211	121,953	2,575	717,820 19 0
„ American coasting	75	24,784	813	..
Total	286	146,737	3,388	717,820 19 0

Monthly Rates of Exchange in 1882, 1883, and 1884.

Month.	1882. Per £ Sterling.		1883. Per £ Sterling.		1884. Per £ Sterling.	
	Dol. c.	Dol. c.	Dol. c.	Dol. c.	Dol. c.	Dol. c.
January	4 76 to	4 83	4 76½ to	4 81	4 78 to	4 84
February	4 81¾	4 83	4 79¼	4 81	4 83	4 85
March	4 52¼	4 85	4 77½	4 80	4 84	4 85
April	4 84	4 85¾	4 79	4 81	4 84	4 85
May	4 84½	4 87	4 80½	4 83	4 79	4 85
June	4 83	4 85½	4 81½	4 83	4 77	4 82
July	4 82	4 84	4 80	4 83	4 77	4 80
August	4 82	4 83	4 79	4 81	4 79	4 80
September	4 76	4 83	4 79	4 80	4 79	4 80
October	4 76	4 78½	4 78	4 80	4 78	4 79
November	4 76¾	4 78½	4 77½	4 80	4 76	4 78
December	4 75½	4 77¾	4 78	4 80	4 77	4 78

Mobile Bay and Harbour Improvements.

Under the recent appropriations made by the United States Congress, the present improvements, in the new channel in Mobile Bay seem to be confined to the maintaining of the present depth of water, which is said to be from 16 to 17 feet, and of the widening of the said channel from 100 to 200 feet.

Finances of Alabama for 1884.

The total debt of the State of Alabama amounts to 9,169,100 dol., and the annual interest on the same to 323,923 dol., which was paid punctually half-yearly on the bonds. The receipts from taxes from all sources amounted in 1884 to 820,831 dol., and the disbursements to 928,619 dol. 7 c., leaving a balance in the State Treasury at the end of the past year of about 200,000 dol.

Mobile, February 12, 1885.

NEW ORLEANS.

Report by Consul De Fonblanque on the Trade and Commerce of New Orleans for the Year 1884.

AGRICULTURE.

THE year 1884 has been in all respects a bad one for this port and district. The three principal crops—cotton, sugar, and rice—have been more or less unremunerative, and the financial difficulties, felt all through America, have made these shortcomings more disastrous than they might otherwise have been. Coming immediately after another bad year the feeling of depression was very marked. In its summary of the business year the "Times-Democrat" finds a cause for this in the lack of available local capital thus:—

"An inspection of the statistics of the commercial and financial history of the United States for the past three decades, amid all the changes that have come over the country, are calculated to excite both interest and wonder at the punctuality of recurring commercial events. Cycles of depression in trade occur with remarkable regularity, and in obedience to causes which are the result of the laws of trade; and to their violation is clearly traceable the depression of the past ten years ending in the recent financial disasters, which would have been much more serious had they not been averted by remarkably conservative financial skill.

"The necessity of rehabilitating the situation should induce our capitalists, bankers, and merchants to raise our city financially and commercially to her natural and proper standard; but this can only be done by augmenting our working capital. When we speak of working capital, we mean capital for furnishing means separately and respectively to facilitate our local trade, cultivate our crops, and assist the various manufacturing industries which are rapidly springing up here and in the environs. Taking capital from one institution to put it in another is not what is wanted, but some combined energetic effort to bring more capital here.

"Our banks are accustomed to lend money to the merchants very liberally during the early spring and summer months, who in turn lend to their customers, the planters. The banks draw largely on New York for money for these purposes, and just previous to the late financial troubles in that city they put out their money freely, expecting, as heretofore, to obtain funds from there as needed for summer business; but the financial disturbances in that market rendered this impossible. Hence our banks have had to shorten their accommodations to the merchants, and the merchants have had to refuse to assist many of their best customers.

"There is a lesson to be learned from these facts, however, and our business men should appreciate its importance, and to avoid such trouble as this in the future we must be less dependent on New York; and this can only be done by making New Orleans a great Southern trade and financial centre, which can, of course, only be accomplished slowly. This is a subject which should receive the earnest attention of all our Southern business men, and especially of bankers of the South.

"The rapid increase of the wealth of the South, the enormous development of her manufacturing and mining interests, and the steady growth of her population require a corresponding advance in her banking facilities, and certainly no better or more convenient financial centre can be found for this section than New Orleans, especially as the credit of the State is improving, owing to the result of the late election, whereby an amendment to the debt ordinance of the Constitution of 1879 was adopted, repealing the 3 per cent. for 15 years' clause, and fixing the interest at 4 per cent. on the State debt from January 1, 1885. There is no record where any other State in the Union has voluntarily increased the rate of interest upon its debt."

It is undoubtedly true that cycles of depression in trade " will recur with remarkable regularity," even when trade is carried on in a legitimate manner; but I think that the recent troubles may be traced to the prevalence of what may be termed gambling transactions, by which riches have been suddenly amassed and ruin as speedily inflicted, without adding one cent to the national wealth, and disturbing credit at its foundations. With capitalists forming " pools " and making " corners " at one extremity of the commercial scale, and the workman using his political power to force up the rates of labour at the other, the old-fashioned conditions under which business was conducted have sadly changed. With the exceptions to be presently mentioned, New Orleans knows little of " pools " and " corners," for the reasons suggested by the above quotation: there is not sufficient capital to get them up; but she suffered by the speculation of other cities, notably by the grain gambling in St. Louis and Chicago, under which an export trade, which promised at one time to be remunerative, has considerably diminished. Thus, taking the amount of grain carried by British ships (which will not be an unfair test), we find:—

	Bushels.	Sacks.
1878	4,439,997	..
1879	4,821,807	..
1880	11,922,741	90,855
1881	9,568,691	180,369
1882	4,353,571	65,729
1883	7,716,139	166,009
1884	4,014,398	1,154,066

No share of the blame is due here, because the facilities for loading corn have been ample and prices reasonable. It has also been demonstrated that the old objections respecting the heating of corn in a voyage round the Florida Keys are without foundation, and that corn of an ordinary good quality arrives at Liverpool or Havre in better condition that it was at the time of loading. Still combination, which benefits a few to the detriment of the port, is not unknown. The proprietors of cotton presses have their " pool," under which only about a third of the machinery is in operation. The tug-boats have also established a monopoly, and all the workers engaged in the handling of cotton are organised into a society so strong, that all the commercial exchanges in the city and the Chamber of Commerce combined could not break it. Its most formidable enemy is its own methods, which are diverting the weighing, bagging, marking, and compressing of cotton from New

Orleans to interior towns, where these operations can be performed at reasonable rates. Thus the weighing, which here costs 29½ c. a bale, is done in the country at from 5 c. to 10 c. There is a corresponding saving in compression, and the wasteful drayages from boat or railway station to the press and back again to the ship is avoided. As this is comparatively a new business it might be supposed that special care would be taken to conduct it to the satisfaction of all concerned, but, unfortunately, here again the fatal tendency to make illegitimate profits is felt. Complaints of false weighings, by which the Liverpool buyer has suffered, are not unknown.

Upon the subject of diversion a committee of the Cotton Exchange reported as follows:—

"Very near the same relative proportions are shown in the quantity of cotton handled in presses and supervised, the latter representing closely the amount received and sold in this market. In a word, although the season has been unfavourable, and the business of New Orleans proper has decreased 193,841 bales, the loss has not been occasioned by diversion to other points, or an increase in the proportion of through shipments. These facts are demonstrated by the annexed figures of the New Orleans cotton movement:—

| | Year ending August 31. ||
	1884.	1883.
	Bales.	Bales.
Gross receipts	1,709,381	2,013,586
Decrease from last year	304,205	..
Increase over year before last	336,206	..
Received in presses and supervised	1,103,379	1,296,220
Decrease from last year	193,841	..
Decrease from year before last	1,487	..
Received in transit	606,002	717,366
Decrease from last year	111,364	..
Increase over year before last	337,693	..
Percentage of transit cotton to gross receipts	35 5/10	35 6/10

"While the statement embodied above sets forth that in the competition for trade we have not our proportion of the crop compared with last year, it is necessary to carry the comparisons back, so as to cover the four years past and in greater detail, in order to show the position of the trade and judge of future possibilities. This is done as follows:—

	1883–84.	1882–83.	1881–82.	1880–81.
Cotton crop of the United States	5,713,200	6,949,756	5,456,048	6,605,750
Gross receipts at New Orleans	1,709,381	2,013,586	1,373,175	1,883,849
Per cent. gross receipts at New Orleans to cotton crop of United States	29·92	28·97	25·16	28·52
Transit cotton passing through New Orleans	606,002	717,366	268,309	466,170
Per cent. of transit to gross receipts at New Orleans	35 5/10	35 6/10	19 4/10	24 7/10
Number of bales handled in presses of New Orleans, or, in other words, received and sold in this market	1,103,379	1,296,220	1,104,866	1,417,679
Per cent. of cotton crops of United States received and sold in New Orleans	19 3/10	13 6/10	20 2/10	21 4/10

"These figures indicate that we have lost since 1880–81 nearly 120,000 bales; that is, with the same percentage of the crop as in

1880-81, the quantity received for sale in this market for 1883-84, out of a crop of 5,713,200 bales, should have been within a fraction of 1,223,000 bales instead of 1,103,000 bales. While local causes, such as the partial failure of crops or vice versâ, in the section tributary to this market may affect the result exceptionally, the deductions from a series of years cannot be doubted. For a certain percentage of the supply of the Northern and Eastern mills, the trade must necessarily be direct from the interior to mill doors by rail, avoiding the inevitable cost of handling at delivery ports. This overland movement, which (including the deliveries to Northern seaports) amounted to $16\frac{2}{10}$ per cent. of the crop in 1880-81, $19\frac{9}{10}$ per cent. in 1881-82, $16\frac{9}{10}$ per cent. in 1882-3, and $17\frac{3}{10}$ per cent. in 1883-4, is undoubtedly more at the expense of other seaport markets than of New Orleans, the main causes affecting our trade being arbitrary local rates, by which cotton is shipped from the interior through New Orleans to foreign and domestic ports at a fraction of what is charged from the same points on consignments to this city proper.

"Looking at these questions from a purely business standpoint, the committee are not disposed to cavil at the handling of through cotton, when such cotton is a clear diversion in favour of a New Orleans route. All such diversion is a gain in favour of New Orleans, aiding towards the support of its labouring population; but when the completion of a line of railroad, instead of bringing an addition actually leads to a curtailment of our trade, the results are too serious not to demand searching investigation, and the most powerful efforts of the community for their correction. How far the cost of handling cotton in New Orleans may affect the question should also be considered in all its branches. Investigations show but little difference in the rates current at nearly all the leading Southern delivery ports, but it also shows, as will be seen by the following, that they suffer even in a greater degree than New Orleans by being converted into way stations for the transfer of a large percentage of their gross receipts:—

1883-4.

	Gross Receipts.	Transit Cotton.	Per cent. of Transit.
			Dol. c.
New Orleans	1,709,381	600,002	35 5
Mobile	265,458	98,517	37 1
Galveston	605,703	333,266	55 0
Savannah	655,784	315,000	48 0
Norfolk	582,872	284,759	48 8 "

It is now ascertained that the extension of railway communication with Texas and the new route north, known as the "Queen and Crescent" line (New Orleans to Cincinnati viâ Meridian), is of no appreciable advantage (so far as the cotton trade is concerned) to this city.

During the past year I have received several letters from persons anxious to do business with this city in the cotton seed oil trade. I made inquiries, and the result gives me to understand that this business is one into which outsiders are not invited. It is therefore, probably, a very good one, and so the following details may prove interesting:—

"Previous to 1855 the cotton seed had no commercial value whatever, and the planters were very much annoyed to know what to do with this superfluous and bulky product, and were put to considerable inconvenience to haul it miles away, and dump it in streams or in the woods.

"Experiments made in 1834 to extract the oil from the seed proved a failure, and it was not until after the war that this industry was completely successful. In 1867 there were but seven mills in the whole country, three of which were located in New Orleans; in 1870 there were 26 mills; in 1880, 47 mills, six of them in New Orleans. These mills are now scattered throughout the South in all the important cotton centres on the rivers and on the railroads—108 in all.

"The only material used is the cotton seed, which yields not only a number of valuable products, such as cotton seed cake, meal, oil, ash, soap-stuff, &c., but actually furnishes the fuel to convert itself into three various substances. The cotton plant averages about 3½ lbs. of seed to every lb. of lint. The cotton crop, therefore, of last year yielded about 9,200,000 lbs., or 4,600,000 tons of seed, sufficient to have produced 160,000,000 gallons of oil.

"The amount of seed annually crushed in the United States averages about 420,000 tons, or 10 per cent. of the total product. Indeed, the only cotton seed brought to the mill for crushing is from the country in its immediate neighbourhood, or from that lying along the banks of some stream where transportation is cheap and easy.

"A ton of cotton seed yields the following products: 35 gallons of crude oil, 22 lbs. of cotton, 750 lbs. of cake of average value of 19 dol., making the total value of the cotton seed product of the South 8,000,000 dol., or 3 per cent. of that of the cotton crop.

"The product of the cotton seed mills are—1st. *Cotton Seed Cake*, which is the residue of the cotton seed after the oil has been pressed from it. The cake is shipped in sacks containing 200 lbs. each. It is of a rich golden colour, quite dry, and has a sweet, nutty, oleaginous taste. Its principal uses are for stock-feeding and fertilising purposes. It is generally ground for this purpose to the consistency of corn meal, when it becomes known as 'cotton seed meal.' Most of it used for feeding purposes is shipped to Great Britain, where it is extensively employed in fattening stock. For this purpose it is the best food in the world, yielding a larger proportion of meat to the lb. than any other animal food. Cotton seed cake is also a splendid food for cows, causing a rich and plentiful flow of milk.

"As a fertiliser, cotton seed cake is the best known for a larger number of plants.

"2nd. *Cotton Seed Oil.*—Cotton seed oil is of two kinds—the crude oil, and the clarified or refined oil. The refined oil is generally clarified by the use of some strong alkali—caustic soda being the most used. The precipitate which falls to the bottom in the process of clarifying is termed 'soap stock.' It is frequently used also in the manufacture of gas, and a number of mills in this country are lighted by gas made from the cotton seed itself. In the refining process about 10 to 20 per cent. of the crude oil is lost, according to seasons.

"Cotton seed oil has been put to a variety of uses. It is employed in the manufacture of soap, making the finer varieties, such as glycerine, castile, mottled, &c. It is used also by painters, but being a non-drying oil it is somewhat unsatisfactory for this purpose, drying very slowly. It is not good for lubricating purposes, for the reason that it is too gummy. Its great use, however, is as a substitute, or adulterant, for olive oil, whose place it is rapidly supplying. It is nearly impossible to detect good cotton seed oil from the best brands of olive oil by taste, smell, or any other process. This the olive growers of Italy have been unwillingly compelled to acknowledge. An instrument, called the oleometer, has been invented to distinguish between the two oils by means of their different specific gravity; but this is confessedly an uncertain and unreliable test.

"3rd. The 'hulls' are the shell, or skin, of the cotton seed. The hull constitutes about one-half of the seed, the product of a ton of seed being 1,000 lbs. of hulls and 1,000 lbs. of kernel. A good use has been found for these hulls by employing them as fuel for running the mill. Some oil being still left in them, they burn well and furnish all the fuel necessary, the mills finding it unnecessary to purchase a bushel of coal. The ashes left by the hulls when burned yield a cheap and valuable fertiliser, containing the salts needed in the production of many plants. When bleached they furnish a good lye, used in the manufacture of soap. It is said that the hulls of cotton seed will furnish stock for the manufacture of paper, but nothing practical has been done in this line.

"Another product of the cotton seed oil, but which has been very little attended to as yet, is glycerine. One gallon of crude oil will make $3\frac{1}{2}$ lbs. of glycerine.

"4th. Soap stock is the deposit left after the oil has been refined. A large amount of this is shipped to Liverpool, New York, Key West, and Havanah for the manufacture of soap; but several of the cotton seed mills are now saponifying their own stock.

"In the late session of the Cotton Seed Association, one of the members claimed that at some early day cotton seed would yield all the grape sugar demanded by the commerce of the world. The average annual yield of the cotton seed products of the South is 8,000,000 dol. This, however, represents only 10 per cent. of the cotton seed raised in this country. If all the seed was used and crushed, this little article, once despised and deemed of no value at all, would be worth between 80,000,000 dol. and 100,000,000 dol. annually."

It will be seen in another part of this report that the export of these products in British ships is on the increase.

Sugar.—As I have been accused of taking a pessimist's views on this subject, I will quote from a local publication, which confirms all I have reported from my own information, and gives a true statement of the position. It is dated October 20th, when the outcome of the crop could be estimated:

"Last Sunday's papers inform us that the first shipment of new sugar to the New Orleans market was sold at 5 c. per lb. The news has fallen like a pall upon the sugar planters of the State, the most hopeful of whom expected $6\frac{1}{2}$ c., or at least 6 c.

"Nearly all claim that sugar cannot be grown profitably for less than these figures, and the only hope that remains under present prices is to secure from the sale of the growing crop the amount actually expended in making it.

"The outlook for sugar planters is so gloomy that planters are inquiring for new methods of manufacture and new crops to substitute for cane. They are cutting down expenses in every direction. Cane cutters, who at this time last year were paid 1 dol. 25 c. per day, are now paid from 75 c. to 90 c. The labourers, appreciating the situation, are generally working for what the planters can afford to give. The crop throughout the State is far below the average, the cane being small, hard, and dry, from the long drought.

"Those planters who have supplemental rollers, with saturators, are fortunate such a season as this, many claiming from their use 25 per cent. additional results. The new methods of sugar manufacture in England

and Germany, which greatly increase the yield of sugar, have proved of great interest to our State planters, but new and expensive machinery is at this time beyond the means of all except a few.

"We have heard it publicly stated among the sugar planters that numbers of them will not be able another year to obtain the advances necessary to make a crop. These, of necessity, will cease to plant sugar. Renters and tenants will in time occupy lands thus vacated, and other crops will in part be planted; but such an inviting field will soon attract foreign and northern capitalists, who will build central factories, operated by the latest improved methods and machinery, whereby the yield over that now obtained will be so largely increased as to allow the manufacturers to pay the farmer a good price for his cane and work it up at a profit, even at present prices.

"The subject of retrenchment in expenses is now given serious attention by our sugar planters. Something must be done to prevent bankruptcy. One of our largest planters, who has annually used thousands of dollars' worth of cotton seed meal on his cane to great advantage, was recently heard to remark that he would curtail that expense hereafter. This economy is about as wise as cutting down the rations of the work animals of the plantation would be.

"It would be much better to buy up a number of thin steers, and stall-feed them with cotton seed meal, rice straw and parings, and apply their manure to the canes, thus making the cotton seed meal achieve a double end."

The following is quoted from "Boucherous" report:—"There were 172,430 acres of cane (excluding ditches and headlands) ground last season, which is 51,865 acres, or 43 per cent. more than the previous year. Planters using the vacuum pan obtained an average of 2,646 lbs. of sugar per acre, or 126 lbs. per ton of cane, and 21 tons of cane per acre; and those using other apparatus 1,290 lbs. of sugar per acre. An increase in vacuum pans in two years amounts to 35, making a total of 155 vacuum pans now in use. The number of sugar houses in operation in 1883-84 was 998, of which 840 used steam, and 158 were worked by horse-power, yielding a total production of 221,515 hogsheads, weighing 287,712,230 lbs., or 143,855 tons of 2,000 lbs., and 15,277,316 gallons of molasses. Of this, 105,812 hogsheads, weighing 148,868,630 lbs. net, or 74,434 tons, were refined sugar. This is the largest crop of refined sugar that has been made since the war. Planters are beginning to understand the wants of the consumer, and are making an article to meet the requisites of the market. The balance of the crop, 115,703 hogsheads, weighing 138,843,600 lbs. net, or 69,421 tons, was made by the old process. In making up the total amount of the crop in lbs., 1,400 net is taken for clarified sugar, and 1,200 lbs. net for brown sugar."

The first arrivals of new sugar in 1883 came in on September 20, in 1882 on October 6, and in 1881 on October 18.

"The sugar market opened in September with no stock on hand. In October the new crop came in in sufficient quantities to slightly depress prices. The market for the first half of November was weak and declining, but the rest of the month was steady owing to the improved demand. December was active in the early part of the month, but was weak and easy during the rest. In January the demand was good, especially for the better grades of open kettles and yellow clarifieds. Although the receipts began to fall off in February, the market showed little briskness. The prices of sugar were heavily depressed in March owing to the ratification of the Mexican treaty. The depressed condition of foreign markets, overflows and large local stocks, considerably augmented by heavy receipts, the feeling in April was a little better until refineries commenced importing large quantities of foreign sugars. The defeat of the Tariff Bill in May and an improvement in New York slightly stimulated the market, only to be followed throughout the rest of the season by the greatest depression ever known in our local sugar circles."

Public Works.

The World's Cotton Centennial and Industrial Exposition, held in this city, will form the subject of a special report, belonging to another series.

It is deeply to be regretted that political differences and a conflict of rival systems have prevented the appropriation of adequate sums for the improvement of the Mississippi river, and the prevention of overflows, by which the States forming this Consular district have suffered severely. This subject was treated at some length in my report for the year 1883, and it would now appear that the "outlet" system is gaining favour, a proposal having been made by a syndicate to perform the necessary work and take payment by results, so much for every foot of depth gained.

Shipping.

My registers show the following movements of British ships:—

Entered.

	Ships.	Tonnage.	Crews.
Direct	123	157,823	3,185
Indirect	208	217,741	4,921
Total	331	375,567	8,106

Cleared.

	Ships.	Tonnage.	Crews.
Direct	134	197,198	4,799
Indirect	146	159,153	3,244
Total	280	356,351	8,043

This shows a falling off compared with the average of the five preceding years, the returns being—

Entered.

Years.	Ships.	Tonnage.
1879	301	304,671
1880	437	436,175
1881	353	354,140
1882	306	338,331
1883	353	402,673
1884	331	375,567

But it must be remarked that the clearances during last year were unusually small in comparison to the entries. A number of ships held over until January, 1885, in which month 53 ships cleared, as against 39 during the corresponding period of 1884.

The principal articles exported in British ships in the year 1884 were—

Articles.		Quantity.
Cotton	Bales	876,482
Cotton products—		
Cake	Sacks	331,180
Meal	,,	387,901
Seed	,,	8,885
Oil	Barrels	8,821
Wheat (in bulk)	Bushels	1,161,746
,,	Sacks	53,959
Corn (in bulk)	Bushels	2,852,652
,,	Sacks	100,107
Rosin	Barrels	4,085
Staves	Pieces	710,707
Borax	Barrels	170
Beef	,,	10
Bran	Sacks	25
Building material	Packages	1,263
Copper	Lbs.	18,670
Cigars		15,000
Coffee	Sacks	5,143
Coal	Tons	300
Cross ties	Pieces	53,752
Flour	Barrels	133
,,	Sacks	1,282
Grease	Tierces	40
,,	Barrels	70
Hops	Bales	747
Hay	,,	750
Honey	Cases	2,927
Hides	Bales	20
Hogs (live stock)		20
Lumber	Feet	124,831
Lime	Barrels	10
Lard	Cases	225
Lead	Packages	3,657
,,	Bars	5,086
,,	Pigs	13,641
Ore	Sacks	238
Pecans	Barrel	1
Potatoes	Barrels	25
Rice	Sacks	150
,, (Polish)	,,	192
Red wine	Cases	3,715
Soap stock	Barrels	3,517
Shingles		105,000
Shells (pearl)		116
Tallow	Tierces	105
Tar	Barrels	2
Timber	Pieces	3,488
Tobacco	Cases	113

The cotton carried by British ships during the last five years was—

COTTON.

		Bales.
1880	.. ..	872,309
1881	.. ..	774,014
1882	.. ..	792,685
1883	.. ..	920,527
1884	.. ..	876,482

The total exports during the same period, according to Customs accounts, were—

Whither Exported.	1880.	1881.	1882.	1883.	1884.
Liverpool	901,031	939,441	672,164	852,376	782,787
Queenstown, Cork, &c.	6,576	4,960	7,902	13,267	...
Havre	265,320	327,092	271,714	294,682	360,361
Nantes, Cette, and Rouen	9,592	8,612	2,241	2,906	1,750
Amsterdam	...	2,843	...	...	...
Rotterdam and Ghent	6,151	9,124	...	2,849	1,300
Bremen	71,153	124,008	68,218	126,277	12,020
Antwerp, &c.	9,855	8,304	...	8,519	4,605
Hamburgh	...	1,963	783	87	1,457
Gottenburg and Stockholm	5,831	2,000	...	3,014	...
Spain, Gibraltar, &c.	26,462	31,736	19,533	57,828	65,245
Mexico, West Indies, &c.	20,656	20,787	22,377	15,199	7,632
Genoa, Trieste, &c.	30,021	57,100	31,867	55,188	31,947
Russia	86,085	97,672	82,637	168,295	75,876
New York	211,666	177,339	234,324	325,888	275,415
Boston, &c.	26,475	8,908	...	11,379	2,130
Providence, &c.	12,981	9,078	9,530	4,365	5,974
Philadelphia	3,572	...	...	...	...
Other coastwise ports	...	...	...	10,899	2,805
By river and rail	3,291	2,906	17,508	1,117	...
Total	696,718	1,833,882	1,440,748	1,957,605	1,739,304

The shipments of grain have already been given. About two-thirds of that for the past year was carried in British ships. Indeed, I am glad to say that we have the preference—for insurance, for speed, and for delivery in good order—and so secure the lion's share of any freight that is going.

Seamen.—During the year 1884, with 8,106 seamen entered, the desertions have been 424 and the discharges 185. As there has been no material change in the rates of wages, and local inducements were about the same, this shows an improvement.

Desertions were principally from sailing ships; and in the fact that these have given way to steamers, which obtain rapid despatch, and not unfrequently give promises to their crews for continued service, one reason for this may be found. Another, if I am correctly informed, is that deserters have learned to pay the crimps back in their own coin, breaking their engagements to these as they have induced them to break theirs with the ships.

I do not think that the United States law forbidding advances has had much effect. I also notice that the diminution in desertions began in the first six months of the year, and were marked before this law came into operation. The statistics on this subject for the last five years are:—

Year.	Number of Crews.	Number of Desertions.
1880	9,605	1,159
1881	9,958	1,041
1882	7,647	986
1882	8,987	884
1884	8,106	424

Quarantine.—It is understood that the new Board of Health will relax the hard-and-fast geographical lines and fixed periods of detention adopted by its predecessor to the extinction of foreign commerce during the summer months, and deal with each ship, so to speak, on her merits, considering the sanitary condition of the ports at which she has touched and her own, and allowing cargoes to be removed subject to disinfection. The material provisions for this change of system have been made, but it is too soon to offer details, lest they should prove to be misleading.

New Orleans, February 14, 1885.

UNITED STATES.

BOSTON.

Report by Consul Henderson on the Trade and Commerce of Boston and the Boston Consular District for the Year 1884.

The year 1884 has been one of continuous and increasing depression in trade, no less in Boston and this Consular district than throughout other parts of the country.

This condition of things is in great measure attributed to abundant harvest and over-production of manufactured goods, coupled with a demand which, though not very much below the average, was sufficiently sluggish in an overstocked market to produce a sensible decline in prices. Once inaugurated and unchecked by the occurrence of any countervailing influence, this decline was all the more firmly established by the indisposition of purchasers to supply more than their immediate wants in a falling market, and was thus prolonged and intensified as weeks and months succeeded each other.

The indisposition to purchase was at the same time accompanied by an objection to sell to any but those whose credit was above suspicion, whilst the occurrence of numerous though not very heavy failures, and the apparently hopeless collapse of railway and other securities, extended the growing want of confidence to the loan market, and shut out from legitimate employment a vast amount of idle and consequently unremunerative capital.

The closing of many mills and factories, partial suspension of work in others, and the occurrence of numerous and generally unsuccessful strikes against an almost universal reduction of wages, whilst producing much distress amongst the labouring classes, had moreover a very material influence on consumption and prices.

A slight improvement began to show itself towards the end of the year, and a confident hope is generally entertained in a revival of business and prosperity; but whether this improvement will be permanent or transitory must, to a great extent, depend on the feasibility of maintaining a low standard of prices and wages, and of disposing in foreign markets of the surplus agricultural products, the proceeds of which, whether leaving a profit or not, materially contribute to the payment of wages and the purchasing power of the population.

Review of Boston Trades and Markets in 1884.

Cotton.—Receipts of cotton were 80,000 bales less than during the previous year. Owing to the comparatively short crop, the price was well maintained throughout the year, with but one temporary break in October.

Wool.—The production of wool shows an annual increase, and is expected soon to exceed the demand for home consumption, and almost entirely to supersede importations from abroad. Receipts at Boston were however considerably less than in 1883, and prices lower, whilst imported wools did not in some instances cover the cost of importation.

Dry Goods.—This trade was very much depressed during the year. Demand was so much reduced and prices declined so materially that mills were forced to suspend or curtail production, and most of them have lost money. "Jobbers," or middlemen, bought sparingly, and sold as close to cost as possible; but the retail houses made some profit on their sales. The value of cotton goods exported (630,000 dol.) was 400,000 dol. less than in 1883. Woollen mills were somewhat more successful, for though some goods sold at a loss, others left a small profit, and on the whole they more than covered expenses.

Ready-made Clothing.—This branch of trade and industry suffered less from the general depression than any other in Boston. Whilst the competition of other cities left but a small margin for profit, sales were larger than in the previous year, and no losses of importance were incurred from bad debts.

Boots and Shoes.—Sales, amounting to nearly 2,500,000 cases (each case averaging 24 pairs of boots and shoes), were less by about 80,000 cases than in 1883. Profits were small, but the business of the year was not altogether unsatisfactory.

Hides and Leather.—Receipts of foreign hides show a slight falling off, but native were largely in excess of the previous year, and prices ruled somewhat higher. The leather market was nevertheless very dull, and with the exception of a sharp advance in sole leather in February and March, prices were unremunerative.

Iron.—The price of iron, which had fallen considerably in the previous year, continued to fall in 1884, and foreign imports were very small. In American pig the decline in the two years was 8 dol., viz., from 24 dol. to 16 dol; in bar $\frac{7}{8}$ c., or from $2\frac{1}{4}$ c. to $1\frac{3}{8}$ c.; and in steel rails 12 dol., or from 40 dol. to 28 dol. A considerable decline also occurred in copper, tin, and lead.

Flour and Grain.—Flour continued to fall till December, when it was from 1 dol. 50 c. to 1 dol. 75 c. per barrel lower than in January, and the lowest price ever known. A slight rise then took place, and has been since maintained. Wheat, maize, and oats also declined considerably. Receipts and exports of flour were somewhat larger than in 1883, whilst those of wheat and maize were smaller. The oat crop was more abundant than for many years past, and the maize crop was the largest on record, but as the previous one was small there is not more than will be required.

Cattle.—Exports of horned cattle were three times as large as in 1883, whilst those of fresh meat amounted to 20,500,000 lbs. against 12,750,000 lbs. in that year.

Fish.—The season's catch of mackerel was remarkably abundant, but the fish were mostly of small size, and prices fell so low as not to cover expenses in some cases, and many vessels hauled up in November, although mackerel continued plentiful till December. But whilst fishermen did not succeed in making any money, the demand was very brisk at low figures, and dealers and packers did a large and not unprofitable business. Receipts at Boston were 130,000 barrels from the native fleet, and 60,000 imported from Canada, being a total excess of 43,500 barrels over the previous year. The total catch by the New England fleet, including 20,358 barrels caught in Canadian waters, was 479,659 barrels. Codfish was also very abundant, the supply at Boston being 30,000 quintals more than in 1883. The price however was lower than for 50 years past, and left no profit to fishermen.

Sugar, Molasses, and Groceries.—Imports of raw sugar, though showing a large increase over the previous year at all ports in the

United States, were smaller at Boston. Prices of both raw and refined, which were lower in January than ever before, continued to fall during the year, but were firm with an upward tendency in December. Molasses also declined, but in tea, coffee, spices, and other groceries there was little charge.

Butter and Cheese.—Receipts and exports of butter and cheese were somewhat larger than in 1883, with more fluctuation, but generally lower prices.

Money Market and Exchange.—Money was in abundant supply, but was only obtainable on the best security. Discount rates fluctuated between 4 and 6 per cent., against 5 to 7 per cent. in 1883. Clearing-house exchanges amounted to 3,243,000,000 dol. against 8,515,000,000 dol. the year before. Foreign exchange was somewhat higher, ranging for bankers' sight bills between 4 dol. 83¼ c. and 4 dol. 90¼ c. per pound, against 4 dol. 83 c. and 4 dol. 89¼ c. in 1883.

Ocean Freights.—Freights were generally lower than in 1883, and fluctuated considerably. On inward freights, pig iron ranged from 6d. to 4s., and bar from 5s. to 7s. 6d.; chemicals from 4s. 6d. to 12s. 6d., and measurement goods from 10s. to 25s. per ton. The highest rates were in May and the lowest in December. Outward freights ranged from 35s. to 75s. per head on cattle, 15s. to 20s. per 40 cubic feet of space on dead meat, ½d. to 5½d. per bushel on grain, 4s. to 20s. per ton on flour, and 6s. to 27s. 6d. per ton on provisions. The highest rates on cattle were in January and the lowest in September. On other exports the rates were lowest in May and highest in December.

Building and Building Materials.—The price of all building materials, as well as of labour employed in building, was lower than for many years past. This circumstance, added to the want of other safe means of investing capital and to the occurrence of an almost unprecedented number of fires, led to extensive building operations. The number of permits granted in Boston for new buildings was 1,438, and the valuation of these buildings was 7,500,000 dol.

IMMIGRATION.

The number of immigrants in Massachusetts (none having arrived in Vermont or New Hampshire) during the year to June 30th, 1884, was 35,633, or 6·88 per cent. of the total at all ports in the United States, against 48,849 or 8 per cent. in 1883, and 58,963 or 7·5 per cent. in 1882.

The quantities and ruling prices at Boston of the most important articles received from and exported to other States of the Union and foreign countries in 1884 were:—

Articles.	Units.	Received.	Exported.	Ruling Prices.
Boots and shoes	Cases	..	2,487,822	..
Coal, native	Tons	2,178,201	..	Anthracite, 5 to 6 dol. per ton.
„ foreign	„	27,876	..	..
Coffee	Bags	50,269	..	..
Cotton, raw	Bales	466,080	150,215	9⅞ to 12¼ c. per lb.
„ goods	Value	..	630,567	Sheetings 6¼ to 7½ c.
Fish—				
Mackerel	Quintals	380,000	..	2 dol. 50 c. to 20 dol. per barrel of 2 quintals.
Cod	„	200,000	..	2 to 4 dol. per quintal.
Flour	Barrels	3,687,181	2,306,198	2 dol. 50c. to 6 dol. 25 c. per barrel.
Corn meal	„	86,283	82,153	..
Bran	Bushel	3,457,638	..	..
Grain—				
Wheat	„	1,949,137	1,665,804	..
Barley	„	500,722	..	..
Maize	„	9,078,308	4,143,641	47 to 73 c. per bushel
Oats	„	5,840,310	..	32 to 52 c. per bushel.
Rye	„	57,090	..	67 to 85 c per bushel.
Hemp and jute	Bales	45,956	..	..
Hides	„	1,570	..	..
„	Number	1,974,513	..	21 to 26 c.
Ice	Tons	..	38,690	..
Iron—				
Bar	„	127	..	36 to 50 dol.
„	Bars	642,219	..	..
Railroad	„	2,403	..	..
„	Tons	187	..	..
Bundle	Bundles	553,678	..	..
Plate	Plates	53,434	..	..
Scrap	Bundles	7,749	..	..
„	Tons	525	..	..
Pig	„	24,704	..	16 to 24 dol.
Leather	Sides	2,587,124	..	..
„	Bundles	1,050,910	..	..
Lumber	Feet	98,272,377	35,579,000	..
Petroleum	Gallons	7,406,920	..	..
Provisions—				
Beef	Barrels	13,817	18,559	11 to 14 dol.
Pork	„	22,369	26,697	12 to 20 dol.
Tongues	„	3,920	..	..
Hams	„	4,445	..	..
„	Casks	9,787	..	..
Bacon	Boxes	70,883	127,989	..
Cheese	„	331,129	183,954	1 to 15½ c. per lb.
Lard	Tierces	83,964	96,593	7½ to 11¼ c. per lb.
„	Cases	105,593	79,439	..
Butter	Packages	751,963	46,245	8 to 36 c. per lb.
Canned provisions	„	4,431	..	..
Horned cattle	Number	139,465	63,464	..
Sheep	„	568,041	20,632	..
Veal	„	38,979	..	..

UNITED STATES.

Articles.	Units.	Received.	Exported.	Ruling Prices.
Live hogs	Number	786,110	..	..
Dressed ,,	,,	5,992	..	..
Fresh meat	Lbs.	..	20,576,148	..
Spirits, native	Gallons	..	1,514,938	..
,, foreign	,,	159,772	..	..
Sugar, raw	Tons	199,848	..	4¾ to 6¼ c. per lb.
,, refined	Barrels	..	60,740	6 to 8⅛ c. per lb.
Molasses	Hogsheads	40,493	3,996	..
Tin	Pigs	10,720	..	..
,, plates	Boxes	226,652	..	..
Tobacco	Hogsheads	10,583	..	..
,,	Bales	1,078	..	..
,,	Boxes	5,546	..	..
Wine	Gallons	162,241	..	..
Wool, domestic	Bales	431,919	..	Ohio, 36 to 42 c. per lb.
,, foreign	,,	56,852	..	..

FOREIGN COMMERCE.

VALUE in Dollars of Foreign Imports and Exports of Merchandise at Boston in the Year to December 31, 1884.

From and To	Imports.	Exports.
United Kingdom	29,291,530	54,997,056
Canada and Newfoundland	2,713,237	2,516,714
Australia and New Zealand	850,182	2,652,881
British West Indies and Guiana	2,093,629	320,270
British Africa	819,605	669,684
British East Indies and Hong Kong	1,005,593	..
Total from and to British empire	36,773,776	61,156,605
,, ,, ,, other countries	22,544,955	3,674,115
Total imports and exports in 1884	59,318,731	64,830,720
,, ,, ,, 1883	70,181,896	65,292,430
Average for five years, 1878 to 1882	57,845,887	61,304,117

VALUE in Dollars of Foreign Imports and Exports of Merchandise at Ports in the Boston Consular District in the Fiscal Year to June 30, 1884.

Into and From	Imports.	Exports.
Massachusetts ports	66,227,548	63,543,270
Vermont	5,882,221	1,782,985
New Hampshire	11,864	76
Total for year to June 30, 1884	72,121,633	65,326,331
,, ,, June 30, 1883	81,056,971	64,218,381
Average for five years, 1878 to 1882	61,382,328	60,271,405

The total imports and exports in 1884 were 9·76 per cent. of those at all ports in the United States. Of the total exports in 1884, 970,103 dol. was the value of foreign imports re-exported.

COMMERCIAL FAILURES IN 1884.

The number of firms in business and of failures and amount of liabilities in 1884 were respectively 57,925,839 dol. and 11,598,899 dol. in the Boston Consular district, against 56,963,746 dol. and 31,612,753 dol. in 1883, and an average of 54,004,638 dol. and 11,342,311 dol. for five years from 1878 to 1882. The figures for 1884 were respectively 6·4, 7·65, and 5·124 per cent. of totals for the United States.

FOREIGN SHIPPING TRADE.

NUMBER and Net Register Tonnage of British Vessels Entered and Cleared at the Boston Consulate in the Year to December 31, 1884.

From and To.	Entered. Vessels.	Entered. Tons.	Cleared. Vessels.	Cleared. Tons.
British ports	1,566	707,371	1,637	752,676
Foreign ports	247	126,457	190	87,737
Total in 1884	1,813	833,828	1,827	840,413
,, 1883	1,976	834,414	1,979	834,834
Average five years, 1878 to 1882	2,079	737,925	2,072	735,462

NATIONALITY, Number, and Tonnage of Vessels in the Foreign Trade Entered Inwards at the Boston Custom-house in the Year to December 31, 1884.

Nationality.	Number.	Tonnage.
British	1,800	830,761
American	617	275,737
Belgian	13	26,820
German	20	15,187
Norwegian	28	11,852
Austrian	6	3,640
Spanish	4	2,994
Portuguese	7	2,271
Swedish	6	2,107
Danish	6	2,004
Dutch	8	1,382
Italian	3	1,345
French	6	968
Haytien	1	234
Total entered in 1884	2,526	1,177,302*
,, ,, 1883	2,734	1,262,741*
Average five years, 1878 to 1882	2,803	1,320,722*

* Exclusively gross tonnage up to August, 1882; partly gross and partly net from August, 1882, to August, 1883; and exclusively net tonnage from August, 1883, to December, 1884.

Number and Tonnage of American and Foreign Vessels in the Foreign Trade Entered and Cleared at Ports in the Boston Consular District in the Fiscal Year to June 30, 1884.

Entered and Cleared at Ports in	Entered. American. Vessels.	Tons.	Entered. Foreign. Vessels.	Tons.	Cleared. American. Vessels.	Tons.	Cleared. Foreign. Vessels.	Tons.
Massachusetts	733	324,296	2,313	933,172	696	290,879	2,181	790,237
Vermont	107	9,007	750	93,118	95	7,819	743	92,375
New Hampshire	5	1,249	26	4,329	17	4,602	24	4,031
Total year to June 30, 1884	845	334,552	3,089	1,030,619	808	303,300	2,948	886,643
,, ,, 1883	956	345,380	3,531	1,214,532	901	313,728	3,429	1,052,344
Average four years, 1879 to 1882	798	290,174	3,355	1,243,090	779	259,710	3,262	1,169,969

As shown in this table, American tonnage at ports in the district decreased in 1884 as compared with 1883, but increased as compared with the average of four years to 1882, whilst foreign tonnage decreased in comparison to both the preceding epochs.

The total tonnage entered and cleared at ports in the district in the year to June 30, 1884, was 8·44 per cent. of the total entered and cleared at all ports in the United States.

Boston, February 28, 1885.

UNITED STATES.

LOS ANGELES.

Report by Vice-Consul Mortimer on the Trade and Commerce of Los Angeles and Wilmington, California, for the Year 1884.

Los Angeles is advancing rapidly in business, in wealth, and in population, and although the progress is so rapid as to be startling, there is every indication that the prosperity of her people is permanent and substantial. The facts and circumstances which militate in favour of and against this view are adverted to below in their proper order. The county records show that most of the land purchased during the year was paid for in cash, and that where a mortgage was given in part payment, the amount of the cash payment was generally in excess of the amount secured by the mortgage, thus relieving the transaction of any taint of speculation. During the years 1883-84 the four leading architects of this city furnished plans for buildings worth 2,525,000 dol., all of which have been constructed. In addition, a large number of buildings have been constructed from plans furnished by builders and architects of lesser note.

Trade and Commerce.

Exports.—The principal exports of this district are wheat, barley, wine, canned-dried and green fruits, and honey.

Wheat and Barley.—Ordinarily the quality of the grain of this district is of the best. Owing to unusually late rains in June most of the wheat rusted, and the quantity and quality, especially the former, were alike deficient. I have not got accurate returns of the wheat production of this vice-consular district: the yield of Los Angeles county, as appears by the books of the county assessor, amounts to 4,500,000 bushels; this is an increase of 2,500,000 bushels over the yield of 1883. The yield of barley amounts to 2,500,000 bushels, or an increase over the yield of 1883 of 1,500,000 bushels. There is a corresponding increase in the root and fruit crops, raisins, nuts, olives, &c.

Wine.—It appears from the books of the county assessor that the product of wine this year in Los Angeles county amounts to 5,350,000 gallons, being an increase of 1,350,000 gallons over last year. There are about 30,000 acres planted in vines in Los Angeles county, of which 5,500 acres were planted in 1884. Mr. Charles A. Witmore, chief viticultural officer for this State, wrote to me recently as follows:—" It has been stated that there are 25,000 acres of vines now planted in Los Angeles county, but I cannot yet verify the estimate. If you say that our progress bewilders the newsgatherer you will be telling the truth: say also that Los Angeles county has paid less attention to improving her selection of vine stocks than any other leading viticultural district, and that she will in consequence have a great deal of grafting to do hereafter in order to bring up the standard of quality." A good sound claret can be purchased at the vineyards here for 10*d.* per gallon; with the addition of some spirit this wine would bear shipment to Europe direct from this port. The best wines of California are really good: large quantities of adulterated wine are manufactured in New York and other Eastern States, and sold as California wines. British purchasers should deal directly with the producers here. The Phylloxera has not appeared in Southern California; it is, however, doing some damage in counties about 400 miles north of Los Angeles. Care is being taken to prevent the pest spreading, and this district may escape.

Canned-Dried and Green Fruits.—Large quantities of canned and dried fruits, principally apricots, peaches, pears, figs, and raisins are exported from this district, and recently some of these goods have been put upon the London market. Oranges and lemons are sent in large quantities to the Eastern States. The Southern California Packing Company have canned 750,000 pounds of fruit this season, and are sending some large consignments to England. The fruit is put up in two-and-a-half pound cans, which sell at the cannery here for from 8s. to 11s. per dozen. The fruit is excellent, and will bear transportation anywhere. The fruit business is as yet in its infancy here. The following figures show the increase in the export of green fruits:—

Year	Lbs.
1881	111,100
1882	1,120,700
1883	5,918,660

The above figures represent the shipments by rail; in addition considerable amounts were shipped by sea.

Honey.—Honey of the finest quality is produced here in large quantities; several large shipments have been made recently to the United Kingdom. 500 tons of honey will form part of the cargo of the British ship "The Douglas," now loading at this port. The dealers here are selling to the exporters at 2d. per lb.

Imports.

The principal imports from the United Kingdom are Portland cement, coal, paints, tin, coke, iron, crockery, salt, sal soda, caustic soda, saltpetre, &c.

Portland Cement.—This article is largely used here, and several miles of sidewalk have been constructed with it in this city in the past year; it is also used in the construction of sewer pipe and pipes for irrigation: the price during the year has varied from 16s. to 20s. per barrel of 400 lbs. in car-load lots. The present price is 17s. per barrel.

Coal.—The imports of coal in British ships from England, New South Wales, and British Columbia during the year aggregate 35,300 tons. Price here in car-load lots, 2l. 4s. to 2l. 8s. per ton. Retail price, 3l. 2s. to 3l. 6s. per ton, or 4s. per cwt.

Paints.—Cookson's Venetian red is used largely here. Messrs. Newton, Chaplin, and Co. of this city tell me that they sell about 100 tons a year. Wholesale price 10l. 10s. per ton; retail price 12s. 6d. per cwt. Other English paints are used here, but not in large quantities.

Coke.—The demand for English coke is increasing. The supply shipped direct to this port is exhausted, and consumers are now purchasing in San Francisco, and paying 1l. 12s. per ton freight from San Francisco to Los Angeles (482 miles by rail). The present price here is 4l. 10s. per ton.

Iron.—The foundries here are paying 7l. 3s. per ton for Glengarnock pig iron. Of this amount 1l. 12s. represents the freight from San Francisco to Los Angeles, which would be saved by shipping direct to this port.

Crockery.—English crockery and delf ware are used here almost exclusively. To illustrate prices I may say that the 8-inch dinner plate (ironstone china) sells here retail for 4s. 4d. per dozen. C. W. Gibson and Co. of this city tell me that they are also selling large quantities of English porcelain and other decorated goods in that line. All goods of this class are imported viâ New York; if shipped direct to this port the English exporter could make most of the profit now reaped by the railways from New York to this city.

Salt.—A good deal of English salt is used here, price 4l. 14s. to 5l. 2s. per ton. Heretofore this article has been imported viâ San Francisco. The freight by rail from San Francisco to Los Angeles is 1l. 14s. per ton. One of the wholesale dealers here recently imported a quantity direct from this port, but the ship "Rotomahana" was lost on the voyage.

The following extract from the *Weekly Record*, a paper published here by the Collector of Customs, shows the importations at the port (21 miles south of the city) since it was made a port of entry:—

"We present in this number of the *Record* the statistics of business at port of Wilmington, California, from November 1, 1882, to December 31, 1884, the 26 months that Wilmington has been a port of entry."

A summary of the business shows importations as follows:—

Foreign coal		Tons	126,182
American coal		"	26,487
Total		"	152,669
Lumber		Feet	135,426,792
Salt		Lbs.	448,000
Tinplate, 1,500 cases		"	162,000
Cement		Casks	10,188
Coke		Tons	1,322
Pig iron		"	102
Sheep dip		Gallons	3,020

The collections at the Custom-house during the 26 months have been 118,028 dol. 32 c.

The imports of lumber and 80,000 tons of coal were made in American ships; the balance of the business, with some small exceptions, was done in British ships.

CARRIAGE OF GRAIN.

In my report for the year 1883 I stated that the Southern Pacific Railway were carrying grain from this district to Liverpool, viâ New Orleans, for 36s. per ton, and that that rate would not pay them. This year the company's rate from this district to Liverpool has been 45s. per ton. In consequence of this increase in the railway rate, more British ships have obtained cargoes this year than in 1883, and at somewhat better rates.

MEXICAN TREATY.

A treaty has been entered into between the United States and Mexico, which will admit into the United States the fruit products of Mexico, free of duty. A Bill to carry this treaty into effect will shortly come before Congress. The treaty, if carried, will be disastrous to California. Oranges, lemons, limes, grapes, and raisins can be raised in Mexico at much less cost than here, both land and labour being very much cheaper. The distance, too, from the points in Mexico where these products are raised to markets in the Eastern States is less than from California. Efforts are being made to defeat the Bill by California and Arizona. The Bill is supported by railway and land speculators who have acquired large interests in Mexico, and may be carried.

SHIPPING AND NAVIGATION.

The following is a synopsis of the amount and tonnage of shipping at the port during the year 1884:—

British Vessels.—Entered 21, total tonnage 30,276, total value of cargoes discharged 89,235*l*. Cleared 19, total tonnage 28,682. Of the 19 clearing, four obtained cargoes of grain valued at 52,576*l*., five cleared in ballast, and 10 retained sufficient cargo to proceed without taking ballast.

American Steamers.—12 passenger and freight steamers plying between this port and San Francisco made during the year 177 trips.

American Ships.—Entered 12, total tonnage 26,630. These ships are engaged in the coal trade; several of them made more than two voyages to the port from the mines of Washington territory. They brought altogether 21 cargoes.

American Schooners.—A large number of schooners are engaged in the lumber trade between this port and ports to the north; during the year they brought 168 cargoes of lumber, averaging 292,000 feet each. Average value of cargo 16,000*l*.

Wilmington Harbour.—Wilmington, 21 miles south of the city of Los Angeles, is the port for the city. The outer harbour is protected from all winds except the south-east. During the winter it is not a safe anchorage, as at that season violent gales from the south-east are not uncommon. The inner harbour is well protected on all sides; it is about three miles long, and has a depth of from 20 to 25 feet at low water. All the coasting schooners and steamers cross the bar and reach the wharves in the inner harbour. Foreign-going ships anchor in the outer harbour and discharge cargo into lighters. Since 1870 improvements have been made by the Government with a view to making the inner harbour available for foreign-going ships. About 660,000 dol. have been expended in dredging the bar and in constructing training walls, 6,700 feet in length, to direct the current and concentrate the flow of the ebb-tide. The result of these operations has been to increase the depth of water on the bar, at mean low water, from one foot to 10 feet; as the tide rises six feet, this gives at mean high water 16 feet on the bar. The Government engineer states that 225,000 dol. will be required to complete the work, and secure a channel 300 to 400 feet wide, with a depth at mean high water of 19 feet. Of the required amount 50,000 dol. of the last appropriation is unused, and "it is confidently expected that Congress will grant the remainder at its present session." Wilmington is the best port south of San Francisco, in which harbour facilities and economical railroad transportation combine. The collection district of Wilmington includes as ports of delivery Santa Barbara, San Buenaventura, and Hueneme. The area of the countries, of which these are the ports, aggregates 39,740 square miles.

Casualties.—The British ship "Rotomahana," from Liverpool, bound for this port, laden principally with coal, was destroyed by fire on the voyage. The cargo—coals—of the "Scottish Tar" from Hull, bound for this port, ignited spontaneously on the voyage: the fire was fortunately extinguished, and the ship reached this port with the loss of about 200 tons of her cargo. The cargo—coals—of the "Strathblane," also from Hull, ignited spontaneously after her arrival at this port; the damage was trifling.

AGRICULTURE.

This district produces every variety of fruit grown in the Northern and Eastern States; its specialty however is semi-tropical fruits, such as the orange, lemon, lime, pomegranate, and fig. Every year the acreage in fruit is increased very largely. Peaches of the finest quality sell here at the orchards for one halfpenny per pound; even at this low price a good peach orchard will pay 60*l.* per annum per acre. Grapes sell at from 3*l.* to 5*l.* per ton. The products of the orchards are either dried, evaporated, canned, preserved, crystallised, or sold green. Recently a firm here commenced the crystallisation of fruits, as practised in the south of France, and are meeting with good success. The following figures of the cost of planting and probable receipts from a 10-acre orange orchard are said to be correct:—

COST.

	Dollars.
10 acres of land	1,000
1,000 trees, budding	750
Planting and curing for same first season, at 25 dol. per acre	250
Caring for orchard, second year, at 15 dol. per acre	150
Caring for orchard, third year, at 15 dol. per acre	150
Fourth year, 20 dol. per acre	200
Fifth year, 25 dol. per acre	250
Other expenses incidental to work	550
Total	3,300
Interest on investment	1,000
Grand total	4,300

RECEIPTS.

The yield and prices are placed at the lowest possible estimate:—

	Dollars.
Third year, crop scattering oranges, a few hundreds or thousands not counted	
Fourth year, an average of 50 oranges to the tree, 50,000 oranges, at 20 dol. per thousand	1,000
Fifth year, 200 to the tree, 200,000 oranges, at 20 dol. per thousand	4,000

I am advised that the following corrections should be made in the above estimate. The cost of land suitable for oranges should be put at 2,000 dol. instead of 1,000 dol. In the estimate of receipts the yield is put at too early a date by at least two years; with these corrections the estimate is about correct.

White Scale.—The cottony cushion scale, commonly called the "white scale," has appeared on the orange trees here, and is doing some damage. It has been stated that the "white scale" destroyed all the orange trees at the Cape of Good Hope. Dr. S. F. Chapin, State Inspector of Fruit Pests, in a recent communication to the "Los Angeles Herald," states with reference to it as follows: "It is surely the case that, in particular, the citrus interest is threatened with destruction, unless some active measures are devised and carried into execution to

stay the spread of one of the worst pests ever known to horticulture. . .
Since my visit to infected orchards a year since, it has spread rapidly to
many orange trees, remote from those first affected."

Population and Industries.

The population of the city of Los Angeles, according to the census of 1880, was 11,183. The population now is about 34,000. The population of the county is about the same. In this district there are about 7,000 persons of British birth, of whom about 4,000 reside in this city and county. There are several thousand French, German, and Italian subjects in this district. Newspapers are published here in four different languages.

Industries.

The following comprises a complete list of the manufactories in operation in this city:—One woollen mill, four foundries, five planing mills, three flour and feed mills, one cracker factory, two soap factories, eight carriage and wagon shops, three breweries, one distillery, ten wineries, one vinegar factory, one salt-making establishment, two ice factories, one gas-manufacturing establishment, one electric light works, five harness and saddle-making establishments, two soda-water factories, three coffee and spice mills, five upholstering establishments, six tin and iron working shops, one macaroni factory, one cannery, one Alden fruit drier, one fruit-preserving establishment, three candy manufactories, two windmill factories, ten cigar manufactories, four brickyards, two cooper shops, four marble works, two pipe-making works, one wireworks, one paper box manufactory, one trunk manufactory, two brush and broom factories, one tannery, one cornice factory, and four furniture factories.

Rate of Wages.—Unskilled labourers receive from 6s. to 8s. per day; skilled labourers from 8s. to 1l. per day. The labour market is overcrowded here at present.

Paper Factory.—An English company recently purchased a large tract of desert land in this county, and are successfully engaged in converting the yucca tree, with which it is covered, into paper.

Mines.—Los Angeles is the distributing centre for the mines in the counties of Los Angeles, Ventura, and San Bernardino, in this vice-consular district. The output of bullion from these mines in 1884 exceeded 6,000,000 dol. Besides gold and silver, there are very valuable tin and copper mines in this district. The tin mines are not being worked at present owing to litigation; they are represented to be of enormous value.

Oil.—The output of oil from the mills of Los Angeles and Ventura counties in 1883 was valued at 1,000,000 dol. I have not got the figures for 1884, but understand that there has been a considerable increase.

Public Works.

Los Angeles is connected with New Orleans and the Eastern States by the Southern Pacific Railway and connections. The same railway has also lines in operation from Los Angeles, west to Santa Monica 16 miles, south to Wilmington 21 miles, east to Santa Anna 32 miles, and north to San Francisco 482 miles. A railway is being constructed from Los Angeles in a north-easterly direction to Duarte, 20 miles.

The land grant to the Atlantic and Pacific Railway, made by Congress in 1866, provided for the construction of a railway from

Missouri to the Pacific coast. The company constructed to the Needles, on the Colorado river, and then purchased from the Southern Pacific Railway this branch line from the Needles to Mojave. This has not been held to be in compliance with the terms of their charter. To prevent a forfeiture of their land grant, the Atlantic and Pacific Company are now constructing from Daggett, a point on the Mojave desert, between Mojave and the Needles, through the Cajou pass to this county. This will give Los Angeles another through line to the east in competition with the Southern Pacific Railway.

The Southern Pacific Railway constructed their line from this city to San Francisco, in places at the bottom of the dry bed of old mountain watercourses. The exceptionally heavy rainfall of last winter, the heaviest ever recorded here, filled these watercourses and destroyed the line for many miles, interrupting communication with San Francisco for several weeks, and entailing a loss of several million dollars to the company. The line has now been reconstructed in a substantial manner.

General Remarks.

Emigration.—Large numbers of emigrants continue to arrive here from all parts of the world. At a recent meeting of the British Benevolent Society of this city, a resolution was passed to the effect that the only emigrants likely to succeed here at the present time are practical farmers, having a capital to the amount of 700*l.* and upwards, and domestic servants. The term "domestic servants" must be understood to mean cooks, housemaids, &c. Butlers and coachmen are almost unknown here. Good servants can readily get 5*l.* per month; domestic services are at present performed almost exclusively by Chinamen, who receive from 4*l.* to 6*l.* per month; white servants are difficult to get; they think domestic service degrading. Many female domestics here preserve their dignity by requiring their employers to address them with the prefix "Miss."

Financial.—The rate of interest here on the best mortgage security is from 10 per cent. to 12 per cent. per annum. The mortgagee pays the taxes on his mortgage about $1\frac{1}{4}$ per cent. The nett interest is therefore from $8\frac{3}{4}$ per cent. to $10\frac{3}{4}$ per cent. On large sums the rate is less: on one transaction recently, a loan of 40,000*l.*, the rate was 6 per cent. nett. Loans on mortgage are generally made by the banks, of which there are six in this city. There is a good opening here for a mortgage company. A great deal of English capital has been invested here recently. The stock of one large wine company is held largely in England. A very large vineyard and winery has just been purchased by an English company for 150,000*l.*

Intending emigrants are cautioned against purchasing land here before seeing it. I am informed that parties in Scotland are selling to intending emigrants desert land in the northern part of this county, valueless for purposes of cultivation, for 1*l.* per acre, representing it to be valuable arable land. Good land here is worth from 5*l.* to 60*l.* per acre. Emigrants should not purchase land until they have lived here for six or eight months.

Land Transfer Reform.—In the large cities of the United States the accumulation of the records of deeds, mortgages, wills, &c., has become so rapid that it is now generally admitted that the present system of transfer of real estate must be altered and improved. Some interest has been manifested in this district in a proposal to adopt a system, similar to that in use in Australia, known as "The Torrens System of Land Transfer." The important differences between the present system and the one proposed to be introduced are as follows. The proposed system is a register of title, and not as at present simply a register of deeds. Parties owning land will have to prove their title before a Government officer to be appointed for that purpose, who will thereupon take possession of the title deeds, and issue an indefeasible certificate to the rightful owner. Thereafter upon any transfer being made, the last certificate will be cancelled and a new one issued to the new owner. If the officer whose duty it is to issue certificates issues one to a person who is not entitled, and a transfer of it be made to an innocent purchaser, the Government will be liable in damages to the rightful owner. The matter is now before the New York Legislature, and this State will probably await action there. The proposed reform would be a great boon to the people at the expense of the legal profession.

Climate.—The climate of this district is attracting persons suffering from consumption from all parts of the world, in many cases with beneficial results. The following article on Southern California as a health resort was prepared recently by a committee of competent physicians resident in this city.

While the climate of the whole State has many features in common, as the wet and dry seasons, instead of the Eastern winter and summer, and the prevalence during the summer or dry months of the great north-west trade winds, sweeping steadily from the sea over the land, yet there are many points of divergence in different localities. This difference in climate is especially marked between Northern and Southern California. The mountain ranges and the valleys of all the northern portion of the State have a general north-westerly trend, leaving the country open to the harsh sweep of the north winds. In Southern California, however, the trend of both mountains and valleys is from east to west, and the high sierra, like a wall, shelters the land from these cold northerly currents. The result is a climate much milder and more equable than in the upper portion of the State. It might be supposed that the country, lying in the same latitude as the Carolinas, would have the same oppressive and debilitating summer heat. From this it is saved, however, by the tempered westerly trade wind, which daily blows inward to the land, bringing with it the coolness of the sea. There is a peculiar stimulus to this air coming in from the thousands of miles of salt water. One has to live by the sea to understand it. The key to the climate lies in this that it has a warm sun and a cool air; hence the cool nights. One picks ripening figs and bananas grown in his own dooryard, and then goes to sleep under a blanket. The warm yet not debilitating day furnishes one of the requisites in a climate for invalids; the cool restful night, with its possibility of refreshing sleep, furnishes the other. The question is asked daily in letters from the east what diseases and what classes of invalids may hope for benefit in coming to Southern California. In reply it might be stated:—

1st. Persons of delicate constitution, either inherited or acquired, and who resist poorly the extremes of heat or cold; persons who need a warm, equable, yet rather bracing climate.

2nd. Persons inheriting consumption, but in whom the disease has not yet developed, or only to a slight degree. Many such persons seem to throw off the tendency, and remain strong and well. Even if parents coming with the disease do not in the end recover, their children, growing up in this climate, have a strong chance in their favour of eliminating the inherited tendency entirely from their blood, and casting off the family taint.

3rd. Persons well advanced in consumption are often temporarily

[525]

benefited. Such persons should think well, however, before leaving the comforts of their own homes and undertaking the fatigue of even a week of travel by railroad. It should not be done unless under the advice of the family physician; and if they do come, it should be accompanied by friends. The despondency of loneliness and home sickness diminishes greatly the chance of benefit.

4th. Persons suffering with bronchial troubles are often much benefited. Such cases, however, and indeed many others, too often make the mistake of remaining for weeks or months without seeking the advice of a physician as to the particular locality suited to their complaint. The varieties of climate in Southern California are many. Some portions of the country have nightly a heavy fog; other portions only a few miles away have no fog. Some sections are exposed to strong winds; others are sheltered.

Some are low and damp; others high, warm, and dry. Other persons go away disappointed, possibly the worse, who had they sought proper advice as to the especial locality suited to their complaint, might have received much benefit from their sojourn in the country. There are certain precautions, also, rendered necessary for invalids by the coming on of the cool night air after the warm day, and by the cool breeze from the sea, which can only be learned by experience, which to an invalid is a costly teacher, or from the advice of a physician familiar with the climate and the peculiarities of the different localities.

5th. Those coming from malarious sections of the country, with systems depressed by the dregs of fever, are especially benefited. It is a common custom with the people here to go down to various pleasant points upon the seacoast, and camp out for weeks upon the beach, enjoying the surf-bathing. There are also well-furnished and well-kept hotels at different localities by the sea. This seaside life is especially beneficial to the persons suffering from the various compilations of malarial poisoning.

6th. The open air life which is here possible, and the great variety of fresh vegetable foods to be had at all seasons, help to break up the dyspeptic troubles which make life a burden to so many overworked men.

7th. Many persons suffering from asthma have derived much benefit from climate. The capricious character of the malady—no two persons suited by the same surroundings—makes it difficult to give advice in most countries to the sufferer, because of the limited range of elevation and climatic differences from which to choose. Here, however, within a circle of 150 miles, one may find spots below the sea level, at the sea level, or with an elevation of 10,000 feet above it; spots with nightly a heavy fog, and spots that never know the presence of a fog; places swept by an almost constant breeze, and others sheltered from all wind; the odours and gases of asphaltum and petroleum springs, or the air of the mountain pineries; the scent of the orange blossom, or the balsamic odour of the plants of the desert. Differences of elevation, which elsewhere one travels 1,000 miles to find, here he finds within a radius of 50 miles.

8th. Some cases of chronic rheumatism are benefited by the climate. Certain hot mineral springs and iron-sulphur springs have gained quite a reputation in such affections. The climate of the coast-line, however, has rather too much fog. Such cases do better in the portion of the country back from the sea and among the mountains. There are points along the line of the Southern Pacific Railroad, as it crosses the Colorado desert, where the hot, dry air, both night and day, and the warm springs for bathing, offer the very best climatic requisites for the relief of such affections.

9th. Chronic kidney and bladder troubles find in the mild climate, with its possibility of constant out-door life and the equable winter and summer temperature, the surroundings best suited to at least stay the course of the disease.

10th. Cases of nervous prostration, and all the innumerable train of tormenting ills that come to an overtaxed or deranged nervous system, may hope for relief by a residence in some one of the many pleasant spots that dot the land. The warm, clear day tempts to the out-door life, and the cool night gives the refreshing sleep so needed in this class of maladies. Strangers speak almost invariably of the restful slumber of the night.

I cannot advise persons to come here for the benefit of their health unless possessed of sufficient means to maintain themselves until renewed health will admit of their seeking employment.

Railroad Freight Movement.

The following Table of the Freight Movement by the Southern Pacific Railroad to and from Los Angeles for 1883 has been compiled by Mr. J. M. Davies, Secretary of the Board of Trade, from official sources. The statement for 1884 is not yet completed:—

UNITED STATES.

Local Freight.

Articles.	Forwarded.	Received.
	Lbs.	Lbs.
Merchandise	35,654,970	34,261,230
Agricultural implements	42,059	180,510
Barley	14,788,410	9,987,740
Base Metals	90,000	90,000
Beans	..	189,950
Beer	999,720	808,030
Bluestone	199,660	..
Borax, crude	..	684,140
Box material	117,410	2,539,490
Brandy	183,540	232,400
Bricks	277,080	121,706
Calves	6,500	3,500
Canned goods	45,860	288,000
Cattle	228,500	2,997,500
Cement and plaster	966,320	3,198,690
Coal and coke	115,740	10,196,790
Coal oil	1,115,840	1,868,900
,, crude	623,880	108,780
Corn	317,730	1,390,720
Doors, sashes, &c.	29,580	513,350
Farm products	132,240	213,980
Flour	2,142,080	3,669,540
Forest products	..	51,130
Fruit, dry	66,000	106,090
,, green	6,150,530	5,947,630
Hay and straw	967,390	1,501,860
Hides	809,040	545,290
Hogs	71,040	264,500
Honey	198,790	180,560
Horses	172,500	710,500
Ice	238,450	316,630
Iron and its manufactures	2,250,140	821,770
,, pig	..	431,520
Lath	218,940	4,770,100
Lime	20,250	5,271,420
Lumber	7,838,330	114,082,740
Machinery	199,400	41,420
Mill stuffs	1,018,610	131,780
Oats	21,030	21,000
Potatoes	426,810	2,745,790
Posts, fences, &c.	40,000	1,013,460
Quicksilver	15,000	20,240
Raisins	47,540	282,310
Rye	..	82,850
Salt	897,840	81,300
Sewer pipe	86,090	744,160
Shakes	60,630	1,830,540
Sheep	957,900	6,175,000
Shingles	118,060	3,258,090
Staves and headings	237,310	43,130
Vegetables	30,820	126,590
Wheat	2,155,760	14,152,200
Wine	2,427,340	4,132,370
Wood	54,920	6,592,540
Wool	421,270	1,735,090
Vehicles	102,620	20,500
Total	86,407,560	251,773,900

LOS ANGELES.

TOTAL of East-bound Freight from Los Angeles, 1883, including Through and Through Local.

Articles.	Lbs.
Barley	376,390
Borax	685,130
Brandy	694,590
Cattle	60,000
Canned goods	417,710
Fruit, dry	314,690
,, green	8,010,220
Flour	86,500
Hay	156,520
Horses	82,000
Honey	177,090
Hides	576,740
Lumber	358,100
Mill stuffs	20,040
Potatoes	1,319,830
Raisins	221,030
Sheep	6,941,200
Vegetables	20,030
Wheat	5,140,230
Wine	2,945,450
Wool	2,615,340
Merchandise not otherwise specified	871,570
Total	32,070,400
,, west-bound freight	38,572,890

RECAPITULATION.

	Forwarded.	Received.	Total.
	Lbs.	Lbs.	Lbs.
Local	86,407,560	251,773,900	338,181,460
East-bound	..	..	32,070,400
West-bound	..	..	38,572,890
Grand total for 1883	..	..	408,824,750

1192

UNITED STATES.

AMOUNT Received at and Forwarded from Wilmington from January 1, 1883, to December 26, 1883.

Month.	Forwarded.	Received.
	Lbs.	Lbs.
January	2,273,904	4,688,008
February	3,474,932	292,713
March	10,016,870	676,245
April	7,768,210	334,900
May	12,860,395	217,530
June	2,390,030	197,175
July	522,700	287,540
August	560,350	846,250
September	1,804,650	3,578,980
October	262,580	2,061,341
November	679,820	415,010
December 1st to 26th	2,194,510	424,080
Totals from January 1 to December 26, 1883	44,808,951	14,019,772

Los Angeles, California, February 3, 1885.

NEW YORK.

Report by Consul-General Booker on the Trade, Navigation, and Commerce of New York for the Year 1884.

The past year has been one of great depression throughout the Union: commercial, manufacturing, and financial interests have suffered alike. Importers and the wholesale trade have been receiving and purchasing goods upon continuously falling markets, and the profits, if any, have been reduced to the minimum. Manufacturers have had to close, or partially close, their works, and wages of operatives have had to be reduced. Notwithstanding the low prices and reduced stocks there has been no disposition, at any period of the year, to purchase more than what was wanted for immediate necessities. The time will arrive, and probably before long, when it will be recognised that prices have declined to a point which will admit of no further shrinkage, and some activity will be the result. The harvest was exceptionally good, but prices have ruled so low for all cereals that, except in well-favoured localities, the agriculturists have not been able to realise their crops to any advantage to themselves; and the same cause—low prices in grain-importing countries—which has operated against the farmer, has also had the effect of withholding the advantages usually derived by transporting agencies and all classes in the free circulation of money.

At the close of 1883 it was considered that prices of railroad stocks had reached a very low point, but later events proved that the over-construction of roads, and the extravagances in connection with many of them, were to have a much more disastrous effect than was apparently looked for by the most cautious and far-seeing. In May last there was a panic in financial circles, under which there was a ruinous fall in prices, extending, for the time, to securities about the intrinsic value of which there could be no question; the panic, although not of long duration, caused many failures of magnitude, but the disasters did not extend, except in a very few instances, beyond the limit of finance. Upon its subsidence the better class of stocks recovered, in some measure, their value, but the decline in all others has been maintained and under reduced dividends, which will probably be continued, there is no present prospect of any considerable advance. The statistics presented in an appendix will show the extent of the depreciation. The failures, as exhibited in the following table from the circular of Dun's Commercial Agency, do not show such an increase either in numbers or liabilities as might have been expected from the almost unprecedented depression experienced in every State and territory of the Union.

Failures in the United States.

Division.	1884. Number of Failures.	1884. Amount of Liabilities.	1883. Number of Failures.	1883. Amount of Liabilities.	1882. Number of Failures.	1882. Amount of Liabilities.	1881. Number of Failures.	1881. Amount of Liabilities.	1880. Number of Failures.	1880. Amount of Liabilities.
		Dollars.		Dollars.		Dollars.		Dollars.		Dollars.
Eastern States	1,375	17,223,831	1,197	37,861,897	772	13,491,400	772	11,071,156	723	6,460,117
Middle ,,	2,592	112,856,060	2,136	57,108,534	1,667	41,385,652	1,372	32,924,538	1,472	33,953,292
Southern ,,	2,291	28,318,557	1,844	19,785,607	1,618	20,998,123	1,439	16,469,412	835	8,813,442
Western ,,	3,369	54,872,983	2,961	46,878,403	1,950	19,019,175	1,504	15,594,732	1,171	11,519,419
Pacific States and Territories	1,341	13,071,996	1,046	11,239,731	731	6,653,214	495	5,096,094	534	5,005,730
Totals	10,968	226,343,427	9,184	172,874,172	6,738	101,547,564	5,582	81,155,932	4,735	65,752,000

NEW YORK.

The values of imports and exports of merchandise and coin and bullion for the past three years is given in the following table:—

MERCHANDISE.

	1884.	1883.	1882.
	Dollars.	Dollars.	Dollars.
Imports..	629,227,000	687,020,000	752,843,000
Exports..	749,304,000	795,092,000	767,982,000
Excess of exports over imports	120,077,000	108,072,000	15,139,000

COIN AND BULLION.

	1884.	1883.	1882.
	Dollars.	Dollars.	Dollars.
Imports—			
Gold..	28,113,000	22,056,000	13,402,000
Silver..	15,350,000	14,153,000	9,098,000
Total	43,463,000	36,209,000	22,500,000
Exports—			
Gold..	41,331,000	6,048,000	38,890,000
Silver..	29,117,000	25,793,000	17,148,000
Total	70,448,000	31,841,000	56,038,000
Excess of imports over exports	..	4,368,000	..
Excess of exports over imports	26,985,000	..	33,538,000

TOTAL MERCHANDISE AND COIN AND BULLION.

	1884.	1883.	1882.
	Dollars.	Dollars.	Dollars.
Imports..	672,690,000	723,229,000	775,343,000
Exports..	819,752,000	826,933,000	824,020,000
Excess of exports over imports	147,062,000	103,704,000	48,677,000

The foregoing statistics show that—

	Dollars.
Merchandise imports in 1884 were less than those of 1883 by..	57,793,000
Treasure imports in 1884 exceeded those of 1883 by	7,254,000
Combined merchandise and treasure imports in 1884 were less than those of 1883 by..	50,539,000

	Dollars.
Merchandise exports in 1884 were less than those of 1883 by	45,788,000
Treasure exports in 1884 exceeded those of 1883 by	38,607,000
Combined merchandise and treasure exports in 1884 were less than those of 1883 by	7,181,000

In a report on the commerce of New York, so largely that of the whole country, it seems proper to preface it by a reference to the trade and general condition of the United States, hence the foregoing brief summary is given.

Port of New York.

The value of the imports of merchandise from foreign countries in 1884 was, according to the Custom-house books, 429,380,956 dol., a decrease of nearly 45,000,000 dol. on that of 1883. Of the above 315,474,080 dol. comprised general merchandise and 113,905,976 dol. dry goods. 69½ per cent. was dutiable and 30½ per cent. free. The specie imports in the year were 26,666,865 dol., an increase of 5,854,831 dol. on the previous year.

The following table classifies the specie and gives the countries from which it came:—

	Gold.	Silver.
	Dollars.	Dollars.
Great Britain	7,114,739	2,723
France	3,975,152	843
Germany	6,337,568	46,590
West Indies	5,340,408	1,080,702
Mexico	30,657	1,988,038
South America	372,168	280,071
Other countries	30,686	64,520

The imports at New York in 1884 were over 68 per cent. of those of the United States. The Customs receipts at this port were 132,416,697 dol.

Imports from Great Britain and British Possessions are furnished in the table below:—

	Dollars.
From Great Britain and Ireland	100,589,190
Dominion of Canada	832,385
Newfoundland and Labrador	287,271
British West Indies, British Guiana, and Honduras	8,232,494
British East Indies	15,285,213
Hong-Kong	1,207,939
British Possessions in Africa	1,226,407
Australasia	1,614,600
Gibraltar	4,640
Other possessions	875,739
Total imports	130,155,878
Total in 1883	145,125,906
1882	155,041,132
1881	135,264,194
1880	165,305,351

NEW YORK.

Imports at New York from the under-mentioned countries during the year 1884 (exclusive of specie):—

	Dollars.
Argentine Republic	4,110,038
Austria	7,744,965
Belgium	10,923,160
Brazil	50,265,889
Central American States	6,161,227
China	15,616,793
France	70,842,413
Germany	65,019,163
Italy	16,706,357
Japan	11,274,485
Mexico	9,016,486
Netherlands (and Dutch East and West Indies)	4,872,933
Russia	2,779,659
Spain	6,207,520
„ Possessions, Cuba	57,181,497
„ „ Porto Rico	6,890,456
„ „ all others	12,339,351
United States of Colombia	3,891,843
Uruguay	2,128,981
Venezuela	6,674,041

The values of leading articles of foreign imports in 1884 and 1883 are given in the following table:—

	1884.	1883.
	Dol.	Dol.
Animals	1,347,178	1,143,904
Bristles	871,528	1,324,727
Buttons	2,564,257	3,120,514
Cocoa	1,179,265	1,057,789
Coffee	34,730,337	35,451,270
China, glass, and earthenware	8,116,609	9,588,047
Cotton	1,062,831	827,627
Drugs, &c.—		
Acids	376,340	1,133,387
Aniline colours	1,218,825	1,276,964
Argols	2,708,179	2,842,305
Bleaching powder	677,377	580,573
Brimstone	1,042,416	901,369
Camphor	271,770	315,332
Cochineal	97,043	205,835
Cutch	269,967	305,200
Gambier	385,706	367,650
Glycerine	476,844	578,996
Gum arabic	318,753	441,434
Gum copal	313,293	431,409
Indigo	1,301,277	1,709,356
Liquorice root and paste	917,639	872,546
Manuring salts	272,351	217,572
Oil—		
Cocoanut	714,405	555,618
Lemon	171,140	178,830
Olive	371,407	453,230
Rose	169,790	123,180
Paints	966,888	1,176,256
Potash, all kinds	787,948	855,654
Plumbago	235,972	416,290
Quinine	888,509	557,127
Saltpetre	286,956	376,835
Shellac	407,413	854,993
Soda—		
Ash	1,366,550	1,958,902

UNITED STATES.

	1884.	1883.
	Dol.	Dol.
Soda, continued—		
Caustic	720,000	573,734
Nitrate	1,135,562	1,318,621
Sponges	297,085	265,600
Sumac	178,910	175,864
Vanilla beans	357,885	372,326
Dry goods—		
Manufactures of cotton	22,842,717	25,918,700
„ flax	15,869,015	17,115,046
„ silk	35,869,781	36,891,942
„ wool	28,861,874	31,462,217
Miscellaneous	10,462,589	10,120,912
Fancy goods	1,065,982	1,312,197
Feathers	2,868,598	3,316,911
Fish	1,081,888	1,055,814
Furs	5,458,298	5,709,657
Fruits	14,913,795	15,276,479
Hair	1,286,988	1,609,340
Hemp	5,966,742	5,603,705
Hides, dressed	5,064,498	5,300,970
„ undressed	16,456,787	17,118,674
Hops	350,282	554,906
India-rubber	9,509,604	14,107,386
Ivory	565,093	670,431
Jewellery, watches, and precious stones	7,947,831	11,836,770
Jute	626,531	449,459
Jute butts	1,737,022	2,207,734
Linseed	3,566,798	1,489,930
Metals, &c.—		
Brass goods	205,896	261,806
Bronzes	181,122	203,740
Cutlery	1,589,313	2,141,452
Iron, pig	2,343,399	3,406,860
„ other	2,689,497	2,679,832
Metal goods	1,340,916	1,226,148
Platina	187,426	284,044
Steel	3,083,016	4,964,120
Spelter	148,590	264,146
Tin plated	8,860,239	10,239,384
„ slabs	3,964,524	5,577,248
Molasses	1,739,600	2,722,900
Paintings	1,338,503	1,461,824
Paper stock	3,900,948	3,219,704
Plaster	591,317	538,280
Salt	482,265	549,872
Soap	289,335	283,935
Spices	2,517,963	3,033,022
Stationery, books	4,074,179	4,143,010
Sugar	46,975,249	57,851,506
Tea	11,188,199	11,979,800
Tobacco and cigars	7,136,074	8,984,572
Toys	805,783	839,278
Wines, liquors, &c.—		
Beer	529,773	753,425
Bitters	94,117	95,864
Brandy	981,496	1,119,276
Champagne	2,230,737	3,001,050
Gin	166,855	177,787
Mineral waters	246,026	297,790
Rum	66,067	84,271
Whisky	124,101	277,960
Wines	2,481,750	3,246,042
Wood	7,015,295	7,769,643
Wool	4,334,937	4,882,947

NEW YORK

Exports.

The value of the exports to foreign countries from New York amounted to 385,271,949 dol., classified as follows:—

	Dollars.
Domestic merchandise	321,400,682
Foreign ,,	9,460,694
Specie and bullion	54,410,578

The exports of merchandise to Great Britain and Ireland amounted to 155,076,037 dol., and to British Possessions 24,061,425 dol., full particulars of which will be found in Appendix No. 13.

The following table shows the distribution of exports, not including specie, other than to Great Britain and British Possessions:—

	Dollars.
France	19,806,704
French, West Indies	1,101,005
,, Possessions in Africa	802,980
,, Guiana	53,212
Other French possessions	44,216
Germany	32,184,960
Russia	317,499
Denmark	3,089,537
Danish, West Indies	423,679
Netherlands	10,373,336
Dutch, East Indies	2,237,506
,, West Indies and Guiana	652,144
Belgium	16,308,302
Sweden and Norway	1,894,682
Spain	4,522,683
Spanish Possessions in West Indies	8,972,433
Other ,, ,,	142,987
Austria	1,891,034
Turkey in Europe	373,004
,, Asia	276,318
Italy	4,390,203
Greece	101,611
Egypt	348,869
Mexico	3,566,075
United States of Colombia	7,607,326
Central America	687,652
Hayti	2,964,880
St. Domingo	1,065,643
Venezuela	2,720,472
Brazil	3,767,409
Argentine Republic	3,046,676
Uruguay	1,178,515
Chili	1,580,804
Peru	487,952
Ecuador	92,170
Hawaiian Islands	
China	2,392,616
Japan	1,250,519
Siam	63,320
Madagascar	37,156
Arabia	129,439
Liberia	65,656
Africa	229,214
Portugal	3,187,054
Sicily	305,412
Sardinia	39,235
Sandwich Islands	175,519

1200 UNITED STATES.

The destination and classification of specie is given below:—

	Gold.	Silver.
	Dollars.	Dollars.
Great Britain	26,487,370	12,766,872
France	4,352,824	914,940
Germany	1,660,420	187,886
West Indies	3,889,577	69,337
Mexico	7,800	211,117
South America	879,105	76,613
Other countries	789,542	92,517

GRAIN.

The following table gives the quantity of grain shipped to Great Britain and the Continent of Europe, also the nationalities and description of vessels employed in its carriage:—

SHIPMENTS of Grain in 1884.

Nationality.	By Steamships.		By Sailing Vessels.	
	Number of Vessels.	Bushels.	Number of Vessels.	Bushels.
American	..	..	2	69,354
Austrian	..	..	24	744,385
Belgian	73	5,074,773	..	..
British	661	25,033,842	3	143,167
Danish	28	1,388,205	..	..
Dutch	54	1,917,564	..	..
French	65	2,283,770	1	12,537
German	216	6,442,330	2	35,004
Italian	16	498,463	35	447,604
Norwegian	..	..	9	254,815
Portuguese	2	107,989	24	442,022
Spanish	5	214,863	..	..
Swedish	..	..	1	23,010
Total	1,120	42,961,799	101	2,171,898

In order to show the changes in the carrying trade, I give below a statement of the numbers of ships of the different nationalities, with the quantity of grain each carried in the two past years; the percentages are also furnished:—

	1884.			1883.		
Nationality.	Number of Ships.	Bushels.	Per Cent.	Number of Ships.	Bushels.	Per Cent.
American	2	69,354	0·15	2	25,650	0·05
Austrian	24	744,385	1·65	51	1,498,684	3·10
Belgian	73	5,074,773	11·25	93	5,734,018	11·86
British	664	25,177,009	55·78	797	29,704,042	61·43
Danish	28	1,388,205	3·07	30	1,137,382	2·35
Dutch	54	1,917,564	4·25	52	1,587,762	3·28
French	66	2,296,307	5·09	45	1,532,093	3·16
German	218	6,477,334	14·35	119	4,290,018	8·87
Italian	51	946,067	2·10	61	1,704,768	3·52
Norwegian	9	254,815	0·56	24	650,594	1·34
Portuguese	26	550,011	1·22	18	406,747	0·84
Spanish	5	214,863	0·48	..	..	..
Swedish	1	23,010	0·05	3	50,443	0·14
Russian	..	..	..	2	31,760	0·06
Total	1,221	45,133,697	100·00	1,297	48,353,961	100·00

The shipments in 1884 comprised:—

	Bushels.
Wheat to Great Britain	13,378,405
„ „ Continent	15,282,435
Maize to Great Britain	6,623,455
„ „ Continent	3,087,373
Rye „ „	4,846,088

Exports of Flour and Grain from New York to all Countries for the past Five Years.

Articles.		1884.	1883.	1882.	1881.	1880.
Flour	Barrels	3,907,021	4,481,153	4,623,956	4,510,454	4,220,612
Corn meal	„	114,516	123,502	112,316	199,541	203,716
Oatmeal	Packages	33,637	31,048	9,538	10,422	62,902
Wheat	Bushels	28,687,362	21,712,652	37,620,103	41,788,708	61,909,929
Indian corn	„	11,862,158	25,445,262	9,012,373	31,614,480	49,875,430
Oats	„	2,456,219	147,835	170,586	434,337	427,959
Barley	„	76,343	8,313	6,616	7,442	254,833
Rye	„	4,846,088	5,088,084	1,980,586	1,074,163	2,181,183
Total grain		47,928,170	52,402,146	48,790,264	74,919,130	114,649,334
„ flour		15,628,084	19,985,188	20,807,802	20,297,043	18,992,831
„ meal		861,708	866,584	563,720	923,228	1,599,688
Grand total		64,417,962	73,253,918	70,161,786	96,139,401	135,211,853

VALUE of Exports of Breadstuffs in 1884 and Two previous Years.

	Dollars.
In 1884	57,591,322
1883	66,855,522
1882	76,902,493

RECEIPTS of Flour, Meal, and Grain at New York for the past Five Years.

Articles.		1884.	1883.	1882.	1881.	1880.
Flour	Barrels	5,988,855	6,305,268	5,909,145	5,730,436	5,422,252
Corn meal	,,	370,767	351,074	319,923	370,424	319,730
Oatmeal	Packages	77,967	66,644	53,459	45,796	112,650
Wheat	Bushels	36,864,761	27,087,779	44,857,341	44,297,112	59,492,246
Corn	,,	19,488,523	35,659,359	16,839,504	45,232,950	61,076,810
Oats	,,	18,167,287	19,041,085	16,040,989	14,684,857	13,997,960
Barley	,,	4,223,732	4,194,421	4,063,773	3,664,102	3,929,517
Rye	,,	4,284,831	5,049,633	1,859,581	1,730,104	2,045,758
Peas	,,	284,305	244,654	580,415	290,833	297,896
Beans	,,	270,900	1,041,200	228,388	403,140	418,488
Malt	,,	4,046,137	3,878,796	2,951,660	2,820,244	2,815,853
Buckwheat	,,	8,850	11,676	19,196	17,184	19,747
Total grain		87,639,326	96,208,683	87,440,847	113,140,526	144,094,275
,, flour		26,949,848	28,973,706	26,590,753	25,786,962	24,407,134
,, meal		1,948,510	2,000,614	1,824,174	1,837,778	2,421,398
Grand total		116,557,684	126,582,923	115,855,774	141,165,266	171,152,807

The visible supply of grain, comprising the stocks in granary at the principal points of accumulation at lake and seaboard ports, and in transit by rail and water, December 27, 1884, was as follows:—

In Store at	Wheat.	Corn.	Oats.	Barley.	Rye.
	Bushels.	Bushels.	Bushels.	Bushels.	Bushels.
New York	8,992,912	355,979	654,986	169,370	65,441
,, ,, afloat (estimated)	112,613	117,280	...	184,490	224,538
Albany	1,600	26,000	59,000	167,000	13,300
Buffalo	2,455,000	21,000	10,000	350,000	27,000
Chicago	13,479,785	1,475,219	489,431	86,872	104,403
Newport News	238,180	...	...	...	...
Milwaukee	3,640,190	...	4,473	95,861	15,511
Duluth	4,435,370	...	...	...	...
Toledo	2,805,735	34,205	28,466	...	58,663
Detroit	549,743	21,853	8,007	9,825	467
Oswego	212,000	110,951	...	520,259	2,200
St. Louis	2,502,253	357,194	65,690	44,630	39,814
Cincinnati	51,978	12,898	52,011	44,507	7,510
Boston	145,961	491,728	484,191	33,108	2,000
Toronto	188,579	1,179	875	123,221	1,101
Montreal	282,333	2,562	6,555	38,770	3,874
Philadelphia	1,108,135	120,939	99,440	...	...
Peoria	7,922	8,054	89,006	368	1,695
Indianapolis	59,100	6,400	102,500	...	2,000
Kansas City	844,609	55,345	2,612	...	1,350
Baltimore	871,190	302,666	4,769	...	31,256
On rail	396,932	903,430	158,052	70,000	22,211
Total, Dec. 27, 1884	43,382,190	4,424,812	2,319,974	1,938,281	624,343
,, ,, 29, 1883	35,507,400	9,695,044	6,229,342	3,292,196	2,673,349
,, ,, 30, 1882	21,048,017	9,104,137	4,423,374	3,010,154	1,470,685
,, ,, 31, 1881	17,762,769	16,861,137	2,747,274	2,972,274	1,301,723

The crop of wheat and other grain was far beyond an average, but the low range of prices since it was harvested has been very discouraging to the farmers. No. 2 red wheat sold on the spot at 1 dol. 12½ c. to 1 dol. 13½ c. per bushel during January, February, and the first week of March, when it fell to 99 c., and ranged between that figure and 1 dol. 5 c., acted upon more or less by a speculative feeling until it was known that the harvest here and in England was to be more than ordinarily productive, when there was a sensible decline, and in August 90 c. was the ruling figure. After this, there was a further gradual decline until the close of the year, when No. 2 red was quoted at 83 c. per bushel. Indian corn sold at 60 c. to 64 c. per bushel, until it was ascertained that the crop was to be a very large one, when it fell to 54 c. to 56 c., rallying at times, but closing at something under those figures.

Export of Provisions from New York in 1884 and 1883.

Articles.		Quantity.
		1884.	1883.
Pork	Barrels	133,038	182,167
Beef	"	129,968	145,539
Bacon and hams	Lbs.	200,188,089	275,581,355
Butter	"	11,883,540	17,612,679
Cheese	"	103,958,569	109,485,199
Lard	"	155,290,189	208,334,821
Stearine	"	6,862,641	5,509,709
Grease	"	34,014,063	42,044,521
Tallow	"	30,336,241	35,944,920

Petroleum.

The production of petroleum for the past five years is given below:—

	Barrels.
1880	20,048,000
1881	29,638,000
1882	30,460,000
1883	24,000,000
1884	23,690,000

Monthly Average Prices in New York in 1884.

Months.	Average Price per Barrel.		
	Crude.	Refined Standard White.	Naphtha.
	Dol. c.	Dol. c.	Dol. c.
January	8 02	9 47	6 92
February	8 11	9 11	7 41
March	7 88	8 51	7 50
April	7 74	8 58	7 50
May	7 45	8 47	7 50
June	7 09	8 03	7 50
July	6 21	8 81	7 50
August	7 06	8 04	7 50
September	7 00	7 89	7 50
October	6 76	7 86	7 50
November	6 81	7 76	7 50
December	6 83	7 83	7 50
Average for 1884	7 25	8 28	7 44
" 1883	7 44	8 14	5 96
" 1882	7 04	7 41	6 54
" 1881	7 15	8 05	9 52
" 1880	7 21	9 12	7 73

[525]

UNITED STATES.

The National Petroleum Exchange gambled in the enormous amount of 3,171,405,000 barrels of oil, as represented by pipe line certificates during the year, and the New York Petroleum Exchange handled 2,898,876,000 barrels.

The export of crude, refined, and naphtha from New York amounted to 9,613,036 barrels, 73½ per cent. of the total from the United States. In Appendix No. 7 will be found a table showing the destination of these exports, and the total exports for the past five years.

Sugar.

The foreign imports and domestic receipts at New York during 1884 and 1883 are shown in the following table:—

From	1884.	1883.
	Tons (2,240 lbs.)	Tons (2,240 lbs.)
Cuba	302,858	304,803
Porto Rico	18,391	13,106
British West Indies	91,961	65,940
St. Croix	2,732	1,040
Martinique and Guadaloupe	20,784	19,045
Other West India Islands (Peru and Mexico)	24,599	15,265
Brazil	120,738	83,081
Manila	69,580	82,700
China	6,251	6,715
Java	715	244
Other East Indies	14,487	5,816
European and other foreign ports (chiefly beet)	81,361	40,274
Receipts of Melado	896	1,454
From Southern United States	10,388	7,362
Total receipts	765,741	646,845

The prices of raw and refined sugar for the several months of the year, together with the average prices for the different descriptions in 1884 and 1883, will be found in the subjoined table:—

Raw Sugar.

1884.	Cuba, Fair to Good Refining.	Porto Rico, Refining Grades.	Havana, White.	Havana, Brown, Nos. 10 to 12.	Manila.	Brazil, Nos. 9 to 11.	Melado.
	Dollars.	Dollars.	Dollars.	Dollars.	Dollars.	Dollars.	Dollars.
January	$5\frac{3}{4}$ to $6\frac{13}{16}$	$5\frac{3}{4}$ to $6\frac{1}{8}$	$7\frac{1}{4}$ to $7\frac{1}{8}$	6 to $6\frac{5}{8}$	$5\frac{1}{8}$ to 6	$5\frac{1}{4}$ to $6\frac{1}{8}$	$3\frac{1}{4}$ to $4\frac{1}{2}$
February	$5\frac{13}{16}$ $6\frac{13}{16}$	$5\frac{1}{8}$ 6	$7\frac{1}{4}$ $7\frac{1}{2}$	6 $6\frac{1}{4}$	$5\frac{1}{8}$ $5\frac{3}{4}$	$5\frac{1}{4}$ $6\frac{7}{8}$	$3\frac{1}{4}$ $4\frac{1}{4}$
March	$5\frac{1}{2}$ $5\frac{7}{8}$	$5\frac{1}{8}$ 6	7 $7\frac{1}{2}$	$5\frac{3}{4}$ $6\frac{1}{4}$	$4\frac{5}{8}$ $5\frac{3}{4}$	5 $6\frac{7}{8}$	3 $4\frac{1}{4}$
April	$5\frac{3}{16}$ $5\frac{3}{8}$	$5\frac{1}{4}$ $5\frac{5}{8}$	7 $7\frac{1}{4}$	$5\frac{3}{4}$ 6	$4\frac{5}{8}$ $5\frac{1}{8}$	5 $5\frac{1}{2}$	3 4
May	$4\frac{15}{16}$ $5\frac{7}{16}$	5 $5\frac{5}{8}$	7 $7\frac{1}{4}$	$5\frac{5}{8}$ $6\frac{1}{8}$	$4\frac{1}{2}$ $5\frac{1}{8}$	$4\frac{7}{8}$ $5\frac{1}{2}$	3 4
June	$4\frac{3}{4}$ $5\frac{1}{16}$	5 $5\frac{3}{4}$	7 $7\frac{1}{4}$	$5\frac{5}{8}$ $6\frac{1}{8}$	$4\frac{1}{2}$ $5\frac{1}{8}$	$4\frac{7}{8}$ $5\frac{1}{4}$	3 4
July	$4\frac{13}{16}$ $5\frac{1}{2}$	5 $5\frac{3}{8}$	..	$5\frac{5}{8}$ $6\frac{1}{8}$	$4\frac{1}{2}$ 5	$4\frac{7}{8}$ $5\frac{1}{4}$	3 4
August	$4\frac{11}{16}$ $5\frac{1}{16}$	5 $5\frac{3}{8}$	..	$5\frac{5}{8}$ $6\frac{1}{8}$	$4\frac{1}{2}$ 5	$4\frac{7}{8}$ $5\frac{1}{4}$	3 4
September	$4\frac{13}{16}$ $5\frac{1}{8}$	5 $5\frac{3}{8}$	..	$5\frac{5}{8}$ $6\frac{1}{8}$	$4\frac{1}{2}$ 5	$4\frac{7}{8}$ $5\frac{1}{4}$	3 4
October	$4\frac{3}{4}$ $5\frac{1}{8}$	5 $5\frac{3}{8}$	..	$5\frac{5}{8}$ $6\frac{1}{8}$	$4\frac{1}{2}$ 5	$4\frac{7}{8}$ $5\frac{1}{4}$	3 4
November	$4\frac{13}{16}$ $5\frac{1}{4}$	5 $5\frac{3}{8}$	..	$5\frac{5}{8}$ $6\frac{1}{8}$	$4\frac{1}{2}$ 5	$4\frac{7}{8}$ $5\frac{1}{4}$	3 4
December	$4\frac{3}{4}$ $4\frac{15}{16}$	5 $5\frac{3}{8}$	..	$5\frac{5}{8}$ $6\frac{1}{8}$	$4\frac{1}{2}$ 5	$4\frac{7}{8}$ $5\frac{1}{4}$	3 4
Average for the year ..	5·29	5·33$\frac{1}{3}$	7·25	$5\frac{15}{16}$	$4\frac{15}{16}$	5·25	$3\frac{9}{16}$
,, 1883	6·79	6·62$\frac{1}{2}$	8·25	7·0	6·33	6·32$\frac{1}{2}$	4·60

Refined Sugar.

1884.	Hard Descriptions.				Soft Descriptions.			
	Cut Loaf.	Crushed.	Powdered.	Granulated.	Grocer's White, Standard A.	Small A.	Extra C.	Yellow, Extra C.
	Dollars.	Dollars.	Dollars.	Dollars.	Dollars.	Dollars.	Dollars.	Dollars.
January	$8\frac{1}{4}$ to $8\frac{3}{4}$	$8\frac{1}{4}$ to $8\frac{3}{4}$	$7\frac{7}{8}$ to $8\frac{1}{4}$	$7\frac{3}{4}$ to $7\frac{7}{8}$	$7\frac{5}{16}$ to $7\frac{1}{2}$	$6\frac{3}{4}$ to $7\frac{1}{4}$	$6\frac{1}{2}$ to $6\frac{7}{8}$	6 to $6\frac{5}{8}$
February	$7\frac{7}{8}$ $8\frac{1}{4}$	$7\frac{7}{8}$ $8\frac{1}{2}$	$7\frac{3}{4}$ 8	$7\frac{1}{2}$ $7\frac{3}{4}$	7 $7\frac{5}{16}$	$6\frac{5}{8}$ $7\frac{1}{4}$	$6\frac{3}{8}$ $6\frac{5}{8}$	6 $6\frac{7}{16}$
March	$7\frac{5}{8}$ 8	$7\frac{5}{8}$ 8	$7\frac{1}{2}$ $7\frac{3}{4}$	$7\frac{3}{16}$ $7\frac{7}{16}$	$6\frac{3}{4}$ $7\frac{1}{16}$	$6\frac{3}{8}$ $6\frac{3}{4}$	$6\frac{1}{8}$ $6\frac{3}{8}$	$5\frac{3}{4}$ $6\frac{1}{8}$
April	$7\frac{1}{2}$ $7\frac{3}{4}$	$7\frac{1}{2}$ $7\frac{3}{4}$	$7\frac{1}{4}$ $7\frac{1}{2}$	$6\frac{13}{16}$ $7\frac{3}{16}$	$6\frac{1}{2}$ $6\frac{3}{4}$	6 $6\frac{5}{8}$	$5\frac{5}{8}$ $6\frac{1}{8}$	$5\frac{1}{4}$ $5\frac{7}{8}$
May	$7\frac{1}{2}$ $7\frac{7}{8}$	$7\frac{1}{2}$ $7\frac{7}{8}$	$7\frac{1}{8}$ $7\frac{1}{2}$	$6\frac{13}{16}$ $7\frac{1}{8}$	$6\frac{3}{8}$ $6\frac{15}{16}$	$5\frac{7}{8}$ $6\frac{1}{2}$	$5\frac{5}{8}$ 6	$5\frac{1}{4}$ $5\frac{5}{8}$
June	$7\frac{1}{2}$ $7\frac{5}{8}$	$7\frac{1}{2}$ $7\frac{5}{8}$	7 $7\frac{3}{8}$	$6\frac{1}{2}$ $6\frac{3}{4}$	$6\frac{3}{16}$ $6\frac{11}{16}$	$5\frac{3}{4}$ $6\frac{1}{2}$	$5\frac{1}{2}$ $5\frac{7}{8}$	$5\frac{1}{4}$ $5\frac{5}{8}$
July	$7\frac{1}{4}$ $7\frac{5}{8}$	$7\frac{1}{4}$ $7\frac{5}{8}$	7 $7\frac{3}{8}$	$6\frac{5}{8}$ $6\frac{15}{16}$	$6\frac{1}{8}$ $6\frac{3}{16}$	$5\frac{7}{8}$ $6\frac{1}{2}$	$5\frac{3}{8}$ $6\frac{3}{16}$	$5\frac{1}{4}$ 6
August	$6\frac{7}{8}$ $7\frac{1}{4}$	$6\frac{7}{8}$ $7\frac{1}{4}$	$6\frac{11}{16}$ 7	$6\frac{1}{2}$ $6\frac{5}{8}$	6 $6\frac{1}{4}$	$5\frac{5}{8}$ 6	$5\frac{3}{8}$ $5\frac{3}{4}$	5 $5\frac{1}{2}$
September	$6\frac{7}{8}$ $7\frac{1}{8}$	$6\frac{7}{8}$ 7	$6\frac{1}{2}$ 7	$6\frac{1}{4}$ $6\frac{11}{16}$	$5\frac{15}{16}$ $6\frac{3}{4}$	$5\frac{5}{8}$ $6\frac{1}{2}$	$5\frac{3}{8}$ $5\frac{5}{8}$	$5\frac{1}{8}$ $5\frac{3}{8}$
October	$6\frac{5}{8}$ $6\frac{7}{8}$	$6\frac{5}{8}$ $6\frac{7}{8}$	$6\frac{1}{4}$ $6\frac{3}{4}$	6 $6\frac{3}{8}$	$5\frac{5}{8}$ 6	$5\frac{3}{8}$ $5\frac{3}{4}$	$5\frac{1}{8}$ $5\frac{3}{8}$	$4\frac{3}{4}$ $5\frac{1}{8}$
November	$6\frac{1}{4}$ 7	$6\frac{3}{4}$ 7	$6\frac{1}{4}$ $6\frac{5}{8}$	$6\frac{1}{16}$ $6\frac{5}{16}$	$5\frac{5}{8}$ 6	$5\frac{3}{8}$ $5\frac{3}{4}$	$5\frac{1}{8}$ $5\frac{3}{8}$	$4\frac{3}{4}$ $5\frac{1}{8}$
December	$6\frac{1}{2}$ $6\frac{3}{4}$	$6\frac{1}{2}$ $6\frac{3}{4}$	$6\frac{1}{3}$ $6\frac{1}{2}$	$5\frac{11}{16}$ 6	$5\frac{1}{2}$ $5\frac{5}{8}$	$5\frac{1}{8}$ $5\frac{1}{2}$	$4\frac{7}{8}$ $5\frac{1}{4}$	$4\frac{1}{2}$ 5
Average for the year.	$7\frac{7}{16}$	$7\frac{7}{16}$	$7{\cdot}12\frac{1}{2}$	6·75	$6{\cdot}37\frac{1}{4}$	$6{\cdot}12\frac{1}{2}$	5·50	5·50
" 1883 ..	$9{\cdot}12\frac{1}{2}$	9·17	8·89	8·65	8·74	$6{\cdot}87\frac{1}{2}$	6·59	7·22

There were taken for consumption in 1884 738,715 tons, an increase over the previous year of 100,624 tons. The exports of raw were 8,519 tons, and of refined 55,878 tons, of which 48,408 tons were shipped to Great Britain. It has been estimated that the consumption in the whole country was 8½ per cent. in excess of that of 1883. The increased production in sugar-growing countries and the enormous supply of beet-root sugar in Europe, under the fostering care of the different Governments, have caused a continuous decline in the value, until the price has reached a point below the cost of production, in any part of the world, of cane-grown sugar. The export of refined sugar has been far in excess of any previous year, which has been caused by the anxiety of refiners to relieve the market; and to do so to offer their stock for export at rates below what they were willing to take for the home trade; the concessions would not have been sufficient to allow of the export had the drawback not been in excess of the duty paid on the raw article, which amounted to a bounty variously estimated at from 25 c. to 42 c. per 100 lbs.

Molasses.

There has been a falling off in the receipts of foreign molasses at this port during the year of 1,848,720 gallons, and of domestic of 3,927,025 gallons.

The following table gives the sources of our supply:—

	Gallons.
From Cuba	7,740,995
Porto Rico	2,173,130
Barbadoes	174,375
Demerara	90,310
Trinidad	67,140
St. Croix	47,720
Antigua	64,740
Nevis	14,300
St. Kitts	4,250
St. Domingo } Surinam and other foreign countries	163,670
Total receipt of foreign	10,540,630
Received from Louisiana and Southern ports	3,927,025
Total supply	14,467,655

The consumption was estimated at about 13,000,000 gallons.

COFFEE.

FOREIGN Imports and Coastwise Receipts at New York in 1884 and 1883.

From	1884.	1883.
	Lbs.	Lbs.
Brazil	250,887,663	281,840,196
Maracaibo	32,198,528	28,681,549
La Guayra	20,552,220	14,531,040
Central America	13,725,180	8,547,840
Savanilla	6,545,920	6,851,520
Angostura	160,640	285,750
Island of Hayti	21,369,740	19,825,830
Jamaica	6,001,200	6,865,410
Porto Rico	1,446,885	4,762,395
Curaçoa	..	..
Cuba	34,320	4,370
Manila	402,280	59,520
Java and Sumatra	18,336,624	14,267,130
Singapore	13,206	406,410
Macassar	837,744	791,492
Ceylon	241,500	74,060
Holland	5,900,580	12,830,535
Other Europe	11,104,560	15,395,940
Mexico, Africa, and other foreign countries	5,175,600	5,509,350
Total direct	394,934,390	421,530,337
Received coastwise From Southern ports	1,043,955	1,644,860
Total receipts	395,978,345	423,175,197

STOCK at New York on the 31st December.

Countries.		Quantity.
Brazil	Bags	209,488
Maracaibo	,,	49,545
La Guayra	,,	7,514
Mexican	,,	5,288
Savanilla	,,	4,807
Central America	,,	5,615
Jamaica	,,	2,063
Angostura	,,	303
Singapore	Mats	2,314
Java	,,	8,200
Sumatra	,,	86,669
Ceylon	Packages	630
Africa	,,	3,000
Total at New York		385,436

The imports at New York have been about 75 per cent. of what has been received at the Atlantic ports of the Union.

The price for each month of the past year is given as follows:—

1884.	Fair to Prime Cargoes.			Java (Padang).
	Brazil.	Maracaibo and La Guayra.	St. Domingo.	
	Dol. c.	Dol. c.	Dol. c.	Dol. c.
January	12 62½	12 25	10 75	18 25
February	13 12½	12 25	10 75	18 25
March	12 25	12 25	10 75	18 25
April	10 71	12 25	10 75	17 25
May	10 37½	12 18·7	10 00	17 50
June	10 12½	10 37	8 75	17 00
July	10 12½	10 25	8 75	15 75
August	10 25	10 12½	8 75	15 50
September	10 87½	10 87½	8 75	15 12½
October	10 62½	10 87½	8 75	15 12½
November	10 06	10 66·6	8 75	15 12½
December	10 00	10 05	8 75	15 12½
Average for the year	10 92	11 18	9 77	16 56·2

The past year was an unfavourable one for the trade, but during the later months the jobbers were able to make small profits. The consumption appears to have been increassd 10 per cent., which is difficult to account for with the general depression. The speculative phase of the market, as represented by the option dealings carried on at the Coffee Exchange, has not been so prominent a feature of the course of trade, so far as the volume of transactions is concerned, as during 1883, but the Exchange has been no less an important factor of the market. Jobbers have found the buying or selling of options against actual coffee a convenient and safe way of protecting their supplies, whether spot or afloat, and have generally resorted to the Exchange for this purpose. In addition to this there has been the purely speculative element in the market, represented by operators in Rio and Europe, as well as at home, and who at times have been heartily interested in the market; and last, there has been a small clique of room traders, who might be aptly termed the camp followers of the Exchange. These three elements combined have transacted a large amount of business during the year under review, and their operations have been the barometer of the market, keenly sensitive to changes, and quick to indicate the set of the current. There has been no such heavy speculative movement during 1884, however, as was witnessed in 1883, partly because the course of the market has not afforded favourable opportunities for such operations, and partly because the sentiment of the times has tended toward a contraction rather than an expansion in every department of speculative activity. There is no data for making a comparison between the relative volume of trading during the past two years, as the managers of the Exchange have ceased making up their monthly abstracts of the business transacted, but there is no doubt but that the volume of business has been considerably less than in 1883.

WOOL.

There was drawn for consumption at this port in 1884—

	Lbs.
Clothing wool	3,462,722
Combing „	290,268
Carpet „	27,292,514

In Appendix No. 8 will be found a statement of the imports of foreign wool at New York during the years 1883 and 1884.

METALS.

IMPORTATIONS at New York in 1884 and 1883.

		1884.	1883.
Tin plates	Boxes	2,049,420	2,274,117
Tin—Straits	Tons	8,211	8,896
Billiton	"	137	70
Banca	"	350	394
Australian	"	1,056	1,585
English	"	132	225
Pig iron	"	70,963	128,388
Bar iron	"	14,812	15,999
Sheet iron	"	2,417	4,142
Scrap iron	"	6,511	19,596
Iron ore	"	35,732	36,640
Spiegel eisen	"	57,714	56,374
Steel and iron rods	"	115,627	102,136
Steel rails	"	23,828	37,111
Steel blooms	"	3,604	1,186
Steel—bars, tires, and forgings	"	8,860	11,838
Old rails	"	549	6,924
Crop ends	"	4,878	13,936
Spelter	"	2,040	2,687
Pig lead	"	2,287	867
Russia sheet iron	Packs	13,635	12,910
Antimony	Casks	3,044	3,406
Sheet zinc	"	2,393	2,615

RECEIPTS of Domestic Lead and Spelter at New York in 1884.

	Tons.
Lead	18,117
Spelter	2,886

BONDED Stocks of Foreign Irons, Rails, and Metals in New York on 1st January, 1884 and 1883.

		1884.	1883.
Pig iron	Tons	2,506	2,822
Spiegel eisen	"	1,422	3,005
Old rails	"	1,135	4,522
Scrap iron	"	1,177	694
Steel rails	"	121	2,603
Iron "	"	58	5,638
Steel rods	"	5,666	5,253
Iron "	"	546	707
Swedish iron	"	2,649	1,566
Sheet "	"	42	85
Russian sheet iron	"	77	416
Spelter	"	140	425
Lead	"	130	63
Antimony	Casks	128	143
Zinc (1,120 lbs.)	"	25	50
Tin plates	Boxes	42,542	32,759

The production of pig iron in New York State in 1884 was 239,486 tons, against 331,964 in 1883.

THE following gives the Prices of Various Metals in January and December of 1884.

	January.			December.		
	Dollars.		Dollars.	Dollars.		Dollars.
No. 1. American pig iron ..	20	to	21			18
Steel rails	34		35	28	to	29
Tin plates, Melyn grade, ICChl.	$6\frac{1}{8}$		$6\frac{1}{4}$	5·65		5·70
Tin plates, Allaway's grade, ICChl.	5·45		$5\frac{1}{2}$	5		5·10
Tin plates, Dean grade, roofing	5·15		5·20	4·50		$4·57\frac{1}{2}$
Tin plates, B. V. grade, coke	$4\frac{5}{8}$		4·85			4·50
Tin, straits	17·90		$19\frac{1}{4}$	16·10		$16\frac{1}{2}$
Copper, Lake	$14\frac{7}{8}$		15	$11\frac{1}{4}$		12
Copper, Baltimore	14		$14\frac{1}{4}$	$10\frac{3}{4}$		$11\frac{1}{8}$
Lead, common	$3\frac{3}{4}$		4·35	$3\frac{1}{2}$		$3\frac{3}{4}$
Spelter, ordinary domestic ..	$4\frac{1}{4}$		$4\frac{1}{2}$	$4\frac{1}{8}$		4·30
Spelter, Silesian	5		$5\frac{1}{8}$			4·90
Antimony, Cookson's ..	11·15		12	$10\frac{1}{2}$		11
Antimony, Hallett's	10·20		11	10		$10\frac{1}{4}$

DRY GOODS.

IMPORTS of Dry Goods at the Port of New York from Great Britain and Ireland in 1884 and 1883.

	1884.	1883.
	Dollars.	Dollars.
Manufactures of—		
Wool	12,783,489	12,579,819
Cotton	10,311,961	13,120,085
Silk	4,459,764	4,199,249
Flax	14,462,157	12,442,169
Total	42,017,371	42,341,322

The imports from all points in 1884 and the preceding year are given in the following table:—

	1884.	1883.
	Dollars.	Dollars.
Manufactures of—		
Wool	28,861,874	31,462,217
Cotton	22,842,717	25,918,700
Silk	35,869,781	36,891,942
Flax	15,869,015	17,115,046
Miscellaneous	10,462,589	10,120,912
Total	113,905,976	121,508,817

In the following Table will be found a Classification of the Leading articles of Dry Goods imported in 1884.

		Dollars.
Manufactures of Wool—		
Woollens	.. ..	12,893,209
Worsted fabrics	.. ..	9,021,360
Shawls..	.. ..	2,407,377
Carpetings	.. ..	856,737
Manufactures of Cotton—		
Cottons	.. ..	4,031,001
Coloured cottons	.. ..	560,206
Embroidered muslins	.. .. ..	4,376,206
Laces ..	.. ..	4,182,339
Manufactures of Silk—		
Piece silks	.. ..	15,489,833
Velvets	.. ..	3,221,021
Satins..	.. ..	291,677
Ribbons	.. ..	1,981,573
Laces ..	.. ..	1,861,487
Silk and cotton	.. ..	3,384,883
Manufactures of Flax—		
Linens	.. ..	11,681,963
Handkerchiefs	.. ..	1,384,383
Linen and cotton	.. ..	545,312
Miscellaneous manufactures—		
Leather gloves	.. ..	2,159,904
Kid gloves	.. ..	550,974
Feathers and flowers..	.. .. ..	823,934
Straw goods	.. ..	3,532,556

The course of trade in foreign goods at the hands of importers was irregular; the spring trade was scarcely satisfactory; and stocks were disposed of at a heavy loss in some cases, especially silks. The autumn trade proved to be good in some respects, but exceptionally dull on the whole. There was an active demand for velvets, velveteens, lustre dress goods, novelties in fine dress goods, and fine worsted cloths for men's wear, but many staple articles dragged heavily, as silks, laces, &c., which suffered severely from domestic competition, and from the general depression of trade. The stocks carried over, therefore, while not large in the aggregate, were rather full in these instances. The importation of Huddersfield goods has been gradually increasing, the imports in 1884 having been fully 50 per cent. over what they were five years ago. A leading dry goods journal in reference to this says:—

"The increasing demand for these Huddersfield goods is of such momentous importance to our domestic woollen manufacturers, whose retrospective and prospective condition has been, and is, with few exceptions, extremely unsatisfactory, that we deemed it proper to institute a few inquiries on the subject.

"It appears that the Huddersfield mills were so well employed during the major portion of the past year, that in addition to many of the leading manufacturers running overtime, they have been compelled to employ extra machinery outside their own establishment. The principal productions have been plain and fancy worsteds, for suitings and pantaloonings, corkscrews being the most popular kind of weave in plain and solid-coloured goods, as well as fancies, the styles of which have been neat and small in design. Silk is extensively introduced, and forms a very important element. The styles are always clear, and the colours bright, and when several shades are combined, the effects produced are most satisfactory. The special features have been a greater variety of patterns than usual, and increased boldness of design in response to the change in public taste, the fashion at present running on livelier and more decided colourings than in any previous years. Meltons have also done well.

"The corkscrew pattern grows steadily in favour, and is being developed into a variety of sizes and effects. Black has been perhaps the colour mostly prevailing, but there has been considerable enquiry for browns, wine colours, as well as for olives, greens, and grey mixtures, all of which have been in demand, not only for overcoatings, but also for suitings. Fancy worsteds have been largely sold for pantaloonings in checks and stripes. Imitation sealskins have not sold well, but astrachans, and goods of that order, in bright colours, have fared pretty well. Large checks for ladies' ulsters and dresses, as this journal frequently predicted would be the case, have given place to neat patterns in fancy makes, as with plain beavers and meltons. Black doeskin cloths have moved very slowly, and medium fancy goods have been much neglected.

"This trade with Huddersfield, which is rapidly increasing at the very time our own mills are so poorly employed, ought to be not only a matter of casual interest, but the facts concerning it might well engage the most serious attention of our domestic woollen manufacturers."

The new tariff came into operation in July, 1883, and the imports of woollen goods increased considerably; stocks became very heavy, and large sales had to be made at the auction houses. Local mill-owners suffered, and importers derived little or no benefit from the increased foreign supplies. What has been said in regard to woollens applies also to silk goods which were imported freely on the reduction of duty. With the increase of stocks, the demand for them decreased in consequence of the general depressed condition of trade, and the substitution of a cheaper material for dresses, &c.

Domestic Dry Goods Trade in 1884.

The past year may safely be chronicled as the least satisfactory to manufacturers and distributors of dry goods that has been experienced since 1878. During all the spring months, and until summer was nearly ended, the demand for consumption was checked by unseasonably cold weather, and the spring trade was therefore disappointing. In spite of bounteous crops, the trade movement was slow throughout the fall, and considerably less than an average business was done by jobbers here and in most parts of the country. While overproduction was largely responsible for the poor outcome of the year's business, by causing a steady shrinkage in values, and consequent lack of confidence, there were other depressing influences which cannot be ignored. The discussion of the Morrison Tariff Bill in Congress had a most disquieting effect upon business, and the May panic in Wall-street, with the subsequent impairment of banking facilities and resultant failures, caused merchants to adopt a very conservative policy, to which they adhered with more or less tenacity during the remainder of the year. The presidential campaign was greatly detrimental to trade interests during several of the autumn months, business having been practically at a standstill for a short time after the election, owing to the suspense then existing. Toward the close of the year there was a somewhat better and more hopeful feeling in the trade; and the outlook, if not particularly bright because of the industrial depression still prevailing, is at least fairly encouraging. There was an over-supply of cotton goods from the beginning of the year, and an unsuccessful effort was made in April to obtain the consent of three-quarters of the New England mills to stop production one day in each week for two months, in order to relieve the market. The May panic, and the subsequent stagnation in business, however, led to a partial stoppage of the mills, many of which continued to run on short time during the summer and early fall time, while some shut down entirely, and nearly one half the spindles in the country were idle for a time. The demand continued very slack until after the result of the Presidential election was definitely ascertained. Then manufacturers' agents determined to close out their surplus stocks of staple cotton goods, and succeeded in doing so, but at prices which probably left little, if any, margin of profit to the mills. The tone of the market became firmer before the year closed, owing to a continued advance in raw cotton; but prices are still very low, making due allowance for the lessened cost of production arising from reduced wages. The export trade in domestics has made a poor exhibit in spite of the exceptionally low prices which prevailed, the shipments from this port for the year having been 130,464 packages, against 142,516 in 1883, and 140,677 in 1882.

In the woollen goods market, the year opened with trade unusually depressed and sluggish, the only encouraging feature being the improved distribution of heavy clothing and woollens occasioned by the seasonably cold weather then prevailing. There was, indeed, an element of strength in the situation, owing to comparatively light stocks, and a marked disposition on the part of manufacturers to work closely to the orders in hand. It was found, however, that these beneficial influences were counter-balanced by threats of tariff disturbance, which, combined with some curtailment of banking facilities, tended to produce an indisposition on the part of the trade to anticipate wants. Values, however, remained more or less steady, owing to the determination of many of the manufacturers to close their mills rather than suffer any serious break in prices. The demand for spring styles lasted well on into the months of March and April, but it was early apparent that clothing houses did not intend to make their preparations for heavy woollens as early as usual. During the spring season sales were lighter than for some years past, distributors throughout the country being evidently determined to pursue a very cautious policy, leaving manufacturers the alternative of carrying much heavier stocks than usual, or curtailing production forthwith. The latter expedient was adopted to a very considerable extent, and the necessity for the step became more apparent as the season advanced. The "street" panic of May last, though without immediately disastrous effect on well-established dry goods houses, prevented the resumption of active business for which the commission houses had looked; and the policy of contraction pursued by the banks tended still further to the same end. These influences continued to operate with increasing force as the months passed away, the full trade entirely failing to recoup manufacturers for the losses sustained during the earlier months. Prices of spring goods were fixed at a large reduction from the previous year's rates, but buyers were not inclined to speculate, and none but first-class styles received attention. The year closed without any material modification of the trading conditions now indicated, and the results, it is to be feared, will be anything but satisfactory to the manufacturing interests. These remarks apply to dry goods, woollens generally, as well as to men's wear goods. Sales at auction have been large and frequent, and prices as a whole have been easy, while confidence has been impaired by the failure of several clothing and jobbing houses whose repute throughout the trade was of the highest.

VALUES of Imports by Sea of Raw Silk into New York in 1884 and 1883.

	1884.	1883.
	Dollars.	Dollars.
Shipments from Europe—		
Strictly European	3,955,887	3,766,551
Re-shipped Asiatics	142,841	164,051
Shipments from Asia—		
Japan	873,762	1,193,080
China	240,798	696,828

In addition to the above there were imported in 1884, viâ San Francisco, under "through Bills of Lading," raw silk:—

	Dollars.
From Japan, of the value of	5,047,616
„ China „ „	3,517,304

TEA.

IMPORTS at New York from China and Japan in the past Three Years.

	1884.	1883.	1882.
	Lbs.	Lbs.	Lbs.
From China	35,112,894	39,407,448	34,168,156
From Japan	15,072,431	16,370,368	19,641,542
Total imports	50,185,325	55,777,816	53,809,698

Of the receipts from China 13,503,743 lbs. were green tea and 21,609,151 lbs. black tea. The trade was unfavourably affected to a greater or less extent by the wide-spread depression that influenced every department of trade and industrial enterprises throughout the year, thereby neutralising favourable features that under other circumstances would have proved more advantageous; furthermore, a speculative deal early in the year proved disastrous to all interested, and contributed greatly to unsettle the trade throughout the country, and for a time so demoralised the market that it was many months before its influence was wholly eradicated. The unfortunate deal was in course of liquidation when the financial panic of May occurred, and consequently the market was not in a very fit condition to welcome the first arrivals of new crop which came to hand almost immediately afterwards; they accordingly met with a very cool reception, and the market continued almost pulseless until the warlike operations of the French in China imparted a little vigour to Oolongs, and the detention of two Suez steamers early in August temporarily improved the situation of Japan, but the improved demand developed by these features was short-lived and a reaction took place, which was scarcely neutralised until the last month of the year when the market began to respond to the favourable features which had been gradually developing, so that the year closed with a promise of better things.

Green Teas.—At the beginning of the year the situation of these kinds was exceptionably favourable. As the season in China had closed it was found that the total shipments to this country for the season would not exceed 11,500,000 lbs., which, with possible shipments from Great Britain of about 3,000,000 lbs., would leave a probable decrease of from 2,000.000 lbs. to 3,000,000 lbs. compared with usual receipts. With so good a showing as this, supplies were held with much confidence, and although not "called" upon the Exchange, values sympathised keenly with the speculative advance in Japans and China blacks, and steadily strengthened to such an extent that in March it became questionable how far consumption would be affected by the high prices that sellers demanded. There was very little disposition shown by dealers to purchase except the cheap lines, which were offered moderately through the auction room. These conditions were changed, however, by the collapse in Japans, and the sluggishness of the demand caused sellers to gradually yield, until in May an average decline of fully 15 per cent. on all kinds had taken place, the lower grades of round teas selling relatively higher than any other sorts, and the auction room proving the chief outlet for supplies. Trade dragged along heavily through June, the country buying slowly, and values gradually melting away, and the favourable features with which the year opened became so far neutralised by the conservative buying of dealers throughout the country, that holders at last determined to close out their supplies as rapidly as possible. Accordingly, during July the offerings at auction increased, as this seemed to be the only available channel through which sellers could market their stocks. Prices necessarily weakened, and transactions showed a heavy loss. New crop Pingsueys were shown by overland sample in July, but although quality was good they awakened but little real interest. This condition of affairs continued through August, and in September the near arrival of new teas caused the continued free offering of old crop by auction at prices that were still more unsatisfactory to importers. The offerings of new teas met with no better fate, and during October and November the market was depressed by the large increase in shipments from China as compared with last year. There was some improvement during December, in consequence of the scarcity of really choice Moyunes, while low grade Young Hysons were firmer in sympathy with an advance in common and good medium Japans, for which, in many instances, they are made to do duty.

Black Teas.—The year opened with Formosas selling on the basis of 30 c. for superior. In February it rose to 32 c., while March options at the Exchange sold at $32\frac{1}{2}$ c. and May at $37\frac{1}{4}$ c.; this was the highest point reached, and after the collapse referred to elsewhere, the course of the market was steadily downward until in May superior sold at 26 c.; in June there was a further decline of 1 c. to 2 c. Overland shipments of new crop came upon the market at this time in limited quantities and sold at 31 c. for good and 33 c. for superior, 36 c. for fine, 40 c. for finest, and 50 c. for choice, and the demand was limited, and these proved to be the top prices, for subsequent sales in July of parcels received viâ San Francisco were made on the basis of 34 c. for fine and 44 c. for choice, while for invoices to arrive per "Glenavon," the first Suez steamer, sales were made at 29 c. to 30 c. While the market was in this condition, the operations of the French caused some little stir and developed more disposition to buy, resulting in an advance of 2 c. to $2\frac{1}{2}$ c. from the lowest point, superior selling readily at 32 c. This advance had scarcely been established, however, when the prospect of a peaceful solution of the war relaxed the demand, and the market again became stale and unprofitable, with stocks pressed for sale through the auction room, and superior sold down again to 26 c. to 27 c. Belief that supplies would be materially affected by the war again revived in October, and the market once more showed improvement with an advance of about $1\frac{1}{2}$ c. in prices; but notwithstanding the subsequent partial occupation of the island by the French, the general dulness of trade neutralised the strong feature, and up to the close of the year they hung rather stubbornly and resisted further improvement, desirable fully superior second crop selling at 29 c., while low superior late crop sold slowly at 28 c.

The market for Amoy and Foochow Oolongs pursued much the same course except that the reaction for Amoys was not so marked as for Formosas. At the commencement of the year stocks were concentrated, and as a consequence importers obtained full prices, which advanced with the general upward movement in all black teas. At the Exchange as high as $32\frac{1}{2}$ c. was paid for No. 4 spot Amoys. After this there was the same story of dull trade and low prices detailed above. The first Suez arrivals of new crop sold at 22 c. for good, and 24 c. to 25 c. for superior. The war flurry in August brought about a slight advance in prices, and considerable business was transacted on the basis of 23 c. to 24 c. for cargo Amoy, while a fair business in Foochows took place on the basis of 25 c. for good cargo. Stocks, however, concentrated and confidently held notwithstanding the subsequent dulness of trade, but in November a disposition on the part of a few receivers to resort to the auction room resulted in a decline of $1\frac{1}{2}$ c. to 2 c. There was again a straightening up of the market in December, and the year closed with a very steady feeling for these descriptions, and a good demand for the lower grades.

The supply of Congous has been about the same as last year, but the general course of the market has not been favourable, naturally following the London market, from which supplies are chiefly drawn. Values have been low, quality considered, the demand running mostly upon grades costing 16 c. to 18 c.

Japan Tea.—The speculative movement in this description during the first three months of the year supplied the keynote of the whole market during the first six months; for Japans led the advance and caused the break that subsequently carried everything else down with it. Considerable speculative trading in Japan options had already taken place when the year commenced, buyers having been attracted by the unusually low point to which values had been depressed. There was not much activity in spot for actual trade demand, but the trading in options steadily increased in volume, and prices constantly advanced, until in February Standard No. 4, which the month previous had been sold at 20 c. to 21 c., brought $27\frac{1}{2}$ c., with 30 c. offered for the same teas delivered in June. But this was not the highest point; for in March, when the market was apparently "cornered," No. 4 Standard, equal to fully good medium first crop, sold at 30 c. net, while 34 c. and $34\frac{1}{2}$ c. was offered for June delivery. It was here that the crash came with a decline of 8 c., which was partially recovered, but the effects of this speculative boom hung about the market for months during which time the speculative holdings were being slowly absorbed, resulting in a further heavy decline in values, No. 4 selling as low as 16 c., and averaging during the month of June $16\frac{1}{2}$ c. to 17 c. Upon such a market as this, overland new crop teas met with a cool reception, and sold slowly at steadily declining prices after the first few parcels had been placed. The market for new teas thus opened sluggishly, but late in July intelligence was received that two Suez steamers bringing about 2,500,000 lbs. had met with detention on their voyage, and that their arrival would be deferred at least a month or six weeks. Up to this time the large receipts expected early in August imparted a dull and heavy feeling, but under the influence of this detention the market at once brightened and prices strengthened, establishing better prices for "Glenavon" teas and all railroad supplies, which sold readily during August at 26 c. to 27 c. for good medium. In September, however, this improvement was in a measure lost on account of the heavy supplies that commenced to arrive, as well as owing to liberal sales by private contract and large offerings through the auction room. Values steadily declined, and in November showed a falling off of 8 c. to 9 c. for good medium from the highest point in August. Towards the end of December there was some improvement, and values advanced about 2 c. from the lowest point, good medium selling at 22 c. to 23 c.

The quality of the teas has not differed materially from that of the previous season. The early Formosas were rather light, but later arrivals showed improvement, while the last crop was very undesirable. Greens were fully up to the average of previous seasons, which was especially marked in Pingsueys, although choice Moyune chops were really scarce. The choicest grades of Japans were in rather light supply, but "Exchange Standard No. 4" appears to have been a standard around which the bulk of the crop was fixed. The sales at public auction during 1884 amounted to 350,600 packages against 333,500 packages in 1883, and 530,000 in 1882. This method of disposing of stocks is the natural outlet for over supply at any particular juncture; it furthermore results from a stringent money-market and a disposition to afford shippers in China and Japan the opportunity of open sales in a declining market. I referred in my last annual report to a "tea call" having been commenced in the Importers' and Brokers' Exchange; it has not developed into anything of magnitude and it is doubtful if it will realise the expectation of those who took such a deep interest in its adoption.

Hemp.

The imports into New York in 1884 were 327,611 bales, against 289,201 in 1883. The highest price for Manila hemp was 11 c. in August, and the lowest 8¼ c. in May. The highest price for Sisal was 5¼ c. in March, and the lowest 4⅛ c. in June. The total consumption in 1884 of Manila was 201,953 bales, and of Sisal 161,759 (equal to 215,680 bales Manila).

Cattle Trade of New York.

Receipts for the year—600,947 beeves, 4,606 milch cows, 199,235 calves, 2,010,606 sheep and lambs, and 1,705,001 hogs. Receipts of Chicago dressed beef for New York and surrounding cities were 2,130 car loads, or 67,200 carcasses.

Exports of live stock and fresh meat from this port for the year were 49,252 beeves, 3,639 sheep, 411,981 quarters of beef, 57,805 carcasses of mutton, and 1,184 dressed pigs.

Selling prices of beeves have ruled fairly steady and about 1 c. per lb. dressed weight higher than during the year 1883. Sheep and lambs have been plenty, and with the prevailing low price of wool have been sold at lower figures than during any of the previous twenty years

Hogs have fluctuated with the fluctuations of pork and pork products as sold on the Produce Exchange. For the last quarter of the year the ruling prices have been very low.

The quality of the cattle, sheep and lambs, and hogs offered here for the year past would compare favourably with the offerings of previous years. The large demands for light and cheap cattle for canning and packing purposes in the West has kept out of this market the larger part of the Texas and range cattle from the far West, and our supplies have been more largely than in any former year drawn from the cattle-breeding States of Virginia, Pennsylvania, Ohio, and Kentucky.

City-trade slaughterers have been forced to contend with a steady and by no means small offering of Chicago-dressed fresh meats, and their profits have been small; but the failures have not been important, and their financial condition is thought to be fairly strong.

Drovers who have bought their cattle in Chicago and St. Louis have not made any money, but operators in Pennsylvania, Virginia, Ohio, and Kentucky have had a fairly good year's business.

American live stock and fresh meat exporters have lost a great deal of money—not less than 500,000 dol. in the aggregate—and the prospect of recovering even a part of this loss during the ensuing year is not flattering. Prices must advance materially in England and Scotland, or decline considerably in America, to leave a margin for profit above the cost of freight, shipping expenses, and insurance.

RECEIPTS of Live Stock at New York during the past Three Years.

	1884.	1883.	1882.
Beeves	600,947	670,297	639,408
Cows	4,606	4,335	5,073
Calves	199,235	190,327	193,672
Sheep and lambs	2,010,606	2,036,018	1,993,819
Hogs	1,705,001	1,586,243	1,418,189

EXPORTS of Live Cattle and Fresh Meat from New York.

Years.	Live Cattle.	Quarters of Beef.	Live Sheep.	Carcasses of Mutton.	Dressed Hogs.
1884	49,252	411,981	3,639	57,805	1,184
1883	68,300	384,735	31,027	68,187	496
1882	18,939	222,413	18,180	47,216	1,395

PRICES in each Month of Prime Beeves, Sheep, Lambs, and Hogs, in 1884.

1884.	Cents per lb.			
	Beeves.	Sheep.	Lambs.	Hogs.
January	12½ to 13¼	6¼ to 6¾	7½ to 7¾	7½ to 8¼
February	13 13½	6⅝ 7	7¾ 8	8 8¾
March	12 13	6¾ 7	7¾ 8¼	8½ 9
April	12¼ 13	7 7½	8¼ 8⅝	7¼ 8
May	12 13	6⅞ 8¼	7½ 9	7⅛ 7⅜
June	12½ 13¼	6 6½	7½ 9	7 7¼
July	12 13¼	5⅛ 5¾	6½ 7	6¾ 7½
August	12 12¾	5 5½	6¼ 6½	7¼ 8¼
September	12 12½	4¾ 5	6 6¼	8⅛ 8½
October	12 12½	5 5⅜	5⅝ 5¾	7 7½
November	11¼ 12¼	4⅝ 4⅞	5½ 5¾	6¼ 6½
December	11 12¼	4¾ 6	4¾ 6⅛	5⅞ 6⅛

MONEY MARKET.

The money market was easy throughout the year, the first five months ranging from 4 per cent. to 5 per cent. for loans on first-class paper, and the remaining seven months from 4½ to 5½ per cent. For call loans there was a wide range, according to the demand for Stock Exchange purposes. The first week of the year 2 to 3½ per cent. had to be paid, but after this money was plentiful at from 1 to 2 per cent. until May, when there was a crash in stock circles, and for a few days all rates were paid for temporary assistance, but the range may be said to have been between 2 per cent. and 8 per cent. per annum. In June there was at times a great demand, and high rates were paid, though the bulk of the loans were made at from 1½ to 4 per cent. In July there was less disturbance in stock operations, and the range was from 1 to 3½ per cent., after which to the end of the year rates varied from 1 to 2½ per cent.

NEW YORK.

Exchange, 1884.

The following table shows the highest and lowest quotations for bankers' sterling at 60 days' sight, and sight:—

	Sixty Days. Dol. c.	Sight. Dol. c.
January—		
Highest	4 86½	4 89
Lowest	4 82	4 85½
February—		
Highest	4 87½	4 90½
Lowest	4 86½	4 89
March—		
Highest	4 88	4 90½
Lowest	4 87½	4 90
April—		
Highest	4 88½	4 90½
Lowest	4 88	4 90
May—		
Highest	4 88	4 90
Lowest	4 84	4 86
June—		
Highest	4 86	4 88
Lowest	4 82	4 84½
July—		
Highest	4 84	4 86½
Lowest	4 82½	4 84
August—		
Highest	4 84	4 86
Lowest	4 82½	4 85
September—		
Highest	4 84	4 86
Lowest	4 83	4 85
October—		
Highest	4 83	4 85
Lowest	4 80½	4 84
November—		
Highest	4 82	4 86
Lowest	4 80	4 84
December—		
Highest	4 82½	4 86½
Lowest	4 80	4 85

Savings Banks.

The report of the superintendent of the banking department shows that the increase in the aggregate resources of the State was much less in 1884 than in the two preceding years. The following is a statement of the respective periods:—

	Dollars.
January 1, 1882	443,047,414
January 1, 1883	472,927,319
January 1, 1884	499,242,641
January 1, 1885	505,927,496

	Dollars.
Gain in 1882	29,879,905
„ 1883	26,315,322
„ 1884	6,684,855

A statement of the resources and liabilities, with some statistics in connection therewith, will be found in the following table:—

RESOURCES.

		Dollars.
Bonds and mortgages		141,944,250
Stock Investments:—		

	Dollars.
United States bonds	134,628,660
Discount of Columbia 3·65 bonds	3,159,000
Bonds, State of New York	4,073,250
Other States' bonds	15,713,166
Bonds of cities in this State	90,015,058
„ of counties „	10,142,096
„ of towns „	3,985,145
„ of villages „	1,123,625
Total par value	262,840,000
Total cost of stock investments	276,559,949
Estimated market value being	308,949,368

	Dollars.
	450,893,618
Loaned on stocks as authorised by chap. 409, Laws of 1882	6,217,044
Banking houses and lots at estimated market values	6,225,859
Other real estate at „ „ „ „	1,890,954
Cash on deposit in banks and trust companies	29,406,729
Cash on hand	5,889,270
Amount loaned on collaterals	185,806
Other assets	5,218,216
Total	505,927,496

LIABILITIES.

	Dollars.
Amount due to depositors	437,107,501
Other liabilities	150,994
Surplus	68,669,001
Total	505,927,496

STATISTICS.

Number of open accounts, January 1st, 1885	1,165,174
Accounts opened and reopened in 1884	237,568
Accounts closed in 1884	220,183
	Dollars.
Deposits received in 1884, exclusive of interest credited	152,521,462
Deposits withdrawn in 1884	161,516,369
Interest credited and paid for in 1884	15,023,236
Salaries paid in 1884	1,057,329
Other expenses in 1884	437,466
Unauthorised investments at market value to January 1, 1885	265,741
Average of each account, January 1, 1885	375·14

The aggregate surplus of the savings banks January 1, 1885, was 68,669,001 dols. on market values of real estate and stock investments. On par value of stocks and market value of real estate the surplus at the same date was 22,559,633 dol. The increase on market value basis during the year was 659,442 dol., and on par value basis 2,716,489 dol. For the year 1884 the sum of 15,023,236 dol. in interest was credited and paid to depositors. Of the 117 banks engaged in active business 10 paid 3 per cent., 16 paid 3½ per cent., 47 paid 4 per cent., 4 paid 3 and 3½ per cent., 35 paid 3 and 4 per cent., 3 paid 3½ and 4 per cent., 1 paid 3½ and 4½ per cent., and 1 paid 4 to 5 per cent. The nine banks in process of liquidation paid no interest to depositors. The total expenses of the savings banks for the year 1884 were 1,494,794 dol.; for the year 1883 they were 1,444,809 dol. The cost of the care of each account for the last year was 1 dol. 28 c.; an increase of 2 c. per account over each of the two years immediately preceding.

The average annual increase in deposits for the five years immediately preceding January 1, 1884, was 26,404,074 dol., but during 1884 the increase was only 6,027,491 dol. This great falling-off of course indicates the lessened earning capacity of the depositors, and is a very striking feature of the business depression. Two-thirds of the increase in deposits, too, occurred in the first six months of last year, which shows that the pecuniary situation of the depositors became worse as the year advanced.

We learn also that since the beginning of the present year depositors in very considerable numbers are drawing on their savings, evidently to tide over the hard times, for the total of the unemployed is much greater than usual. Mutual benefit societies and unions organised by the workmen are further helping to ward off distress by making allowances to their members out of work.

Yet bad as the times were last year, the number of savings banks' depositors increased from 1,147,585 to 1,165,174, a gain of 17,586, and the average of each deposit was only slightly less in 1884 than in 1883—375 dol. 14 c. as against 375 dol. 64 c. The strength and careful management of the banks, too, were satisfactorily demonstrated in a year when they were put to a strain of great severity. Last May, when there was so much alarm regarding the ordinary banks of deposit, several of the savings institutions in this city and Brooklyn were subjected to runs, and many depositors drew out the entire sums to their credit; but, to use the words of the superintendent, not a single savings bank was even momentarily embarrassed. Of course, the greater part of this money, drawn out under the influence of temporary distrust, was afterwards returned, but enough of it was probably kept by the unreasonably timid to exercise a very considerable influence on the revenues of the banks at the close of the year.

That there should have been any increase in the total amount on deposit in a year like the last is proof that the condition of business was better than it was supposed to be. With the savings banks owing 1,165,174 people 437,137,501 dol., the situation of our prudent workers is for from discouraging.

The number of savings banks in the State is 126, of which 25 are in this city.

	Dollars.
The total deposits in the State are	437,137,501
Of which is held by New York City banks	244,425,371
The total surplus of the banks is	68,669,001
Of which is in this city	40,229,681
Total open accounts in State banks	1,165,174
Of which are in this city	618,094
Total interest credited to depositors	15,023,236
Of which was by city banks	8,285,720

In Appendix No. 9 will be found a statement of the resources and liabilities of the several city banks

NEW YORK CITY BANKS.

The statement of the associated banks of New York City on the 3rd January, 1885, gives the following information:—

	Dollars.
Loans	297,887,700
Specie	87,867,800
Legal tenders	37,356,900
Nett deposits other than United States	340,816,300

The detailed statement will be found in Appendix No. 10.

STATE BANKS.

The annual report of the superintendent of the State Bank Department exhibits growth in the State bank interest, the number of banks having increased from 84 to 89 during the year ended October 1st, 1884, and the amount of their capital and business also showing a substantial increase.

The following is a comparative statement of condition:—

RESOURCES.

	Condition Sept. 22, 1883.	Condition. Sept. 20, 1884.
	Dollars.	Dollars.
Loans and discounts	92,495,044	88,515,326
Due from directors	3,843,919	3,595,641
Overdrafts	145,212	260,434
Due from trust companies, national, State, private banks, and brokers	12,958,753	11,504,281
Real estate	2,277,849	2,732,910
Bonds and mortgages	521,665	510,129
Stocks and bonds	2,903,559	4,310,684
Specie	6,608,161	11,298,772
United States legal tender notes and circulating notes of national banks	5,785,423	7,787,784
Cash items	32,192,097	25,504,478
Loss and expense account	361,765	384,010
Assets not otherwise included above	622,946	1,041,826
Total	160,716,393	157,446,275

NEW YORK.

Liabilities

	Condition Sept. 22, 1883.	Condition Sept. 20, 1884.
	Dollars.	Dollars.
Capital	21,761,700	22,150,700
Surplus fund	6,401,976	6,579,456
Undivided profits	4,744,442	5,213,446
Circulation	23,241	63,658
Due depositors on demand	113,914,963	109,560,334
,, trust companies, State, national, and private banks, and brokers	10,812,056	11,692,388
,, individuals and corporations, other than banks and depositors	2,171,845	1,506,839
,, treasurer of the State of New York	61,065	12,677
Amount due not otherwise included above	825,105	666,777
Total	160,716,393	157,446,275

Trust, Loan, and Guarantee Companies.

The superintendent of the department reports as follows:—
"The aggregate resources of the trust, loan, mortgages, and guarantee companies of the State on July 1, 1883, were 160,137,764 dol., and on July 1, 1884, 151,629,464 dol."

Each of the trust companies engaged in the business of receiving deposits of money has securities to the amount of 10 per cent. of the paid-up capital of the company deposited with the superintendent of the banking department as security for the payment of its depositors and creditors, such deposit in no instance being less than 50,000 dol. Trust, loan, mortgage, and guarantee companies were first placed under the supervision of the superintendent by chapter 324 of the Laws of 1874, since which date they have reported semi-annually to this department, and been subjected to regular annual examinations. The marvellous growth of the business transacted by the corporations of this class is shown in the fact that within seven years their aggregate resources have increased 87,100,025 dol., while the increase in deposits during the same period has been 68,903,336 dol.

The superintendent repeats his recommendation for a general law to regulate the organisation of this class of institutions to check their dangerous multiplication. He makes the same recommendation as to safe deposit companies.

Stocks.

The total sales at the New York Stock Exchange during 1884 were 96,865,325 dol. shares, as against 96,037,905 dol. in 1883, and 113,720,665 dol. in 1882. In Appendix No. 11 will be found a table giving the highest and lowest prices in 1884, the last price in 1883, and exhibits the decline and advance in the several stocks between the final quotations of the last two years.

UNITED STATES.

FAILURES in New York City and Brooklyn.

Dun's Annual Circular gives the following information:—

Year.	Number of Failures.	Amount of Liabilities.
		Dollars.
1884	718	77,875,721
1883	545	28,210,225
1882	455	21,212,308
1881	388	14,674,314
1880	415	19,459,744

SHIPPING.

The number of British ships which entered at this port in 1884 was 2,573, measuring 4,079,782 tons. Of these 1,409 were steamers, measuring 3,594,140 tons, and 1,164 sailing vessels, measuring 485,642 tons. The total tonnage shows an increase of 154,637 tons over 1883 and of 179,291 tons over 1882. The number of British vessels engaged in the direct trade between Great Britain and British Possessions in 1884 was 1,659, measuring 3,298,536 tons, and in the indirect or carrying trade between foreign countries and New York 878 vessels, measuring 781,246 tons. The total number of seamen composing the crews of British vessels entering the port was 90,869.

Appendices Nos. 1, 2, and 3 exhibit the entries and clearances of British vessels engaged in the direct and indirect trade with this port. Appendix No. 4 gives the number and tonnage of British vessels arriving at this port during the past 10 years, distinguishing sailing and steam ships.

Appendix No. 5 gives the number of seamen in British vessels engaged, discharged, deserted, &c.

Appendix No. 6 gives the number of ships and tonnage of all nations arriving from and departing for foreign ports, and the direct and indirect trade of each nationality.

NEW YORK.

OFFICIAL Statement of Foreign Arrivals at the Port of New York in 1884, with the Total Arrivals in the Seven Previous Years.

Nationality.	Steamers.	Ships.	Barques.	Brigs.	Schooners.	Total.
American	241	108	283	288	845	1,765
British	1,327	131	452	218	483	2,611*
German	236	113	166	16	..	531
Norwegian	..	30	269	19	1	319
Italian	21	3	182	27	..	233
French	88	..	6	2	..	96
Belgian	85	..	1	..	..	86
Spanish	57	..	16	7	3	83
Austrian	..	3	71	3	..	77
Dutch	48	2	5	8	..	63
Swedish	..	4	47	7	..	58
Danish	31	..	5	11	1	48
Portuguese	2	1	19	8	..	30
Russian	..	1	7	..	..	8
Haytien	..	..	..	4	4	8
Mexican	1	..	..	..	5	6
Colombian	..	..	2	2	2	6
Costa Rican	..	..	..	4	..	4
Brazilian	..	..	..	2	..	2
Venezuelan	..	..	..	1	..	1
Total 1884	2,137	396	1,531	627	1,344	6,035
,, 1883	1,979	438	1,744	758	1,457	6,376
,, 1882	1,945	407	1,857	896	1,371	6,476
,, 1881	1,953	408	2,350	883	1,385	6,979
,, 1880	1,895	575	2,893	1,007	1,447	7,827
,, 1879	1,591	681	3,234	1,023	1,548	8,077
,, 1878	1,310	540	2,919	1,021	1,528	7,318
,, 1877	1,074	389	2,254	1,076	1,451	6,244

NEW YORK HARBOUR.

The shallowing of the water on the bar has caused considerable uneasiness to be felt in view of the increasing size of the steamships coming to the port, and a report has been submitted by Major Gillespie, of the United States Engineers, to the Chief of the Corps, relative to the deepening of Gedney's Channel through Sandy Hook Bar, in which he says:—"The project which I submit for present consideration is to open a channel through the single shoal lying across the western entrance to Gedney's Channel, between the 30 feet curves low stage, by dredging, or by any other method providing for the raising of the obstructing material, and carrying it elsewhere to an assigned place of deposit; or by any well-developed plan of removal by artificial currents. The proposed cut will extend along the axis of the channel for an approximate distance of 4,000 feet; will be 1,000 feet wide, and will carry 30 feet at mean low stage. The maximum depth of cutting will be 6½ feet, and the amount of material required to be removed will be 700,000 cubic yards, measured in place. The tonnage of the largest vessel using the port in 1830 was 600 tons, draught 10 feet; increased in 1860 to 3,000 tons, draught 21 to 24 feet; and in 1884 to 8,000 tons draught 26 feet and over.

"The commercial importance of the city of New York demands, it seems to me, that the depth of the bar at low tide should be greater

* The Consular Register shows 2,573.

than the loaded draught of the largest vessel coming to the port, so that a crossing may be made at all times without regard to tides. The latest construction is the 'Umbria,' of the Cunard line. It has a light draught of 26 feet, and loaded of 28 feet. The 'Great Eastern,' which came here in 1863, had a tonnage of 18,000 tons, and drew 27 feet. She is an exceptional vessel, and no vessel of her type will probably be built again. I do not know that the cut once opened will be self-maintaining, but the present appropriation being small, it is well enough to experiment with it, and if the experiment is moderately successful the use of large sums for construction by stone structures may be avoided, and the annual appropriation for maintenance may be placed at comparatively low figures."

AGRICULTURE.

There is nothing of interest specially to report upon the agriculture of this State. I had hoped to have received in time the State Diary Commissioners' report, as it would, no doubt, have given interesting statistics in regard to a very important feature connected with it, but it has not yet been published. I give in Appendix No. 12 a table, compiled from official sources, showing the product in 1883 of the principal crops of the several States and territories in this Consular district.

CANALS.

The report of the superintendent of Public Works shows that the expenditures of the department for the fiscal year ending September 30 last were 737,346 dol. 3 c., and for extraordinary repairs 33,096 dol. 42 c. The canals were opened on May 6 and closed on December 1, the tonnage for the season being 5,000,488 tons, a decrease of 654,568 tons from the previous year. During the past season the levels have been kept to the standard depth of water, and there have been no interruptions except those caused by breaks. Of the 30,000 dol. appropriated for removing obstructions in and improving the navigation of the Hudson river between Troy and Coxsackie, 17,990 dol 71 c. have been expended, exclusive of the cost of engineering. The work of lengthening Lock No. 50 of the Erie Canal has been begun, and will be completed before the opening of navigation this year. The superintendent recommended the passage of a Bill for the construction of a dam and reservoir at Forestport to supply water to what is known as the "long level," between Utica and Syracuse, so as to supply a much-needed increase of storage capacity. He recommends the substitution of a lift bridge for the swing bridge at Albion, which is a serious obstruction to navigation, on the level between Lockport and Rochester, and the digging out, root and branch, of the eel grass, which is constantly growing in this section of the canal, and is a source of considerable annoyance and expense. The superintendent also suggests the construction of one or more reservoirs of sufficient capacity to overcome any emergency that may arise from lack of water in the Champlain Canal.

NEW YORK.

LABOUR MARKET.

The following are the current wages in this city and neighbourhood:—

	Dol. c.	Dol. c.	
Carpenters	2 50 to	3 00	per day.
Plasterers	3 50	..	,,
Painters	2 75	..	,,
Stonemasons	4 00	4 50	,,
Stonecutters	4 00	..	,,
Bricklayers	4 25	4 50	,,
Stair builders	3 50	..	,,
Marble cutters	2 50	3 50	,,
,, furniture workers	2 00	..	,,
Brickmakers	2 50	3 00	,,
Burners	3 50	4 00	,,
Grist millers	18 00	25 00	per week.
Engineers	2 00	3 50	per day.
Firemen	12 00	14 00	per week.
Cattle slaughterers	40 00	45 00	,,
Sheep ,,	20 00	30 00	,,
Cigar hand workers	12 00	13 00	,,
Maltsters, ordinary	11 25	11 50	,,
Brewers, ,,	11 00	13 00	,,
Bakers	13 00	15 00	,,
Sugar boilers	55 00	100 00	per month.
,, filtermen	1 45	1 50	per day.
Machinists	2 50	3 50	,,
Pattern makers	3 00	3 50	,,
Moulders	3 25	3 50	,,
Blacksmiths	15 00	..	per week.
,, helpers	8 00	10 00	,,
Brass workers, skilled	17 00	18 00	,,
,, unskilled	10 00	11 00	,,
Tinsmiths	10 00	10 50	,,
Planers in planing mills	14 00	..	,,
Sawyers	15 00	17 00	,,
Boys in planing and saw mills	4 00	..	,,
Garment cutters, men	16 00	25 00	,,
,, women	12 00	..	,,
Cloak-makers, ,,	7 00	..	,,
Labourers, unskilled	1 00	1 50	,,

Attached to Castle Garden (emigrant landing depôt) is a Labour Bureau, which found employment in 1884 for 23,687 immigrants, of whom 15,302 were males and 8,385 females. The female immigrants were, with but few exceptions, engaged for household work of various kinds. Of the males, 11,768 were engaged for agricultural or common labour and 3,534 for the following occupations:—

Apprentices	44
Bakers	220
Barbers	14
Barkeepers	210
Basket makers	6
Boiler smiths	2
Bookbinders	10
Brass finishers	21
Brass moulders	16
Brewers	12
Brushmakers	2
Butchers	123
Cabinet makers	222
Carpenters	144
Cigar makers	33
Compositors	2
Confectioners	34
Cooks	22

Coopers	38
Coppersmiths	5
Dyers	3
Druggists	4
Engravers	5
Florists	64
File cutters	1
Gardeners	254
Gilders	5
Glaziers	4
Goldsmiths	3
Grocery clerks	111
Hatters	42
Horse shoers	52
Iron moulders	24
Lithographers	2
Locksmiths	154
Masons	115
Machinists	151
Miners	60
Millers	15
Musicians	6
Painters	74
Plasterers	27
Potters	7
Saddlers	44
Shoemakers	237
Spinners	5
Stone cutters	10
Tailors	210
Tanners	18
Tawers	6
Tinsmiths	66
Turners	17
Upholsterers	16
Wagon smiths	104
Waiters	312
Wheelwrights	66
Weavers	60

The wages of the females varied from 8 dol. to 10 dol. 50 c. per month; those of ordinary labourers, 1 dol. to 1 dol. 25 c. per day. Farm labourers varied greatly in the different months, as will be seen in the following table:—

	Per Month.
	Dol. c.
January	7 50
February	8 50
March	12 00
April	13 00
May	14 00
June	15 00
July	14 00
August	12 00
September	11 00
October	10 00
November	9 00
December	7 00

The following, copied from a local paper, gives a good report of the labour market:—

"*Wages and Cost of Living.*—We begin a new year with a general sense of depression. This is due, probably, as much to the general reduction in wages of labour as to any other cause. All over the country, during the past few months, there has been a readjustment of the terms of labour. Employers, in a great number of instances, have found themselves unable to continue operations in view of the decline in the prices of their products, without a corresponding reduction in the cost of producing them. Accordingly, they have notified their workmen that it would be impossible for them to avoid more or less prolonged suspension of labour, unless lower wages should be accepted. In many other cases establishments have been closed without any attempt to secure new arrangements, because employers deemed it safer not to add to the stock of goods unsold, which already clogged the market. The great number of persons thus thrown out of employment, by seeking work elsewhere, rendered the readjustment of wages inevitable, and in consequence the reduction proposed by those employers who were willing to continue work at all has been generally accepted. A late statement, prepared by 'Bradstreet's Commercial Agency' from reports of its correspondents in all parts of the country, indicates that only about 17,000 persons are on strike and about 316,000 unemployed, while most of the remainder, fully 80 per cent. of the whole, have accepted lower wages. It is supposed that the reduction in rates averages from 10 to 15 per cent.

"These figures, however, apply only to the manufacturing and mechanical pursuits, and give little idea of the condition of labour in agriculture, in transportation, or in that large class of persons known to the Census Bureau as 'personal or professional services.' The wages of farm labour change more slowly than in other branches of employment, and depend more directly upon the immediate local demand and supply. In the wages of persons employed in transportation a change as great, probably, as in manufactures has already taken place. On the other hand, the rate of wages for ordinary labour by the day depends so largely upon individual needs and circumstances, and is, at all events, so low that it can hardly be said to have undergone much change. One large class of persons employed in domestic service seems to be more nearly independent of all human vicissitudes than any other. The wages of that class have a faculty of rising, but no perceptible faculty of falling. Depression there is felt, however, perhaps quite as much as anywhere else; not in the reduced rates of wages, but in the material diminution of the number of persons employed. In hard times families contrive to get along with one servant instead of two, or with none instead of one, and find it a good deal easier than to cut down wages.

"Thus, on the whole, there has been a very important decrease in the sum of money paid for labour in the aggregate. Probably, considering the number of persons unemployed, the sum paid for labour weekly is more than 15 per cent. lower than it was six months ago. This, by itself, would imply a very great change in the relative positions of different elements of society and in the cost of production. It causes, too, more general and widespread dissatisfaction than any other of the many consequences of industrial disorder. Unhappily the people who work for wages do not always consider that the cost of what they have to buy has also diminished. Taking wholesale prices as a guide, there has probably been so great a change that, in the aggregate, the dollar will now buy as much as 1 dol. 15 c. would have bought six months ago. A considerable part of this decline, moreover, is reflected in retail sales, so that the actual cost of living to all labouring people has been reduced, though probably not so much in proportion as the aggregate sum paid for wages. The discrepancy is due to the inertia of retail prices. These do not yield in correspondence with a decline in wholesale prices, and the consequence is that some part of the compensating advantage of a lower cost of living is lost to the labourer, who has to accept a lower rate of wages. But the remedy for this he has largely in his own hands. The buyers make retail prices. No combination of dealers has ever existed or probably ever will exist powerful enough to resist a general determination on the part of those who buy to go where they can get prices most closely agreeing with those of the wholesale market. The ignorance of many buyers, the indifference of many others, the want of concert between them, the tyranny of habit which moves most people to buy just where they have been in the habit of buying, all give the retail dealer an advantage of which he is sure to avail himself.

"This adjustment of prices and wages to a lower level, however, has been absolutely necessary to a revival of prosperity. Those who suffer most by it are, after all, the capitalists, whose interests and dividends vanish, and whose property at the same time sinks tremendously in market value. Those who live by the wages of labour are, as they ought to be, in a measure compensated for any loss of income by a decrease in the cost of living, and it rests mainly with them to determine whether the compensation shall in part be defeated by excessive retail charges. Meanwhile, the adjustment to a lower cost of production prepares the way for a more healthy and profitable industry hereafter; and when wages have touched a point at which producers can make a profit, an increase of production naturally follows, which, in this case, would mean a revival of trade and resumption of work by the unemployed."

IMMIGRATION.

There were 320,197 immigrants landed at this port in 1884, and they came from the following countries:—

England	25,917
Ireland	40,829
Scotland	5,569
Wales	1,880
Germany	142,139
Austria	3,581
Hungary	15,962
Sweden	17,317
Norway	10,231
Denmark	7,147
Netherlands	2,867
Belgium	1,862
Switzerland	7,154
France	3,122
Italy	13,993
Roumania	73
Greece	54
Spain	85
Portugal	6
Russia	12,678
Bohemia	7,221
Luxemburg	243
Turkey in Europe	67
British North America	36
West Indies	14
South America	11
Australia and New Zealand	5
Sandwich Islands	3
British East Indies	10
China	5
Japan	4
Other Asiatics	21
Africa	91
	320,197

of whom 15,162 were citizens of the United States.

NEW YORK.

The total number landed at Castle Garden	320,197
Of whom are citizens	15,162
Aliens, steerage passengers	305,035
„ cabin „	24,995
	330,030
Comprising, adult males	207,158
„ adult females	76,360
„ children under 12	46,512
	330,030

The avowed destination of the immigrants was as follows:—

Arizona	193
Arkansas	297
Alabama	148
Australia	13
British Columbia	48
Connecticut	6,159
Colorado	1,942
Cuba	21
California	5,588
Canada	1,838
Delaware	295
District of Columbia	198
Dakota	3,900
Florida	245
Georgia	217
Indiana	7,648
Illinois	27,750
Idaho	151
Iowa	11,110
Indian Territory	5
Kentucky	1,380
Kansas	5,279
Louisiana	434
Maine	385
Maryland	1,538
Michigan	13,271
Missouri	6,389
Minnesota	14,100
Mississippi	85
Montana	471
Mexico	55
Massachusetts	8,814
Manitoba	5
New Hampshire	363
North Carolina	55
Nebraska	6,725
New Mexico	106
New Brunswick	10
Nevada	487
New York	111,472
New Jersey	8,062
Ohio	13,818
Oregon	689
Pennsylvania	33,992
Rhode Island	2,161
South Carolina	125
Tennessee	309
Texas	4,845
Utah	1,893
Vermont	321
Virginia	194
West Virginia	256
Wisconsin	14,608
Washington Territory	135
Wyoming	499
West Indies	9

1234   UNITED STATES.

These figures, however, only approximately represent the number who actually settled in each State, since many who declare their destination to be in the Eastern States design remaining only temporarily, preparatory to removing further west.

In 1883 405,909 alien passengers arrived at this port, of whom 379,460 were immigrants.

During 1884 there were returned to the countries whence they came, through the agency of the Board of Commissioners of Emigration, 1,144 immigrants under the Act of Congress, which forbids the landing of any convict, idiot, or any person unable to take care of himself or herself without becoming a public charge.

Castle Garden is the legal landing-place of immigrants (steerage passengers being designated as such) arriving from foreign ports. It is situated at the southern extremity of the city, and is well adapted for the uses to which it is devoted. It is about one-third surrounded by the waters of the harbour, which furnish sufficient space for the wharves required for the reception of immigrants: the interior contains ample space for the accommodation of 3,000 immigrants and their baggage, and for all the offices required for the Commissioners and their officers. Attached to Castle Garden is a labour bureau maintained at the expense of the German and Irish emigrant societies, which provided employment in the past year for 23,687 immigrants, of whom 15,302 were males and 8,385 females.

New Buildings.

Plans Filed during the Year: the City's Growth.—Inspector Esterbrook, of the Department of Buildings, and his staff of assistants, to-day close one of the most active years in the history of the Bureau. Examination of the records show that during 1884 plans for 2,905 new buildings have been filed. The estimated cost of these new buildings is 44,160,423 dol. The actual cost, however, far exceed these figures, as the expense of construction generally goes above figures estimated by the architect. In some cases the estimated cost is not given on the plans, and therefore is not included in the above figures. These buildings are located in all parts of the city, but the majority are to be built in the upper part. The following table shows the number of plans filed each month during the year, with the estimated cost for the same:—

Month.	Plans Filed.	Estimated Cost.
		Dollars.
January	277	3,956,423
February	269	4,846,821
March	270	3,743,010
April	266	4,881,542
May	259	4,324,285
June	260	3,844,510
July	238	3,981,230
August	264	3,946,028
September	232	3,513,151
October	209	3,355,390
November	191	2,194,533
December	170	1,574,500
Total	2,905	44,160,423

The number of plans filed last year was 2,748, which was an increase for 1884 of 157. The estimated cost of buildings last year was

43,214,346 dol.: increase of estimated cost over last year 946,077 dol. In a number of the plans filed there are from five to 20 buildings included that are not specified. Plans for the alteration of 2,279 old buildings have been filed during the year, representing an estimated cost of about 5,000,000 dol. against 4,540,885 dol. last year.

1,734 buildings were reported as unsafe, and complaints were received against 1,900 others.

The following figures are given to show the rapid growth of the city as represented annually for the last 11 years in the number of plans filed:—

Year.	Estimated Cost.
	Dollars.
1874	16,667,414
1875	18,226,870
1876	15,903,880
1877	13,365,114
1878	15,219,680
1879	22,507,322
1880	29,115,335
1881	43,391,300
1882	44,793,186
1883	43,214,346
1884	44,160,423

Fire Department.

The work that the New York Fire Department has accomplished during the past year fully entitles it to the credit of being second to none in the world. During the entire year the department has been actively employed day and night fighting conflagrations and making experiments and plans for its better equipment. In no previous year has the department been kept so busy as during 1884. There have been more fires to attend, more duties to perform, and a smaller loss of property than in any single year before. Some interesting facts and figures regarding the work of the department are given below. The present department was established in 1865 by Act of Legislature. There are now 1,027 persons connected with it, including those employed in the several bureaus. The Board of Fire Commissioners, three in number, are in full charge. They have an executive staff of 18. The uniformed force at present numbers 879, and is under the command of Chief Charles Shay. There is an assistant chief, 12 battalion chiefs, 160 company officers, 109 engineers, and 595 firemen and privates. In connection with the department there are the Bureau of Combustibles, inspectors of buildings, the fire alarm and telegraph service, the repair shops, and the hospital and training stables. In these 119 persons are employed.

The Fire Department now consists of 52 engine companies, 18 hook and ladder companies, and two water towers. Two of the engine companies are stationed on the fireboats "William F. Havermeyer" and the "Zophar Mills." There are about 300 engines, hose carriages, hook and ladder trucks, and other vehicles of various kinds in use in the department. The hose lines are 120,000 feet in length.

During the past year there have been several new buildings erected, and almost every engine-house has undergone repairs. Extra engines, and a second company, consisting of an assistant foreman, an assistant engineer, and four privates, have been placed in the houses of each com-

[525]

pany Nos. 5, 18, and 26, and Hook and Ladder Company No. 5. With these there are now, all told, eleven engine-houses with double companies. The duties of these extra companies are to answer calls that may come in while the regulars are out on duty. They are situated in engine-houses most conveniently equipped and located to accommodate the number of men. It is the intention of the Commissioners to so scatter this extra service as to guard against all possible contingencies.

One entire new company has been established during the year. It is located at Riverdale, and consists of two officers and 10 men, with an engine, hose carriage, and a hook and ladder truck.

During the year there have been 2,381 fires, causing a loss of property valued at 3,450,309 dol. Although the number of fires for 1884 have been increased 230 above that of last year the loss of property has been 55,356 dol. less.

The area of the district in which these fires occurred covers about $41\frac{1}{2}$ square miles, or 26,500 acres. The tract covered extends from the battery to the city of Yonkers, and is 16 miles long, but varies in width from a few hundred yards to $4\frac{1}{2}$ miles. Ward's, Randall's, and Blackwell's Islands are also within the limits of the department. There is a network of telegraph wires, about 900 miles in length, stretched on 6,200 poles, which connects this territory with Fireman's Hall, No 155, Mercer-street. About 700 alarm boxes are scattered throughout this entire district.

During the coming year a hundred of improvements are to be made that will greatly improve the department. A six-story building is to be erected on the north side of Sixty-seventh-street, near Third Avenue. The two lower floors will be fitted up for a hook and ladder house. The third and fourth floors will be used as a training school and gymnasium for the life-saving corps, while the upper part of the house will be arranged with electrical apparatus. As all applicants for position must pass a physical examination, such an institution will be of great utility. The system of alarums is also to be changed. Under the present arrangement, when a call is sent out at night, it awakens every fireman in the city, no matter where the fire occurs. It is proposed to divide the department into four divisions, each of which is to have a separate line of wires. As the telegraph wires are to be put under ground the department will not immediately make this important change. A number of improvements are also to be made in the life-savings corps, which has proved remarkably efficient during the past year. There are now about 400 members in active service as lifesavers.

State Prisons.

The annual report of the superintendent of State prisons, which was submitted to the Legislature to-day, commences with a tabulated statement of the earnings and expenditures of the three prisons—Sing Sing, Auburn and Clinton—for the last fiscal year, showing a net surplus of earnings amounting to 10,657 dol. 97 c. It sets forth that the financial statement for the year ending September 30, 1883, was the most favourable exhibit which had been made in the history of the State prisons; but the result accomplished in 1883-84 surpasses that of the previous year. The expenditures were reduced 7,454 dol., which approximates 2 per cent. of the total expense of 1882-83. The net surplus is 1,551 dol. 74 c. larger than it was in the previous year.

A table is submitted showing the progress which has steadily been made in the financial affairs of the State prisons since the present system of management and employment was adopted.

Results of Prison Reform.—The report goes on to state that in the matter of moral improvement the existing system continues to produce gratifying results. Thus, the Warden of Sing Sing prison reports that the discipline there is in the highest sense satisfactory. But the particularly gratifying feature of this good discipline is that the *morale* of the convicts makes the maintenance of the discipline easy. Out of an average population in that prison of 1,522 during the year, only eight men were locked in cells for refractory disposition, and not one man in all has been disobedient so as to require discipline beyond a day or two. The health of the convicts in all three prisons is reported as being unusually good. As a body the convicts have gained in intelligence, in moral character, in physical strength, in habitual industry, and in willing obedience to authority.

A table is submitted showing a marked decline in the number of convicts during the past 10 years in proportion to the gain in population. For the past year, however, there has been an excess of commitments over discharges, which is accounted for by the fact, established by experience, that penal offences multiply during hard times in any country.

Contract Labour System.—Touching the employment of the labour of the convicts, the report say:—" The last Legislature repealed the contract labour system in the prisons and prohibited its use by the superintendent. It not only repealed the present system, but prohibited the contracting of the labour of the convicts in any manner. The superintendent can renew no contracts, can make no contracts, either like those hitherto made or upon the 'piece price plan,' which is regarded with so much favour by many prison reformers. When it did this act the Legislature did not make any provision for the employment of the convicts in the only legal manner under the existing laws. The Legislature failed to make a large appropriation of money from the treasury to meet the necessary expenditures, to buy machinery and stock for engaging in manufacturing on State account, and for hiring and paying for the citizens' skilled labour, which will be needed to begin and direct extensive manufacturing operations in the prisons. The establishment of this system has been precipitated upon the superintendent, since the close of the fiscal year, by the abandonment of one contract and by the failure of one large contracting firm. As other contracts will soon expire, it is plain that the question of adopting some legal system, and making sufficient appropriations of money to carry it out effectively cannot be prudently and safely deferred any longer.

"*Urgent need of Legislation.*—The possible prospective embarrassment of the superintendent was apprehended by him before the last Legislature adjourned. In reply to the inquiry of the Senate he stated his views in respects to the necessity and the advantage of action by the Legislature. There is not sufficient money to enter upon the State account system thoroughly and economically. There is no other legal mode of working the convicts whose labour is not contracted for. Further, the superintendent is unable to foretell what the action of the Legislature may be, what plan for employing the convict labour may be adopted. The present situation should be well understood. Until the passage of the law by the last Legislature, repealing the contract system in the prisons, the superintendent had the right to work convicts by State account or by contract, or partly by one and partly by the other, as in his discretion he should deem best. By the act of the last Legislature (chap. 21, Laws of 1884) no discretion is granted to the superintendent. He is compelled to work the convicts on State account."

Pursuing this subject, Superintendent Baker goes on to state that during the month of September he asked the opinion of the Attorney General upon the question of his legal power to employ labour of prisoners upon the "piece price plan," as that mode of working convicts is regarded with special approbation by many of the most earnest prison reformers. The reply of the Attorney General, which is submitted, stated that in the opinion of that official the superintendent, under chapter 21 of the Laws of 1884, would have no authority to enter into any contract which would bind him for any specified time or to do any specified amount of work for a definite price.

Only State Accounts System permitted.—In view of this condition of affairs the report says:—"Until there shall be further legislation the labour of all prisoners in the State prisons not contracted must be employed on State account. The appropriation which was made by the last Legislature 'for care and maintenance' is wholly insufficient to work the prisons on State account. The Legislature must decide two questions:—

"*First*—Will it adhere to the State account system?

"*Second*—How much money will be necessary to carry on that system, with the energy and activity demanded to keep the prisoners at work, with the industry which their self-support, the mandate of the law, and their welfare in the prisons compel?

"It is not safe, as it is not economical, to undertake such business in a feeble, desultory, and half-hearted manner. In order to spare the people from heavy taxation on account of the prisons, and more important, in order to preserve the efficacy of the reformatory influences which are now working so admirably in the prisons, the regularity and the diversity of the present labour system must be maintained just as constantly as it has been under the existing system."

Gravity of the Question.—The superintendent has a most profound sense of the perplexities and the difficulties of the existing situation. He has studied the problems which are presented; he knows well what disastrous results attended the operation of the State account system, which became so intolerable that the people, by their suffrage, swept it away. He has borne witness to the success of the system which has stood every test applied to it. He has seen it improve year by year and come closer to the ideal standard. He regards it superior to any other ever practised in the State, when it is measured by actual attainments, whether they be material or moral and reformatory. He deemed it a grave mistake to rashly and abruptly change the system with no well-considered plan to take its place. He has the opinion now which he expressed in his last annual report, to wit:—

"The prisons of New York are doing well—better in all respects than they ever have done before the last five years. Before any change is made in the system their condition, operations, tendencies, and capacities for useful work should receive the most considerate investigation. The people of the State have great interests at stake; the prisoners who fill the prisons have also. At the same time new plans, new theories, or exploded systems in new forms or guises should be brought to the test of the most critical examination. It is easy to make a mistake; but it may cost millions of money to pay for it and years of time by the suspension of the system now working so admirably and effectively. It should be made very clear that a change will be beneficial."

Convicts must be Employed.—"The convicts in prison must be kept at labour. It is necessary for their physical and moral well-being. The experience of the last hundred years in every enlightened nation in the world positively affirms this fundamental principle. The conspicuous prison administrators and the greatest prison reformers declare that productive labour by the inmates of prisons is a vital condition of success in reforming the convicts, and is the corner-stone in any practical and humane system. Besides, every week in the year, several men are sent by judicial sentences to the State prisons to be confined and to be engaged 'at hard labour' during the term of their sentences. Unproductive labour is a curse to the prisoners; it fails to reform, but debases, hardens, and brutalises. For this reason it is not to be tolerated; and it less tolerable because the majority of the convicts in our State prisons are young men, many of whom can be saved from continued lives of crime by the moral influences of judicious discipline, industrial training, and humane treatment in the prisons.

"If it be true that the prime ends of penal punishment in prison can be reached in the highest degree by a system whose material results will repay the pecuniary cost of the prison maintenance and care, shall this fact be ignored? That is, shall the people be taxed several hundred thousand dollars every year when there is not only no need of it, but there is no advantage in doing so? There is not so much prosperity at this time; there is not such redundance of money and such surplus of income as to recommend this policy to any servant or representative of the people."

Charity Organisation Society.

The following, taken from *Bradstreet's Weekly Journal*, gives a good account of the working of the society in its endeavour to suppress mendicancy and reduce pauperism, which, it is well known, are stimulated by indiscriminate almsgiving both by societies and individuals:—

To bring order out of the chaos of poverty-stricken domestic life in New York is the most serious problem America presents to the benevolent mind. With an Irish population more than twice as great as that of the city of Cork, and a German population greater than that of Bremen, there is injected annually at Castle Garden a foreign immigration from every part of Europe at the rate of from a fifth to a third of the entire number of its inhabitants. While a larger part of this immigration passes on to the interior, the baser elements linger in the metropolis, and a strange speech and strange manners render them almost inaccessible to the beneficent influences of the city. It is estimated that there are 30,000 strangers transiently in New York every day of the year, and thither gravitate the dissolute from all quarters, either to enjoy the facilities of a great city for self-indulgence, to secrete themselves from observation, or to share the gains of easy imposture and petty depredations. The distribution of the population in tenement houses is another serious obstacle to efficient work amongst it, for this system of habitations implies that the occupants of the apartments are only leaseholders and therefore temporary, while the enforced neighbourhood of families of different habits tends to bring them all to one level of uncleanliness. How great the field is that requires the observation of philanthropy may be gathered from the first two years of the work of the New York Charity Organisation Society. Numerically this association has the record of 48,768 cases of persons and households on its books, and estimates that these indicate a population of 195,000 brought to its notice. Some of the significant features of this statement are these: This aggregate is far from being an exhaustive canvass of the city, but is only the accumulation of such names as individuals, churches, institutions, and other societies actively co-operating, report to the central office, a co-operation which as yet does not cover half the charitable agencies at work among the poor. This record is not made up by spontaneous examinations of poor districts to learn the condition and habits of their population, but only from those applications for aid by which the parties confess themselves to be in need, and therefore voluntarily invite scrutiny to themselves. Geographically these people are distributed among 17,658 houses, which, as the secretary of the society says, would line a street like one of the avenues from the Battery to Fairfield, Conn. This partial view of the substratum of New York shows one-seventh of the population as the objects of either police or charitable administration.

Now, the purport of this article is to exhibit the methods taken to bring some order into this unhappy mass of humanity, to set recuperative forces to work among them, or to impose upon them such restraints as may make them amenable to laws of decent living. This is the aim of the Charity Organisation Society, and herein lies its distinctive character. Before its appearance on the field the good people of the city had set up hundreds of relief centres, and to them these 200,000 went at will, extracted what they could, and disposed of it as they would. In some fitful, superficial way emissaries of these relief agencies followed a few applicants to their retreats, and endeavoured by appeals to their individual characters to put them in a better way of life, while at the same time enticing them by the prospect of further gifts to pursue their old career. But practically nothing was done of a systematic sort to bring the whole baksheesh, clamouring community under regimen, to sift it out into classes requiring different treatment. Under that system the people went to the fountains for water; under the new the water is carried to their homes and distributed as they have need. It was impossible, of course, for any voluntary society to take the government of a population as large as that of the city of Buffalo, especially when it had no coercive authority, and that population was particularly devoid of self-regulating promptings and in need of restraint. But the old methods had provided a powerful constituency in the shape of societies and agencies controlling the apparatus of an endlessly varied relief, and rooted in the sympathy of the more intelligent and humane part of the community.

If these could be brought to act in concert, were it ever so limited, at once the importunate would be confronted with a system, and that in itself would oblige them to conform, and conformity to rule meant the beginning of regulated lives. Moreover, the investigations of the Charity Organisation Society have emphasised, if they have not discovered, a fact of no small importance—it is the tendency of the supplicant classes to congregate and form a community. The first effect of disaster upon an ingenuous nature leads to isolation and the careful secreting of a sorrow, just as a sick cow leaves the herd and goes off by herself until regained strength permits her to appear again as qualified for gregarious life. In that stage of misfortune, private and personal handling is good and necessary. But when misery has become a stock-in-trade, quite a new phase of social life is reached. It then becomes a basis of association and a source of corruption.

One of the earliest movements of the Charity Organisation Society in New York was to make a registry of streets, in which the building standing upon each lot was described, if there were one at all, and the character of the inmates of each tenement was recorded. The primary object of this record was to detect at once, and in the office, a false address furnished by an applicant for aid, or the character of its neighbourhood, whether the resort of criminals, or of professional beggars, a nest-hole of gin shops, or a house of decent repute. But this investigation also revealed that particular tenements and quarters of the city were purlieus of habitual beggars. Of some 12,000 tenements registered as the abodes of those who had openly sought relief or whose names were recorded on the books of penal institutions, the secretary writes: "The average number of charitable recipients in all the houses reported is $3\frac{1}{4}$ families, or 13 persons to each house. We believe this teaches that the habit of looking to charity for support is contagious, that it rapidly becomes the fashion in localities."

The infected quarters of the city thus marked out, a correlative step was to register the inmates, and from their history and circumstances to gather the material for their proper classification and appropriate treatment. The process of accomplishing this was contemporaneous with and intimately related to the plan of the street register. The principal agents of the Commission of Charities and Correction, of the relief societies and the churches, were requested to send for confidential use reports of the persons and families whom they assisted, giving their names, residences, members of the family, professed occupation, and stating the nature of the relief bestowed. It will be seen at a glance that the simple assorting into alphabetical order of these reports brought out not only the discrepancy of statements made by the same person in different quarters, but the number of distinct places to which he had applied for aid and the total product of his begging. If the system could be applied to all the charitable disbursements of the city from all sources, the whole condition of the supplicant class would be laid bare. In the first two years, ending in 1884, the society received 61,303 reports, relating to nearly 50,000 persons and households. Now, two uses of this centralised registration immediately become apparent. First, it is only necessary to return to each relieving agency the consolidated reports concerning any of its beneficiaries to enable it to judge whether it has been imposed upon, or whether its treatment of a case has been adequate and wise; secondly, the record becomes a point from which to trace the career of any particular solicitor of alms. It must not be supposed, however, that as soon as instances of duplicated relief are thus detected the inference is drawn that the perpetrator of it is a fraud. On the contrary, often this disclosure points to a necessity which ought to have more abundant and systematic aid. So, also, this accumulated personal information goes far to discriminate between genuine necessity and professional pretence; and if the register perpetuates the bad record of some, it also becomes the credential of others —a result of infinite moral gain in the administration of charity. The contents of this register, it should be said, are not available to curious eyes. It is not open to inspection, but any one who wishes to befriend an unfortunate case may, on evidence of that intention, learn what is known in the office concerning that particular object of solicitude—no more. The reserve is practised in defence of the reputation of the poor, and that a reformed person may not be hereafter confronted with an old record of ill odour.

Beyond this clerical work the society sets up an agency for pursuing these investigations still further, endeavouring to learn all those circumstances upon which a successful treatment of any case depends, and it is involved at times in correspondence with cities of Europe and frequently over all parts of America. It also provides a mechanism by which different charitable organisations may co-operate with each other toward a common discipline or a common method of emancipation from dependence. It provides still further means of friendly counsel and guidance in all cases where no proper arrangement exists to meet the exigencies of poverty. Such is the machinery wherewith the society confronts 200,000 avowed beggars, and says to them, " You need not and you must not beg; you must look forward to conforming to rule, and to bringing your lives under an orderly regimen, which is your only hope of deliverence from misery. What is requisite to reinstate you in usefulness or in honourable place we will undertake, but re-entrance upon normal and proper relations to society we shall resolutely enforce upon you."

Of the outcome of these measures only two characteristic illustrations can be here given. Last year 7,000 cases were taken from the register, being those concerning whom the information was most explicit and analysed, with this result, 65 per cent., or over 4,500 of them, comprised men with or without dependent children, who were apparently able-bodied; the rest were instances of widowhood or sickness or of spinsterhood. Now the inference was not drawn that these men were dissolutely idle, but that they may have been temporarily thrown out of employment by sickness, strikes, or fluctuations in trade. The conclusion was reached that some means of placing these men in the industrial organisation of society was first required, and prominent administrators of relief societies were summoned into council, who there determined that the assistance to be given in such cases should be such as would enable them to find permanent work either in or out of the city. The productive capacity of these men could not be less than 1 dol. per day, and under severest pressure it is hard to see how they could live and support their families on a less average than 50 c. a day. By transferring them from the list of idle dependents to self-maintained labourers the community would gain 6,750 dol. a day, or 175,500 dol. each month of 26 working days. That economical result was worth aiming at, even if the moral effects of the transfer upon the men and their families were left out of account.

In the year preceding its last summary the society claimed to have procured the translation of 539 cases, comprising 2,500 persons, from the dependent to the self-maintained list. These cases were sifted out of the mass of suppliants by the discriminative effects of the society's measures. The pecuniary estimate of the consequences of this transition measured by Professor Thorold Rogers' standard is equivalent to the lucrative investment of 1,875,000 dol., the interest on which sum, at 5 per cent., is 93,750 dol., or nearly five times the entire disbursements of the Charity Organisation Society during that year.

Of the collateral methods pursued to make fruitful order encroach on the disintegrated mass of 200,000 souls, fallen out of the useful state, there is no room to speak. That some inroads have been made upon it is evident, and the large economical results are apparent. The hope of the rest depends upon the steady pressure which breaks up the undistinguishable mass of paupers into distinctive groups, each of which, according to its requirements, shall be confronted with practicable measures for living reputably and serviceably.

State Finances.

The receipts and payments show the finances of the State to be in a most gratifying condition. It was estimated by the State comptroller that the actual surplus at the end of the fiscal year, September 30, would be 2,207,941 dol., but it has been exceeded by 341,169 dol.

Setting aside the general fund debt for Indian annuities, the principal of which amounts to 122,695 dol., the State has no debt except the canal debt, the last instalment of which falls due in 1893. This debt was decreased in the year 1,576,284 dol., and was on the 30th September 4,276,323 dol.

Valuations and tax rate for the past five years are given in the following table:—

Year.	Valuation.	State Tax.
	Dollars.	
1884	3,014,591,372	2·575 Mills.
1883	2,872,257,325	3¼ ,,
1882	2,783,682,567	2·45 ,,
1881	2,681,257,606	2¼ ,,
1880	2,637,869,238	2·86 ,,

CITY FINANCES.

The total funded debt of New York on January 1st, 1885, was 126,871,138 dol., but there is to be deducted from this 34,823,735 dol. sinking fund (investments and in cash), leaving a net debt of 92,047,403 dol.

Valuations and tax rate for the past five years are given in the following table:—

	Real Estate.	Personal.	City Tax.
	Dollars.	Dollars.	Per cent.
1884	1,119,761,597	218,536,746	2·25
1883	1,079,130,669	197,546,495	2·29
1882	1,035,203,816	198,272,582	2·25
1881	976,735,199	209,212,899	2·26
1880	942,571,690	201,194,037	2·22

1244. UNITED STATES.

Temperature, New York City.

The following is taken from the records of the Signal Service Bureau for 1884:—

	Highest. °	Lowest. °
January	47	8
,, Average	32·75	19·50
February	61	2
,, Average	42·50	27·625
March	63	5
,, Average	44·25	30·67
April	73	32
,, Average	55·875	40·125
May	84	42
,, Average	67·25	51
June	92	49
,, Average	78·67	60
July	90	53
,, Average	78·625	62·67
August	92	56
,, Average	79	64·50
September	92	50
,, Average	79	61·50
October	84	32
,, Average	65	48·50
November	62	24
,, Average	51	35·66
December	60	1
,, Average	40·875	28

Vital Statistics, New York City, 1884.

Births	30,527
Still births	2,908
Marriages	11,805
Deaths	35,034

The causes of death were principally as follows:—

Zymotic diseases	9,263
Constitutional	7,941
Local	14,246
Developmental	2,224
By violence	1,340
Small-pox	—
Measles	762
Scarlatina	608
Diphtheria	1,090
Remittent, intermittent, typho-malarial, and other fevers	395
Diarrhœal diseases of children under five years of age	3,160
Diarrhœal diseases, all ages	3,679
Phthisis pulmonalis	5,235
Bronchitis	1,485
Pneumonia	3,159
Heart diseases	1,645
All diseases of brain and nervous system	3,016
Bright's disease and nephritis	1,928

The estimated population of the city on July 1st, 1884, was 1,356,958.

The death rate per 1,000 inhabitants 25·82.

New York, March 31, 1885.

APPENDIX.

Contents.

No. 1. A summary of British shipping at the port of New York, showing the entrances and clearances in both direct and indirect trade.

No. 2. An analysis of the direct trade.

No. 3. An analysis of the indirect or carrying trade.

No. 4. Number and tonnage of British vessels arriving at this port during the past 10 years, distinguishing sailing and steam vessels.

No. 5. Number of seamen in British vessels engaged, discharged, deserted, &c.

No. 6. Number of ships and tonnage of all nations arriving from and departing for foreign ports, and the direct and indirect trade of each nationality.

No. 7. Statistics of petroleum trade, 1884.

No. 8. Statistics of wool trade, 1884.

No. 9. Resources and liabilities of the savings banks of New York.

No. 10. Condition of the associated banks of New York City at the close of 1884.

No. 11. Highest and lowest prices of stocks in 1884: comparisons with 1883.

No. 12. Return showing the product of each principal crop of the several States and territories named, the total acreage, and the value of each crop for 1883.

No. 13. Exports of merchandise, &c., to Great Britain and British Possessions during the year 1884.

Appendix No. I.—DIRECT Trade in British Vessels from and to Great Britain and the British Colonies.

ENTERED.

Total Number of Vessels.			Total Tonnage.			Total Number of Crews
With Cargoes.	In Ballast.	Total.	With Cargoes.	In Ballast.	Total.	
1,645	50	1,695	3,218,234	80,302	3,298,536	76,505

CLEARED.

Total Number of Vessels.			Total Tonnage.			Total Number of Crews.
With Cargoes.	In Ballast.	Total.	With Cargoes.	In Ballast.	Total.	
1,637	115	1,752	3,302,916	31,620	3,334,536	77,301

INDIRECT or Carrying Trade in British Vessels from and to other Countries.

ENTERED.

Total Number of Vessels.			Total Tonnage.			Total Number of Crews.
With Cargoes.	In Ballast.	Total.	With Cargoes.	In Ballast.	Total.	
774	104	878	673,386	107,860	781,246	14,364

CLEARED.

Total Number of Vessels.			Total Tonnage.			Total Number of Crews.
With Cargoes.	In Ballast.	Total.	With Cargoes.	In Ballast.	Total.	
634	138	772	707,483	2,646	710,129	11,797

TOTAL British Shipping at the Port of New York (both Direct and Indirect Trade) during the Year 1884.

ENTERED.

Total Number of Vessels.			Total Tonnage.			Total Number of Crews.
With Cargoes.	In Ballast.	Total.	With Cargoes.	In Ballast.	Total.	
2,419	154	2,573	3,891,620	188,162	4,079,782	90,869

CLEARED.

Total Number of Vessels.			Total Tonnage.			Total Number of Crews.
With Cargoes.	In Ballast.	Total.	With Cargoes.	In Ballast.	Total.	
2,271	253	2,524	4,010,399	34,266	4,044,665	89,098

NEW YORK.

Appendix No. II.—DIRECT Trade in British Vessels from and to Great Britain and British Possessions.

Entered.

Ports whence Arrived.	Number of Vessels. With Cargoes.	Number of Vessels. In Ballast.	Number of Vessels. Total.	Tonnage. With Cargoes.	Tonnage. In Ballast.	Tonnage. Total.	Total Number of Crews.
United Kingdom	721	36	757	2,583,756	65,124	2,648,880	62,387
Gibraltar	94	...	94	184,654	...	184,654	2,394
British East Indies	79	...	79	100,735	...	100,735	1,774
Australia and New Zealand	3	...	3	1,224	...	1,224	32
Cape of Good Hope and other African ports	6	...	6	2,711	...	2,711	36
Dominion of Canada	420	9	429	82,997	8,278	91,275	2,979
Newfoundland	13	1	14	12,978	688	13,666	268
Bermuda	39	3	42	55,300	3,839	59,139	1,350
Jamaica	114	...	114	100,486	...	100,486	2,791
Barbados	8	...	8	5,147	...	5,147	145
Other British West Indian ports	148	1	149	88,246	2,373	90,619	2,349
Total	1,645	50	1,695	3,218,234	80,302	3,298,536	76,505

Cleared.

Ports to which Departed.	Number of Vessels. With Cargoes.	Number of Vessels. In Ballast.	Number of Vessels. Total.	Tonnage. With Cargoes.	Tonnage. In Ballast.	Tonnage. Total.	Total Number of Crews.
United Kingdom	897	...	897	2,831,883	...	2,831,883	65,107
Gibraltar	33	...	33	60,506	...	60,506	936
British East Indies	46	...	46	63,050	...	63,050	1,106
Australia and New Zealand	17	...	17	13,421	...	13,421	268
Cape of Good Hope and other African ports	4	...	4	3,721	...	3,721	67
Dominion of Canada	295	114	409	64,155	30,120	94,275	2,946
Newfoundland	33	1	34	19,400	1,500	20,900	385
Bermuda	45	...	45	60,130	...	60,130	1,470
Jamaica	127	...	127	111,692	...	111,692	3,018
Barbados	16	...	16	6,937	...	6,937	160
Other British West Indian ports	124	...	124	68,021	...	68,021	1,838
Total	1,637	115	1,752	3,302,916	31,620	3,334,536	77,301

Appendix No. III.—INDIRECT or Carrying Trade in British Vessels from and to other Countries.

Entered.

Countries whence Arrived.	Number of Vessels. With Cargoes.	Number of Vessels. In Ballast.	Number of Vessels. Total.	Tonnage. With Cargoes.	Tonnage. In Ballast.	Tonnage. Total.	Total Number of Crews.
Argentine Confederation	3	...	3	1,563	...	1,563	31
Austria	2	...	2	4,096	...	4,096	49
Belgium	51	4	55	64,055	6,180	70,235	1,090
Brazil	183	3	186	148,639	2,319	150,958	3,160
Central America	34	...	34	36,770	...	36,770	812
Chili	10	...	10	8,802	...	8,802	150
China	8	...	8	14,981	...	14,981	280
Denmark and colonies	25	...	25	10,376	...	10,376	28
France and colonies	48	31	79	37,824	25,002	62,826	1,090
Germany	26	...	26	20,692	...	20,692	472
Greece	...	...	...	...	...	...	...
Hayti and San Domingo	28	...	28	15,336	...	15,336	275
Italy	26	...	26	46,231	...	46,231	702
Japan	6	...	6	12,471	...	12,471	205
Mexico	35	...	35	32,630	...	32,630	577
Netherlands and colonies	32	...	32	28,480	...	28,480	528
Peru	...	...	...	...	...	...	...
Portugal	2	...	2	1,937	...	1,937	35
Russia	1	...	1	1,513	...	1,513	24
Spain and colonies	230	3	233	156,026	2,275	158,301	3,006
Sweden and Norway	...	...	...	...	...	...	...
Turkey	1	...	1	700	...	700	13
United States of America	10	63	73	10,376	72,084	82,460	1,397
Uruguay	9	...	9	5,227	...	5,227	102
Venezuela	4	...	4	4,658	...	4,658	75
Total	774	104	878	673,386	107,860	781,246	14,364

Cleared.

Countries to which Departed.	Number of Vessels. With Cargoes.	Number of Vessels. In Ballast.	Number of Vessels. Total.	Tonnage. With Cargoes.	Tonnage. In Ballast.	Tonnage. Total.	Total Number of Crews.
Argentine Confederation	14	...	14	43,321	...	43,321	169
Austria	...	...	...	...	...	...	...
Belgium	70	1	71	82,459	1,912	84,371	1,394
Brazil	59	...	59	32,305	...	32,305	882
Central America	9	...	9	8,135	734	8,869	180
Chili	2	...	2	1,563	...	1,563	69
China	5	...	5	8,403	...	8,403	157
Denmark and colonies	27	...	27	10,886	...	10,886	301
France and colonies	123	...	123	103,257	...	103,257	1,557
Germany	21	...	21	22,327	...	22,327	325
Greece	1	...	1	1,612	...	1,612	24
Hayti and San Domingo	42	...	42	39,336	...	39,336	736
Italy	8	...	8	15,313	...	15,313	221
Japan	6	...	6	8,156	...	8,156	122
Mexico	22	...	22	25,934	...	25,934	407
Netherlands and colonies	45	...	45	45,450	...	45,450	723
Peru	...	...	...	...	...	...	...
Portugal	6	...	6	8,152	...	8,152	119
Russia	1	...	1	1,698	...	1,698	24
Spain and colonies	147	7	154	100,692	...	100,692	1,709
Sweden and Norway	4	...	4	3,162	...	3,162	59
Turkey	3	...	3	3,655	...	3,655	58
United States of America	5	130	135	3,104	...	134,104	2,394
Uruguay	7	...	7	2,776	...	2,776	64
Venezuela	7	...	7	4,787	...	4,787	103
Total	634	138	772	707,483	2,646	710,129	11,797

Appendix No. IV.—NUMBER and Tonnage of British Vessels arriving at the Port of New York: Comparison for the last Ten Years distinguishing Sailing and Steam Vessels.

Year.	Sailing Vessels. Number.	Sailing Vessels. Tonnage.	Steam Vessels. Number.	Steam Vessels. Tonnage.	Total Number of Vessels.	Total Number of Crews.	Total Tonnage.
1875	1,219	485,553	569	1,603,174	1,788	57,196	2,088,727
1876	1,231	561,503	590	1,588,113	1,821	55,683	2,149,616
1877	1,518	555,121	655	1,819,595	2,173	59,899	2,374,716
1878	1,579	751,053	873	2,338,009	2,452	73,528	3,089,062
1879	1,720	940,341	1,108	2,772,003	2,828	82,166	3,712,374
1880	1,687	919,991	1,284	3,073,946	2,971	87,088	3,993,937
1881	1,574	859,855	1,271	3,171,916	2,845	88,760	4,031,771
1882	1,501	673,650	1,162	3,217,841	2,663	89,606	3,891,491
1883	1,385	665,599	1,192	3,250,546	2,577	89,633	3,916,145
1884	1,164	485,642	1,409	3,594,140	2,573	90,869	4,079,782

UNITED STATES.

Appendix No. V.—RETURN of the Number of Seamen who have been Engaged, Discharged, Left Behind, Reported Dead, or Deserted, or who have been Relieved at the British Consulate-General, New York, and showing the Total Number of British and Foreign Sailors who were Engaged, Discharged, &c., from British Ships, with the Total Amount of Wages paid at the Consulate to Seamen on Discharge from their Ships, and from Hospital or Gaol; and also showing the Number of New Agreements entered into during the Year 1884.

Seamen.											Nationality.		Total Number of Seamen.	Wages.			Agreements.
Engaged.	Dis-charged.	Left Behind.			Died.			Deserted.	Relieved.		British.	Foreign.		Paid on Discharge from Vessels.	Paid on Discharge from Hospital or Gaol.	Total Wages Paid.	Number Opened.
		In Gaol.	In Hospital.	Total.	At Sea.	On Shore.	Total.										
11,944	7,981	11	125	136	48	31	79	4,207	456		15,886	8,917	24,803	Dol. c. 373,225 84	Dol. c. 3,400 41	Dol. c. 376,626 25	427

Appendix No. VI.—The following gives the Number of Ships and Tonnage of all Nations Arriving from and Departing for Foreign Ports, and exhibits the Direct and Indirect Trade for each Nationality.

NEW YORK.

Entered.

Nationality.	Number of Vessels.			Tonal Tonnage.		
	Steamers.	Sailing Vessels.	Total.	Direct.	Indirect.	Total.
Austria ...	...	78	78	2,417	48,467	50,884
Belgium ...	85	1	86	*	...	...
Brazil ...	1	2	3	1,600	...	1,600
Columbia ...	...	6	6	1,542	...	1,542
Costa Rica ...	...	4	4	560	...	560
Denmark ...	31	16	47	51,880	8,023	59,903
France ...	91	8	99	234,442	...	234,442
Germany ...	233	289	522	911,444	143,614	1,055,058
Great Britain ...	1,409	1,164	2,573	3,298,536	781,246	4,079,782
Hayti ...	...	8	8	1,945	...	1,945
Italy ...	21	222	243	65,725	89,240	154,965
Mexico ...	66	44	110	132,103	...	132,103
Netherlands ...	49	14	63	98,117	2,800	100,917
Norway and Sweden ...	...	382	382	8,600	230,140	238,740
Portugal ...	2	28	30	3,890	2,945	6,835
Russia ...	...	8	8	...	5,761	5,761
Spain ...	57	26	83	84,192	3,204	87,396
United States of America ...	241	1,504	1,745	...	947,304	947,304
Venezuela ...	...	1	1	120	...	120

Cleared.

Nationality.	Number of Vessels.			Total Tonnage.		
	Steamers.	Sailing Vessels.	Total.	Direct.	Indirect.	Total.
Austria ...	...	91	91	13,169	47,505	60,674
Belgium ...	1	...	...	...	...	...
Brazil ...	...	3	4	1,725	...	1,725
Columbia ...	...	5	5	1,430	...	1,430
Costa Rica ...	...	4	4	560	...	560
Denmark ...	31	15	46	49,964	9,765	59,829
France ...	91	8	99	231,488	...	231,488
Germany ...	233	279	512	901,903	2,954	904,857
Great Britain ...	1,398	1,126	2,524	3,334,536	710,129	4,044,665
Hayti ...	...	8	8	1,945	...	1,945
Italy ...	18	226	244	43,669	109,206	152,875
Mexico ...	71	64	135	162,126	...	162,126
Netherlands ...	48	11	59	98,674	2,611	101,285
Norway and Sweden ...	...	380	380	12,100	223,140	235,240
Portugal ...	2	29	31	4,120	2,830	6,950
Russia ...	...	8	8	5,761	...	5,761
Spain ...	58	24	82	83,920	2,876	86,796
United States of America ...	238	1,121	1,359	...	804,936	804,936
Venezuela ...	1	1	2	1,120	...	1,120

* Information not received in time for insertion.

[525]

Appendix No. VII.—EXPORT of Petroleum, &c., from New York to Foreign Ports from Jan. 1 to Dec. 31.

REFINED.

	1884.	1883.	1882.	1881.
	Gallons.	Gallons.	Gallons.	Gallons.
Great Britain—				
London	18,498,831	36,056,955	26,156,756	24,299,664
Liverpool	9,009,430	11,566,634	9,967,113	11,707,668
Bristol	3,824,381	3,855,673	3,961,584	4,270,378
Ireland	5,335,599	5,791,493	5,010,725	9,538,963
Other ports	6,543,519	6,976,948	6,452,053	8,013,306
Germany—				
Bremen	30,327,016	47,053,007	49,177,906	41,350,488
Hamburgh	32,545,982	32,275,401	34,105,649	17,424,648
Königsberg and Stettin	6,768,171	4,766,126	10,548,384	7,413,504
Dantzic	1,102,897	1,110,141	2,120,057	2,584,964
Other ports	1,372,183	835,570	1,282,805	968,614
France—				
Marseilles	...	...	331,945	...
Havre	...	...	188,730	...
Norway and Sweden	5,454,902	7,333,437	6,789,961	7,746,457
Russia	188,822	1,539,156	1,609,272	2,255,402
Denmark	7,780,317	8,718,855	7,254,729	6,614,113
Belgium	32,713,207	37,123,499	26,651,267	30,963,398
Holland	15,657,198	14,509,702	13,091,877	10,994,612
Spain	370,960	282,480	198,733	10,248
Portugal	1,310,612	2,009,420	1,594,388	1,930,550
Gibraltar and Malta	3,337,780	2,679,078	1,314,621	4,501,395
Italy	2,191,084	2,771,556	1,961,912	3,325,772
Austria—				
Trieste, &c.	6,281,043	15,505,652	12,566,256	17,258,957
Greece	1,095,010	1,280,410	379,300	2,675,110
Turkey in Europe	3,572,183	4,165,261	3,876,839	7,136,594
Turkey in Asia	3,463,195	3,080,742	1,231,580	3,455,840
India	28,699,200	16,838,690	20,504,060	12,441,980
China, Japan, &c.	27,306,720	25,188,470	31,637,450	17,985,910
East Indies	28,762,320	31,403,150	25,198,225	24,973,745
Africa—				
Alexandria, &c., Egypt	3,483,440	2,964,550	1,846,380	3,783,270
Canary Islands	182,379	153,849	119,370	214,822
Other ports	6,096,635	4,858,329	3,809,948	4,012,669
Australia	2,813,836	2,284,946	2,622,795	2,196,795
New Zealand	858,451	660,180	749,638	767,196
Sandwich Islands	223,580	242,500	109,565	78,150
South America—				
Brazil	6,110,077	5,997,804	5,266,665	5,895,851
Argentine Confederation	5,893,250	3,820,423	2,989,679	2,701,592
Chili and Peru	1,054,014	1,416,050	1,588,710	758,740
United States of Colombia	465,257	340,654	195,061	152,450
Venezuela	727,596	667,254	517,574	454,005
Other ports	67,101	119,461	136,490	64,090
Central America	306,094	244,340	184,944	200,524
Mexico	1,215,032	1,334,968	1,288,795	1,009,933
British North American Colonies	1,388,097	1,211,126	664,580	312,199
Cuba	420,761	302,396	755,834	505,672
British West Indies and British Guiana	1,545,726	1,630,328	1,492,385	1,522,953
Other West Indies	1,239,512	927,014	1,240,628	1,190,334
Total	317,603,397	353,893,678	330,743,218	307,963,525

CRUDE.

	1884.	1883.	1882.	1881.
	Gallons.	Gallons.	Gallons.	Gallons.
France—				
Havre	9,146,170	10,541,315	8,343,867	9,338,145
Marseilles	4,620,174	3,690,400	1,942,554	3,101,735
Bordeaux	2,434,925	2,451,408	1,929,769	1,654,888
Dunkirk	6,741,170	7,863,408	4,384,725	5,725,189
Other ports	9,883,893	8,922,915	7,937,875	5,014,128
Bremen	425,850	753,616	1,100,621	2,478,364
Norway and Sweden	...	62,374	148,235	115,187
Spain	15,113,436	12,411,383	12,814,730	14,474,224
Cuba	2,857,852	2,171,437	3,203,576	1,796,098
Other ports	6,070,624	2,347,315	...	...
Total	57,294,094	51,215,571	41,805,952	43,697,958

NEW YORK.

NAPHTHA.

	1884.	1883.	1882.	1881.
	Gallons.	Gallons.	Gallons.	Gallons.
Great Britain	4,483,110	5,985,201	6,905,233	7,040,656
France	3,414,282	6,432,361	4,967,089	6,343,997
Germany	521,780	1,668,038	1,235,525	990,711
Other Europe	983,201	1,655,163	1,490,740	1,726,609
Various ports	221,573	98,888	184,313	126,583
Total	9,623,946	15,849,651	14,782,900	16,228,556

RESIDUUM.

	1884.	1883.	1882.	1881.
	Gallons.	Gallons.	Gallons.	Gallons.
To all ports	3,941,795	6,494,597	4,483,109	3,846,575

	Gallons.
Total refined since Jan. 1, actual shipments, 317,603,397 gallons, crude equivalent	423,471,196
Total crude since Jan. 1, actual shipments	57,294,094
Grand total crude and crude equivalent	480,765,290
Same time, 1883	523,073,808

		Gallons.
Total crude, refined, and naphtha,	1884	384,521,437
,, ,, ,,	1883	420,958,900
,, ,, ,,	1882	387,332,070
,, ,, ,,	1881	367,890,039
,, ,, ,,	1880	264,067,119

Appendix No. VIII.—IMPORTS of Foreign Wool at New York in 1883 and 1884.

From—	1883.			1884.		
	Number.	Weight.	Entered Value.	Number.	Weight.	Entered Value.
	Bales.	Lbs.	Dollars.	Bales.	Lbs.	Dollars.
England	56,073	21,353,134	3,136,204	46,854	17,562,744	2,416,424
Argentine Republic	213	167,439	25,192	607	506,749	52,915
France	8,476	2,179,650	272,901	6,590	2,004,862	208,917
Belgium	378	140,323	18,588	946	435,022	55,505
Brazil	1,048	901,761	110,168	562	473,531	53,570
British West Indies	5	242	35	...	...	...
Dutch ,,	101	39,857	3,194	68	24,149	1,654
Chili	986	582,768	50,493	538	151,739	50,138
Venezuela	51	6,845	373	20	4,690	294
China	933	601,766	65,847	1,473	941,997	86,198
Germany	200	68,415	21,284	282	142,060	22,950
Scotland	10,385	2,548,300	307,159	10,124	2,459,511	321,838
Italy	560	353,070	36,244	55	42,017	5,150
British Possessions in Africa	609	278,459	37,882	2,097	924,357	121,053
Austria	343	207,330	26,503	1	75	7
Turkey	275	164,922	22,931	1,397	899,321	98,591
Sicily	1,165	498,263	59,430	99	69,743	7,494
United States of Columbia	...	...	...	44	5,325	679
British Australia	158	60,646	15,275	1,119	368,099	96,238
Uruguay	1,974	2,002,188	304,491	2,442	2,544,907	324,345
Denmark	926	436,868	58,052	1,217	581,516	55,591
Turkey in Asia	886	341,295	36,695	...	...	...
New Zealand	170	59,702	14,463	...	...	...
British East Indies	66	23,875	3,516	...	...	...
Nova Scotia	1	393	96	...	...	...
Russia	3,422	1,382,590	148,550	...	...	...
Total	89,404	34,400,037	4,776,069	76,535	30,142,414	3,979,553

Appendix No. IX.—Resources and Liabilities of the Savings Banks of New York City, with the Dividends paid in 1884.

	Total Resources.	Due Depositors.	Surplus.	Dividends in 1884.
	Dollars.	Dollars.	Dollars.	Per cent.
American Savings Banks	437,887	434,156	3,731	3½
Bank for savings in the city of New York	46,744,770	39,553,685	7,191,085	3½
Bowery Savings Bank	50,191,562	41,360,089	8,831,473	4
Broadway Savings Bank	3,992,478	3,702,239	290,239	4
Citizens Savings Banks	10,042,546	9,152,793	889,753	3½
Dry Dock Savings Institution	12,837,969	11,658,777	1,179,192	3½
East River Savings Institution	11,118,425	9,717,556	1,400,869	3½
East Side Savings Bank for Sailors	6,913	6,325	588	...
Eleventh Ward Savings Bank (closing)	42,359	42,180	179	3½
Emigrant Industrial Savings Bank	33,074,881	28,128,095	4,946,786	4
Equitable Savings Institution (closing)	153	153	...	...
Excelsior Savings Bank	346,861	336,156	10,705	4
Franklin Savings Bank	2,945,692	2,561,978	383,714	3½
German Savings Bank	18,062,752	16,677,227	1,385,525	4
Greenwich Savings Bank	21,915,909	18,715,478	3,200,431	3½
Harlem Savings Bank	2,135,851	1,965,386	170,465	4
Institution for Savings of Merchants' Clerks'	6,041,473	5,327,763	713,710	3½
Irving's Savings Institution	6,068,586	5,344,471	724,115	4
Manhattan Savings Institution	6,615,843	6,059,157	556,686	4
Metropolitan Savings Bank	4,258,883	3,913,044	945,839	3½
New York Savings Bank	6,701,804	5,413,817	1,287,987	4
North River Savings Bank	2,130,207	1,968,671	161,536	4
Seamens' Bank for Savings	32,785,583	26,685,431	6,100,151	3½
Gnion Dime Savings Institution	5,824,030	5,382,024	442,006	4
West Side Savings Bank	333,625	320,711	12,914	3¼

NEW YORK.

Appendix No. X.—NEW YORK City Banks.

The following Statement shows the condition of the Associated Banks of New York City for the week ending January 3rd, 1885.

Banks.	Loans and Discounts.	Specie.	Legal Tenders.	Net Deposits other than United States.	Circulation.
	Dollars.	Dollars.	Dollars.	Dollars.	Dollars.
New York	11,924,000	1,344,000	1,354,000	11,482,000	450,000
Manhattan County	8,298,000	2,658,000	637,000	9,353,000	...
Merchants'	7,195,100	1,075,100	1,388,700	7,593,300	340,000
Mechanics'	7,711,000	2,787,000	1,078,000	8,596,000	...
Union	4,436,400	1,071,400	322,000	4,078,100	...
America	11,538,200	4,094,500	1,138,500	12,862,700	1,100
Phœnix	2,667,000	312,000	268,800	2,221,000	252,000
City	8,109,500	9,550,200	589,000	16,035,400	...
Tradesmens'	2,219,900	404,300	106,400	2,026,900	35,800
Fulton	1,043,500	1,113,000	145,900	1,633,800	...
Chemical	14,246,300	6,766,300	1,014,200	18,938,600	...
Merchants' Exchange	2,752,800	222,900	983,000	2,772,100	292,500
Gallatin National	4,805,600	819,100	739,200	3,517,200	585,600
Butchers' and Drovers'	1,559,200	379,100	276,500	1,739,300	201,500
Mecanics' and Tradesmen's	701,000	204,000	123,000	808,000	...
Greenwich	839,600	98,500	220,500	923,500	2,600
Leather Manufacturers	2,832,000	453,200	199,100	2,139,000	524,005
Seventh Ward	1,025,000	264,500	165,600	1,119,800	29,100
State of New York	2,839,700	907,400	493,600	3,862,800	...
American Exchange	12,433,000	4,573,000	1,807,000	13,135,000	...
Commerce	17,873,300	5,540,300	1,443,700	16,312,600	839,220
Broadway	6,138,200	906,000	376,900	4,872,700	894,200
Mercantile	6,297,100	1,269,300	489,300	6,283,500	854,000
Pacific	2,116,900	724,300	179,300	2,741,900	...
Republic	5,408,300	463,000	976,300	5,097,200	423,000
Chatham	3,325,800	570,900	735,000	3,835,200	45,000
Peoples'	1,484,400	221,000	139,800	1,729,400	5,400
North America	3,010,800	108,500	558,600	3,232,700	...
Hanover	8,581,600	2,360,000	818,200	9,844,600	360,000
Irving	2,537,000	556,200	685,000	2,917,000	319,200
Citizens'	2,427,600	863,500	361,700	3,360,900	265,000
Nassau	2,036,600	261,800	398,100	2,547,300	...
Market	2,680,400	373,500	435,000	2,357,400	443,500
St. Nicholas	2,063,400	160,400	218,700	1,901,600	...
Shoe and Leather	2,716,000	356,000	407,000	2,774,000	442,000
Corn Exchange	4,716,700	542,700	268,000	4,154,700	...
Continental	3,991,900	1,481,300	625,500	5,455,900	63,600
Oriental	2,011,600	106,200	330,900	1,864,100	...
Importers' and Tradesmen's	16,672,500	6,671,700	2,773,700	23,141,100	1,106,900
Park	16,921,000	5,894,500	1,680,300	22,703,700	45,000
North River	1,600,000	20,000	224,000	1,579,600	...
East River	1,020,700	122,700	235,200	949,700	220,700
Fourth National	13,175,000	5,912,500	1,764,500	17,011,600	360,000
Central National	6,880,300	1,037,000	1,723,000	8,102,000	297,000
Second National	2,042,900	401,000	297,000	2,397,000	45,000
Ninth National	4,524,400	1,487,600	671,300	5,671,400	45,000
First National	15,581,400	3,924,800	941,100	16,680,700	449,900
Third National	5,010,000	1,519,800	697,700	6,029,700	...
New York National Exchange	1,198,000	179,700	244,300	1,136,200	179,500
Bowery	1,910,600	326,000	221,800	2,092,000	221,000
New York County	1,757,300	225,500	409,900	2,237,200	180,000
German American	2,595,600	553,000	182,100	2,631,300	...
Chase National	3,071,800	797,600	548,600	4,179,000	45,000
Fifth Avenue	2,226,800	780,200	241,500	2,619,200	...
German Exchange	1,653,300	112,000	498,000	2,264,100	...
Germania	1,877,000	272,000	146,000	2,284,100	...
United States	3,377,400	802,900	185,300	3,608,700	180,000
Lincoln	1,352,500	289,000	187,700	1,617,000	44,000
Garfield	1,019,900	93,100	150,200	919,300	178,000
Fifth National	1,117,600	145,300	175,800	1,153,800	133,500
Bank of the Metroplis	2,708,500	337,500	660,900	3,688,300	...
Total	297,887,700	87,867,800	37,356,900	340,816,300	11,398,800

The following are totals for several weeks past :—

1884.	Loans.	Specie.	Legal Tenders.	Deposits.	Circulation.	Aggregate Clearings.
	Dollars.	Dollars.	Dollars.	Dollars.	Dollars.	Dollars.
December 20	294,342,400	86,852,200	37,695,200	335,443,100	11,686,300	558,051,647
,, 27	295,874,200	88,170,500	36,592,300	335,272,100	11,618,600	408,361,823
1885.						
January 3	297,887,700	87,867,800	37,356,900	340,816,300	11,398,800	520,508,470

Appendix No. XI.—HIGHEST and Lowest Prices of Stocks in 1884, last Quotations in 1883, and an Exhibit of the Decline and Advance between the final Quotations of the Two Years.

	Highest.	Lowest.	Last.	Last, 1883.	Decline.	Advance.
Adams Express...	137	127	132	128	...	4
American Express	102	88	88	91⅛	3⅛	...
Albany and Susquehanna	134	128	130	132½	...	2½
Alton and Terre Haute	47½	18	22½	44	21½	...
,, ,, preferred	96	70	75	87	12	...
Atchison, Topeka, and Santa Fé	76¾	62	76¾	83¾	7	...
American Telegraph and Cable Company	60½	49	54	60	6	...
Bankers' and Merchants' Telegraph Company	127¾	1	4½	119¾	115¼	...
Buffalo, New York and P. preferred	10	10	10	...	...	...
Boston Air Line preferred	90	81¾	88	82	...	6
Burlington, Cedar Rapids, and Nor.	73	55	60	83	23	...
Canton	40	39½	40	50	10	...
Cameron Coal	5	3	5	16¾	11¾	...
Canadian, Southern	57⅞	24¾	29	50	21	...
,, Pacific	58¼	39	44	54⅝	10⅝	...
Cedar Falls	12	8	11½	12	½	...
Central Iowa	16	9	9	13	4	...
,, Arizona	¼	¼	¼	¼	...	...
,, Pacific	67¾	29¾	34	63⅝	29⅝	...
Cleveland, Colorado, Cincinnati, and Indianapolis	69½	28	31⅜	65	34⅜	...
Chesapeake and Ohio	15	5	5¾	14⅛	8⅜	...
,, ,, 1st preferred	28	9½	9⅞	24	14⅛	...
,, ,, 2nd preferred	17	6½	8½	16¾	8¼	...
Columbus, Chicago, and Indiana C.	1½	1	1¼	1½	¼	...
Chicago, Burlington, and Quincy	127¾	107	115⅛	120¼	5⅛	...
,, and Alton	140	118	127½	132½	5	...
,, ,, preferred	150	144	150	140⅛	...	9⅞
,, St. Louis and Pittsburg	13¼	6¾	7⅛	12	4⅞	...
,, ,, ,, preferred.	35	16½	17	33¼	16¼	...
,, and North-Western	124	81½	84⅛	116½	32⅜	...
,, ,, ,, preferred	149½	117	119½	144⅛	24⅝	...
,, Milwaukee, and St. Paul	94¼	58¼	71½	92⅝	21½	...
,, ,, ,, preferred	119	95⅞	103	116½	13½	...
Cincinnati, Sandusky, and Cleveland	24½	24½	24½	40	15½	...
Cleveland and Pittsburg	141	130	137	138¾	1¾	...
Columbia and Greenville preferred	33	33	33	31	...	2
Consolidation Coal	23	18	20	29	9	...
Colorado Coal	17½	7	8	15⅛	7⅛	...
Danbury and Norwalk	50	50	50	66	16	...
Delaware, Lack., and Western	139½	86¾	87½	116¾	29¼	...
,, and Hudson	114	67	68	105½	37½	...
Denver and Rio Grande	25⅝	6⅜	8½	24¾	16¼	...
Dubuque and Sioux City	89	55	58	77	19	...
East Tennessee	8¼	3	3¼	5¾	2½	...
,, ,, preferred	14½	4¾	4¾	11½	6¾	...
Evansville and Terre Haute	51	30	33	51	18	...
Elizabeth, Lexington, and B. S.	25	25	25	...	...	...
Green Bay	8½	3¾	3¾	5	1¼	...
Gold and Stock Telegraph	76	75	75	82	7	...
Harlem	198	188	191	192	1	...
Homestake Mining	11	8	9¼	12	2¾	...
Houston and Texas	51	20	32½	50⅛	17⅝	...
Illinois Central	140	110	115¾	131½	15¾	...
,, ,, leased line	85	80	82	81¾	...	¼
Indiana, Bloomington, and Western	20¼	9	12	17¾	5¾	...
Iron Steamboat Company	15	15	15	35	20	...
Joliet and Chicago	145	137	140	138	...	2
Keokuk and Des Moines	5	5	5	...	...	...
Lake Shore	104¾	59½	61⅝	94⅞	33¼	...
,, Erie and Western	19¾	6⅞	8¾	18½	9¾	...
Louisiana and Missouri River	24	19½	19¾	25	5¼	...
,, ,, ,, preferred	40	38	40	...	...	...
Louisville and Nashville	51⅜	22½	25¼	44⅜	19½	...
,, New Albany and Chicago	35	10	17	33	16	...
Log Island	78¼	62	62½	66	3½	...

	Highest.	Lowest.	Last.	Last, 1883.	Decline.	Advance.
Manhattan	67	40	64½	42	...	22½
,, new	65	42	65	46	...	19
,, 1st preferred	93½	88	90	86	...	4
,, Consol	79	64½	65½	...	...	...
Maryland Coal	15	7	7	12	5	...
Manhattan Beach	24	10	11½	15½	4	...
Memphis and Charleston	40	23	29	32	3	...
Milwaukee and Lake Shore	16	10	10	12¼	2¼	...
,, ,, ,, preferred ...	41	31	32	38½	6½	...
Metropolitan	105	80	90	90	...	...
Michigan Central	91½	51¾	55	85½	30½	...
Mobile and Ohio	13⅜	6¼	7¼	10⅛	2⅞	...
Minneapolis and St. Louis	18¼	7½	11	17½	6½	...
,, ,, preferred ...	36½	17	25¾	35	9¼	...
Mutual Union Telegraph	17⅜	10	14	18	4	...
Missouri, Kansas, and Texas...	23¼	9¼	15⅜	21¾	6⅜	...
,, Pacific	100	63½	90⅝	87½	...	3⅛
Morris and Essex	127	116	115	123¾	8¾	...
Nashville, Chattanooga, and St. Louis ...	56	30	36	54	18	...
New Central Coal	10¼	5	5⅛	9	3⅞	...
,, Jersey Railroad	193½	185½	192½	195	2½	...
,, ,, Central	90	37½	39⅛	84	44⅞	...
,, York Central	122	88¾	86⅛	112	25⅞	...
,, ,, and New England	18⅛	9	13¼	18⅛	4⅞	...
,, ,, ,, Haven	182	175	175	183	8	
,, ,, Lackawanna and W.	94	83	85½	85½	...	...
,, ,, and Texas Land Company ...	138¾	122½	138	124	...	14
,, ,, Elevated	130	115	130	105	.	25
,, ,, Lake Erie, and Western... ...	28½	11⅛	14⅛	26⅞	12¾	...
,, ,, ,, ,, preferred	70	20	28½	77⅛	48⅝	...
,, ,, Susquehanna, and Western ...	5¾	1⅞	1⅐	5	3⅛	...
,, ,, ,, ,, preferred	18¼	4½	4½	16½	12	...
,, ,, Ontario, and Western	16½	7	12	16⅜	4⅜	...
,, ,, Chicago, and St. Louis	10⅛	4¼	4¼	8⅞	4⅝	...
,, ,, ,, ,, preferred	20¾	7½	7⅝	18	10⅜	...
Norfolk and Western	11	10	11	13½	2½	...
,, ,, preferred	42	17	21	40	19	...
Northern Pacific	27	14	16¼	24¼	8	...
,, ,, preferred	57⅝	37¼	39¾	51⅜	11⅝	...
Ohio Southern	11¾	6½	9½	9½	...	...
,, and Mississippi	25⅞	14⅝	17¾	23	5¼	...
,, ,, preferred	64	45	64	112½	48½	...
Oregon Improvement Company	65⅛	8¾	21	62	41	...
,, Transcontinental	34⅝	6¼	13¾	30¼	16½	...
,, Railroad and Navigation	119	60	69½	93½	24	...
,, Short Line	24½	8¾	16	20½	4½	...
Ohio Central	4½	1¼	1½	2½	1	...
Ontario Mining...	29½	20	20	29¼	9¼	...
Pacific Mail	56¾	31	55¼	41	...	14¼
Philadelphia and Reading	60⅝	16⅞	18	55⅛	37⅛	...
Pennsylvania Coal	264	264	264	260	...	4
Pittsburg, Fort Wayne, and Chicago ...	135	121	126¾	133	6¼	...
Pullman Car	116½	90¾	106	115	9	...
Peoria, Decatur, and Evansville	17¾	7	12	13½	1½	...
Quicksilver	6½	3¾	5¾	6	¼	...
,, preferred	34	20	33	30	...	3
Rensselaer and Saratoga	145	138	144	141	...	3
Rochester and Pittsburg	16⅛	1⅞	3	14½	11½	...
Rock Island	126¾	100¼	105	116½	11½	...
Rome, Watertown, and Ogdens	24	17	18½	20¾	2¼	...
Richmond and Danville	61	32	45	57	12	...
,, West Point	32	12	19	28	9	...
,, Allegheney	5	2½	2⅛	4½	2⅜	...
St. Paul and Duluth	32¾	15	24½	34	9½	...
,, ,, preferred	90	65	79	94	15	...
Standard Mining	7¼	1¼	1¼	7	5¾	...
South Carolina	11	9	9	24½	15½	...
Sutro Tunnel	⅛	⅛	⅛	¼	⅛	...
St. Louis and San Francisco	29½	11½	20½	26	5½	...
,, ,, preferred ...	50	25½	38½	40	1½	...
,, ,, 1st preferred...	95½	70	83	87⅝	4⅝	...
St. Paul, Minneapolis, and Minnesota ...	99	76⅛	78½	94¼	15¾	...
,, and Omaha	38⅛	21⅞	23⅛	33⅜	9½	...
,, ,, preferred	100	80¾	82¼	92½	10¼	...
Spring Mountain Coal...	51	29½	49¾	29½	...	20¼
Texas and St. Louis	2	2	2	13	11	...
,, New Orleans	93	90½	90½	...	...	...
,, Pacific	22⅜	5½	12⅝	17⅛	4½	...
Union Pacific	84⅝	28	46	70⅛	24½	...
United States Express...	60½	45	51	56	5	...
,, Trust Company	505	505	505	...	...	...
Virginia Midland	21	15	17¾	23	5¼	...
Wabash, St. Louis, and Pacific	19¾	4	5	17⅛	12½	...
,, ,, ,, preferred ...	32	9	13	29⅜	16⅜	...
Wells Fargo Express	110	100	108	115½	7½	...
Western Union Telegraph	78⅛	49	54	74	20	...
Warren Railroad	122½	121	121	118	...	3

Appendix No. XII.—Table showing the Product of each Principal Crop of the Several States and Territories named, the Total Acreage, and the Value of each Crop for 1883.

States and Territories.	Indian Corn.			Wheat.			Oats.			Rye.			Wheat.		
	Bushels.	Acres.	Value.	Bushels.	Acres.	Value.	Bushels.	Acres.	Value.	Bushels.	Acres.	Value.	Bushels.	Acres.	Value.
			Dollars.			Dollars.			Dollars.			Dollars.			Dollars.
New York	17,512,000	761,423	12,784,271	8,035,200	780,124	8,919,072	42,071,400	1,344,637	16,828,560	2,703,816	241,685	1,946,748	8,649,218	357,662	6,485,913
New Jersey	9,715,100	346,971	6,814,815	2,063,600	154,000	2,269,960	4,265,800	130,873	1,706,320	1,028,976	101,488	771,732	4,198	249	3,190
Connecticut	1,710,000	57,001	1,385,100	34,300	2,171	42,875	1,100,700	37,141	528,336	441,303	30,302	361,868	14,344	626	10,758
Delaware	3,822,200	212,346	1,911,100	966,700	93,860	1,073,037	517,600	21,664	207,040	6,669	840	4,001	...	...	...
Rhode Island	414,300	12,947	352,155	460	30	644	179,100	5,882	85,968	15,837	1,372	13,145	21,266	808	17,651
Kansas	172,800,900	4,708,473	44,928,234	26,851,100	1,534,350	20,943,858	27,560,000	699,476	5,787,600	4,583,500	269,280	1,695,895	347,490	18,794	138,996
Nebraska	101,278,900	2,813,303	24,306,936	27,481,300	1,772,990	19,236,910	21,630,000	540,161	4,326,000	1,026,080	64,176	359,128	3,623,880	163,800	1,340,836
Colorado	532,100	21,287	452,285	2,394,000	114,000	2,298,240	1,209,000	31,046	725,400	31,046	1,783	24,837	157,080	6,064	117,810
Dakota	4,915,055	270,058	2,211,775	16,128,000	1,008,000	11,612,160	9,000,000	210,000	2,520,000	174,167	8,014	95,792	731,013	31,100	292,405
Wyoming	...	...	...	26,500	1,747	25,970	63,000	2,100	37,800	...	...	...	...	...	...
Utah	280,100	13,340	246,488	1,579,400	83,130	1,453,048	546,000	24,050	311,220	22,821	2,220	18,257	296,396	12,114	198,585

States and Territories.	Buckwheat.			Hay.			Potatoes.			Tobacco.			
	Bushels.	Acres.	Value.	Bushels.	Acres.	Value.	Bushels.	Acres.	Value.	Lbs.	Acres.	Value.	
			Dollars.			Dollars.			Dollars.			Dollars.	
New York	2,360,634	290,896	2,030,145	6,053,833	4,962,158	63,565,247	38,742,768	400,758	15,004,380	9,068,789	5,440	1,178,943	
New Jersey	244,608	35,026	220,147	610,751	508,959	8,397,826	4,275,857	44,081	2,351,721	...	...	...	
Connecticut	89,206	10,977	73,149	625,856	568,960	9,575,597	3,625,700	36,257	1,921,621	9,576,824	8,145	1,292,871	
Delaware	6,515	428	4,886	56,213	49,142	734,669	292,810	4,183	137,621	...	...	...	
Rhode Island	1,204	126	1,023	81,708	71,050	1,348,182	845,185	6,985	507,111	...	...	...	
Kansas	27,720	2,999	23,285	5,075,000	3,500,000	19,031,250	6,361,520	79,519	3,307,990	...	...	...	
Nebraska	20,808	2,029	16,646	1,123,601	749,067	3,932,604	3,467,124	42,282	1,040,137	There is no separate return for these States and Territories.			
Colorado	...	...	...	114,505	81,789	1,545,818	506,515	5,959	329,235			
Dakota	2,931	553	2,638	585,200	418,000	2,194,500	1,265,335	12,285	379,607			
Wyoming	...	...	...	21,450	16,500	278,850	104,500	1,045	71,060			
Utah	...	...	...	174,720	124,800	628,992	949,416	9,129	683,580			

Appendix No. XIII.—Exports from the Port of New York to Great Britain and British Possessions during the Year 1884.

1884.		England.	Scotland.	Ireland.	Gibraltar.	Canada.	New-foundland.	British West Indies.	British Guiana and British Honduras.	British Possessions in Africa.	Australasia.	British Possessions in East Indies.	Other British Possessions.	Nova Scotia and New Brunswick.
January	Domestic	10,976,710	2,014,525	70,278	58,730	...	146,711	596,861	100,896	68,674	540,266	102,654	132,384	73,593
	Foreign	137,090	8,648	...	374	77,053	35	30,325	5,726	980	1,184	...	...	4,642
February	Domestic	9,552,268	1,743,108	702	148,500	...	32,969	517,214	59,942	109,210	278,772	233,592	10,518	48,303
	Foreign	175,904	27,890	...	79	87,480	707	17,439	986	286	5,740	...	30	14,200
March	Domestic	8,666,303	1,513,027	131,324	31,239	...	100,117	593,744	116,226	97,141	513,869	444,065	57,017	42,149
	Foreign	138,179	5,921	...	701	110,554	...	37,484	5,780	635	8,382	...	...	2,645
April	Domestic	8,270,179	1,634,249	2,637	41,854	3,201	139,392	585,942	77,619	33,818	450,002	531,753	251,915	51,929
	Foreign	248,678	24,004	...	581	119,361	5,209	26,943	257	66	1,440	...	...	15,774
May	Domestic	8,840,728	1,979,478	32,448	27,875	6,774	165,356	569,317	127,254	52,212	321,050	245,447	33,400	57,898
	Foreign	142,211	4,537	...	9,604	140,139	799	22,224	1,498	...	6,779	...	...	14,620
June	Domestic	12,098,040	2,055,139	52,092	26,873	108,997	104,597	642,114	111,291	85,251	415,167	391,881	201,252	64,318
	Foreign	166,003	15,150	350	176	...	104	23,222	4,344	1,448	342	...	...	16,210
July	Domestic	13,468,067	1,875,575	175,579	23,495	100,553	130,286	575,028	127,470	89,174	434,069	581,702	56,812	50,202
	Foreign	214,013	67,034	...	693	...	3,113	23,247	275	1,450	4,767	...	...	11,669
August	Domestic	12,258,850	1,965,495	397,840	50,711	99,680	93,399	598,162	78,979	45,608	380,020	248,291	93,106	69,917
	Foreign	134,711	15,160	720	...	...	1,335	15,695	...	454	6,388	...	...	19,645
September	Domestic	11,897,570	1,740,132	68,190	26,713	115,294	169,174	417,563	133,730	105,251	725,580	300,918	35,118	65,075
	Foreign	168,584	4,270	85	...	...	389	21,794	471	82	7,301	...	...	19,511
October	Domestic	11,890,448	1,911,878	56,006	37,368	119,622	141,672	408,158	82,202	92,787	862,147	413,430	61,960	72,125
	Foreign	58,542	4,547	...	...	...	552	20,440	115	74	4,734	352	...	3,045
November	Domestic	9,339,354	1,477,041	77,043	937	85,108	131,291	511,181	135,478	60,072	425,824	251,050	129,525	56,468
	Foreign	72,648	2,497	...	27	...	3,150	19,069	472	3,853	7,880	2,892	...	6,213
December	Domestic	12,121,489	2,631,423	148,917	80,632	104,683	93,151	540,116	95,704	58,253	457,256	141,556	33,740	41,043
	Foreign	101,228	3,801	...	1,246	...	489	17,276	742	787	9,254	916	...	10,807
Domestic		129,380,006	22,540,570	1,213,056	554,927	1,268,524	1,448,115	6,555,400	1,246,791	897,451	5,864,022	3,886,339	1,096,747	693,020
Foreign		1,757,791	183,459	1,155	13,481	9,975	13,332	275,158	20,666	10,115	64,191	4,160	30	138,981
Total		131,137,797	22,724,029	1,214,211	568,408	1,278,499	1,461,447	6,830,558	1,267,457	907,566	5,928,213	3,890,499	1,096,777	832,001

Report from Vice-Consul Ashley, Providence, Rhode Island.

DIRECT Trade in British Vessels from Great Britain and British Colonies, 1884.

	Total Number of Vessels.	Tonnage.	Crews.
Entered	36	3,691	189
Cleared.	36	3,712	191

INDIRECT or Carrying Trade in British Vessels from and to other Countries.

	Total Number of Vessels.	Tonnage.	Crews.
Entered	4	1,959	38

TOTAL British Shipping at the Port of Providence (both Direct and Indirect) during the Year 1884.

	Number of Vessels.	Total Tonnage.	Number of Crews.
Entered	40	5,650	227
Cleared	36	3,712	191

UNITED STATES Vessels Entered from Foreign Ports, 1884.

From—	Number.	Tons.	Crews
Dominion of Canada	4	508	25
Hayti	5	785	38
Porto Rico	3	769	24
West Indies (British)	7	3,153	70
Total	19	5,215	157

UNITED STATES Vessels Cleared for Foreign Ports, 1884.

For—	Number.	Tons.	Crews.
Cuba	4	751	31
West Indies (British)	1	555	12
Total	5	1,306	43

NEW YORK.

Direct Importations.

		Quantity.
From Dominion of Canada—		
Lumber	Feet	3,102,455
Shingles	Number	2,790,500
Laths	,,	6,599,000
From Hayti—		
Logwood	Lbs.	2,035,570
From Great Britain (England)—		
Scrap iron	,,	1,411,340
From Italy—		
Brimstone	Tons	1,129
From Porto Rico—		
Molasses	Gallons	157,602
From West Indies (British)—		
Salt	Lbs.	10,477,679

Value of direct importations, 167,670 dol.

Imports viâ New York and Boston transported without Examination and Duties Paid here.

Hides
Madder
Polishing stone
Cotton lace
Dress goods
Colours
Linen cloths
Buttons
Silk lace
Purses
Steel tools
Dye assistant
Damask
Towels
Tape
Thread
China ware
Pins
Jewellery
Gloves
Furniture
Pipes
Porcelain ware
Brandy
Metal manufactures
White paste
Webbing
India-rubber manufactures

Acids
Cudbear
Nut galls
Manufactures of cotton
Paper-hangings
Machinery
Steel bars
Woollen cloths
Manufactures of wool
Endless belts
Handkerchiefs
Tin
Cotton quilts
Drapers
Borax
Logwood extracts
Bisqui ware
Britannica ware
Papier-maché
Ink stands
Paintings
Musical instruments
Flannels
Bottles
Suspenders
Button covers
Cords
Cloaks

Seeds—oil
Indigo
China galls
Manufactures of linen
Cotton cloth
Garden seeds
Bar iron
Soda ash
Hair pencils
Lapping
Steel pens
Tiles
Needles
Steel wire
Sheetings
Bead iron
Buckles
Glass ware
Fancy boxes
Furs
Manufactures of brass
Dolls
Puff boxes
Wood manufactures
Machine teeth
Lace nets
Clocks
Charcoal iron

Chemicals
Safflower
Gums
Manufactures of silk
Glue
Yarns
Linen crash
Earthenware
Shawls
Skins
Hosiery
Wool
Copper rollers
Soda
Extracts
Clothing
Toys
Artificial flowers
Combs
Doylies
Braids
Baskets
Wine
Size
Trimmings
Books
Logwood black
Chemicals

Value of above, 369,048 dol.

1262 UNITED STATES.

MERCHANDISE Warehoused at other United States Ports transported to this Port in Bond and Duties Paid.

Description.		Quantity.
Brandy, whisky, gin, rum, and wines	Gallons ..	6,947
Shingles	Number ..	524,500
Lumber, statuary, and paintings ..	Feet ..	16,000
Total value	Dollars ..	10,001

Collections.		Dol.	c.
Duties on imports		211,322	72
Duties on tonnage		839	64
Marine hospital dues		2,387	95
Steamboat fees		542	10
Customs fees		1,243	95
Storage		629	35
Miscellaneous		671	09
Total		217,636	80

ARRIVALS from other United States Ports 4,209 Vessels laden with

Cargoes.		Quantity.
Cotton	Bales ..	142,876
Wool	,, ..	27,941
Flour	Barrels ..	4,349
Grain	Bushels ..	816,172
Coal	Tons ..	766,165

TONNAGE of the Port, December 31, 1884.

	Number.	Tonnage.
Sail vessels	107	$14,544\frac{47}{100}$
Steam ,, ...	34	$19,564\frac{79}{100}$

Receipts by Vessels and Cars from Domestic Ports.

Description.		Quantity.
Cotton	Bales	227,933
Wool	,,	100,434
Coal	Tons	821,837
Flour	Barrels	253,085
Corn	Bushels	1,658,091
Oats	,,	469,061
Meal and bran	,,	402,962
Meal	,,	183,247
Oil	Barrels	107,088
Beef	Lbs.	22,156,800
Hay	Bales	334,796
Liquors	Gallons	77,437

Exports to British West Indies.

Description.		Quantity.
Flour	Barrels	41
Bread	,,	10
Pork	,,	2
Beef	,,	2
Lard	Tierces	2
Oats	Bags	40
Soap	Boxes	10
Starch	,,	5
Butter	Lbs.	150
Salt	,,	100
Bags	Bales	1
Tomatoes	Case	1
Condensed milk	,,	2

Total value, 526 dol.

Exports to Dominion of Canada.

Description.		Quantity.
Engines	Number	2
Piping	..	..
Cement	Barrels	200

Total value, 24,770 dol.

Manufactures.

Business has been very dull through the year, with very little prospect of a revival at its close.

Iron Foundry.—The business during the year has been much less than that of 1883; there has been a gradual decrease. For the greater part of the year prices have remained about the same as last year.

Print Cloths.—The market has been much more depressed than in 1883. The prices have been lower than they have been for 20 years or more.

1264 UNITED STATES.

Sales, 1,414,800 pieces. The range of prices for 56 × 60's has been from $2\frac{3}{4}$ c. to $3\frac{3}{16}$ c.

Woollen Goods.—More machinery was idle than in 1883; at least one-half of the mills was run on part time. The demand for goods was not steady. Profits have been small. Prices were fully 5 per cent. lower than in 1883; worsted goods and clothing wools fell off considerably. A better trade is expected in the spring.

The yarn business has been fair; the prices have been low and the profits small.

Steam Engines.—Business has not been quite as good as it was last year. Works have run the full number of hours each day with the usual number of men most of the year. No reduction has been made in wages. Manufacturers are confident that the present year will show a much larger business.

Vital Statistics.

Whole number of deaths	2,232
Males	1,083
Females	1,149
	2,232
White	2,117
Coloured	115
	2,232
United States	1,682
Ireland	370
England, Scotland, and Wales	99
Germany	22
British America	32
Portugal and Western Islands	5
Other countries	22
	2,232

No epidemic has prevailed during the year, and the health of the city has been good.

PORT TOWNSEND.

Report by Vice-Consul Rev. J. B. Alexander on the Trade and Commerce of the Puget Sound District for the Year 1884.

The data contained in this report are taken partly from the report of the Governor of Washington Territory, and partly from such other sources as I have had at my command. The imports and exports and shipping statistics are official from the Custom-house at Port Townsend.

This being the port of entry for the district of Puget Sound, all vessels entering from foreign ports, or clearing from the Custom-house are obliged to come to this place, thus indicating it to be the proper locality for the Vice-Consulate.

Washington Territory.

Washington Territory is bounded on the north by British Columbia, on the east by Idaho, on the south by Oregon, and on the west by the Pacific Ocean, comprising an area of 69,994 square miles, of which 3,114 is water, leaving 66,580 square miles of land surface, of which it is estimated about 20,000,000 acres are in timber lands, 5,000,000 acres rich alluvial bottom lands, and 10,000,000 acres are prairies and plains. It is divided by the cascade range of mountains into two sections, wholly dissimilar in climate, soil, and resources. The climate of the eastern section is colder and drier than that of the western section: the Japanese current flowing from the warm South Pacific Ocean lending a portion of its wildness to the lands west of the cascades from the California line to Alaska. The fertile cereal-producing prairie lands and plains are situated in the eastern part, and nearly all the rich alluvial bottom lands are in the western part of the territory.

Natural Resources, Fertility of Soil, and Climate.—Washington Territory is one of the richest in natural resources. The fertility of the soil and climate in the eastern section favours the production of cereals, and probably the yield of wheat, oats, barley, and rye cannot be excelled anywhere in the United States. The average yield of wheat is 25 bushels per acre, but 40 and 50 bushels have been raised. In the western section the yield of potatoes varies from 200 to 650 bushels per acre; hops average one ton to the acre, but 3,000 and 4,000 pounds have been raised, and the quality is exceptionally fine; of the grasses, timothy, redtop, and clover grow abundantly. Timothy has averaged $3\frac{1}{2}$ tons per acre. Many kinds of apple, pear, quince, peach, plum, and cherry, with the smaller fruits, flourish in great abundance in each section.

Puget Sound.

Puget Sound is a great, deep inland sea, extending nearly 200 miles from the ocean, having a surface of about 2,000 square miles, and a shore line of 1,594 miles, indented with numerous bays, harbours, and inlets, and containing numerous islands inhabited by farmers, lumbermen, herdsmen, and those engaged in quarrying lime and building stone. The waters of Puget Sound are remarkably rich in food-fish, the curing of which in various forms has already become an important adjunct of the commerce of the territory. Salmon, halibut, cod-fish, black-cod, smelt, and herring abound; a small oyster of fine flavour is found along the north-west coast in marketable quantities, and attempts are being successfully made in cultivating the same. Some few barrels of Baltimore oysters were shipped out here and planted, but the attempt was a failure, principally on account of the long time the oysters were in reaching the Sound, and the unsuitable locality when planted. Clams and other edible fish are plentiful, and dog-fish, a species of shark, from which an oil is produced, are very numerous.

Minerals.

Washington Territory is also very rich in mineral resources. The coal fields, so far as have been discovered, are situated on the eastern side of Puget Sound, although indications have been found in various other parts. Six of the principal mines yielded at the end of this year 412,149 tons, which was shipped principally to the Oregon and California markets. A superior quality of limestone and sandstone are found; a brown namatita iron-ore of excellent quality and magnetic ore have also been discovered, and are being successfully worked. Gold, silver, copper, lead, and cinnabar are found in paying quantities, and more recent discoveries and developments show that the more precious metals are very rich: the gold product of the territory for the year ending 30th June, 1884, was 64,000 dol.

Manufactures.

The manufacturing interests of Washington Territory have attained a highly gratifying degree of development, that of lumber taking the lead. In Western Washington, between the cascade range on the east and the coast, or Olympic Range on the west, and between the 47th and 49th degrees of north latitude, is a thickly-timbered belt of fir, cedar, alder, maple, ash, and other woods. Of these probably fir represents three-fourths. In the midst of this timber region lie the waters of Puget Sound, whose irregular shore line forms innumerable harbours splendidly adapted for the erection of saw mills and other wood-working factories, and also for the establishment of ship-yards. In this timber belt there are 20,000,000 acres covered with timber, which will average 25,000 feet of lumber to the acre, or a total of 500,000,000,000 feet of lumber. Fir trees frequently attain the height of 250 feet, and the mills sometimes turn out planks 100 feet in length. There are 24 mills on Puget Sound, which cut in the aggregate 1,300,000 feet per day. These mill corporations own mill property, including town sites, amounting to 6,320,000 dol.; have 150,930 acres of timber lands, which are valued at 754,650 dol.; and represent a total investment of 7,074,650 dol. Two counties are missing from this list of timber lands, the figures not being obtainable. Very many of these mill corporations own sailing vessels, which are engaged in carrying lumber from the various mill ports to San Francisco and foreign countries, besides having agencies in San Francisco, and owning property there in the shape of timber yards. Seven mill corporations own between them about 30 vessels and 12 tig-boats. The business of furnishing logs for these mills gives employment to a great many "camps," and in prosperous times it requires 300 camps, or 1,200 men. The lumber made from fir is splendidly adapted for mills, and the fir spars make the finest masts known. The future of the lumber business of the Sound district is closely linked with the progress of California, Central and South America, Australia, and the islands of the South Pacific, with occasional shipments to the Hawaiian Islands and China.

COMMERCE.

The commercial relations of Washington Territory are widely diversified. The commerce of Puget Sound, although confined chiefly to the two great products—lumber and coal—gives employment to a arge fleet of vessels. Only two ports in the United States—New York and San Francisco—exceed Port Townsend, the port of entry for this district, in the number of registered American sailing vessels in foreign trade. During the year vessels have cleared from this port for ports in British Columbia, Mexico, Hawaiian Islands, Australia, Fiji Islands, China, Japan, South America, Central America, Peru, England, and Ireland, besides a coastwise trade with California and Alaska.

The surplus grain, wool, and salmon of the eastern and southern portions of the territory have been principally shipped by way of the Oregon Custom-house at Portland, although shipments of grain have been made by the Northern Pacific Railroad, direct to the Eastern States. Many herds of cattle have been driven or shipped by rail also to the east. It is believed that this commerce is on the increase, and that upon the completion of the cascade branch of the Northern Pacific Railroad, exchanges will not only be more frequent and extensive between the eastern and western sections of the territory, but that direct communication by ocean steamers will be established between Puget Sound and the ports of Asia.

CUSTOM-HOUSE STATISTICS.

During the year 1884 merchandise was imported direct from foreign countries into the Puget Sound district as follows: Goods subject to duty, 36,665 dol.; free goods, 173,283 dol.: total, 209,938 dol. Imports of 1883 were 23,120 dol. free goods, and 99,796 dol. dutiable: total 122,916 dol. The increase of 1884 was 87,022 dol.

Exports of domestic merchandise for 1884 were as follows:—

IN AMERICAN VESSELS.

Articles.		Quantity.	Value.
			Dol.
Lumber	Feet	39,385,000	501,221
Laths and pickets		2,778,000	8,617
Shingles		3,200,000	7,633
Wheat	Bushels	14,545	12,749
Flour	Barrels	38,560	178,020
Oats	Bushels	44,814	17,751
Horses	Numbers	315	53,038
Cattle	,,	267	11,363
Sheep	,,	16,868	41,889
Hogs	,,	1,740	11,070
Other articles	Articles	..	572,287
Total			1,415,638

IN FOREIGN VESSELS.

Articles.		Quantity.	Value.
			Dol.
Lumber .. .. .. Feet ..		17,661,000	227,003
Laths and pickets		3,100,000	11,039
Other article		..	5,456
Total		..	243,498

Of the above there was carried in American vessels to British Columbia exports to the value of 824,049 dol.; British Possessions in Australasia, 235,285 dol.; Hawaiian Islands, 234,729 dol.; Peru, 53,634 dol.; Chili, 23.234 dol.; United States of Columbia, 30,607 dol.; Mexico, 3,344 dol.; China, 10,706 dol.

And in foreign vessels, to Chili, 76,755 dol.; Peru, 16,476 dol.; China, 10,706 dol.; British Possessions in Australasia, 129,647 dol.; United States of Columbia, 12,389 dol.; and Bolivia, 4,895 dol.

The exports of the Puget Sound district to foreign countries during the past five years compare as follows:—

Years.						Amounts.
1880	..	..	..	..	..	445,067 dol.
1881	..	..	..	..	..	529,887 ,,
1882	..	..	..	..	..	1,460,725 ,,
1883	..	..	..	..	..	1,601,147 ,,
1884	..	..	..	..	..	1,659,133 ,,

Of exports by sea coastwise no official record is made, but exceed those to foreign countries five or six times. During this year 175,000,000 feet of lumber were shipped to California ports, and more than 400,000 tons coal to California and Oregon. The aggregate value of all exports coastwise could not have been far from 8,000,000 or 9,000,000 dol.

SHIPPING.

During the year 1884 arrivals and departures of vessels in the foreign trade were much more numerous than in 1883. Of American vessels alone 867 entered, of the aggregate tonnage of 350,659, and of foreign vessels 30 of 18,871 tons. 36 foreign vessels of 25,452 tons, cleared for foreign ports, and 901 American vessels, of 362,553 tons.

The foreign arrivals of 1884 were represented by 587 American vessels of 261,260 tons, and 32 foreign vessels of 25,971 tons; while the departures foreign included 587 American vessels of 262,172 tons, and 50 foreign vessels of 40,865 tons

Of the coastwise traffic nothing satisfactory can be obtained, as vessels are not required to report; probably 138 vessels entered last year, and 100 cleared, the tonnage being 133,934 of the entered vessels and 85,359 of the cleared vessels.

LIGHTHOUSES, ETC.

To facilitate the navigation of the coast and the inland waters in this district there are 10 lighthouse stations, most of them supplied with powerful steam fog horns and numerous buoys, which require a staff of 18 keepers.

In addition to these there are life-saving stations at convenient points and quite a number of signal stations, from the latter of which reports of the weather, &c. are received two or three times a day.

The attention of the United States Government has lately been called to the defenceless condition of the entrance of Puget Sound. Suitable sites for batteries and defensive works have been reserved by the Government for a number of years, and it has been recommended that the more important of these, at the entrance of Puget Sound, be occupied and put in proper condition for use.

Financial Condition.

The assessed property of the territory is estimated at over 51,000,000 dol. The rate of taxation is $2\frac{1}{2}$ mills on the dollar, with a special tax of $\frac{1}{4}$ of a mill on all property for penitentiary purposes. The territory is out of debt, having last July a sum of 47,901 dol. 81 c. in the territorial treasury. The population is estimated to be 150,000.

Port Townsend, March 23, 1885.

SAN DIEGO.

Report by Vice-Consul Winchester on the Trade and Commerce of San Diego for the Year 1884.

The year 1884 has been characterised by steady growth in population and development in the resources of the district for which San Diego is the seaport and principal town. The early months were remarkable for excessive rainfall, which on the coast reached 19·46 inches, in the four months January to April; the largest rainfall previously recorded in the same period being 10·60 inches, and the average for 13 years, during which observations have been taken, being 6·54 inches. In the interior the rainfall was twice to three times as heavy. As a result there were damaging floods and such injury to the railroad that a partial change in its location had to be made, and through traffic was suspended till the end of the year.

The yield of honey reached 1,100 tons, but grain crops were injured by the excessive and protracted rains. Wheat matured imperfectly, was shrunken, and below the shipping standard. One cargo was shipped by a British vessel comprising 1,380 tons of wheat, and 41 tons abalone shells, value 9,068*l*.

There were no arrivals of British shipping.

Shipments to San Francisco, principally by steamers, were as follows:—

Description.		Quantity.	Value Free on Board.
Honey (extracted)	Lbs.	933,912	16s. to 21s. per cwt.
,, comb	,,	888,420	32s. 46s. ,,
Bees wax	,,	54,415	116s. per cwt.
Wool	,,	684,816	3d. to 8d. per lb.
Wheat	,,	379,605	4s. 2d. per 100 lb.
Dried fish	,,	1,138,000	14s. to 23s. per cwt.
Dried abalones	,,	160,000	28s. per cwt.
Abalone shell	,,	437,000	£11 per ton.
Whale oil	Gallons	13,990	1s. 6d. to 1s. 9d. per gallon.
Seal skins	Lbs.	134,700	2d. per lb.
Dry and salt hides	,,	88,807	
Dry and salt skins	,,	73,093	
Lemons	Boxes	429	
Oranges	,,	1,537	
Raisins	,,	1,227	
Olives	Kegs	68	

Of the extracted honey included in this return, 576,997 lbs. are known to have been transhipped for Liverpool and London. The abalone shells were principally exported to England and Germany. The remaining articles enumerated would probably not reach English markets.

Shippers of honey have been informed that a prejudice exists against San Diego honey in the Liverpool market, as it is reported that shipments have been made hence of adulterated or imitation honey, but on careful enquiry the evidence appears conclusive that no adulteration has been or is practised here. The reports mention glucose or corn syrup as the adulterant. This material, at a minimum cost of 17s. 6d. per cwt. in San Francisco, would cost, including delivery, tanking, and packages not less than 26s. per cwt. free on board here, while the highest grades of pure honey were procurable last year at 21s. per cwt. The adulterated article would thus cost more than the genuine.

Railroad Extension.

The extension of the California Southern railroad to a connection with the Atlantic and Pacific road, referred to in the report for 1883, is now in progress and is expected to be completed by 1st January, 1886, when San Diego will be a terminus for the important system of railways forming a trans-continental route controlled by or in alliance with the Atchison Topeka and Santa Fè railroad. The expectation of the early completion of this connection and of resulting business activity, together with the increasing reputation of San Diego as a winter resort has attracted numerous settlers and visitors. Town property is in fair demand at enhanced prices, and country lands are being settled up rapidly. The population of the county stated as 12,000 a year ago is now probably 14,500 to 15,000.

Enquiries are often received as to the advantages offered by San Diego to settlers, and a few words on this subject may be appropriate. San Diego is a pleasant place in which to live. The writer is not acquainted with any health resort where the climate is so uniformly healthful and enjoyable. On the average of five years there have not been more than nine days per annum when the temperature has fallen below 40 deg., and not quite 12 days per annum on which it marked over 80 deg. At no time did it fall below 32 deg., and only on one day in five years did the minimum temperature reach 70 deg. Cold spells and heated terms are alike unknown, the heat of the day is tempered by ocean breezes and nights are always cool and pleasant. The average humidity from sunrise to sunset is 65 per cent. The daily range of temperature from April to September averages $12\frac{1}{2}$ deg. and for the rest of the year $16\frac{1}{2}$ deg. In the interior the climate changes according to distance from the coast and elevation. Inland valleys are drier; hotter in the daytime and cooler at nights, elevation is gradually gained till at 50 miles distance the pine belt is entered 5,000 to 6,000 feet above sea level. Malaria is unknown. As a summer residence it is as desirable as in winter.

Openings for profitable business in the town are not easily found. Many persons whose own health or that of some member of their family renders residence in such a climate a necessity, eagerly watch for business opportunities and are content with smaller gains than are considered adequate in a more rigorous climate. In the country large tracts of land are being subdivided and sold at low prices compared with those ruling in other parts of the State. There is little Government land worth occupying remaining open for settlers. Near the coast the rainfall is too uncertain for general farming to succeed, but lands are adapted for fruit culture, particularly the grape (raisin and wine), olive and apricot. Where the fruit farmer understands his business, is careful in selecting good land with adequate water supply, plants, good trees, and vines of suitable varieties and cultivates carefully, he may on an average of years expect fair if not handsome returns Published estimates of results of fruit farming are often grossly misleading, exceptional yields of fruit are assumed together with maximum prices, and drawbacks are not mentioned, but the average results appear satisfactory where the business is carried on with thoroughness and skill. At a distance of 20 to 30 miles from the coast the rainfall is sufficient to ensure good crops of grain, and apples, pears, cherries, and other fruits are raised to perfection. Probably fully the average rate of farming profits in the State are realised in this section, but distance from a market is so great that large profits are out of the question. A considerable number of cattle are kept in this district. Good ranges have advanced in price materially. The disease known as Blackleg has prevailed to a slight extent among young cattle, and there have been a few cases of Texas fever, but on the whole stock has been healthy and very profitable. Sheep have paid moderately well in spite of low prices for wool. Bee-keeping gives employment during six or eight months of the year to a considerable number of persons and on an average of years yields fair returns for labour and the small capital required. Wages of the labouring class are high; carpenters, bricklayers and other artizans receive 12s. to 16s. per diem., unskilled labourers 6s. to 8s. per diem.; the cost of living is about 4s. per diem. Farm hands receive 5l. to 6l. per month with board. Large numbers of workmen are now unemployed in neighbouring districts, and the supply of labour is likely to be above rather than below requirements.

Capitalists can find opportunities for investments in moderate amounts. For loans the rate of interest is 8 to 12 per cent.

A good future for San Diego seems assured, and though its progress may not be as rapid as was at one time expected, it is confidently believed that the magnificent harbour will soon be utilized and a considerable shipping and general business, both local and transfer, be ultimately developed.

San Diego, March 11, 1885.

SAN FRANCISCO.

Report by Consul Stanley on the Trade and Commerce of California for the Year 1884.

CALIFORNIA has shared in the general depression which has prevailed during the past year, and there are as yet no definite indications of substantial improvement.

The great depression which has taken place in the value of almost all articles of commerce has had its natural effect on the mercantile interests of this coast, intensified moreover by certain circumstances, which have exercised a specially adverse, though probably only temporary, influence on the trade of San Francisco, the distributing centre for this State. I refer to the opening of new overland railroads to which I adverted in my last report.

The Northern Pacific enables eastern merchants and manufacturers to compete successfully with San Francisco for the trade of Oregon and Washington Territory, and the Southern Pacific has brought about a similar result with respect to Southern California and Arizona. In due time, however, trade will accommodate itself to the changes with which it has to deal, and the gradual development of this coast, and increase of population, which will be materially encouraged by the increased facilities afforded by these new lines of railway will together contribute to the growth of San Francisco, which from its commanding position enjoys so many advantages.

Unfortunately the completion of the California and Oregon railway has been delayed in consequence of the general depression and stringency in money matters; the opening of this road would give direct railway communication between the two States, and doubtless be of material mutual advantage. One hundred and fifty miles through a most difficult country have still to be made.

The wheat crop, the principal industry of the country, was fortunately greatly above the average, and this, so far as the producing classes are concerned, has to some extent mitigated the adverse circumstances of exceptionally low prices. The surplus of wheat available for export from last crop has been variously estimated at 1,250,000 tons to 1,500,000 tons of 2,000 lbs. each. The actual exports of wheat and flour for the first six months of the cereal year, July to December, have been together about 500,000 tons, and the estimated stock on 31st December was 800,000 tons.

In consequence, however, of the low price ruling, it is to be expected that farmers will carry over a considerable quantity into next crop, and the indications at present are, that the actual exports of wheat and flour for the cereal year, July to June, may fall short of 1,000,000 tons.

The exports of flour, though fairly maintained, do not show continued increase. Millers on this coast find they cannot compete in the English market with English millers so successfully as heretofore, the probability is that there will be some falling off in the shipments of flour to the United Kingdom. An increased market for flour is, however, expected in China.

The English wheat market during the past year has been unsatisfactory to Californian shippers, prices having steadily declined to the extent of 6s. or 7s. per quarter. Present prices must be extremely unsatisfactory to producers in this state, and probably involve actual loss to those farming the poorer classes of land, and to those subject to heavy charges for mortgage interest. The average price during the past few months has been about 26s. to 27s. per 500 lbs., free on board at San Francisco, including bags.

It is difficult to ascertain to what extent the production of wheat on this coast would be reduced in the event of continued low prices. It may be assumed, however, that under such circumstances farmers would endeavour to grow crops more likely to yield them a satisfactory result. They may, however, give increased attention to summer fallowing their land, which can be done in this climate with considerable advantage, and farmers would thus give their land a desirable rest; the results being, of course, a reduced aggregate production, but probably at some saving in cost per quarter, and with a better average production per acre.

It is hardly likely, however, that a few seasons of low prices will bring about any material change in the situation. Farmers will look upon the present low prices as exceptional, and they will probably continue to grow wheat as heretofore until they have further evidence as to the prices they are likely to get for their produce. It is not easy for farmers to make rapid changes in their crops, and beyond the limited amount of land which can be profitably used for vineyard and orchard purposes, it is doubtful if they can readily place their lands under profitable cultivation otherwise.

It is quite impossible to forecast the prospects for the coming year's wheat crop, everything depending completely on the weather during the next two months.

The winter rainfall was sufficient to enable farmers to put in a fair average crop, but the spring has been exceptionally dry, and though the ground has till now retained sufficient moisture to prevent any material damage, yet rain is now urgently needed to ensure a satisfactory growth. At the moment of writing a nice soft rain is falling, with indications of a continuance. Should it last two or three days with another good shower in April, and no subseqeunt hot-blighting winds, a big crop would result.

The question of irrigation in all the great interior valleys is engaging much attention at this time. The necessity of irrigation in this climate is admitted on all hands, but there are many conflicting interests, and serious questions have arisen as to the right of appropriating water from the rivers for irrigation purposes in dry districts of the State. Legislation will be necessary to settle these questions, which should be dealt with without delay, as without irrigation a large portion of the State is comparatively unsuitable for settlement in small farms.

Great interest is felt on this coast in the prospects of the Panama and the projected Nicaraguan canals. The opening of one or both of them would be of the greatest importance to the prosperity of this coast, and would especially encourage the trade of San Francisco, as the superiority of its harbour and other business advantages could not fail to concentrate at it the shipping trade, and make it the distributing point for a large amount of country.

Shipping interests are generally depressed, and local owners have not greatly added to their fleets during the year. A vigorous attempt is being made to establish the business of building iron and steel vessels here, and the Union Iron Works, which have spent a large sum of money in having the best appliances for shipbuilding, have just completed a steel steamer for the coasting trade. This is an entirely new departure, and I fear the cost of material and labour is too high to make the enterprise successful.

Freights have been extremely low during the year, the condition of the English wheat market rendering it impossible for vessels to secure satisfactory rates of freight.

There were charatered during the year for the United Kingdom 468,183 tons, of which 279,137 tons were British and 155,806 American.

American owners have, however, pursued the policy more largely than English owners of laying up their vessels during the continuance of unprofitable rates of freight, and San Francisco, being an American home port, accounts in some measure for the large amount of American tonnage disengaged here.

No shipments of importance have been made viâ the Southern Pacific Railway and New Orleans, but the managers still give out that they can carry a large proportion of the wheat crop by this route. It is not, however, generally believed that this can be done profitably, and certainly not at the present low prices. At high prices it is very possible a considerable amount of wheat might go overland, and this may in the future become a point of some importance, and tend to prevent the recurrence of the high rates which have sometimes prevailed.

Manufacturing industries are not in a satisfactory position, and the past year has been generally unprofitable. There is increasing competition from the Eastern States, where wages are lower, and it would appear to be only a question of time when wages on this coast must also fall; as indeed may be said of the whole of the United States. In the meantime Californian manufacturers are placed at a great disadvantage.

The following table shows the value of the principal productions of California during the last three years:—

Articles.	1882.	1883.	1884.
	Dollars.	Dollars.	Dollars.
Wheat	51,000,000	42,500,000	55,000,000
Barley	10,000,000	10,000,000	12,000,000
Other cereals	4,000,000	4,000,000	6,000,000
Gold and silver	17,500,000	16,500,000	15,275,000
Base bullion and lead	1,000,000	750,000	} 782,000
Other base bullion	1,250,000	1,500,000	
Wine and brandy	5,000,000	4,000,000	6,000,000
Wool	7,500,000	8,000,000	7,000,000
Lumber	5,000,000	5,500,000	5,000,000
Quicksilver	1,450,000	1,215,000	1,000,000
Fruit	5,000,000	7,500,000	7,500,000
Cattle, slaughtered	22,000,000	23,000,000	23,000,000
Dairy produce	7,500,000	8,000,000	8,000,000
Coal	700,000	700,000	650,000

EXPORTS.

The following shows the value of the exports by sea during the past five years:—

Countries.	1880.	1881.	1882.	1883.	1884.
	Dollars.	Dollars.	Dollars.	Dollars.	Dollars.
Great Britain	17,598,000	33,000,000	34,000,000	26,147,000	19,231,624
Domestic ports	5,656,000	5,400,000	5,559,000	3,756,000	2,865,658
British Columbia	1,235,700	1,109,000	1,583,000	1,595,300	1,305,655
Australia	822,500	999,000	1,650,000	1,200,000	1,420,011
China, including Hong Kong	3,347,000	5,505,000	4,700,000	4,239,700	2,960,681
Belgium	...	...	2,342,400	919,600	1,499,061
Japan	593,500	466,000	476,300	373,500	456,757
Hawaiian Islands	2,178,600	2,662,200	2,606,000	3,007,700	2,566,745
Mexico	1,852,000	2,227,000	2,546,000	1,877,900	1,555,351
France	...	...	...	...	836,286
Central America	...	...	...	...	1,097,560
British India	...	...	...	...	15,256
Other countries	2,277,700	2,295,800	289,300	2,650,300	1,353,271
Total	35,563,000	53,664,000	55,752,000	45,767,000	37,163,916

The following goods went east by rail:—

	Tons.
Barley and grain	11,500
Beans	3,420
Borax	1,560
Canned fruit	10,490
Dried "	1,660
Fruit	6,500
Hides and pelts	2,360
Hops	1,500
Leather	1,140
Salmon	4,760
Lumber	1,070
Sugar	27,860
Tea	8,770
Wine and brandy	12,670
Wool	12,280
Total	107,540

The exports to Great Britain were:—

Articles.		Quantity.	Value.
			Dollars.
Wheat	Centals	10,410,622	14,822,000
Flour	Barrels	653,253	2,944,000
Barley	Centals	303,227	340,000
Cotton	Lbs.	1,151,224	250,000
Timber	Feet	9,693,000	219,000
Salmon	Cases	43,000	189,000
Tinned fruits	"	290,000	149,000
Honey	Lbs.	1,471,000	75,000
Borax	"	736,000	52,400
Others			191,224
Total			19,231,624

The principal exports to other countries were as follows:—

Articles.		Quantity.	Value.
			Dollars.
To China—			
Flour	Barrels	292,369	1,301,069
Ginsing	Lbs.	324,000	650,000
Cartridges and arms	Cases	3,850	169,623
Cotton goods	..	..	230,000
To Australia—			
Tinned salmon	..	..	483,000
Timber	..	..	162,900
To Hawaiian Islands—			
Flour	Barrels	42,337	1,965,560
Dry goods	..	..	318,700
Provisions	..	..	153,000
To Belgium—			
Wheat	Centals	958,112	1,430,000
To France—			
Wheat	Centals	561,007	810,000
To Mexico—			
Quicksilver	Flasks	5,502	160,300
Dry goods	..	..	124,000
Machinery	..	..	254,000

WHEAT AND FLOUR.

Receipts during the Year ended December 31.

Articles.		Quantity.
Wheat	Centals	13,708,814
Flour	Barrels	1,209,022

A barrel of flour being reckoned as three centals of wheat, the total receipts of wheat are equivalent to 17,323,541 centals.

The exports during 1884 were:—

Articles.		Quantity.
Wheat	Centals	12,158,714
Flour	Barrels	1,201,761

equivalent to 15,763,998 centals.

The combined value of wheat and flour exported was 22,618,023 dol.

The exports of flour and grain was as follows:—

Nationality.	Flour.	Wheat.	Barley.	Oats.
	Barrels.	Centals.	Centals.	Centals.
Great Britain	669,381	10,542,638	303,653	..
France	5,200	565,030	..	..
Belgium	1,250	958,111	..	..
China	298,167	..	..	805
Hawaiian Islands	43,006	4,667	67,075	23,143
Others	184,757	88,268	84,635	4,964
Total	1,201,761	12,158,714	455,363	28,912

The cost of wheat, free on board, including freight to the United Kingdom, was as follows per 500 lbs. :—

	s.	d.		s.	d.
January	41	0	to	42	0
February	40	0		41	0
March	40	0		41	0
April	40	0		41	0
May	39	0		40	0
June	37	6		38	6
July	38	0		39	0
August	36	6		37	6
September	34	0		36	0
October	34	0		36	0
November	33	6		34	6
December	34	6		36	0

The following shows the exports and values of wheat and flour during the last five years :—

Year.	Wheat. Quantity.	Wheat. Value.	Flour. Quantity.	Flour. Value.
	Centals.	Dollars.	Barrels.	Dollars.
1880	9,452,099	15,243,378	560,770	2,754,267
1881	20,006,540	30,821,996	785,078	3,569,190
1882	18,756,239	31,355,452	959,889	4,801,298
1883	12,960,540	22,978,539	1,246,618	6,220,627
1884	12,158,714	17,329,448	1,201,761	5,288,575

The prices throughout the year ranged as follows :—

Month.	Wheat		Wheat		Barley		Barley	
	Dol.	c.	Dol.	c.	Dol.	c.	Dol.	c.
January	1	70	to 1	82½	1	2½	to 1	20
February	1	55	1	77½	0	87½	1	20
March	1	52½	1	65	0	82½	1	00
April	1	52½	1	62½	0	75	1	00
May	1	45	1	62½	0	77½	0	97½
June	1	45	1	52½	0	80	0	97½
July	1	37½	1	47½	0	80	1	7½
August	1	25	1	45	0	80	1	10
September	1	15	1	3½	0	80	0	91¼
October	1	22½	1	30	0	85	1	10
November	1	20	1	30	0	90	1	12½
December	1	22½	1	35	0	90	1	12½

WOOL.

The wool trade may be considered among the diminishing trades of California. Its decline has been steady since 1876, when it reached its largest dimensions, viz., 56,000,000 lbs. Californian wool being dirty and inferior in staple is not used by Californian manufacturers, who require the best wool, and the supply of superior wool in the United States being limited, the great bulk of that used in California comes from Australia. There being a considerable amount of mountainous land in California unsuitable for anything but sheep farming, the wool industry must always have a certain importance, a market being found in the east, where inferior fabrics are manufactured. All the good land in California is now taken up for grain and fruit, and land which a few years ago was thought only fit for sheep-farming now sells at prices far too high for sheep pasturing. Australia, the Cape, and South America, where land is cheap and grass perennial, undersell Californian wool in this market.

The production for the last five years has been:—

	Lbs.
1880	46,100,000
1881	45,100,000
1882	40,100,000
1883	40,850,000
1884	37,410,000

There were exported by sea and rail 34,600,000 lbs. to be used in the manufacture of inferior woollen fabrics. The amount in hand is about 6,000,000 lbs.

TIMBER.

Several cargoes of redwood timber have been exported to the United Kingdom during the past year, and this may become an important business. Redwood is very well adapted to finishing purposes, and is only found in considerable quantities in Humboldt and Mendocino counties in this State.

CANNED GOODS.

Salmon.—The pack of salmon on the coast amounted to 930,000 cases against 1,120,000 cases in 1883. The receipts in San Francisco were only 185,000 dol., being much less than in recent years, a very large proportion having been sent overland by the Northern Pacific. A very small quantity remains in stock throughout the coast. The amount exported by sea and land was 283,800 cases, of the value of 1,271,600 dol. Very low prices have ruled, and the business has been unprofitable to all concerned except to the fishermen.

Fruits.—The late and unusual rains in June having destroyed much of the fruit, there was a considerable falling off in the production, the amount having been 650,000 cases against 1,000,000 cases in 1883. Little of the stock remains unsold. This is likely to be an increasing and profitable industry, for though Californian fruits cannot be said in general to have the fine flavour of European fruits, they are produced cheaply and in abundance, and there is a large market in the interior for canned fruits among those who have never eaten better fruit, and abroad for those to whom the price of European fruit renders it a prohibited luxury. There is also a fair prospect that the railways may reduce their rates for fresh fruit and place it in the eastern market more quickly. This will be a great encourgement to fruit growers.

GOLD, SILVER, AND ORES.

The following table, prepared by Mr. Valentine, manager of Wells, Fargo, and Company, shows the value of the bullion produced in the States, west of the Missouri River, in 1884:—

	Gold Dust and Bullion	Silver Bullion, Ores, and Base Bullion.	Total.
	Dol.	Dol.	Dol.
California	12,896,594	2,376,394	15,272,988
Nevada	1,527,859	7,361,080	8,888,939
Oregon	552,472	2,695	555,167
Washington territory	68,946	1,179	70,125
Alaska	115,041	..	115,014
Idaho	1,160,077	2,382,100	3,542,177
Montana	1,875,000	9,987,000	11,862,000
Utah	35,635	7,354,201	7,389,836
Colorada	2,575,861	17,657,888	20,233,749
Arizona	460,791	6,595,588	7,056,379
New Mexico	217,688	3,442,926	3,660,614
Takota	2,876,847	110,000	2,896,847

Of this amount 25,183,587 dol. consisted of gold, 43,529,925 dol. of silver, 6,086,252 dol. of copper, and 6,934,091 dol. of lead.

Mining operations during the year were on the whole satisfactory. Work with good wages was given to 30,000 miners: no losses of any magnitude occurred in California, and generally fair profits were made by owners and investors.

The total production of the above-mentioned States for the past 10 years has been as follows:—

Year.	Gold.	Silver.	Lead.	Copper.	Total.
	Dollars.	Dollars.	Dollars.	Dollars.	Dollars.
1875	39,968,194	31,635,239	5,100,000	..	76,703,433
1876	42,886,935	39,292,924	5,040,000	..	87,219,859
1877	44,880,223	45,846,109	5,085,250	..	95,811,582
1878	37,576,030	37,248,137	3,452,000	..	78,276,167
1879	31,470,262	37,032,857	4,185,769	..	72,688,888
1880	32,559,067	38,033,055	5,742,390	898,000	77,232,512
1881	30,653,959	42,987,613	6,361,902	1,195,000	81,198,474
1882	29,011,318	48,133,039	8,018,155	4,055,037	89,207,549
1883	27,816,640	42,975,101	8,163,550	5,683,921	84,639,212
1884	24,362,784	44,250,708	6,834,091	6,086,252	81,633,835

It will thus be seen that though the yield of gold has greatly decreased, owing in some measure to the legislature of 1883 relative to mines worked by hydraulic power, the total production of metals is brought nearly up to the average by the increased yield of silver, copper, and lead.

It is said that Mr. Valentine has greatly underestimated the yield of silver last year in California. He, however, adheres to the figures he has given.

The treasure exported was as follows:—

Countries.	1883.	1884.
	Dollars.	Dollars.
China	9,595,188	13,079,770
New York	1,569,743	1,782,544
Japan	708,977	1,253,947
Hawaiian Islands	556,753	1,175,700
Calcutta	..	273,500
Other places	68,430	33,548
Total	12,299,091	17,599,009

A Bill is in progress in the Californian Legislature, which if passed will give a fresh impetus to hydraulic mining, by enabling it to be pursued under certain regulations. Its main features are that it may be undertaken provided the company forms dams or otherwise prevents the debris from coming down the rivers, the company to be answerable for any damage that may be caused to the land by inadequate dams. The agricultural interest will strongly oppose the Bill, the damage that might be caused to the land by breakage of dams being certain, while their security for indemnity by the companies appears uncertain.

Quicksilver.

There were produced in California 31,913 flasks against 46,725 flasks in 1883; indeed there has been a steady annual decrease since 1881, when the production was 60,851 flasks, and it is expected that before long California will import the quicksilver she needs. The working expenses are so great that no profit can be made, and though December quotations at 32 dol. show a rise of 6 dol per flask, the rise ought to have more corresponded with the rise in London, when from 5l. 2s. 6d. in January it rose to 6l. 15s. in December.

The exports were 21,901 flasks, against 38,031 flasks in 1883.

Imports.

The total value of the imports was 35,000,000 dol. less than it has been for many years, as is shown by the following table, giving the value of the imports from different countries during the past five years:—

From	1880.	1881.	1882.	1883.	1884.
	Dollars.	Dollars.	Dollars.	Dollars.	Dollars.
China	10,865,000	11,023,800	8,592,000	9,208,000	6,843,000
Japan	9,576,000	6,868,000	11,240,000	9,185,000	6,665,000
Hawaiian Islands	4,834,000	6,306,000	7,655,000	7,834,000	7,962,000
Great Britain	3,442,000	4,324,000	6,601,000	4,248,000	3,215,000
Australia	559,000	1,025,000	2,158,000	1,636,000	1,188,000
Central America	2,622,000	1,882,000	1,954,000	1,440,000	1,782,000
British India	1,627,000	1,576,000	51,000	1,120,000	1,537,000
British Columbia	1,092,000	1,064,000	1,000,000	710,000	1,425,000
France	721,000	838,000	1,308,000	804,000	1,164,000
Spanish possessions	...	...	6,000	538,000	798,000
Others	3,571,000	5,005,200	5,143,000	3,277,000	2,421,000
Total	38,909,000	39,912,000	46,176,000	40,000,000	35,000,000

There entered free from duty goods to the following value:—

From	Value.	Remarks.
	Dollars.	
China	4,325,000	Chiefly raw silks and teas.
Japan	6,430,000	,, ,, ,,
Hawaiian Islands	7,963,000	Sugar.
Great Britain	237,000	.. .. ..
Australia	290,000	.. .. ..
Central America	1,732,000	Nearly all coffee.
British India	312,000	Chiefly gambier.
British Columbia	365,278	,, raw hides and furs.
France and possessions	467,000	,, raw cotton.
Spanish possessions	3,700	.. .. ..

The value of the principal articles from Great Britain during the past five years has been as follows:—

Articles.	1880.	1881.	1882.	1883.	1884.
	Dollars.	Dollars.	Dollars.	Dollars.	Dollars.
Manufactured steel	...	726,800	1,960,800	355,600	98,000
Tin plates	704,000	679,400	935,000	683,300	590,000
Coals	98,500	593,300	402,700	400,000	357,000
Cement	...	...	161,200	202,000	64,700
Earthenware	159,300	178,500	217,000	166,000	159,000
Pig iron	133,000	63,300	218,000	281,100	100,000
Manufactured iron	424,800	301,100	472,000	186,000	255,000
Steel ingots	180,000	83,100	224,000	210,000	15,300
Cotton goods	65,000	116,000	142,000	110,000	213,000
Flax goods	175,000	245,000	178,500	78,200	198,000

Iron.

I quote at some length, as dealing with one of the articles in which British industry is largely concerned, the report of Mr. J. W. Harrison.

He says the past year proved disastrous to importers of pig iron, there having been a steady decline for the first nine months, and the quotation of the last three months shows sales of foreign iron at fully 2 dol. per ton less than importation cost.

To the American manufacturer there was this redeeming feature, that less foreign pig iron by 17,821 tons was imported than in 1883.

Previous to last year at least 75 per cent. of the pig iron melted here was Scotch, but now Eastern iron is a most formidable rival, the low prices ruling in New York, assisted by recent railway freight reductions, enabling Californian manufacturers to obtain American iron at the same price as Scotch iron.

This stagnation of the metal trade has been universally felt, and there appears little prospect of this year showing an improvement on last. Foundrymen here are acting cautiously, buying only to suit probable demand.

Glengarnock iron has fluctuated during the year between 22 dol. and 25 dol. per ton on the spot, whereas the cost delivered has never been under 24 dol. 50 c., and at the beginning of the year was over 26 dol. per ton.

The following table shows the pig iron trade for the past five years:—

Year.	Prices.	Stock, 31st December.	Consumption.	Importation.	Afloat, 31st December.
	Dollars.	Tons.	Tons.	Tons.	Tons.
1880	26 to 38	14,862	11,749	13,200	2,080
1881	24·50 30	8,275	15,187	8,600	2,880
1882	28 35	8,108	20,159	20,000	4,340
1883	24·50 27·50	16,038	21,850	25,000	1,620
1884	22 26	16,864	118,60	12,700	4,230

The above shows the stock on hand to be 826 tons more than at the end of 1883. Of this stock 9,100 tons are Scotch and English, and 7,768 tons American manufacture.

Were it not for the present state of stagnation among foundrymen the above stock would be deemed a very light one, whereas taking the consumption of 1883 as a standard, and considering the quantity due here shortly, it is probably sufficient for all the requirements of the trade.

Wrought Iron.—The total importation amounted to 13,880 tons, being 3,000 tons less than in 1883. There has been since the beginning of the year a fall of 3 dol. 50 c. per ton, the price being now 22 dol. 50 c. against 26 dol. at the end of 1883.

TIN.

The price of pig tin remained fairly steady throughout the year, from 18 dol. to 20 dol., closing at 18 dol. These prices were in favour of the buyer.

Tin Plates.—Good coke tin varied in the market from 5 dol. to 5 dol. 50 c. At a trade sale in July 1,300 boxes were sold at 4 dol. 75 c. to 5 dol. Charcoal and coal were 1 dol. higher. The consumption at San Francisco was about 175,000 boxes.

The imports of 1884 being higher than in 1883, while the demand was less, prices fell, coke tin of common brands selling as low as 5 dol.

CEMENT.

The imports were the lightest known for many years, and among them were many German and Belgian cements. The year opened with a large stock, and the price was low. Portland sold as low as 3 dol.; Belgian and German were freely offered at 2 dol. 75 c.

A California cement lately introduced bids fair to be a rival in quality to Portland cement, while it can be brought to this market much cheaper.

COAL.

The tonnage imported was the largest yet brought here in one year, as is shown by the following table:—

Whence Arrived.	1880.	1881.	1882.	1883.	1884.
Great Britain	66,660	281,313	188,771	174,173	129,951
British Columbia	169,162	158,629	157,762	120,528	291,546
America	358,424	333,212	376,882	438,835	423,082
Australia	59,872	126,296	158,901	162,185	190,497
Other countries	...	230	580	735	...
Total	654,118	899,680	882,896	896,456	1,035,076

[525]

Comparatively little Eastern Cumberland and Lehigh coal has been received, the depression in business generally, especially in foundry business, having made its importation unremunerative. No great advance in prices can be expected in view of the new mines lately discovered in Washington territory, and the increased and increasing outport from the mines in Vancouver Island. The prospect, however, of an increased foundry business will probably somewhat raise the price of Eastern coal and English coke. The large coast supply has an adverse influence on British shipping interests, as it greatly reduces the import of coal from the United Kingdom and Australia, and prevents vessels obtaining satisfactory rates of freight in this direction.

The average price per month of coal was:—

Month.	Australia.	English Steam.	Scotch Splint.	West Hartley.
	Dol. c.	Dol. c.	Dol. c.	Dol. c.
January	8 50	8 00	9 25	9 50
February	8 25	8 00	9 00	9 25
March	8 00	7 50	9 00	9 50
April	7 50	7 00	8 50	9 00
May	7 25	7 00	8 00	8 50
June	7 50	7 00	7 50	9 00
July	7 75	7 00	7 50	8 00
August	7 75	7 00	7 50	8 00
September	7 50	7 00	7 50	8 00
October	7 25	7 00	7 50	8 00
November	7 00	7 00	7 35	8 00
December	7 00	6 75	7 00	8 00

English coke ruled from 11 dol. to 13 dol. per ton, according to quality.

TEA.

Prices remained generally firm, though early in the year there was a sudden but shortlived rise. Teas classed as No. 1 have rated 18 dol. to 20 dol. in the primary markets, and closed at 18 dol., with a tendency to rise.

The tea was brought by 26 steamers and 14 sailing vessels, the latter almost exclusively from Hong Kong. The use of sailing ships was a new feature in this trade, and materially reduced the price by steamers, the steamer rate which was formerly 18 dol. having been reduced to 8 dol.

The imports for the past five years have been:—

Year.	China.	Japan.	Total.
	Lbs.	Lbs.	Lbs.
1880	4,997,527	17,081,997	22,079,524
1881	5,278,766	12,704,741	17,983,507
1882	4,701,588	19,469,028	24,170,616
1883	3,483,563	17,184,448	20,668,011
1884	3,058,111	15,255,463	18,313,574

SUGAR.

The total imports were 165,919,335 lbs., of the value of 8,130,000 dol. and exceeded by 25,000,000 lbs. the importation of any previous year. Of this amount the Sandwich Islands supplied 139,000,000 lbs.

Nearly all the sugar received was contracted for by one of the local refineries on prices based upon the value in New York. The imports under the head of China comprise sugar to the value of 243,000 dol. from Hong Kong.

The very large increase in the deliveries for consumption is due to the enlargement of the local refineries, which are able to sell their products along the line of the transcontinental roads, which were formerly compelled to get their supplies from the East.

The greater part of the Hawaiian crop of 1885 has already been contracted for by a San Francisco refinery. This is estimated at a little more than the crop of 1884. For the large quantity required beyond this the refineries will have to look to other sources of supply, either by direct importation or by purchase in the open market. Prices during the year gradually declined. Refined opened at $10\frac{1}{2}$ cents. per lb. for crushed, and $8\frac{1}{2}$ cents. for extra yellow, but in December they fell to $7\frac{3}{4}$ cents. for the former and $6\frac{1}{4}$ cents. for the latter. The best Hawaiian raw grocery sugars opened at 8 cents. to $8\frac{1}{4}$ cents., and are now sold at $5\frac{1}{2}$ cents. to $5\frac{3}{4}$ cents., whilst refining sugars, polarising 91 degrees, which sold at the beginning of the year at 6 dol. 4 c., declined in June to 3 dol. $\frac{7}{8}$ cent. They are now at $4\frac{1}{2}$ cents. to 5 cents.

The past five years have shown the following imports of sugar:—

From	1880.	1881.	1882.	1883.	1884.
	Lbs.	Lbs.	Lbs.	Lbs.	Lbs.
Hawaiian Islsnds	64,301,865	88,175,671	104,150,909	103,932,158	139,787,963
Manilla	9,884,660	16,462,269	1,528,136	20,183,302	21,378,719
China	1,894,564	2,566,422	940,956	4,157,392	1,197,104
Others	2,001,089	9,692,237	12,424,558	7,326,204	3,555,549
Total	78,082,178	116,896,599	119,044,559	135,599,056	165,919,335

COFFEE.

The year opened with nominally good prices, but dealers were shy at giving the prices demanded. In March the New York and European markets falling, a corresponding fall took place here.

Guatemala was imported in moderate quantities, and the well-washed qualities found ready sale at good prices.

The imports from Salvador consisted mainly of good unwashed qualities. The abundant supply eventually had a depressing effect on prices, which from $12\frac{1}{2}$ per cent. gradually fell to 10 per cent. at the close of the year.

Costa Rica receipts were large and consisted mainly of good qualities, for which at the opening $13\frac{1}{4}$ cents. were obtained; at the end of the year the price was $11\frac{1}{2}$ cents. Some inferior qualities of Costa Rica sold well for their value.

Rio coffee was imported solely from New York, and sold at New York prices with the freight added.

The following table shows the amount imported in the last few years and the prices obtained:—

From	1881.	1882.	1883.	1884.
	Lbs.	Lbs.	Lbs.	Lbs.
Costa Rica	2,300,000	4,949,000	1,756,000	3,907,000
Nicaragua	384,000	606,000	425,000	228,000
Salvador	5,198,000	6,964,000	6,252,000	7,749,000
Guatemala	6,420,000	7,317,000	7,218,000	6,394,000
Rio	185,000	524,000	475,000	178,000
Singapore	..	..	1,500	776,000
Others	828,000	1,360,000	1,166,500	273,000
Total	15,315,000	21,720,000	17,294,000	19,505,000

Average prices:—

Year.	Guatemala.	Salvador Unwashed.	Costa Rica.	Rio in New York.
	Dol. c.	Dol. c.	Dol. c.	Dol. c.
1881	13 04	12 20	13 16	11 78
1882	11 57	10 21	11 31	9 77
1883	11 88	10 57	12 03	10 36
1884	11 77	10 54	11 66	10 92

SHIPPING.

British shipping, which had gradually risen during the last five years to exceed that of all other nationalities, including the American foreign trade, was this year surpassed in number and tonnage by American shipping trading from foreign ports. The low freights kept many British ships from coming here, while the sailings of the American mail steamers to Australia, the Sandwich Islands, Mexico, and Panama were not influenced by the freights.

British shipping showed a great decrease as compared with the three preceding years, the arrivals here having been as follows since 1881:—

Year.	Ships.	Tons.
1881	369	493,993
1882	403	592,936
1883	320	485,793
1884	256	405,672

Of these, 27 arrived in ballast, 278 cleared, of which 215 left with cargoes for Great Britain or British Possessions; 40 left in ballast, mostly for Victoria, where they loaded with coal for this market; and 23 left for foreign countries, including four which went to take in cargo at other United States ports.

The British tonnage disengaged in port at the end of the year was 89,044 tons, and that on the way 111,352 tons.

The total disengaged tonnage in port was 182,000 tons; that on the way 186,000 tons.

The following statement regarding the tonnage duty collected in the United States shows that San Francisco ranks second in the amount of tax collected, and that the amount received from British shiping at all United States ports equals that received from the shipping of all nations, including America:—

Ports.	Number of Vessels.	Amount Collected.
		Dollars.
New York	2,117	490,299
San Francisco	385	137,983
Baltimore	253	64,203
New Orleans	304	82,830
Boston	671	83,299
Philadelphia	413	84,277
Pensacola	254	50,119
Others	2,882	302,763
Total	7,279	1,295,773

Nationality.	Amount.
	Dollars.
America	272,113
British	626,141
German	97,111
Italian	62,074
Norwegian	99,903
Others	138,431
Total	1,295,773

The following shows the entries made at this office regarding seamen during the past four years:—

Year.	Engaged.	Discharged.	Deserted.	Sent to Hospital.	Reported Dead.
1881	3,786	1,113	2,948	62	45
1882	4,159	1,775	3,275	80	43
1883	3,263	1,436	1,939	35	28
1884	2,815	1,087	1,822	49	28

Freights.

Freights to the United Kingdom during the year have been so low as to leave little if any profit. Iron ships have accepted 30s. per ton, and 45s. has been the highest paid throughout the year. The rate at the end of the year was 2l. 2s. 6d., with some prospect of a rise.

Wines and Viticulture.

This is one of the leading industries of California, and as the wines become better known in Europe the demand will increase, but until cheaper methods of manufacturing it here are found, the ordinary wines cannot be sold as cheaply in Europe as French and Rhenish wines of the same qualities. There is, however, a sufficiently large market in America for all the wine California is likely to produce for many years, and that the taste for it is increasing here is shown by the continually decreasing quality of French wine imported. The production in California in the last five years has been as follows:—

	Gallons.
1880	8,500,000
1881	7,000,000
1882	10,000,000
1883	8,500,000
1884	15,000,000

The price of grapes for wine-making was 15 dol. to 20 dol. for California grapes, and 20 dol. to 32 dol. for foreign grapes grown here per ton.

California wine suffers abroad, owing to many vineyard cultivators manufacturing their wine without any experience, and having thus placed a quantity of poor wine in the market.

The tendency hitherto shown to produce quantity not quality is disappearing. Large cellarage for storage is being made, and greater care than formerly is taken in selecting the grapes. The climate and soil are most favourable for grape-growing, hence it can hardly be doubted that California has a great future before it as a wine-producing country.

Mr. Wetmore, the chief executive viticultural officer of California, in his report for 1884, states that at first the cultivation of grapes here, as regards their wine-making qualities, was a failure, as the wine grapes of France and Germany, with few exceptions, require long pruning, special care, and adaptability to soil and climate, in order to produce profitable results, whilst here the old method received from the Mexicans of pruning on arms with short spurs was applied to all grapes alike. The aim sought after was to acquire the largest crops. At one time even the Riesling, now recognised as one of our best wine-making grapes, was almost abandoned as an unprofitable wine. The Riesling wines were therefore largely blended with coarser products, and the true capacity of California to furnish Rhenish wines of good quality is hardly known outside the State.

Mr. Wetmore goes on to mention other reasons that have given California wines a bad reputation, and then proceeds to state his reasons for believing that within the next three years the trade will place in the hands of retailers at New York wine much better than the ordinary classes of imported French wines at a price not exceeding 1 dol. per gallon, or 10 c. the regulation pint bottle, and good sound ordinary wine at 75 c. per gal., or $7\frac{1}{2}$ c. per bottle.

Among the reasons given are better knowledge of vineyarding, produced through the agency of numerous associations in the State, a better selection of grapes, and more extensive cellarage. Old vines have been pulled up, and those which experience has shown to be the most successful planted in their place, so that in a few years there will be a veritable revolution of general average quality.

The improvement will be specially noticeable in dry reds of Bordeaux and Burgundy commercial types, sweets reds of true Oporto character —the Trousseau a Bastardo having been specially and extensively propagated for this purpose—Rhenish whites, fair substitutes for light Sauternes from Colombar and Folle Blanche, with appropriate blends, and good approximation to high-classed young Cognacs.

These words are used critically, and the brands he refers to as the certain results of the next few vintages will be far superior to the average imported wines of similar pretension.

In my last report I quoted from Mr. Wetmore to the effect that

60,000 acres were planted previous to 1881. He now believes that 50,000 is nearer the truth, and that last year 20,000 were added, bringing the total acreage under wine cultivation to be about 156,000 acres, of which about 60,000 contain vines of five years old and upwards.

The price paid for grapes at wineries where distillation and sweet wines are not the chief products, but where dry wine is generally attempted, varies from 25 dol. to 35 dol. per tun, according to quality, and from 30 dol. to 35 dol. for certain select qualities. In the same districts the new wines of recent vintages have correspondingly varied from 25 c. to 30 c. per gallon, delivered at the railway stations in cooperage furnished by the purchasers.

It is very difficult to determine what the value of the wine would have been if aged one year at the vineyards. Those who have kept such wine generally do also a mercantile business, and sell direct to the consumers, retailers, and jobbers. In such cases the wines may range from 30 c. to 75 c. per gallon.

The cases where 1 dol. per gallon has been reached are rare, and are only to be found among high-classed Rieslings.

Considering the prices as for average bulk lots, grapes or new dry wines naked, in well-established districts, and for vineyards of the best average quality yielding about four tuns per acre, an estimate of income may be arrived at as follows:—

Grapes sold to the wineries 100 dol. to 120 dol. per acre; cost of good culture, picking and delivering crops, 30 dol.; net profit 70 dol. to 90 dol. per acre.

Wine (estimated at 135 gallons per tun and 8 gallons of pomace brandy) sold new and naked, 135 dol. to 162 dol. per acre; add 32 gallons of brandy at 75 c., or 24 dol. per acre. The cost of making the wine has to be deducted, but some of the large establishments make the brandy pay nearly the whole cost of making the wine.

From these statements it will be seen how profitable it is to combine wine-making with grape-growing. This is especially so in the case of small vineyards where the crop does not exceed three tuns to the acre, and where the finest varieties are grown, for to get the full benefit of fine varieties the grower should carefully ferment them and keep them separate from inferior stocks.

It is very unlikely that the choicest varieties will bring less prices than the better average varieties do now, say 30 c. a gallon for wine, for though the tendency may be for less prices for inferior wines, the prices will assuredly rise for the most select varieties, and that of the good averages will remain as now.

On the whole it would be safer rather to aim at a good average class than at the highest class, the consumption of these being limited to the tables of the rich.

I have quoted at considerable length from the pamphlet of Mr. Wetmore, as he has an intimate knowledge of the subject, and because I believe that in grape-growing and wine-making in California many Englishmen can find profitable employment, and a healthy and not unpleasant life.

Those who would be successful should study the subject theoretically as well as practically.

A higher class of education is required than for ordinary farming, as a knowledge of chemistry is indispensable, and it would be very advantageous to be able to read the French and German publications as they appear.

I would also advise them to procure the reports of the chief executive viticultural officer of California.

Population and Immigration.

The excess of arrivals over departures in the State of California last year was about 20,000; the greater part of the arrivals had sufficient money to purchase private lands, or at least to take up Government lands.

The town of San Francisco is said now to contain 300,000 inhabitants.

I wish to repeat most emphatically, and to extend the warning given in my last report against British subjects coming here to seek employment.

I then excepted mechanics, stating they could find work and good wages, but a longer experience shows me that they should be included in the number of those who ought not to come.

California, which is much larger than Great Britian, has not above 1,000,000 inhabitants; of these the great majority are, as elsewhere, of the wage-earning class, and the employers are not sufficiently numerous to give work to those already here.

There is much actual distress, and not a day passes without British subjects applying to me for relief.

Gardeners who would look after the horses and cows, and make themselves generally useful could probably find places.

Wages are so high that work is concentrated in as few hands as possible. Household female servants can generally find places and get good wages, but their work is harder than it is in England. For instance, in all except large establishments the cook does the washing, and what is called the parlour-maid acts as butler, footman, and housemaid. An indifferent cook gets 75*l*. a year, a parlour-maid 50*l*.

To those who have, say 1,000*l*. and are steady, industrious men, and fairly good agriculturists, the country offers a good opening in the purchase of private lands, as it also does to men of less means, who can bring with them from 200*l*. to 300*l*., and are prepared to work hard for some years on Government grants; but Government lands conveniently situated for a market, and otherwise desirable, get scarcer every year.

To a man with a little capital, vineyard cultivation and wine-making appear to offer the best chances of securing a competency without exceedingly hard manual labour.

The price of suitable vine land unprepared is not less than 100 dol. per acre, and no returns can be expected till the fourth year. The usual plan with purchasers is to place on it an experienced vineyard cultivator to bring it into bearing order. With the small profit such manager can make during his four years' charge, he does not expect a high salary. From 20 dol. to 30 dol. per month will get a good man.

Meanwhile, the owner can either reside on the spot and help to bring his vineyard into cultivation, or he can apprentice himself to or take service with a viticulturist.

When he finally enters on his own vineyard, to be successful he should combine wine-making with vine cultivation.

I do not recommend any one to cultivate an ordinary orchard; the price of such fruit hardly repays the cost of growing it.

Those accustomed to work in an office or shop should by no means come here, except under a definite arrangement. This has been applicable for the last 20 years, but more especially now, when there is great trade depression, and all business men are reducing their establishments. Many who have come out with the highest testimonials and with a considerable sum of money have waited vainly for months in the hope of getting employment, and have finally returned home, bitterly regretting they had been induced to leave it. These are fortunate compared with those who have remained till they have spent their all: their lot then is a hard one.

It must be remembered that though the rate of wages is high measured by the English standard, yet the cost of keeping house is in proportion high, and though what at first may be considered luxuries can be obtained cheap, they soon cease to be luxuries.

There are some trashy publications, unfortunately of considerable circulation, which, among many misleading statements, continually represent California as the land for a poor man. I know no country more unsuited to a poor man than California. I would strongly advise all intending emigrants to consult the California Emigration Association, whose address is 10, California-street, San Francisco. They should explain their wants and their qualifications, and should mention the amount of money at their disposal on arrival. Those who come prepared to buy private lands, or to take up Government land, and to expend money, time, and labour on it will be warmly welcomed by this association, and they can rely on the advice they will receive from it, and on every assistance being given them in the selection of suitable land. The association discourages, and properly as yet, the emigration of labourers or mechanics without means.

The number of Chinese in the State has greatly diminished, and under the present restrictive law will yearly diminish; and as they were largely employed in vineyard and orchard culture, it is possible a somewhat larger field may soon be available for white labour, but as yet the Chinese departures have been fully counterbalanced by increased ship emigration.

San Francisco, March 30, 1885.

Appendix No. I.—RETURN of British Shipping at the Port of San Francisco for 1884.

Direct Trade in British Vessels from and to Great Britain and British Colonies.

Entered.

Total Number of Vessels.			Total Tonnage.			Total Number of Crews.	Total Value of Cargoes.
With Cargoes.	In Ballast.	Total.	With Cargoes.	In Ballast.	Total.		£
216	...	216	358,445	...	358,445	7,004	...

Cleared.

Total Number of Vessels.			Total Tonnage.			Total Number of Crews.	Total Value of Cargoes.
With Cargoes.	In Ballast.	Total.	With Cargoes.	In Ballast.	Total.		£
215	40	255	351,038	65,352	416,390	8,133	3,790,806

Indirect or Carrying Trade in British Vessels from and to other Countries.

Entered.

Countries whence Arrived.	Number of Vessels.			Tonnage.			Number of Crews.	Value of Cargoes.
	With Cargoes.	In Ballast.	Total.	With Cargoes.	In Ballast.	Total.		£
Peru	...	7	7	...	7,643	7,643	129	...
Germany	4	...	4	3,360	...	3,360	73	...
Japan	1	2	3	795	3,507	4,302	74	...
Spain	4	...	4	5,112	...	5,112	100	...
Belgium	3	...	3	3,977	...	3,977	69	...
Chili	...	6	6	...	6,982	6,982	114	...
Brazil	...	7	7	...	9,993	9,993	179	...
Others	1	5	6	499	5,359	5,858	112	...
Total	13	27	40	13,743	33,484	47,227	850	...
Total direct and indirect	229	27	256	372,188	33,484	405,672	7,854	...

Cleared.

Countries to which Departed.	Number of Vessels.			Tonnage.			Number of Crews.	Value of Cargoes.
	With Cargoes.	In Ballast.	Total.	With Cargoes.	In Ballast.	Total.		£
France	6	...	6	5,805	...	5,805	122	66,040
Chili	...	6	6	...	7,102	7,102	130	...
Spain	1	1	2	1,858	1,200	3,058	49	13,400
Belgium	2	...	2	3,138	...	3,138	53	24,510
Peru	1	...	1	750	...	750	18	100
United States of America	...	4	4	...	4,570	4,570	86	...
Mexico	...	1	1	...	749	749	13	...
Whaling voyage	...	1	1	...	63	63	8	...
Total	10	13	23	11,551	13,684	25,235	479	104,050
Total direct and indirect	225	53	278	362,589	79,036	441,625	8,612	3,894,856

SAN FRANCISCO.

Appendix No. II.—STATEMENT showing the Number and Tonnage of all Vessels trading from Foreign Ports with San Francisco in 1884.

ENTERED.

Nationality.	Number of Ships.			Total Tonnage.		
	Direct.	Indirect.	Total.	Direct.	Indirect.	Total.
British..	216	40	256	358,445	47,227	405,672
American	..	416	416	..	429,379	429,379
French..	4	8	12	892	6,615	7,507
German	..	16	16	..	16,279	16,279
Others..	12	17	29	6,487	10,514	17,001
Total	232	497	729	365,824	510,014	875,838

CLEARED.

Nationality.	Number of Ships.			Total Tonnage.		
	Direct.	Indirect.	Total.	Direct.	Indirect.	Total.
British..	255	23	278	416,390	25,235	441,625
American	..	440	440	..	478,545	478,545
French..	5	5	10	1,266	2,684	3,950
German	1	19	20	198	21,982	22,180
Others..	10	21	31	2,262	12,695	14,957
Total	271	508	779	420,116	541,141	961,257

Appendix No. III.—STATEMENT showing the Number and Tonnage of all Vessels trading with San Francisco from Foreign Countries during the Five Years ended December 31, 1884.

ENTERED.

Year.	British.		American.		Others.		Total.	
	Number.	Tonnage.	Number.	Tonnage.	Number.	Tonnage.	Number.	Tonnage.
1880	197	257,042	374	414,780	78	74,442	649	719,264
1881	369	493,993	390	422,543	86	59,060	845	975,596
1882	403	592,936	391	428,326	104	68,369	898	1,089,631
1883	320	485,793	409	388,940	77	48,516	806	923,249
1884	256	405,672	416	429,379	57	30,887	729	865,938

CLEARED.

Year.	British.		American.		Others.		Total.	
	Number.	Tonnage.	Number.	Tonnage.	Number.	Tonnage.	Number.	Tonnage.
1880	183	239,733	423	474,349	64	35,949	670	750,031
1881	365	488,135	444	509,373	100	63,723	909	1,061,631
1882	389	568,174	438	508,035	99	66,055	926	1,142,264
1883	290	438,467	425	438,320	66	38,998	781	915,785
1884	278	441,625	440	478,545	61	41,087	779	961,257

1294 UNITED STATES.

Appendix No. IV.—Comparative Statement showing the Condition of California Savings Banks on January 1, 1883, 1884, and 1885.

Liabilities.

	Savings Banks of California.			San Francisco Savings Banks.		
	January 1, 1883.	January 1, 1884.	January 1, 1885.	January 1, 1883.	January 1, 1884.	January 1, 1885.
	Dollars.	Dollars.	Dollars.	Dollars.	Dollars.	Dollars.
Capital paid up	3,284,311	3,482,915	3,521,431	1,647,985	1,650,400	1,650,855
Reserve fund	1,906,736	2,057,654	2,315,343	1,690,678	1,774,284	1,890,825
Due depositors	55,223,985	59,923,949	59,142,630	47,949,755	51,896,856	52,424,681
Other liabilities	433,180	346,982	361,750	209,145	246,494	205,758
Total liabilities	60,848,212	65,811,300	65,341,154	51,497,563	55,568,034	56,172,119

Resources.

	Savings Banks of California.			San Francisco Savings Banks.		
	January 1, 1883.	January 1, 1884.	January 1, 1885.	January 1, 1883.	January 1, 1884.	January 1, 1885.
	Dollars.	Dollars.	Dollars.	Dollars.	Dollars.	Dollars.
Bank premises	665,770	665,852	675,676	507,705	507,705	483,606
Real estate by foreclosure	5,093,854	4,405,854	3,764,916	4,763,104	4,182,879	3,541,132
Invested in stocks and bonds	17,332,950	18,240,484	15,902,726	16,153,889	17,326,505	15,074,326
Loans on real estate	30,356,515	31,568,213	34,804,584	25,686,046	26,300,487	29,499,584
Loans on stocks, bonds, &c.	3,899,161	7,425,578	5,894,392	2,541,336	5,563,512	5,690,273
Money on land	1,542,989	1,876,489	1,900,529	992,507	894,445	1,125,679
Money in other banks	1,228,797	1,353,489	715,078	353,160	554,260	309,400
Other assets	728,176	275,341	1,683,253	499,816	238,241	448,119
Total assets	60,848,212	65,811,300	65,341,154	51,497,563	55,568,034	56,172,119

UNITED STATES.

ASTORIA.

Report by Consular-Agent Cherry on the Trade and Commerce of Astoria for the Year 1884.

In comparing the past year with the preceding one there will be found a decrease of trade: this has been caused by the general depression which has been prevailing over the business-world during the past year, and has materially affected prices of the staple products that leave this river, together with the almost total cessation of railroad building and consequent stoppage of large sums paid out.

Exports and Imports.

The values of the commerce of the port show some diminution, some of which is due to the opening of the Northern Pacific Railway, which has taken some of the canned salmon overland, instead of its going by sea as heretofore; but I have no doubt that in the near future the tide of immigration that the same railroad is pouring into the country drained by the Columbia River will bring the amount of produce to be exported by sea up to a very much greater amount than it will take away from the exports.

The practice of vessels going up river 110 miles for their cargoes still prevails, causing detention in time and some material expense, when it would be more advantageous for the shipowner to have the cargo lightered; the only thing preventing its being done cheaply is that each vessel pays for her own lighterage instead of its being done by the exporters who then having a heavy expense and interest at stake, would very quickly take measures to have it done for a more reasonable figure than now existing.

The following statement shows the number of vessels which have leared at Astoria during the past five years:—

Year.	Number.		Value of Cargo in Dol.
In 1880	63	Foreign	4,181,352
1881	126	,,	7,414,516
1882	136	,,	10,873,697
1883	383	,, and domestic.	14,031,467
1884	403	,, ,,	15,600,000

Foreign exports from the Columbia for 1884 are 95 vessels, whose cargoes comprise, as taken from the records of the Astoria Custom-house:

Articles.		Quantity.	Value.
			Dol.
Wheat	Bushels ..	3,799,183	2,941,187
Salmon	Cases ..	353,786	1,591,937
Flour	Barrels ..	249,648	1,136,955
Lumber	1,000 feet ..	4,153	46,654
			5,716,733

Of the above amount the direct exports were:—

Articles.		Quantity.	Value.
			Dol.
Salmon	Cases ..	296,057	1,468,207
Flour	Barrels ..	19,047	96,712
Wheat	Bushels ..	561,503	455,354
Lumber	Feet ..	284,000	34,568
			2,054,841

of which amount there were taken by

	Dollars.
British vessels	1,490,540
American ,, ...	564,301

Of this quantity 1,450,740 dol. went to the British Islands, and 38,800 dol. to the continent of Europe.

Foreign imports for the year were:—

	Dollars.
From the British Islands	160,220
,, British colonies	44,466
	204,688

All of which arrived in British bottoms. The above imports consisted of coals, tinplates, salt, and other cannery supplies.

The amount collected for duties in this Custom-house during the past year was 54,815 dol., the total collections being 66,000 dol.

Salmon Canning Industry.

This industry has not been a profitable one for the past year to the proprietors of the salmon-canning establishments. Various causes have brought this about; of which actual lower values for all descriptions of food over production of canned salmon on the Pacific coast, and the injury to the reputation of the pack of the Columbia River by the putting up of outside and inferior salmon under Columbia River brands, are the chief. Proprietors of canning establishments know the reasons, but are unable to agree among themselves as to the proportionate quantity that each cannery should limit itself to, and to united measures in putting a stop to the piracy of brands.

Notwithstanding that the season of 1884 was ushered in under the unsatisfactory circumstances of a poor demand from the two great markets for the product, and with very few contracts, and those of limited extent, the packers, regardless of this, put up a larger catch than ever before, aggregating something under 650,000 cases, and consequently the price in some instances has been forced to less than 4 dol. per case.

The price paid for fish was however materially lower, being from 60 c. to 70 c. as compared with from 80 c. to 90 c. for the year before. I cannot find that the bonâ fide fisherman was any the worse for this reduction in price, but it certainly had the effect of keeping away a number of men who looked to the fishing season for a means to indulge in their habits of dissipation.

The importance of this industry to this town and the surrounding country may be more correctly estimated by the following figures of the pack of the canneries in the town alone.

In 1882 19 canneries put up 341,000 cases, paying 614,520 dol. for fish.

In 1883 24 canneries put up 410,000 cases, paying 1,096,200 dol. for fish.

In 1884 24 canneries put up 475,200 cases, paying 855,350 dol.

This important industry was begun by a noted fisherman of this coast, William Hume, in the spring of 1866, who commencing some 30 miles up the river in a small way, and with very primitive appliances for making cans and cooking the fish, put up at that time 4,000 cases of four dozen one-pound tins each, the price for fish at that time being 15 c., but each succeeding year saw the price of fish rising, and the materials and prices of manufactured articles decreasing. However, a greater number of fishermen divided the increased catch and price amongst themselves, the number increasing faster than the price and the number of fish caught, till the quantity caught by each boat averaged a far smaller return in money.

The accompanying table gives the results of prices of product and the raw fish :—

Year.	Total Product.	Price Received	Cost of Fish.
			Cents.
1866	4,000	16·00	15
1867	18,000	13·00	15
1868	28,000	12·00	20
1869	100,000	10·00	20
1870	150,000	9·00	20
1871	200,000	9·50	22½
1872	250,000	8·00	25
1873	250,000	7·00	25
1874	350,000	6·50	25
1875	375,000	5·60	25
1876	450,000	5·00	25
1877	460,000	5·20	37½
1878	460,000	5·00	40
1879	480,000	4·60	50
1880	530,000	4·80	50
1881	550,000	5·00	60
1882	544,000	5·00	60
1883	629,000	4·60	85
1884	648,000	4·35	65

The materials chiefly used in this industry are imported mostly from the British islands, and consist of net twine, block tin and lead, tin-plate, caustic soda and salt. The values and quantities of each are :—

Description.				Quantity.	Value.
					Dollars.
Net twine	..	..	Lbs. ..	360,000	380,000
Block tin	..	..	,, ..	255,000	63,000
Tin plates	..	..	Boxes..	66,500	425,000
Fine salt	..	..	Sacks..	10,000	8,000
Caustic soda	..	..	Lbs. ..	25,000	1,000
Total	..	..	..	..	877,000

The twine for netting comes mostly from Great Britain, viâ New York and Boston, and then by overland railway.

Block tin almost altogether from Australia, viâ San Francisco.

Block lead comes from the San Francisco refineries.

Tin-plates, about two-thirds of the quantity, comes directly by sail to this port; from Liverpool in British vessels the other third, viâ San Francisco, where there are better facilities for storing in bond.

Salt and caustic potash arrived in sailing vessels direct from Liverpool, and the quantity imported is estimated by the proposed amount of the pack of salmon.

Of the future of the business but little can be said with certainty; it is evident that there has been too much competition. During the past year there has been considerable dissatisfaction, and some litigation between some of the canning companies and their financial and business agents. In commenting on the result of last season's business the Press sensibly remarks: "The best solution of the problem of the rival interests of packers and the middlemen is the establishment of a salmon exchange right here, where the article which now commands a a world-wide sale is put up. . . . . If properly managed it would appear that the establishment of an exchange would be to the interests of all concerned."

The total value of all property invested in the canning business in this Consular district is not less than two million of dollars, and includes 37 canneries.

From May 1st to October 16th there was shipped direct from Astoria to the United Kingdom canned salmon as follows:—

Month.			Cases.	Value.
				Dollars.
In May ..	..	..	9,500	47,500
June ..	..	..	43,868	219,340
July ..	..	..	58,624	293,120
August	..	..	95,20	474,600
September	..	..	86,534	432,670
October	..	..	9,311	46,555
			303,457	1,513,785
Besides	..	..	29,658	To New York by sail.
			101,871	California by steamer.
And ..	..	..	171,734	By rail to the interior of the United States.
Total ..		..	606,720	

Of the three last items of shipments it is very difficult to trace how much goes to the United Kingdom, but it is certain that some of it does.

Previously to last year the Australian colonies came next to the

United Kingdom as customers for the canned salmon, but the domestic demand of the United States has increased so as to put itself second on the list and the colonies third.

It is proper here to mention the great waste of material that seems incident to all new countries where labour is high. It seems to me that it would be a profitable business to save it.

The first is the loss of tin in the clippings, &c., from tinplate, which from lack of knowledge how to save or make use of, and the price of labour and freight is now thrown into the river from the windows of the can shops of the canneries: making a mound of glittering tin scrap, which attracts the eye of every visitor; this eventually rusts down into a bank of iron rust.

The other, with a far better prospect of profit, is the utilisation of the offal of the salmon that is unfit to be put up. At present it is mostly thrown into the river to pollute the stream, the smaller portion being taken by one small oil factory for expressing the oil: the process is a crude one, and results in a gummy oil, which brings but a small profit to the manufacturer, as it has to be shipped to San Francisco to be refined. The refuse, after the oil is extracted, is thrown into the river. As the number of fish caught is over 2,000,000, and one-third of each is unfit for canning, I estimate the amount of this refuse to be 3,000 tons after the oil is extracted. Every inducement seems to offer to put it up in the shape of guano. Chinese labour is fairly cheap and industrious: material for barrelling and charcoal dust to absorb the drainage are both cheap and to be readily had, and the handiness to the ship for export all seem to show where money could be invested with profit.

Lumber Industry.

In the last report from this district it was stated it cannot be long before the resources of the great forest region will be developed as it should be. Facts now justify the assertion. During the past year there has crossed out of the Columbia River 40 vessels lumber-laden to San Francisco, seven to other ports in California, two to Monte Video, and three to Panama, this last for the Panama Canal construction.

The county, of which Astoria is the county seat, is one of the largest of the lumber-producing of this Consular district, and the chief forest trees are hemlock, spruce, fir, and cedar. But the whole extent of the coasts of Oregon and Washington territory are covered with the same description of forest, and with but comparatively small clearings in it.

Hemlock has only been used to a very small extent for its bark for tanning purposes. Spruce is used where lightness is wanted, and must be kept from the wet, salmon cases and other boxes are made from it.

Fir is the most generally used of all the different kinds of woods; its strength, durability, and the ease with which it is manufactured brings it into use for all the general purposes of house building, boat building, planking of roads and bridges; and piling, for the support of bridges and buildings over water; ships' spars and deck planking, some thousands of feet of selected lumber being sent to New York for trial for this purpose.

Cedar is the wood used in finishing where lightness and ease of of working is wanted. It is a very durable wood, lasting for years as fence posts, house sills, window jambs, &c.; it is also much used as finishing in river steamer cabins, being light; it is, however, quite brittle.

The only reason I can give that this industry does not command a higher position in the list of exports is the great distance it is from centres of population, where the demand is far greater than the supply, and the early building of large saw-mills on the shores of Puget Sound, which have hitherto supplied the foreign trade.

At present the waste from forest fires and settlers' clearing homesteads is far greater than the drawing on the forests by the legitimate demands of commerce.

DEEP-SEA FISHING.

The existence of cod banks off this coast was not an assured point till last autumn. Cod, hake, halibut, and other cold-water fish are known to be in large numbers to the north of the Straits of de Fuca, off the British possessions, and extending to the Alaskan waters.

In October last a company was organised in Astoria to prospect the bank known to be off the coast, with a view to establish a permanent industry in supplying the towns of Oregon and Washington territory with fresh sea fish, and if practicable to put up works to dry the cod and any other fish that could be secured. A small schooner was procured (not the best adapted for the purpose) and supplied with a trawl net, as used on the English coasts, and under the management of a practical English fisherman having the advantage of several years' experience in English waters. The venture was highly successful in the catch: the cast was made some fifteen miles west of this port, and on the first haul enough was taken to establish the fact that there was plenty of cod, hake, flounders, soles, and tom cods, and numerous other smaller fish, some of them of most extraordinary shapes and appearances.

The attempt, however, was made too late in the season for a vessel of her build: the next trip being stormy, the venture had to be given up. Whether it will be revived this season, or wait till better business conditions will warrant the trying is as yet undecided; but the fact remains that the makings of a valuable industry lies at the door of this port.

COAL MINES.

The existence of coal deposits in the limits of the district of this Consular agency has been long known. Numerous croppings have been discovered at distances varying from 10 to 60 miles, extending along the western face of the coast range of mountains; and evidently the same bed crops out at Coos Bay, a distance of nearly 200 miles, where it worked altogether in the interests of San Francisco, and for the part supply of that city. The handy supply of forest wood for fuel, and the covering of such an extent of country with forests, making the construction of roads expensive, has so far put a stop to the development of the coal deposits. However, since the Act of Congress forfeiting the land grant so long held by a railroad corporation, lying between this port and the interior valley, which prevented all enterprise in that direction, has gone into effect, there is some talk of building a narrow gauge railroad to tap the extensive cedar forests in the Nehalem Valley, and which will go through the area known to contain coal. At present the coals used for steaming and domestic purposes have come in part from Great Britian, New South Wales, and from the coal mines in Puget Sound, Washington territory. This last, however, is of an inferior quality: the company owning the mines have steam colliers of their own, which has enabled them to carry the coals at small freight charges, and being domestic mines, have also the advantage of not paying the duty of 75 c. per ton, which foreign coals have to pay; they are therefore enabled to undersell the foreign article quite materially for house purposes, but steamers depend mostly on the New Castle (N.S.W.) coal.

Casualties.

I have fortunately none to report as having occurred to British vessels, and only one as worthy of mention as having occurred to an American vessel dragging her anchors and taking the ground near the entrance to the river, which necessitated the discharge of her cargo and repairs to her keel: her injuries were comparatively slight.

Columbia River Bar Improvements.

As mentioned in my last report the petitions of citizens and chambers of commerce resulted in an appropriation by Congress for the improvement of the mouth of the river by the construction of a training wall to contract the present wide mouth. The plan adopted by the United States' engineers in charge consists in commencing a dyke at the most northerly point of the south bank of the entrance to the river, and continuing it on the ridge of a bank known as Clatsop Spit, north-west for two miles, then curving to the west, north-west, and west a mile more. This when finished will contract the present entrance from five and a-half miles to about three: it is then expected that the contracted entrance will cause a scour on its sand-bed enough to make a deeper channel, and giving a permanent increase to the bar entrance; the training dyke will at the same time collect the moving sands on its outward face, and gradually build a permanent bank of sand, reproducing conditions existing some 35 years ago, when the present submerged Clatsop Spit extended as a sand dune covered with forest trees of fair size. The present depth of the bar is 19 feet at low water, which allowing for mean high water at seven feet makes 26 feet; it is expected, when finished, the result will be at least 32 feet of water on the present bar. The estimated cost of the improvement is 3,000,000 dol. This then will give this port all the advantages of the Golden Gate, enabling a larger class of vessels to come to the port, and consequently the freighting of produce at less cost.

Directions for Sailing Vessels.

My attention has been called to the want of proper directions in the immediate vicinity of the port. I gather most of my information from old pilots. From the end of October to the end of spring the prevailing winds are from the south-east, south, and south-west; this almost blowing from the southward affects the currents along shore, giving it a northerly set during all these months, and in fact till the summer north-west winds prevail. From Cape Blanco to the Straits of de Fuca in the north the current increases as it runs north, generally stronger inshore and with a shoreward set to it. Directly off the Columbia the current is affected by the tides ebbing and flowing, and the stage of the water in the river. As soon as the master of the vessel bound to this port finds himself to the northward of Cape Disappointment (or Hancock), the current, evidently augmented by the flow of the river, sets his vessel northward and inshore; this current is the cause of much delay and anxiety to the shipmaster first making this port. The large extent of Shoal Water and Gray's Harbours to the northward cause a strong suck shoreward during the flood tides, and seem to augment it during the ebbs.

Under these circumstances it is always better for the shipmaster coming to this port to make the land at Tillamook Head. This head is a bold one, and about a mile off it is a high rock, on which is a first-class light, and on a line between this light and that on Point Adams is the position for a master seeking pilots, or waiting for towage, or tides, should keep his vessel.

British Sailors.

Year.	No. of Crews.	Engagements.	Alterations.	Discharged.	Desertions.
1884 ..	1,512	238	2	14	183

Seven deaths reported and five permits for hospital; the total desertions make 12 per cent. of the crews.

General Remarks.

The general business of Astoria, owing to its being a combination of a seaport and a manufacturing place, has suffered less in proportion than any other town on the Pacific coast from the present depression, consequent on the finishing of the different railroads, and also of the general business depression of the commercial world.

The climate of Western Oregon and Washington territory is very similar to that of the British islands, and is well adapted to British emigrants. As shown the leading industries are agriculture, salmon fishing, and preserving, and the manufacture of sawn lumber.

To the emigrant of good health, accustomed to work, and industrious, no place brings more certain chance of remunerative employment and eventual competence, but excepting in the towns a great deal has to be foregone in the way of want of conveniences. There are few roads, and those only in the better-settled counties, and isolation in farm life more than in most farming countries.

In towns the unmarried labourers generally live in cheap hotels and boarding-houses, and lead a very restless and changing life, being almost constantly on the move, looking for something better, shifting from town to country, and engaged successively in all kinds of employment—steam-boating, longshore lumbering, mining, fishing and farm labour, as circumstances and an empty purse may lead.

The growth of the town of Astoria has been steady, depending on the increase of commerce and the salmon interest. It is the stopping-place of steamers from San Francisco, running every five days, of which there are three of good passenger and carrying capacity, and for the steamers to British Columbia and Alaska, besides the smaller coasting craft for the immediate vicinity.

The health of this district has been uniformly good for the past year; no disease of an epidemic nature has manifested itself.

Astoria, Oregon, March 3, 1885.

NEWPORT NEWS.

Report by Vice-Consul Warburton on the Trade and Commerce of Newport News for the Year 1884.

The commercial history of Newport News dates from 1st May, 1882, when the port was formally opened. Its conception dates from 1872, just previous to the great commercial panic which caused the postponement of many incipient enterprises, and wrecked many of the strongest houses.

Railways.

The railway connecting Newport News with Richmond was commenced early in 1881, in expectation of being completed in time for the Yorktown Centennial celebration of the surrender of Cornwallis, held in October of that year, but this expectation was not realised. It is 75 miles long, while the Yorktown branch is seven miles; but the rails have been removed. As the railway was being constructed many improvements and preparations for the reception of vessels were carried on at the port itself. Since its completion the expansion of trade has pressed closely upon the facilities afforded by the port and railway, which latter is called the Chesapeake and Ohio, and is the last addition to the list of Grand Trunk Railways which carry the exports and imports of the United States between the Atlantic and the interior, and connect the former with the Pacific Ocean.

It may not be out of place here to review the ramifications of this line, the facilities it offers, the waterways which intersect and are tributary to it, and the produce which it will convey to the port.

The Chesapeake and Ohio System.—The Chesapeake and Ohio system comprises the roads tabulated below, which are either owned, controlled, or operated by the company or its directors.

Chesapeake and Ohio System Proper.

	Miles.
Chesapeake and Ohio main line and branches, extending from the Atlantic to the Ohio Railway	519
Elisabeth, Lexington, and Big Sandy River	134
Kentucky and South Atlantic	20
Chesapeake and Ohio South-Western	397
Kentucky Central	150
" " Knoxville extension	100
Indianopolis, Cincinnati, Chicago, and St. Louis	360
Scioto Valley	140
	1,820

Sunset or Trans-Mississippi System.

	Miles.
Galveston, Harrisburg, and St. Antonio branch	256
,, ,, Mexican and Pacific	600
,, ,, Eagle Pass branch	22
Texas, New Orleans	106
Louisiana, Western	112
,, Sabine branch	104
St. Louis and San Francisco and branches, Atlantic and Pacific leased lines	700
	1,910

Central Pacific System.

	Miles.
Central Pacific main line and branches	1,215
Central Pacific Oregon extension	150
California Pacific	116
Northern Railway	117
Stocton and Copperopolis	49
Sacramento and Placerville	74
Berkeley branch and Vacca valley	33
	1,802

Southern Pacific System.

	Miles.
Southern Pacific main line and branches in California	712
Southern Pacific main line in Arizona	384
,, ,, New Mexico	170
,, ,, St. Louis branch	250
Monterey and Santa Cruz	36
Los Angeles and San Diego	28
,, ,, Independence	17
Atlantic and Pacific, Western division	700
	2,297
Grand total	7,829

Water Carriage.

This system of railways is intersected by the Ohio River, navigable from the heart of Pennsylvania, and its Birmingham Pittsburg, to Cairo, where it joins the Mississippi.

That river, with its confluent the Missouri, is navigable from St. Paul's, Minnesota, and the territory of Dakota, to New Orleans on the Gulf of Mexico. Westward of the Great River the Chesapeake and Ohio system is intersected by the Arkansas, Red River, Rio Grande, and Colorado, all navigable, before it reaches its western terminus at San Francisco.

Cities, States, and Territories included in the Chesapeake and Ohio System.—Among the cities it connects are Richmond, Lexington, Louisville, Columbus, Toledo, Cincinnati, Indianapolis, Chicago, Peoria, Cairo, St. Louis, Memphis, New Orleans, Kansas, Omaha, Cheyenne, Denver, Topeka, Galveston, El Paso, Los Angeles, Sacramento, and San Francisco; and among States and territories, Virginia, West Virginia, Kentucky, Ohio, Indiana, Illinois, Tennessee, Missouri, Arkansas, Mississippi, Louisiana, Texas, Mexico, New Mexico, Colorado, Nebraska, Wyoming, Utah, Nevada, Arizona, and California; while the controllers of the line own largely the river lines and steamships trading to New York and New Orleans, on the Sacramento and Colorada rivers, as well as those trading to Japan, China, and the Australian colonies.

[1431]

Ocean Steamers.—From its terminus at Newport News steamers ply regularly between that port and Boston, New York, Baltimore, Washington, Richmond, Norfolk, and Rio Janeiro.

Produce conveyed by the Chesapeake and Ohio System.—It will be seen that this system, extending over 7,829 miles, drains the principal areas of production for cattle, sheep, hogs, corn wheat, coal, iron, gold, silver and lumber, while it taps the cotton districts west of the Alleghanies, and nearly all the tobacco-growing States. Neither is it improbable that the southern chain of railways, of which the Richmond and Danville is the northern link, will eventually find in Newport News a most favourable exit for southern cotton.

NEWPORT NEWS.

Newport News Geographical Position is in Warwick county, Virginia, near the extremity of the peninsula formed by the York and James rivers, and situated on the latter in latitude 37° north, and longitude 76° 30′ west of Greenwich. By the ocean route, which steamers usually adopt, it is 3,250 miles from Liverpool, although many put the distance at 3,120, and they are probably correct.

Distance by Water from Important Points.—The port and city is by water 110 miles from Richmond, 12 from Norfolk, 180 from Washington and Baltimore, 388 from New York, 260 from Philadelphia, and 28 from Cape Charles City. It is eight miles from the lighthouse on Old Point Comfort, at the entrance of Hampton Roads and Chesapeake Bay, and 23 from Capes Henry and Charles, between which the Chesapeake Bay with its confluent rivers joins the Atlantic Ocean.

The Channel.—The channel, which is easily navigable, has a depth of 27 feet at low water, which is increased to $30\frac{1}{2}$ feet at high tides, and though pilotage is at present compulsory, it is unnecessary. A Bill to render it optional was defeated in the State Legislature this year in the interests of Norfolk.

The Harbour.—The harbour is land-locked and perfectly secure, as are the roads, of which I have had ocular evidence during a severe gale blowing from the worst quarter on the 8th January of this year.

Soil and its Capabilities—The soil of Warwick county and the peninsula generally is sandy and poor, but easily drained and capable of growing garden produce. It is raised from 20 to 50 feet above the highest level of the river, which is salt here. At a depth of 35 feet abundance of excellent water is found by driving artesian wells. That which supplies the Warwick Hotel has given 120,000 gallons a day. There is an abundance of timber, principally pine of an inferior kind, which, with the adjacent land, is almost altogether owned by the Old Dominion Land Company, which owns the port.

Population, Buildings, and Wharves.—The population at present amounts to about 1,200, composed principally of officials and workmen employed by the Railway, Land, and Elevator Companies, and their families. These three companies have expended over 1,000,000*l.* in wharves, hotels, houses, workshops, and other works, including a grain elevator, which contains 1,600,000 bushels.

The City.—The city is laid out in avenues and streets upon the usual American plan. These are macadamised with oyster shells, which form an excellent roadway.

Building lots are sold at prices varying, according to location, from 80*l.* to 250*l.*, having a uniform frontage of 25 feet, and a depth of 100 feet.

Centres of Population and Manufacture.

Hampton.—About 6½ miles eastward of the city is the village of Hampton, containing about 3,000 inhabitants. It is one of the oldest settlements in the United States, and gives the name to Hampton Roads. It contains the coloured and Indian schools and the soldiers' home, which with their picturesque grounds and buildings add considerably to its importance and appearance. The small bay, by which it is approached seaward, is shallow, and affords shelter to fishing craft and others of small tonnage. The railway connects it with Newport News.

Fortress Monroe.—Three miles further to the east, at the extremity of the peninsula, is Fortress Monroe, an antiquated fort, with wet ditches, and occupied as a school of artillery. Close by, under the walls of the fort, is the Hygeia Hotel, a large, irregular building, capable of containing 800 people, frequented during nine months of the year by visitors from all parts of the Northern and Southern States.

Norfolk.—The city of Norfolk is situated on the right bank of the Elisabeth River, at four miles from its confluence with the James, and 12 from Newport News. It numbers 27,000 inhabitants. Divided by the Elisabeth from Norfolk is Portsmouth, a naval dockyard, and these two, with their suburbs within a radius of two miles, have 55,000 inhabitants, an increase of 10,000 during the past four years.

After New Orleans and Savannah, Norfolk exports the largest quantity of cotton, amounting to one-sixth of the total export and one-ninth of the crop, as will be seen by the table below. The value of its export is about 8,000,000*l.*

Export of cotton in bales:—

Season of	Foreign.	Coastwise.	Total.
1880–1	328,818	391,843	720,661
1881–2	331,871	289,032	620,849
1882–3	372,529	414,833	787,362

The total exports to foreign ports in 1882–3 were 4,766,597; total crop, 6,949,756 bales.

The principal railroads communicating with Norfolk are the Norfolk and Western, formerly the Atlantic, Ohio, and Mississippi; the Richmond and Danville, which joins the first-named at Burkesville: the Seaboard and Roanoke Railway, which communicates with Beaufort, Wilmington, Charleston, and the south and cotton districts. Besides cotton, there is a large trade in lumber and staves.

Norfolk is approached by a channel 20·8 inches deep at low water, and very narrow in some places, but it is capable of great improvement.

A coal pier is being constructed to deep water at Lambert's Point, three miles from the city, and excellent coal is obtainable for steam or other purposes from the same formation as that whence Newport News is supplied.

York Town.—York Town, on York River, about 20 miles from Newport News, is a small village with a few hundred inhabitants. It is celebrated for the surrender of Cornwallis in 1781, and at one time divided with Newport News the prospective honour of becoming a maritime city, but the overwhelming advantage of the latter secured its adoption as the terminus of the railway. It has a depth of 30 feet of water at low tides.

Williamsburg.—Williamsburg, on the James River, just opposite, is one of the earliest settlements, and contains about 1,500 inhabitants, being the seat of the State infirmary. It is in a dilapidated condition, and has none of the elements of improvement.

West Point.—West Point, on the York River, is the salt water terminus of the Richmond and Danville Railway, which drains Georgia and North and South Carolina, and carries a great deal of cotton lumber and tobacco. The port is accessible for vessels of 2,000 tons, and not unfrequently they load there in part and finish at Newport News or Norfolk. The channel of York River is somewhat difficult of navigation.

Cape Charles City.—Cape Charles, the terminus of the New York, Pennsylvania, and Norfolk Railway, which is on the point of completion, has been recently named and laid out as a city. It is situated on the eastern shore of Chesapeake Bay, in Northampton county, about 35 miles from Norfolk by water, and 25 from Newport News. Communicating with Baltimore and the Northern cities by rail, this route will shorten the transport of truck produce to New York by 12 hours, and will probably become a favourite passenger line to Norfolk and the South.

City Point and Claremont.—City Point and Claremont are small ports on the James River, which do a considerable local trade, and admit vessels drawing 18 feet of water.

Richmond.—Richmond, with a population of 70,000, is at the navigable head of the James River—110 miles by water and 75 by land from Newport News. At high tides there is 16 feet of water, which admits of considerable coastwise traffic, but the latter, as well as foreign trade, is surely abandoning the port for deeper water at the ocean terminus. Its present relative importance as a port will appear in the table of shipping given hereafter. Richmond, which is the capital of Virginia, and at one time was the capital of the Confederacy, enjoys a valuable and extensive water power from the fall of the James River, over the granite rocks, which form the basis of the geological structure of the Alleghany range of mountains. Beyond them, extending to the sea, the formation is post-pliocene, or quarternary. Richmond has large manufactories of flour, which is said to have peculiar qualities, which enable it to stand tropical climates, and is largely exported to Brazil. It has also extensive iron works, the principal of which is the "Tredegar;" but its largest industry is tobacco, which is manufactured and exported in various forms.

The table below indicates the extent of the above industries:—

Nature of Industries.	Number of Hands Employed.	Capital in the Business.	Annual Sales.
		£	£
Flour and corn meal.. ..	272	'50,000	120,000
Iron and nail works.. ..	2,486	65,000	125,000
Tobacco	4,058	105,000	340,000
Total of all manufactures	16,597	500,000	1,150,000

Alexandria, Fredericksburg, Port Royal, Petersburg, Smithfield, and Suffolk.—Alexandria, on the Potomac, a few miles below Washington; Fredericksburg and Port Royal, on the Rappahannock; Petersburg, on the Appomattox; Smithfield, on Pagan Creek; and Suffolk, on Nausemond River, are all ports in Virginia, situated within Capes Henry and Charles; but being frequented principally, if not altogether, by coasters, and not being likely to attract foreign trade, I have not deemed it necessary to relate any particulars regarding them.

It may be said of them, however, as of all Virginian ports, that they are never obstructed by ice, as in the case of northern harbours.

Climate.

The climate of Newport News is comparatively mild and equable, and has none of the extremes met with in the interior, or in the large seaport towns. This is principally due to the cooling and warming ocean breezes, which modify the temperature in summer and winter. This summer the temperature has not risen above 90°, nor fallen below 9°. The summer nights usually average 73° throughout. The inhabitants are subject to the usual chills which prevail on all the Eastern coast, but these are in a great measure due to bad food, bad drainage, and uncleanliness, and disappear with generous living and a proper attention to hygiene.

Advantages which Newport News holds out to Shipping.

Advantages as a Port.—I now propose to enumerate the advantages which British vessels gain by trading to this port in comparison with other ports, and also to set forward any disadvantages which may have come under my notice.

Freedom from Ice.—As stated above, vessels are never obstructed by the formation of ice in the severest winters, and consequently may be certain of making this port without delay from that cause. This advantage will be sufficiently appreciated by those masters and owners who have experience of Northern ports during the winter.

Superior Steam Coal.—The coal supplied to steamers is of a very superior description, and is equal to the best Welsh. It is uniform in quality, and has received the approval of every vessel which has consumed it. It is supplied f.o.b. at 3 dol. 50 c., or 14s. 7d. per ton, with an additional charge for trimming of 5d. per ton.

Subjoined is an analysis of the various coals supplied to steamers:—

Mine.	Carbon.	Volatile Matter.	Ash.	Water.	Sulphur.
Nuttalberg	69·00	29·59	1·07	0·34	0·78
Lewell	72·32	21·38	5·07	1·03	0·20
Quinemont	75·59	18·19	4·68	0·94	0·30
New River	71·33	22·53	4·33	1·81	Nil.

In 1883, 157 British and 21 foreign steamers, and in 1884, 143 British and 6 foreign steamers called at this port for coal.

In addition to the above-mentioned steam coal, very large quantities of gas, splint, and cannel coal is exported, principally coastwise. In 1883 the amounts were in tons:—

Steam.	Gas.	Splints.	Cannel.	Total.
110·119$\frac{1210}{2240}$	98·512$\frac{270}{2240}$	7·698$\frac{2230}{2240}$	7·650$\frac{2200}{2240}$	223·811$\frac{430}{510}$

1492   UNITED STATES.

Convenience of the Harbour.—There is no harbour in the United States so easy of access. The channel has a depth of 27 feet at lowest tides, with a rise of 3 to 3½ feet, and there is 35 feet alongside of the wharves. Steamers arriving or departing or moving from one pier to another experience no difficulties, and do not require assistance from tugs. There is no charge for wharfage, and expenses are less than at any port with which I am acquainted. A list of those incurred is subjoined.

Hampton Roads.—Hampton Roads is a spacious and secure anchorage, completely land-locked, and with excellent holding ground; it is distant 15 miles from the sea. Vessels can lie here awaiting orders without any considerable loss of time or distance, as they are southward or northward bound. Steamers from the Gulf of Mexico and the West Indies, laden with cotton, sugar, mahogany, &c., call here for coal to complete their voyage to Europe.

Pilotage.—The charges for pilotage are as follows:—

		Dol.	c.
Vessels drawing 10 feet of water, per foot		2	50
„ „ 13 „ „		3	00
„ „ 14 „ „		3	50
„ „ 15 „ „		4	00
„ „ 16 „ „		4	50

Charges other than pilotage:—

	Dol.	c.
Customs—		
Survey, with cargo	3	00
„ coming for coal only	0	67
Entry, coastwise	2	00
„ foreign	2	50
Official oaths and certificates, each	0	20
Permit to unload	0	20
Port charges—		
Wharfage	Nil.	
Doctor's certificate	7	00
Coal, per ton	3	50
Trimming, per ton	0	10
Stevedoring, plank per 1,000 feet	0	50
Logs „ „	0	70
„ staves „	0	50
Trimming bulk wheat, 1,000 bushels, single deck	2	00
Double deck, 1,000 bushels	3	00
Bags, stowage, „	5	50
Sewing bags, per 1,000 bushels	5	00
Cotton, screwing in per bale	0	40
Handstowing	0	25
Consular fee	1	25

No tugs required.

It may not be out of place here to allude to a few of the industries which find an outlet for their products at this port, and which are likely by their future development to affect its progress and increase its importance.

Cattle and grain will no doubt find their way in large quantities from the inland States, where they are produced, to the seaboard at this point, for the reason that it is the shortest and most favourable route than can be obtained. It is 120 miles nearer than New York to St. Louis, which is one of the most, if not the most important of centres for cattle and grain in the United States; while the rich grazing lands of Kentucky and Tennessee are still more favourably situated, and as regards the varied productions of Missouri, Kansas, Illinois, and Indiana, Newport News has an advantage over any Eastern port.

It no doubt takes time to divert trade from its accustomed channels, and it may be some years before through traffic prefers the shortest and cheapest route; but undoubtedly local products, and especially all new and rising industries, will seek an outlet at once where circumstances are most favourable.

The industries which have made the Northern States rich have in the Virginias only recently been undertaken, notwithstanding that natural advantages exist in those States, which the former cannot claim; and it is not improbable that a revival of trade will witness a transfer of labour and capital to the more favoured localities; notably in the case of the iron manufactures, which now languish in Pennsylvania, but notwithstanding the extreme depression now existing are thriving fairly in Virginia and West Virginia.

Iron Industries.

Iron Industries of the Virginias.—On the 1st January, 1884, the following was the number and condition of the charcoal and bituminous or coke furnaces of Virginia, West Virginia, and the United States:—

Charcoal Furnaces.

State.	In Blast. No.	In Blast. Weekly Capacity.	Out of Blast. No.	Out of Blast. Weekly Capacity.
		Tons.		Tons.
Virginia	3	135	28	1,352
West Virginia	..	..	6	625
United States	78	8,936	169	16,008
Total	81	8,936	203	17,985

Bituminous or Coke Furnaces.

State.	In Blast. No.	In Blast. Weekly Capacity.	Out of Blast. No.	Out of Blast. Weekly Capacity.
		Tons.		Tons.
Virginia	6	3,021	7	1,740
West Virgina	6	2,480	1	160
United States	101	45,365	123	41,967
Total	113	52,866	131	43,867

In addition to the above there are in the United States 231 furnaces using anthracite coal, of which 109 were in blast on the 1st January, 1884, having a weekly capacity of 28,824 tons; and 122 out of blast, having a weekly capacity of 25,555 tons.

Anthracite Furnaces.—There are no anthracite furnaces in the Virginias where that coal does not exist.

Charcoal Iron.—It appears from the foregoing table that the manufacture of charcoal iron in Virginia and West Virginia is diminishing as compared with the United States, and that of bituminous or coke iron is greatly increasing.

Position of the Virginias as Iron Producers.—Thus, in 1870, Virginia ranked thirteenth in production among the States, sixteenth in 1880, and seventh in 1883; West Virginia tenth, seventh, and eleventh respectively in those years; while both together produced in 1870 one thirty-third of the output in the United States of coke or bituminous iron, one-eighteenth in 1880, and one-eighth in 1884, the amounts produced in that year being 280,000 tons and 2,300,000 tons respectively, a ton being 2,000 lbs.

Iron Ores.—The ores principally employed are specular and brown hematite, which are found in inexhaustible quantities, yielding from 30 to 60 per cent. of metallic iron, with a very small percentage of sulphur and phosphorus. I refrain from giving analyses of these ores, because I consider that those presented to the public are the most favourable, and do not represent an average of the ore, the best specimens being selected for analysis.

Limestone.—Abundance of excellent limestone is found in close proximity to the ore beds, and coal of good quality at distances of 50 to 100 miles.

Cost of Iron.—The cost of a ton of pig iron in Virginia is said to be 12 dol. 50 c., or 52s., while in Pennsylvania it cannot be produced for less than 17 dol., or 69s. 5d. Pig iron on the Clyde is delivered (free on board) at 44s. 7d. per ton, and freight costs 4s.—total 48s. 7d.—while the duty at three-tenth of 1 cent. per lb. is 6 dol. 72 c., or 28s., making a grand total per ton of 2,240 lbs. of 76s. 7d. in port. These facts account for the rapid development of the manufacture of pig iron in the Virginias, and promise well for its future.

Magnetic Ore.—Large quantities of magnetic iron ore of very high quality are found in the south-western portion of Virginia, but from want of railway facilities remain undeveloped. They are localised in the geological systems, termed laurentian and huronian, which underlie the lower silurian and overlie the granite. These rocks are partially stratified, and at first were ranked with the azoic, but traces of animal life have been discovered therein. These strata are, as far as I can ascertain, peculiar to this continent.

It may not be out of place to give a slight sketch of the nature, locality, and characteristics of the iron and coal deposits in Virginia and West Virginia, especially of those along the Chesapeake and Ohio Railway, and which it assists principally in developing. Thereby a rough estimate may be formed of the capacities of this region for the production of iron, and of the various constituents employed in its manufacture, in their relation to quantity, distance, and quality, together with other considerations which affect cost of production and distribution.

IRON ORES OF THE VIRGINIAS AND FACILITIES FOR THE MANUFACTURE OF IRON AND STEEL.

The extensive and valuable deposits of iron ore and coal in the country traversed by the Chesapeake and Ohio Railway have attracted the attention of capitalists and experts, who now rank this field of production among the most important in the United States.

Advantages for Manufacture.—The advantages for the manufacture of iron (and in due time of steel) are certainly somewhat exceptional, for at this time of extreme depression in the iron and coal trade, almost the only ore mines and iron furnaces operated in Virginia are those along the Chesapeake and Ohio Railway; and this fact is the more significant when it is considered that the furnace construction upon this railway was commenced about the date of its opening for traffic in the summer of 1873, was prosecuted through the commercial panic which followed, and was completed upon falling markets.

Yet in this short period, and in the face of these difficulties, enough has already been accomplished to demonstrate that very superior iron can be made at low cost from the ores, fuel, and fluxes which abound upon the line of this railroad—a result only possible with unusual local advantage.

The revival of American iron manufacture will be attended with the certain development of those localities which afford the greatest facilities for conducting this industry, and among them may be numbered the valleys of the New River and Kanawha, which contain practically inexhaustible deposits of coal and iron. These are notable no less for their extent than for their diversity and quality.

For a distance of 375 miles along the Chesapeake and Ohio Railway are found in workable seams, at frequently recurring intervals, magnetic and specular ores (as locally termed), the hematites in their usual varieties, and fossiliferous, red shale, slate, block and black band ores. Many of these cross the railway, and nearly all are cheaply accessible.

The ores in several counties along the central and eastern division of the railroad have long been worked in the charcoal furnaces of the past, and have produced excellent iron, ranking very high in the Government records of gun metal. Since then, however, the conditions of iron-making have greatly changed. Charcoal has ceased to be an economical fuel in the greater part of Virginia, as will be seen from the fact that on the 1st January, 1884, only three charcoal furnaces out of 31 in that State were in blast, and none out of six in West Virginia. The present low price of pig iron renders more general the use of the larger coke and coal furnaces, with their complete blast machinery and their labour and fuel-saving improvements.

The favourable conditions of cost and supply, and of transmission afforded by the Chesapeake Ohio Railway, have caused the leading iron-masters of the Ohio Valley to examine the deposit east of the Blue Ridge, as a substitute for the rich steel (or Bessemer) ores, brought at a cost of 7 dol. 50 c. to 10 dol. per ton, from Lake Superior and the Missouri iron mountains; and this examination has resulted in favourable reports from the mining chemists, and in business orders subject to favourable transportation rates.

The first important iron ore belt crosses the Chesapeake and Ohio Railway in Louisa county, 56 miles from Richmond, with a north-east and south-west strike, and can be traced for long distances. It is described as a "fissure vein of hematite ore 30 feet wide" by Professor Ridgeway, who adds that two and a half tons of this ore make a ton of pig iron. The Louisa ores tend to "red shortness," while beyond the Blue Ridge "cold short and neutral ores abound."

The next well-defined formation of iron ores is passed immediately beyond Gordonsville. Here an excellent hematite, analysing 57 per cent. metallic iron and 10 per cent of phosphorus, has been mined and supplied in considerable quantity. The same formation embraces also micaceous ores, with specular and magnetic characteristics. In Nelson and Amherst counties the ore exposures are very large, and are described by Professor J. W. Mallet, of the University of Virginia, as an intimate mixture of specular iron and magnetite, merging into red hematite, and finally limonite or brown hematite. Fourteen analyses of these ores varied from 31 per cent. to 66 per cent. of metallic iron, with little phosphorus or sulphur.

This deposit is considered by some identical with the magnetic ore belt in New Jersey, which in 1867 furnished 1,300,000 tons of ore.

Limestone flux is found in Louisa and Albemarle county, and of a very superior quality west of the Blue Ridge.

Crossing into the valley of Virginia, the railway passes through another group of hematite deposits, and considerable masses of what is locally styled "specular ironstone." The hematites here give analysis of from 43 per cent. to 58 per cent. of metallic iron, with phosphorus ranging from 14 per cent. to 24 per cent., and in one instance 52 per cent.

The specular iron ore of the Blue Ridge is entirely free from phosphorus.

The hematites of this section of the valley are silurian, and lie close to the pure limestones of that period. This is considered to be an extension of the same formation as the iron ores of the Cumberland, Reading, and Lehigh valleys of Pennsylvania.

Rising above the silurian deposits of the Shenandoah valley, the line of railway enters the Northern Mountain belt, especially noticeable for large masses of brown hematite. Professor Ridgeway says of these: "There is an immense amount of iron ore reposing at a low angle to the horizon, in a stratified form, and in good mining condition: the aggregate mass of hematite iron ore at these points surpasses anything which I have ever seen elsewhere."

These deposits are traced continuously for miles along the mountain slopes; they lie favourably for excavation and easy removal down to the railroad, and are mainly mined in open cutting, though occasionally with shafts and drifts.

Near the Elisabeth furnace there is presented an ore front of over 1,200 feet, which has been exposed and worked irregularly for years with no indication of failure.

A large number of the mountain ores, analysed by the first chemists, give 40 per cent. to 58 per cent. of metallic iron. The analyses referred to show no sulphur, but phosphorus is present, the average being one-half of 1 per cent., suggesting advantageous mixtures with the magnetic ores previously referred to.

The Victoria Iron and Steel Mining Company.—Passing westward, 168 miles from Richmond and 243 miles from Newport News, the railway crosses occasional deposits of argilaceous hematites in the vicinity of Goshen, where there is a large furnace belonging to an English company (the Victoria Steel and Iron Company), one of which is fossil ore 18 inches thick; and further on is the Longdale Iron and Coal Company, which has had great prosperity in the worst times. It is managed by Pennsylvania ironmasters, and derives its coal and coke from its own mines at Sewell, in West Virginia.

Lowmoor Foundry.—The Lowmoor Iron Company, 276 miles from Newport News, works a seam of hematite ore, 30 feet to 60 feet in thickness, containing 59 per cent. of iron, 0·106 per cent. of phosphorus, and 0·02 per cent. of sulphur. The supply of coal is derived from the New River 100 miles distant, and excellent limestone is found on the spot containing 90 per cent. to 95 per cent. of carbonate of lime. Surface indications of iron are found at Hinton, 347 miles from Newport News, and between that place and Lowmoor important deposits of hematite and fossil ores have been discovered.

Coal.

Extent of the Deposits.—Authorities agree that the largest carboniferous deposits of the American continent, and in many respects the most important, are the "Great Alleghany," "Appalachian," or Cumberland coalfields, as variously designated, extending from Alabama, through the intermediate States, into Ohio and Pennsylvania. The greatest ascertained development of these deposits is in the State of West Virginia, where the surface area was estimated by Professor W. B. Rogers to cover 16,000 square miles. The Alleghany coalfield is entered by the Chesapeake and Ohio Railway, a few miles beyond Hinton, and the seams are traced 108 miles westward.

Mr. Howell Fisher on the Coal Facilities.—As regards this district Mr. Howell Fisher, of Pennsylvania, has written as follows: "In respect to conditions most essential to cheap and profitable working, this region stands unrivalled. It has been stated that the chasm of the river renders it most peculiar service in its relation to the coal. Cutting all the coal strata for nearly its whole length entirely through, and getting down among the shales under the coal, the river has caused the numerous streams which pierce this whole coal region to cut down through most of the coal bearing strata on their courses, leaving the coal entirely above water level, accessible at hundreds of points by simply scraping off the surface soil, so that, so far as the mere coal-getting is concerned, 2,000 dols. will open a mine ready to ship 1,000 tons per week. There is no region in the world where less physical labour will prepare a mine for the delivery of coal at the drifts mouth.

"This will be made clear by a comparison of the position of coal here and in Great Britain in this respect. In Great Britain, and in fact in almost all the European coalfields, the coal is deep below the water level. To reach the seams requires the expenditure of years of labour, and vast sums of money in sinking shafts or pits, and in erecting pumping and hoisting machinery, to be maintained and renewed at heavy annual expense. It is authoritatively stated that the cost of sinking shafts in the Newcastle region of England to the depth of 1,000 feet has been, in many instances, 1,000 dol. (200*l.*) per yard. In the Great Northern coalfield of Great Britain, producing 20,000,000 tons per annum, there are 200 pits or shafts, costing in first outlay, for sinking and machinery, 50,000,000 dol., to which must be added the necessary expense of constructing and of maintaining proper air-courses and their accessories requisite for the safety of the employés.

"There is now invested, simply in pits and machinery for pumping and hoisting the 100,000,000 tons produced in Great Britain, 200,000,000 dol., which is destined to utter destruction in serving the purposes for which it was used.

"Now, in this great coalfield, crossed by the Chesapeake and Ohio Railroad, nature has already sunk all the necessary pits and shafts, which need neither repair, removal, or labour to work them. The laws of gravity have provided the most perfect, permanent, and costless pumping machinery; and the most perfect ventilation of the mine and safety of the employés, instead of requiring scientific knowledge and anxious thought, is simply a matter of ordinary care, the almost perfect freedom from noxious gases being the natural results of the position of the coal strata."

An Englishman reading the above can reflect with pardonable pride upon the energy and skill exhibited by his countrymen, which enables them, under so many disadvantages, to compete successfully in the production of coal; and with the additional disadvantage of an ocean transit of 3,300 miles, obliges the United States to impose a protective duty of 3s. 1½d. per ton to enable their coal to hold its own in Eastern cities and seaports.

Wages and their Purchasing Power.—And here it is desirable to state that, though the wages of the miner in America are considerably in excess of those obtained in England, they do not procure him more of the necessaries and comforts of life; far less indeed, if my observation is correct, than he can obtain for a lesser wage at home. This result is brought about by the fiscal policy of the United States, which robs the many for the benefit of the few, and both raises the price and lowers the quality of almost every article of consumption.

As will be gathered by the remarks of Mr. Fisher, the coal strata are practically in a horizontal plane.

Mining Plant.—The mining plant is of the simplest kind, viz.: side or branch tracks, inclines and tipples, and occasionally bins. In many cases the coal is deposited on the railway track by self-acting inclines, where the empties are pulled up by the full descending bins on a tramway at various inclinations to the horizon, laid with 20 lbs. to the yard, rails of iron or steel, and worked in the usual way by a large drum.

Cost of Coal Getting.—In reference to the cost of coal getting, at least three mines have been opened for less than 400l. The Coal Valley mine, 418 miles from Newport News and 343 from Richmond, which weekly ships 1,000 tons from a seven-foot vein, 80 feet above the railways, was opened and equipped for less than 900l.

For particulars as to the coal seams refer to the writings of Rogers, Ansted, Stevenson, Hildreth, and McFarlane, and to the report of M. F. Maury to the State Centennial Commission, upon the mineral resources of West Virginia.

New River Cokes.—As regards the manufacture of iron, the New River cokes rank first for blast furnace and cupola use. They have supplied most of the furnaces along the Chesapeake and Ohio Railway.

Below are a few analyses of the cokes from the principal mines:—

COKES.

	Carbon.	Volatile Matters.	Ash.	Sulphur.	Water.	Hydrogen.	Oxygen.	Nitrogen.
Nuttalburg	91·22	..	7·53	0·92	..	..	..	..
Sewell	93·00	..	6·73	0·27	..	..	..	..
Quinnemont No. 1	93·00	..	5·85	0·30	..	..	..	..
,, ,, 2	91·72	2·71	5·09	0·48	..	..	..	..
,, ,, 3	91·14	..	6·65	0·42	0·23	0·38	1·17	0·01
Connellsville	87·46	..	11·36	0·69	0·49	..	..	..

In blast furnaces one-and-half tons of this coke is the usual allowance for one ton of iron made from the raw ores.

Kanawka Coals.—The Kanawka coals differ from the New River coals in several important characteristics. They are harder, have less fixed carbon, more volatile combustible matter, and generally less ash; and in variety they meet a somewhat wider range in the requirements of the mechanical arts.

At Canneltown there are 38 feet 6 inches of these coals; at Paint Creek, 38 feet 10 inches; near Coalburg, 41 feet 3 inches. These seams become thicker as they recede from the Kanawha. The Ridgeway Section at Canneltown gave five workable seams and an aggregate thickness of 41 feet.

Cannel Coal.

	Volatile Matter.	Fixed Carbon.	Ash.	Water.
Canneltown, average	46·50	41·30	12·20	..
Kirkless Hall, England	40·30	56·40	3·30	..

Semi-Cannel Coking and Gas Coals.

	Volatile. Matter.	Fixed Carbon.	Ash.	Water.
West Virginia, average	36·88	58·88	3·79	0·63
Newcastle, England	32·70	65·55	1·75	..

Splint or Bituminous Coals.

	Volatile Matter.	Fixed Carbon.	Ash.	Water.
West Virginia, average	32·98	62·29	3·70	0·96
Clyde Splint, Scotland	36·80	59·00	4·20	..

The foregoing averages are taken from numerous analyses of coal in different localities.

Mr. J. Bowron, of Newcastle, on the Virginian Coalfields.—In references to the capabilities of this district, whose iron and coal capacities I have shortly attempted to describe, Mr. J. Bowron, of Newcastle-on-Tyne, during a session of the Society of Arts in 1873, said that two years ago he spent some months in Virginia, more particularly for the purpose of investigating its mineral resources, and he could concur with the remarks of Professor Ansted, F.R S.

There was no doubt of the regularity of the coalfields throughout the whole of West Virginia, while the country was so intersected by valleys that it was very easy indeed to open up at any point coal seams which could be readily identified with the same seams occurring 20 or 30 miles off. He had himself followed one seam a long distance, and he could hardly have believed it if he had not traced it. On approaching the Appalachian region he found such immense deposits of hydrated hematite ore as he had never seen before, though he was familar with deposits of a similar kind in Cumberland and Spain. Besides these resources, the capabilities of Virginia as a paper-producing country were greater than he believed existed anywhere else. It had the materials at hand for which, at present, America depended mainly on England, being well supplied with metallic sulphurets, salt, limestone possessing 98 per cent. of carbonate of lime, manganese, pure water and coal, and having these it could not lack anything for chemical manufactures. It possessed besides such a growth of non-resinous trees and plants suitable for the manufacture of paper, that he had no hesitation in saying that one State alone could easily supply paper for the whole civilised world.

Lumber Capacities.

Species of Lumber.—The lumber capacities of Virginia and West Virginia are very great, especially the latter, and comprise immense growths of white, black, red and chestnut oaks, black and white hickory, black walnut, ash, poplar, wild cherry, and chestnut, interspersed with maple, white pine and chestnut.

White oak is the most important and plentiful, and can be placed upon the railway cars at a cost of about 12 dol. 50 c. per 1,000 feet superficial (83·3 cubic feet), the items being as below within a mile or two of the railway:—

	Dol.	c.		£	s.	d.
Stumpage per 1,000 feet	2	50	=	0	10	5
Logging ,, ,,	4	00	=	0	16	8
Sawing ,, ,,	4	00	=	0	16	8
Carriage to cars ,,	2	00	=	0	8	4
Cost of Shipment to England—						
Freight to Newport News at 8 c. per cubic foot	6	66	=	1	7	9
Ocean at 12 c. per cubic foot	9	99	=	2	1	7½
Charges at Liverpool, insurance, &c.	4	99	=	1	0	9½
Total	34	158	=	7	2	3

or 1s. 8d. per cubic foot.

The present price of white oak is, delivered in Liverpool, 2s. 5d. per cubic foot.

The above calculations refer to the choicest lumber in pieces, 16 feet to 20 feet × 10 inches to 12 inches × 4 inches to 6 inches.

I have selected white oak as an example, because its value is intrinsic, not affected by fashion, as in the case of black walnut and other woods, and likely to increase in consequence of the large and regular consumption.

Agriculture.

There are millions of acres in Virginia and West Virginia available for corn and grass culture, as well as for sheep and cattle, and which may be had at from 1 dol. to 10 dol. per acre, but they are in my opinion unsuited to the emigrant who is not possessed of a fair amount of capital, and even for him better opportunities offer further west. The winters in the mountains are, moreover, long and severe, and militate against profitable agriculture and farming.

Copper.

Copper ores are found in great quantities in the south-western portion of the State, especially in the counties of Grayson, Carroll and Floyd; generally in the form of oxides and sulphurets, in veins varying from 6 to 60 feet thick. The percentage of metal is from 8 to 30. These deposits are found at distances from the nearest point on the Norfolk and Western Railway, of from 16 to 63 miles, the cost of transportation being 25s. to 85s. per ton. They have hitherto been wastefully and unskilfully worked, and this circumstance, coupled with the difficulties of communication, have prevented their development. The valley of the New River, near whose head waters they are found, is of great beauty, and singularly favoured both as to soil and climate.

Tin.

Tin has recently been found in paying quantities in West Virginia, but I have been unable to procure reliable information as to the richness or extent of the deposits.

FISHERIES.

Among the most important resources of Virginia are the fisheries, which are free to all.

Through the courtesy of Mr. McDonald, State Inspector of Fisheries, I am enabled to append some valuable statistics, showing the quantities and varieties of fish taken off the coast of Virginia, together with their respective values, the capital and means employed in their capture, and other particulars. To these I have added similar particulars for the adjoining States of Maryland and North Carolina, whose waters blend together and form a common fishing ground, with some diversity as to State laws. Quite recently, however, the Virginia legislature has adopted the Maryland fishing laws with great advantage to both States.

Sea Fishing.—Sea fishing is carried on by trawlers which use no nets, but long ropes garnished with baited lines.

Line Fishing.—Line fishing is profitable, and is carried on principally during the oyster close season which commences on 15th May. The fish most esteemed is "sheepshead," which fetches 5d. to 6d. per lb., and is caught up to 20 lbs. in weight.

Hogfish are next in demand, and weighing from $\frac{1}{2}$ lb. to 1$\frac{1}{2}$ lbs. fetch from 8s. 4d. to 10s. per dozen. "Spot-trout," flounders, mackerel, and some other varieties are caught in great abundance, and fetch lower prices.

Success in this pursuit of course depends principally on the skill of the fisherman. I have seen one man in six hours catch 60 lbs. of "sheepshead," value 25s. There is a good sale for the better kinds of fish, which are packed in ice and sent to Richmond, Baltimore, and New York.

Net Fishing.—This is principally carried on in the shallow waters of the rivers and estuaries with fixed nets into which the fish are conducted as they ascend or descend along the shores in search of food. Countless quantities of herring and menhaden are secured in this way, the latter being oily and unfit for food, but form excellent manure. Shad, which is quite a superior fish, and rock, somewhat resembling cod, are also caught in large quantities. These latter kinds fetch 3d. to 5d. per lb., at retail.

Oysters.—The oyster fisheries are however by far the most important, and give employment to the largest number of persons. Dredging is not permitted, as it is said to injure the beds by covering the young oysters with sand, and thus smothering them. The oysters are generally procured with long double rakes, armed with iron teeth, which close like a pair of scissors. Two men can procure 20 to 30 bushels a day, valued at 25 c. to 30 c., or 1s. to 1s. 3d. per bushel wholesale, according to quality. These retail at from 45 c. to 80 c. (1s. 10$\frac{1}{2}$$d$. to 3$s$. 4$d$.) per bushel. The close season extends from 15th May to 15th September. The oystermen fish out of canoes or small boats, and generally sell their catch to the oyster sloops, which vary from 20 to 100 tons, and cruise about or anchor alongside the fishing boats.

An estimate of the number of oysters taken may be formed by observing the vast quantities of shells used for macadamizing the roads, for building and filling in wharves, for lime, and for other purposes.

The take is however yearly diminishing in consequence of the wasteful and unscientific conduct of the fisheries, and for an adequate supply in the future, scientific oyster culture is indispensable, and opens a profitable field for the investment of capital.

1502   UNITED STATES.

Table I.—TABLE of Species showing, by States, the Quantity in Pounds of each of the more important Food Fishes and other Aquatic Species taken in 1880.

	Maryland.	Virginia.	North Carolina.
	Lbs.	Lbs.	Lbs.
Alewives, *Clupea vernalis*, Mitch., and *C. æstivalis*, Mich.	9,203,959	6,925,413	15,520,000
Black bass, *Micropterus salmoides* (Lac.), Henshall		130,000	175,000
Black drum, *Pogonias chromis*, Lacep.	75,000	60,000	150,000
Blue fish, *Pomatomus saltatrix* (Linn.), Gill	10,000	1,546,417	600,000
Catfish, *Amiurus*, sp., and *Ichthelurus*, sp.	420,000	500,000	300,000
Charleston porgies, *Pagellus*. sp.	..	..	50,000
Clams (quatrangs or little necks), *Venus mercenaria*, Linn.	40,000*	363,820	309,600
Crabs, *Callinectes hastatus*, Ordway	1,166,667†	2,139,200	11,200
Cravallé, *Carangus* (several species)	..	..	..
Croakers, *Micropogon undulatus* (Linn.), C. and V.	20,000	450,000	350,000
Eels, *Anguilla vulgaris*, Turton	15,000	125,000	50,000
Flounders, *Paralichthys*, and other genera	5,000	40,000	20,000
Green turtle, *Chelonia mydas*, Schw.	..	..	6,000
Groupers, *Epinephelus* (several species)	..	..	..
Grunts and pig-fish, *Hæmulon* (several species)	3,000	100,000	400,000
Menhaden, *Brevoortia Tyrannus* (Latr.), Goode	3,903,000	88,213,800	50,000
Mixed fresh water fish	778,518	243,140	39,025
Mixed salt water fish	163,000	195,139	2,061,500
Moonfish or banded porgy, *Chætodipterus faber* (Brouss.), J. and G.	5,000	180,000	30,000
Mullet, *Mugil albula*, Linn., and *M. brasiliensis*, Ag.	30,000	25,000	3,368,000
Oysters, *Ostrea virginiana*, Lister	74,200,000	47,861,240	1,190,000
Pompano, *Trachynotus Carolinus* (Linn.), Gill.	..	8,000	25,000
Perch, *Perca fluviatilis*, Linn., and *Morone americanas* (Gmelin), Gill.	890,000	745,000	430,000
Red drum, *Sciænops ocellatus* (Linn.), Gill.	10,000	40,000	175,000
Sailors' choice, *Lagodon rhomboides* (Linn.), Hol.	2,000	10,000	70,000
Scup, *Stenotomus argyrops* (Linn.), Gill.	..	..	20,000
Sea-bass, *Cerebropristis atrarius* (Linn.), Barn.	5,000	20,000	125,000
Shad, *Alosa sapidissima* (Wilson), Storer	3,774,426	3,171,953	3,221,263
Sheepshead, *Archosargus probatocephalus* (Walb.), Gill.	12,000	503,666	80,000
Shrimp, *Peneus retiferus* (Linn.), Edwards	..	..	63,000‡
Spanish mackerel, *Scomberomorous maculatus* (Mitch.), J. and G.	18,000	1,609,663	10,000
Spot, *Liostomus obliquus* (Mitch.), De Kay	20,000	700,000	520,000
Squeteague, *Cynoscion regalis* (Bl.), Gill	60,000	1,107,000	170,000
Starfish and butter-fish, *Poronotus triacanthus* (Peck), Gill	1,000	115,000	200,000
Striped bass, *Roccus Lineatus* (Schn.), Gill.	700,000	625,000	770,000
Sturgeon, *Acipenser sturio*, Linn.	144,000	411,558	436,900
Terrapin, *Malacoclemmys palustris*, Gmel.	30,000§	165,600	123,000
Turtle (various salt and fresh water species)	..	..	30,000
Whiting and king-fish, *Menticirrus alburnus* (Linn.), Gill., and *M. littoralis* (Hol.), Gill.	3,000	175,000	150,000
Total	95,712,570	158,874,609	32,249,488

* 10 lbs. of meat to a bushel of clams.
† 3 crabs to the pound.
‡ 35 lbs. to the bushel.
§ 3½ lbs. each.

Table II.—PARTICULARS of Maryland, Virginia, and North Carolina Fisheries for 1880. Latest Return.

	Maryland.	Virginia.	North Carolina.
Persons employed	26,008	18,864	5,274
Fishing vessels	1,450	1,446	95
Fishing boats	2,850	6,618	2,714
Capital in fishing industries	1,270,000*l*.	385,000*l*.	113,150*l*.
Pounds taken, including oysters	80,281,667	146,122,545	11,357,300
Value of the same	970,000*l*.	570,000*l*.	56,150*l*.
Pounds of river produce	15,430,903	12,752,064	20,892,188
Value of the same	80,560*l*.	54,565*l*.	111,000*l*.
Total value to fishermen	1,050,000*l*.	625,000	1,655,000

Table III.—OF Persons.

State.	Fishermen.	Shoresmen.	Factory Hands.	Total.
Maryland	15,873	1,256	8,879	26,008
Virginia	16,051	628	2,185	18,864
North Carolina	4,729	520	25	5,274

Table IV.—OF Capital in £ Sterling, showing, by States, the Amount of Capital employed in various ways.

State.	Total Capital Invested.	Value of Vessels.	Value of Boats.	Value of Gear and Outfit.	Value of Traps. Pound Nets.	Value of Traps. Pot and Bass Nets.	Value of Netting. Gill Nets.	Value of Netting. Seines.	Value of Netting. Dipnets and Castnets.	Value of Factories and other Shore Property.	Additional Cash Capital.
	£	£	£	£	£	£	£	£	£	£	£
Maryland	1,270,000	350,000	37,300	35,500	2,680	1,320	9,000	10,800	142	820,500	1,000
Virginia	385,000	115,000	60,000	72,000	21,000	181	7,200	14,200	...	100,000	...
North Carolina	103,150	8,000	25,000	10,900	6,300	235	1,900	19,400	330	20,900	4,400

OYSTER Industry of Maryland, Virginia, and North Carolina.

Table V.—OF Persons employed in 1880, showing, by States, the Number of Persons Engaged.

State.	Fishermen.	Shoresmen.	Factory Hands.	Total.
Maryland	13,748	790	8,864	23,402
Virginia	14,236	501	1,578	16,315
North Carolina	1,000	20	..	1,020

[1431]

Table VI.—Of Apparatus and Capital.

State.	Total Amount of Capital Invested.	Vessels. Number.	Vessels. Tonnage.	Vessels. Value.	Boats. Number.	Boats. Value.	Gear and Outfit. Value.	Shore Property. Value.
	£			£		£	£	£
Maryland	1,210,000	1,450	43,500	355,000	1,825	27,000	35,000	800,000
Virginia	275,000	1,317	13,170	95,000	4,481	46,000	67,000	68,000
North Carolina	14,000	90	1,350	4,600	800	3,300	3,100	31,000

Table VII.—Oyster Products.

State.	Number of Bushels* of Native Oysters Produced.	Value to Fishermen.	Enhancement in Value of other Oysters in Preparation for Market.‡ Number of Bushels Re-handled.	Enhancement in Value of other Oysters in Preparation for Market.‡ Amount of Enhancement.	Total Value as Sold.
	Bushels.	£	Bushels.	£	£
Maryland	10,600,000†	540,000	7,653,492	430,000	970,000
Virginia	6,827,000	200,500	1,622,130	54,000	254,000
North Carolina	170,000	13,000	..	..	13,000

Emigration.

Effects of Slavery and the War on Virginia.—The price Virginia has paid for slavery has been heavier than that of any other State. Besides the injuries she sustained from the ravages of war, which from her geographical, political, and strategical position she felt most heavily of all the Confederate States, her soil and climate is well suited to white, and to none of her products is coloured labour indispensible; nor is the negro so well adapted to the rigours of a Virginian winter as to the milder seasons of more southern latitudes. Consequently while the cotton, rice, and sugar-growing States absolutely require coloured labour, Virginia would be more prosperous were its place supplied by an influx of those emigrants who are now building up the western country. But the presence of the African acts as a deterrent to the white labour, and this State has not the inducement of free land to offer to the surplus population of Europe.

Land.—A great deal of the land is low in price, but it is lower in value, having been exhausted by the pernicious system of cultivation, which seems everywhere to have accompanied slavery, and requires time and capital to restore it to even moderate fertility. Good land being scarce is abnormally high priced. One of the most successful

---

* Each bushel of oysters is estimated to yield 7 lbs. of meat.

† Many oysters landed by Maryland fleet are taken in Virginia waters, thus increasing the total for the former at the expense of the latter.

‡ This includes transportation to other markets in oyster vessels; also increase in value due to fattening, canning, and planting.

farmers on the James River, whose land is estimated at the value of 10*l.* per acre, told me that he only made 6 per cent. on his capital invested, and he considered very few people made that.

Truck Farming.—Truck farming, which is carried on to a great extent in the vicinity of Norfolk, is said to be very profitable, but requires a gardener's experience. Nearly all the vegetables grown here are sent to the northern cities where, being early, they fetch high prices.

Roads.—The roads in Virginia are very bad, and in winter almost impassable. There is, I believe, only one macadamised road in the State extending through a portion of the "valley," and in consequence of the apathy of the landowners, it is impossible to make any improvement in this particular.

Timber and Mineral Lands.—There is a considerable amount of virgin land now covered with fine timber, and underlaid with minerals in the mountainous part of the State, but it is held by speculators for mining and other purposes, and is not available for the emigrant.

Condition of the Labouring Classes.—The condition of the labouring classes is good. Skilled labour is paid from 6*s.* 6*d.* to 10*s.* a day; unskilled, which is principally coloured, 3*s.* 6*d.* to 4*s.* 6*d.*, and in the Virginian mines 5*s.* to 6*s.* Female coloured servants get from 20*s.* to 40*s.* a month, with board and lodging.

Cost of Necessaries of Life.—The necessaries of life are cheap, but clothing and luxuries are dear and bad. From the Richmond market return I take the following prices:—

Beef	2½*d.* to 1*s.* per lb.
Mutton	5*d.* ,,
Flour	10*s.* 6*d.* to 1*l.* 6*d.* per barrel of 196 lbs.
	But some grades are 1*l.* 13*s.* per barrel.
Tea	1*s.* 1*d.* to 4*s.* 2*d.* per lb.
Sugar, refined	4½*d.* ,,
Potatoes	1*s.* 6*d.* to 2*s.* 6*d.* per bushel of 60 lbs.
Eggs	9*d.* to 1*s.* 1*d.* per doz.
Butter	9*d.* to 1*s.* 1*d.* per lb.
Onions	6*s.* 4*d.* per barrel.
Lard	5½*d.* per lb.
Bacon	4½*d.* to 5*d.* ,,
Hams	7½*d.* to 11½*d.* ,,
Coffee	5*d.* to 1*s.* 2*d.* ,,
Fowls	8*d.* to 1*s.* 1*d.* each.
Cheese	4½*d.* to 10*d.* per lb.
Whiskey	6*s.* 3*d.* to 12*s.* 6*d* per gallon.
Timber, white oak	3*l.* 10*s.* to 4*l.* 12*s.* per 1,000 feet.
,, yellow pine	1*l.* 17*s.* 6*d.* ,,
,, white pine	3*l.* 2*s.* 6*d.* to 7*l.* 5*s.* ,,
Kerosine oil	5*d.* per gallon.

Climate.—The climate of the State varies considerably. In all but the tidewater section it is hot and cold, measured by the temperate standard of England. It rises as high as 100° in the shade in towns and cities, and falls to several degrees below zero. I have myself seen it at 7° below, that is to say 39° of frost. In the eastern section it seldom falls lower than 10° below freezing point (Fahrenheit). The climate is healthy, except as stated before on the eastern coast, but the extremes of temperature are trying to English constitutions, and sojourners here, as in most other sections of the United States, lose the bloom and freshness they brought from Europe, without, at the same time, suffering from bad health.

Virginia as a Field for Emigrants.—It will be seen from the above remarks that I do not recommend Virginia as a field for the ordinary emigrant, and my reasons may be summed up in the fact that it does not offer sufficient inducements either to the labour which conducts the operations of agriculture or to that which fills the wants of manufacturing communities. A time will come, however, when the latter class will find a large demand and a profitable reward for its services. For nature has bestowed upon Virginia more than her share of the various elements above and beneath the soil, which build up the wealth of communities, and every day northern and English capital are being gradually but surely attracted to this section of the United States.

RETURN of British Shipping at the Port of Newport News in the Year 1884.

Direct Trade in British Vessels from and to Great Britain and British Colonies.

Entered.

Total Number of Vessels.			Total Tonnage.			Total Number of Crews.	Total Value of Cargoes.
With Cargoes.	In Ballast.	Total.	With Cargoes.	In Ballast.	Total.		£
10	3	13	9,692	3,035	12,727	268	...

Cleared.

Total Number of Vessels.			Total Tonnage.			Total Number of Crews.	Total Value of Cargoes.
With Cargoes.	In Ballast.	Total.	With Cargoes.	In Ballast.	Total.		£
96	...	96	99,684	...	99,684	2,145	...

Indirect or Carrying Trade in British Vessels from and to other Countries.

Entered.

Countries whence Arrived.	Number of Vessels.			Tonnage.			Number of Crews.	Value of Cargoes.
	With Cargoes.	In Ballast.	Total.	With Cargoes.	In Ballast.	Total.		£
Russia	...	...	...	...	...	...	...	...
Denmark	1	...	1	1,271	...	1,271	23	...
Germany	...	...	...	...	...	...	...	...
France	...	1	1	...	1,094	1,094	18	...
Spain and colonies	4	2	6	3,617	1,445	5,062	127	...
Brazil	1	...	1	885	...	885	21	...
Mexico	4	...	4	4,118	...	4,118	127	...
Portugal	...	...	...	...	...	...	...	...
Total	10	3	13	9,891	2,539	12,430	316	...

Cleared.

Countries to which Departed.	Number of Vessels.			Tonnage.			Number of Crews.	Value of Cargoes.
	With Cargoes.	In Ballast.	Total.	With Cargoes.	In Ballast.	Total.		£
Russia	1	...	1	1,179	...	1,179	22	...
Denmark	4	...	4	3,468	...	3,468	71	...
Germany	21	...	21	23,626	...	23,626	484	...
France	7	...	7	8,797	...	8,797	227	...
Spain and colonies	20	...	20	16,728	...	16,728	435	...
Brazil	4	...	4	4,008	...	4,008	111	...
Mexico	...	...	...	...	...	...	...	...
Portugal	1	...	1	1,097	...	1,097	24	...
Total	58	...	58	58,901	...	58,901	1,374	...

1508 UNITED STATES.

TOTAL of all British Vessels Entered and Cleared in 1883 and 1884.

Year.	Entered. Number.	Entered. Tonnage.	Cleared. Number.	Cleared. Tonnage.
1883	168	187,624	165	184,743
1884	150	163,612	154	168,585

EXPORTS.

The principal articles exported from Newport News for the years 1883 and 1884 were as below:—

		1883.	1884.
Lumber, to Europe	Tons	18,123	8,262
Flour, to Brazil	Barrels	132,371	73,079
Lard, to Brazil	Packages	33,175	13,860
Whisky, to Bremen	Barrels	11,386	29,154
Cotton, to Liverpool	Bales	9,061	42,581
Wheat, to Europe	Bushels	197,878	534,237

The values of exports from this port for the year 1884 are as below, excluding coastwise merchandise:—

Articles.		Quantity.	Value.
			Dollars.
Cotton	Bales	30,491	1,562,298
Coal	Tons	41,000	156,425
Walnut logs			46,670
Staves			76,393
Bark			1,740
Oak plank and poplar			50,630
Flour			451,533
Linseed cake			4,000
Lard and bacon			65,427
Whisky			1,020,390
Wheat			517,463
Cotton seed			7,737
Sundries			36,500
Total			4,005,406

Nearly all this was carried in British vessels.

A summary of the number and tonnage of British vessels which in 1883 cleared from the principal ports in the United States shows Newport News to be in importance as regards British shipping:—

Ports.	Number of Ships.	Tonnage.
New York	2,577	3,897,689
Boston	1,979	834,834
Baltimore	396	445,327
San Francisco	290	438,467
New Orleans	356	413,041
Newport News	165	184,743
Portland, Maine	260	133,774
Savannah	91	97,825
Pensacola	116	86,348
Portland, Oregon	71	68,576
Beaufort, South Carolina	80	61,372
Galveston	65	59,910

All ports above 50,000 tons, except Philadelphia, are given above, and show Newport News to have attained the seventh position in the United States as regards the magnitude of British tonnage.

In reference to the exports shown in the preceding return, it is well to remark that it by no means shows the actual value of goods destined for Europe, but only those exported and cleared for foreign ports. For instance, tobacco, which forms one of the principal articles exported, is sent to Liverpool through New York, and being shipped coastwise to the care or order of New York agents, is not recognised in the Newport News Customs as an export, but is credited to New York.

The depression of trade caused the abandonment of a line of steamers, which had been put on in the end of 1883 for a few months, between this port and Liverpool. When direct communication is re-established, the export list will more fairly represent the trade of the port.

Newport News, May 8, 1885.

PORTLAND, OREGON.

Report by Vice-Consul Laidlaw on the Trade and Commerce of Oregon and Washington Territory (East of the Cascade Mountains) for the Year 1884.

The past year has been one of severe depression in all branches of business, which is attributable to the cessation to a great extent of expenditure for railway construction, to the heavy shrinkage in railway securities, in which most of our capitalists had invested, and to the very low market prices for wheat, canned salmon, wool, and other products of this section. The money market has been very stringent throughout the year, and failures from overtrading during more prosperous years have been numerous.

The number of buildings erected in Portland and suburbs was considerable, although much smaller than during 1883. Many of the buildings for business purposes are very handsome, and the dwellings built of late years are vastly superior both in appearance and convenience to those of former years. A very large proportion of the tonnage employed in the foreign trade of the Columbia River was British, the proportion being 73 per cent., as against 83 per cent. last year.

Import Trade.

The value of direct imports from foreign countries during the year is given below:—

	Dollars.
Entered at Portland	477,778
at Astoria	191,171
Total	668,949

This is a decrease of about 26 per cent. as compared with 1883. Some proportion of these imports were brought from the Eastern States by rail in bond, which is a new feature consequent upon the opening of the Northern Pacific and Oregon short lines of railway to the Eastern States, and increased imports of the finer classes of goods may be expected in this way during subsequent years.

The imports were from the following countries:—

	Dollars.
From Great Britain	451,245
Hong-Kong	131,468
Australia	31,117
British Columbia	32,677
Germany	3,769
Sandwich Islands	7,416
Miscellaneous	11,257
Total	668,949

PORTLAND, OREGON.

The articles imported consisted of—

Articles.		Portland. Quantity.	Portland. Value.	Astoria. Quantity.	Astoria. Value.
			Dollars.		Dollars.
Tin and tinplate	Lbs.	1,833,017	65,895	5,147,789	183,319
Coal	Tons	26,662	74,479	2,170	6,066
Rice	Lbs.	3,569,353	64,025	..	..
Earthenware and glass	,,	..	30,900	..	..
Salt	,,	9,358,279	29,521	276,007	884
Cement	Barrels	14,933	25,592	29	87
Pig iron	Tons	1,658	22,692	..	..
Beer, porter, and ale	Gallons	18,603	16,395	..	..
Liquors	,,	24,062	13,123	..	..
Soda and chemicals	Lbs.	1,084,159	10,772	..	..
Cigars and tobacco	,,	10,611	10,268	..	..
Fire bricks and fire clay	Number / Tons	429,020 / 473	11,260	..	..
China nut oil	Gallons	19,600	8,335	700	302
Sugar	Lbs.	79,984	5,885	..	..
Tea	,,	25,012	5,617	..	..
Sheet iron	,,	25,088	1,819	..	..
All other articles	..	..	81,195	..	513
Total	..	..	477,778	..	191,171

The estimated value of imports from Atlantic and Pacific ports of the United States during the year (including shipments by rail amounting to 35 per cent. of the whole) was 20,051,470 dol. against 27,668,780 dol. during 1883. The actual decrease is not so great as would appear from these figures, for in 1883 supplies for interior towns all passed through Portland, and the value could thus be estimated, whereas this year a large proportion of such supplies were delivered directly from the Eastern States by rail, and necessarily the value could not be ascertained.

The principal articles so imported into Portland were—

Articles.	1884.	1883.
	Dollars.	Dollars.
Groceries and provisions	3,867,658	3,950,014
Dry goods, clothing, hats, &c.	2,833,295	3,569,790
Railroad material	1,137,051	2,600,766
Hardware, iron and steel	1,662,514	3,104,814
Boots and shoes	1,619,880	2,220,442
Wines and liquors	952,456	835,876
Cigars and tobacco	912,835	1,125,560
Waggons, carriages, &c.	786,214	794,178
Paints, oils, and glass	752,381	755,198
Bags, bagging and twine	705,401	721,631
Crockery and glassware	632,315	856,536
Books and stationery	414,907	393,026
Musical instruments	400,126	230,110
Drugs and medicines	403,895	894,149
Fruits, nuts, candies, and vegetables	366,074	241,598
Powder, shot, guns, &c.	318,174	1,031,636
Agricultural implements	295,662	517,394
Stoves and tinware	244,642	149,388
Coal and coke	244,630	261,503
Furniture	231,150	460,657
Tin, copper, and lead	220,762	242,900
Harness and saddlery	193,414	127,720
Wooden ware	147,963	163,525
Carpets, oilcloths, &c.	123,700	247,773
Building materials	106,083	284,496
Chinese merchandise	8,642	77,885

Coals.—The following are the imports during the past three years:—

From—	1882.	1883.	1884.
	Tons.	Tons.	Tons.
Puget Sound, and domestic	3,350	25,495	35,423
British Columbia	11,080	4,410	7,289
Australia	9,445	16,107	11,462
Great Britain	3,147	2,255	4,898
Total	27,022	48,267	59,252

The imports of coke from Great Britain during last year were only 513 tons.

The consumption of coal continues to increase year by year. The price of coals during the year was low.

Cement.—At the close of 1883 stocks were very heavy, and the imports have been light, being only 14,962 barrels as against 46,317 barrels in 1883. Value per barrel is now only 3 dol., which leaves no profit to the importer.

Metals.—The imports of pig iron this year have been much lighter, yet the stocks at the close of the year are unusually heavy and market prices low. Glengarnock, which may be taken as the standard, is worth only 23 dol. 50 c. per ton. The following are the imports for the last three years:—

	Tons.
1882	2,601
1883	5,025
1884	1,658

The product of the Oregon iron and steelless furnace during the last seven years has been—

	Tons.
In 1878	1,310
1879	2,500
1880	5,000
1881	6,100
1882	6,750
1883	7,000
1884	3,640

The rolling mills referred to in my last report have not been built, as several stockholders failed to take up their stock. The imports of metals (other than pig-iron) are as under:—

Articles.		Quantity.	
		1883.	1884.
Iron bars	Number	57,798	39,152
,, ,,	Bundles	55,431	17,100
,, sheet	,,	11,766	6,722
,, pipe	Pieces	40,871	16,132
Steel bars	Number	1,765	1,429
,,	Bundles	3,680	2,235
Tinplate	Boxes	77,964	88,200
Tin	Ingots	5,315	5,178
,,	Tons	..	26
Copper	Packages	373	425
Iron rails	Number	57,068	943
Steel ,,	,,	64,314	19,331
Spikes	Lbs.	1,078,820	643,600
Fish plates	,,	1,156,909	317,547
Bolts	,,	1,076,150	229,664
Lead	Pigs	5,016	3,075
,,	Packages	835	1,092

The consumption of tinplates was even greater than in 1883, more especially of the grades used in salmon canning. Prices were low, ranging from 5 dol. 50 c. to 6 dol. for lower grades, and 6 dol. 50 c. to 7 dol. 25 c. for the higher grades of coke and charcoal:—

	Boxes.
Direct importation was	63,461
Viâ San Francisco	22,653
By rail overland	2,086

Sugar.—At one time a steady direct trade was done with the Sandwich Islands, but the Hawaiian Reciprocity Treaty killed it, as the crops there have ever since been controlled by Mr. Claus Sprechles of San Francisco. The direct importation during the year was only 57,155 lbs., other receipts being:—

	Barrels.	Half Barrels.	Kegs.	Mats.	Boxes.
From San Francisco	26,449	42,665	2,815	16,267	13,693
By rail overland	305	311	32	6	267

1514 UNITED STATES.

Rice.—Fully one-half of the imports during the past year have come viâ San Francisco, direct trade being impeded by the partial stoppage of the passenger traffic with China. The imports were:—

	Lbs.
From Hong-Kong	3,519,353
Sandwich Islands	50,000
Viâ San Francisco	3,887,350
Total	7,456,703

Tea.—Imports viâ San Francisco were 13,415 chests; from Hong-Kong, 25,012 lbs.

MANUFACTURES OF COTTON, WOOL, SILK, FLAX, AND JUTE.

Under the existing tariff there can be little trade with foreign countries in articles of cotton and wool, as nothing but the finer fabrics can be imported at a profit. The following Custom-house entries were made from foreign countries:—

	Value. Dol.
Manufactures of wool	3,693
,, cotton	5,878
,, silk	6,348
,, flax and jute	8,981

Bags and Bagging.—The trade was supplied from Calcutta viâ San Francisco. Prices were very low. The total imports were about 6,027,000 yards and bags.

EXPORT TRADE.

Although our exports have actually been greater than in 1883, yet values were so low that there has been a very considerable decrease in the total valuation.

The following table gives the destination and value of exports by sea (except coastwise):—

	£
To Great Britain, wheat, flour, salmon, and ores	1,038,554
Belguim, wheat	52,960
France, wheat	7,514
British Columbia, flour and provisions	5,703
Hong Kong, flour and timber	6,236
Panama, timber	6,434
Uruguay, timber	4,490
Atlantic ports of United States, wool, hides, and salmon	30,638
	1,152,529

The shipments of produce east, by way of the Northern Pacific and Oregon short line (Union Pacific), were as under:—

Hops	3,154,531 lbs.
Wool	2,583,353 ,,
Hides	221,722 ,,
Salmon, canned	153,297 cases.
,, salt	1,370 barrels.
,, fresh	1,013 packages.
Green fruit	2,955 boxes.
Dried ,,	493 ,,

PORTLAND, OREGON.

In addition to the above, 24,517 cases of British Columbia tinned salmon were shipped by rail, in transit for Canada.

Exports (Coastwise).—The total value of all exports coastwise from the Columbia River is estimated at 5,593,000 dol., and the principal articles are—

Articles.		Quantity.	Value.
			Dollars.
Salmon, tinned	Cases	115,053	} 517,030
,, salted	Lbs.	273,800	
Wool	,,	6,208,233	987,141
Flour	Barrels	236,981	956,659
Wheat	Centals	354,272	434,286
Woollen goods	,,	..	311,600
Timber	M. feet	29,605	307,475
Hides, pelts, &c.	Lbs.	2,190,092	179,303
Copper ore	Sacks	73,908	127,800
Flax seed	,,	33,876	102,345
Bran and millstuffs	,,	112,334	80,294
Oats	Centals	64,406	63,920
Potatoes	Sacks	73,342	38,346
Pig iron	Tons	1,836	33,090
Leather	,,	..	30,960
Fruits, green and dry	Boxes	28,796	24,636

TOTAL EXPORTS.

	£
Foreign	1,116,190
Domestic, by sea	1,149,200
,, by rail	404,800
Total	2,670,190

The following gives the values of the principal articles of home produce and manufacture exported by sea :—

	£
Copper ores	26,053
Flax seed	20,469
Flour	384,804
Fruit	3,930
Hides	37,042
Hops	14,855
Iron, pig	6,620
Oats	12,138
Potatoes	7,320
Salmon and fish	402,789
Timber	74,400
Wheat	653,753
Wool	201,588
Woollen goods	62,322

The following is the average cost of leading articles of export, free on board, including freight to England by iron ships, for the different months of the year:—

Months.	Wheat, per Quarter of 500 lbs.	Flour, per 280 lbs.	Salmon, per Case of 48 1-lb. Tins.
	£ s. d. £ s. d.	£ s. d.	£ s. d.
January	2 4 0 to 2 6 1	1 14 11	1 1 11
February	2 2 6 2 3 9	1 14 9	1 2 1
March	2 0 6 2 2 2	1 13 0	Nominal.
April	.. 2 1 4	1 12 8	1 2 6
May	1 19 2 2 1 3	Nominal.	1 2 0
June	1 17 7 1 19 10	1 11 2	0 19 2
July	Nominal.	Nominal.	0 19 2
August	1 13 9 to 1 15 4	1 14 6	0 19 4
September	1 13 5 1 15 4	1 13 0	0 19 4
October	1 13 2 1 14 10	1 11 4	0 18 6
November	1 12 6 1 13 9	1 9 1	0 18 4
December	1 14 10 1 16 2	1 10 2	0 18 4

Wool averaged about 15 c. per lb. for Willamette Valley and Southern Oregon, and 13 c. to 18 c. per lb. for Eastern Oregon. The Valley wools are running down year by year, while Eastern Oregon wools are improving.

Hops varied very much in price during the year, and although as high as 30 c. per lb. was paid, the average was not over 10 c. to 15 c. per lb.

The following are the exports of wheat and flour from Columbia River during the entire year:—

To	Wheat. Quantity.	Wheat. Value.	Flour. Quantity.	Flour. Value.
	Centals.	Dollars.	Barrels.	Dollars.
United Kingdom	2,034,856	2,576,669	271,486	1,241,435
France	35,781	37,570	..	..
Belgium	202,697	264,860	..	..
Hong-Kong	..	..	5,250	21,000
British Columbia, Puget Sound, &c.	34,126	44,558	72,997	294,873
San Francisco and Southern ports	320,146	389,728	163,984	661,786
Total	2,627,606	3,313,385	513,717	2,219,094

The exports of wheat during the harvest year were from Portland and Astoria, in centals—

	To United Kingdom.	To France.	To Belgium.	To San Francisco.	To Puget Sound.	Total.
From August 1, 1883, to July 31, 1884	2,129,792	24,753	122,264	239,027	72,914	2,588,750
Five months ending December 31, 1884	1,430,660	35,781	119,577	199,301	12,973	1,798,292

The exports of flour during the same period were from Portland and Astoria, in barrels—

	To United Kingdom.	To San Francisco and Alaska.	To British Columbia and Puget Sound.	To China.	Total.
From August 1, 1883, to July 31, 1884	329,142	156,920	61,926	5,392	553,380
Five months ending December 31, 1884	33,668	36,083	32,328	5,250	107,329

The following table of receipts at Portland shows the relative production of the two great wheat-growing sections, the surplus from which is exported by way of the Columbia River:—

Year.	Willamette Valley. Wheat.	Willamette Valley. Flour.	Eastern Oregon and Washington Territory. Wheat.	Eastern Oregon and Washington Territory. Flour.	Total Wheat and Flour reduced to its equivalent in Wheat.
	Centals.	Barrels.	Centals.	Barrels.	Centals.
1884	826,583	332,923	2,061,469	172,902	4,405,527
1883	1,442,290	327,788	617,535	146,228	3,481,873

The total exports of wheat and flour, reduced to its equivalent in wheat (at the rate of three centals per barrel of flour), were 4,248,890 centals.

Salmon.—The number of canneries in operation during 1884 was 37 and the product was nearly as given below. The value of the pack is estimated at 516,000*l*. The season opens April 1 and closes July 31, and during the past year the business was carried on at a loss. Fishermen are paid so much per fish irrespective of weight, but the meshes of the nets are made of such a size that only fish of a certain size can be taken. During the season the price ranged from 70 c. at the beginning to 25 c. per fish at the close, or during a heavy run. The average price of canned salmon, free on board, here or at Astoria, did not exceed 4 dol. 20 c. per case. In addition to the fish canned, a considerable quantity is annually packed in barrels, salted. The product and distribution from the Columbia River canneries during the last five years are given below:—

Year.	Product.	To England.	To Eastern States by Rail and Sail.	To San Francisco.	Estimated Stocks on December 31, 1884.
	Cases.	Cases.	Cases.	Cases.	Cases.
1884	645,000	303,926	179,559	105,321	53,500
1883	632,500	286,033	97,183	245,205	..
1882	548,760	352,882	..	191,869	..
1881	544,500	370,016	..	178,947	..
1880	533,000	237,371	..	290,083	..

1518 UNITED STATES.

Wool.—The receipts of Valley wools at Portland during 1884 were 1,404,967 lbs., and of Eastern Oregon and Washington wools 7,168,953 lbs.

The exports were—

	To San Francisco.	To Atlantic States.	Total.
	Lbs.	Lbs.	Lbs.
By sea	6,206,153	150,931	} 8,942,517
„ rail		2,585,433	

The total clip of Eastern Oregon and Washington was about 11,000,000 lbs., of which about 20 per cent. was Valley. The quality of Valley wools was very inferior, with the exception of the product of the more southern counties of the State; that from Eastern Oregon was also poor, but better than Valley, which has hitherto been superior. The sheep in the Valley are deteriorating year by year.

Hops.—Receipts at this port were 3,894,171 lbs. of Oregon and Washington Territory hops. Quality was only fair. Shipments were: to San Francisco by sea, 423,374 lbs.; to Atlantic States and Europe by rail, 3,154,700 lbs.

Timber.—Throughout the year this trade has been in a very depressed condition, and values have been fully 20 per cent. below those of 1883. This is owing to the lessened consumption for railroad purposes and the comparatively small demand for building lumber. Several shipments were made to Panama on order from the Canal Company. The following are the exports from the Columbia River:—

	Spars. Number.	Quantity.	Value.
		1,000 Feet.	Dollars.
To San Francisco and coast ports	484	29,605	307,475
Panama		2,601	32,171
Monte Video		1,973	20,259
Hong-Kong	450	256	9,460
Other places		134	3,245
Total	934	34,569	372,610

Besides the above a large quantity of rough lumber is annually shipped to San Francisco from Coos Bay, Port Orford, Coquille, Umqua, and other ports in Southern Oregon, which have only a coasting trade.

Money Market.

Throughout the whole year the money market has been very stringent, and loans on the security of real estate have been with difficulty obtained even at 10 per cent., the highest legal rate of interest. Banking facilities are ample. In Portland there are two National banks, two British joint stock banks, two private banks, besides several savings banks and mortgage loan banks. Nearly every town of 2,000 or 3,000 inhabitants has one or more banks. Short loans for business purposes have been obtainable during the year at from 8 to 9 per cent., and savings banks allow from 3 to 6 per cent. on time deposits.

PORTLAND, OREGON.

The following are the average monthly rates of exchange on London for the different months of the year:—

Month.	Exchange on London, 60 days. Bank.		Merchant.	
	Per Dollar.		Per Dollar.	
January	$49\frac{11}{16}$ to	$49\frac{5}{8}$	$49\frac{3}{4}$ to	$49\frac{13}{16}$
February	$49\frac{1}{2}$	$49\frac{7}{16}$	$49\frac{9}{16}$	$49\frac{5}{8}$
March	$49\frac{3}{8}$	$49\frac{5}{16}$	$49\frac{1}{2}$	$49\frac{9}{16}$
April	$49\frac{1}{4}$	$49\frac{3}{16}$	$49\frac{3}{8}$	$49\frac{7}{16}$
May	$49\frac{3}{8}$	$49\frac{5}{16}$	$49\frac{1}{2}$	$49\frac{9}{16}$
June	$49\frac{5}{8}$	$49\frac{9}{16}$	$49\frac{11}{16}$	$49\frac{3}{4}$
July	$49\frac{3}{4}$	$49\frac{11}{16}$	$49\frac{13}{16}$	$49\frac{7}{8}$
August	$49\frac{13}{16}$	$49\frac{3}{4}$	$49\frac{7}{8}$	$49\frac{15}{16}$
September	$49\frac{3}{11}$	$49\frac{11}{16}$	$49\frac{7}{8}$	$49\frac{15}{16}$
October	$49\frac{7}{8}$	$49\frac{13}{16}$	50	..
November	$49\frac{15}{16}$	$49\frac{7}{8}$	$50\frac{1}{16}$	$50\frac{1}{8}$
December	$49\frac{1}{2}$	..	$50\frac{1}{8}$	..

SHIPPING.

The improvement in river channels is shown by the fact that while in 1883 37 per cent. of exports of wheat and flour was entered at the Astoria Custom-house, during the past year only 22 per cent. was so entered. I believe that next year there will be little or no cargo lightered an account of shoal places in the Willamette and Columbia rivers.

The following shows the grain-carrying trade of the last two years:—

Nationality.	1883.		1884.	
	Number of Ships.	Registered Tonnage.	Number of Ships.	Registered Tonnage.
British	65	63,376	64	64,366
American	12	16,505	16	21,557
German	4	3,977	1	932
Swedish and Norwegian	1	730	1	656
Total	82	84,588	82	87,511

61 British ships registering 60,878 tons entered at this port, against 74 ships of a registered tonnage of 72,696 tons in 1883. The arrivals and departures of all ships and steamers during 1884 were:—

Countries from which Arrived or to which Departed.	Arrivals.	Departures.
	Registered Tons.	Registered Tons.
Great Britain	21,824	84,315
Australia and New Zealand	9,662	..
British Columbia	3,088	..
European ports	..	5,949
Mexico and Central America	1,613	3,188
China and Japan	3,875	2,722
East Indies	1,308	..
South America	36,658	1,898
Islands of the Pacific	2,648	..
Atlantic ports of the Union	10,275	..
Pacific ,, ,,	270,285	253,549
To domestic ports to load	..	1,200
Total	361,236	352,821

Further tables showing the movements of British and foreign shipping are given in the appendix to this report.

BRITISH SAILORS.

The following gives the number and changes in crews of British ships entering this port during the past three years:—

Year.	Total Number of Crews.	Deserted.	Discharged.	Engaged.	Reported Dead.	Percentage of Desertion.
1882	1,905	455	87	455	9	24
1883	1,390	182	47	182	3	13·9
1884	1,153	201	43	216	1	18

Until 1883 all desertions were reported here, but a large proportion of desertion takes place at Astoria, where vessels report on entering the river. Seamen's wages have averaged 5l. 11s. 9d. for able seaman: highest rate paid 7l., lowest 2l. 15s.

Although the latest United States Shipping Act renders it illegal and prescribes severe penalties against any one giving advances to seamen directly or indirectly, it has had no effect in abolishing crimping or advances. The only apparent effect has been to lower wages, but I am satisfied that this is not an actual result, and that the difference is paid as an advance and goes into the pockets of boarding-house keepers. The failure of this Act to protect seamen from imposition is principally due to the fact that provision is only made for punishing those who pay, and not those who receive such advances. I have not yet seen one seaman who would confess that an advance was being paid, although he might be engaging himself at a rate of wages obviously intended to cover such advance. There is a fine Sailors' Home at this port, built by subscription, but I regret that owing to the strong opposition of the rascally crew engaged in crimping sailors, the Home does not receive the support it deserves.

PORTLAND, OREGON.

TONNAGE ENGAGEMENTS

The engagements of tonnage during the past year have been as under (not including coasting voyages):—

	Reg. tons.
Grain cargoes	94,914
Salmon and assorted cargoes	10,257
Timber cargoes	5,716
Miscellaneous voyages	3,994
Total	114,040

Although a proportion of the grain ships were chartered before arrival, the great majority of charters were effected after arrival. Rates were very low on account of the depressed condition of the home markets. The following table shows the rates of original charter, the average rate for the year being 2l. 4s. 10d.:—

Number of Ships. To Great Britain.	To Continent.	Tonnage.	Rate per ton of 2,240 lbs.
			£ s. d.
1	..	944	3 2 6
1	..	701	3 0 0
12	..	10,177	2 12 6
2	..	2,032	2 11 3
11	..	10,695	2 10 0
1	..	446	2 8 9
1	..	810	2 8 3
7	1	7,920	2 7 6
1	..	844	2 7 3
1	..	1,279	2 3 3
2	..	2,010	2 5 6
14	2	15,588	2 5 0
4	..	3,851	2 3 6
11	..	11,737	2 2 6
1	..	954	2 1 3
9	1	12,049	2 0 0
2	..	2,686	1 18 9
2	1	3,722	1 18 6
2	..	2,916	1 17 6
1	..	1,491	1 16 3
1	1	2,980	1 12 6

The year opened with an exceedingly dull market, and during January rates for wooden vessels were 1l. 12s. 6d., and for iron ships 2l. 1s. 3d. to a port in the United Kingdom; in February, 2l. 2s. 6d.; in March 1l. 18s. 6d. for wood, and 2l. 2s. 6d. for iron ships; in April, the same rates; in May there was an improvement, and the rate for iron ships was 2l. 5s.; in June 2l. 2s. 6d. was the rate for wooden vessels; in July 2l. 5s. was paid for wooden vessels, and some charters to arrive were made at 2l. 12s. 6d.; in August rates were lower nominally, 2l. 12s. 6d. for iron vessels; in September rates were 2l. 8s. 3d. to 2l. 10s.; in October 2l. 12s. 6d., dropping to 2l. 6s. 3d.; in November, 2l. 5s. to 2l.; in December rates advanced, and on the last days of the years 2l. 12s. 6d. was the rate for iron vessels. Throughout the year there was a good demand for wooden ships at better rates in proportion to those paid for iron, as the owners of this class of vessel were generally willing to give a large range of continental ports at the same rate as for the United Kingdom.

Two very fine new American-built iron vessels of large capacity visited this port during the year: one of these registered 1,899 tons, length 273 ft. 6 in.

STEAMSHIP LINES.

There have been no additions to the fleet of deep-sea steamships trading to this port; but the Oregon Pacific Railroad Company purchased an iron steamer for trading between Taquina Bay and San Francisco. Steamers run between this and San Francisco now only once every five days, as the trade between the Columbia river and that port decreases yearly. The following is the freight in tons carried from and to San Francisco throughout the year:—

	From San Francisco.	To San Francisco.
	Tons.	Tons.
Oregon Railway and Navigation Company	38,028	37,070
Pacific Coast Steamship Company	37,480	30,698
Total	75,508	67,768
During 1883	177,491	39,877
Decrease	101,983	..
Increase	..	27,891

RIVER AND HARBOUR IMPROVEMENTS.

In view of the large number of British ships passing annually up and down the Columbia river, a short account of the extensive works in progress may prove of interest.

Under the superintendence of Captain Powell, of the United States Engineers, the river channels have been much improved, and but few vessels have been compelled to incur lighterage charges during the year from Portland. The following information is furnished me by the above-named officer:—The present project for the improvement of the Lower Willamette and Columbia rivers is to afford a channel of 20 feet depth at low water. The amount expended to June 30, 1884, is 505,363 dol., and has resulted in maintaining a channel of 17 feet to 18 feet at low water from Astoria to Portland, a distance of 100 miles. The project consists in contraction of waterway by low dykes and cut-off dams, and inshore protection for improvement of the river channels at the four bars from Portland to St. Helen's, Oregon; in dredging and stirring up the bottom at these bars during construction of permanent works, and also at shoal places below St. Helen's. On July 5, 1884, the United States Congress appropriated 100,000 dol. towards continuing these improvements.

Swan Island Bar and Post-Office Bar.—Dredgers were employed during the working season on these bars, and a depth of 22 feet in the channel obtained. These bars are in the Willamette river, about 12 miles below Portland.

Saint Helen's Bar (Columbia River).—This bar is 27 miles below Portland. Propeller sluicing is now a recognised method for temporary improvement on the Columbia, and this bar was again sluiced during the year, a depth being obtained of 22 feet at extreme low water, with a breadth of 150 feet in the channel across the bar. Permanent improvements have been commenced.

Walker's Island Bar is on the Columbia river, about 40 miles below Portland. The channel at this point was also sluiced, a depth of 19 feet at extreme low water being obtained.

Mouth of the Columbia River.—On 5th July last the United States Congress appropriated 100,000 dol. to begin the work of improving the mouth of this great river. The plan of this improvement is the construction of a low tide jetty about $4\frac{1}{2}$ miles long, from near Fort Stevens on the South Cape to a point about 3 miles south of Cape Hancock. The natural channel is shifting, sometimes good and sometimes poor, but always unreliable. Of late years the channel has carried about 19 feet at low water and for an insufficient width : 26 feet are required in the bar in a wide and direct channel, and 30 feet are desirable, on account of the heavy seas of the locality, for the deep vessels needed by the Columbia river trade. The amount estimated by the United States engineers for completion of the project is 3,100,000 dol., and the appropriation now granted is being used for construction of tramways, purchase of plant, and generally for preparations for work on the jetty.

Taquina Bay.—This harbour is the terminus of the Oregon Pacific Railway from Coovallis in Benton county, Oregon. The length of jetty is now 2,042 feet, depth of water at low tide 12 feet, a gain of 2 feet since my last report: mean rise of tide 7 feet. The amount expended to June 30 last is 109,990 dol.

Coos Bay.—This harbour has a considerable coasting trade, and exports timber and coal; vessels drawing 13 feet cross the bar without difficulty. The jetty is now 1,760 feet long, and the amount expended on construction to June 30 last is 301,884 dol.

Coquille River.—The depth of water over the bar has lessened during the year, being now only $6\frac{1}{2}$ feet : rise of tide 4 feet. The jetty is now 1,815 feet long, and 19,990 dol. had been expended at June 30 last.

Signal Service Station, &c.—There is a signal service station close to the lighthouse on Cape Hancock, connected with Astoria and Portland by telegraph. Vessels are now regularly reported upon arrival at or departure from the Columbia river. The signals used are those of the international code and the Government cautionary signals. There is also a life-saving station at Cape Hancock, and the Columbia and Willamette rivers are lighted by stake, beacon, and range lights from Astoria to Portland. A tidal gauge is operated at Astoria, which furnishes indications of the state of the Columbia river bar with regard to its roughness, and is of service to pilots, masters, and fishermen.

Pilotage and Port Charges.

The Act referred to in my last report to impose a special tonnage tax to be used in improvement of the Columbia river failed to pass Congress. River pilotage rate will probably be raised from 3 dol. to 4 dol. per foot when the State Legislature meets in January, as the pilots say they cannot live at the former rate.

The tug and pilot service has been efficient throughout the year, and there are few complaints of detention on this account.

Casualties.

The only serious casualty during the year in or near this district was the stranding of the American ship "Chesebrough," wheat-laden, which dragged her anchors during a heavy gale, and went ashore on Clatsop Spit. She was got off in about nine hours, and towed to Astoria leaking, where she was discharged and repaired.

Agriculture.

The year 1884 has not been profitable to the agriculturist; although crops were generally above an average, prices of all staple produce has been very low. The winter and spring were all that could be desired for grain crops, but rain, during harvest, did some damage.

Wheat.—From 15 per cent. to 20 per cent. of the crop was damaged and discoloured by rains, but this damaged grain was generally used for feeding purposes. Estimates of the exportable surplus varied from 1,100,000 quarters to 1,200,000 quarters, both of which estimates are evidently much too high, shipments from all sections to the end of the year being only 424,056 quarters, and stocks are not large. The average yield per acre in the great Willamette Valley was probably about 20 bushels (60 lbs.), but farming is generally of very low class. In Eastern Oregon and Washington Territory the average yield was probably over 25 bushels per acre. Quality was good average.

Oats were an immense crop, far above an average both in quantity and quality, but this crop suffered severely from rains during harvest, and probably 50 per cent. was damaged. The average yield per acre, I am told on excellent authority, must have exceeded 65 bushels (36 lbs.) per acre. Market prices were however very low and unremunerative.

Hops.—The crops of Oregon and Washington Territory were fully double those of 1883, but the quality was only fair. The crop of Western Washington Territory was about 20,080 bales, and the Oregon crop 8,100 bales, or 5,072,400 lbs. in all. No crop is subject to more violent fluctuations than this. Before picking time there were contract buyers at from 20 c. to 30 c. per lb., but fortunately for such speculators the growers generally were disinclined to sell. After picking was finished the market dropped as low as 8 c., and the average price to the grower hardly exceeded 12½ c. to 15 c. per lb. The yield in some instances was as high as 4,000 lbs. per acre, and the average was about 2,000 lbs.

Flax Seed.—Very little is grown in the Willamette Valley, the receipts being almost entirely from Eastern Oregon and Washington. The export was small, as two-thirds of the product was used by a local oil mill.

Fruit Culture.—Much more attention is being paid to orchards, as through the opening of new lines of railroad a ready market has been ound for green fruits in Montana, Dakota, Minnesota, and other States. The crop was a very heavy one. Apples, pears, cherries, plums, prunes, currants, raspberries, and strawberries grow in great profusion and perfection, and the crop of all fruits was a very heavy one last year and of superior quality. Peaches grow to great perfection in Eastern Oregon.

Potato Crop.—This crop was very large, but values were so low that a considerable proportion lies in farmers' hands, not being worth the cost of hauling to market.

Sheep and Cattle.—Stock farmers have not suffered so much as others in the general depression, though prices were lower than last year. Few cattle were driven to the Eastern States during the year, and the increase must be very considerable. A well-informed dealer gives the following as average prices of ordinary cattle and sheep on the ranges: Yearlings, 10 dol. to 15 dol.; two-year-olds, 20 dol. to 25 dol.; three-year-olds, 25 dol. to 35 dol. Sheep, 1 dol. 75 c. to 2 dol. In December occurred the severest snowstorm that has ever been experienced in this State, the railroads being blocked for several weeks, but the loss of sheep and cattle was small.

Population and Industries.

According to estimates based upon latest election returns the population of Oregon is between 250,000 and 260,000. There is a State Board of Immigration, with headquarters in Portland, the business of which is to give reliable information to immigrants and assist them with advice. The arrivals by sea were 13,762 and the departures 18,360. It is difficult to procure reliable information as to immigration by land, but there has been a small steady immigration principally into Eastern Oregon and Washington, and the gain in population from this source was as nearly as can be ascertained about 9,000. I do not think that the city population has increased much throughout the year, and there has been a lessened demand for skilled labour at lower wages. House rents have fallen considerably, and living expenses are somewhat lower. I would not advise professional men, clerks, or shopmen to come here, but there is certainly a good opening for labourers, mechanics, farmers, and stock farmers. These must also be prepared for hard work and the sacrifice of some conveniences in order to be successful in their pursuits.

Besides Portland, which has a population including its suburbs of about 45,000, there are many towns in the State having from 1,000 to 2,000 inhabitants, and many small villages. Salem, the capital of the State, has 2,500, Astoria 6,000, The Dalles 3,000, and Pendleton 2,300; and in Eastern Washington, Walla Walla has 5,000, Spokane Falls 3,000, and Dayton 2,000 inhabitants.

Manufactories.—There has been a slight decrease in value of the product of factories in the city of Portland, the total value of manufactured produce being estimated at 11,232,000 dol. for the year. About 5,270 hands have been employed in various industries, but Portland cannot as yet be called a manufacturing city, and the State is pre-eminently a producing and not a manufacturing one. The three woollen mills at Oregon City, Brounsville, and Ashland employed between 300 and 400 hands, and consumed about 1,500,000 lbs. of wool.

Mining.

The mineral deposits of Oregon and Eastern Washington are both large and diversified. Several counties are not only rich in gold and silver, but in coal, iron, copper, lead, zinc, cinnabar, &c. These deposits have not however been worked to any extent, but only need capitalists to develop them.

Gold and Silver.—The report of the director of the Mint gives the production of this State as 830,000 dol. gold and 135,000 dol. silver, but as much of the mining is done by the Chinese, who are reticent as to their operations, the total product is estimated at fully 1,500,000 dol. The gold mines of the new Coeur D'Alene district in Idoto are proved to be very rich, but the nature of the deposits is such that they can only be worked to a profit by corporations or individuals possessed of abundant capital to carry on extensive works.

1526 UNITED STATES.

Coal.—Coos Bay mines produced and shipped during 1884, 25,217 tons, a slight increase over last year.

Iron.—The product of the Oregon Iron and Steel Company during the last seven years is given in another portion of this report. The iron produced is a fine quantity of charcoal pig. These mines are not worked with energy at present, the market value of pig iron being so low.

Copper.—The mines of Montana have shipped some quantity of rich ores through this port, only a smal lproportion of which was shipped to the United Kingdom.

Public Works.

Railways.—The Northern Pacific has done some construction work on the division from Ainsworth on the Snake River, through the Takima country towards Puget Sound, and also on the division west of the Cascades Mountains, but as there is a tunnel of nearly two miles in length, necessary to pierce this range it will be several years before this line is completed.

The Oregon Railway and Navigation Company completed its line to a junction with the Oregon short line branch of the Union Pacific and opened it for traffic on the 25th November. This completes the second trans-continental line terminating in Portland.

The Oregon and California Railroad completed its line as far as Ashland, 341 miles from Portland. Farther construction is suspended for want of funds. The lease referred to in my last report has been abrogated, and the Company is in the hands of a receiver. Between Ashland and Delta, the present terminus of the Central Pacific, there is a gap of 129 miles.

The Oregon Pacific Railway has finished its line between Corvallis, in Benton county, and Taquina Bay.

The Columbia and Puget Sound Railway, which is a narrow gauge running to the coal fields tributary to Seattle on Puget Sound has also completed 22 miles this year.

The railroad lines in operation, and in course of construction throughout Oregon and Washington territory are as under (not including sidings):—

Broad Gauge Railways.

Companies.	Miles Completed.	Miles under construction.
Northern Pacific Railroad	490	65
Oregon Railway and Navigation	657	..
„ and California	448	..
„ Pacific Railroad	71	..
„ and Trans-continental	14	..
Total miles..	1,680	65

PORTLAND, OREGON.

Narrow Gauge Railroads.

Companies.	Miles Completed.
Oregon Railway Company (Limited)	148
Columbia and Puget Sound	42
Olympia and Tenino Railroad	15
Total	205

The traffic over the lines of the Oregon Railway and Navigation Company (which also includes all through traffic of the Northern Pacific and Union Pacific) and of the Oregon and California Railroad during 1884 is given below:—

	Forwarded.	Received.
	Tons.	Tons.
Oregon Railway and Navigation	149,534	227,490
" and California, East Side	21,916	49,999
" " " West Side	8,875	42,701

Terminal Facilities.—None of the buildings referred to in my report of 1883 as in course of construction have been completed by the Northern Pacific Terminal Company, but this company has spent 30,000 dol. on temporary wooden stations and a round house for the use of the Northern Pacific Railroad's Puget Sound division.

Canals.—A canal and locks around the Willamette Falls at Oregon City, for the passage of river steamers, was opened in 1871, which has been of great service ever since.

I am indebted to Major Jones, United States engineer in charge of the Government works at the canal and locks in course of construction around the cascades of the Columbia River, for the following information:—

The plan of this improvement is to give lockage around the main rapid, and an open river navigation through the minor rapids below for stages of 20 feet of water at the foot of the canal.

Since 1883 the open river work has been completed substantially over a distance of $3\frac{1}{2}$ miles, known as the Lower Cascades. The total expenditure has been about 100,000 dol., and it has resulted in making the river navigable, probably at all stages of the water, for steamboats alone, and for boats with barges in tow, for all seasons except during three of the summer months. Work has been continued on the canal prism, and preparations made for building the locks. The expenditure upon this work to June 30 last has been 799,252 dol., and the estimated amount still required for completion of the project is 1,505,400 dol.

CITY AND STATE FINANCES.

The receipts by the State Treasurer during two years and a quarter ending December 31 were, from all sources, 652,693 dol.; after deducting expenditure, there was a balance of nearly 300,000 dol. at the close of the year. The bonded debt of the city of Portland at the close of the year was 76,500 dol., bearing interest at 6 per cent., with a floating debt of 31,931 dol. The total receipts were 310,444 dol., and expenditure 257,634 dol. In addition to this, 140,737 dol. were paid by property owners for street improvements, sewers, &c.

TAXATION.

The State, county, and city taxes during the year were as under:—

	Per Cent.
State tax	0·80
„ school tax	0·56
County tax	0·40
City tax	1·10
School district tax	0·35
Total	3·21

The city tax levy for 1885 is 0·90 per cent.

REAL ESTATE.

There has been very little speculation in city property during the year owing to the dearness of money, but there exists a strong conviction in the minds of property holders that values will advance materially when the existing depression passes over.

Since September 1, 1882, the State has sold the following lands:—

	Acres.
University lands	2,218·26
Agricultural College lands	4,559·69
Common school lands	122,646·17
Internal improvements	32,743·13
Total	162,167·25

School lands are sold at 2 dol. per acre. The following were the entries at two of the principal United States land offices in Washington Territory during 1884:—

	Acres.
At Vancouver	67,726·41
Walla Walla	223,544·00

The sales of railroad lands during the year were—

	Quantity.	Average Price.
	Acres.	Dol. c.
Northern Pacific	89,241·02	4 00
Oregon and California	19,861·74	2 77·7

These prices are on long credit, not cash. Government land is sold at 2 dol. 50 c. and 1 dol. 25 c. per acre. The average price of improved land in Oregon is from 20 dol. to 22 dol. 50 c. per acre. Unimproved land in the valleys averages 10 dol. to 15 dol. per acre, and in the foothills 8 dol. to 15 dol. per acre. A large proportion of the best lands in the Willamette Valley is held by original settlers in large parcels and at high figures.

Remarks.

Among the most valuable trees in this State is the spruce, often rising to a height of 200 feet, and 200 inches in diameter; also the sugar pine, silver pine, common pine, block pine, larch, cedar, redwood, hemlock, white fir, and many others. The forests are often very dense, and the cascade and coast ranges are frequented by elk, deer, and antelope, also by yellow and silver foxes, mink, and marten. Black, cinnamon, and grizzly bear, wildcat, wolf, and the congar are to be found in the mountains. Pheasant, grouse, quail, and snipe abound in parts of the valleys, and the rivers and streams abound in fish.

The climate of Oregon is mild and genial, and in winter the thermometer rarely falls below 20° in the valleys or foot-hills, while in summer it seldom rises above 80°. According to the records of the health officer in Portland, the number of deaths during 1884 was 252 males and 127 females; of these, 104 were of children under 10 years of age. Malarial sickness is very prevalent in this city, no doubt caused by the inefficient system of drainage.

During the year 208 dwellings were built, costing 391,700 dol. On wharfs 64,000 dol. were disbursed, and on gas and water improvements 300,000 dol. The total amount spent in new buildings and in improvements on old ones was 2,063,300 dol.

The business portion of this city is now well lighted by electricity, and the fire department is very efficient and thoroughly equipped.

Every town of any pretensions throughout the State has a volunteer fire brigade, and generally one or two steam fire-engines. Losses by fire have, however, been especially severe during the past year, and a large proportion of these losses were borne by British corporations, nearly all the larger companies having agencies here.

Portland, Oregon, May 15, 1885.

Appendix No. 1.—STATEMENT showing the Number and Tonnage of all Vessels arriving at Portland, Oregon, and departing for Foreign Ports during 1884.

| | Entered. ||||||| Cleared. |||||||
| | Number of Vessels. ||| Total Tonnage. ||| Number of Vessels. ||| Total Tonnage. |||
	Direct.	Indirect.	Total.	Direct.	Indirect.	Total.	Direct.	Indirect.	Total.	Direct.	Indirect.	Total.
British	26	35	61	27,497	33,381	60,878	60	3	63	59,288	3,667	62,955
United States	..	10	10	..	10,694	10,694	..	26	26	..	31,366	31,366
German	..	3	3	..	2,190	2,190	..	2	2	..	1,349	1,349
Norwegian and Swedish	..	1	1	..	656	656	..	1	1	..	656	656
	26	49	75	27,497	46,921	74,418	60	32	92	59,288	37,038	96,326

Appendix No. II.—RETURN of British Shipping at the Port of Portland, Oregon, for the Year 1884.

Direct Trade in British Vessels from and to Great Britain and British Colonies.

Entered.

Number of Vessels			Tonnage			Total Number of Crews.	Total Value of Cargoes.
With Cargoes.	In Ballast.	Total.	With Cargoes.	In Ballast.	Total.		
21	5	26	22,279	5,218	27,497	550	£ 47,235

Cleared.

Total Number of Vessels			Total Tonnage			Total Number of Crews.	Total Value of Cargoes.
With Cargoes.	In Ballast.	Total.	With Cargoes.	In Ballast.	Total.		
60	...	60	59,288	...	59,288	1,044	£ 525,827

Indirect or Carrying Trade in British Vessels from and to other Countries.

Entered.

Countries whence Arrived.	Number of Vessels			Tonnage			Number of Crews.	Value of Cargoes.
	With Cargoes.	In Ballast.	Total.	With Cargoes.	In Ballast.	Total.		
Chili	1	11	12	1,308	9,060	10,368	198	£ 299
Peru	...	7	7	...	5,585	5,585	116	...
Argentine Republic	...	5	5	...	4,999	4,999	86	...
Brazil	...	4	4	...	4,707	4,707	68	...
Uruguay	...	3	3	...	2,733	2,733	49	...
Sandwich Islands	...	1	1	...	945	945	17	...
Coastwise	...	3	3	...	4,044	4,044	69	...
Total	1	34	35	1,308	32,073	33,381	603	299
Total direct and indirect	22	39	61	23,587	37,291	60,878	1,153	47,534

Cleared.

Countries to which Departed.	Number of Vessels			Tonnage			Number of Crews.	Value of Cargoes.
	With Cargoes.	In Ballast.	Total.	With Cargoes.	In Ballast.	Total.		
Belgium	3	...	3	3,667	...	3,667	48	£ 24,760
Total	3	...	3	3,667	...	3,667	48	24,760
Total direct and indirect	63	...	63	62,955	...	62,955	1,092	550,587

UNITED STATES.

ST. PAUL.

Report by Vice-Consul Treherne on the Trade and Commerce of Minnesota for the Year 1884.

THE general course of trade during the year 1884 has been remarkably steady in every prominent line within this Vice-Consular district. At no time in the twelve months has there been any rush for goods, and at no time has there been any significant falling off in the demand. The heavy Wall-street failures in May and the accompanying panic in the East disturbed confidence for a time, and had the effect of increasing the reserve of the merchants. Business was also affected for a brief period during the Presidential campaign, and for about ten days was almost at a standstill. Yet merchants quite generally agree in saying that business has been much better than they could have reasonably anticipated last winter. There is no doubt that but for the very marked depreciation which has taken place in the prices of nearly all kinds of goods, the volume of sales, as expressed in money value, would have been very much larger in 1884 than in the year 1883; in other words, that there were actually more goods sold than in 1883. As it was, the goods handled in the city of St. Paul amounted in value to 74,829,700 dol., showing an increase of 2,780,929 dol. over the previous year. Notwithstanding the depression of trade throughout the country, it is generally conceded by all that collections are good, and the commercial agencies state that country merchants are paying better now than they were at this time last year.

No fears are expressed among the merchants for the future. While no marked revival of trade is looked for during the year 1885, the general belief is that there will be no falling away in trade, in other words, the belief is quite general that there will continue to be a steady business—such as has characterised the markets of the past year—for several months to come. Prices are now regarded as about as low as they are likely to go, and some improvement is looked for in that direction. The condition of trade is certainly healthful. Merchants claim that they were never in better condition to do business, and bankers corroborate their statements in that regard. Their stocks have been reduced, and, as has been observed before, they have been extremely conservative and cautious in all their dealings. The number of new houses established in St. Paul during the past year is 881. This does not seem to betoken much lack of confidence in the future of business. Failures in the meantime have been very rare, and have included only two or three of any importance whatever; and, generally speaking, it has been the concerns that have been weak from the start that have failed. The sentiment is quite general, especially among the heavy wholesale dealers, that within the next twelve months there will be a turn in the tide; that there will be, however, a continuation of the general dulness and depression for several months yet, and a continuation of the "weeding-out" process which has been driving weak concerns, with small capital and loose credit, to the wall; that things will probably not grow any worse, and will not immediately grow much better.

This district being essentially an agricultural one, the New York financial troubles of last May and the industrial depression prevailing in the Eastern States were not the only cause of the quietude of trade. The principal cause was the extremely low price of wheat, which has partially paralysed agricultural interests, and has extended more or less to all allied interests.

Bradstreet's "Commercial Agency Summary" for the year 1884 shows that there are 21,836 firms engaged in business in Minnesota and Dakota combined, of which number 2,111 are located in St. Paul.

In his message to the Minnesota State Legislature, which convened in St. Paul in January, 1885, Governor Hubbard said in regard to freight tariff: The producers of our State have been greatly disappointed by the failure of the railroad companies to adjust their tariffs the past year to conform to the changed conditions in the general business of the country. They justly complain that charges for transportation are out of proportion to the value of the commodities transported. While the prices of grain have declined to a point that affords no profit to the farmer under the most favourable conditions for marketing his crop, the charges for transportation prevailing in former years have been substantially maintained. A slight reduction may have been made in some instances as a grudging concession to popular clamour, yet it has not been sufficient to afford appreciable relief in this regard. From many points in the State one-half the value of a bushel of wheat is taken for its transportation to Chicago, while from remote stations the freight and accompanying charges upon certain kinds and grades of grain amount almost to a confiscation of the property.

The amount of exchange dealt in by the banks of St. Paul alone during 1884 approaches 109,000,000 dol. The good showing made by the banks was not entirely unexpected, as the addition of 800,000 dol. to the banking capital of the city since last year certified to the increasing demand for the machinery of banking in St. Paul's business. An increase in surplus was expected, as a result of the conservative policy adopted by banks everywhere since the alarm of the early summer, and the increase of loans and exchange is a natural consequence of the growth of the city and the increase of its business. The increase of nearly 300,000 dol. in deposits is not so much a matter of course, but is evidence of financial ease and comparative abundance in the community, as well as of general confidence in the security of the banks. The decrease in circulation, amounting to 25 per cent.—a larger proportion of decrease than is found anywhere else in the country—is new evidence of the profitableness of the general banking business, which encourages the surrender of circulation and the employment of capital in loans.

The indication of general prosperity found in the banking review is more than confirmed by the statistics of the jobbing trade, which is the foundation and bulwark of St. Paul's material growth and success. The aggregate money value of the business done is a trifle less than a year ago, but the decline in prices of all kinds of merchandise shows that the volume of goods handled must be vastly larger. The actual amount of goods handled must be from 10 to 20 per cent. more than last year. In spite of this decline, the value of the trade in these important items has increased. Again, the wholesale houses have purposely limited their trade to safe and legitimate transactions, while country merchants, on the other hand, have limited their purchases, especially toward the close of the year, to the actual needs of the present season. I therefore consider the business as represented in the year's statistics to be actual and sound, and to constitute a foundation for a solid and profitable increase, when a revival of business activity shall strengthen confidence and stimulate trading.

SHIPPING AND NAVIGATION.

Except the traffic with points on the Lower Mississippi River the shipping interests of Minnesota are centered in Duluth, at the head of the navigation of Lake Superior. The record of this port for 1884 shows a large increase over 1883 in the number of arrivals and clearances, the tonnage and freight receipts, and shipments. Navigation opened on Lake Superior May 1st, and closed about December 1st.

Agriculture.—The number of acres sown in wheat in Minnesota increased 393,071 acres over 1882, and 215,831 acres over 1883. There was no injury to crops, and the result was a bountiful harvest, but the low price of farm products has caused dissatisfaction among the farmers, because they cannot obtain adequate returns for their labours. Some of the farmers in this State are not now depending entirely upon growing wheat, as was largely the case in past years. The raising and improvement of stock is attended to more, and the tendency of this change has already increased the demand for Minnesota butter, cheese, and beef in Eastern markets.

POPULATION AND INDUSTRIES.

The national census of 1880 gave Minnesota a population of 780,806. A comparison of the vote cast at the Presidential election of that year, with the poll in November last, shows beyond question a present population of over 1,000,000—an increase of 30 per cent.—much the larger part of which has been realised within the past two years. The number of immigrants arriving in St. Paul during the past year was somewhat less than it was in 1883. About 60,000 foreigners have settled in the North-western country tributary to St. Paul during 1884. Of this number about 20,000 were Scandinavian, 20,000 German, 10,000 British, and 10,000 from all other countries. It is impossible to make an estimate of the number of domestic immigrants to the north-west, as none of the railroads have prepared any data from which any figure could be estimated. In former years, however, the proportion has been three domestic to one foreign immigrant, and it is fair to presume that such a proportion was maintained last year. From this there appears to have been a falling off to the extent of about 25 per cent. last year in the aggregate immigration, the Germans alone keeping up their reputation as immigrants.

The increase in the assessed valuation of real and personal property has been about 25 per cent. within two years, and 50 per cent. since 1880, as appears from the following statement of property valuation, as fixed by the Minnesota State Board of Equalisation:—

		Dollars.
Valuation for 1880	.. .. ..	268,517,736
,, 1881	.. .. ..	283,277,386
,, 1882	.. .. ..	322,157,615
,, 1883	.. .. ..	348,603,486
,, 1884	.. .. ..	401,028,587

This showing will be accepted as evidence that the State is making substantial progress.

During the year the iron mines in the Lake Vermillion dstrict of Minnesota commenced their output, and the reported discovery of paying quantities of gold near Duluth has caused a rush of emigration to that point. Tin in large quantities has been discovered in the Black Hills in Dakota, and wells have been sunk in both Dakota and Minnesota, from which a steady and abundant flow of natural gas has been obtained. The output of bituminous and lignite coal in portions of Dakota is largely increasing, and is becoming a standard article of commerce in that territory. Gypsum is now being manufactured in large quantities in the Black Hills in Dakota, and a cement claimed to be equal in strength to Portland cement is being very largely manufactured at Mankato, in Minnesota. The precious metals are still largely mined in Dakota, and the yield of the principal mines in the territory of Montana, situated to the west of Dakota and tributary to St. Paul and Minneapolis, for the first 10 months of 1884, was 4,994,284 dol.

The manufacture of lumber takes a prominent place among the industries of the North-west. The total cut in 1884 in the North-western lumber region (which includes Northern and Eastern Minnesota and Western Wisconsin) was 2,534,298,361 feet of lumber, 1,059,354,300 shingles, and 630,090,780 lath—an increase over the cut of 1883 of 447,811,966 feet of lumber, 202,994,030 shingles, and 85,799,850 lath. The stock on hand December 1 aggregated 1,795,708,522 feet of lumber, 424,998,406 shingles, and 310,276,900 lath; an increase over the total of December 1, 1883, of 600,078,686 feet of lumber, 50,011,556 shingles, and 199,513,700 lath. The anticipated log supply from this winter's operations is placed at 2,619,866,000 feet, of which 1,522,500,000 represent new logs.

Public Works.—From the report of the Commissioners appointed by the State of Minnesota to examine and report upon the improvement of the Mississippi river, and other rivers and harbours in Minnesota, I learn that 2,538,000 dol. were expended during the last 10 years for public improvement on Minnesota rivers and harbours.

In railroad construction in 1884, Minnesota and Iowa added to their mileage 279 miles each, and Dakota 269 miles. No other States built so many miles of road, Pennsylvania approaching the nearest, having built 252 miles. The mileage here given is taken from the "Railway Age," and, I think, includes side tracks and spurs. The State Commissioner of Railroads, in his annual report, states that 256·84 miles of railway were added to the mileage of the State in 1884, as against only 137·45 miles of new line in 1883. In the country tributary to St. Paul and Minneapolis, within the last year 1,033 miles of railroad were built, while in 1883 1,219 miles, and in 1882 2,400 miles were built. Nearly 30 per cent. of all the new road constructed in the country in 1884 was built in the North-west, as against about 22 per cent. in 1883, and about 25 per cent. in 1882. The total expenditure on railroad construction in this territory for the year 1884 was 21,603,716 dol.

General Remarks.—The biennial report of the State Superintendent of Public Instruction shows an enrolment of 223 undergraduates at the University of Minnesota in 1882-3, and 279 in 1883-4. In the 49 high schools located in 33 counties there are 2,343 pupils. The permanent school fund, July 31, 1883, amounted to 5,779,930 dol. 35 c., and July 31, 1884, to 6,246,321 dol. 15 c. The permanent University fund was 644,731 dol. 71 c. in 1883, and 663,630 dol. 25 c. in 1884.

Trade and Commerce.

The following is a statement of the transactions of the Custom-house at St. Paul for the year 1884, as well as the receipts for the past five years:—

ST. PAUL.

Months.	1884.		1883.		1882.		1881.		1880.		1879.	
	Dol.	c.	Dol.	c.	Dol.	c.	Dol.	c.	Dol.	c.	Dol.	c.
January	7,143	96	3,631	36	2,009	37	1,711	90	1,025	97	489	64
February	4,046	35	7,337	41	4,022	65	3,847	55	831	25	155	35
March	4,081	25	6,070	21	2,740	60	1,126	96	942	30	705	28
April	7,202	18	2,500	31	3,512	49	2,471	37	1,194	66	575	96
May	3,396	16	4,972	57	1,442	17	3,570	65	940	24	1,139	28
June	2,533	48	3,782	74	3,468	68	2,324	67	1,104	58	1,213	60
July	4,383	59	8,520	75	2,843	75	4,466	53	2,010	57	1,597	91
August	12,350	61	7,951	28	7,792	96	1,257	20	1,560	67	1,082	35
September	9,370	78	9,630	86	5,129	09	3,582	26	3,040	25	1,064	13
October	2,519	30	3,233	07	3,434	45	754	96	1,289	55	1,175	25
November	4,009	18	3,010	08	5,477	50	3,581	78	1,806	01	1,851	54
December	2,812	11	3,375	42	3,574	57	2,114	02	1,042	58	771	27
Total	63,848	95	64,016	06	45,248	28	30,809	85	16,788	63	11,821	56

A recent report to the Secretary of the Treasury from Special Agent Martin shows the following as the value of merchandise imported directly, without appraisement to the principal interior cities of the country during the year ending June 30, 1883, where duties are assessed and collected.

	Dol.
Chicago	8,950,044
St. Louis	2,600,248
Cincinnati	1,810,826
Buffalo	512,645
Cleveland	378,434
Rochester	351,576
Milwaukee	341,408
Detroit	339,045
Louisville	257,151
St. Paul	201,022
Indianapolis	196,019
Kansas City	88,549
Denver	49,440
Toledo	24,263

At the St. Paul Custom-house 8,688 packages of goods were received upon which 55,771 dol. was collected in duties.

The statistics for 1884 of the Custom-house at Duluth, Minn., are as follows:—

ARRIVALS.

Countries.	From American Ports.			From Foreign (Canadian) Ports.		
	Number of Vessels.	Tonnage.	Number of Men.	Number of Vessels.	Tonnage.	Number of Men.
American	625	489,087	12,852	109	12,045	1,181
Foreign	..	..	..	163	81,296	3,348

CLEARANCES.

Countries.	To American Ports.			To Foreign (Canadian) Ports.		
	Number of Vessels.	Tonnage.	Number of Men.	Number of Vessels.	Tonnage.	Number of Men.
American	633	499,869	12,607	107	11,577	1,231
Foreign	..	..	..	164	82,251	3,405

UNITED STATES.

IMPORTS AND EXPORTS—PORT OF DULUTH, 1884.

	Duties.	Value.
	Dol.　c.	Dol.
Imported commodities from foreign countries..	..	14,977
Commodities from foreign countries for transit and transhipment to other foreign countries	8,501　34	18,822
Exported foreign commodities to foreign countries ..	..	333
Exported domestic commodities to foreign countries ..	..	763,033

The wheat receipts from Duluth for the lake season were as foll by months:—

	Bushels.
May	1,562,440·20
June	670,420·40
July	936,471·50
August	440,891·00
September	2,039,736·10
October	3,147,226·50
November	2,300,313·00
Total	11,097,499·50

During the same time there were 350,000 bushels shipped by rail, making the total shipments for the season 11,447,499·50 bushels, against 6,313,645·10 the previous year, being an increase in shipments of 5,133,854 bushels. The total receipts of the crop of 1884 up to January, 1885, were 10,637,276 bushels, and of this amount 7,847,276 were shipped, leaving 3,150,000 bushels in store.

The internal revenue collections of the Minnesota district for the year 1884 were:—

	Dol.　c.
Miscellaneous	3,554　66
Beer stamps	260,113　99
Cigars and tobacco	87,673　43
Special taxes	140,020　71
Total	491,462　79

DOMESTIC TRADE.

The bulk of trade and commerce of the State of Minnesota is transacted in the cities of St. Paul and Minneapolis; in fact, the amount of trade done at other points is so small that it will be a waste of time to attempt to classify it. I will therefore give only a general description of outlying cities and villages, and enumerate more particularly the trade of St. Paul and Minneapolis. The eastern boundary of the latter city is now conterminous with the western boundary of the former, and for all practical purposes of growth exhibit they form one city. Of course, there are preponderances in each case. In the grain and commission combination, Minneapolis, owing to its immense milling interests, has 50,000,000 dol., representing chiefly the various transactions in wheat before reaching the mills, against St. Paul's 8,000,000 dol., which represents simply the sales of wheat for shipment, while in bank exchange St. Paul shows 108,000,000 dol. to 34,000,000 dol. for the sister city. But the 4,700 new structures, costing nearly 15,000,000 dol., the many miles of streets, sewers, sidewalks, &c., may be grouped in perfect fairness. Following are the combined results of 1884:—

Assessed valuation of city property	136,000,000 dol.
Number of residences erected	3,880
Number of business and public buildings	844
Total number of buildings erected	4,724
Value of buildings erected	14,888,427 dol.
Miles of new streets graded	29·6
Miles of sewers laid	10·9
Miles of conduits and water mains	34⅔
Miles of sidewalk laid	55
Miles of tramway track laid	26¼
Miles of new railway tributary	1,037
Value of local railway improvements	2,146,247 dol.
Number of new business firms	1,712
Volume of straight jobbing trade	106,278,992 dol.
Amount grain and commission trade	58,356,000 ,,
Banking capital	12,383,000 ,,
Bank exchange	143,462,365 ,,
Real estate transfer transactions	33,367,964 ,,

St. Paul.

It has been a matter of surprised comment among business men in this city that, despite what are generally accepted as hard times, the ratio of growth over previous years is almost universally kept up. The statistics of the jobbing trade show an increase, though certainly not so decided as in previous years. Although the record does not furnish any grounds for elation in the business community, the merchants, as a rule, appear to be very well satisfied with the outcome of the year's dealings. In the face of a depreciation in values, which has been general, and has brought the prices of goods in many leading lines down to figures that have never before been touched in the history of the wholesale trade of St. Paul, there has been an increase in the aggregate money value of the goods handled, as compared with last year's figures, amounting to 2,780,929 dol. It is the opinion of all the leading dealers that, while the money value of the goods handled is less than last year, the quantity of goods—by themselves considered—is fully as large, if not larger, than in 1883. This opinion is freely expressed. Several of the leading lines show a monetary decrease, but it is owing, in every case, almost wholly to the great depreciation which has taken place in prices. Trade has been severely depressed all over the country, and the excitement and uncertainty begotten of a Presidential contest have added to the general suspense and demoralisation. St. Paul has necessarily shared somewhat in the general depression, but it is doubtful if there is a city in the country that has been less affected. Again, there has been in the North-west the local factor of the low price of wheat in addition to the general influence entering into the situation. This has had some effect on the country trade, and, by reflection, on the business of the city. Still, taken with all the other factors, it has not proved powerful enough to carry the volume of goods handled below last year's showing. There has been a tendency to growth in spite of all adverse circumstances, on account of the setting up of new territory at the West.

The following figures for the wholesale trade of St. Paul have been prepared by the Secretary of the Chamber of Commerce:—

Wholesale Business.	Number of Establishments.	Number of Employés.	Amount of Sales, 1884.	Increase over 1883.
			Dollars.	Dollars.
Agricultural implements	8	148	2,550,000	..
Barrels	7	68	94,400	..
Blank books, paper, and church goods	11	90	1,000,000	..
Beer	14	168	1,114,000	..
Boots and shoes	6	116	3,275,000	365,000
Brewers' supplies	3	26	231,800	..
Bricks and tiles	16	275	300,000	..
Cigars and tobacco	33	65	1,343,000	76,000
Clothing	3	73	900,000	75,000
Coffees, teas, spices, &c.	3	92	595,000	..
Confectionery and bakers' products	4	142	696,500	..
Crockery and glassware	4	59	517,000	38,000
Drugs, paints, and oils	11	223	3,717,200	1,217,200
Dry goods	6	518	8,915,000	..
Fuel and pig iron	17	484	4,607,800	..
Furniture	7	75	460,000	..
Fruits	3	25	395,000	..
Grain, flour, feed, and commission	53	147	7,931,000	1,631,000
Groceries	10	404	11,565,000	..
Guns and sporting goods	2	22	162,000	52,000
Hardware, stoves, and heavy iron	14	278	3,400,000	..
Hats, caps, and furs	6	132	1,404,000	154,000
Hides and furs	6	67	742,000	25,400
Jewellery	7	27	207,000	128,500
Junk	3	34	87,000	..
Leather saddlery and findings	6	99	1,017,000	36,000
Lime and cement	3	10	128,000	..
Live stock	2	28	1,040,000	..
Lumber	21	684	3,714,000	54,000
Machinery and mill supplies	14	263	1,460,000	152,000
Millinery and lace goods	3	58	385,000	..
Musical instruments	7	64	408,000	..
Notions, toys, and hosiery	9	116	820,000	..
Printing materials	2	21	224,000	43,000
Provisions and dressed meats	12	340	3,710,000	2,397,000
Sash, doors, and blinds	6	153	726,000	..
Trunks and valises	2	16	200,000	..
Waggons and carriages	3	45	71,000	..
Wines and liquors	15	72	2,296,000	236,000
Miscellaneous*	34	333	2,421,000	..
Total	396	6,060	74,829,700	6,652,100

Nett increase over 1883, 2,780,929 dol.

* Miscellaneous includes bar supplies, billiard tables, brooms, brushes, carpets, fireworks, fish, ice, mantels and grates, mineral waters, photographic materials, rubber goods, safes, seeds, soap, stoneware, tailors' trimmings, undertakers' goods, vinegar, wooden and willow ware.

The difference between the apparent and real increase.

MINNEAPOLIS.

The past year has not been one of large increase in the jobbing trade of Minneapolis. Probably no one conversant with the depression, which has prevailed throughout the country anticipated any kind of an increase. All classes of goods entering into the straight jobbing trade shrunk in value from 10 to 15 per cent. The merchant, therefore, who has sold 2,000,000 dol. worth of goods this year, as he did last, has been called upon to put out from 10 to 15 per cent. more goods. A comparison with the tabulated statement of the preceding year shows that commodities, such as dry goods, groceries, drugs, and hardware have kept very even pace with the business of the year before. There has been some increase in the trade in dry goods and drugs, but in the articles of luxury there has been a falling off, and in many other lines there has been a diminution, traceable to one cause or another.

STILLWATER.

Stillwater is "a city set upon a hill," at the head of Lake St. Croix, an hour's ride from St. Paul or Minneapolis, in one of the most productive regions of the State, possessing numerous facilities for trade. From the days of the old pioneers of the St. Croix Valley to the present time, Stillwater has been one of the centres of the lumber trade of Minnesota, as it is a natural distributing point for all the logs cut on the numerous tributaries of the St. Croix river. The amount of capital invested by the different lumbermen in mills is computed at about 1,200,000 dol. The 10 mills have a daily capacity of 1,029,000 feet, and during the season just closed cut 143,000,000 feet of lumber, 16,000,000 laths, and 9,100,000 shingles. In 1884, 287,224,770 feet of logs were scaled at this point, while the yearly cut probably reached 300,000,000 feet.

The following will serve to give a general idea of the business done in the city during 1884:—

SALES.

	Dollars.
Dry goods	300,000
Groceries	275,000
Clothing	200,000
Boots and shoes	100,000
Hardware	300,000
Other branches (not including milling)	900,000
Total	2,075,000

The banking interest is represented in Stillwater by the First National and the Lumbermen's National Banks. Each has a paid-up capital of 250,000 dol., and a surplus fund of 60,000 dol. and 50,000 dol. respectively.

Principal Cities of Minnesota.

Name.	County.	Population.	Manufacturing Industries.	Assessed Valuation. Real Estate.	Assessed Valuation. Personal Property.	Remarks.
Albert Lea	Freeborn	3,000	Flour, beer, waggons, and brick	Dollars. 403,800	Dollars. 118,723	Improved farm lands in vicinity are valued at from 25 dol. to 40 dol. per acre, and wild lands from 15 dol. to 25 dol. This is a favourite watering-place, and a headquarters for sportsmen.
Alexandria	Douglas	3,000	Flour, woollen goods, butter, cheese and other farm products, beer, and brick	...	...	The surrounding country is very rich for stock-raising, and large quantities of stock are shipped from this point. There is a good water-power here, and a wood-pulp and straw-paper mill would do well.
Anoka	Anoka	6,000	Flour, lumber, and brick	887,660	641,790	Good water-power, considerably improved. Annual trade of city exceeds 1,000,000 dol.
Austin	Mower	3,000	Flour and feed, butter, cheese, canned goods, waggons, and carriages	399,092	223,819	
Brainerd	Crow Wing	13,000	Lumber, bricks, flour, and beer	1,420,165	400,949	Hard woods and iron are found in vicinity.
Crookston	Polk	5,000	Waggons, lumber, flour, and beer	...	...	United States Land Office and County Seat are located here. There is a good water-power, slightly developed.
Duluth	St. Louis	15,000	...	...	...	The principal port of Minnesota is on Lake Superior. Wheat shipments from this point, in 1883, amounted to 7,655,438 bushels. Gold, silver, iron, and copper are found in the vicinity; very little, however, of the first-named.
Faribault	Rice	7,000	Flour, furniture, woollen goods, blankets, syrup, honey, iron industries, waggons and carriages, and stone and marble works	1,189,732	892,357	The flour manufactured in 1884 was valued at 1,000,000 dol. There is an excellent unimproved water-power. Land in the vicinity is valued at from 15 dol. to 40 dol., according to improvements.
Fergus Falls	Otter Tail	7,500	Flour, lumber, and building paper	...	...	There is one of the best water-powers in the west at this point. A United States Land Office is located here. The country around is noted for its wheat farms.
Hastings	Dakota	4,000	Flour, beer, lumber, furniture, and iron works	647,409	571,230	Has a good water-power.
Lake City	Wabasha	3,500	Flour, lumber, agricultural implements, and furniture, and also some wholesale or jobbing trade	341,177	238,211	

Principal Cities of Minnesota—continued.

Name.	County.	Population.	Manufacturing Industries.	Assessed Valuation. Real Estate.	Assessed Valuation. Personal Property.	Remarks.
				Dollars.	Dollars.	
Mankato	Blue Earth	...	Flour, butter, beer, linseed oil, and brick	1,488,373	497,050	Has large creameries and extensive stone quarries.
Minneapolis	Hennepin	110,000	See elsewhere	...	...	
Moorhead	Clay	5,000	Flour, beer, lumber, brick, and car and agricultural machinery	656,872	190,112	Situated at the head of navigation of the Red River of the North.
Northfield	Rice	3,030	Flour and lumber	634,117	456,757	Has good water-power.
Owatonna	Steele	4,000	Flour, agricultural implements, waggons, stone, brick, and butter	632,249	414,735	There are several good mineral springs in the vicinity.
Rochester	Olmsted	5,500	Flour, lumber, furniture, butter, canned goods, patent medicines, and waggons	994,295	661,995	Land in vicinity ranges in price from 15 dol. to 20 dol. per acre for wild land, and from 30 dol. to 50 dol. for improved.
Red Wing	Goodhue	7,000	Flour, lumber, furniture, stoneware, waggons and carriages, machinery, brick, sugar, and agricultural implements	1,280,791	793,300	White sand suitable for the manufacture of plate glass is found in abundance at this point.
St. Paul	Ramsey	108,000	See elsewhere	...	...	
Stillwater	Washington	15,000	Lumber, carriages and waggons, flour, railway carriages, machinery, and beer	...	...	An annual business of over 5,000,000 dol. is transacted in this city.
St. Cloud	Stearns	6,000	Flour, lumber, waggons and carriages, brick, marble, and agricultural implements	1,194,212	412,433	Has a good water-power, now being improved, and large granite quarries are situated in the vicinity.
St. Peter	Nicollet	4,000	Furniture, cigars, flour, butter, vinegar, beer, stone, and brick	...	...	
Sauk Centre	Stearns	2,700	Furniture, carriages, lumber, and flour	213,614	157,719	
Wabasha	Wabasha	3,300	Flour, lumber, iron and agricultural implements, and furniture	350,794	148,244	
Waseca	Waseca	3,000	Flour, lumber, waggons, furniture, brick, butter, and agricultural implements	255,510	139,345	Annual retail business estimated at 310,000 dol.
Winona	Winona	17,000	Lumber, flour, agricultural implements, paper, cotton, wool, boots and shoes, leather, linseed oil, sewing machines, watches, and canned meats	...	...	Value of sales in 1883, 12,136,936 dol.; banking business in 1883, 2,193,438 dol.; building improvements in 1883, 794,256 dol.

Principal Villages of Minnesota.

Name.	County.	Population.	Assessed Valuation. Real Estate.	Assessed Valuation. Personal Property.	Value of Land in Vicinity per Acre. Unimproved.	Value of Land in Vicinity per Acre. Improved.	Manufacturing Industries.	Remarks.
			Dollars.	Dollars.	Dollars.	Dollars.		
Ada	Norman	1,000	88,982	121,832	...	...	Flour and lumber.	County seat.
Aitken	Aitken	1,300	...	...	...	...	,,	...
Appleton	Swift	600	...	...	...	...	,,	Good unimproved water-power.
Argyle	Marshall	500	...	...	...	...	,,	...
Belle Plaine	Scott	1,000	...	...	...	...	Flour.	...
Benson	Swift	800	...	...	...	...	,, butter, and woollen goods.	...
Bird Island	Renville	600	...	...	...	...		...
Blooming Prairie	Steele	500	84,527	51,966	...	...	,,	Stock-raising is carried on largely at this point.
Blue Earth City	Faribault	1,500	157,319	176,763	...	...	Flour, brick.	...
Breckenridge	Wilkin	800	121,200	60,133	...	...	,,	Good unimproved water-power.
Brown's Valley	Traverse	600	...	...	...	...	,,	...
Caledonia	Houston	1,000	98,404	170,199	...	...	Flour and lumber	Good water-power.
Cannon River Falls	Goodhue	1,600	87,583	60,624	10 to 35	...	,, lumber, and brick.	...
Carmen	Polk	500	...	...	...	...	,, and brick	This is a large brick shipping point.
Carver	Carver	800	43,810	48,911	...	...	,, brick, and stone	Large quantities of brick shipped from here.
Chaska	Carver	1,400	61,709	75,426	8 to 16	20 to 40	,, and woollen goods.	Has extensive water-power.
Chatfield	Fillmore	1,500	96,319	124,407	...	...	Lumber and woollen goods.	...
Dassel	Meeker	500	...	...	...	...		Good unimproved water-power.
Delano	Wright	800	...	...	...	...	Flour	...
Detroit	Becker	1,500	90,386	102,184	...	...	Butter and waggons.	Two mineral springs near here.
Dodge Centre	Dodge	800	50,525	...	10 to 40	...	Flour, lumber...	Extensive water-power. Would make a good point for manufacture of wooden ware.
Dundas	Rice	900	88,150	36,208	...	...		Excellent water-power.
Elk River	Sherbourne	1,200	...	...	...	...	,, and lumber	
Excelsior	Hennepin	500	...	...	...	...	,, and staves.	
Eyota	Olmsted	400	52,300	29,961	...	...	Grain, pork, and live hogs	Annual business, 385,000 dols.
Fairmont	Martin	1,000	126,714	75,280	...	...	Flour, butter, cheese.	...
Farmington	Dakota	1,000	77,700	87,629	...	...	Feed and butter.	...
Glencoe	McLeod	1,500	...	...	...	...	Lumber.	...
Glenwood	Pope	500	42,909	55,456	...	...	Flour.	...
Glyndon	Clay	900	656,872	190,112	...	...	Flour and lumber.	...
Graceville	Big Stone	500	...	...	...	...	,, butter.	...
Grand Meadow	Mower	500	53,265	32,752	...	...	Butter.	...
Granite Falls	Yellow Medicine	1,250	...	...	...	...	Flour, waggons	Large water-power.
Hancock	Stevens	400	...	...	...	...		...

Principal Villages of Minnesota—continued.

Name.	County.	Population.	Assessed Valuation. Real Estate.	Assessed Valuation. Personal Property.	Value of Land in Vicinity per Acre. Unimproved.	Value of Land in Vicinity per Acre. Improved.	Manufacturing Industries.	Remarks.
			Dollars.	Dollars.	Dollars.	Dollars.		
Henderson	Sibley	1,100	144,010		...	...	Flour and agricultural implements.	...
Hokah	Houston	900	66,772	23,996	...	...	,, and butter	...
Houston	Wright	800	49,219	38,930	3 to 12	20 to 50	,, ,, ,,	Annual business, 250,000 dol.
Howard	McLeod	600	...	...	...	...	,, and lumber	...
Hutchinson	Jackson	1,000	...	...	...	...	,, and beer.	Good water-power.
Jackson	Waseca	...	63,471	32,604	...	...	,, hardwood, lumber, and brick	Retail annual business, 300,000 dol.
Janesville	Scott	1,300	72,583	263,223	...	...	,, brick, beer	Good water-power.
Jordan	Dodge	1,400	55,050	...	...	...	Butter, cheese, sash and doors, waggons	Annual business, 500,000 dol. Good brick clay near.
Kasson		1,200	141,795		10 to 60			
Lanesborough	Fillmore	1,200	105,142	121,808	8 to 10	20 to 40	...	...
Le Roy	Mower	1,200	33,100	35,000	...	...	Flour and brick	...
Le Sueur	Le Sueur	2,000	...	...	...	...	,, waggons, lumber, brick	Annual mercantile business, 450,000 dol.
Litchfield	Meeker	1,800	294,620	219,772	...	...	Lumber	1,000,000 bushels of wheat shipped annually.
Little Falls	Morrison	2,000	164,790	72,922	...	...	Flour and lumber.	Good water-power.
Long Prairie	Todd	700	...	...	...	...	...	
Lu Verne	Rock	1,500	...	...	...	...	,, cheese, beer.	
Madelia	Wantonwan	700	...	...	...	...	Beer and stone.	
Mantorville	Dodge	600	...	...	...	...	...	
Marshall	Lyon	1,200	...	...	...	...	Flour	Good water-power.
Melrose	Stearns	550	...	...	...	...	Butter	
Montevideo	Chippewa	1,100	...	...	...	...	Flour, brick	Good water-power. Large stock farms in vicinity.
Morris	Stevens	1,200	172,327	135,182	...	...	...	
Morristown	Rice	500	...	...	...	...	,, butter, barrels, feed, lumber and sugar	...
New Richland	Waseca	500	31,770	24,689	...	...	,, lumber, beer, brick, vinegar	A very thriving place.
New Ulm	Brown	3,500	292,708	180,929	...	...	Stone	County seat.
Ortonville	Big Stone	1,000	...	...	...	...	Flour, lumber.	
Osakis	Douglas	600	...	...	...	...	,, ,,	Good water power.
Perham	Otter Tail	750	...	...	...	...	Lumber	Large lumber mills. Good unimproved water-power.
Pine City	Pine	800	18,057	44,076	...	...		
Pine Island	Goodhue	850	24,511	89,017	...	...	Flour and lumber.	Business estimated at 150,000 dols. per annum.

Principal Villages of Minnesota—continued.

Name.	County.	Population.	Assessed Valuation. Real Estate.	Assessed Valuation. Personal Property.	Value of Land in Vicinity per Acre. Unimproved.	Value of Land in Vicinity per Acre. Improved.	Manufacturing Industries.	Remarks.
			Dollars.	Dollars.	Dollars	Dollars.		
Plainview	Wabasha	900	62,277	134,603	20 to	50	Creamery and small factories.	Yearly business about 500,000 dols.
Preston	Filmore	1,200	104,180	132,741	20 to	30	...	...
Princeton	Mille Lacs	1,500	...	...	...	...	Flour, lumber	Good water-power.
Red Lake Falls	Polk	1,250	...	...	...	...	,, lumber, honey	Apiary of 75 hives, yielding 4,500 lbs. of honey yearly.
Redwood Falls	Redwood	1,200	...	...	...	...		
Reeds Landing	Wabasha	600	37,890	26,512	...	...	Lumber.	...
Bush City	Chicago	...	42,469	45,251	8 to	40	...	...
Rushford	Fillmore	1,400	168,706	65,008	10 to	50	Agricultural implements and flour.	...
St. Charles	Winona	1,250	...	...	12 to 25	20 to 40	Creamery and flax.	...
St. James	Watonwan	600	72,543	21,448	...	...	Beer and brick	Large business, with British possessions north.
St. Vincent	Kittson	...	168,213	43,042	...	...	Flour, cheese	Good water-power.
Sauk Rapids	Benton	750	155,901	...	...	...	,, waggons, iron, brass, lime, and brick	Annual business, 855,000 dols.
Shakopee	Scott	2,000					,, and machinery.	
Sleepy Eye	Brown	1,800	147,960	83,366	...	...	Furniture and small manufactures.	...
Spring Valley	Fillmore	1,300	157,495	138,392	...	...	Lumber.	...
Taylor's Falls	Chicago	1,000	85,276	93,469	5 to 15	20 to 40		Mining settlement.
Tower	St. Louis	2,000	...	...	...	...	,,	United States Land Office.
Tracy	Lyon	1,800	...	...	...	...	,,	Commodious docks.
Two Harbours	St. Louis	...	...	...	...	...	Flour	Good water-power. Lumbermen's local supply point.
Verndale	Wadena	600	...	...	...	...		
Waconia	Carver	500	...	...	...	...	,, lumber.	...
Wadena	Wadena	500	...	...	...	...	,,	...
Warren	Marshall	600	...	...	...	...	,,	Uninproved water-power.
Waterville	Le Sueur	800	57,629	35,600	...	...	lumber, furniture, and woollen goods	
Wells	Faribault	1,200	118,170	86,285	10 to 25	...	,, butter, vinegar, cheese.	Large lake. Summer resort.
White Bear	Ramsey	700	...	...	...	...	,,	...
Willmar	Kandiyohi	1,300	149,889	248,015	...	...	,, syrup, and creameries.	Annual shipments of cattle valued at 500,000 dols.
Windom	Cottonwood	700	...	...	...	...	,,	
Winnebago City	Faribault	1,200	...	...	...	...	,,	
Worthington	Nobles	1,500	...	...	...	...	,, and butter.	...

ST. PAUL.

Market Prices.

The relative condition of the farmers in the Red River Valley and Northern Dakota, as compared with their position a year ago, is now a subject of some inquiry, as it is asserted by some that the low price of wheat has reduced their ability to buy. Herewith are appended the figures charged for the several principal commodities in Moorhead in the autumn of 1882, when wheat was 80 c. per bushel, and now (1884) when wheat sells at 50 c :—

Articles.	Quantity.	1882.	1884.
		Dol. c.	Dol. c.
Best patent process flour	Per sack	3 75	2 25
Buckwheat flour	Per pound	0 08	0 05
Oatmeal	,,	0 07	0 05
Cornmeal	,,	0 03	0 02$\frac{1}{2}$
Ham	,,	0 18	0 15
Potatoes	Per bushel	0 75	0 30
Beans	Per pound	0 08	0 05
Eggs	Per dozen	0 35	0 25
Butter, best creamery	Per pound	0 45	0 35
Boneless codfish	,,	0 12$\frac{1}{4}$	0 10
Venegar, best	Per gallon	0 50	0 40
Carbon oil, best	,,	0 30	0 20
Pickles, best	,,	0 50	0 30
Cut-loaf sugar	Per pound	0 14	0 10
Granulated sugar	,,	0 12$\frac{1}{4}$	0 08
Best Rio coffee	,,	0 20	0 15
Best O.G. Java coffee	,,	0 40	0 35
Best roasted coffee	,,	0 25	0 20
Best basket F. Japan tea	,,	1 00	0 75
Best Japan tea	,,	0 75	0 50
Japan tea	,,	0 25	0 20
Apples, green	Per package	0 75	0 40
Larger raisins	Per pound	0 25	0 20
Currants	,,	0 10	0 07
Raspberries	,,	0 45	0 40
Alden apples		0 20	0 12$\frac{1}{2}$
Corn	Per can	0 20	0 12$\frac{1}{2}$
Tomatoes	,,	0 20	0 12$\frac{1}{2}$
Peaches	,,	0 30	0 20
Fall apples	,,	0 50	0 35
California fruit	,,	0 35	0 35
Fancy soda biscuits	Per pound	0 12$\frac{1}{3}$	0 10
Oyster pearl biscuits	,,	0 10	0 08
Washing powder	Per package	0 15	0 10
Matches	Per box	0 08$\frac{1}{3}$	0 02$\frac{1}{4}$
Chow-chow	Large bottles	0 90	0 75
Nutmegs	Per pound	1 25	0 75
Cloves	,,	0 75	0 39
Cinnamon	,,	0 60	0 40
Ginger	,,	0 40	0 30
Pepper	,,	0 40	0 25
Pepper	Per box	0 15	1 10
		18 89$\frac{7}{8}$	12 60$\frac{1}{4}$

Percentage of former price, 66$\frac{3}{8}$.

The above table shows that while a few of the articles show great reductions, the aggregate shrinkage is 33$\frac{1}{3}$ per cent. on all the articles considered together. According to these figures, everything else being equal, a bushel of wheat now at 50 c. has as much purchasing power as a bushel of the same commodity had in 1882 at 80 c. per bushel. While it is possible the same comparison would not hold out regarding other articles, as of dress, &c., inquiry shows that it will at least approximate the figures on provisions.

Trade Laws.

During the first two months of 1885 the State Legislature met in regular biennial session. The most important laws passed were those regulating railway companies, and the warehousing and inspection of grain. Of the former, the provisions relied on to open a free market to the farmer are sections 15 and 16. The former requires every railroad company to permit any person or company, for an annual rental of one dollar, to construct, maintain, and operate any elevator or warehouse at any of its regular way stations, to be used for the purpose of receiving, storing, and handling grain—and this without regard to the capacity of such elevator, and without discrimination as to persons, and in the order of application—and that such railway company shall provide reasonable track facilities and running connections between its main track and such elevators or warehouses on its own land, &c. Such warehouses shall not be constructed within 100 feet of any existing structure, and shall be at a safe fire distance from the station buildings, &c. The latter section requires the company, upon reasonable demand, to furnish transportation for all grain stored in such elevators or offered for shipment in bulk or otherwise from any established side track at any regular station on its line, promptly, and without discrimination, &c. Appended to this report I give the full text of the two bills.

Banks.

Banking statistics of Minnesota (taken from the message of Governor Hubbard to the Legislature, January, 1885) are summarised as follows:—

	1884.	Increase since 1882.
Number of banks	214	36
Capital stock (149 banks)	15,904,754 dol.	6,553,537 dol.
Surplus fund (84 banks)	2,300,144 ,,	699,167 ,,
Deposits (86 banks)	27,284,117 ,,	4,573,812 ,,
Loans and discounts (86 banks)	37,572,756 ,,	10,425,432 ,,

Of the above banks, 48 are national, 32 State, 6 savings, and 128 private. The figures given being for less than one-half the banks of the State are not very satisfactory as showing the resources and liabilities of these institutions. The increase in the several items will indicate to some extent, however, their growth in business.

Shipping and Navigation.

The record of Duluth port for the year 1884 was a good one, showing a large increase over 1883 in the number of arrivals and clearances, the tonnage and freight receipts, and shipments. Navigation opened May 1, the first boat arriving May 2, and closed with the lower lakes about the 1st of December, and for local vessels about the third week in December. The arrivals and clearances by months were as follow:—

ST. PAUL.

ARRIVALS.

May	94
June	135
July	135
August	123
September	134
October	134
November	99
December	10
Total	887
Total, 1883	789
Increase	98
Total tonnage, 1884	583,328
,, ,, 1883	529,043
Increase	54,285

CLEARANCES.

May	104
June	130
July	148
August	128
September	128
October	149
November	111
December	5
Total	903
Total, 1883	784
Increase	129
Tonnage, 1884	583,673
,, 1883	520,834
Increase	62,842

Among the principal articles received by the lake were 95,000 bricks, 377,000 tons of coal, 141,948 barrels of cement, salt, lime, &c., 1,941 packages of crockery and glassware, 2,698 packages of furniture, 11,752 packages of groceries, 13,116 packages of hardware, 10,730 pieces of iron, 7,463 tons of steel rails, 1,481,000 feet of lumber, 15,836 packages of merchandise, 13,092 kegs of nails, &c., 34,066 cases of oil, 27,038 barrels of sugar, and 4,000,000 shingles. Among the shipments were 33,893 tons of ore and 13 cars of silver bullion, 60,000 brick, 414,435 barrels and 385,089 sacks of flour, 10,218 bundles of hides, 5,035,321 feet of lumber, 141,340 sacks of ore, 4,000 barrels of poultry, 6,315 sacks of wool, and 11,097,399 bushels of wheat.

The receipts of coal are a falling off of over 43,000 tons from 1883.

The harbour improvements cost about 44,000 dol., and greatly increased its conveniences. Vessels of the largest draught can now move about in it with ease.

UNITED STATES.

AGRICULTURE.

The State statistical agent of the United States Agricultural Department makes the following returns of acreage and product of the several crops of Minnesota, revised from the monthly reports:—

Crops.	Acres.	Bushels.
Corn	688,840	22,731,720
Wheat	2,780,539	44,488,624
Rye	27,542	578,382
Barley	301,410	8,618,524
Oats	1,027,509	41,293,742
Buckwheat	8,560	98,440
Potatoes	67,430	7,215,010
Hay	381,247	648,120*
Sorghum	4,726	463,148†

* Tons.   † Gallons.

The numbers and average values per head of farm animals in the State on January 1, 1885, were as follow:—

Animals.	Number.	Average Value.
		Dollars.
Horses	310,775	81·20
Mules and asses	10,450	93·78
Milch cows	352,748	28·99
All other cattle	361,947	23·88
Sheep	283,486	3·28
Swine	349,328	5·08

Total yield of all crops for the last six years:—

Crops.		1879.	1880.	1881.	1882.	1883.	1884.
							Estimated.
Wheat	Bushels	31,218,634	39,399,068	32,947,570	32,176,570	36,042,752	44,488,624
Oats	,,	20,667,933	22,867,932	21,954,126	26,480,842	30,934,393	41,293,742
Corn	,,	12,939,901	13,125,255	14,654,646	16,605,379	5,886,427	22,731,720
Barley	,,	2,423,932	2,751,638	4,215,715	6,109,140	5,770,946	8,618,524
Rye	,,	172,887	170,817	170,053	308,379	319,647	578,382
Buckwheat	,,	33,163	29,736	42,847	81,758	85,910	98,440
Potatoes	,,	3,915,890	3,782,243	3,997,187	5,074,736	7,113,813	7,215,010
Beans	,,	24,434	20,904	22,294	43,929	34,707	...
Sugar cane syrup	Gallons	446,946	662,837	684,066	509,634	159,261	463,148
Cultivated hay	Tons	194,994	175,595	227,432	269,925	417,099	648,120
Flaxseed	Bushels	99,378	397,190	435,517	762,117	826,281	...
Wild hay	Tons	1,200,506	1,263,472	1,261,089	1,564,597	1,617,307	...
Timothy seed	Bushels	39,376	60,940	96,214	200,809	281,744	...
Clover	,,	18,460	8,371	27,715	6,930	21,166	...
Apples	,,	124,261	147,803	158,058	176,038	120,736	...
Grapes	Lbs.	135,086	141,731	200,616	203,727	152,678	...
Tobacco	,,	65,089	48,437	79,631	62,859	14,744	...
Honey	,,	208,018	221,255	144,162	163,999	254,964	...
Maple syrup	Gallons	10,670	12,449	13,418	12,923	11,638	16,771
,, sugar	Lbs.	58,462	47,712	49,577	54,512	47,697	35,687
Butter	,,	15,638,069	15,693,283	16,052,020	17,136,788	20,525,357	...
Cheese	,,	586,448	417,994	522,456	335,793	615,497	...
Wool	,,	948,184	923,170	1,083,775	1,122,625	...	...
,, fall, 1883	,,	...	...	...	...	859,337	...
,, spring, 1884	,,	...	...	...	...	...	1,195,665

ST. PAUL.

Average bushels per acre of crops for the last eleven years:—

Crops.	1874.	1875.	1876.	1877.	1878.	1879.	1880.	1881.	1882.	1883.	1884. Estimated.
Wheat	14·23	17·05	9·61	16·78	12·50	11·30	13·30	11.42	13·81	14·37	16·00
Oats	28·61	34·38	23·04	32·19	38·65	36·42	33·49	30·14	34·44	34·65	40·28
Corn	28·64	24·81	25·84	23·47	34·90	33·95	31·07	30·91	26·42	11·10	33·00
Barley	21·17	30·15	22·70	26·37	26·95	24·87	23·21	21·40	23·73	21·76	28·59
Rye	12·15	16·42	14·21	14·38	15·99	14·98	13·89	12·99	15·81	15·46	21·00
Buckwheat	9·65	12·70	7·23	11·67	9·99	9·80	10·06	12·02	14·47	13·07	11·50
Beans	7·83	9·06	7·48	4·70	12·52	11·33	13·66	13·09	14·19	9·80	...
Potatoes	80·90	120·76	75·75	62·00	97·12	103·26	98·87	95·84	105·93	120·71	107·00

ACREAGE of the Principal Cultivated Crops for the last Seven Years.

Crops.	1878.	1879.	1880.	1881.	1882.	1883.	Estimated. 1884.
	Acres.	Acres.	Acres.	Acres.	Acres.	Acres.	Acres.
Wheat	2,365,775	2,762,521	2,961,842	2,884,160	2,329,969	2,507,209	2,780,539
Oats	474,557	567,371	682,520	728,367	769,133	892,649	1,027,509
Corn	324,174	379,776	422,461	474,030	628,512	530,220	688,840
Barley	55,423	96,951	118,488	196,917	257,385	265,207	301,410
Rye	13,813	11,534	12,312	13,091	19,500	20,666	27,542
Buckwheat	3,766	3,380	2,955	3,564	5,650	6,570	8,560
Potatoes	35,559	37,910	33,254	41,707	47,904	58,930	67,430
Beans	2,280	2,156	1,538	1,703	3,095	3,539	...
Sugar cane	3,207	5,033	6,914	7,396	6,192	3,834	4,726
Hay	121,228	145,150	135,722	171,512	198,183	286,951	381,247
Flax	2,183	12,966	40,004	73,649	79,547	70,880	...
Miscellaneous	27,199	18,336	24,844	19,685	22,605	39,080	...
Total	3,429,164	4,043,074	4,417,846	4,615,781	4,367,675	4,685,735	...
Increase over preceding year	444,510	613,910	404,772	167,935	...	318,060	...

The wheat crop of 1884, on an average, was considered much better in quality than the crop of 1883.

Farm animals are reported to have been in a healthy condition generally during the entire year. Several cases of glanders among horses were reported early in the season, and about the same time a few correspondents mentioned instances of sickness among cattle; but the latter were apparently slight disorders, as no reports of deaths resulting from them reached this office.

On the 1st of January, 1885, the number of horses of all ages in the State were reported to be 310,775, an increase of 23,735 during the year. The average value per head was placed at 81 dol. 20 c., making a total of 25,234,930 dol. This indicates a remarkable shrinkage in values of this kind of stock during the year. On January 1, 1884, the average value per head was reported to be 103 dol. 25 c. I thought at the time that that figure was from 8 to 10 dol. too high, and believe the one given for this year to be about as much too low. There has been some depreciation in values of this class of stock, but I do not believe that it will exceed 10 per cent.

The number of mules and asses reported this year was 10,450, being an increase of only 303 head, and the average value given per head was 93 dol. 78 c., or 18 dol. 22 c. per head less than on the preceding January 1st. My impression is that in this instance, also, last year's valuation was too high, and this year's is too low. The depreciation is more probably from 7 to 10 per cent.

There were 352,748 milch cows reported this year, at an average value of 29 dol., against 280,861 last year, at a valuation of 27 dol. per head; being an increase of 71,887 head and of 2 dol. per head in the value. Both of these results are easily accounted for by the circumstance that butter and chese manufacture, or dairy farming, as it is called, is rapidly becoming one of the most important branches of agriculture in this State; and there is good reason to believe that this will continue to grow in importance, because the demand for Minnesota butter is constantly and rapidly increasing, and the recent awards of the New Orleans World's Exposition of prize medals and premiums to the Minnesota butter exhibit will, most likely, tend to make this demand very much greater in the early future.

The total number of neat cattle, other than cows, reported on January 1st, was 361,947, and the average value given 23 dol. 38 c. per head. This is an increase of 34,838 head, and the average value per head reported for 1885 is 3 dol. 13 c. more than that given for 1884. The demand for Minnesota cattle, both for beef and for stocking ranches in Dakota and Montana, has been good throughout the year, and that for beef is growing continually.

The number of sheep reported on January 1, 1885, was 283,486, and the value per head 3 dol. 28 c.; and of hogs 349,328, at 5 dol. 8 c. per head. This indicates an increase of the former during the year of 18,094, and an increased value of 33 c. per head; and of the latter of 61,711, at a reduced value of 2 dol. 42 c. per head.

The total values of farm animals in the State, as reported to this office at the beginning of the current year, was as follows, viz.:—

	Dollars.
Horses	25,234,930
Mules and asses	973,001
Milch cows	10,229,692
Other neat cattle	8,462,521
Sheep	930,824
Hogs	1,774,426
Total	47,605,394

Population and Industries.

Mines.—Quite an excitement has been caused during the past year by the reported discovery of gold and silver in large quantities near Duluth, Minnesota. The gold discoveries are in townships 64, 65, 66, and 67, east of the fourth (surveyor's) meridian, the silver lying to the south. Assays are claimed to have been made giving from 40 dol. to 2,900 dol. gold to the ton, and silver assays from 200 dol. to 1,160 dol. per ton. How much sulphur is in the gold ore, or iron pyrites and copper in the silver, I am unable to state. The general feeling in St. Paul regarding the discoveries and assays is one of smiling incredulence.

ST. PAUL.

Factories.—The manufacturing exhibit of St. Paul is as follows:—

Manufactures, 1884.	Number of Establishments.	Number of Employés.	Value of Product, 1884.	Increase over 1883.
			Dollars.	Dollars.
Agricultural implements	2	375	725,000	..
Barrels	7	68	94,400	..
Blacksmiths and wheelwrights	30	94	98,000	42,000
Bookbinding	7	93	120,000	30,000
Boots and shoes	28	635	1,300,000	275,000
Brass works	4	25	51,600	..
Brewers and maltsters	12	185	945,000	30,377
Bricks and tiles	16	320	211,000	41,000
Brooms and brushes	6	44	61,000	5,500
Cigars	49	962	1,156,000	356,000
Clothing	81	1,500	1,879,000	..
Confectionery	7	78	197,000	..
Contractors and builders	153	4,111	5,023,000	76,000
Crackers and bakery products	30	300	947,000	..
Drugs, chemicals, and oils	5	122	575,000	170,000
Engraving	8	46	68,000	..
Flour and grist milling	5	71	1,296,000	..
Furniture and upholstery	9	138	173,000	..
Furs	8	199	435,000	9,000
Harness and saddlery	15	130	240,000	..
Iron, architectural	3	173	290,000	25,000
Jewellery and watches	13	38	62,000	9,600
Machinery, foundries and boilers	20	472	1,001,000	256,000
Marble and stone cutting	22	1,000	800,000	624,000
Millinery, lace, and fancy goods	18	120	109,000	12,000
Painting and glazing	45	270	290,000	65,000
Photography	14	40	72,000	9,000
Pictures and frames	4	19	35,000	10,000
Printing and publishing	33	1,200	1,800,000	102,000
Railroad repairs and car making	4	1,050	1,193,000	..
Slaughtering and meat packing	60	250	1,675,000	..
Sash, doors, boxes, and planing mills	11	322	506,000	22,000
Tin, hardware, stoves and plumbing	29	301	560,000	110,000
Trunks and valises	2	87	100,000	..
Waggons and carriages	19	311	1,000,000	388,000
Miscellaneous*	64	576	1,574,000	272,200
Total	843	15,725	26,662,000	776,520

* Miscellaneous includes awnings and tents, artificial limbs, boats, carpet weavers, carriage trimmers, cutlery grinding, dyeing, dry plates, fence works, fireproof building material, fireworks, hair goods, hoop and skirt factory, knit goods, lighting companies, lumber, mineral waters, musical instruments, nickel plating, optician, plastering, sewer and drain pipes, show cases, taxidermists, terra cotta lumber, type foundry, vinegar and catsup, and wine works.

Population.

During the year 1885 the State of Minnesota takes a census of the population. Until this is compiled, statistics of population are merely guesswork. The people of St. Paul claim to have now a population of 120,000, and Minneapolis claims 125,000. These figures, however, I would be inclined to reduce from 5,000 to 10,000.

Public Works.

Messrs. Platt B. Walker, of Minneapolis; E. W. Durant, of Stillwater; and William Crooks, of St. Paul, State Commissioners, appointed by Governor Hubbard to examine and report upon the improvement of the Mississippi river and other rivers and harbours in Minnesota, reported under date of December 25, 1884, and state that as far as possible the information is obtained from official sources. The following statement is taken from their report, and shows the amount of money expended in Minnesota during the last 10 years for public improvements on Minnesota rivers and harbours:—

	Amount Expended.	Amount Required to Complete.	Amount Required in 1885.
	Dollars.	Dollars.	Dollars.
Lake Superior	415,000	600,000	170,000
Mississippi River, above St. Anthony Falls	35,000	20,000	10,000
Chippewa River	110,000	100,000	55,000
St. Croix River	50,000	27,000	27,000
Reservoir system	418,367	1,225,000	50,000
St. Anthony Falls	400,000	75,000	50,000
Red River of the North	110,000	275,000	30,000
Mississippi River, below St. Paul	1,000,000	..	..

That the streams are worth the expenditure the Commission is well assured. The St. Croix river has three steamers and 25 barges engaged exclusively in the freight and passenger business. The Commission says: "There are no means by which the amount of tonnage moved on the Mississippi below St. Paul can be ascertained, but it is safe to assert that the tonnage on our rivers far exceeds that on all the railroads doing business in the State. This, of course, includes the movement of the immense quantities of logs and lumber produced upon the headwaters of the Mississippi and its tributaries."

While believing that the improvement of the Upper Mississippi—from St. Paul to Grafton, commenced in 1878—is in its infancy, the Commission thinks that great good has already been secured, the value of the improvements to lumbermen alone being incalculable.

Railroads.—The record of railroad building in the territory tributary to St. Paul and Minneapolis, within the last year, is given below. The North-west has built 1,033 miles of railroad in 1884, for 1,319 miles in 1883 and 2,400 in 1882. This means that it has built nearly 30 per cent. of all the new roads in the country this year, for about 22 per cent. in 1883 and about 25 per cent. in 1882. Thus, if the North-west is falling behind its own record, it is gaining upon the rest of the country.

The following table gives the amount of railroad building in the North-west tributary to St. Paul and Minneapolis:—

	Miles.	Cost.	Improvements.
		Dollars.	Dollars.
New trackage	1,033	15,428,011	3,395,705
New grading	327	2,780,000	..
Local improvements	..	..	2,146,247

Making a total expenditure of 21,603,716 dol. on railroad construction in the territory, apart from local improvements in St. Paul and Minneapolis.

The "Railway Age" gives the following record of railway contruction for the year 1884:—

States.	Miles.
Maine	41
New Hampshire	..
Vermont	4
Massachusetts	19
Rhode Island	..
Connecticut	11
New York	20
New Jersey	19
Pennsylvania	252
Delaware	24
Maryland and D. C.	17
West Virginia	70
Ohio	105
Indiana	29
Michigan	96
Illinois	40
Wisconsin	224
Virginia	118
Colorado	34
Montana	9
New Mexico	48
Utah	7
Wyoming	..
California	66
North Carolina	184
South Carolina	7
Georgia	111
Florida	153
Alabama	74
Mississippi	246
Tennessee	72
Kentucky	40
Minnesota	279
Iowa	279
Missouri	118
Arkansas	32
Louisiana	120
Dakota	269
Nebraska	79
Kansas	160
Indian territory	..
Texas	72
Nevada	..
Oregon	218
Arizona	5
Idaho	39
Washington territory	62

GENERAL REMARKS.

Meteorological.—A review of the weather, as observed and recorded at the United States Signal Office, St. Paul, Minn., during the year 1884, shows an annual mean temperature of 43·7°. The average of the last 14 years is 45·2°, consequently the year in question was 1·5° cooler than the average, and was much cooler than 1873, 1877, and 1878, and decidedly warmer in than 1883.

The total rainfall, included melted snow, for 1884 is 26·11 inches. The average for the last 14 years is 28·98.

90° was the highest temperature observed during the year; 1884 is the only year on record that the temperature did not go above 90°.

Insurance.—The fire and inland insurance business transacted in the State of Minnesota for the year 1884 was as follows:—

	American Companies.	Foreign Countries.	Township Mutuals.	Total.
	Dol. c.	Dol. c.	Dol. c.	Dol. c.
Risks written	157,284,613 00	36,923,376 00	1,863,364 00	196,071,353 00
Premiums received	2,093,082 40	434,398 31	11,611 38	2,539,092 09
Average premium rate	1 33	1 53	..	1 36
Losses paid	1,472,900 04	358,478 15	4,174 41	1,835,552 60
Losses incurred	1,548,919 35	334,887 78	4,753 41	1,888,560 54
Ratio of losses incurred to premiums received	0 74	0 77	0 41	0 75

St. Paul, April 11, 1885.

UNITED STATES.

Report on the Production of Borax in the United States.

No. 6.

Mr. West to Earl Granville.—(Received January 20.)

My Lord,   Washington, *January* 6, 1885.

I HAVE the honour to inclose to your Lordship herewith a Report on the production of borax in the United States.

I have, &c.
(Signed)   L. S. SACKVILLE WEST.

Inclosure in No. 6.

Report.

IT may be said in general terms that all California south of the Chon-chilla and Tresno region and east of the coast range, is a silver and borax region. Southern Nevada is much the same. The counties of Mono, Juyo, and San Bernardino, with part of San Diego, are the chief localities, though a remarkable line of borax deposits extends across Nevada from west of Humboldt Sink to Desert Wells and Fish Lake, 140 miles south-east. The first discovery of borax in California was made in 1856 near Red Bluff, in the northern part of the State. The first deposits, however, successfully worked, were those of the Borax and Hachinhama Lakes in Lake County, and 100 miles north of San Francisco. At present the supply comes from the more easily worked and richer deposits in the sandy deserts about Death Valley and south-east of Pyramid Lake in Nevada.

The first shipment of borax was made in 1864.

The crystals of borax in the mud were removed by the use of cofferdams, 4 feet square, and often nearly 1,000 lbs. were taken from one such space. In the deepest mud stratum the small crystals disappeared and immense ones, often 7 inches and 4 inches thick, were discovered.

These needed only solution and recrystallization to render them fit for market.

About 1868, operations ceased at Borax Lake, but continued at Hachinhama till 1873, producing annually 250,000 lbs. In 1866 the borax still remaining was estimated at 54,000,000 lbs.

In San Bernardino deposits of tincal and borated sands have attracted much attention. The product is of the finest quality, and its manufacture has been highly profitable. The marsh is 12 miles long and 8 miles wide, and is worked by several English and American Companies.

Borax minerals are found throughout this region in a great variety of forms, as native borax or tincal, as boratic acid, as ulexite or borate of lime, as pricute, pandermite and colemnite. Of all these the silky white balls of ulexite, often 1 foot in diameter, compressible, cotton-like, and similar to the Tarapacá produce, is the most attractive form.

The crude boraxes of the Pacific Coast are usually of high quality, but the chief problem is to economize labour and cost of transportation, and the effort is being made to produce the highly concentrated "boratic acid glass," 1 lb. of which is equal to 3 lbs. of common borax. The Basin of Nevada, in which the alkaline lakes or marshes of Mono, Owens, Walker, Carson, Humbolt, are situated, is covered in many parts with dry efflorescent salts, washed in the course of ages from the soda feldspar of the volcanic rocks and ridges of yellow lava which cover the country for miles. The waters of the lakes are heavy, appear like thin oil, smell like soap, possess great detersive qualities, are caustic as potash, and easily saponify.

Teel's Marsh, in Nevada, is the most productive borax field on the Pacific Coast, and its tincal deposit covers 10 square miles of surface. Dr. La Conte visited Rhode's Marsh in 1882, and found it to contain chemically pure common salt borax in three forms, sulphate of soda and carbonate of soda, all in great quantities, and within a space of 3 miles square.

Boracic acid is imported into the United States in large quantities, about 2,600,000 lbs. being consumed annually, nearly every pound of which was of Italian production. Since 1842 the duties have been as high as 20 per cent. The consumption of American produce is about 1,800,000 lbs. annually, and importation, therefore, may be said to have ceased. The total yield last year on the Pacific Coast was 2,800,000 lbs. The total product of the West for the last twenty years has been 41,809,785 lbs. The supply of borax is very large, and its price will probably remain close to the margin of cost. The price of simple borax has fluctuated greatly since 1864. It has been as high as 85 cents, and as low as $7\frac{1}{4}$ and 10 cents per pound. The demand is increasing both in the the United States and Great Britain, whose annual consumption reaches 25,000,000 lbs., supplied, it is said, chiefly from the Italian marshes. The supply from the Pacific Coast seems inexhaustible, but the difficulty of working it in the desert regions which yield the product is great, and as the market price nears the margin of the cost of production the industry cannot be highly remunerative.

(Signed)   L. S. SACKVILLE WEST.

No. 7.

Notes from the Reports of the Governors of the Territories of Idaho, Montana, Dakota, New Mexico, Arizona, and Alaska.

Idaho.

THE Territory of Idaho contains a population of 32,610, and comprises an area of 84,800 square miles.

The Revenue receipts for the year 1884 amounted to 32,146 dollars. The assessed valuation of real and personal property was 13,938,412 dollars, an increase of nearly 50 per cent. over the previous year.

This Territory is rich in mineral deposits, but many of the rich mining districts are idle. The mining laws are imperfect and there is a general lack of scientific knowledge.

The out-put of mineral wealth was 7,000,000 dollars.

The yields from all crops are generally abundant. Wheat last year yielded from 35 to 55 bushels to the acre; barley, 45; oats, 55; and potatoes, 250. Potatoes weighing 2 lbs. each are not uncommon, and cabbages weighing 15 lbs. each are often seen.

The Report says that a capital of 10,000,000 dollars is invested in stock-raising yielding a profit of 300 per cent.

There are 820 miles of railway completed.

Montana.

The Report gives the population at 84,000. The Territory has an area of 146,080 square miles, and is well calculated for stock-raising. It is estimated that there are 900,000 head of cattle.

The assessment list when completed will show between 50,000,000 and 60,000,000 of taxable property.

This Territory suffers much from Indian depredations.

Dakota.

This Territory has a population of 135,177 (1880), and its area is 149,100 square miles. The wheat crop last year is estimated at from 20,000,000 to 25,000,000 bushels; flax, 3,000,000 bushels; corn, 2,500,000 bushels; barley, 2,000,000 bushels; and oats, 10,000,000 bushels.

The region known as the Black Hills is rich in gold, silver, mica, lead, copper, and iron. The gold shipments for the year 1884 amounted to 4,500,000 dollars and silver, 2,000,000 dollars. This Territory is perhaps the richest and most thriving of the Territories, and is likely soon to obtain State rights.

New Mexico.

New Mexico has a population of 119,565 and an area of 122,580 square miles, and is chiefly adapted to stock-raising. It is estimated that there is 1,000,000 head of cattle and fully as many sheep. A great want of water exists, and the Report recommends a liberal appropriation to sink wells and build reservoirs. Ranches have no legally defined boundaries, and, there being equal right on the part of all to occupy the public lands, animals roam and graze in common. It is anticipated that trouble will ensue when the country becomes, as it must do sooner or later, overstocked. The administration of this Territory is attended with much difficulty.

Arizona.

Arizona has a population of 40,440 and an area of 113,020 square miles. The Report says that the population is steadily increasing, and that great progress is being made in mining, grazing, and agriculture.

The yield of wheat and barley per acre is from 25 to 35 bushels. Apples, peaches, pears, plums, figs, quinces, apricots, and every variety of fruit yield largely.

Sugar cane and cotton are also grown.

Land can be had at from 5 to 10 dollars per acre; improved land at from 15 to 30 dollars. Water is scarce also in this Territory.

Alaska.

Alaska has a population of 33,426 and an area of 577,390 square miles.

There are only 430 white persons in this Territory, the remaining portion being composed of Creoles, Innuites, Aleuts, Tinnehs, Thlinkets, and Hydas (see Census of 1880).

From the Report it would seem that the administration of this Territory is much neglected, and that proper measures are not taken for the development of its almost unknown resources.

The Alaska Seal and Fur Company carry on a most profitable trade under the protection of the Federal Government.

The fur seal islands are 1,500 miles to the westward of Sitka, and it may be presumed, therefore, that the Company carry on their operations much as they please. It is manifest that it is not the interest of a fur Company to civilize or develop the resources of their fur regions.

The Report points out that the boundary-line from Portland Canal to Mount St. Elias should be speedily and definitively determined by joint survey of the English and American Governments.

Report of the Utah Commission on Polygamy.

The Report says that since the passage of the Edmunds' Act, making polygamy illegal, 196 males and 263 females have adopted it.

During the year 1884 there appears to have been a polygamic revival.

The institution is boldly and defiantly defended and commended by the spiritual teachers, and plural marriages have increased. Three-fourths or more of the Mormon adults, male and female, have never entered into the polygamic relation: yet every orthodox Mormon, every member in good standing in the Church, believes in polygamy as a Divine revelation. Several trials have taken place under the Edmunds' Act, and although convictions were obtained, the proceedings showed the hold which polygamy has obtained.

At one trial for unlawful cohabitation, in order to empanel a jury, the question was asked of each juror under the Act:—

"Do you believe it right for a man to have more than one living and undivorced wife at the same time?" Each and every Mormon in the box answered, "Yes," so that the panel was completed by the selection of twelve non-Mormons. This trial, of course, resulted in a verdict of guilty.

The defendant in the case maintained that the Edmunds' Act was unconstitutional inasmuch as the Constitution of the United States expressly states that Congress shall make no law respecting the establishment of religion or prohibiting the free exercise thereof, and this view is in conformity with the sentiments of all the Mormon people.

The Report concludes by recommending measures for the better enforcement of the Act.

UNITED STATES.

Report by Consul Fonblanque on the World's Cotton Centennial Exhibition at New Orleans.

No. 5.

Consul Fonblanque to Earl Granville.—(Received March 17.)

My Lord, New Orleans, March 3, 1885.

I HAVE the honour to inclose a Report upon the World's Cotton Centennial Exposition.

I have, &c.
(Signed) A. DE G. DE FONBLANQUE.

Inclosure in No. 5.

Report.

THE principal events of the past year, so far as New Orleans is concerned, were the preparation and opening to the public of the World's Industrial and Cotton Exposition.

This enterprise was conceived in a Resolution passed at a Convention of the National Cotton Planters' Association held in the year 1882, and given legal existence by an Act of Congress approved February 10, 1883, of which it may be interesting to note the preamble and the following sections:—

"Whereas it is desirable to encourage the celebration of the one hundredth anniversary of the production, manufacture, and commerce of cotton, by holding, in the year 1884, in some city of the Union, to be selected by the Executive Committee of the National Cotton Planters' Association of America, an institution for the public welfare, incorporated under the laws of Mississippi, a World's Industrial and Cotton Centennial Exposition, to be held under the joint auspices of the United States, the said National Cotton Planters' Association of America, and of the city in which it may be located, and in which cotton, in all its conditions of culture and manufacture, will be the chief exhibit, but which is designed also to include all arts, manufactures, and products of the soil and mine; and

"Whereas such an Exhibition should be national and international in its character, in which the people of this country and other parts of the world who are interested in this subject should participate, it should have the sanction of the Congress of the United States: therefore,

"Be it enacted by the Senate and House of Representatives of the United States in Congress assembled, That a World's Industrial and Cotton Centennial Exposition, to be held in the year 1884, under the joint auspices of the United States' Government, the National Cotton Planters' Association of America, and the city where it may be located."

Sections 2 to 7 provide for a United States' Board of Management.

"Sec. 8. That whenever the President shall be informed by the said Board of Management that provision has been made for suitable buildings, or the erection of the same, for the purposes of said Exposition, the President shall, through the Department of State, make proclamation of the same, setting forth the time at which the Exhibition will open, and the place at which it will be held, and such Board of Management shall communicate to the Diplomatic Representatives of all nations copies of the same, and a copy of this Act, together with such regulations as may be adopted by said Board of Management, for publication in their respective countries.

"Sec. 9. That the President be requested to send, in the name of the United States, invitations to the Governments of other nations to be represented and take part in said World's Industrial and Cotton Centennial Exposition, to be held in some city of the United States to be hereafter selected as aforesaid.

"Sec. 10. That medals, with appropriate devices, emblems, and inscriptions commemorative of said World's Industrial and Cotton Centennial Exposition, and of the awards to be made to exhibitors thereat, be prepared at some mint of the United States, for the said Board of Management, subject to the provisions of the 52nd section of the Coinage Act of 1873, upon the payment of a sum not less than the cost thereof; and all the provisions, whether penal or otherwise, of said Coinage Act against the counterfeiting or imitating of coin of the United States shall apply to the medals struck and issued under this Act.

"Sec. 11. That all articles which shall be imported for the sole purpose of exhibition at said World's Industrial and Cotton Centennial Exposition, to be held in the year 1884, shall be admitted without payment of duty, or of customs fees or charges, under such regulations as the Secretary of the Treasury shall prescribe: Provided, that all such articles as shall be sold in the United States, or shall be withdrawn for consumption therein at any time after such importations, shall be subject to the duties, if any are imposed on like articles by the Revenue Laws at the time of importation; and provided, further, that in case any articles imported under the provisions of this Act shall be withdrawn for consumption, or shall be sold without payment of duty as required by law, all penalties prescribed by the Revenue Laws shall be applied and enforced against such articles, and against the persons who may be guilty of such withdrawal or sale."

On the 24th April, 1883, the location of the Exposition was fixed at this city, and subscriptions to its stock opened shortly afterwards. The city of New Orleans gave 100,000 dollars to build a Horticultural Hall which should be a permanent structure, the State gave 100,000 dollars, and we now know that the total derived from all other sources, including railways, &c., did not exceed 380,583 dollars.

With this capital the Direction commenced work in March 1884, as their own contractors and builders.

The reasons for placing the Exposition in this spot, 6 miles from the centre of the city, are thus given in the Director-General's organ in the local press:—"The wisdom of this selection is perceived in the manifold advantages offered on every hand. It placed the Exposition upon the great waterway of inland navigation of the United States, the Mississippi River, and opened direct communication with the towns and cities along 20,000 miles of navigable streams. By railway it is connected with every State, and Mexico as well as Canada. The Eads system of jetties has opened the mouth of the river, so that now the largest ships afloat can come to the park and discharge their freight within a few feet of the Exposition buildings."

The wharf, without which the Mississippi River was useless, was not constructed until about a month before the "opening" of the Exposition. Existing railways were connected with it by a single line in the month of November, and no steam communication with the city has as yet been made.

Thus every piece of lumber and all other building materials had to be carted out a distance of 5 or 6 miles along streets which were frequently in such a condition as to render it impossible to do the journey in less than two hours. The first work taken in hand, the main building, which covers 33 acres of ground, was constructed with sheer manual labour. During at least a dozen visits which I made, extending over a period of five months, I did not see one labour-saving appliance, not even a tramway for moving timber.

In this manner the original capital was seriously depleted. Congress was applied to for a loan of 1,000,000 dollars, which was granted; and 300,000 dollars appropriated for a Government exhibit.

This caused an expansion of the project which was fatal to its ultimate success.

The following are the principal buildings:—

Main building (wood)	1,378 × 905 feet.
Government building (wood)	885 × 565 „
Factories and mills (wood and iron)	350 × 180 „
Machinery (iron)	300 × 120 „
Art Gallery (iron)	330 × 100 „
Horticultural Hall (glass)	600 × 194 „

There are also live stock stables, saw-mill, and wood-working sheds, houses of public comfort, i.e., for refreshments, retiring rooms, &c., belonging to the Exposition, and besides a very handsome barrack built by the Mexican Government for its troops, and an iron pavilion for some of its exhibits.

The main building is a masterpiece of construction, light, airy, and, considering the immense expanse of its roofs, wonderfully open and free from obstructions to the view. It is also much more rain-proof than even friendly critics expected. It contains a music-hall with a seating capacity for 11,000 persons, and an orchestra for 600 performers. The Government building is built upon the same plan as the main, but being somewhat lower, the effect of lightness above mentioned is not so conspicuous.

The Horticultural Hall is a vast conservatory (said to be the largest in the world). This is the property of the city, and will remain.

The Art Gallery is built entirely of sheet iron, and is practically fire-proof. Its interior arrangements are admirably suited for their purpose.

There is nothing about the other structures to call for mention.

The park, which, when first taken possession of by the Exposition authorities, was a piece of rough waste land, with a grove of handsome live oaks upon it, has been levelled, drained, and planted in the immediate vicinity of the buildings, and laid off with broad asphalte walks. It can never present the appearance promised in the too flattering pictures which have been published of it, and halts far behind the descriptions which fervent journalists have thought it wise to present for the attraction of strangers; but taking things as they are, a vast improvement has been made which the touch of spring may develop into a sufficiently beautiful display.

In this connection I may observe that immense damage has been done to the interests of this Exposition by its inconsiderate friends in the press. From the first the people of New Orleans have been told that everything was going as by magic, and that a splendid success was assured. They, therefore, kept their money in their pockets, and thought it quite unnecessary to work for what was progressing in so satisfactory a manner without their help. Later on, they read in their newspapers that this or that work was progressing rapidly, or that this or that building was finished; but saw with the same eyes on the spot that the writer had drawn his facts from his imagination, or his instructions. As an example I quote the following:—

"The City Park has been assigned for the uses of the Exposition. It is a beautiful stretch of ground lying between St. Charles Avenue on the north and the Mississippi River on the south. The buildings front east towards the main portion of the city. Magnificent groves of live oaks are scattered over the grounds, and with the embellishment given by the Exposition management, the conversion of large tracts into beautiful and elaborate gardens (many of them several acres in extent) tropical trees and verdure meeting the vision in nearly every direction, miniature lakes and huge fountains dotting the landscape, flowers in profusion and luxuriant vegetation on every side, the park presents a scene unrivalled in this country and with hardly a parallel in the world."

This was published on the 1st September. At that time there was not a tropical tree, or a lake, or a fountain, or a flower, or any growing thing except the live oaks and the grass; and one-third of the space was a vast sheet of ploughed-up mud!

With an imagination almost as daring the public were thus invited to the opening of the Exposition:—

"Even as the eyes of the Mussulman faithful turn towards sacred Mecca, so the gaze of the whole world is to-day bent on the Crescent City, the warm and lovely Princess of the American Mediterranean. Toward her capital the argosies of the Princes, Potentates, and Powers of the earth plough their lordly way through the azure waters of many seas; and great armadas of Imperial and Royal battleships, clothed in all the splendid panoply of naval warfare, sail grandly hither to salute the sovereign lady of the blazing crescent with courtesy of huge guns and homage of gallant men, and all roads lead to the new Rome. Far and wide of the length and breadth of the Colombian continent the giant iron horses are harnessed and rush along over mountain and plain under whip and spur of fire and steam, bringing to the festa our honoured guests, and the hearty offerings of 60,000,000 freemen, our brothers in the Union.

"The temple of the goddess may present an aspect of confusion to the uninformed and inexperienced, nevertheless, order underlies all this apparent confusion, and magician hands are directing the myriad gnomes who delve away by day and night in the giant palaces by the mighty river. Despite outward appearances, they will be prepared and decked in all their promised gorgeousness when, on the 16th proximo, our 'Lord King Arthur' shall take his good sword Escalibur and cut the cord that binds the arms of the steel and iron Titans."

The Exposition was opened on the 16th December (by postponement from the 1st) in the presence of some 14,000 visitors, more than half of whom were strangers, and although the "confusion" above mentioned had in no wise yielded to order, but on the contrary was worse confounded, there was in the buildings themselves and in the portions of the State exhibits which were in order enough to repay a visit if expectation had not been unduly heightened; and if the ordinary and palpable provisions for the comfort of people who had come 6 miles from their houses or lodgings had been made. There was not a retiring-room for either sex, or a restaurant, or a buffet, or (except in the music hall) a seat. The consequences were clearly marked in a sudden slackening of the tide of visitors which had set in coincident with the arrival of letters in the north-east and west, and the publication in the newspapers of the true condition of affairs.

On the 17th March, 1884, the following Circular for the information of foreign exhibitors was issued by the United States' Treasury Department, and on the 14th April it was published by the Department of Transportation of the Exposition:—

"*Washington, D.C., March* 17, 1884.

"The following section of an Act of Congress, approved the 10th February, 1883, is published for the information and guidance of Customs officers:—

"'Section 11. That all articles which shall be imported for the sole purpose of exhibition at the said World's Industrial and Cotton Centennial Exposition, to be held in the year 1884, shall be admitted without the payment of duty, or of customs fees or charges, under such regulations as the Secretary of the Treasury shall prescribe: Provided that all such articles as shall be sold in the United States, or withdrawn for consumption therein, at any time after such importation, shall be subject to the duties, if any are imposed on like articles by the Revenue Laws in force at the date of importation; and, provided, further, that in case any articles imported under the provisions of this Act shall be withdrawn for consumption, or shall be sold without payment of duty as required by law, all penalties prescribed by the Revenue Laws shall be applied and enforced against such articles and against the persons who may be guilty of such withdrawal or sale.'

"In pursuance of this Act the following Regulations are prescribed:—

"Invoices will be required which shall recite the fact that the goods embraced therein are intended for this Exhibition. Each shipper shall be required to make such invoice in triplicate, giving a description of his goods, their value, and the marks and numbers thereon, but any number of such invoices may be embraced in one declaration by the agent, such declaration to be taken before a Consular officer of the United States, and certified in the usual manner. One copy of the invoice will be sent to the Collector of Customs at the port of first arrival, one copy to the Collector of Customs at New Orleans, and one copy to the consignee or agent of the shipper.

"Articles intended for this Exhibition, and arriving at the ports of Philadelphia, New York, Baltimore, or San Francisco, or any port on the Canadian frontier at which goods may be shipped for immediate transportation under the Act of the 10th June, 1880, entitled "An Act to amend the Statutes in relation to immediate transportation of dutiable goods, and for other purposes" (Synopsis, 4582), may be shipped by bonded common carriers from the port of first arrival to New Orleans. On the arrival of such goods at New Orleans, either direct or viâ either of the ports named, due notice of such arrival will be given to the Collector by the consignee, whereupon the Collector will take possession of the same. Entry for warehouse in the usual manner will be permitted, and the usual bond taken to secure the duties, and after the building shall have been duly bonded, the goods will be stored in the Exhibition building. Upon completion of the warehouse entry and storage of the goods in the Exhibition building the packages will be opened and due examination and appraisement of the contents, with proper allowance for damage sustained on the voyage of importation, if any, will be made by the appraiser at such Exhibition building, which shall, for that purpose, be regarded as a public store. After the appraisement shall have been completed, the entry will be liquidated as usual, and proper record made of the same.

"To identify the articles a ticket will be pasted on each article, giving the name of the shipper stated in the invoice, and the number of the warehouse entry. A store-keeper will be stationed at the Exhibition building, at the expense of the Exhibition, who will keep a register of the goods received in a debit and credit account, checking against the receipts the deliveries as they may be made. The goods may be withdrawn for exportation at any time within three years from the date of importation without payment of duty or customs fees or charges. On withdrawal for consumption, however, the usual fees accrue. If not withdrawn for consumption or exportation within that time the goods become liable to sale to realize the duties. On the sale of any of the goods for consumption in the United States, withdrawal entry will be permitted on payment of duties at the rates in force at the dates of importation of the several articles respectively. On such withdrawal for consumption after one year from date of original importation, an additional duty of 10 per cent. on the duties originally assessed will be exacted.

"Attention is invited to the provisions of law inflicting penalties and forfeitures for violations of the Revenue Laws of the United States.

"By the President's Proclamation, dated the 10th September, 1883, it was declared that the Exposition will be opened on the first Monday in December 1884, and will continue to the 31st May, 1885. No importations made after the date last mentioned will be admitted under these instructions.

(Signed) "CHAS. J. FOLGER, *Secretary*."

Foreign exhibits began to arrive about the end of November, the owners being under the impression that they would be allowed to sign "the usual bond," and have their goods immediately transferred to the bonded warehouse which was also the World's Cotton Centennial Exposition; but although a good deal of vexation had been caused at the Centennial for want of definite instructions on this point, the Customs authorities here were left without guidance. They had to enforce the hard and fast rules of ordinary importation, and the Exposition was not bonded until the 3rd December, two days after the date originally fixed for opening it! The difficulties about individual bonds were removed on the 8th. It is no matter for wonder, therefore, that the Foreign Sections were bare on the opening day.

This deadlock removed, and proper force applied to the unloading of home products, the Exposition began to fill up with most creditable rapidity, but it soon became apparent that the Management were in difficulties. Early in January 1885 it was admitted that all their capital and a sum of 130,028 dollars received for "Installation receipts and admissions" have been expended, that the gate-money was not sufficient to pay running expenses, and that the Exposition was 250,000 dollars in debt.

A mass meeting to consider measures of relief was held on the 8th January, at which the Director-General (Mr. E. A. Burke) said:—"The question that I want to discuss with the people of New Orleans is not the possibility of a failure of this Exposition—that thought never enters my mind, because I know the forces that can be invoked, that stand ready and willing, if needs must be, to take up this grand work and carry it on—but the question that I want to discuss as a citizen of New Orleans, not only as a man whose whole heart is in the work before him, but as a citizen of New Orleans, proud of my city, and loth to feel the humiliation that I would feel, and that you would feel, if any others than yourselves were to take up this work and go on with it. (Applause.) In inverse ratio to the grand and glorious benefits that will result to the people of this community would be the result of apathy or neglect or any character of indifference in holding up the hands of your own chosen agents in the administration of this trust, and I have no fear— and that is the reason why this vast meeting of citizens is called—I have no fear as to what this people will do; I have had aid offered me from different quarters, and I have said to them, 'No, gentlemen; wait. Give the people of New Orleans an opportunity to know the truth, to realize the situation, and they will push away the difficulties, take up the responsibilities, and there will be no occasion to call for outside aid in this great enterprise.' Now, what is the situation?"

This was following up the mistake upon which I have already commented. No people in the world are likely to make sacrifices when they are told that there is some one pressing for permission to relieve them of the necessity. The people of New Orleans took the hint, and the results of this particular meeting were *nil*.

"The situation," according to Mr. Burke, was simply this—"that we undertook with 1,600,000 dollars to overcap the results of the great Centennial which cost some 7,000,000 or 8,000,000 dollars. Our plans, we thought, were well laid, and so they were. Up to the first day of November our expenditure had been 921,364 dollars, leaving us over 600,000 dollars to prosecute our work. It is natural that we should have met with some difficulties in carrying on the enterprise; but it will be no doubt a surprise to the people of this community to learn that the majority of all these great results that have been produced and laid before you have been brought about from the 7th day of August last, for, notwithstanding that the loan was made by Congress on the 22nd May, it was the 7th day of last August before one dollar of the funds became available for the purposes of the Management; and thus all of these results have been produced since that date, except the original plans, all of which were changed and expanded. New buildings had to be devised, new plans of the park undertaken, and a wider scope given to all of the departments; and we found when the day appointed for the opening approached, although we were very nearly in readiness with our buildings at that time, that we were confronted by a difficulty that had never been anticipated, and that we had no right to anticipate. We believed, with the exhibitors who were sending forward their exhibits to the Exposition, that a brief ten days' time would be sufficient for the transport of the shipments, a few days' extra time was allowed for putting them in place; and so it had been anticipated that by the 1st December shipments sent forward from the 1st November to the 15th November would be ready for the opening.

"We found, very much to our regret, some fifteen days before the day named for opening, that owing to the movement of the cotton crop and sugar crop, and the influx of freights of winter goods from various cities, the capacity of our railroads was taxed to the utmost, and as a consequence very many of the shipments were delayed in transit. We found the facilities quite inadequate for the rapid transit of these exhibits to the grounds, and notwithstanding the extraordinary outlay which the Management had to undertake in the purchase and equipment of a railroad to assist in carrying the freight, we found it was utterly impossible to make the shipments in the proper time, and we were compelled to postpone the opening for sixteen days, thinking then that we could formally open and continue under full receipts. But it so happened that many of the exhibits that were shipped in the early part of December or in the latter part of November did not get into the Exposition grounds until within the past week or ten days.

"Then, again, extraordinary difficulties were encountered in respect to the Customs. I do not say this was due to the gentleman who have charge of the Customs here, who have offered and extended every facility in their power, but owing to some misunderstanding or lack of adequate regulations, the very Government that invited all the nations of the earth to its National Exposition placed great difficulties in the way of their installation. These are things we could not have provided against. In the breadth and liberality of their action the Board of Management undertook to take from the railroad stations 5,000 car-loads of freight, to carry them to the Exposition grounds, unload the cars, carry the exhibits to the spaces of the exhibitors, and place them in readiness for the opening.

"We never conceived the enormous expense, the vast labour attaching to this undertaking. There was a machinery department 2,000 feet long, the heaviest machinery of the world, pouring in upon us, with comparatively inadequate facilities for handling the same, having, as it were, to be dragged by physical force from the cars and put in place. Hundreds of thousands of dollars have been expended, and necessarily so, in carrying on this work of transportation and installation over what had been contemplated. Then, again, at the time when we had hese buildings to finish here was the whole world pouring its treasures down at our doors at one time. We had announced that we would be in readiness, and it was our duty to exhaust every effort to be prepared.

"As the date approached it became more and more important that every nerve should be strained, and every hour of the day and night was utilized. Our labourers, mechanics, clerks, and officers, in fact, everybody connected with the Management, were driving forward under circumstances such as have never beset an undertaking of this kind before. In a city and in a location of a character unequalled in the site of any former World's Exposition, with inadequate facilities for transportation and handling and for conveying the very materials essential for completing the building, amid rain and storm and mud, these men worked that they might be ready, worked by day and by night, and even violated the Sabbath.

"Hundreds of thousands of dollars more than had been anticipated were spent in this way, because the forces had to be doubled, and double pay had to be paid for night work and Sunday work; 200,000 dollars had to be expended in motive power for the machinery alone. Thus the expenses were piled up with frightful rapidity, but all were necessary to the accomplishment of the work.

"From the 1st November to the 1st December, in that one month of awful exertion, the sum of 503,000 dollars was added to the previous expenditure of 921,000 dollars, and from the 1st December to the 1st January the actual cash outlay amounted to 250,898 dol. 8 c., making a total actual disbursement up to the 1st January of 1,675,602 dol. 94 c., or a total exhaustion of the entire means at the command of the Board of Management, with a very large number of contracts and obligations uncared for. So that we were brought face to face with this fact, that on the 1st January the amount of operating expenses and unpaid obligations were 250,000 dollars.

"This amount would never have troubled the Management if we had had fair weather from the date of the opening; but it seems that for some thirty days and nights we had almost incessant storms of rain, and the stranger was warned from our doors. As a consequence, instead of having the benefit of large receipts to provide for the operating expenses, and a surplus for a portion at least of the accumulated indebtedness, we have, during more than twenty days of terrible weather, been getting further and further behind."

The opening sentence contains the mainspring of the mistake: the Directors undertook an impossibility.

Honourable gentlemen, for the most part eminently successful in their respective callings, they were yet without technical knowledge or experience in the business before them collectively. From a condition almost of despair, caused by the apathy of New Orleans, they were suddenly elevated into triumph by the loan of a million from the United States. Their ideas expanded and ran away with them.

On the 21st January a special appeal was made to the Cotton Exchange and the following Schedule published:—

RECEIPTS.

	Dol.	c.
Government loan	1,000,000	00
Stock and donations	580,583	00
Installation receipts and admissions	130,028	20
Total	1,710,611	20
Expenditure to the 12th January, 1885	1,980,523	33
Receipts	1,710,611	20
	269,912	13
Less margins in bank	34,000	00
	235,912	13

DISBURSEMENTS.

	Dol.	c.
Construction	979,048	44
Machinery account	223,956	72
Park improvement	125,464	83
States and Territories	178,970	94
Department of—		
Agriculture	25,440	09
Education	12,279	28
Installation	47,626	68
Transportation	12,985	90
Information and Accommodation	9,607	80

Department of—								Dol.	c.
Art								1,683	83
Woman's work								6,016	66
Coloured exhibits								12,369	55
Miscellaneous account in process of collecting and settlement								3,272	06
Operating expenses, railroad included								136,235	16
Salaries								38,799	22
Furniture, stationery, office expenses, hauling and general expense account								51,830	10
Special Commissioners, foreign and domestic agencies, travelling expenses								35,148	11
News, advertisements and subscriptions to press								21,637	93
Posters, circulars, lithographs, folders, posting and mailing expenses								40,286	71
Commissions								4,239	97
Interest and discount								5,155	90
Telegraph								2,629	94
Postage								2,337	00
Music								9,500	51
Grand total								1,980,523	33

The mysterious capitalists before mentioned were again held up as an incentive to home aid, but only 43,000 dollars (secured upon the admission money and to be repaid at the rate of 1,000 dollars a-day) was raised. This made it quite clear that New Orleans would not, or could not, provide the necessary assistance; and this being so, it might be supposed that the mysterious capitalists who were so eager to assist would have been gratified, but they are again doomed to disappointment, as a Committee has gone to Washington to ask a further loan of 500,000 dollars from Congress. At this time (5th February) it was admitted that the debt was 360,000 dollars.

I now come to the much pleasanter task of noticing what has been done by exhibitors, and will commence with the Government building, the construction and size of which has already been given. The central portions are occupied by scientific exhibits from the Smithsonian Institute, the United States' Medical Department, and a large and varied collection from the Patent Office. These, although of great value from an educational point of view, and capable of forming the texts for popular lectures which might prove highly attractive, share the usual fate of similar objects when left dumb and lifeless, so to speak, in their cases. The space they occupy is not frequented, and those who wander into it by accident hurry out again or pass on with listless gaze.

On the flanks of this building on all sides are exhibits from the various States, each having a show of its own under the direction of its own Commissioners. Now, considering that this display is made up, practically speaking, of raw material, of which 80 per cent. is Indian corn, grains, grasses, fruit, vegetables, coal, minerals, and wood, it might be supposed that the result would be monotonous and ineffective. I must admit that I anticipated little pleasure from this part of the Exposition, and that I am most agreeably disappointed. I found an ingenuity of construction, a grace in design, and a dexterity of arranging what I had considered unmanageable materials, which was simply a revelation.

The States of Dacota and Kansas are especially to be commended for their trophies—structures of 50 feet high, surmounted the one by a colossal female figure and the other by a gigantic eagle, composed entirely (except the face of the figure) of corn (Indian), grains, and grasses. Viewed at a distance these works of art (for such they are), with their flutings, and mouldings, and cornices, appear to be made of some plastic composition highly decorated. It is only when the visitor has approached within a few yards that he finds at once his mistake, and his admiration. Nebraska also has some most ingenious and effective decorations in this style. It would seem as though there were no limit to the uses of Indian corn for these purposes. As used in the exhibit now under consideration, it ranges from white to a purple which may do duty for black, and passes through almost every shade of yellow, orange, and red. The "cob" is used as a whole, is cut vertically for one effect, horizontally for another. It is "shucked" and the grains arranged as beads in numberless ways and patterns. Much ingenuity is also displayed in the arrangement of wheat and barley ears, and feathery grasses which still retain their verdure. The North-west has several other exhibits of a like nature, and only second to those I have described. If it does not take the palm for grain, it undoubtedly excels in its methods of displaying it. From this district comes also a fine show of vegetables and fruits, some rich specimens of iron and copper ore, and a quantity of the most beautiful agate and onyx that I have ever seen. With regard to fruits and vegetables, one of the most striking lessons taught by this Exposition is that (with the exception of a few varieties which Nature only allows to exist in tropical or sub-tropical climates) you can find all you want in more or less perfection in the exhibits of almost every State. Arkansas sends some of the finest apples and pears in the building. The sunny birth-land of the potato has to yield to icy Michigan in the show of this esculent. Nearly the same thing may be said of coal. I am informed that the variety found in this exhibit is a surprise to the best informed on this subject; that the wealth of the United States in this particular is for the first time fully demonstrated, and that there is not one sort known to the commerce of Europe that is not to be found in the exhibit of one State or another. More, the monopoly of production conceded to certain States for certain qualities has been broken down. Pennsylvania finds a rival in Alabama for hard coal, and in Virginia for the anthracite which was supposed to be her speciality. I should imagine that in many other respects this Exposition will open new markets and suggest new fields of labour and of wealth. Take woods suitable for furniture as an example. For many years the popular taste has run upon black walnut till the supply has become almost exhausted. There are to be found in the exhibits of twenty States specimens of wood quite as suitable for the purpose in question, and obtainable in any quantities at reasonable prices.

It is in this building that the most competent lessons taught by the Exposition will be learned. Those who run can read them. They are lessons not only of what is, but what may be. If, for instance, Arkansas can produce such fruit, why should Louisiana, which lies very little to the south of her, and Mississippi, which is parallel and has nearly the same soil and climate, not do likewise, instead of placing their main dependence upon a precarious cotton crop and the foredoomed culture of sugar?

Amongst the riches of Tennessee will be found an exhibit from the Rugby Colony founded by "Tom Brown," and a relic interesting (if genuine) which claims to be a baluster from the old "Tabbard Inn" in which Sir Geoffrey Chaucer and nine-and-twenty pilgrims took their ease on their famous journey to Canterbury. Tennessee also shows some excellent native made wine and specimens of marble.

Several States, notably Ohio, send exhibits of "women's work" in the shape of decorated china and embroidery in which great taste and skill is shown. The principal exhibit of "women's work" (which was made a feature of the Exposition, but is delayed for want of funds) will be placed in one of the galleries of this (the Government) building, next to a very complete show of educational materials contributed by the United States and France, and facing a paleontological and geological display which does not call for special notice.

In the United States' Educational Department will be found a model, belonging to the city of Bath, of its modern bathing establishment and the ancient Roman baths over which it is built.

I now come to the main building. Right and left of its principal entrance, with passages running parallel with that, are ranged exhibits of American manufacturers occupying spaces containing—plus passages—159,064 square feet, and which according to the prospectus should contain the articles enumerated in Groups 3, 5, 7, and 8, as follows:—

Group 3.—*Raw and Manufactured Products, Ores, Minerals, and Woods.*

Mining and metallurgy.
Products of the cultivation of forests and of the trades appertaining thereto.
Products of hunting, shooting and fishing, spontaneous products, machines, and instruments connected therewith.
Agricultural products not used for food.
Chemical and pharmaceutical products.
Chemical processes for bleaching, dyeing, printing, and dressing.
Leather and skins.

Group 5.—*Textile Fabrics, Clothing and Accessories.*

Cotton thread and fabrics.
Thread and fabrics of flax, hemp, &c.
Worsted yarn and fabrics.
Woollen yarn and fabrics.
Silk and silk fabrics.

Shawls.
Lace, net, embroidery, trimmings, &c.
Hosiery and underclothing, and accessories of clothing.
Clothing for both sexes.
Jewellery and precious stones.
Portable weapons, and hunting and shooting equipments.
Travelling apparatus and camp equipage.
Toys.

Group 7.—*Alimentary Products, Cereals, Farinaceous Products, and Products derived from them.*

Bread and pastry.
Fatty substances used as food.
Milk and eggs.
Meat and fish.
Vegetables and fruit.
Condiments and stimulants.
Sugar and confectionery.
Fermented drinks.

Group 8.—*Education and Instruction, Apparatus and Processes of the liberal Arts.*

Education of children, primary nstruction, instruction of adults.
Organization and appliances for secondary instruction.
Organization, methods, and appliances for superior instruction.
Printing and books.
Stationery, bookbinding, painting, and drawing materials.
General application of the arts of drawing and modelling.
Photographic proofs and apparatus.
Musical instruments.
Medicine, hygiene, and public relief.
Mathematical and philosophical instruments.
Maps and geographical and cosmographical apparatus.

This portion should be the centre of attraction, but the display made is not a representative one. We miss altogether some objects in which American enterprise has obtained a high state of perfection during the last decade and find others unworthily presented. In this category are watches, gold ornaments, and jewellery; electro-plated goods, picture-frames, and bookbinding; guns and pistols; artificers' tools, locks, and other fastenings; cutlery, surgical and dental instruments; and india-rubber goods. There are three displays of watches (one from Waltham), all small and not in any way remarkable. There are no gold ornaments of any value, and no jewellery. There are two exhibits of electro-plate, one large and one small. The larger contains some artistic designs and pretty treatment in turning, but judged by what American manufacturers can and do produce, this would not be classed as more than fourth-rate. All iron work (with the exception of stoves for cooking and heating, of which there is really a magnificent collection) is badly represented. The exhibition of fire-arms made by Messrs. Remington, the Winchester Rifle Company, Colt and Co., and Ballards, is not worthy of a World's Exposition. The best show of fowling-pieces (the only one of hammerless guns) is made by Messrs. Westley, Richards, and Buckley, of Birmingham, through their agents. It is a pity these were not sent to the British section. No steel goods worth mention will be found, and if there be any india-rubber it must be hidden away in some corner where it cannot assert its presence.

The display of stoves deserves more than a passing word of praise. Their beauty may perhaps be that of youth, the brightness of their steel ornaments and talc fronts may fade; but for the more enduring and useful qualities, construction, compactness, and the variety of purposes which they serve, they are as good as can be. Opposite to them, at the other end of this section, is a large and handsome exhibit of pianos and harmoniums, into the merits of which I am not competent to enter. The only other articles which (in an Exposition having the pretensions of this) I can single out for praise are the lamps—table, hanging, and standard—made of embossed metal work and coloured glass by Idour and Co., and Donnell and Co., of New York, and Nosburg and Co., of Brooklyn. These are in all respects admirable.

Mr. Lowell has said that if the United States should adopt the principles of free trade, we shall find them our most powerful competitor in all the markets of the world. This may be so, but we shall not be hard pressed by such articles as have been sent to New Orleans. The displays of silks, satins, and velvets, of muslins and laces, and of woollen goods are poor. So are those of glass and ceramics. The carpets and rugs are emphatically bad. The best houses in these lines are conspicuously absent, but there are in this section, twenty-four stalls at which pseudo-Oriental goods, and articles such as are met with in the Lowther Arcade and the Passage des Panoramas, are sold.

As a practical proof that this criticism is not prejudiced or unjust, I will cite the fact that there is no exhibit here in front of which one may depend upon finding (say) six spectators. This does not include the operations of a young man who executes an oil painting (subject to order) in fifteen minutes. He has always a crowd of admirers.

My reason for saying that this portion should be the centre of attraction is that it is next to the main entrance, is laid out with wider walks than are to be found elsewhere, leads to the music hall, and is the most direct road to and from the Government building, the Art Gallery, and the Agricultural Hall. It might have been made a pleasant lounging-place, but nothing whatever has been done in this direction.

There are, so to speak, no auxiliary attractions. No statuary, no flowers, no fountains, no birds, no bright drapery, and not a single seat. For some time there was no music; now it is promised twice a-week. The organ in the music hall is of moderate calibre. The so-called restaurants are bad, and dear. The facilities for transport are deficient. It is therefore clear that this will never become a popular resort.

On the extreme right wing, with paths going east and west, is a large exhibit of agricultural machinery, which merits a good deal more attention than it receives. Further on we find some very gorgeously fitted up railway sleeping and drawing-room cars.

In the gallery to the left is the Art Furniture Department, and here certain exhibitors have unconsciously set an object-lesson in colour which may be studied with advantage. The carpets are the principal offenders. The representative American carpet is a composition of vermilion red and chrome yellow, aggravated by blue flowers and green leaves. Such is to be seen in some of the first stands in the gallery now under notice, and upon it chairs and sofas covered in delicate coloured plush and velvet are placed in cruel disregard of a discord which almost speaks. A little further on we come to a series of exhibits in which details have been carefully attended to and the harmonies pleasantly conserved. These are rooms fitted up by the R. Mitchell Company of Cincinnati. The woodwork is as good as anything I have seen anywhere. The representative American carpet is discarded. Indeed, in two cases the mistake (if any) is in the want of colour, but this would be supplied with drapery, china and glass, &c., if the room were fully furnished for occupation.

There is a separate display of furniture from Michigan in a house in the grounds, and here, again, there is much to admire, especially the pieces made from Honduras mahogany, which is darkened and given a very rich appearance. In point of design all this is excellent, but the prices are high. There is nothing that people of moderate incomes could buy; and here is, I think, a mistake which American manufacturers make: they seem to think that lack of wealth bespeaks want of taste, which is not true, and that cheap goods must necessarily be made of ugly shapes and upholstered in glaring colours, which is again a fallacy.

I now come to the foreign sections, which run east and west at right angles to the Groups 3, 5, and 7 already mentioned, and taking them from right to left we find *Belgium*. This exhibit is first in excellence as it is first in place. It was arranged at Brussels by Government authority, and sent out here and fitted up in charge of Government officials. The consequence is a very perfect and representative display, comprising specimens of iron and tin ware, glass in sheets and tubes, and very handsome mirrors, full lines of linen and cotton goods, crockery, watches and clocks, pianos, ecclesiastical ornaments, gloves, guns, lace, graduating from the commonest sorts to the finest, Brussels and Mechlin rugs and carpets, and a fine collection of woollens, flannels, kerseymeres, and fine broadcloths.

Russia, which is her neighbour, exhibits some handsome malachite tables and bronzes of more than average artistic merit. Also enamelled woodwork, samovars, liqueurs and conserves, leather, carriages, and some fine hangings for portières.

[565]

On the other side of the music hall we come to *Austria*, where the first exhibit that presents itself is a large, but not remarkable, collection of bent wood chairs with cane and wicker seats. After this little is to be found but meerschaum pipes, glass ware, and ceramics, all for sale.

Italy, her neighbour, has a very similar display, shell cameos, trinkets, majolica and bisque faience, and a very handsome show of Venetian glass chandeliers and mirrors.

France, which comes next, with the exception of some wines and some ormolu candelabra and groups of a rather old fashion, and a small case of shoes, artificial flowers, and dolls, presents anything but a characteristic show.

Great Britain and Ireland, the next in order, and our manufacturers who have gained glory in other Expositions, and contributed to their success, are conspicuously absent. The best things we have are cutlery from Wolstenholm, Field, and Rogers, all first rate; woollen goods from Apperley, Curtis, and Co., and the Blarney Tweed Company, and the art furniture of Felix and Wyman, of London. This, which is exhibited in three rooms, is quite the best in all the Exposition—more, it is the best I have ever seen in America.

There is a delicacy of design, a novelty of arrangement, a modulation of colours, which will at once catch the eye of the connoisseur; and the richness of the materials will commend itself to those who look for a tangible value for their money. In this section and the Belgian alone can the public find seats.

Close at hand are two very creditable displays from *Jamaica* and *British Honduras*. These are admirably arranged and characteristically decorated under the personal supervision respectively of Mr. Morris, M.A., F.L.S., F.G.S., Director of Public Gardens at Jamaica, and of Mr. Agar of Belize. Great credit is due to these gentlemen for the ability they have shown in setting up and arranging the products of these respective Colonies.

Japan, Siam, and China show the objects with which we are all familiar, and as these are for sale, they must be included in the bazaar element.

We are now at the end of this line, where *Mexico* occupies a large space very handsomely decorated, and containing some 300 ebonized cabinets glazed on all sides, which, set out in rows, give rather a funereal appearance. I think that the contents of half of them, at least, would have made a better show in more humble surroundings. Still, it is a very complete and interesting display, ranging from specimens of morbid anatomy to satin slippers, and including pottery, artistic and domestic, the latter in very quaint forms, waxwork (highly characteristic), harness, models of artillery, arms, uniforms, dresses, boots, blankets, and rugs (very substantial), sombreros (silver-mounted, worth 20*l.*), and straw hats that could be bought for as many cents. All sorts of straw, wicker, and rush goods, rope and twine sacking, coffee, seeds, sugar, candied and bottled fruit, liqueurs. &c. These in the cabinets. Outside we find woods of all sorts, some beautifully carved wooden frames for glasses or pictures, and a street tramway car. I am sorry if I have omitted any items, but the manner in which some of the cabinets are packed is somewhat confusing. The Government of Mexico has been a warm and powerful ally of the Exposition. It has sent a splendid band to New Orleans and a squadron of cavalry; and, as before mentioned, is building itself a handsome iron pavilion (nearly finished) in which the minerals of the country will be exhibited.

After having gone carefully over the ground thus explored, the inquiring visitor, having the origin and constitutional objects of this Exposition in view, will surely ask himself, "Where is the cotton?" It is the "World's 'Cotton' Centennial Exposition." It was originated by the Cotton Planters' Association. Its opening could not be postponed because it was to commemorate the export of the first batch of cotton to Europe. In the Act of Congress creating it it is to be an Exposition "in which cotton in all its conditions of culture and manufacture will be the chief exhibit." Where, then, is the cotton?

North Carolina exhibits six bales and a few bushes for decoration.

South Carolina has five bales, some stubbed cotton, a few samples of inferior grey cloth, and some fair sheetings.

Arkansas shows four bales, and a few bushes for decoration. Mississippi has an archway decorated with picked cotton, and some samples of drills. Missouri exhibits three bales of cotton. Alabama one bale, and a few bushes for decoration. Texas uses picked cotton for decoration, has some graded in glass jars, and shows drills and what appear to be pickings. Missouri shows three bales and fourteen small boxes of graded samples. Louisiana presents a group of an old man and woman and their dog, composed of ginned cotton, and uses some bushes for decoration.

I could not find any cotton from Tennessee.

Turning northward for manufactured cotton, Massachusetts reserves herself for the main building. New York has no show of textile goods. Maine has some very handsome plush and pile velvet goods, but no cotton. New Hampshire makes far the largest and the best display in point of variety and material, but the designs and colours of printed cotton goods do not commend themselves to the artistic eye.

In the main building the space devoted to textile fabrics does not present what I take to be a representative Exhibition of American goods, and, with reference to the subject immediately under discussion, *i.e.*, cotton in all forms, is decidedly poor. In one block (100 yards) of Canal Street (our principal shopping thoroughfare), in the windows of five dry goods stores, can be seen any day a better collection of printed calicos, cretonnes, muslins, lawns, &c., than is offered in the whole Exposition. Sir P. Coates, of Paisley and New York, exhibits spool thread in all colours, and so does Clarke, of New York.

In the Machinery Department the Willowmantic Spool Cotton Company show the entire process of manufacturing thread. The Maginnis Company, of this city, show two spinning machines, and the Hopedale Company, of Massachusetts, one. Evan A. Leigh and Co., of Manchester and New York, have one mule, one slubber, one intermediate, one roving, and two carding machines, all English. There are two very small weaving machines, one for grey cloth and the other for duck. There is a small machine for making bobbins. In the Machinery Hall are one large compress, two ginning machines, and an exhaust cotton-opener and finisher lapper, by Lord, Brothers, of Todmorden. And that is all. There is no weaving worth mention, no "small ware" frames, and no printing. In my Trade Report I have described at some length the character and value of the products of the cotton-seed after it has left the gin. To recapitulate shortly, they are:—

1. Lint.
2. Husks used for fuel and fertilizing.
3. Oil. (Its residuum, soap stock.)
4. Cotton-seed cake.
5. Cotton-seed meal.

None of the machinery employed in this industry is shown, and there is no display of oil-cake or meal.

Cotton figures, I should say, in a proportion to other materials in the three main departments, as follows:—

Raw material, 1 to 2,000; machinery, 3 to 100; manufactured, 30 to 100.

This, therefore, is not an Exposition in which "cotton in all its conditions of culture and manufacture is the chief exhibit." It is not a "World's" Industrial Exposition, because, with the sole exception of Belgium, no European country is adequately represented. It is not even a fairly representative American Exposition in point of manufactured goods, or of machinery.

So far as the main building is concerned, it is, in sober sadness, little more than a large bazaar, but without any of the extraneous attractions which sometimes make bazaars agreeable, and which have been found necessary to attract the public to places of far higher pretensions.

UNITED STATES.

Report by Mr. West on the Fish Commission.

No. 4.

Mr. West to Earl Granville.—(Received July 6.)

My Lord, Washington, June 14, 1885.

I HAVE the honour to inclose to your Lordship herewith a Report on the Fish Commission, which I have drawn up from the printed documents already transmitted to your Lordship's Office.

I have, &c.
(Signed) L. S. SACKVILLE WEST.

Inclosure in No. 4.

Report on the United States' Fish Commission.

THE United States' Fish Commission was created by a joint Resolution of Congress in 1871. State legislation for the preservation of food fish had previously existed, and had given rise to much difference of opinion as to its salutary effects. The Commission was therefore authorized to prosecute investigations and inquiries with a view of ascertaining whether any or what diminution in the quantity of the food fishes of the coasts and lakes had taken place, and if so, to what causes the same were due, and also what protective, prohibitory, or precautionary measures should be adopted. This Commission was to consist of one member to be appointed by the President, and the amount appropriated by Congress to prosecute these inquiries was 8,500 dollars. Professor Spencer F. Baird was appointed Commissioner, and had soon a corps of trained specialists engaged in intelligent and systematic investigation. Stations were established at Wood's Holl (Massachusetts) and Cape Hatteras, and the results were so valuable that Congress appropriated for the ensuing year 30,500 dollars, and subsequently larger sums, until the total amount expended has reached nearly 1,500,000 dollars. The division of the work of the Commission is as follows:—

1. The systematic investigation of the waters of the United States and the biological and physical problems which they present.

2. Investigation of the methods of fisheries, past and present, and the statistics of production and commerce of fishery products.

3. The introduction and multiplication of useful food fishes throughout the country, especially in waters under the jurisdiction of the general government, or those common to several States, none of which would undertake to spend money for this purpose.

These separate branches of the work have been pursued carefully and diligently, and the life, character, and habits of various species of fish have become fully known.

The fishery industry of the United States, according to the last census, gives employment to 131,426 persons, and in it the capital invested amounts to 37,955,349 dollars.

It became necessary, therefore, that this industry should be properly protected and developed, on account of the decrease of many varieties of fish. The work of propagation has been carried on assiduously, and species have been acclimated to rivers in which previously they did not exist.

The central station is in Washington. The following are the hatching stations:—

Grand Lake stream (Maine), where the eggs of the schoordic salmon are collected. Bucksport (Maine) for collecting and hatching the eggs of the Atlantic salmon and white fish (*Coregonus*). Cold Spring Harbour (Long Island, New

[566]

York), for collecting and hatching various species of the salmon, cod, and other sea fishes. Havre de Grace (Maryland), for collecting and hatching shad eggs. Whyteville (Virginia), for hatching eggs of the brook and California trout. St. Jerome's Creek (Maryland), for the artificial propagation of the oyster, Spanish mackerel, and the banded porgy. Avoca (North Carolina), for shad, alewife, and striped bass. Northville (Michigan), for the development and distribution of the eggs of the white fish (Coregonus). There are two stations west of the Rocky Mountains for the Californian salmon. During the present year about 130,000,000 white fish (*Coregonus*), 3,000,000 salmon, and 27,000,000 shad have been developed and distributed.

The most important work, however, of the present year, is the attempt to stock the Columbia River and the system of streams emptying in Paget Sound with shad.

1,500,000 shad have already been sent to Portland (Oregon) for this purpose. It is proposed also to stock the tributaries of the Gulf of California with the same fish, and 1,000,000 young shad are on their way to be placed in the Republican and Colorado Rivers. This interesting experiment of transferring the fish of the Atlantic to the Pacific will be watched with great interest.

An immense number of fish have also been sent to France, Germany, and other European countries. The Commission has three ships fitted for the service, viz., the "Fish Hawk," "Albatross," and "Lookout," and three railway cars specially arranged for transportation. In connection with the establishment of the station at St. Jerome's Creek for oyster breeding, it would appear from a Memorandum in the Bulletin of the Fish Commission, vol. iv, 1884, that in order to arrest the deterioration of the oyster beds extensive measures should be taken. The last census gave 22,195,370 bushels (1880).

The exportation of oysters from the Chesapeake and Delaware has fallen from nearly 1,000,000 bushels in 1880 to 500,000 bushels in 1883. In the Chesapeake prices have doubled within the last five years, and, judging by them, the product must have fallen off since 1880 between 4,000,000 and 6,000,000 bushels. The Report of the Maryland Oyster Commission states that the oyster beds are in imminent danger of complete destruction, and that in the last three years they have lost 40 per cent. of their value. The Virginia beds have fallen off two-thirds. The area of the great beds of the Chesapeake and Delaware Bays is 471,171 acres, and the product in 1880 was 41 bushels per acre. At present the yield is certainly not more than 25 bushels.

Remedial measures are therefore necessary, and systematic cultivation is recommended, as initiated at St. Jerome's Creek upon the French system. The artificial breeding of the oyster has thus become a matter of great importance to the fishing industry of the United States, and will, no doubt, be extensively developed under the superintendence of the Commission.

The successful results which Professor Baird has obtained are universally appreciated, and it may be anticipated that Congress will continue to make liberal appropriations for carrying on the work.

Report by Sir L. Sackville West on the Consumption of Spirits, Wine, and Beer, and on Wine Production in the United States.

No. 5.

Sir L. West to the Marquis of Salisbury.—(Received July 13.)

My Lord,   Washington, June 30, 1885.

I HAVE the honour to inclose to your Lordship a Report on the consumption of spirits, wine, and beer, and the wine production in the United States, which I have drawn up from statistics which have been published.

I have, &c.
(Signed)   L. S. SACKVILLE WEST.

Inclosure in No. 5.

Report on the Consumption of Spirits, Wine, and Beer in the United States.

REFERENCE to the Reports of the Bureau of Statistics of the Treasury show that the increase in the consumption of distilled spirits, wine, and beer since 1840, taken by decades on the scale of 100, has been as follows:—

	Distilled Spirits.	Wines.	Beer.
1840	100	100	100
1850	120	130	157
1860	209	227	435
1870	185	251	878
1880	148	581	1,777
1884	188	423	2,531
1881 1882 1883 1884	176	492	2,266

Per centage consumption of distilled spirits, wine, and beer.

The year 1880 being exceptional in the unusual amount of domestic wine produced, as also in the unusual decrease in the production of distilled spirits, the average consumption for 1881, 1882, 1883, and 1884, together with the statistics for 1884, is given; *e.g.*, the amount of distilled spirits consumed in 1850 was 20 per cent. greater than in 1840, and, in 1884, 88 per cent. In like manner the amount of wine in 1880 was 581 per cent. of that consumed in 1840.

The following Table shows the amount in gallons of spirits, wine, and beer consumed for the years 1840, 1850, 1860, 1870, 1880, and 1840:—

(Table No. 1.)—TABLE showing the consumption of Distilled Spirits, Wine, and Beer in the United States for the Years 1840, 1850, 1860, 1870, 1880, and 1884.

Year.	Distilled Spirits. Domestic.	Imported.	Total.	Wines. Domestic.	Imported.	Total.	Beer. Domestic.	Imported.	Total.
	Gallons.	Gallons.	Gallons.	Gallons.	Gallons.	Gallons.	Gallons.	Gallons.	Gallons.
1840	40,378,090	2,682,794	43,060,884	124,734	4,748,362	4,873,096	23,162,571	148,272	23,310,843
1850	46,768,083	5,065,390	51,833,473	221,249	6,094,622	6,315,871	36,361,708	201,301	36,563,009
1860	83,904,258	6,064,393	89,968,651	1,860,008	9,199,133	11,059,141	100,225,879	1,120,790	101,346,669
1870	78,490,198	1,405,510	79,895,708	3,059,518	9,165,549	12,225,067	203,743,401	1,012,755	204,756,156
1880	62,132,415	1,394,279	63,526,694	23,298,940	5,030,601	28,329,541	413,208,885	1,011,280	414,220,165
1884	81,128,581	1,511,680	81,128,581	17,402,938	3,105,407	20,508,345	588,005,609	2,010f908	590,016,517

In order to estimate the actual increase or decrease in the *per capita* consumption, comparison is made with the statistics of population since 1840, as follows:—

Actual increase o decrease in *per capita* consumptio

1840	100	1870	226
1850	136	1880	294
1860	184		

As will be seen, the population nearly trebled between 1840 and 1880. If the actual number of gallons of each consumed in the successive decades is taken, and for purposes of comparison, the population from 1881 to 1884 inclusive is estimated at 52,000,000, the actual *per capita* consumption of distilled spirits, wine, and beer will be found to have been as follows:—

GALLONS consumed *per Capita*.

	Spirits.	Wine.	Beer.
1840	2·52	·29	1·37
1850	2·23	·27	1·58
1860	2·86	·35	3·23
1870	2·07	·32	5·31
1880	1·24	·56	8·26
1881 1882 1883 1884	1·46	·46	10·16

[566]

From the above, it will be seen that the percentage of *per capita* consumption for the several decades is as follows:—

	Spirits.	Wine.	Beer.
1840	100	100	100
1850	89	93	115
1860	114	121	236
1870	82	110	388
1880	49	193	603
1881			
1882	} 58	159	742
1883			
1884			

Increase and decrease in *per capita* consumption.

During the past forty years, therefore, there has been a decrease in the *per capita* consumption of distilled spirits of fully 40 per cent., an increase in the *per capita* consumption of wines of 60 per cent., and an increase of 642 per cent. in that of beer and other malt liquors. In 1880, 513,192,120 gallons of beer were brewed in the United States, which gave a consumption of 10½ gallons per head. The decrease in the consumption of spirits, of which whiskey may be considered the type in the United States, would seem to argue the success of the temperance movement, while the increase in the consumption of beer and light wines is a decided gain to the community.

Percentage of imported beverages.

By reference to the statistics, it will be found that the percentage of the total amount consumed of spirits, wines, and malt liquors produced in the United States has undergone a great change during the last forty years.

The following Table of imported beverages represents the percentage of each consumed for each decade:—

	Spirits.	Wine.	Beer.
1840	6·2	97·4	·63
1850	9·8	96·5	·55
1860	6·7	83·2	1·11
1870	1·8	75	·49
1880	2·2	17·8	·24
1884	1·9	15·1	·34
1881			
1882	} 2·1	23·3	·31
1883			
1884			

It will be seen from the above that only about 2 per cent. of the distilled spirits consumed are imported, while not over one-third of 1 per cent. of the malt liquors consumed are imported, and yet the amounts consumed are so great that even these small percentages amounted, in 1884, to 1,511,680 gallons of distilled spirits and 2,010,908 gallons of malt liquors.

Wine industry.

The statistics of the wine industry are deserving of notice. It has been shown that the increase in the *per capita* consumption during forty years equals 60 per cent.; but, owing to the rapid development of this industry, the average importation during the last four years has been only 23·3 per cent. of the total consumption, while in 1840 it was 97·4 per cent., and, even so recently as 1870, equalled 75 per cent. The total importation is at present about the same as in 1840, notwithstanding the fact that the population has trebled, and that there has been an increase of 60 per cent. in the *per capita* consumption. In 1840 the amount of domestic wine produced was only 124,734 gallons, and during the last five years the average annual production has been 19,994,916 gallons, and the average importation 5,473,467 gallons.

Internal revenue taxes.

The internal revenue taxes on spirits, wine, and malt liquors are as follow:—

	Dol. c.
Liquors, fermented, per barrel	1 00
,, distilled, per gallon	0 90
Whiskey, per gallon	0 90

		Dol.	c.
Imitation wines		2	40
Wholesale liquor dealers		100	00
Wholesale malt		50	00
Retail liquor dealers		25	00
Retail malt		20	00
Manufacturers of stills		50	00

The amount of revenue derived therefrom last year was— *Amount of revenue.*

	Dollars.
Spirits	76,905,385
Fermented liquors	18,084,954
Total	94,990,339

The total proceeds of the internal revenue taxes were 121,586,072 dollars, and the ordinary customs duties on the imports amounted to 6,263,887 dollars.

For some time past there has been a movement in favour of a reduction of the internal revenue taxes, which, if effected, would, it is argued, render any reduction of the customs duties out of the question. The loss to the revenue by a reduction of the duty on spirits would be considerable, while it would not really benefit the mass of the consuming population, the increased purchase power of which depends upon remunerative production and marketable facilities more than upon relief from indirect taxation. *Proposed reduction of internal revenue taxes.*

Grape Culture and Wine Production in the United States.

It will be seen from the foregoing Report that the production of wine in the United States has greatly increased during the last five years, but since 1880 the Agricultural Department has furnished no statistics. In the Report for that year the following Table showing the total average yield and the value of the production is given :—

(Table No. 2.)—TABLE showing the Total Average Yield and Value of Wine produced in the several States.

States.	Area in Vines.	Production.	Value.
	Acres.	Gallons.	Dol. c.
Alabama	1,111	422,672	399,705 00
Arkansas	893	72,750	112,401 87
California	32,368	13,557,155	4,046,865 80
Connecticut	64	5,336	6,076 75
Delaware	125	4,050	4,050 00
Florida	83	11,180	15,415 00
Georgia	2,991	903,244	1,335,521 62
Illinois	3,810	1,047,875	809,547 20
Indiana	3,851	99,566	91,719 40
Iowa	1,470	334,970	346,398 60
Kansas	3,542	226,249	190,330 75
Kentucky	1,850	81,170	80,908 75
Maine	71	1,500	2,850 00
Maryland	699	21,405	19,151 00
Massachusetts	227	6,338	10,050 50
Michigan	2,266	62,831	75,617 30
Minnesota	63	2,831	2,446 00
Mississippi	432	209,845	310,532 75
Missouri	7,376	1,824,207	1,320,050 40
Nebraska	280	5,767	8,982 00
New Jersey	1,967	215,122	223,866 70
New Mexico	3,150	908,500	980,250 00
New York	12,646	584,148	387,308 83
North Carolina	2,639	334,701	268,819 25
Ohio	9,973	1,632,073	1,627,926 88
Oregon	126	16,900	9,240 00
Pennsylvania	1,944	114,535	128,097 00
Rhode Island	55	262	516 50
South Carolina	193	16,988	22,356 25
Tennessee	1,128	64,797	90,796 00
Texas	850	35,528	44,704 87
Utah	658	114,975	175,825 00
Virginia	2,099	232,479	200,045 25
West Virginia	466	71,026	61,461 80
Wisconsin	217	10,968	15,559 85
Total	181,583	23,453,827	13,426,174 87

Production in California.

It will be seen from this Table that California takes the lead in the **area** planted and amount of production, and Table No. 3 gives the acreage and production by Counties.

(Table No. 3.)

Counties.	Acres in Vines.	Total Production.
		Gallons.
Sonoma	..	2,180,000
San Francisco	..	250,000
San Mateo	..	90,000
Alameda	..	270,000
Santa Clara	..	580,000
Santa Cruz	..	172,000
San Benito	..	60,000
El Dorado	1,100 or 1,200	350,000
Nevada	400	..
Placer	800 to 900	..
Amador	600	..
Calaveras	400	..
Tuolumne	400	..
Mariposa	500	..
Los Angeles	5,713	3,800,000
Napa	..	2,460,000
Contra Costa	..	25,000
Solano	..	160,000

There does not appear to have been much change in the kind of grape planted. The red grapes are the Concord and Ives Seedling, and the white the Catawba and the Dedalvare. The Labrusca vine very generally prevails, and the Nortons, Virginia, and other varieties of the *Æstivalis* family, have given good results. In the States south of the 35th parallel the *Vulpina* and *Candicans* are the favourites. In some counties in California foreign vines have been introduced with success, principally the "Gutedel," "Berger," and "Zinfandel." "Zinfandel" cuttings planted in March 1878 gave, in 1880, 2½ tons per acre. It is stated that in Sonoma county the grape crop returns from 45 to 120 dollars per acre, while the wheat crop only returns 15 dollars per acre. The vineyards of California have been threatened with phylloxera, but it does not appear that any great damage has as yet ensued. It is certain, says the Commissioner of Agriculture in his Report (1880), that the table wines of low alcoholic strength made in the United States are more free from adulteration, and consequently more healthy, than the wines ordinarily imported in casks, but there is much to be done in the improvement of the culture of the vineyards before the native can supersede the foreign production.

(Signed)   L. S. SACKVILLE WEST.

UNITED STATES.

No. 1.

Mr. West to Earl Granville.—(*Received May 9.*)

My Lord,   *Washington, April* 23, 1884.

I HAVE the honour to inclose to your Lordship the Report of the debate in the House of Representatives upon a Resolution for inquiry into adulterated food and drugs from the Committee on Public Health. The Resolution, however, was not agreed to.

I have, &c.
(Signed)   L. S. SACKVILLE WEST.

Inclosure in No. 1.

Extract from the "Congressional Record" of April 22, 1884.

Adulterated Food and Drugs.

Mr. Beach.—I am instructed by the Committee on Public Health to move to suspend the Rules and adopt the Resolution which I send to the desk.

The Clerk read as follows:—

"*Resolved,*—That the Committee on Public Health be and it hereby is authorized to inquire into the extent and character of the adulterated food and drugs imported into the United States or exported therefrom; and to this end the said Committee is authorized to send for persons and papers and to sit during the recess, if in its judgment it be necessary in the proper execution of this inquiry; and the sum of 2,000 dollars, or so much thereof as may be necessary, is hereby appropriated out of the contingent fund of the House to defray the expenses of the said inquiry."

Mr. Mills.—I demand a second on the motion to suspend the Rules.
Mr. Beach.—I ask unanimous consent that a second be considered as ordered.
Mr. Mills.—Oh, no; I object to that.
Mr. Beach and Mr. Mills were appointed tellers.
The House divided; and the tellers reported—ayes 93, noes 51.
So the motion to suspend the Rules was seconded.

[587]

The Speaker.—Under the Rules debate is now in order for thirty minutes—fifteen minutes in support of the motion to suspend the Rules and fifteen minutes in opposition to it.

Mr. Beach.—Mr. Speaker, the object of this investigation is to gather facts upon which to formulate such legislation as may be necessary to check the evils resulting from our foreign commerce in adulterated commodities. The proposed inquiry relates solely to exports and imports. There is no intention to investigate adulterations in the States or the commerce in adulterated articles between the States. We propose simply, in the language of the Resolution, to inquire into " the extent and character of the adulterated food and drugs imported into the United States or exported therefrom."

The subject, Mr. Speaker, is one of very great importance. It is particularly so at the present time by reason of the attitude assumed by foreign Governments. I trust that I may have the attention of the House for a few moments, so that we may get an intelligent vote on this proposition.

A few days since I found in the " New York Herald " the following article:—

" [By cable to the 'Herald.']

"*London, March* 31, 1884.

" In the House of Commons to-day Right Honourable George J. Dobson, Chancellor of the Duchy of Lancaster, replying to Mr. Thomas Duckham, Liberal Member for Herefordshire, said that the Foreign Office had been instructed to obtain information from America regarding the importation into England of American adulterated butter and cheese."

The reading of this article suggested to my mind that probably England had in contemplation a course of action towards American dairy products similar to that which France and Germany have pursued toward our hog products. If my suspicions are well founded the urgency of the inquiry sought by this Resolution is apparent. It will not do for us to abide the results of the English investigation. Commercial honesty as well as regard for the interests of our farmers and dairymen require that we ourselves should embark upon the investigation, and if we find, as I feel confident we shall, that there is just cause for the complaint, Congress should at once so regulate our foreign commerce in butter and cheese, and in fact all other articles which are the subject of adulteration, that the spurious article may be detected and not come in deceptive competition with the genuine.

In this matter of butter and cheese the statistics will justify the present action of England. We find in the Report of the Chief of the Bureau of Statistics the facts in relation to our exportations of butter and cheese.

In the year 1880 we exported butter to the value of 6,690,687 dollars. In 1881 it was about the same, or to be exact 6,256,024 dollars. In 1882 it suddenly dropped to 2,864,570 dollars, and in 1883 it fell off to 2,290,665 dollars.

Our exportation of cheese for the year 1881 was valued at 16,380,248 dollars, and in 1882 at 14,058,975 dollars. In 1883 it dwindled to 11,134,526 dollars.

These are indeed startling facts, and it behoves us to inquire into the cause of this great decrease in the exportation of our dairy products. It is openly charged that the decline is owing to the spurious butter and cheese which have taken the place of the genuine article.

Upon consulting Mr. Nimmo, the Chief of the Bureau of Statistics, to ascertain, if I could, the cause, I found that during the year 1881 we exported close on to 4,000,000 dollars' worth of oleomargarine butter. In 1882 the exportation of this imitation butter fell off to 308,427 dollars, but in its stead we shipped abroad an entirely new article of commerce, called oleomargarine (the oil), to the value of 2,666,197 dollars. In 1883 we shipped of this oil 4,143,748 dollars. This oil was exported to Holland and other countries to be manufactured into butter.

I inquired of Mr. Nimmo whether the article exported under the name of " butter " was genuine or in part spurious. He said he was unable to tell, that even the Customs officers could not tell, for under a decision of the Attorney-General they had no right to break packages for the purpose of inspection. He furthermore said that nothing but a thorough investigation would reach the facts, and he deemed such an investigation of great importance.

The same remarks will apply to cheese. Public attention has been directed mainly to the adulterations of butter, but cheese is adulterated in an equally villainous way. They have a sort of emulsifying process whereby lard is injected. The value of the adulterated article is far inferior to that of the genuine, and it is supposed to be detrimental to health. It is charged that we are exporting large quantities of this adulterated cheese, and it is openly asserted that the decline of 5,000,000 which occurred during the last year in our exportation of cheese is owing to the sensitiveness of foreign markets upon this subject of adulterations. This is a matter the Committee proposes to investigate, and at the same time it proposes to ascertain to what extent England is sending us adulterated cheese. Our importation of foreign cheese during the last year was valued at about 1,000,000 dollars. That much of it was adulterated is publicly asserted. In proof of the assertion I may read an article I cut from the "New York World" of last Friday:—

"Dr. Bartley, the chemist of the Brooklyn Health Department, has adopted a method of determining the deleteriousness of suspected edibles that surpasses the most critical analysis in reliability. A man having complained that 'English dairy' cheese was prejudicially adulterated, Dr. Barkley was directed by his department to make an analysis. He pooh-poohed the idea, and to prove that it was all a matter of imagination ate some of it. It made him so ill that he had to prescribe for himself. This testimony is worth more than a thousand white-washing certificates."

Now, while England is investigating the adulterated cheese which it is alleged is shipped to that country from America, I think it is well for us to profit by her example and inquire into the adulterated cheese which England is sending over to us.

We might also look into the adulterations which are practised in the manufacture of lard by the intermixture of tallow, and we would probably ascertain the reason why our exportations of lard, which were valued in 1881 at over 34,000,000 dollars, fell in 1883 to about 24,000,000 dollars, a decline of 10,000,000 dollars in two years.

I regret, Mr. Speaker, that in the few moments allowed for this debate I can not take up and consider the various adulterated articles which enter into our foreign commerce. Those who have given the subject but little attention have no conception of the extent to which these adulterations prevail. Among our exports we find the principal adulterations to be in butter, lard, and cheese. There are others, however, to which public attention has not yet been called, but which will be brought to light by the labours of this Committee. Why, only last night, in glancing over the February number of the Consular Reports issued by the State Department, I find that Consul Tanner, the Consul at Liege and Verviers, writes under date of 6th November last in regard to petroleum, of which we exported last year about 45,000,000 dollars' worth, as follows:—

"Petroleum is imported into this Consular district from Antwerp. It comes here to the wholesale dealers, and from them to the retail. Now, I am confident in my own mind that if petroleum is adulterated it is not done in the United States, and it looks, from the fact of the complaints in this instance coming from the retail dealers here, that it is doctored before it reaches their hands. By whom or when it is doctored is no business of mine, so that it is not done in the United States, and this brings me to the point. I respectfully ask the Department to have me supplied with a statement as to the quality and general condition, &c., of petroleum, such as we export for general use to Belgium, in order to vindicate our dealers from all suspicion of unfairness and adulterations.

"If I can succeed in doing this by the aid of the Department, I am sure that it will redound greatly to the interest of American exporters in many other articles, and will go far toward removing prejudices here against other of our products."

Now, Mr. Speaker, I would like to call attention to the principal articles of import which are the subject of adulteration. During the last year we imported drugs and chemicals to the value of 43,716,090 dollars, upon which we received a duty of 6,053,574 dollars. For the same period we imported spices to the value of 2,018,630 dollars, upon which we received a duty of 873,886 dollars. In the same year we imported spirits, wine, and malt liquors to the value of 13,733,666 dollars, upon which a duty of 9,253,341 dollars was paid. There was imported during last year of oils of all kinds 1,045,051 dol. 29 c., with a duty of 421,077 dol. 29 c. It is commonly believed that in most all of these articles which go to make up a vast commerce adulterations are practised to a greater or less extent.

It is strange that my protectionist friends on the other side of the House have not seen before now the necessity of the action we propose to take under this Resolution. They insist upon high duties to protect the American labourer against the pauper wages of Europe. They seem to have overlooked the fact that if we shut out by legislation these adulterated articles, we would practically put an end to their importation. Under the existing high rate of duties foreign countries can not send us the pure article. They are obliged to resort to adulteration to compete with our home producers.

Now, Mr. Speaker, if it is found upon this investigation that our exports and imports are adulterated, as is charged and commonly believed, it is obviously the duty of Congress to take some action. What that action may be remains for future consideration. The paramount duty now is to get at the facts. There are two ways in which we should look at this question. The one as it affects our duty to foreign nations with which we have commercial relations; the other as it concerns our own people and the general Government. For one, I believe that honesty and fair dealing are just as important among nations as among individuals. For this reason I would require that all exported articles should be just what they profess to be. If they are adulterated let them be so marked. We can not afford to have our commercial honesty as a nation assailed.

With regard to the duty we owe our own people in the matter of imports I think there will be no dispute. The protection of the public health is a legitimate function of the Government. We would be authorized, therefore, in prohibiting the importation of all adulterated articles which are detrimental to health, and we would be equally authorized in exacting absolute purity in the foreign drugs upon which we have to rely for the cure of sickness.

Another legitimate function of Government is to protect the people against deception, where the deception is general and can be prevented only through Government action. If adulterated goods are shipped to us from abroad with a view to be sold in this country at the price of genuine goods, it is the duty of the Government to stop them at the custom-house and see that they are properly branded before they are scattered among the people.

I have an illustration in point. It is well known that we have been exporting cotton-seed in large quantities. It is publicly charged that the oil is expressed from the seed and shipped back to this country as "olive oil." Now the difference between pure olive oil and the adulterated article can not be detected by the great mass of consumers. It requires an expert or a chemist to distinguish the genuine from the spurious. The people, however, buy the inferior article and pay the superior price. They are robbed and plundered, and the only way to stop the deception is through Government interference.

I have only time, Mr. Speaker, to allude to one other branch of this subject, and that is a highly important one. I refer to the effects of the importation of adulterated articles upon the revenues of the Government. About thirty years ago, when England was deeply agitated upon this question, and a Committee of Parliament was raised for investigation, it was estimated that the loss to the British revenues by reason of adulterations exceeded 2,000,000*l.* annually. I have no doubt whatever in my own mind that our revenues are defrauded in a much larger sum from our foreign trade in these adulterated goods, and I am anxious to gather the facts for the information of Congress.

The Speaker.—The time for debate in favour of the motion to suspend the Rules has expired. The gentleman from Texas (Mr. Mills) is recognized to control the remaining fifteen minutes.

Mr. Mills.—I yield five minutes to the gentleman from Maryland (Mr. McComas).

Mr. McComas.—Mr. Speaker, if, as one Member, I can get nothing better in this direction than the Resolution now proposed I must take that, but I protest, with all respect toward the Committee and the House, that there is now pending in this House a Bill introduced during the first two weeks of the Session which is already far in advance in the direction in which the mover of this Resolution would go—a proposition which is far beyond the point at which this Resolution starts, and there I think we ought now to start. This Bill was introduced in the Senate during the last Congress by Senator Miller, of New York, and in the House by Mr. Flower, of that State. It was referred to the Committee on Commerce of this House, and my distinguished friend from Michigan (Mr. Horr) made an exhaustive and elaborate Report upon it from that Committee. That Report has done more in reference to this important subject than this whole investigation can do during the brief life of the present Congress.

What is the immediate purpose of the Resolution? Is it intended to call the attention of the people of the country to the adulterations of food and drugs? It does not include medicines along with foods and drugs. Why, Sir, the country is already far ahead of this House in reference to this question. They are fully aroused to the need of a remedy for adulteration, and want you to apply the remedy. While we have been waiting for five months the public sentiment, as shown by the very extracts which the gentleman from New York has read from the press of the country, and by letters and personal inquiries of constituents which other gentlemen as well as myself have received, has gone already far in advance of this Resolution. Is it proposed to investigate to find out whether indeed there be adulteration? Who on this floor doubts or denies it? Everybody knows it. If this House is to undertake any remedy, the Bill which I hold in my hand, introduced here on the 11th December by the gentleman from Missouri (Mr. O'Neill), the same Bill *in totidem verbis* which was approved by the Committee on Commerce in the last House, and which I had intended to reintroduce because of its merits, ought to be passed instead of this tentative Resolution, which will prolong investigation through the coming summer and perhaps on through the short Session of Congress, when the measure must die.

There is at hand the exhaustive investigation recently had in England, and on which the Adulteration of Foods Acts are based, and on which this Bill is modelled.

This Bill I hold in my hand protects the territories and the district of Columbia, and indirectly the country at large, from the importation of adulterated food, medicines, and drugs. It does more than that. The State of New York, which has by legislation and investigation attempted to meet these evils, especially with respect to certain foods, has only State power and State action; but the Bill I hold in my hand does that which is more important than all laws of that character either by State or national action.

This Bill was referred to the Committee on Agriculture at the present Congress. It was reported favourably by the Committee of the last Congress. It does what is just and philosophical. It does what is most practical. It fixes a standard to define and classify everything coming into this country. It declares, Mr. Speaker, what is a food, what is a drug, and what is a medicine. But the Resolution on that table, for which I will vote if I can get nothing better, does not include medicine, and the word "drug" does not include it.

The Speaker.—The gentleman's time has expired.

Mr. McComas.—I ask the gentleman from Texas to yield me two minutes longer.

Mr. Mills.—Certainly.

Mr. McComas.—The Bill I hold here sets forth eight different classifications for the information of the people of the country and of the officers of the States and of the several national Departments. It includes under medicine all things which are known and recognized as to strength, purity, and quality as medicines. It includes under food those things which have not been mixed or injuriously affected as to quality or strength, from which nothing has been abstracted or into which improper substances have not been injected, or to which inferior or cheaper substitutes have been added, as well as all imitations. It excludes food partly diseased or rotten, or, as in case of milk, the product of diseased animals, or anything coloured, polished, or powdered whereby damage is concealed. It excludes all poisonous ingredients, or matter injurious to health. It excludes all matters like butterine, oleomargarine, and other adulterated foods; and it excludes all medicines which in an extreme moment may be given by a physician, but which may be a sham and a fraud upon the doctor and patient. All these things are provided for in the Bill which I hold in my hand, and the Secretary of the Treasury is empowered to employ analysts and inspectors and to investigate, and its provisions, as well as the decisions of the Treasury Department, would go everywhere throughout the country to give correct standard to trade, to commerce, and agriculture. Yet, Sir, we are to be told after five months of a Session of Congress, when we ought to be passing that Bill approved thus by so many members of this body, we are to be content with the pending Resolution, when we now and here should be taking care of the consumer throughout the land. This Bill has been on the Calendar for a long time, and we ought to correct the evils which confessedly exist, for which this is a remedy.

[587]

If, however, I am not permitted to vote for that Bill now I must vote for the pending proposition. I should prefer, however, going far in advance, and doing now fully and completely that which, sooner or later, we will be compelled to do.

I thank the gentleman from Texas for his courtesy.

Mr. Mills.—Mr. Speaker, I am not in favour of the Government interfering in the regulation of what its people eat, drink, or wear. I believe that the people of the United States are competent to determine for themselves what they ought to eat and how they will have it. I believe in that doctrine of our fathers, that the people are competent to build Governments and to administer them so as to take care of themselves. I do not believe the Government of the United States is inspired with any superior intelligence over the people who sent us here to make laws for them. I do not believe the Government of the United States can better determine what the people shall eat than the people can determine for themselves. Hence I am opposed to this constant interference on the part of the law-making power of the Government with the habits, food, and customs of the people at home. There is too much sumptuary legislation, as a friend has just whispered to me here.

Now, if it be wise for us to depart from this old fundamental idea in our Government, and it is necessary for the Government to examine into butter or oleomargarine, or whiskey or anything else which enters into the consumption of the people, this is not the proper way to do it. If we are going to have an examination made about butter imported into the United States, or exported to other people, the better way for us to do is to authorize the Secretary of the Treasury to have the investigation made at the custom-house. He can do it infinitely better than a floating Committee of this House. He can have his inspectors and his experts, who can make examination of goods coming in and going out.

Suppose some butter is presented for examination before this Committee, and they have an expert to pass upon it, how can he know what is coming in at New York on that day or the next day, or what is going out? The proper plan would be manifestly not to deputize the Committee, but to authorize the Secretary of the Treasury to take such steps as in his wisdom may be necessary to have an examination made through the custom-houses, and make his annual Reports to Congress. Therefore, there is no necessity for the passage of this Resolution.

The Speaker.—The question is on the motion of the gentleman from New York to suspend the Rules and pass the Resolution.

The question was taken. The House divided, and there were—ayes, 64; noes, 80.

Mr. Beach.—I ask for the yeas and nays on this proposition.

The yeas and nays were not ordered, only fourteen members voting in favour thereof.

So the Resolution was not agreed to.

Mr. Scales.—I ask unanimous consent that my colleague, Mr. Green, who is absent on account of sickness, be permitted to print some remarks on this subject.

There was no objection.

No. 2.

Mr. West to Earl Granville.—(*Received May* 17.)

My Lord, Washington, *May* 4, 1884.

WITH reference to my despatch of the 23rd ultimo, I have the honour to inclose to your Lordship herewith copies of two Bills* which have been introduced into the House of Representatives: one to prevent the fraudulent manufacture and sales of imitations of or adulterations of butter, and for other purposes, and the other to regulate the exportation of articles made in imitation of butter and cheese. The first has been referred to the Select Committee on Public Health, and the second to the Committee on Commerce.

I also inclose copies of a Resolution and of the Report thereupon from the Committee of Agriculture on oleomargarine and imitations of butter.

I have, &c.
(Signed) L. S. SACKVILLE WEST.

---

* These Bills have not yet become law in the United States.—*Foreign Office, April* 1885.

29

Inclosure 1 in No. 2.

48th Congress, 1st Session.—*House of Representatives*, 1995.

IN THE HOUSE OF REPRESENTATIVES.

January 7, 1884.

Read twice, referred to the Select Committee on the Public Health, and ordered to be printed.

MR. WELLER introduced the following Bill:—

A Bill to prevent the fraudulent Manufacture and Sales of Imitations of or Adulterations of Butter, and for other purposes.

Be it enacted by the Senate and House of Representatives of the United States of America in Congress assembled, that no person or persons shall manufacture for sale, sell, or keep for sale, any adulterated article imitating butter, composed in part of butter mixed with fats, or fats and other substances; and no person or persons shall manufacture for sale, sell, or keep for sale, any substance (known as oleomargarine) composed of fat of animals, as tallow, lard, oil, or other similar substances, in whole or in part; and no person shall manufacture any of said substances in combination to imitate butter, save and except that each and all said person or persons so manufacturing, selling, offering for sale, or keeping for sale, the same shall keep the same in, and only offer the same for sale and sell the same from, original packages, having plainly, and in a place outside to be easily and readily observed by the public, on said original packages, a formula of the materials, substances, and also the proportions of each entering into and composing the said imitation of butter.

Section 2. That any person or persons convicted of violating any of the provisions of this Act shall be fined in a sum not exceeding 5,000 dollars, but not less than 100 dollars, and, at the discretion of the Court, subject to imprisonment at hard labour not exceeding ten years.

Inclosure 2 in No. 2.

48th Congress, 1st Session.—*House of Representatives*, 2421.

IN THE HOUSE OF REPRESENTATIVES.

January 8, 1884.

Read twice, referred to the Committee on Commerce, and ordered to be printed.

MR. GEORGE W. RAY introduced the following Bill:—

A Bill to regulate the exportation of Articles made in Imitation of Butter and Cheese.

Be it enacted by the Senate and House of Representatives of the United States of America in Congress assembled, that every person who shall export to any foreign country any article or substance in the semblance of butter or cheese, not the actual product of the dairy, and not made exclusively of milk or cream, but into which the oil or fat of animals not produced from milk enters as a component part, or into which melted butter or any oil thereof has been introduced to take the place of cream, shall distinctly and durably stamp, brand, or mark upon every tub, box, firkin, or case containing such article the words "oleomargarine butter" or "butterine," or "oleomargarine cheese," when either is made from oleomargarine; the words "lard butter" or "lard cheese," when either is made from a mixture of lard and dairy butter, or of a mixture of lard and milk or cream, and the words "vegetable-oil butter" when it is made from a mixture of vegetable oils with dairy butter or oleomargarine, in plain Roman letters, not less than half an inch square, and shall file in the custom house a manifest accurately describing such commodities, which manifest shall be verified by oath or affirmation, and on failure to file such manifest shall forfeit 100 dollars for each offence.

Section 2. That all shipments of articles in the semblance of butter or cheese mentioned in the first section of this Act, from interior points in the United States to foreign countries, on through bills of lading, shall be accompanied by an invoice or list of such commodities, made out under the hand of the shipper thereof, which manifest or list shall be certified to under the hand of the agent of the shipper at the port at which such commodities are to be exported to any foreign country, and shall be filed in the custom-house at that port, as in the case of merchandize originally shipped from seaports and from frontier ports.

Section 3. That every person who shall export to any foreign country or place, or cause to be placed upon any vessel, car, or vehicle for exportation to any foreign country, any of the said articles or substances required by the first section of this Act to be stamped, marked, or branded as therein stated, without first stamping, marking, or branding the same as by said first section provided, and filing in the custom-house at the seaboard or frontier port a manifest thereof as aforesaid, shall, for each and every such offence, forfeit and pay a fine of 1,000 dollars, to be recovered in any Court of competent jurisdiction, one-half of such fine, when paid, to go to the informer, and the other half to be paid into the Treasury of the United States.

Section 4. That whenever there is found on board of any vessel, car, or vehicle, for exportation to a foreign country, any of the articles in the semblance of butter or cheese mentioned in the first section of this Act, and not distinctly and durably stamped, branded, or marked as therein provided, the Collector of Customs is hereby authorized to impose upon the shipper thereof a fine of 5 dollars upon each and every tub, box, firkin, or case containing such articles in the semblance of butter or cheese, and to retain the same in his custody until such fine is paid.

Section 5. That the Collectors of Customs at the several ports of the United States are hereby authorized to employ, with the approval of the Secretary of the Treasury, proper persons as special inspectors of dairy products, whose duty it shall be, under such regulations as the Secretary of the Treasury shall prescribe, to attend to the execution of the provisions of this law; and the said inspectors shall be paid, in the discretion of the Secretary of the Treasury, a per diem compensation not to exceed 6 dollars a-day when actually employed.

Section 6. That the special inspector of exports shall, before entering upon the duties of his office, take and subscribe an oath faithfully and diligently to perform the duties imposed upon him by this Act, which oath shall be administered by the Collector of the Port; and the said inspector shall receive as a salary the sum of   dollars per annum.

Inclosure 3 in No. 2.

48th Congress, 1st Session.—Mis. Doc. No. 31.

HOUSE OF REPRESENTATIVES.

Oleomargarine and Imitations of Butter.

January 22, 1884.—Referred to the Committee on Agriculture.

February 7, 1884.—Referred to the House Calendar and ordered to be printed.

MR. PARKER submitted the following, which was referred to the Committee on Agriculture:—

Whereas it is alleged that the interests of the American agriculturists and dairymen are greatly and unjustly injured by the manufacture, sale, and use of oleomargarine, butterine, suine, and imitation, artificial and adulterated butters of different kinds, and of adulterated and imitation compounds and mixtures sold and consumed as dairy products; and

Whereas it is alleged that fat and oils of hogs and cattle and of other animals, and also that vegetable oils, are used in the making and compounding of suine, oleomargarine butter, butterine, and adulterated and imitation dairy products; and also that such fats and oils are used and are imported, and are exported to be used for the making and compounding of such artificial, adulterated, and imitation dairy products, and that such adulterated imitation compounds are surreptitiously sold in this country and elsewhere in competition with genuine dairy products, greatly to the injury of the agriculturists and dairymen of the United States; and

Whereas it is alleged that the manufacture, sale, and exportation and disposition of said compounds, materials, and commodities is so conducted as to avoid general publicity and to prevent the obtaining of accurate or desirable statistics in relation thereto, and to mislead and deceive the consumer as to the actual character, composition, and ingredients thereof: Therefore,

Resolved,—That the Committee on Agriculture be, and hereby is, instructed to inquire into, and investigate the said allegations, and ascertain the facts relating thereto, and the facts and statistics of the adulterated and imitation compounds and mixtures of dairy products, and of the materials composing the same.

Attest:
(Signed)   JNO. B. CLARK, Jun., *Clerk.*

Inclosure 4 in No. 2.

48th Congress, 1st Session.—Report No. 251.

HOUSE OF REPRESENTATIVES.

Oleomargarine and Imitations of Butter.

February 7, 1884.—Referred to the House Calendar and ordered to be printed.

Report.

[To accompany Mis. Doc. No. 31.]

MR. BEACH, from the Committee on Agriculture, submitted the following:—

The Committee on Agriculture, to which was referred the Resolution relative to oleomargarine and imitations of butter, begs leave to report that it has considered the same, and recommends its passage with the following amendment:

At the end thereof add the following words:—

"And to this end the said Committee is hereby empowered to send for persons and papers."

UNITED STATES.

BALTIMORE.

Report by Consul Donohoe on the Trade and Commerce of Baltimore for the Year 1885.

SHIPPING AND NAVIGATION.

THERE has been a very considerable falling off in the number of British steamers at this port during the year. This has arisen from the low freights that have prevailed and the falling off in the grain export trade, which seems to have diminished at all the Atlantic ports.

The following table shows the movement of shipping at this port during the past year, not however taking into account the coasting trade, which is entirely confined to vessels under the American flag. The return of American vessels represents the entries and clearances to and from foreign ports only.

RETURN of all Shipping at the Port of Baltimore in the Year 1885.

ENTERED.

Nationality.	Sailing. Number of Vessels.	Tons.	Steam. Number of Vessels.	Tons.	Total. Number of Vessels.	Tons.
British	59	27,926	306	424,140	365	452,066
American	169	56,132	7	1,568	176	57,700
German	20	20,493	30	74,450	50	94,943
Spanish	...	...	11	25,689	11	25,689
Italian	25	14,900	...	...	25	14,900
Norwegian	13	8,663	2	2,192	15	10,855
Total	286	128,114	356	528,039	642	656,153

Total for 1884 724,639,139

CLEARED.

Nationality.	Sailing. Number of Vessels.	Tons.	Steam. Number of Vessels.	Tons.	Total. Number of Vessels.	Tons.
British	53	25,322	309	429,024	362	454,346
American	189	66,471	9	3,532	198	70,003
German	21	18,108	30	76,651	51	94,759
Spanish	...	...	11	25,689	11	25,689
Italian	24	14,490	...	...	24	14,490
Norwegian	13	8,619	2	2,192	15	10,811
Total	300	133,010	361	537,088	661	670,098

Total for 1884 764,706,316

UNITED STATES.

TRADE AND COMMERCE.

I annex a table showing the principal articles of export and import at this port during the last two years.

RETURN of Principal Articles of Export from Baltimore during the Year 1885, calculated at $5 to the £1 sterling.

		1885.		1884.	
Articles.		Quantity.	Value (in sterling).	Quantity.	Value (in sterling).
Wheat	Bushels	4,537,922	Total value of exports, £6,977,259 sterling.	16,524,524	Total value of exports, £8,471,888 sterling.
Corn (maize)	,,	13,528,857		5,051,695	
Flour	Barrels	1,051,262		444,941	
Cotton	Bales	107,028		209,291	
Petroleum	Gallons	11,847,556		15,158,733	
Tobacco	Hogsheads	37,630		43,192	
Bacon	Pounds	11,299,277		3,009,121	
Quercitron bark	Bags	58,042		53,602	
Live cattle	Head	17,897		15,221	
Coal	Tons	71,527		59,289	
Lard	Pounds	15,838,524		4,338,922	
Rosin	Barrels	38,490		58,749	

IMPORTS.

		1885.		1884.	
Articles.		Quantity.	Value (in sterling).	Quantity.	Value (in sterling).
Coffee	Bags	501,527	Total value of imports, £2,275,180 sterling.	471,977	Total value of imports, £2,392,395 sterling.
Tin plates	Boxes	455,902		475,599	
Iron ore	Tons	78,882		185,930	
,, pg	,,	6,178		7,527	
Salt	Sacks	354,653		339,446	
,,	Bushels	103,564		64,464	
Chemicals	Packages	30,623		30,033	
Brimstone	Tons	14,796		18,219	
Nitrate of soda	Bags	13,412		34,468	
Guano	Tons	11,423		19,464	
Oranges and lemons	Boxes	43,638		62,589	

Grain.

The quantity received by the four lines of railway at this port has been 25,271,766 bushels, about half of which has been carried by the Baltimore and Ohio line.

Wheat.

The short crop and small demand for export with speculation running up the price to a fictitious value has caused a large falling off in the export trade.

Corn.

There has been more demand for corn for exportation, and there has been a considerable increase in the quantity sent forward.

Flour.

Flour has been exported in much larger quantities than in former years.

There has always been a considerable trade in this article with Brazil, but now a demand for it seems to have sprung up in Great Britain, and a great deal has been exported during the year.

The export of bacon and lard has very much increased. *Bacon and lard.*

The export of cotton has fallen off considerably; it never amounted to much from Baltimore, but is now considerably reduced in consequence of railway discrimination in favour of other ports, and the steamer connection with the southern ports not being as efficient as in former years. *Cotton.*

The table of imports does not call for any particular remarks, as it shows but little change from the quantities of the few articles imported in 1884. As long as the American tariff remains as at present, not much improvement can take place in the way of imports, and as far as this port is concerned there has been a tolerably steady decrease in the value of imports for the last eighteen years. *Gradual decrease in imports.*

The exports at this port, which in 1879 and 1880 were large, are since then gradually dwindling away. *Decrease in exports.*

The grain trade, which was once very extensive, is now much diminished, and I see but little chance of its increasing when so many of the vessels engaged in it have to come here light, so that the low freights that have prevailed for outward cargoes give little inducement to owners of steamers to send their vessels to this port.

I find it is not possible to obtain at this port the statistics necessary for a table giving the values of the imports from and exports to each country, as I am informed by the Custom authorities that the foreign trade is not kept by countries. *Foreign trade.*

The principal trade with Great Britain consists in the importation of tin plates, chemicals, dry goods, earthenware, salt, and manufactures of iron and steel, and the exportation of grain, tobacco, cotton, and provisions. *British trade.*

Population and Industries.

The trade which employs the greatest number of hands in this State is the packing trade for oysters, fruit, and vegetables. In Baltimore there are 132 establishments employing 23,000 hands. *Packing trade.*

There are 32 tobacco factories, employing about 2,750 hands. *Tobacco factories.*

There are 21 cotton mills in the State, with 4,300 hands employed. *Cotton mills.*

There are a large number of hands employed in building. *Building trade.*

There were 8,222 deaths in Baltimore during 1885; of these 3,250 were of children under five years. The births were 7,797 for the year. The greatest number of deaths were from consumption, and amounted to 1,290 persons. *Health and vital statistics.*

The number of immigrants landing here were 8,285 in 1885, and 30,820 in 1884. The great falling off at this port was occasioned by the low railway fares from New York to the West, immigrants being taken to Chicago for one dollar. *Immigration.*

Baltimore, February 5, 1886.

NEW ORLEANS.

Report by Consul De Fonblanque on the Trade and Commerce of New Orleans for the Year 1885.

AGRICULTURE.

I GATHER from intelligent observers, who have formed their opinions upon personal experience of the agricultural resources of this State, and by comparison with what has been done elsewhere, that four things are necessary for its prosperity :—

1. Scientific inquiry into the best manner of increasing the yield of its crops per acre.
2. Premiums to farmers for the encouragement of experiments in the above direction.
3. An extension of banking facilities.
4. Summary jurisdiction in cases of petty theft.

I will consider these in their turn :—

1. *Scientific Inquiry, &c.*—This has already been commenced with regard to the cultivation of the sugar cane and the manufacture of its produce—under the auspices of the University of Louisiana at Baton Rouge—and good results are expected. But there remain many other problems; such, for example, as the use and choice of fertilisers for other crops, the protection of these against insects, the prospects of fruit (and notably grape) culture, &c., to be considered, with careful note of results, under skilled supervision.

2. *Premiums to Farmers.*—In other States the yield per acre has been wonderfully increased by these inducements. The value of land is comparatively low, and there is plenty of it to be obtained; but it is obvious that in a country where good main roads (or indeed any roads worthy of the name) are, to say the least, scarce, where those which exist are frequently impassable, and time is of importance in gathering and sending crops to market, the more compact a farm is made the more profitable it is likely to be.

3. *Banking Facilities.*—The terms of credit for plantation supplies are about 40 per cent. to 50 per cent. In other States farmers' banks abound, and money can be obtained for 8 per cent. to 10 per cent. With money in his hand the farmer can go into the market and buy exactly what he wants at the current rates, whereas in the hands of a New Orleans factor he has to take what the latter pleases and pay what he demands. Here I may say that the capital employed by the banks is by no means adequate to the general commercial wants of the district.

4. *Summary Jurisdiction, &c.*—The law of Louisiana requires that every larceny shall be tried before a jury, and here this mode of trial is fraught with delays, objections, and adjournments. The practical result is, that it is found better policy to keep nothing liable to be stolen than to rely upon the law for the protection of property that can be easily filched. Thus, in many rural districts, such pursuits as breeding poultry and cultivating fruit and vegetables, which are valuable to the farmer's wife and children elsewhere, cannot be taken up.

Necessity for other crops than cotton, sugar, and rice.

For many years agricultural Louisiana has relied upon her cotton and her sugar to the exclusion of all other produce, and farmers have bought food for themselves and fodder for their mules. Lately a wiser system has prevailed, and rice has been added to the list of staple products with great success. But there are strong indications that the duties on foreign sugar will be so lowered as to make its manufacture in this country unprofitable, and rice has already received a serious blow, as will hereafter appear. It seems, therefore, that great changes must be made in the cultivation of this State, and that the four principles stated at the head of these remarks should have immediate attention. She would do well to take a lesson from her once despised sister Arkansas, whose agricultural display at the World's Cotton Centennial Exposition was in quality and variety second to none in the whole building.

The cotton crop.

Cotton.—The crop of 1885-6 is now estimated at 565,000 bales. The manner in which it profits New Orleans will be made the subject of remark further on.

Rice.

Rice.—This crop, which produced 73,424 barrels in 1872-3, is estimated for 1885-6 at 392,360, but some of this is of inferior quality owing to unfavourable weather in the summer. The "blow" above referred to was delivered in the form of a decision by the Secretary of the Treasury in the case of a shipment of so-called "granulated rice" imported in June last, fixing the duty at 20 per cent. ad valorem, instead of at $2\frac{1}{2}$ c. a lb., the rate fixed for clean rice. Upon this subject I beg to quote as follows from a remonstrance made by a delegation of rice planters at Washington in October:—" Without questioning the evidence as to this particular parcel having been subjected to some intentional process or other by which the grains were broken, it is submitted that rice precisely similar to this, and undistinguishable from it, may be obtained by the simple process of screening a parcel of the same grade of rice, as it used to be imported into the United States prior to 1883. There is nothing but the evidence in this particular case (furnished by certificates of the European shippers) to show that this parcel has not been obtained by screening, and that it bears precisely the same relation to the foreign rice, now imported at $2\frac{1}{4}$ c., that middling or broken, or No. 2 rice, bears to whole rice in the classifications of the Charleston, Savannah, and New Orleans markets respectively for the domestic article.

" This being the case, it is submitted that whatever may have been the process to which this particular parcel of rice was subjected, such process was not a necessary means of reducing rice to that condition, although it may have been intentionally resorted to in this case for the purpose of bringing this parcel into the United States at a less duty than $2\frac{1}{4}$ c. a pound. That the resort to such process, whatever it may have been, could have been induced for no other purpose is rendered obvious by the consideration that, at the locality where the process was performed, the effect of the application of the process must have been to reduce the market value of the article so treated, since broken rice is worth less than whole all the world over; and no rice, foreign or domestic, is ever intentionally subjected to any similar process here, because its value would be thereby diminished.

" If, therefore, all the rice in the 1,000 bags in question was really subjected to an intentional special process, such process was not adapted to any purpose whatever, except to serve as a pretext for escaping the duty imposed by law. Again, since the process employed in this particular has made no change in the physical, chemical, or edible properties of the rice subjected to it, since its whole effect has been to reduce the entire parcel to that broken condition to which a considerable part of every parcel of clear rice is reduced by the ordinary process of cleaning, it is submitted that the fact of such a process having been resorted to cannot suffice to take the cleaned rice subjected to it out of the category of 'rice cleaned,' and put it into the category of the manufactured article not otherwise enumerated or provided for. To illustrate this in a practical way reference is asked to the sample of Louisiana rice herewith. This sample represents rice as it comes upon the market from the mills at New Orleans. It will be seen that a certain proportion of the grains are broken.

"Owing to the softer character of the East India rice, a much larger percentage of it is broken in cleaning—probably one-third in weight. These things being so, it is manifest that when the law was passed by Congress fixing a duty of $2\frac{1}{4}$ c. upon clean rice, it was known and considered that foreign rice consisted of, say, two-thirds whole grains and one-third broken grains; but now, if the broken grains separately imported are admitted at a duty of 20 per cent. ad valorem, which is less than half a cent a pound, and twice their weight comes in in whole grains obtained by screening at $2\frac{1}{4}$ c. a pound, the total quantity of foreign rice brought into the country will pay an average duty of only 1·66 c., instead of $2\frac{1}{4}$ c. a pound, as the law requires. It is immaterial whether the rice imported as 'broken' is obtained by screening or by special process devised for the purpose.

"An ordinary parcel in England or Germany being once screened, and the whole grains separated, these whole grains may be imported into New York two-thirds whole at a duty of $2\frac{1}{4}$ c. a pound, and one-third broken by special process at a duty of less than half a cent a pound. It is notorious that in New York the foreign whole and the foreign broken are purchased for the purpose of being again mixed together; so that, commercially, the effect is precisely the same as if the original parcel, as it came from the mill, had been imported at a duty of 1·66 c. a pound.

"This result is a practical nullification of the law to the detriment of the interests intended to be protected by it, and, so long as the importations remain constant in quantity, to the detriment also of the public revenue. If, however, the effect of the reduction of duty thus obtained should be to so increase the importations of foreign rice as to raise the revenue derived from the $2\frac{1}{4}$ c. and the 20 per cent. ad valorem duties to an aggregate equal to the average of former years, then the injury inflicted upon the interests intended to be protected by the law will be immeasurably intensified; and it is the manifest tendency toward this disastrous result that has caused the present respectful remonstrance to be made."

Sugar.—This precarious crop has turned out much better than was expected. The acreage planted was less than the preceding years, but the yield per acre is better and the expenses less than in any year since the war. The crop is estimated at 200,000 hogsheads, or (about) 250,000,000 lbs.; and prices range from 1 c. to $1\frac{1}{3}$ c. better than last year, owing to increased demands from refiners. Whether the duty on foreign sugar (beet and other), which renders this profit possible, can be kept up, is a question which causes much anxiety to planters, as it would seem that some Northern protectionists are prepared to jettison some of this impost in case of a storm. *Sugar crop.*

Ramie.—The possibility of utilising this plant is again under discussion, and I am told that the difficulties which have stood in the way of its decortication and manufacture are in a fair way to be removed; but as this has been said several times during the last twelve years, I suspend my remarks on the subject. *Ramie.*

MINERALS.

Of the discovery of iron fields in North Louisiana and the prospects of working them, Mr. Enderin, a mining expert, reports:—

Report of mining engineer.

"I have confined my investigations to the northern tier of parishes, viz., Caddo, Webster, Claiborne, Lincoln, Union, and Bienville.

Iron industry in North Louisiana.

"From my observations in those parishes, carried on during the last three months, during which time I have been some 65 or 70 days in the saddle, I believe the iron industries of North Louisiana can be made profitable if they are properly managed, but I do not believe they will become equal to those of Alabama.

"The most profitable way of working them would be first and foremost by the establishment of small furnaces of 15 or 18 tons. These small furnaces would supply material to hollow-ware and stove-foundries, nail works, car-wheel factories, &c. The manufacture of these articles from the iron produced by such furnaces would give all the profits that the iron is capable of yielding. In this way, also, other industries connected with and dependent upon the first would be created, and we should get factories for carriages, wagons, agricultural implements, &c.

"Then, again, timber of excellent quality abounds throughout this iron section of Louisiana. The ash, the hickory, and the walnut are found everywhere, and this abundance offers great advantages to persons desirous of engaging in other businesses.

"If iron manufacturers were to go into Northern Louisiana and establish large furnaces such as they have in Alabama, the iron being so scattered, covering the entire surface, more or less, the cost would be very great, and the field would probably be exhausted sooner than is desirable: therefore it is that I advocate the erection of small furnaces only.

Character of iron ore.

"The iron goes to a depth of about five feet on an average, not compact, but percolated through the earth to that depth, and its quality is the best, as good as can be found anywhere. Then there is found here another kind of iron that will perhaps be eventually used—that is, silicious iron. This cannot be used alone, because the amount of slag arising from the too great abundance of silex would clog the furnace, although silex is necessary to a certain extent for fluxing. But this silicious iron may some day be used in the same furnace with other iron free of silex.

Fuel.

"I think no coal can be found in Louisiana. But fortunately this iron should be treated with no other fuel than charcoal, and of this there is the greatest abundance to be obtained from the enormous supply of pine in this section.

Limestone.

"Limestone is another essential in the manufacture of iron, and plenty of this is to be found in the region immediately surrounding Shreveport. There is cause for congratulation in this, because the lack of limestone frequently places a great hindrance in the way of manufacturing iron. It is absolutely necessary for fluxing purposes. Now there is a good deal of limestone in many other parts of the State, but in places from which it would be difficult to transport it to the iron section of Louisiana. The limestone around Shreveport has not been tried yet, but I have no doubt as to its answering the purpose very well. If so, it would be ready to hand within a mile or two of many of the furnaces that would probably be established along the Vicksburg and Shreveport Railway, which would no doubt be the line of transportation for the limestone. I fully believe that if these small furnaces were started as I have suggested, the other industries that I have named would soon follow in their train, and Northern Louisiana would manufacture her iron into goods that would be distributed all through Southern Arkansas, North and East Texas, part of Mississippi, and the whole state of Louisiana, and that would be the means of adding greatly not only to the capital of our State, but to her population."

Marble of a fair quality has also been discovered.

The Labour Question.

The future of New Orleans as a seaport appears to me to depend upon a solution of this most important and difficult question.

A veritable "burning" question, which has not been touched (except in these reports) until very recently, on account of the political danger incurred. The Press is now obliged to take it up, but does so with gloved hands on account of the fate ("boycotting") which befell a newspaper which dared to offend the working men's counsel by speaking out.

The following is from the "Times Democrat" of October 25th, 1885:—"Almost every day our commercial columns contain items like the following, taken from the 'Times Democrat' of yesterday: 'The shipments of cotton on Friday to vessels loading for all ports amounted to 10,431 bales, of which 4,890 were in transit, and 5,541 shipped from city presses.' We have recently given statistics to show the great change which has taken place in the cotton trade of New Orleans during the last five years, and have called attention to the momentous fact that New Orleans is annually becoming, to a greater and greater extent, a mere point for export of cotton, instead of being a market for the actual handling and sale of the great staple. Is it not time that some steps were taken to inquire into the real causes of this state of affairs, and to arrest this diversion of our trade? While cotton passing through this port in transit leaves some money in the community, yet it leaves much less than would the same quantity of cotton handled in the usual way. The tendency of modern commerce is to take the most direct routes, and to avoid all charges, as far as possible; yet there are other considerations besides mere cost which govern merchants in the transaction of their business. First among these considerations is safety—an element which the transit cotton business, at present, conspicuously lacks. A new Orleans exporter, who purchases 1,000 bales of cotton from a country buyer, and lets the cotton pass through this port in transit, avoids a very considerable expense in the way of handling, but he also runs a risk which he would not take if the inducements were not very great; for in that case he has no opportunity to examine the cotton he has bought, or to verify the weights of the invoice for which he pays. During the last two seasons, when the crop was almost entirely devoid of grades below low middling, and the difference of value between the various grades were small, the risk as regards classification was slight. But the case is different now. The present crop contains an abundance of very undesirable low cotton, and the exporter may easily lose more from deficient classification and weights in cotton bought in the country than he saves in the cost of handling. Yet, so long as the difference between the cost of handling cotton in transit and selling it here remains what it now is, the temptation to adopt the apparently cheaper method will be most irresistible."

The real causes of this state of affairs are patent to all: they are the arbitrary regulations and excessive prices imposed by the powerful labour organisations. Here are details of the consequences given by the Cotton Exchange and its President:—

[254]

"The outlook for our cotton trade is anything but cheering, and if we are to judge by the figures for the past few years there is abundant cause for alarm. During the past season the percentage of our receipts, both net and gross, that has passed through the port without stopping has been larger than ever before known, and it looks as if the custom of buying in the interior, and using New Orleans only as a means of exit, is likely to increase largely in the near future, unless means can be devised to stem the current.

<small>Loss of local trade.</small>
"Referring to the business of the seven months, to March 31st of this year, we find that the number of bales handled in presses has fallen off nearly 100,000. This decrease is not warranted by failure of the crops in this section, nor is it due to diversion of trade tributary to New Orleans in favour of other ports. It represents almost wholly a loss of local trade. Compared with former years we find that from 1880-81 to 1883-84 the proportion of the crop handled in New Orleans decreased 120,000 bales—that is, had our percentage of the crop in 1883-84 been the same as in 1880-81 we should have handled about 1,223,000 bales instead of 1,103,000 bales.

"This year the crop is said to point to between 5,650,000 and 5,700,000 bales; at all events, it will not vary much from those figures. Assuming 5,650,000 as a basis, we shall not handle more than $17\frac{1}{2}$ per cent. of the crop. In other words, our trade will fall below 1,000,000 bales, and we have lost of our trade proper during the last five years nearly 220,000 bales.

"The situation of the cotton trade of New Orleans demands the most serious consideration of those interested, including the labourers, pressmen, and merchants. There is a difference between what is called 'croaking' and a plain statement of stubborn facts, and I am candid in my answers, because I consider that the truth should be known, and if possible the proper correctives applied.

<small>Through shipments f.o.b.</small>
"The startling increase of through shipments this year at the expense of our local trade indicates how strong a hold this f.o.b. business, as it is called, has taken. Facilities for buying, compressing and shipping from interior points are multiplying on all sides, and there is an undoubted disposition manifested by the railroads to discriminate against New Orleans in favour of through business.

"The main causes for this condition of our business may be summed up in three words, 'dollars and cents.' Buyers and shippers state that it costs them less to handle cotton direct from the interior than in New Orleans. It is not necessary to argue this point; the facts are that the transit cotton has increased within the past five years 38 per cent. In the years 1880-81 we had gross receipts of 1,883,849 bales, of which 466,170 were in transit. For the first seven months of 1884-85 we had gross receipts of 1,609,941, of which 646,907 were in transit. The latter is for the seven months ending March 31st, 1885. During April this year our receipts were 39,805 bales, of which only 11,366 bales went to presses, and last month (May) we received 17,572, of which 5,088 went to presses. This is a matter in which labourers, pressmen, and merchants are all concerned. In fact, I may say that the entire city of New Orleans is most deeply concerned, as cotton is the principal mainstay of this community. The labourers are the first to seriously feel the effects. There is no knowing how much deprivation may be caused among that class during the ensuing dull season, because of the falling off there has been in their work. Whatever they may do, if this condition of a steadily diminishing trade goes on, it is only a matter of time before there will not be sufficient work to go round. The number of labourers is not decreasing, while the work is. Every inch we lose now will count doubly against us in our efforts to regain our trade. Each year, unfortunately, the system of buying in the interior becomes more perfect, and some of our best people are making arrangements to engage in it."

Warning to labour.

Respecting these f.o.b. (free on board) shipments the "New York Shipping List" says:—"It is but a few years ago that the chartering of all cotton tonnage, steam as well as sail, and from whatever port shipments were made, was accomplished at this port. It was here that agents always sought employment for their vessels, and that shippers sent their orders for tonnage. With the advent of what is known as the 'tramp' steamer this business, however, gradually drifted to the other side of the Atlantic, where these steamers were owned and managed, and until quite recently the greater portion of the business which had centred here was transacted in Liverpool, Havre, and other European ports. These steamers were enabled to accept such low rates of freight that so long as tramp steamers monopolised so large a share of the ocean-carrying traffic there seemed to be little change of the engagement of any considerable part of the cotton tonnage returning to this side; but it appears that in this respect a new departure has been taken, and another radical change is taking place. Arrangements have been completed with the railroads running to the principal cotton shipping ports of the South, the several lines of coast steamers coming from them to New York, and the great Transatlantic line of ocean steamers, whereby a shipment of cotton can be brought now almost from the point of production, and carried to its European destination with better despatch and promptness, as well as at lower rates of freight than is possible by the former method of shipping by direct steamer. This is on account of the larger and more powerful steamers now employed upon our coast lines, increased facilities for loading and transhipment, and the enormous capacity of the powerful boats that now regularly ply on the Transatlantic ferry. Thus a shipment brought by rail from the interior is put on board the coast steamer the same day, comes hither on schedule time, can be readily transferred into the Atlantic steamer in a few hours, and then crosses to Liverpool in from seven to eight days. It is said that in this way shipments are not more than 15 or 18 days *en route*, and can be delivered with time-table regularity. The advantages offered by this method in the saving of expense and time have already resulted in diverting large shipments into this channel, and the probabilities are that a very considerable proportion of the present crop will reach European markets in this way. Furthermore, it is said that the Atlantic steamers are enabled to make close connections with the railroads running to the manufacturing towns in England and upon the Continent, so that in reality the raw material is almost taken from the field to the foreign mill upon a single bill of lading and a single rate of freight, without further trouble or expense to the shipper or spinner. This brings back to us a share in an important carrying trade, and will prove a great benefit to our lines of coast steamers; but it is in the nature of cold comfort to those who heretofore have participated in the benefits of chartering tonnage for this special line of trade."

Changes in carrying trade. The "tramp" steamship.

Through all this it will be observed that though the fact that business has left the city and port is admitted, the causes which induced the European importers of cotton to adopt the new system are but lightly touched. In other reports I have noticed the almost total absence here of labour-saving machinery. I have shown how a bale of cotton from its arrival to its departure is "handled," and

UNITED STATES.

Labour-saving machinery. perhaps I need not repeat the statement. It is now for the first time suggested publicly by leading merchants that the port charges might be lessened by reducing the mere manual work. It remains to be seen how this proposition will be met by the Trades Assembly, and I regret to state that the question is embittered by the action of a recent grand jury in indicting for libel three of its leaders on account of certain placards carried in its annual procession.

It does not, of course, matter to our manufacturers how or whence they procure their cotton, so that they can obtain it at a remunerative price and in good order; but the new system is not without its risks, and the old one presented several advantages. It is to the advantage **Risks to transit of cotton.** of the importer that his cotton should be shipped under the auspices of such an institution as the New Orleans Cotton Exchange. The risks of incorrect weighing and classing, bad packing, loading in wet weather or condition, pilfering in transit, &c., are reduced to a minimum under its supervision. I therefore hope, in the interests of our own people, that a *modus vivendi* between labour and its employers will be found, and that this port may regain its business to the benefit of all.

EXPORTS AND IMPORTS.

The principal exports in British ships during 1885 are as follows:—

Exports in British ships.

Articles.		Quantity.
Cotton	Bales	889,023
,, seed oil	Barrels	5,397
,, ,, ,, cake	Sacks	383,143
,, ,, meal	,,	368,453
,, seed	,,	6,875
,, ,, soap stock	Barrels	3,738
Corn	Bushels	6,810,749
,,	Sacks	55,450
Rye	Bushels	54,583
Wheat	,,	20,147
,,	Sacks	2,472
Flour	Barrels	1,225
,,	Sacks	2,100
Staves	Pieces	559,765
Lumber (oak)	Feet	160,500
,, ,,	Pieces	51,604
Lead	Bars	26,237
,,	Pigs	52,700

Small quantities of copper ore, rosin, moss, honey, shingles, lard, tallow, and tobacco have also been exported in our ships.

Comparison with last year. Compared with last year, the export of cotton shows an increase of 2,641 bales, and there is a slight decrease in cotton seed products, except meal. In corn there is a considerable increase; in round numbers 6,000,000 bushels against 2,000,000 bushels, but in wheat there is a great falling off.

Imports. *Imports.*—I have stated in previous reports the reasons why the importation of British goods has fallen away so as to be at present hardly appreciable. The World's Cotton Centennial Exposition gave our manufacturers a chance of making a market, and I pointed out the particular objects which would be most likely to gain attention. This **"Comptoir Industriel Belge."** chance was not taken; but the Belgians, who made an admirable display representative of all their products, took the hint, and have established an agency in which 32 firms are represented, and where the following articles can be sampled and priced:—

Ladies' cloth, encaustic tiles, Courtrai linens, handkerchiefs, cambrics, tapestry for furniture, table-covers, cap robes, linen ticking, religious books, chromo-lithographs, flannels, woollen cloths and cashmeres, real laces, knit goods, tweeds, portable narrow-gauge railways, perfumery and fruit extracts, sheet zinc and lead, lamps, gas fixtures and bronzes, railway materials, brass and reed musical instruments, veterinary products, marble clocks, confectionery and pharmaceutical products, firearms of all descriptions, liquors and cordials, kid gloves, toilet soaps, paving stones, window glass, looking glasses and frames, table linen, buttons and trimmings, enamelled ironware, and printing. *Articles from Belgium.*

This is the way, in my humble judgment, to make a market. It is the way in which we might have kept and increased that which we once had in this district, but our trades do not seem to understand that the day in which the manufacturer or the wholesale house might wait at home to be dealt with has passed. The producer must now go out and meet the retailer more than half-way, or he will be intercepted by some more enterprising rival. An American lock gains a gold medal at the "Inventions," and is sold freely in the city of Chubb and Bramah! During a recent leave of absence I met a gentleman who has eight agencies for the sale of American goods in England, and he can be met in Long Acre with orders for American carriages and carriage materials in his pocket! The fact that there is nothing about the New Orleans of to-day to render it impervious to foreign goods is proved by the establishment of the Belgian agency, and the success which it has met with; I therefore venture to repeat what I wrote in March, 1884, on the subject of the World's Cotton Centennial Exposition, and which (substituting the words "trader" for "exhibitor," and "competition in" for "display of") applies, I think, to the present:— *Pushing American goods in London.*

"The intending exhibitor will do well to give up preconceived ideas as to what will suit the American market. The time in which expense and gaudiness were the principal qualities looked for has passed. For every one person who had the means and taste to buy objects of decorative art, or who appreciated art in the shape or colouring of common things ten years ago, there now are a hundred." *Advice to British manufacturers.*

Writing especially of this city and the south generally, "I recommend a display of the following articles in the best designs and at all prices: china and earthenware, table and bedroom services, furniture of all sorts, table decorations, wall papers, hangings, carpets, rugs, house decorations and ornaments, oleographs, prints, &c., and kitchen and dairy utensils; all sorts of printed calicoes, cretonnes, chintz; all sorts of fine cutlery, toilet articles, dressing case and bags (mounted), workboxes and fancy stands, screens and holders; all sorts of sporting (shooting and fishing) tackle, garden ornaments, window gardening materials, tents and awnings, stable fittings and utensils, school furniture and appliances; designs for street pavement, cleaning, and drainage, drainage pipes, traps, valves, tanks, &c.; cotton carding, spinning, and weaving machinery, machine tools, hospital furniture (surgical appliances, not instruments), and steam cranes and winches for loading and discharging ships from the wharf." *Articles recommended for this market.*

SHIPPING.

Returns with which I am favoured from the Custom-house and by my colleagues show the following movements of ships:—

ENTERED.

	Number.	Tons.	Crew.
British	335	389,279	8,076
American	477	435,359	11,100
Austrian	28	18,051	361
Belgian	1	2,101	..
Danish	..	..	..
French	16	28,536	584
German	21	22,845	147
Italian	85	42,128	1,228
Mexican	23	17,783	..
Russian	5	3,748	79
Spanish	53	76,361	1,680
Swedish and Norwegian	13	8,175	..

CLEARED.

	Number.	Tons.	Crew.
British	323	374,383	8,564
American	410	417,534	10,359
Austrian	20	14,647	260
Belgian	1	2,101	..
French	16	28,536	584
German	17	19,355	356
Italian	72	32,975	1,095
Mexican	28	37,369	..
Russian	3	2,104	44
Spanish	58	69,374	1,088
Swedish and Norwegian	16	8,176	..

Trips of regular lines. Of the above the British, American, and Mexican have regular lines of steamers. The British (2), from Liverpool, indirect and direct back, and the same ship will make about four trips in the course of the year; the American (2) to New York and back, and each ship will make the round voyage about once a month; the Mexican (1) plies to Vera Cruz and back pretty regularly.

Increase of sailing ships. There has been a remarkable increase of sailing ships of all nations at this port during the latter part of the year. During the three months ending December 31st, 1884, we had 39 British sailing ships, of 34,266 tons, as against 53 ships, 55,618 tons, during the corresponding period of last year.

PUBLIC WORKS.

The "American" Exposition. *The American Exposition.*—This successor (or continuation) of the World's Cotton Centennial Exposition of 1884–5, though started with good prospects of success, is (so far) a failure. The original plan of making it an exhibition of goods manufactured in the various cities of the Union could not be carried out.

Electric Light.—The city of New Orleans, lighted partially by electricity for some time, is now almost entirely illuminated by this agent: the suburbs by tower lights, and the streets by lamps on cranes. As this system only came into full operation on the 1st January, the subject will more properly belong to the present year.

<small>Electric lighting.</small>

IMMIGRATION.

I have again to give a note of warning against the highly-coloured inducements offered to immigrants in pamphlets, purporting to describe the resources of the States within this Consular district. My colleague in Texas will no doubt have done the like, but as many poor people who have been ruined there by misrepresentation come back more or less destitute through this city, and make their complaints to me, I may perhaps be allowed to mention the fact. These pamphlets are generally published in the interests of railroad companies that have lands to dispose of along their lines, and steamship agents who desire to obtain outward passengers sometimes join in the project. I have tested the *bona fides* of a so-called emigration society founded as above-described, and find that its exertions are not to be obtained for the protection of the emigrant. The vagrant laws of Louisiana and Mississippi are severe. There is nothing in the nature of poor-law relief, and if from sickness or any other cause the foreign labourer becomes destitute, there is only a gaol before him. Vagrants are defined as "idle persons who, not having visible means to maintain themselves, live without employment; all persons wandering abroad and lodging in groceries, taverns, beer-houses, market places, sheds, barns, uninhabited buildings, or in the open air, and not giving a good account of themselves; and all persons wandering abroad and begging." The practice is to impose a fine, which the "vagrant" has to work out at a certain rate per day.

<small>Warning to emigrants.</small>

<small>Vagrant laws.</small>

PUBLIC HEALTH.

The health of the city of New Orleans during the past year has been good. Its death rate, notwithstanding the large accession to its population caused by visitors to the Exposition, has been below the average.

<small>Death rate.</small>

New Orleans, February 5, 1886.

UNITED STATES.

BOSTON.

Report by Consul Henderson on the Trade and Commerce of Boston and the Boston Consular District for the Year 1885.

THE foreign trade of Boston for 1885 (constituting 94 per cent. of that of the whole Consular district) shows a decrease in imports of 950,000*l*.,* and in imports of over 1,500,000*l*.† This was principally due' as regards imports, to a previous falling off in the demand for fore'ign goods, and the indisposition of importers to lay in larger stocks than they expected to dispose of readily; and, in respect to exports, to the low prices and short demand abroad for agricultural products. *Foreign trade.*

With the exception of the iron market, which only began to show signs of improvement towards the end of the year, domestic trade was on the whole more active than for several years past, and in spite of a general decline in prices was, with few exceptions, fairly remunerative. *Domestic trade.*

The majority of domestic industries did not suffer materially from lack of work, but, whilst compelled to submit to low prices, were injuriously affected by numerous and some prolonged strikes against the reduction of wages, and which, though in most cases compromised or settled by arbitration, seriously interfered with the execution of work which had been contracted for, and produced some distress amongst the strikers. *Domestic industries.*

Meanwhile the following statistical data, published recently for the State of Massachusetts, evince a progressive and prosperous condition of the population generally, and lead to the inference that the prevalence of low prices, so much complained of, have mainly contributed to the well-being of producers and consumers alike, by reducing the cost of living and stimulating consumption, and the employment of capital and labour. These statistics show that, according to the census taken in 1885, the population of the State was 1,941,465, being an increase of 8 per cent. in five years since 1880, when the previous census was taken; whilst, as compared with 1884, the valuation of real and personal property shows an increase of 5,000,000*l*., the amount of savings banks deposits an increase of 2,450,000*l*., the number of firms in business an increase of over 2,000*l*., and business failures a decrease of 64 in number and of 550,000*l*., or 30 per cent., in the amount of their liabilities. *Increase and condition of the population.*

The following is a review of the most important Boston trades and markets in 1885:—

Receipts of cotton at this port were 399,000 bales, or a decrease of 67,000 bales; and exports 119,400 bales, or a decrease of about 30,000 bales. Mills in the Northern States, which receive most of their cotton direct from the South, took 890,000 bales, or an increase of 200,000. Prices averaged $5\frac{3}{4}d$. from January to April, but fell gradually to $4\frac{3}{4}d$. *Cotton.*

---

* The rate of conversion of dollars into sterling in this report is 4*s*. to the dollar.

† In statements of increase or decrease in quantities or values, the comparison, unless the date is given, is with the previous year.

UNITED STATES.

by the end of the year, principally owing to the universal decline in the consumption and price of cotton goods, and the prospect of a large forthcoming crop.

Wool.
Receipts of wool were 480,000 bales domestic, and 60,500 bales foreign, or an increase altogether of about 57,000 bales. With the exception of a temporary decline in July, prices of fine domestic wool were as high as 1s. 7d. per lb. throughout the year, which closed with an upward tendency and a comparatively small stock in dealers' hands.

Cotton and woollen goods.
Sales of cotton and woollen goods show a large increase, but whilst woollens sold at a profit as fast as they could be produced, cotton goods were in many cases disposed of at a loss, and after curtailing production barely above cost. The value of cotton goods exported was 120,000l.

Clothing trade.
The clothing trade continues to grow in importance, and to give employment to an increasing number of the working class, principally women. The year's trade was very large in volume, and, notwithstanding low prices, profitable.

Boot and shoe trade.
The boot and shoe trade, like ready-made clothing, assumes larger proportions every year. In spite of some interruption from strikes, shipments to different parts of the country amounted to 64,000,000 pairs of boots and shoes, being an increase of 3,500,000 pairs.

Hides and leather.
Receipts of hides exceeded 2,000,000 in number, or an increase of 220,000. Prices were lower, whilst leather was in good demand, and improved in price towards the end of the year.

Iron.
The iron market was in a very depressed condition during the greater part of the year, and owing to short demand and low prices, both imports and home production were considerably reduced. Towards the close of the year, however, there was a better demand, and prices had an upward tendency. The lowest quotations were:—For pig iron, 3l. 12s. and 4l. 4s., according to grade; and for bar iron, 6l. 15s. and 9l.

Flour and grain.
Notwithstanding a short wheat crop, a large surplus from 1884 and a short demand for export made the flour market sluggish. Prices for home consumption, however, averaged a fraction higher. Receipts of flour and wheat show a decrease of 600,000 barrels and 73,000 bushels respectively, and exports a decrease of 250,000 barrels and 66,000 bushels. Maize and oats were abundant, but exports were very small in either case. Maize was very low in price, but oats, which are virtually limited to home consumption, did not vary from the previous year.

Cattle, meat, and dairy products.
There was a large decrease in exports of cattle and sheep, but in fresh beef, as well as in packed beef and pork products, the increase was considerable. Exports of cheese decreased largely, whilst in butter and lard there was little change. Prices in all cases were lower than in 1884.

Fish.
In consequence of the termination of the Fisheries Articles of the Treaty of 1871, imports of mackerel from Canada decreased nearly one-half. The supply of fish was nevertheless abundant, and, whilst prices were excessively low, leaving little or no profit to owners of fishing vessels and fishermen, dealers and packers did a large and paying business.

Sugar.
Imports of raw sugar show a decrease of 35,000 tons, or 17½ per cent., and sales of refined for consumption and exportation a decrease of 22,000 tons. Owing to a reported deficiency in the supply of beet sugar, prices of both raw and refined were fractionally increased.

Shipping and shipbuilding.
Shipping interests at this port are, if possible, in a more depressed condition than they have been for some years past, and Boston ship-owners find it, under the existing circumstances of the carrying trade,

BOSTON. 397

more difficult than ever to compete with. Foreign flags' shipbuilding is, as a necessary consequence, almost entirely suspended, and but for the coasting trade, which is exclusively carried on by ships built in the country, would be virtually extinct. Freights were low, but fluctuated less than in 1884.

The value of real estate has been much enhanced by an increased demand for safe investments, and by extensive building operations, which, whilst required to meet the growing wants of the population, have served to give employment to capital and labour, and impart some activity to the trade in building materials. Rents have not advanced, but new buildings, both for dwelling and business purposes, have been occupied as fast as they were completed, and at the existing low cost of materials pay a fair interest on the money invested. *Real estate and house building.*

The money market was in an unsettled condition during the year, owing to the uncertainty which has continued to hang over the question of the perpetuation of the coinage of debased silver currency as unlimited legal tender, and to the want of confidence engendered by the long-continued depression in the railway stock and bond market, and other interests affected by it. Money was nevertheless abundant, and with occasional momentary fluctuations generally obtainable, on good security, at very low interest, whilst clearing-house returns show a large increase in the movement of capital. *Money and stock markets and exchange.*

The stock market has been gradually recovering its tone and healthy condition, and stocks and bonds, including those of railways known to be sound, but which had been more or less affected by its general demoralisation, have regained their former position and legitimate market value.

Foreign exchange showed a somewhat narrower range than in 1884. Bankers' light bills rose gradually, with slight fluctuations, from 4 dol. 84½ c. per £ in January, to 4 dol. 90 c. in December.

The following tables (Annexes A, B, and C) are returns of shipping and of exports and imports at ports in the Boston Consular district, and in the State of Maine, for the fiscal year ended on June 30, 1885, this being the latest date to which reliable statistics are obtainable:—

Annex A.—RETURN of all Shipping in the Foreign Trade* at Ports in the Boston Consular District, and in the State of Maine, in the Fiscal Year ended June 30, 1885.

ENTERED.

Nationality.	Sailing. Number of Vessels.	Sailing. Tons.	Steam. Number of Vessels.	Steam. Tons.	Total. Number of Vessels.	Total. Tons.
Foreign†	3,122	393,146	474	784,615	3,596	1,177,761
American	834	248,077	464	229,758	1,298	477,835
Total	3,956	641,223	938	1,014,373	4,894	1,655,596
,, fiscal year, 1884	4,437	694,270	817	1,063,421	5,254	1,757,691

CLEARED.

Nationality.	Sailing. Number of Vessels.	Sailing. Tons.	Steam. Number of Vessels.	Steam. Tons.	Total. Number of Vessels.	Total. Tons.
Foreign†	3,042	364,478	391	667,586	3,433	1,032,064
American	1,211	331,785	466	229,121	1,677	560,906
Total	4,253	696,263	857	896,707	5,110	1,592,170
,, fiscal year, 1884	4,854	782,836	725	943,362	5,579	1,726,198

Annex B.—RETURN of Principal Articles of Export from Ports in the Boston Consular District, and Ports in the State of Maine, during the Fiscal Year ended June 30, 1885.

Articles.		1885. Quantity.	1885. Value.	1884. Quantity.	1884. Value.
			£		£
Meat and dairy products	..	..	3,471,758	..	3,862,494
Horned cattle	Number	55,684	1,107,409	79,412	1,577,905
Corn, flour, and other breadstuffs	..	..	3,455,338	..	3,983,818
Cotton, raw	Bales ..	145,971	1,611,616	122,497	1,431,773
,, manufactures of	..	..	218,003	..	276,747
Tobacco, in leaf and manufactured	..	..	501,335	..	563,508
Iron ore, iron, steel, and manufactures of	..	..	294,441	..	298,645
Sugar and molasses	..	..	244,159	..	167,331
Coin and bullion	..	..	15,340	..	30,000
Foreign goods re-exported	..	..	178,071	..	249,215
All other articles..	..	..	2,589,435	..	2,232,542
Total..	..	..	13,686,905	..	14,673,978

* No statistics obtainable in regard to the coasting trade.

† The nationality of foreign vessels can only be ascertained in the aggregate for the whole of the United States. It is approximatively estimated, however, that British tonnage, entering and clearing in the Boston Consular District, and in the State of Maine, during the year 1885, was over 95 per cent. of the total foreign tonnage.

BOSTON.

RETURN of Principal Articles of Import to Ports in the Boston Consular District, and Ports in the State of Maine, during the Fiscal Year ended June 30, 1885.

Articles.	Value.	
	1885.	1884.
	£	£
Sugar and molasses	2,605,182	4,106,440
Wool	1,472,721	2,017,289
Hides, goat, and fur skins and furs	1,061,085	1,087,864
Chemicals, drugs, and dyes	856,447	982,890
Iron ore, iron, steel, and manufactures of	840,680	979,938
Flax, hemp, and jute	783,719	724,243
Fish	460,228	502,249
Cotton goods	311,488	228,779
Coin and bullion	33,808	60,093
All other articles	4,078,228	4,518,241
Total	12,503,586	15,208,026

Annex C.—TABLE showing the Total Value of all Articles Exported from and Imported to Ports in the Boston Consular District, and Ports in the State of Maine, during the Fiscal Years to June 30, 1885 and 1884.

Country.	Exports.		Imports.	
	1885.	1884.	1885.	1884.
	£	£	£	£
United Kingdom and colonies	12,190,872	13,652,012	6,733,662	8,178,923
Spain and colonies	162,636	163,423	2,173,355	3,358,923
France and ,,	124,220	181,220	628,419	856,423
Argentine Republic	89,753	83,484	626,903	558,235
Germany	7,723	39,427	626,167	399,258
Brazil	6,806	4,505	304,322	226,043
Italy	18,721	9,336	268,296	334,073
Netherlands and colonies	62,339	49,221	211,540	206,971
Belgium	112,224	99,802	147,703	179,496
Sweden and Norway	12,077	1,200	189,599	185,569
Chili	120,277	148,920	32,078	26,679
Turkey	23,577	16,559	102,905	109,333
All other countries	755,680	224,869	458,637	588,100
Total	13,686,905	14,673,978	12,503,586	15,208,026

Boston, February 19, 1886.

MOBILE.

Report of Consul Cridland on the Trade and Commerce of Mobile, United States, for the Year 1885.

It could hardly be expected that the trade of Mobile during the past year, marked by business depression all over the United States, would exhibit a rapid growth or greatly increased prosperity. When it is seen then that the port held its own in the face of most unfavourable circumstances, it has reason to congratulate itself that its trade has been a fair average one.

The changed conditions of the cotton trade are affecting all the southern seaports; each one has to face the facts presented by empty warehouses and silent presses. A large portion of the cotton credited to the cotton ports is compressed in the interior, and merely passes through on its way to shipment. Mobile has also suffered by this changed condition of affairs, but a larger proportion of the cotton that reaches this city is handled by the population than is the case at any other southern port. Therefore, while the gross receipts at this port exhibit a decrease of about 14,000 bales, the actual cotton handled in this market, compared with the previous year, shows an increase of 10,000 bales.

Weight and Value of Cotton Receipts at Mobile for the past Two Years.

	1885.	1884.
Total receipt	236,871 Bales.	254,651 Bales.
Total weight	117,670,407 Lbs.	126,075,163 Lbs.
Total value, in sterling	2,429,901*l.* 13*s.* 6*d.*	2,635,088*l.* 11*s.* 6*d.*
Average weight, per bale	496·77 Lbs.	495·09 Lbs.
Average value, per bale	49 dol. 24 c., or 10*l.* 5*s.* 2*d.*	49 dol. 67 c., or 10*l.* 7*s.*
Average value, per lb.	9·91 c., or 5*d.*	10·03 c., or 5⅛*d.*
	Exchange at 4 dol. 80 c. per £	Exchange at 4 dol. 80 c. per £

The decrease in the receipts is owing to the fact that the staple finds its way to other points.

Comparative View of the Exports of Cotton from Mobile for the past Two Years.

	1885. Bales.	1884. Bales.
To Great Britain	43,130	56,157
Foreign ports	700	1,380
United States ports	203,146	204,795
Total	246,976	262,332

The acreage planted in cotton in the State of Alabama in 1885 was 2,823,000 acres, and the total crop 825,000 bales.

Cotton Freights, &c.

Cotton weights.

Cotton freights during the past year ruled at $\frac{3}{8}d.$ to $\frac{11}{32}d.$, until the latter part of the season, when they became easier, and closed at $\frac{5}{16}d.$

The supervision of cotton at Mobile continues as last reported, and is found to protect all interests.

The charges on cotton at this port are in all respects as reported in the Commercial Report for 1884.

The Timber and Lumber Trade of Mobile.

Timber and lumber trade.

The timber and lumber trade of Mobile is becoming one of its leading features as a business centre. In 1885 there was a decrease in the shipments of timber, owing to the fact that hewn timber has become unpopular in the trade. An increased demand for sawn timber is, however, expected in the future, which will make up for any loss from the cause referred to. The shipments of lumber were, during the past year, slightly in excess of the previous year. It is hoped that this trade will increase, as the supply of various woods in the forests that border the rivers that flow towards the Gulf of Mexico are practically inexhaustible. This trade will increase yearly if the new channel in Mobile Bay is widened and made deeper.

Shipments of lumber.

The shipments of lumber from Mobile to Great Britain and foreign countries for 1885, compared with 1884, were as follows:—

Countries.	1885.	1884.
	Feet.	Feet.
To the United Kingdom	4,525,661	6,435,736
„ Continent	3,408,382	2,736,404
„ British West Indies	1,423,185	3,130,744
„ South America	1,110,845	931,829
„ Central America	862,723	610,843
„ Cuba	2,844,057	736,761
„ other countries	1,292,688	2,519,785
Total exports	15,467,541	17,102,102
Value in sterling, at 4 dol. 80 c. per £	38,556*l.* 1*s.* 3*d.*	47,529*l.* 17*s.* 4*d.*

The shipments of lumber from Mobile to the coast ports, and into the interior of the United States for the past two years, has been as follows:—In 1885, 6,798,263 feet: total shipments, 22,265,804 feet. In 1884, 5,149,989 feet: total shipments, 22,252,091 feet.

The supply of pitch pine, oak, cedar, cypress, and other woods seems abundant for many years to come, and the trade is evidently, though slowly, on the increase. Capitalists from the Western States and Canada are investing in timber lands in Alabama with the intention of cutting the timber for exportation from this port.

Shipments of Hewn and Sawn Timber from Mobile for the past Two Years in Cubic Feet.

Countries.	1885.	1884.
	Feet.	Feet.
To the United Kingdom	2,769,285	2,852,915
Continent of Europe	353,540	957,799
Total	3,122,825	3,810,714
Value in sterling, at 4 dol. 80 c. per £	77,266*l.* 9*s.* 1*d.*	105,204*l.* 0*s.* 8*d.*

Shipments of timber.

The fact of large vessels being able to come up to the port of Mobile through the new channel in the bay, and take on board a large portion of their cargoes of timber or lumber, has been very beneficial to the trade of the port. Vessels drawing over 16 feet, when partially loaded, have to be towed down to the lower bay to complete their cargoes.

Export of Staves in the last Two Years.

	Number.	Value.
		£ *s. d.*
In 1885	107,884	2,772 18 4
1884	70,803	1,425 4 2

Staves.

Manufacture and Export of Shingles.

During the past year some 50,000,000 shingles were made in Mobile and vicinity, and shipped to the West Indies, the coast ports of the United States, and to the Western States, where the demand was quite large. Machine made ranged from 2 dol. 50 c. (10*s.* 5*d.*) to 3 dol. (12*s.* 6*d.*) per 1,000 for No. 1, and 1 dol. 50 c. (6*s.* 3*d.*) to 2 dol. (8*s.* 4*d.*) per 1,000 for No. 2.

Shingles.

Naval Stores.

A fair business was transacted in this department during the past year, and satisfactory prices realised.

The receipts from the interior to Mobile were:—

Naval stores.

	1885.		1884.	
	Barrels.	Value at 4 dol. 80 c.	Barrels.	Value at 4 dol. 80 c.
		£ *s. d.*		£ *s. d.*
Rosin	200,608	83,618 4 7	210,512	76,713 9 4
Turpentine	41,718	130,365 9 6	41,801	126,247 15 1

RESIN Exported.

	1885.	1884.
	Barrels.	Barrels.
To United Kingdom	27,175	23,440
Continent of Europe	34,442	52,757
Total	61,617	76,197
Value	24,026*l.* 18*s.* 1*d.*	24,650*l.* 14*s.* 11*d.*

Exchange 4 dol. 80 c.

IMPORTS OF SALT INTO THE PORT OF MOBILE.

Salt.

The Liverpool salt seems to be the favourite article, as it dissolves quicker than the rock salt of Louisiana. The cargoes brought here direct in ships seem to find a ready sale.

	1885.	1884.
	Sacks.	Sacks.
Imports from Liverpool ..	16,324	26,582
„ „ other ports ..	14,025	8,245
Total	30,349	34,827

IMPORTS of Alabama and Pennsylvania Coal into Mobile for the past Two Years.

	1885.	1884.
	Tons.	Tons.
Alabama coal	40,301	17,808
Pennsylvania coal	715	891
Total	41,016	18,699

Coal.

The demand for Alabama coal continues good, and the receipts from the mines last year show an increase of 100 per cent. over the previous year, but so far the price and freight prevents a competition with English coal carried to the West Indies, the Gulf of Mexico ports, and Central America. The price of steam coal ranges at Mobile at 14*s.* 7*d.* per ton of 2,000 lbs., free on board. The bituminous coal used for household purposes costs now 1*l.* 3*s.* per ton.

The following extract in reference to the coal, coke, and iron industries of Alabama shows what has been done for some years past in the mineral district of the State, and is of much interest:—

Alabama coal, coke, and iron industries.

"*Alabama Coal, Coke, and Iron Industries.*

"(From the *Birmingham Age* of January, 1886.)

"The world now knows something of the magnitude and extent of the coal and iron ore deposits of the State of Alabama, though we believe the accepted reports greatly underestimate the extent of both. But the general public does not know how much is doing, and has been done, towards developing resources that are to be the basis of the future greatness of our State.

"The coal output of Alabama since 1873 is as follows:—

Year	Tons.
1873	40,000
1874	45,000
1875	60,000
1876	100,000
1877	175,000
1878	200,000
1879	200,000
1880	340,000
1881	375,000
1882	800,000
1883	1,400,000
1884	2,000,000
1885	2,225,000

"In 1872 only 10,000 tons of coal were mined in this State. In 1879 a great impetus was given to coal mining by the opening up of the Pratt seam by the Pratt Coal and Coke Company for steam, coke, and gas purposes, and the working of the Helena seam for grate purposes. Since that time many mines have been opened, and, as seen from the above table, the output has steadily increased.

"Six years ago the Louisville and Nashville road hauled only 2,000 tons of Alabama coal, now the Pratt mines alone have a daily average output of more than 2,000 tons. New mines are being opened up every year throughout the coal-fields, wherever convenient access to transportation can be had. The opening-up of the Warrior river and the deepening of Mobile harbour would give a great impetus to coal mining; and Alabama, instead of ranking as the fifth or sixth coal-producing State, would in a few years rank next to Pennsylvania.

"In 1880 Alabama had 316 coke ovens; in 1884 the number had increased to 976; and it is safe to say that on the 1st of January, 1886, there were 1,200 coke ovens in operation in the State.

"These 1,200 coke ovens consumed the following number of tons of coal for each year named:—

Year	Tons.
1880	106,283
1881	184,881
1882	261,839
1883	359,699
1884	413,184
1885	515,550

"The coke produced from this half million tons of coal for each year named was as follows:—

Year	Tons.
1880	60,781
1881	109,033
1882	152,941
1883	217,531
1884	244,009
1885	304,509

"This coke sells at from 2 dol. 50 c. to 3 dol. a ton, and the output for 1885 was therefore worth nearly 900,000 dol. It is a fact not generally known that Alabama, within the past few years, has grown to be the second coke-producing State in the Union. Pennsylvania comes first, Alabama second, and West Virginia third. No other State, unless we except Pennsylvania, has better coking coal, and we may look for this industry to grow gradually into immense proportions.

"The production of pig iron since 1876 is as follows:—

	Tons.
1876	24,732
1877	41,241
1878	41,482
1879	49,841
1880	77,190
1881	98,081
1882	112,765
1883	172,465
1884	189,660
1885	189,660

"We have placed the output of pig iron in 1885 at the same as 1884, because no additional furnaces were built during that year.

"Here we have some idea of the growth of these three leading industries in Alabama, the products of which were worth for 1885 about 7,000,000 dol., or about one-fourth the value of the entire cotton crop of the State. Four more furnaces will be built in or around Birmingham during the present year, others will no doubt be built in other parts of the State; hundreds more of coke ovens will be built; mines will be opened and the coal output be increased; indeed, in the history of the State the future of these industries were never brighter."

Agriculture.

Agriculture.

The cultivation of vegetables in Mobile county for export to the northern and western markets in the early spring of the year, one of the leading branches of business in this section, has been steadily on the increase for past years, but the growers have met with many disadvantages in protracted droughts and severe frosts, and consequently much loss. However, notwithstanding such disadvantages, the production of vegetables in Mobile county in 1885 produced 34,538*l*. 2*s*. 6*d*., and in the year 1884 49,592*l*. 5*s*. 10*d*.

Wool.

Wool.

This trade suffered last year in the general depression of business, the manufacturers buying only what was absolutely necessary for their business. The receipts at Mobile for the past year show an increase of 90 per cent. over the year previous.

Exchange 4 dol. 80 c.

Articles.	Weight.	Value.
	Lbs.	£ s. d.
Wool received at Mobile in 1885	465,000	17,437 12 0
Ditto ditto in 1884	245,875	10,500 18 2

MOBILE.

FISH AND OYSTER TRADE.

Value of fish and oysters taken in and off Mobile Bay and brought to the city, sold or exported during the past two years:—

Articles.	1885. £ s. d.	1884. £ s. d.
Fish	21,979 3 4	20,833 6 8
Oysters	23,958 6 8	22,916 13 4
Total	45,937 10 0	43,750 0 0

RETURN of all Shipping at the Port of Mobile, United States, in the Year 1885.

ENTERED.

Nationality.	Sailing. No. of Vessels.	Sailing. Tons.	Steam. No. of Vessels.	Steam. Tons.	Total. No. of Vessels.	Total. Tons.
British	66	53,033	4	4,101	70	57,134
American	125	34,454	7	1,863	132	36,317
Swedish and Norwegian	49	31,511	...	...	49	31,511
Other countries ...	23	12,355	1	1,008	24	13,363
Total	263	131,353	12	6,972	275	138,325
,, for the year preceding ...	309	150,554	5	3,265	314	153,819

CLEARED.

Nationality.	Sailing. No. of Vessels.	Sailing. Tons.	Steam. No. of Vessels.	Steam. Tons.	Total. No. of Vessels.	Total. Tons.
British	64	51,295	3	2,949	67	54,244
American	118	31,723	8	2,070	126	33,793
Swedish and Norwegian	56	34,133	...	...	56	34,133
Other countries ...	17	8,756	1	1,008	18	9,764
Total	255	125,907	12	6,027	267	131,934
,, for the year preceding ...	279	142,566	7	4,171	286	146,737

UNITED STATES.

RETURN of Principal Articles of Export from Mobile, United States, during the Years 1884 and 1885.

Articles.	1885. Quantity.	1885. Value (in Sterling).	1884. Quantity.	1884. Value (in Sterling).
		£		£
Cotton in bales	246,976	2,533,583	262,332	2,714,570
Lumber, feet	15,467,541	38,556	17,102,102	47,529
Timber, feet	3,122,825	77,266	3,810,714	105,204
Resin, barrels	61,617	24,026	76,197	24,650
Vegetables, packages	100,655	34,538	157,299	49,529
Other articles, packages, tons, barrels, and pieces	856,722	7,724	751,814	6,241
Total		2,715,693		2,947,723

RETURN of Principal Articles of Import to Mobile during the Years 1884 and 1885.

Articles.	1885. Quantity.	1885. Value (in Sterling.)	1884. Quantity.	1884. Value (in Sterling).
		£		£
Salt in sacks, and	30,349		34,827	
Coffee in bags are the only articles of any importance brought to Mobile from foreign ports	7,900	26,884	10,500	52,719
Total		26,884		52,719

TABLE showing the Total Value of all Articles Exported from and Imported to Mobile from and to Foreign Countries during the Years 1884 and 1885.

Country.	Exports. 1885.	Exports. 1884.	Imports. 1885.
	£	£	The statements published in reference to the imports into Mobile are not reliable. Neither country or article is mentioned. In all probability the total value of imports from Great Britain during the last two years did not exceed 5,000l. in each year.
United Kingdom and colonies	603,569	639,823	
Russia	..	14,005	
Germany	14,012	11,100	
France	8,173	8,055	
Spain	7,255	5,773	
	6,991	15,051	
	..	7,966	
	10,842	13,430	
Total	650,842	715,203	

As previously stated the only imports for years past from England to Mobile have been salt, iron ties, and malt liquors. Coffee is now and then brought direct from Brazil, and fruit, principally bananas and cocoa nuts, from Honduras, but the quantity or value cannot be ascertained correctly.

PENSACOLA.

Mr. Vice-Consul Howe reports as follows:—

RETURN of all Shipping at the Port of Pensacola in the Year 1885.

ENTERED.

Nationality.	Sailing. Number of Vessels.	Sailing. Tons.	Steam. Number of Vessels.	Steam. Tons.	Total. Number of Vessels.	Total. Tons.
British	65	51,612	8	9,477	73	61,089
American	130	57,558	...	...	130	57,558
Swedish and Norwegian	110	80,250	...	...	110	80,250
Italian	87	54,583	...	...	87	54,583
Russian	26	16,198	...	...	26	16,198
Austrian	10	8,481	...	...	10	8,481
Netherlands	6	3,450	...	...	6	3,450
German	5	3,014	...	...	5	3,014
Other countries	6	2,235	...	...	6	2,235
Total	445	277,381	8	9,477	453	286,858
,, for the year preceding	605	352,165	3	3,396	608	355,561

CLEARED.

Nationality.	Sailing. Number of Vessels.	Sailing. Tons.	Steam. Number of Vessels.	Steam. Tons.	Total. Number of Vessels.	Total. Tons.
British	67	53,265	8	9,477	75	62,742
American	158	67,310	...	...	158	67,310
Swedish and Norwegian	106	75,702	...	...	106	75,702
Italian	86	56,851	...	...	86	56,851
Russian	36	22,449	...	...	36	22,449
Austrian	11	8,047	...	...	11	8,047
German	7	5,027	...	...	7	5,027
Other countries	10	5,120	...	...	10	5,120
Total	481	293,771	8	9,477	489	303,248
,, for the year preceding	567	320,676	3	3,396	570	324,072

RETURN of Principal Articles of Export from Pensacola during the Year 1885.

Articles.	1885. Quantity.	1885. Value.	1884. Quantity.	1884. Value.
		£ s. d.		£ s. d.
Pitch pine lumber	100,950,573	252,376 8 7	101,442,000	253,605 0 0
Sawn pitch pine timber	7,556,522	173,170 5 11	8,140,377	186,550 6 2
Hewn pitch pine timber	2,055,609	42,825 3 9	2,288,608	47,679 6 8
Cotton	12,787	133,197 18 4	14,443	142,925 10 5
Pig iron	2,083	8,679 3 4	..	..
Other articles	..	930 4 2	..	1,137 14 2
Total	..	611,179 4 1	..	631,897 17 5

RETURN of Principal Articles of Import to Pensacola during the Year 1885.

Articles.	1885. Quantity.	1885. Value.	1884. Quantity.	1884. Value.
		£ s. d.		£ s. d.
Chief articles	*	*	*	*
Other ,,	..	26,189 11 8	..	14,248 15 0
Total	..	26,189 11 8	..	14,248 15 0

The following, as regards the above table of exports, is descriptive of the values, quantities, weights, and measures, the conversion of money into sterling being at the rate of 4 dol. 80 c. per £ :—

    Lumber, at average of 12 dol. (2l. 10s.) per 1,000 superfical feet.
    Sawn timber ,, ,, 11 c. (5½d.) ,, cubic foot.
    Hewn ,, ,, ,, 10 c. (5d.) ,, ,,
    Cotton ,, ,, 9½ c. (4¾d.) ,, lb. for year 1884.
    ,, ,, ,, 10 c. (5d.) ,, ,, ,, 1885.
    ,, in bales of 500 lbs. average weight each bale.
    Pig iron, in tons, at 20 dol. (4l. 3s. 4d.) per ton.

* As regards the above table of imports, the quantities and values of the chief articles of trade cannot be ascertained, there being no regular chamber of trade. Breadstuffs, groceries, hardware, and such-like goods are received from the large northern and western markets.

TABLE showing the Total Value of all Articles Exported from Pensacola and Imported to Pensacola from and to Foreign Countries during the Years 1884 and 1885:—

Country.	Exports. 1885.			Exports. 1884.			Imports. 1885.			Imports. 1884.		
	£	s.	d.	£	s.	d.	£	s.	d.	£	s.	d.
United Kingdom	233,410	4	2	247,501	0	10	25,658	6	8	10,429	11	8
France	36,970	8	4	34,918	6	8	..			..		
Argentine Republic	35,172	10	0	28,809	15	10	..			..		
Netherlands	17,898	19	2	27,319	7	6	..			..		
United States of Colombia	20,221	17	6	24,334	11	8	..			..		
Uruguay	21,884	3	4	22,594	11	8	..			..		
Spain	20,406	0	10	23,732	5	10	..			..		
Italy	19,368	15	0	21,839	3	4	..			..		
Belgium	12,707	5	10	6,614	11	8	..			..		
Germany	4,430	8	4	12,793	2	6	..			..		
Portugal	4,966	17	6	6,126	13	4	..			..		
Other countries	7,459	11	8	12,540	4	2	531	5	0	3,819	3	4
Total	434,897	1	8	469,123	15	0	26,189	11	8	14,248	15	0

Imports and exports generally.

The difference between the total value of exports given above, and the total value of all exports given in the second table of this report, relating to export and imports, is accounted for by the explanation that during the year 1885 articles valued at 176,282*l*. 2*s*. 5*d*., and during the year 1884 articles valued at 162,774*l*. 2*s*. 5*d*., were shipped to ports in the United States.

As shown by the tabulated statements in this report, the export trade of Pensacola for the past year was not equal to the average yearly export trade of the place for some years previous: depressed markets abroad, particularly in the United Kingdom, in pitch pine wood—the staple product of this part of the State of Florida—having been the chief cause of the falling off in the trade. The value of the imports given, as from the United Kingdom, is mostly for superphosphate, for fertilising purposes, and salt—which articles, on arrival, are sent forward (the fertilising compounds) to surrounding cotton-planting districts, and much of the salt is also sent to various surrounding places in trading transactions. From countries other than the United Kingdom the imports consist mostly of wines and fruits.

Mobile, February 20, 1886.

UNITED STATES.

CHARLESTON.

Report by Consul Walker on the Trade and Commerce of his Consular District, embracing the States of North and South Carolina, for the Year 1885.

RETURN of all Shipping in the several Collection Districts within the Consular District of North and South Carolina in the Year 1885.

ENTERED.

Collection Districts.	Nationalities.	Sailing. Number of Vessels.	Sailing. Tons.	Steam. Number of Vessels.	Steam. Tons.	Total. Number of Vessels.	Total. Tons.	Grand Total. Number of Vessels.	Grand Total. Tons.
Charleston, South Carolina	British	38	20,880	48	49,436	86	70,316	..	..
Wilmington, North ,,	,,	28	10,714	8	11,512	36	22,226	..	92,542
Charleston, South ,,	American	429	*	470	*	899	532,334	..	..
Wilmington, North ,,	,,	184	50,303	55	46,908	239	97,211	1,138	629,545
Charleston, South ,,	Norwegian	40	18,232	..	..	40	18,232	..	..
Wilmington, North ,,	,,	48	18,038	..	..	48	18,038	88	36,270
Charleston, South ,,	Other countries	89	37,719	3	3,182	92	40,901	..	..
Wilmington, North ,,	,,	77	29,472	..	..	77	29,472	169	70,373
Beaufort, South Carolina									
,, North ,,	⎫ No returns have been furnished by the collectors of these several districts.								
Edenton, ,, ,,	⎬								
Georgetown, South ,,									
Newberne, North ,,	⎭							1,517	828,730

* The books at the Custom-house do not furnish the information needed for these blanks.

RETURN of all Shipping in the several Collection Districts within the Consular District of North and South Carolina in the Year 1885—continued.

CLEARED.

Collection Districts.	Nationalities.	Sailing. Number of Vessels.	Sailing. Tons.	Steam. Number of Vessels.	Steam. Tons.	Total. Number of Vessels.	Total. Tons.	Grand Total. Number of Vessels.	Grand Total. Tons.
Charleston, South Carolina	British	35	19,252	45	46,957	80	66,290	..	..
Wilmington, North "	"	28	10,714	8	11,512	36	22,226	116	88,516
Charleston, South "	American	429	* 46,410	*	* 46,908	899	532,334	..	..
Wilmington, North "	"	172	46,410	55	46,908	227	93,318	1,126	625,652
Charleston, South "	Norwegian	51	23,709	..	..	51	23,709	..	..
Wilmington, North "	"	46	17,512	..	..	46	17,512	97	41,221
Charleston, South "	Other countries	72	28,932	1	742	73	29,674	..	..
Wilmington, North "	"	75	28,028	..	..	75	28,028	148	57,702
Beaufort, South Carolina									
Edenton, North "	No returns have been furnished by the collectors of these several districts.								
Georgetown, South "									
Newberne, North "									
								1,487	813,091

* The books at the Custom-House do not furnish the information needed for these blanks.

CHARLESTON.

Return of the Principal Articles of Export from the several Collection Districts of the United States of America within the Consular District of North and South Carolina in the Years 1885 and 1884.

Articles.		1885. Charleston. Quantity.	1885. Charleston. Value.	1885. Wilmington. Quantity.	1885. Wilmington. Value.	1885. Total. Quantity.	1885. Total. Value.	1884. Charleston. Value.	1884. Wilmington. Quantity.	1884. Wilmington. Value.	1884. Total. Value.
			£		£		£	£		£	£
Upland cotton	Lbs.	130,286,323	2,887,077	31,010,763	478,229	161,297,086	3,365,306	..	27,452,502	568,045	..
Sea Island cotton	,,	579,841	35,584	..	..	579,841	35,584	..	..	..	..
Phosphate rock	Tons	14,422	20,927	..	..	14,422	20,927	..	..	..	..
Spirits of turpentine	Gallons	1,381,320	75,922	2,267,445	160,054	3,648,765	235,976	..	2,854,160	178,385	..
Other naval stores	Barrels	86,153	24,734	314,473	90,283	400,626	115,017	..	461,633	132,532	..
Lumber	M. feet	2,854	20,936	11,991	40,792	14,845	61,728	..	15,472	53,756	..
Other articles	..	..	..	..	2,830	..	2,830	..	..	4,697	..
Total	..	..	3,065,180	..	772,188	..	3,837,368	4,350,713	..	937,415	5,288,128

TOTAL Value of the Principal Articles of Import to the several Collection Districts of the United States of America within the Consular District of North and South Carolina in the Years 1885 and 1884.

	1885.	1884.
	£	£
Charleston	117,143	104,478
Wilmington	26,486	32,034
Total	143,629	136,512

TABLE showing the Total Value of all Articles Exported from and Imported to the several Collection Districts of the United States of America, within the Consular District of North and South Carolina, from and to Foreign Countries during the Years 1885 and 1884.

EXPORTS.

Countries.	Charleston.		Wilmington.	
	1885.	1884.	1885.	1884.
	£	£	£	£
The United Kingdom	1,302,660	..	..	..
Other foreign countries.	1,762,520	..	..	..
Total	3,065,180	4,350,713	772,188	937,415

IMPORTS.

Countries.	Charleston.		Wilmington.	
	1885.	1884.	1885.	1884.
	£	£	£	£
Total	117,143	104,478	26,486	32,034

The several Collection Districts of the United States of America within the Consular District of North and South Carolina are Beaufort, Edenton, Newberne, Wilmington (North Carolina), and Beaufort, Georgetown, Charleston (South Carolina).

It has not been practicable to obtain returns from the collectors of the several districts above-named, other than from those of Charleston in South Carolina, and Wilmington in North Carolina. The returns from Beaufort, in South Carolina, should show the employment of nearly 100,000 tons, British, arriving in ballast and carrying phosphate rock to British and other European ports, exclusive of coastwise trade in American vessels.

The records of the several Custom-houses are not so kept as to furnish readily the figures necessary for the forms prescribed by the Foreign Office. Such records at the best are insufficient, for they fail to record all coastwise traffic, whether inward or outward, and such

CHARLESTON.

traffic far exceeds in volume and value the foreign traffic of some of the ports (see Table A. for the number and tonnage of American vessels).

The customs officers at Charleston having but recently taken office, the details of foreign imports required by the foregoing table are not accessible. Their aggregates, however, are given.

The foreign imports at Wilmington direct have been inconsiderable.

General Remarks.

The city of Charleston claims to have a population of 60,000, with trade to the extent of 13,000,000*l.*, and to receive annually 500,000 bales of cotton, worth from 4,000,000*l.* to 5,000,000*l.*, rice to the extent of 350,000*l.*, naval stores to the value of 370,000*l.*, and lumber to the value of 100,000*l*. *[Commercial outlook, viz., population. General trade. Cotton receipts.]*

Phosphate of lime in inexhaustible beds, producing annually to the value of nearly 600,000*l*. *[Rice receipts.]*

There are many mills for the preparation of commercial fertilisers. *[Naval stores.]*

There is a cotton factory working 15,500 spindles on cloth, 5,500 on yarn, 464 looms, and numerous factories of minor importance. *[Lumber. Phosphate rock.]*

A company has been organised and in operation, the business of which is the importation of coffee from Brazil by cargo for transmission into the interior. *[Factories. Coffee import.]*

Banking capital has undergone reduction, until there is no more than 150,000*l.*; meanwhile deposits in savings banks reach 700,000*l.*, and much private capital besides is employed in banking operations. *[Banking capital.]*

Money for commercial purposes commands 7 per cent. *[Cost of commercial accommodation.]*

7 per cent. is the legal rate recognised by the State law of South Carolina. *[Legal interest]*

To meet the expenses attendant upon the execution of the port regulations, the following tax or fee is imposed upon all vessels arriving, viz.:— *[New tax on shipping.]*

	Dol.	c.
Coastwise—		
Steamships, yearly	20	0
Schooners, per trip	2	0
Brigs, per trip	2	50
Foreign—		
Steamships, per trip	12	0
Barks, per trip	6	0
Brigs ,,	3	0

Charleston, March 29, 1886.

NEW YORK.

Report by Consul-General Booker on the Trade, Navigation, and Commerce of New York for the Year 1885.

In the last six months of 1885 a decided improvement manifested itself in the domestic trade of New York, and there was an active demand for all descriptions of dry goods, with a general rise in value, though not of so decided a character as to leave a profit to the manufacturers; but after the depression which had existed for over two years it was a great satisfaction to them to find relief in the reduction of their accumulated stocks. Low prices had increased the consumption, and the stocks in interior points had become materially reduced. In the produce market there was no material change for the better in prices, but there was an increased demand generally. The Custom-house returns show that while about the same value of merchandise was withdrawn from the bonded warehouses in the first half of the year as was warehoused, the withdrawals in the last half were in excess of the receipts over 600,000*l.* {General report on trade.}

In railroad stocks there was a marked appreciation, though the returns of the year did not show any actual increase in the earnings. There was a considerable falling-off in regard to the movement of cereals, which, with the low rates caused by the active competition of the different lines engaged in their transporation, proved a very important factor in keeping down the earnings. A combination of the different companies in regard to rates has increased considerably the earnings since the commencement of this year.

During the year money was plentiful, the banks having large amounts of unemployed funds: rates on call loans varied from 1 to 2 per cent., until towards the close, when they ranged from $1\frac{1}{2}$ to 4 per cent. Commercial paper was discounted from 3 to 5 per cent., 4 to 5 per cent. being the current rate in the last two months of the year. The condition of the associated banks of the city is shown in the following table: it will be observed that the loans and discounts increased 7,416,000*l.* since the end of June:—

ASSOCIATED Banks of New York City. {Bank returns.}

Week ending	Loans and discounts.	Net deposits, other than U.S.A.	Circulation.
	£	£	£
January 3	61,364,865	70,208,158	2,348,153
March 28	62,002,127	72,809,443	2,245,338
June 27	62,569,513	77,613,281	2,041,604
September 26	67,792,355	79,511,303	2,020,983
December 26	69,409,290	77,034,112	2,047,426

Sterling exchange.

The following table gives the rates of sterling exchange during the year:—

BANKERS.

	60 days.	Sight.	Commercial.
	Dol. c.	Dol. c.	Dol. c.
January—			
Highest ..	4 84	4 88	4 81½
Lowest ..	4 81½	4 85½	4 79½
February—			
Highest ..	4 84½	4 88	4 81¾
Lowest ..	4 83½	4 87	4 81½
March—			
Highest ..	4 85½	4 88	4 82½
Lowest ..	4 83½	4 86½	4 81¼
April—			
Highest ..	4 87	4 89	4 85⅜
Lowest ..	4 85½	4 88	4 82½
May—			
Highest ..	4 88	4 90	4 86¼
Lowest ..	4 87	4 89	4 85¼
June—			
Highest ..	4 87½	4 89	4 85¾
Lowest ..	4 85	4 86	4 83¾
July—			
Highest ..	4 86	4 87½	4 84¼
Lowest ..	4 84½	4 86	4 83¼
August—			
Highest ..	4 86½	4 88½	4 84¼
Lowest ..	4 84	4 86	4 82⅜
September—			
Highest ..	4 84½	4 86½	4 82⅞
Lowest ..	4 83	4 85	4 81⅛
October—			
Highest ..	4 85	4 87	4 83⅛
Lowest ..	4 83½	4 85½	4 82⅛
November—			
Highest ..	4 84	4 86	4 82¼
Lowest ..	4 83	4 85½	4 81⅜
December—			
Highest ..	4 87	4 90½	4 84¾
Lowest ..	4 83½	4 86	4 81⅞

Failures in district.

The Failures, as exhibited in the following table taken from Dun's Commercial Agency, show a large reduction both in number and liabilities in 1885 on those of the previous year in this city and the Eastern States of this Consular district:—

	Number of Failures.		Amount of Liabilities.	
	1885.	1884.	1885.	1884.
			£	£
New York City and Brooklyn	506	718	4,094,249	16,042,398
New York State (outside of cities of New York and Brooklyn)	677	706	1,647,865	2,255,677
Connecticut	176	169	353,185	301,665
New Jersey	122	119	195,628	271,784
Rhode Island	126	136	257,209	676,765
Delaware	23	27	40,220	114,103
Total	1,630	1,875	6,588,356	19,662,392

The import returns in Annex B. show a falling-off in merchandise receipts compared with 1884 of about 8,500,000*l*., of which 2,700,000*l*. comes under the heading of dry goods: of these the receipts of silk manufactures show by far the greatest decrease, approximating to 1,430,000*l*.; the next largest decrease is in metals, being close upon 450,000*l*. The only articles of English manufacture in exceptionably large demand have been laces, curtains, &c. In connection with the decrease in British imports, I may point out that there was a falling-off of nearly 7,000,000*l*. between 1880 and 1884, and that we were unable to keep up our imports to those of 20 years ago, although in that period the consumption of such goods as we received from Great Britain had been augmented by the wants of nearly 20,000,000 additional people. As this port continues to receive about the same percentage (70 per cent.) of all the merchandise imported into the United States as it did 20 years ago, its trade, now as then, represents very fairly that of the whole country. The cause of the reduced imports is to be attributed to the vast strides that have been made in the manufacturing industries of this country, fostered as they have been by high and, in some instances, prohibitory duties, and by the competition of other European countries. *Imports generally.*

The export returns in Annex B., excluding specie, show little variation in gross upon those of 1884, but there are material variations. The exports of refined sugar increased from 1,656,000*l*. to 3,249,000*l*. domestic cottons from about 1,815,000*l*., to 2,283,000*l*.; and Indian corn, in consequence of the unprecedentedly large crop in this country, from 1,491,000*l*. to 2,960,000*l*. (11,862,000 bushels to 26,260,000 bushels). Wheat decreased from 5,364,000*l*. to 3,170,000*l*. (28,690,000 bushels to 16,286,000 bushels), whilst the export of flour decreased only from 4,040,000*l*. to 3,603,000*l*. (3,907,000 barrels to 3,705,000 barrels). The last is important, as showing the increased export of wheat in its manufactured state. *Exports generally.*

In the carrying of grain to Great Britain and the Continent, British ships increased their lead from 55·78 per cent. in 1884 to 64·48 per cent. in 1885. Of the quantity shipped, Germany comes next with 10·41 per cent., Belgium with 9·59 per cent., France and the Netherlands with about 3 per cent. each, the remainder being divided between ships of different European nations. No grain was transported across the Atlantic in American bottoms. In 1884, 101 sailing vessels carried grain cargoes to Europe; in the past year 93, of which 73 were Belgian. Ocean outward freight rates were lower than at any previous *Carrying of grain.*

UNITED STATES.

period, ranging from 2d. to 4½d. per bushel by steamers from this port to Liverpool.

Agriculture.—The product valuation and average yield per acre of wheat, maize, and oats in 1885, in the States and territories within my Consular district, are furnished in the following tables taken from the report of the United States Commissioner of Agriculture:—

Article.	Quantity.	Value.	Average Yield.
	Bushels.	£	Bushels.
New York—			
Wheat	10,565,000	2,089,333	15·2
Maize	22,448,000	2,680,273	30·7
Oats	38,676,000	2,840,412	28·0
New Jersey—			
Wheat	1,395,000	274,001	9·7
Maize	11,212,000	2,234,426	32·0
Oats	3,556,000	271,038	26·7
Connecticut—			
Wheat	31,000	6,705	14·1
Maize	2,033,000	26,533	35·0
Oats	1,090,000	94,307	28·5
Rhode Island—			
Wheat	..	..	..
Maize	429,000	63,630	33·5
Oats	167,000	15,136	26·3
Delaware—			
Wheat	957,000	187,284	10·7
Maize	4,174,000	643,814	19·3
Oats	501,000	41,072	23·7
Colorado—			
Wheat	2,395,000	404,563	11·5
Maize	959,000	134,336	34·4
Oats	1,698,000	160,902	37·3
Kansas—			
Wheat	11,197,000	7,830,678	10·6
Maize	158,390,000	1,499,278	32·4
Oats	27,145,000	1,286,130	32·0
Nebraska—			
Wheat	19,828,000	2,328,204	11·3
Maize	129,426,000	5,065,733	36·7
Oats	24,028,000	940,456	34·3
Dakota—			
Wheat	27,913,000	3,622,530	12·8
Maize	15,345,000	885,099	29·0
Oats	13,229,000	626,790	37·5
Utah—			
Wheat	1,926,000	242,010	20·0
Maize	979,000	157,095	20·6
Oats	845,000	62,665	30·5
Wyoming—			
Wheat	66,000	10,877	21·0
Maize	..	..	..
Oats	84,000	7,615	32·0

New York has grown, in addition to the cereals in the foregoing table, large quantities of barley, rye, and buckwheat, but the reports of last year's crops have not yet been published: for some years there have been about 350,000 acres in barley, 240,000 in rye, and 285,000 in buckwheat. The potato crop has averaged 1,000,000 tons. The total area of land in the State is 30,476,800, of which about 78 per cent.

is cultivated or used for grazing purposes; the remainder is timber land, which has been decreasing year by year. There are in the State 1,510,300 milch cows, the product of which was estimated to be in 1885 about 1,070,000 cwt. of butter and 1,160,000 cwt. of cheese. The business of supplying milk to the inhabitants of this city and Brooklyn is a very large one, and the State dairy commissioner, in his report, states that the product of over 100,000 cows comes daily over the railroads of the State for this trade. The dairy interests have been seriously interfered with by the manufacture of oleomargarine, but since the passage of an Act by the Legislature of this State in 1884, making it a misdemeanour to manufacture an article out of any oleaginous substance designed to take the place of butter or cheese produced from pure unadulterated milk or cream, or to offer the same for sale as an article of food, the reduction of sales of oleomargarine has decreased nearly 75 per cent. from what it was before the Act went into effect, which has kept up the price of butter in this market in the face of larger receipts and a diminished export. There is a constant improvement in the breed of cattle. The herd-book registers more Jerseys than any other breed, the next being Holstein-Fresian, the Aryshire and Devon following. The natural basis of stock-breeding has changed in this State, owing to the steady supply of dressed meat from the West. Feeding in the winter, or stall-feeding, as the practice is termed, cannot be followed any longer with a profit except under very favourable circumstances. There has also been a marked improvement in the breed of horses, by the introduction of European draught horses, especially the Norman and Percheron, and to a considerable extent the English shire horse and the Clydesdale.

Labour Market.—The rates of wages in the Eastern States of my district—New York, Delaware, New Jersey, Rhode Island, and Connecticut—have, of late, had an upward tendency, in many cases brought about by strikes under the direction more frequently of the Knights of Labour than of the Trades' Unions. In the cotton and woollen mills the established advance has been about 10 per cent., but it is doubtful if the operatives have really received a benefit to that extent. There are more hands employed in the factories than there were a year ago. Of the States referred to, New York, New Jersey, and Connecticut have labour bureaux. The reports of the Commissioners of New York and New Jersey have not yet been published; the first report of the Commissioner for Connecticut was issued in November, and gives a good deal of valuable information. There are Bills before the Connecticut and Rhode Island Legislatures to improve the condition of operatives, and one of the Connecticut Bills provides that no miners shall be employed over 10 hours, that those between 15 and 18 years of age shall not be employed without a physician's certificate of physical capacity for the work, and that none under 16 years of age shall be employed about dangerous machinery, or in certain unhealthy occupations.

Labour.

The governor of this State in his last message recommended that provisions should be made by law for a Commission to have the power to investigate the labour question generally, especially the system of courts or boards of arbitration, and to report to the present or some future Legislature such a law as would secure the benefits of the system of arbitration to those interested.

An attempt is being made by the Knights of Labour to reduce the working hours to eight a day on and after the 1st of May, but the chief of the association (general master workman) has recently, in a secret circular, issued in consequence of the disposition on the part of local assemblies in the West to act independently of the chief executive officer, stated that the Knights of Labour must not strike for the eight hours' system on the 1st of May under the impression that they are obeying orders from headquarters, for such an order has not been and will not be given. He adds, "Out of the 60,000,000 people in the United States and Canada our order has possibly 300,000. Can we mould the sentiments of the millions in favour of the short hours' plan before the 1st of May? It is nonsense to think of it." The intention of the order is that wages shall be reduced in proportion to the reduction in the hours of labour, and the main object is stated to be to make room for the large number of unemployed, caused, as it is asserted, by the increased introduction of labour-saving machinery. The Knights of Labour insist that they have no affiliation with Communism, and that the tendency to harmony between labour and capital is becoming more marked daily, notwithstanding the numerous strikes and "boycotting" under its direction. In the secret circular referred to he states: "My duties to the order and humanity must not be measured by the standard of dollars and cents. My policy must no longer be misunderstood. While I, as the chosen mouthpiece of the order, am proclaiming to the world that the Knights of Labour do not advocate or countenance strikes until every other means has failed, the wires from a thousand cities and towns are bearing the news of as many strikes by Knights of Labour in which arbitration and conciliation were never hinted at. Not that alone, but they were in many cases scorned and rejected by our own members. In some cases these strikes were entered upon against the advice of the general executive board. It is claimed by our members that arbitration is one-sided. That may be true of the past, but the voluntary concessions made to us within the last three months prove most conclusively that the just claims of labour will be listened to if we go forward in the way we started. It is claimed that this is a year for concessions and advances. Be that as it may, we cannot force them by striking.

"I am aware that the machinery of our order is not capable of performing the work required by the large gains in membership; and this fact must have a restraining influence on our members until the next general assembly meets. Five hundred assemblies were added to the roll in February—as many as were organised in the first eight years of the order's existence. It is not within the bounds of human possibility to expect that all these new recruits can be properly trained before the assemblies are founded. The organisers seldom visit them for instructions more than once, and this is not enough. They must devote their spare moments to educating those already organised before adding any more new assemblies to the order. To attempt to win concessions or gains with our present raw, undisciplined membership would be like hurling an unorganised mob against a well-drilled regular army. Again, it is not fair to the older assemblies to bring in new members, pick up their quarrels as soon as organised, and have them expect pecuniary aid from those who helped to build the order for a noble purpose. It is not wise to give men and women a premium for joining us. It is wrong to encourage them in the idea that they have nothing to do themselves; that they are to lean upon others. They must depend upon themselves, and in any case cannot receive assistance inside of six months; and I will hold out no inducements that will encourage them in the belief that they will receive assistance even then.

"We must not fritter away our strength, and miss the opportunity of present success in the struggle against capital by rushing into useless strikes. To the cardinal principles of our order we must add another—'patience.' You have had patience for years, and had not the Knights of Labour appeared upon the scene you would still be waiting. Your scales of prices must stand as they are for the present if you cannot raise them by any other process than a strike. You must submit to injustice at the hands of the employer in patience for a while longer. Bide well your time. Make no display of organisation or strength until you have every man and woman in your department of industry organised, and then do not strike, but study, not only your own condition, but that of your employer. Find out how much you are justly entitled to, and then the tribunal of arbitration will settle the rest."

The "Knights of Labour" differ from the older "trades unions in forming mixed assemblies," organised by localities rather than by trades. The importance of this is in the power of "boycotting." *Wages in New York.*

The following table gives the wages paid in this city per day, the number of hours employed, and the average earnings per week:—

	Wages per Day.	Hours.	Wages Average Per Week.
	£ s. d.		£ s. d.
Carpenters	0 14 5¼	9	4 6 7
Plasterers, work 4½ days	0 16 6	9	3 14 2
Painters „ 5 „	0 14 5¼	9	3 12 2
Stone masons „ 4 „	0 14 5¼	9	2 17 9
„ cutters „ 5 „	0 16 6	8	4 2 6
Bricklayers „ 4 „	0 16 6	9	3 6 0
Stair builders	0 14 5¼	9	4 6 7
Marble cutters	0 14 5¼	9	4 6 7
„ furniture workers	0 10 3¾	9	3 1 10
Bricklayers	Per Month 6 3 8 and found.	..	..
Engineers	0 12 4½	10	3 14 3
Firemen	0 8 3	10	2 9 6
Maltsters, ordinary (do not work during June, July, August, and September)	0 8 3	14	2 17 9
Machinists, full	0 14 5¼	10	4 6 7
Pattern makers	0 14 5¼	10	4 6 7
Moulders	0 10 3¾	10	3 1 10
Blacksmiths	0 12 4½	10	3 14 3
„ helpers	0 8 3	10	2 9 6
Tinsmiths, full	0 14 5¼	9	4 6 7
Planers in planing mills, full	0 14 5¼	10	4 6 7
Sawyers, full	0 14 5¼	10	4 6 7
Boys in planing and saw mills, full	0 4 1½	10	1 4 9
Labourers, unskilled	0 6 2¼	10	1 17 1
„ masons	0 10 3¾	9	3 1 10
Cabinet-makers	0 14 5¼	10	4 6 7

Population.

Population.—The undermentioned States and Territories of this Consular District have taken a census in 1885, and the population is given below, together with that of 1880:—

Country.	1880.	1885.
New Jersey	..	1,278,033
Rhode Island	276,531	304,284
Colorado	194,327	243,910
Kansas	996,096	1,268,562
Nebraska	452,402	740,645
Dacota	135,177	415,263

Immigration.

Immigration.—There were 281,177 immigrants landed at this port in 1884, and they were of the following nationalities:—

England	25,657
Ireland	35,277
Scotland	5,796
Wales	1,111
Germany	97,913
Austria	10,882
Hungary	11,605
Sweden	16,045
Norway	9,974
Denmark	7,507
Netherlands	2,273
Belgium	1,702
Switzerland	5,739
France	3,814
Italy	15,740
Roumania	284
Malta	68
Greece	44
Spain	199
Portugal	25
Armenia	16
Russia	16,835
Bohemia	6,812
Finland	16
Luxemburg	272
Turkey	96
India	8
China	80
Japan	5
East Indies	74
Arabia	26
Canada	104
West Indies	221
Mexico	6
Central America	32
South "	17
Australia	19
Iceland	14
United States	4,869
	281,177

The avowed destination of the immigrants was as follows:—

Arizona	85
Arkansas	174
Alabama	157
Australia	8
Alaska	4
British Columbia	91
Connecticut	5,269
Colorado	2,189
California	5,638
Canada	2,134
Cuba	23
Delaware	196
District of Columbia	332
Dakota	4,936
East Indies	29
Florida	23
Georgia	248
Indiana	4,189
Illinois	35,308
Iowa	10,304
Idaho	50
Indian Territory	21
Kentucky	1,243
Kansas	5,383
Louisiana	663
Maine	229
Maryland	1,715
Michigan	8,733
Missouri	7,521
Minnesota	12,564
Mississippi	35
Montana	431
Mexico	56
Massachusetts	7,162
Manitoba	12
New Hampshire	183
North Carolina	41
Nebraska	6,013
Nevada	364
New Jersey	8,211
New York	83,839
New Mexico	77
New Brunswick	8
New Zealand	1
Ohio	13,228
Oregon	618
Pennsylvania	26,621
Rhode Island	2,213
South Carolina	162
South America	86
Tennessee	317
Texas	3,575
Utah	1,788
Vermont	262
Virginia	238
West Virginia	292
Wisconsin	15,330
Washington Territory	175
Wyoming	159
West Indies	11
Total	281,177

During the year there were returned through the agency of the Board of Commissioners of Emigration 1,172 immigrants to the countries whence they came, under the Act of Congress, which forbids the landing of any convict, idiot, or any person unable to take care of himself or herself without becoming a public charge.

The operations of the Board commence on the arrival of a ship from a foreign port, which is boarded by an officer from Castle Garden, who examines and reports to the Commission as to the cleanliness of the vessel, the number of steerage passengers, the number of births and deaths if any, particulars of any sickness during the voyage, and the nature of any complaints the immigrants may have to make. After examination of their luggage on board ship by the Customs officers, the immigrants are transferred to the landing depôt by barge or steamboat, and are examined as they enter by the officers of the Bureau, whose object is to discover, in accordance with the law, if any are likely to become a public charge. Upon arrival, the immigrants pass into the rotunda of Castle Garden, where everything possible under the circumstances is provided to secure the comfort of the new arrivals—responsible brokers to exchange foreign money at the current rates without deduction, interpreters speaking and writing every European language, a telegraph office for the forwarding of despatches, and a restaurant supplying food at reasonable prices.

Attached to Castle Garden is a labour bureau, maintained at the expense of the German and Irish Immigrant Societies, through which last year 15,539 persons obtained employment—8,643 men and 6,896 women—the latter, with few exceptions, being engaged as domestic servants.

Vital statistics.

VITAL Statistics, New York City, 1885.

Births	30,030
Deaths	35,696
Marriages	11,716

The causes of death were principally as follows:—

Zymotic diseases	9,003
Consumption	5,120
Pneumonia	3,588
Diarrhœal diseases	3,414
Diphtheria	1,261
Bronchitis	1,574
Heart disease	1,774
Diseases of brain and nervous system	3,176
Bright's disease	2,066
Apoplexy	713
Cancer	746
By violence	1,329
Small-pox	25
Typhus fever	11
Typhoid fever	293
Cerebro-spinal meningitis	200
Measles	735
Croup	837
Whooping cough	482
Scarlet fever	555

City finances.

City Finances.—The total funded debt of the City of New York on the 1st of January, 1886, amounted to 26,604,025*l.*, against which there is a sinking fund on hand of 7,059,145*l.*

Valuations and tax rates for the past six years are given in the following table:—

NEW YORK.

Year.	Real Estate.	Personal.	City Tax.
	£	£	Per cent.
1885	240,699,285	41,750,816	2·40
1884	230,670,888	45,018,570	2·25
1883	222,300,918	40,694,578	2·29
1882	213,251,986	40,854,151	2·25
1881	201,207,450	43,097,857	2·26
1880	194,169,770	41,445,971	2·22

Annex A.—RETURN of all Shipping at the Port of New York for the Year 1885.

ENTERED.

Nationality.	Sailing. Number of Vessels.	Sailing. Tons.	Steam. Number of Vessels.	Steam. Tons.	Total. Number of Vessels.	Total. Tons.
Great Britain ...	1,337	731,054	1,314	3,426,048	2,651	4,157,102
United States ...	1,523	594,212	243	385,262	1,766	979,474
Germany	200	111,846	243	539,117	443	650,963
France ...	3	1,240	85	213,641	88	214,881
Sweden and Norway...	378	258,249	27	10,524	405	268,773
Belgium	1	750	85	235,223	86	235,973
Italy ...	172	97,308	20	33,457	192	130,765
Mexico ...	8	1,223	1	950	9	2,173
Netherlands ...	8	3,100	44	95,460	52	98,560
Austria...	...	...	74	49,151	74	49,151
Spain ...	35	12,697	67	89,318	102	102,015
Denmark ...	17	4,600	33	61,424	50	66,024
Other European countries ...	34	19,310	3	2,814	37	22,124
South America	4	917	...	...	4	917
Central America	3	537	...	...	3	537
Other countries	5	690	...	...	5	690
Total...	3,728	1,837,733	2,239	5,142,389	5,967	6,980,122
,, for the year preceding...	3,805	2,113,153	2,286	5,284,694	6,091	7,397,847

CLEARED.

Nationality.	Sailing. Number of Vessels.	Sailing. Tons.	Steam. Number of Vessels.	Steam. Tons.	Total. Number of Vessels.	Total. Tons.
Great Britain ...	1,250	557,737	1,236	3,222,508	2,486	3,780,245
United States ...	1,079	454,927	204	323,430	1,283	778,357
Germany	213	192,069	239	529,050	452	721,139
France ...	4	1,653	83	208,615	87	210,268
Sweden and Norway...	367	250,734	14	5,457	381	256,191
Belgium	...	...	85	235,223	85	235,223
Italy ...	173	96,747	21	35,130	194	131,877
Mexico...	5	778	...	...	5	778
Netherlands ...	8	3,328	45	97,590	53	100,918
Austria...	77	51,144	...	...	77	51,144
Spain ...	36	12,354	67	89,318	103	101,672
Denmark ...	17	4,776	30	55,841	47	60,617
Other European countries ...	33	18,742	1	938	34	19,680
South America	5	1,146	...	...	5	1,146
Central America	4	716	...	...	4	716
Other countries	3	414	...	...	3	414
Total...	3,274	1,647,285	2,025	4,803,100	5,299	6,450,385
,, for the year preceding ...	3,403	1,669,799	2,190	5,194,463	5,593	6,864,262

[354]

Annex B.—Return of Principal Articles of Import to New York during the Years 1885 and 1884.

Articles.		1885. Quantity.	1885. Value. £	1884. Quantity.	1884. Value. £
Cocoa	Bags	58,550	232,063	...	242,928
Coffee	Cwts.	3,770,147	6,818,077	3,526,200	7,154,449
China, glass, and earthenware	...	...	1,441,059	...	1,672,020
Cotton	...	...	114,825	...	218,943
Dry goods—					
Manufactures of cotton	...	...	4,330,565	...	4,705,599
,, flax	...	...	3,068,904	...	3,237,279
,, silk	...	...	5,968,834	...	7,389,175
,, wool	...	...	5,349,832	...	5,945,555
,, miscellaneous	...	...	1,993,589	...	2,155,292
Fancy goods	...	...	214,810	...	219,591
Furs	...	...	916,381	...	1,124,410
Fruits	...	...	3,071,909	...	3,072,240
Hair	...	...	315,935	...	265,118
Hemp	...	...	1,151,348	...	1,229,150
Hides, dressed	...	...	1,063,460	...	1,143,285
,, undressed	...	...	3,382,173	...	3,357,184
India rubber	...	...	1,975,938	...	1,958,977
Jewellery, watches, and precious stones	...	...	1,489,517	...	1,637,253
Jute and jute butts	...	...	459,644	...	496,345
Linseed	...	...	378,707	...	734,760
Molasses	Gallons	...	275,681	10,540,630	358,358
Paper stock	...	...	786,410	...	803,593
Metals—					
Cutlery	...	...	276,704	...	327,398
Iron, pig	Tons	86,821	340,237	...	482,739
,, other	...	...	390,912	...	554,036
Metal goods	...	...	390,719	...	276,227
Steel	...	...	542,070	...	635,101
Tin plates	...	...	1,657,664	...	1,825,210
Tin slabs	...	...	869,299	...	816,691
Soda, ash	...	...	323,671	...	281,509
,, caustic	...	...	150,830	...	233,925
Spices	...	...	518,031	...	518,700
Stationery and books	...	...	857,913	...	839,280
Sugar	Tons	797,269	10,090,505	755,353	9,676,901
Specie and bullion	...	...	3,527,802	...	5,493,374
Tea	Lbs.	...	2,493,263	50,185,325	2,304,770
Tobacco and cigars	...	...	1,869,006	...	1,470,030
Wines, spirits, &c.	...	...	1,655,327	...	1,425,710
Wood	...	...	1,551,637	...	1,445,150
Wool	Lbs.	44,729,255	1,008,772	30,142,414	819,787
Other articles	...	...	12,265,293	...	15,397,808
Total	...	...	85,579,316	...	93,945,850

Annex B.—Return of Principal Articles of Export from New York during the Years 1885 and 1884.

Articles.		1885. Quantity.	1885. Value. £	1884. Quantity.	1884. Value. £
Bacon and hams	Lbs.	264,380,796	4,605,963	207,003,137	4,322,048
Butter	,,	14,542,382	466,390	16,212,126	579,251
Cotton, domestics	Packages	198,150	2,282,914	140,136	1,815,379
,, raw	Bales	739,981	7,866,755	680,079	7,328,144
Cheese	...	79,607,405	1,357,357	90,090,329	1,860,422
Flour	Barrels	3,705,029	3,603,366	3,907,021	4,040,815
Indian corn	Bushels	26,259,228	2,963,988	11,862,158	1,490,930
Lard	...	214,809,076	3,260,886	155,214,411	2,753,061
Pork and beef, salt	Lbs.	70,077,624	960,564	55,869,152	738,153
Petroleum, refined	Gallons	313,980,239	5,787,453	314,486,421	5,970,802
,, crude	,,	49,496,978	764,796	61,281,018	990,643
,, lubricating	,,	11,835,668	501,455	10,508,375	439,536
Sugar	Lbs.	247,090,990	3,249,379	118,730,282	1,656,353
Specie and bullion	...	...	4,955,286	...	11,208,577
Wheat	Bushels	16,286,200	3,170,564	28,687,362	5,364,056
Other articles	...	...	27,212,000	...	28,817,850
Total	...	...	73,009,116	...	79,366,020

Annex C.—TABLE showing the Total Value of all Articles Exported from and Imported to New York from and to Foreign Countries during the Years 1885 and 1884.

Countries.	Exports. 1885.	Exports. 1884.	Imports. 1885.	Imports. 1884.
	£	£	£	£
Great Britain	35,523,364	39,948,607	18,005,175	22,187,569
British possessions	4,723,489	4,956,653	5,209,317	6,090,737
Germany	6,798,438	7,133,445	12,148,906	13,183,289
France and possessions	3,950,853	5,156,530	11,263,707	12,293,400
Belgium	3,135,388	3,424,743	1,185,110	1,847,849
Spain and possessions	2,903,372	3,595,530	9,201,130	10,859,840
Netherlands and possessions	2,898,456	2,732,176	2,251,120	835,992
United States of Columbia	1,339,044	1,567,110	351,343	801,720
Central American States	..	..	610,562	1,269,212
Italy	1,321,104	904,381	2,619,000	3,441,510
Brazil	757,175	776,086	6,963,706	7,433,595
China	688,752	492,878	2,027,758	1,944,886
Denmark	687,638	636,443	71,084	..
Venezuela	636,406	560,416	1,227,208	1,374,852
Portugal	618,024	656,532	220,290	..
Argentine Republic	600,632	627,625	326,746	846,667
Mexico	586,212	814,493	1,062,559	1,427,647
Hayti	578,563	610,766	377,220	..
Sweden and Norway	509,562	390,304	283,270	..
Japan	311,387	257,609	745,313	1,201,929
Chili	210,098	325,647	30,570	..
St. Domingo	193,351	219,522	314,680	..
Uruguay	174,933	242,774	553,600	438,570
Austria	104,364	286,552	1,196,545	1,595,462
Russia	38,730	..	599,013	572,610
Other countries	3,719,781	3,049,198	6,734,384	4,298,514
Total	73,009,116	79,366,020	85,579,316	93,945,850

	£
Total specie and bullion exports comprised in 1885	4,953,288
In 1884	11,208,577
Total specie and bullion imports—	
In 1885	3,696,718
In 1884	5,493,372
Specie and bullion exports to Great Britain—	
In 1885	2,953,764
In 1884	8,086,373
Specie and bullion imports from Great Britain—	
In 1885	130,120
In 1884	1,466,197
Specie and bullion imports—	
From France in 1885	1,000,086
„ Germany in 1885	1,698,877
„ France in 1884	819,055
„ Germany in 1884	1,315,137
Specie and bullion exports—	
To France in 1885	150,683
„ Germany in 1885	78,095
„ France in 1884	1,085,158
„ Germany in 1884	380,750

UNITED STATES.

Annex D.—Return of the Number of Seamen who have been Engaged, Discharged, Left Behind, Reported Dead, or Deserted, or who have been Relieved at the British Consulate General, New York, and showing the Total Number of British and Foreign Sailors who were Engaged, Discharged, &c., from British Ships, with the Total Amount of Wages paid at the Consulate to Seamen on Discharge from their Ships and from Hospital or Gaol; and also showing the Number of New Agreements entered into during the Year 1885.

Seamen.											Wages.			Agreements.
Engaged.	Discharged.	Left Behind.			Died.			Deserted.	Relieved.	Nationality.		Total Number of Seamen.	Paid on Discharge from Vessels.	Paid on Discharge from Hospital or Gaol.	Total Wages Paid.	Number Opened.
		In Gaol.	In Hospital.	Total.	At Sea.	On Shore.	Total.			British.	Foreign.					
11,651	7,176	25	144	169	64	28	92	4,692	484	15,533	8,731	24,264	Dol. c. 331,672 30	Dol. c. 3,774 70	Dol. c. 335,447 00	333

PROVIDENCE.

Mr. Vice-Consul Stockwell reports as follows:—

During the year 1885 nothing of extraordinary interest has been developed with respect to the commerce at this port or the general trade of the city.

The volume of business transacted by the Custom-house is about the same as in 1884.

Direct importations for the most part come from Canada, and consist chiefly of lumber in various stages of manufacture—from cord wood to finished lumber.

The indirect importations comprise the greater receipts, coming under the revenue laws of the 14th July, 1870, and the 10th July, 1880, providing for bonded cars and boats. The goods received in New York or Boston, in unbroken packages, are shipped under bond to their destination. During the year 1885 goods to the value of 103,624*l.* were received from foreign countries, England furnishing the largest amount, Germany the next largest, and France the next. The amounts given in the annexes do not include the goods received free of duty. The aggregate of such importations is not accessible.

The exports were very light as usual, and, as before, consist of naval stores, lumber, provisions, &c., taken out by returning vessels clearing directly for some near foreign port. The exports for the year 1884 were made unusually larger by the shipment of machinery to New Brunswick.

The ten hour law was agitated in 1885, and at the May session of the General Assembly at Newport the law was passed, and went into operation on the 1st January, 1886. The Knights of Labour became very prominent as an organisation before the close of the year. Generally, what has been done by the Knights of Labour has been advantageous to both the employer and the employé. Strikes and "boycots" have been averted by arbitration, and money and ill-feeling saved. There has been an advance generally of 10 per cent. in the wages of the skilled and unskilled labourers. This advance, however, in all cases has not been the result of the interference of the Knights of Labour; many manufacturers have granted the increase voluntarily. Although wages are higher, yet it is true that in some cases there has been a corresponding increase in fines, so that no gain was made. There is now before the General Assembly a law to correct the evils connected with the system of fines. The great argument of the protectionist of the manufacturing class is based partly on the benefits claimed to accrue to the labourer. The protectionist declares that free trade will bring pauper labour. Why, pauper labour is here already, in spite of the vaunted protection to labour. Protection always robs, but does not always protect.

POPULATION.

	1850.	1860.	1870.	1880.	1885.
Providence	41,513	50,666	68,904	104,857	118,070
Newport	9,563	10,508	12,521	15,693	19,566
State	147,545	174,620	217,353	276,531	304,284

UNITED STATES.

Annex A.—RETURN of all Shipping at the Port of Providence in the Year 1885.

ENTERED.

Nationality.	Sailing. Number of Vessels.	Sailing. Tons.	Steam. Number of Vessels.	Steam. Tons.	Total. Number of Vessels.	Total. Tons.
British	57	5,752	1	1,043	58	6,795
American	29	6,922	...	...	29	6,922
Italian	2	1,014	...	...	2	1,014
Total	88	13,688	1	1,043	89	14,731
,, for the year preceding	59	10,873	...	...	59	10,873

CLEARED.

Nationality.	Sailing. Number of Vessels.	Sailing. Tons.	Steam. Number of Vessels.	Steam. Tons.	Total. Number of Vessels.	Total. Tons.
British	46	4,312	...	...	46	4,312
American	5	1,914	...	...	5	1,914
Italian	...	...	...	...	...	...
Total	51	6,226	...	...	51	6,226
,, for the year preceding	37	4,894	...	...	37	4,894

Annex B.—RETURN of Principal Articles of Export from Providence during the Years 1885-84.

Articles.	1885. Value.	1884. Value.
	£	£
Miscellaneous	180	..
Machinery	..	5,149
Total	180	5,149

RETURN of Principal Articles of Import to Providence during the Years 1885-84.

Articles.	1885. Value.	1884. Value.
	£	£
Dry goods	39,385	42,112
Chemicals, &c.	25,749	13,711
Metals, and manufactures of	13,945	18,555
All others	24,545	29,473
Total	103,624	103,851

Annex C.—TABLE showing the Total Value of all Articles Exported from Providence, R.I., and Imported to Providence from and to Foreign Countries during the Years 1885–84.

Country.	Exports. 1885.	Exports. 1884.	Imports. 1885.	Imports. 1884.
	£	£	£	
P. E. Island	64	..	..	
Turks Island	116	107	..	Imports not returned by countries till July 1, 1884.
New Brunswick	..	5,042	..	
England	..	..	49,567	
Germany	..	..	17,494	
France	..	..	6,463	
All others	..	..	30,100	
Total	180	5,149	103,624	

New York, April 2, 1886.

SAN FRANCISCO.

Report by Consul Stanley on the Trade and Commerce of California for the Year 1885.

CALIFORNIA has, in a measure, felt the benefit of the general improvement in trade which has occurred throughout the United States during the past year, though it can scarcely be said to have fully emerged from the depression which characterised my last report.

The loss of the Oregon and Northern trade, occasioned by the opening of the Northern Pacific railroad, which removed the distributing centre for numerous commodities from San Francisco to Eastern cities, has not yet been made good to San Francisco merchants and manufacturers by the increase of demand within the borders of the State itself, though a steady moderate increase of population is already yielding promise of this.

The most important railroad work completed within the State during the past year has been that of the California Southern railroad, from the city and port of San Diego to a point of connection with the Atlantic and Pacific Railway system. This gives the extreme southern port of California a through and independent connection with the East, which will doubtless tend to the prosperity of all that portion of the State.

The wheat and grain crops generally throughout the State proved to be very deficient as compared with the previous and several former years.

The surplus of wheat estimated available for export from the crop of 1885 was about 750,000 tons; but as a considerable surplus of the previous season's crop remained on hand at the opening of the harvest year in July, it is estimated that there was then not less than 1,000,000 tons of 2,000 lbs. available for export.

The actual exports of wheat and flour from 1st July to the 31st December, 1885, have been together equal to about 280,000 tons of wheat, and the estimated stock remaining on hand at the latter date was probably about 600,000 tons of 2,000 lbs.

Farmers were unwilling sellers of their wheat during the autumn months, while a considerably higher range of prices existed in Europe than has since been current.

The result is that they are left in very many instances with their wheat on hand, and have to face a very indifferent out-look. Were it not that farmers generally throughout the State are exercising the extreme economies in farming, which improved machinery and the low prices of almost all material now permit of, it is improbable that they could have more than paid expenses from their crops of last year.

As it is, the debtor class have probably, in many instances of wheat farming, got still more into debt.

The exports of flour are only tolerably maintained.

The improved roller process now being adopted in England is interfering with the ready sale of the manufacture of this coast in that market.

The Pacific Islands and China are in part filling the void which this is occasioning; and it seems probable that the latter country will, more especially during periods of low prices, continue to be a large customer for the flour product of California.

The English wheat market, except for a brief period during the autumn, when prices were enhanced by fears and rumours of war, has again been most unsatisfactory to Californian shippers.

Under the influence of large Indian supplies the Liverpool market has declined from about 1*l*. 17*s*. 2*d*. per imperial quarter, which was for a short time current during the autumn for Californian wheat, to the present ruling price of about 1*l*. 13*s*. 7*d*. per imperial quarter.

Average price of wheat in California. The average price of wheat in California during the past few months has been about 1*l*. 8*s*. 6*d*. per 500 lbs., free on board at San Francisco, including bags.

In a measure perhaps the low prices ruling for wheat during the past few years is causing certain Californian farmers to direct their attention to the growing of other crops, though so far this is not occurring to any material extent.

Good crop expected in 1886. The autumn and winter season has been especially favourable this year, and it is estimated that the average now under wheat is considerably in excess of a year ago, and should the season maintain its favourable character through the spring there will almost certainly be a very large wheat harvest next June and July.

The question of irrigation in certain districts of the State, where the average rainfall is deficient, continues to receive much attention.

It is generally admitted, however, that the prices current and likely to rule for wheat cannot admit of an expensive system of irrigation, and in cases where this is being undertaken and contemplated it is with a view rather to varied farming, including most largely the cultivation of fine fruits.

More attention paid to fruit growing. Each year greater attention is being devoted to this branch of cultivation, and it is probable that within a few years the fruit product of California will show great improvement both in quality and variety.

The improved varieties of grapes resulting from the importation of fine foreign cuttings is most noticeable, and will become more apparent each year.

Wine. It seems certain that these improved varieties of wine and table grapes will ultimately result in driving the Mission grape entirely out of the market, which was, until a few years ago, almost exclusively cultivated, and I have little doubt that before long California wine will be largely imported to the East and even to Europe.

Viticulturists are largely grafting foreign cuttings upon the Mission vine, and it is claimed with great success.

The vintage of California last autumn was very much below the estimates formed of it earlier in the year. This may be attributed generally to an unfavourable spring, and perhaps more particularly to a late frost, which did much injury in the important valleys of Napa and Sonoma.

An expected and material fall in the value of wine has in consequence been averted for the present.

Shipping interests depressed. Shipping interests continue very depressed, and many of the vessels owned locally and employed in the coast, timber, and coal trades have been laid up to await the advent of better times.

Shipbuilding. I mentioned in my last report that the Union Iron Works have by a large investment of money secured the best appliances and position for carrying on iron shipbuilding, and had just finished a steel steamer for the coasting trade. It is understood that this steamer has proved a complete success so far as her work is concerned, and has demonstrated the ability of this company to build and equip such craft. The times have, however, been unfavourable to this industry, and until general shipping interests improve it is improbable that the company will be called upon to do much work of this description.

Foreign freights again ruled very low during the entire year, and must have proved quite unremunerative to shipowners. There were chartered for the year to the United Kingdom 362,532 tons, of which 234,924 tons were British, and 127,608 tons belonging to other nations, mostly American.

Freights very low.

Should the present outlook for a large wheat crop be fulfilled it is thought that the extreme depression in ocean freights may shortly be somewhat ameliorated.

The various overland railways cut no figure in the carriage of cereals from this coast for Europe, nor is it likely they can do so, unless wheat should attain to a very much higher range of prices in Europe than at present seems probable.

Railways cannot carry grain at present low prices.

Manufacturing industries are not generally in a satisfactory condition on the coast, though they are probably less depressed than was stated in my last report.

Manufacturing industries not generally satisfactory.

High wages for both skilled and unskilled labour, as compared with the Eastern States, militate against successful competition here in very many instances.

The tendency of wages, however, is towards a decline, and it seems hardly probable that they can be maintained for many years more above the parity of Eastern cities.

Wages high as compared with the East, but will almost certainly fall.

In the city of San Francisco during the past year building operations have shown an activity not equalled for many years past. This has probably been induced more by the very moderate prices ruling for all building material, than the moderate measure of increased prosperity which I have indicated as prevailing.

The statistics given in the appendix show a slight increase in the value of the exports as compared with 1884.

Exports.

The items that are of special interest to England are cereals, tinned salmon, and tinned fruits and vegetables. Of these, cereals immensely preponderate.

Specially interesting to England.

I would add to my opening remarks regarding wheat cultivation that great attention is being paid to the production of a first-rate article, with a special view to competition with Russia and India for the English market, and last year an association of the principal millers was formed, called the Millers' Association of the Pacific Coast. Its main objects are to improve the method of the purchase of wheat, and to bring the miller more directly in contact with the farmer who grows high-class wheat.

Endeavours to beat English made flour.

The following remarks made by some of the leading authorities on the coast, referring specifically to the English market, may have an interest for English farmers and millers.

Various opinions on flour.

Mr. Bannister, vice-president of the Corporation Starr and Company, who since 1876 have had a branch establishment at Liverpool, and who make it their specialty to send cargoes of the finest flour, takes a very hopeful view of California prospects as supplying England with flour, and says that it is very difficult for English millers to compete with California millers, as the former, tempted by the cheapness of Indian wheat, generally use it, the consequence being a bitter taste to the flour and a dirty colour, whereas California flour is white, sweet, and generally superior.

Opinion of Mr. Bannister.

Even when English millers make flour from California wheat their machinery is, he states, so inferior to that in use in California, that the flour is not equally good. Again he states that English millers grind the wheat too much.

He adds that, after careful calculation, he is confident that wheat can be laid down by small growers at tide water at 3s. per cental of 100 lbs., and that large wheat growers can afford to do it at 2s. per 100 lbs.

This firm shipped to England during the first four months of the harvest year nearly 150,000 barrels of flour.

Mr. Horace Davis thinks English millers can compete with California millers.

A somewhat different view of the prospects of English millers is taken by Mr. Horace Davis, of Golden Gate Mills, and president of the Farmers' Association.

He states that the margins of profits were never so close as throughout 1885, owing to many new mills having been erected and improved machinery having been placed in others, causing greatly increased production; hence sharp competition among millers.

He considers that Russia and India are forestalling the United States, and that the wheat world was quite taken aback at the enormous quantity India has shown herself capable of supplying; her surplus for 1885, excluding the reserves, being 1,300,000 tons.

With this amount of grain thrown on the markets of the world prices must continue to fall, and those producers who cannot compete with India in profitable production must go to the wall.

The English farmers must inevitably do so unless they change their line of products.

With regard to flour he thinks English millers can hold their own, for though much of the India wheat is doubtless dirty, English ingenuity is equal to the handling of it, and their millers make excellent flour out of what appears to Californians very poor stock.

All India wheat, moreover, is not to be classed as of inferior quality No. 1 Bombay wheat being equal to the finest wheat produced in California.

Salmon and other tinned goods Imports.

There is a large sale of these in England, the combined value exported having been 275,000l. against 331,000l. in 1884.

The total value of the imports is 100,000l. more than in 1884.

The articles in which England takes a leading part are iron, tin plates, Portland cement, salt, and chemicals, and I will deal briefly with each of these.

Manufactured iron and steel ceased.

The imports from England of manufactured iron and steel have almost ceased, owing to the very high duty charged.

They are now brought from Pittsburgh and Pennsylvania, or manufactured here.

Eastern pig iron sold cheaper than English pig iron.

Pig iron is still imported to some extent, but it is yearly decreasing, large quantities of Eastern pig iron being brought here, which, owing to the heavy duty of 1l. 6s. 10½d. (6 dol. 72 c.) per ton, can compete with British pig iron. Indeed, and it is a matter of special importance to British exporters, during 1885, for the first time on record, American Eastern iron sold here below Scotch iron. It is also said that Glengarnock and Thomas iron are not so carefully selected for this market as they used to be, and that should greater care not be taken these hitherto favourite brands will be superseded by others.

Scrap iron.

From 8,000 to 10,000 tons are annually imported, the local product being insufficient to meet the requirements of the rolling mills, nail works, &c. About two-thirds of the imports come from England. The duty is the same as on pig iron.

Tin plates.

These all come from Great Britain, no tin plate manufactories having hitherto been successfully worked in the United States.

It is very possible, however, that they may succeed, the saving of the high duty of one halfpenny (1 cent) per pound being a great incentive to American manufacturers to use their best endeavours.

Probability American tin plates competing with English.

The production of the mines in California, Washington territory, and British Columbia has increased so largely and steadily that it is evident the importation of foreign coal must materially diminish within a very few years.

Coal.

At the present time the price of coal is lower than ever known, the best grades of steam coal selling here, duty paid, at 1*l.* to 1*l.* 4*s.* (5 dol. to 6 dol.) per ton, so that after deducting 3*s.* (75 c.) per ton and the freight, very little margin for profit is left on the original cost of the coal.

This is one of the few articles from England whose importation has steadily increased during the last 10 years.

Portland cement.

Previous to that the annual importations did not exceed 15,000 barrels, while it now amounts to 120,000 to 150,000 barrels annually. The duty on this is 20 per cent. of its original cost, yet English Portland cement has almost driven American cement out of the market.

English still holds the market.

In former years large quantities of Rosendale cement, manufactured in the Eastern States, were used here, but its importation has almost ceased.

To keep this large trade low freights from England are necessary, so as to be able to place the cement in this market at a price not higher than 12*s.* (3 dol.) per barrel of 100 lbs.

Freights must be low to keep it.

Considerable quantities are imported here and to Oregon from Great Britain, the total quantity averaging annually from 7,000 to 10,000 tons. It is principally used for dairy purposes and for family consumption, the cheaper kinds of salt manufactured here being almost exclusively used for meat packing. The duty on foreign salt is 6*d.* (12 c.) per 100 lbs., and therefore a considerable item in an article which sells here at 44*s.* (11 dol.) per ton of 2,000 lbs. in white sacks.

Salt.

Rough chemicals are imported in large quantities, such as soda ash, soda crystals, alum, bleaching powder, caustic soda, bicarbonate of soda, &c.

Chemicals.

The aggregate importation of these is large, amounting to about 10,000 tons a year, but prices have been very low, caused by increased competition of American chemicals, especially of soda crystals and bicarbonate of soda.

The duties are as follows:—

Articles.		Duty.
		c.
Soda ash	per lb.	¼
Caustic soda	,,	1
Bicarbonate of soda	,,	1½
Soda crystals	,,	¼
Alum	per 100 lbs.	60
Bleaching powder		free

The following table has been compiled by Mr. John Valentine, vice-president and general manager of Wells, Fargo, and Company.

Precious metals.

The following is the annual product of lead, copper, silver, and gold in the States west of the Missouri River, excluding British Columbia and Mexico:—

Year.	Lead.	Copper.	Silver.	Gold.	Total.
	£	£	£	£	£
1885	1,713,000	1,568,000	8,903,000	5,277,000	17,461,000
1884	1,367,000	1,217,000	8,706,000	5,017,000	16,307,000

Of these my Consular district, California, Oregon, and Washington territory, contributed to the value of 3,150,000*l.*

Freights. — Grain freights have during the past year ranged lower than ever before known. The range for iron vessels to Cork, the United Kingdom, and the Continent of Europe has been from 27*s.* 6*d.* to 35*s.*, and for wooden vessels about 2*s.* 6*d.* lower.

Shipping. — English and foreign shipping generally has decreased, and American shipping has increased. During the year the Union Iron Works turned out the first steel vessel for deep-sea service built on the Pacific Coast, the "Arago," a steamer of 827 tons.

The following table shows the entries made at this office regarding seamen during the years 1884–85.

Year.	Engaged.	Discharged.	Deserted.	Sent to Hospital.	Reported dead.
1885	2,461	1,034	1,474	36	58
1884	2,815	1,087	1,822	49	28

Railways. — No material change has occurred during the year, beyond the entrance to San Francisco of the Atlantic and Pacific railroad, partly by purchase and partly by lease from the Southern Pacific Company.

While rates of freight and passenger traffic are the same over both roads, the tendency is to secure better attention, care, and despatch in the transportation of passengers and freight.

Work has been resumed on the California and Oregon Railway, with a fair prospect of its speedy completion. This road, it is thought, will materially benefit San Francisco, by placing it in rapid communication with Northern California and Oregon.

Note.—The values are reduced to sterling, at the rate of 5 dol. to the pound. The current value of the pound sterling is 4 dol. 84 c.

In mentioning the duty, I have given both currency and sterling. The currency is the duty charged, and to get the exact figure it should be estimated at about 4 dol. 84 c.

San Francisco, March 17, 1886.

Annex A.—RETURN of all Shipping at the Port of San Francisco in the Year 1885.

ENTERED.

Nationality.	Sailing. Number of Vessels.	Sailing. Tons.	Steam. Number of Vessels.	Steam. Tons.	Total. Number of Vessels.	Total. Tons.
British	177	263,586	58	135,148	235	398,734
American	257	195,537	158	230,661	415	426,198
,, from Atlantic ports of the Union	40	66,702	...	...	40	66,702
,, sealing and whaling voyages	53	13,084	...	...	53	13,084
German	20	23,971	4	1,472	24	25,443
French	3	1,206	...	...	3	1,206
Other countries	25	14,799	3	762	28	15,561
Total	575	578,885	223	368,043	798	946,928
,, for the year preceding	504	496,605	226	378,181	730	874,786

CLEARED.

Nationality.	Sailing. Number of Vessels.	Sailing. Tons.	Steam. Number of Vessels.	Steam. Tons.	Total. Number of Vessels.	Total. Tons.
British	191	277,631	54	126,886	245	404,517
American	265	211,149	162	235,992	427	447,141
,, Atlantic ports of the Union	10	13,979	...	...	10	13,979
,, sealing and whaling voyages	60	13,314	...	...	60	13,314
German	17	19,312	4	1,472	21	20,784
French	3	1,206	1	2,263	4	3,469
Other countries	29	17,238	7	978	36	18,216
Total	575	553,829	228	367,591	803	921,420
,, for the year preceding	552	590,824	230	382,438	782	973,262

The entries and clearances of American ships do not include the coasting trade.

Annex B.—RETURN of the Principal Articles of Export from San Francisco during the Years 1884-85.

Articles.		1885. Quantity.	1885. Value.	1884. Quantity.	1884. Value.
			£		£
Wheat and flour	Tons	777,000	4,216,000	788,000	4,523,000
Wine	Gallons	1,184,000	365,000	1,194,000	320,000
Tinned salmon	Cases	180,900	165,000	284,000	254,000
Tinned fruit and vegetables	,,	121,000	110,000	89,000	77,000
Quicksilver	Flasks	16,000	92,000	21,900	130,000
Timber	Feet	19,266,000	90,000	20,232,000	98,000
Borax	Lbs.	7,506,000	89,000	4,279,000	65,000
Other articles	...	...	2,255,000	...	1,966,000
Total	...	...	7,382,000	...	7,433,000

RETURN of the Principal Articles of Import to San Francisco during the Years 1884–85.

		1885. Quantity.	1885. Value.	1884. Quantity.	1884. Value.
			£		£
Raw silk	Lbs.	2,690,000	1,748,000	3,305,000	1,720,000
Sugar	Tons	76,500	1,644,000	74,100	1,626,000
Coals	,,	568,400	348,000	546,500	364,000
Coffee	Lbs.	22,600,000	420,000	19,505,000	344,000
Rice	Tons	19,300	210,000	24,550	250,000
Tea	Lbs.	7,000,000	214,000	6,664,000	214,000
Tin plates	Boxes	119,000	83,800	155,530	118,000
Cement	Barrels	66,400	18,000	52,300	15,000
Pig iron	Tons	11,120	20,000	9,000	19,000
Scrap iron	,,	9,600	19,000	13,880	30,000
Other articles	...	...	2,375,200	...	2,300,000
Total	...	...	7,100,000	...	7,000,000

Annex C.—TABLE showing the Total Value of all Articles Exported from San Francisco, and Imported to San Francisco, from and to Foreign Countries during the Years 1884–1885.

Country.	Exports. 1885.	Exports. 1884.	Imports. 1885.	Imports. 1884.
	£	£	£	£
Great Britain	4,185,000	3,846,000	630,000	643,000
China	740,000	592,000	1,200,000	1,367,000
Hawaiian Islands	500,000	513,000	1,800,000	1,592,000
Australia	272,000	284,000	180,000	238,000
Canada	250,000	261,000	250,000	285,000
Central America	140,000	219,000	560,000	356,000
Japan	121,000	91,000	1,300,000	1,333,000
France	51,800	167,000	300,000	233,000
Germany	14,000	13,000	161,000	120,000
Belgium	3,600	300,000	62,000	60,000
Spanish possessions	3,000	2,000	108,000	160,000
India	500	3,000	240,000	308,000
Domestic ports and other countries	1,101,100	1,142,000	309,000	305,000
Total	7,382,000	7,433,000	7,100,000	7,000,000

SAN FRANCISCO.

Consul Stanley to the Earl of Rosebery.

My Lord, San Francisco, April 7, 1886.

I HAVE the honour to transmit herewith commercial reports on Portland (Oregon), San Diego, Los Angeles and Wilmington, and on Astoria.

Mr. Mortimer, Vice-Consul at Los Angeles, states that owing to the delay in publishing the statistics he is unable to furnish them in the form required by the Instruction of 22nd December.

He also gives as a reason for Including in his report several matters that are apparently of only local interest, that attention has been largely called to the south of California as a field for English emigration, and that he thinks the information he gives may be useful to intending immigrants. I have, &c.,
(Signed) G. E. STANLEY.

PORTLAND, OREGON.

Report by Vice-Consul Laidlaw on the Trade and Commerce of Portland (Oregon) for the Year 1885.

The trade of this district shows a great improvement over that of 1884. The harvest in all sections of the State has been large, and the receipts here of all leading articles of produce increased very much during the year, while the imports have been much lighter than for years past. Market prices of all produce have, however, been very low; still money has been much more plentiful, and business failures have been at least 50 per cent. less than during 1884. *Trade. Harvest. Imports.*

As usual the most of the tonnage employed in the foreign trade of this district was British: the proportion being 84 per cent. of the whole, as against 73 per cent. last year. *Tonnage.*

IMPORT TRADE.

Statistics of direct imports from foreign countries, as given in the tables annexed, show a decrease of about 36 per cent., but only a very small proportion of imports are received direct, mainly coals, rice, salt, tin plates, earthenware, and chemicals. Trade is chiefly supplied by steamer from San Francisco, and by sail and rail from the Eastern States; and it is impossible to estimate the value of the imports by these routes with any degree of accuracy. The direct importations of coals increase year by year, but, owing to the competition of domestic *Imports.*

	Coals.	coals, prices of foreign have been so low that in many instances cargoes have been brought from Australia as ballast, either free of freight or at a merely nominal rate. The total receipts were 60,096 tons, of which 31,768 tons were domestic, 6,281 tons from British Columbia, 15,863 tons from Australia, and 6,185 tons from Great Britain. Australian coal was sold as low as 4 dol., or 16s. 6d., per ton.

Coals.

coals, prices of foreign have been so low that in many instances cargoes have been brought from Australia as ballast, either free of freight or at a merely nominal rate. The total receipts were 60,096 tons, of which 31,768 tons were domestic, 6,281 tons from British Columbia, 15,863 tons from Australia, and 6,185 tons from Great Britain. Australian coal was sold as low as 4 dol., or 16s. 6d., per ton.

Salt.

The imports of salt have been smaller than last year, but this is a steady trade.

Tin plates.

The consumption of tin plates, though somewhat smaller than that of 1884, was still very large. A very large proportion of the imports is used in the district of Astoria for salmon canning purposes.

Rice.

The business of importing rice is principally in the hands of Chinese merchants.

Pig-iron.

Imports of pig-iron have been trifling, and stocks are heavy. The Oregon Iron and Steel Company produced 4,137 tons in 1885, sold only 2,957 tons, and had a stock at the close of the year of 3,598 tons. This company shipped 1,965 tons to San Francisco during the year.

Jute bags and bagging.

One of the largest indirect imports is of jute bags and bagging, and this trade of late years has been entirely supplied from Calcutta viâ San Francisco. The imports of burlaps and burlap grain bags alone exceeded 7,000,000 yards and bags. Market prices were unusually low, averaging about 3d. for standard 22 bags by 36 bags.

EXPORT TRADE.

Exports generally.

The value of exports to foreign countries, by sail and by rail to the Eastern States and coastwise, increased 20 per cent. last year. Some trade formerly tributary to this district has been diverted to San Francisco by the opening of the Oregon Pacific Railway viâ Taquina Bay, a small port in Middle Oregon.

Of the total exports of wheat, 30 per cent. has been shipped either to San Francisco or Puget Sound, the greater proportion of which was reshipped at these points to Great Britain: 45 per cent. of the flour exported was also similarly disposed of.

Coastwise exports.

The tables annexed to this report give the foreign shipments in detail. Coastwise exports and shipments by sail and rail to Eastern States of wheat, flour, salmon, wool, oats, barley, flax-seed, hides, hops, timber, fruits, and farm produce, pig-iron, &c., are valued at 1,674,680l., against a valuation of 1,256,940l. during 1884.

Breadstuffs.

Breadstuffs.—The increase of production has been very rapid of late years, as the following comparison of receipts at Portland from the two great wheat-growing sections tributary to this port will show. The figures are for the cereal years ending 31st July each year:—

Year.	Willamette Valley.		Eastern Oregon and Washington Territory.	
	Wheat.	Flour.	Wheat.	Flour.
	Quarters.	Sacks.	Quarters.	Sacks.
1882–1883	288,458	229,451	123,507	102,359
1883–1884	165,317	233,046	412,294	121,031
1884–1885	361,422	135,949	438,674	103,442
Aug.–Dec., 1885	154,376	54,098	677,064	56,525

Willamette Valley wheat is known in the British markets as Oregon wheat, and takes a high position in the trade. Eastern Oregon and Washington wheat is known as Walla Walla, the difference in value being about 2s. per quarter.

The total shipments of breadstuffs during the past year both to foreign ports and coastwise were 909,296 quarters of wheat, valued at 1,128,730l., and 321,411 sacks of flour, valued at 350,316l.

Salmon.—Shipments are generally made at Astoria, with the exception of those destined for the Eastern States by rail. The product of the Columbia River Canneries during 1885 was 557,000 cases of 4 dozen 1 lb. tins, and the shipments by railway from this district were 231,063 cases. Of British Columbia salmon, 28,172 cases passed through in transit for Canada.

Wool averaged about $8\frac{1}{2}d.$ per lb. for Valley, and 8d. for Eastern Oregon. Both were tender in staple. The clip was very large, and receipts here were 12,481,962 lbs.; shipments, 11,558,427 lbs. In 1884 receipts were 8,577,054 lbs., and shipments 8,942,517 lbs.

Hops.—The following were the receipts here and shipments viâ San Francisco and Atlantic States during the last two years:—

Year.	Receipts.	Shipments.
	Lbs.	Lbs.
1885	5,210,837	5,561,381
1884	3,894,171	3,578,074

Timber.—This branch of trade has continued in a depressed condition throughout the year, and shipments from this port to foreign countries were small, as given in the tables

Money Market.

There has been much more ease in the money market throughout the year, and banking facilities have been increased. There are now in Portland two British joint stock banks, four national banks, one private bank, besides several savings and mortgage loan banks.

Exchange on London, 60 days, has varied from $4s.\ 1\frac{3}{8}d.$ to $4s.\ 2\frac{1}{8}d.$ per dol. for bank, and $4s.\ 1\frac{1}{2}d.$ to $4s.\ 2\frac{1}{4}d.$ per dol. for mercantile bills.

Shipping.

Throughout the year the river channels have been kept in good condition, and the expense of lighterage has been very small.

The very large increase in grain exports attracted a correspondingly increased number of ships to this port, 113 British ships registering 111,101 tons entered here. During 1884 only 61, with a registered tonnage of 60,878 tons, so entered.

The engagements of tonnage during the past year (not including coasting voyages) have been as under:—

	Registered tons.
Grain cargoes	105,026
Salmon and assorted cargoes	6,288
Lumber cargoes	2,885
Miscellaneous voyages	803
Total	115,002

UNITED STATES.

Rates of freight.
Rates of freight were very low on account of the abnormally depressed condition of home markets, and the average rate for the year was 2*l*. 4*s*. to a port in the United Kingdom.

Steam tonnage.
There has been no increase in the steam tonnage employed in the coasting trade during the year. The freight carried from and to San Francisco by the allied lines was—

	From San Francisco.	To San Francisco.
	Tons.	Tons.
During 1885	75,863	132,260
1884	75,508	67,768

Sailors.
British Sailors.—Seamen's wages have averaged 4*l*. 5*s*. for able seamen: highest rate paid 7*l*., lowest 2*l*. 18*s*. 4*d*.

Working of United States Shipping Act.
The latest United States Shipping Act, which has now been in force 18 months, has proved an unmixed evil, and from my observation of its workings here, its only effect has been to increase the evils it aimed at suppressing. Were a Consular convention concluded with the United States, it would have a good effect upon the discipline of British crews in this port, and enable Consular officers better to protect sailors from the impositions of the rascals engaged in crimping seamen in Untied States ports. I very much regret that, for some reason which is not apparent, masters of British ships do not generally support the Mariners' Home here, but seem to prefer to engage crews from the boarding-house keepers here and at Astoria, who fatten upon the cash advances of the sailors, and pander to their vices.

Hospital endowment.
It may not be out of place to mention here that, principally through the voluntary subscriptions of British shipmasters, the Consular officer at this port has now an endowed bed in the Good Samaritan Hospital always at his disposal, and also that a suitable plot of ground has been purchased for the purpose of burying there such deceased British subjects as he may think proper.

Graveyard.

Changes in crews.
The following gives the number and changes in crews of British ships entering this port during the year:—

Total Number of Crews.	Deserted.	Discharged.	Engaged.	Reported Dead.	Percentage of Desertion.	Hospital Permits.
1,977	256	47	191	3	13	24

RIVER AND HARBOUR IMPROVEMENTS.

River and harbour.
Very little has been done in this respect during the past year. Propeller sluicing was again resorted to for the temporary improvement of the Columbia River, where some of the bars were silting up. Some addition was made to the wharf accommodations of this port.

Pilotage.
The rate of river pilotage was raised at last session of the Legislature from 3 dol. to 4 dol. per foot draft. A new pilot schooner was also built by the State for use of the pilots of the Columbia River bar. The rate of pilotage at the mouth of the Columbia River was also restored to the old figure of 8 dol. per foot draft for the first 12 feet, and 10 dol. per foot for any excess.

AGRICULTURE.

Although crops all over this State were unusually large and of excellent quality, prices of produce have been so low that farming has been far from profitable. The crops were got in in splendid condition.

Wheat.—Quality was good average. Judging by the quantity so far marketed the exportable surplus will not exceed 1,600,000 quarters, though estimates made during harvest were very much higher.

Oats.—The crop was very large, and of fine quality. Receipts here were 444,892 centals against 177,673 centals last year.

Hops.—The experience of growers during the past year again proved the danger of relying entirely upon this crop. At harvest time prices were so low that many growers would not go to the expense of picking. Nevertheless receipts here were 28 per cent. in excess of the previous year.

Fruit Culture.—Crops of apples, pears, prunes, plums, and other fruits were very large receipts here, being fully 50 per cent. greater than in 1884. There is a large market by rail east, which is encouraging to growers.

Sheep and Cattle.—According to census returns from all counties in the State, the number of animals were as under: Sheep, 1,686,929; cattle, 373,247; horses, 165,909; hogs, 202,612; mules, 3,591. There has been a large increase of sheep on the ranges, but a large number of cattle have been shipped to the Eastern States, so that their increase cannot be great. The business has been profitable and the losses very light.

POPULATION AND INDUSTRIES.

Arrivals at this port by sea during the year were 9,955, while departures were 11,788. There has been a steady immigration by rail principally into Eastern Oregon and Washington, but I do not think the population of Portland and vicinity has increased, and there has been a lessened demand for labour and some distress among the labouring population.

Manufactories.—The estimated value of manufactured produce during the year in this city is 1,982,000*l.*, a decrease of about 12 per cent. as compared with 1884.

MINING.

The mineral deposits of Oregon and Washington Territory are being slowly developed, and from present prospects there will be much more done in the way of mining during the next year.

PUBLIC WORKS.

A narrow gauge railway is being built from Portland to connect with the system of the Oregonian Railway Company. This will give a competing line to the great Willamette Valley. It is expected to be completed about July.

The traffic over the lines of the Oregon Railway and Navigation Company (which includes all through traffic of the Northern Pacific and Union Pacific Railways), and of the Oregon and California Railroad, is given below and compared with that of 1884:—

	Forwarded.		Received.	
	1885.	1884.	1885.	1884.
	Tons.	Tons.	Tons.	Tons.
Oregon Railway and Navigation	157,836	149,534	312,978	227,490
Oregon and California, east side	20,154	21,916	75,318	49,999
Oregon and California, west side	7,310	8,875	55,695	42,701

City Finances and Taxation.

City finances. The bonded debt of the city of Portland at the close of the year was 76,500 dol., or 15,300l., bearing interest at 6 per cent., with a floating debt of 20,000 dol., or 4,000l. The total revenue was 395,768 dol., or 79,154l., and the expenditure 411,802 dol., or 82,360l.

Taxation. The State county and city tax rate was as under:—

	Per cent.
State tax	0·40
,, school tax	0·37
County tax	0·70
City tax	0·90
School district tax	0·50
Total	2·87

The city tax levy for 1886 is 1 per cent.

Remarks.

City improvement. Although there have been many transactions in city property during the past year, purchases for merely speculative purposes have been very few, and values have been maintained. 200 dwellings were built, which, with improvements on old ones, cost about 78,000l. On wharves 8,000l. was spent, and on brick business buildings about 89,000l., a total of 192,900l.

Caution to immigrants. There has been a good deal of distress amongst the labouring population this year, and I have had many applications from British subjects for relief. Those in actual want have been relieved by the British Benevolent Society and other similar organisations. There is no opening here for clerks, shopmen, and professional men, unless they are in such circumstances that they can afford to wait some time while looking after employment. Even labourers and mechanics might not find work for some time, and they should not come here unless prepared for this contingency. Under the operations of the Restriction Act the Chinese population is diminishing.

SAN FRANCISCO.

Annex A.—RETURN of all Shipping at the Port of Portland, Oregon, in the Year 1885.

ENTERED.

Nationality.	Sailing. Number of Vessels.	Sailing. Tons.	Steam. Number of Vessels.	Steam. Tons.	Total. Number of Vessels.	Total. Tons.
British...	113	111,101	...	...	113	111,101
United States (Foreign)	3	3,743	...	...	} 181	} 285,026
,, (Atlantic)	3	4,162	...	...		
,, (Coasting)	34	13,061	141	264,060		
German	3	2,673	...	...	3	2,673
Norwegian and Swedish	1	901	...	...	1	901
Total	157	135,641	141	264,060	298	399,701
,, for the year preceding ...	...	...	...	...	...	361,236

CLEARED.

Nationality.	Sailing. Number of Vessels.	Sailing. Tons.	Steam. Number of Vessels.	Steam. Tons.	Total. Number of Vessels.	Total. Tons.
British...	101	99,942	...	...	101	99,942
United States (Foreign)	12	15,629	...	...	} 174	} 282,447
,, (Coastwise)	28	5,337	134	261,481		
German	4	3,614	...	...	4	3,614
Total	145	124,522	134	261,481	279	386,003
,, for the year preceding ...	...	...	...	...	...	352,821

Annex B.—TABLE of Principal Articles of Export from Portland, Oregon, during the Years 1885 and 1884.

Articles.		1885. Quantity.	1885. Value.	1884. Quantity.	1884. Value.
			£		£
Wheat	Quarters ...	628,958	791,900	465,529	583,288
Flour	Sacks ...	175,796	198,172	193,715	252,487
Lumber	Mil. feet ...	2,375	5,698	1,470	3,608
Salmon in tins	... ...	...	2,390	...	7,961
Other articles	... ...	...	3,430	...	2,621
Total	...	...	1,001,590	...	849,965

RETURN of Principal Articles of Import to Portland, Oregon, during the Years 1885 and 1884.

Articles.		1885. Quantity.	1885. Value.	1884. Quantity.	1884. Value.
			£		£
Coals	Tons	28,328	17,294	26,662	14,896
Rice	Lbs.	3,316,336	11,390	3,569,353	12,805
Salt	,,	6,764,019	4,572	9,358,279	5,904
Oils	Gallons	49,160	3,296	19,600	1,667
Tin and terne plates	Lbs.	787,995	5,090	1,833,017	13,179
Soda and chemicals	,,	720,919	1,887	1,084,159	2,155
Earthenware and glass	...	...	2,084	...	6,180
Pig iron	Tons	226	571	1,658	4,538
Cement	...	...	...	14,933	5,118
Beer, porter and ale	Gallons	5,467	1,001	18,603	3,279
Wines and liquors	,,	...	1,320	24,062	2,626
Fire bricks	...	...	...	429,020	} 2,252
Fire clay	...	...	...	473	
Other articles	...	...	12,405	...	20,957
Total	...	...	60,910	...	95,556

N.B.—The above return does not include exports or imports, coastwise or by rail.

Annex C.—TABLE showing the Total Value of all Articles Exported from Portland and Imported to Portland, Oregon, from and to Foreign Countries during the Years 1885 and 1884.

Country.	Exports 1885.	Exports 1884.	Imports 1885.	Imports 1884.
	£	£	£	£
Great Britain	973,315	814,682	23,429	52,015
Denmark	17,300	..	..	..
Belgium	..	15,618	..	..
British Columbia	6,655	5,705	7,252	6,535
China	595	4,162	18,015	26,293
Australia	..	..	9,029	6,223
Holland	..	6,400	..	..
Other countries	3,725	3,398	3,185	4,490
Total	1,001,590	849,965	60,910	95,556

SAN DIEGO.

Report by Vice-Consul Winchester on the Trade and Commerce of San Diego for the Year 1885.

The trade and commerce of San Diego during the year 1885 has shown a considerable improvement over that for the previous year, as will be seen on reference to the annexed tables.

Imports, coal. *Coal Imports.*—In 1885 four cargoes from Australia and two from British Columbia, aggregating 7,211 tons, were imported, all in American ships. In 1884 the importation was one cargo from British Columbia by a French vessel.

Coal is imported into this district principally for railroad use. San Diego is now connected with important railroad systems whose requirements are large. Five cargoes are already arranged for arrival in 1886 mostly Australian, in English ships. Coal is being mined extensively in New Mexico, and though of inferior quality to that imported, is largely used for railroad purposes, though it is probable that imported coal will continue to be used on the coast sections of the roads.

General merchandise of British origin, consisting of cement, tin plates, glass, earthenware, salt, &c., is in good demand, and is now supplied from San Francisco. Importers there have the co-operation of transportation companies in making efforts to retain control of the markets of this district, but it is probable that direct importations will not be long deferred, as the district for which this port is the natural base of supply is large and growing rapidly. *(Imports, general.)*

Exports.—Honey and wheat are the principal articles available for English markets. For the last two years there has been no surplus wheat for export, but the coming season promises favourably for large crops and a shipping surplus. The district produces honey largely, in some years exporting over 1,000 tons, and considerable supplies already find their way to English markets. *(Exports.)*

This district is undergoing rapid development owing to the completion of communication with trans-continental systems of railroad, and the influx of settlers attracted by the low prices of fruit lands and the growing popularity of the place, owing to its remarkably fine climate. Former reports have given full information as to the climate, which is probably the best known for permanent residence. *(Progress of district.)*

The population of the town has nearly doubled within the year, and its growth continues without check. Country lands are becoming settled, and building, colonising, and irrigating enterprises, involving large capital outlay, are being prosecuted vigorously.

The cultivation of the raisin grape promises to become a leading industry, and the wine grape and other descriptions of fruit can be cultivated with good pecuniary results. To practical men with capital, fruit culture promises satisfactory returns, but as a rule men without moderate capital or special skill in such business ought not to undertake it. Persons contemplating settlement here should be careful not to accept the highly-coloured descriptions and estimates frequently put out in England by the agents of land schemes. Invalids find the climate enjoyable all the year round, and particularly beneficial in throat and pulmonary affections. In addition to favourable opportunities for investment, money can be loaned on good security to return 8 to 10 per cent. free of taxation. *(Prospects for settlers.)*

A.—RETURN of Shipping at the Port of San Diego in the Year 1885 (Trade with adjoining Coast of Mexico not included).

ENTERED.

Nationality.	Sailing.		Steam.		Total.	
	Number of Vessels.	Tons.	Number of Vessels.	Tons.	Number of Vessels.	Tons.
United States of America	6	4,771	...	...	6	4,771
Total for the year preceding	1	501	...	...	1	501

UNITED STATES.

B.—Return of Principal Articles of Production in San Diego District, Shipped therefrom, during the Years 1885 and 1884, comprising Shipments Coastwise and by Rail in 1885, and Coastwise in 1884.

Articles.		1885. Quantity.	1885. Value.	1884. Quantity.	1884. Value.
			£		£
Wool	Lbs.	1,404,190	32,179	684,816	17,120
Honey	,,	1,723,662	21,546	1,822,332	20,881
Bees'-wax	,,	29,120	1,396	54,415	2,720
Wheat		1,067,603	2,780	379,605	790
Abalove shells		106,470	380	437,000	2,146
Hides		109,704	3,428	88,807	2,590
Sheep skins		94,111	1,960	73,093	1,370
Oranges	Cases	2,057	823	1,537	461
Lemons	,,	536	214	429	128
Raisins	Boxes	3,214	1,125	1,227	307
Total			65,831		48,513

Return of Principal Articles of Import into San Diego during the Years 1885 and 1884.

Articles.	1885. Quantity.	1885. Value.	1884. Quantity.	1884. Value.
	Tons.	£	Tons.	£
Coal from Australia	5,151	6,438	..	..
,, from British Columbia	2,060	2,472	800	1,000
Total	7,211	8,910	800	1,000

Los Angeles and Wilmington.

Report by Vice-Consul Mortimer on the Trade and Commerce of Los Angeles and Wilmington, California, for the Year 1885.

Introductory remarks. The rapid progress of this district in wealth and population, to which I adverted in my last report, has continued with slight abatement during the year 1885. Probably the best illustration of the productiveness of the country is to be found in the fact that the farmers find it to their advantage to borrow money on mortgage for the improvement of their properties, at so high a rate of interest as 12 per cent. per annum. In this (Los Angeles) county the population numbered 34,000 in 1880, and the number of acres of land cultivated was 130,000. In 1885 the population had increased to 70,000, and the number of acres of land cultivated to 450,000.

Chief exports. During the year 1885 buildings have been erected in this city of an aggregate value of 250,000*l*. In the years 1883 and 1884 the total value of the buildings erected exceeded 500,000*l*. The books of the County Recorder show that upwards of 6,000 transfers of real property, situated in this city and county, were made during the year 1885. The value of the property so transferred exceeded 2,000,000*l*., an increase on the number and value of the transfers of 1884 of about 20 per cent.

SAN FRANCISCO.

Trade and Commerce.

Exports.—The chief exports form this district are grain, oranges, and other fruits, wine and honey.

Grain.—The crop of wheat and barley was a light one. This country produced about 100,000 tons, a considerable decrease on the product of the previous year.

Oranges and other Fruits.—During the season of 1885 over 1,400 car loads of oranges were shipped from this district; 300 car loads (3,000 tons) found a market in San Francisco, and the remainder in the large cities of the Eastern States and Canada. Shipments are now being made to Manitoba. A very strong association ("The Orange Growers' Union") has been formed here recently. Its object is to so regulate the shipment of oranges to the cities of the Eastern States that an over-supply shall not be sent to any point.

Apricots, pears, peaches, and other fruits are canned here in ever-increasing quantities, and shipped to the Eastern States and Europe. The manager of the Southern California Packing Company tells me that his company packed about 600,000 lbs. of fruit last season, and that this amount is less than one-tenth of the product of the county. The average price paid for the fruit by the packing companies is $\frac{1}{2}d.$ per lb.; it is packed in $2\frac{1}{2}$ lb. cans, and sells in car-load lots at 8$d.$ per can.

Wine.—The wine product of Los Angeles county for 1885 amounted to 5,500,000 gallons, a slight increase on that of 1884. Mr. L. J. Rose, an officer of the State Board of Viticulture, in a recent report, estimates that there are 35,000 acres of land in this district in bearing grapes. At four tons of grapes to the acre, which is a fair average here, this would give 140,000 tons of grapes as the present product of this district.

By a combination of the wine makers the price of grapes was reduced last season 50 per cent. Large producers refused to sell at this reduced price, and hastily constructed wineries in which they manufactured their grapes into wine. Most of them had so little knowledge of wine-making that their product is of inferior quality.

The action of the wine-makers in reducing the price of grapes will operate to their disadvantage in that the large amount of bad wine made this season will do much to injure the character of California wine. Mr. Rose states that grapes purchased at 2$l.$ per ton, which was the standard price last season for common varieties, can be manufactured into wine which can be sold at a profit for 5$d.$ per gallon.

Honey.—The yield of honey is increasing; it is of the finest quality, and is being shipped to England in considerable quantities—wholesale price here 2$d.$ per lb.

Imports.

The chief imports from the United Kingdom are: coal, Portland cement, tin plate, coke, iron, crockery, paints, soda, salt, &c.

Coal.—The average price here in car-load lots is from 2$l.$ 4$s.$ to 2$l.$ 8$s.$ per ton.

Paints.—I am advised on good authority that the consumption of English paints has more than doubled here in the past year.

Coke.—The consumption of English coke in this city is not large, not more than 500 tons per annum. Large quantities pass through here, however, from San Francisco for Arizona.

With the exception of coal the articles named as the chief imports from the United Kingdom have heretofore generally been imported by way of San Francisco. The railway freight to Los Angeles (482 miles) increases the cost to the consumer here by from 30$s.$ to 40$s.$ per ton. An American ship brought a general cargo from England a few months ago, and an English ship is now discharging a general cargo, comprising most of the articles named below, under the heading "Other Importations from England." In previous reports I suggested that these articles could profitably be imported direct to this port. I am glad to see that this is now being done. The following extract from a report of the collector of customs shows the business done at Wilmington since it became a port of entry:—

Amount of business done at the port of Wilmington since it became a port of entry.

The port of Wilmington became a port of entry in November, 1882.

From November 1, 1882, to February 28, 1886, three years and four months, the imports have been as follows:—

	Tons.
Foreign coal—	
From Departure Bay, B.C.	63,914
Sydney, Australia	51,967
Newcastle, Australia	47,123
Liverpool, England	17,555
Hull, England	4,197
Total	184,756
American coal—	
From Tacoma, W.T.	22,965
Seattle, „	8,522
Coos Bay, Oregon	450
Total	31,937
Total tons, coal	216,693
Lumber, feet	191,811,000
Other importations from England—	
Flour sulphur, lbs.	25,612
Rock salt „	142,255
Salt in sacks, „	998,000
Soda crystals, „	278,896
White caustic soda, lbs.	81,518
Caustic potash, „	2,354
Carbonated soda ash, „	35,124
Tin plate, „	216,000
Coke, tons	1,322
Pig iron, tons	177
Portland cement, casks	10,188
Sheep dip, gallons	3,020
Bath brick, dozen	398
Exports to Great Britain—	
Wheat, sacks	237,957
Honey, cases	3,239
„ lbs.	482,191
Canned fruit, cases	3,240
„ dozen 2½ lb. cans	6,480
Flour, sacks	3,679
Paper pulp, lbs.	479,789

Total amount of freight handled at the city of Los Angeles by the Southern Pacific Railway in 1885.

The total amount of freight forwarded from Los Angeles by the Southern Pacific Railway during the 12 months ending November 1, 1885, exceeded 70,000 tons, an increase on the business of the previous 12 months of a little over 30 per cent. The total amount of freight received and forwarded by the same company during the 10 months ending November 1, 1885, exceeded 183,000 tons.

SHIPPING AND NAVIGATION.

Decrease in British shipping.

There has been a marked decrease in the amount and tonnage of British shipping at the port of Wilmington during the year 1885, and a proportionate increase in American shipping. With the exception of one Norwegian ship, the business of the port has been carried on in British and American ships. I cannot get accurate returns of the amount and tonnage of the American shipping. In connection with what has been heretofore stated, however, the following summary will sufficiently indicate the business of the port:—

British Vessels.—Entered in 1884, 21—total tonnage, 30,276; in 1885, 13—total tonnage, 19,330. Cleared in 1884, 19—total tonnage, 28,682; in 1885, 15—total tonnage, 22,514. {British shipping in 1884 and 1885.}

American Steamers.—Passenger and freight steamers plying between this port and San Francisco made about 200 trips during the year 1885 as against 177 in 1884.

American Ships.—In 1884, 21 American ships entered the port. I am informed that there has been a considerable increase in the number and tonnage of American ships in 1885. As before stated, I have not got the exact returns. {American shipping increased.}

Wilmington Harbour.—Wilmington, 21 miles south of the city of Los Angeles, is the port for the city. The Government has expended 140,000*l.* in the last 15 years in improving the harbour. The Government engineer estimates that 50,000*l.* more will be required to so complete the improvements as to admit foreign-going ships to the inner harbour. At present vessels drawing 16 feet can enter the inner harbour at high water. The expenditure of 30,000*l.*—for which amount Congress is now being petitioned, and will probably grant—will, it is estimated by the Government engineer, give access to the inner harbour to vessels drawing 23 feet. At present foreign-going vessels anchor in the outer harbour, and discharge cargo into lighters. This answers very well in summer; in winter, however, they lose much valuable time, owing to the bay being too rough to admit of lighters coming alongside. The British ship "Holt Hill," now discharging cargo, has, the master informs me, lost 12 days in the past five weeks, owing to the bay being too rough to bring lighters alongside. Owners should consider this in chartering for this port in winter. Since writing the foregoing, I learn that an order has just been made for a re-survey of the harbour, with a view to the formation of an outer breakwater for the protection of deep draft vessels. {The improvement of Wilmington Harbour. Wilmington Harbour. Delays in discharging and receiving cargo in winter.}

Agriculture.

Oranges and grapes are the specialties of this district. There are about 12,000 acres planted in orange trees in Los Angeles county now bearing fruit, and several thousand acres in young trees, which will begin to bear fruit in from two to five years' time. In San Bernardino county the orange crop has, at intervals of from three to four years, been greatly damaged by frost. At less frequent intervals the same trouble has been experienced in this county. {Oranges and grapes the chief products of this district.}

Oranges are being shipped from Mexico to the Eastern States. Should the reciprocity treaty referred to in my last annual report go into effect, the consequences will be very serious to orange growers here. The present duty is sufficient to protect Californian orange growers from competition with the cheaply-produced Mexican article. As the Mexican oranges are of better quality, their admission free of duty would cripple the industry here. {Mexican oranges in competition with Californian.}

The "white scale" referred to in my last report is still doing immense damage to the orange trees. Some of the oldest orange orchards in the county are being topped and pruned to such an extent that they will not bear any fruit for several years. In some cases the trees are being cut down. No cheap effectual remedy has as yet been discovered to destroy the insect; it is stated, however, that another insect has appeared which preys on the "white scale," and is not {Destructive pest attacking the orange trees.}

Legislative protection required for the fruit interests.

injurious to the orange trees. At the fifth annual session of the State Board of Horticulture, held at Los Angeles in November last, the following resolutions were carried:—" Resolved, as the sense of this convention, that the fruit interests of this State require the support of legislative enactments—both State, county, and municipal—especially in the direction of quarantine regulations, backed by requisite appropriations to make them efficient." "Resolved, that it is the sense of this convention—first, that the scale bug can be eradicated; second, that this can be done only by universal and simultaneous action in infested districts."

Memorial to Congress requiring an increase on the duty on prunes, olives, and raisins.

At the convention of the fruit growers of California, held at Los Angeles in September, 1885, a memorial to Congress was adopted asking that body to increase the duty on prunes, olives, and raisins, on the ground that these industries, now in their infancy here, could not otherwise successfully compete with the products of the cheap labour of Southern Europe. I direct attention to these matters owing to the steady influx of Englishmen intent on making their fortunes in fruit culture. Fruit farming here, though unquestionably profitable, has risks and drawbacks to which attention is not directed in the emigration pamphlets so widely distributed in England. The value of land in this district suitable for fruit culture is dependent upon the nature and extent of the supply of water for irrigating it. Dry land, worth 2*l.* per acre, is, with an adequate supply of water, worth from 30*l.* to 40*l.* per acre. Irrigation works here have not been attempted by the Government as yet. Companies and private individuals have carried to completion some extensive irrigation works in San Bernardino county. The Bear Valley reservoir has been constructed at an altitude of 6,300 feet above the sea; it covers 20,000 acres, and has a watershed of 65 to 70 square miles. The Ontario colony, also in San Bernardino county, have tunnelled into the mountains, and have obtained a flow of water of upwards of 800 miner's inches. An inch of water will irrigate eight acres, and is worth from 100*l.* to 300*l.* I am satisfied that the storage of water in this district, now just beginning to be practised, offers a good field for the remunerative investment of capital on a large scale.

Value of land.

Irrigation.

Water.

Value of water.

Government land.

American citizens, and those who have declared their intention to become citizens, can obtain Government land for a nominal sum. There is very little good Government land in this district still open for settlement. The records of the Government Land Office in this city show the acreage of public lands disposed of in the last three years as follows:—

	Acres.
1883	139,151
1884	132,319
1885	257,913
Total	529,383

Live Stock.—The aggregate value of the live stock in this county amounts to about 1,000,000*l.* Sheep farming is a waning industry here, owing to the fact that the land is becoming too valuable for sheep runs. What sheep there are—about 200,000—are exclusively wool-bearers.

POPULATION AND INDUSTRIES.

Increase in population.

I have little to add to my remarks under this heading in my report for the year 1884. The population of this city has increased from 34,000 in 1884 to about 40,000. Some additional factories have been started in the past year: the list given in my last report is, however, substantially correct.

Rate of Wages.—The rate of wages has not varied in the past year; the labour market is overcrowded here at present. A determined effort is being made by the labour unions and others to force the Chinese to leave this district; notice has been given that after May 1st next employers of Chinese labour will be "boycotted." It is probable that in the immediate future the Chinese will be driven from this district. Should this prove to be the case, the demand for all classes of labourers will be very good for some time thereafter. {Labour market.}

Domestic servants, who are willing to do the work that two or three servants would be employed to do in England, can readily get employment at from 5*l*. to 6*l*. per month, and board. {Wages of domestic servants.}

Paper Factory.—The English company referred to in my last report as being engaged in converting the Yucca tree into pulp for the manufacture of paper, has suspended operations for the present, the venture, I am informed, having proved unsuccessful. Notwithstanding the failure of this company to make the enterprise pay, I am advised by competent authorities that the business can and will yet be made to pay handsomely. {Manufacture of paper pulp.}

Mines.—The output of bullion from the mines of this district has not increased in the past year.

Oil.—The output of oil from the wells of this county is estimated at 600 barrels per day. Value at the wells 8*s*. per barrel. {Output of oil.}

Tramways.—There are four tram car lines in this city, having a total length of 15 miles. They carry 2,500,000 passengers per annum. {Tramways and cable roads in Los Angeles.}

Cable Roads.—A cable road, one and a quarter miles in length, was constructed during the year at a cost of 20,000*l*. Another cable road of the same length, and which will cost the same amount, is now being constructed.

Public Schools.—There are 20 common schools here, attended by 5,000 male and female children. Grave charges of immorality resulting from the co-education of the sexes have been made by opponents of the public school system. {Public schools in Los Angeles.}

Public Works.

In my report for 1884 I stated that the Southern Pacific Railway controlled the two main and three branch lines running out of this city. During the year 1885 two new railways have entered the city. The Atlantic and Pacific constructed, from a point between Mojave and the Needles, in San Bernardino county, through the Cajon Pass to a junction with the Southern Pacific at Colton, 60 miles east of Los Angeles, and then acquired a right of way over the Southern Pacific to this city. This gives Los Angeles another through line to the Eastern States in competition with the Southern Pacific. The value to this district of this competition cannot be over-estimated. At the present time, and for some weeks past, a war of rates has been going on between these competing lines: waged with such fierceness that for some time the Southern Pacific carried passengers from this city to the Missouri River, a distance of upwards of 2,000 miles, for 4*s*. {Railway construction in 1885. Temporary reduction in railway fares.}

The other new line is the Los Angeles and San Gabriel Valley Railway: 14 miles of this line are being operated, and the construction is being proceeded with in the direction of the Cajon Pass, 80 miles east of this city, the intention probably being to form a junction there with the Atlantic and Pacific. {Further railway construction.}

Riverside and Los Angeles.—A railway is also being constructed from Riverside, in San Bernardino county, to connect with the Los Angeles and Santa Ana line.

Santa Monica and Los Angeles.—Surveys are being made for another railway from this city to Santa Monica, a sea-side resort, 16 miles west of Los Angeles. It is stated that this line, and the Los Angeles and San Gabriel Valley line, are being constructed in the interest of the Atlantic and Pacific Railway, and that it is the intention of the latter corporation to make Santa Monica a port by the construction of a floating breakwater.

The Southern Pacific Railway from Los Angeles to San Francisco (482 miles) is constructed for many miles through the dry bed of old mountain watercourses. The heavy rainfall of March, 1884, filled these watercourses, and did great damage to the road bed for nearly 100 miles, entailing a loss to the company of several millions of dollars. Notwithstanding the fact that the company reconstructed their line in a very substantial manner, the damage was to some extent repeated in November, 1885, and again a few weeks ago. As the mountains at the points where the damage occurred are very precipitous and the soil friable, it would appear that the damage and consequent loss is liable to be repeated whenever the rainfall is exceptionally heavy.

General Remarks.

Emigration.—My attention has been directed to the advertisements of railway agents in London, advising prospective settlers that they can obtain 320 acres of good Government land in this country. The object of these persons is simply to get passengers for the railways they represent. The land they send their victims to is desert land, described by a newspaper here as "less valuable for agriculture than the Nubian desert." There is a great deal of distress among many of these emigrants in the northern part of this country. Persons coming here to settle should not purchase land without seeing it, as many do; nor should they purchase until, by residence here of six or eight months, they have acquired some knowledge of the country.

Financial.—There are six banks in this city—aggregate resources, 1,000,000*l.*; aggregate deposits, 700,000*l.* In the last 20 years the rate of interest on the best first mortgage security has steadily declined from 5 per cent. per month, the current rate 20 years ago, to 1 per cent. per month, which is the current rate now. The debt of Los Angeles county, 90,000*l.*, has been refunded in the past year, and now bears interest at 4½ per cent. per annum, a reduction in interest of 2½ per cent. per annum. The city debt, 50,000*l.*, bears interest at 7 per cent. per annum. There are good openings here for the profitable investment of capital as follows:—

1. *A Mortgage Company.*—A very large sum could readily be invested here on the best first mortgage security, at a rate of interest sufficient to pay 10 per cent. per annum nett. An English company could pay their shareholders 12 or more per cent. by borrowing on debentures in England, on the security of loans made here, and re-investing here the sums so borrowed. The influx of a large amount of capital for investment on mortgage would probably still further reduce the rate of interest here, by operating as I have indicated; large profits could be made, however, even if the current rate here fell to 8 per cent.

2. *Water Companies.*—Water supply is the chief factor in determining the value of land here. The storage of water for sale to land-owners offers immense inducements to capitalists. With the exceptions

noted herein, local capitalists have not entered this field, owing, I believe, to lack of sufficient capital.

3. *Fruit-canning, Wine-making, Marmalade.*—In all these industries more capital is needed for their further development. If well-directed, very large sums can be profitably employed.

4. *Paints.*—A great variety of mineral paints are to be found in this district. No attempt has as yet been made to develop this source of wealth. I am assured that there is money to be made in their manufacture.

Climate.—The climate of this district, though by no means perfect, is probably the best in the civilised world. As in the South of France, there is a sudden change of temperature at sunset, and people who are not careful are apt to contract severe colds. Persons suffering from consumption and kindred diseases are likely to recover if they come here when the disease is in its initial stage. The average rainfall for the last eight years has been 17 inches. For full information as to this climate I beg to refer to my report on this district for the year 1884. *[margin: Climate good for persons suffering from consumption and kindred diseases.]*

Land Transfer.—Deeds, mortgages, &c., are recorded in the office of the County Recorder, and are there open to public inspection without charge. Publicity is further given by the publication in the daily papers of a synopsis of the transfers, mortgages, &c., of the previous day. To illustrate this plan I give, in Appendix A., some extracts from the report of yesterday's transactions, as contained in to-day's issue of the "Real Estate Record" of this city. The system of transfer of land in use here, though inferior to the Torrens system, has much to recommend it. *[margin: Publicity in transfer of real estate.]*

NOTE.—In this report dollars have been converted into pounds at the rate of 5 dol. per pound.

APPENDIX A.

Extracts from the "Daily Real Estate Record," Saturday, April 3, 1886:—

CONVEYANCES.

	Dol.	c.
1. Silas Bond to Alda L. Harper—N 2 acs. of W 4 acs. of N½ of lot 5, blk. B, Oge and Bond trt.	200	00
2. Silas Bond to Mrs. Elizabeth B. Harper—S 2 acs. of W 4 acs. of N½ of lot 5, blk. B, Oge and Bond trt.	200	00
3. Williamson D. Vawter to Edwin J. Vawter—Lots H and I blk. 171 Santa Monica	1,600	00
4. Ed. T. McGinnis to Richard R. Tanner—Lot 61 Central add. Santa Monica	10	00
5. Charles G. Jones to J. Jacobson—S½ of lot 2, blk. N, San Pascual trt.	3,500	00
6. Edward Evey, assignee of J. W. Clark and Co., to J. W. Clark—W½ of NW¼ of NW¼ of sec. 16 T 4 S R 10 W	1	00
7. William H. Hounsom to J. W. Clarke—Trt. in NW¼ of NW¼, sec. 16 T 4 S R 10 W	1	00
8. Cordelia A. Boynton to Rhoda F. Dickey and Anna Dickey—W½ of N 66 ft. of lot 9, blk. C, San Pascual trt.	656	00
9. Chas. W. Bell to Anna F. Thompson—Lot 3, Washburn's subd. of lot 12, blk. N, San Pascual trt.	500	30
10. J. S. Allison to W. D. Root—Mines in San Gabriel Mining District.	1	00

MORTGAGES.

William Kahlstorf to James Booth—Lot in or adjoining lot 5, blk. 4, Lamanda Park; 7 months, 1½ per cent. per month	50	00
Rhoda F. Dickey and Anna Dickey to Cordelia A. Boynton—W½ of N 66 ft. of lot 9, blk. C, San Pascual trt.; 3 years, 10 per cent. per annum	656	64
Arbelle O. Blanchard and E. L Blanchard her husband, to Peter Warner—6·12 acs. in lot 5, blk. 73 H S; April 30, 1887, 10 per cent. per annum	3,500	00
E. E. White to Savings Bank of Southern California—Lots 7, 8, 9, 10, 11, 12, blk. 25 E L A; 1 year, 1 per cent. per month	1,000	00
François Riebout to C. Dassian de Paye—Lots 3 and 4, blk. X, Aliso trt.; 1 year, 1 per cent. per month	800	00
H. A. Willis to George R. Thomas—Lot 11 and part of lots 9 and 12 blk. N San Pascual trt.; 1 year, 12 per cent. per annum	3,000	00
Maria J. Moorhead to James Cuzner—Lot in lot 5, blk. J, San Pascual trt.; 90 days, 10 per cent. per annum	541	70
Thomas A. Saxon and Josephine A. Saxon, his wife, to Andrew Glassell—N 45 acs. of E½ of NW¼ sec. 24 T 1 S R 12 W; 2 years, 11·85 per cent. per annum	1,600	00
Anson Pitcher to Mrs. Isa M. Patterson—Lot 12, blk. P, Mott trt.; 1 year, 10 per cent. per annum	500	00
Sarah D. Wilson to James F. Towell—W½ of Farm lot 177, American Colony trt.; 1 year, 12 per cent. per annum	1,000	00
E. W. Doss and Martha A. Doss, his wife, to A. W. Worm—SE¼ of NE¼ and E½ of SE¼ and SW¼ of SE¼ of sec. 6 T 1 S R 14 W; 3 years, 1 per cent. per month	1,500	00

ATTACHMENTS, LIENS, &c.

Samuel H. Sampson to H. M. Russell—Constable certificate of sale of und. int. in lots B and C, blk. 196, Santa Monica.

MISCELLANEOUS.

C. N. Wilson, W. A. Brophy, James Barrett, and F. M. Brophy—Notice of location of "Hidden Treasure" mine in fractional N½ of NW¼ of sec. 30 T 1 S R 13 W.
Otto F. Brant to Curtis and Sweetser—General power of attorney.
Stephen Bush to W. E. Willmore—Assignment of mortgage, bk. 63, p. 601.
Matilda Brodtbeck to Otto Brodtbeck—General power of attorney.
A. J. Copp and Carrie B. Copp to E. R. Richmond—Assignment of mortgage, bk. 63, p. 12.
H. W. Sanborn to H. G. Conner—Satisfaction of mortgage, bk. 66, p. 122.

JUDGMENTS.

John Mansfield v. Thomas F. Pepper and Clara Pepper—Foreclosure 10 acs. in Ro Santiago de Santa Ana.

ASTORIA, OREGON.

Report by Vice-Consul Cherry on the Trade and Commerce of Astoria for the Year 1885.

General business. Imports and exports. Imports.
  General Business for the past year can be briefly stated as bad.
  Imports and Exports.—As may be seen by Annex B., a material reduction in amounts and values may be found.
  Imports.—This reduction is partly due to the smaller demand for the materials in putting up the pack of salmon, owing to causes mentioned under *Salmon packing*, and also to the decline in the price of materials.

Tin plates.
  Tin Plates.—The retail prices varied from 1*l*. 1*s*. to 1*l*. 3*s*.—the first

price ex ship for quantities, and the second in smaller jobbing lots: all the plate was of i.c. coke grades.

Salt.—The price in jobbing lots was from 3*l.* 6*s.* per ton to 3*l.* 10*s.* 6*d.* per ton for Factory F., Liverpool. {Salt.}

Twine.—This article does not appear in the customs reports, as it comes invariably either from Boston or New York, directly by rail or viâ San Francisco, but is of British manufacture; selling price 3*s.* 9*d.* per pound. {Twine.}

Block Tin.—This, although of British colonial production, comes from Australia viâ San Francisco; the retail price varies from 10*d.* to 11*d.* per pound. {Block tin.}

Coals are mostly imported from Newcastle, N.S.W., but some from Great Britain; the general price, by the quantity of 500 tons or more, was 1*l.* 5*s.* per ton (English), duty paid. {Coals.}

Exports.—The reduction on exports are mainly in lower prices of products, and the decrease in the preserved salmon export, owing to the increased demand for the article in the domestic markets, as well as a smaller pack. The supply for the markets of the United States going by rail and not by sailing vessels is as heretofore. The main exports are still breadstuffs from the interior, and preserved salmon from this town and vicinity, with a slight lumber export trade. {Exports.}

Canned Salmon.—As shown in Annex B., only 222,500 cases of this product left here by sailing vessels, all of which was to the United Kingdom. {Canned salmon.}

Wheat and Flour—The same may be said of the breadstuffs, which go mainly to the United Kingdom manufactured. {Wheat and flour.}

Lumber.—The total quantity of this export was to countries on the Pacific Ocean, south of the United States. {Lumber.}

Agriculture.—Owing to the mild, humid climate making a heavy forest growth, and preventing the ripening of the chief cereals, with the exception of oats, agriculture is in a backward condition. {Agriculture.}

Submerged Lands.—A good deal of low land now submerged at high water is being reclaimed by dyking, which is however an expensive undertaking, but is highly remunerative, as immense crops of hay, root crops, and oats can be raised on the rich loam. {Submerged lands.}

Cattle and Dairying.—The district adjacent to this Consular office is pre-eminently a dairy country; the extent of open and cleared lands is, however, so small relatively that the increase of cattle barely supplies the local markets, and there is no export either by sea or land: a steady increase in blooded stock purchased in the Eastern States is to be noted. Small attempts at cheese and butter factories have been made with profitable results. {Cattle and dairying.}

Deep-Sea Fishing Interests.—In my last report I mentioned the probability of the putting on of a vessel for deep-sea fishing: this was done, and the results were fairly satisfactory to the owners till the vessel was lost on the beach. Another venture is to be made, but the general impression is that a steamer is required so as to enable the catch to be taken up river with despatch and without handling. {Fishing interests.}

Salmon Fishing.—The depressed state of the markets, both in the United Kingdom and the United States, confirmed the canners in their determination not to put up the usual quantity, and, together with the really smaller run of fish, made a comparatively small and dull business in this line: the price of fish received by fishermen was about 2*s.* for each fish, which represents an aggregate of 84,000*l.* for 100 days' fishing. {Salmon fishing.}

Canning Salmon.—Again I have to report a generally unprofitable year in this the most import industry of this town and district. The overstock of the foreign markets, especially that of the United {Canning salmon.}

Kingdom for the year 1884, has been presumably the chief cause which has forced the price gradually down to the limits of actual cost for these goods. The market was slightly improved by the loss of some 60,000 cases of the pack of 1884, and 20,000 of the pack of 1885 at sea, which materially lessened the stocks, and to those packers that did not realise on their pack at an early date, the better prices ruling later in the year gave some remuneration, but it is generally acknowledged that the purchasing houses took the chief part of what profits there were in the business.

The total pack of the Columbia River was close to 560,000 cases of 48 one lb. tins, showing a falling off of more than 90,000 cases from the year 1884.

The price of the pack brought on an average about 16s. per case; it is however difficult to procure exact figures.

Shipping.

Shipping.—An increase in numbers and tonnage will be found as compared with 1884, and vessels of a larger class are more often making their appearance, the very low freights prevailing making it unremunerative for vessels of small carrying capacity to come to the Columbia River. The great majority of the foreign trade is still done under the British flag.

Freights.

Freights have fluctuated between the extremes of 50s. and 38s. 9d. for the United Kingdom, but making about 42s. 6d.; on the average fully 10s. per ton more than in San Francisco. I gather that of this 10s. no more than 6s. has been incurred in extra expenses, detention, &c., making a difference of 4s. in favour of the port.

Internal improvements.

Internal Improvements.—The work on the locks of the Cascades of the Columbia proceeds slowly, but when completed will add about 80 miles to the present steamboat navigation. A ship railway is projected around another rapid, which will add a further 200 miles of river navigation through a rich grain-growing country, thereby materially reducing the expense of moving the grain crop to this port.

Railway wanted.

Railway Wanted.—The country between this port and the interior valley of the Willamette and the general railway system is without a railway.

A lucrative opening for capital lies in the reach of the person or company that may open up this line, which would pass through country known to contain a rich mineral deposit of coal lying on both sides of the coast range, besides the valuable cedar forests, and some country available for settlement: this tract has, till within six months, been held by a railroad grant, the interest of the grantees being against the opening up the line; the grant has been forfeited.

Labour.

Labour.—This subject, owing to late troubles, requires a few remarks. Owing to the rapid extension of railroad building, ending in 1884, a large number of men, mostly without family ties, were attracted to the country by the prospects of high wages; on the stoppage of railroad building these men have been left without resources, and have helped to glut the unskilled labour market, reducing prices; and the matter is not helped by the constant immigration of new comers, by the facilities of travel made by the newly-opened railroads with the Eastern States. All this has contributed to keep idle a large body of men, who are too ready to listen to any plan that promises relief. The popular mind has been directed against the Chinese, who are accused of being the chief cause of the low prices obtainable for labour, when on a calm review it is clearly shown that the work they perform is of such a nature as to open up a great many channels of better paid employment to white men.

Prospects for the coming year.

Prospects for the Coming Year.—The prospects for the coming year are brighter for the material prosperity of the town; the canners are already making preparations for putting up a larger pack of salmon, which of itself will put a great deal of money into circulation; the influx of immigrants is making itself felt in increased demand for lands and opening up the country.

Health.—The health of the town and surrounding district has been uniformly good for the past year, being remarkably free from the usual milder forms of sickness usual in all communities.

Annex A.—RETURN of all Shipping at the Port of Astoria, Oregon, during the Year 1885.

ENTERED.

Nationality.	Sailing. Number of Vessels.	Tons.	Steam. Number of Vessels.	Tons.	Total. Number of Vessels.	Tons.
British	104	104,451	...	...	104	104,451
American	11	12,802	3	2,373	14	15,175
German	3	2,613	...	...	3	2,613
Norwegian	1	910	...	...	1	910
Total	119	120,776	3	2,373	122	123,149

CLEARED.

Nationality.	Sailing. Number of Vessels.	Tons.	Steam. Number of Vessels.	Tons.	Total. Number of Vessels.	Tons.
British	94	92,944	...	...	94	92,944
American	9	10,886	3	2,373	12	13,259
German	3	2,613	...	...	3	2,613
Total	106	106,443	3	2,373	109	108,816
,, for the year preceding...	...	...	...	...	95	...

Annex B.—RETURN of Principal Articles of Export from Astoria, Oregon, during the Year 1885.

Articles.		1885. Quantity.	Value.	1884. Quantity.	Value.
			£		£
Preserved salmon	Cases...	222,594	229,426	296,060	301,987
Wheat	Bushels	395,843	60,836	561,508	93,695
Flour	Barrels	13,525	13,088	19,044	19,900
Lumber	M. feet	558	1,232	2,744	5,800
Sundries	...	...	85	...	1,472
Total			304,667		422,854

UNITED STATES.

RETURN of Principal Articles of Import to Astoria, Oregon, during the Year 1885.

Articles.		1885.		1884.	
		Quantity.	Value.	Quantity.	Value.
			£		£
Tin plates	Boxes	32,800	25,889	47,127	37,720
Salt	Tons	200	260	123	182
Coals, &c.	,,	1,297	1,420	2,467	1,806
Total		...	27,569	...	39,708

Annex C.—TABLE showing the Total Value of all Articles Exported from Astoria, Oregon, and Imported to Astoria, Oregon, from and to Foreign Countries during the Years 1885–1884.

Country.	Exports.		Imports.	
	1885.	1884.	1885.	1884.
	£	£	£	£
Great Britain	303,359	396,979	26,105	38,405
British colonies	77	..	266	548
Other countries	1,232	25,878	1,198	755
Total	305,668	422,857	27,569	39,708

UNITED STATES.

GALVESTON.

Report by Consul Lyall on the Trade and Commerce of Galveston (Texas) for the Year 1885.

History and description. The city of Galveston is built on an island (the apex of a sand bank in the Gulf of Mexico) 30 miles long, and from two to four miles broad. It was discovered in the 16th century by the followers of Hernando de Soto, in returning from their unlucky Mississippi river enterprise. It was then but a small island, occupied by the remnant of a tribe of Indians. At the commencement of this century it was still a rendezvous for pirates, of whom Lafitte (who assisted General Andrew Jackson in defending New Orleans against the British forces in 1814) was the last recorded. Galveston is neatly laid out, the streets being at right angles; and the houses, 95 per cent. of which are of wood, are tastefully built and constructed, but the roads are execrable, or rather (excepting in the business portion of the town) are non-existent. Galveston is tolerably healthy during the winter months, but the six months of hot weather is very trying. Dengue fever, liver complaints, sunstroke, &c., are then in season on the island, with the addition on the mainland of malarial fevers of a deadly type. Pneumonia, from the sudden changes of temperature, is very prevalent in the cold season, and is often fatal. Commercially Galveston has, for the last six or seven years, been declining. Before the present network of railways, some 8,000 miles, intersected the State, all produce, especially cotton, necessarily found its outlet at this port, and was brokered and handled here.

Since then, in consequence of the immense immigration to the interior of the State, towns have sprung up which eclipse Galveston in population, and the railway companies, who have erected cotton presses at the principal centres of industry, take cotton through to New York, Boston, Philadelphia, &c., without change of cars. It is true that Galveston has this season shipped 600,000 bales against 426,000 at the same period last year, but at least two-thirds came down already compressed, and was loaded direct from the railway trucks to the vessels.

Population. The population of Galveston was computed a short time ago at 30,000, but as its diminishing trade will not at present support more than 20,000, it follows that there are always from 8,000 to 16,000 people out of work. The only hope for the place is the obtaining sufficient water on the bar to enable vessels, drawing 18 feet and upwards, to come in and load from the wharves, instead of, as at present, finishing their loading in the roads—at a distance of seven or eight miles from the shore—at enormous expense and trouble for lighterage, tugs, &c. There is at present often only 12 to 12½ feet of water on the bar, so that no average-sized ocean steamer can get out loaded.

Harbour works. From time to time some 150,000 dol. has been spent altogether by the United States Government in deepening the waterway, but, up to date, with little or no result. A fresh attempt is to be made this year, having been, I believe, already sanctioned by Congress, which will consist in throwing two long breakwaters, or jetties, on the plan of the

Port Said entrance, some five or six miles out to sea. If this succeeds, Galveston will become the Atlantic outlet for the produce of an enormous extent of territorry, comprising California, Nevada, Colorado, Kansas, New Mexico, and other rapidly-developing central States, and Territories, and will take rank as a rich and important city. The local trade of Galveston, chiefly groceries and dry goods, is mainly in the hands of German Jews, not a few of whom have accumulated considerable wealth. There are no manufactures, and the water supply, entirely from the rainfall, is collected in cisterns and tanks. Some years ago they sank an artesian well to the depth of 730 feet, which, however, produced undrinkable water. The pipe became, and remains, full to the summit, and is highly magnetic. Another source of decay in the trade of this city

Strikes and labour. is the frequency of strikes: all classes banding together for the enforcement of higher wages, though they are actually receiving the same rates of pay as five or six years ago, when the commerce of the place was prosperous and flourishing. They also insist that no negro labour shall be employed on the wharves, and are threatening to "boycott" any merchants, shipping goods by railway or steamer companies, who will not submit to their terms. The State Government appears helpless in this, as in other contingencies, to remedy the evil. The view taken by the merchants and wholesale traders of the city is that these strikes are lawless and predatory combinations, which should be forthwith suppressed by the Executive, under the statute of "Conspiracy to Injure and Intimidate;" but this is, after all, only their side of the question, to say nothing of the fact that the Government has no actual force at its disposal, the few soldiers in the State being fully employed several hundred miles off on the frontiers in watching the Indians, and keeping the Cow-boys and Mexican banditti under some sort of control, while the police of the town, few and inefficient, are virtually elected by the working men, whom they would have to deal with.

Prices. The argument of the strikers and labouring population is that provisions and necessaries, always dear, are, through the action of the merchants in combining to form "rings" and "corners," and thereby to run up prices, getting still dearer; consequently that, unless they receive wages in proportion, they cannot earn a subsistence.

Meat. It remains a fact that in this land of plenty, bullocks, which cost on the hoof 16 dol. to 20 dol., are sold retail at 50 dol. to 60 dol. Beef is here 15 c. to 20 c. per lb., *i.e.*, 7*d*. to 10*d*., and American beef, which comes from Texas, can be sold in Liverpool at 10 c., or 5*d*. per lb.

Bread. Bread costs here about double what bread costs in England, and is of inferior quality to English bread; yet the English bread is made mainly of American imported flour.

Spirits. Whiskey, sold wholesale by the distillers at 50 c. the gallon, with 1 dol. for revenue, making 1 dol. 50 c., is retailed at 4 dol. 50 c. to 5 dol. per gallon, or about 300 per cent. profit: beer in the same proportion.

Fish. It is no uncommon occurrence in the summer to find large quantities of fish in the market, but however extensive the catch, the prices are never lowered. If the fish don't sell at the usual exorbitant rates, they are thrown away and left to rot. Fish in these waters are year by year getting scarcer, and prices becoming higher.

Cost of living. This "high price," "ring and corner" system recoils on, damages, and demoralises the entire community. It sounds well to be told in Europe that working men in Texas get 8*s*. to 16*s*. per diem. in a country which can sell first-class beef in England at 5*d*. per pound, and make a profit on it, while underselling all Europe in breadstuffs.

But this will not help the working man, if it costs him 8*s*. to 10*s*. a day to live, at the rate he has been accustomed to live in England, on

25s. a week. Still less if, as is the case here, employment is difficult to get, there being always some 8,000 to 10,000 working men (in a population of 30,000 to 35,000) out of work, who of course have to live somehow or other, and actually do live on those who are in receipt of wages, and those who own property.

An industrious working man comes here (as hundreds have done) from England or from Germany, works hard, and by strict self-denial saves money, while his mates are enjoying themselves and spending their wages in saloons, &c. It is hardly safe or judicious to keep his savings in a bank for any length of time, so he purchases two or three vacant lots, and builds dwelling houses on them, working from morning till night, in a burning sun, to get them finished. When completed his acquaintances offer to rent them from him, and for some months all goes well. At the end of a certain period, however, he finds great difficulty in realising his rents: one of his tenants is out of work, another is "on strike," a third is a regular "beat," *i.e.*, a man who never pays anybody, making perpetual excuses. Distraining and seizing furniture for rent cannot be done in Texas; furniture being unattachable, also tools, or indeed anything a man is supposed to get a living by. The man finds it a difficult matter to turn his non-paying tenants out of his houses (the tenant having a right to remain until he has got another lodging ready to move into), and is lucky if he manages to do so without law expenditure. *Rent.*

Grocers and storekeepers, again, have to charge enormous prices to cover their bad debts; in effect, the whole system is a vicious circle, and a striking example of the absurdity of trying to "get ahead of the nature of things," and of ignoring, as obsolete, the political economy of our forefathers.

The wholesale merchants combine to run up prices; the shopkeepers are obliged to charge at a still higher rate, because credit is the rule, and half their customers don't pay; the working men, in consequence of these high prices, have to demand double and treble the wages they would receive in Europe, and strike (aggressively) to get it, thereby upsetting business in general; and this state of things is the outcome of what, in America, is called "freedom, enlightenment, and progress."

I make these remarks in no carping spirit towards America, but that British interests and intending immigrants may be able to consider both sides.

In the prospectuses of Texan immigration offices, land agencies, &c., in London, the above circumstances are discreetly left to conjecture, while the high rates of wages, the cheapness of living, the fertility of the soil, and the rapidly increasing prosperity of the State are depicted in glowing colours. There is no doubt but that Texas is a marvellous country, and will eventually become one of the richest and most powerful, if not the richest and most powerful, State in the Union. Its resources are boundless, and its soil as fertile, with proper cultivation, as any in the world. It is yet in its infancy. Although 12,000 miles of actually railway have been constructed and are in working order, there are not yet more than six persons to the square mile. This estimate, as its population has already reached 750,000, will give some notion of its immense area. It is a vast semi-tropical amphitheatre, rising gradually towards the north and west from the sea level, capable of producing the staples of the temperate and some of those of the torrid zone. Its produce and material wealth are yearly increasing, its mineral resources are being developed, and could labour be obtained at moderate (certain and fixed) rates, provisions be sold at reasonable prices, the laws properly enforced, and the improvement of its harbours be made an immediate *Hints to emigrants.* *Resources.*

sine qua non, Galveston, its principal port and commercial outlet would have a brilliant future. This last item of harbour improvement is especially important, as without it this city, whose trade is already steadily falling off, will fail inevitably to take its place, as it would otherwise assuredly do, as the principal industrial centre and leading city of the Gulf of Mexico. In the lower coast districts south of Galveston cotton and sugar were formerly extensively and profitably cultivated, the low-lying bottom lands of the Rio Brazos de Dios being enormously fertile. Unfortunately these lands have become, since the war and emancipation of slaves (from want of regular cultivation), exceedingly unhealthy; many rich plantations have been abandoned owing to the difficulty of obtaining controllable labour. Such plantations as are working are mostly supplied with convict labour: great opposition has, however, been already made by the working classes to this utilisation of criminals, they preferring to see any industrial enterprise fail rather than see it carried out by labour competing with their own. These Brazos lands would be a mine of wealth could coolie labour be imported and utilised: the "people," however (who, by the way, refuse to settle or work upon these lands which are at present a sort of squatting ground for negroes who don't work at all), would soon raise the same cry as they do against the Chinamen, besides which there is a law prohibiting the importation of Chinese labour.

Cattle raising. The great industry of the interior, for men of capital, is purchasing waste land and cattle raising. Any man of ordinary judgment, with 5,000*l.* to 10,000*l.* to invest, can make a good thing of it.

15 or 22 years ago such a man, who had then invested 4,000*l.* to 5,000*l.* in land and cattle, would now be worth 40,000*l.* to 50,000*l.*, all got too without toil or application, merely by judiciously investing in waste land (then averaging 25 cents, or 1*s.* per acre), and allowing it and his cattle to increase both in value and numerically. It is now not such a good speculation, but is even yet about the best enterprise that offers to young men of a certain capital, gifted with a fair amount of brains, and not afraid to "rough it" for a few years. The great thing now is to properly adopt the ways and means of the business, which is still "in the rough," so to speak, by importing races, both of cattle and sheep, exactly suitable to the climate (which in my opinion has not yet been effected), and by properly housing and feeding the animals during the winter months.

Climate. The piercing north winds which suddenly set in from time to time on the vast cattle plains of Western Texas during the winter months, often lower the temperature 30 or 40 deg. in a few hours, causing terrible destruction to unsheltered flocks. The cattle, on any run unprotected either by belts of trees, or by abrupt hills, under the lee of which they can shelter, die by thousands during these "cold spells," as they are called. This mortality arises not so much from actual cold and starvation, but from the animals not being sufficiently hardy, especially the sheep. The fat-tailed breed of sheep from Northern Asia, Asia Minor, &c., will be, I believe, the "breed of the future" for Western Texas, Colorado, and in fact the whole immense cattle country east of the Rocky Mountains.

Not only the breeds, but the methods of sheltering cattle practised by the Northern Asiatic shepherds on the Caspian and Turcoman steppes, Armenia, Asia Minor, &c., will have to be adopted, *i.e.*, of digging subterranean sheepfolds, &c., on the steppes, under the lee of hillocks where these are available, into which refuges the flocks and herds are driven at night, or whenever bad weather sets in. These would, in my opinion, produce admirable results.

The drawback to Englishmen holding large tracts of land, cattle ranches, &c., in Texas, is a certain "uncertainty," or insecurity, owing to the nature of the government.

Laws may be passed at any time prohibiting "aliens" from holding landed estates, or indeed prohibiting any one, even a citizen, from holding land as cattle pasture which is fit for cultivation: add to this the insecurity of life and property, which is a consideration with some people. It is commonly computed that in Texas 80 per cent. of white murderers, when not in turn assassinated (on the vendetta principle) by friends or relatives of the deceased, die of natural causes. Of the remaining 20 per cent., about two-thirds are lynched, leaving a balance of 5 per cent. to the Executive. *Insecurity.*

The "strong arm of the law" may be said to reach negro murderers, horse thieves, &c., with tolerable regularity; still of these criminals, quite seven-eighths of those executed are lynched. Indeed, it is computed that, taking criminals all round, white and black, about five lynchings occur to each regular judicial execution. *Lynch law.*

Texan "desperadoes" are often popular, well-known men, with money and friends to back them. These continue by various "legal" expedients, by appealing for new trials, on the ground of animus against the delinquent, by changing the name, squaring juries, getting important witnesses out of the way, &c. (all which is quite "in order"), to so prolong the trial that the culprit eventually escapes punishment altogether.

This "procedure" forms, of course, the *raison d'être* of the frequent lynchings. Texan Government officials, again, appear to be elected not so much to control crime as to hold office, as it were, "on sufferance."

So long as they respect the divers whims and crotchets of the popular mind they may retain their positions, and keep up the similitude of authority. A mayor is a mayor, a recorder is a police magistrate by the will of the people (duly ascertained after some weeks of wirepulling, manipulation of election papers, "lobbying," and "ward" bumming), but must not always expect to be obeyed or respected. If he does not give decisions in accordance with the views of the "people" or of his subordinates, his policemen and constables will contradict and defy him in open court, and refuse to carry out his orders, so that he will have either to resign his post, or stomach their insults. A case of this sort happened here a few days ago. *Administration of justice.*

In cases of stolen property, the action (or inaction) of the police may be said to be determined by the amount of money to be made by the affair, without any reference to the orders of superior (?) authority.

If a sum of money they think sufficient is offered for recovery, the police will set to work; if only a moderate reward, they will not move in the business.

The same principle holds good as to criminal cases, murders, assassinations, cattle robberies, horse stealings, &c., all over the State.

When 200 dol. or 300 dol. is offered for the arrest of a noted assassin or horse thief, he becomes worth hunting up, but not before.

The "modus operandi" of arresting is usually (after discovering the haunts of the culprit by bribing some aider and abetter) to lie in ambush for him with a double-barrelled gun, and (the object being by disabling the man completely to facilitate his capture) to "shoot him on sight," either with or without the preliminary of calling upon him to surrender. There is another element of uncertainty and insecurity (in the future), which it is as well to consider before investing capital in Texas, which is that the machinery of the State Government, not being apparently calculated to stand any severe strain, the authorities are apt to virtually abdicate when any moment of crisis happens to arrive. This tiding over of disagreeable and anxious incidents, such as the systematic assassination of Mexican employés on the frontier, because they work for less pay, and are more sober and civil than United States citizens; the massacre and expulsion of Chinese contrary to treaty for the same reasons; the ignoring of the aggressive and illegal action of labour unions (because too powerful to be conveniently meddled with, &c.), are "signs of the times."

When these things happen unpunished and unchecked, a country may fairly be said to be on the verge of anarchy. With anarchy will come suspension of all business, and, in all probability, civil war.

Galveston, Texas, February 25, 1886.

SAN FRANCISCO.

Consul Stanley to the Earl of Rosebery.

My Lord,   San Francisco, April 24, 1886.

I HAVE the honour to enclose a report on the trade and commerce of Washington territory by Mr. Alexander, British Vice-Consul at Port Townsend.

This report contains much that has no special interest for Great Britain, but I venture to transmit it in its entirety for the following reasons:—

1st. Were it to contain only matter of direct commercial interest to Great Britain I should have to ask Mr. Alexander to rewrite it.

2nd. There is no direct trade between Great Britain and Washington territory.

3rd. As a description of Washington territory, the fullest given in the Consular series, the report is most interesting, and may be valuable to intending immigrants, the territory offering a specially inviting field for British immigrants. Mr. Alexander has evidently taken great pains to obtain correct data, and the report throughout shows that it has been conscientiously written.

I have informed Mr. Alexander that in his future reports he need not dwell at length on what interests mainly the residents of Washington territory and the United States Government, but should confine them to the points specified in Foreign Office Instructions.

I have, &c.,
(Signed)   G. E. STANLEY.

PORT TOWNSEND.

Report by Vice-Consul Alexander on the Trade and Commerce of the Puget Sound District and Washington Territory for the Year ending March 31, 1886.

The subject-matter contained in this report has been taken principally from the elaborate and very complete report of the Governor of Washington territory to the Secretary of the Interior, and for the statistical and commercial returns I am indebted to the collector of customs at Port Townsend. These two sources, both being official, we may presume ought to give a not very inaccurate statement of the trade, resources, and commercial relations of the Puget Sound district and Washington territory as far as they are obtainable.

Washington Territory.—The territory during the last year has not escaped the great stagnation in trade and depression in business which has been almost universally felt by every civilised country in the world, but despite many drawbacks the year may be considered as having been one of substantial advancement and improvement. Although specula-

[395]

tion has been temporarily checked, the entries of public lands less numerous, and the influx of emigrants less rapid, yet the important industries of the country, such as wheat-raising east of the mountains, and lumbering and coal-mining on the western coast, have moved forward with increased impetus, so that the aggregate production has far surpassed that of any former year in the history of the territory.

The new population has largely betaken itself to the country to engage in agricultural pursuits; an immensely increased acreage in wheat has been tilled, and the yield per acre of this crop the present year is almost unparalleled in the world. Immense new lumber mills have been constructed, and the forest has been penetrated with railroads and steam engines, which supersede the horse and ox teams for procuring timber. The most valuable veins of coal yet worked have been reached by railway, and their production has been shipped in increasing quantities to the seaboard. Important discoveries of iron and other ores have recently been made. Stock-raising, dairying, and fruit culture have progressed under the most favourable circumstances of soil, climate, and good markets; the crop of hops has been great and excellent in quality.

Many miles of railway have been built by the Oregon Railway and Navigation Company, running into the wheat-fields of Eastern Washington, and the Northern Pacific Railroad Company has been almost constantly at work on its Cascade division, which now lacks less than 80 miles of grading to complete this most important connection between the two great sections of the territory divided by the Cascade mountain range.

Numerous manufacturing enterprises have been started, and commercially the importance of the territory is better understood since the recent landing of tea from China and Japan upon the shore of Puget Sound for transportation by railway to the Atlantic States; train-loads of tea travelling across the continent to New York in eight days and four hours.

Population and financial condition. *Population and Financial Condition.*—The present population of the territory will amount to almost 175,000 persons; its financial condition has improved, the rate of taxation for territorial purposes being two and a half mills on the dollar; the assessed valuation of the territory is over 10,000,000*l.*; the territory is now said to stand free from any financial obligation, with an available surplus of nearly 20,000*l.* at its command.

Public health and diseases of animals. *Public Health and Diseases of Animals.*—The people of the territory have been comparatively free from epidemic and infectious diseases; and so far no contagious or infectious diseases among the cattle have made their appearance in this territory.

Education. *Education.*—In this territory the 16th and 36th sections in every township are reserved for school land by the Government. This will aggregate over 2,000,000 acres, worth about 10*s.* per acre, but a large portion of these lands being valuable for timber and agricultural purposes, and close to towns or settlements, are worth now about 2*l.* The public school system is supported by a tax levied by the county commissioners of each county, together with the fines for breaches of certain laws. Besides the public schools, there are several private institutions of learning and a territorial university.

Law, order, militia, &c. *Law, Order, Militia, &c.*—Stirring events connected with the anti-Chinese agitation, which has now as far as the Chinese are concerned almost subsided, except the bitter feeling, have recently attracted the attention of almost the entire civilised world to a portion of this territory, and have induced the general government to take vigorous measures for the preservation of order, and of respect for its treaty obligations.

I hear unexpected disturbances of the peace, got up by irresponsible, unreasonable, lawless, and ignorant man, have doubtless instigated the better and more thoughtful portion of the community to take more active and efficient measures for the future preservation of life and property, for we find that in most of the larger towns militia and volunteer organisations have been formed, and the force of the territory consists at the present time of seven companies, mustering 400 officers and men, almost fully equipped.

There is no doubt that one of the unfortunate results of the agitation in progress throughout the north-west is the discouragement and depression of business. It has brought industrial enterprise to a standstill, and has greatly checked mercantile activity. Capitalists hesitate before making investments, and every form of agitation that threatens disorder deters investments and causes capital to withdraw.

Mineral Resources.—The most important coalfields up to the present time have been found in Western Washington territory, and these chiefly in and near the Puget Sound Basin: of these the most valuable and the most extensively-worked mines are those situated near the towns of Seattle and Jacoma, and it is from these two points that the coal shipments of the territory are made. The coal in the Seattle district appears to be lignitic in character, while that in the Jacoma region is bituminous. Until more thorough explorations have been made, it cannot with any degree of certainty be learned what is the extent of the mineral resources of the territory; yet sufficient is known at the present time to justifiy the claim which has been made that Washington territory is one of the most extensive and valuable coalfields of the United States, the Pennsylvania of the Pacific coast.

The total shipment for the territory during the year was 380,000 tons; adding to this the home consumption, the output was over 400,000 tons. Both sail and steam vessels are employed in this coal-carrying trade.

During the last part of the year there has been a check put on the output of the mines and the quantity of coal carried, partly for the reason that the only market for this coal is in California and Oregon, where it must sell in competition with the best quality of coal from England and Australia, which is brought out in the grain ships for ballast at nominal rates, and consequently sold very cheap. It is against this competition that the poorer coal of Puget Sound must be sold in a market where the demand is limited. The secondary cause is that the market being very dull wages have had to be reduced, and a strike amongst the colliers was the result, which lasted some time.

Other Minerals.—Limestone is found in great abundance in the Puyallup Valley, and also on some of the islands of the San Juan Archipelago, where it is extensively worked.

A brown hematite iron ore of the very best quality exists in almost inexhaustible quantities throughout the Puget Sound Basin, and magnetic ore has been found in the Suoqualmie Pass.

Valuable discoveries of copper have also been made in the Suoqualmie Pass region.

In the eastern part of the territory extensive silver deposits have lately been discovered in the Chewelah and Colville districts, and are now being rapidly developed, quartz mills being placed in operation, and producing very gratifying results.

Of the other valuable ores, gold, lead, cinnabar, &c., have been found. Marble and gypsum are found in King county. Sandstone of an excellent quality has been extensively quarried on Bellingham Bay, in Pierce and King counties, and in many other localities. Remarkable specimens of kaolin have been exhibited, and clay suitable for brickmaking is plentiful and well distributed.

Strong indications of petroleum are found in some parts, principally in the Puyallup Valley; and boring for oil has been commenced, but no very satisfactory results so far have been obtained.

Food fishes, &c.

Food Fishes, &c.—The whole of the tide waters of Puget Sound, as well as all the waters along the coast of the territory, abound with food fishes and mollusks.

The principal fish are salmon, of which there are five varieties—halibut, several kinds of cod, sturgeon, skate, smelt, herring, and salmon trout.

The canning of salmon is one of the most valuable industries of the territory.

These waters also abound with dog-fish and ground shark, from the livers of which great quantities of excellent lubricating oil are extracted by the Indians and sold to traders; but within the last year a manufactory has been established with great success on San Juan Island, where the oil is extracted from the fish, fish glue manufactured from the heads and fins, and guano from the offal.

Whales are plentiful off Cape Flattery, and numbers are caught by the Indians, who use the oil and blubber as food. When traded off, three gallons of dog-fish oil are bartered for one gallon of whale oil.

Of the edible mollusks, oysters are plentiful in many localities, and their cultivation is carefully carried on.

Clams of several varieties abound, and canneries have been established, where they are put up most successfully.

Seals and sea-otters may be classed under this heading. The most valuable is the fur-seal, for the capture of which quite a number of schooners are fitted out every spring, which cruise off Cape Flattery. At the end of the season the catch is sold, and generally sent at once to London to be cured.

Sea-otters—one of the most valuable fur-bearing animals—are now only occasionally taken along the west coast of the territory, principally in the neighbourhood of Gray's Harbour.

Trout are found usually in most of the freshwater lakes and rivers. Recently the United States Fish Commissioner has introduced carp into many of the lakes and ponds, where it is expected they will thrive and become a good article of food.

Manufactures.

The principal manufacturing interests of Washington territory are connected with the manufacture of lumber. There are several large mills, possessing first-class machinery, which each turn out a product of lumber valued at from 100,000*l*. to 200,000*l*. annually, and there are several smaller ones which do an important local business. There are also large furniture factories, planing mills, sash and door factories, and barrel factories. In metal working there are important foundries, iron works, boiler works, and copper shops. Very extensive ore smelting works have been erected in Jefferson county, the capital stock of the company being fixed at 100,000*l*. There are match, stair, ice and soda factories, brickyards, breweries, fish canneries, bookbinderies, gas and waterworks, ship and boat building yards, and other minor industries. The business of canning and packing salmon for foreign and domestic markets has assumed large proportions. There are nine canneries on the Washington territory side of the Columbia River, and other establishments are situated on Gray's Harbour and on Puget Sound.

Shipbuilding is a prominent manufacturing industry of Western Washington. The fir timber, especially the yellow fir of Puget Sound, is peculiarly well-adapted for shipbuilding: its strength, durability, general superiority, and cheapness over that of other regions is fully established. 11 new vessels have been built on the Sound this year, and were registered at this port of entry, aggregating a total tonnage of 1,559. Several others have been rebuilt and remodelled, and many more are on the ways.

There are numerous flouring mills scattered throughout the country, especially the western portion; and in the eastern portion this industry is rapidly growing in importance.

The facilities for employing water power are numerous and especially favourable.

The paper-making industry has been established during the past year at La Camas, and is now turning out an excellent product on a very large scale.

Commerce.—No adequate estimate can be made of the entire commerce of the territory, for the reason that the surplus grain, wool, and salmon of the eastern and southern portion of the territory have hitherto been principally shipped by the way of the Oregon Customhouse, at Portland and Astoria, and no separate account has been taken of the productions of this territory, which, for the purpose of a full showing, would belong to its credit. By careful computation it is ascertained that 250,000 tons of wheat, flour, and barley, the surplus product of the territory, are shipped to Portland, Oregon, and thence to be exported.

Thousands of cattle are being driven or shipped by rail direct to the east, without any Custom-house record being taken of their number and value; it is estimated that the Northern Pacific Railroad Company alone carried from the territory to eastern points 26,640 head of cattle, 22,000 head of sheep, and 3,000 head of horses; the prices obtained for this stock have been satisfactory, and will encourage further shipments. It is estimated that over 100,000 cattle and 8,000,000 lbs. of wool are annually shipped from the territory.

Shipments of grain for this season have been made by rail in the same direction, the Northern Pacific Railway Company carrying to Duluth and other eastern points 4,161 tons of wheat and 1,600 tons of other grain. It is expected that these shipments will assume larger proportions. Of other products there were shipped to eastern points 1,783 tons of flour, 1,700 tons of hops, 67 tons of green fruit, 10,019 tons of lumber, and 500 tons of wool, so that the aggregate exports of the territory cannot be accurately computed. Still the Northern Pacific Railway Company, pushing to completion their line of road across the Cascade mountains direct to the waters of Puget Sound, and the fact that capacious elevators will shortly be erected at Jacoma to handle the wheat products of this eastern portion of the territory, will doubtless make a perceptible change in the amount of the export of grain by rail east, as well as by the way of Portland and Astoria, Oregon.

The output of coal for the year was over 400,000 tons.

The head office of the collection district for Puget Sound is at Port Townsend, and there vessels are constantly arriving and departing for ports in British Columbia, Australia, Hawaiian Islands, China, Japan, Mexico, Central America, South America, Peru and Great Britain, besides for all important points in California and Alaska, and the ports on the Atlantic side of the United States, thus rendering it one of the most important seaports in the United States.

The appended tables, marked Annex A., B., and C., fully corroborate this statement.

Railroads.

Railroads.—The construction of railroads has steadily increased. The principal are the Oregon Railway and Navigation Company, which operates 259·5 miles of line within the territory: this road, by its connections east through the Oregon short line and Union Pacific, is doing much for the development of the territory.

The Northern Pacific Railroad Company operates 455·9 miles of line within the territory, and during the year it completed 62 miles, which were accepted by the President of the United States. Grading and bridging of 37 additional miles is finished, and it is expected that this part will be in operation shortly. The people of the territory begin to see near at hand direct railroad connection between the western and eastern parts of the territory. The influence of the opening of this line in the extension of the commerce of the territory is making itself felt to a constantly growing extent. Many of the products of the territory, for which there was no outlet before the completion of the road, find a ready market in the Atlantic and Western States and territories. This company have established a wheat rate, which they promise to keep in force, of about 1s. 6d. per 100 from all points along its line in Washington territory to Duluth, on Lake Superior. This rate enables wheat to be sold at a profit.

The Columbia and Puget Sound Railroad Company now has in operation 44·6 miles of main line, with a short branch of eight miles. This road carried over its lines 210,000 tons of freight during last year, and now opens one of the most valuable coalfields yet discovered.

There are now in all 866 miles of railroad in the territory, of which 804 miles are in working order.

Climate.

Climate.—There is an important difference between the climates of the eastern and western parts of the territory; the mean temperature in the eastern division being in summer 73°, and in winter 34°; while that of the western division is 63° in summer, and 39° in winter. This difference in two sections lying contiguous in the same latitude, and with but little difference in elevation, is owing, in great part, to the range of mountains running north and south separating the two sections, thus warding off from the eastern portion of the territory the immediate effects of ocean currents and ocean breezes.

There is also a great difference between the two sections in respect to the amount of rainfall; the climate of Western Washington affording a greater quantity of moisture. Variations in temperature are less in the western than the eastern part of the territory.

Soil and production.

Soil and Production.—The soil of the eastern section of the territory is prolific in the production of wheat and other cereals; the average yield of wheat being over 25 bushels to the acre.

Tobacco is cultivated to some extent, and grapes, peaches, and melons do remarkably well.

The central and northern region, east of the Cascades, is less developed, owing to lack of railroads until lately; but it has many of the same characteristics. Sweet potatoes, sorghum, tobacco, eggplant, melons, corn and hops, thrive in the Yakima and Wenatchee valleys. Much of this country has hitherto been devoted to stock-raising.

At a comparatively few localities only is artificial irrigation needed; and in most of these it is readily obtainable at moderate expense.

Western Washington is especially adapted to all the grasses, and to oats and the root crops. Some wheat is grown on the uplands, but the rich alluvial bottom lands are most sought for by the farmer. Two and one-half to four tons of hay per acre each year are frequently obtained. The following vegetables and fruits grow in perfection in the counties bordering on Puget Sound:—Cabbages, asparagus, beans, beets, cauliflower, carrots, celery, cucumber, kale, parsnips, peas, potatoes, rhubarb, turnips, squash, currants, and the different varieties of berries growing upon vines and bushes. Many kinds of apple, pear, quince, peach, and the smaller fruits, such as plums and cherries, flourish in great perfection, and attain a large size and superior flavour. The climate is so mild that protection of trees and vines is never thought of, and it is very rarely that any are injured; blight and other diseases have not yet made their appearance in this part of the country. Certain parties have recently interested themselves largely in the production of beet sugar, and recent investigations and experiments have developed the fact that there is here the soil and climate suitable for cheaply producing a choice quality of sugar beets upon a very large scale. On Puget Sound there have been 27,000 acres of tide lands diked and reclaimed with great profit. Wonderful crops of oats are obtained on these lands; probably 150,000 acres more can be reclaimed. The crop of hops for the year has been less than an average, reducing the yield to about 13,000 bushels; but it has been more satisfactory than was anticipated at the beginning, and more remunerative than was expected: this result has been attained entirely upon the score of quality. The best soil adapted to the growing of hops is the alluvial deposit found in the river-bottom land adjacent to Puget Sound, yet good results have been obtained on the table lands in certain localities. Since the opening of the Northern Pacific Railroad, direct shipments have been made to all parts of the United States and Europe, particularly to London.

It will not be out of place in this report to mention that few countries possess such a promising field for emigration as this territory. The intending emigrant, always presuming he has some capital, can choose for himself the particular line he would like to follow. Should he wish to pursue more especially wheat-growing and stock-raising, he will select the extensive prairie lands and bunch grass country of the eastern section; or should he prefer more general farming, dairying, fishing, or lumbering, he will betake himself to the western slope of the Cascade mountains. 700 Welsh families, aggregating 3,000 persons, from Pennsylvania, have recently settled upon land in Douglas county, in what is known as the Big Bend country. It is this section, closely followed by the Palouse country, which is now receiving the largest number of emigrants, reaching up to 100 a day, principally from the East and California. The bonâ fide settler is afforded every facility for procuring land by the homestead, the pre-emption, the timber culture, the coal, stone, and mining laws, &c. United States Land Offices are situated at convenient places. There is a total of 26,631,928 acres of unsurveyed land in the territory, of which one-half is good agricultural and timber land. As yet, no board of emigration has been created. *Emigration.*

The navigation of the coast and inland waters of the territory is facilitated by lighthouse stations, where, in some cases, in addition to the light, powerful steam foghorns and bells are used when required. Numerous buoys are also anchored to mark dangerous rocks and intricate passages. During the last year a steam foghorn has been placed on Point Robinson, Puget Sound, and a lighthouse is to be erected at once on Destruction Island, on the west coast. Life-saving stations are placed at convenient places on the coast, and from the numerous signal stations, weather reports, &c., are frequently received *Lighthouses, &c.*

746   UNITED STATES.

The United States Coast Survey has been carried on very successfully this year—three parties with vessels having been engaged by the Government in this important work—and it is expected soon that an accurate and complete chart of these waters will be published, which is much needed to meet the demands of the growing commerce.

Rates of interest and wages.

The ordinary rate of interest is 1 per cent. per month, but it will range from $8\frac{3}{10}$ to 18 per cent. per annum. The field for investment is wide. Lands in great variety, agriculture, mines, stock-raising, manufactures, railroads, commerce, fisheries, and town improvements all offer great inducements, but great caution is necessary. The rates of wages range from 6s. to 1l. a day. Labour appears to be plentiful, with the exception of domestic female servants.

Annex A.—RETURN of all Shipping at the Port of Port Townsend for the Year ending March 31, 1886.

Shipping.

ENTERED.

Nationality.	Sailing. Number of Vessels.	Tons.	Steam. Number of Vessels.	Tons.	Total. Number of Vessels.	Tons.
British	27	25,923	15	1,981	42	27,904
United States	162	129,077	739	371,160	901	500,237
Bolivia	1	859	...	...	1	859
Chili	9	8,362	...	...	9	8,362
France	2	810	...	...	2	810
Germany	3	1,972	...	...	3	1,972
Hawaiian Islands	5	4,290	...	...	5	4,290
Italy	1	508	...	...	1	508
Norway	7	4,922	...	...	7	4,922
Total	217	176,723	754	373,141	971	549,864
,, for the year 1884	175	120,075	869	371,941	1,044	492,016

CLEARED.

Nationality.	Sailing. Number of Vessels.	Tons.	Steam. Number of Vessels.	Tons.	Total. Number of Vessels.	Tons.
British	27	26,515	15	1,981	42	28,496
United States	166	126,659	755	366,266	921	492,925
Bolivia	1	972	...	...	1	972
Chili	8	7,817	...	...	8	7,817
France	2	810	...	...	2	810
Germany	3	1,972	...	...	3	1,972
Hawaiian Islands	5	4,290	...	...	5	4,290
Italy	1	508	...	...	1	508
Norway	7	4,922	...	...	7	4,922
Total	220	174,465	770	368,247	990	542,712
,, for the year 1884	176	113,728	873	350,675	1,049	464,403

To this total number of vessels and tonnage must be added about one-third, which will cover the number of vessels and tonnage employed in the coasting trade: these vessels being under enrolment and license are not required to report at the Custom-house. This would make the tonnage which came into this district 733,153, and the tonnage which left will be 723,616, making a grand total of all tonnage for the year 1,456,768.

A comparison of the years 1884 and 1885 will mark a decrease in the number of vessels but a great increase in the tonnage, indicating that a larger and better class of vessels are engaged in the commerce of Puget Sound.

From present indications it is expected that there will be a considerable increase in commerce during the coming year, an unusual large number of vessels being on the way to the Puget Sound ports for cargoes.

Annex B.—RETURN of Principal Articles of Export from Port Townsend during the Year 1885.

Articles.		Quantity.	Value.
			£
Horses	Number of head	516	11,606
Cattle	”	521	4,171
Sheep	”	21,774	10,912
Hogs	”	2,703	3,376
Wheat	Bushels	273,421	41,831
Oats	”	62,126	3,703
Potatoes	”	14,434	943
Lumber	M. feet	89,171	194,910
Laths	”	10,133	3,900
Pickets	”	1,566	2,762
Shingles	”	1,944	959
Oil, illuminating	Gallons	181,653	7,500
Bacon, hams, and lard	Lbs.	640,913	12,601
Butter, cheese, eggs, breadstuffs	”	55,353	18,959
Flour	”	43,747	35,500
Iron, steel manufactures			9,068
Other articles			108,785
Total, 1885			471,486
,, 1884			340,929

RETURN of Principal Articles of Import from Port Townsend during the Year 1885.

Articles.		Quantity.	Value.
			£
Tea	Lbs.	2,705,663	83,628
Rice	”	838,307	3,527
Sugar	”	15,106	175
Beef	”	3,549	93
Liquors	Gallons	3,405	589
Other articles			37,667
Total, 1885			125,679
,, 1884			43,139

NOTE.—The rate of £ sterling of Great Britain is reduced from the Custom-house standard at 4.86 dol., as fixed by Act of Congress, approved 3rd March, 1873.

[395]

Annex C.—TABLE showing the Total Value of all Articles Exported from Port Townsend and Imported to Port Townsend from and to Foreign Countries during the Years 1884 and 1885.

Country.	Exports.	Imports.
	£	£
Great Britain	39,449	..
British Possessions in Australia	98,675	5
British Columbia	239,086	40,410
Argentine Republic	2,182	..
Bolivia	1,572	..
Chili	38,986	6
China	2,673	1,391
Hawaiian Islands	27,867	300
Japan	..	83,543
Mexico	123	..
New Caledonia	982	..
Norway	1,199	..
Peru	5,563	34
Uruguay	5,845	..
United States of Columbia	7,284	..
Total, 1885	471,486	125,679
„ 1884	340,929	43,139

From the preceding tabular statements the total value of exports and imports was 597,165*l.*, and to this amount must be added the coasting trade, of which no record is readily obtainable, estimated to be 1,600,000*l.*; thus making a grand total of all exports and imports of 2,197,165*l.* for the year 1885, showing a marked increase over the previous year and extension in trade, in spite of the general commercial depression.

San Francisco, April 24, 1886.

(137)

No. 5.

United States.

Report by Sir L. West on the Coinage of the United States and Depreciation of the Silver Dollar.

Sir L. West to the Marquis of Salisbury.

My Lord, *Washington, December* 29, 1885.

WITH reference to previous correspondence on the coinage question, I have the honour to inclose to your Lordship herewith a Report accompanied by tabular statements, which I have drawn up in connection therewith.

I have, &c.
(Signed) L. S. SACKVILLE WEST.

Inclosure in No. 5.

Report.

BY the first Coinage Act of 1792 one ounce of gold was made the equivalent of fifteen ounces in silver, and the gold eagle eleven-twelfths fine weighed at that time 270 grains. This, however, proved to be an undervaluation of silver up to 1834, when the gold eagle was reduced in weight to 258 grains, and subsequently by alloy to a fraction below nine-tenths fine, or to eight hundred and ninety-nine and two-tenths thousandths. This reduction made the new gold eagle 66·68 cents less than the old one. The half eagle of 129 grains and the quarter eagle of $64\frac{1}{2}$ grains were of the same fineness (see Table 1). In 1837 the gold coinage was raised to nine-tenths fine, and the ratio to silver has since been one to sixteen. The double eagle first appeared in 1849 and the gold dollar in 1853.

The silver dollar of 1794 weighed 416 grains, and contained $371\frac{1}{4}$ grains of pure silver. The Act of 1837 reduced it to $412\frac{1}{2}$ grains, but the amount of pure silver

History of the coinage.

was unchanged. In 1851 the three cent silver coin was authorized, 750 fine weighing 12⅜ grains. By the Act of 1853 all the fractions of the silver dollar were reduced to the ratio of 384 grains to the dollar, nine-tenths fine, and regulated by the metric system of weights; or for halves, 12½ grains; quarters, 6¼ grains; and dimes, 2$\frac{1}{12}$ grains; and the weight of the 3 cent piece was changed to three-fiftieths of the half-dollar, or to 11·52 grains. In consequence of this 7 per cent. shortage of silver in the half-dollars, the demand for them in South America and the West Indies ceased, and they became worthless for commercial transactions in those markets.

The trade dollar was authorized by Act 12th February, 1873,* in consequence of the demand of merchants engaged in the trade with China, and who paid the Mint the cost of its manufacture. It weighed 420 grains, nine-tenths fine, and was worth as bullion 3 or 4 per cent. more than its legal tender value. In 1876 the legal tender power of the trade dollar was withdrawn, and with the decline in the price of silver the exported dollars returned to the country, and there are, it is supposed, at present 6,000,000 dollars, more or less, in circulation which are useless in foreign markets.

Standard dollars. According to the last Report of the Director of the Mint, the number of standard silver dollars in the Treasury on the 1st October, 1885, was 165,483,721 dollars (see Table 2). The average price paid for silver purchased during the year was 1·08977 dollars + per ounce fine, equal to 0·98079 dollars + per ounce standard. The rate of issue of silver dollars being 1·16$\frac{4}{11}$ dollars per ounce standard, the seigniorage to the Government was over 18 per cent. There were consumed during the year 1884 in the coinage of 28,526,715 standard dollars 24,515,145·70 standard ounces, costing 24,171,436·16 dollars.† It would appear that although 2,000,000 dollars a-month have been absorbed, under the Coinage Act, to purchase silver bullion for the annual coinage of 28,000,000 dollars, silver has steadily gone down in relative market value. In 1878, **Price of silver.** the first year of the operation of the Act, one ounce of fine silver was worth 1·18 dollars, or the silver in the

---
* See Mr. West's Report of July 5, 1883 ("Commercial No. 41, 1883.")
† Senator Sherman's Speech, 1884.

silver dollar was worth 91 cents. In 1884 an ounce of fine silver was worth 1·11 dollars, and the silver in the dollar was worth 85 to 86 cents, so that, instead of $412\frac{1}{2}$ grains of silver being equal to a dollar in gold, it requires, as near as may be, one ounce or 480 grains of standard silver to be equal in market value to a gold dollar. Senator Sherman goes on to say: "Not only has this Law not restored silver to its former ratio, but it has gone down gradually in the face of a determined effort on the part of the United States to prevent that depreciation. . . . . . Should we not, therefore, change our ratio as other nations have done before us, and seek, by adapting our coinage to the relative market value of the two metals, to check the depreciation of silver, or at least to coin silver at the same value we pay for it, and not try to make a delusive profit out of our own citizens?" *Senator Sherman's views.*

On the other hand, it is argued by the silver ring that the suspension of the silver coinage would still further depreciate the price of silver bullion by the sudden stoppage of the Government purchases, which now take about one-half of the production of the American mines. *Views of the silver ring.*

The Mint demand for silver is, as aforesaid, 28,000,000 dollars per annum. The total production in the world is about 110,000,000 dollars, of which the United States produces a little more than 46,000,000 dollars. But as the price of silver bullion is governed generally by the law of supply and demand, it would seem that a purely artificial demand, such as is created under the Coinage Act and which rests upon political rather than commercial considerations, is not the kind of demand which determines the price of an article in the market, and that it is moreover quite uncertain whether the demand of India and other silver standard countries will increase or decrease or remain stationary. The bullion dealers, however, in both hemispheres have doubtless anticipated the probability that the United States' Government will, ere long, cease to buy silver bullion for arbitrary coinage, and foresee a plethora of it in the markets of the world, which will still further reduce its price. It is scarcely possible that the Government can continue for ever to buy metal which the people refuse to take off its hands in coin, or to use the *Annual production and coinage.*

Operation of Coinage Act.

public funds to keep up the price of an article in the market in the interest of a particular class of producers at the expense of all others. The Comptroller of the Currency in his last Report stated that he believed the operation of the present Law, which compels the coinage of 2,000,000 silver dollars per month, weighing only 412½ grains each, with unlimited legal tender quality, would eventually bring financial disturbance upon the country, and that it seems doubtful if the Government of the United States should attempt to issue a circulation based upon silver, even at its bullion value, until the relative value of this metal is more definitely settled throughout the world. If the Government should pay its interest and other obligations, and redeem its bonds in standard dollars, the business of the country would immediately go to a silver basis. Gold would go to a premium, which would compel its being held, to a certain extent, as an article of merchandize, and it would not circulate as money. Indeed, it would seem that a large portion of the gold in the United States does not so circulate, as appears from the statistics of exports, imports, and coinage collected during a number of years past by the Director of the Mint.

Stock of gold coin.

The stock of gold coin in the country in 1884 was estimated to be 552,000,000 dollars; of this stock there was held by the Treasury 89,000,000 dollars; by national banks, 98,000,000 dollars; in other hands, 365,000,000 dollars; total, 552,000,000 dollars. Of this amount only the 187,000,000 dollars held by the Treasury and national banks can be really ascertained to exist. "But, in fact," says Professor Newcombe, writing on monometallism and bimetallism, "no gold at all is in actual circulation from hand to hand in the Eastern States, and probably very little in any part of the country east of the Rocky Mountains." And he asks: "What has become of it? Is it hoarded or melted down? If the latter, the state of affairs is serious, since it would lead to the conclusion that fully the entire annual gold product of the world is absorbed for other than monetary purposes."

Gold production.

For the year ending the 1st November, 1885, the production of gold by the mines of the United States is estimated to have been 30,800,000 dollars. During the period from the 1st November, 1884, to the 1st October, 1885, the amount of foreign and domestic gold coin and bullion imported in excess of the amount exported has been 12,315,915 dollars, making an increase in the stock of gold in the country of 43,115,915 dollars. From this amount must be deducted 12,000,000 dollars, estimated to have been used in the arts, leaving the increase, therefore, at 31,115,915 dollars.

Table 3 shows the amount of coin and currency in the country on the 1st January, 1879, and on the 1st November of the year named. Table 4 shows the amount of coin, bullion, and currency held by the Treasury, State, and national banks, and Table 5 the amount in the hands of the people.

Market ratios of gold and silver. — The whole question of the market ratio of the two metals would seem to turn upon how the influence of the demand for them for other purposes than that of money compares with the influence of their demand for the purpose of coinage. While, however, the monometallists and bimetallists are discussing these questions, the practical issue of the situation for the bondholder is that he has the prospect of having his interest paid in silver dollars worth only 85 cents; for the merchant of being forced to transact business with a depreciated currency which is worthless abroad, and for the workingman, of a diminution in the purchasing power of his wages to the extent of 15 or 20 per cent.

Bank note circulation. — The report of the Comptroller of the Currency states that while the bank note circulation is steadily decreasing, there has been no deduction in the total circulating medium in the United States, the reduction in the national bank currency outstanding having been more than met by the coinage of the standard silver dollar, and the issuance of certificates thereon.

Silver certificates. — Under section 3 of the Act of 1878 silver certificates have been issued which are represented by standard dollars in the Treasury to the amount of 125,053,286 dollars. Of the certificates thus issued 31,906,514 dollars remain in the Treasury, leaving 93,146,772 dollars of them in circulation (1st November, 1885).

Gold certificates. — The gold certificates issued under section 12 of the Act of 1882, outstanding in the hands of the people and banks on the 1st November, 1882, 1883, 1884, and 1885, not including amount in Treasury, were 6,962,289 dollars, 48,869,940 dollars, 85,301,190 dollars, and 106,465,420 dollars respectively.

142 UNITED STATES.

Coinage Bills before Congress.

A Bill has now been introduced into the Senate to provide for the further issue of silver certificates on the deposit of the standard silver dollar of 412½ grains in sums of not less than 10 dollars, the depositors to receive certificates therefor of 1 dollar, 2 dollars, or 5 dollars. This Bill appears to have no other object than to insure the continuance of the operation of section 3 of the Act of 1878, above alluded to, and to replace by 1 and 2 dollar certificates the suspension of the 1 dollar and 2 dollar notes which was resorted to to facilitate the circulation of the silver dollar. At the same time a Bill has been introduced to suspend the coinage of the standard silver dollar under the Act of 1878, and also one to provide for the free and unlimited coinage of the silver dollar. By the Act 12th July, 1882 (section 12), legal tender notes are redeemable in gold; but it would be difficult for the Government with its present stock of gold to redeem the outstanding legal tender notes, or such portion of them as might be presented if gold, as it seems likely to be, were held at a premium, and it is scarcely likely that the banks will again come forward, as they did on a late occasion, with a loan to the Treasury of 6,000,000 dollars gold, to help it again out of its difficulties.

The question is not, however, whether the Government should redeem its obligations in gold or silver, but whether it employs a currency for this purpose which commands the confidence of the commercial world in its stability.

Depreciation of silver.

The present depreciation of silver is not generally thought to be permanent, but to be mainly owing to its demonetization in Europe, which has forced its sale as a commodity upon the world's market. It would appear that from 1857 to 1873 the variations in the market price of bar-silver in London were between $60\frac{5}{16}d.$ and $61\frac{11}{16}d.$ per standard ounce, so that during this period the United States' silver dollar of 412½ grains was worth more than its gold dollar, and, indeed, for a period of six years (1858 to 1864) exceeded it in value by over 4 per cent. Since 1873, however, the decline in value has been rapid, the fall being from $59\frac{1}{4}d.$ in 1873 to an average of 50·79 for 1883, and to 49½ in April 1885, which is equivalent to a reduction in the value of the silver dollar, in comparison with gold, from

100·45 in 1873, to 85·57 in 1885. But it is asserted that even if silver should cease to be a legal tender throughout the world, it would still continue to be used as money until a substitute in the form of gold could be obtained, and would continue at its market value in exchanges which, in relation to gold, is regulated by the amount of labour expended in producing either metal.

It is held, therefore, that the demonetization of silver would not produce a sudden vacuum of metallic currency, or a demand for gold more than sufficient to cause its production to the extent required; that, in fact, the relative values will ultimately adjust themselves, since the market value of both metals, even if not used as money, is determined by natural laws. The cause, therefore, of the depreciation of silver, according to the above theory, has been the discarding and sale of its silver currency by Germany; and as the great commercial nations of the world did not require this discarded silver, and would not purchase it for any purpose, depreciation has been the inevitable temporary result. However much the commerce of the East Indies may require silver, it cannot suddenly receive and pay for large quantities of it. *Cause of depreciation.*

Those who take this view object to a silver currency chiefly on the ground that it is inconvenient both for general circulation and for bank reserves. They argue that the value of a redeeming currency consists largely in its adaptability to general circulation, and is diminished by the difficulties of handling, transport, and deposit. In this connection it may be stated that the space required for storing the gold and silver coin in the Treasury is 417 cubic feet, and that the weight of 300,000 dollars is 16,534·66 lbs. avoirdupois. *Inconvenience of silver coinage.*

The advocates of the gold standard maintain that it is a necessity for the United States. The great commercial nations, they say, with which the United States are in intimate relations, and which recognize the single gold standard, have great reservoirs of gold, and ability, through their foreign commerce, to either receive surplus gold and pay for it, or send their surplus gold and receive products in exchange. These great reservoirs of gold, furthermore, immediately respond to any deficiencies or demands for gold in the various commercial countries using gold as a standard, and so, by the law of supply *Gold standard advocated.*

[698]

and demand, keep the volume of gold in equilibrium with the volume of commodities to be measured, and greatly aid in maintaining, in respect to most articles, a uniformity of prices. By adopting another standard, therefore, or two standards, great loss and inconvenience would be entailed, and the future industrial and commercial development of the country be arrested.

Contention of the silver interest.

The silver interest, on the other hand, maintains that whatever temporary inconvenience may be caused by the plethora of silver coin, created under the Coinage Act, no check ought to be given to the silver production of the country such as would result from a sudden suspension of the monthly purchase by the Government of that metal, for which it provides; and upon these conflicting opinions Congress is called upon to pronounce.

(Signed)   L. S. SACKVILLE WEST.

Authorities cited in Report.

Report of Comptroller of the Currency (1885).
Report of the Director of the Mint (1885).
Simon Newcombe (Principles of Political Economy).
Hon. Justin Morrill (Speech in Senate, 1883).
Hon. John Sherman (Speech in Senate, 1883).
Daniel Wells (Political Economies).

UNITED STATES.

(No. 1.)—TABLE showing the Legal Weight and Fineness of the Coins of the United States.

	Legal Weight.	Fineness.
	Grains.	Thousandths.
Gold—		
Double eagle	516	900
Eagle	258	,,
Half eagle	129	,,
Three dollars	64·5	,,
Quarter eagle	77·4	,,
Dollar (new)	25·8	,,
Silver—		
Trade dollar	420	,,
Standard dollar	412·5	,,
Half dollar	192·9	,,
Quarter dollar	96·45	,,
Twenty cents	77·16	,,
Dime	38·58	,,
Half dime	19·2	,,
Three cents	11·52	,,
Minor—		
Five cents	77·18	{ 75 per cent. copper. 25 ,, nickel.
Three cents	30	Ditto.
Two cents	96	{ 95 per cent. copper. 5 ,, tin and zinc.
One cent	48	Ditto.

(See Sections 3511, 3512, 3513, 3514, 3515, Revised Statutes of United States.)

(No. 2.)—COMPARATIVE Statement of the Coinage Movement and Circulation of Standard Silver Dollars at the end of each Six Months from July 1, 1884, to July 1, 1885, and for the Three Months ending October 1, 1885.

Period.	Total Coinage	Held for Payments of Certificates Outstanding.	Held in Excess of Certificates Outstanding.	Total.	In Circulation.
	Dollars.	Dollars.	Dollars.	Dollars.	Dollars.
July 1, 1884	175,355,829	96,427,011	39,133,905	135,560,916	39,794,913
January 1, 1885	189,561,994	114,865,911	31,636,954	146,502,865	43,059,129
July 1, 1885	203,884,381	101,530,946	63,882,166	165,413,112	38,471,269
October 1, 1885	210,759,431	93,656,716	71,827,005	165,483,721	45,275,710

146 UNITED STATES.

(No. 3.)—TABLE showing the Amount of Coin and Currency in the United States on January 1, 1879, and on November 1 of the Years named.

	January 1, 1879.	November 1, 1882.	November 1, 1883.	November 1, 1884.	November 1, 1885.
	Dollars.	Dollars.	Dollars.	Dollars.	Dollars.
Gold coin and bullion	278,310,126	547,356,262	581,970,254	585,611,872	586,727,787
Silver coin	106,573,803	208,744,424	242,701,932	275,735,439	307,658,827
Legal tender notes	346,681,016	346,681,016	346,681,016	346,681,016	346,681,016
National Bank notes	323,791,674	362,727,747	352,013,787	333,559,813	315,847,168
Total	1,055,356,619	1,465,509,449	1,523,366,989	1,541,588,140	1,556,914,798

(No. 4.)—TABLE showing the Amount of Coin, Bullion, and Currency held by the Treasury, State, and National Banks.

	January 1, 1879.	November 1, 1882.	November 1, 1883.	November 1, 1884.	November 1, 1885.
	Dollars.	Dollars.	Dollars.	Dollars.	Dollars.
Gold	158,680,355	260,455,297	273,179,117	277,784,954	335,251,499
Silver	38,879,908	131,411,701	157,933,165	185,012,536	199,744,216
Currency	211,375,639	160,580,475	175,570,682	187,504,997	192,126,306
Total	408,935,902	552,447,473	606,682,964	650,302,487	727,122,021

(No. 5.)—TABLE showing the Amount of Gold, Silver, and Currency in the Hands of the People.

	January 1, 1879.	November 1, 1882.	November 1, 1883.	November 1, 1884.	November 1, 1885.
	Dollars.	Dollars.	Dollars.	Dollars.	Dollars.
Gold	119,629,771	286,900,965	308,791,137	307,126,918	251,476,288
Silver	67,693,895	77,332,723	84,768,767	90,722,903	107,914,611
Currency	459,097,051	548,828,288	523,124,121	492,735,832	470,401,878
Total	646,420,717	913,061,976	916,684,025	891,285,653	829,792,777

UNITED STATES.

No. 6.

Report by Sir L. West on Imports and Exports in the United States.

Sir L. West to the Marquis of Salisbury.

My Lord, Washington, February 2, 1886.

I HAVE the honour to inclose to your Lordship herewith a Memorandum with reference to the Returns of Imports and Exports for the year 1885, which I have drawn up, suggested by a pamphlet which has been published and entitled "Home and International Trade."

I have, &c.
(Signed) L. S. SACKVILLE WEST.

Inclosure in No. 6.

Memorandum on the Decrease in the Total Values of the Imports and Exports of Merchandize during the Twelve Months ended the 31st December, 1885.

THE Chief of the Bureau of Statistics reports that the total values of the exports of merchandize for the twelve months ended the 31st December, 1885,* were 688,846,556 dollars, and for the twelve months ended the 31st December, 1884, 749,366,428 dollars, showing a decrease of 60,519,872 dollars. [Value of exports.]

The values of the imports of merchandize for 1885 were 587,551,506 dollars, and for 1884, 629,261,860 dollars, showing a decrease of 41,710,354 dollars, or a total decrease in the value of exports and imports of 102,230,226 dollars. This decrease must give rise to serious apprehensions for the future prosperity of the Western States, and indeed for the commercial interests of the Union in general. How important a part the wheat crop of the country constitutes of the grand total of exports is shown by the fact that from 1873 to 1883 about one-fourth of the whole agricultural exports was made up by wheat and flour. The export of those articles for this period was over 1,200,000,000 bushels. It is calculated that fully one-half of this great aggregate was due to the deficiency of crops in Europe during [Value of imports.] [Cause of decline.]

* See Returns of Imports and Exports (in Sir L. West's despatch of January 28).

those years, for taking the average quantity exported a few years prior to 1873 and the present rate of exportation as a joint basis of estimate, the result would be, for ten years, at least 600,000,000 bushels less than was actually sent abroad. Fortuitous circumstances, therefore, have been the cause of the enormous exportation of produce since 1873. It is estimated that this export trade for the ten years ended 1882 has given 80,000,000 tons of freight to be carried by rail and water eastward, a distance of over 1,000 miles, worth to the carrying Companies 400,000,000 dollars, and has given to the Transatlantic carrying capacity a like amount.

What, however, will be the situation upon the cessation of these fortuitous circumstances, which the decrease in the value of the exports during the past year seems to indicate? It must be borne in mind that, as above stated, one-fourth of all the agricultural produce finds a market abroad, and that the price of the whole crop is fixed in foreign lands. Moreover, that by reason of the higher price which the American farmer has to pay for what he consumes, but does not produce, his necessary outlay, independent of the cost of labour and fixed investment, is calculated to exceed that of a like number of agriculturists in Europe and Asia by more than 500,000,000 dollars a-year, a sum greater than the estimated average annual net profits of all the manufacturers in America during the past ten years.

To meet this excess of outlay over his agricultural competitors in Europe and Asia, it is estimated that for the period of the last six years he has had a net increase of 15 per cent. as compared with the results of his industry in former years, as appears from the following statement of Mr. Bookwalter:—

"The value of the total product of the United States was in 1875, 1,740,000,000 dollars, and in 1880, 2,500,000,000 dollars. It is therefore," he says, "quite within the bounds of the most reliable testimony to place the average annual production from 1875 to 1880 inclusive at 2,000,000,000 or 12,000,000,000 dollars for the period of six years. A gain, therefore, of 15 per cent. upon this total sum shows a net increase of income of 1,800,000,000 dollars. By that much the farmer was enriched in consequence of an almost unbroken succession of good crops, the concurrent failure of crops in

Europe, the resulting maintenance of a steady demand for his surplus at fair and generally high prices, and what constitutes the peculiar significant feature of the case, his ability to purchase his supplies in a market which had not yet rallied from its depression, and in which he was a welcome buyer at the lowest prices known for a generation."

He then proceeds to compare this unexampled period of prosperity with the actual situation which the American farmer has now to face. {Outlook for the future. Wheat.}

Wheat, which had risen in price in 1878 to 1 dol. 32 c. per bushel, and in 1880 stood at 1 dol. 24 c. per bushel, has been gradually falling, and is now under 90 cents a bushel, at which figure cultivation is generally considered unremunerative; while, at the same time, the price of all articles of his consumption has increased. But not only has he to contend with this reverse of his former prosperous condition, but he is threatened with the partial, if not total, loss of the European grain market; for of the 80,000,000 to 85,000,000 bushels calculated to be the average export of grain to Europe, India can easily supply 40,000,000 bushels at a lower price, and, according to Mr. Bookwalter, will ere long double that quantity. In a letter dated Madras, 26th February, 1883, he states that over 25,000,000 acres are annually under wheat cultivation, with an out-turn of 300,000,000 bushels. These assertions seem to be borne out by the latest Returns. For the three weeks, January 1886, the export of wheat was only 984,264 bushels, against 4,094,997 for the same period of 1885. Flour, 334,868 barrels in 1886, against 701,826 barrels in 1885. The railway movement last week* showed only 25,000 tons freight from Chicago, against 75,000 tons for the same period of last year, and grain is bought and sold in Europe at several cents below New York prices.

Mr. Bookwalter also states that American cotton will soon find a formidable competitor in the Egyptian, as well as Indian, produce, for which he predicts a still more extensive area of cultivation. {Cotton.}

"There are," he says, "already from 5,000,000 to 6,000,000 acres under tillage, and in a single year Egypt has exported to the value of 60,000,000 dollars, and even in 1885 exported 800,000 bales. India has

* February 1, 1886.

7,000,000 acres under cotton, and in 1884 exported 1,000,000 bales, valued at 70,000,000 dollars. No revision of the laws, by which American trade is bound, can," he says, "restore American supremacy in the grain markets of the world. The American farmer no longer holds, as he once did, the position of dictator in in the European market. It is rather the 6 cents ryot of India who now takes precedence at that Board, and who is able, if not to supply all the wheat which Europe requires, at least so to load the market with his cheap product as to depress the price below what, to the American wheat grower, is a living figure, and thus," he continues, "while we have been vaingloriously assuring each other of our commercial independence of Europe, regarding it as bound by its necessities in any event to contribute to our enrichment, Europe has been daily drawing towards a position in which it will be, in a sense, most injurious to our financial and industrial interests, independent of the United States. This is America's great and imminent danger."

To corroborate this statement he shows that the purchasing power of the vast populations of Asia, Africa, and Australia is greater, as regards Great Britain, than that of the United States, and that, therefore, the current of capital and enterprise tends towards them.

The amount which the people of the United States buy of Great Britain averages only 2 dol. 50 c. per head; Australia, 35 to 40 dollars per head; Straits Settlements and Hong Kong, 45 to 70 dollars per head; Cape Colony, 30 dollars per head.

The range for the British Colonies, exclusive of India, is from 10 to 50 dollars per head, and in South America it is: Uruguay, 18 dollars per head; Chile, 4 dol. 50 c. per head; and the Argentine Republic, 9 dollars per head.

"We shall have no cause to wonder or complain if Great Britain and Europe generally under the dictates of this impulse choose to trade with 800,000,000 people in the East who will eagerly take European commodities in exchange for their products, rather than with 55,000,000 in the West, who refuse to deal on a basis of reciprocity."

America, by her restrictive commercial policy, has

effectually excluded herself from the great markets of the world; while the necessities of Europe for her surplus agricultural produce, the mainstay of her prosperity, no longer exist.

Another informant spoke to me to the following effect, on the subject of wheat cultivation in the Western States :—

Wheat could not be cultivated with any profit under a dollar a bushel, and the price was now 84 cents. It was, he said, no use concealing the fact that the United States had lost the command of the grain markets of Europe and would never recover it.

The prosperity of the country had hitherto depended and still depends upon a profitable market for its surplus agricultural produce, and when, as at present, this market is wanting, the Western farmer must necessarily forego his present social status. He must live more cheaply, he must clothe himself in coarser garments, he must economize cents where he spent dollars. Such a change in his condition will be rendered necessary, and even then he will scarcely be able to compete with the cheap labour produce of India and Europe in the grain market. He designated the Legislature as narrow-minded. It had acted as if there was no other country in the world but the United States, and as if what took place abroad could not affect their interests. It had at the same time traded on bad harvests and commotions in Europe as a normal condition for profitable agricultural pursuits in the United States, and seemed incapable of appreciating the fact that no nation can commercially isolate itself. The result has been the loss of the markets of the world, and the dependence upon home consumption, which is insufficient for the surplus produce. This state of things he regarded as most serious, as it must inevitably produce a conflict between the Western and Eastern States, which latter, under a restrictive Tariff, have amassed wealth at the expense of the former by enhancing the cost of material life. He seems to think that the only hope for the Western States is in an expansion of the home market by increased immigration and consequent increased demand for agricultural produce; but in the meantime the situation was fraught with danger to the prosperity of the country.

The Western farmer must retrench.

United States.

No. 7.

Sir L. West to the Earl of Rosebery.

My Lord, Washington, *May* 20, 1886.

I HAVE the honour to acknowledge the receipt of your Lordship's despatches, calling for a Report upon the subject of Labour Unions in the United States, and on the economical and social causes of the recent railway and other strikes, and I have now the honour to transmit to your Lordship, herewith, a report which I have drawn up thereupon.

The Report refers to the organization of the "Knights of Labour," their publications, their doctrines and proposals, articles in the Press regarding them, their methods of action and results therefrom, hours of labour, legislative restrictions thereto, State Legislation regarding labour, trades unions, criminal law relating to trade combinations, the action of the Executive, the tendency to invoke federal legislation, and to other circumstances connected with these questions.

I have, &c.
(Signed) L. S. SACKVILLE WEST.

Inclosure 1 in No. 7.

Report on the Constitution of the Order of the Knights of Labour in relation to Labour Movements and Strikes.

THE preamble to the published Constitution* of the Order states that "the alarming aggressiveness of great capitalists and corporations, unless checked, will inevitably lead to the pauperization and hopeless degradation of the toiling masses."

* Pamphlet forwarded to House of Commons Library.

Aims of order.

The aims of the Order are, therefore, declared to be:

" I. To make industrial and moral work, not wealth, the true standard of individual and national greatness.

" II. To secure to the workers the full enjoyment of the wealth they create, sufficient leisure in which to develop their intellectual, moral, and social faculties, and all of the benefits, recreation, and pleasures of association: in a word, to enable them to share in the gains and honours of advancing civilization."

How they propose to secure them.

In order to secure these results, the Knights of Labor demand at the hands of the State:—

" III. The establishment of Bureaus of Labor Statistics, that we may arrive at a correct knowledge of the educational, moral, and financial condition of the laboring masses.

" IV. That the public lands, the heritage of the people, be reserved for actual settlers; not another acre for railroads or speculators, and that all lands now held for speculative purposes be taxed to their full value.

" V. The abrogation of all laws that do not bear equally upon capital and labor, and the removal of unjust technicalities, delays, and discriminations in the administration of justice.

" VI. The adoption of measures providing for the health and safety of those engaged in mining, manufacturing, and building industries, and for indemnification to those engaged therein for injuries received through lack of necessary safeguards.

" VII. The recognition by incorporation of trades' unions, orders, and such other associations as may be organized by the working masses to improve their condition and protect their rights.

" VIII. The enactment of laws to compel corporations to pay their employees weekly, in lawful money, for the labor of the preceding week, and giving mechanics and laborers a first lien upon the product of their labor to the extent of their full wages.

" IX. The abolition of the contract system on National, State, and Municipal works.

" X. The enactment of laws providing for arbitration

between employers and employed, and to enforce the decision of the arbitrators.

" XI. The prohibition by law of the employment of children under 15 years of age in workshops, mines, and factories.

" XII. To prohibit the hiring out of convict labour.

" XIII. That a graduated income tax be levied.

" And we demand at the hands of Congress :—

" XIV. The establishment of a National monetary system, in which a circulating medium in necessary quantity shall issue direct to the people, without the intervention of banks ; that all the National issue shall be full legal tender in payment of all debts, public and private ; and that the Government shall not guarantee or recognize any private banks, or create any banking corporations.

" XV. That interest-bearing bonds, bills of credit, or notes shall never be issued by the Government, but that, when need arises, the emergency shall be met by issue of legal tender, non-interest-bearing money.

" XVI. That the importation of foreign labour under contract be prohibited.

" XVII. That, in connection with the post-office, the Government shall organize financial exchanges, safe deposits, and facilities for deposit of the savings of the people in small sums.

" XVIII. That the Government shall obtain possession, by purchase, under the right of eminent domain, of all telegraphs, telephones, and railroads, and that hereafter no charter or license be issued to any corporation for construction or operation of any means of transporting intelligence, passengers, or freight.

" And, while making the foregoing demands upon the State and National Government, we will endeavour to associate our own labors.

" XIX. To establish co-operative institutions such as will tend to supersede the wage system by the introduction of a co-operative industrial system.

" XX. To secure for both sexes equal pay for equal work.

" XXI. To shorten the hours of labor by a general refusal to work for more than eight hours.

[704]

" XXII. To persuade employers to agree to arbitrate all differences which may arise between them and their employees, in order that the bonds of sympathy between them may be strengthened and that strikes may be rendered unnecessary."

The following are the Headings of the Articles of the Constitution of the General Assembly.*

ARTICLE I.

Name. Jurisdiction. Membership.

Articles of the Constitution.

ARTICLE II.

Meetings and representation.

District Assemblies and local assemblies send one representative for one thousand members to the General Assembly, which meets once a year.

ARTICLE III.

Officers and term of office, and provides for an Executive Board of "five."

ARTICLE V.

Duties of officers.

ARTICLE VI.

Revenue; under this system large sums must be collected.

ARTICLE VII.

No document valid without the seal.

ARTICLE VIII.

Co-operative fund.

ARTICLE IX.

Organizers.

* The text in full of these Articles will be found in a pamphlet which has been forwarded to the House of Commons Library.

Article X.
Isolated members.

Article XI.
Relates to admission of window glass workers.

Article XII.
National trade assemblies.

Article XIII.
Journal of United Labour.

Article XIV.
Secrecy (only when necessary).

Article XV.
Assistance fund.

Article XVI.
Benefit insurance.

Article XVII.
Practical co-operation. Production and distribution.

Article XVIII.
Special appropriations.

Article XIX.
State assemblies.

Article XX.
Repealing laws.

Then follow the Rules of Order of the General Assembly, the constitution for the district assemblies, and the constitution for the local assemblies.

In the preamble to the last it is stated " that the local assembly is not a mere trade union or beneficial society ; it

Local Assembly.

is more and higher. It gathers into one fold all branches of honourable toil. It aims to assist members to better their condition morally, socially, and financially........ While acknowledging that it is sometimes necessary to enjoin an oppressor, yet strikes should be avoided whenever possible. Strikes at best only afford temporary relief, and members should be educated to depend upon thorough organization, co-operation, and political action, and through these the abolishment of the wage system."

Rules. Articles I., II., III., IV., and V. relate to rules, membership, officers.

Article VI. establishes local courts for the trial of grievances, misdemeanours, and violations of the laws of the Order.

Articles VII., VIII., IX., and X. relate to internal organization.

Article XI. relates to discussions for the local assemblies. Subjects, "Labour Question, Child Labour. How can the toiler receive a just share of the wealth he creates?"

The doctrines and proposals of the organization are fully set forth in the preamble of the printed constitution as above given, and of which a copy is annexed to this report.*

Not subversive of social order. They cannot be considered as subversive of social order or opposed to the authority of the law. But at the same time there are three points distinctly stated in the preamble to the constitution for the local assemblies, which it is important to bear in mind in connection with what has recently occurred. These are :—

1. Strikes are admitted to be sometimes necessary.
2. Political action is recommended. And
3. The "abolishment" of the "wage system" is insisted on. Although the members of the Order do not call themselves Socialists, the affinity to Socialism of this manner of treating the labour question is apparent, and may, therefore, ultimately result in an alliance with it, as well as with the subversive doctrines of Communism as propagated in Europe.

Powderly's manifesto. A recent manifesto of the General Master Workman (Powderly) points in this direction. He says: "The men of 1776 broke the power of monarchy and dethroned

* Forwarded to House of Commons Library.

the king. The power which they wrested from the hands of a king was not so great as that which is now held by one man" (Jay Gould), " who through the corrupt use of money has brought manufacturers and workmen to ruin. The power of the king has passed away; the power of wealth is passing away, and it must now be determined whether man shall rule, or whether illegitimate wealth shall rule."

The theory, however, at present propounded by the organization, is only to limit the liberty of any man to acquire all the wealth he can, and to employ it in the way he chooses, but the means by which this restraint is to be put upon the accumulation of wealth are not as yet indicated, further than by a scheme of forced arbitration on questions concerning the share which the workmen may claim for the product of their labour, and which it is pretended they have a right to insist upon. This theory is combated by all employers, on the ground that any such restraint put upon the profits which they are enabled to make from any branch of industry, or from railway transactions, cannot conduce to the general good, as it must necessarily limit the power of production and means of transport, and thereby diminish the material well-being of the whole community. The more moderate party, who are in sympathy with the Knights of Labour, do not object to the legitimate acquisition of wealth, but they contend that, in the case of railway corporations, it has not been legitimately acquired, but by stock jobbery, by stock watering, and other similar devices, and, in the case of manufacturers, by means of a high protective tariff, and the creation thereby of monopolies which rob the mass of the consuming population of a free market. It is wealth dishonestly obtained, say they, that hurts the labouring man as it hurts the whole community. It is the immunity and reward given to dishonesty and fraud on a grand scale which presses heavily on the labouring interests of the country.

Limit of present theories.

On this subject the New York "Times" writes: "The legislation of the United States has for the past generation discriminated directly and powerfully, not in favour of capital, but in favour of certain classes of men possessing considerable amounts of capital, and against small capitalists and working men. This has been the unavoidable effect, and in many cases the intended effect.

New York "Times."

of the high protective tariffs, which have done more to demoralize labour, to render it dependent and uncertain, and to deprive it of the full return due to it, than any other one thing. And this has not only been the case, but this legislation, more than any other on the Statute Books, has been suggested, enacted, controlled, and maintained by the influence of organizations of capitalists who have added to their offence the element of hypocrisy in pretending that they were seeking the interests of labour."

In the above-mentioned manifesto, Mr. Powderly says: "Do not pass resolutions condemning capital, for we are not fighting capital. Do not antagonize the contest we have before us . . . . The battle against the man who represents monopoly must be fought out." An element, however, has been introduced into the organization which he did not anticipate, and which he now finds it difficult to control. It is the importation and partial adoption of the "boycott" system, which has resulted from the Irish immigration, and the influence which it has acquired. He says in a circular to the Order: "If the Order is to perform its mission as intended by its founders, a radical change must be effected. A stop must be called, and the ship brought back to her moorings. It has always been, and is at the present time, my policy to advocate conciliation and arbitration between employers and working men. Thousands of men who had become disgusted with the ruinous policy of the strike, as the only remedy for the ills we complain of, were drawn to us, because we had proclaimed to the world that we had discarded the strike until all else had failed . . . Strikes are often the forerunner of lawless action. One blow brings on another, and, if a single act of ours encourages the anarchist element, we must meet with antagonism. Strikes must be avoided; we must stamp out every effort of the party man to use us for political purposes." Mr. Powderly evidently sees the necessity of restraining the precipitate action of his followers. On this subject the New York "Tribune" writes: "Freedom of labour is the grandest result of the great civil war. But some who have been subjected to oppression all their lives, when they reach a free country where all have equal rights, do not know what to do with their freedom. In politics, they are apt to mistake freedom for license to

Boycotting.

Strikes.

New York "Tribune."

tyrannize over others. In labour, they are apt to employ the unjust, cruel, and brutal methods to which labourers have resorted for their defence in overcrowded lands. To be free, they imagine, embraces the right to domineer over somebody else. So they bring to this country the strike and the boycott, and organizations to deprive other working-men of their bread and means of livlihood, who do not please to subject themselves to rules which associations make. This is not freedom, but slavery of labour. It threatens not only social order, but that very freedom and equality of rights which make this country a refuge for the oppressed . . . Few men of American birth and training are found in the ranks of coercionists and boycotters . . . Organization is welcome in this country, as is every other agency by which the interests of labour may be advanced, so long as it does not assail the freedom of other labourers who are not organized. But, the instant their freedom is assailed, whether by the use of force or terrorism, to support strikes, or by excluding from work men not members of unions, or by the boycott or other foreign methods hostile to American institutions, then suddenly the organization finds itself frowned upon by the vast majority of American citizens . . . . The question for the Knights of Labour is whether that organization has started on the same downward road."

Mr. Powderly's language to his followers, at all events, seems to indicate that great care must be taken in order to prevent it from so doing. His efforts, however, to avert the great strike of railway operatives, which has caused the present complications, as well as his endeavours to have the questions in dispute submitted to arbitration, were unavailing, and, after an unfortunate misunderstanding with the Railway Company, he was forced to acquiesce in the continuance of the strike. The situation thus created is described, as follows, in the "Nation" of New York:—"The strike of the Knights of Labour in the South-West has now reached the point to which it has been plainly running from the start, an armed conflict with the Government of three, perhaps five, States. Great satisfaction is proclaimed by the so-called Executive Committees that they are again united, and that Mr. Powderly's order to return to work has been rescinded. No right-thinking person can feel satisfaction while contemplating public tumult and

"The Nation."

probable bloodshed, but, if there is a widespread conspiracy in the United States against law and order, no time can be considered too early for confronting it. By conspiracy we mean a secret society whose object is to prevent anybody but the conspirators from earning a living, not because they object to any man's earning a living outside the employments they are engaged in, but because they are unable to coerce employers if the unemployed are allowed to work when they see fit to strike. The situation in the South-West has reached this pass, that nobody is allowed to represent labour except those who refuse to work or allow anybody else to work."

Inability of Executive Board to exercise restraint.

It is clear that the organization of the Order of the Knights of Labour leaves the methods of action for which it provides without the control which it was sought to vest in the Executive Board, but which events have shown it is unable to exercise. The language of the above-quoted article, therefore, seems justified in view of the results of the strike which has rendered the position of the Knights of Labour as a law-abiding beneficent association untenable, and that of the Railway Corporations secure in their opposition to the organization. Once committed to the strike, Mr. Powderly, having failed to obtain arbitration, writes to Mr. Gould:—

Powderly to Gould.

"You can settle this strike. The continuance rests with you, and you alone. Every act of violence, every drop of blood that may be shed from this term forth, must be laid at your door." He goes on to say that Mr. Gould has called the Order a conspiracy and a secret menace, and that he is willing to lay everything connected with the Order before the world if he will lay open to the public the methods whereby he has made his fortune, and let the world judge which is the conspiracy.

It is unnecessary to enter into further details of a controversy carried on under such circumstances, and which could have no satisfactory issue. The failure, however, to settle the dispute by arbitration created a situation fraught with danger to social order, and which therefore induced Congress to take action in the matter, with the view of mediation. Accordingly a Bill, copy of which is annexed (Appendix I.), was introduced into and passed by the House of Representatives to this end, and a Committee was also appointed to investigate the nature of the strike and labour movement which accom-

Committee of Inquiry into strike.

panied it. The Committee immediately commenced its task, and the following is a summary of the evidence given by the most important witnesses:—

Mr. W. O. McDowell (Knight of Labour), *sworn*. McDowell's evidence.

Q. State what are the objects of the organization of the Knights of Labour?—*A.* To elevate the members by helping them to educate themselves, by helping them to save that which the average workman has wasted through bad habits, and to lift him from the condition into which he has fallen through such habits, and make him hereafter an employer instead of an employé.

The witness here made a detailed statement of the attempt to arbitrate between the Knights of Labour and the railways interested.

Q. What was the original cause of this strike?—*A.* Causes of strike. The difference between the principle of payment by day-work and by piece-work. The general cause of this strike and of the recent ones all over the country had been the successful strike on the horse-car lines in New York last February. An additional reason was the universal system of watering railway stock, which made it necessary for railway managers to screw down the rates of labour as much as possible.

Q. What remedy could you suggest?—*A.* The remedy Remedy. was to enforce the law. The law of every State required that dollar for dollar should be paid for railway stock, but that provision of the law was evaded by railroad managers forming themselves into a Crédit Mobilier or Construction Company, and issuing to themselves $100 of stock for every $1 or $10 of work.

Q. Is not the great evil in all this the fact that railroad stock is watered?—*A.* That is the evil, and there is great irritation about it all over the country.

Q. Does not trouble arise partly from competition of labourers?—*A.* No. The great difficulty has not been a demand for increase of wages.

Mr. Powderly, *sworn*.

Q. State the origin of the organization of the Powderly's evidence. Knights of Labour?—*A.* It emanated from the garment-cutters of Philadelphia, which was disbanded to give place to the new organization which was perfected in 1869. No man was to know anything about it. It was to be a secret in all its workings. The man who joined it was not permitted to mention the name of the association outside the meeting-room, nor was it spoken inside. The idea was to bring in every department of productive industry.

Q. It is a benevolent society for the protection of all people who toil, and is entirely within the law?—*A.* Yes.

Q. What is the number of its present membership?—*A.* Our present number does not exceed 500,000.

Q. Are women admitted?—*A.* Yes, on an equal footing with men.

Q. Do you make any difference as to the admission of coloured men?—*A.* There is no distinction in regard to colour, creed, sex, or condition.

MR. McDOWELL, *recalled.*

Q. There is nothing that you know of in the organization inconsistent with obedience to law and with the administration of Government?—*A.* Nothing whatever. On the other hand, it is a perfect supporter of the law in every particular.

MR. FRED TURNER (of the Executive Board), *sworn.*

Turner's evidence.

Witness stated, in reply to questions, that the Knights of Labour had no political object, and did not seek to influence legislation. That the treatment of them by the railway managers had been very discourteous, and that they had refused to recognise or treat with the organization, although they were willing to do so with them as simple citizens.

Q. Can the central power of your organization order men to work or order them to quit work?—*A.* The general laws do not contemplate strikes.

Powers in relation to strikes.

Q. Have you power to order a strike?—*A.* Yes. There is no law in our constitution governing strikes. We do not believe in strikes.

Q. Then where do you derive your power to order strikes?—*A.* We have no power directly to order a strike, but we have the power to approve or disapprove a strike.

Q. Was this strike approved or disapproved?—*A.* We never knew anything about it; it has never been approved.

Q. Is the power vested in you to direct men to return to work?—*A.* Yes.

Q. Who ordered the strike?—*A.* District Assembly No. 101.

Q. When a strike is ordered, what is the first action taken by the Executive Board?—*A.* It takes no action in the matter unless appealed to.

Q. And do you then seek to investigate the right or wrong of the matter?—*A.* Yes.

Q. Do you also seek to have the differences compared?—*A.* Yes.

Q. If you do not succeed, what is the next step?—*A.* If we approve it, we have to lend it a hand financially.

Q. Do you ever direct financial assistance to a strike without first investigating it?—*A.* No.

Mr. Jay Gould, *sworn*, said that the roads which he controlled were actually doing more work now than they did last year at the same period, and that, therefore, he presumed that they did not come under the rule of the Committee. Upon being informed that the Committee proposed to examine him with regard to antecedent proceedings, Mr. Gould proceeded to explain the position in which he stood in regard to the Knights of Labour, and the nature of the strike from his point of view. {Jay Gould's evidence.}

"We had," he said, "at the date of the strike, 14,315 operators. The Knights of Labour—the strikers—numbered 3,717, but they were not the men who were necessary to work the roads. We should not have missed them. But when they left our employment, what did they do? They exercised more than the right of eminent domain. They took forcible possession of St. Louis, Sedalia, Atchison, Kansas City, Parsons, Fort Worth, Little Rock, and Texas Kana, and said, 'no man shall run a train over that road.' What was to be done? we had no earnings. Payments were therefore suspended, and thus 10,000 men who were loyal to the Company, who could run our trains every day, were deprived of their work and of their power to earn their wages. That was what followed the strike, the seizure, you can call it by no other word, forcible seizure, something that the Czar of Russia would hesitate to do with his millions of soldiers behind him." On the subject of arbitration, he said that he had consented to meet Mr. Powderly and discuss with him the matter as individuals. He was induced to do so because he could not reconcile the moderate sentiments expressed by Mr. Powderly with the acts of the Association. The Company, he said, had been willing to discuss arbitration, but not on the terms proposed by the organization. In consequence of what passed at the interview with Mr. Powderly, the Knights thought their end was gained and counselled moderation. When, however, the negotiations failed, they issued an address to the workingmen of the world, which said: "There stands before us a giant of corporate wealth, impersonated in the great fiend—the enemy—Gould the Giant Fiend. He dances as he climbs over the ruins of our houses and the blight of our lives. Monster Fiend Gould must be overthrown. We must not rest until this giant is dead at our feet."

This, said Mr. Gould, is the response which three assemblages of the Knights of Labour made to our continuing the hand of fellowship which we had held out to them.

Mr. Gould was then asked:—

Q. Have you considered the question as to whether there is any mode by which the whole working force of a railroad can be put under the control of the people?— *A.* Yes. The laws do that now. On roads operated by receivers strikes are rapidly overcome, because there is respect for the United States Courts. The public has a right to have railways operated. Any law which defines that right and couples with it provisions for arbitration would be a practical solution of the question.

Q. Why were not your views, which are friendly to arbitration, carried out at St. Louis?—*A.* We have always been ready to arbitrate any grievances between the Company and its operators, but the interpretation which Mr. Powderly put upon this disposition was that the Knights of Labour were to step in and oversee this arbitration. We did not propose to deal with the Knights of Labour as an organization. I stated this distinctly to Mr. Powderly at our interview.

Mr. Gould was then asked to explain the ways of Construction Companies in issuing stock to themselves out of proportion to the work done, but he denied any knowledge of such dark and questionable transactions.

Hopkins's evidence. Mr. HOPKINS, the Vice-President of the Missouri Pacific, was then sworn and examined. He corroborated generally Mr. Gould's evidence. He had always believed in arbitration as a means of settlement, and he saw no objection even to compulsory arbitration, provided it was made compulsory on both sides. But he said such arbitration would have to be between operators themselves (actually at work) and the Company. That was the point in the whole matter.

The Committee has now adjourned, and will resume the investigation at St. Louis and other places which were the scenes of the late disturbances.

From the above evidence it would appear—

1. That the methods supplied by the organization of the Knights of Labour were employed for the purpose of bringing about the strike.

2. That the strike was not contemplated or approved by Mr. Powderly.

3. That Mr. Powderly endeavoured to arbitrate, but upon terms which were deemed inadmissible.

4. That the continuance of the strike and illegal acts committed place the railway companies in the right. But the investigation, as far as it has hitherto gone, only establishes the fact of the existence of an organized labour association, which has power to work either for good or for evil, and it does not seem to have elicited the causes which have brought it into being. During the debate, however, on the Labour Bill, it was boldly asserted in the House of Representatives that the very fact that the United States was one great military camp of opposing forces, of organised capital and organised labour; the very fact of oft repeated uprisings of the people in warlike protest against corporate greed and rapacity; the very fact that these corporations and their stockholders have grown enormously rich, and the working people wretchedly poor, show that there is something radically wrong in the economical system, which must therefore be changed before the industrial problem can be solved. In thirty years, from 1850 to 1880, the net product of manufactures increased 400 per cent., while during the same period the average annual wages increased only 40 per cent. This was generally the language of those who opposed the Bill, as being inadequate to meet the evil which, it is asserted, permeates the whole industrial system, and which mere arbitration cannot cure.

Summary of evidence.

UNITED STATES.

President's Message. The importance of the questions which have arisen out of the recent disturbances has been recognised by the President in a Message to Congress, copy of which will be found in Appendix No. II., in which he recommends the creation of a Commission of Labour to be ingrafted upon the Bureau of Labour, already constituted by the Act of 1884, and which, under federal authority, shall be charged with the consideration and settlement, when possible, of all controversies between labour and capital. It will be observed that the President attributes the discontent of the employed to the "grasping and heedless exactions of employers, and the alleged discrimination in favour of capital as an object of governmental attention."

Views of Jeff Davis. Coincident with the President's Message there has appeared a letter from Mr. Jefferson Davis, giving his views on the same subject. He says:—"Self-interest and free competition for labour will, wherever labourers are abundant, give to the rich the power to oppress the poor. We cannot legislate to destroy the motive of self-interest, for that lies at the foundation of progress, and our efforts must therefore be directed to unifying the interest and labour and capital as far as this may be done by the Legislature of the State."

He is in favour of a Court of Arbitration, whose decisions, he says, "should be based on something like a co-operative principle of industrial partnership, in which the wages of the workmen should be measured by the profits of the corporation."

"Evening Post" on President's Message. With regard to the President's Message, the New York "Evening Post" says:—"The vagueness of the President's message on the labour question is greatly to be regretted. He does not explain in what consists the grasping and heedless exactions of employers, to which he says the discontent of the employed is due, nor where we are to look for the alleged discrimination in favour of capital as an object of governmental attention. This is all the more unfortunate because the vagueness of statement on the labour side is already the curse of the labour controversy." The great mass of capital which has grown up under the tariff, which is upheld as in the interest of the workmen, has been used for political purposes. "It has ended by almost transforming American society. It has drawn into the country a vast mass of labourers of a very low order of intelligence to be employed in the huge enterprises, corporate or other, owing their growth to Congressional legislation." The rate of wages was said to depend on the success, in the last Presidential election, of the political party to which the capitalists belonged, and that, in event of defeat, wages would go down to 35 cents a day. "In the labour troubles, by which the industry of the country and its politics are so much disturbed to day, we are witnessing the result of this stupendous experiment. We have the country swarming with labourers of foreign birth, brought over here with the wildest notions about the comfort which awaited them, and now bitterly disappointed and ready to wreak vengeance on the employers. These new-comers have found out that our industrial system has been built up on politics, and they have heard from their employers that wages are raised and lowered on election day, and they now hear from politicians that the greedy capitalists have pocketed during the past twenty years, by means of steady importation of labour, the superb profits of the war tariff, and ought to be made to disgorge."

A general idea of the nature of the disturbance in the labour market, which culminated in the strike on the Western Lines of Railway, may be formed from the foregoing statements. It will be observed that the alleged grievances of labour are very vaguely stated, and that it is the unfair position of labour with regard to capital which is mainly insisted on as justifying a movement in favour of an equalization of profits, and of a limitation being put upon the accumulation of wealth by manufacturers and railway corporations. Herein seems to consist the great grievance of the labour party, and for which it seeks legislative redress in measures which, however, are deemed inconsistent with freedom of contract and free labour. It is a movement, in fact, to coerce employers and force them to recognize the power of organized labour to dictate terms. It is asserted that the unequal distribution of wealth is becoming greater every day, and that, while the rich are growing richer, the poor are growing poorer. Although it is admitted that capital ought not to be antagonistic to labour, the advantages which it enjoys give it a power of oppression which, under existing circumstances, renders it

[704]

Labour grievances.

374 UNITED STATES.

so, and therefore justifies labour in endeavouring to restrain its operations. The grievances, therefore, of the working men, which in some instances are real, are made use of by those who hold these doctrines for the furtherance of other objects than the increase of wages and settlement of disputes with employers; and, as has been seen by the result of the strike, the labouring man has been the victim of designing persons by trusting too much to the means for the bettering of his social and moral condition so plausibly proposed in the constitution of the labour union of which he had been induced to become a member.

Press animus. The animus of the Press in the present labour dispute is clearly indicated in the articles which have been quoted, and may be taken as a protest against strikes and boycotts as remedies for evils which have grown up under the fiscal system imposed upon the country since the Civil War, and which it is asserted can only be changed by the requirements of the mass of the consuming population bearing irresistibly on the Legislature.

The special information which has been called for in this Report relates to—

1. The hours of labour on railways and in such other employments as have recently been the theatre of strikes.

2. The movement for shortening the hours of labour.

3. The principles generally applied to State legislation regarding labour.

4. The particular grievances alleged by the employers to exist.

5. The action of Trades Unions.

6. The criminal law relating to trade combinations, and its enforcement by the Courts.

7. The action of the Federal Government in the suppression of disorders.

8. The tendency to invoke Federal legislation in order to deal with strikes and disturbances.

The scope of the information required under the foregoing heads is such as to render it impossible to compile it for each State of the Union within a reasonable time, and the States of Massachusetts, New York, Pennsylvania, and Maryland are therefore taken as typical in their character and circumstances in relation to them.

UNITED STATES.

1. The chief of the Maryland Bureau of Labour in his last report gives the following information respecting the hours of labour and wages of railroad mechanics procured from the men on the Baltimore-Ohio line :—

The hours of labour on railways and in such other employments as have recently been the theatre of strikes.

Ten hours constitutes the usual working day, but the railway shops have, as a rule, been working eight and nine hours, and wages have been reduced proportionately.

Lumber Yard.—Hands employed in loading and unloading lumber. Ten hours, $1·10 per day.

Saw Mill.—Hands are paid $1·50 to $1·80 per day for 10 hours.

Carpenters' Shop.—Hands engaged on repair work receive $1·50. Hands on new work, $2 per day for 10 hours; helpers, $1·10.

Passenger Car Shops.—Hands engaged on repair from $1·80 to $2 per day for 10 hours.

Tin Shop.—Hands employed in roofing cars and buildings, $1·70 to $2 per day. Ten hours.

Yard.—Loading and unloading coke, coal, iron, &c. Hands receive $1·10 per day, 10 hours. Overtime paid proportionately.

Paint Shop.—Hands receive from $1·50 to $1·75. Ornamental painters $2 per day, 10 hours.

Wheel and Iron Foundry.—Wheel moulders are paid by the piece, 25 cents per wheel for all perfect work cast. During 1883–84 hands made as much as $3·50 and $4 per day. During the last year the average was $2 per day, 10 hours.

Brass Moulders.—Hands receive $1·75 to $2 per day, 10 hours.

Axle Shop.—Hands are paid by the piece. During 1885 average earnings were $1·40, in busy seasons $2 per day.

Blacksmiths' Shops.—Hands receive from $1·75 to $2·25 per day.

Machinery Department.—Machinists receive $1·60 to $2 per day, 10 hours.

Boiler Shop.—Hands receive from $2·25 to $2·50 per day. The report states that much distress was experienced by the workmen in 1885, resulting from a reduction in the hours of labour and a corresponding reduction in the pay from $1·10 per day to 99 and 85 cents.

A peculiarity with workmen in railway shops is the effect of constant employment in one line. A railroad

[704]

hand will be laid off for weeks together and seldom seek any other work. He seems indeed incapacitated for outside work. The Chief of the Bureau says that he has noticed men to hang about the shops for days together, waiting for a resumption, or continue to work on short time at greatly reduced wages, without making any effort to find occupation in other directions; and he remarks, "Herein lies one of the causes of the condition of labour to-day, and will prove the source of trouble in the near future.

"Individual independence among mechanics is practically extinct, and all legislation, to be effective, must be based on a recognition of the fact that great bodies of labour are to-day dependent absolutely on large corporations for their very existence."

The hands employed in the construction of railroads are nearly all Italians. Under the contract system they seldom receive more than $1 per day, and are subject to deductions for rent and medical attendance.

The mechanics and labour employed in the shops are largely of Irish nationality.

The movement for shortening the hours of labour.

"The leaders of the movement, in order to rally their discouraged followers, had recourse to the cry for a law limiting the day's work to eight hours, which has now been raised amongst all trades unions in the country. Upon this subject Mr. Atkinson has an article in the last number of "Bradstreet's." He shows that in each thousand workers in the United States only one hundred are engaged in occupations upon which an eight-hour law could be enforced, and that consequently the passage of such a law would simply operate to depress the trades upon which it could be enforced relatively to all other trades. In the first place, he says agricultural labour, cattle and sheep growing, horticulture and fishing, could not be subjected to an eight-hour law; and if they could, it would ruin them. Blast furnaces, gas works, bakeries, restaurants, and all other employments requiring continuous heat, could not be subjected to the eight-hour rule without instant destruction. Paper mills require continuous operation. So do railways. There are then the great multitude of employments that the officers of the law can never reach or know anything about, the people who work at home, such as seamstresses, washerwomen, carpenters, blacksmiths; in short, everybody who is his own employer. The only trades that could be reached are those where large numbers of workers are collected together for the purpose of attending machinery, such as cotton and woollen mills, rolling mills, boot and shoe factories, and the like. These number not more than one in ten of the people in the United States who work with their hands. If the advocates of an eight-hour law should get it passed, the first efforts of the men who had promoted it would be to find out how to work overtime to the best advantage in order to gain a better subsistence. "The logical result," he says, "of all such acts by which the free conduct of adults is restricted in certain specific cases is to limit the full use and benefit of labour-saving machinery, and thus to lengthen the necessary hours of work of the great mass of the people."

Section 3,738 of the Revised Statutes of the United States provides as follows:—

"Eight hours shall constitute a day's work for all labourers, workmen, and mechanics who may be employed by or on behalf of the Government of the United States."

In the State of New York there is an Act making eight hours a legal day's work, but it only applies to those employed by the State or any Municipal Corporation.*

In the State of Pennsylvania there is an Act (1868) enacting that eight hours, between the rising of the sun and the setting of the sun, shall be a legal day's labour.†

In the State of Maryland there is also legislation affecting the hours of labour as well as employers and working men.‡

The "eight-hour" movement appears to have been coincident with the enormous development of productive machinery, and consequent displacement of manual labour. Since 1870 the whole power of mechanism has doubled, having risen from 2,300,000 horse-power to 4,500,000. But it will be found that the operatives most active in the agitation in favour of it are those employed in trades least affected by machinery. The outcome of the present agitation cannot be predicted. Many political economists are in favour of the eight-hour law, while others, as Mr. Ed. Atkinson, endeavours to show its inutility.

* See Consul-General Booker's Report annexed.
† See Consul Clipperton's Report annexed.
‡ See Consul Donohoe's Report.

UNITED STATES.

Among the former a new theory of the effect of shortening the hours of labour has been propounded. Estimating the number of wage labourers at 9,472,159, and taking 11 hours to be the average length of the working day, a reduction of 3 hours' labour would have the effect of withdrawing from the market the product of 28,416,477 hours' labour a day, without discharging a single labourer. The commercial vacuum thus produced would, in its effect upon labour and business, be equal to increasing the present demand over one-fourth; that is to say, without increasing the home or foreign market, but simply to supply the present nominal consumption, it would create employment for 3,500,000 labourers.

Principles generally applied to State Legislation regarding labour.

The State legislation regarding labour in New York, Pennsylvania, and Maryland has already been alluded to, and will be found in the Consular Reports.

The Act in the State of New York, providing for liens of mechanics, labourers, and others who perform labour for buildings and other improvements, is perhaps the most notable feature of State legislation.*

The labour laws of the State of Massachusetts,† which, together with a digest and a synopsis of labour legislation in the United States, are framed in the interest of labour.

The grievances alleged to exist.

Neither labourers nor mechanics have, generally speaking, any just cause of complaint against the employer. "There never was a time in the history of this country," says Mr. Ed. Atkinson, "when the general rate of wages was as high as it is now, the general product so large, the cost of living so low, and the proportionate profit of capital so small. The average wages to-day are $285 to $290 a year for $10\frac{1}{2}$ hours per day, as against $175 to $180 in 1840 for 13 to 14 hours." The labour movement has been taken advantage of by those interested in the spread of socialism, and who are in close connection with it in Europe to propagate their doctrines. The improvement of the social and moral condition of the labourer, which is the avowed object of Labour Unions, conceals dangerous designs, to which the mass of those who are induced to join them become unconscious victims. Once committed to strikes, they are

---

* See Mr. Booker's Report.

† These laws have been forwarded to the Library of the House of Commons.

compelled by necessity to follow them up, and soon find themselves in the meshes of their leaders, from whom they dare not escape. There are doubtless honest and well-meaning men among them, as Mr. Powderly, and others, men who desire to see harmony instead of antagonism established between labour and capital, but recent events have demonstrated their inability to direct the movement to this end, or to control designs clearly directed against capital. The foreign populations, who are strongly imbued with revolutionary ideas, form a most dangerous element in all the labour unions, for, not content with the impunity and liberty which is accorded to them, they seek to attack the institutions of their adopted country under the cloak of social improvement for the masses by an organized system of political agitation. It is not, however, so much against the great capitalists, as against the "Bosses" or employers of labour, that the wrath of the labour party is now directed, and to whom, it is to be presumed, the President alluded in his message. The "strikes" on the Western lines, which involved a loss to the country of millions of dollars, had clearly for object to force the recognition of the organization of the Knights of Labour on the Railway Companies as a body to be consulted on all operating matters. The petty grievances concerning piece-work and day-work were soon lost sight of in the excitement of the war which was to be declared against capital, but public opinion emphatically condemned proceedings which caused the suspension of ordinary business and actual bloodshed.

The action of the Trades Unions does not differ much from that of other organizations with which they are more or less affiliated and work in common. The Central Labour Union of New York, composed of 160 organizations, representing 150 members, is cosmopolitan, and therefore more socialistic; and Socialists, Communists, Anarchists, of all shades are to be found in it. It proclaims that, the soil being the inheritance of all the people, everyone should have free access to it, without tribute to landlords and monopolists; that, as by labour all wealth is produced, the labourer is entitled to a full share; that when the wealth-producers live in poverty, and the idlers in luxury, it is very evident that the social and industrial system which permits such conditions

The action of Trades Unions.

must be wrong and immoral, and requires a thorough change; that certain persons have been given the legal sanction to wring from the workers all the benefits secured by labour organizations by high rents, costly transportation, gigantic corners in grain and provisions, and by monopolizing the issue of money. The Union does not believe in strikes, excepting as a last resort, and the older Unions associated with it very rarely have a strike. It is stated that the Union raised, during the first year of its existence, $60,000 for the relief of strikers; that thousands of dollars have since passed through its treasury annually for the benefit of the workers in New York. The action of such an organization, which includes Trades Unions, has other objects in view than the mere adjustment of the wage system, which is only made a pretext for the prosecution of them.

<small>The Criminal Law relating to Trade Combinations and its enforcement by the Courts.</small>

The Penal Code of New York declares that the orderly and peaceable assembling " or co-operation of persons employed in any calling, trade, or handicraft, for the purpose of obtaining an advance of wages or compensation, or of maintaining such rate, is not a conspiracy." A peaceable orderly strike is therefore not unlawful, nor is an organization of workmen who unite in a strike unlawful.

Section 168, however, of the Penal Code provides " that if two or more persons conspire to prevent another from exercising a lawful trade or calling, or doing any other lawful act, by force, threats, or intimidation, or by interfering or threatening to interfere with tools, implements, or property belonging to or used by another, or with the use or employment thereof, or to commit any act injurious to trade or commerce, or for the perversion or obstruction of justice, each of them is guilty of a misdemeanour;" and Section 653 declares that " a person who, with a view to compel another person to do, or abstain from doing, an act which such other person has a legal right to do or to abstain from doing, wrongfully or unlawfully uses, or attempts the intimidation of such person by threats or force, is guilty of a misdemeanour."

Under these provisions boycotters and strikers have lately been arrested, but whether they can be punished under both or either is a question which has not yet been decided by the Courts.

The Pennsylvania Act, 1872, declares it to be lawful for any labourer or labourers, acting as individuals or as members of any club, society, or association, to refuse to work or labour for any person or persons whenever, in his, her, or their opinion, the wages paid are insufficient. . . . . "Provided that nothing herein contained shall prevent the prosecution and punishment under existing laws of any person or persons who shall in any way hinder persons who desire to labour for their employers from so doing, or other persons from being employed as labourers."

The law of the State of Michigan provides :—

Section 2.—"If two or more persons shall wilfully and maliciously combine or conspire together to obstruct and impede by any act or by means of intimidation the regular operation and conduct of the business of any railroad company or any other corporation, firm, or individual, or to impede, hinder, or obstruct, except by due process of law, the regular running of any locomotive, engine, freight, or passenger train on any railroad, or the labour and business of any such firm, corporation, or individual, such persons shall on conviction thereof be punished by imprisonment in the county jail not more than 3 months or in the State prison not exceeding one year."

The statutes of the States of Illinois and Missouri are in the same sense.

The "Boycott," therefore, which, as aforesaid, has lately been imported from Europe, would seem to be punishable under these acts as conspiracy.

The Federal Government takes no action in the suppression of disorders in any particular State, unless called upon by the State Authorities to assist them in so doing. *The action of the Federal Government in the suppression of disorders.*

The tendency to invoke federal legislation in order to deal with strikes is shown by the passage of the Arbitration Bill, the appointment of a Committee of Investigation, and the general tone of the President's message to Congress. It was urged in the House of Representatives during the debate upon the labour question that the legislative interference of Congress in matters relating to labour disputes would be unconstitutional, as the State legislature was alone competent to deal with them. On the other hand, it was agreed that, if Congress has the constitutional power to regulate inter-State commerce, it certainly has the power to enquire into the *The tendency to invoke Federal legislation in order to deal with strikes and disturbances.*

causes of its partial or total interruption, more especially as it is a matter which concerns governmental roads, railroads to which Government has given land and money, and where the Government has an interest in seeing peace and order prevail, instead of discontent and disorder. Moreover, if the working men are wronged, it is the duty of Congress to see that they are righted. Although there was clearly an expression of opinion in favour of the legislation proposed, it was generally considered inadequate to meet the situation. If, it was said, questions of supply and demand will not regulate themselves, if labour is weak and unable to compete against the power of money, if the money power has acquired a hold upon the legislation of the country which it requires the masses of the people by their votes to break, then Congress must step in and legislate effectively. But it was not stated what legislative measures could regulate supply and demand, enable labour to compete against the power of money, and abolish the hold which the money power has acquired in the Legislature, nor were the causes which called for such legislation admitted. The principle of voluntary arbitration, therefore, has been recognised and adopted by Congress, and a second Bill has been introduced into the House of Representatives, which will be found in Appendix III., in consequence of the President's suggestions "to establish a Department of Labour, and to create a Board for the arbitration of controversies between labour and capital." It will be seen that Section 4 provides that "in all controversies or disturbances which may interfere with transit and commerce between the States it shall be the duty of the Commission of Labour to act as a Board of Arbitration for the peaceful settlement of such controversies whenever the conciliatory offices of said Commission may be invoked by the parties thereto," and that there is therefore no compulsory clause to enforce arbitration. But at the same time Congress has thus admitted the demand of the labour party for Federal Legislation, which may lead to important consequences.

Bill for establishing Department of Labour.

The following is a summary of the Report of the Special Agent and Expert of the Census Bureau upon strikes and lockouts occurring within the United States during the calendar year 1880 :—

UNITED STATES. 383

The total number of separate strikes was 765, the largest number, 304, occurring in the State of Pennsylvania, New York 104, and Ohio 93.

The number of strikes in certain of the prominent trades is as follows:—

Iron and Steel Industries	236
Coal Mining	158
Textile Trades	46
Cigar Making	43
Building Trades	36
Transportation	36
Printing Trades	28
Glass Industries	27
Piano Making	14
Boot Trade	11

Strikes in 1880.

The total number of causes reported for the 765 strikes was 813. This greater number of causes is due to the fact that some strikes involved more than one question or cause. Much the greater proportion ($7\frac{1}{2}$ per cent.) of strikes were caused by differences as to the rates of wages. A total of 503, or about 86 per cent. of those relating to rates of wages, or 2 per cent. of all, were for an advance, and 77, or 14 per cent. of those relating to rates of wages, or $9\frac{1}{2}$ per cent. of all, were against a reduction. Strikes growing out of demands for an advance are much more uniformly successful than those against a reduction. In conditions of trade that justify an advance it is much more to the interest of the employer to give in than to have his works stopped. Workmen as a rule do not make their demands for an advance on a rising market much before they are warranted, and it may also be said that in many cases they refuse to accept a reduction when the circumstances of trade fully justify the employer in asking it. Of the total number of strikes 35 per cent. were successful, 18 per cent. were compromised, and 47 per cent. were unsuccessful. Strikes for advance of wages were the most successful. From 414 of the 765 strikes, reports were received, showing the number of men idle in those cases to have been 128,262, making an average of about 310 men to each strike. As to wages lost, it appears that 64,779 workmen lost $3,711,197. This would be at the rate of $57 each. As the entire number of workmen

Causes.

Results.

estimated was 228,138, the total loss of wages on this average would be $13,003,866—that is, for the time lost the wages which would have been received, had the works run constantly, is the amount named.

<small>Prime movers in strikes.</small>

The Commissioner states that the testimony taken from the employés shows that only in very rare instances are strikes favoured or encouraged by the working men of the State. The official leaders of Trades Unions prefer to see the difficulties of labour settled in some less destructive way, and they admit that many strikes are ill-advised. The older organizations rarely enter upon a strike until after giving the subject mature consideration and weighing the chances of success or failure, but those which are just beginning to try the power of union are anxious " to receive the baptism of fire," and enter upon strikes upon the slightest provocation. Yet, says the Commissioner, strikes may be considered on the decrease, or rather every attempt is made to prevent them. Union men, in fact, dread a strike as much as the employer does. The richer the Union, the less chance of a strike, and therefore he says that the establishment of strike funds will serve to discourage strikes, and that the experience of the English unions sustains this opinion. The legislation of Trades Unions, he adds, which there is every reason to believe will be a thing of the near future, will give ample protection against the misappropriation of these funds

A Bill, in fact, has already been introduced into the House of Representatives for this purpose, a copy of which will be found in Appendix IV. The last annual report of the New York Bureau of Statistics of Labour gives official information as to 222 strikes which occurred in the States during the year ending November 1st, 1885. Of these strikes 97 were successful, 34 failed, 32 were compromised, and 59 were still pending. The number of persons engaged in them was 26,866, and they involved an expenditure of $206,159, a sum which does not include the heavy loss in wages to the strikers or the great loss borne by the employers. It is indeed almost impossible to estimate the loss to the country in general involved in the labour troubles, or the amount of injury which local trade has suffered by the partial suspension of business consequent thereon. In this connection the "eight-hour" movement previously mentioned is especially responsible, for it discourages enterprise on the part of the employers of labour in different trades, and produces a stagnation of business detrimental to all local interests. Some employers have conceded, others have resisted. The question, therefore, seems to be this. Are there certain special branches of industry so favourably situated and having such advantages over other trades that they can sustain themselves (for this is what it amounts to) on 20 per cent. less labour than is now applied to them? If there are such trades, the "eight-hour" movement will succeed as to them, but there will be, nevertheless, a struggle between employers and workmen in these special branches of industry. It is an experiment as to whether any particular trade can be carried on with the proceeds of eight hours' labour. Bradstreet's collection of statistics of the eight-hour movement shows that the total number of workmen engaged in it in all parts of the country is 325,000. The demand for shorter hours has been conceded to 150,000 without a strike, and to 35,000 after striking, leaving 140,000 still on strike or defeated. The trades in which the movement has been most successful are those connected with house building, agricultural implement makers, furniture makers, and machinery building. Inconvenience may be experienced in many industries, but the daily work will more or less be carried on as before, for indeed it would seem that only a moiety of the trades susceptible of being affected by an "eight-hour" rule are at present menaced by the movement.

But while the experiment lasts there will be a general depression in industrial business, and a consequent loss of earnings on both sides, which, as aforesaid, cannot be estimated. In a circular lately issued by Mr. Powderly to the organization he makes no mention, however, of the "eight-hour" movement, but confines himself to re-iterating the principles upon which it is founded, and from which, he says, it has lately unfortunately departed. *More of Powderly's sentiments.*

"We have been losing ground, so far as public opinion is concerned, for some time. We have allowed things to be done under the name of the Knights of Labour for which the organization was in no way responsible."

He inveighs against strikes and boycotts, and urges the assemblies to repudiate them. With regard to capital, he says:—

"Men who own capital are not our enemies. If that theory held good, the workman of to-day would be the enemy of his fellow toiler on the morrow, for, after all, it is how to acquire capital, and how to use it properly, that we are endeavouring to learn. No, the man of capital is not necessarily the enemy of labour; on the contrary, they must be brought closer together."

A copy of this circular will be found in Appendix V.

The object now in view is to perfect the organization and harmonise it with the trades unions in such a manner as to secure united action, and to establish a control over the dangerous elements which recent events show to exist in its composition.

L. S. SACKVILLE WEST.

Washington, 20th May, 1886.

Summary.

1. The organization of the order of the "Knights of Labour" is a powerful factor in the present industrial situation.

2. The professed aims and objects are not revolutonary, but tending to socialism in its milder form.

3. The alleged grievances which it seeks to redress are attributed to the fiscal system which has obtained since the Civil War.

4. Recent events prove the leaders unable to restrain the action of their followers in endeavouring to obtain their ends by violent and illegal means, against which both public opinion and the Press are strongly pronounced.

5. The advantage in the controversy between the organization and the Railway Companies is with the latter.

6. The labour troubles give rise to legislation in Congress on the subject of arbitration and investigation.

7. The examination of the parties to the controversy before a Committee of the House of Representatives not at present satisfactory as regards the application of practical remedies.

8. Both in Congress and by the President "corporate greed and rapacity" and the "grasping and heedless

exactions of employers" require investigation and remedy. The principle of voluntary arbitration under federal control admitted.

9. The credulity of the associations in the objects to be attained taken advantage of by those who have other designs, of a political nature, to further. Special information will be found under the following heads:—

>Hours of labour.
>Movement for shortening hours of labour.
>Particular grievances.
>Action of Trades Unions.
>Criminal Law.
>Action of Federal Government.
>Federal Legislation.

Inclosure 2 in No. 7.

Digest of the Labour Laws of Massachusetts.*

Chapter 48. Employment of children.
Section 1. Child under ten years not to be employed in manufactories.
Penalties.
Chapter 74. Employment of Labour.
Section 1. Persons employed in factories to receive forfeiture if discharged without notice.
Section 2. Penalty for intimidating labourers.
Section 3. Employers of labour not to contract for exemption from liability for injuries.
Section 4. Minors under 18 and women not to be employed in manufacturing establishments more than 10 hours a day, except, &c.
Chapter 103. District and Police Officers.
Chapter 104. Inspection of buildings.
Chapter 106. Formation of Co-operative Corporations.
Chapter 112, Section 143. Action against owner for labour and materials.
Section 145. Statement of amount of debt for labour.
Chapter 183. Trustee Process.
Chapter 191. Liens on buildings and land.

* See Note, p. 378.

Section 1. Certain mechanics and others to have liens on buildings and land for amount due them for labour and materials.

Chapter 16. Security against mechanics' liens on public buildings.

Chapter 157. Payment of wages in cases of insolvency.

Chapter 106. Liability of members or stockholders in Corporations for wages.

Chapter 86. Importation of Labourers.

Chapter 243. An Act fixing the responsibility of Railway Corporations for negligently causing the death of employees.

Act 1886. To provide for weekly payment of wages by Corporations.

It will be observed that the labour laws of Massachusetts are very elaborate, and framed in the interest of the labourer and mechanic.

APPENDICES.

Appendix I.

49TH CONGRESS.   1ST SESSION.   [Calendar No. 553.
H. R. 7479.

IN THE SENATE OF THE UNITED STATES.

April 5, 1886.—Read twice and referred to the Committee on Education and Labour.

April 6, 1886.—Reported by Mr. Blair without Amendment.

An Act to provide a method for settling controversies and differences between railroad corporations engaged in inter-State and Territorial transportation of property or passengers and their employees.

Be it enacted by the Senate and House of Representatives of the United States of America in Congress assembled, That whenever differences or controversies arise between railroad companies engaged in the transportation of property or passengers between two or more States of the United States, between a Territory and State, within the Territories of the United States, or within the District of Columbia, and the employees of said railroad companies, which differences or controversies may hinder, impede, obstruct, interrupt, or affect such transportation of property or passengers, if, upon the written proposition of either party to the controversy to submit their differences to arbitration, the other party shall accept the proposition, then and in such event the railroad company is hereby authorized to select and appoint one person, and such employee or employees, as the case may be, to select and appoint another person, and the two persons thus selected and appointed to select a third person, all three of whom shall be citizens of the United States, and

[704]

wholly impartial and disinterested in respect to such differences or controversies; and the three persons thus selected and appointed shall be, and they are hereby, created and constituted a board of arbitration, with the duties, powers, and privileges hereinafter set forth.

Sec. 2. That the board of arbitration provided for in the first section of this Act shall possess all the powers and authority in respect to administering oaths, subpœnaing witnesses and compelling their attendance, preserving order during the sittings of the board, and requiring the production of papers and writings relating alone to the subject under investigation now possessed and belonging to United States Commissioners appointed by the Circuit Court of the United States; but in no case shall any witness be compelled to disclose the secrets or produce the records or proceedings of any labour organization of which he may be an officer or member; and said board of arbitration may appoint a clerk and employ a stenographer, and prescribe all reasonable rules and regulations, not inconsistent with the provisions of this Act, looking to the speedy advancement of the differences and controversies submitted to them to a conclusion and determination. Each of said arbitrators shall take an oath to honestly, fairly, and faithfully perform his duties, and that he is not personally interested in the subject-matter in controversy, which oath may be administered by any State or Territorial officer authorized to administer oaths. The third person so selected and appointed as aforesaid shall be the president of said board; and any order, finding, conclusion, or award made by a majority of such arbitrators shall be of the same force and effect as if all three of such arbitrators concurred therein or united in making the same.

Sec. 3. That it shall be the duty of said board of arbitration, immediately upon their selection, to organize at the nearest practicable point to the place of the origin of the difficulty or controversy, and to hear and determine the matters of difference which may be submitted to them in writing by all the parties, giving them full opportunity to be heard on oath, in person and by witnesses, and also granting them the right to be represented by counsel; and after concluding its investigation said board shall publicly announce its award, which, with the findings of fact upon which it is based, shall be reduced to writing and signed by the arbitrators concurring therein, and, together with the testimony taken in the case, shall be filed with the Commissioner of Labor of the United States, who shall make such award public as soon as the same shall have been received by him.

Sec. 4. That it shall be the right of any employees engaged in the controversy to appoint, by designation in writing, one or more persons to act for them in the selection of an arbitrator to represent them upon the board of arbitration.

Sec. 5. That each member of said tribunal of arbitration shall receive a compensation of ten dollars a day for the time actually employed. That the clerk appointed by said tribunal of arbitration shall receive the same fees and compensation as clerks of United States circuit courts and district courts receive for like services. That the stenographer shall receive as full compensation for his services twenty cents for each folio of an hundred words of testimony taken and reduced to writing before said arbitrators. That United States marshals or other persons serving the process of said tribunal of arbitration shall receive the same fees and compensation for such services as they would receive for like services upon process issued by United States commissioners. That witnesses attending before said tribunal of arbitration shall receive the same fees as witnesses attending before United States commissioners. That all of said fees and compensation shall be payable by the United States in like manner as fees and compensation are payable in criminal causes under existing laws: Provided, That the said tribunal of arbitration shall have power to limit the number of witnesses in each case where fees shall be paid by the United States: And provided further, That the fees and compensation of the arbitrators, clerks, stenographers, marshals and others, for service of process, and witnesses under this Act, shall be examined and certified by the United States district judge of the district in which the arbitration is held before they are presented to the accounting officers of the Treasury Department for settlement, and shall then be subject to the provisions of section eight hundred and forty-six of the Revised Statutes of the United States; and a sufficient sum of money to pay all expenses under this Act, and to carry the same into effect, is hereby appropriated out of

[704]

392 UNITED STATES.

any money in the Treasury not otherwise appropriated: Provided, however, That not exceeding one thousand dollars shall be paid out of the Treasury of the United States to defray the expenses of any single arbitration under this Act.

Passed the House of Representatives April 3, 1886.

Attest: JNO. B. CLARK, Jr., *Clerk.*

APPENDIX II.

49TH CONGRESS.   1ST SESSION.   [Ex. Doc. No. 130.

SENATE.

Message from the President of the United States relative to the disputes between laboring men and employers.

April 22, 1886.—Read and ordered to be printed.

To the Senate and the House of Representatives:

The Constitution imposes upon the President the duty of recommending to the consideration of Congress from time to time such measures as he shall judge necessary and expedient.

I am so deeply impressed with the importance of immediately and thoughtfully meeting the problem which recent events and a present condition have thrust upon us, involving the settlement of disputes arising between our laboring men and their employers, that I am constrained to recommend to Congress legislation upon this serious and pressing subject.

Under our form of government the value of labor as an element of national prosperity should be distinctly recognized, and the welfare of the labouring man should be regarded as especially entitled to legislative care. In a country which offers to all its citizens the highest attainment of social and political distinction its working men cannot justly or safely be considered as irrevocably consigned to the limits of a class and entitled to no attention and allowed no protest against neglect.

The laboring man, bearing in his hand an indispensable contribution to our growth and progress, may well insist, with manly courage and as a right, upon the same recognition from those who make our laws as is accorded to any other citizen having a valuable interest in charge; and his reasonable demands should be met in such a spirit of appreciation and fairness as to induce a contented and patriotic co-operation in the achievement of a grand national destiny.

While the real interests of labor are not promoted by a resort to threats and violent manifestations, and while those who, under the pretexts of an advocacy of the claims of labor, wantonly attack the rights of capital, and for selfish purposes or the love of disorder sow seeds of violence and discontent, should neither be encouraged nor conciliated, all legislation on the subject should be calmly and deliberately undertaken, with no purpose of satisfying unreasonable demands or gaining partisan advantage.

The present condition of the relations between labor and capital is far from satisfactory. The discontent of the employed is due in a large degree to the grasping and heedless exactions of employers, and the alleged discrimination in favor of capital as an object of governmental attention. It must also be conceded that the laboring men are not always careful to avoid causeless and unjustifiable disturbance.

Though the importance of a better accord between these interests is apparent, it must be borne in mind that any effort in that direction by the Federal Government must be greatly limited by constitutional restrictions. There are many grievances which legislation by Congress cannot redress, and many conditions which cannot by such means be reformed.

I am satisfied, however, that something may be done under Federal authority to prevent the disturbances which so often arise from disputes between employers and the employed, and which at times seriously threaten the business interests of the country; and in my opinion the proper theory upon which to proceed is that of voluntary arbitration as the means of settling these difficulties.

But I suggest that, instead of arbitrators chosen in the heat of conflicting claims, and after each dispute shall arise, for the purpose of determining the same, there be created a Commission of Labor, consisting of three members, who shall be regular officers of the Government, charged among other duties with the consideration and settlement, when possible, of all controversies between labor and capital.

A Commission thus organized would have the advantage of being a stable body, and its members, as they gained experience, would constantly improve in their ability to deal intelligently and usefully with the questions which might be submitted to them. If arbitrators are chosen for temporary service as each case of dispute arises, experience and familiarity with much that is involved in the question will be lacking, extreme partisanship and bias will be the qualifications sought on either side, and frequent complaints of unfairness and partiality will be inevitable. The imposition upon a Federal court of a duty so foreign to the judicial function as the selection of an arbitrator in such cases is at least of doubtful propriety.

The establishment by Federal authority of such a Bureau would be a just and sensible recognition of the value of labor, and of its right to be represented in the departments of the Government. So far as its conciliatory offices shall have relation to disturbances which interfered with transit and commerce between the States, its existence would be justified, under the provisions of the Constitution, which gives to Congress the power " to regulate commerce with foreign nations and among the several States." And in the frequent disputes between the laboring men and their employers, of less extent, and the consequences of which are confined within State limits and threaten domestic violence, the interposition of such a Commission might be tendered, upon the application of the legislature or executive of a State, under the constitutional provision which requires the General Government to " protect " each of the States " against domestic violence."

If such a Commission were fairly organized, the risk of a loss of popular support and sympathy resulting from a refusal to submit to so peaceful an instrumentality would constrain both parties to such disputes to invoke its interference and abide by its decisions. There would also be good reason to hope that the very existence of such an agency would invite application to it for advice and counsel, frequently resulting in the avoidance of contention and misunderstanding.

If the usefulness of such a Commission is doubted because it might lack power to enforce its decisions, much encouragement is derived from the conceded good that has been accomplished by the railroad commissions which have been organized in many of the States, which, having little more than advisory power, have exerted a most salutary influence in the settlement of disputes between conflicting interests.

In July, 1884, by a law of Congress, a Bureau of Labor was established and placed in charge of a Commissioner of Labour, who is required to " collect information upon the subject of labor, its relations to capital, the hours of labor and the earnings of laboring men and women, and the means of promoting their material, social, intellectual, and moral prosperity."

The Commission which I suggest could easily be engrafted upon the Bureau thus already organized by the addition of two more Commissioners, and by supplementing the duties now imposed upon it by such other powers and functions as would permit the Commissioners to act as arbitrators when necessary between labor and capital under such limitations and upon such occasions as should be deemed proper and useful.

Power should also be distinctly conferred upon this Bureau to investigate the causes of all disputes as they occur, whether submitted for arbitration or not, so that information may always be at hand to aid legislation on the subject when necessary and desirable.

GROVER CLEVELAND.

EXECUTIVE MANSION, *April* 22, 1886.

APPENDIX III.

49TH CONGRESS. 1ST SESSION.

H. R. 8119.

IN THE HOUSE OF REPRESENTATIVES.

April 26th, 1886.—Read twice, referred to the Committee on Labor, and ordered to be printed.

Mr. Springer introduced the following Bill:

A Bill to establish a Department of Labor and to create a board for the arbitration of controversies between labor and capital.

396 UNITED STATES.

Be it enacted by the Senate and House of Representatives of the United States of America in Congress assembled that there shall be at the seat of Government a Department of Labor, the general design and duties of which shall be to acquire and to diffuse among the people of the United States useful information on subjects connected with labor, in the most general and comprehensive sense of that word, and especially upon its relation to capital, the hours of labour, and earnings of laboring men and women, and the means of promoting their material, social, intellectual, and moral prosperity. There shall also be established in said Department a Commission of Labor, consisting of three members, who shall be charged, among other duties, with the consideration and settlement, by means of arbitration, when possible, of all controversies between labor and capital.

Sec. 2. That the Department of Labor shall be under the charge of a Commissioner of Labor, who shall be appointed by the President, by and with the advice and consent of the Senate, and who shall be entitled to a salary of four thousand dollars a year. There shall also be two Assistant Commissioners, appointed by the President, with like advice and consent, who shall each be entitled to a salary of three thousand dollars a year. The Commissioner of Labor and the two assistants shall constitute a Commission of Labor. The Commissioner of Labor shall appoint a chief clerk of said Department and a clerk of said Commission, who shall each receive a salary of two thousand dollars per annum, and such other employees as may be necessary for said Department and Commission: Provided that the total expense of said Department and Commission shall not exceed one hundred thousand dollars per annum. During the necessary absence of the Commissioner, or when the office shall become vacant, the Assistant Commissioner first named, and in his absence the other Commissioner, shall perform the duties of Commissioner; and in the absence of all the Commissioners the chief clerk shall perform such duties.

Sec. 3. That the Commission of Labor shall have power to investigate the causes of all controversies and disputes between labor and capital in the United States, as they may occur, whether such controversies and disputes are submitted for arbitration or not, and to report thereon to the President of the United States, who shall, from time to time, transmit such reports to Congress. In making such investigation, and all other investigations authorized by this Act, said Commission may, in its discretion, proceed to the place where such controversies exist, and shall have the power to send for persons and papers, to administer oaths to witnesses, and shall have such other powers as are possessed by United States Commissioners appointed by circuit courts of the United States in making preliminary examinations.

Sec. 4. That in all controversies or disturbances which may interfere with transit and commerce between the States, it shall be the duty of the Commission of Labor to act as a board of arbitration for the peaceful settlement of such controversies whenever the conciliatory offices of said Commission may be invoked by the parties thereto ; and in all controversies between laboring men and their employers, the consequences of which are confined within the limits of any State, and which may threaten domestic violence, the interposition of said Commission may be tendered by the President of the United States for the purpose of settling such controversies by arbitration, on the application of the legislature of such State, or of the executive when the legislature cannot be convened.

Sec. 5. That the Commission of Labor shall prescribe all needful rules and regulations, not inconsistent with the Constitution and laws of the United States, for governing its proceedings in making investigations, and hearing and determining all questions and controversies submitted to it for arbitration or settlement under the provisions of this Act. All questions submitted for arbitration shall be in writing and signed by the parties respectively ; and the decision or award shall have such force and effect only as is provided in the articles of submission. All awards and decisions made by said Commission shall be entered of record in its proceedings, and a copy thereof furnished to each of the parties thereto ; and one copy shall be transmitted to any court which by the terms of submission may be authorized to take any action thereon. The said Commission, when sitting as a board of arbitration, shall permit each party to appear in person or by counsel and to examine and cross-examine the witnesses; and it shall transact all its proceedings in public, except when in consultation, after hearing all the evidence and arguments in the case. The members of the Commission of Labor shall take and subscribe an oath, in each case submitted to them, to honestly, fairly, and faithfully perform their duties, and that they are not personally interested in the subject-matter in controversy, which oath may be administered by the clerk of the Commission, who is hereby authorized to administer oaths in such cases, and to witnesses in all investigations by said Commission.

Sec. 6. That it shall be the duty of the Commission of Labor, whenever any controversy is submitted to it for arbitration, to meet as soon as possible, at the nearest practicable point to the place of the origin of the difficulty or controversy, and to hear and determine the matters of difference which may be submitted in writing, giving all parties full opportunity to be heard on oath, in person and by witnesses; and after concluding its investigation the Commission shall publicly announce its decision or award, which, with the findings of fact upon which it is based, shall be reduced to writing and signed by each member of the Commission concurring therein, and, together with the testimony taken in the case, shall be entered of record and furnished to the parties in interest as herein required.

Sec. 7. That the Commission of Labor shall employ one or more stenographers, who shall take down and transcribe the testimony of witnesses, but not the arguments of counsel, in each case submitted or investigated, and shall allow as full compensation for such services twenty cents for each folio of one hundred words. The United States marshal of the district where the meetings of the Commission may be held shall assign one or more deputy marshals to serve the processes of said Commission, who shall each receive for such services the same compensation as is now allowed by law for serving the processes of United States Courts and Commissioners. The witnesses attending before said Commission shall receive the same fees as witnesses attending before United States Commissioners. The members and clerk of the Commission shall be allowed their actual and necessary travelling expenses when absent from the capital in performance of their official duties. That all of said fees, expenses, and compensation shall be paid by the Commission out of the funds appropriated for the payment of its expenses, under such rules and regulations, and under such limitations as to the number of witnesses in each case to be paid by the United States, as said Commission may prescribe. All such accounts shall be approved by the Commission and attested by the oath of the person making the same.

Sec. 8. That the Commissioner of Labor, the two Assistant Commissioners, the chief clerk, and the clerk of said Commission shall, before entering upon their duties, severally give bonds to the Treasurer of the United States, each in the sum of ten thousand dollars, conditioned to render a true and faithful account to the Treasurer quarter-yearly of all moneys which shall be by them received by virtue of their office, with sureties to be approved by the Solicitor of the Treasurer. Such bonds shall be filed in the office of the First Comptroller of the Treasury, to be by him put in suit upon any breach of the conditions thereof.

Sec. 9. That the Commissioner of Labor shall, on or before the fifteenth day of December in each year, make a report in detail to Congress of all moneys expended by him and by said Commission. He shall also make a general report in writing of his acts and the investigations required by this Act, and of all the investigations, proceedings, decisions, and awards of the Commission of Labor; and he may recommend the publication of papers forming parts of or accompanying his report. He shall also make special reports and recommendations on particular subjects whenever required to do so by the President or either House of Congress, or when he shall think the subject in his charge requires it.

Sec. 10. That the Act of Congress "to establish a Bureau of Labor," approved June twenty-seventh, eighteen hundred and eighty-four, is hereby repealed; but the Commissioner of Labor appointed by said Act, and all clerks and employees in the Bureau of Labor authorized to be appointed by said Act, shall continue in office and employment as if appointed under the provisions of this Act, and until a Commissioner of Labor and other clerks and employees are appointed and qualified as herein required and provided.

Appendix IV.

49TH CONGRESS. 1ST SESSION.

H. R. 7621.

IN THE HOUSE OF REPRESENTATIVES.

April 5, 1886.—Read twice, referred to the Committee on Labor, and ordered to be printed.

Mr. John J. O'Neill introduced the following Bill:

A Bill to legalize the incorporation of National Trades Unions.

Be it enacted by the Senate and House of Representatives of the United States of America in Congress assembled, That the term National Trades Union, in the meaning of this Act, shall signify any association of working people having two or more branches in the States or Territories of the United States for the purpose of aiding its members to become more skilful and efficient workers, the promotion of their general intelligence, the elevation of their character, the regulation of their wages and their hours and conditions of labor, the protection of their individual rights in the prosecution of their trade or trades, the raising of funds for the benefit of sick, disabled, or unemployed members, or the families of deceased members, or for such other object or objects for which working people may lawfully combine, having in view their mutual protection or benefit.

Sec. 2. That National Trades Unions shall, upon filing their articles of incorporation in the office of the recorder of the District of Columbia, become a corporation under the technical name by which said National Trade Union desires to be known to the trade, and shall have the right to sue and be sued, to implead and be impleaded, to grant and receive, in its corporate or technical name, property, real, personal, and mixed, and to use said property, and the proceeds and income thereof, for the objects of said corporation as in its charter defined.

Sec. 3. That an incorporated National Trade Union shall have power to make and establish such constitution, rules, and by-laws as it may deem proper to carry out its lawful objects, and the same to alter, amend, add to, or repeal at pleasure.

Sec. 4. That an incorporated National Trade Union shall have power to define the duties and powers of all its officers and prescribe their mode of election and terms of office, and to establish branches and sub-unions in any Territory of the United States.

Sec. 5. That the headquarters of an incorporated National Trades Union shall be located in the District of Columbia.

Appendix V.

NOBLE ORDER OF THE KNIGHTS OF LABOR OF AMERICA.

Philadelphia, May 3, 1886.

To the Order Everywhere, Greeting:

The response to the secret circular issued on March 13th has been so generous, and the endorsement of the sentiments contained in it has been so unanimous, that I feel encouraged and strengthened in the work. Nearly four thousand Assemblies have pledged themselves to act on the advice contained in the circular of the 13th ult. I feel that it only requires the coming to the front of the real men of our Order to set us right before the world. We have been losing ground, so far as public opinion is concerned, for some time. One of the causes is that we have allowed things to be done under the name of the Knights of Labor for which the organization was in no way responsible. I ask of our members to keep a jealous eye upon the doings of the labor men who never labor, and, when they charge anything to our Order in your locality, set the seal of your condemnation upon it at once by denying it.

If a paper criticises the Knights of Labor or its officers, do not boycott it; and, if you have any such boycotts on, remove them. A journal not long since made some uncomplimentary allusions to the General Master Workman of the Knights of Labor, and at the next meeting of the nearest Assembly a motion was passed to boycott the paper; not that alone, but every merchant who advertised in the columns of the paper. I wrote to the Assembly, asking that they remove the boycott, and it was done. We must bear in mind that our General Master Workman is only a man, and is not above criticism. We demand for ourselves the "right of free speech." We cannot consistently deny it to others. We must tolerate fair, open criticism. If a reply is necessary, make it in a gentlemanly, dignified manner. If we are criticised or abused by a blackguard sheet, treat it as you would the blackguard himself—in silence.

That our aims and objects are good is no reason why our members should be regarded as beings of superior build or material. We are no more the salt of the earth than the millions of unknown toilers who do the work of the world. In our dealings with laborers and capitalists we must deal justly and fairly by them. If we would have equity done to us, we in turn must do equity to others. This is the aim of the Knights of Labor, and must not be lost sight of in future.

Let me direct your attention to a few little abuses :—

I find that, wherever a strike occurs, appeals for aid are scattered broadcast among the Assemblies. Do not pay one cent for such purposes in future unless the appeal comes from your own District Assembly or the General Assembly. If boycott notices are sent to you, *burn them*. I have in my possession over four hundred boycott notices which were sent to Assemblies with a request that they be acted on. Let me mention some of them :—A member is editing a paper. He fears a rival, and proceeds to get into an altercation with him, boycotts him, and then asks of the Order to carry it out. A certain paper is influential in one or the other of the political parties. Members of the opposing party conceive the idea of getting rid of the paper, and they invoke the aid of the Knights of Labor, first taking the precaution to have the paper in question say something uncomplimentary of the Knights of Labor. In fact, our Order has been used as a tail for a hundred different kites, and in future it must soar aloft free from all of them. I hate the word boycott. I was boycotted years ago; I could not get work at my trade for months. It is a bad practice; it has been handed to us by the capitalist. I have no use for it, only when everything else fails.

Appeals for aid, circulars, petitions, advertisements of every kind, are scattered everywhere through the Order. I copy a letter which comes to me on the subject: " A large part of our time has been spent in reading boycott notices and appeals for aid, keeping us until 12 o'clock. We were led to believe the Knights of Labor to be an educational institution, but this kind of education is not productive of good. We have no time for instruction. What do you advise us to do?" I advised them to either burn or table these matters, and now ask of the Secretary of each Assembly to do the same. If our JOURNAL were not boycotted by our members, it could be made the medium of communication between the General Officers and the Order, but the JOURNAL is not read in one-quarter of the Assemblies. Some Assemblies send out documents in envelopes, addressed to " Secretary of Assembly, No. ——." In many places the Secretaries have been discharged because of this practice. No member has the right to address another in that way, and if it is ever practised again the offender will be punished.

In future the General Executive Board must not be interfered with in the performance of its duty. If you have confidence in them, sustain them and obey them; if not, ask for their resignations. While the Board was endeavouring to settle the Southwest trouble, Assemblies in some places, with the best of intentions no doubt, were passing and publishing resolutions condemning Jay Gould. These things did no good; on the contrary, they were injurious. In the settlement of troubles it becomes the duty of the Executive Board to meet everybody and go everywhere. While they are doing this they must not be hampered by the actions of those who do not know what their task is. Keep quiet; let your officers do their best, and, if you cannot find a way to aid them, do not retard their progress. Resolutions do not prevent land-stealing, stock-watering, or gambling in the necessaries of life. If I had my mind made up to rob a bank at midnight, a string of resolutions as long as the moral law, protesting against my contemplated action, would not influence me a particle; but, if some interested party would take the trouble to study up the question and would inform himself as to my right to rob the bank, and would stand guard at the door of the vault, I would not rob it at midnight if he did his duty. What we want from our members is not gush or windy resolutions about our rights. We know we have rights without passing resolutions. Men who think, study, and act are required.

The General Assembly will meet in special session on the 25th of May, in the city of CLEVELAND.

From the receipt of this letter you must not address any communication to me, nor need you expect an answer if you do. I have thousands of letters piled up around me now, and they never can be read, much less answered, by one man. During and since my illness the mail delivered at my house has exceeded four hundred letters a day. They come from everybody and everywhere. I must play the part of wheel-horse instead of leader of a great movement, and our own members are responsible for it. I asked through the JOURNAL to send no letters to me. I am told by some to get help. If I had fifty assistants it would do no good, for it takes my whole time to read one-half of the letters, and in the middle of my work I am waited on by some committee, who generally misrepresents me after they leave, for every member of the committee will tell a different story. From now until the General Assembly meets I will receive no committees, answer no letters. I must formulate a plan for the future, and will not be interfered with. Let me repeat, *I will meet no committees, answer no letters, nor will I go anywhere at the request of members or Assemblies.* This is imperative. I must have a chance to do something of benefit for the Order, and I cannot do it if I am to sit for eighteen hours a day reading letters which have been answered and re-answered in the JOURNAL and Constitution. What I will say to the General Assembly will be said to the whole Order, and you must give me time to prepare it.

We have had some trouble from drinking members and from men who talk about buying guns and dynamite. If the men who possess money enough to buy guns and dynamite would invest it in the purchase of some well-selected work on labor, they would put the money to good use. They will never need the gun or dynamite in this country. It is my opinion that the man who does not study the politics of the nation and the wants of our people would make but little use of a rifle. The man who cannot vote intelligently, and who will not watch the man he votes for after he is elected, cannot be depended on to use either gun or dynamite. If the head, the brain of man, cannot work out the problem now confronting us, his hand alone will never solve it. If I kill my enemy I silence him, it is true, but I do not convince him. I would make a convert rather than a corpse of my enemy. Men who own capital are not our enemies. If that theory held good, the workman of to-day would be the enemy of his fellow-toiler on the morrow, for after all it is how to acquire capital and how to use it properly that we are endeavouring to learn. No! the man of capital is not necessarily the enemy of the labourer; on the contrary, they must be brought closer together. I am well aware that some extremist will say I am advocating a weak plan, and will say that bloodshed and destruction of property alone will solve the problem. If a man speaks such sentiments in an Assembly, read for him the charge which the Master Workman repeats to the newly-initiated who joins our "army of peace," and, if he repeats his nonsense, put him out.

"In the hands of men entirely great the pen is mightier than the sword."

To that I add: in the hands of man entirely mouth the gun is harmless as his word.

To our drinking member I extend the hand of kindness. I hate the uses to which rum has been put, but it is my duty to reach down and lift up the man who has fallen a victim to the use of liquor. If there is such a man within sound of the Secretary's voice when this is read, I ask of him to stand erect on the floor of his Assembly, raise his hand to heaven, and repeat with me these words:

"I am a Knight of Labor. I believe that every man should be free from the curse of slavery, whether that slavery appears in the shape of monopoly, usury, or intemperance. The firmest link in the chain of oppression is the one I forge when I drown manhood and reason in drink. No man can rob me of the brain my God has given me unless I am a party to the theft. If I drink to drown grief, I bring grief to wife, child, and sorrowing friends. I add not one iota to the sum of human happiness when I invite oblivion over the rim of a glass. If one moment's forgetfulness or inattention to duty while drunk brings defeat to the least of labor's plans, a lifetime of attention to duty alone can repair the loss. I promise never again to put myself in such a position."

If every member of the Knights of Labor would only pass a resolution to boycott strong drink, so far as he is concerned, for five years, and would pledge his word to study the labor question from its different standpoints, we would then have an invincible host arrayed on the side of justice.

We have, through some unfortunate misunderstanding, incurred the enmity of several trades unions. While I can find no excuse for the unmanly attack made upon us by some of these people at a time when we stood face to face with a most perplexing question, neither can I see any good reason why there should be any cause for a quarrel. We must have no clashing between the men of labor's army. If I am the cause of the trouble, I stand ready at a moment's notice to make way for any one of my rivals whom the General Assembly may select. When I joined the Knights of Labor I left the trade union. I believe the aims and objects of our Order come first; I believe in combining all the scattered battalions of labor's mighty host in one grand whole. Labor-saving inventions, steam and electricity, have for ever broken the power of one trade or division of labor to stand and legislate for itself alone; and with the craft that selfishly legislates for itself alone I have no sympathy. Well may we say of the men who are fighting us, "Forgive them, Father, for they know not what they do." Break the power of the Knights of Labor, and you hand labor, bound hand and foot, over to its enemies. Years ago I extended an invitation to men of all trades to become a part and parcel of the Knights of Labor. To-day I stand ready to make every honorable concession, to do everything in honor to bring about a better feeling between trades unions and the Knights of Labor. At the special session of the General Assembly the entire trouble can and must be settled. If mistakes have been made they must be rectified; if wrongs have been inflicted they must be righted. But there is one thing that will not be done while I stand at the head of this organization—it will not be used to further the schemes of individuals, cliques, or parties, and it will be subordinate to no other organization on earth.

T. V. POWDERLY,
General Master Workman.

Appendix VI.

Report by Consul-General Booker.

There has been comparatively little legislation in this State in regard to labour.

Liens of mechanics, labourers, and others who perform labour, for buildings or other improvements are provided for and regulated by an Act of 1885. Under this, any person who with consent of the owner or contractor performs labour or furnishes materials in erecting, altering, or repairing any building or structure may have a lien upon the premises for the value of such labour or materials to an amount not exceeding the agreed price or the value of such labour and materials remaining unpaid at the time of filing the lien. Notice of lien must be filed within ninety days after completion of the work; the lien continues for one year only, unless within that time an action to enforce it is commenced and notice of pendency filed or other proceedings taken according to the statute.

There is an Act making eight hours a legal day's work, but it only applies to those employed by the State or any Municipal Corporation, or by persons contracting with the State or Corporation for performance of public work. This Act embraces all classes of mechanics, working men, and labourers, excepting those engaged in farming and domestic labour, but overwork for an extra compensation, by agreement between employed and employer, is permitted. By a division in the Court of Appeals in April, 1884, it was decided that the intent of the Act was to place the control of the hours of labour within the discretion of the employé, giving him the privilege at his option to refuse to work beyond the eight hours, or to secure extra compensation for extra work by stipulation in the contract of employment. In the absence of any such stipulation, the language of the Act repels any inference of an intent to confer a right upon an employé to charge for more than one day's labour for services rendered in any calendar; and for such services he may not demand any extra compensation. The case was one in which the employé worked in the department of Docks in the city of New York with knowledge that the custom of the department and the nature of the services required ten hours' work each day. He worked for two years without objection or claim for extra compensation, giving

[704]

receipts purporting to be full up to date; he subsequently sued for extra pay for the extra work over eight hours per calendar day.

The manufacture of cigars in tenement houses is prohibited by an Act of the Legislature. There is an Act to protect labourers engaged in the construction of railroads, and there are special laws for the protection of female employees and minors; children between the ages of eight and fourteen have to attend some private or public day school, or receive instruction at home, at least fourteen weeks in each year, eight of which must be consecutive.

Appendix VII.

Report by Consul Clipperton.

The Knights of Labour were constituted as a permanent organization in 1869 in this city (Philadelphia). The body was strictly secret for a considerable time, but can now be considered as no longer a secret organization in the true sense of the word. Secrecy, it is claimed, was necessary in the early stage of the Society to protect the members from personal persecution and loss of labour by belonging to it. At a later period, when the Society became strong and able to hold up its head, the tendency was, and is now, to give it as much publicity as is consistent with the administration of its functions. The organization extends throughout the United States, England, and Belgium, and in this country its growth is very rapid. But few names at the present time are dropped from the rolls or withdrawn, while, on the other hand, sixty or seventy assemblies are organising daily throughout the country. The number of assemblies exceeds 6,000 and the membership half a million. The pecuniary support of the organization is by nominal tax upon the membership, each assembly supporting itself, and the assemblies paying a tax to the Executive Board. The Executive Board announce the minimum sum required for general expenses, the assemblies their rateable proportion and as much additional contribution as they voluntarily tender. The Executive Board is composed of General Master Workman, General Secretary and Treasurer, and three members selected from the membership at large in general assembly, held annually.

The paramount doctrine of the Society is to conciliate all relations between capitalists and working men; to adjust differences and the clashing of interests between them; to foster a system of mutual advantage between Capital and Labour; to prevent, not to encourage, strikes, and to elevate the moral character of the working men of all classes.

There has been little legislation by the State of Pennsylvania on the subject of employers and working men. But two Acts, one of April 14th, 1868, and the other of April 23rd, 1883, are of any consequence.

The Act of April 14th, 1868, enacts that eight hours between "the rising of the sun and the setting of the sun shall be a legal day's labour in all cases of work or service by the day, where there is no contract or agreement to the contrary." This enactment is not to affect farm or agricultural labour, or by the week, month, or year; nor is it to affect making as much overtime as any person may think fit, the compensation to be agreed upon between the employer and employed. And all settlements of pay in coal mining, iron foundries, &c., shall be at least once a month, and the employé shall have the right to assign his claim, or any part thereof, against the employer and employed. And all settlements of pay in coal mining, iron foundries, &c., shall be at least once a month, and the employé shall have the right to assign his claim, or any part thereof, against the employer. The eight hours clause has been inoperative up to this date. From May 1st, however, by agreement between employers and employés, nine hours in some and eight hours in other trades will become a day's work.

The Act of April 23rd, 1883, gives power to establish Courts of Conciliation which are tribunals appointed by county judges, with power to settle disputes between employers and employés in the iron and steel, glass, textile fabrics, and coal trades. Their decision is final, and the Courts to consist of not less than two employers and two employés. The expenses of such Courts to be paid by voluntary subscriptions, and attorneys and litigants have no appeal.

The working of the organization appears to be effective. The offices of Grand Secretary and Treasurer, Frederick Turner, in this city, are capacious rooms, and his staff consists of twenty-two persons The Executive

Board visits different sections of the country and do all in their power to settle by arbitration all differences between employers and employés. They use a moral power to prevent strikes in the different sections, and especially in such cases where it is apparent that they are fraught with great loss to both sides.

At the last Convention, held at Hamilton, Ontario, Canada, in October, 1885, an effort was made to change the Constitution so as to leave the power to strike solely in the hands of the Executive Board. This was a direct reversal of the Constitution, and the movement was lost by a large vote. At the special sessions to be held at Cleveland, May 25th, it is almost certain that the change will be made. With this power within the absolute control of the Executive Board it is held that the day for serious strikes will be over.

The Knights of Labour have a system of life insurance, of $500, payable at once on the proof of death of the member. This fund is raised by a personal assessment, and since its organization the cost to each member has been half a cent. per day, or $1 84 cents per annum. Two policies of $500 each are allowed to be taken by a single member on paying double rates. I enclose copy of the circular issued by the order on this subject.

BENEFIT INSURANCE ASSOCIATION, KNIGHTS OF LABOR OF AMERICA.

OFFICE OF SECRETARY, 217 S. MAIN ST.,
PITTSBURGH, PA., MARCH 1, 1886.

TO THE ORDER WHEREVER FOUND,
  GREETING:

Owing to the large and unexpected increase in the membership of our Order in the past few months, I deem it necessary that this circular be issued and read at several successive meetings of every L. A. in the Order, so that every member of the Order may have an opportunity to know that within the Order life insurance can be obtained at a cost which has not exceeded* one cent per day for $500.00 indemnity. A summary of the affairs of the Association, March 1, 1886, is as follows:—

Number of certificates issued	6,462
„ of members in good standing, of which 1,400 have not yet been assessed	4,210
„ of members deceased, suspended, and dropped	2,252
„ of certificates of deceased members paid	55
„ of assessments levied, at 25 cents each	38
Amount of benefits paid	$23,370,00

*Average cost per day, one cent.

---

* Later returns have reduced the costs to ½ cent per day.

The membership is increasing at the rate of over 300 per month, and benefits are paid as rapidly as the money from assessments is received.

Any member (male or female) in good standing, in average good health, of temperate habits, and between 18 and 50 years, can become a member by making application and paying a fee of $1.25.

Supplies such as application blanks, circulars, &c., are furnished free from this office.

Quite a number of applications for benefits have been received, and payment refused, from the representatives of deceased persons who had been members, but had been suspended, and had died in bad standing, and consequently were not entitled to benefits. The refusal to honor such claims has caused the report to be circulated that this Association had failed to meet its engagements, and I take this opportunity to contradict all such reports, and to say that the certificates of every deceased member who had complied with the laws of the Order, and died in good standing (except a few recent deaths which have not yet been assessed for), has been paid or is in process of settlement, and that since January 1, 1885, $500.00 has been paid on each certificate.

Sisters and Brothers, the insurance feature of our Order is in successful operation, and all that is needed to make it a grand success is the support of every member of the Order who has the welfare of his or her dependent ones at heart by enrolling themselves as members.

The payment of nearly $25,000.00 in benefits to its widows and orphans ought to be a sufficient guarantee for the future, and the trifling cost of about one cent a day places it within the reach of all. Drop a nickle or two a week in a toy bank and you will always have the money ready to pay your assessments. Curtail your expenses a cent or two a day and you can carry a certificate and never miss the money, besides giving to yourself the peace of mind that, if you should die, you had provided for your dependent ones.

Do not defer this matter, but act on it at once, and if your Local has no insurance supplies order what is needed on the inclosed blank, stating also the number desirous of joining.

Please see that every member of your Local is furnished with a circular and application blank, and that all have an opportunity to join. If this is done, and the officers bring the subject of insurance before the L. A. at frequent intervals, thousands will be advised of the existence of the Insurance Association, who might otherwise never hear of it. Trusting that you will lend your influence and assistance in furthering the good work, I am

Fraternally Yours,
HOMER L. McGAW,
General Insurance Secretary.

Appendix VIII.

Report by Consul Donohoe.

Copy of Acts of Maryland affecting Employers and Working Men.

Laws of Maryland, Chapter 266.

An Act to amend Article thirty of the Code of Public General Laws of this State, title "Crimes and Punishments," by adding thereto, and an additional section under the new sub-title of "Conspiracy."

Section 1. Be it enacted by the General Assembly of Maryland that Article thirty of the Code of Public General Laws of this State, title "Crimes and Punishments," be and the same is hereby amended by adding thereto the following additional section, under the new sub-title of "Conspiracy."

Section *a*. An agreement or combination by two or more persons to do or procure to be done any act in contemplation or furtherance of a trade dispute between employers and workmen shall not be indictable as a conspiracy if such act committed by one person would not be punishable as an offence. Nothing in this section shall affect the law relating to riot, unlawful assembly, breach of the peace, or any offence against any person or against property.

Chapter 267.

An Act to provide for the formation of "Trade Unions" under the provisions of Article twenty-six of the Code of Public General Laws of this State, as the same was enacted by the Act of 1868, chapter 471, and under the supplements thereto, and to define the powers of the Corporations so authorized to be formed. Approved April 8th, 1884.

Section 1. Be it enacted by the General Assembly of Maryland that any five or more persons, citizens of the U.S., a majority of whom are citizens of this State, who are engaged in the same occupation or employment, or in similar occupation or employment, may organize and form as a Corporation, to be known as a "Trade Union," with such additions to the said name as they may adopt and set forth in their certificate, to promote the well-being of their everyday life, and for mutual assistance in securing the most favourable conditions for the labour of its members, and as a beneficial society under the provisions of Article 26 of the Code of Public General Laws of this State, as the same was enacted by the Act of 1868, chapter 471, and its supplements, in the manner in which other corporations provided for in said Act are authorized to be formed, each of said Trade Unions so organized and formed as a corporation sahll possess all the powers and be subject to all the regulations in said Act and in its supplements authorized to be incorporated under the provisions of said Act and its supplements.

1886.
Chapter 163.

An Act to regulate the hours of work of Conductors, Drivers, and Employees of Horse Railway Companies of this State.

Section 1. Be it enacted by the General Assembly of Maryland that no Horse Railway Company incorporated under the laws of this State, and no officer, agent, or servant of such Corporation, and no person or firm owning or operating any line or lines of horse railways within the limits of this State, and no agent or servant of such firm or person, shall require, permit, or suffer its, his, or their conductors or drivers, or any of them, or any employees in its, his, or their service, or under its, his, or their control, to work for more than twelve hours during each or any day of twenty-four hours, and shall make no contract or agreement with such employees, or any of them, providing that they or he shall work for more than twelve hours during each or any day of twenty-four hours.

Section 2. And be it enacted that any Corporation which shall in any manner violate any of the provisions of this Act shall be deemed to have misused or abused its corporate power and franchise, and the Attorney-General of the State, upon the application in writing made by any citizens of this State, accompanied by sufficient proof of the violation of any of the provisions of this Act, shall forthwith without further authorization institute proceedings for the forfeiture of the charter of such Corporation by petition, in the name of the State, in the manner provided by the laws of this State for the enforcement of the forfeiture of the charters of any Corporations which have abused or misused their corporate powers or franchises.

Section 3. And be it enacted that, if any Corporation, or any officer, agent, or servant of such Corporation, or any person or any firm managing or conducting any horse railway in this State, or any agent or servant of such person or firm, shall do any act in violation of the provisions of this Act, it, he, or they shall be deemed to have been guilty of a misdemeanour, and shall, on conviction thereof in a court of competent jurisdiction, be fined 100 dollars for each offence so committed, together with the costs of such prosecution.

Section 4. And be it enacted that this Act shall take effect from the date of its passage (approved April 1, 1886).

All the leading industries in Baltimore are organized, and some of them, such as the Horse-shoers', Printers', Cigar Makers', Cabinet Makers', Carpenters', Tin-can Makers', Bricklayers', Granite Cutters', and Glass Blowers' Unions, are strong in numbers; most of these Unions are connected with the national organization of the Knights of Labour, but it is not possible for an outsider to tell, except when a strike occurs, what Societies belong to the "Knights." I understand that, from the want of success of the "Knights" in the management of the great strike on the Southern lines of railway from St. Louis, many of the local Unions here are holding aloof from them. There have been several strikes in this district; the most important occurred in the bituminous coal region of Western Maryland, where the miners struck about seven weeks ago and are still holding out.

The passage recently of the "Twelve-hour Law" by the Maryland Legislature was the cause of a strike on most of the tram lines in this city, but the men, after holding out for some short time, have been fairly beaten, and street-car lines are now running. There is a strike still pending on the question of the employment of Union or Non-Union men, and an attempt to boycott the manufacturer has met with but little success. The question now that appears to be agitating the minds of the working-men is the eight-hour one, and a strong fight may be expected, when they become thoroughly organized throughout the country, upon it.

Baltimore, April 30, 1886.

No. 8

UNITED STATES.

Sir L. West to Earl of Rosebery.

My Lord, Washington, May 21, 1886.

WITH reference to your Lordship's despatch of the 6th ultimo, requesting me to cause a report to be drawn up by one of the members of Her Majesty's Legation in answer to questions respecting co-operation in the United States, I have the honour to enclose herewith a report on the subject which has been drawn up by Mr. Helyar.

I have, &c.,
(Signed) J. L. SACKVILLE WEST.

Inclosure 1 in No. 8.

Report by Mr. Helyar on Co-operation in the United States.

Question I.—Co-operative stores in the United States have hitherto been few in number, and mostly unsuccessful. Mr. Barnard, in a useful little work called "Co-operation as a Business,"* states that distributive co-operation in the United States has been marked by almost utter failure. Stores few and unsuccessful.

The causes of this want of success are chiefly to be found in bad methods, in a misunderstanding of the objects sought, and in American impatience at results. Only a slow-thinking, penny-counting, frugal, and painstaking people could bring co-operation to a success. The average American has thought it beneath him to consider the details of dimes, and experiments in co-operative distribution have generally miscarried through carelessness, inattention, and neglect. Reasons for failure.

There are, however, some exceptions, notably the Philadelphia Industrial Co-operative Society, which, though only six years old, has already cash sales of over 100,000 dol. and a total income of over 116,000 dol., and a disposable profit of 6,520 dol., the larger part of which is paid as a cash dividend on the members' purchases. Philadelphia co-operative society an exception.

Other co-operative stores are now being established in different parts of the country, but the idea is in its infancy. A Central Co-operation Board has been started in New York, for the purpose of advising co-operative societies generally, and it has drawn up a scheme of by-laws for general use. Movement spreading. A Co-operative Dress Supply Association, recently started in New York, proved however a complete failure, and collapsed disastrously. Dress society a failure.

Question II. (a)—Co-operative workshops, on the other hand, have been established with success in various parts of the United States. Mr. Carroll Wright, in his Report as Chief of the Massachusetts Labour Workshops.

* Sent to Library of House of Commons.

[386]

Bureau for 1886,* under the head of "Profit-Sharing," gives some instructive examples.

Profit sharing.
I. Profit-sharing in addition to wages:—

Steam pumps.
Messrs. A. S. Cameron and Co., of New York, steam-pumping manufacturers, from 1869 to 1877 divided 10 per cent. of their profits among their workmen, and only dropped the plan on Mr. Cameron's death. This bonus amounted to an increase of $4\frac{1}{2}$ per cent. on wages, and is stated to have had a salutary effect on the men, and to have been a commercial success.

Carriages.
Messrs. Brewster, carriage builders of New York, established the same system in 1869, and continued it with success until the strike of 1872 broke it down.

Woollen manufactures.
The Peace Dale (Rhode Island) Manufacturing Company, with a capital of 200,000 dol., which manufactures shawls, worsted coatings, cassimeres, and other woollen fabrics, began profit-sharing in 1878, and continues it with success. Bonuses of varying amount were given as voluntary encouragement to employés from 1880 to 1883, but since then the depressson of trade has caused their suspension.

Chemical works.
Messrs. Lister, of the Passaic Chemical Works, Newark, New Jersey, have for some years given voluntary bonuses in addition to wages. The largest example of this kind is the Pillsbury Flour Mills, Minneapolis, with a capital of 2,500,000 dol. The company give a certain percentage of the profits (exact percentage not revealed) to the employés—(a) to all of five years' standing; (b) to the superior employés of any standing. The wages of the former class were thus advanced 50 per cent., and the latter 65 per cent. The system is stated to be a great moral and material success.

II. Profit-sharing through stockowning:—

Tailoring.
The statistics given relate only to Massachusetts. The Boston Tailors' Association Union of 1849, the first co-operative association in Massachusetts to engage in production, divided profits in proportion to labour performed; but at the present time the co-operative manufacturing corporations do not in practice divide on any other basis than that of capital invested. They are, therefore, only profit-sharing through the distribution of their capital stock.

Statutory position.
Co-operative corporations were authorised by chapter 290 of the Acts of 1866, by which any seven or more persons, of lawful age and inhabitants of Massachusetts, might, by articles of agreement, associate themselves for commercial or agricultural purposes, and become a corporation with the usual rights and liabilities, comprising a board of three or more directors, a president, and a treasurer, chosen annually by the stockholders. Further particulars of this law will be found on pp. 290–91 of Mr. Carroll Wright's Labour Report for 1886 (Massachusetts).*

1870–75.
Between 1870 and 1875 13 co-operative manufacturing corporations were organised, only two of which are now existing.

Somerset Foundry Company.
The oldest association of all, the Somerset Co-operative Foundry Company, dating from 1867, is still existing and successful. Including this company, there are now ten such associations in the State, of which a brief description will be given. (See also p. 202, et seq., of Mr. Wright's report above mentioned.)

From 1875 to 1885 several new companies were started, while others disappeared, producing the above result.

1. The Somerset Co-operative Foundry, started in 1867 on the ruins of the old Boston Store Foundry, gradually made its way, and

* 17th Annual Report of the Bureau of Statistics of Labour, March, 1886 Wright and Potter, Boston. Sent to Library of House of Commons.

has raised its capital stock to 30,000 dol., besides 50,000 dol. invested in new plant, made in the business. The annual product amounts to 75,000 dol., and the dividend, except in bad years, has been recently 10 per cent.

The stock is held almost entirely by the workmen, and there is a gradual tendency towards larger holdings. The company is stated to enjoy excellent credit, and to be completely successful.

2. The Kingston Co-operative Foundry, established 1877, with a present capital of 11,900 dol., has had a severe struggle for existence through want of sufficient capital at first, want of credit, and various adverse circumstances. It has now an annual output of 20,000 dol., and yields a dividend of 3 per cent. per annum. *Kingston Co-operative foundry.*

3. The Leonard Co-operative Foundry.—This foundry was purchased in 1877 by a number of moulders at Taunton, and has been successful. The first three years' profits went into the 30 per cent. reserve required by law; since then, dividends of 6 per cent. have been paid. The capital is 25,000 dol., and the annual product 75,000 dol. The effect of stockholding is stated to have been marked on the amount and quality of the work. "The men take pains to do well, and have a pride in the reputation of their goods." *Leonard Co-operative Foundry.*

4. The East Templeton Co-operative Chair Company was organised in 1872 by some skilled workmen thrown out of employment, and started with a capital of 10,000 dol. This has now increased to 20,000 dol., and the value of the annual product is 45,000 dol. to 50,000 dol., and dividends of 5 to 6 per cent. are paid. The company has been successful, and the effect on the work done good. In 1880 the shop and contents were destroyed by fire, but the loss has been nearly made good. *East Templeton Chair Co.*

5. The Athol Co-operative Furniture Company was formed in 1879 also by men thrown out of employment, with a capital of 2,500 dol. It began badly, and in 1882 the shop was destroyed by fire. A new start was made, but the company has never been prosperous. It has now a capital of 5,000 dol., and an annual product of 15,000 dol., but pays no dividends. The non-success is attributed to bad management and want of capital. *Athol Furniture Company.*

6. The Stoneham Co-operative Shoe Company, started by temporarily unemployed men in 1872, with a capital of 10,000 dol. The management was good, and the company has been very successful. It has now a capital of 20,000 dol., an annual product of 150,000 dol., and has recently yielded dividends of 15 to 20 per cent. *Stoneham Shoe Company.*

7. The Middlesex Co-operative Boot and Shoe Company, Stoneham, organised in 1875 by unemployed men. It began with a capital of 10,000 dol., and met with great difficulties at first, being worked for three years at a loss. It has, however, turned out a success. The capital has risen to 15,000 dol., the annual product to 90,000 dol., and recent dividends have been as high as 20 and 25 per cent. *Middlesex Boot and Shoe Company.*

8. The American Co-operative Boot and Shoe Company, Stoneham, organised in 1882, with a capital of 10,000 dol. It enjoys good credit, but has not been strikingly successful financially. The capital has risen to 30,000 dol. and the annual product to 50,000 dol. but no dividends are paid at present. *American Boot and Shoe Company.*

9. The Franklin Co-operative Boot and Shoe Company, Stoneham, started in 1883 by men thrown out of work by failures. It began with a nominal capital of 10,000 dol., and met with many difficulties. The capital is now 20,000 dol., and the annual product 50,000 dol., but no dividends are paid. *Franklin Boot and Shoe Company.*

10. The Wakefield Co-operative Shoe Company, organised after *Wakefield Boot and Shoe Company.*

the example of the last-named in 1883, with 15,000 dol. capital. It has been fairly successful, has an annual product of 35,000 dol., and paid 8 per cent. dividend in 1884.

Cosmopolitan element. A mixture of nationalities is noticeable in these associations, which appears to cause no inconvenience, but efforts are made to keep the stock in the hands of native Americans.

Varied results of co-operative enterprises. (2*b*.) It will be noticed that the commercial success of these societies varies greatly. Some, like the Somerset Co-operative Foundry, have been very prosperous, while many have been as distinct failures. The necessary conditions for success appear to be:— 1, a sufficient capital, with regard to which Mr. Carroll Wright states that the necessary amount is very generally underestimated; 2, efficiency and regularity of management; and 3, accurate separation of wages from profits in practice. There have also been many failures from crude ideas and unreasonable expectations on the part of the artisan stockholders. Still the system has made a beginning, and several successful societies exist.

Two prosperous societies outside Massachusetts may be added to the list.

Beaver Falls Foundry Association. The Beaver Falls Co-operative Foundry Association, at Beaver Falls, Pennsylvania, started in 1872 with a nominal capital of 25,000 dol., and has prospered steadily. The larger part of the stockholders are employed in the foundry, and dividends of 12 to 15 per cent. are paid.

Equitable Foundry Co., Rochester. The Equitable Co-operative Foundry Company of Rochester, New York, started in 1867, with a capital of 30,000 dol. It has greatly prospered, and the paid-up capital increased to 100,000 dol.: 12 per cent. is paid to the shareholders, and the rest to those members who work in the company in proportion to wages. Nearly all the workers are also stockholders.

No influence on strikes. These societies do not appear to have attained sufficient importance and weight in the country at large to influence strikes one way or the other.

Modes of profit-sharing. (2*c*.) Summarising the above facts, we find that profit-sharing in connection with wages is done in two ways: the percentage of profits is either given to labour after a dividend on capital has been paid, or such percentage is allotted to labour without first paying a fixed dividend on capital. The latter place has the merit of giving something to labour, however small the profits may be, and it has, therefore, a greater educational effect than the other, under which, in years of very small profits, labour receives no additional percentage. Such percentage is also distributed in two ways:—1. By classes. 2. In proportion to wages earned. The former plan, however, is liable to excite jealousies and dissatisfaction. This extra percentage may be considered as extra pay for extra services (*i.e.*, increased efficiency), and it is this which constitutes its educational value.

Profit-sharing in connection with stock-owning is also twofold. Profits are either divided on the basis of capital alone, or partly on the basis of capital and partly on that of labour. But the Massachusetts co-operative manufacturing societies come entirely under the former head; but, of course, the dividends thus paid act as an indirect reward to labour.

Co-operative banks. *Question III.*—Co-operative banks have been in operation in the United States for many years, and have spread from Pennsylvania over a large part of the Union. They are recognised and protected by the laws of many of the States. In Pennsylvania alone they are reported to number 1,700.

133

A few may be cited as showing their general progress. It is difficult to keep the co-operative banks entirely distinct from the building societies, as the two are often united.

Building societies, Philadelphia.

The Union Savings and Building Association of West Philadelphia reports 32 series of shares, 15 of which were paid off on maturity. The assets are 188,881 dol.

The Randolph Bank and Loan Association had in 1879 a business of 40,000 dol. The Working Men's of Wilmington, Delaware, had assets of 143,364 dol. in that year. The Second National Savings Fund and Loan Association of Morris Town showed half-yearly receipts of 13,836 dol. The Tradesmen's Building and Loan Association of Philadelphia reported in 1880 an income of 71,792 dol. The State Mutual Sinking Fund, Loan, and Building Association of Philadelphia had a business of 45,402 dol. in 1879.

Randolph Bank and Loan Association.

The co-operative banks have never obtained a fair foothold in New York city. In Massachusetts, where they have now made great progress, they had no legal status till recently, but in 1879 an Act was passed for their constitution and supervision, which is considered a a model for other States, under which they are placed on the same footing as the savings banks. From the latest report of the Savings Banks Commissioners, it appears that there are now 30 co-operative banks in Massachusetts—

Their total assets were	$2,512,335
The number of shares	78,565
„ members	11,836
„ borrowers	2,482
The amount of deposits	$274,998,412
„ surplus	$5,210,525
The guaranty fund	$6,604,464
The number of open accounts	848,787
Average of each account	$324
Amount of deposits during the year (including dividends)	$60,248,180
And the number of such deposits	896,078
Giving an average of each deposit of (a decrease of 2 dol. 82 c. on the previous year)	$67·24
Amount of withdrawals	$48,172,172
Number of withdrawals	534,882
And average of withdrawals	$90·06

The above totals nearly all show a large increase except the surplus, and the amount of withdrawals, which both decreased.

Investments in the United States bonds tend to decrease, while investments in bank stock, railroad bonds, and State and municipal bonds increase largely. The earnings of these banks were 13,869,466 dol., being 294,418 dol. more than the previous year, and the dividends 10,284,661 dol., an increase of 406,947 dol., giving the different banks' dividends, varying from 3 to 5 per cent., according to their prosperity, an average dividend of 4·14 per cent. There have been several failures in recent years, but the losses to investors have not been large in proportion to the whole.

Investments.

The following table gives statistics respecting the 12 largest co-operative banks in Massachusetts:—

Largest banks in Massachusetts.

TABLE of Twelve Largest Banks in Massachusetts.

Name.	Place.	Incorporated.	Number of Shares.	Number of Members.	Number of Borrowers.	Assets.	Increase of Assets from last Year.
						Dollars.	Dollars.
Campello	Brockton	Oct. 3, 1877	3,595	500	13	136,097	30,926
Fitchbury	Fitchbury	,, 27, ,,	5,141	659	273	207,171	46,013
Haverhill	Haverhill	Aug. 20, ,,	3,259	418	98	101,603	29,804
Homestead	Boston	Sept. 11, ,,	5,564	783	114	150,314	28,321
Mechanics	Taunton	,, 14, ,,	4,250	643	211	208,911	30,027
Pioneer	Boston	July 26, ,,	4,740	716	139	165,952	15,101
Security	Brockton	Dec. 17, ,,	2,725	479	99	118,038	24,373
Taunton	Taunton	March 2, 1880	3,959	572	216	187,899	36,639
Troy	Fall River	July 10, ,,	3,042	424	91	107,341	13,688
Waltham	Waltham	Oct. 13, ,,	6,294	976	187	224,502	50,200
Worcester	Worcester	,, 19, 1877	5,226	703	143	161,174	25,769
Working Men's	Boston	June 9, 1880	3,753	531	101	110,388	25,605

Savings bank.

These loan associations and co-operative banks appear likely to take the place of the savings banks, at any rate to a great extent.

Each system has its advantages and defects.

The savings bank receives money at any time during business hours, in such sums as the depositor chooses to pay; it gives interest on the money while in the bank, and permits the depositor to take it out any time under slight restrictions. This is good, and teaches the people to save. But the savings bank takes no personal interest in the investor, who pays his money to an irresponsible and indifferent clerk.

Loan association.

In the loan association the money must be paid in a fixed sum at regular intervals, and there are fines in case of neglect. He cannot draw his money out so easily as in the savings bank, but this is really for his good. He is in personal contact with the president, directors, and his fellow members, and has the same interest in the disposal of the money. He has the annual report and a vote, and no one has more.

Mr. Barnard's suggestions.

Mr. Barnard, in his work, suggests that each class of bank might adopt the good features of the other. The loan associations, for instance, should issue much fuller and more complete reports, and those quarterly. The attendance of directors at meetings should be noted, and fines imposed for absence. The Massachusetts plan of paying the premium monthly, with the interest, is preferred to the Philadelphia plan of deducting the premium from the loan, as being juster and less likely to create ill-feeling. Fixed tables of payments are better than the uncertain bidding at an auction. Similarly, the savings banks might adopt with advantage many of the features of their rivals. But in any case the co-operative banks have a great future before them.

Philadelphia.

Question IV.—The enclosed report by Consul Clipperton* shows that while Philadelphia, the great centre of co-operation generally in the United States, contains many working men's societies, clubs, &c., they are none of them, strictly speaking, on the "co-operative" basis. The Order of the Sons of St. George for Englishmen in the United States, of which he gives a description, may be described as more or less co-operative and charitable, and is doing a very useful work in many of the States of the Union. With regard to education, Mr. Clipperton points out that the great system of Government free schools in Philadelphia defies rivalry from private co-operative associations. This is also true of most of the States of the Union, the free school system being almost universal.

* See page 59.

Question V.—Consul Clipperton, in this report, gives a clear description of the purchase of his home by the working man, through the Philadelphia building societies, which have been so successful, and have been the parents of similar societies now scattered throughout the Atlantic States. The result of this system in Philadelphia is that through it the great majority of working men in that city own their own homes, without incurring a burden of debt. {Purchase of the working man's home.}

The system encourages thrift and industry, real estate rises continually, the taxable property grows, and the drink bill is checked. Mr. Barnard describes the actual position of one of these societies, the Artisans' Building and Loan Association of Philadelphia, as follows:—"It was incorporated in 1870, with a capital of 1,000,000 dol. A meeting was called by 15 persons: 420 shares were then subscribed for, and the society started. In its 11th annual report the repayment in cash of the first series of shares is announced. They are 130 in number, and will be paid at a valuation of 204 dol. 49 c. each. There has been paid on each share 1 dol. for 132 months, and the share has earned 72 dol. 49 c., making up the foregoing total. The following year the shares of the second series, now valued at 181 dol. 70¾ c., will mature and be paid. Any loans made on such shares are settled on maturity, by giving a release for the amount of the debt in place of so much cash. The business done in 11 years amounted to 800,990 dol., or over 6,000 dol. a month. Loans on 489 shares were made during the period to the amount of 97,800 dol. The total number of the shares is 1,135, valued at 133,439 dol. 46 c." {Advantages of system.}

The sources of income in these banks are fivefold. The capital is increased each month by a sum equal to the number of shares. Each new member becomes a winner for them all. The fines and premiums bring money in addition to the dues and interest on the loans. For instance, a borrower bids at a meeting for 1,000 dol., at a premium of 30 dol. per cent. He receives 700 dol. The Association offers the remaining 300 dol. for auction, and gains a further 30 per cent., or 90 dol. This money again makes 27 dol., so that the association makes a total profit of 417 dol., and the entire 1,417 dol. begins to draw interest at once. All the dues, premiums, fines, and interest received are put up for auction each month, and draw further interest. Then there are the profits or withdrawals; a two-year-old share is worth 39 dol., and is bought on withdrawal by the association for the dues paid, and a premium of 3 dol., the association making 12 dol., which go to swell the general capital. {Sources of income.}

In Philadelphia the ground rent system gives a special character to these transactions. Any person desiring to build on a lot of land can, instead of buying, hire it for all time. He can offer to pay the price for it at any time, and the owner cannot decline to sell. The owner can never claim payment during the lease if the rent is regularly paid. {Ground rent system.}

In New York the great value of land and the system of tenement houses have given rise to another class of building society, called the "Hubert Home Club Associations." A number of intending housebuilders form a club and erect an apartment house, which they lease to themselves. Eight families, for instance, put up a house of ten flats. Each gives the others a bond for 1,000 dol., forming the capital. Land is bought and the house built: total cost 12,000 dol. Each member is assessed for money as required, and a mortgage raised to make up the whole sum. The house becomes the joint property of the members, each holding one-eighth. The members hold an auction for the choice of rooms, the money received being equaly divided among all. Then the club leases to each member his flat for 99 years at 1 dol. {Hubert Home Club Associations.}

a year. Each member transfers the fee to the club on signature of the lease, in order to prevent danger to the club from the financial embarrassment of any member. The member may sublet by permission, but in this way the fee cannot be lost or forfeited. The extra flats are let to outsiders, and the rent thereof pays wholly or in part for the running expenses of the house, interest on mortgage, &c.

Spread of building societies.

These building societies, under whatever form, have met with a distinct commercial success, and are spreading throughout the great cities of the United States. They also undoubtedly enable the working man, and also the class above him, to obtain better and more comfortable houses than would otherwise be possible.

Agriculture.

Question VI.—Co-operation has not as yet been applied to agriculture in the United States to any extent. The "Agricultural Chemical Works" mentioned above, and one or two co-operative "creameries" and milk associations (the stockholders of which are, as a rule, independent farmers), are of course in no sense instances of "co-operative agriculture." I am informed on official authority that co-operation has not as yet taken this direction in this country.

Massachusetts fisheries.

Question VII.—The best and I believe the only striking instance of co-operation under this heading, is that of profit-sharing without wages in the Massachusetts Fisheries.

The system is the following :—It is not customary in this business to pay wages. The crews are rewarded for their labour in direct proportion to the value of the catch.

In cod-fishing by hook and line the plan is carried out with extreme nicety: each man keeps a separate account of the fish he takes, and is paid accordingly. In mackerel and other seine fishing all the members of each crew share equally. At Gloucester the profits are divided as follows :—

The owners furnish the vessel complete, also provisions and fishing gear. After certain charges and expenses have been deducted from the gross value of the catch, the net value is divided one-half to the owners and one-half to the crew, and from the latter half is paid the cook's wages, cost of medicine, and a small payment to the widows and orphans' fund.

The men share equally in seine fishing, and according to success in cod-fishing.

In the haddock fishery the owners find the vessel only and pay the skipper, receiving a quarter of the gross proceeds. The crew pay for everything else, but take three-quarters of the proceeds.

It is generally agreed that the wages system would be impracticable in this business. The most skilful men are found in the cod-fishery, where merit is rewarded; while the least skilful are in the seining line, where all share equally.

Fluctuations in earnings.

The fluctuations in the sums earned are great and frequent, the business being an uncertain one; but this form of profit-sharing gives superior men a perfect opportunity to benefit themselves proportionally. The average pay per man per voyage seems to run from 15 dol. to 40 dol., roughly speaking, according to the length and success of the trip, but in some very successful trips sums of 100 dol. and 120 dol., and in one case over 220 dol. per man, were earned.

From the above statement I think it will be seen that co-operation in the United States is as yet in its infancy.

Concluding remarks.

In the form of the building societies and co-operative banks it has been very successful and is growing rapidly; in production it is progressing, but only to a limited extent; while applied to distribution, to agriculture, and in other directions it has not been a success.

137

The enclosed report by Mr. Wright on labour, and by the Massachusetts Commissioners on Savings Banks, and Mr. Barnard's work on co-operation as a business, already mentioned, contain much valuable information, and have been freely made use of in this Report.*

Washington, May 21, 1886.

H. A. H.

Inclosure 2 in No. 8.

Consul Clipperton to Sir L. West.

Sir,
Philadelphia, May 7, 1886.

IN reply to your despatch of the 20th ult., requesting a Report on the subject of co-operative building and kindred subjects in Philadelphia, I beg to inform you that I have not learnt that there are any co-operative building societies in this city beyond those known as building and loan associations, the principles of which are well known in England, and are practically conducted as follows:—The association is regularly incorporated under an Act of the State Legislature, having a president, secretary, and treasurer, and a board of directors. Each share of stock deposits a monthly payment of 1 dol., and is entitled to a loan of 200 dol. upon giving real estate security, and the payment of another 1 dol. per month (6 per cent. interest per annum), together with any "premium" incurred by the borrower in consequence of competition among members for the loan of the money to be put out at each monthly meeting. The building and loan associations are very popular in Philadelphia, and enormous sums of money are paid out on loans to be used in the construction of houses, in the main, for working classes. These houses, and the plot on which they are built, stand in the name of the borrower, in fee-simple, he giving a first bond and mortgage to the association upon the same for the money borrowed. In most instances the money borrowed is paid to the builder in instalments as the building progresses towards completion. These run on an average of 10 years, when they are wound up, the mortgages cancelled, and the borrower becomes absolute owner of his property, the cost of which has been but a little more than an annual rent he must have paid had he rented the dwelling from year to year. Thus, the working man decides to build up a home for himself by means of a building and loan association, and he proceeds as follows:— {Building societies.}

1. Purchase the ground for, say, 50*l.*

2. Take nine shares in an association, for which he pays 9 dol. (1*l.* 16*s.*) dues per month.

3. Contracts to build his house of six or seven rooms (a parlour, dining-room, kitchen, three bedrooms, a bath-room with hot and cold water, and gas throughout house) for 1,500 dol. (300*l.*).

4. Obtains a loan from his building and loan association of 1,800 dol., which is paid in instalments to the builder as the building progresses towards completion, under the immediate supervision of a "Committee on Loans," who protect the interests of the society, and render every facility to the borrower. He now pays the interest on this loan at the rate of 6 per cent. per annum, which is another 9 dol. (1*l.* 16*s.*) per month, and any premium that may have arisen, which, as a rule, is a small sum, say 5 per cent., or 45 cents per month additional.

* These works have been forwarded to the Library of the House of Commons.

5. He pays his taxes, repairs, and water rent, amounting to about 30 dol. per annum, making his total payments per annum:—

	Dol.	c.
Building and Loan Association, 9 shares	108	00
Interest on loan	108	00
Premium	5	40
Taxes, repairs, and water	30	60
	252	00

In 10 years the association payments cease, the bond and mortgage are cancelled, and the borrower is absolute owner in fee of the property, and on the payment of an annual sum of not more than 72 dol. over and above what he would have paid for his rent, had he rented and not built.

There are no co-operative societies providing social, educational, and recreative facilities for the working people in this city founded on the basis referred to in your despatch.

The Government free schools of Philadelphia are so extensive, and cover such a wide field of education, that co-operation and combination of certain classes of the community for educational purposes is quite unnecessary. There are societies, clubs, choirs, bands, circles in every section of the city for the purposes of recreation, sociability, and mutual improvement, but they are in no sense co-operative, each club or guild paying his own expenses by *pro ratâ* and stated dues levied upon its members. These social guilds are very numerous in Philadelphia, extending to all walks of life, and cover every vocation—religion, temperance, music, all classes of amusements and beneficial objects. The male population, almost entirely, belong to some one or many of these clubs or guilds, while the female organisations are circumscribed chiefly to the church societies and family circles for amusement strictly, such as dancing and singing.

Order of the Sons of St. George.

The only society, not American, that has a strictly beneficial, social, and national character about it in this city is one of recent origin, and is known as the "Order of the Sons of St. George." It is composed of working men exclusively English of birth or descent. It was started in 1870, when three Englishmen were brutally murdered in the coal regions of Pennsylvania. Two of the known murderers and their families were quietly spirited off from the processes of the law. It was in the days of the well-remembered "Mollie Maguires," an organisation of assassins, said to be a wing of the "Ancient Order of Hibernians," which required summary measures both by the civil courts and the State militia to put down. The Order of the Sons of St. George has grown rapidly, extending from State to State wherever English working men congregate: there is a "sick benefit" of from 12s. to 20s. per week during sickness, and a funeral allowance of from 10l. to 20l. for a member, and half that sum for the funeral of a member's wife. The weekly dues of membership are from 5d. to 7½d. per week, and the fundamental principle of the Order is to make provision for sickness and death, thus preventing any member's family becoming an object of charity. In addition to this the families of the various lodges meet together socially on stated occasions, thereby keeping alive the English love of country and the festivities of her fête days. This organisation, non-political, unsectarian, and exclusively English, is growing rapidly: to its own membership it is of great advantage; it lends a helping hand, and its officers are always ready to advise and to assist them when landing on these shores. The praiseworthy work of this beneficial and social organisation of English working men in the United States cannot be too highly commended.

There are but one or two co-operative stores for the trade of working men and their families in this city. In Trenton, New Jersey, there is one which is quite successful. These societies are not on a large scale, and as they are supported almost exclusively by English membership, the principles and methods of conducting the business are precisely the same as co-operative societies and stores at home.

Co-operative work, as one of the simplest and most direct methods of aiding the working man in the improvement of his condition, has not, as yet, taken good hold in this country. "Profit-sharing," a step towards co-operative labour, such as that advanced by M. Godin, who founded the "Familistère" of Guise, France, has not, thus far, deeply interested the American working man. Superior individual qualifications, personal ambition, and that recognised inordinate desire for immense wealth and family aspirations stand in the way of extended co-operation. Mercantile speculation by men of superior abilities in their respective vocations will not give way to the higher end of the general good of the working classes: personal independence and personal desire for wealth, conflict with the common interest of permanent benefit to the independence of workers, and their guarantee against want and misery. Co-operation in the commercial, industrial, and proprietary sense is far distant as an established institution of this country.

I have, &c.,
(Signed)   ROBT. CHAS. CLIPPERTON, H.M.'s Consul.

92

No. 9.

UNITED STATES.

Sir L. S. Sackville West to the Earl of Rosebery.

My Lord,   Washington, June 9, 1886.

I HAVE the honour to acknowledge the receipt of your Lordship's Circular despatch of the 30th March last, calling for information on the liability of employers in the United States to compensate workmen injured in their service, and to forward to your Lordship herewith a report which I have drawn up on the subject. It will be seen that the existing law in this connection is the common law, and does not depend on special legislation, and that the Commissioner of Labour is about to direct the attention of his department to the points set forth in your Lordship's above-mentioned despatch.

I have, &c.,
L. S. SACKVILLE WEST.

Inclosure in No. 9.

Report of the State of the Law in the United States relating to the Liability of Employers to compensate Workmen injured in their Service.

IN reference to the particular points upon which the report is called for, it may be stated that there are no statutory provisions in any of the States of the Union except the State of Iowa.

The common law rules in all such matters. The common law doctrine in the United States is that common employment relieves the employer from responsibility for the injuries which one employé may receive through the negligence of a co-employé, unless negligence can be shown in the employment of unfit agents. This doctrine is the law of the United States, the single exception being in the State, as aforesaid, of Iowa, in which the statute law provides "that every railway company shall be liable for all damages sustained by any person, including employés of the Company, in consequence of any neglect of its agents, or by any mismanagement of its engineers or other employés of the Company."

But this law applies only to railways, the common law applying in all other cases. Parties seeking work in factories or on railroads can make a special contract relative to damages in case of accident through the negligence of co-employés, but this privilege throws the burden on the shoulders of the workman.

The employer is now liable, under the common law, for two classes of injuries caused by fellow-workmen: when he has directly interfered in the Act which caused the injury; and when by his negligence in selecting he has employed an incompetent workman. In all other cases, except where special legislative restriction exists, he is not liable for injuries to co-workmen unless by special contract he assumes to become liable.

It is now, however, sought to change the "status" of the parties by legislative action, and to make the employer also liable for all injuries caused by his authorized agents in the legitimate performance of the duties which he has prescribed, such regulation to apply to industrial works and railroads. Such a law would place the necessity of proposing a special contract upon the employers instead of upon the workmen seeking employment. With reference to the question, "How far does a system of insurance by workmen themselves against accident prevail, compulsorily or otherwise?" the Commissioner of Labour informs me that a system of insurance against accident by workmen themselves prevails to a certain extent in the United States, but to what extent he is unable to indicate. Such a system is, however, in practical work on the Baltimore and Ohio Railway, where the company guarantees a certain rate of interest upon a given capital which has been set aside by it for the benefit of an insurance association among the men. It is not made compulsory, but in fact is so, because of the inability to secure employment unless the workman participates in the system. The Commissioner adds that he will, during the present year, collect the fullest information relative to just this class of material. With regard to the liability of shipowners, they are liable in the same manner under the general common law as other employers for injuries occasioned by themselves, but not for those caused by the act of an employé. A sailor who is injured in the course of his duty is entitled to his wages, and to be cured at the expense of his ship. There is a special statute in the State of New York for cruel and unusual punishment of sailors, but this is a criminal law and confined to American ships and crews. The shipowners' liability extends to all sailors employed in American ships.

L. S. SACKVILLE WEST.